This outstanding book is based on two decades of education and experience in mental health practice at the Divine Mercy University. It presents a Catholic Christian understanding of the human person, and it shows in detail how this understanding can inform the work of psychologists, counselors, social workers, and clergy and laity involved in pastoral work. The authors are trained in the practical aspects of the psychological sciences, but they also bring a deeper philosophical and theological tradition to bear on the relationship between the practitioner and the client. . . . The result is a richer and a truer picture of what it is to be human, and what human happiness and well-being are. Knowing what is normative and what is excellent in human being is essential to those who hope to heal and guide others.

> —Msgr. Robert Sokolowski, PhD, Elizabeth Breckenridge Caldwell
> Professor of Philosophy, The Catholic University of America.
> Author of *Phenomenology of the Human Person* (2008).

The editors and authors are to be commended for their timely and visionary work, *A Catholic Christian Meta-Model of the Person*. They have created a volume that speaks directly to the concerns of Archbishop José Gomez of Los Angeles when he said, "The crisis I see today is this: In our society, we no longer seem to share any coherent or common understanding about what it means to be a human being. . . . As I see it, this problem is rooted in our society's broader loss of the awareness of God." The editors and authors of this important book are re-capturing the essence of humanity based on Biblical principles, Catholic philosophical tradition, and natural law, which they integrate with psychological science. They are reclaiming the objective essence of what it means to be a person. Recommendations in the book for psychological treatment, then, are based on this premise that there is an objective essence to humanity. The advice on how to help clients flows from what constitutes a person. I highly recommend this work as one that will endure for many decades and probably for centuries.

> —Robert D. Enright, PhD, Professor of Educational Psychology,
> University of Wisconsin-Madison, and Founder of International
> Forgiveness Institute. Co-author of *Forgiveness Therapy: An
> Empirical Guide for Resolving Anger and Restoring Hope* (2015).

Just as Peterson and Seligman's *Character Strengths and Virtues* helped a virtue-based view of the person secure a place in mainstream psychology, *A Catholic Christian Meta-Model of the Person*, by Vitz, Nordling, Titus, and colleagues, takes the fields of psychology and mental health a giant step forward—by presenting an integrative vision of personhood and human flourishing grounded in insights from the psychological sciences and wisdom from Catholic philosophy and theology. As a character psychologist, I am especially grateful for its rich, multidimensional analysis of virtues and vices and their role in the quest for character and a purposeful life. This extraordinarily comprehensive handbook is sure to command attention worldwide as a landmark interdisciplinary contribution to both psychology and mental health practice.

> —Thomas Lickona, PhD, Director of the Center for the 4th and
> 5th Rs (Respect and Responsibility) at the State University
> of New York at Cortland, Emeritus Professor of Education.
> Author of *How to Raise Kind Kids* (2018).

I applaud the work of Divine Mercy University and, in a special way, your work in creating the Catholic Christian Meta-Model of the Person. This model incorporates the wisdom of theology, philosophy, and psychology in a manner that acknowledges all dimensions of our humanity. I am most grateful for this important contribution of our Church.

> —Most Reverend William E. Lori, Archbishop of Baltimore

Much psycho-therapy today is based on antiquated theories of the human person, which take nothing from the rich heritage of Christian teaching, and which succumb to the crude scientisms of our age. Teaching at the Institute for the Psychological Sciences (now Divine Mercy University) I came to see how much more can be given to people in trouble by the Christian view of inter-personal being than by much current therapeutic practice. This book, written by prominent faculty at DMU, develops a Catholic Christian Meta-Model of the Person in terms that will be profitably studied by all with an interest in genuine healing, whatever their faith. It embodies the fruits of a teaching experience that I have observed to have a transforming effect on a great many lives, mine included.

> —Sir Roger Scruton, PhD, Senior Fellow, Ethics and Public
> Policy Center, Washington, DC, and Professor, University of
> Buckingham, London. Author of *On Human Nature* (2017) and
> *Beauty* (2009).

Studies of the body-soul composite need a clear understanding of the healthy human person. This can derive only from philosophy and theological anthropology, from which practical psychological implications have to be drawn out. This book does precisely this, and so it may serve all those who come in contact with the psychological sciences.

> —Fr. Wojciech Giertych, OP, Theologian of the Papal Household. Author of *The Spark of Faith: Understanding the Power of Reaching Out to God* (2018).

In an age when threats to the human person have reached proportions hitherto unimaginable, these highly competent scholars have set out into the deep. They have done so boldly and with acumen. The book exudes catholic sensibilities. Nothing human, including sound therapy, escapes divine instruction. Mental health professionals will find these chapters an elixir for their practices. Instead of their only remedying symptoms, they will find consolation in liberating persons.

> —Fr. Romanus Cessario, OP, PhD, LHD, Saint John's Seminary, Boston, MA. Author of *The Moral Virtues and Theological Ethics* (2009) and *Christian Faith and the Theological Life* (1996).

The Meta-Model is clearly stated and well defined, with its hierarchical structure of the human person based on updated Thomistic concepts and principles. The book provides a well thought out and very worthwhile proposal for an interdisciplinary program of study and practice. It would serve very well as a starting place for an integrated program to educate Catholic mental health practitioners both in the theoretical and in the practical side of the psychological sciences with a focus on psychology and mental health practice. Congratulations on this work of integration, which pushes out the limits of each of the corresponding fields of study: psychology, philosophy, and theology.

> —Sr. Mary Prudence Allen, RSM, PhD, Member of the International Theological Commission. Author of *The Concept of Woman* (Vol. 1, 1997; Vol. 2, 2006; Vol. 3; 2017).

This book succeeds in an unusual and very necessary feat: to propose a meta-model that offers an integral vision of the person, considering the contributions that psychology, philosophy and theology make for clinical practice. The main merit of this work is to cover the relevant topics, from the most theoretical to the case study, because the most difficult thing is to span the distance between theoretical premises and practical application. Many congratulations to the authors for this magnificent contribution to the development of a Christian psychology.

> —Martín F. Echavarría Anavitarte, PhD, Professor and Director
> of the Department of Psychology, Universitat Abat Oliba CEU,
> Barcelona, Spain. Author of *Corrientes de Psicología Contemporánea*
> (2011) and *La praxis de la Psicología y sus niveles epistemológicos
> según santo Tomás de Aquino* (2009).

The "two truths" theory—that something could be "true in science" but "false in theology," or vice versa—was confronted and defeated centuries ago. Whatever is really true is true for everyone and for every discipline. Yet one wouldn't know it from Catholic psychological practice, which all too often neglects its own resources and relies on fractured, fragmented, and incomplete views of the human person taken over from secular theories and outlooks. I applaud this effort to bring all the pieces together. It will not be the last word. It is an excellent first word.

> —J. Budziszewski, PhD, Professor of Government and Philosophy,
> University of Texas at Austin. Author of *Commentary
> on Thomas Aquinas's Treatise on Happiness and Ultimate
> Purpose* (forthcoming) and *On the Meaning of Sex* (2012).

A Catholic Christian
Meta-Model of the Person

A Catholic Christian Meta-Model of the Person

Integration with Psychology & Mental Health Practice

Edited by

PAUL C. VITZ, WILLIAM J. NORDLING,
AND CRAIG STEVEN TITUS

DIVINE MERCY UNIVERSITY PRESS
Sterling, VA

Published by Divine Mercy University Press.

Sterling, Virginia, 20166

www.divinemercy.edu

Cataloging-in-Publication Data

A Catholic Christian meta-model of the person: Integration

with psychology & mental health practice /

edited by Paul C. Vitz, William J. Nordling, & Craig Steven Titus.

713 p.; 18 x 25 cm.

Includes bibliographical references and index.

LCCN 2019944307

ISBN 978-1-7331235-0-1 (Casebound)

ISBN 978-1-7331235-1-8 (Paperback).

Subjects: 1. Psychology. 2. Philosophy. 3. Theology.

4. Psychology—Personality.

5. Mental health in practice.

Classification: LCC BF698 | DDC 150—dc23

Printed in the United States of America

The paper used in this publication meets

the requirements of American National Standards for

Information Science— Permanence of Paper for

Printed Library materials, ANSI Z39.48-1992.

∞

To Jesus, Mary, and Joseph, the Holy Family,
and to our families

—PCV, WJN, & CST

CONTENTS

PART IV. THEOLOGICAL SUPPORT

PART V. THEORETICAL AND CLINICAL APPLICATIONS
OF THE META-MODEL

PREFACE

A basic assumption of this present volume is that our understanding of the nature of the person is fundamental to all aspects of mental health practice. Such a vision of the person defines the scope of what we see as human problems, our understanding of how such problems develop, and what is to be done to promote healing, growth, and even flourishing. Another major assumption of this book is that the most complete and true understanding of the person will serve as the foundation for the best psychological theory-building, for improvement of psychological research, and for development of the most effective intervention strategies, methodologies, and practices.

Not surprisingly, much of the relatively short history of modern psychology has consisted of attempts to understand the person. However, many of these efforts have consisted of the development of what could be termed "partial" theories of the person, which examine one aspect of the person and personality in depth, but ignore many other aspects of the person. Such partial theories include psychoanalysis, behaviorism, client-centered therapy, family systems theory, cognitive and neuroscience approaches, and existentialism. Again, such approaches make significant contributions to our understanding of the person, but are inadequate both theoretically and therapeutically when taken alone.

Fortunately, in the last few decades some efforts have been made to integrate two or more of these partial theories to develop a broader perspective of the person. Nonetheless, these integrative efforts have not succeeded in producing a comprehensive understanding of the person, even from a purely psychological perspective based on what is actually available in the field.

However, another assumption of this volume is that an understanding of the person based solely on psychological perspectives of the person and the collective wisdom of the mental health field is itself still too reductionistic to fully express the complexity of human nature. Psychology is but one of the major wisdom traditions that have sought to understand the person. Other sources of wisdom, such as the long-standing Western philosophical tradition and the three-thousand-year-old Judeo-Christian theological tradition, have also made significant contributions to our understanding of the person. Collectively these three wisdom traditions—psychology, philosophy, and theology—offer unique and complementary insights into the person, and the exclusion of any of the three diminishes or distorts our understanding of human nature. The first major goal of this volume is to employ these three wisdom traditions to develop an integrative, synthetic, comprehensive, realist framework for understanding the person: the Catholic Christian Meta-Model of the Person (CCMMP). Therefore, the end goal of this volume is to demonstrate how the Meta-Model can greatly enrich the psychological sciences and mental health practice.

Because of the multidisciplinary nature of the theoretical foundations of the CCMMP and its applications to clinical practice, the volume places some unique demands on the reader. It requires that one develop a competency in thinking about the person not only psychologically, but also philosophically and theologically. The editors have arranged the text in a logical order to make the learning process more manageable, but nonetheless there will be times when the reader may be challenged with new language, assumptions, concepts, and methods unique to the other disciplines.

The overall structure of the volume consists of five parts. Part I (Chapters 1–2) orients the reader to the work as a whole. These two chapters in combination provide a compact introduction to the Catholic Christian Meta- Model of the Person and its broad implications for the mental health field.

Part II (Chapters 3–6) describes a rationale for how psychology, philosophy, and theology can make unique complementary and corrective contributions to our understanding of the person, while avoiding each discipline's limitations. This part of the volume also provides specific psychological support for the Meta-Model.

Part III (Chapters 7–16) presents the philosophical method and premises of the Meta-Model regarding the person as a unified whole, embodied as man or woman, interpersonally relational, sensory-perceptual-cognitive, emotional, rational, and volitional and free. These chapters also identify the ways in which the person is fulfilled through vocational callings and commitments, and through virtues and the moral and spiritual life.

Part IV (Chapters 17–19) discusses the three theological premises of the Meta-Model, specifically the person as created in the image of God (foundationally good), with innate dignity; fallen (sinful), needing to struggle against pervasive evil and weakness; but offered redemption (salvation), with hope for new meaning and holiness.

Part V (Chapters 20–26) introduces some of the ways that the Meta-Model can provide par-

ticular contributions to the psychological sciences and mental health practice. These chapters examine implications of the Meta-Model for the training of mental health professionals, for case conceptualization, assessment, and diagnosis, for individual and group psychotherapy, as well as the Meta-Model's influence on psychological research.

As was mentioned earlier, because of the multidisciplinary approach of this volume, many readers will find challenges as they engage material that is not primarily associated with their particular discipline. Readers from different backgrounds may want to take different approaches to studying the CCMMP volume. Below are three strategies for engaging with the volume.

Mental health professionals who have little training in philosophy and theology may find it helpful to read Part I and Part II of the volume, and then skip to Part V. Although all of the chapters in Part V will be of interest to most mental health professionals, Chapters 20–22, which cover the areas of training, case conceptualization, and group psychotherapy, collectively provide a foundational introduction to the implications of the Meta-Model for mental health practice. However, ultimately one must thoroughly understand the vision of the person presented in the Meta-Model in order to understand possible contributions it can make to the psychological sciences and mental health practice. Therefore, mental health professionals will eventually need to immerse themselves in Parts III and IV of the volume.

Those trained more in philosophy may want to employ another strategy for reading this book. After starting with Part I, to get the overview and foundational premises of the Meta-Model, they may wish to address Part III, which presents the philosophical method and premises. It provides a vision of the person that is wider and deeper than a rationalist one, because of its realist approach. The Meta-Model presents a framework for the three disciplines to reflect together on reality in order to identify the ultimate meaning and truth of the person. Next, these readers may want to investigate the theological supports and premises (Part IV) to grasp how the moral and spiritual nature of the person is integrated in the Meta-Model. Moreover, many of these readers will have chosen this volume because of its philosophical and theological bridging with the psychological sciences and mental health practice, and therefore may be eager to get to the psychological premises and supports (Part II) and theoretical and clinical applications of the Meta-Model (Part V). In particular, Chapters 20–22 collectively provide a foundational introduction to the implications of the Meta-Model for mental health practice.

Those experienced more in theological and spiritual considerations may take still another tack in engaging the Meta-Model. As with the others, they will want to start with the big picture described in Part I. Then, they may want to read Part IV on how the Meta-Model incor-porates Catholic Christian theology (revelation and faith-based reflection) and practice (Christian moral and spiritual life), and the difference it makes that the person is created, fallen, and offered redemption. But since such reflections on the person and divine grace require a deep understanding of the person, these readers may also be eager to address the psychological (Part II) and philosophical (Part III) supports and premises. Then these readers may have an interest in the clinical implications of the Meta-Model (Part V). As mentioned above, Chapters 20–22 collectively provide a foundational introduction to the implications of the Meta-Model for mental health practice.

In conclusion, this volume presents a Catholic Christian Meta-Model of the Person, which is a synthetic and systematic, realist framework for understanding the person, a framework that is rooted in three wisdom traditions: psychology, philosophy, and theology. The book's goal is to make explicit the most significant assumptions and principles of the Meta-Model that are needed for integration with psychological science and mental health practice.

HISTORY AND ACKNOWLEDGMENTS

The history of the development of the Meta-Model began in 1999 with the founding of the Institute for the Psychological Sciences, which became one of the two schools of Divine Mercy University (DMU) in 2016. Under the visionary leadership of its first academic dean, Gladys Sweeney, the faculty began to meet regularly to develop a Christian vision of the person, a vision that could serve as a grounding framework for the psychological sciences and mental health practice. After much development, this framework was named the Catholic Christian Meta-Model of the Person (CCMMP).

A significant intellectual influence in the creation of the Meta-Model was St. John Paul II's philosophical and theological anthropology and his then recently published encyclical, *Faith and Reason* (*Fides et Ratio*, 1998). This work of John Paul II was important in that it initiated increased interest in the person as understood from within the long Christian theological tradition, while also integrating the Christian vision of the person with the philosophical tradition and contemporary social sciences. In his work, John Paul II advocated for the mutual interdependence of faith and sciences in the development of a comprehensive and enriched vision of the person.

Throughout its development, the Meta-Model has been a multidisciplinary effort, which includes mental health professionals, theologians, philosophers, and social scientists. As central to the mission of DMU, it has also been a wide, collaborative effort that has included continual discussion and feedback from students and alumni, members of the administration, and outside scholars.

The earliest foundational work on the Meta-Model was initiated under the guidance of Fr. Benedict M. Ashley, who assisted the faculty in the development of the initial core courses in philosophy and theology that constituted the integration curriculum. Fr. Ashley later served as a faculty member, a friend, and a consultant to the Institute.

In the early development of the model, a considerable focus was placed on grounding the Meta-Model's vision of the person both theologically and philosophically. Leadership and significant contributions toward these ends were made by Craig Steven Titus, Christian Brugger, and Michael Pakaluk.

More recent developments involved focusing on the contributions of the psychological sciences to the Meta-Model and, more specifically, how the model could be integrated with research, theory building, and clinical applications. Important efforts in the theoretical grounding of the psychological sciences with the Meta-Model were initially contributed by Paul C. Vitz. Additional initial important contributions to examining both theoretical and clinical applications were made by William J. Nordling, Phil Scrofani, Frank Moncher, Su Li Lee, and G. Alexander Ross.

Although the contributors listed above deserve special mention, it is important to note that ultimately the development of the Meta-Model was supported and enriched by a much larger community consisting of faculty, students, alumni, and outside scholars. One of the most important communal efforts in the development of the Meta-Model has been the work of the DMU group over a 20-year period. The DMU Group includes all of the university's full-time faculty members and many of its part-time faculty members. Current members of the group meriting recognition for their contributions and length of service to the development of the model include Antony Bond, Ana Buenaventura, Kathleen Dudemaine, Christopher Gross, Stephen Grundman, Suzanne Hollman, Benjamin Keyes, Julia Klausli, Lisa Klewicki, Su Li Lee, Timothy Lock, Matthew McWhorter, Rebecca Morse, William Nordling, Helena Orellana, Harvey Payne, Anna Pecoraro, Fr. Robert Presutti, Phil Scrofani, Craig Steven Titus, and Paul C. Vitz.

The names of former faculty members participating in the DMU Group or contributing to the model in the past are too numerous to list. However, those meriting special recognition include Kathryn Benes, Christian Brugger, Michael Donahue, Fr. Benedict Groeschel, John Haldane, Steven Hamel, Margaret Laracy, Frank Moncher, Michael Pakaluk, Carlton Palmer, Edmund Pellegrino, Holiday Rondeau, G. Alexander Ross, Fr. Peter Ryan, Sir Roger Scruton, Sr. Mary Clare Smith, and Gladys Sweeney.

Throughout the development of the Meta-Model, eminent scholars also made significant contributions, especially Fr. Romanus Cessario, Fr. Benedict Groeschel, William May, Daniel Robinson, Kenneth Schmitz, and Sir Roger Scruton.

A number of integrative projects sponsored by DMU have also influenced the Meta-Model. These include the Anthropology Project and the ongoing Newman Lecture Series. The Anthropology Project, under the direction of Fr. Romanus Cessario, Fr. Benedict Ashley, Kenneth Schmitz, Roger Scruton, and Paul C. Vitz, produced the well-reviewed book titled *Philosophical Virtues and Psychological Strengths* (2013, Sophia Press). Other contributors to this project include John Cuddeback, Matthew Cuddeback, David Franks, Paul Gondreau, Tobias Hoffmann, Daniel McInerny, and Christopher J. Thompson.

The students of Divine Mercy University have greatly enriched the development of the Meta-Model and the material presented in this book. Much of the material in this volume has been preserved in the "oral" tradition and taught in classes for two decades. Through many class discussions and from feedback on drafts of foundational documents, the students have helped to deepen and to clarify important aspects of the model. Students have also provided valuable service to the preparation of the manuscript in their capacity as research assistants.

We would also like to thank the many people who have provided their expertise and service both in the development and promotion of this volume. A very special mention should be made of Anne Needham, for her skilled copyediting. The production of the book was greatly facilitated by Anne Kachergis. Other important contributors to the promotion of the book include Thomas Brooks, Ebony Shamberger, and Jessie Tappel. Special appreciation goes to Andrea Cassar, for his expertise on the design of promotional material.

Finally, it is important for us to express our great appreciation for the continuous support of Fr. Charles Sikorsky, the current President of DMU, and his predecessors, Fr. John Hopkins, and Fr. Richard Gill. We also wish to express our deep gratitude for the ongoing support we have received from the Board of Directors of DMU under the leadership of Board Chair Mr. Thomas Cunningham, as well as his predecessors.

If we have missed acknowledging someone who has contributed to this project, we regret the omission. In closing, we would like to thank Our Lord, who has constantly sustained us all these years.

Part I

The Meta-Model of Integration

Introduction to a Catholic Christian Meta-Model of the Person for Mental Health Practice

William J. Nordling, Paul C. Vitz,

and Craig Steven Titus

ABSTRACT: This chapter introduces the Catholic Christian Meta-Model of the Person (CCMMP) and its implications for mental health practice. In doing so, it begins to respond to five basic questions, which are answered more fully in the rest of the volume. (1) What is the Catholic Christian Meta-Model of the Person? (2) Why is the CCMMP's enriched vision of the person necessary for the mental health field? (3) How does the use of the Meta-Model enrich clinical practice in general? (4) How does the CCMMP's vision of the person benefit the client? And (5) how does the Meta-Model's vision of the person benefit the clinician's understanding of his or her identity as a Christian mental health professional? In addition to these questions, the chapter presents three foundational documents of the Meta-Model: (a) its *Definitions of the Person*, (b) its *Psychological Premises*, and (c) its *Framework for Mental Health Practice*. Finally, this chapter orients the reader to the structure of the book and suggests strategies for its use by readers of different backgrounds.

The two major goals of this book are to provide a comprehensive understanding of the Catholic Christian Meta-Model of the Person (CCMMP) and to explore ways in which this vision of the person can enrich theory and practice within the mental health field. This introductory chapter assists in the accomplishment of this goal by orienting readers to the volume as a whole and by giving a brief introduction to the Meta- Model and pointing out some broad indications of its significance for the mental health field.

To orient the reader, the chapter will introduce three foundational documents that succinctly summarize the CCMMP and implications of its application within mental health practice. These documents include: (a) the *Catholic Christian Meta-Model's Definitions of the Person*, (b) the *Psychological Premises*, and (c) the *Catholic Christian Meta-Model Framework for Mental Health Practice*.

In addition to introducing these major foundational documents, this chapter will give context, or "the big picture," for study of the entire volume by providing preliminary answers to the following questions, which will be answered more comprehensively in the remaining chapters: (1) What is the Catholic Meta-Model of the Person? (2) Why is the CCMMP's enriched vision of the person necessary for the mental health field? (3) How does the use of the Meta-Model enrich clinical practice in general? (4) How does the CCMMP's vision of the person benefit the client? And (5) how does the Meta-Model's vision of the person benefit the clinicians' understanding of their identity as Christian mental health professionals?

The chapter will then provide further orientation to the volume for the reader by overviewing the structure of the book, as well as strategies that readers may wish to adopt in approaching their study of the volume given their different familiarity with the fields of psychology and mental health practice, philosophy, and theology.

What Is the Catholic Christian Meta-Model of the Person?

The Catholic Christian Meta-Model of the Person is a framework that gives a rich comprehensive understanding of the nature of the person. The Meta-Model is developed from core premises or propositions about dimensions of personhood that have been contributed by the wisdom of the psychological sciences, as well as by the two ancient wisdom traditions of philosophy and theology. The core theological, philosophical, and psychological premises of the Meta-Model are introduced in Chapter 2 ("Theological, Philosophical, and Psychological Premises for a Catholic Christian Meta-Model of the Person"). The premises of the Meta-Model are then discussed in a comprehensive way throughout this volume, in Part II, Psychological Support (Chapters 3–6), Part III, Philosophical Support (Chapters 7–16), and Part IV, Theological Support (Chapters 17–19).

The Meta-Model's vision of the person can be summarized succinctly in its three-part definition, which represents its fundamental premises about the person from theological, philosophical, and psychological perspectives, found in Table 1.1 below.

Each of the dimensions or capacities of the person identified in the definitions is explored thoroughly in a chapter of its own: personal wholeness (Chapter 8); uniqueness as man or woman (Chapter 9); fulfilled through vocational callings (Chapter 10); fulfilled in virtue (Chapter 11); interpersonally relational (Chapter 12); sensory-perceptual-cognitive (Chapter 13); emotional (Chapter 14); rational (Chapter 15); volitional and free (Chapter 16); created in the image of God and thus fundamentally good and possessing dignity (Chapter 17); fallen (Chapter 18); and redeemed (Chapter 19).

However, some general comments here about the Meta-Model will provide context and prevent possible misunderstandings from developing. First, it is important to note that the Meta-Model posits that psychology, philosophy, and theology are all sources of truth about the person (John Paul II, 1998; and Chapter 6, "Person as an Integrated Laminate"). They make integrative and complementary contributions to a realist understanding of the person. These disciplines act as "lenses" for viewing the person and together provide the possibility of a richer, clearer vision of the person than is possible when only one lens is utilized. As will be examine in more depth later, these different disciplines use different methodologies (Chapter 7, "Methodology and Presuppositions") and examine the person from different levels of analysis or "laminates" (Chapter 6). Each of these levels of analysis has its own important contributions to

Table 1.1. Definitions of the Person

From a theological perspective, (Scripture, tradition, and the Magisterium), the human person is created in the image of God and made by and for divine and human love, and—although suffering the effects of original, personal, and social sin—is invited to divine redemption in Christ Jesus, sanctification through the Holy Spirit, and beatitude with God the Father.

From a philosophical perspective, the human person is an individual substance of a rational (intellectual), volitional (free), relational (interpersonal), sensory-perceptual-cognitive (pre-rational knowledge), emotional, and unified (body-soul) nature; the person is called to flourishing, moral responsibility, and virtue through his or her vowed or non-vowed vocational state, as well as through life work, service, and meaningful leisure.

From a psychological perspective, the human person is an embodied individual who is intelligent, uses language, and exercises limited free-will. The person is fundamentally interpersonal, experiences and expresses emotions, and has sensory-perceptual-cognitive capacities to be in contact with reality. All of these characteristics are possible because of the unity of the body and unique self-consciousness, and are expressed in behavior and mental life. Furthermore the person is called by human nature to flourishing through virtuous behavior and transcendent growth; through interpersonal commitments to family, friends, and others; and through work, service, and meaningful leisure. From their origins (natural and transcendent), all persons have intrinsic goodness, dignity, and worth. In the course of life, though suffering from many natural, personal, and social disorders and conditions, persons hope for healing, meaning, and flourishing.

understanding the truth about the human person, and when integrated together they result in an enriched and more accurate understanding.

For example, the theological premise that we are made in the image of God gives faith-based certainty that we are interpersonally relational and called to love each other. Theology also provides us with an understanding of the nature of marriage and family life as a calling to self-giving love, and our interpersonal relationship with God as a source of hope, especially for an afterlife.

The philosophical tradition, for its part, gives us deep insight, broad analysis, and a systematic synthesis concerning existential meaning in life, truth and beauty, and ethical aspects of vocations and flourishing. This includes many types of relationships ranging from family relationships, types of friendships, and our relationship with community.

The psychological sciences contribute theories and empirical data that provide developmental perspectives and psychodynamic understandings, but in addition often provide a specificity allowing for the development of clear treatment plans and interventions. For example, the psychological sciences have identified that distressed couples are often characterized by a disproportionate response to criticism and by certain "demand/withdraw" behaviors. Such characteristics of the interpersonal nature of the person would not be identified nor would interventions be developed to address them through the methods utilized by theology and philosophy. In short, adopting a multidisciplinary perspective for the development of the CCMMP allows for a framework for an understanding of the person that is comprehensive and accurate, while also allowing for more specificity and applicability.

In parallel with the theological and philosophical premises of the Meta-Model, there are the eleven psychological premises (see Table 1.2). These psychological premises are the basis for the Meta-Model's psychological definition of the person (see above). The reader should note that in brackets after each psychological premise is an indication of the corresponding philosophical or theological premise with which the psychological premise is associated. In short, the table presents a brief illustration of how the psychological, philosophical, and theological "laminates," lenses, or levels of understanding are supportive and complementary of each other.

A second important clarification about the Meta-Model that may prevent misunderstandings pertains to the relationship between the Meta-Model and personality theories and models of therapeutic intervention already existing within the mental health field. It is important for the reader to be mindful that the Meta-Model does not replace traditional personality theories or theories of the person found in intervention models. Instead, the Meta-Model is an overarching comprehensive view of the person, which provides a framework for integrating the rich understandings about various dimensions of the person that are explored in existing personality theories, while avoiding the reductionism that results when a vision of the person is based on one or only a few of these personality theories. Similarly, the Meta-Model does not replace existing therapeutic models in the field, but instead provides a framework for the thoughtful selection of one or more interventions based on its comprehensive view of the person.

A final clarification to prevent misunderstandings centers on the claim that the Meta-Model provides a more comprehensive vision of the person. Although the three-part theological, philosophical, and psychological definition may seem to the reader to be rich and complex, it may still come across as missing some essential characteristics of the person. It should be noted that this definition of the person is derived from eleven major premises concerning the person. However, within the individual chapters discussing these eleven major premises of the Meta-Model there are many "sub-premises" or characteristics of the person that fall under each these broad premises. For example, that personhood is characterized by having a spiritual soul, existing as either a man or woman, and developing and maturing over time are all discussed under the premise that the person is a personal unity. The importance of the person as embedded in a family and culture is covered under the premise that the person is interpersonally related. In short, if there seems to the reader to be something missing in the definition, by the end of the book it will be discovered that the Meta-Model framework addresses many aspects of the person not included at the broader definitional level or even at the more specific level of the theological, philosophical, or psychological premises.

Table 1.2. A Psychological Vision of the Person Consistent with the Theological and Philosophical Premises of the Catholic Christian Meta-Model of the Person

The following eleven psychological premises represent a psychological understanding of the person consistent with the theological and philosophical premises of the CCMMP and with the psychological sciences. They serve as an outline that will be augmented with sub-premises that further elucidate the Meta-Model's theoretical and clinical implications for psychology and counseling. Together with the CCMMP's theological and philosophical premises, they deepen and help fill out our understanding of the person, for use in mental health practice. (In parentheses is found the name of the corresponding theological and philosophical premise.)

I. The person has an essential core of goodness, dignity, and value and seeks flourishing of self and others. This dignity and value is independent of age or any ability. Such a core of goodness is foundational for a person to value life, develop morally, and to flourish. (Created)

II. The person commonly experiences types of pain, suffering, anxiety, depression, or other disorders in his or her human capacities and interpersonal relationships. The person is also distressed or injured by natural causes and by others' harmful behavior. People have varying levels of conscious and nonconscious distorted experience, which express that they do not respect and love themselves or others as they should. Moreover, they often do not live according to many of their basic values. (Fallen)

III. The person, with the help of others, can find support and healing, correct harmful behaviors, and find meaning through reason and transcendence, all of which bring about personal and interpersonal flourishing. In short, there is a basis for hoping for positive change in a person's life. (Redeemed)

IV. Each human being is a body-soul unified whole with a unique personal identity that develops over time in a sociocultural context. This unity pertains to the person's whole experience. For instance, physical abuse affects the person's bodily, psychological, and spiritual life. (A Personal Unity)

V. The person flourishes by discerning, responding to, and balancing three callings: (a) called as a person to live a value-guided life while focusing on love and transcendent goals; (b) called to live out vocational commitments to others, such as being single, married, or having a distinct religious calling; and (c) called to participate in socially meaningful work, service, and leisure. (Fulfilled Through Vocation)

VI. The person is fulfilled and serves others through the ongoing development of virtue strengths, moral character, and spiritual maturity, including growth in cognitive, volitional, emotional, and relational capacities. Through effort and practice, the person achieves virtues that allow the attainment of goals and flourishing. For example, a father or a mother who develops patience, justice, forgiveness, and hopefulness is better able to flourish as a parent. (Fulfilled in Virtue)

(table continues)

7

Table 1.2 (*continued*)

VII. The person is intrinsically interpersonal and formed throughout life by relationships, such as those experienced with family members, romantic partners, friends,
co-workers and colleagues, communities, and society. (Interpersonally Relational)

VIII. The person is in sensory-perceptual-cognitive interaction with external reality and
has the use of related capacities, such as imagination and memory. Such capacities
underlie many of our skills, allowing us to recognize other people, communicate
with them, set goals, heal memories, and appreciate beauty. (Sensory-Perceptual-
Cognitive)

IX. The person has the capacity for emotion. Emotions, which involve feelings, sensory
and physiological responses, and tendencies to respond (conscious or not), provide
the person with knowledge of external reality, others, and self. The excess and
deficit of certain emotions are important indicators of pathology, while emotional
balance is commonly a sign of health. For example, when balanced, the human
capacity for empathy can bring about healing for self and others, while a deficit or
excess produces indifference or burnout. (Emotional)

X. The person has a rational capacity. This capacity involves reason, self-consciousness, language, and sophisticated cognitive capacities, expressing multiple types
of intelligence. These rational capacities can be used to facilitate psychological
healing and flourishing by seeking truth about self, others, the external world, and
transcendent meaning. (Rational)

XI. The person has a will that is free, in important ways, and is an agent with moral
responsibility when free will is exercised. For instance, the human being has the capacity to freely give or withhold forgiveness and to be altruistic or selfish. Increases
in freedom from pathology and in freedom to pursue positive life goals and honor
commitments are significant for healing and flourishing. (Volitional and Free)

Why Is the CCMMP's Enriched Understanding of the Person Necessary for the Mental Health Field?

As stated previously, a basic assumption of this volume is that our understanding of human nature and the person is fundamental to all aspects of mental health practice. Our vision of the person defines the scope of what we see as being human problems, our understanding of how such problems develop, and our construal of what is to be done to promote healing and even flourishing. Another previously mentioned major assumption of this book is that the more complete and accurate our understanding of the person is, the better a foundation it provides for psychological theory building, improvement of psychological research, and development of more effective intervention strategies and methodologies for mental health practitioners.

The fields of psychology, philosophy, and theology have each made major contributions to our understanding of the person. In a relatively short period, a hundred years or so, psychology has developed a large collection of "partial" theories for understanding the person. They are referred to here as partial theories because in many cases these theories have examined one aspect of the person in depth, but have neglected other important dimensions of the person. These partial theories include, for instance, the psychoanalytic tradition with its emphasis on the interior or psychodynamic life of the person; behaviorism with its emphasis on how the environment influences human behavior; interpersonal theory and its emphasis on the importance of relationships; cognitive approaches, which examine the importance of thought processes; and existentialism with its emphasis on human freedom and the importance of meaning in the life of the person.

This list includes only some of the major theoretical schools existing within the mental health field. If taken individually, these theoretical schools provide an important but limited understanding of the person. In the last few decades, notable efforts have been made to bring two or more of these partial theories of the person together to enhance clinical practice. Examples include Cognitive-Behavioral Therapy (Beck, 1979), Rational Emotive Behavioral Therapy (Ellis & Ellis, 2011), Multimodal Therapy (Lazarus, 1989), and the Biopsychosocial Model (Campbell & Rohrbaugh, 2006). A number of contributors to the field of counseling and psychotherapy have also integrated multiple theories and research about the person, which has resulted in an enriched vision of the person in their therapy models, for example: Emotion-Focused Therapy (Greenberg & Goldman, 2018), the Gottman Method of couples therapy

(Gottman, 1999), Relationship Enhancement Therapy (Guerney, 1977; Scuka, 2005).

At this point a number of questions could be raised about whether there really is a need for the Catholic Christian Meta-Model of the Person to serve as a new framework for the mental health field. If we are just patient, might not most of the "neglected" aspects of personhood covered in the Meta-Model be discovered and finally included? Might not the forces of integration existing within the mental health field eventually bring all the partial theories together? We believe that this is not forthcoming, for reasons we now briefly explore. More well-developed answers to these questions are provided throughout the text.

There is a need for a unifying framework. Partial theories of the person existing in the mental health field are not simply like pieces cut from the same puzzle and waiting to be combined. Without a unifying framework, which the Meta-Model represents, the pieces cannot so readily be fit together. The numerous partial theories or perspectives on the person offered by the mental health field sometimes contradict one another in terms of their fundamental assumptions about the person, and even more frequently disagree about the relative emphasis that should be placed on various abilities of the person. For example, when it comes to the issue of whether the person has volition or freedom, the conclusion has ranged from a view of the person as completely determined (in the case of radical behaviorism), to having significantly impaired freedom (in the case of both modern behaviorism and classic psychoanalytic theory), to the person's being essentially free (in the case of existentialist schools).

Even more common is the disagreement across personality theories and therapy models with regard to the emphasis that should be placed on various dimensions of the person. For example, in both theory and clinical practice there is the divide between those who advocate the individual as the most important level of analysis and those who would see the dyadic level, or even the family system, as the most important level of emphasis. This distinction is not a small issue within the field, and these two perspectives have not always peacefully coexisted. One need only consider that during the first fifty years of the history of psychotherapy, when individual psychotherapy dominated, no significant theories or models for couples, marital, or family therapy existed (Gurman, 2002). This divide is also evidenced by the not-uncommon choice made by clinicians to work almost exclusively with individuals—from a psychodynamic or other interior-focused perspective—or, alternatively, to work mostly with couples, parents, families (and individuals)—from a family systems perspective—even when similar problems are being addressed.

The more comprehensive understanding of the person provided by the CCMMP allows the clinician to adjudicate and contextualize the important truths about the person that are contained within the various partial theories. Therefore, the Meta-Model can incorporate the valuable insights from behaviorism, concerning human learning, and acknowledge the important impact of the person's environment, while moderating a view that would excessively limit human freedom. It can also acknowledge the important insights regarding human freedom that are drawn from the existentialist schools, while excluding the idea of some of these schools that the person is almost completely free and able to create his or her own nature. The Meta-Model also advocates for mental health professionals to be trained to assess, conceptualize, and in-

tervene at both the individual interior and dynamic level as well as at the dyadic or systems level, rather than being limited to only one level of analysis.

There is a need for a broad framework. We need to have a framework or meta-model that is broad enough to encompass all of the current personality theories, as well as the understandings of the person coming from both integrative therapeutic models and existing and emerging valid research. In addition, such a meta-model must also include the essential domains of the person that the psychological sciences have either neglected or, without the help of philosophy and theology, are not capable of adequately exploring. These broader domains include vocation and virtue, a normative human nature, relationship with God (the Transcendent), the importance of living a moral life, and the meaning contained within suffering. The CCMMP posits that a synthetic integrated framework for understanding the person can be based on the three wisdom traditions: the psychological sciences and the mental health field, the broader philosophical tradition (a Christian philosophical tradition), and the Catholic-Christian theological tradition. This resulting synthetic integrated framework, the Meta-Model, can then serve to unify the many partial existing psychological theories of the person and provide a broader framework for grounding mental health practice.

There is a need for an integrated approach to clinical training and practice. It is commonly the case in graduate training that personality theories are presented in a survey style with no overarching framework, and that graduate students are introduced to only a few integrated therapeutic methods in depth. This educational approach results in new clinicians' lacking a comprehensive framework for understanding the person (such as is represented by the Meta-Model), as a foundation for practice. Postgraduate training in new psychotherapy and counseling models, along with ongoing clinical experience, do provide some broadening of a clinician's understanding of the person, but this is often countered by the tendency of clinicians to become experts in certain areas of practice, as well as the tendency to become increasingly reliant on a few selected therapeutic intervention models. The need for the CCMMP as framework for mental health training and professional practice therefore is given support by a combination of factors: the failure of graduate training to provide the mental health professional with a comprehensive understanding of the person; the limited integration occurring within even the most integrated therapeutic models; the fact that even mature clinicians master only a few of these integrated models, so that collectively these many small efforts at integration do not result in the acquisition or use of a rich understanding of the person in clinical work; and

finally, the limitations created by professional specialization. (See Chapter 20, "Principles for Training," for discussion of how the Meta-Model can enrich the training of mental health professionals.)

One final question that might be raised in this section is whether such a multidisciplinary framework, which aims at integrating the truths about the person from psychological, philosophical, and theological perspectives, is methodologically possible. This question immediately initiates a need for exploration of the nature of truth and the relationship between faith, reason, and the scientific method adopted by contemporary psychology. This brief introductory chapter can only state the conclusion that it is possible; satisfactory development of the argumentation of this conclusion is left to the entire book. However, a significant foundation for this conclusion is explored especially in Chapter 5 ("Basic Psychological Support"), Chapter 6 ("Person as an Integrated Laminate"), and Chapter 7 ("Methodology and Presuppositions").

How Does the Use of the Meta-Model Enrich Clinical Practice in General?

Part V of this volume examines both broad and specific ways in which the CCMMP enriches various aspects of clinical practice, such as assessment, diagnosis, case conceptualization, individual psychotherapy, and group psychotherapy. Other chapters in Part V examine how the Meta-Model shapes the training of mental health professionals and how it can influence the conducting of psychological research. This section seeks only to highlight a few of the most important ways the Meta-Model enriches clinical practice.

First, the Meta-Model's vision of the person

greatly expands what is meant by diagnosis. In short, if we ask the question, "what is wrong with this client?" contemporary mental health practice approaches to answering this question range from (a) identifying a biochemical cause, to (b) identifying a symptom cluster associated with a specific diagnostic label, to (c) understanding what is wrong with certain personality features of the client, to (d) identifying dysfunctional interpersonal or family-system patterns of interaction. Taking all four of these levels of analysis for diagnosis of the client's problem can result in a moderately rich understanding of what needs to be addressed in a treatment plan. However, it is common that mental health professionals stop at a symptom-based diagnosis. In other cases mental health practitioners who are psychodynamically trained will seek to understand the personality structure, and those who work with couples and families will also emphasize obtaining a family systems perspective, but seldom are all four levels of analysis utilized.

The Meta-Model encourages the use all four of the aforementioned levels of analysis. In addition, the Meta-Model, with its emphasis on the client as fulfilled through vocational callings and through virtue, adds important characteristics beyond these four levels of analysis in order to arrive at an adequate diagnosis. For example, the Meta-Model would require that an assessment and diagnosis of how a married client is functioning in his or her call to be a spouse and parent; how this married client is functioning in his or her call to serve others in their life work; whether there is a balance between work and family life; what virtues are needed by this married person to live out commitments to spouse and children, and what other virtues are needed for flourishing. It would require also an exploration of the client's spiritual functioning and desired relationship with God, as well as how the client lives out a moral life consistent with his or her beliefs.

Although clinicians may be able to identify cases in which a majority of these areas were assessed, the benefit of the Meta-Model as a framework is that it seeks to safeguard the consistency of such thoroughness with each client. Seldom do counseling and therapy address every problem or lack of flourishing. However, the Meta-Model benefits the clinician and client by making sure that all important areas of the client's life are assessed and prioritized in the treatment plan.

Note that the vocational approach adopted by the Meta-Model ultimately sees flourishing in one's vocational callings as the highest level of analysis, one that is well beyond the diagnosis made at the symptom level, or even at the personality or family system level. The Meta-Model, instead, sees these other levels as important primarily because they affect the person in his or her current vocational callings. For example, in the case of a married client, his or her depression, rigid personality characteristics, and dysfunctional family of origin, as well as his or her strengths, are seen ultimately in the light of how they impede or promote efforts to be a loving spouse and caring parent, and to be successful in serving God and neighbor through one's life work and living a morally good life.

It follows from the Meta-Model's implications for diagnosis that other clinical activities, such as the intake interview and other formal assessment processes, are also influenced. A Meta-Model approach to interviewing and assessment does not mean that clinicians have to change their preferred initial approach to gathering information and building the therapeutic relationship in the intake process. However, it does mean that clinicians need to be aware of what gaps in the comprehensive vision presented by the Meta-Model remain unknown and still need to be explored at a later time.

A Meta-Model assessment process does require that clinicians know the limitations of their preferred therapeutic modalities and the specific theoretical orientations of these modalities. For example, marital therapists may need to be aware that although their intake and assessment process will generally yield much information about interpersonal functioning and the clients' functioning in their vocational callings as spouse and perhaps parent, it may not be as effective for assessing each client's personality or spiritual functioning. In short, each therapeutic modality and even each school of therapy has strengths and weaknesses when it comes to using the Meta-Model for developing an understanding of clients and for planning and implementing treatment.

Another benefit of the Meta-Model for the mental health field is its effect on the role of the practitioner. Generally, there has been a distinction made between clinicians who mostly work with individuals and those who work with dyads or families. There will likely always be specializations based on a clinician's preferences, but the use of the Meta-Model advocates for basic-level training in theory and practice at understanding the person both as an individual and also as interpersonally relational. The Meta-Model also requires the clinician to understand how individual flourishing and interpersonal flourishing are fundamental to vocational flourishing.

How Does the CCMMP's Vision of the Person Benefit the Client?

The Meta-Model's vision of the person improves client care in some ways that are both unique and profound. The Meta-Model's premise that each client is made in the image of God, and thus is foundationally good and possesses innate dignity, has significant implications for the therapeutic relationship. The Meta-Model's vision of the person helps to focus the clinician's awareness that this client, who has made poor life choices, has committed evil acts, exhibits a personality disorder, displays psychotic symptoms, or has racist views, is still foundationally good and possesses dignity. Certainly most clinicians of good will, whether or not they use the Meta-Model, struggle to maintain this awareness when confronted with challenging clients. These efforts of clinicians to struggle to keep in mind the dignity of the person are not generally explicitly motivated by any personality theory or understanding of the person formed during their graduate training. The point being made is that the Meta-Model is explicit about the goodness and dignity of the client in a way not generally present in existing personality theories or therapeutic interventions. And yet, the mental health professional's firm hold on the reality of the goodness and dignity of the client can foster true charity and compassion, which maintains and strengthens the relationship.

The Meta-Model also benefits the client by promoting a deep respect for the uniqueness of each client. An important advancement in the mental health field is its increasing recognition of the fundamental goodness of culture, and more broadly its incorporation of respect for diversity. The Meta-Model supports this development by adding some insights into both the uniqueness of the person and the importance of culture. In the case of the Meta-Model, respect for diversity begins at the level of the individual. This specific client is recognized as a unique and unrepeatable person who has unique vocational callings. For example, this client, a married woman, is created uniquely by God, she is uniquely called to be a spouse to this man and a mother to this child. She has a unique set of talents, is called to a unique life of service aimed toward bringing goodness into the world. She is loved by God and is called to respond to a unique relationship with God (the Transcendent).

In addition, the Meta-Model adds to client care by its adding nuance to the understanding and valuing of the client's culture and other aspects of diversity. In the Meta-Model culture is seen as being foundationally good, since it both teaches about and bestows many basic human goods aimed at flourishing, such as relationship and community; moral norms and what it means to live a good life; and meaningful work, leisure, and celebration. However, the Meta-Model has a realist understanding of culture in that, although culture is seen as vitally important in forming the identity of the client and promoting his or her flourishing, cultures are nonetheless imperfect in their teaching about and promotion of flourishing.

The Meta-Model therefore encourages the mental health professional to value and respect culture, but it is also a corrective to the idealization of culture. Aspects of the client's culture that foster flourishing are seen as good, but aspects of culture that hinder flourishing are seen as barriers to the client's well-being. For example, if one culture supports faithfulness in marriage and another does not, then with respect to fostering the client's vocational commitment to marriage, one culture can be seen as a better teacher and aid for both client and clinician.

In short the Meta-Model does not accept a relativistic view that all aspects of a given culture are unequivocally good or that there is no way to evaluate influences of a given culture as positive or negative. However, such judgments about culture are not left to the subjective life experiences and possible cultural biases of either the client or the clinician, but instead are grounded both by objective human nature recognized by the Meta-Model as well as by each client's healthy experiences of his or her culture.

Finally, the Meta-Model helps benefit the client by fostering a deep respect for the client's right to make life decisions and to seek flourishing by following his or her conscience. In the mental health field, one of the most important ethical principles is the imperative for the clinician to avoid exercising undue influence in their relationship with their client or to compromise the client's autonomy and right to make life decisions. Temptations to violate these ethical principles are strongest when the clinician believes the client is making a mistake that will have negative consequences, or when the clinician believes there exists a better solution to a problem. The Meta-Model emphasizes that each client is foundationally good, has inherent dignity, is volitional or free, is a moral being, and is responsible for discerning his or her vocational callings (for example, to marry or not marry, and what life work to pursue). When the client is seen in this light, it can help the clinician to avoid the temptation to use undue influence, since this would do violence to the client's freedom to flourish by following conscience. It also helps clinicians to accept humbly that they cannot reliably know how God is calling this unique client to flourish.

How Does the CCMMP's Vision of the Person Benefit the Clinician's Understanding of His or Her Identity as a Christian Mental Health Professional?

Much of this book examines the Meta-Model's rich understanding of the person, which can be used to understand clients and assist them in healing, growth, and flourishing. However, because the Meta-Model's vision of the person is also equally applicable to the life of each clinician, it can also greatly benefit his or her understanding of what it means to be a Christian mental health professional.

The Meta-Model emphasizes that client and

clinician alike are fulfilled through vocational callings and a life of virtue. Although for all clinicians both vocation and virtue are important dimensions of being a person, they especially highlight for the Christian the realities that (a) there is a call to relationship with God that aims at a holy, just, virtuous life; (b) there is a call to a vocational state that involves deep relational commitments, love, and sacrifice (e.g., marriage); and (c) there is a call to one's life work and other forms of service as a means of loving neighbor. Although these three types of vocational callings are distinguishable, they are ultimately unified in the life of the Christian, supportive of one another, and in need of a balance among them for flourishing. These truths have important implications for what it means to be a Christian mental health professional.

First, the Meta-Model's emphasis on vocation as a fundamental dimension of the person has important implications for the identity of the mental health professional. Christian mental health professionals view professional work as a calling from God and not simply a job. Service to their clients is seen as a way of loving both God and neighbor. While the secular ethical codes of the mental health professions present aspirational principles of doing no harm as well as promoting the best interest of clients and patients (beneficence) (see the codes: American Association for Marriage and Family Therapy, 2015; American Counseling Association, 2014; American Psychiatric Association, 2013; American Psychological Association, 2017; National Association of Social Workers, 2017), Christian mental health professionals experience themselves as called to the even more self-giving ethic of charity (1 Cor 13; Benedict XVI, 2005: American Association of Christian Counselors, 2014; United States Conference of Catholic Bishops. 2009). In practical ways love motivates them to give of themselves and to persevere for the good of their clients. For example, while doing pro-bono work may be seen, by the secular clinician, as being civic minded, promoting justice and serving the poor is seen as a commandment from Jesus that is embraced as a way of life for the Christian mental health professional.

Second, Christian mental health practitioners, while valuing the development of professional skills, recognize that to be true to their Christian identity and their calling as mental health professionals, they must seek to be holy and virtuous. Indeed, with humility, they recognize that they need to constantly develop the virtues, such as empathy, compassion, patience, and practical wisdom, that are needed in their professional work. In addition, Christian mental health professionals pray for and work to develop the supernatural virtues of faith, hope, and charity. They also seek to help their clients at a natural level to be faithful to their life commitments; hopeful for healing, growth, and flourishing; and compassionate toward self and others.

Third, by recognizing the importance of each of their callings, mental health professionals understand that they must have balance in their lives. For example, a Christian mental health professional who is married recognizes that the calling to professional work must be in balance with and not harm his or her marriage and its accompanying commitments and responsibilities to spouse, children, and family life. Christian clinicians also recognize that their relationship with God, their work for justice, and their growth in holiness not only are good in themselves, but also support and allow growth in all their vocational callings, including their professional life.

In addition, the Meta-Model benefits the Christian mental health professional's awareness of his or her identity by providing clear Christian ethical principles based on the nature of the person (natural moral law and divine law). These principles both augment traditional professional ethics and allow for resolution of ethical conflicts by mental health professionals in a way that is true to their Christian identity and conscience, while respecting the dignity, rights, and conscience of clients.

Additional insights into how the Meta-Model is used in the training and formation of Christian mental health professionals are given in Chapter 20. Chapter 10, which covers vocational callings, and Chapter 11, which examines the importance of virtue development and moral reasoning, also provide valuable insights crucial for clinicians to understand their calling to be Christian mental health practitioners.

A Summary of the Benefits of the Catholic Christian Meta-Model Framework for Mental Health Practice

This chapter has introduced the Catholic Christian Meta-Model of the Person as a framework for mental health practice. A document summarizing the four major benefits of the model presented in this chapter is found in Table 1.3.

The Structure of the Book and Some Guidance for Mental Health Professionals, Philosophers, and Theologians

Information about the overall structure of the book and the specific content of chapters has been introduced throughout this chapter. In addition, a short, systematic introduction to the structure of the book as a whole, as well as guidance for readers of different backgrounds has been provided in the preface to the book. However, since some readers may not have read the preface, this information is presented again below, since it helps to orient the reader to the volume.

The book has five parts. Part I (Chapters 1–2) orients the reader to the overall work as a whole. The two chapters in combination provide a compact introduction to the Catholic Christian Meta-Model of the Person and its broad implications for the mental health field.

Part II (Chapters 3–6) describes a rationale for how psychology, philosophy, and theology can make unique, complementary, and corrective contributions to our understanding of the person, while recognizing each discipline's methodological limitations. This part of the volume also provides specific psychological support for the Meta-Model.

Part III (Chapters 7–16) presents the philosophical method and premises of the Meta-Model regarding the person as a unified whole, embodied as man or woman, interpersonally relational, sensory-perceptual-cognitive, emotional, rational, and volitional and free. These chapters also identify the ways in which the person is fulfilled through vocational callings and commitments, and through virtues and the moral and spiritual life.

Part IV (Chapters 17–19) discusses the three theological premises of the Meta-Model, specifically the person as created in the image of God (foundationally good), with innate dignity; fallen (sinful), needing to struggle against evil and weakness; but offered redemption (salvation), with hope for new meaning and holiness.

Table 1.3. A Catholic Christian Meta-Model Framework for Mental Health Practice

The following text identifies four ways that the Catholic Christian Meta-Model of the Person (CCMMP) contributes to and benefits mental health practice.

....

The CCMMP expands the vision of the person. The Catholic Christian Meta-Model of the Person presents a systematic, integrative, nonreductionist understanding of the person, marriage and family, and society, an understanding that is developed from the psychological sciences, philosophy, and the Catholic theological tradition and worldview. The Meta-Model integrates the methods and findings of these three disciplines to understand eleven essential dimensions of the person. These include the narrative of the person as (1) existing and fundamentally good (created), (2) affected by disorders (fallen), and (3) capable of healing and flourishing (redeemed). The person is (4) a unified whole, (5) fulfilled through three types of vocational callings (individual goodness and relationship with the transcendent; vocational states; and life work), (6) fulfilled in virtue strengths and character development, (7) and fulfilled in interpersonal relationships. The person is (8) sensory-perceptual-cognitive, (9) emotional, (10) rational and intelligent, and (11) volitional and free.

The CCMMP enriches mental health practice. The Meta-Model serves as a framework for mental health practice and for understanding the person. Mental health practitioners can use the Meta-Model to assess and diagnose client strengths and weaknesses, psychological disorders, and problems of everyday living; to explain how problems have developed; to establish treatment goals; and to select and implement evidence-based treatment interventions. Adopting the integrative perspective of the CCMMP as a framework benefits clinical practice, because the Meta-Model provides the structure to integrate existing personality theories and evidence-based therapeutic interventions to fulfill its comprehensive view of persons and the treatment of their problems. Furthermore, the Meta-Model approach also brings benefits by identifying the importance of life callings and vocations of clients and of the development of virtue and character to fulfill them. Finally, the Meta-Model enhances ethical practice by grounding traditional professional ethical principles and the respect for diversity in a moral normative understanding of the person, who possesses innate goodness and dignity in being created unique and in the image of God.

The CCMMP benefits the client. The Meta-Model approach to mental health practice helps the clinician and client to understand the client's life narrative and its challenges through this nonreductionist framework. This framework requires consideration of personal development, interpersonal relationships, values, character strengths and weaknesses, vocational commitments, existential issues, diversity, social contexts, and spiritual life. The client is viewed as a unique person, essentially good and possessing dignity. The practitioner acts collaboratively with the client to understand and implement treatment. In doing so, the clinician acts for the client's healing and flourishing in a manner that reflects love of neighbor and respect for the client's conscience and freedom to make life decisions.

The CCMMP clarifies and supports the clinician's Christian identity. The CCMMP clarifies how practitioners' lives and faith are integrated with their professional practice. Becoming a mental health professional is experienced as a calling by God to serve his people. In accepting this call the clinician becomes responsible for developing the professional competencies and virtues (such as empathy, patience, practical wisdom) needed for effective practice. The Meta-Model's worldview motivates a capacity and willingness to generously and unselfishly help all people, especially poor and disadvantaged populations. It also motivates working with Church ministries and brothers and sisters in the faith.

Christian practitioners integrate both professional and Christian ethics in their clinical work to promote their client's freely chosen goals aimed at psychological, moral, and spiritual flourishing. When some aspects of the clients' goals are contrary to Christian ethics and to their ultimate welfare, the practitioner works in a compassionate and nonjudgmental way to assist with as many of their goals as is allowable, according to professional and Christian ethics. This ethical attentiveness allows respect for the client's dignity, conscience, character development, and freedom, while also enabling practitioners to remain faithful to their own consciences.

Part V (Chapters 20–26) introduces ways that the Meta-Model can enrich the psychological sciences and mental health practice. These chapters examine implications of the Meta-Model for the training of mental health professionals, case conceptualization, assessment, diagnosis, and individual and group psychotherapy, as well as how it might influence psychological research.

Because the content of this volume is drawn from psychology and the mental health field, philosophy, and theology, some readers will find challenges as they engage material that is not primarily associated with their particular discipline. Therefore, readers from different backgrounds may wish to take varying approaches to studying the CCMMP volume. Below are three strategies for engaging with the volume according to each reader's background.

First, mental health professionals who have little training in philosophy and theology may find it helpful to read Part I and Part II of the volume, and then skip to Part V. Although all of the chapters in Part V will be of interest to most mental health professionals, Chapters 20–22, which cover the areas of training, case conceptualization, and group psychotherapy collectively, provide a foundational introduction to the implications of Meta-Model for mental health practice. However, ultimately one must thoroughly understand the whole vision of the person presented in the Meta-Model in order to understand possible contributions it can make to the psychological sciences and mental health practice. Therefore, mental health professionals will eventually need to read the philosophical and theological parts of the volume as well (Parts III and IV, respectively).

Second, those trained more exclusively in philosophy may want to employ another strategy for reading this book. After starting with

Part I, to get the overview and foundational premises of the Meta-Model, they may wish to engage Part III, which presents the philosophical method and premises in more detail. This part provides a vision of the person that is wider and deeper than a rationalist one, because of its realist approach. It also presents the Meta-Model as a framework for the three disciplines to reflect together on reality in order to identify the ultimate meaning and truth of the person. Next, these readers may want to turn to Part IV, which investigates the Meta-Model's theological supports and premises and how the Meta-Model integrates the moral and spiritual nature of the person. Those who have chosen this volume because of its philosophical bridging with the psychological sciences and mental health practice will be prepared to explore the psychological premises and supports (Part II) and theoretical and clinical applications of the Meta-Model (Part V). In particular, Chapters 20–22 collectively provide both a foundational introduction and representative sampling of the implications of the Meta-Model for mental health practice.

Last, those readers with theological and spiritual backgrounds, but little preparation in the mental health field, may take still another tack in engaging this book. Similarly to the others, they will want to start with the big picture described in Part I. Then, they may want to read Part IV on how the Meta-Model incorporates Catholic Christian theology (revelation and faith-based reflection) and practice (Christian moral and spiritual life) regarding the difference it makes to propose that the person is created, fallen, and offered redemption. But since such reflections on the person and divine grace require a deep understanding of the person, this reader will also want to explore the psychological (Part II) and philosophical (Part III) supports and premises of the CCMMP. Then these readers will also be prepared to explore the clinical implications of the Meta-Model (Part V). Again, Chapters 20–22 collectively provide both a foundation-al introduction and representative sampling of the implications of the Meta-Model for mental health practice.

REFERENCES

American Association of Christian Counselors. (2014). *AACC code of ethics*. Forest, VA: Author.

American Association for Marriage and Family Therapy. (2015). *AAMFT code of ethical principles for marriage and family therapists*. Washington, DC: Author.

American Counseling Association. (2014). *ACA code of ethics*. Alexandria, VA: Author.

American Psychiatric Association. (2013). *The principles of medical ethics: With annotations especially applicable to psychiatry*. Washington, DC: Author.

American Psychological Association. (2017). *Ethical principles of psychologists and code of conduct*. Washington, DC: Author.

Beck, A. T. (1979). *Cognitive therapy and the emotional disorders*. New York, NY: Penguin.

Benedict XVI. (2005). *Deus caritas est* [Encyclical, on Christian love]. Vatican City, Vatican: Libreria Editrice Vaticana.

Campbell, W. H., & Rohrbaugh, R. M. (2006). *The biopsychosocial formulation manual: A guide for mental health professionals*. New York, NY: Routledge.

Ellis, A., & Ellis, D. J. (2011). *Rational emotive behavior therapy*. Washington, DC: American Psychological Association.

Gottman, J. M. (1999). *The marriage clinic: A scientifically based marital therapy*. New York, NY: Norton.

Greenberg, L., & Goldman, R. (2018). *Clinical handbook of emotion-focused therapy*. Washington, DC: American Psychological Association.

Guerney, B., Jr. (1977). *Relationship enhancement*. San Francisco, CA: Jossey-Bass.

Gurman, A. (2002). The history of couple therapy: A millennial review. *Family Process, 41*, 199–260.

John Paul II. (1998). *Fides et ratio* [Encyclical, on the relationship between faith and reason]. Vatican City, Vatican: Libreria Editrice Vaticana.

Lazarus, A. (1989). *The practice of multimodal therapy: Systematic, comprehensive, and effective psychotherapy*. Baltimore, MD: John Hopkins University Press.

National Association of Social Workers. (2017). *Code of ethics of the National Association of Social Workers*. Retrieved from https://www.socialworkers.org/About/Ethics/Code-of-Ethics/Code-of-Ethics-English.

Scuka, R. (2005). *Relationship enhancement therapy: Healing through deep empathy and intimate dialogue*. New York, NY: Routledge.

United States Conference of Catholic Bishops. (2009). *Ethical and religious directives for Catholic health care services*. Washington, DC: Author.

Chapter 2

Theological, Philosophical, and Psychological Premises for a Catholic Christian Meta-Model of the Person

CRAIG STEVEN TITUS, PAUL C. VITZ, WILLIAM J. NORDLING, AND THE DMU GROUP

ABSTRACT: This chapter presents an integrated Catholic Christian Meta-Model of the Person (CCMMP). The Meta-Model is a framework that explicitly employs major theological and philosophical premises (foundational principles) and briefly identifies the basic corresponding psychological premises. The Meta-Model proposes a view that is informed by Christian faith and by reason and the psychological sciences. The text outlines and organizes the distinctive qualities of complex human nature and the dynamic human person. The intention is to produce a richer and truer understanding of the person for the mental health field, one that will enhance theory, research, and practice. How it does this is addressed in the chapters that follow. This chapter also provides a specific, synthetic, Christian definition of the person using theological, philosophical, and psychological perspectives for a deep understanding of the person.

We start with a three-part definition of the person that informs the integrated project presented in this volume. This definition is derived from theological, philosophical, and psychological premises that are introduced in this chapter and are developed throughout the entire book.

The Catholic Christian Meta-Model's Definition of the Person

From a theological perspective (Scripture, tradition, and the Magisterium), the human person is created in the image of God and made by and for divine and human love, and—although suffering the effects of original, personal, and social sin—is invited to divine redemption in Christ Jesus, sanctification through the Holy Spirit, and beatitude with God the Father.

From a philosophical perspective, the human person is an individual substance of a rational (intellectual), volitional (free), relational (interpersonal), sensory-perceptual-cognitive (pre-rational knowledge), emotional, and unified (body-soul) nature; the person is called to flourishing, moral responsibility, and virtue through his or her vowed or non-vowed vocational state, as well as through life work, service, and meaningful leisure.

From a psychological perspective, the human person is an embodied individual who is intelligent, uses language, and exercises limited free-will. The person is fundamentally interpersonal, experiences and expresses emotions, and has sensory-perceptual-cognitive capacities to be in contact with reality. All of these characteristics are possible because of the unity of the body and unique self-consciousness, and are expressed in behavior and mental life. Furthermore the person is called by human nature to flourishing through virtuous behavior and transcendent growth; through interpersonal commitments to family, friends, and others; and through work, service, and meaningful leisure. From their origins (natural and transcendent), all persons have intrinsic goodness, dignity, and worth. In the course of life, though suffering from many natural, personal, and social disorders and conditions, persons hope for healing, meaning, and flourishing.

Part I of this volume (this chapter and the prior chapter) gives a foundational introduction to the CCMMP. The remaining parts of the volume provide systematic support for the Meta-Model: Part II, psychological theory and research; Part III, philosophical rationale; Part IV, theological support; and, finally, Part V, theoretical and practical applications of the Meta-Model in mental health practice.

[A] *A Theological Vision of the Person* that is based on Christian faith and tradition (the teaching of the Bible and the Catholic Magisterium) and accords with a tripartite ordering of salvation history.

The Person Is . . .

I. CREATED

Humans are created by God "in the image" and "after the likeness" of God (Gen 1:26); "in the image of God he created them; male and female he created them" (Gen 1:27).

1. *Goodness and dignity.* They are good (as is everything created by God) and have special, intrinsic dignity and value as persons (Gen 1:31).

2. *Gift of love.* Their lives (and every good thing) are ultimately a gift of love that has been given and is continually sustained by God (Jas 1:17). In turn, acceptance of the gift, gratitude, worship, service, and self-gift (love of God and of others as oneself) are appropriate responses to the original gift.

3. *Unity of person.* Human persons are created as a unified whole, constituted of a material body and a spiritual soul (Gen 2:7).

4. *Communion with God.* By knowledge and by love, humans are created as persons to enter into communion with God (Jn 17:26), who is a knowing and loving communion—a Trinity of Persons.

5. *Communion with others.* They are created to enter into communion and friendship also with other persons. In the beginning, Adam experienced loneliness in original solitude, which was overcome by an original unity when God created Eve to be Adam's wife, "a helper fit for him," and "the mother of all the living" (Gen 2:18–20). The nuptial meaning of the body (its basic structure to receive and give, to know and love) informs all vocations to married and celibate life. Being created in the image of God is the basis for all vocations.

6. *Flourishing.* Human persons are called to flourishing, that is, perfection and holiness, through the interpersonal accepting and giving of love: "be perfect, as your heavenly Father is perfect" (Mt 5:48). Although perfect flourishing is reserved for heaven, human persons are called at present to flourish in the integrity of the individual (psychological, moral, and spiritual level), as well as in the integrity of relationships with God and neighbor (including the distinct relationships related to one's vocational state in life and the application of the virtues needed for that state).

7. *Divine order and natural law.* Creation is marked by a divine order that humans can know in terms of the divine law (e.g., the Decalogue, Ex 20:1–17) and the natural moral law (which is the human rational participation in the eternal law; see Rom 2:14). Divine law and natural law are made concrete in the Christian life. Even the happiness of the non-believer is dependent on living in accord with natural law.

II. FALLEN

Because of the sin of Adam and Eve, the divine likeness in mankind is wounded and disfigured (Gen 3:16–19).

1. *Disorder and trials.* Experiences of sin, weakness, decay, death, and disorder constitute the difficulties and trials experienced in human temporal life (1 Pet 1:6).

2. *Consequences of sin.* Original sin and the consequences of every personal and social sin pit mankind against God, each human person against himself, person against person, and mankind against nature (Ps 78:19).

3. *Goodness is foundational and evil is not.* The tendency toward evil is a disordering of inclinations that are themselves basically good. While the wounds of evil are not foundational, the enduring goodness of God's creation is: "where sin increased, grace abounded all the more" (Rom 5:20).

4. *Our struggle with evil.* Evil and sin put human flourishing in peril. Evil is a disordering and privation of what should be, according to human nature created in the image of God: emotions (hatred), thoughts (lies), choices (harming self or others), commitments (adultery instead of fidelity), or development (failures to develop one's human capacities or to fulfill other responsibilities). Evil opposes God through disobedience to the law of love, through demonic obsessions, and through spiritual opposition, for example. In the context of struggles with evil and the restlessness that results from sin, God offers redemption and can make all things work for the good (Rom 8:28).

III. REDEEMED

In Jesus Christ's incarnation, God gives a new dignity to human nature and, through Christ's death and resurrection, redeems mankind, calling each person to communion with God and neighbor and to interior healing and growth (Titus 2:14).

1. *Eternal happiness and beatitude.* Human persons are called to the communion with God that is fully granted only through divine assistance in the loving presence and beatific vision of God in the life to come. However, this communion is already received, as a foretaste, in this life, through the gifts of faith, hope, and love (the theological virtues) and through the flourishing experienced in our vocations (1 Jn 3:2; Mt 5:8).

2. *Faith.* Through faith in God and union with Jesus Christ in Baptism, every human person is invited to become God's son or daughter (Gal 4:5; 1 Jn 3:1) and to receive the Gift of the Holy Spirit (Acts 2:38; Jn 14:26). They are called to partake in the redemptive work of evangelization and sanctification that Christ achieves through his Body the Church.

3. *Hope.* Sin, death, and disorder are definitively overcome by Jesus' redemption (1 Cor 15:54–55). Moreover, the suffering caused by their effects can be turned to salvific purposes (Rom 5:3). Supported by hope and spiritual sacrifice in the midst of suffering (1 Pet 2:5; Rom 12:1), human persons participate in overcoming the effects of sin through the redemptive work of Christ, who has promised the guidance of the Holy Spirit, eternal beatitude with God, the resurrection of the body, and the other promises of the Kingdom of God at the end of time (Rom 6:3–6; Mt 4:17).

4. ***Love.*** The whole law and the prophets depend on two commandments: to love God, "with your whole heart, with all your soul, and with all your mind … and to love your neighbor as yourself" (Mt 22:37–40; see also Deut 6:5; Lev 19:18; Mk 12:30; Lk 17:33). Jesus Christ makes mankind known to itself, making clear the supreme calling through his definitive gift of self, which is love (Vatican Council II, 1965, *Gaudium et spes* [GS] §22); having a likeness to God, man "cannot find himself except through a sincere gift of himself" (*GS* §24). Self-gift is rooted in communion and often involves a form of self-sacrifice.

5. ***Nature and grace.*** Human nature always remains weakened by sin (*concupiscence*—disordered emotions, weakness of reason and will) but can be assisted, and in certain ways healed and divinized, by divine grace (1 Thess 5:23). Persons can become holy through a life of faith, hope, and love as well as through the other infused virtues and the Gift of the Holy Spirit. They can become "participants in the divine nature" (2 Pet 1:4). All people are called to live a morally good life and are offered divine assistance to do good.

6. ***Vocation.*** A vocation is often understood as a religious phenomenon, in which people respond to a "calling" from God to fulfill a spiritual function or life work. From a Christian perspective, vocations or callings take three basic forms: (a) a person's call to relationship with God—through a pursuit of holiness; (b) a person's committed state in life—single, married, ordained, or religious; and (c) a person's work and service—through paid work, volunteer efforts, and everyday service within families and among friends. They are all forms of self-gift and are all graced transformations of human capacities. (On the philosophical underpinning of vocations, see Premise V.1–4, this chapter.)

7. ***Vocation to holiness.*** The common vocation to holiness is based upon the call in this world to love God and neighbor as oneself, and to live a life of good works, which God prepared beforehand for each person (Lk 10:27; 1 Thess 4:3; Eph 2:10). God gives to each a personal vocation: the unique and unrepeatable role God calls each person to play in carrying out the divine plan (2 Tim 1:9; Vatican Council II, 1964, *Lumen gentium* [LG] §39).

8. ***Vocational States.*** All people start life as single and may continue their lives as single in love and service to God and neighbor. In general, being a member of a family is the first vocational state, and it is within the family that receiving and giving of love are taught. There are also committed

vocations to a state in life, that is, vocations to commit oneself to be married, ordained, or consecrated (religious). All these states involve collaboration in God's work of sanctifying oneself and other people (1 Pet 5:1–4; LG §41–43).

9. **Work and service.** Through a third level of vocation, human persons engage in work and service, paid or not, and this serves their personal flourishing and sanctification, while contributing to the good of the family, of other persons, and of the world (Gen 2:15; Mt 25:20). It is through such work that one can exercise the divine command to reach beyond one's friends and family to love one's neighbor, to welcome the stranger, to exercise justice for the poor, and to do good to one's enemy.

10. **Prayer and sacraments.** Each person is called to communion with God through prayer. Religious practices of prayer unite individuals to community and to God. Because of the importance of the whole person, worship involves the body (through silence and song, standing and kneeling, eating and drinking) and relationship (through greetings and signs of peace, through blessings and communal responses). In this way, our body participates in and even knows the faith. God offers not only eternal salvation but also temporal support, healing, and guidance through the sacraments, which are available to Christian believers. Starting with Baptism, the sacraments are the seven efficacious signs of divine grace, instituted by Jesus Christ, offered through the work of the Holy Spirit, and entrusted to the Church (2 Cor 5:17; Lk 22:19–20; *Catechism of the Catholic Church* [CCC], 2000, §1210). God's grace is not limited to the sacraments though, for it enables the baptism of desire, which through God's justice and mercy is offered even to unbelievers.

This Christian theological vision of the person (outlined through the premises in sections A.I–III) refers to an ontological, existential, and teleological reality for all temporal human life. The following section addresses metaphysical or ontological, epistemological, and ethical issues in a synthetic approach to the person that is grounded in human experience and reason and that comes from a perspective of Christian philosophy.

[B] *A Christian Philosophical Vision of the Person* that is based on human experience, reason, and Christian philosophical tradition in dialogue with the sciences and other forms of knowledge.

The Person Is ...

IV. A PERSONAL UNITY

The spiritual soul, created by God, is the animating principle and substantial form of the living human body (Ps 139:13; CCC §§362–68). Because of their body-soul unity, all humans have the capacity for a distinctively human personal consciousness, as different from merely animal consciousness.

1. *Human dignity*. Every living human being has basic dignity and a complete human soul, including human intellectual powers, even if a person is permanently or temporarily not able to express them because of disorders or lack of development (Gen 1:31; GS §§14–15).

2. *Body-soul unity as gift of life*. A human person is a complete, wholly unified, living being constituted of a material body and an immaterial, incorruptible, and immortal soul. The body-soul unity constitutes the gift of life that is always dependent on God. Since the person's spiritual intellect subsists in a body, without being reduced to the bodily aspect per se, a person's soul survives the body's death. The human soul is so deeply united to the body that it is considered the substantial form of the body (Gen 1 & 2; GS §14; CCC §§364–365). The deepest aspect of the person is sometimes called the *soul*, the *spirit*, the *heart*, or the *mind* (Mt 22:37–40; Lk 10:27; Mk 12:30; Deut 6:5).

3. *Either male or female*. Males and females are complementary embodiments of human nature. Sex differences are not mere social conventions. While equal in dignity and worth, and while bearing many characteristics in common, male and female persons are not identical at the levels of the physical body or at the level of mental and emotional life. Their complementarity has a nuptial significance, which is revealed and actualized through a *disinterested gift of self*, typified not only in marital sexual love

but also in celibate forms of self-giving and service to others. Sex differences reach beyond the marital relationship and the home, inasmuch as there are masculine and feminine characteristics that influence behavior in society (Eph 5:28–33).

4. *Natural law and the personalist norm.* The natural (moral) law grounds professional ethics—such as the principles of conscience and responsibility, respect for individual freedom, doing no harm, beneficence, and respect for a person's basic dignity regardless of differences. It also grounds the additional demands of Christian ethics by rooting them in the natural inclinations—such as seeking good and avoiding evil, or loving God and neighbor—which lead to both social justice and worship of God. As expressed in the personalist norm, the person is a self-possessing subject with distinct personal ends and should not be used instrumentally as a mere object or as a mere means to someone else's ends (Mt 7:12). From a philosophical perspective and an experiential basis, natural law is a human, rational participation in the normative dimension of reality, which directs humans to their final end of flourishing through a law written in their inner being. However, it can be difficult to discern the ordering of the natural inclinations and the related principles of the natural law, or the best way to apply them in everyday settings. From a faith-based perspective, natural law is a rational participation in the wisdom and love of God's eternal law (Rom 1:19–20, 2:14–15). Its divine origin is confirmed and its content clarified in divine revelation, for example in the two tablets of the Decalogue, that is, in love of God and love of neighbor as self (Ex 20:1–17; Lev 19:18; Mt 22: 38–39; Rom 13:9). However, sinfulness and the other effects of the fall often hinder knowledge and awareness of the principles of natural moral law and their application.

5. *Multiple capacities.* Animate human nature includes multiple capacities at the organic (vegetative and motoric), cognitive (sensation-perception and reason or rational intellect), and affective (emotion and will or volitional intellect) levels of the person (Lk 10:27).

6. *Organic living beings.* Humans are capable of bodily health and flourishing. They possess a natural inclination to preserve and promote their bodily well-being. Bodily health (at its different levels) is known to influence, without being equated to, overall personal flourishing (Ps 16:9).

7. *Behaviors and actions.* Persons express themselves through behavior and are moved in response to cognitions (pre-rational, intellectual, and intuitive), and affections (emotional, intellectual, and intuitive) regarding things to be sought and avoided (2 Tim 4:7).

8. ***Culturally, historically, and ecologically located.*** Human beings are situated in history and culture. They shape and are shaped, but not totally determined, by their sociocultural and physical environment (Gal 4:4; Lk 2:1–2).

9. ***Wholeness.*** A unified notion of the whole person includes a transcendent and personal dimension and recognizes that flourishing (through virtue and vocation) requires an interconnection between the five domains: relationality, sensory-perception (including imagination), emotion, reason, and will (Prov 20:7). This view of wholeness also avoids distorted understandings of the person that develop as a result of individualist, materialistic, reductionist, relativist, determinist, dualist, or behaviorist conceptualizations. All of the identified capacities and qualities of the person work together in a holistic way in the healthy person. To understand and serve persons requires keeping in mind their integrated wholeness.

V. FULFILLED THROUGH VOCATION

Human flourishing also involves a teleological (purposeful) development through three levels of vocation: (a) distinct responses to the call to personal goodness and holiness, (b) different vowed and non-vowed vocational states, and (c) work and service.

1. ***Calling or vocation.*** In the strict sense, "vocation" means the personal response to the call of goodness and truth that characterizes a person's life globally, but especially through the personal development of the *gift of self.* The basic notion of a calling comes from a source: from the world, a person, or God that attracts as intrinsically good. For example, people report being attracted to a *soul mate*, committing themselves in marriage, and, thus, finding their true calling. The callings are perfective of the human person (Deut 6:18; Mt 19:16–21). (For an explicitly theological treatment of these callings or vocations, see Premise III.6–9, this chapter.)

2. ***Calling to goodness.*** Through a first type of calling or vocation, each person is attracted to and perfected through existence (being), truth (knowledge), goodness (love), relationship (family, friends, and society), and beauty (integrity, ordering, and clarity). Such goods underlie human experiences of the world, which is, nonetheless, a place not only of wonder and good, but also of fatigue and evil. A fitting human response requires, first, affirming the goodness and beauty that one finds and, then, contributing to the goodness through choices, before experiencing some sense of flourishing in the act. For example, one can choose to be compassionate instead of cruel, to defend the weak instead of taking advantage of their plight, to help families in need, and to enrich human culture.

Such responses to the many faces of goodness contribute to one's both everyday and ultimate flourishing (Mt 5:2–12).

3. *Calling to committed vocational states.* Through a second type of calling, a human being responds to natural and transcendent desires to enter into committed vocational states: (a) to commit oneself to a husband or a wife in order to form a family through the marriage bond; (b) to commit oneself to ultimate goodness in service of God and others through ordained or religious commitments; as well as (c) to seek, in integrity of life, to contribute one's intelligence, goodwill, and resources to others and society as a single person (Gen 2; Eph 5).

4. *Calling to work, service, and meaningful leisure.* Through a third type of calling, a person engages in the diverse kinds of work and service that one must do in order to flourish personally and to contribute to the well-being of other members of one's family, community, and society. For example, people report being attracted to the beauty, purposefulness, and useful nature of work with wood, and commit themselves to learn and practice carpentry in an honest manner, creating goods for others, and, thus, finding meaning in their call to work and service (Gen 2:15; Mt 25:20). Work has great value in itself, but non-work does as well. There is the call to types of leisure, that is, to the meaningful non-work that allows not only rest, exercise, and self-care, but also family, interpersonal relationships, and cultural activities, as well as contemplation of truth and beauty, and finally participation in the worship of God and the life of the Church (Ps 46:10).

VI. FULFILLED IN VIRTUE

Human flourishing involves a teleological (purposeful) development of the person's capacities and relationships, through virtue, vocation, and related practices that aim at the good life. By contrast, much of human languishing and suffering results from experiences of trauma, misdirected choices, unsuitable practices, or damaged relationships, which may often be outside of the person's full responsibility.

1. *Inclined toward flourishing and God.* From a Christian philosophical perspective, every human person, from the first moment of existence, has a capacity to grow toward temporal well-being, moral goodness, and ultimate flourishing. This teleological movement shapes human life from conception until death. The human person has a natural capacity to know that there is an ultimate source and purpose of human life (the creator God); in this way, humans express a natural desire for God (Mt 5:8; Acts 17:27; GS §19).

2. *Natural inclinations.* Human capacities express basic positive inclinations toward existence (being), truth (knowledge), goodness (love), relationship (family, friends, and society), and beauty (integrity, ordering, and clarity). These natural inclinations are the seeds of the natural human virtues, callings, and flourishing. They are also a basis for recognizing the natural law as a rational participation in eternal law (Rom 1 & 2).

3. *Development over time.* The person comes into existence when his or her living body-soul unity comes into existence at conception. The unfolding of the multiple capacities of human nature is subject to development over time through biological growth as well as through family and social experiences, which prepare for growth understood in terms of virtues and vocations. This mature development is manifest in relationships, especially marriage and family, friends and community, work and service, and religion. Through this moral and spiritual development, the person seeks to overcome a divided heart, social discord, and religious indifference (1 Cor 13:11).

4. *Health and illness.* Health can be conceived in terms of integral human development. It is a function of the expression, at the proper time and to the proper degree, of bodily, psychological, and spiritual capacities. Illness is a function of some privation or deterioration of the proper fulfillment of one or more of these three capacities (Ps 1:3).

5. *Virtues.* Virtues are distinguished by the capacities that they perfect and the ends that they attain. For example, the moral virtue of prudence perfects the human inclination to act in the light of truth and the intellectual capacity to attain reasonable goals through fitting action, as when a mother and father take counsel, make decisions, and act concretely in order to raise their children to be honest and caring. The nature of the person demands that virtues be expansive and interconnected, for example, that prudence also be loving (1 Cor 13:1–3) and that the criteria for justice and mercy be met together.

6. *Types of virtue.* Virtues perfect human capacities, as they aim at full flourishing. They are differentiated in three major types. First, theological virtues (faith, hope, and charity or love) are divine gifts that also influence the other virtues (see Premise III.2–4, this chapter), for example, as when theological hope encourages a person's confidence in daily activities. Second, the natural virtues are acquired. These virtues are called cardinal virtues (prudence, justice, courage, and temperance or self-control), which draw together related virtues or character strengths, such as patience and perseverance. Third, the intellectual virtues are theoretical (wisdom, un-

derstanding, and knowledge or science) or practical (art and practical wisdom).

7. ***Connection of the virtues through practices.*** The basic virtues, associated virtues, and practices create the interconnected paths of intellectual, moral, and spiritual development. The virtues are known best in performance. For example, the natural virtue of courage (a basic or cardinal virtue), along with the natural virtues of hope and perseverance (two of its associated virtues) must be formed through particular practices, such as when a person is being trained to experience hope, to practice self control, and to show courage and perseverance when confronted with emergency situations. While each of the virtues primarily perfect one of the human capacities (listed later, in the chapter on virtue), they interrelate in a dynamic connection of intellectual, moral, and theological strengths (1 Cor 13:13; Gal 5:22–26).

8. ***Moral disorder and evil.*** Often people make evil choices as if they were good, because of prior distorted interpretations and actions (defensive interpretations, denials of compromise, rationalization of ideologies, etc.). Because of moral disorders at personal and social levels, humans tend to inordinately seek pleasure, power, and recognition. Distorted emotions, cognitions, or volitions impede flourishing—as when fear results in the failure to act rightly, or when anger blocks true love and justice (Gal 5:19–21).

9. ***Vice.*** The Christian tradition identifies pride as the root of all sin, and the seven capital sins or deadly vices as vanity, envy, hatred (and wrath), sloth, greed, gluttony, and lust. In the face of moral evil and vice, human beings are in need not only of development, but also of healing, forgiveness, and reconciliation at personal, interpersonal, and religious levels (Lk 15; Mt 1:21).

10. ***Prevention.*** Integral human development in virtue helps to prevent and overcome inadequacies in moral judgment such as relativism (the denial of objective truth), emotivism (the construal of ethical judgments as mere expressions of positive or negative emotions about a thing), subjectivism (the affirmation that one's own perception or knowledge is necessarily correct), consequentialism (the determination of goodness by an act's consequences alone, and the denial that any acts are intrinsically evil), and materialism (the reduction of the person to biological determinants, such as genetic and neural processes).

Although the human body and spiritual soul are naturally inseparable and purposeful and always in relationship with other persons, for the sake of analysis we distinguish the following structures or capacities of human nature, which are available to each person in the search for purpose and flourishing.

VII. INTERPERSONALLY RELATIONAL

Humans are naturally social, with inclinations and needs for family, friendship, life in society, and other interpersonal relationships.

1. ***Receptive and interpersonal.*** Human persons are intrinsically receptive and oriented toward other persons. This orientation is expressed through communicative acts of receiving and giving. Furthermore, social acts serve personal flourishing only inasmuch as they serve the good of other persons and the common good (1 Jn 3:17–18).

2. ***Centered in love.*** The highest expression of interpersonal communication is the self-giving love that is also known as the virtue of charity (*philia* and *agapē*). While having a unity of purpose, love takes different forms depending on the type of interpersonal relationship at hand. It informs and interconnects all the other virtues, while being served by them as well, especially the virtues that concern relationships, such as justice, religion, chastity, courage, and obedience (1 Jn 4:8) (see Premise XI.3, on the "Types of human love").

3. ***Relationship with God.*** Humans have a natural desire to know, love, and be united with God, who is not only the creator (first cause) and sustainer (efficient cause) of human life, but also its ultimate end (final cause). It is therefore fitting that human persons enter into religious practices (such as prayer, rituals, scriptural readings and sacraments, and other expressions of faith, hope, and love) in order to worship, respect, and love God (Jn 1:12–13).

4. ***Spousal relationships and the spousal meaning of the body.*** The natural institution of marriage is built upon the spousal complementarity of the sexes and an attraction to the opposite sex (see Premise IV.3, "Either male or female"). This type of marriage involves a lifelong covenantal commitment and gift of self (union). This love is formalized in monogamous marriage that is open to the gift of new life (procreation) and committed to the goods of family, including the holiness of spouses. In the sacrament of marriage, God provides graces for the spouses to face the challenges of intimacy, fidelity, and family. In response to a call to holiness, some persons commit themselves to celibate spousal relationships with God to love and serve God and his people (Gen 2:18–24).

5. *Family.* Interpersonal relationality is first developed in the family, which is the basic unit of society. Humans have both a natural need for family and natural inclinations to establish families, that is, inclinations toward the goods of marriage and the procreation and education of children (Lk 2:51). All families, regardless of structure, deserve support, including assistance for the difficulties that they face.

6. *Friends.* Human friendship contributes to human fulfillment. It underlies the relationships of affection, companionship, and intimacy that are grounded on a mutual gift of self and a common sharing of the good, in ways other than through sexual love (Jn 15:15).

7. *Communities.* Humans are situated in a community of persons, expressed in sociocultural, civic political, and faith based contexts, all of which shape persons but do not totally determine them. Humans contribute to community by working and expressing responsibility for others. Friendship serves as the bonding force for community (Eph 4:4–13; Ps 122:1–2).

VIII. SENSORY-PERCEPTUAL-COGNITIVE

Each human exercises pre-rational sensory-perceptual-cognitive capacities as a body-soul unity. These pre-rational capacities serve as important foundations for the rational human linguistic, interpersonal, and moral dimensions, and the higher cognitive capacities so central to the unique character of human life.

1. *Receptive to the external world.* The human person receives and seeks basic knowledge of other people, the world, and oneself through instincts, primary senses, and higher-order perceptions and pre-rational and rational cognitions.

   a. The bio-physiological bases for knowledge include instincts, such as visual, tactile, and survival instincts, as well as intrinsic curiosity. In this Meta-Model, these characteristics serve the natural inclinations for goodness and relationship that aim at flourishing.

   b. The five primary senses and their organs or systems provide unique contact with the perceivable world and reality. They are biologically based means of gathering particular information and interpreting stimuli.

   c. Higher-order perceptions and pre-rational cognitions process instincts and the primary senses. The higher-order internal perceptions, along with the simpler sensory perception experience, provide the human person a means to be receptive to objects, persons, and meaning. The higher-order pre-rational perceptions and cognitions are, however, distinct from and yet contribute to still higher order rational cognition.

2. *The five primary senses.* Traditionally called "external senses," the five primary senses are identified as vision, hearing, smell, taste, and touch. Each of these senses gathers particular information, and together they serve the larger, unique, and active experience of people.

a. *Vision* is the most abstract of these senses. It is prized for the information that it gives of sources of life and danger, and, at higher levels, it is instrumental in the communication of meaning and beauty.

b. *Hearing* adds a greater experience of external reality, especially through its basic role in communication, which it serves, at higher levels, in spoken language and music.

c. The sense of *smell* is a capacity that provides distinct smell of objects and various means for self-preservation (e.g., fire and food) and, at a higher level, it serves the knowledge and memory of others (e.g., scent of cookies and memory of Grandma).

d. The sense of *taste* is useful in determining whether food is good or spoiled. Its pleasure incites people to one of the most necessary human activities, namely, eating, and at a higher level it is an integral part of ritual and celebration.

e. *Touch* and *pain* involve generalized tactile and pain systems. Touch provides the most concrete type of sensory contact with other people and the world. And at a higher level, it mediates the connection and attachment with other people that is necessary for life and flourishing. Pain has great relevance for knowledge of limits and physical survival.

Science provides a rich understanding of the working of these primary senses, their organs, and the neurological systems through which they function. It has also provided further knowledge of related or complementary sensory perceptions and processes, such as the perception of balance and motion, known as the vestibular sense. There is, in addition, a proprioceptive-kinesthetic sensory perception, which gives us an understanding of our body's movement and position and is especially operative in dance and music.

3. *Higher-order perceptions and pre-rational cognitions.* There are, of course, higher levels of knowledge based on the information of sensory-perceptual-cognitive input. Classical realist philosophical sources recognize examples of higher-order, pre-rational types of knowledge or cognition: the synthetic perception of embodied identity, memory,

imagination, and the evaluative sense. In this realist approach, these systems have been called the *internal senses* or *passive intellect*, because they passively receive sense data about particular things and form perceptual judgments that influence sensory affect (emotional reactions) and active intellectual rational and affective processes (e.g., intuition, abstraction, intention, reasoning, and choice).

a. *Synthetic capacity.* There is the *synthetic perception of identity* or wholeness, that is, the capacity to know oneself, another person, or a thing as a single object of different primary senses, for example, the sight of hair, sound of crying, smell of dampness, and feeling of pressure on your leg all belong to one thing, namely, your child. There is also a related proprioceptive (or kinesthetic) perception of feeling whole and having a sense of the position of one's whole body in space.

b. *Memory capacity.* There are pre-rational and rational types of *memory.* There are memories based on time, such as immediate, short-term, and long-term memories. There are memories of a different kind, such as episodic memory (autobiographical details) and semantic memory (factual memory). There are also emotional memory (memory of fear based on earlier experiences) and "muscle" memory (memory of how to perform certain acts).

c. *Imaginative Capacity. Imagination* is the capacity to employ particular images in spontaneous or rational and willfully evoked (negative or positive) ways, for example, in the experience of dreaming, in planning for one's wedding, in the creative flow of a jazz musician, and in a soldier's reaction, evoked by a past trauma, to a loud noise.

d. *Evaluative capacity.* There is also an *evaluative capacity,* that is, the attractions and repulsions that draw on instinctual reactions, memory of related experiences, and past thoughts and choices, in order to make a type of pre-discursive or pre- rational judgment about what is sensed. This has also been called "gut sense" or "a gut feeling." This sense is also called "particular reason," by philosophers, because it involves the recognition of the meaning of particular things, such as, the immediate reaction to a baby's smile.

4. ***Cognitive habitual dispositions.*** The plasticity of these perceptual and cognitive capacities allows the development of habitual dispositions, which include memory and the evaluative capacity. The cognitive habitual dispositions activate, organize, and extend the higher-order perceptions and cognitions mentioned above. In particular, sensory-perceptual-

cognitive knowledge is solidified through activity, that is, through behavior that uses sensory-perceptual cognition. This type of disposition formation requires the activation of response systems, as referred to by the ideas of "muscle memory," "practice makes perfect," and "neurons that fire together wire together."

5. ***Basis for active knowledge.*** From a realist perspective, there is a unity and distinction in the types of human knowledge. Human knowledge is rooted in the unity of reality's intelligible order. There are, however, distinct types of knowledge. For example, there are the hierarchically ascending types of sensation, perception, and cognition, which ground still higher mental capacities and action:

> a. *primary sensation* (e.g., the visual cortex's recognition of the contrast of black and white, and of the form of an "A");
>
> b. *higher-order perception* (recognition of "A" as a letter in the alphabet);
>
> c. *rational cognition* (reasoning about the meaning of "A" in the context of a narrative, as in *The Scarlet Letter,* where "A" was used as a sign to identify a person as an adulterer);
>
> d. *spiritual intuition* (understanding of a need for personal forgiveness and interpersonal reconciliation in cases of adultery); and
>
> e. *practical action* (practical commitment to forgive and to work toward reconciliation in such situations, and to "go, and do not sin again" [Jn 8: 11]).

The more complex and active types of reason are not epiphenomena of the higher-level pre-rational capacities that are of concern here. The higher forms of reason are considered nonmaterial and qualitatively distinct from these lower capacities, as discussed in Chapter 15, on the person as "Rational."

6. ***Active encounter with the world and its conditions.*** Through reflection on sensory perceptions and cognitions, persons gain knowledge of objects to study. Moreover, such perceptions are a basis for the process of metaphysical discovery of the un-sensed conditions or causes of existence, goodness, truth, interpersonal relationality, and beauty. That is, they provide a basis for further rational reflection, and they are needed to know the world and to encounter others, oneself, and God (Rom 1:20).

IX. EMOTIONAL

Human emotional capacities (sensory affect) are significant for personal self-understanding, interpersonal relations, moral action, and spiritual life. Humans are emotional in a unique and personal way because of their body-soul spiritual unity. There are other differences in the emotional life of humans, differences that reflect their being created as man or woman, that are based on biological predispositions, and that are rooted in experience.

1. ***Emotionally aware.*** In response not only to sensations and perceptions, but also to rational intentions and commitments, humans experience emotional appraisals (initial reactions and responses) and can become aware of their emotions. The emotions are a passageway between the sensations and conscious thought, and they influence both. Although a person is often not initially responsible for the first movements of emotion (such as joy at seeing a friend, anger at being hurt, or sadness at the loss of a loved one), humans can develop enduring emotional dispositions or ways of regulating emotions. On the one hand, emotions can impair the free exercise of reason or will, and emotional dispositions can be harmful and even pathological. Addressing harmful and pathological emotions is an important part of psychotherapy. On the other hand, emotions can be useful and even necessary indicators of personal goods, and important aids in understanding the world and acting morally. For example, sorrow can aid one in becoming contrite, fear can make one attentive to danger, and so on. Furthermore, emotions can be ordered in accord with reason and vocations, and with the flourishing of the person and others.

2. ***Emotions are inherently good.*** Emotional capacities are inherently good. Nonetheless, particular emotions can strengthen or can harm a person—they can aid in flourishing or lead to languishing. In terms of morality, depending on the way they relate to love, reason, choice, truth, and flourishing of self and others, emotions can become good or evil. They are a basic human capacity that opens a way to understand other people, the world, and oneself. There are two types of emotion. First, there are sensory-perceptual, pre-rational judgments or automatic reactions (first movements). These emotions are neither good nor evil. Second, there are the emotions that are attributable to the effects of rational choices (volitional stimuli), social interactions, and spiritual conditions, or reactions to other emotions (second movements). These emotions (at the level of action and disposition) can become good or evil, that is, they can lead to flourishing or languishing through choices. There are different sensory-perceptual-cognitive affects (as distinct from the will), including

emotions or feelings, moods, sentiments, and temperaments. They are rooted in the biopsychosocial and spiritual experience of the person.

3. **Emotions influence intellectual and spiritual capacities.** Emotions have an influence on intellectual and spiritual capacities either positively and negatively; for example, positively when righteous anger aids one to act justly, or negatively when a strong reaction of anger in the face of an injustice blinds a person to his rational and charitable commitments and prevents him from seeing the person who committed the injustice and the conditions that may have made the injustice less than fully voluntary.

4. **Intellectual and spiritual capacities influence emotions.** Emotions are influenced by intellectual judgments and spiritual commitments. Emotions are created or refined, for example, when a reasonable decision to right a wrong gives rise to righteous anger, which motivates the person to be attentive to the injustice, to face opposition courageously, and to persevere to the end (Mk 7:11).

5. **Social influence on emotions.** Emotions have an interpersonal and cultural context. Emotions are influenced by other people and by groups, both in the present and from early experience. For example, a person's emotional life is influenced by experiences with spouses, parents, family, friends, colleagues, political settings, and religious communities, and, of course, in our model, by grace. Furthermore, an individual does not only depend upon the emotional balancing that comes through social networks, an individual also aids others to regulate their commitments and choices. This two-way street of regulating emotions requires that individuals and groups seek to understand emotion and to employ it for the good of themselves and others.

6. **Emotion-based virtues.** A person may develop habitual dispositions (virtues) that help to regulate emotions in seeking the good. Distinctions are made among the other virtues, that is, cognitive-based (practical reason) and will-based (hope, charity, and justice) virtues. The primarily emotion-based virtues aim at integrating the person by using reason, will, and interpersonal commitments. Recognition of the plasticity of emotions, of their capacity to be involved in habitual dispositions and to be influenced by reason and will, underlies the conviction that emotional capacities can be formed into moral virtues. The characteristics of emotion outline the emotion-based virtues (e.g., as acts, as dispositions to act, as reasons to act, and in the transcendent dimension of acts). Emotion-based virtues include courage, patience, righteous anger, perseverance, hope, and self-control. Emotion-based vices include cowardice, impatience, destructive anger, indifference, despair, and indulgence (Jn 2:15 & 11:35).

7. *Significance of emotions in moral action.* Emotion is necessary but not sufficient for moral action. Well-regulated emotions, along with the contributions of reason, volition, and other people, are necessary for virtuous moral action. Emotions make one aware of important goods, values, and goals. They motivate one to attend to moral choices and to realize them. They contribute to development and healing by connecting basic essential capacities and by linking us interpersonally. They constitute a part of everyday flourishing and a foretaste of divine beatitude. Well-ordered emotions, moreover, serve as a contrast and corrective to tendencies toward vices, such as pride, greed, adultery, presumption, fearfulness, or impatience. Disordered emotions play different roles in immoral action or in blocking moral acts. They blind or distort one's vision of the truth of what is good, for example, through self-serving bias and rationalizations. They make concentrating on the purpose and fulfillment of virtuous moral action more difficult. They tend to distract a person from the moral and spiritual goals that form the call to goodness, life commitments, and work.

8. *Unity yet distinction of affect (emotion and will).* Human affect is understood in the philosophical tradition as involving both emotional affect and volitional affect. Sensory affect (emotion) is the type of attraction mediated by sensory-perceptual experience, for example, when we feel hope of attaining a distant and difficult good, such as the hope of finding a meal in the midst of a famine. Intellectual affect (will or volition) is the type of attraction mediated by reason, as when we choose a good means to a good end proposed by reason, such as a truly good and satisfying solution to a troubling family conflict. As sensate and intellectual capacities respectively, emotion and will express different dimensions of affect, for example, the distinction between love (as emotion) and charity (as willed). (This distinction is discussed further in Premise XI, on the human person as volitional and free.)

9. *Religious or spiritual emotion.* There is a special type of emotion found in spiritual emotion. Since the theological virtues, such as charity, are rooted in the whole person, religious emotion overflows from the transcendent life of grace. God's gift of grace informs and perfects nature, and, in this case, it informs the nature of emotions. People feel confident, encouraged, and attached in the midst of experiences of faith, hope, and charity for God, neighbor, and self. However, the volitional motivation and commitment of charity influences the emotion of love without being reduced to it. Charity does not always accompany feelings of tenderness or bonding, nor do tender feelings necessarily come with charity. Nonetheless, a firm commitment of charity helps to mediate both everyday and religious experiences of emotion.

X. RATIONAL

Human persons are intelligent and actively seek truth and freedom. In being rational, they have different levels and types of intelligence and knowledge. They express rationality in language, often in a narrative form.

1. **Rational inclinations.** Humans have rational inclinations to seek and know the truth and to find flourishing (Jn 8:31–32).

2. **Objects of knowledge.** Humans are capable of knowing (a) themselves, others, and God (Rom 1:19–20); (b) the created order (Ps 8:6–7); (c) truth, including divinely revealed truth (Lk 8:10); (d) the beauty of all creation and of God (Ps 8:1–2); and (e) good and evil, and that good is to be done and pursued and evil avoided (Jn 14:15).

3. **Sense and intellectual knowledge.** Human knowledge is sensory (including instinct), perceptual, cognitive, and intellectual, the last of which can be intuitive (e.g., insight), discursive (e.g., reasoning), and infused (or graced). Self-knowledge and knowledge of the world are supported by bottom-up and top-down influences, which can come even from sources that are originally non-conscious. Examples of non-conscious bottom-up influences are natural inclinations to family involving instincts (e.g., the sexual urge) and other non-conscious cognitive schemas and defenses concerning family life. Examples of non-conscious top-down influences are of two sorts. One involves the natural top-down influences such as the spiritual inclination to know the truth, which is made conscious, for example, in the intellectual intuitions about good and evil that ground moral decisions. The other involves top-down influences of grace, such as intuitions (e.g., about divine mercy that affect one's being merciful) and other movements of grace (e.g., inspiration that supports the giving of good counsel) (Lk 1:77–78).

4. **Types of belief.** Belief, in general, requires the witness of a trusted authority. It involves assent, choice, or judgment that first arises from cognitive (sensory-perception or thought) or affective (emotion or will) engagement with a trusted source. On the one hand, an everyday belief requires some intelligible object (e.g., a friend saying: "I am suffering") and an affirmation concerning the authority found in oneself or the other person (e.g., I have confidence in my friend). On the other hand, religious belief or faith is directly a gift of grace that entails that we ponder with assent God and his authority (and related intelligible objects, such as the propositions that Jesus of Nazareth is the Christ and head of his Body the Church, and that the human person is created in the image of God).

Religious faith is communicated indirectly through witnesses (e.g., Sacred Scripture and tradition) (2 Cor 5:7).

5. ***Self-knowledge and self-control.*** Through a realist knowledge of oneself and the world, human persons can knowingly choose to influence their emotions indirectly and their behavior directly. The aim of developing rational beliefs and virtues is to aid the person in making free choices that contribute to their flourishing (Eph 5:8–9).

6. ***Rational virtues and natural law.*** Rational inclinations can be further developed in knowledge, beliefs, and enduring dispositions of mind called intellectual virtues, at theoretical and practical levels (wisdom, understanding, and knowledge or science). On the moral side, right practical reason, concerning self and others, is manifested through the cardinal virtue of prudence and its associated virtues, which aid in discerning and counseling, adjudicating, and performing moral action. Moral norms guide human judgment (conscience) and action in accordance with good and away from evil. These norms are rooted in the natural law and divine law (Jn 14:26; Rom 2:15).

7. ***Beauty.*** Humans are aesthetic and seek beauty. They are drawn to the deeper levels of beauty, as found in beautiful persons, nature, actions, or things, through the classical properties of luminosity, harmony, and integrity. Beauty has these qualities, and they are expressed in culture, creation, and God. The experience of beauty also elicits a thirst to contemplate the ultimate source of beauty (Ps 27:4).

XI. VOLITIONAL AND FREE

Humans are the subject of moral action, capable of responsible volition and free choice.

1. ***Responsibility.*** To a large degree, human persons are capable of responsibility for their own actions concerning themselves and in regard to others (Jn 8:10–11).

2. ***Self-determination.*** They can act so as to shape their moral characters, that is, the enduring dispositions of their minds, wills, and affect (Rom 12:2).

3. ***Types of human love.*** They are capable of loving natural and divine goods and persons. Although exhibiting a basic common structure, human love is manifest distinctly in affection (*storgē*), friendship (*philia*), romance, courtship, and marriage (*eros*), and the virtue of charity (*agapē*), which can purify and rightly order all the other loves (1 Cor 13:4–13).

4. ***Creativity.*** Like God (by analogy), humans are able to conceive of and deliberately bring into existence things that once were not, although not from nothing, that is, not *ex nihilo* (Gen 2:15). For example, we find human creativity in the procreation of and caring for children, the making of art and literature, and the development of knowledge, science, and technology.

5. ***Limitation.*** There are two types of limitation. First, humans are naturally very limited in the number and quality of our interpersonal relations. Our bodies are quite limited, our rational capacities are prone to error, and our will is often weak. We are greatly limited in time. Second, we experience moral and spiritual limitations due to original, social, and personal sin (Rom 7:19).

6. ***Volitional inclinations.*** Human persons have natural volitional tendencies or inclinations to actualize diverse human goods and, through grace and faith, divine goods. Even in the midst of the challenges of negative influences of family, friends, and society, humans have a natural tendency toward virtues related to love and justice (Mt 6:19–21).

7. ***Capacity for growth in freedom.*** The human capacity for freedom can be developed in two ways. The *freedom for excellence* and flourishing involves growth in the human capacities to know truth and reality, to choose good, and to avoid evil, and ultimately to love God and neighbor. Freedom for excellence is intimately linked to truth and cannot be reduced simply to the second type of freedom, which involves attaining *freedom from* things that limit our human capacities, such as psychological disorders, or from outside influences (e.g., unjust laws, poverty). Freedom develops over time and, obviously, has certain limits. It requires both growth and healing as found in the intellectual and moral virtues, especially justice, self-control, courage, and forgiveness, as well as in the theological virtues, especially faith, hope, and charity. True freedom, therefore, is an expression of the whole person (Phil 4:8–9).

[C] *A Psychological Vision of the Person* that is consistent with the theological and philosophical premises of the Catholic Christian Meta-Model of the Person (CCMMP).

The following eleven psychological premises represent a psychological understanding of the person consistent with the theological and philosophical premises of the CCMMP and with the psychological sciences. They serve as an outline that will be augmented with sub-premises that further elucidate the Meta-Model's theoretical and clinical implications for psychology and counseling. Together with the CCMMP's theological and philosophical premises, they deepen and help fill out our understanding of the person, for use in mental health practice. (In parentheses is found the name of the corresponding theological and philosophical premise.)

I. The person has an essential core of goodness, dignity, and value and seeks flourishing of self and others. This dignity and value is independent of age or any ability. Such a core of goodness is foundational for a person to value life, develop morally, and to flourish. (Created)

II. The person commonly experiences types of pain, suffering, anxiety, depression, or other disorders in his or her human capacities and interpersonal relationships. The person is also distressed or injured by natural causes and by others' harmful behavior. People have varying levels of conscious and nonconscious distorted experience, which express that they do not respect and love themselves or others as they should. Moreover, they often do not live according to many of their basic values. (Fallen)

III. The person, with the help of others, can find support and healing, correct harmful behaviors, and find meaning through reason and transcendence, all of which bring about personal and interpersonal flourishing. In short, there is a basis for hoping for positive change in a person's life. (Redeemed)

IV. Each human being is a body-soul unified whole with a unique personal identity that develops over time in a sociocultural context. This unity pertains to the person's whole experience. For instance, physical abuse affects the person's bodily, psychological, and spiritual life. (A Personal Unity)

V. The person flourishes by discerning, responding to, and balancing three callings: (a) called as a person to live a value-guided life while focusing on love and transcendent goals; (b) called to live out vocational commitments to others, such as being single, married, or having a distinct religious calling; and (c) called to participate in socially meaningful work, service, and leisure. (Fulfilled Through Vocation)

VI. The person is fulfilled and serves others through the ongoing development of virtue strengths, moral character, and spiritual maturity, including growth in cognitive, volitional, emotional, and relational capacities. Through effort and practice, the person achieves virtues that allow the attainment of goals and flourishing. For example, a father or a mother who develops patience, justice, forgiveness, and hopefulness is better able to flourish as a parent. (Fulfilled in Virtue)

VII. The person is intrinsically interpersonal and formed throughout life by relationships, such as those experienced with family members, romantic partners, friends, co-workers and colleagues, communities, and society. (Interpersonally Relational)

VIII. The person is in sensory-perceptual-cognitive interaction with external reality and has the use of related capacities, such as imagination and memory. Such capacities underlie many of our skills, allowing us to recognize other people, communicate with them, set goals, heal memories, and appreciate beauty. (Sensory-Perceptual-Cognitive)

IX. The person has the capacity for emotion. Emotions, which involve feelings, sensory and physiological responses, and tendencies to respond (conscious or not), provide the person with knowledge of external reality, others, and self. The excess and deficit of certain emotions are important indicators of pathology, while emotional balance is commonly a sign of health. For example, when balanced, the human capacity for empathy can bring about healing for self and others, while a deficit or excess produces indifference or burnout. (Emotional)

X. The person has a rational capacity. This capacity involves reason, self-consciousness, language, and sophisticated cognitive capacities, expressing multiple types of intelligence. These rational capacities can be used to facilitate psychological healing and flourishing by seeking truth about self, others, the external world, and transcendent meaning. (Rational)

XI. The person has a will that is free, in important ways, and is an agent with moral responsibility when free will is exercised. For instance, the human being has the capacity to freely give or withhold forgiveness and to be altruistic or selfish. Increases in freedom from pathology and in freedom to pursue positive life goals and honor commitments are significant for healing and flourishing. (Volitional and Free)

Part II

Psychological Support

The Advantages That the Catholic Faith Provides for Development of an Integrated Meta-Model of the Person for Psychology and Mental Health Practice

Paul C. Vitz

ABSTRACT: This chapter identifies major reasons the present situation in the field of psychology is favorable to how a Christian understanding of the person can be meaningfully integrated with contemporary secular psychology and mental health practice. Present advantages include the marked decline of secular confidence that the future would be necessarily secular, along with the growth of religion in most of the world, including the United States, and the absence, over the last several decades, of new major psychological theories hostile to Christianity and the growth of psychological theory and practice compatible with Christianity, including Cognitive-Behavioral Therapy, positive psychology focused on the virtues, the acceptance of forgiveness as a factor in psychotherapy, psychology's changed and more positive attitude toward spirituality and religion. Another advantage for faith and psychology integration is the present existence of many Christian psychotherapists and the many Christians who now use mental health services; both groups desire such an integration. In addition, this chapter presents the special advantages provided by a Catholic understanding of psychology: the explicit, readily available official Catholic theology, the clear, official Catholic moral positions, the well-developed Catholic integration with major philosophical traditions and the many varied Catholic cultures that work against any capture by a particular culture.

Perhaps the most general major reason that the present time is a favorable one for the task of integrating a Christian understanding of the person with modern psychology is that the enthusiasm and confidence that the world's future, and especially that of America, would be secular has greatly declined; indeed in many respects it has disappeared. Younger psychologists may not be aware that the era of the 1940s, '50s, and '60s had an incredible secular confidence about what

This chapter is an expanded and revised version of a text that was originally published as "Christian and Catholic advantages for connecting psychology with the faith," P. C. Vitz, 2011, *Journal of Psychology and Christianity*, 30(4), 294–306.

the future would be like. At the time, the secular humanist scenario was assumed as inevitable, positive, and for the world, at least all the developed world. In liberal Protestantism, this was represented by writers like Harvey Cox (1965) and his thesis that the Church as an institution would disappear and Christians would become indistinguishable from positive change agents in the ongoing evolution of secular history. *Time Magazine* (April 8, 1966), catching this spirit, in the next year had its famous issue titled, "Is God Dead?" The secular humanist future was based on assumptions, derived from the Western Enlightenment, about the nature of truth—which was to be understood as part of "rational" Western philosophy—and of course on science. This view also assumed the intrinsic goodness of the secular vision and its development.

Since the 1960s a major critique of the Western secular future has come from the secular intellectuals now well known as Postmodernists (See Derrida, 1964, 1973, 1976, 1978; Foucault, 1970, 1972; Lyotard, 1984; Rorty, 1979, 1982, 1987). This movement has deconstructed the truth claims of much of Western Enlightenment secular thought, although not science itself. Postmodernists have also deconstructed the moral legitimacy of the previously unexamined secular philosophies—especially grand narratives such as the idea of progress. Although Postmodern thinkers are themselves secular, usually of a nihilistic type, their critique has greatly undermined the secular humanist assumption of its dominant future and an inevitable religion-less future.

The other major critique of and surprise for the secular vision has been the obvious growth and energy of religion around the world. Both for better and for worse, almost all major religions seem to be growing in their cultural and political significance. Christianity, especially in its Evangelical and Catholic expressions, is alive and well in this country and around the world (Jenkins, 2007). With the fall of Communism, Christianity has revived in Eastern Europe, and, most especially, Eastern Orthodoxy has revived in Russia. Meanwhile, both in the United States and in Israel, Orthodox Judaism has also revived. And of course, the starkest example of religious energy is probably that of Islam, with its explicit attack on secularism of the Western and especially European variety (Scruton, 2002). In short, Postmodern thought from within Western secularism, and the revival of religion outside and even within it, are the two needles that have popped the secular humanist bubble.

Another contributor helping to make the intellectual environment of psychology favorable to a Christian response to psychology has been the absence of any major new psychological theories of the person—especially theories critical of religion—for some thirty or forty years. When Freud, Jung, Adler, and others were proposing new theories of the person from 1900 to 1950, it would have been hard to address these usually critical interpretations from a Christian perspective: psychology was dynamic and growing—often in ways that could not be anticipated at that time. In the period of 1940 to 1970 or so, the humanistic and self psychologies were also being proposed and developed with great enthusiasm (see Rogers, 1961; and Maslow, 1970). With psychology being such a moving and often critical target, approaching it from a religious perspective would have been very difficult.

In the subsequent forty years, there have been important developments in psychology, but none as dramatically novel as the early theories and, above all, none that represent worldviews basically hostile to Christianity. Indeed, Christian therapists have readily integrated these more recent theories into their practice.

Cognitive-Behavioral Therapy (CBT) treated the human being as a relatively rational and free agent and dealt differently with the various specific mental problems that were brought into therapy. It was not a grand theory of the personality. In cognitive and behavioral psychology, the understanding of the person was not that different from the premodern emphasis on the conscious mind and reason. As a result, Christian psychotherapists, along with many others, have easily adapted to this kind of psychotherapy and have admired the useful theoretical and methodological innovations developed by its major founders, such as Aaron Beck (1979) and Albert Ellis (1962) while bracketing off their broader less-than-Christian-friendly worldviews. Albert Ellis was himself personally very hostile to religion, and he was often surprised at the enthusiasm and support his cognitive and behavioral approach received in Christian circles. Besides CBT, attachment theory (Cassidy & Shaver, 2018) has been a major, more recent contribution to psychology. This now well-established understanding initiated by John Bowlby (1969, 1973, and 1980) and first measured by his student Mary Ainsworth (1978) focuses on the mother-child attachment bond and identifies its importance for the later healthy mental functioning of the child. The attachment between mother and child or father and child is a particular way of explaining the importance of love or positive human bonding, and again this literature has been easily accepted by Christian psychologists; indeed, they have welcomed it as validating the importance of parent-child, marriage, and family relationships in human development.

The recent introduction of the concept of forgiveness into psychotherapy is another important contribution to contemporary psychology, and obviously it is supportive of a Christian understanding both of the person and of the way to effectively resolve many forms of mental suffering. The contributions of the Protestant psychologist Everett Worthington (1998, 2003, 2006) and the Catholic psychologist Robert Enright (Enright & Fitzgibbons, 2015) make them arguably the two major founders of this approach. Both Worthington and Enright have been able to formulate theoretical and methodological approaches to forgiveness therapy that are accepted within both Christian and secular circles.

Yet another new and important development in psychology has been the positive psychology movement begun and led by Martin Seligman (1990, 2003; Seligman & Csikszentmihalyi, 2000; Peterson & Seligman, 2004). This movement has identified certain qualities—which approximate, sometimes closely and sometimes less so, the traditional virtues—as important for the psychological flourishing of all humans. These psychologists have not introduced new basic ideas, but are introducing a new way to measure the virtues and to understand the conditions whereby humans learn and are able to practice the different virtues. Philosophy and theology have long conceptualized the virtues, and this has been true in both Western and non-Western traditions (see Peterson & Seligman, 2004, Chapters 1–3). But for all their theoretical importance, relatively little was empirically known about what conditions and practices develop the understanding of virtues, enable their reliable expression in everyday life of clients, and present the virtues as a way of addressing mental health problems. Thus, contemporary psychology has much to contribute to our knowledge of the virtues and their use in psychotherapy. But a general emphasis on the virtues themselves has long been part of the Christian tradition, which has offered spiritual and liturgical practices to heal and develop the person through the virtues across different vocations and ways of life.

Still another favorable contributor to intellectual support for Christians in psychology is that the understanding of the effects of religion on people's lives has changed greatly in the last generation. In the early years of modern psychology, religion was often seen as a mental pathology or as a large-scale cultural neurosis or illusion (for example, Freud's *The Future of an Illusion*, 1927). Even those psychologists, such as Jung, who had some sympathy for religion, especially of a spiritual type, were commonly critical of Christianity. (For relatively recent revelations of Jung's Gnostic and anti-Christian positions, see Jung's recently published correspondence with White, in Lammers & Cunningham, 2007; Noll, 1994, 1997.) Those psychologists who were not personally very opposed to religion typically had the secular humanist's view that religion was an immature understanding of life and was in the process of withering away. Over the last few decades, however, there have been many studies showing that the religious person with an intrinsic religious motivation is happier, healthier, and lives longer than those who are not religious (see Bergin, 1983; Larson & Larson, 1991; Koenig, King, & Carson, 2012). This research on the positive benefits of religion on medical and psychological well-being is now generally accepted.

Finally, there has been a change in the kind of people who choose to become mental health professionals and also in the kind of people who seek assistance with mental health problems. When psychotherapy was first starting, mental health professionals tended to come from a relatively narrow, secular background. As a result, most clinicians were secular or agnostic, and in any case, they were dramatically less likely to be religious than most people, especially in the United States. In the early years of psychotherapy most patients also tended to be from a skeptical or highly diluted religious background, whether Christian or Jewish. In recent decades, however, the range of mental health professionals expanded beyond psychiatry and psychology to include clinical social work, professional counselors, and marital and family therapists, and an increasing number of integrative Christian psychology training programs have developed (e.g., at Fuller Theological Seminary, Wheaton College, Regent University, the Institute for the Psychological Sciences at Divine Mercy University). This new situation has produced many more mental health professionals who are religious—in particular, Christian. Although on average, mental health practitioners still tend to be less religious than the population at large, there now is a very significant group of Christian practitioners with their own professional associations (e.g., the Christian Association for Psychological Studies, American Association of Christian Counselors, Society of Christian Psychology and the Catholic Psychotherapy Association). These professional training programs and associations have also founded scholarly journals (such as *Journal of Psychology and Religion, Journal of Psychology and Christianity, Journal of Psychology and Theology, Edification*, and recently the e-journal *Christian Psychology around the World*, and, also forthcoming, *The Catholic Journal of Psychology and Mental Health Practice*, from Divine Mercy University).

In addition, with the growth of the field of psychotherapy, more and more patients are themselves religious. Indeed, clergy refer many church members to psychotherapy. With direct experience of religious clients, many psychologists have dropped their previous, rather prejudiced, set of categories and have come to understand religion either as potentially an aid for psychotherapy, or at least in most cases as not harmful. It has also helped that many contemporary psychologists truly admire and respect their clients, even when they come from quite different backgrounds. In addition the American Psychological Association and other related organizations have accepted spirituality as a form of diversity to be respected in therapy.

In summary, because of (1) the decline of secular confidence, (2) the growth of religion around the world, (3) the end of new theories hostile to religion, (4) the growth of psychological theories compatible with Christianity, (5) the understanding of serious religious and spiritual life as an aid to human flourishing, and (6) the increase in the number of Christian psychotherapists and Christian psychotherapy patients, the time is ripe to develop further Christian and explicitly Catholic models of psychology.

Advantages of Catholic Christianity for Addressing the Integration Problem

In the task of integration I believe that the Catholic faith has special and powerful advantages. It should be understood that any attempt to show the advantages of a Catholic model will inevitably invite contrasts between the Catholic model and the Protestant tradition, but such an attempt is not meant to detract from the very substantial positive Protestant contributions (see below) to Christian integration with the mental health field over the past fifty years. Therefore, the interpretation that follows should be seen as a friendly challenge to my Protestant friends and colleagues, from whom I have benefited so much over the years. It is a challenge also to many Catholics who have followed a secular model of psychology for want of confidence in a Catholic model that would be not only coherent but also academically and professionally respectable.

1: The Theological Issue

Perhaps the most important issue is that if one is going to relate psychology and Christianity, one needs an explicit and broadly conceived theology. That is, one has to know what one is connecting *with* or integrating *with* psychology. It is, of course, well known that Protestant theology differs from denomination to denomination, and that these differences are often far from trivial. In particular, the nature and extent of human sinfulness or "depravity" have been hotly debated. Perhaps the most systematic and extensive Protestant theology is that found in the Reformed tradition, but of course there are very significant differences among the Reformed, Lutheran, Baptist, and Methodist traditions. The specificity of, commonalities with, and differences between the Catholic Church and these confessions are the subject of continuing dialogue (Congregation for Doctrine of the Faith, 2000). On top of that, there is the more recent trend to be "nondenominational" and thus theologically vague. More importantly, there is no equivalent to the Catholic Magisterium in Protestant denominations, thus it is often unclear what a particular official Protestant theology is. For Catholics the *Catechism* and the pronouncements of the Magisterium provide clear guidance. (The Magisterium is the official teaching authority of the Church, embodied in the bishops of the Church in union with the pope.) The entire focus of the Magisterium is on the Word of God as found in Sacred Scripture and tradition. A readily available example is the official *Catechism of the Catholic Church* (2000), which offers a genuine and systematic presentation of Catholic doctrine on faith and morals and which unites all Catholics even across various rites, cultures, and geographical areas (e.g., Roman Catholic, Byzantine Catholics, Coptic Catholics, etc.).

There is arguably a core "orthodox" Christian theology, common to all forms of Christianity—the kind of thing that C. S. Lewis called "mere Christianity" (Lewis, 1952/2001) and found in the above-mentioned ecumenical dialogues. But it is not obvious that this core is a living theological tradition, and there is a question whether this "mere Christianity" actually exists in a form separate from specific confessional traditions. In any case, even if "mere Christianity" were to be identified in detail, it would not be official for any group of Christians, and since it is a minimal theology it would have little to say about many issues, especially moral ones. In short, a serious problem for Protestant efforts to relate psychology and theology is that the multiplicity and often ambiguity of theological traditions makes integration particularly difficult or limited to an oversimplified "mere Christianity." If there is to be a Protestant integration of psychology, it will, I believe, have to come from within a well-specified Protestant theological tradition. I believe that such a clearly defined Christian position is the ambition of the Society for Christian Psychology (SCP) approach. (Also see Johnson, 2007.)

In contrasting the multiplicity within Protestantism to Catholicism I do not mean that orthodox Catholic theology is static or without its own internal controversies. There are biblical, patristic, Augustinian, Dominican, Franciscan, and Jesuit schools of Catholic thought that would rightfully be identified as sharing the common tradition but having divergent perspectives and accents with regard to some aspects of the person. It is in such perspectives

that are found further reflections on the Christian faith. Catholic thinkers who represent diverse contemporary schools include Marie Joseph Lagrange, OP (1905), Henri de Lubac, SJ (1987, 1996, 1998), Marie-Dominique Chenu, OP (1950), Karl Rahner, SJ (1961–92,1994a, 1994b), Yves Congar, OP (2011); Bernard Lonergan, SJ (1957, 1972); Hans Urs von Balthasar (1982–1989), and René Girard (1977, 2001; see also Bailie, 1995, and Fleming, 2004). Moreover, at least since John Henry Newman, the concept of the historical development of Catholic theology has been known and widely accepted. Nevertheless, in spite of its dynamic aspect, Catholic theology has a breadth, consistency, and specificity—especially with regard to basic doctrines—that makes it possible to know, much more clearly than is the case with much of Protestant theology, exactly what is being integrated with psychology.

If there were to be such a Protestant denominational integration it would, of course, have much overlap with other Protestant denominations as well as considerable overlap with any Catholic integration. In any case, when one is developing a Christian model of psychology, psychology itself is complex enough without the addition of uncertainties about the kind of Christian framework to which it is being related.

2: The Moral Issue

There is no doubt that all those who think seriously about psychology agree that psychology is intimately connected with many moral issues. One simply cannot intervene in a person's life—particularly in the context of interpersonal and emotional problems—without recognizing a moral context. As one large example, consider the problem of sexual ethics. It is a commonplace that many psychological problems involve sexual values and sexual behavior. And dealing with them requires that both the psychotherapist and theoretical psychologist take a moral stance. Most secular psychologists tend to let the patient determine the morality of the relevant sexual behaviors, but this stance is not reliable. For example, secular psychologists sometimes advocate pre- and even extramarital sexual behavior as therapeutic responses to certain kinds of problems; also it is common for psychologists to have a positive attitude toward masturbation and often suggest it as a psychologically useful behavior. Many have an equally positive attitude toward abortion, and of course today the official attitude of most psychologists toward homosexual genital acts is one of acceptance, typically of a supportive kind. These are clearly moral attitudes that are not part of any kind of scientific knowledge.

It is significant that all of these secular moral positions are also often advocated within the major Protestant denominations, at least in modern Western countries and with the exception of many Evangelicals. The official acceptance by many Protestant sects of premarital sex, contraception, abortion, divorce, and homosexual genital acts is well known. The acceptance of this "new" morality goes against the moral standards of their own Protestant tradition, which for hundreds of years were essentially the same for all Christians. At the start of the twentieth century the major Protestant denominations condemned birth control, divorce, abortion, and could not have imagined homosexual clergy and same-sex marriage. When, at the Lambeth Conference of 1930, the Anglicans first broke with the long-established Christian moral position on birth control, the other Protestant denominations condemned them. But as the years went by these moral changes were slowly accepted. Apparently the reason for this acceptance has been the secular culture's wide acceptance and approval of them. Today a number of the so-called liberal or mainline Protestant churches, at least in Western societies, have a sexual morality that is indistinguishable from the surrounding neo-pagan culture. Some conservative Protestant denominations still reject the more recent changes in sexual morality, but there is reason to be skeptical that these positions will hold, in view of the long-term Protestant response to birth control and divorce, which they also initially rejected.

The substantive problem, from a Catholic position, is that in making these changes many Protestants have accepted views that Catholics (and most Eastern Orthodox and many Evangelicals) understand as contrary to Scripture and that violate the tradition of Christian morality already well established in the early history of the Church. In addition, these changes, from a Catholic perspective, are contrary to the nature and best interests of the human person. One should add that there is some evidence, which I believe will grow in the years ahead, to show that breaking the moral law with respect to such sexual issues often leads to psychological harm, which the Christian psychologist should seek to alleviate—for example, post-abortion trauma, the harm done to children by divorce, and the harm done by promiscuity and pornography (Fagan, 2009; Eberstadt & Layden, 2010); such harm is done not only to individuals but also to families and to society.

The point is that without an agreed upon, broadly relevant and basic moral framework and its associated normative understanding of the person, no substantive integration of psychology and theology seems possible, since the nature of human flourishing around which a psychological system would be formulated is not clear. On all of the above moral issues the Catholic position is officially clear and systematically articulated and defended (Paul VI, 1968; John Paul II, 1993, 1995). Of course, there are large numbers of individual Catholics who reject the Church's morality either in theory or in practice. There are also some intellectual dissidents who challenge these positions, but they have no official status in the Church, and like other such proposed historical challenges, theirs have rarely led to any significant doctrinal changes within Catholicism. Part of the support for the traditional Catholic morality also has come from the large number of Catholics who live in non-Western societies and who see these moral changes as the peculiar heresies of a rich, self-indulgent, dying, and no longer admired Western culture.

In any case, although changes in Catholic moral positions are possible, these are rare and, if made, are made clearly and explicitly. The result is that Catholic moral theology has a specific and internally consistent quality that enables it to be integrated, at least potentially, with psychology. In contrast, the diversity of views around moral issues among Protestant denominations assures that integration attempts will be divided and sometimes contradictory. In short, in both theory and application, it is at least possible for a common integrative framework to be accepted and used throughout the entire Catholic world.

3: The Philosophical Issue

The Catholic theological tradition has long appreciated the importance of philosophy for its defense and support. Catholics have known since the early patristic period that rational and philosophical support for the faith is both necessary and possible. Without such philosophical and rational support, there is no way to address the surrounding non-Christian society—a social condition that now is obviously evident again (John Paul II, 1998). Thus, Catholic tradition has always been able to defend itself at least

in part in the language of philosophical and rational discourse—a language much more open to the non-Christian than that of pure theology with its faith-based acceptance of Christian revelation, beliefs, and practices.

There have, of course, been different philosophical contributions to Catholic theology. For example, Augustinian and Thomist approaches are two of the major traditions. More recently, Karol Wojtyła (1993) introduced what he calls a Thomistic Personalism, a philosophical understanding that has become prominent in the Church through a renewed focus on the dignity of the human person and on interpersonal relationships (see Crosby, 2004; Williams, 2009). We need philosophy and sometimes psychology to unpack much of the latent meaning present in God's revealed truth. For example, what is the nature of love? How does love relate to our bodies? How do Christ's commandments lead to human flourishing? What is forgiveness, and how does a person go about giving and receiving it?

In principle, philosophical support could be brought to bear by Protestants who relate psychology and theology. Indeed valuable contributions have been made by Mark McMinn and Clark Campbell (2007) in their work "Integrative Psychotherapy," but this work offers integration with only a few schools of psychotherapy and does not encompass a level of integration that provides a ground for theoretical development of a "grand" personality framework, nor does it illustrate broadly how this integrative model can be used in intake interviewing, case formulation, and treatment planning. The development from a Protestant theology of such a broad integrative framework capable of addressing all of these areas seems unlikely, in part because, in spite of growing appreciation in some Evangelical circles of the value of philosophical reasoning in supporting theology, there still remains in many others suspiciousness toward philosophy and its relationship to religion.

Nevertheless, the question of philosophy and theology and their use in integration is an open question mainly because so many Protestants have already contributed so much to integration over a roughly fifty-year period (Entwistle, 2015; Johnson, 2007; Moriarty, 2010; Roberts, 2007; Stevenson, Eck, & Hill, 2007; Tietjen & Evans, 2011).

However, for the reasons noted above I generally think that a Catholic psychology, really a Catholic model or framework of the person, can be developed to provide a grand personality theory or meta-model of the person, which can synthetically unite existing secular schools of psychotherapy and be widely applicable in clinical practices such as interviewing, assessment, case formulation, treatment planning, and delivery. That is, of course, the proposal of the present volume.

4: The Cultural Issue

A final major Catholic advantage is that, relatively speaking, Catholics are found in a very wide range of different cultures, societies, and social classes, thus the particular distortions of the faith dominant in any one cultural environment do not become generally accepted by the Catholic Church. As noted above, today's Western sexualized culture is seen by millions of other Catholics as the peculiar cultural preoccupation of a dying and no longer impressive society. Likewise, possible future pressures for polygamy from some African countries would be balanced by many other Catholics living where polygamy is not a part of any social pressure; a tendency toward a caste-like treatment of different groups or to some kind of religious syncretism from a future influence stemming from India would be balanced by Catholics from other regions of the world. In short, this wide cultural range of Catholics is a good antidote to religious parochialism and to the faith's becoming a victim of what might be called "cultural capture."

Examples of Two Theological and Philosophical Issues

Catholic Anthropology

As an example of the importance of general philosophical contributions, let us consider what is known as Catholic anthropology. In fact, the term "anthropology," or "study of man," is pretty close to what Americans know as "psychology." The word "anthropology" in this Catholic sense has no connection to what is meant by "anthropology departments" in most American universities. Catholic anthropology has been very influential, especially at the Institute for the Psychological Sciences (IPS), now part of Divine Mercy University, with professors and students who are working to relate psychology to the faith. It refers to an understanding of the person that has emerged in the work of various Catholic writers.

This framework has been strongly influenced by personalist, phenomenologist, and Thomist philosophers, including Max Scheler (1970), Étienne Gilson (1950), Jacques Maritain (1985), Gabriel Marcel (1949, 1963, 1967), Emmanuel Mounier (1952), Maurice Nédoncelle (1966, 1984), Dietrich von Hildebrand (2009), Robert Spaemann (2006), Joseph Ratzinger (1990) and Karol Wojtyła/John Paul II (see Connor, 1992; Williams, 2009). The emphasis of this approach has been on persons as developing out of interpersonal relationships, especially those that require self-giving love, and on the phenomenology of human experience. Relationships are understood as first expressed by God's very creation of man and as imaged in the Trinity itself. This personalist Catholic tradition has strong similarities to the writings of the Protestants Thomas Torrance (1983, 1985) and John Macmurray (1961), and of the Orthodox theologian John Zizioulas (1985), as well as those of certain Jewish philosophers, initially Martin Buber (1971) and more recently Emmanuel Levinas (1998). However, this framework for philosophically and theologically understanding the person as heavily indebted to relationships with others is in opposition to much of modern philosophy and psychology, which focus on the autonomous individual. Other critical contributions to the renewed Catholic understanding of the person have come through revivals in biblical studies (Lagrange, 1905, 1931; Brown, 1965/2010) and in natural law and virtue theory (Pieper, 1966; Anscombe, 1981; Pinckaers, 1978; MacIntyre, 1984). There has been some significant integration of this personalist approach with traditional Thomism. For example, Norris Clarke (1993) identifies a dynamic and relational aspect of Aquinas that he believes has been neglected. Clarke concludes that a person is a rational substance in active relationship to God and others. (Also see the CCMMP in Chapter 2, above.)

Although many of these writings have been at a philosophical and theological level, they have been of direct relevance to psychology, and at IPS they have made an important contribution. For example, they provide a solid foundation in both theology and philosophy for understanding the importance of object relations theory (see the work of Melanie Klein and Donald Winnicott), attachment theory (e.g., Bowlby, 1969, 1973, 1980, Ainsworth, Blehar,

Waters, & Wall, 1978) and the findings on early interpersonal relationships and neurological development (e.g., Siegel, 2012).

Importance of the Body

The Catholic tradition has long emphasized the importance of the body for understanding both the person and religion itself. Examples of this emphasis are found in the importance given to such things as the sign of the cross, kneeling or standing for prayer, and the importance given to relics and to the bodily portrayal of Christ, especially in the crucifix with its emphasis on the body of Christ. Other emphases on the body include the importance given to sacraments, and most especially the real presence at Communion, which involves eating and drinking the Body and Blood of Christ. There are many ramifications of this emphasis in the practice of Catholicism.

The importance that the Catholic Church accords to the body also shows up in the interpretation of sexuality from a Catholic theological and philosophical perspective. A major recent expression of this concern is the *Theology of the Body* by Pope John Paul II (2006; also see Ashley, 1985). Here the emphasis is on male and female as bodily different and as complementary. This difference and complementarity is often summarized under what is called "the nuptial meaning of the body." Thus a Catholic psychology recognizes that God created male and female persons as different, complementary, and of equal dignity (see Chapter 9, "Male and Female"; see also Allen, 2015). Most secular psychologies of the person, with the exception of early Freudian oedipal theory, have totally neglected any differences between male and female persons. The emphasis on the theology of the body, which is rooted in ancient Hebrew respect for the body, has been important in supporting

Catholic moral theology especially with respect to sexuality. The Catholic rejection of contraception, abortion, divorce, and same-sex marriage are all directly related to the bodily meaning of human relationships and to the Church's understanding of the nature of body and soul as integrally connected. Much contemporary neuroscience has made many psychologists more aware of this importance of the body for understanding the person, but this understanding has yet to be extensively recognized in psychology. However, in this volume the body will be given due importance.

A clearly developed and specifically Catholic Christian approach to the project of relating psychology and Christianity is, of course, the main theme of this book. The various chapters, especially the early theoretical chapters, spell out in some detail a reasonably full-fledged model of integration, namely the Catholic Christian Meta-Model of the Person. It is also assumed that such integration is possible without any violation of the independence of scientific psychological knowledge or the theological integrity of Christianity. For more on this important claim see, in this volume, Chapter 2, "Theological, Philosophical, and Psychological Premises for a Catholic Christian Meta-Model of the Person," and Chapter 7, "The Method and Presuppositions of the Catholic Christian Meta-Model of the Person"; see also Ashley, 2000, 2013; Brugger, 2008, 2009.

REFERENCES

Ainsworth, M. D. S., Blehar, M. C., Waters, E., & Wall, S. (1978). *Patterns of attachment: A psychological study of the strange situation.* Hillsdale, NJ: Erlbaum.

Allen, M. P. (2015). Four principles of complementarity: A philosophical perspective. In S. Lopes & H. Alvaré (Eds.), *Not just good, but beautiful: The complementary relationship between man and woman* (pp. 49–59). Walden, NY: Plough Publishing.

Anscombe, G. E. M. (1981). Modern moral philosophy. In P. Unger (Ed.), *Collected philosophical papers* (Vol. 3, pp. 26–41). Oxford, United Kingdom: Oxford University Press. (Original work published 1958)

Ashley, B. M. (1985). *Theologies of the body: Humanist and Christian.* Braintree, MA: Pope John Center.

Ashley, B. M. (2000). *Choosing a world-view and value-system: An ecumenical apologetics.* New York, NY: Alba House.

Ashley, B. M. (2013). *Healing for freedom: A Christian perspective on personhood and psychotherapy.* Arlington, VA: The Institute for the Psychological Sciences Press.

Bailie, G. (1995). *Violence unveiled: Humanity at the crossroads.* New York, NY: Crossroad Publishing.

Beck, A. T. (1979). *Cognitive therapy and the emotional disorders.* New York, NY: Penguin.

Bergin, A. E. (1983). Religiosity and mental health: A critical reevaluation and meta-analysis. *Professional Psychology: Research and Practice, 14*(2), 170–184.

Bowlby, J. (1969). *Attachment and loss: Vol. 1. Attachment.* London, United Kingdom: Hogarth Press.

Bowlby, J. (1973). *Attachment and loss: Vol. 2. Separation: Anxiety and anger.* London, United Kingdom: Hogarth Press.

Bowlby, J. (1980). *Attachment and loss: Vol. 3. Loss: Sadness and depression.* London, United Kingdom: Hogarth Press.

Brown, R. E. (2010). *New Testament essays.* Milwaukee, WI: Bruce. (Original work published 1965)

Brugger, E. C., & the Faculty of the Institute for the Psychological Sciences. (2008). Anthropological foundations for clinical psychology: A proposal. *Journal of Psychology and Theology, 36,* 3–15.

Brugger, E. C. (2009). Psychology and Christian anthropology. *Edification, 3*(1), 5–18.

Buber, M. (1971). *I and thou.* New York, NY: Scribners. (Original work published in German, 1923)

Cassidy, J., & Shaver, P. R. (Eds.) (2018). *Handbook of attachment: Theory, research and clinical applications* (3rd ed.). New York, NY: Guilford.

Catechism of the Catholic Church (CCC) (2nd ed.).

(2000). Vatican City, Vatican: Libreria Editrice Vaticana.

Chenu, M. D. (1950). *Pour une théologie du travail.* Paris, France: Seuil.

Clarke, W. N. (1993). *Person and being: The Aquinas lecture, 1993.* Milwaukee, WI: Marquette University Press.

Congar, Y. (2011). *True and false reform in the Church* (P. Philibert, Trans.). Collegeville, MN: Liturgical Press. (Original work published in French, 1950)

Congregation for Doctrine of the Faith (2000). *Dominus Iesus* [Declaration on the unicity and salvific universality of Jesus Christ and the Church]. Vatican City, Vatican: Libreria Editrice Vaticana.

Connor, R. (1992). The person as resonating existential. *American Catholic Philosophical Quarterly, 66*(1), 39–56.

Cox, H. G. (1965). *The secular city.* New York, NY: Macmillan.

Crosby, J. F. (2004). *Personalist papers.* Washington, DC: The Catholic University of America Press.

de Lubac, H. (1987). *Paradoxes of faith* (P. Simon, S. Kreilkamp, & E. Beaumont, Trans.). San Francisco, CA: Ignatius Press. (Original work published 1948)

de Lubac, H. (1996). *The discovery of God* (A. Dru, Trans.). Grand Rapids, MI: Eerdmans. (Original work published 1956)

de Lubac, H. (1998). *The mystery of the supernatural* (R. Sheed, Trans.). New York, NY: Crossroad. (Original work published 1946)

Derrida, J. (1964). Violence et metaphysique: Essai sur la pensée d'Emmanuel Levinas. *Revue de Metaphysique et de Morale, 3*, 322–354.

Derrida, J. (1973) *Speech and phenomena, and other essays on Husserl's theory of signs.* Evanston, IL: Northwestern University Press.

Derrida, J. (1976). *Of grammatology.* Baltimore, MD: Johns Hopkins University Press.

Derrida, J. (1978). *Writing and difference.* Chicago, IL: University of Chicago Press.

Eberstadt, M., & Layden, M. A. (2010). *The social cost of pornography: A statement of findings and recommendations.* Princeton, NJ: Witherspoon Institute.

Ellis, A. (1962). *Reason and emotion in psychotherapy.* New York, NY: Lyle Stuart.

Enright, R. D., & Fitzgibbons, R. P. (2015). *Forgiveness therapy: An empirical guide for resolving anger and restoring hope* (2nd ed.). Washington, DC: American Psychological Association.

Entwistle, D. N. (2015). *Integrative approaches to psychology and Christianity: An introduction to worldview issues, philosophical foundations, and models of integration* (3rd ed.). Eugene, OR: Cascade Books.

Fagan, P. F. (2009). *The effects of pornography on individuals, marriage, family and community* (Research Synthesis No. RS09K01). Retrieved from Family Research Council website: https://www.frc.org/issuebrief/the-effects-of-pornography-on-individuals-marriage-family-and-community

Fleming, C. (2004). *René Girard: Violence and mimesis.* Cambridge, United Kingdom: Polity.

Foucault, M. (1970) *The order of things.* New York, NY: Random House (Original work published in French, 1966)

Foucault, M. (1972). *Archaeology of knowledge.* New York, NY: Random House. (Original work published in French, 1969)

Freud, S. (1927). The future of an illusion. *Standard Edition, 21*, 3–56.

Gilson, E. (1950). Christian personalism (A. H. C. Downes, Trans.). In *The spirit of medieval philosophy* (Chapter 10, pp. 189–208). London, United Kingdom: Sheed & Ward. (First delivered as the Gifford Lectures, 1931–1932).

Girard, R. (1977). *Violence and the sacred* (P. Gregory, Trans.). Baltimore, MD: The Johns Hopkins University Press.

Girard, R. (2001). *I see Satan fall like lightning.* Maryknoll, NY: Orbis Books.

Jenkins, P. (2007). *The next Christendom: The coming of global Christianity.* New York, NY: Oxford University Press.

John Paul II. (1993). *Veritatis splendor* [Encyclical, on certain fundamental questions of the Church's moral teaching]. Vatican City, Vatican: Libreria Editrice Vaticana.

John Paul II. (1995). *Evangelium vitae* [Encyclical, on the value and inviolability of human life]. Vatican City, Vatican: Libreria Editrice Vaticana.

John Paul II. (1998). *Fides et ratio* [Encylical, on the relationship between faith and reason]. Vatican City, Vatican: Libreria Editrice Vaticana.

John Paul II. (2006). *Man and woman he created them: A theology of the body* (M. Waldstein, Trans.). Boston, MA: Pauline Books & Media.

Johnson, E. L. (2007). *Foundations for soul care: A Christian psychology proposal*. Downers Grove, IL: InterVarsity Press.

Koenig, H. G., King, D. E., & Carson, V. B. (Eds.). (2012). *Handbook of religion and health* (2nd ed.). New York, NY: Oxford University Press.

Lagrange, M.-J. (1905). *Historical criticism and the Old Testament* (E. Myers, Trans.). London, United Kingdom: Catholic Truth Society.

Lagrange, M.-J. (1931). *Le Judaïsme avant Jésus-Christ*. Paris, France: J. Gabalda et fils.

Lammers, A. C., & Cunningham, A. (2007). *The Jung-White Letters*. London, United Kingdom: Routledge.

Larson, D. B., & Larson, S. S. (1991). Religious commitment and health: Valuing the relationship. *Second Opinion: Health, Faith & Ethics, 17*(1), 26–40.

Levinas, E. (1998). *Entre nous: On thinking-of-the-other* (M. B. Smith & B. Harshav, Trans.). New York, NY: Columbia University Press. (Original work published in French, 1991)

Lewis, C. S. (2001). *Mere Christianity*. New York, NY: Harper Collins. (Original work published 1952)

Lonergan, B. (1957). *Insight: A study of human understanding*. New York, NY: Philosophical Library.

Lonergan, B. (1972). *Method in theology*. New York, NY: Herder and Herder.

Lyotard, J-F. (1984). *The post-modern condition: A report on knowledge*. Minneapolis, MN: University of Minnesota Press.

MacIntyre, A. (1984). *After virtue: A study in moral theory* (2nd ed.). Notre Dame, IN: University of Notre Dame Press.

Macmurray, J. (1961). *Persons in relation*. Atlantic Highlands, NJ: Humanities Press International.

Marcel, G. (1949). *Being and having*. London, United Kingdom: Dacre Press.

Marcel, G. (1963). *The existential background of human dignity*. Cambridge, MA: Harvard University Press.

Marcel, G. (1967). *Problematic man*. New York, NY: Herder and Herder.

Maritain, J. (1985). *The person and the common good* (J. F. Fitzgerald, Trans.). Notre Dame, IN: University of Notre Dame Press. (Original work published in French, 1947, as *La personne et le bien commun*)

Maslow, A. (1970). *Motivation and Personality* (2nd ed.). New York, NY: Harper & Row.

McMinn, M. R., & Campbell, C. D. (2007). *Integrative psychotherapy: Toward a comprehensive Christian approach*. Downers Grove, IL: IVP Academic.

Moriarty, G. L. (Ed.) (2010). *Integrating faith and psychology: Twelve psychologists tell their stories*. Downers Grove, IL: IVP Academic.

Mounier, E. (1952). *Personalism*. London, United Kingdom: Routledge & Kegan Paul.

Nédoncelle, M. (1966). *Love and the person*. New York, NY: Sheed & Ward.

Nédoncelle, M. (1984). *The personalist challenge*. Allison Park, PA: Pickwick.

Noll, R. (1994). *The Jung cult: The origins of a charismatic movement*. New York, NY: Free Press.

Noll, R. (1997). *The Aryan Christ: The secret life of Carl Jung*. New York, NY: Random House.

Paul VI. (1968). *Humanae vitae* [Encyclical, on the regulation of birth]. Vatican City, Vatican: Libreria Editrice Vaticana.

Peterson, C., & Seligman, M. E. P. (2004). *Character strengths and virtues: A handbook and classification*. New York, NY: Oxford University Press.

Pieper, J. (1966). *The four cardinal virtues*. Notre Dame, IN: University of Notre Dame Press. (Original works published 1954–1959)

Pinckaers, S. (1978). *Le renouveau de la morale*. Paris, France: Téqui.

Rahner, K. (1961–92). *Theological investigations* (23 Vols.). New York, NY: Herder and Herder.

Rahner, K. (1994a). *Hearer of the word*. New York, NY: Continuum.

Rahner, K. (1994b). *Spirit in the world*. New York, NY: Continuum.

Ratzinger, J. (1990). Concerning the notion of person in theology. *Communio, 17*(3), 439–454. (Original work published in German, 1973)

Roberts, R. C. (2007). *Spiritual emotions: A psychology of Christian virtues*. Grand Rapids, MI: Eerdmans.

Rogers, C. R. (1961). *On becoming a person*. Boston, MA: Houghton Mifflin.

Rorty, R. (1979). *Philosophy and the mirror of nature*. Princeton, NJ: Princeton University Press.

Rorty, R. (1982). *Consequences of pragmatism*. Minneapolis, MN: University of Minnesota Press.

Rorty, R. (1987). *Contingency, irony and solidarity*.

Cambridge, United Kingdom: Cambridge University Press.

Scheler, M. (1970). *The nature of sympathy* (P. Heath, Trans.). Hamden, CT: Archon Press.

Scruton, R. (2002). *The West and the rest*. Wilmington, DE: Intercollegiate Studies Institute.

Seligman, M. E. P. (1990). *Learned optimism*. New York, NY: Knopf.

Seligman, M. E. P. (2003). Positive psychology: Fundamental assumptions. *The Psychologist, 16*, 126–127.

Seligman, M. E. P., & Csikszentmihalyi, M. (2000) Positive psychology: An introduction. *American Psychologist, 55*, 5–14.

Siegel, D. J. (2012). *The developing mind: How relationships and the brain interact to shape who we are* (2nd ed.). New York, NY: Guilford.

Spaemann, R. (2006). *Persons: The difference between "someone" and "something"* (O. O'Donovan, Trans.). Oxford, United Kingdom: Oxford University Press. (Original work published in German, 1996)

Stevenson, D. H., Eck, B. E., & Hill, P. C. (Eds.) (2007). *Psychology & Christianity integration: Seminal works that shaped the movement*. Batavia, IL: Christian Association for Psychological Studies.

Tietjen, M. A., & Evans, C. S. (2011) Kierkegaard as a Christian psychologist. *Journal of Psychology & Christianity, 30*(4), 274–283.

Torrance, T. (1983). *The mediation of Christ*. Grand Rapids, MI: Eerdmans.

Torrance, T. (1985). *Reality and scientific theology*. Edinburgh, United Kingdom: Scottish Academic Press.

von Balthasar, H. U. (1982–1991). *The glory of the Lord: Theological aesthetics* (Vols. 1–7). San Francisco, CA: Ignatius Press.

von Hildebrand, D. (2009). *The nature of love* (J. F. Crosby & J. H. Crosby, Trans.). South Bend, IN: St. Augustine's Press. (Original work published in German, 1971, as *Das Wesen der Liebe*)

Williams, T. D. (2009). What is Thomistic personalism? *Alpha Omega, 7*(2), 163–197. Retrieved from http://www.uprait.org/archivio_pdf/a042_williams1.pdf

Wojtyła, K. (1993). Thomistic personalism (T. Sandok, Trans.). In A. N. Woznicki (Ed.), *Catholic thought from Lublin: Vol. 4. Person and community: Selected essays* (pp. 165–76). New York: Peter Lang. (Original paper presented in Polish, 1961)

Worthington, E. L., Jr. (1998). An empathy-humility-commitment model of forgiveness applied within family dyads. *Journal of Family Therapy, 20*, 59–76.

Worthington, E. L., Jr. (2003). *Forgiving and reconciling: Bridges to wholeness and hope*. Downers Grove, IL: InterVarsity Press.

Worthington, E. L., Jr. (2006). *Forgiveness and reconciliation: Theory and application*. New York, NY: Routledge.

Zizioulas, J. D. (1985). *Being as communion*. Crestwood, NY: St. Vladimir's Seminary Press.

Chapter 4

Modern Personality Theories

A Critical Understanding of Personality from a
Catholic Christian Perspective

PAUL C. VITZ

ABSTRACT: Major secular theories of personality (e.g., Freudian, Jungian, Rogerian) are briefly identified, and their typically unnoticed and undefended philosophical presuppositions made explicit (e.g., atheism, determinism, moral relativism, subjectivism). These presuppositions are contrasted with Christian presuppositions for understanding the person. The major characteristics of the person, as they are understood in a Catholic Christian perspective, are then identified and, when it's needed, briefly defended. These characteristics include embodiment, which is based on body-soul unity and takes account of male and female differences; interpersonal relationships throughout the life span; a significant amount of free will; reason, that is, human intelligence; sensory-perceptual-cognitive experience, including imagination; emotions; vocations; and the virtues. The general relevance of such a Catholic Christian theory for understanding psychological problems, and finally its theological connections to Trinitarian theology are presented.

This chapter first characterizes what the existing modern secular theories of personality are. Next these theories are compared and contrasted with the assumptions and characteristics of a proposed Catholic Christian theory of the person and personality. Finally the chapter presents distinctive aspects of such a new theory, identified in this volume as the Catholic Christian Meta Model of the Person (CCMMP).

First, what are the major personality theories in psychology, and how do they function in the discipline? Examples of such theories are those developed by Sigmund Freud, Carl Jung, Alfred Adler, H. S. Sullivan, the neo-Freudians such as Erik Erikson, and others like Carl Rogers, Abraham Maslow, and Gordon Allport. (Presentations and discussions of these theories are found in almost all personality theory

Parts of this chapter appeared in the chapter "A Christian Theory of Personality," in R. C. Roberts & M. R. Talbot, Eds., 1997, *Limning the Psyche* (pp. 20–40), Grand Rapids, MI: Eerdmans. The chapter presented here is an expanded and revised version of a text that was originally published as "Reconceiving personality theory from a Catholic Christian perspective," by P. C. Vitz, 2009, *Edification: Journal of the Society for Christian Psychology*, 3(1), 42–50. Copyright 2009 by Christian Counseling Resources. Adapted with permission.

textbooks, examples are Feist, Feist, & Roberts, 2018; Schultz & Schultz, 2013; Sollod, Wilson, & Monte, 2009.) Most of these theories were developed inductively from experience with mentally troubled persons in a psychotherapeutic setting. As such, these theories took shape over many years in various publications and were seldom systematized and summarized by their originators. A few, such as those proposed by Maslow and Allport, did focus on normal and positively functioning individuals, but these theories left out pathological aspects of personality. Some theorists focused on the first three years of life, others on the ideal mature adult, still others on the self and self-realization as providing the answer to mental health problems and purpose of life itself. Only Freud and Erikson provided a theory of personality development, and only Erikson included early adulthood, maturity, and old age. However, Erikson (1959, 1964, 1968, 1978) left out religious life and other important aspects. In short, all these theories are useful, but limited, interpretations of the person. Although some contradictions and conflicts among different theories remain, many of the basic contributions have been accepted and are now part of how most theorists and mental health practitioners view the person.

Taken together, these theories represent what is meant by the psychological understanding of the person for our culture at large—a viewpoint that emerged and became common during the twentieth century. This is especially true in the United States, but is now found in many countries. These theories underlie the popular psychology that dominates most discussions about the person today. It is hard to remember the older, much simpler, understanding of the person, which existed in the nineteenth century and earlier, that emphasized the conscious mind, reason, and doing what was morally right.

One issue to address concerning these theories is whether they can be considered scientific. Many psychology courses and textbooks implicitly treat these modern, secular theories as part of traditional natural science. This is, however, a serious mistake. Very limited aspects of these theories have a genuinely scientific basis. For example, anxiety and depression when described as part of a personality theory can often be reliably identified. But even then, such symptoms have many possible causes in addition to what might be postulated by the theory. In any case, by the time one gets to personality concepts such as the Oedipus complex, an animus archetype, or self-actualization, the standard scientific understanding, and especially the positivistic experimental paradigm of modern psychology, have been left behind. No knowledgeable psychologist today understands Freudian or Jungian theory as based on science or even as likely to become so. These personality theories are really theoretical interpretations with no reliable methodology for scientific verification. They may lead to pragmatic and intuitive truths, but these truths are more like the knowledge found in the experience of most practical work. Practical knowledge of materials, tools, and techniques is important and is genuine knowledge, but it is not the result of repeated public experiments with independent and dependent variables, nor is it part of an explicit, coherent, usually quantitative system. In short, practitioners using these personality theories are operating with what can be called "applied philosophies of life."

Any attempt to present an integrative understanding of the person from a Catholic Christian perspective must, however, take both the personality theories and the mental health professional's applied knowledge into account. For example, much "outcome research" is being done today, and evidence-based practice is a standard.

This important research systematically evaluates the effectiveness of different therapeutic methodologies and identifies those interventions that are associated with client improvement. The scientific measurement of positive outcomes justifies some psychotherapeutic procedures and provides some indirect evidence for the guiding theoretical framework. Such studies, however needed and useful, are like correlational studies that show a general association between a set of ideas, assumptions, and procedures and a beneficial outcome.

Different Presuppositions

All theories of personality make a number of different major assumptions about the person. These are needed as foundations to the theoretical system that is then built on them. In most cases, these assumptions are never made explicit, much less defended. The assumptions need to be identified and contrasted to those that underlie a Catholic Christian representation of the person. As examples, here are some of the underlying concepts most relevant to our topic. (For an early but largely neglected discussion of presuppositions in personality theories, see Arnold & Gasson, 1954; also relevant, Vitz, 1997.)

Atheism versus Theism

All the major modern theories of personality and counseling are secular and either explicitly or implicitly assume that God does not exist. The major theories, regardless of the personal positions of their founders, are atheistic in the sense that God is omitted from the theory, and religious motivation, when it does come up, is usually ignored or sometimes treated as pathological. Gordon Allport's (1937) moderately important trait and self theory was open to religious aspects of personality, and he was a believer, but religious concepts were not central to his approach and are not the major ideas for which he is known. The negative, ignorant, or critical reaction of the typical psychologist to the important paper of Allen Bergin (1980), in which he criticized the absence of religion in mainstream psychology and especially psychological theory, is still common today.

The claim here is that the rejection or omission of God, and the omission of the importance of religious and spiritual beliefs and practices, is a central error of any personality theory. Religion at the very least is a psychological reality of importance for many millions of Americans and for billions around the world. To omit such a significant aspect of personality is simply bad clinical science. Since the Gallup Poll began asking the question in the 1940s, over 85% of Americans have consistently said they believe in God. For countless people this belief in God with its ramifications is a major part of their personality and is important to them on a daily basis. Even adult unbelievers were often reared religiously, and this has often affected their personalities. The revival of traditional religions and New Age spirituality in the last few decades continues to demonstrate the power and persuasiveness of religious life for Americans. Of course, throughout the world from Russia to India to the Islamic societies, religion is alive and expanding.

In contrast, a Christian interpretation of personality begins by assuming that God exists and that he is a person with whom one is in a relationship. This relationship has psychological consequences, to which we shall return. The assumption of theism is no less rational than the assumption of atheism. After all, atheists cannot prove that God does not exist. One psychological advantage of accepting the existence of God and the validity of most religious life is that one can then treat a religious client both more honestly and with a greater respect. Although many mental health professionals now view religion and spirituality as one form of diversity, and at least in theory are expected to respect such beliefs of the client, nonetheless when they are not believers themselves, they may steer clear of exploration of what may be of central importance to their believing client. The average mental health professional who is not a believer is often quite comfortable in exploring and affirming a client's homosexual orientation and lifestyle, even if the clinician is heterosexual. But such a nonreligious practitioner would be much less comfortable exploring and affirming a client's traditional Christian lifestyle.

Subjectivity versus Realism

Many secular theories, especially humanistic psychology, are based on the assumption that all we can really know are the states of our own minds. Sometimes these theories also accept the kind of knowledge found in the physical sciences, although that kind of knowledge is normally less relevant to humanistic psychology, which has ignored even the importance of human biology for understanding personality. With the exception of Freud's much-criticized oedipal theory, even sex differences in personality have been almost completely ignored, along with such hereditary factors as temperament.

Closely related to the assumption of subjectivity is the notion that the important thing is to express, understand, and communicate one's own thoughts and feelings, whatever they are; to affirm them, whatever they are; and to be open to the same thing in others. "Truth" is therefore fundamentally psychological, and there are as many "truths" as there are individual psychol-

ogies. Our subjective world is the only significant one, and the final court of appeal for something's validity is what we think—or rather, how we feel—about it. The view that feelings can be transitory, that they can be illusory or even false, is not acknowledged or discussed in such personality theories. In this psychology, our feelings are always authentic even if they change constantly as the self changes. Any unchanging moral basis for genuine flourishing is ignored. (However, some recent psychologies, e.g., positive psychology, have begun to address this problem directly in their study of the virtues.)

The objective nature of God as external to us, and of the external world created by him, is assumed by a Christian understanding of personality theory. Although our own particular thoughts and feelings are of legitimate importance, they do not define reality and cannot be given ultimate existential and ontological priority. For example, Christians must submit not only to God, but also to the lawful world that God has created and that science has often identified. As noted above, this realism is at odds with the dominant modern philosophies. It is, however, in profound sympathy with the general assumption of realism found throughout science since its origin. (Obviously I am not defending logical positivism, which was never very strong among scientists and is no longer much of a force even in philosophy.) From a Catholic perspective, a biblical, personalist, and neo-Thomist realism is often assumed, as is the case here.

Determinism versus Freedom

Many modern secular theories of personality—such as Freud's—explicitly reject human free will; other theories do so implicitly. Determinism is usually part of a materialist philosophy; but it need not be, since some believe that the mind, though different from body, is nevertheless strictly determined. Although these secular theories interpret, and consider important, such cognitive and emotional mental states as perceptions, thoughts, memories, and feelings, they generally ignore the will.

But in practice mental health professionals, from the days of Freud on, have not been consistent determinists. After all, psychoanalysis and other forms of psychotherapy and counseling assume that the client will freely choose to enter into treatment and to freely return for new sessions and as a consequence of therapy he or she will become less controlled or less bound by unconscious thoughts, automatic reactions, schemas, habits, addictions, and early learned patterns of relating, such as attachment styles. A psychotherapy that does not assume common-sense understandings of free will can hardly function.

A Christian perspective does not deny a proper role to causal factors: witness its emphasis on making decisions, such as getting married, free of coercion. However, Christianity does accentuate both human freedom and the will expressing it. The emphasis on voluntary agency entails a strong focus on positive character traits—virtues—that support the will as it chooses a response. Some important secular theories, such as those of Carl Rogers and Abraham Maslow and the existential theorists, affirm human freedom. In doing this, they made important early anti-determinist statements. But, with the exception of Maslow, they largely ignored the traditional virtues as traits that support the will.

Relative Morality versus Moral Standards

Modern secular psychology assumes that values are relative to the individual. Wallach and Wallach (1983) have shown that every prominent modern psychology, from Freud and Jung to cognitive dissonance theory, assumes that the only good is what is good for the individual self. This view can take a variety of forms, ranging from the moral philosophy of ethical egoism to individual relativism of a radical kind. The nature and consequences of these views are rarely acknowledged or defended. Taken together, these moral views have helped to undermine traditional religious teachings. They have also helped to bring about the "individualistic morality" still so prevalent today and so frequently bemoaned by social critics (Bellah, Madsen, Sullivan, Swidler, & Tipton, 1985; Benedict XVI, 2009, 2012; Francis, 2017; MacIntyre, 1999; Vitz, 1994). It is worth noting that most relativistic systems of morality are absolutist about something—typically about moral relativity itself, and about those psychological processes that support moral relativism.

The existence of enduring moral principles that are revealed by God or found in nature is fundamental to Catholic Christianity and thus to any Catholic personality theory. The two great commandments summarize Divine Revelation: Love God and love others. Love as understood here (i.e., as self-giving) is a high value, and is clearly superior to hate. Christianity also assumes the moral truth and psychological validity of the Ten Commandments. It is also understood that, based on the natural law tradition, all people can come to know that there are certain actions we should do, and others we should not do (Budziszewski, 2009; George, 1999; May, 2013; Pinckaers, 1995).

Within a Catholic framework much morality is clearly spelled out, and it is assumed that this morality is for the benefit and flourishing of the person. Finally, it is understood that some psychological problems can arise from violating the moral law and that many aspects of psychological flourishing develop from keeping the moral law. This Catholic framework does not deny that psychological problems are in some cases heavily related to genetic, biochemical, or other deterministic factors outside of the will of the client, but nonetheless, even in such cases the meaning given to one's suffering and the actions taken (bitterness and hatred versus seeing suffering as redemptive and offering forgiveness) may facilitate psychological well-being or reduce the development of psychological disorders.

Here again, some deeply relativistic systems have (paradoxically) "absolute" implications. For example, Rogers assumes that psychological pathologies can arise from disobeying the absolute principle that individuals should create and follow their own values and rules. There is, then, a similarity between a Rogerian and a Christian theory. The difference—*and it is major*—is that the latter presumes that the law comes from God and from nature, not from the self.

Reductionism versus Constructivism

Modern secular personality theory commonly assumes that "higher" things, especially religious experience and moral ideals, are to be understood as caused by underlying lower phenomena. For example, love is reduced to sexual desire; sexual desire to physiology; spiritual life or artistic ideals are reduced to sublimated sexual impulses (as in Freud); and much of consciousness is assumed to be caused by unconscious forces (again, as in Freud or in Jung).

A Christian theory is constructionist. It emphasizes the higher aspects of personality as containing, and often causing or transforming, the lower aspects, and sometimes as being in conflict with them. Thus, my conscious thought causes me to seek what is good or true or beautiful. Searching for and experiencing the self-giving love of God and others motivates a desire to transcend everyday reality. Constructionist thinking is synthetic, bringing things together in an integrated pattern of coherence, while reductionist thought is analytic—breaking whatever is being studied into parts. Of course, good analysis is an important requirement for any successful integration or construction. However, much modern psychology has provided only the analysis, with its reductionist consequences. Integration often results in a hierarchical understanding, whereas the modern mentality is generally anti-hierarchical. One of the few modern constructionist personality theorists is Viktor Frankl (1960, 1963), with his emphasis on the search for higher meaning. Recently however, the work of Seligman (Peterson & Seligman, 2004; Seligman & Csikszentmihalyi, 2000) and many others in the positive psychology movement have brought back an emphasis on the higher aspects with their focus on the virtues and character strengths.

In short, these five pairs of contrasting principles clarify two things: many fundamental assumptions of modern personality theories are not grounded in empirical or scientific evidence, and these assumptions are often inconsistent with a Catholic Christian interpretation of person and personality.

Different Psychological Characteristics of Personality Are Emphasized

Embodiment

Almost no personality theory identifies our body as important in understanding personality.

The closest any theory comes to representing embodiment in its theoretical concepts is Freud's distinctive male and female differences, expressed in the Oedipus and the Electra complexes. These representations have been seriously critiqued, but at least Freud was willing to address the issue of sex differences in personality. Jung did propose opposite sex archetypes as present in each sex, but the consequence of this was to emphasize the unisex psychology of both men and women. After Freud, no major personality theorist seems to have even addressed differences in male and female personality!

The recent findings about the powerful effects of bodily processes on everything from early mother-child attachment (Siegel, 1999, 2012), to language development and mirror neurons (Friederici, 2017; Obler & Gjerlow, 1999; Rizzolatti & Sinigaglia, 2008), to the effects of the body on the content of even abstract and mathematical thinking make the neglect of the body a glaring oversight in all the modern personality theories (Lakoff & Johnson, 1999). No doubt, ignoring the body and how, through maturation and experience, it develops such important but limited capacities as walking, seeing, and hearing, much less language, allowed certain theories of the person to consider the self as autonomous and self-created, that is, without regard to bodily limits and the contributions of others to our formation. Given this "oversight," it even seemed possible for some existentialists to conceive that a self could create its own essence after its existence, create its own meaning without reference to external, objective reality.

As other chapters in this volume make clear, the emphasis on body derives from the Catholic assumption that the person is a body-soul unity or whole (see Chapter 2, "Theological, Philosophical, and Psychological Premises," and Chapter 8, "Personal Wholeness"). This idea, of course, introduces another new concept for understanding personality: namely, the long-ignored soul. So, with the reintroduction of the soul (see Chapter 5, "Basic Psychological Support") and the introduction of vocation (see Chapter 10, "Fulfilled Through Vocation"), in particular the vocation to holiness, a Catholic psychological approach also includes an emphasis on the spiritual life.

In addition, other chapters in this volume present a well-developed Catholic Christian understanding of the person and personality with a heavy but appropriate emphasis on both common embodiment and on the complementary nature and equal dignity of male and female (see Chapter 9, "Man and Woman").

Relationships

Much secular personality theory has tended to assume that the personality, at least when it is mature and healthy, is an isolated autonomous self. These psychologies, for example that of Rogers (1961), and many existential psychologists, focus on how the individual becomes independent—how the individual separates from its mother, father, community, religion, and everything else upon which it was previously dependent. Individuation leading to autonomous self-fulfillment is seen as the basic goal or purpose of all human life

Since Christianity does not assume that the goal of life is independence, and even sees a dark side to independence in the common pathologies of alienation and loneliness, a Christian approach to personality gives a central role to the place of relationship in the formation of personality. The Christian view also sees the positive and often inevitable nature of dependence, for example, in babies, children, the disabled, and the elderly. The seriously infirm, even most adults when sick or injured, are all dependent in crucial ways on others for their well-being; and everyone is dependent on God. However, Christianity postulates *interdependence* and mutual and freely chosen caring for the other as the primary type of adult relationship. Personality is fulfilled in self-giving love and not in isolation: in ultimate union with God, and in love of other humans.

Interdependence is neither dependency nor independence. It is not dependency, which in adults can be an inappropriate need for the other rather than a freely chosen bond. Nor is it independence, since, in an interdependent relationship, persons choose to relate to another, and to give themselves to each other. As conceived by most modern psychologies, the notion of independence ignores the importance of relationships in bringing the truly mature person into existence.

Emotions

The emotions have always been an important aspect of modern psychology, although for a time they were relegated mostly to what was called motivation. Today, however, emotions are a central part of contemporary psychology. For example, there has been the development of therapies such as Emotion-Focused Therapy (Greenberg, 2002; Johnson, 2004). There are also the major contributions in neuroscience by Antonio Damasio (1994), Joseph LeDoux (1996) and Michael Gazzaniga (1994). And, not surprisingly, emotions are an important part of any Catholic Christian approach (see Chapter 14, "Emotional").

Sensation-Perception-Imagination-Cognition

Again, this major component or characteristic of the person has always been a standard part of modern psychology since the study of psychophysics began, in the nineteenth century. Later, Gestalt psychology initiated the still-active study of visual pattern perception. Other some-

what more recent research has focused on face perception, aesthetic perception, speech perception, preverbal cognition, and so forth. This emphasis also includes accepting the importance of imagination especially as it relates to human involvement in the arts. And again, a Catholic Christian approach includes this noncontroversial component (see Chapter 13, "Sensory-Perceptual-Cognitive").

Will

The will, or human agency, in the past has been given only modest emphasis in psychological theories of the person. Freud, at the theoretical level, denied the free, acting will in personality formation. As noted above, many psychologists have ignored or downplayed the importance of human agency. This is not true of the humanistic and existential psychologists, nor is it true of relatively recent models of the person such as Cognitive Behavioral Emotional Therapy (CBET) proposed Albert Ellis (1962, 1994) and Cognitive-Behavioral Therapy (CBT) developed by Aaron Beck (Beck, 1975; Beck, Freeman & Davis, 2003) or by the social learning theorist Albert Bandura (1989) with his emphasis on human agency.

The emergence of positive psychology, with its rediscovery of the virtues and character strengths as major contributors to personality, also bodes well for the importance of free will and agency in secular psychology's new understanding of the person.

The traditional Christian emphasis on the person's freedom to choose the good is well known and, as already noted, is a central part of any Catholic Christian model of person and personality (see Chapter 16, "Volitional and Free").

Reason

From Freud and Jung to Rogers, reason or intellectual cognition, especially in the sense of the search for truth, has been given little emphasis. Of course, Freud did postulate an ego, but it was not master in its own house, since it was primarily controlled by the unconscious nonrational drives of the id and superego. Rogers put the emphasis on getting in touch with feelings. The big exceptions are the more recent cognitive and behavioral theories noted above.

However, in the Catholic tradition, reason has long been an important aspect of the person; indeed the Catholic Church borrowed much of its philosophical understanding of reason from the Greek philosophers. Because of the importance given to truth (e.g., as expressed in the words of Christ "I am the way, and the truth, and the life" Jn 14:6 [RSV]), reason was understood as central to personality from the beginning of the faith. The Gospel writers and St. Paul also spoke frequently of speaking and knowing the truth.

Vocations

Existing theories rarely mention that a person has a calling to some kind of personal flourishing, to a state in life like marriage, or to a kind of work, paid or unpaid, that benefits both the person and his society. The contribution of vocation or calling or personal *telos* is an important Catholic contribution to understanding personality and especially to flourishing. Alfred Adler, an exception to the majority of theorists, did strongly emphasize what he called "social interest" as necessary for healthy personality. Similarly, Frankl (1963) in various ways makes clear if a man has a "why" to life he can bear with any "how."

Virtues

Secular theories of personality seldom mention the traditional virtues. Instead they focus on what might be called the modern "virtues" of suspicion and doubt, of independence and autonomy, of breaking away from inhibitions and getting in touch with and expressing feelings and sexual behaviors. An important exception was Erik Erikson, who introduced virtues (or ego strengths) into his eight psychosocial stages of development. Erikson anticipated, along with some of the concepts associated with the self-actualization of Maslow, the present positive psychology movement that has brought virtues back into contemporary psychology (e.g., Seligman & Csikszentmihalyi, 2000.)

A Catholic Christian representation of the person has always given the traditional virtues importance in understanding personality. In a Christian model of personality, the natural virtues such as justice, courage, wisdom, and temperance are understood as needed for a naturally flourishing life, but also as the ground for the theological virtues of faith, hope, and charity. This importance is maintained and given emphasis in the framework developed in Chapter 11, "Fulfilled in Virtue."

The Origin of Mental Pathologies

A major theoretical proposition of the Catholic Christian Meta-Model of the Person is that mental disorders and pathologies can be usefully interpreted as distortions or weaknesses in the model's domains of the person: body-soul unity, interpersonal relationships, the will, reason, emotions, and sensory-perceptual-cognitive capacities, plus vocations and virtue. Specifically, understanding a mental disorder can begin by first observing its effect or expression in the *body*. This obviously allows medical treatments aimed at intervention in the body, including the use of medication and special diets. Being embodied means that all mental activity has a biological base, and thus a first thing to investigate with patients is their bodily state.

The next important domain to evaluate is the condition of a client's *interpersonal relationships* both past and present. Here, theory and research on early attachment becomes especially relevant. In addition, a person's adult attachments or interpersonal relationships need to be evaluated to gain an adequate grasp of the person's psychological disorder.

The person's *will* also becomes a focus for evaluating mental state. The self-determining quality of free choice is so central to personality that the strength of, the freedom of, and the patient's understanding of the will are to be evaluated. In particular, any restriction of will, as found in addictive behavior, is to be noted. Weakness and limitations of will caused by fear and anxiety is an additional aspect to be identified. In short, how much freedom of will, how much capacity for agency, does the person have?

A further dimension to evaluate is the state of the person's *reason*. Central aspects of such evaluation include the sophistication of rational capacities (Piaget, 1952; Piaget & Inhelder, 1969), ability to engage in moral reasoning (Kohlberg, 1981, 1984), and types of irrational thinking patterns identified so well by the cognitive-behavioral therapists Beck and Ellis. The point is to get an understanding of the rational capacities of a person and their distortions. An integrated Catholic approach can bring into therapy also the development of reason and the knowledge of truth and goodness—not only with respect to the self and others, but also with respect to a general knowledge of God and self-giving love.

Pathologies of the *emotions* are, of course, common, with anxiety and depression being the most obvious. Here the Catholic Christian Meta-Model acknowledges many of the important contributions of the existing secular approaches.

Pathologies in the *sensory-perceptual-cognitive* domain are usually neurological, and the model has nothing special to contribute here except to acknowledge the importance of this domain, especially with regard to imagination.

Does the person have an inability to discern their callings or *vocations*, or are there blocks to them, such as the inability to make commitments? An additional characteristic to evaluate is the presence and strength of the major *virtues* in the patient's personality. What virtues seem to be almost absent? What virtues could be strengthened to help overcome psychological problems? Some personality disorders, for example, can be conceptualized at least partially as being related to the absence of certain virtues (e.g., lack of empathy and justice in the "antisocial" personality).

A final aspect of the person to consider when evaluating the nature of a disorder is implied by the Catholic assumption of the existence of objective *morality*. Here the Catholic position is that some mental disorders are a consequence of breaking the moral law. These disorders often may be sexual in character, for example, promiscuity. However, a failure of committed love to a spouse or child, an absence of good works done for others—these are also moral failures that can have negative psychological consequences. The Catholic position is that the morality relevant to issues that might come up with most clients and mental health professions is clearly addressed in the social and moral teaching of the Church (*Catechism of the Catholic Church*, 2000, and various documents of Vatican II and the Church's Magisterium).

Catholic Christian Contributions to an Integrative and Synthetic Understanding of Person

Relationship and Theology

As many know, the word "person" comes from the Latin word *persona*, which means "mask," as worn in the Roman theater, and also from the theatrical role that went with the mask. The Latin term translated the Greek word *prosōpon*, which had the same meaning.

But this etymology of the word "person" is not very important or revealing. It is more important that the concept of a person rose to prominence, as a major philosophical and theological issue, in early Christian thought. Müller and Haider (1969) have gone so far as to claim that the concept of a person was "unknown to ancient pagan philosophy, and first appears as a technical term in early Christian theology" (p. 404). We do not need to agree with this extreme assertion to recognize that Christianity had a seminal place in the development of the concept of the person, and the Christian origins help us understand what a Christian model of the person and personality will entail.

The concept of a person was developed to help formulate the doctrine of the Trinity—God as three persons. This early theological use placed a strong emphasis on dialogue; it was largely through the proposition of a dialogue of mutual love within the Trinity that the plurality of persons in God was recognized. Dialogue as explicit interpersonal communication was central to God the Father's relationship with Israel and the prophets, and, of course, with Christ himself. Because we are made in the image of a Trinitarian—and thus interpersonal—God, we ourselves are interpersonal by nature and intention. Human beings are called to loving, committed relationships with God and with others, and we find our full personhood in these relationships. According

to the Protestant theologian T. F. Torrance (1983, 1985), the essential feature of the Christian conception of the world, in contrast to the Hellenic, is that it regards the person, and the relations of persons to one another, as the essence of reality, whereas ancient Greek thought conceived of personality, however spiritual, as an accident of the finite—a transitory product of a life that as a whole is impersonal (Torrance, 1985, p. 172). Torrance identifies two basic understandings of God as a person. The first view, which has dominated Western philosophy, comes from Boethius, who defined a person as "an individual substance of a rational nature." Such a definition places the emphasis on the differentiation of substances. The second understanding derives primarily from the patristic, primarily Greek, period of the Church, and also from the twelfth-century French philosopher and theologian, Richard of St. Victor. The Fathers of the Church and Richard of St. Victor derive their concept of the person from the idea of the Trinity. Torrance describes Richard's understanding of a person "not in terms of its own independence as self-subsistence, but in terms of its ontic relations to other persons, i.e., by a transcendental relation to what is other than it, and in terms of its own unique incommunicable existence"; so "a person is what he is only through relations with other persons" (Torrance, 1985, p. 176). The early Fathers' view of relationship as essential to personality is found also in Augustine, but it was largely displaced in the Latin West by a narrow interpretation of Boethius as laying stress on the individual.

The Catholic theologian Joseph Ratzinger (1970, 1990; later Benedict XVI) took a position strikingly similar to Torrance's. Ratzinger (1970) wrote,

Christian thought discovered the kernel of the concept of person, which describes something other and infinitely more than the mere idea of the "individual." Let us listen once more to St. Augustine: "In God there are no accidents, only substance and relation." Therein lies concealed a revolution in man's view of the world: the relation is discovered as an equally valid primordial mode of reality. It becomes possible to surmount what we call today "objectifying thought"; a new plane of being comes into view. (p. 132)

According to Ratzinger, substance and relationship are each jointly necessary, but not individually sufficient, determinants of personality. In today's historical context, however, special emphasis needs to be laid on the place of relationship in personality. Like Torrance, Ratzinger (1990) pointed out that the dominant interpretation of Boethius's definition of "person" as an "individual substance of a rational nature" had unfortunate consequences for the Western understanding of the person because of its emphasis on a person as an isolated individual, an autonomous being. If substance dominates our thinking about persons, we may lose the earlier Christian insight that personality also essentially involves relationship.

Finally, in a way similar to both Torrance and Ratzinger, the Eastern Orthodox theologian J. D. Zizioulas (1985) in his book, *Being as Communion*, reiterates the Eastern Church's understanding of the importance of relationship, which had never gone into eclipse. One should also note the important philosopher of religion John Macmurray (1991), who strongly emphasized relationship as central to the person.

There is now an enormous amount of psychological evidence for the importance of relationship in the formation of the person. Relationships are essential for basic human existence and development (see Siegel, 1999,

2012). A newborn child who lacks a mothering relationship with another human will die, even if its physical needs are met. A person learns to speak through loving relationships that begin in the first weeks after birth, when the infant first listens to its mother's voice. In fact, for many this relationship begins in utero when the fetus first hears its mother's voice. Language-learning requires relationships, and is foundational to the human person. The field of developmental psychology has provided evidence that the individual's sense of his own language and individual thought processes derives developmentally from responding to the mother and her use of language, and from interaction starting in infancy and continuing through childhood. Vygotsky (1978) said, "An interpersonal process is transformed into an intrapersonal process" (p. 57).

Additional Psychological and Theological Characteristics

In light of these considerations, from the Christian perspective, it is clear that Carl Rogers's well-known book *On Becoming a Person* (1961) is mistitled. His book is about becoming not a person but an individual, and in particular, an autonomous, self-actualizing, independent individual. An individual is created by separating from others, by concentrating psychological thought, energy, and emotion on the self, not on God and other people.

Becoming an individual—that is, separating and distancing yourself from others—has a logical progression. First, you break the "chains" that linked you to your parents, and then to others, and then to society and culture. Finally, you reject the self itself: that is, you separate consciousness from the illusion of the self. You reject the self and all its desires—and thus the process of separation culminates in an experience of a state of nothingness. Radical autonomy ultimately means separation from everything; it means total or ultra-autonomy, where even the self is gone.

Let me offer a brief sketch to illustrate the distinction between a person and an individual:

A Person is created by God in the image of God.
An Individual is created by the self in the image of self.

A Person loves and trusts God, and loves others as self; Persons forgive those who have hurt them.
An Individual loves and trusts the self, trusts others, and rejects or ignores God; Individuals forget hurts, and those who have hurt them.

A Person has the goal of committed relationships with others and union with God.
An Individual has the goal of separating from others, and, in the extreme, of separating even from the self.

For a Person, true freedom is choosing complete dependence on God, who is free.
For an Individual, true autonomy is choosing complete dependence on the self.

A Person accepts the reality of God, other people, and the physical world.
An Individual rejects everything outside of the self as subjective and a nonreality.

Putting the Individual in Perspective

These contrasts overstate the case in the sense that no individual is apt to take these modern principles to such an extreme. Reality does not let us. Most of us have enough common sense to protect us from taking psychological theories too seriously. The image of a person is also idealized. We are all aware how poorly most Christians live

up to such ideals. In the everyday world, it can be hard to distinguish who is operating from which of these two theoretically very different models.

The secular emphasis on independence and individuation can be good and historically has brought about major benefits, such as the notion of individual rights. Independence from the unexamined views of others is also an important virtue, not just for the secular world but in the Christian world as well. Christian theology emphasizes free will or free choice. God gives us freedom to choose him or not. Throughout Scripture, this is a central theme. The emphasis placed on freedom by the world in the last few centuries can be understood as a basic Christian principle translated into the social and political world where, often as a result of the secular Enlightenment, it has accomplished much good.

The Actual Process of Becoming a Person: "Personagenesis"

What is the process of becoming a person, within such a Catholic Christian theory of personality? What is "personagenesis," as Robert Connor calls it (1992, p. 45–49)? Although the following describes a process of becoming a person, it is really a process of how *the person, who is already present at conception*, develops in increasingly complex ways throughout a normal life span.

First, a Christian theory does not reject the claim that a person is a substance as represented by embodiment, but gives equal or greater emphasis to the person as relation. In the language of Karol Wojtyła (later John Paul II), a person is constructed on the "metaphysical site" of substance, but the process of construction involves the dynamics of relationships (Connor, 1992, p. 47).

For Wojtyła, the first step in personagenesis "seems to be passivity, receptivity of love from another" (Connor, 1992, p. 45). In the natural world, this is usually the love a newborn receives from its mother and father. In the spiritual realm, which is at the core of personality, it is listening to the call and love of God. Once initiated, the process of becoming a person continues as a "vertical transcendence" in which the person gives "the self to another" (Connor, 1992, p. 47). The process of lovingly giving the self to another both transcends and determines the self in its act of performing service. The giving of the self to another is how the individual self is transcended; it is also how one comes to know both the other and, from the perspective of the other, to know oneself much more "objectively" than one ever can from inside an autonomous self. Thus, one becomes a person, or, more accurately, one fulfills in actuality the person who was there from the beginning.

Wojtyła (1979) noted that free will is at the center of a person's self-gift to another, for while man freely determines his actions, he is "at the same time fully aware" that his actions "in turn determine him; moreover they continue to determine him even when they have passed" (Connor, 1992, p. 48).

When the other person receives one's gift of love and gives him- or herself in return, the highest form of intimacy results. Intimacy with God and others thus becomes a major characteristic of a person.

Relationship and Philosophy

Some have interpreted Aquinas as failing to appreciate and recognize the importance of relationships as central to the concept of person (cited by Clarke, 1993, "Introduction"). However, a significant Thomist response to this problem has come from Norris Clarke (1993), who argued that relationship was always implicit in the Thomist understanding of the person as a rational substance. Clarke draws out the Thomist appreciation of relationship and concludes: "All being, therefore, is, by its very nature as being, dyadic, with an 'introverted', or in-itself dimension, as substance and an 'extroverted', or towards-others dimension, as related through action.... to be is to be substance-in-relation" (pp. 15–17).

In conclusion, the preceding Catholic Christian theory of personality, presented here in short form, is a distinctive model that includes some of the assumptions and emphases of existing theories, but without many secular presuppositions, combined with new assumptions and new basic aspects of personality. In addition, unlike existing secular theories, the present approach has an explicit listing and defense of the assumptions underlying the theory.

REFERENCES

Allport, G. W. (1937). *Personality: A psychological interpretation*. New York, NY: Holt.

Arnold, M. B., & Gasson, J. H.(1954). *The human person: An approach to an integrated theory of personality*. New York, NY: Ronald Press.

Bandura, A. (1989). Human agency in social cognitive theory. *American Psychologist, 44,* 1175–1184.

Beck, A. T. (1975). *Cognitive therapy and emotional disorders*. Madison, CT: International Universities Press.

Beck, A. T., Freeman, A., & Davis, D. D. (2003). *Cognitive therapy of personality disorders*. New York, NY: Guilford.

Bellah, R., Madsen, R., Sullivan, W., Swidler, A., & Tipton, S. (1985). *Habits of the heart: Individualism and commitment in American life*. New York, NY: Harper & Row.

Benedict XVI. (2009). *Caritas in veritate* [Encyclical, on integral human development in charity and truth]. Vatican City, Vatican: Libreria Editrice Vaticana.

Benedict XVI. (October 17, 2012). General audience. Vatican City, Vatican: Libreria Editrice Vaticana.

Bergin, A. E. (1980). Psychotherapy and religious values. *Journal of Consulting and Clinical Psychology, 48*(1), 95–105.

Budziszewski, J. (2009). *The line through the heart: Natural law as fact, theory, and sign of contradiction.* Wilmington, DE: ISI Books.

Catechism of the Catholic Church (2nd ed.). (2000). Vatican City, Vatican: Libreria Editrice Vaticana.

Clarke, W. N. (1993). *Person and being: The Aquinas lecture, 1993.* Milwaukee, WI: Marquette University Press.

Connor, R. (1992). The person as resonating existential. *American Catholic Philosophical Quarterly, 66*(1), 39–56.

Damasio, A. (1994). *Descartes' error: Emotion, reason and the human brain.* New York, NY: Putnam.

Ellis, A. (1962). *Reason and emotion in psychotherapy.* New York, NY: Lyle Stuart.

Ellis, A. (1994). *Reason and emotion in psychotherapy, revised and updated.* Secaucus, NJ: Carol Publishing Group.

Erikson, E. H. (1959). *Identity and the life cycle: Selected papers.* Psychological Issues. Monograph No. 1, Vol. 1. New York, NY: International Universities Press.

Erikson, E. H. (1964). *Insight and responsibility.* New York, NY: Norton.

Erikson, E. H. (Ed.). (1968). *Identity: Youth and crisis.* New York, NY: Norton.

Erikson, E. H. (Ed.). (1978). *Adulthood.* New York, NY: Norton.

Feist, J., Feist, G. T., & Roberts, T.-A. (2013). *Theories of Personality* (8th ed.). New York, NY: McGraw-Hill.

Francis. (April 28, 2017). Message from the Holy Father to the participants in the Plenary Session of the Pontifical Academy of Social Sciences (28 April–2 May 2017). Vatican City, Vatican: Libreria Editrice Vaticana.

Frankl, V. (1960). *The doctor and the soul: An introduction to logotherapy.* New York, NY: Knopf.

Frankl, V. (1963). *Man's search for meaning.* New York, NY: Simon & Schuster.

Friederici, A. D. (2017). *Language in our brain: The origins of a uniquely human capacity.* Cambridge, MA: MIT Press.

Gazzaniga, M. (1994). *Nature's mind: Biological roots of thinking, emotions, sexuality, language and intelligence.* New York, NY: Basic Books.

George, R. P. (1999). *In defense of natural law.* Oxford, United Kingdom: Oxford University Press.

Greenberg, L. (2002). *Emotion-Focused Therapy: Coaching clients to work through feelings.* Washington, DC: American Psychological Association Press.

Johnson, S. M. (2004). *The practice of emotionally focused couples therapy* (2nd ed.). New York, NY: Brunner-Routledge.

Kohlberg, L. (1981). *Essays on moral development: Vol. 1. The philosophy of moral development.* San Francisco, CA: Harper & Row.

Kohlberg, L. (1984). *Essays on moral development: Vol. 2. The psychology of moral development.* San Francisco, CA: Harper & Row.

Lakoff, G., & Johnson, M. (1999). *Philosophy in the flesh: The embodied mind and its challenge to Western thought.* New York, NY: Basic Books.

LeDoux, J. (1996). *The emotional brain: The mysterious underpinnings of emotional life.* New York, NY: Touchstone.

MacIntyre, A. (1999). *Dependent rational animals: Why human beings need the virtues.* Chicago, IL: Open Court.

Macmurray, J. (1991). *Persons in relation.* Atlantic Highlands, NJ: Humanities Press. (Original work published in 1961.)

May, W. E. (2013). *Catholic bioethics and the gift of human life* (3rd ed.). Huntington, IN: Our Sunday Visitor Press.

Müller, M., & Haider, A. (1969). Person: Concept. In Karl Rahner (Ed.), *Sacramentum mundi* (Vol. 4, pp. 404–409). New York, NY: Herder & Herder.

Obler, L. K., & Gjerlow, K. (1999). *Language and the brain.* Cambridge, United Kingdom: Cambridge University Press.

Piaget, J. (1952). *The origin of intelligence in children.* New York, NY: International Universities Press.

Piaget, J., & Inhelder, B. (1969). *The early growth of logic.* New York, NY: Norton.

Pinckaers, S. (1995). *The sources of Christian ethics* (M. T. Noble, Trans.). Washington, DC: The

Catholic University of America Press. (Original work published 1985)

Peterson, C., & Seligman, M. E. P. (2004). *Character strengths and virtues: A handbook and classification.* New York, NY: Oxford University Press.

Ratzinger, J. (1970). *Introduction to Christianity.* New York, NY: Herder & Herder.

Ratzinger, J. (1990). Concerning the notion of person in theology. *Communio, 17*(3), 439–454. (Original work published in German, 1973.)

Rizzolatti, G., & Sinigaglia, C. (2008). *Mirrors in the brain: How our minds share actions and emotions.* Oxford, United Kingdom: Oxford University Press.

Rogers, C. (1961). *On becoming a person.* Boston, MA: Houghton Mifflin.

Schultz, D. P., & Schultz, S. E. (2013). *Theories of personality* (10th ed.). Belmont, CA: Wadsworth.

Seligman, M. E. P., & Csikszentmihalyi, M. (2000) Positive psychology: An introduction. *American Psychologist, 55,* 5–14.

Siegel, D. J. (2012). *The developing mind: How relationships and the brain interact to shape who we are* (2nd ed.). New York, NY: Guilford.

Siegel, D. J. (2012). *Pocket guide to interpersonal neurobiology: An integrative handbook of the mind* (1st ed.). New York, NY: W.W. Norton.

Sollod, R. N., Wilson, J. P., & Monte, C. F. (2009). *Beneath the mask: An introduction to theories of personality* (8th ed.). Hoboken, NJ: Wiley.

Torrance, T. (1983). *The mediation of Christ.* Grand Rapids, MI: Eerdmans.

Torrance, T. (1985). *Reality and scientific theology.* Edinburgh, United Kingdom: Scottish Academic Press.

Vitz, P. C. (1994). *Psychology as religion: The cult of self-worship* (2nd ed.). Grand Rapids, MI: Eerdmans.

Vitz, P. C. (1997). A Christian theory of personality. In R. C. Roberts and M. R. Talbot (Eds.), *Limning the psyche: Explorations in Christian psychology* (pp. 20–40). Grand Rapids, MI: Eerdmans.

Vygotsky, L. S. (1978). *Mind in society: The development of higher psychology processes.* Cambridge, MA: Harvard University Press.

Wallach, M. A., & Wallach, L. (1983). *Psychology's sanction for selfishness: The error of egoism in theory and therapy.* San Francisco, CA: W.H. Freeman.

Wojtyła, K. (1979). *The acting person* (A. T. Tymieniecka, Ed.; A. Potocki, Trans.). Boston, MA: D. Reidel Publishing Company. (Original work published 1969)

Zizioulas, J. D. (1985). *Being as communion.* Crestwood, NY: St. Vladimir's Seminary Press.

Chapter 5

Basic Psychological Support for the Catholic Christian Meta-Model of the Person

Paul C. Vitz

ABSTRACT: This chapter identifies how contemporary psychology serves to support the major theological and philosophical properties of the Catholic Christian Meta-Model. The narrative theological premises of created, fallen, and redeemed are similar to narrative aspects of existing approaches to personality and psychotherapy. For example, we as persons are good but harmed by experience and can find healing and fulfillment through self-actualization. Some narrative psychologists describe successful therapy as constructing a new and redemptive life-story. The teleological premises of the Meta-Model parallel those found in positive psychology with its focus on virtue development and the emphasis on higher meaning found in existential psychology. The structural dimensions of the person also receive psychological support. For example, the idea of the person as a body-soul unity or whole is similar to many holistic psychologies. The emphasis on relationship parallels attachment theory and other contemporary interpersonal theories. Traditional scientific psychology has long studied and known the importance of the person's reason, that is, intelligence and language, as well as the importance of emotions and of sensory-perceptual-cognitive capacities. Recently, after neglect, the will is receiving a new emphasis as well.

Chapter 2 presented the Catholic Christian Meta-Model of the Person (Meta-Model for short), with its systematic theological and philosophical foundations, as well as a preliminary list of psychological premises associated with the Meta-Model. Here we present theory and evidence from the field of psychology that underlie and support the basic philosophical and theological premises of the Meta-Model.

Part 1: Support from Secular Psychology for the Narrative Structure of the Meta-Model's Theological Premises

A major feature of the person in the Meta-Model is the person's narrative character, the theological narrative structure of the person as created, fallen, and redeemed, and then the person's response to his or her vocations or callings. For significant Christian treatments of the topic of narrative and theology see the work of Goodson (2015), Hauerwas & Jones (1997), MacIntyre (1981), and Ricœur (1984).

What the Model assumes by the term "narrative" is as follows: To begin, a narrative is a sequence of events presented by a narrator, or storyteller, to one or more people. A narrative is intrinsically social and involves a community of at least two people, but more commonly many more. This interpersonal quality means that narratives are also interactive, dialogic. A narrative has both a general theme and a goal or *telos*. As it moves toward the goal, there are both people and events that aid the movement and people and events that work to prevent reaching the goal. As a result, a narrative has a moral character in which there is a struggle between good and evil, usually, but not always, between those supporting the goal and those hostile to it. This struggle encourages people to develop virtues rooted in wisdom and truth based on contact with reality. This often leads to character development and always has an implicit message for the audience. Humans in all cultures appear to need narratives or storytelling, and it is now commonly accepted in psychology that understanding and responding to stories are foundational properties of human nature, specifically of how all humans find much of the meaning in their lives (this idea will be further developed in the next section). Even pre-verbal infants seem to have a rudimentary capacity for interpreting external events in a moral narrative framework (Hamlin, 2013).

The general Judeo-Christian narrative, which is for all persons, is not found, as far as I know, in any of the narrative approaches to the person in contemporary psychology. Underneath the general model, the Christian narrative does emphasize that each person has a distinctive and particular story and calling. This specific narrative of each person follows from the assumption that each person is unique and has a unique vocation or calling from God; that is, in psychological parlance, a role he plays in the narrative of his life.

Putting God into the Meta-Model is, no doubt, something of a novelty for psychology, but there is a rationale for it. First, keep in mind that all the existing psychological theories of the person, by leaving God out, are atheistic; yet this omission is simply an assumption that is seldom, if ever, defended. The absence or non-relevance of God is not something that scientific psychology has established. Let us briefly revisit an important debate in psychology that occurred some decades ago between two very prominent psychologists, Albert Ellis (1980), an atheist, and Allen Bergin (1980), a Mormon theist. Bergin explicitly argued that values followed from the psychologist's worldview, and he contrasted theistic values with the humanistic values often expressed in psychotherapy. Ellis accepted that values followed from worldviews and not directly from scientific psychology. He contrasted his particular atheistic humanistic views with some of Bergin's interpretations. And, of course, he argued that his atheistic views were more rational. But the upshot of the debate was an agreement that the psychologist's values do not come from an objective science of psychology but from the therapist's own personal assumptions, religious or nonreligious worldview, and general philosophical assumptions.

The secular theories often have an implicit general theory in which they stress a particular or individualistic narrative for each patient or client. Although such approaches do not specify an *explicit* general narrative for all patients, since they have no normative model of the person, I will describe briefly the implicit narrative theory actually present in them. And, as we will see below, the secular narrative approaches have many analogies or implicit similarities to the general Christian narrative.

We begin with Sigmund Freud, who understood the person as coming out of a vague evolutionary past and as determined by biological instincts, primarily sex and aggression. These innate forces, located largely in the unconscious, were presumed to cause much psychological conflict throughout most of our life. The purpose of psychoanalysis was to reduce our conflicts to a manageable level, that is, to what can be called the normal level of human misery. Thus, Freud rejected any psychological synthesis of life's problems. He claimed that to do so, as Jung and Adler proposed, was to change psychology from a science into a religion. Freud wrote that analysts "cannot guide patients in their 'synthesis'; we can, by analytic work, prepare them for it" (quoted in Roazen, 1975, p. 204). As is noted below, the Christian therapist, in many ways, respects Freud's view in the process of therapy or counseling, at least with non-Christians. Freud saw people like Adler (1931) as "buffoons.... publishing books about the meaning of life (!) ..." (Freud, E. L., 1960, p. 401.) Freud did leave a place in normal life for love and a life instinct and for sublimated sexuality, but his basic understanding of human nature was that it was primarily characterized by dangerous or harmful motives. Because there was no ultimate synthesis or answer to life's problems, Freud's vision of the person, like that of many psychoanalysts, was essentially tragic (Schafer, 1976).

Carl Jung proposed that our initial state was rooted in a universal inherited collective unconscious, with a smaller personal unconscious on top of it, capped with a still smaller amount of consciousness. The collective unconscious consisted of a large number of inherited archetypes that came from our primate and early human life.

Some of these archetypes were negative or bad (e.g., the shadow, aspects of the persona, trickster) but most were positive (e.g., the self, animus or anima, wise old man, earth mother). Our problem was the failure to make these archetypes conscious, integrated, and developed. Jungian therapy aimed at doing this, and the process was called individuation or self-realization and was itself both the goal of therapy and the spiritual purpose of life. Jung explicitly claimed that self-realization was the purpose of his therapy, and he accepted self-realization as the ideal, highest form of human spiritual striving. For example, in a book by a prominent follower of Jung and endorsed by him (Jacobi, 1973, p.60), we find the following claim about Jungian psychotherapy: "It is a *Heilsweg*, in the twofold sense of the German word: a way of healing and a way of salvation." And, "Jungian psychotherapy is thus a system of education and spiritual guidance"; "Only a few are willing and able to travel a path of salvation." Jung's psychology also has a significant narrative component. Many of his archetypes are well known as mythological or legendary characters (e.g., the wise old man, earth mother, hero, princess, king, shadow, etc.) found throughout the literature of most cultures. In certain respects, Jung's psychotherapy requires the patients to understand the meaning of their archetypes so as to create a new narrative understanding of their life. Jung's work has often been applied to describe and conceptualize narratives applicable to life outside of therapy. See, for example, the writers behind much of the "Men's Movement" such as Bly, 1990 and Moore & Gillette, 1990.

In a different context, both Carl Rogers (1961) and Abraham Maslow (1970a) proposed a widely known psychological kind of redemption or salvation termed "self-actualization." For Maslow (1970b), the highest expression of this was what he called the "peak-experience." Viktor

Frankl's (1960, 1970) existential "logotherapy" emphasized that some kind of transcendent higher meaning, selected by the client, is the answer to a person's ultimate purpose and is a major goal of psychotherapy. Frankl's position probably is the closest to the Meta-Model's assumption of redemption.

Erik Erikson's (1950, 1959, 1968,1982) implicit narrative is based on his eight psychosocial stages of human development ranging from birth to old age. Each stage has its own goal, starting with basic trust and the virtue of hope (infancy), then autonomy and the virtue of will (early childhood), then initiative and the virtue of purpose (childhood, play age), next industry and the virtue of competence (childhood, school age), next identity and the virtue of fidelity (adolescence), next intimacy and the virtue of love (young adulthood), next generativity and the virtue of care (mature adulthood), and finally ego integrity and the virtue of wisdom (old age). Erickson therefore has an explicit narrative for each stage and an implicit one for the complete life cycle.

Also, there is now Seligman's positive psychology (2012), in which the human's purpose is to flourish through cultivating the virtues. Seligman (Peterson & Seligman, 2004, pp. 51–52) appears to accept an evolutionary origin of the virtues. That is, the worldwide, almost universal emphasis on the virtues stems from their contribution to individual and especially to group and culture survival. This understanding fits other psychologies that assume that the person's origin is only material, or at least does not involve God. The secular approaches all neglect transcendence and assume only immanence. The Meta-Model's emphasis on flourishing through virtues and vocation means that the flourishing being advocated is based on self-giving to God and to others. This flourishing begins on earth and ends in eternal joy in the afterlife.

Evidence for the various kinds of analogous support from secular psychology for the Meta-Model's basic narrative understanding of the person, discussed above, is summarized in Table 5.1.

It is important to emphasize that though some secular psychologies address the meaning of life within therapy, it is never the goal of psychotherapy, based on the Meta-Model, to even suggest the Christian narrative to clients, much less to convert them. A Christian therapist or counselor seeks to heal pathology, remove symptoms, and to emphasize growth through response to the client's freely chosen vocation and practice of virtue. The goal is always to respect the client's freedom and when possible to increase their freedom. Redemption in Christ is a religious choice and not a part of therapy. Any involvement in an issue of life goals should be freely introduced by the client and should remain free of any pressure from the therapist. Although therapy and counseling with Christian clients may occasionally allow the therapist to mention Christ, even the confused and uncertain Christian must make their choice of faith freely. This admonition applies also to secular therapists who may be tempted to imply, or even impose, various ideologies on clients.

Recent Rationale for Narrative Psychology

There are now important psychological approaches committed to narrative models that provide interpretations of human personality within an explicit narrative framework. For example, several major arguments for the relevance of narratives to psychology came to prominence in the '80s and '90s and were aimed at creating a paradigm shift in psychology away from the mechanistic, deterministic interpretation of the person toward a more humanistic, literary, and

Table 5.1. The Meta-Model's Explicit and Secular Implicit
General Narrative Understanding of Person: A Brief Summary

Theory	Human Origin	Our Problem	The Answer
Catholic Christian Meta-Model of the Person	Created by God: in image of God; person originally good; all persons have equal dignity & worth	Disobedience of Adam & Eve and now our own sinful actions with pervasive bad consequences.	Redeemed by Christ: freely seek & follow Christ for love of him & others; transcendent focus.
Sigmund Freud	Just exist with biological drives from evolution; person is mostly bad.	Biological drives/instincts in conflict with each other, reality, & society.	Reduce pathology to normal level; No synthesis or purpose; tragic view of life; focus on self & this world.
Carl Jung	Just exist with archetypes from primitive past; archetypes (& person) mostly good, some bad.	Anxiety, depression, & lack of meaning become a major problem in adult life.	Integrate by expressing archetypes as Gnostic spiritual process of self-realization; focus on self & this world.
Alfred Adler	Just exist as biological and mostly as a social being; person has mostly good potential.	Inferiority feelings with solution focused on the individual ego overcoming inferiority.	Express creative self: often focused on others/ social interest; self- & other-focused; but always this world.
Carl Rogers and Abraham Maslow	Just exist; humanistic interpretation of self as all good.	Inhibitions & bad experiences created by family & society.	Remove inhibitions; autonomous expression of self-actualization; focus on self & this world.
Viktor Frankl	Just exist; existential interpretation of person as mostly good.	Lack of higher meaning; existential angst over fear of death, non-being.	Therapy-guided search for a personal higher, sometimes transcendent meaning; focus usually on self & this world.
Erik Erikson	Just exist as biological and social being; mix of good & bad.	Failure to successfully progress through one or more of eight psychosocial stages.	Go through the stages & build the associated virtues, esp. adult virtues; focus on self, others, & this world.
Martin Seligman	Exist via evolution; person not good or bad; life, virtues based on chance & personal or group survival.	Failure to develop virtues.	Flourishing through developing virtues; focus on self & this world. Not explicitly ethical.

teleological framework. An important pioneer was Jerome Bruner with his influential publications (1986, 1990, 1991). A theoretical work with more than a dozen contributors, edited by Theodore Sarbin (1986), was also influential. Turning specifically to psychotherapy, we find many narrative theorists. A good example is Don Spence (1982), with his emphasis on narrative truth—as contrasted with the patient's reported and presumed historical truth—as the appropriate model for understanding a patient. Psychoanalysis itself has developed something of a similar position in the nonreductionist writings of Roy Schafer (1992), with his advocacy of narrative models that use psychoanalytic concepts in psychoanalytic sessions. It has long been noted that psychoanalytic case histories often had a kind of narrative character, and indeed Freud once mentioned that his case histories were often responded to as though they were short stories. (Perhaps this is why Freud got the Goethe Prize for literature but never the Nobel Prize for science.)

There is also the narrative understanding of counseling described within a Christian framework by Vitz (1992a, 1992b) that partly prefigures the present Meta-Model approach. Another, more recent and very comprehensive narrative approach to counseling and psychotherapy is presented in the work of John McLeod (1997) who claims "all therapies are narrative therapies" (p. x; also see Angus & McLeod 2003; McLeod, 2004; White, 2007). A closely related narrative understanding involves conceptualizing personality itself, outside of any kind of psychotherapy, as based on the story of a person's life. This sometimes comes close to traditional biography and is found in the writings of the personality theorist Dan McAdams (1988), in his focus on a person's life story as a framework for understanding personality. McAdams explicitly considers these stories as "redemptive" (2013).

The narrative approach has not only been increasingly important in the field of psychotherapy and counseling, but has long been present in the qualitative research methodologies of the phenomenologists that seek a rich understanding of psychological functioning (e.g., depression, anxiety, loneliness) and human phenomena through the analysis of narrative accounts of human subjects who have experienced them (Giorgi, 1970). In short, the general idea of conceptualizing the person and psychotherapy within a narrative framework is now well established in psychology and needs no special rationale.

We turn now to psychological support for the specific three theological stages of the Meta-Model: *created*, *fallen*, and *redeemed*. Each stage must be considered by itself, that is, separate from the others. That the person is created by God and in the image of God obviously has no similar direct expression in secular psychology. Most practicing psychotherapists assume the person just *is*, and usually, as a result of their humanistic and existentialist psychologies, therapists simply assume the person is valuable and is basically good. As already noted, some psychologists assume, with Rogers, Maslow, and a few others, that the self or person is entirely good. Others, such as Melanie Klein, seem to assume the person is entirely bad and born so. The Meta-Model, by contrast, does not simply assume the basic value of the person but derives the dignity and value of the person explicitly from the premise that we are made by God and in God's image and as "very good" (Gen 1:31).

In spite of our original and still significant goodness, the Meta-Model claims we are fallen. Now, of course, existing psychology does not speak of "fallenness" or original sin, although Sigmund Freud explicitly identified oedipal motivation as an expression of original sin (Freud, 1913/1957, p. 153; Vitz, 1988, pp. 166–169). Never-

Table 5.2. **The Meta-Model's Theology and Its Relation to a Traditional Catholic Christian Psychology**

Meta-Model's Theology		
Created	*Fallen*	*Redeemed*
Created by God: in the image of God	Fallen by our actions: disobedience of Adam & Eve and consequences for us	Redeemed by Christ: must seek & follow Christ
Original state: justice; solitude; innocence; happiness	Original sin: Vices and many negative effects	Called to: redemption, sanctification, & communion, & theological virtues
Traditional Catholic Christian Psychology		
Original psychology, i.e., pre-fall	*Fallen psychology: The major vices*	*Redeemed & transcendent psychology: Love of Christ*
Intrinsic goodness and great value of person; life as a gift; unity of person; desire to flourish; marked by divine & natural moral order. Person lived in an ongoing union with God, thus our original Catholic Christian psychology was a mixture of natural positive psychology (the virtues) and a transcendent psychology.	Resulted from loss of transcendent contact with God; our dominant motivation became egocentric. The vices express and symbolize the nature of the traditional Catholic Christian understanding of the source of much human suffering. 1. Pride & vanity 2. Envy 3. Wrath 4. Greed 5. Sloth 6. Lust 7. Gluttony	Called by Christ to love of God & others; helped by virtues (1–3 are transcendent) and vocations to holiness, state in life, work. The virtues are the traditional Catholic Christian psychological answers. 1. Faith 2. Hope 3. Love (charity) 4. Humility 5. Practical wisdom (prudence) 6. Justice 7. Courage 8. Self-control (temperance)

theless, contemporary psychology does provide many detailed descriptions of negative states that are commonly observed by psychologists and are apparently intrinsic to humanity. These negative states often can be easily understood as strong evidence for the human propensity to sin. As examples, consider the ease with which people show interpersonal hatred and violence; the tendency many people have to envy what they don't possess, especially what is good and possessed by others; the predisposition toward pride and arrogance; the overabundance of harmful narcissism; the frequency of rape and sexual abuse; and the ubiquitous self-serving bias. At the interpersonal level, Gottman (1999) has summarized the literature on married couples and noted how easily distressed couples fall into negative and distorted perceptions, behave in maladaptive ways, and even find themselves physiologically dysregulated.

All these can be seen as expressions of our fallen nature. In short, we humans have many deep and serious problems. This Catholic Christian psychology is briefly summarized in Table 5.2.

Table 5.3. Traditional Christian Mental Pathologies (the Vices) and
Their Contemporary Psychological Descriptions

---

1. Pride & vanity: self-centeredness, neglect of others, narcissism, anxiety

2. Envy: hating the good in others; resentment, jealousy, anxiety, depression

3. Wrath: violence, interpersonal hatred of others, lack of forgiveness, disrespecting others, self-hatred

4. Greed: injustice, self-serving bias, anxiety

5. Sloth: Indifference to others or self, lack of commitment, depression, despair

6. Lust: depersonalization & objectification of others, rape, sexual abuse of children

7. Gluttony: self-indulgence & inordinate pleasure in eating, drinking, drugs; often resulting in addiction

---

For an insightful and rich discussion of the psychology of the major vices, listed in Table 5.2, see Dennis Okholm (2014).

Table 5.3 presents a brief characterization of how the Catholic Christian psychology of Table 5.2 connects with or integrates the Meta-Model with existing secular clinical psychology. It should be emphasized that Table 5.3 notes the greater scientific utility of the secular characterizations of the majority of pathologies and of their treatments, for they are more specific and better for identifying treatment procedures. The present Meta-Model thus acknowledges and accepts within its integration the many valuable and positive contributions of secular modern psychology. The theological and philosophical vocabulary of the Model is often too general and abstract to be very useful in the therapy setting, at least until it gets unpacked in clear psychological terms, which is the point of many of the other chapters in this volume.

The Meta-Model is not simply a theoretical model, but also serves as the foundation for Catholic Christian approaches to psychotherapy. Because it is comprehensive in nature, the Meta-Model is able to integrate truths contained in the existing secular personality theories or to incorporate the existing effective methodologies of secular therapy into itself. Of course, the Meta-Model may reject some of the assumptions or values in a given theory or consider some aspects of the therapeutic methodologies to be illicit, but by and large the Meta-Model, and the approach to therapy derived from it, actually requires such integration. For example, psychoanalytic, Jungian, Adlerian, Cognitive-Behavioral Therapy, and Emotion-Focused Therapy are examples that have been, or can be, used within the Meta-Model framework. The first goal of a Catholic Christian approach to psychotherapy is to free the person of pathologies and dysfunctional behavior, which threaten human freedom. A second goal, usually emerging near the end of therapy, is to encourage the client to choose freely to develop virtues in the process of expressing his or her vocational commitments. As mentioned before, such a Catholic Christian approach to mental health practice does not seek to religiously influence the client, but instead creates the conditions of greater freedom, which later may be used by the client to give himself to others and God.

Part 2: Support from Secular Psychology for the Meta-Model's Philosophical Premises

We begin by recalling the eight philosophically based properties or components of the person as identified in the Meta-Model. These properties are foundational elements, which Catholics and Christians use in their discussions, that identify a community of enquiry that is formed around a narrative philosophical tradition. Philosophers who have developed this understanding include MacIntyre (1981, 1990) and C. Boyd (2007). The properties are: (1) the person is a whole, a body and soul unity; (2) the person is called to flourishing through a threefold vocation to personal holiness, to vowed or non-vowed vocational states (e.g., married), and to work and service in support of community and society; (3) the person is motivated toward fulfillment through growth in the virtues; (4) the person is relational, that is, significantly the result of interpersonal relationships throughout the lifespan; (5) the person has sensory-perceptual-cognitive capacities; (6) the person is emotional, that is, emotions strongly influence who we are; (7) the person is rational, using reason and intelligence; and (8) the person has a will, a significant part of which is free, and thus the adult person is morally responsible for much of his or her behavior. In Chapter 2, the theological and especially the philosophical rationale and understanding of these properties has already been given.

As shown below, all of these properties already have significant support within the existing field of psychology; however, the Meta-Model adds important new psychological characteristics or emphases to each property and provides an integration or synthesis of all of them.

1. The Person Is Whole, a Unity

This assumption about the person has been emphasized by many major personality theorists. It is important to keep in mind that this holistic and nonreductionist emphasis does not deny that there are important traits and components, lower psychological or biological aspects of the whole person, but states that in most settings, such as the psychotherapy session, the person responds as an integrated whole. This holistic property should never be forgotten even when attending to a person's test scores measuring aspects of their personality or behavior.

The Importance of the Body. Since the person is a **body-soul unity**, the biological body is a significant contributor to the person and personality. All psychological functions are influenced by our body and take place in it. As a general rule the major psychological theories of personality developed in the twentieth century ignored the human body, especially sex differences, as a significant factor in understanding the person. Sigmund Freud is an exception, since he did distinguish between male and female psychology with the Oedipus and Electra complexes. But this interpretation has been rejected by most mental health professionals. Carl Jung also distinguished between male (animus) and female (anima) archetypes, but primarily to attribute them to the opposite sex and thus to emphasize the unisex or androgynous personality of the person.

The psychologist William Sheldon (1940) was a genuine exception to this lack of interest in the psychology of the body. In the 1940s he proposed three major body types as determinants of personality. Endomorphs, ectomorphs, and mesomorphs were very roughly equivalent to overweight, very thin, and muscular types, respectively, and they were identified by measuring a person's nude body shape. A person's score on these three measures was then related to various personality traits and to behaviors. Sheldon's work received some empirical support but it has fallen out of favor, mostly because such gross body measurements are no longer viewed as sensitive to the many ways human bodies differ. In addition, his theory was insensitive to environmental and experiential effects on personality. Sheldon's model also was based only on male subjects.

Psychologists apparently neglected the body's influence because so little relevant knowledge about the body was available and because the existing, somewhat politically correct, attitude toward sex differences was that no such differences were significant. As a result, a unisex interpretation of personality was assumed to be true rather by default. In addition, in the twentieth century, the tradition of biological or body-based determinants of behavior was associated with unpopular conservative or non-liberal interpretations of people and society.

However, there is now a truly enormous amount of accepted evidence that the body is an inextricable part of a person and of personality. Consider the huge amount of evidence from developmental neuroscience and from the related position of evolutionary theory. See, for example, the work of David Buss (2008). Another small sample of this material will refresh our memory of how major this change has been. Daniel Siegel (2012) pioneered much of this understanding of the developing mind with his books on "how relationships and the brain interact to shape who we are." There are now important contributions to the neuroscience of human relationships (Cozolino, 2006) and the neuro-

science of psychotherapy (Cozolino, 2010). For example, it has long been known that the mother's physiology influences the developing fetus, but recent work shows that such influences work both ways, as cells from the fetus migrate to the mother to influence her immune system and even help repair damaged organs in the mother (See Dawe, Tan, & Xiao, 2007; Khosrotehrani & Bianchi, 2005).

Along with this explosion of neuroscience knowledge has come a large amount of evidence for important sex differences. Starting, perhaps, with Anne Moir and David Jessel (1991), this research is now very well established. See, for example, books on the female (2006) and male brain (2010) by Louann Brizendine; Steven Rhoads (2004) has another major contribution and so has Simon Baron-Cohen (2003). More recently, scientists have put forth an interpretation that sex differences complement each other in a positive and synergistic way. (See Allen, 2014, 2015; Ingalhalikar et al., 2014; Vitz, 2018; see also Chapter 9, "Man and Woman"). New findings on biological differences are published almost weekly in the medical world.

One important understanding to be drawn from the assumption of embodiment is that attempts by some in the field of artificial intelligence to fully model human intelligence will fail unless they include our body as well. Human intelligence is based on more than some abstract, digital, left-hemisphere intelligence; it includes the emotions found in the right hemisphere, the mid-brain, and even lower areas; it includes our sensory and perceptual and imaginative capacities and perhaps even such organs as the heart. In short, to simulate the human mind, one must also simulate the human body.

One often-overlooked characteristic of wholeness is the integration of our basic capacities so that meaning or interpretation is intrinsic to human understanding of most experience. Even so-called facts are always understood in terms of our worldview. And values arise out of the integration of the experience of the person, which involves the emotions, imagination, reason, will, and relationships.

The Issue of the Soul.   There is a significant aspect of this Catholic Christian unity that is quite different from secular holistic psychologies and even from those psychologies that recognize the importance of the body. The Meta-Model explicitly proposes that the person is a unity of body and soul. Modern psychology almost universally omits any reference to the soul, and as far as I know, no established psychological approach even addresses the soul as a relevant issue.

However, there were two important pioneers of modern psychology that did address this issue: Otto Rank (1930/1998) and Carl Jung (1933/1955). Rank's book is a rather long historical treatment with a generally positive position about the soul's relevance to modern psychology. Jung's discussion was brief and similar to the notion of soul as spirit, without the Christian understanding of its unity with body. In spite of these early expressions, the soul never became an aspect of any major psychological theory of personality or psychotherapy. A quite relevant discussion of modern "soulless" psychology is presented by Hendrika Vande Kemp (2007).

A recent attempt to bring back the relevance of the soul is a book by the Christian psychiatrist Jeffery Boyd (1996), appropriately titled *Reclaiming the Soul*. In his intelligent cry in the wilderness, Boyd identifies the absence of this concept even in holistic and humanistic psychology and notes many of the problems that arise from ignoring the soul. And more recently, there is a strong implication of the soul's

relevance in the work of Eric Johnson (2007), and most importantly, in the studies of Mario Beauregard (Beauregard, 2012; Beauregard & O'Leary, 2007), who provides a well-presented neurological case for the soul understood in a way compatible with Christianity.

In the case of the Meta Model, the term soul means the *animating spiritual form of the human body*. This is also the traditional Catholic position (*Catechism of the Catholic Church*, 2000, §365; John Paul II, 1993, §48); and also the position of Aristotelian philosophical psychology. It is proposed here that the soul as the spiritual or ontological form of the body can be usefully understood by a comparison with the DNA code that expresses the material form or biological structure of the body.

How might one understand the "form of the body"? One way is to note that the majority of the cells of the human body are replaced, often every few days or months, although sometimes it takes longer. (Brain neurons are the exception; they are not replaced.) Such cell replacement represents a restoration of most of the body. Each older cell must be exactly replaced in the newer cell. Given this cell replacement, there must be a latent pattern, blueprint, or form in the body that allows the body to restore itself so that it keeps the recognizable unique configuration of each person's body. Presumably the DNA code contains this blueprint for cell restoration and replacement. Keep in mind that in replacing a cell even the very complex DNA code itself must also be replaced or duplicated in every new cell. Such a massive, complex and continuously repeated, detailed replacement is remarkable.

It is also important to note that the DNA that will express the form of the body does not have to look like or be similar in shape to the body, that is, a code does not have to look like what it later expresses. Our genetic code even contributes substantially to a person's personality (Plomin, DeFries, Knopik, & Neiderhiser, 2016).

Putting aside the issue of cell replacement, it is well known that our DNA plus other yet-to-be-identified properties is a biological code for our whole body, brain included. The DNA plus code, which, as noted, does not look like our body, is that part of our nature known to science, and it contains the material form of our body that will be expressed starting at conception and in our subsequent bodily development and existence. However, our material code will have various identifiable imperfections that are birth defects—usually of a minor nature, but, of course, sometimes they are significant. Our recognition of bodily defects is a sign that a better code can be conceptualized. It is thus not difficult to conceptualize a perfect, spiritual and unique "code" for each person, a code that has no defects and that lies behind a person's imperfect material code.

We suggest that a perfect, *spiritual code* or *soul* exists at a transcendent level and it both animates and structures the form of our body. Keep in mind, however, that there are not two human souls, one material and one spiritual. Our material code is not our soul. Instead, the divinely created and animated transcendent "spiritual DNA plus" or real spiritual code is the soul; this soul both animates and structures the material aspects of the body and integrates these bodily processes with human consciousness (Vitz, 2017) and our spiritual capacities into a body-soul unity. Therefore, there are reasons to believe that such a spiritual soul serves as the animating principle and substantial form of the living body.

Our spiritual, perfect code might furthermore be understood as a source of the glory that the spiritual body-soul unity will express when a person is resurrected. If we have glorious bodies in heaven and, as so many near-death reports

claim (Alexander, 2012; Spitzer, 2015), we are recognizable to others in heaven, then our heavenly bodies could be more fully and completely expressed by our spiritual code (form) without the defects experienced when it was expressed in this material world as our DNA. Putting such speculation aside, it is important to remember that the Meta-Model has reintroduced the soul into psychology and along with it the transcendent spiritual realm.

There are ways in which this proposed integrative unity of a spiritual code with the human body can be illuminated by comparison to familiar human experience. Consider a well-trained pianist who has a complete conceptual grasp of a piece of music. This conceptual understanding is a kind of nonmaterial mental or spiritual code of the music, and this mental experience transcends both its neural and bodily representation, and it also transcends the physical, acoustic properties of the music, which the musician hears and compares to the conceptual code of the music. Nevertheless, this qualitatively different higher understanding *in the act of performance* creates a unification of the transcendent mental code of the music and the musician's neuro-bodily response, including the musical sounds heard by the pianist.

Somewhat analogous to the soul, the musical performance is a mind-body unity, since the nonmaterial, higher-level conceptual understanding of the piece gets embodied through the performance. Often the embodiment, like material DNA, contains imperfections known as mistakes. In the same sense, many human responses represent the integration of a mental thought with an embodied response, again often with a failure to fully represent the original mental concept or code.

Holistic Psychologies. Many of the psychologists who advocated the holistic position were reacting to both behaviorism and traditional psychoanalysis. Behaviorism, in theory, reduced the person to a small number of primary biological drives and behaviors that were reinforced by drive reduction or by the reduction of learned anxiety associated with the primary drives. Traditional psychoanalytic theory also reduced the person to a small number of unconscious motives that were based on sex, aggression, or defense mechanisms. Though Adler (See Carlson, Watts, & Maniacci, 2012) was an early psychologist to assume a holistic position, most of the effective "holistic" emphasis came from humanistic and existential psychologists. Among the many who championed understanding the person as a whole were Gordon Allport (1960), Viktor Frankl (1960, 1970), Rollo May (1983), Abraham Maslow (1970a), Carl Rogers (1961), and Adrian van Kaam (1966).

A few quotes from some of these well-known theorists should suffice. The Harvard psychologist Gordon Allport (1937) was one of the early personality psychologists to make such a claim:

> The chief tenet of [personalistic psychology] is that every mental function is embedded in personal life. In no concrete sense is there such a thing as intelligence, space perception, color discrimination or choice reaction; there are only *people* who are capable of performing such activities and of having such experiences.... Nor can motives ever be studied apart from their personal setting; they represent always the striving of the total organism toward its objective. (p. 18)
>
> The personologist seeks to understand individual consistency, that is, uniformities and regularities in individual behavior. The concern is always for the whole personality as it exists in real people. (Allport, 1960, pp. 146–147)

Abraham Maslow (1970) adds a similar nonreductionist and holistic perspective:

> If I had to condense the thesis of this book into a single sentence, I would have said that in addition to what psychologists of the time had to say about human nature, man also had a higher nature and that this was instinctoid, i.e., part of his essence. And if I could have had a second sentence, I would have stressed the profoundly holistic nature of human nature in contradiction to the analytic-dissecting-atomistic-Newtonian approach of the behaviorisms and of Freudian psychoanalysis. (p. ix)

And with Viktor Frankl (1978) we have the following example supporting the above positions:

> A scientist may stick to his science and stay in one dimension, but he should also remain open, keep his science open, at least to the possibility of another, higher dimension. As I have said, a higher dimension is higher in that it is more inclusive. If, for example, you take a square and project it vertically so that it becomes a cube, then you may say that this square is included in the cube. Anything occurring in the square will be contained as well in the cube, and nothing that takes place in the square can contradict what occurs in the higher dimension of the cube. The higher dimension does not exclude; it includes. And between the higher and lower dimensions of truth there can be only inclusiveness. (p. 62)

The holistic emphasis is also clearly expressed by the psychoanalyst W. W. Meissner (1993) with his concept of "self as agent," which he interprets as a superordinate structural construct representing the whole person and containing the willing or responsible self as agent. Meissner's concept also supports the Meta-Model's emphasis on the person as having a free will and thus moral responsibility.

At present it appears that the majority of practicing mental health professionals now accept that, at least in actual practice, understanding the person as a whole is a necessary part of good mental health practice. As a consequence, the Meta-Model of the Person, with respect to this holistic nonreductionist assumption, is quite consistent with much contemporary psychotherapy and indebted to both the important contributions of modern secular psychologists and the long Catholic personalist philosophical tradition—for example, Gilson (1932); Stein (1932/1996); Mounier (1938); Maritain (1985); Wojtyła (1995); Marcel (1963); Nédoncelle (1966); and von Hildebrand (2009).

Integrative Approaches to Psychology.   In addition to its holistic emphasis, the Meta-Model also integrates different psychological theories and applications into its general framework. There are already a number of secular integrationists who have argued that therapy practice should include a combination of different psychological perspectives. Indeed, there is a *Journal of Psychotherapy Integration* and a Society for the Exploration of Psychotherapy Integration (SEPI). An important example is Lazarus (1989), who includes all the following in his integration: sensation, imagery (**sensation-perception-cognition**, and higher cognition (**reason**); emotion (**emotion**), drugs, and biology (**body**); person to person relationality (**interpersonal relationships**); and behavioral aspects (**will**) of the person. This is integration in practice, but it does not specify a general psychological model of the person, nor, of course, is there a philosophical integration. A cognitive-affective integration of personality has been proposed by Mischel & Shoda (2008), but it is rather limited, because it is focused only on interpreting normal personality and its consistency over time. They do not address application to narratives, psychotherapy, philosophy, or theology.

Within Protestant Christianity there are several important integrative theories, and the Meta-Model has benefited from them and from discussion with some of their authors. An edited

volume, Stevenson, Eck, & Hill (2007), reprints many of the most insightful contributions to the problem of integrating Christianity and psychology made over the last fifty years or so. A serious discussion of the integration task, often very relevant to the Meta-Model's assumptions, is presented by David Entwistle (2015). Mark R. McMinn and Clark Campbell (2007) have a made a significant contribution to an integrative psychotherapy from a Christian perspective; their approach is consistent with our model's clinical implications. Robert C. Roberts has given an introduction to a Christian integration (1997) as well as much material on the relevance of the virtues (2007). Eric Johnson (2007) has provided an integrative and also primarily Protestant Christian interpretation of psychology. His model is not especially focused on psychotherapy but is more a theoretical conceptualization well-supported in Scripture and basic theology. Neither McMinn & Campbell nor Johnson explicitly addresses philosophical integration, nor do the virtues or a person's vocation get an explicit treatment. The narrative character of the Meta-Model is not a major characteristic of most of the Protestant integrative approaches. And, of course, the Catholic perspective is not developed in these previously cited works. Nevertheless, it is clear that integrating psychology with Christianity is hardly a novel undertaking, most especially among Protestant Christians, who have clearly successfully pioneered this important project since the 1960s.

2. Flourishing in the Virtues

For many years psychology more or less ignored the virtues, in spite of some theorists who tried to keep interest alive. Erikson, noted earlier, associated a virtue with each of his stages, but they were often referred to as ego strengths. Maslow, in his treatment of the higher values, or higher needs, associated with self-actualization, mentioned several attributes that could be understood as virtues. But somehow these proposals never really caught on among the great majority of psychologists. However, support for the importance of the virtues is now widely recognized, thanks especially to the positive psychology movement of Martin Seligman and his colleagues. A brief summary of this now-widespread and growing movement will be useful. Perhaps Seligman's *Learned Optimism* (1990) can mark the beginning of psychology's rediscovery of the virtues, followed by *What You Can Change and What You Can't* (1994). Next (2000) is the well-known article with Mihalyi Csikszentmihalyi that introduces the name "positive psychology." Then comes *Authentic Happiness* (2002) and the very influential book by Christopher Peterson and Seligman, *Character Strengths and Virtues: A Handbook and Classification* (2004). At present, all kinds of publications on the virtues have come out. Some important examples are S. J. Lopez & C. R. Snyder, Eds., *Oxford Handbook of Positive Psychology* (2011); Stephen Joseph, Ed., *Positive Psychology in Practice* (2015); Blaine J. Fowers, *Virtue and Psychology* (2005); and A. C. Parks, *The Wiley-Blackwell Handbook of Positive Psychological Interventions*, 2014. As a result, psychology has made contributions to our understanding of almost all the traditional virtues and character strengths ranging from courage (Pury & Lopez, 2010), to gratitude (Emmons & McCullough, 2004), to resilience (Reich, Zautra, & Hall, 2010) and self-control (Mischel & Ayduk, 2002).

At IPS some of our students have made theoretical contributions by proposing virtue training in psychotherapy, with a specific virtue addressed to particular mental pathologies. For example, Eric Gudan (2010) has developed an approach to moderate ruminative depression

using gratitude as an intervention; Leslie Trautman (2006) has proposed that humility and altruism can be used to address narcissistic personality disorder.

3. Flourishing Through Vocation

Although the term "vocation" is not used in contemporary psychology and the expression "a calling" is rarely used, the basic idea has now become rather common in the framework of virtue theories, where the focus is on "flourishing" and developing a personality characterized by virtue. And, of course, for decades what is known as career counseling has been an active part of psychology. Both of these approaches exhibit some of what the Meta-Model proposes under the concept of vocation (for a full articulation of the Meta-Model's understanding of vocations, see Chapter 10, "Fulfilled Through Vocation"). The field of career counseling focuses on the Model's consideration of vocation to one's work in the world that contributes to society. The goal of developing virtues so as to flourish is quite close to the Model's treatment of personal vocation to holiness and flourishing (see Seligman, 2012). Only the vocation to state in life seems to be generally ignored in the field, though countless individuals certainly grapple with the question, especially on the subject of marriage. (It should be noted, however, that Otto Rank, anticipating us, addresses vocation in something like the way we do here; see Rank, 1968, pp. 171–172).

There are many psychological concepts proposed as important human attributes that can be interpreted as representing a kind of psychological calling or vocation in a specific and often rather narrow sense. Certainly the concepts of self-realization and self-actualization were often presented as a kind of calling relevant for many people. Maslow's "peak-experience" (1970b) had a vocational meaning. Becoming independent or becoming creative (May, 1975) were often presented as significant "callings" for people in general as well as for those in psychotherapy. Another example is Kohlberg's (1981) advocacy of post-conventional moral thinking. The Meta-Model, however similar to secular notions of "calling" or "profession," is based on the understanding of a calling as coming from God; even in the case of many non-believers, they understand they have a special kind of calling, though not, of course, from God.

4. Interpersonal Relationships

There are now many major psychological theories that emphasize the foundational importance of interpersonal relationships in the formation of the person both in childhood and in adulthood. However, the first major psychologist to develop such an emphasis was probably Alfred Adler (1938), especially with his concept of social interest as central to mental health, as well as his focus on such things as birth order as a factor in personality formation. Somewhat later H. S. Sullivan (1953) proposed his still-influential "interpersonal theory" of personality addressed, in particular, to schizophrenia. Within psychoanalysis the interpersonal emphasis began with the contributions of object relations theorists, first M. Klein (1975) and then W. R. N. Fairbairn (1952) and D. W. Winnicott (1958). At roughly the same time John Bowlby (1969, 1973, 1980, 1988) was initiating what is now well known as attachment theory, with his interpretation of separation anxiety and related issues. This was followed by Mary Ainsworth's (1985; with Blehar, Waters, & Wall, 1978) and Mary Main's (2000; Main, Kaplan, & Cassidy, 1985) contributions to attachment styles. There were also others, such as Jay Greenberg and Stephen Mitchell (1983) and more recently Lorna Smith Benjamin (2003), who give a strong interpersonal empha-

sis in a psychoanalytic framework. And quite recently the prominent emotion-focused theorist Susan M. Johnson (2013) has come out with a special emphasis on the maintaining of long-term, stable relationships, especially monogamy, as essential for psychological well-being.

In short, the day when psychology routinely assumed an isolated, autonomous individual as the basis for conceptualizing the person is now rapidly fading before the strong evidence that interpersonal relationships are foundational.

5. Sensation-Perception-Cognition

Sensory and perceptual and elementary cognitive aspects of the person have been a basic part of psychology, and thus of our concept of the person, since modern psychology began in the mid-nineteenth century. Indeed psychophysics and, later, pattern perception (e.g., Gestalt psychology) were early and major recognitions of our sensory-perceptual-cognitive nature. Freud's emphasis on dreams also very early addressed this essential characteristic of personality. Today the psychological study of sensory experience, pattern perception, artistic ability, imagination, simple learning, episodic memory, and many related phenomena identify the sensory-perceptual-cognitive component of the person as a universally accepted and foundational property of the person.

6. Emotion

There is now a great deal of evidence supporting the importance of emotions and feelings to human psychology. Les Greenberg (Greenberg, 2002; Greenberg & Paivio, 1997; Greenberg & Safran, 1987) is a major theorist who brought emotion into a prominent focus in psychotherapy, and was followed up by emotion-focused therapists such as Susan M. Johnson (2004). Albert Ellis, with his strong rational emphasis, did eventually change the name of his therapy from "Rational Behavior Therapy" or RBT to "Rational Emotive Behavior Therapy" or REBT. Emotions are simply central in understanding mental problems and how to heal them. Often a major problem in psychotherapy is a difficulty in changing negative or harmful emotions even after an intellectual understanding of their pathological origin has been established. The present emphasis on training therapists to be empathic with their client acknowledges the importance of emotion in understanding the person.

Psychologically oriented neuroscientists like Antonio Damasio (1994), Joseph LeDoux (1996), and Michael Gazzaniga (1994) initiated much of the new research on emotions. Their research and publications have had a major impact not only on psychology but on the society at large. In short, the study of the emotions has become a large, lively, and standard part of psychology. (For recent expressions of this interest see Ekman, 2016; Volz & Hertwig, 2016).

7. Reason-Intelligence

This is something of a "no brainer," if you'll pardon the expression. Psychology, since the first IQ tests, now over a hundred years old, has had a major focus on human intelligence and the use of language—in short, on reason. The conscious mind and the use of reason are, as already noted, given great emphasis in the Rational Emotive Behavioral Therapy (REBT) of Albert Ellis (1962, 1994) and other such approaches (including Beck, 1975). The emphasis on reason and intelligence is simply a commonplace in the field of psychology. There is also now good evidence, on both the psychological and neuronal (brain) levels, on how reason and emotion often interact, published in the work of Daniel Kahneman (2003, 2011; and Kahneman, Slovic, & Tversky, 1982).

8. Will

This topic, important in early psychology—see William James (1890/1950, 1897/1956) and Rank (1936)—fell into neglect for many decades, especially in the behaviorist psychology period. It was brought back by existential psychology (May, 1969), by research on delay of gratification (Mischel, 1974), and even more strongly by academic social psychology, with the emphasis on self-efficacy or agency (Bandura, 1986, 1997). Also, the return of a strong interest in the psychology of the virtues requires that a person must willingly choose virtues in order to flourish. Seligman (2002) has explicitly emphasized the will: "To be a virtuous person is to display, by acts of will, all or at least most of the six ubiquitous virtues: wisdom, courage, humanity, justice, temperance, and transcendence" (p. 137). Hence, along with the study of virtues came a clear focus on the study of willpower and self-regulation, or self-control, by such important psychologists as Roy Baumeister and John Tierney (Baumeister & Tierney, 2011) and, as noted above, Walter Mischel (Mischel & Ayduk, 2002; Mischel et al., 2011).

Reflection on Some Aspects of the Model

It is important to consider a new and innovative emphasis of the Meta-Model found in three of the preceding properties of the person: they each focus on a *reality* outside of the self. To attend to the virtues, to attend to vocations or callings, and to recognize the significance of the other, of interpersonal relationships, is to make the external world of foundational importance for the person. This contrasts greatly with so many secular psychologies that focus inward on the self. Perhaps starting with Descartes (who certainly had no idea how others would respond to his work) and culminating in such psychologies as that of Carl

Rogers, the retreat from reality, especially the retreat from the other, in understanding the person has been extreme. (Rogers, in his theory, strongly emphasized the independent, autonomous individual who has a self that creates its own values and reality. However, in practice, he introduced the importance of relationship—indeed, his focus on the relationship between therapist and client was a major contribution to psychology.) In any case, it is clear from work of the preceding psychologists that the times have changed, and the concept of interpersonal relationships as a formative factor throughout a person's life is now widely accepted.

Conclusion

Recalling the major properties of the Catholic Christian Meta-Model of the Person, we can understand, from the previously mentioned references, that all of them have substantial support in today's secular psychology. However, these are the more important contributions of the CCMMP:

1. The selection of the eleven specific components of the person who is: theologically and narratively created, fallen, redeemed; and philosophically a body-soul unity who seeks vocations and virtues, who is formed by interpersonal relationships, by sensory-perceptual-cognitive experience, by emotion, by reason, intelligence, and a will that is partly free.

2. The explicit Catholic Christian moral framework, which allows ethical issues to be addressed.

3. The idea that the synergistic interaction and integration of these components is always part of the person.

4. The addition of some new aspect to a component, for example, the addition of the soul to the whole person, or the spiritual, transcendent calling to the human vocation.

5. The addition of a new emphasis on a component, such as the importance given to relationships, the virtues, and vocations.

6. The emphasis on work, service, and meaningful leisure as aspects that contribute significantly to flourishing.

7. The clearly developed theological and philosophical rationale for the model.

8. The general narrative of the person with its capacity to be made into a specific narrative for each person.

9. The combination of the truth of psychological science with philosophical truth and the Catholic Christian theological truth about the person. Therefore, considered in its totality, the Catholic Christian Meta-Model of the Person represents an important, and genuinely new, interpretation of the person and personality.

REFERENCES

Adler, A. (1931). *What life should mean to you.* Boston, MA: Little, Brown.

Adler, A. (1938). *Social interest: A challenge to mankind.* London, United Kingdom: Faber & Faber.

Ainsworth, M. D. S. (1985). Attachment across the lifespan. *Bulletin of the New York Academy of Medicine, 61,* 792–812.

Ainsworth, M. D. S., Blehar, M. C., Waters, E., & Wall, S. (1978). *Patterns of attachment: A psychological study of the strange situation.* Hillsdale, NJ: Lawrence Erlbaum.

Alexander, E. (2012). *Proof of heaven: A neurosurgeons journey into the afterlife.* New York, NY: Simon & Schuster.

Allen, M. P. (2014). Gender reality. *Solidarity: The Journal of Catholic Social Thought and Secular Ethics, 4*(4), 1–36.

Allen, M. P. (2015). Four principles of complementarity: A philosophical perspective. In S. Lopes & H. Alvaré (Eds.), *Not just good, but beautiful: The complementary relationship between man and woman* (pp. 49–59). Walden, NY: Plough Publishing.

Allport, G. W. (1937). *Personality: A psychological interpretation.* New York, NY: Holt.

Allport, G. (1960). *Personality and social encounter.* Boston, MA: Beacon Press.

Angus, L. E., & McLeod, J. (Eds.). (2003). *Handbook of narrative and psychotherapy: Practice, theory, and research.* London, United Kingdom: Sage.

Bandura, A. (1986). *Social foundations of thought and action: A social cognitive theory.* Englewood Cliffs, NJ: Prentice-Hall.

Bandura, A. (1997). *Self-efficacy: The exercise of control.* New York, NY: Worth.

Baron-Cohen, S. (2003). *The essential difference: Male and female brains and the truth about autism.* New York, NY: Basic Books.

Baumeister, R. F., & Tierney, J. (2011). *Willpower: Rediscovering the greatest human strength.* New York, NY: Penguin.

Beauregard, M. (2012). *Brain wars: The scientific battle over the existence of the mind and the proof that will change the ways we live our lives.* New York, NY: HarperCollins.

Beauregard, M., & O'Leary, D. (2007). *The spiritual brain: A neuroscientist's case for the existence of the soul.* New York, NY: HarperCollins.

Beck, A. T. (1975). *Cognitive therapy and emotional disorders.* Madison, CT: International Universities Press.

Bergin, A. E. (1980). Psychotherapy and religious values. *Journal of Consulting and Clinical Psychology, 48*(1), 95–105.

Benjamin, L. S. (2003). *Interpersonal reconstructive therapy.* New York, NY: Guilford.

Bly, R. (1990). *Iron John: A book about men.* Reading, MA: Addison-Wesley.

Bowlby, J. (1969). *Attachment and loss: Vol. 1. Attachment.* New York, NY: Basic Books.

Bowlby, J. (1973). *Attachment and loss: Vol. 2. Separation: Anxiety and anger.* New York, NY: Basic Books.

Bowlby, J. (1980). *Attachment and loss: Vol. 3. Loss: Sadness and depression.* New York, NY: Basic Books.

Bowlby, J. (1988). *A secure base: Parent-child attachment and healthy human development.* New York, NY: Basic Books.

Boyd, C. (2007). *A shared morality: A narrative defense of natural law ethics.* Grand Rapids, MI: Brazos Press.

Boyd, J. (1996). *Reclaiming the soul: The search for meaning in a self-centered culture.* Cleveland, OH: Pilgrim Press.

Brizendine, L. (2006). *The female brain.* New York, NY: Broadway Books.

Brizendine, L. (2010). *The male brain.* New York, NY: Broadway Books.

Bruner, J. S. (1986). *Actual minds, possible worlds.* Cambridge, MA: Harvard University Press.

Bruner, J. S. (1990). *Acts of meaning.* Cambridge, MA: Harvard University Press.

Bruner, J. S. (1991). The narrative construction of reality. *Critical Inquiry, 18,* 1–21.

Buss, D. M. (2008). *Evolutionary psychology: The new science of the mind* (3rd ed.). Boston, MA: Allyn & Bacon.

Carlson, J., Watts, R. E., & Maniacci, M. (2012). *Adlerian therapy: Theory and practice.* Washington, DC: American Psychological Association Press.

Catechism of the Catholic Church (2nd ed.). (2000). Vatican City, Vatican: Libreria Editrice Vaticana.

Cozolino, L. (2006). *The neuroscience of human relationships.* New York, NY: Norton.

Cozolino, L. (2010). *The neuroscience of psychotherapy* (2nd ed.). New York, NY: Norton.

Damasio, A. (1994). *Descartes' error: Emotion, reason and the human brain.* New York, NY: Putnam.

Dawe, G. S., Tan, X. W., & Xiao, Z.-C. (2007). Cell migration from baby to mother. *Cell Adhesion and Migration, 1*(1), 19–27.

Ekman, P. (2016). What scientists who study emotion agree about. *Perspectives on Psychological Science, 11*(1), 31–34.

Ellis, A. (1980). Psychotherapy and atheistic values: A response to A. E. Bergin's "Psychotherapy and religious values." *Journal of Consulting and Clinical Psychology, 48,* 635–639.

Ellis, A. (1962). *Reason and emotion in psychotherapy.* New York, NY: Lyle Stuart.

Ellis, A. (1994). *Reason and emotion in psychotherapy, revised and updated.* Secaucus, NJ: Carol Publishing Group.

Emmons, R. A., & McCullough, M. E. (Eds.). (2004). *The psychology of gratitude.* New York, NY: Oxford University Press.

Entwistle, D. N. (2015). *Integrative approaches to psychology and Christianity: An introduction to worldview issues, philosophical foundations and models of integration* (3rd ed.). Eugene, OR: Cascade Books.

Erikson, E. H. (1950). *Childhood and society* (2nd ed.). New York, NY: Norton.

Erikson, E. H. (1959). *Identity and the life cycle: Selected papers.* Psychological Issues, Monograph No. 1, Vol. 1. New York, NY: International Universities Press.

Erikson, E. H. (Ed.) (1968). *Identity: Youth and crisis.* New York, NY: Norton.

Erikson, E. H. (1982). *The life cycle completed.* New York, NY: Norton.

Fairbairn, W. R. N. (1952). *An object-relations theory of the personality.* New York, NY: Basic Books.

Fowers, B. J. (2005). *Virtue and psychology: Pursuing excellence in ordinary practices.* Washington, DC: American Psychological Association Press.

Frankl, V. (1960). *The doctor and the soul: An introduction to logotherapy.* New York, NY: Knopf.

Frankl, V. (1970). *The will to meaning: Foundations and applications of logotherapy.* New York, NY: Penguin.

Frankl, V. (1978). *The unheard cry for meaning: Psychotherapy and humanism.* New York, NY: Simon & Schuster.

Freud, E. L. (Ed.). (1960). *Letters of Sigmund Freud.* New York, NY: Basic Books.

Freud, S. (1957). *Totem and taboo.* In J. Strachey (Ed. and Trans., in collaboration with A. Freud, A. Strachey), *The standard edition of the complete works of Sigmund Freud* (Vol. 13). London, United Kingdom: Hogarth Press and the Institute of Psychoanalysis. (Original work published 1913)

Gazzaniga, M. (1994). *Nature's mind: Biological roots of thinking, emotions, sexuality, language and intelligence.* New York, NY: Basic Books.

Gilson, E. (1932). Le personnalisme chrétien. In *L'espirit de la philosophie médiéval* (pp. 195–215). Paris, France: Librairie Philosophique J. Vrin.

Giorgi, A. (1970). *Psychology as a human science: A phenomenologically based approach.* New York, NY: Harper & Row.

Goodson, J. L. (2015). *Narrative theology and the hermeneutical virtues: Humility, patience, and prudence.* London, United Kingdom: Lexington.

Gottman, J. (1999). *The marriage clinic.* New York, NY: Norton.

Greenberg, J. R., & Mitchell, S. A. (1983). *Object relations in psychoanalytic theory.* Cambridge, MA: Harvard University Press.

Greenberg, L. (2002). *Emotion-focused therapy: Coaching clients to work through feelings.* Washington, DC: American Psychological Association Press.

Greenberg, L., & Paivio, S. (1997). *Working with emotion in psychotherapy.* New York, NY: Guilford.

Greenberg, L., & Safran, J. D. (1987). *Emotion in psychotherapy.* New York, NY: Guilford.

Gudan, E. (2010). *Gratitude-based interventions for treating ruminative depression* (Unpublished doctoral dissertation). Institute for the Psychological Sciences, Arlington, VA.

Hamlin, J. K. (2013). Moral judgment and action in preverbal infants and toddlers: Evidence of an innate moral core. *Current Directions in Psychological Science, 22*(3), 186–193.

Hauerwas, D., & Jones, G. L. (1997). *Why narratives? Readings in narrative theology.* Eugene, OR: Wipf & Stock.

Ingalhalikar, M., Smith, A., Parker, D., Satterthwaite, T. D., Elliott, M. A., Ruparel, K., Hakonarson, H. Gur, R. E., Gur, R. C., & Verma, R. (2014). Sex differences in the structural connectome of the human brain. *Proceedings of the National Academy of Sciences of the United States of America, 111*(2), 823–828.

Jacobi, J. (1973). *The psychology of C. G. Jung.* New Haven, CT: Yale University Press.

James, W. (1950). *The principles of psychology* (Vol. 2). New York, NY: Dover. (Original work published 1890)

James, W. (1956). *The will to believe, and other essays in popular philosophy.* New York, NY: Dover. (Original work published 1897)

John Paul II. (1993). *Veritatis splendor* [Encyclical, on certain fundamental questions of the Church's moral teaching]. Vatican City, Vatican: Libreria Editrice Vaticana.

Johnson, E. L. (2007). *Foundations for soul care: A*

Christian psychology proposal. Downers Grove, IL: InterVarsity Press.

Johnson, S. M. (2004). *The practice of emotionally focused couples therapy* (2nd ed.). New York, NY: Brunner-Routledge.

Johnson, S. M. (2013). *Love sense: The revolutionary new science of romantic relationships.* New York, NY: Little, Brown.

Jung, C. (1955). *Modern man in search of a soul.* New York, NY: Harcourt. (Original work published 1933)

Kahneman, D. (2003). A perspective on judgment and choice: Mapping bounded rationality. *American Psychologist, 58*(9), 697–720.

Kahneman, D. (2011). *Thinking, fast and slow.* New York, NY: Farrar, Straus and Giroux.

Kahneman, D., Slovic, P., & Tversky, A. (Eds.). (1982). *Judgment under uncertainty: Heuristics and biases.* Cambridge, United Kingdom: Cambridge University Press.

Khosrotehrani, K., & Bianchi, D. W. (2005). Multilineage potential of fetal cells in maternal tissue: a legacy in reverse. *Journal of Cell Science, 118,* 1559–1563.

Klein, M. (1975). Love, guilt and reparation. In R. E. Money-Kyrle (Ed.), *The writings of Melanie Klein* (Vol. 1, pp. 306–343). New York, NY: Free Press. (Original work published 1937)

Kohlberg, L. (1981). *Essays on moral development: Vol. 1. The philosophy of moral development: Moral stages and the idea of justice.* New York, NY: Harper & Row.

Lazarus, A. A. (1989). *The practice of multimodal therapy: Systematic, comprehensive, and effective psychotherapy.* Baltimore, MD: Johns Hopkins University Press.

LeDoux, J. (1996). *The emotional brain: The mysterious underpinnings of emotional life.* New York, NY: Touchstone.

Joseph, S. (Ed.). (2015). *Positive psychology in practice: Promoting human flourishing in work, health, education, and everyday life* (2nd ed.). Hoboken, NJ: Wiley.

Lopez, S. J., & Snyder, C. R. (2011). *Oxford handbook of positive psychology* (2nd ed.). New York, NY: Oxford University Press.

MacIntyre, A. (1981). *After virtue: A study in moral theory.* Notre Dame, IN: University of Notre Dame Press.

MacIntyre, A. (1990). *Three rival versions of moral enquiry.* London, United Kingdom: Duckworth.

Main, M. (2000). The organized categories of infant, child and adult attachment: Flexible vs. inflexible attention under attachment-related stress. *Journal of the American Psychoanalytic Association, 48*(4), 1055–1096.

Main, M., Kaplan, N., & Cassidy, J. (1985). Security in infancy, childhood and adulthood: A move to a level of representation. *Monographs of the Society for Research in Child Development, 50,* (1-2, Serial No. 209), 66–104.

Marcel, G. (1963). *The existential background of human dignity.* Cambridge, MA: Harvard University Press.

Maritain, J. (1985). *The person and the common good* (J. F. Fitzgerald, Trans.). Notre Dame, IN: University of Notre Dame Press. (Original work published in French, 1947)

Mounier, E. (1938). *A personalist manifesto* (The monks of St. John's Abbey, Trans.). New York, NY: Longmans Green.

Maslow, A. (1970a). *Motivation and personality* (2nd ed.). New York, NY: Harper & Row.

Maslow, A. (1970b). *Religion, values and peak-experiences.* New York, NY: Viking.

May, R. (1969). *Love and will.* New York, NY: Norton.

May, R. (1975). *The courage to create.* New York, NY: Norton.

May, R. (1983). *The discovery of being: Writings in existential psychology.* New York, NY: Norton.

McAdams, D. P. (1988). *Power, intimacy, and the life story.* New York, NY: Guilford.

McAdams, D. P. (2013). *The redemptive self: Stories we live by.* New York, NY: Oxford University Press.

McLeod, J. (1997). *Narrative and psychotherapy.* London, United Kingdom: Sage

McLeod, J. (2004). The significance of narrative and storytelling in postpsychological counseling and psychotherapy. In A. Leiblich, D. P. McAdams, & R. Josselson (Eds.), *Healing plots: The narrative basis of psychotherapy* (pp. 11–28). Washington, DC: American Psychological Association Press.

McMinn, M. R., & Campbell, C. D. (2007). *Integrative psychotherapy: Toward a comprehensive Christian approach.* Downers Grove, IL: InterVarsity Press.

Meissner, W. W. (1993). *The therapeutic alliance: A vital*

element in clinical practice. Northvale, NJ: Jason Aronson.

Mischel, W. (1974). Processes in delay of gratification. In L. Berkowitz (Ed.), *Advances in experimental social psychology* (Vol. 7, pp. 249–292). New York, NY: Academic Press.

Mischel, W., & Ayduk, O. (2002). Self-regulation in a cognitive-affective personality system: Attention control in the service of the self. *Self and Identity, 1*(1), 113–120.

Mischel, W., Ayduk, O., Berman, M. G., Casey, B. J., Gotlib, I. H., Jonides, J., Kross, E., Teslovich, T., Wilson, N. L., Zayas, V., & Shoda, Y. (2011). 'Willpower' over the lifespan: Decomposing self-regulation. *SCAN, 6*, 252–256.

Mischel, W., & Shoda, Y. (2008). Toward a unified theory of personality: Integrating disposition and processing dynamics within the cognitive-affective processing system. In O. P. John, R. W. Robins, & L. A. Pervin (Eds.), *Handbook of personality: Theory and research* (3rd ed., pp. 208–241). New York, NY: Guilford.

Moir, A., & Jessel, D. (1991). *Brain sex: The real difference between men & women*. New York, NY: Delta.

Moore, R., & Gillette, D. (1990). *King, warrior, magician, lover: Rediscovering the archetypes of the mature masculine*. San Francisco, CA: Harper.

Nédoncelle, M. (1966). *Love and the person*. New York, NY: Sheed & Ward.

Okholm, D. (2014). *Dangerous passions, deadly sins: Learning from the psychology of ancient monks*. Grand Rapids, MI: Brazos Press.

Parks, A. C. (2014). *The Wiley-Blackwell handbook of positive psychological interventions*. Hoboken, NJ: Wiley.

Peterson, C., & Seligman, M. E. P. (2004). *Character strengths and virtues: A handbook and classification*. New York, NY: Oxford University Press.

Plomin, R., DeFries, J. C., Knopik, V. S., & Neiderhiser, J. M. (2016). Top 10 replicated findings from behavioral genetics. *Perspectives on Psychological Science, 11*, 3–23.

Pury, C. L. S., & Lopez, S. J. (Eds.). (2010). *The psychology of courage: Modern research on an ancient virtue*. Washington, DC: American Psychological Association Press.

Rank, O. (1936). *Will therapy*. New York, NY: Knopf. (Original work published 1929)

Rank, O. (1998). *Psychology and the soul: A study of the origin, conceptual evolution, and nature of the soul*. Baltimore, MD: Johns Hopkins University Press. (Original work published 1930)

Rank, O. (1968). *Modern education: A critique of its fundamental ideas*. New York, NY: Agathon Press. (Original work published 1932)

Reich, J. W., Zautra, A. J., & Hall, J. S. (Eds.). (2010). *Handbook of adult resilience*. New York, NY: Guilford.

Rhoads, S. E. (2004). *Taking sex differences seriously*. San Francisco, CA: Encounter.

Ricœur, P. (1984). *Time and narrative, Vol. 1* (K. McLaughlin & D. Pellauer, Trans.). Chicago, IL: Chicago University Press.

Roazen, P. (1975). *Freud and his followers*. New York, NY: Knopf.

Roberts, R. C. (1997). Parameters of a Christian psychology. In R. C. Roberts & M. R. Talbot (Eds.), *Limning the psyche: Explorations in Christian psychology* (pp. 74–101). Grand Rapids, MI: Eerdmans.

Roberts, R. C. (2007). *Spiritual emotions: A psychology of Christian virtues*. Grand Rapids, MI: Eerdmans.

Rogers, C. R. (1961). *On becoming a person*. Boston, MA: Houghton Mifflin.

Sarbin, T. R. (Ed.). (1986). *Narrative psychology: The storied nature of human conduct*. New York, NY: Praeger.

Schafer, R. (1976). *A new language for psychoanalysis*. New Haven, CT: Yale University Press.

Schafer, R. (1992). *Retelling a life: Narration and dialogue in psychoanalysis*. New York, NY: Basic Books.

Seligman, M. E. P. (1990). *Learned optimism*. New York, NY: Knopf.

Seligman, M. E. P. (1994). *What you can change and what you can't*. New York, NY: Knopf.

Seligman, M. E. P. (2002). *Authentic happiness: Using the new positive psychology to realize your potential for lasting fulfillment*. New York, NY: Atria.

Seligman, M. E. P. (2012). *Flourish: A visionary new understanding of happiness and well-being*. New York, NY: Free Press.

Seligman, M. E. P., & Csikszentmihalyi, M. (2000). Positive psychology: An introduction. *American Psychologist, 55*, 5–14.

Sheldon, W. (1940). *The varieties of human physique:*

An introduction to constitutional differences. New York, NY: Harper & Brothers.

Siegel, D. J. (2012). *The developing mind: How relationships and the brain interact to shape who we are* (2nd ed.). New York, NY: Guilford.

Spence, D. (1982). *Narrative truth and historical truth: Meaning and interpretation in psychoanalysis.* New York, NY: Norton.

Spitzer, R. (2015). *The soul's upward yearning: Clues to our transcendent nature from experience and reason.* San Francisco, CA: Ignatius Press.

Stein, E. (1996). The separate vocations of man and woman according to nature and grace. In L. Gelber & R. Leuven (Eds.), *Essays on woman: The collected works of Edith Stein* (2nd ed., pp. 59–85) (F. M. Oben, Trans.). Washington, DC: Institute for Carmelite Studies Publications. (Original work published 1932)

Stevenson, D. H., Eck, B. E., & Hill, P. C. (2007). *Psychology & Christianity integration: Seminal works that shaped the movement.* Batavia, IL: Christian Association for Psychological Studies.

Sullivan, H. S. (1953). *The interpersonal theory of psychiatry.* New York, NY: Norton.

Trautman, L. (2006). *Virtue as a support for psychological health in the treatment of narcissistic personality disorder* (Unpublished doctoral dissertation). Institute for the Psychological Sciences, Arlington, VA.

Vande Kemp, H. (1982). The tension between psychology and theology: An anthropological solution. *Journal of Psychology and Theology, 10,* 205–211. Reprinted in Stevenson, Eck, & Hill (2007).

vanKaam, A. (1966). *Existential foundations of psychology.* New York, NY: Lantham.

Vitz, P. C. (1988). *Sigmund Freud's Christian unconscious.* New York, NY: Guilford.

Vitz, P. C. (1992a). Narratives and counseling, Part 1: From analysis of the past to stories about it. *Journal of Psychology and Theology, 20*(1), 11–19.

Vitz, P. C. (1992b). Narratives and counseling, Part 2: From stories of the past to stories for the future. *Journal of Psychology and Theology, 20*(1), 20–27.

Vitz, P. C. (2017). The origin of consciousness in the integration of analog (right hemisphere) & digital (left hemisphere) codes. *Journal of Consciousness Exploration & Research, 8*(11), 881–906.

Vitz, P. C. (2018). Men and women: Their differences and their complementarity: Evidence from psychology and neuroscience. Unpublished paper, Institute for the Psychological Sciences, Arlington, VA.

Volz, K. G., & Hertwig, R. (2016). Emotions and decisions: Beyond conceptual vagueness and the rationality muddle. *Perspectives on psychological science, 11*(1), 101–116.

von Hildebrand, D. (2009). *The nature of love* (J. F. Crosby & J. H. Crosby, Trans.). South Bend, IN: St. Augustine's Press. (Original work published in German, 1971, as *Das Wesen der Liebe*)

White, M. (2007). *Maps of narrative practice.* New York, NY: Norton.

Winnicott, D. W. (1958). *Through paediatrics to psychoanalysis.* London, United Kingdom: Hogarth Press.

Wojtyła, K. (1995). *Love and responsibility* (H. T. Willets, Trans.). New York, NY: Farrar, Straus & Giroux. (Original work published in Polish, 1960, *Miłość i odpowiedzialność*)

Chapter 6

The Meta-Model and the Concept of the Person as an Integrated Laminate

Paul C. Vitz and Su Li Lee

ABSTRACT: A hierarchical model of the concept of person is proposed. The model consists of different levels of abstraction and understanding. The levels include three objective, observable levels: biochemistry, neuroscience, and behavior; three subjective levels of personal experience: simple awareness (*qualia* 1), human self-consciousness (*qualia* 2), transcendent or mystical experience (*qualia* 3); and the following four higher, rational levels: psychological theory, sociocultural theory, philosophical theory, and theological theory. The emotional response of fear of snakes, the nature of a person's embodiment, and the nature of a person's interpersonal relationships are all described within the model, which is based on the converging, supporting evidence about these properties of the person in the fields of science, psychology, and other disciplines, especially philosophy and theology. The mutually supporting evidence is more than scientific consilience, for it includes a hierarchical connectedness, or integration, among the different levels, many of which are not kinds of natural science, and each of which has its own epistemology.

It is widely understood that different ways of thinking about the concept of person exist. A person can be understood from a theological, philosophical, or psychological perspective. Increasingly, these days, the person is understood in terms of such reduced representations as observable behavior or, now especially, as observed brain processes. Each of these perspectives has its own vocabulary and its own procedures for recognizing truth and meaning—in short, its own epistemology.

Our first proposal with respect to the concept of person is to place the different relevant disciplines within a natural hierarchy of understanding. The major levels of this hierarchy, in a top down order are: theology (Level 7), philosophy (Level 6), sociocultural theory (Level 5), psychological (Level 4), mystical experience (Level 3), self-conscious personal experience (Level 2), simple awareness (Level 1), observed behavior (-1), neural activity (-2), and biochemical activity (-3). This hierarchy is *not* one of importance or value but rather of levels of human understanding. All of the levels contain aspects of truth and reality. All levels ultimately are interconnected, and this interconnectedness is especially apparent between adjacent levels. Some levels are above, that is, higher than, our normal conscious mental experience; others are understood to exist at levels below that of our normal, ordinary, conscious experience. At the higher levels of understanding (e.g., psychological theory or philosophy) the representation of the person is more general and less particular than in ordinary mental life; at lower levels, beneath conscious experience, the knowledge about the person is reduced to a smaller but more objectively measureable and scientific understanding.

As an example of a levels of analysis or laminate model of the person, consider the various interpretations of the human experience of fear, something familiar to us all. At the general psychological level, fear is a particular and unpleasant experience that occurs in many settings. In the present case, our example will be fear of a snake. This fear experience normally has two levels that need to be represented. (For a more detailed discussion of *qualia* 1, 2, and 3 see Vitz, 2017.) The first level, which will be called Level 1, is the elementary or basic experience of the perception of the snake and certain immediate feelings and sensations. This level of basic percepts or images and associated feelings and sensations is found as a form of elementary awareness or consciousness in the higher animals as well as in human beings. The second psychological level we call Level 2, and it is, as will become clear, by far the level more characteristic of human experience. Level 2 refers to human self-conscious experience, and by that we mean a language-based response to the Level 1 experience as well as a cognitive understanding of the situation that is causing the fear. Such self-consciousness, as discussed in some detail below, refers to the fact that when persons interpret a given experience or reality, they must reflect outside of what they are experiencing at the time, in this case outside of the immediate Level 1 experience. This Level 2 response might involve the realization that the snake is a harmless garden snake—no cause for alarm—or perhaps it is a big python mov-

ing toward one—flee and warn others. Such self-consciousness exists at a level above Level 1.

This capacity for interpretive self-awareness is based on language. Consider the famous change in consciousness experienced by the blind and deaf Helen Keller, when she suddenly understood the nature of language. In order to understand the contrast more fully, we begin with a description of her experience of her world prior to her insight, which occurred when she was six. She described her previous mental life, what we call Level 1, as follows:

> I know I was impelled like an animal to seek food and warmth. I remember crying but not the grief that caused the tears; I kicked, and because I recall it physically, I know I was angry. I imitated those about me when I made signs for things I wanted to eat … But there is not one spark of emotion or rational thought in these distinct yet corporeal memories.… There was nothing in me except the instinct to eat and drink and sleep. My days were a blank without past, present or future, without hope or anticipation, without interest or joy. (Keller, 2000. p. 5)

Note how she describes awareness without rational thought, and also awareness of emotional behavior without any notion of why the emotion was caused. There is also not even awareness of time, for there was no past or future. It is assumed that a human infant's early and preverbal mental experience is of this Level 1 character.

Here is Helen's description of her language insight:

> We walked down the path to the well-house.… Someone was drawing water and my teacher placed my hand under the spout. As the cool stream gushed over one hand she spelled into the other the word *water*, first slowly, then rapidly. I stood still, my whole attention fixed upon the motions of her fingers. Suddenly I felt a misty consciousness as of something forgot-

ten—a thrill of returning thought; and somehow the mystery of language was revealed to me. I knew then that "w-a-t-e-r" meant the wonderful cool something that was flowing over my hand. That living word awakened my soul, gave it light, hope, joy, set it free! ...

I left the well-house eager to learn. Everything had a name, and each name gave birth to a new thought. As we returned to the house every object which I touched seemed to quiver with life. That was because I saw everything with the strange, new sight that had come to me. On entering the door I remembered the doll I had broken. I felt my way to the hearth and picked up the pieces. I tried vainly to put them together. Then my eyes filled with tears, for I realized what I had done, and for the first time I felt repentance and sorrow.

I learned a great many new words that day.... I do know that *mother, father, sister, teacher* were among them—words that were to make the world blossom for me.... It would have been difficult to find a happier child than I was as I lay in my crib at the close of that eventful day and lived over the joys it had brought me, and for the first time longed for a new day to come. (Keller, 2003, p. 26–27)

This interpretive or reflective ability creates a new quality of experience: *qualia* 2, which is different from *qualia* 1, the characteristic immediate subjective experience at Level 1. (We will use the philosophical term *qualia* to refer to proposed qualitative differences in human subjective experience taking place at different levels.) The capacity for interpretation at Level 2 can proceed to more abstract levels, where the person reflects on the variety of past situations—in the example of fear of snakes, a person might recall having experienced snakes or read or seen movies about them, and so forth. The experienced character of this more abstract level—with its deliberate use of memory and its comparison of different fearful experiences—and all such higher levels,

however, is not proposed as a new qualitative level like the difference between Levels 1 and 2, because these more abstract experiences are still based on the use of language and are assumed to be, likewise, Level 2 experiences.

Consider, as an example of the difference between *qualia* 1 and 2, the following situation: a person wakes up in an unfamiliar situation. He opens his eyes and is immediately aware of the light and physical shapes and colors of what he sees—*qualia* 1—but he doesn't know where he is. This normally short-lived state is then replaced by the experience of something like "Oh, that's right, I fell asleep last night on the couch at the Jones house." This new level of experience or awareness is *qualia* 2, because it involves interpretation using language.

Another example of the Level 1 *qualia* is the experience sometimes reported by adults who face an unexpected threat, as when an automobile suddenly starts to spin out of control. They often report an experience of the event without emotion, as though they were watching it happen while being emotionally and cognitively separated from it. It is as though the sudden threat reduced them to Level 1's simple awareness. I (the first author) recall a man who reported his experience of being suddenly attacked by lions—an attack from which he eventually escaped. Onlookers described his cries of fear and his frantic efforts at escape, but he said that his actual experience was without emotion or thoughts. He was aware of the scene as it transpired, but his experience was only the awareness of being there. Perhaps such "regression" to *qualia* 1 is a sudden return to basic right hemisphere experience, a before-language condition. In any case we propose it as a return to the more primitive or basic Level 1 experience.

In sum, Level 2 is understood generally as the typical psychological level of emotional, cognitive, and intellectual experience that a person has, as in the language insight of Helen Keller and in our example of the experience of fear of snakes. The evidence for the existence of both Level 1 and Level 2 is based on verbal reports of others and their agreement with our own experience. It is important to note that Level 2 has transcended Level 1 and is to be understood as true human self-consciousness created by the language insight. (See Vitz, 2017 for a more detailed discussion.)

There is, however, potentially a still higher level that is qualitatively distinct from Level 2. This new Level 3 is the level of mystical experience often described as ineffable. Perhaps the well-known near-death experiences can be considered as examples of *qualia* 3. There are many closely related ineffable experiences, usually less intense or dramatic than mystical or peak experiences, that represent a qualitative change from *qualia* 2 and thus indicate a Level 3. Examples include the sense of awe that comes as a response to the transcendent experience of beauty, of truth, of love, and sometimes to the power of nature or of the sublime. (For a recent descriptive treatment of awe that supports the notion of its qualitatively distinct nature, see Pearsall, 2007.) It is possible that some of this *qualia* 3 experience of awe might be part of a response to a snake, especially a very large and impressive python. Level 3 is therefore also assumed as a different *qualia* experienced at some time by many, perhaps most, people. Again, this Level 3 experience transcends Level 2.

We now turn to the lower levels in understanding fear, continuing the example of fear of a seen snake. The first lower level, Level -1, is the person's behavior as it could be noted by an external observer; this is potentially an elementary objective scientific description. This level consists of describing a person's fear behaviors, such as startle, backing or running away, per-

haps a shriek. These responses indicating fear are well known. However, Level -1 is a lower, and, of course, objective and public level, unlike either Level 1 or 2. Specifically, Level -1 no longer includes any of the complex invisible internal feelings or cognitions or language-based thoughts—it omits subjective experience or even reports of it; it omits any *qualia* of the experience. Level -1 with its behavioral description is not concerned with describing human experience but identifies only a limited but moderately precise set of external observables.

To move down another level: the neuropsychological level of fear as an emotion is known to involve the amygdala. This level, let us call it Level −2, is obviously still more narrowly focused, as it involves neural circuitry (−2a) and neural cells (−2b), but it is a more particular level and more precise, compared to observations of general behavioral responses, in its identification of features characteristic of fear. It is also not evident that Level −2 relates to fear, since only evidence from higher levels can clearly link neural activity with a particular emotion. A still lower level, Level −3, would involve biochemistry (e.g., hormones, neurotransmitters, etc.). It should be noted that Level -1 and lower are all in a sense public, and open to natural scientific experimentation and theory.

Now let us turn to the levels that can exist above that of our direct psychological experience—that is, above Levels 1, 2, and 3. Certain theorists in psychology have proposed interpretations of fear, describing it at a level that exists above any person's actual particular experience. This level, Level 4, is the level of psychological theory or understanding of fear (or, for that matter, of any other emotion). Level 5 describes any social or cultural interpretation of fear. A yet higher understanding, Level 6, would involve any philosophical theory of fear. This could be,

Table 6.1. Levels of Knowledge and Integrated Laminate Representation of Fear

Level 7 (L 7)	Any theological understanding of fear, e. g., fear of snake in Eden as a sign of spiritual temptation and evil.
Level 6 (L 6)	Any philosophical understanding of fear, e.g. fear of snake as a sign of danger and human fragility.
Level 5 (L 5)	Any sociocultural understanding of fear of snake or fear in general, e.g. snakes as a symbol of danger.
Level 4 (L 4)	Any psychological theory of fear of snake or fear in general, e.g. fear of snake as a protective stimulus of evolution.
Level 3 (L 3)	Conscious experience of awe or other transcendent reality, as described by the individual: qualia 3. For instance, the snake can be awesome.
Level 2 (L 2)	Self-conscious experience based on linguistic/cognitive understanding of a particular snake situation, as described by the individual: qualia 2. For instance, this particular snake is a poisonous copperhead.
Level 1 (L 1)	Conscious awareness of feelings or sensations, as described by the individual: qualia 1. This feeling is the animal-like fear of a snake.
Level −1 (L −1)	Behavioral description of fear-response to a snake.
Level −2a	Brain areas activated by fear (e.g., amygdala; brain circuitry).
−2b (L −2)	Brain cells.
Level −3 (L −3)	Biochemical activity underlying fear.*

(*One could go to still lower levels such as chemistry or physics, but these seem without relevance to the emotion of fear.)

for example, an Aristotelian approach, or an approach with a strong phenomenological, existentialist, or personalist emphasis. Such philosophical theories present general descriptive interpretations of mental experience of different emotions and thoughts, especially of complex mental experiences, including such phenomena as guilt, the search for meaning, and so on. Level 7 would correspond to any theological interpretation of fear. This understanding could be derived from but not restricted to Sacred Scripture, revelation, and religious tradition.

The theological level might address fear or awe of God.

Note that Levels 4 and higher are interpretations that lie outside of and above qualitative experience; they are public and open to reason and discussion. Only Levels 4 and 5 are open, and then in limited ways, to the methods of natural science; but all these levels are open to scientific evidence.

Our proposed hierarchical ordering is summarized in Table 6.1. The levels represented in Table 6.1 are considered as layers of understanding the person and, taken together, are called a "laminate." The seven different levels fall into three distinct groupings: Level 4 and above (reason); Levels 1 to 3 of human experience (described mental experience); and Levels −1 to −3 (objective observation). Taken together (see discussion of resonance below) they enrich our understanding, much as the different laminates of a ski improve its performance: one layer for strength, one for flexibility, and one for smoothness against snow.

To summarize the preceding kinds of levels: we move from the biochemical, Level −3; to neurons and neural circuitry, both in the brain, Level −2; to behavioral psychology, Level −1. Next comes Level 1, with its elementary awareness of certain sights, sounds, and feelings. Then comes human self-conscious awareness of the particular fearful situation at Level 2; and this includes the person's self-conscious reflection on and recall of past experience and knowledge (in this case, of snakes). Then Level 3 with its qualitative experience of awe, of the transcendent. These three levels are based on people's verbal descriptions of their experiences. These descriptions are open to rational evaluation and understanding. The actual experiences themselves may be part of a person's personal history and memory, but the laminate model is based on the descriptions. Keep in mind that this laminate model is an interpretation of one's understanding the levels from the outside as one conceptualizes the person. It is not based on direct experience of Level 1, 2, or 3. After these three levels comes Level 4, any psychological theory of fear. Next is Level 5, any sociocultural understanding of fear. Level 6 is any philosophical understand-

ing of fear. Finally is Level 7, any theological understanding of fear. Clearly these disciplines are placed in an order of increasing abstraction with respect to their representation of the person.

The different levels fall into three types: The minus levels—Levels −1, −2, and −3—are open to the natural sciences. There is no Level 0. Levels 1, 2, and 3 represent types of subjective experience or *qualia*. These *qualia* can usually be described by the person who has them for public evaluation. The still higher laminate levels—Levels 4, 5, 6, and 7—represent public and rational interpretations at higher and higher levels. These higher levels are all open to various amounts of empirical evidence but not to well-controlled scientific experiments.

Although a neuroscientist might use quite abstract mathematics to represent a neurological basis of brain activity, the knowledge of the *person* at such a level has been reduced to a particular and lower level aspect of the body. The level of abstraction proposed here for the ordering of levels refers to the level at which the person is represented, not the degree of abstraction used in understanding phenomena at a given level. A mathematical model of neural connections could be quite abstract, but we are not concerned with the scientific understanding of the level itself.

As a general rule the higher levels often use explicit knowledge from lower levels for explanation, but not vice versa. Lower levels sometimes, of course, contain implicit aspects of higher levels, such as philosophical assumptions. The next problem is to understand what keeps the layers holding together instead of sliding apart.

The Concept of Integration (Resonance)

The levels of understanding the person shown in Table 6.1 are, as noted, normally studied and understood as independent of one another. Scholars and scientists are highly specialized, and their work often has little intellectual relevance even to others working in the same discipline, much less to those working with a different epistemology at a level above or below them. Nevertheless, there are important intellectual connections between levels that can be recognized and that are of real importance. The terms "integration" or sometimes "resonance" will be used to characterize this between-levels support and integrative "glue."

To begin, integration or resonance refers to the obvious way in which the different levels represent different approaches to understanding *the same general phenomenon*—in this case, fear. In our example, Level 2, Level 1, and Level –1 all contribute to an understanding of fear, and they mutually reinforce our understanding. This mutual reinforcement is a major part of what is meant by integration. Normally, this kind of reinforcement is strongest between adjacent levels.

For example, in discussing between-level support with respect to attachment behavior (L –1), the developmental neuroscientist Daniel J. Siegel (2001) writes: "Experience [our L 1] involves the activation of neurons in the brain [our L –2] that respond to the sensory events from the external world" (p. 69) and "the patterns of development of children with distinct attachment classifications [our L –1] suggest that the minds [brains, L –2] of these individuals are functioning in quite distinct manners" (p. 71). Siegel goes on to say: "Recent work also suggests that the prefrontal regions of the brain [L –2] may also be a part of the integrated circuitry that permits social and moral [L 2] behaviors [L –1]" (p. 83). Finally, Siegel writes: "There is an exciting convergence of findings from the neurosciences [L –2 & –3] and from the developmental 'behavioral' sciences [L –1] that allow us to see a unity of knowledge or consilience" (p. 69). However, consilience refers to any kind of unity of scientific knowledge. We use the terms "laminate" and "integration" to refer to hierarchically organized and mutually supporting modes of knowledge of the same general phenomenon; much of this knowledge is not part of natural science, but part of experiential [L 2] or higher level [e.g., L 4] knowledge.

Along the same lines as his colleague Siegel, Allan N. Schore (2002) has identified early abuse causing lasting neurological damage as the right hemisphere develops (L –2) in the first few years. The effects of the damage are observable in a child's behavior (L –1). It also can be assumed that evidence of anxiety in behavior is accompanied by corresponding negative conscious experience at Levels 1 and 2. This subjective experience can also be interpreted at the higher level of psychological attachment theory, Level 4—for example, a pathological internal working model of interpersonal relationships based on early attachment trauma.

In the understanding of integration or resonance, a key concept is that *some aspect* of the *same thing* is being conceptualized at each level. Of course, as one moves to the lower levels, the part of the person that is being examined is of a different nature than what is addressed at higher levels and is a smaller or reduced aspect, but each level is a necessary building block in the full representation of the total person being studied. Often a given level can be subdivided into two or possibly more sub-levels. For example, at

Level –2a the location and responses of brain circuits are studied. (They are, of course, a smaller part of the behavior observable at Level –1.) But it is also possible to subdivide Level –2, as shown in Table 6.1, into a somewhat lower level of the brain, Level –2b, where only cells or neurons would be observed and interpreted. Finally at Level –3, only biochemical processes affecting the relevant neurons would be examined. In any case, the thing that is examined, even though an increasingly smaller part of the original, is still an aspect of the same thing: in the present example, the feeling of fear. And this connection of the part being studied to the adjacent higher and lower levels represents *a kind of vertical thread or fiber connecting the levels*, which serves as the basis or conduit for an integration or "hierarchical consilience" in the present model of the person. This connecting thread can be interpreted as uniting the levels around an essential ontological identity, in this case, fear.

This same kind of thread of continuity exists as one goes to levels that are higher as well. The particular person is understood from different vantage points in each of the different levels. In Levels 1 and 2, we have a particular person being understood in terms of his experience of fear. At the psychological level, Level 4, the person's particular fear response is interpreted within the context of one or more psychological theories of fear. In the sociocultural level, Level 5, we're looking at how that particular person's fear interrelates with his community and its culture. In Level 6, we examine the deeper meaning and *telos* of that person's life within the framework of a philosophy, and in Level 7, we explore the way that person, in the context of the whole of humanity, relates to God.

The lower levels are rather similar to how a microscope moves to greater magnification as it zooms in on smaller and smaller parts of the original material. The higher levels are somewhat analogous to a telescope: whatever is first observed becomes an increasingly smaller part of the total field as magnification increases. This integrated laminate representation of knowledge in a very general sense is shown in Table 6.2. Note that it is assumed that God stands behind all human understanding as a kind of ground or as the light that makes any kind of knowledge available to the human mind.

It is important to keep in mind that this laminate model is a representation of our knowledge or *concept* of the person; it is not a representation of a particular person's actual internal experience. Although the scientist, psychologist, or philosopher who thinks about the concepts shown in Tables 6.1, 6.2, and 6.3 will be operating within their personal subjective experience at Level 2, nevertheless, all the levels in the tables reflect some aspect of reality about the person and are open to reason.

The price or cost of a focus on a lower level knowledge is the loss of higher level knowledge and, of course, vice versa. That is, each level provides some knowledge unique to that level, but a given level is intrinsically incapable of providing the information that can be extracted from the other levels. Of course, information from a higher or lower level can be used to support an interpretation at any other given level. To have a thorough knowledge of a phenomenon, one must step back and consider all or at least several of the levels at the same time.

Let us now turn to representing the person as a collection of qualitatively different sets of integrated laminates considered simultaneously.

Table 6.2. General Model of the Concept of Person Understood as an Integrated Laminate

GOD'S BEING AND REVELATION *Ground of all human knowledge*	
Reason	
Level 7	Theology: Rational interpretation of revelation, Scripture, and tradition. Rational
Level 6	Philosophy: Rationality and experience (e.g., Plato, Aristotle, Thomism, Kant, phenomenological personalism). Rational
Level 5	Sociological/cultural: Social and cultural interpretations of persons. Rational
Level 4	Psychology: Theories of mental processes (e.g., defense mechanisms, ego structures, Bowlby's internal working model, cognitive schemas, etc.). Rational
Described Mental Experience	
Level 3	Personal psychology: Mystical experience of the holy, awe in response to truth, beauty, goodness, nature's power. Subjective but public when a described mental experience (DME). *Qualia* 3
Level 2	Personal psychology: Interpreted experience, normal conscious mental life (e.g., My stomach must be telling me I am hungry since I haven't eaten since breakfast; Oh, there is John; What are they doing?; etc.), basic level of *human* understanding. Subjective but public when described as mental experience with meaning. *Qualia* 2
Level 1	Basic experience of awareness without human meaning, *animal-like*. Subjective but public when described as mental awareness. *Qualia* 1
Objective	
Level −1	Behavioral psychology: observable behavior. Objective
Level −2	Neuroscience: Brain location, circuitry. Objective
Level −3	Biochemical: Hormones, neurotransmitters. Objective

The Concept of Person Understood as an Integrated Laminate

In this final section we will use the integrated laminate model, as just described, to address major dimensions of the person. Starting from the Christian philosophical vision of the person, presented in the Catholic Christian Meta-Model of the Person and explored in other chapters, we assume that a person consists of the following characteristics: (a) a body-soul unity (thus we acknowledge that embodiment is foundational to person); (b) five dimensions or properties: *relationships* with other persons, a *will* (i.e., agency), *rationality* (i.e., human self-conscious intelligence), *emotionality*, and *sensory-perceptual-cognitive* capacities. Recently, psychology, neuroscience, theology, and philosophy have placed great emphases on both the importance of human embodiment and on our interpersonal relationships, and an integrated laminate understanding of these two properties of the person will be developed now.

Modern psychology and philosophy of the nineteenth and twentieth centuries very much tended to emphasize the person as an autonomous self that was intrinsically subjective, in that the self defined its own values and even its very nature. This emphasis can be found in the concept of self held by some humanistic psychologies—for instance, Carl Rogers had no representation of the body as part of personality. Also, the emphasis on autonomy meant a rejection of relationships as intrinsic to the healthy adult personality. Much of the basis for this autonomous model of the person is found in some of the existential philosophy of the last century—in Sartre's work, for example—but not, of course, in the writings of Martin Buber (1958) or of the Catholic personalists, such as Gabriel Marcel (1951, 1952). The present development of the importance of the body is derived from initial presuppositions of the Catholic Christian Meta-Model but is also heavily based on psychological and neurological evidence.

Examples of philosophy's new emphasis on the body include the Lakoff and Johnson (1999) analysis of the body as highly influential in establishing our rational mental life. Their work is essentially based on the research findings of cognitive psychology and especially of neuroscience. Some scientists take this new body emphasis so far as to assume all mental life can be reduced to bodily or material reality; we reject this as an untenable position.

Likewise, the recent understanding of the importance of interpersonal relationships is based both on research and on theoretical developments. Theoretical support in psychology began with Alfred Adler's (1964) notion of "social interest" and with the object relations psychoanalytic contributions. It was firmly established by John Bowlby's well-known theory of separation anxiety and the importance of the early mother-child attachment. His work led to the important research on attachment styles, first done by Mary Ainsworth and Mary Main. There is now a large body of research on the importance of infant and childhood attachment for later personality, and especially on inadequate and anxious attachment as factors in mental pathology. Recently, there also has been the emergence of what is known as interpersonal psychoanalytic theory. In addition, the findings of neuroscience about the importance of oxytocin and vasopressin for establishing bonding support both the interpersonal and body-based conceptualization of the basic nature of the person. The convergence of these two lines of approach has led to what is now called a neurological interpersonal and developmental psychology. Again, see the work of Daniel Siegel (2001, 2012).

In the fields of theology and philosophy, a remarkably similar kind of emphasis has been taking place. In theology, we have the theology of the body, as developed by Pope John Paul II, with its special emphasis on what he called the nuptial meaning of the male and female bodies (see Bachiochi, 2013; Brizendine, 2006, 2010; Gurian, 2011; Hasson, 2015). As noted above, the philosophers Lakoff and Johnson (1999) have brought the body back into the philosophical understanding of the person, with a special focus on conscious rational thought.

As for the focus on the interpersonal aspects of the person, major theologians have been making this point with great clarity. Using Trinitarian theology as a basis and working from the personalist philosophers (e.g., Marcel, 1951, 1952; Mounier, 1952), such major thinkers as Joseph Ratzinger (1990) (now Pope Emeritus Benedict XVI), Pope John Paul II (2006; see Schmitz, 1993), and the Protestant Thomas Torrance (1983, 1985) have come up with remarkably similar understandings of relationship, based on

Table 6.3. Two Dimensions or Properties of the Person from the Catholic Christian Meta-Model, Each Represented as a Qualitatively Different Column of an Integrated Laminate with Its Particular Methodological Lens.

Methodological lens	Types of knowledge/ level	GOD'S BEING AND REVELATION Ground of all human knowledge	
		Focus on body, as in body/soul unity	Focus on relationship
Faith informed by reason	Theology Level 7	Person created out of matter in the image of God; created male & female (Gen, Ch. 1) Theology of the embodied person (John Paul II, [JPII])	Person created as gift to love God and others Trinitarian theology of the person as relational; Self-giving love, (JPII; also Torrance, Ratzinger, Zizioulas; also Buber)
Reason and reflection on experience	Philosophy Level 6	Person as a body-soul unity made for knowing and loving (Thomism) or embodied mind (Lakoff & Johnson)	Person as relationship (Macmurray; personalists; Levinas): Substance in relationship (neo-Thomism)
Reason focused on human social life and culture	Sociology/culture Level 5	Person as embodied in cultural roles and sex roles	Person as interpreted in social and cultural contexts
Reason focused on human psychology	Psychology (theory and practice) Level 4	Theories of sex differences; equality and complementarity; male and female sensitive therapy	Object relations, theories of relationship; attachment theory; interpersonal psychodynamics
Reason reflecting on described personal experience	Psychology (experience) Levels 3, 2, 1	Specific male or female experience of the body	Experience of relationships: attachment, love, friendship, etc.
Reason focused on objective reality	Psychology (behavior) Level −1	Sex-related differences in behavior	Different attachment styles in behavior
Reason focused on biological realities	Biology (brain) Level −2	Sex-related differences in brain circuits, neurons	Effects of attachment on brain structures
Reason focused on chemical realities	Biochemistry Level −3	Testosterone, estrogen, oxytocin, vasopressin	Oxytocin, vasopressin

self-giving love as foundational for the person. The Eastern Orthodox theologian John Zizioulas (1985) has made the same claim, pointing out in particular that the Eastern Church has never lost the interpersonal and communal understanding of the person.

As for more recent philosophers, John Macmurray (1991), the Jewish thinker Emmanuel Levinas (1998), and Alasdair MacIntyre (1981, 1999) have made major statements about the interpersonal and socially embedded nature of the person. Finally, the neo-Thomist philosopher W. Norris Clarke (1993) developed the work of Aquinas so as to explicitly affirm that relationship is just as foundational as substance for understanding the person. This convergence of thinkers is truly remarkable and, we believe,

represents a powerful new and genuinely deep understanding of the person. In Table 6.3, we summarize this understanding by describing the different levels of mutually reinforcing representations of the person as an integrated laminate.

It is important in concluding to note that the Catholic Christian Meta-Model of the Person presented in this volume is itself a type of integrated laminate involving Levels 7, 6, and 4 as shown in Table 6.1. Level 5 could have been included but was omitted for simplicity's sake and because the sociocultural level is on average less relevant to understanding the person in mental health practice. In the future this will be remedied so that all major reason-based (R) levels above the described mental experience (DME) levels are exemplified.

REFERENCES

Adler, A. (1964). *Social interest: A challenge to mankind* (J. Linton & R. Vaughn, Trans.). London, United Kingdom: Faber & Faber. (Original work published in 1933)

Bachiochi, E. (2013). Women, sexual asymmetry, and Catholic teaching. *Christian Bioethics, 19*(2), 150–171. doi:10.1093/cb/cbt013

Brizendine, L. (2006). *The female brain.* New York, NY: Broadway Books.

Brizendine. L. (2010). *The male brain.* New York, NY: Broadway Books.

Buber, M. (1958). *I and thou.* New York, NY: Scribners. (Original work published in German, 1923)

Clarke, W. N. (1993). *Person and being: The Aquinas lecture, 1993.* Milwaukee, WI: Marquette University Press.

Gurian, M (with Stevens, K.). (2011). *Boys and girls learn differently.* San Francisco, CA: Jossey-Bass.

Hasson, M. R. (2015). *Promise and challenge: Catholic reflection on feminism, complementarity, and the Church.* Huntington, IN: Our Sunday Visitor.

John Paul II. (2006). *Man and woman he created them: A theology of the body* (M. Waldstein, Trans.). Boston, MA: Pauline Books & Media.

Keller, H., & Silverman, R. (Ed.).(2000). *Light in my darkness.* West Chester, PA: Chrysalis Books.

Keller, H. (2003). *The story of my life: The restored classic 1903–2003.* New York, NY: Norton.

Lakoff, G., & Johnson, M. (1999). *Philosophy in the flesh: The embodied mind and its challenge to Western thought.* New York, NY: Basic Books.

Levinas, E. (1998). *Entre nous: On thinking-of-the-other* (M. B. Smith & B. Harshav, Trans.). New York, NY: Columbia University Press. (Original work published in French, 1991)

MacIntyre, A. (1981). *After virtue: A study in moral theory.* Notre Dame, IN: University of Notre Dame Press.

MacIntyre, A. (1999). *Dependent rational animals: Why human beings need the virtues.* Peru, IL: Open Court.

Macmurray, J. (1991). *Persons in relation.* Atlantic Highlands, NJ: Humanities Press International. (Original work published 1961)

Marcel, G. (1951). *Homo viator: Introduction to a metaphysic of hope.* Chicago, IL: Regnery.

Marcel, G. (1952). *Metaphysical journal.* Chicago, IL: Regnery.

Mounier, E. (1952). *Personalism*. Notre Dame, IN: University of Notre Dame Press.

Pearsall, P. (2007). *Awe: The delights and dangers of our eleventh emotion*. Deerfield Beach, FL: Health Communications.

Ratzinger, J. (1990). Concerning the notion of person in theology. *Communio, 17*(3), 439–454. (Original work published in German, 1973)

Schmitz, K. L. (1993). *At the center of the human drama: The philosophical anthropology of Karol Wojtyla/Pope John Paul II*. Washington, DC: The Catholic University of America Press.

Schore, A. N. (2002). Dysregulation of the right brain: A fundamental mechanism of traumatic attachment and the psychopathogenesis of posttraumatic stress disorder. *Australian and New Zealand Journal of Psychiatry, 36*(1), 9–30.

Siegel, D. J. (2001). Toward an interpersonal neurobiology of the developing mind: Attachment relationships, "mindsight", and neural integration. *Infant Mental Health Journal, 22*(1-2), 67–94.

Siegel, D. J. (2012). *The developing mind: How relationships and the brain interact to shape who we are* (2nd ed.). New York, NY: Guilford.

Torrance, T. (1983). *The mediation of Christ*. Grand Rapids, MI: Eerdmans

Torrance, T. (1985). *Reality and scientific theology*. Edinburgh, United Kingdom: Scottish Academic Press.

Vitz, P. C. (2017). The origin of consciousness in the integration of analog (right hemisphere) & digital (left hemisphere) codes. *Journal of Consciousness Exploration &Research, 8*(11), 881–906.

Zizioulas, J. D. (1985). *Being as communion: Studies in personhood and the Church*. Crestwood, NY: St. Vladimir's Seminary Press.

Part III

Philosophical Support

Chapter 7

The Methodology and Presuppositions of the Catholic Christian Meta-Model of the Person

Craig Steven Titus, Paul C. Vitz, and
William J. Nordling

ABSTRACT: Every approach to psychological theory, mental health practice, and human flourishing is based upon a vision of the person. Very often, though, the conceptual basis and tradition for such a worldview or value system is only implicit. This chapter explicitly presents an outline of the realist methodology, presuppositions, and tradition that underlie the Catholic Christian Meta-Model of the Person presented in this volume. While drawing from a wide base of theoretical and practical support for an integrated understanding of the person, the chapter also presents the way that this Meta-Model serves to integrate three levels of input: (a) *psychological support*—how personality theories, empirical studies, and evidence-based mental health practices contribute to our knowledge of the person; (b) *philosophical support* (reason-based)—how existential meaning, considerations of truth and beauty, and ethical reflections on goodness, vocations, and interpersonal relationships further enrich our vision of the person; and (c) *theological support* (faith-based)—how the Catholic Christian vision of the person, especially concerning the performative dimension of belief in God, hope in an afterlife, and self-giving love, enriches even more our understanding of the person. This chapter outlines how these three hierarchical disciplines serve each other and point us toward a greater understanding of the person as an object of study and a subject for action.

What is a human person? Why do persons exist? What makes them flourish? Do they need family and friends to be happy? Do they need power, prestige, and wealth to flourish? How do they gain knowledge of themselves and others? Is it possible to avoid these questions or to hold a truly value-free perspective on the human person and relationships, psychology and mental health practice? What difference do a person's psychological, philosophical, and spiritual-religious perspectives make for understanding that person's development and healing, suffering and joy, the meaning of life and death?

Everyone has some notion of what it means to be human, to live a good life, and to flourish (Mt 5; Aquinas, 1273/1981, I, qq. 1–5; Augustine,

401/2007; Frankl, 2000, 1959/2006; Haidt, 2006; Maslow, 1987; Seligman, 2004, 2012). We understand and tell our life narratives based on experiences of and presuppositions about meaning and truth, purpose and goodness, family and community. We also have presuppositions about the nature of our desires for goodness, committed vocational states, and meaningful work and service (Chapter 10, "Fulfilled Through Vocation"). Mental health professionals are no exception. The fact that everyone has a basic understanding of the human person is not always critically recognized though. More recently, there has been some open discussion about the inevitability of basic presuppositions in psychology and mental health practice, including religious-like assumptions (Bergin, 1980; Bergin, Payne, & Richards, 1996; Ellis, 1980; Hamilton, 2013; Miller, 2001; O'Donohue, 2013; Worthington, 1988). In this chapter, we maintain that worldviews and value systems, be they implicit or explicit, influence every theoretical reflection, professional intervention, and interpersonal interaction. This is the case even when the psychological sciences and mental health practices are said to be value-free or when they are presented as generic or without an explicit viewpoint.

This volume seeks to more comprehensively understand the person by integrating the truths of the person that are found in faith-based, reason-based, and psychology- and counseling-focused perspectives at theoretical and practical levels. This Catholic Christian Meta-Model frames personal and interpersonal flourishing and suffering in a worldview and value system that is wider than any of the many partial theories currently existing in the psychological and mental health field, including more recent attempts at integrating different psychological theories.

The project of outlining a Meta-Model does not start from a blank slate. Rather it is part of an ongoing inquiry within the Catholic Christian tradition that has already established a sapiential frame and dialogical methodology, as found in patristic sources and the Doctors of the Church, in addition to Pope John Paul II (1998) and Pope Benedict XVI (2006). These thinkers express a philosophical tradition that continues to offer deep reflections on the nature of reality and our knowledge. In this volume we will use this comprehensive framework to (a) identify the truths of mental health theories and practices, as well as the psychological sciences, in the light of a larger Catholic Christian perspective of the person, (b) ascertain the limitations of these theories, findings, and practices, and (c) use this fuller understanding of the person to enrich case conceptualization, diagnoses, and treatment planning. These innovations, especially, come through the consideration of life-callings, virtue strengths, personal unity, realist understanding of freedom, our divinely given dignity, and our transcendent and redemptive goal.

This particular chapter explicitly presents the integrative method and presuppositions of the Catholic Christian Meta-Model of the Person. It sets the tone for the volume's larger narrative and multidisciplinary approach. The rest of this volume explicitly presents a Catholic Christian vision of the person, for mental health professionals concerned with understanding the larger theological and philosophical context in which psychotherapy can, and very often does, operate.

How Do Reason and Faith Help Us Understand Human Flourishing?

What is the goal of applying the integrative method behind the Catholic Christian Meta-Model of the Person? In short, we maintain that each human is unified, interpersonally relational, perceiving, embodied, emotional, rational, and volitional and free, and each is fulfilled through vocations and in virtue. These complementary dimensions of reality are observed in theoretical and practical ways. The disciplines that we primarily address—psychology, philosophy, and theology—each render different levels of service toward understanding flourishing. The Meta-Model's realist approach addresses these disciplines and their individual presuppositions, methods, and theories. These disciplines, in combination, serve as lenses for enriching our understanding of humans and reality. Each lens utilizes presuppositions and a method. For example, in this volume, we use (a) reason-based lenses to measure the import of what we do as persons with basic dignity, how we relate to other people ethically, and how we aim at everyday goals and ultimate flourishing. We also use (b) lenses of faith and religious practice to see the trajectory and ultimate goal of our life narrative in the light of faith in God. Furthermore, we use (c) lenses of psychology and personality theories to understand human persons and the pathways that lead to flourishing, as well as the hindrances that make them suffer, and we use the lens of mental health practice to identify how to bring support, healing, and hope to people who suffer, for example, from depression, anxiety, or grief. The Meta-Model thus can inform how we observe persons and how we formulate and test hypotheses, which can bring us to a deeper knowledge of the person and interpersonal subjectivity, family, and other systems.

In this chapter, we propose an openly Catholic Christian method of integrating the theoretical, empirical, and experiential bases of mental health practice with a Catholic vision of human beings and interpersonal relationships. We explicitly employ, in a structured way, the major sources of Catholic Christian thought. Scripture and biblical scholarship provide the basic reference for the Meta-Model's theological narrative, starting with the basic conviction (or premise) that humans are created in the image of God and thus are basically good (Gen 1:27–31). The living tradition of the Church and its teaching Magisterium provide a person-based, moral, and spiritual frame. Throughout the volume, the method also intentionally draws upon personal experience, thematized observations, and systematic reflections, with special attention to philosophical sources, the human sciences, mental health theories and practices, and clinical examples.

(Citations and references to ancient and classical sources will use the standard numbering of parts, books, and paragraphs or articles as appropriate. For example, the reference, "Aquinas, 1273/1981, II-II, 17.1," refers to Thomas Aquinas's *Summa Theologiae* [Summary of Theology], Second Part of the Second Part, question 17, article 1)

What Is the Method Behind the Meta-Model?

At its reason-based and faith-based center, the Meta-Model employs a wisdom-based (sapiential) approach. It draws upon reason and faith to search for the deeper meaning that underlies the reality of the person and informs our knowledge of it. The Meta-Model demands attention to the specific methods and sources of these disciplines and contributes to the development of the ongoing tradition of inquiry.

Our realist use of human reason is articulated across the disciplines of the human sciences, philosophy, and theology. Since they each have particular competencies and authorities, their findings, reflections, and doctrine should not be confused with or simplistically translated into the other disciplines. While the disciplines are all expressions of nature or grace, each has its own methodological strengths and limits, as determining distinct but interrelated levels or laminates of reality (Chapter 6, "Person as an Integrated Laminate").

John Paul II's (1998) encyclical *Faith and Reason* (*Fides et Ratio*) describes philosophy's "sapiential dimension as a search for the ultimate and overarching meaning of life" (§81). This search for meaning, purpose, and flourishing is a constant quest across the lifespan and across the millennia, as already documented in ancient cultures (Bellah, 2011). There are relativist and social constructivist presuppositions that seem to call into question the existence of ultimate values. The sapiential dimension of the Meta-Model's method reminds us, however, that human experience is more than particular customs and local values; there are also moral values and religious values that are universal and based on both human nature and interpersonal relationships (John Paul II, 1998, §81). The Meta-Model invites us to reject relativism and to see more, that is, to see the other's brain as a mind, the other's mind as foundational to a person, and the other person as interpersonally relational and called from love and for love. This vision affirms the goodness of the person as a foundation for values, virtues, and vocations.

The Meta-Model employs a theologically and philosophically informed wisdom-based vision of mankind to explore the bases and the limits of the different disciplines and sciences in a search for truth and meaning. This concern for meaning is partially shared in different approaches to psychology, such as existential (Frankl, 1959/2006), humanist (Adler, 1931/2009; May, 2007; Maslow, 1987), psychodynamic (Erikson, 1979), attachment (Bowlby, 1982, 1988; Ainsworth, Blehar, Waters, & Wall, 1978), emotionally focused (Greenberg & Johnson, 1988), marriage (Gottman, 1999), narrative (McLeod, 1997, 2004; White, 2007), and positive psychol-

ogy approaches (Lopez & Snyder, 2009; Peterson & Seligman, 2004; Snyder & Lopez, 2002). However, the Meta-Model's goal-oriented or teleological approach to an ultimate and unified frame of human knowledge and action includes yet goes beyond most psychological perspectives to identify not only the function but also the normative character of human action and the virtues.

How Does the Meta-Model Handle the Unity of Truth and the Diversity of Perspectives?

There are different theories about the origin and end of humanity. Nonetheless, it is a Catholic Christian conviction that through faith and reason we have knowledge of ultimate reality (its origin and end) and the unity of truth, albeit a considerably limited knowledge (Aquinas, 1273/1981; John Paul II, 1998; MacIntyre, 1990, 2007; Popper, 1975, 1983). Furthermore, even though the human species has a common heritage with the rest of creation, what makes humanity distinct is the body-soul unity (understood abstractly as human nature and concretely as the person), which the Meta-Model holds to be God-given. This uniqueness of the human person is partially expressed in abstract thought, self-consciousness, syntactic language, complex tool use, and intentional action (Ashley, 2013).

Basic human nature is the foundation for the true kinship of all humanity, even the unborn and the weak (John Paul II, 1995; MacIntyre, 1999). Human beings nonetheless express diverse perspectives on meaning according to their unique individual, cultural, historic, and religious backgrounds. People's worldviews or cultural traditions are present in the way that people experience the world, think about things, make choices, and live family life. For example, mental health professionals' worldviews influence both their self-understanding and their understanding of the client. Such perspectives influence their understanding of who one is, why one exists, how one should live, the difference it makes how people interrelate, and what makes a person flourish or languish.

Each mental health professional, as a practitioner and a scholar, will benefit from becoming attentive to worldviews, value systems, and traditions of enquiry, since they underlie the psychological sciences and are of utmost importance for the flourishing of the client and the mental health practitioner as well. A Catholic perspective on the ordering of the sciences, thus, recognizes the uniqueness of each person, the methodological diversity of the disciplines, and the unity of truth (Aquinas, 1259/1952, 1259/1986; Ashley, 2006, 2013; Lonergan, 1992). Based on this confidence, the Meta-Model's method humbly seeks to understand more deeply how different theoretical perspectives and practical applications can help us overcome our languishing and promote our flourishing.

What Are the Limits to Faith and Philosophy's Study of Human Nature?

Catholic theological sources affirm that God is the origin of the truth of the tradition's vision of the person. We can know human nature, the person, and God to an important yet limited extent. But a Catholic confidence in the human capacity to appreciate the order of things (existence, goodness, truth, relationship, and beauty) is not without reserve. And although we affirm that it is possible to have true knowledge about many things through our everyday experience, there are limits to some of our knowledge. There is difficulty in coming to surety even about some things we know well (Benedict XVI, 2005). John Paul II's (1998) encyclical on faith and reason

speaks with confidence about human reason's capacity to seek and find truth and the Absolute, even while recognizing that "the disobedience by which man and woman chose to set themselves in full and absolute autonomy in relation to the One who had created them" (§22) diminishes this capacity (Rom 1:20).

MacIntyre (1990) argues that the Catholic tradition—a doctrinally stable yet sapientially expansive worldview—serves as the most coherent tradition for engaging contemporary thought and sciences about human nature and truth. He does so as a philosopher.

What Are the Types of Reductionism to Be Avoided?

The Meta-Model is attentive to knowledge of nature and the methods of science without being a kind of reductionistic naturalism. It seeks to overcome five negative tendencies in modern and postmodern psychology without rejecting the positive contributions of the sciences.

First, it fosters a scientific focus on reality while resisting the reductionism seen in popular atheistic approaches to the biological bases of psychology and the neurosciences, like those of Dawkins (2008) and Dennett (1991, 1995).

Second, it is attentive to biological evolution and comparative studies with other animals, while rejecting the materialism or naturalism that is especially prevalent in uncritical neo-Darwinian evolutionary psychology, which are critiqued by Nagel (2012) and Życiński (2006).

Third, it is conscious of the contributions of the modern founders of the human sciences, such as Sigmund Freud (1900/2010), Ivan Pavlov (1927), John B. Watson (1913, 1924), B. F. Skinner (1938, 1971, 1976), and Max Weber (1904/1992), while simultaneously disallowing the anti-religious or anti-Christian bias found in their works (which are critiqued by Feser, 2008).

Fourth, it recognizes the specific methods of the diverse scientific disciplines and interdisciplinary works without affirming an exaggerated autonomy of the sciences (Ashley, 2013; Ashley & Deeley, 2012; Wallace, 1996).

Last, it also recognizes the importance of the human person, accepting the valid contributions of science (Ellis, 2004; Ellis & Ellis, 2011; Rogers, 1961/2012) without adopting an individualism that would eclipse personal vocations to family and community life. While avoiding these five types of reductionism and providing a constructive alternative, this Catholic philosophical and theological vision of humankind contributes to an enriched and enlarged understanding of psychology and of clinical practice.

What Are the Two Basic Sources for Studying Mankind?

To reiterate the Catholic Christian perspective, there are two sources for the study of the human person: the book of nature or creation and the book of the Word of God. The two books are accessed by "natural reason" and "divine faith," respectively. They aim at two objects: "those things to which natural reason can attain," and the "mysteries hidden in God" (Vatican I, 1870, §3015). John Paul II (1998) distinguishes these two sources as well (§4, §9, §19).

Basic or reason-based (philosophical) knowledge springs from the wonder that is awakened by sense experience and the contemplation of all nature (John Paul II, 1998, §4). For its knowledge of nature, human reason employs the light of intellect and all the natural capacities (John Paul II, 1998, §9); it reveals deep insights through its "analyses of perception and experience, of the imaginary and the unconscious, of personhood and intersubjectivity, of freedom and values, of time and history" (§48).

A faith-based (theological) approach to understanding the person requires the divine assistance of grace. Faith's knowledge of God and redemption is especially nourished by the Word of God, which is committed to the Church in a living tradition. As the Second Vatican Council (1965a) affirms, "Sacred Tradition and Sacred Scripture form one sacred deposit of the Word of God, committed to the Church" (§9).

A Catholic Christian viewpoint, thus, recognizes these two sources of knowledge about the person—knowledge from nature and from the Word of God—and recognizes also that neither knowledge is fully understood without the other; and, even with both, our understanding of the person remains limited. But need for both kinds of knowledge about the person will become clearer only in light of our later discussion of the services that psychology, philosophy, and theology render each other in our self-understanding, interpersonal interaction, and human flourishing.

Discourse, Premises, and Narrative

We will focus on the ordering of these three disciplines in terms of the service that each renders to increasing our understanding of the person. The present Meta-Model accepts valid methods and findings but rejects the metaphysically reductionist interpretations sometimes made by various scientists. In this way, reason-based discourse can serve as a bridge between psychological and faith-based models of the person.

How Does the Discourse of Philosophy Serve the Psychology of the Meta-Model?

The realist and metaphysically open discourse of the Meta-Model is not the idealist movement of

Hegelian dialectic (thesis, antithesis, and synthesis). Rather, the Meta-Model employs a method that recognizes an ordering of the disciplines. It draws upon neurobiology, psychology, social sciences, philosophy, and metaphysics, as well as Catholic Christian ethics and theology. Classically, these different disciplines have been seen to relate to each other in service, as providing—through intuition or insight, analogy, hypothesis formation, deductive and empirical testing, and so on—data for use in understanding the person. For example, there are the services offered by neurobiology (e.g., knowledge of the neurological conditions of opiate drug or alcohol addictions) and psychology (e.g., knowledge of the types of behavior that are indicative of such addiction, even factors more typical of men or women [Nolen-Hoeksema, 2004; Nolen-Hoeksema & Hilt, 2006; Vigna-Taglianti et al., 2016]). Understanding these contributions is more complete with ethical considerations, that is, with recognition of a person's freedom and responsibility. Such discourse enriches the understanding of the person typical of the Meta-Model.

This notion of service among these sciences has been recently revived in interdisciplinary and integrative efforts (for example, in the neurosciences, Siegel, 2012; and in narrative approaches to psychotherapy, McLeod, 1997, 2004). Realist and faith-based discourse requires the framing of the sciences by a meta-model, which through faith and reason addresses the ultimate questions, including the metaphysical and logical principles and presuppositions needed to understand a person's life. The Catholic Christian Meta-Model of the Person serves and supports partial theories of the person by allowing the valid contributions and essential truths of different approaches with the exclusion of their unacceptable and often contradictory metaphysical assumptions.

Other Christian integrated approaches also seek to provide a faith-based frame for mental health practice (Johnson, 2010; McMinn & Campbell, 2007; Entwistle, 2015). To fully understand these models also requires the identification of their ultimate principles and presuppositions, that is, their metaphysical and ethical frame and their ultimate narrative. Amidst a large common ground on the doctrine of salvation, Christian denominations take different emphases and perspectives that make some difference in application. There are divergent theological presuppositions, for example, about whether the person retains a basic dignity and goodness after the fall and in the midst of the influence of evil and sin. Denying that humans have a basic dignity and goodness has significant implications on empathy and love (either each person merits them or not); reason (either it has a potential for leading to good goals or it is always self-serving); volition and free will (either people have at least some measure of responsibility for their actions or they are determined in what they do); emotions (either compassion, patience, and other emotions can aid the person in relating to the world and other people or all emotions are to be distrusted systematically); and so on. The Catholic Christian Meta-Model makes explicit its affirmations, for instance, that each and every human person has a basic dignity and goodness, as well as its other presuppositions that work as premises for applications at the metaphysical, moral, psychological, social, and spiritual levels. Furthermore, it identifies how these premises may serve as a frame for theoretical and practical work.

What Is an Anthropological Premise or Presupposition?

In Chapter 2, the Meta-Model's realist approach to the person is expressed in foundational presuppositions, principles, or premises that are supported by faith-based, reason-based, and psychology-based rationale. In this context, premises are basic presuppositions that pertain to particular domains of knowledge about the person. These premises are truths about reality that the Catholic Christian tradition, in dialogue with contemporary knowledge, has drawn from experience, reflection, or faith, as described in the following chapters.

From these premises, conclusions can be derived by reason or by faith-guided reason. They are not a full description of human nature or experience in themselves but lead to fuller explanations of observable phenomena and fuller narratives of the truth and meaning of human experience. We come to the knowledge of reality needed to formulate a premise either by experience-based induction and intuition, or insight (articulated by the wise and the scientific), or by the authority of the Word of God (expressed in Sacred Scripture, tradition, and the Magisterium, and further articulated in patristic and theological sources), or by both, according to these sources' own competencies and authorities. The project behind the Meta-Model of the Person seeks to engage the sources found in basic experience, psychological theory and findings, philosophical discourse, and theological narrative, to come to an integrated understanding of the person.

What Are the Meta-Model's Philosophical and Theological Premises?

The Catholic Christian Meta-Model's philosophical vision of the person conceptually maps out the natural and spiritual inclinations, the psychological strengths, philosophical virtues, personal vocations, and human goals of flourishing, as expressed in eight reason-based premises. These premises are of two sorts, concerning ei-

ther the anthropological structure of the person or the person's goal of flourishing. The premises affirm that the person is (1) personally unified male or female (a body-soul unity); (2) fulfilled through vocations or callings; (3) flourishing in virtue; (4) interpersonally relational (being in relationship from conception on); (5) sensory-perceptual-cognitive; (6) emotional (having feelings, temperaments, and moods); (7) rational; and (8) volitional and free. These eight presuppositions originate in a common, value-rich humanity and are expansively expressed by each human in search of personal, social, and even ultimate flourishing. They also comprise groups of principles, presuppositions, and findings about the person that we call sub-premises (see a more complete outline of the eight basic philosophical premises in Chapter 2, "Theological, Philosophical, and Psychological Premises").

The Catholic Christian Meta-Model's theological vision of the person identifies, in the light of the Word of God and Christian faith, three major initial premises about human beings; these premises narratively trace salvation history. First, the human person is *created* in the image of God in love and for love; this indelible gift is the basis for each person's dignity and value. Second, humans are *fallen* and affected by sin, as is found in human greed, hatred, self-serving bias, and envy. Third, they are offered *redemption* through God the Father's gift of faith, hope, and love through Jesus Christ and in the Holy Spirit. And they wait to be beatified by the vision of and communion with God, who is humanity's ultimate goal in this life and the next. The heart of the theological perspective is to transform the reason-based levels through infused faith, hope, and charity.

The psychological premises contain no explicitly philosophical or theological presuppositions. But they provide supporting psychological evidence for all the Meta-Model's premises.

For example, the psychological premise, "The person is intrinsically interpersonal and formed throughout life by relationships, such as those experienced with the family, romantic partners, friends, colleagues, and communities," makes no philosophical or theological claims, and it is thoroughly documented in the psychological sciences. This psychological premise supports and parallels the reason-based premise that the person is interpersonal and the faith-based insight that we are created in the image of an interpersonal God and made to love and to be loved (Chapter 4, "Modern Personality Theories," and Chapter 5, "Basic Psychological Support").

The philosophical and psychological premises relate to the theological ones as nature relates to grace. The theological premises assume and build on the psychological and philosophical premises of the person (Chapter 2, "Theological, Philosophical, and Psychological Premises"). The Meta-Model's method explores the basic longings for relationship, knowledge, and love, before examining the specific difference the Christian narrative imparts to an understanding of the person. For example, the natural institution of marriage has been raised by Christ through grace to be a sacrament in light of the original complementarity and union intended in the beginning (Gen 1 & 2; Mt 19). Christian marriage, with its idea of equal dignity for both men and women and its requirement of freely choosing one's spouse, has elevated and enriched the institution of marriage and the lived experience of marriage itself. In the sacrament, God offers strength and clarity to the couple's loving union, openness to family, and growth in holiness, which, in turn, requires their efforts at loving commitment, generosity, justice, and mercy. The interrelation of such basic (philosophical) and spiritual (theological) presuppositions will be more fully presented and explained in the upcoming chapters.

What Is the Meta-Model's Definition of the Person?

In sum, the Meta-Model's synthetic definition of the person is threefold. First, it addresses the nature of the person in a reason-based approach, then it addresses how faith transforms human nature, finally it presents the person as understood in psychology. *From a **philosophical perspective**, the human person is an individual substance of a rational (intellectual), volitional (free), relational (interpersonal), sensory-perceptual-cognitive (pre-rational knowledge), emotional, and unified (body-soul) nature; the person is called to flourishing, moral responsibility, and virtue through his or her vowed or non-vowed vocational state, as well as through life work, service, and meaningful leisure. From an explicitly **theological perspective** (Scripture, tradition, and the Magisterium), the human person is created in the image of God and made by and for divine and human love, and—although suffering the effects of original, personal, and social sin—is invited to divine redemption in Christ Jesus, sanctification through the Holy Spirit, and beatitude with God the Father. Furthermore from a **psychological perspective**, the human person is an embodied individual who is intelligent, uses language, and exercises limited free-will. The person is fundamentally interpersonal, experiences and expresses emotions, and has sensory-perceptual-cognitive capacities to be in contact with reality. All of these characteristics are possible because of the unity of the body and unique self-consciousness, and are expressed in behavior and mental life. Furthermore the person is called by human nature to flourishing through virtuous behavior and transcendent growth; through interpersonal commitments to family, friends, and others; and through work, service, and meaningful leisure. From their origins (natural and transcendent), all persons have intrinsic goodness, dignity, and worth. In the course of life, though suffering from many natural, personal,* *and social disorders and conditions, persons hope for healing, meaning, and flourishing* (Chapter 2, "Theological, Philosophical, and Psychological Premises").

What Is the Context for Developing the Meta-Model's Method?

The next three subsections of this chapter provide reflection on the method behind the Meta-Model, especially on the use of psychology, philosophy, and theology in the service of mental health professionals (there are also other methodological reflections in Chapter 17, "Created in the Image of God"). This chapter seeks to answer the question: "Why are philosophy (reason) and theology (faith) helpful for an in-tegrated approach to psychological theory and mental health practice?" The answer needs to be set in place to understand the difference that the Meta-Model makes not only for case conceptualization but also for assessment, diagnosis, treatment, and other applications (Chapter 21, "Case Conceptualization").

The present chapter next proposes reflections on properly psychological, reason-based, and faith-based premises and their integration. It identifies some methodological considerations of the Meta-Model's premises themselves, as well as considerations for the chapters of Part III and Part IV that describe the Meta-Model's philosophical and theological supports.

Person and Mental Health Practice (Psychology)

Are Psychology and Mental Health Practice Value-Free?

Psychology, as the study of the *psyche*, or soul, is a part of the study of the book of nature and its intelligibility that we can know by reason. Psychology has its own coherency in its methodologies and increasingly in its general understanding of the person. Psychology, as a body of knowledge, also has developed many evidence-based applications in mental health practice. Furthermore, every approach to psychology, to mental health practice, and to the understanding of the person is based on a history, worldview, and value system. The different approaches to psychological theory and mental health practice take different positions on the fundamental nature of the person and role of the practitioners. For example, they differ in terms of their understanding of how free the person is and how much influence the therapist ought to have in the clinical relationship. They differ also in their views of the nature of the world and their espousal of either objective norms or relativist norms. Such awareness of the presuppositions of every model of mental health about human flourishing is also significant for understanding case conceptualization and the whole therapeutic encounter, from intake, assessment, and diagnosis, through treatment, to healing and discharge (Chapter 21, "Case Conceptualization").

Each practitioner and each client, at least implicitly, has a worldview and a personal conscience that have not only philosophical aspects but also an implicitly "religious" one (such as beliefs, traditions, sacred scriptures, worship, and practices). The debate about values in psychotherapy between Bergin (1980) and Ellis (1980) ended with two conclusions: one common and one divergent. Both Bergin and Ellis agreed that every psychology is based on a "faith," or on foundational value-laden presuppositions. They disagreed, however, on the starting points or values. Ellis situated himself in a probabilistic atheist faith, and Bergin, a religious one. Attentiveness to the omnipresence of values and diversity of values has, since this debate, become more widespread (Hicks, 2014; O'Donohue, 2013; Parrott, 1999; Smith, 1978). In Chapter 4, "Modern Personality Theories," we outline the magnitude of these value-based presuppositions in regard not only to atheism and theism but also to subjectivism and realism, determinism and free-will, moral relativism and moral standards, as well as to reductionism and constructivism.

How Has Secularism Influenced Modern Psychology and Mental Health Practice?

The secularization of science, culture, and religion has influenced psychology in theory and practice (Johnson, 2010). The modern secularized worldview has gone beyond seeking autonomy. It has promoted the notion that the human sciences, in order to function scientifically, must be independent of the values of the therapist, and that there is an inherent conflict between science and faith. Charles Taylor (2007), a Catholic philosopher, shows how the history of modern science has become a history of attempts to disengage the study of the sciences from the control of state and religious institutions, but also from traditions of philosophy and religious belief. He explains how modern psychology has separated itself in theory and practice from the constructive and positive resources that are dear to those seeking its assistance, especially from the resources found in their communities of faith and in their hope in God (Rosmarin, 2018).

What Methods Underlie Modern Psychology?

Modern psychology and its various partial theories have often expressed three troubling methodological tendencies that go beyond the necessary discipline-specific methodological reductionism that must focus its observations. First, the scientific method's methodological reductionism is often misused to deny any pertinence of theology for understanding the person. Although science addresses hypotheses that can be falsified (Popper, 1975, 1983), religious faith cannot be quantified and cannot be falsified as is necessary in science. Second, the scientific method is misconstrued to philosophically require a metaphysical reductionism that is materialist. Thus, the sciences are seen as completely independent from philosophy and theology. In such cases, psychology has been practically reduced to one limited scientific focus: in the past, psychology was reduced to sexual drives and behavior (Rieff, 1966/2006), and the current trend is to reduce it to the neurosciences, psychopharmacology, or evolutionary pressures (for a critique of this narrow view see Bennett & Hacker, 2003, and Nagel, 2012). Third, science (including the sciences of the human person) has focused on the accumulation of facts, sometimes the mere accumulation of facts. However, as Poincaré (1905) says, "Science is built up of facts, as a house is built of stones; but an accumulation of facts is no more a science than a heap of stones is a house" (Chapter 9, p. 141).

The contributions of the different disciplines that concern the human person must be rationally interconnected by a house-building or bridge-building discipline. The scientific data require larger theories and a meta-model as a frame to express a coherent understanding of the human person, society, and truth. The Meta-Model is an active framework that serves as an architect's plan in building the house. A coherent explication of the vision is assured by the integrative bridgework, served in part by philosophy (Cessario, Titus, & Vitz, 2013) and, in regard to the human person, by a philosophical psychology. The Catholic Christian Meta-Model of the Person offers such an integrative framework for understanding the person and for the employment of partial theories of the person and mental health practices. Furthermore, there are also partial generic and secular integrated approaches to framing mental health theory and practice. For instance, positive psychology offers a reframing of modern psychology that is more open to the need for a larger vision of the person and purpose in life (see next section). There are also other Christian approaches that often need a larger framework: religiously sensitive counseling, integration, Christian psychology, and biblical counseling (Johnson, 2010; McMinn & Campbell, 2007, p. 23).

What Is Positive Psychology?

Positive psychology has contributed to a revitalized direction for mental health practice (Peterson & Seligman, 2004). It is a relatively new movement that focuses on the need for a goal and end in growth and activity, health and life. It has taken umbrage at exclusively negative or medicalized approaches to psychology that cater to psychological disorders without also attending to the positive goals and resources that are on hand for healing and for prevention. The positive psychology movement has taken an approach that attends to the potential growth of human capacities and skills, especially the emotional, cognitive, self, interpersonal, biological, and coping-based approaches, while also attending to special populations and settings (Lopez & Snyder, 2009; Snyder & Lopez, 2002). It also focuses on the character strengths and virtues that constitute the positive growth that has been missing in much of modern psychology. It has identified the following character strengths—wisdom and knowledge, courage, humanity, justice, temperance, and transcendence—which

are fleshed out by related virtues and practices (Peterson & Seligman, 2004). Peterson and Seligman's (2004) approach to positive psychology recognizes that its recourse to character strengths and virtues does not provide a moral or spiritual account of these qualities. Rather, they recognize that positive psychology (and modern psychology at large) require the services of ethical, metaphysical, and religious traditions in order to understand the mystery of the person with fuller depth and in a way that applies to persons not only as passive objects of study but also as acting subjects in practice and therapy (Peterson & Seligman, 2004; Titus, 2017). What positive psychology has done is to move psychology from an emphasis on determinism (our pathology) to an emphasis on purpose (our goal of healing and flourishing). It has also introduced to modern psychology the beginning of a normative understanding of how the person must live to flourish. The Meta-Model employs deeper foundations and further goals.

What Does a Vocation- and Virtue-Based Approach to Mental Health Practice Contribute?

In the perspective of the Meta-Model, it is the specific task of a philosophical psychology to comprehensively study the human psyche and person. Such a study requires, but goes beyond, empirical efforts, conceptual analysis, systemic considerations, and clinical practices.

It includes an emphasis on vocations and an approach to virtue, both of which are rooted in evidence when applied to mental health. The Meta-Model critically interprets empirical, clinical, systemic, moral, and spiritual observations and reflections. It becomes a bridge-building discipline through its use of the psychological sciences and "philosophical anthropology, including the ethical and religious traditions that inevitably underlie those reflections" (Titus, 2009, p. 2). This approach provides a broader and deeper representation of the person. It goes further than contrastive and dialogical approaches such as that of Bermúdez (2005), who defines the philosophy of psychology as "the systematic study of the interplay between philosophical concerns and psychological concerns in ... the scientific study of cognition and behav-ior" (pp. 1–2). Unlike Bermúdez's approach, the Meta-Model constructively and hierarchically integrates the knowledge, research questions, and resources of biology, neuroscience, human and social sciences, epistemology, ethics, metaphysics, and theology, so as to better understand the person, while recognizing the differences of methodology, sources, and authority among these factors.

Person and Reason (Philosophy)

Philosophy engages the whole reason to understand reality. It aims at the whole of human experience and at a person's being able to act in the light of the whole of truth. As Josef Pieper (2006) says: "To philosophize means to reflect on the totality of that which is encountered with regard to its ultimate meaning, and this act of philosophizing, so construed, is a meaningful, even necessary activity, from which the spiritually existing person can absolutely not desist" (p. 84). This approach to philosophy, reason, and the person is open to all the input of wisdom, understanding, and knowledge from the diverse disciplines and sciences as well.

What Does the Book of Nature Contribute?

Psychology and science interpret "the book of nature" (John Paul II, 1998, §19); they discover and communicate much about the person. Scientific observation of the human person, from conception and birth through growth and decline, contributes much new information about the person. This knowledge of the complexity of the human being is found not only in neuroscience and studies of cognition, affect, and behavior (and their disorders), but also in reflection that yields important and new understandings of human flourishing. Moreover, this study of our nature and of the person requires also the use of reason in the form of philosophy and other disciplines (Ashley, 2006, 2013). It also yields an existential and metaphysical knowledge of the Creator, based in lived experience, reason, and intuition (Rom 1:20; John Paul II, 1998, §22).

Can Reason Be Trusted?

The Meta-Model's vision of the person appeals to reason and Christian tradition. This Christian philosophical view has a deep confidence in reason's capacity to (a) *analyze* experiences and phenomena, intuitions, and concepts, (b) *synthesize* metaphysical and ethical reflections, and (c) *dialogue* with the sciences about the truth of human experience and human nature in advancing the sapiential tradition. In so doing, reason has the capacity to (d) *integrate* scientific sources for a deeper understanding of the person. The Meta-Model is attentive to careful studies of human nature and psychology without reducing the person and experience to observable phenomena alone (e.g., suffering or joy, hatred or love, conflict or peace). Rather, it finds within science indications that there is more to the person than meets our ordinary experience, our personal narrative, or the scientific findings and measurement of neural processes, genes, and human behavior. We can have confidence in the findings of science if we avoid the metaphysically reductionist assumption that only material phenomena exist (Nagel, 2012) and if we avoid assuming that a broader use of reason and faith is not valid (Plantinga, 2011).

Indications of the way to avoid the narrowing of truth have also been provided by the great philosopher theologians of the patristic tradition, both Eastern and Western (such as Justin Martyr, Clement of Alexandria, Basil the Great, Gregory of Nazianzus, Gregory of Nyssa, John Chrysostom, Augustine, and John of Damascus) and the Doctors of the Church (such as Anselm, Bonaventure, Thomas Aquinas, Catherine of Siena, Teresa of Ávila, Thérèse of Lisieux, Hildegard of Bingen), and more recently by John Paul II (1998) and Benedict XVI (2006). These thinkers express a qualified trust in reason, in general, and in a wide, perennial philosophical tradition, in particular. Likewise, other Christian thinkers have offered deep reflections that give trustworthy and true knowledge using philosophical methods (Ashley, 2013; Barbour, 2000; Pieper, 1966; MacIntyre 1990, 1999; McGrath, 2004, 2011; Murphy, 1998; Taylor, 2007; Torrance, 1984, 2002; Zizioulas, 1997; Życiński, 2006).

What Does Philosophy Contribute to an Understanding of the Person?

The search for the ultimate truth about mankind and society requires further philosophical reflection. The study of the biological basis of human experience and behavior is significant, but it does not give a complete rendering of human experience or the larger human condition. The study of the person and human nature (philosophical anthropology) begins with scientific observations but continues with personal encounters, reflections on language, self-consciousness, and culture to uncover deeper layers of being, love and goodness, knowledge and truth, beauty, and interpersonal relationship in our human experience.

The methodological key to philosophical research on the person is found in the principle that human "action follows being" (*agere sequitur esse*). Thus, conversely we come to know someone by what they do, how they tell us about their lives, and what they say they intend to accomplish in life. A person's metaphysical judgments and insights and his or her ethical choices tell us something more, namely, that the person is a spiritual being and a moral agent. This principle of experience, observation, and discourse underlies the philosophical ordering of the sciences in a classical realist perspective (Aristotle, ca. 350 BC/1941; Aquinas, 1273/1981, I, 89.1; I-II, 77.3; III, 19.2). More modern authors such as Anscombe (1981), Foot (2002), Pieper (1966), Ashley (2006), and MacIntyre (1999, 2007) have upheld this tradition, which is experiencing a revival. This approach to causality affirms that in understanding humanity there is a distinct role played by the works of philosophy, the sciences (including psychology), and theology. Each of these three disciplines expresses theoretical dimensions and requires practical applications to help psychologists understand and serve the person.

How Might Basic Human Experience Include Metaphysical Transcendence?

A classical realist philosophy recognizes that humanity cannot be adequately understood without metaphysical references and dialogical narrative. It studies our natural inclinations toward love and goodness, existence and being, knowledge and truth, beauty, and interpersonal relationship. Experiences of these inclinations have transcendent characteristics and lead to God (Aquinas, 1273/1981, I-II, 94.2; Ashley,

2006, 2013; Spitzer, 2010, 2015). These inclinations, while being natural to the person, also transcend the person. They are desires that serve as a common ground for metaphysical intuitions and reasoning and for deeper psychological understanding of the person (Schmitz, 2009). As human beings, we desire to exist and to flourish. We desire love and goodness, knowledge and truth, and beauty. We seek to flourish through transcending ourselves in seeking to be united in friendship and love with others and with the ultimate Other, who is God. We also experience the call to transcend ourselves through various forms of interpersonal relationships and through giving of ourselves in commitment and service.

What Do Experiences of Metaphysical Transcendence Contribute to Being Human?

Experiences of metaphysical transcendence are contested both by atheist scientists who claim that only matter exists and by fundamentalist religionists who claim that reason itself is not to be trusted. Nonetheless, there is a widespread acceptance of the experience and importance of metaphysical transcendence and the need for reason for normal human understanding and ordinary living (Spitzer, 2010, 2015).

The Catholic Christian approach recognizes that there is a mutual and complementary service rendered by scientific, philosophical, and theological methods in understanding transcendence. In an integrative mindset, John Paul II (1995) states that "only a Christian anthropology, enriched by the contribution of indisputable scientific data, including that of modern psychology and psychiatry, can offer a complete and thus realistic vision of humans" (§4). This critical realism draws together these sources expressing the conviction that truth, although complex, is one (MacIntyre, 1990, p. 200). The task of philosophy is to employ human reason to analyze the various expressions about the truth of humanity, to confirm the way that reason has been expressed in the different disciplines, and to build a rational bridge between the disciplines, especially between psychology and theology, so that their complementary contributions to an understanding of the person can be constructively integrated in theory and in practice.

Person and Faith (Theology)

As has been already stated, psychology and mental health practice, philosophy, and theology all have their own expertise and wisdom in providing the knowledge needed for an integrative understanding of the person. Each of them contributes in a particular way, enriching the other disciplines while being enriched by them.

What Does the Word of God Contribute to an Understanding of the Person?

The Catholic tradition maintains that there is one ultimate source for truth, namely the Word of God, which reveals divine wisdom and providence. Through "the book" of the Word of God (John Paul II, 1998, §19; Vatican II, 1965a), we come to know with greater surety the nature of humanity. This approach holds that God is the ultimate source of confidence in the intelligibility of creation.

The Word of God, as found in the Sacred Scriptures and in tradition, complements the philosophical and empirical studies of nature, which are incomplete without reflection on Divine Revelation about the ultimate source and end of created reality (John Paul II, 1998, §34; see also Vatican II, 1965a, §9). The Word of God clarifies basic suppositions about human life—such as the value of human life from conception to death and the meaning of life, human relationships, and suffering (John Paul II, 1995)—that are needed if human science is to be complete.

Both John Paul II (1998) and Benedict XVI (2006) have articulated understandings of reason that have outstripped modern rationalist notions that compartmentalize the sciences. They have presented enlarged notions of reason and rationality that respect the separate natures of science, philosophy, and Christian theology while recognizing the service that each renders the others. This effort is advocated and cogently argued by many Catholic and Christian thinkers who employ a faith-based perspective in critically dialoguing with contemporary science and culture about shortfalls and advances in knowledge, theory, and practice (Johnson, 2007; McGrath, 2004, 2011; Murphy, 1998; Torrance, 1984, 2002; Życiński, 2006). For example, Benedict Ashley (2006; 2013, pp. 92–94), a Catholic bioethicist and theologian, has explored a Catholic notion of the ordering of the sciences and how the sciences serve one another in a way related to psychology and psychotherapy. Furthermore, Ian Barbour (2000), a physicist and specialist in the relationship of science and religion, has identified four models used to interrelate the sciences and religious traditions: conflict, independence, dialogue, and integration.

The Meta-Model of integration, for its part, is committed to dialogue in order to overcome particular notions that tend to pit philosophy, psychology, and theology against one another or that tend to overemphasize their independence. It is through an integrative dialogue between these disciplines that human knowledge becomes more complete. In particular, the task of theology is to assure a fuller communication of the Word of God. This effort is made possible when faith and reason focus on the divine in history, in personal encounters, and in interpersonal relationships, especially in the narrative of human callings, virtues, and flourishing.

What Are the Primary Sources for a Theological Vision of the Person?

The Meta-Model's theological vision of the person (its theological anthropology) is based on a Catholic Christian faith perspective. Thus, it recognizes that God is the source and end of all good and that each person is called to communion with God, other persons, and the rest of creation. This communion is announced and fostered in the law and the prophets (Deut 6:4–5; Lev 19:18; Isa 54:5–8; Hos 14:1–2; Lk 10:27). The free and responsible acceptance of the vocation to love is the acceptance of the ultimate source, God, in whom love finds its true source, who reveals himself through Jesus Christ, and who sustains believers through the gift of the Holy Spirit. As Maurice Zundel (1941/1999) says: "Instead of servants He has preferred to have sons [and daughters], and instead of the terror of creatures crushed by the majesty of their Sovereign Lord, He has awakened in our hearts the love which responds to love, a love that is wholly His free gift" (p. 12).

As mentioned above, the theological vision of the human has been found in listening to God's Word from the heart of the Church (Vatican II, 1965a). The canonical books of Sacred Scripture—especially those found in the Pentateuch (first five books of the Old Testament) and the wisdom books (including the Psalms), the Gospels, and the New Testament epistles (see Cassuto, 1944/2005; Pinckaers, 2005; Wenham, 2000)—offer doctrinal and moral teachings that deeply influence our understanding of the person. That understanding would not be complete without our recognizing the significance of the apostolic tradition and the prayer of the Church (including liturgical prayer and the sacraments), which address the human condition in the light of faith. The ecclesial Magisterium communicates the Word of God to believers, while listening to Sacred Scripture, to people's experience of faith (*sensus fidelium*), and to science (Benedict XVI, 2006; John Paul II, 1998). This theological vision of the person finds support from theologians, philosophers, and scientists (including psychologists), in dialogue with people of good will.

Varied views about the scope of science have evoked statements of caution (and in some cases of rejection) from the Magisterium about the implications of reductionist theories, though it affirms the need for scientific method and metaphysical understandings of the person. For example, while affirming the validity of scientific theories of evolution, Christian thinkers and the Magisterium have rejected materialistic formulations of the theory of evolution that dismiss theological accounts of human experience and the theological dignity of the human person (Benedict XVI, 2006; Chaberek, 2015; John Paul II, 1998; Pius XII, 1950; Schönborn, 2007; Życiński, 2006). The Catholic view of integration expresses a confidence in the complementarity of reason and faith (John Paul II, 1998). It therefore engages philosophical, psychological, and scientific sources either to contrast or, in a particular way, to complement theological sources. The view of integration is attentive to the teaching Magisterium, patristic sources, and Doctors of the Church, according to their different types of authority. It also recognizes the importance of a historical-critical approach to Scripture, read within the Church and a spiritual and metaphysical understanding of grace, providence, and sal-

vation history (International Theological Commission, 2012; Levering, 2008; Vatican II, 1965a).

What Does Christian Faith Contribute to Understanding the Vocation of Each Person?

The calling of each person, family, and community can be understood in terms of God's Word as revealed in the Christian tradition and faith, which are experienced in prayer and sacrament (Vatican II, 1964, 1965a). There is no dichotomy between Divine Revelation and personal experience, in this perspective. The Christian faith contributes answers to questions about the meaning of life and the purpose of suffering, a moral framework for guidance, and a means to forgiveness of enemies; it advocates a belief in the universality of the human family, and it is often a source of hope. In addition, there are certain distortions of faith that need to be understood as psychologically and socially harmful, for example feeling guilty for sins for which you are not responsible (such as the child who feels guilty for causing his or her parent's divorce), or interpreting isolated parts of Scripture for condemning persons or for withholding love and forgiveness.

Furthermore, the Christian commonly finds his or her home in the Body of Christ (the Church) and ultimately in the Kingdom of God. The Catholic Christian view is that the authenticity of a personal experience of faith is corroborated by the living Word of God in the Church, especially through the experience of faith, hope, love, justice, and mercy, and through callings to holiness, vocational commitments, and work. It is the same Word of God who through the Holy Spirit guides the ecumenical councils, the pope and bishops, the believers, and all people of good will. As described in Chapter 18, "Fallen," however, the personal experience of being created in the image of God is seriously troubled by the effects of personal and social sin (Gen 3; John Paul II, 1998). The person and the Church are eschatologically saved, that is, saved at the end of time. Nonetheless, in the meantime, they experience these effects of sin while in the process of being healed, made new, redeemed, and sanctified (Eph 4; Rev 21–22; Vatican II, 1964, §48).

What Is the Place of Faith in the Field of Psychology and Mental Health Practice?

It is well known that the founders of much of modern psychology were often unfriendly to Christianity. Because of the importance of religion for many people, psychology, in recent decades, has become somewhat more open to religion and spirituality (Enright & Fitzgibbons, 2015; Koenig, King, & Carson, 2012; Richards & Bergin, 2005; Schfrankse, 1996; VanderWeele, 2017a, 2017b, 2018; Worthington, 1988, 2006), including Christianity (Chapter 3, "Christian and Catholic Advantages"). There has developed a moral imperative to respect religious belief and practice, since religion is now understood as an important expression of diversity. We believe that this change in attitude in the field of psychology has opened the way for understanding the contributions of the present Meta-Model with its challenge to each school of psychology to identify and defend its own moral and metaphysical assumptions.

Recalling that every ultimate presupposition requires faith, there is a necessary place for consciously acknowledging one's presuppositions in the personal life and professional work of the mental health professional. Our ultimate perspective on values and meaning, which each person has, significantly affects how we understand the nature of persons and their dignity and accordingly how we conduct our personal and professional lives.

How Is the Theological Level Accessible to Science?

As mentioned earlier, our use of the term "science" focuses on observations and measurements of the scientific method, while denying neither the contributions made by personal narrative nor the validity of a Catholic Christian approach to moral and spiritual experience. Human experience is rooted in what is observed in time and schematized in different disciplines (social sciences, history, and personal narrative), but there is more as well. For human experience is rooted also in the reality that underlies yet outstrips measured observations of mankind and the cosmos, conceptual reflections on them, and stories about personal encounters with them. This deep reality is spiritual and metaphysical. Its origin, developmental course, and finality provide the meaning of human life and are in constant interaction with the embodied person and with the "physical" universe (Ashley, 2006; McGrath, 2011; Murphy, 1998; Schmitz, 2007, 2009; Spitzer, 2010, 2015; Życiński, 2006).

In order to do justice to reality, our Meta-Model recognizes that human experience is both historical and transcendent (Ashley, 2013; Levering, 2008; Titus, 2009). The Meta-Model requires analysis of the person and synthesis of the different studies. The Meta-Model uses reason to understand the nature of the person and relationships. Also it assumes that the dominant secular approach, which is materialist and reductionist, seriously limits the methods and scope of science, in general, and the sciences' attempts to understand the human, in particular (Giorgi, 1970; Nagel, 2012; Plantinga, 2011). The Meta-Model, therefore, invites a broader use of reason in opening the theological level of inquiry to a dialogue with science (Benedict XVI, 2006).

What Do the Social Sciences Bring to a Theological Understanding of the Person?

The human and social sciences are generally considered to be cumulative and progressive approaches to gaining knowledge about humans. They record and analyze measured observations and descriptions in scientific methods that are intentionally focused and reductionist. They use scientific methods, which are public and repeatable: hypothesis formulation, experimentation or application, and theory revision (O'Donohue, 2013; Wallace, 1996). They seek to find truthful theories (induction) and to develop useful applied techniques and practices (deduction). The human and social sciences elaborate generalizations. They often involve longitudinal studies and the analysis of data concerning behavior, narrative accounts of one's life, personal responses to questions, and so on. These sciences utilize various experimental and qualitative methods aimed at understanding persons and their social lives. Furthermore, clinical research has made very practical contributions through its identification of evidence-based mental health practices. In sum, the human and social sciences make many new and helpful contributions to understanding the person that complement philosophical and theological understandings.

How Might the Social Sciences Limit a Theological Understanding of the Person?

The scientific method, which is a reductionist methodology, should be contrasted with a materialist secular conception of the scientific method, which includes not only the reductionist nature of modern experimentation but also a metaphysical reductionist assumption. This reductionist naturalism distorts and reduces the nature of truth available for study

(Plantinga, 2011; Życiński, 2006). The secular conception also often presupposes an atheistic or agnostic worldview, denying the possibility of Divine Revelation and God's interaction with the world, even denying those who support top-down influences involving the human nonmaterial mental life and free will (Bandura, 1997, 2006; Beauregard, 2012; Peterson & Seligman, 2004). These secular perspectives on mental health practice commonly interpret social and mental disorders and health in what they assume is a value-free way. Instead they commonly fail to recognize the presuppositions that ground their worldview and value system. This is so even when particular moral and aspirational principles are included in professional codes of ethics: for example, the principles expressed by the American Psychological Association (2017) and by the American Counseling Association (2014). Obviously, these secularized approaches, inasmuch as they count on atheistic or agnostic presuppositions and worldviews, are not consistent with theological worldviews, but they are also not consistent with metaphysically nonreductionist worldviews that are held by many social scientists and mental health professionals (Bandura, 1997, 2006; Beauregard, 2012; Frankl, 1959/2006; Fowers, 2005; Giorgi, 1970; Romanyshyn, 2007) as well as by many positive psychologists (Joseph & Linley, 2006; Lopez & Snyder, 2009).

Nonetheless, a long tradition of studying how presuppositions affect psychology and the person is present, for example, in classical philosophy (Plato, ca. 347 BC/1980; Aristotle, ca. 350 BC/1941; Aquinas, 1268/1994; MacIntyre, 2007; Taylor, 2007), in the phenomenological schools (Buber, 1923/1971; Husserl, 1936, 1913/2012; Merleau-Ponty, 1965; Scheler, 1923/2008; Stein, 1922/2000; Wojtyła, 1993), and other contemporary authors, including many other contemporary Christian philosophers (McGrath, 2004, 2011; Murphy, 1998; Plantinga, 2011; Zizioulas, 1997). In addition, there are many humanistic approaches to psychology and many postmodern philosophical thinkers that reject metaphysical reductionism, but deny or ignore supernatural transcendence as well (Frankl, 1959/2006; Nagel, 2012; Maslow, 1994).

What Does a Christian Nonmaterial and Metaphysical Approach Contribute to Understanding Persons?

A Catholic Christian theological and philosophical perspective seeks to demonstrate how humanity is not fully understood unless its nonmaterial and metaphysical character is taken into consideration at personal and social levels. This approach requires recognition of Divine Revelation as well as openness to metaphysical knowledge of the nature of the cosmos and each unique person, including the dimension of grace. The underlying source of life and meaning is nonmaterial, and the finality of human flourishing is beyond the material dimension of life, though the physical and the nonphysical aspects of human life are intimately connected (Chapter 8, "Personal Wholeness"). Each person participates in the transcendent source of existence, goodness, truth, relationality, and beauty (Aquinas, 1273/1981; Ashley, 2006; Bonaventure, 1259/2002; Schmitz, 2007; Scruton, 2012; von Balthasar, 2013; Wippel, 2011). This transcendent source is the ever-present basis for nonmaterial intellectual and spiritual life. It is especially evident in human capacities, such as complex tool use, syntactic language, creation of beautiful music and art, and mathematical generalizations (Vitz, 2017). It is also found in the experience of freedom, grace, and interpersonal love, including workings of the Holy Spirit in persons of faith and of good will.

A surer, and unique, type of knowledge about the person is found in Revelation, which, while requiring faith, brings a deep conviction about the meaning of life. This knowledge is served by scientific and psychological knowledge about neurobiology, patterns of human development, and psychological health. For example, knowledge of a person's ultimate calling and vocations is complemented by knowledge of his or her level of depressed affect, patterns of interpersonal attachment, and personal strengths.

The Bible, for its part, gives examples of the ways that humans participate in the divine source of life and meaning, for example, in creation (Gen 1 & 2), throughout life (Gen 3; the Gospels; and Acts of the Apostles), through suffering (Job; Rom 5:3; 1 Pet 4:13), through the life of the Holy Spirit (Lk 24:49; Acts 1:1–9 & 2:1–4), as a partaking in the divine nature (2 Pet 1:4), and after death (Ex 3; Lk 20:34–38). This theological level requires a further synthesis if it is to incorporate insights both from the specialized studies of humans and from a wide-ranging wisdom-based framework that is informed by faith and reason concerning our participation in the transcendent source of life (Chapter 15, "Rational," and Chapter 17, "Created in the Image of God").

What Is a Catholic Christian Theological Vision of the Person

A human being is constituted by a body-soul unity and interpersonal relationships, with capacities to truly know and freely love God, others, and self. We offer a three-part definition of a human person: philosophical, theological, and psychological, as mentioned earlier in this chapter and also earlier in this volume (Chapter 2, "Theological, Philosophical, and Psychological Premises," and Chapter 4, "Modern Personality Theories"). Each of the parts completes the others. The Christian philosophical synthetic definition of the person is:

The human person is an individual substance of a rational (intellectual), volitional (free), relational (interpersonal), sensory-perceptual-cognitive (pre-rational knowledge), emotional, and unified (body-soul) nature; the person is called to flourishing, moral responsibility, and virtue through his or her vowed or non-vowed vocational state, as well as through life work, service, and meaningful leisure.

The Christian theological definition of the person reads as follows:

From an explicitly theological perspective (Scripture, tradition, and Magisterium), the human person is created in the image of God and made by and for divine and human love, and—although suffering the effects of original, personal, and social sin—is invited to divine redemption in Christ Jesus, sanctification through the Holy Spirit, and beatitude with God the Father

The Christian psychological definition of the person is:

The human person is an embodied individual who is intelligent, uses language, and exercises limited free-will. The person is fundamentally interpersonal, experiences and expresses emotions, and has sensory-perceptual-cognitive capacities to be in contact with reality. All of these characteristics are possible because of the unity of the body and unique self-consciousness, and are expressed in behavior and mental life. Furthermore the person is called by human nature to flourishing through virtuous behavior and transcendent growth; through interpersonal commitments to family, friends, and others; and through work, service, and meaningful leisure. From their origins (natural and transcendent), all persons have intrinsic goodness, dignity, and worth. In the course of life, though suffering

from many natural, personal, and social disorders and conditions, persons hope for healing, meaning, and flourishing.

The contributions from each field—theological, philosophical, and psychological—serve each other. Furthermore, we find further meaning through a quick historical summary of the term "person" in the Christian tradition and Western culture. The perennial Christian notion of person enriches the ancient notion of *prosopon* (Greek) or *persona* (Latin), which were understood as a mask that Etruscan and Greek actors used to represent mythical characters and social personalities.

Although a latent interpersonal meaning is found in the ancient usage, Christian Sacred Scripture (the Old and New Testaments) in its canonical Greek texts, the Septuagint, already identifies the person (*prosopon*) as represented by one's face or presence. For example, Moses saw God "face to face" (*prosopon kata prosopon*) (Ex 33:11; Num 12:7–8; Deut 24:10). St. Paul says that God's glory shines "in the face (*prosopon*) of Jesus Christ" (2 Cor 4:6). St. Peter speaks of forgiveness of sin coming "from the presence (*prosopon*) of the Lord" (Acts 3:19–20). The Hebrew (Masoretic) text uses analogous terms (such as *adam, nefes, basher, nakar, aner*), as well as the substantive "the do-er of justice" (*nous*), in order to express what we intend by the word "person" (Kittel, 1977; Atkinson, 2014).

An important philosophical source of the Western concept of person has been Boethius (ca. 513/1918a), who defines the person as "an individual substance of a rational nature" (Chapter III), a definition that should not be taken out of the context of his more complete understanding of the person as fundamentally relational, as will be shown. However, Western modern individualist perspectives have obscured the classical and Christian social foundation for understanding the philosophical notion of person defined by Boethius (ca. 513/1918a). They have reduced the person to the individual, and reduced this definition to modern individualist and rationalist categories. They, thereby, presume that this definition is a confirmation of their own moral and social theories. Contemporary and postmodern critiques of Boethius, however, are really critiques of the modern views rather than of Boethius. In reaction to modern individualism, the recent personalist perspectives are more in line with Boethius's complete understanding of the person.

In the classical view, the person is essentially social (Plato, ca. 347 BC/1980; Aristotle, ca. 350 BC/1941). The relational aspect of Boethius's classical and Christian vision of the person is explicitly affirmed in the human community and in the divine Trinity, when, for example, Boethius (ca. 519/1918b) states that: "Every word that refers to the person signifies relation" (Chapter VI). However, the need for further clarity about the relational nature of God as Father, Son, and Holy Spirit led the early Church councils to employ the word "person" (*prosopon*) to identify the one God as a Trinity—one divine substance and three divine persons—in its creeds. (The most pertinent creeds include the Nicene, 325; Constantinopolitan, 381; and especially the Quicumque or so-called Athanasian creed of the fourth or fifth century [Emery, 2010]).

Rich discussions on the nature and action of the person are found in patristic sources, such as Athanasius, Cyril of Jerusalem, John Chrysostom, Gregory of Nyssa, Makarios, and Maximus the Confessor (Larchet, 2005) and the Doctors of the Church. Augustine (426/1991), for example, affirms that "in God there are no accidents, only substance and relation" (V.5.6; see also Aquinas, 1273/1981; Bonaventure, 1259/2002). The Judeo-Christian personalist movement makes significant contributions as well (Barth, 1958/2010; Buber, 1923/1971; Clarke, 1992, 2009; Maritain, 1959; Ratzinger, 1990; Stein, 1932/1996; Torrance, 1984; Wojtyła, 1979; Zizioulas, 1997). In sum, a Catholic Christian approach understands the human person as constituted by the divine gift of life, which is expressed in human nature, capacities, vocations, virtues, moral action, and interpersonal relationships. In the Christological formulation of the Second Vatican Council (1965b, §22), it is Christ who reveals man to himself, and in so doing, reveals the deep meaning of being a person.

Conclusion

General Implications of the Meta-Model's Methodology for Mental Health Practice

First, Christian mental health professionals can use this integrated understanding in clinical practice. For example, evidence-based interventions can be used to build the virtues and character strengths needed to heal and support vocational decisions and interpersonal commitments and to foster healthy spiritual development. In contrast, harmful understandings of theological concepts can contribute to a person's suffering by enhancing irrational guilt, or by fostering violence and hatred of others. These conditions need correction and healing at both theological and psychological levels.

Second, when practical therapeutic methods and objectives are consistent with a full vision of humanity, this larger healing can prepare the way for greater freedom. Distressed persons can be assisted to live in hope and to enjoy some part in the flourishing that God wills for all people. The practical contribution becomes clearer when we understand that theoretical considerations (including theological and metaphysical ones) interrelate in healing the whole person and his or her interpersonal relationships.

Third, it should be reiterated that the Catholic Christian Meta-Model in no way seeks to reduce psychology to a sub-discipline of Catholic theology or faith. It does not mistake piety for therapeutic practice or, conversely, science for salvation and health for holiness, although the Meta-Model provides a basis for good therapy and good therapists. It requires deliberation on human experience in the light of and through the lenses of reason, faith, and the psychological sciences. The Meta-Model's purpose is to render a fuller account of the person and facilitate the use of evidence-based therapies. Neither theology nor philosophy replace psychological theory and its practice. Rather, faith-based doctrine about the person and reason-based reflections contribute to the social sciences as complementary sources of knowledge about human life, love, action, and flourishing.

In sum, we have offered a brief presentation of the Catholic Christian Meta-Model of the Person as a viable realist and faith-based alternative to the secularization of psychology. The Meta-Model also offers aid in the renewal of mental health practice by calling upon more of the client's own personal, interpersonal, religious, and spiritual resources. The Meta-Model supplies a vocation-, virtue-, ethics-, and faith-based understanding of the person for application in an integrated approach that is true to good mental health practice, as well as consistent with the Catholic Christian vision of the person's call to flourishing.

Specific Implications of the Meta-Model's Methodology for Mental Health Practice

The Meta-Model provides a framework for understanding the person and a basis to expand the fundamental questions involved in case conceptualization, which typically include: What happened to the person? (diagnostic issues); Why did it happen? (clinical formulation); What role does diversity play in the case? (cultural and religious issues); and How can what happened to the person be changed? (treatment issues) (Sperry & Sperry, 2012). Within contemporary practice this basic case conceptualization is expressed from a particular theoretical orientation, such as, for example, psychoanalytic theory, cognitive-behavioral theory, or attachment theory.

The present Meta-Model expands such a typical case conceptualization in two major ways. First, it includes the dimensions of the person identified in the Meta-Model, especially its larger human focus on vocations and virtues, including religious issues. Second, it not only permits but requires the use of multiple theoretical approaches for a given case. For example, interpersonal theory may be used to understand the person as interpersonally relational; and cognitive-behavioral theory may be used to understand the person as rational and irrational. The Meta-Model involves an integrative process requiring, not just permitting, different psychological approaches. These qualities make the Meta-Model synthetic and constructive in the case conceptualization of each client. More specifically, the Meta-Model makes three concrete contributions to case conceptualization.

First, by expanding the questions a therapist might ask for case conceptualizations, the Meta-Model broadens the therapist's understanding of important aspects of the clients' lives: (a) Why do the clients live and work?

(life goals, purpose, flourishing); (b) How do their vocations influence their lives? (meaning, committed vocational states, and life work); (c) What personal and relational strengths and competencies do the clients have? (virtue, resource, and character strengths); (d) How do principles and commitments influence their behavior? (ethical side of clinical work and moral implications of vocation).

Second, the Meta-Model is more comprehensive and systematic than partial case models and psychological theories. It understands the person from three complementary disciplines: philosophy (rational and realist discourse); theology (faith-based narrative); as well as psychological theory and mental health practice (Chapter 6, "Person as an Integrated Laminate").

Third, the Meta-Model gives a normative understanding of the person and what is required for true flourishing. The Meta-Model requires a respect for both the subjective view (the client's perspective) and the objective view (the nature of the person) in identifying problems and obstacles to healing and growth, as well as in establishing treatment goals. However, this respect for both subjective and objective understanding contrasts sharply with the almost exclusively relativist and subjectivist approaches to the person commonly seen in theory and practice across different schools of psychology, philosophy, and theology.

Overview and Summary

In this volume, after introducing the Catholic Christian Meta-Model of the Person (Part I), we identified psychological supports for the Meta-Model (Part II). In the present part (Part III), we will explicitly identify how the Catholic Christian reason-based (philosophical) vision of the person can serve as a bridge between faith-based (theological) conceptions and psy-

chological theory and mental health practice (psychological) and contribute to flourishing. The reason-based effort offers focused observations, metaphysical depth, ethical breadth, personal discourse, and interpersonal narrative. Furthermore, in Part IV of the volume, we will identify how the Catholic Christian theological vision of the person offers a spiritual and religious perspective on flourishing illuminated by a multidimensional perspective on life-callings (vocations) and character strengths (virtues). This Christian faith-based or God-centered perspective alone, however, provides a common or "pre-scientific" view of the person (John Paul II, 2006, p. 171). By itself, it is incomplete at a scientific level, but it is enriched by what human reason imports from psychological theory and mental health practice. In Part V of this volume, we will identify some of the theoretical and clinical applications of the Meta-Model, by addressing how its faith-based and reason-based view of the person influences psychological theory, clinical models, and actual practice.

In sum, the psychological support for this integrated vision of the person identifies how personality theories, empirical studies, and experience-based practices expand and complement our understanding of the person, especially as it concerns human disorder and disease, as well as development, healing, and well-being. Reason-based support for the Meta-Model identifies how existential meaning, metaphysical considerations of truth and beauty, and ethical reflections on goodness, vocations, and interpersonal relationships contribute a complementary understanding of the person, especially as it concerns experiences and narratives of the clients' coming to know and love themselves, others, and God. Faith-based support for the Meta-Model identifies how the Catholic Christian vision of the person—especially how belief in

God, hope in an afterlife, and love as self-giving and self-sacrifice—contributes a complementary understanding of the person, especially as it concerns the way that faith, vocations, and virtues influence health and flourishing and enrich an understanding of the lifespan. Last, this chapter has presented the outline of the Catholic Christian Meta-Model of the Person and of its psychological, reason-based, and faith-based supports for its larger vision of the person. Its methodology requires the integration of these three types of methods and the presuppositions that are specific to each of the disciplines.

REFERENCES:

Adler, A. (2009). *What life could mean to you: The psychology of personal development*. Oxford, United Kingdom: Oneworld Publications. (Original work published 1931)

Ainsworth, M. D. S., Blehar, M. C., Waters, E., & Wall, S. (1978). *Patterns of attachment: A psychological study of the strange situation*. Hillsdale, NJ: Erlbaum.

American Counseling Association. (2014). *ACA code of ethics: As approved by the ACA Governing Council, 2014*. Washington, DC: Author.

American Psychological Association (APA). (2017). *Ethical principles of psychologists and code of conduct*. Washington, DC: Author. Retrieved from www.apa.org/ethics/code/ethics-code-2017.pdf

Anscombe, G. E. M. (1981). Modern moral philosophy. In P. Unger (Ed.), *Collected philosophical papers* (Vol. 3, pp. 26–41). Oxford, United Kingdom: Oxford University Press. (Original work published 1958)

Aquinas, T. (1952). *The disputed questions on truth* (Vol. 1) (R. W. Mulligan, Trans.). Chicago, IL: Regnery. (Original work composed 1256–1259)

Aquinas, T. (1981). *Summa theologiae* (English Dominican Province, Trans.). Westminster, MD: Christian Classics. (Original work composed 1265–1273)

Aquinas, T. (1986). *The division and methods of the sciences: Questions V and VI of his Commentary on the* De Trinitate *of Boethius* (4th ed.) (A. Maurer, Trans.). Toronto, Canada: Pontifical Institute of Mediaeval Studies. (Original work composed 1257–1259)

Aquinas, T. (1994). *Commentary on Aristotle's De Anima* (rev. ed.) (K. Foster & S. Humphries, Trans.). Notre Dame, IN.: Dumb Ox Books. (Original work composed 1268)

Aristotle. (1941). *On the soul*. In R. McKeon (Ed.), *The basic works of Aristotle* (pp. 535–606). New York, NY: Random House. (Original work composed ca. 350 BC)

Ashley, B. M. (2006). *The way toward wisdom: An interdisciplinary and intercultural introduction to metaphysics*. Notre Dame, IN: University of Notre Dame.

Ashley, B. M. (2013). *Healing for freedom: A Christian perspective on personhood and psychotherapy*. Arlington, VA: The Institute for the Psychological Sciences Press.

Ashley, B. M., & Deeley, J. (2012). *How science enriches theology*. South Bend, IN: St. Augustine Press.

Atkinson, J. (2014). *Biblical and theological foundations of the family: The domestic church*. Washington, DC: The Catholic University of America Press.

Augustine. (1991). *The Trinity* (E. Hill, Trans.). Hyde Park, NY: New City Press. (Original work composed 399–426)

Augustine. (2007). *Confessions* (2nd ed.) (M. P. Foley, Ed.; F. J. Sheed, Trans). New York, NY: Hackett. (Original work composed 397–401)

Bandura, A. (1997). *Self-efficacy: The exercise of control*. New York, NY: Freeman.

Bandura, A. (2006). Toward a psychology of human agency. *Perspectives on Psychological Science, 1*, 164–180.

Barbour, I. G. (2000). *When science meets religion: Enemies, strangers, or partners?* New York, NY: HarperOne.

Barth, K. (2010). *Church dogmatics: The doctrine of reconciliation* (Vol. 4.2). New York, NY: T&T Clark. (Original work published 1958)

Beauregard, M. (2012). *Brain wars: The scientific battle over the existence of the mind and the proof that will change the way we live our lives*. New York, NY: Harper Collins.

Bellah, R. N. (2011). *Religion in human evolution: From*

the Paleolithic to the Axial Age. Cambridge, MA: Belknap.

Benedict XVI. (2005). *Deus caritas est* [Encyclical, on Christian love]. Vatican City, Vatican: Libreria Editrice Vaticana.

Benedict XVI. (2006, September 12). *Faith, reason and the university: Memories and reflections* [The Regensburg address]. Vatican City, Vatican: Libreria Editrice Vaticana.

Bennett, M. R., & Hacker, P. M. S. (2003). *Philosophical foundations of neuroscience.* Oxford, United Kingdom: Blackwell.

Bergin, A. E. (1980). Psychotherapy and religious values. *Journal of Consulting and Clinical Psychology, 48*(1), 95–105.

Bergin, A. E., Payne, R. I., & Richards, P. S. (1996). Values in psychotherapy. In E. P. Shafranske (Ed.), *Religion and the clinical practice of psychology* (pp. 297–325). Washington, DC: American Psychological Association. doi:10.1037/10199-011

Bermúdez, J. L. (2005). *Philosophy of psychology: A contemporary introduction.* New York, NY: Routledge.

Boethius (1918a). A treatise against Eutychen and Nestorium. In *The theological tractates* (H. F. Stewart & E. K. Rand, Trans.) (pp. 72–127). London, United Kingdom: William Heinemann. (Original work composed ca. 513)

Boethius (1918b). The Trinity is one God not three Gods. In *The theological tractates* (H. F. Stewart & E. K. Rand, Trans.) (pp. 3–31). London, United Kingdom: William Heinemann. (Original work composed ca. 519)

Bonaventure. (2002). Itinerarium mentis in Deum. In P. Boehner & Z. Hayes (Eds.), *Works of St. Bonaventure.* St. Bonaventure, NY: Franciscan Institute. (Original work composed 1259)

Bowlby, J. (1982). *Attachment and loss: Vol. 1. Attachment* (2nd ed.). New York, NY: Basic Books. (Original work published 1969)

Bowlby, J. (1988). *A secure base: Clinical applications of attachment theory.* London, United Kingdom: Routledge.

Buber, M. (1971). *I and thou* (W. Kaufmann, Trans.). New York, NY: Touchstone. (Original work published 1923)

Cassuto, U. (2005). *A commentary on the book of Genesis: Part 1. From Adam to Noah* (I. Abrahams,

Trans.). Skokie, IL: Varda Books. (Original work published 1944)

Cessario, R., Titus, C. S., & Vitz, P. C. (Eds.). (2013). *Philosophical virtues and psychological strengths: Building the bridge.* Manchester, NH: Sophia Institute Press.

Chaberek, M. (2015) *Catholicism and evolution: A history from Darwin to Pope Francis.* Kettering, OH: Angelico Press.

Clarke, W. N. (1992). Person, being, and St. Thomas. *Communio, 19*(3), 601–618.

Clarke, W. N. (2009). *The creative retrieval of Saint Thomas Aquinas: Essays in Thomistic philosophy, new and old.* New York, NY: Fordham University Press.

Dawkins, R. (2008). *The God delusion.* New York, NY: Mariner Books.

Dennett, D. C. (1991). *Consciousness explained.* New York, NY: Little, Brown.

Dennett, D. C. (1995). *Darwin's dangerous idea: Evolution and the meanings of life.* New York, NY: Simon & Schuster.

Ellis, A. (1980). Psychotherapy and atheistic values: A response to A. E. Bergin's "Psychotherapy and religious values." *Journal of Consulting and Clinical Psychology, 48*(5), 635–639.

Ellis, A. (2004). *The road to tolerance: The philosophy of rational emotive behavior therapy.* New York, NY: Prometheus Books.

Ellis, A., & Ellis, D. J. (2011). *Rational emotive behavior therapy.* Washington, DC: American Psychological Association.

Emery, G. (2010). *The Trinitarian theology of Saint Thomas Aquinas* (F. A. Murphy, Trans.). New York, NY: Oxford University Press.

Enright, R. D., & Fitzgibbons, R. P. (2015). *Forgiveness therapy: An empirical guide for resolving anger and restoring hope.* Washington, DC: American Psychological Association.

Entwistle, D. N. (2015). *Integrative approaches to psychology and Christianity: An introduction to worldview issues, philosophical foundations, and models of integration.* Eugene, OR: Cascade Books.

Erikson, E. H. (1979). *Identity and the life cycle.* New York, NY: Norton. (Original work published 1959)

Feser, E. (2008). *The last superstition: A refutation of the New Atheism.* South Bend, IN: St. Augustine Press.

Foot, P. (2002). *Virtues and vices and other essays*

in moral philosophy. Oxford, United Kingdom: Oxford University Press. (Original work published 1978)

Fowers, B. J. (2005). *Virtue and psychology: Pursuing excellence in ordinary practices*. Washington, DC: American Psychological Association.

Frankl, V. E. (2000). *Man's search for ultimate meaning*. Cambridge, MA: Perseus Publishing.

Frankl, V. E. (2006). *Man's search for meaning* (I. Lasch, Trans.). Boston, MA: Beacon Press. (Original work published 1959)

Freud, S. (2010). *The interpretation of dreams*. New York, NY: Basic Books. (Original work published 1900)

Giorgi, A. (1970). *Psychology as a human science: A phenomenologically based approach*. New York, NY: Joanna Cotler Books.

Gottman, J. M. (1999). *The marriage clinic: A scientifically based marital therapy*. New York, NY: Norton.

Greenberg, L. S., & Johnson, S. M. (1988). *Emotionally focused therapy for couples*. New York, NY: Guilford.

Haidt, J. (2006). *The happiness hypothesis: Finding modern truth in ancient wisdom*. New York, NY: Basic Books.

Hamilton, R. (2013). The frustrations of virtue: the myth of moral neutrality in psychotherapy. *Journal of Evaluation in Clinical Practice, 19*(3), 485–492.

Hicks, D. J. (2014). A new direction for science and values. *Synthese: an International Journal for Epistemology, Methodology and Philosophy of Science, 191*(14), 3271–3295.

Husserl, E. (1936). *The crisis of European sciences and transcendental phenomenology* (W. Gibson, Trans.). London, United Kingdom: Routledge.

Husserl, E. (2012). *Ideas: General introduction to pure phenomenology*. London, United Kingdom: Routledge. (Original work published in German, 1913)

International Theological Commission. (2012). *Theology today: Perspectives, principles and criteria*. Vatican City, Vatican: Libreria Editrice Vaticana.

John Paul II. (1995). *Evangelium vitae* [Encyclical, on the value and inviolability of human life]. Vatican City, Vatican: Libreria Editrice Vaticana.

John Paul II. (1998). *Fides et ratio* [Encylical, on the relationship between faith and reason]. Vatican City, Vatican: Libreria Editrice Vaticana.

John Paul II. (2006). *Man and woman he created them: A theology of the body* (M. Waldstein, Trans.). Boston, MA: Pauline Books and Media.

Johnson, E. L. (2007). *Foundations for soul care: A Christian psychology proposal*. Downers Grove, IL: IVP Academic.

Johnson, E. L. (Ed.) (2010). *Psychology and Christianity: Five views* (2nd ed.). Downers Grove, IL: IVP Academic.

Joseph, S., & Linley, P. A. (2006). *Positive therapy: A meta-theory for positive psychological practice*. London, United Kingdom: Routledge.

Kittel, G. (1977). *Theological dictionary of the New Testament*. Grand Rapids, MI: Eerdmans.

Koenig, H. G., King, D., & Carson, V. B. (Eds.). (2012). *Handbook of religion and health* (2nd ed.). New York, NY: Oxford University Press.

Larchet, J. C. (2005). *Mental disorders & spiritual healing: Teaching from the early Christian East*. San Rafael, CA: Angelico Press/Sophia Perennis. (Original work published 1992)

Levering, M. (2008). *Participatory biblical exegesis: A theology of biblical interpretation*. Notre Dame, IN: University of Notre Dame Press.

Lonergan, B. (1992). *Insight: A study of human understanding*. Vol 3 of F. E. Crowe & R. M. Doran (Eds.), *Collected works of Bernard Lonergan*. Toronto, Canada: University of Toronto Press.

Lopez, S. J., & Snyder, C. R. (Eds.). (2009). *The Oxford handbook of positive psychology*. Oxford, United Kingdom: Oxford University Press.

MacIntyre, A. (1990). *Three rival versions of moral enquiry: Encyclopaedia, genealogy, and tradition*. Notre Dame, IN: University of Notre Dame Press.

MacIntyre, A. (1999). *Dependent rational animals: Why human beings need the virtues*. Chicago, IL: Open Court.

MacIntyre, A. (2007). *After virtue: A study in moral theory* (3rd ed.). Notre Dame, IN: University of Notre Dame Press. (Original work published 1981)

Maritain, J. (1959). *Distinguish to unite: or, The degrees of knowledge* (G. B. Phelan, Trans.). New York, NY: Scribner's Sons. (Original work published 1932)

Maslow, A. (1987). *Motivation and personality* (3rd ed.) (R. Frager, J. Fadiman, C. McReynolds, & R. Cox, Eds.). New York, NY: Longman. (Original work published 1954)

Maslow, A. (1994). *Religions, values, and peak expe-*

riences. New York, NY: Penguin. (Original work published 1964)

May, R. (2007). *Love and will.* New York, NY: Norton. (Original work published 1969)

McLeod, J. (1997). *Narrative and psychotherapy.* London, United Kingdom: Sage.

McLeod, J. (2004). The significance of narrative and storytelling in postpsychological counseling and psychotherapy. In A. Leiblich, D. P. McAdams, & R. Josselson (Eds.), *Healing plots: The narrative basis of psychotherapy* (pp. 11–28). Washington, DC: American Psychological Association.

McGrath, A. (2004). *The twilight of atheism: The rise and fall of disbelief in the modern world.* New York, NY: Doubleday.

McGrath, A. (2011). *Darwinism and the divine: Evolutionary thought and natural theology.* Malden, MA: Wiley-Blackwell.

McMinn, M. R., & Campbell, C. D. (2007). *Integrative psychotherapy: Toward a comprehensive Christian approach.* Downers Grove, IL: IVP Academic.

Merleau-Ponty, M. (1965). *Phenomenology of perception* (C. Smith, Trans.). London, United Kingdom: Routledge Kegan.

Miller, R. B. (2001). Scientific vs. clinical-based knowledge in psychology: A concealed moral conflict. *American Journal of Psychotherapy, 55*(3), 344–356.

Murphy, N. (1998). Supervenience and the nonreducibility of ethics to biology. In R. J. Russell, W. R. Stoeger, & F. J. Ayala (Eds.), *Evolutionary and molecular biology: Scientific perspectives on divine action* (pp. 463–489). Berkeley, CA: Center for Theology and the Natural Sciences.

Nagel, T. (2012). *Mind and cosmos: Why the materialist neo-Darwinian conception of nature is almost certainly false.* New York, NY: Oxford University Press.

Nolen-Hoeksema, S. (2004). Gender differences in risk factors and consequences for alcohol use and problems. *Clinical Psychology Review, 24*(8), 981–1010. doi:10.1016/j.cpr.2004.08.003

Nolen-Hoeksema, S., & Hilt, L. (2006). Possible contributors to the gender differences in alcohol use and problems. *The Journal of General Psychology, 133*(4), 357–374.

O'Donohue, W. (2013). *Clinical psychology and the philosophy of science.* Cham, Switzerland: Springer International Publishing.

Parrott, C. (1999). Towards an integration of science, art and morality: The role of values in psychology. *Counselling Psychology Quarterly, 12*(1), 5–24.

Pavlov, I. P. (1927). *Conditioned reflexes: An investigation into the physiological activity of the cortex* (G. V. Anrep, Trans.). New York, NY: Dover.

Peterson, C., & Seligman, M. E. P. (Eds.). (2004). *Character strengths and virtues: A handbook and classification.* New York, NY: Oxford University Press.

Pieper, J. (1966). *The four cardinal virtues* (R. Winston, Trans.). Notre Dame, IN: University of Notre Dame Press.

Pieper, J. (2006). *For the love of wisdom: Essays on the nature of philosophy* (R. Wasserman, Trans.). San Francisco, CA: Ignatius Press.

Pinckaers, S. (2005). *The Pinckaers reader: Renewing Thomistic moral theology* (J. Berkman & C. S. Titus, Eds.). Washington, DC: The Catholic University of America Press.

Pius XII. (1950). *Humani generis* [Encyclical, concerning some false opinions threatening to undermine the foundations of Catholic doctrine]. Vatican City, Vatican: Libreria Editrice Vaticana.

Plantinga, A. (2011). *Where the conflict really lies: Science, religion, and naturalism.* Oxford, United Kingdom: Oxford University Press.

Plato. (1980). *The collected dialogues of Plato: Including the letters* (E. Hamilton & H. Cairns, Eds.). Princeton, NJ: Princeton University Press. (Original work composed ca. 400–347 BC)

Poincaré, H. (1905). *Science and hypothesis.* London, United Kingdom: Walter Scott. (Original work published 1901)

Popper, K. R. (1975). *Objective knowledge: An evolutionary approach.* London, United Kingdom: Oxford University Press.

Popper, K. R. (1983). *Realism and the aim of science.* New York, NY: Rowman & Littlefield.

Ratzinger, J. (1990). Concerning the notion of person in theology. *Communio, 17*(3), 439–454.

Richards, P., & Bergin A. (2005). *Spiritual strategy for counseling and psychotherapy* (2nd ed.). Washington, DC: American Psychological Association.

Rieff, P. (2006). *The triumph of the therapeutic: Uses of faith after Freud.* Wilmington, DE: ISI Books. (Original work published 1966)

Rogers, C. R. (2012). *On becoming a person: A thera-*

pist's view of psychotherapy. Boston, MA: Houghton Mifflin Harcourt. (Original work published in 1961)

Romanyshyn, R. (2007). Wounded researcher: Research with soul in mind. New Orleans, LA: Spring Journal.

Rosmarin, D, H. (2018). Spirituality, religion, and cognitive-behavioral therapy: A guide for clinicians. New York, NY: Guilford.

Scheler, M. (2008). The nature of sympathy (P. Heath, Trans.). New Brunswick, NJ: Transaction. (Original work published 1923)

Schfrankse, E. (1996). Religion and the clinical practice of psychology. Washington, DC: American Psychological Association.

Schmitz, K. (2007). The texture of being: Essays in first philosophy. Washington, DC: The Catholic University of America Press.

Schmitz, K. (2009). Person and psyche. Arlington, VA: The Institute for the Psychological Sciences Press.

Schönborn, C. (2007). Chance or purpose: Creation, evolution, and a rational faith. San Francisco, CA: Ignatius Press.

Scruton, R. (2012). The face of God: The Gifford lectures. London, United Kingdom: Continuum.

Seligman, M. E. P. (2004). Authentic happiness. New York, NY: The Free Press.

Seligman, M. E. P. (2012). Flourish: A visionary new understanding of happiness and well-being. New York, NY: Atria Books.

Siegel, D. J. (2012). The developing mind (2nd ed.). New York, NY: Guilford.

Skinner, B. F. (1938). The behavior of organisms: An experimental analysis. Cambridge, MA: B. F. Skinner Foundation.

Skinner, B. F. (1971). Beyond freedom and dignity. Indianapolis, IN: Hackett.

Skinner, B. F. (1976). About behaviorism. New York, NY: Random House.

Smith, M. B. (1978). Psychology and values. Journal of Social Issues, 34(4), 181–199.

Snyder, C. R., & Lopez, S. J. (Eds.). (2002). Handbook of positive psychology. New York, NY: Oxford University Press.

Sperry, L., & Sperry, J. J. (2012). Case conceptualization: Mastering this competency with ease and confidence. New York, NY: Brunner-Routledge.

Spitzer, R. J. (2010). New proofs for the existence of God: Contributions of contemporary physics and philosophy. Grand Rapids, MI: Eerdmans.

Spitzer, R. J. (2015). Evidence for God from contemporary physics: Extending the legacy of Monsignor Georges Lemaître. South Bend, IN: St. Augustine.

Stein, E. (1996). The separate vocations of man and woman according to nature and grace (F. M. Oben, Trans.). In L. Gelber & R. Leuven (Eds.), Essays on woman: The collected works of Edith Stein (2nd ed., pp. 59–85). Washington, DC: Institute for Carmelite Studies Publications. (Original work published 1932)

Stein, E. (2000). Philosophy of psychology and the humanities (M. C. Baseheart & M. Sawicki, Trans.). Washington, DC: Institute for Carmelite Studies Publications. (Original work published 1922)

Taylor, C. (2007). A secular age. Cambridge, MA: Belknap Press.

Titus, C. S. (2009). Picking up the pieces of philosophical psychology: An introduction. In C. S. Titus (Ed.), Philosophical psychology: Psychology, emotions, and freedom (pp. 1–37). Arlington, VA: The Institute for the Psychological Sciences Press.

Titus, C. S. (2017). Aquinas, Seligman, and positive psychology: A Christian approach to the use of the virtues in psychology. Journal of Positive Psychology, 12(5), 447–458.

Torrance, T. F. (1984). Transformation and convergence in the frame of knowledge: Explorations in the interrelations of scientific and theological enterprise. Grand Rapids, MI: Eerdmans.

Torrance, T. F. (2002). Theological and natural science. Eugene, OR: Wipf & Stock.

VanderWeele, T. J. (2017a). Religious communities and human flourishing. Current Directions in Psychological Science, 26(5), 476–481.

VanderWeele, T. J. (2017b). On the promotion of human flourishing. PNAS, 114(31), 8148–8156.

VanderWeele, T. J. (2018). Is forgiveness a public health issue? American Journal of Public Health, 108(2), 189–190.

Vatican I, Council. (1869–1870). Dei filius [Dogmatic constitution on the Catholic faith]. Retrieved from http://www.ewtn.com/library/COUNCILS/V1.htm

Vatican II, Council. (1964). Lumen gentium [Dogmatic constitution on the Church]. Vatican City, Vatican: Libreria Editrice Vaticana.

Vatican II, Council. (1965a). *Dei verbum* [Dogmatic constitution on Divine Revelation]. Vatican City, Vatican: Libreria Editrice Vaticana.

Vatican II, Council. (1965b). *Gaudium et spes* [Pastoral constitution on the Church in the modern world]. Vatican City, Vatican: Libreria Editrice Vaticana.

Vigna-Taglianti, F. D., Burroni, P., Mathis, F., Versino, E., Beccaria, F., Rotelli, M., . . . Bargagli, A. M. (2016). Gender differences in heroin addiction and treatment: Results from the VEdeTTE cohort. *Substance Use & Misuse, 51*(3), 295–309. doi:10.3109/10826084.2015.1108339

Vitz, P. C. (2017). The origin of consciousness in the integration of analog (right hemisphere) and digital (left hemisphere) codes. *Journal of Consciousness Exploration & Research, 8*(11), 881–906.

von Balthasar, H. U. (2013). *Theo-Drama: Theological dramatic theory, 3 volumes*. San Francisco, CA: Ignatius. (Originally published 1961–1985)

Wallace, W. A. (1996). *The modeling of nature: Philosophy of sciences and philosophy of nature in synthesis*. Washington, DC: The Catholic University of America Press.

Watson, J. B. (1913). Psychology as the behaviorist views it. *Psychological Review, 20*, 158–177.

Watson, J. B. (1924). *Behaviorism*. New York, NY: W. W. Norton.

Weber, M. (1992). *The Protestant ethic and the spirit of capitalism* (T. Parsons, Trans.). London, United Kingdom: Routledge. (Original work published 1904)

Wenham, G. J. (2000). *Story as Torah: Reading the Old Testament narrative ethically*. Grand Rapids, MI: Baker Academics.

White, M. (2007). *Maps of narrative practice*. New York, NY: Norton.

Wippel, J. F. (Ed.). (2011). *The ultimate why question: Why is there anything at all rather than nothing whatsoever?* Washington, DC: The Catholic University of America Press.

Wojtyła, K. (1979). *The acting person* (A.-T. Tymieniecka, Ed.; A. Potocki, Trans.). Boston, MA: D. Reidel Publishing Company. (Original work published 1969)

Wojtyła, K. (1993). Thomistic personalism (T. Sandok, Trans.). In A. N. Woznicki (Ed.), *Catholic thought from Lublin: Vol. 4. Person and community: Selected essays* (pp. 165–76). New York, NY: Peter Lang. (Original paper presented in Polish, 1961)

Worthington, E. L. (1988). Understanding the values of religious clients: A model and its application to counseling. *Journal of Counseling Psychology, 35*, 166–174.

Worthington, E. L. (2006). *Forgiveness and reconciliation: Theory and application*. New York, NY: Routledge.

Zizioulas, J. D. (1997). *Being as communion: Studies in personhood and the Church* (Contemporary Greek Theologians Series, No. 4). Crestwood, NY: St. Vladimir's Seminary Press. (Original work published 1985)

Zundel, M. (1999). *Allusions: Présentations de Bernard de Boissière, André Girard et Marc Donzé*. Paris: Cerf. (Original work published 1941)

Życiński, J. (2006). *God and evolution: Fundamental questions of Christian evolutionism* (K. W. Kemp & Z. Maślanka, Trans.). Washington, DC: The Catholic University of America Press.

Chapter 8

Personal Wholeness (Unity)

CRAIG STEVEN TITUS, PAUL C. VITZ,
AND WILLIAM J. NORDLING

ABSTRACT: This chapter provides philosophical reflection on the Catholic Christian Meta-Model of the Person, which serves as a framework for understanding all persons. The chapter defends the premise that each human being is a personal unity and individual substance, with unique human, moral, and spiritual goals or ends. Employing common experience (including spiritual experience) and philosophical discourse, the chapter endorses the reasonableness of the Catholic Christian vision of personal unity and explores some of its implications for mental health practice. The chapter presents a compelling view of the person's unity or wholeness, which comprises the physical body and the spiritual soul, as a philosophical source for understanding the gift of human life, personal identity, meaningfulness, and dignity. It assumes that men and women are equal in dignity, with significant differences, which makes for their complementarity. Their bodies have nuptial significance and complement each other at the level of physiology and neurobiology, at the level of psychological and social tendencies, as well as at the level of ethical and spiritual dispositions (argument and evidence for this case is made in Chapter 9, "Man and Woman"). The chapter moreover underscores the development over time of the organic whole and unique identity of each person, who also is culturally, historically, and ecologically situated. Last, it challenges the individualist, reductionist, relativist, and dualist approaches to the person, often found in certain strains of philosophy and psychology.

This chapter is the first in a series of nine chapters (Chapters 8 to 16) that present reason-based or philosophical support for the Catholic Christian Meta-Model of the Person (CCMMP). The series will serve as a commentary on the relevance of a robust vision of the person for mental health professionals, who are interested in understanding the continuum and interplay of health and illness, flourishing and languishing. It will also be a welcome contribution for phi-losophers, theologians, and policymakers, who are interested in the contributions of psychology, counseling, and the human sciences to an understanding of the person and interpersonal relationships. One of the challenges this chapter addresses is translating, for non-specialists, the implications of the metaphysical or ontological, teleological, epistemological, and ethical principles that are grounded in a Christian philosophy of the person so as to engage in dialogue with the sciences. This chapter, for the sake of brevity, frames the questions and identifies sources without presenting the arguments extensively.

The Catholic Christian vision of the person (as a Meta-Model, i.e., a model that provides a framework for other models) starts with the premise that each human being is a personal unity or wholeness. This radical, substantial, spiritual unity of the person grounds an exploration of personal dignity, identity, relationships, and flourishing. The history of ideas demonstrates that thinkers who start with duality (extension versus thought, bodily nature versus soul nature, or body versus mind) tend to have difficulty not only (a) accounting for personal unity, but also (b) accounting for experiences of wholeness, continuity, and identity in the midst of change and difference (non-identity), as will be discussed.

In overview, this chapter employs the Catholic Christian vision of the person to address the meaning of innate human dignity and its difference from other types of acquired dignity. It explores a conceptualization of a physical body–spiritual soul unity that differs from the conceptualization inherent to a dualist or reductionist vision of the person. Finally, it situates human persons, as organic living beings, in their cultural, historical, and ecological environment.

How Can We Account for Personal Identity or Character?

First, recent debates about personal identity typically leave out one or more of the following methodological *lenses*, necessary for understanding the person: the *theological*, pointing to God's self-revelation and love; the *existential* and *narrative*, finding meaning in reality and developing one's life story; the *metaphysical* and *ontological*, ascertaining the origin and goal of the person and the human existential, substantial, and physical body–spiritual soul unity; the *sociocultural*, atten-

tive to the influence of social groups; the *psychological*, determining developmental—functional and dysfunctional—patterns of relationality, cognition, motivation, emotion, personality, and behavior; the *ethical*, identifying the professional and personal boundaries of moral responsibility, virtues, and vices; and the *biological* and *neuroscience*, exploring the vitality and characteristics of an organism over time.

In contrast to reductionist or limited approaches that may focus on only one or several of these levels, this chapter, in the light of the Meta-Model, will explore the notion that all of these levels and the whole person must be given a place in an adequate understanding of person. Each of the levels is necessary but not sufficient if we are to understand persons and their flourishing. In particular, this chapter will address questions about the human origin and teleological end of wholeness and dignity: What is more profound, a person's continuity or change, identity or difference, self-consciousness or character? What is the Meta-Model's frame for understanding the origin, development, and ultimate goal of the person? Finally, how do these topics serve mental health professionals by illuminating the continuum and interplay of health and illness, flourishing and languishing?

What Experiential Evidence Is There for the Wholeness of the Person?

The whole person comes to light only in the convergence of one's personal narrative and vocations. It is the person (a physical body–spiritual soul) that unifies all the phenomena found in a single personal event. The basic principles of the Meta-Model remind us of the many interconnected elements found in any single human experience.

The complexity of this example of a single personal experience of a man returning home

Table 8.1. Basic Premises of the Meta-Model as Exemplified in a Typical Human Experience

Basic or Philosophical Premises of the Meta-Model:	A typical example:
Personal Wholeness (Unity)	A man comes home from work.
Fulfilled Through Vocation	He experiences, as husband and father, a convergence of his vocations, leaving behind the people with whom he worked all day, as he meets his family at the front door.
Fulfilled in Virtue	He expresses personal, moral, and spiritual character through the attentive way that he inquires about and cares for each family member.
Relationships	He finds meaning and purpose in being husband to his wife, father to his children, and friend to the neighbor who happens to be visiting.
Sensory-perceptual-cognition	He attends to many details of the concrete needs of each family member and of the house that day.
Emotion	He feels a mixture of exhaustion from efforts outside the home, concern for a parenting situation regarding his daughter but contentment in being with his family.
Reason and Intellect	He considers whether it is wise to allow his daughter to take ballet in light of her other activities.
Will and Freedom	He chooses to relax on the couch with his wife. After dinner, though fatigued, he agrees to read a story to his youngest child and then prays with the child before putting him to bed.

could be described in more fluid fashion. However, here we have simply associated aspects of the experience with the basic principles of the Meta-Model. These principles (and such examples of them) serve as tips of the iceberg of the wholeness of the human being's personhood, moral character, and interpersonal relationships.

What Underlies the Experience of Wholeness?

Most human beings experience a profound sense of self or identity or individual personhood and wholeness (on dissociative and psychotic disorders, see the American Psychiatric Association's *Diagnostic and Statistical Manual of Mental Disorders* and the World Health Organization's *International Classification of Diseases*). Over time, children also come to recognize distinctions between oneself and one's mother, father, siblings, friends, and others (Piaget, 1929; Winnicott, 1958). Such experiences point toward an underlying ontological unifying factor or principle, at the metaphysical and innate level, as the basis for the human capacity and desire for narrative, psychological, ethical, and biological expressions of identity, dignity, and character. Even with the significant biological and psychological changes that individuals go through, from conception to the grave and beyond, a continuity in identity and character is apparent.

There are continuities based on a person's parents, DNA, physical body, birthplace, memory, first language(s), and temperament and emotional dispositions, all of which give rise to an ongoing sense of identity (Neisser, 1993; Snodgrass & Thompson, 1997; Vitz & Felch, 2006) and personal character.

Concerning personal value, Maureen Condic (2009), a professor of neurology and anatomy, has argued that there is scientific evidence about when human life starts, but she has also pointed out that not everyone maintains that human life, as such, is valuable. For example, Princeton philosopher, Peter Singer, recognizes that human life exists from conception (Kuhse & Singer, 1988; Singer, 2011). Nonetheless, he does not attribute to it innate personal dignity, value, or a fundamental right to life. Rather, he asserts that dignity and value are attributed by society and that the lack of health or autonomy (for example, in the case of a gravely and congenitally ill infant, child, or adult) should determine the person's value.

This chapter will also ask the question: How deep is the unity and how extensive the identity? There are several popular models that seek to explain human experiences of continuity and identity in the midst of change and difference. Thinkers have used dualist explanations based on a conceptual distinction between body and soul, understood as extension and thought, which are understood as dual natures: a bodily nature and a nonphysical mental or soul nature. On the one hand, some have applied this distinction to the brain and mind as a brain-mind duality, that is, as two-nature dualism or a separatist dualism, to account for human experience (Gazzaniga, 2006, 2011), while others have reduced the mind to evolutionary epiphenomena of the brain, a mind-brain identity (Churchland, 2001, 2007; Huxley, 1917; Monod, 1971)—this position is a

materialist reductionism. On the other hand, some thinkers see the person as basically a spirit and only accidentally embodied (Descartes, 1641/1996, 1644/1983, Part I, Sect. 63), or they construe the person's identity as a spirit (Berkeley, 1710/2003, Part I, Sects. 17–18); this latter position is idealism or immaterialism. In between these two positions (materialism and idealism), this chapter argues that the basic wholeness of the person is more cogently understood as a physical body–spiritual soul unity, that is, as a single human nature (Aquinas, 1273/1981; Aristotle, ca. 350 BC/1941d; Ashley, 2009; see also Chapter 5, Basic Psychological Support).

From the perspective of the Meta-Model, marked by Judeo-Christian tradition, Aristotle, Augustine, Aquinas, and personalism, the person is animated by a spiritual soul, which is created and sustained in being by the first source of all that exists, which is commonly called God (Gen 1:26–31 & 2:7–24; Ps 139:13; Jn 1:1–5; *Catechism of the Catholic Church* [CCC], §633). In classical and Christian language, the soul is called the substantial form of the body (Aquinas, 1273/1981, I, 76.4). The spiritual soul is the animating principle, or form, of the person and his living human body (Council of Vienne, 1312/2012, Denzinger Schönmetzer (DS) §902; Mt 10:28; Acts 2:27; Rev 6:9, 20:4). This notion of "form" refers not to the shape of the body, but rather to how the physical body is animated by the spiritual soul. Human nature comprises a composite of body and soul, a temple of the Holy Spirit (1 Cor 6:19), created as man or woman (Gen 1 & 2; Mt 19). Death is the separation of the body from the soul, or the returning of the spirit to God (1 Thess 5:23; Mt 10:28; CCC, §§362–368) and resurrection of the dead involves a new spiritual body existence (Mt 22:30; Rm 8:21).

Human Dignity

The Catholic Christian Meta-Model posits that basic dignity is rooted in an innate human core of goodness and relationship, the gift of existence, and the underlying reality of personal unity. A person's awareness of this basic dignity, though, is discovered over time. In addition to the basic dignity, humans acquire a second type of dignity, which they merit by their own contributions to family and society, or disgrace, due to negative actions. Furthermore, we tell our life stories or narratives based on the reality of both basic and acquired dignities, in terms of our personhood, identity, family, and community. Such a narrative involves a whole even when the telling of one's life story is only partial. Confusion about dignity comes when dignity is reduced merely to (a) human, organic well-being and bodily health, (b) cognitive and psychological capacities, or (c) ethical character and spiritual maturity. We need to distinguish basic human dignity, which every person has, from acquired dignity and worth (or dishonor and blame), which depend on moral action.

What Is Basic Human Dignity?

On the one hand, weak notions of the person underlie restricted notions of dignity. For example, in existentialist (Nietzsche, 1885/2006; Sartre, 1946/2007), individualist (Rogers, 1961/2012), and materialist (Churchland, 2001, 2007; Dawkins, 2008; Dennett, 1991, 1995) approaches, basic dignity is not necessarily descriptive of being human and of human nature; rather, it is variable and can be gained and in many cases is lost. For example, defenders of euthanasia often presume that human life does not have intrinsic value and dignity. Rather, they presuppose that dignity should be ascribed to humans who are thriving and healthy and who

are encircled by people who want them as part of their family and as one of their friends. Such a view even defends a right to "death with dignity." This expression is used to defend a supposed right to take one's own life, especially when one is suffering or lonely, and the right to help others do the same. This mercy killing is done in the name of supposedly protecting "dignity," since losing autonomy and the ability to care for oneself, as well as having to depend on others and society for care, can be emotionally stressful for the person, inconvenient for family, and costly for society. Because of the threat of losing one's autonomy, the final autonomous act of such persons is to take their own lives. They mistakenly judge the loss of autonomy as the ultimate loss of their human dignity. The State of Oregon's Death with Dignity Act (1994) exemplifies how the concept of dignity can be misused.

On the other hand, there are strong notions of the person that underlie robust senses of dignity. Based on the experience of life as a gift, classical and Christian philosophical personalist positions state that each person has basic human dignity, no matter one's age or condition. Even before being able to act in ways that typify maturity—such as being able to communicate and speak, care for others, render justice, offer forgiveness, and engage in sacrificial acts—the individual human has basic dignity. It is affirmed that this universal, basic human dignity is innate; it is a permanent gift that is inseparable from human life itself. The physical body–spiritual soul unity constitutes the first gift and the intrinsic ontological and existential footing for the basic human dignity that each human person has, irrespective of his or her physical, psychological, or spiritual state of health or development.

For Aquinas, the human person usually manifests this basic dignity through the common rational nature that underlies our relational capacities to know and to love others and God (1273/1981, I, 29.3 ad 2; III, 4.1 & 2.2 ad 2; see also Berkman & Titus, 2005). Understood philosophically, the spiritual soul or human life form is the basis on which depend all the activities that the person may manifest, including human interpersonal, sensory-perceptual, emotional, rational, and volitional capacities, as well as their related vocations, virtues, and vices. The soul remains the basis of these qualities even when a person is hindered from expressing them because of illness, disorders, or developmental status (Vatican II, 1965a, §§14–15). As difficult as it may be to accept, basic dignity cannot be reduced by a person's physical or intellectual deficits, immoral behavior, or spiritual shortcomings, nor can basic dignity be increased by external beauty, moral goodness, contributions to society, or even holiness.

From a Christian biblical position, dignity is due to the goodness, value, and nature of the person as created in the image of God (Gen 1:28 & 1:31; Vatican II, 1965a, §§14–15). From conception to death, the human rational and interpersonal nature has a basic dignity that springs from this image (see Chapters 9, "Man and Woman," and 17, "Created in the Image of God"). John Paul II (1995, §93, §100) argues strongly for this Christian theological position, that the human person has dignity from conception until natural death. This philosophical and theological notion of basic human dignity has clear psychological and ethical implications—for example, no matter the condition, the person always merits respect.

What Type of Human Dignity or Value Can Be Acquired and Lost?

Basic human dignity, which cannot be lost, is not the only type of value that humans can have

or merit. Further gifts and achievements constitute the grounds for recognizing other levels of value, merit, or honor. Such added dignity can be due to an excellence that is internal to the person (e.g., being virtuous, knowledgeable, wise, or holy). Added dignity may also be merited because of external factors, such as being a good mother or father, or serving a role in society such as teacher, athlete, artist, leader, judge, soldier, or within the religious field (e.g., priests, ministers, and religious). Thus, it is appropriate to honor or praise a person for the artwork they have done, the leadership they have exhibited, or the courage in battle that they have shown. Figure 8.1 represents the basic goodness and innate dignity of the person as a center point of the circular image (signifying the wholeness of the person). The rest of the figure demonstrates areas that represent anthropological capacities (cognition and affect) that can develop and be perfected through vocations and virtues.

Through intentional wrongdoing, however, people can also merit a type of dishonor, shame, or discredit. The person who intentionally commits murder is rightly blamed and punished. Such punishment should be administered justly by a competent public authority with the intention to protect society and rehabilitate the offender (CCC, §§2263–2267; McAleer, 2012).

The basic dignity of each person should always be affirmed, even when one is identifying human faults and shortcomings, including serious ones—that is, it is consistent to recognize that people may merit blame and punishment, while always retaining their basic dignity (Aquinas, 1273/1981; John Paul II, 1995; Berkman & Titus, 2005). Ellis (1980; Ellis & Ellis, 2011) and other cognitive psychotherapists, likewise, hold that a person's behavior can be judged as maladaptive but that the person him- or herself should never be judged. Rogers (1961/2012) also

Figure 8.1. Philosophical Premises of the Catholic Christian Meta-Model of the Person

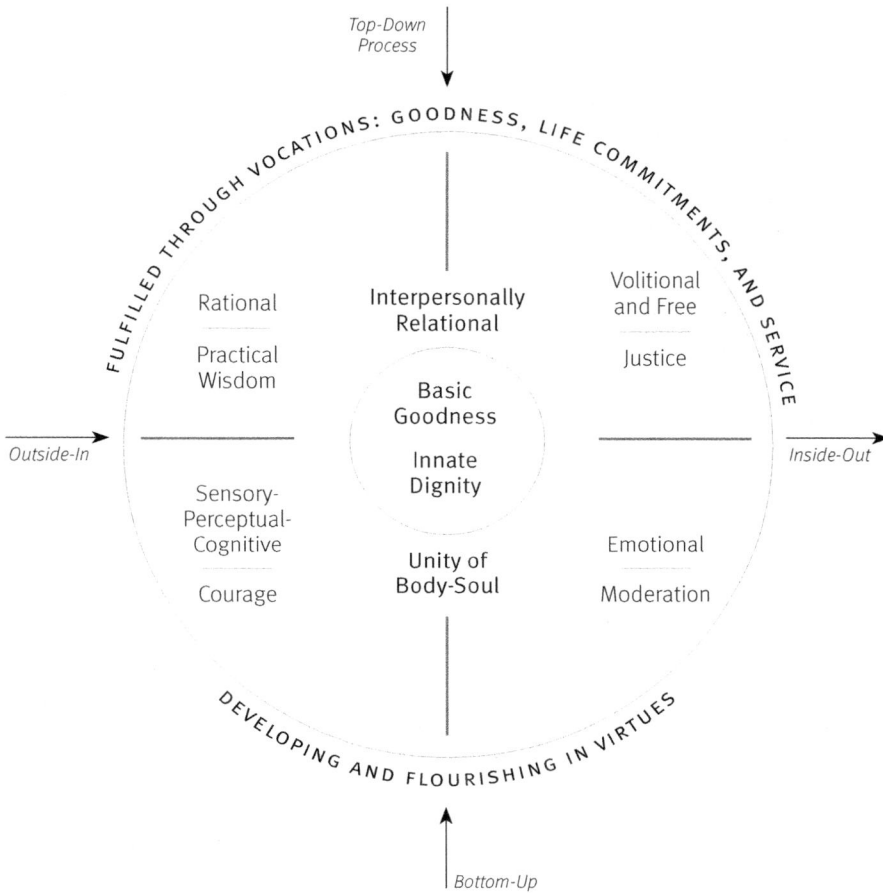

emphasizes the need for unconditional positive regard, even in the face of negative behavior. These thinkers all recognize that negative psychological effects can occur when one judges the person rather than judging the behavior.

What Is the Explicitly Faith-Based Account of Dignity?

From a faith-based perspective, the Bible affirms that "God saw everything that he had made, and behold, it was very good" (Gen 1:31; all quotes in this chapter are taken from the Revised Standard Version—Second Catholic Edition). The very fact of existence (*esse*) is a gift from God, who is the source of all of the goodness of creation (*essentia*). Types of dignity, goodness, or value, beyond basic human dignity, should also be understood in terms of the divine gift that makes them possible and in terms of the added responsibility that demands personal initiative, as found in the parable of the talents (Mt 25:14–46). Even those who have small means, such as the widow with her mite (Mk 12:41–44), can express a Christ-like humility and dignity. Of course, those who have done great things are in need of grace to maintain humility, lest they fall to pride.

By contrast, acquired types of shame or disgrace involve the intentional misuse of human talents and divine gifts. In sum, the original gifted dignity, or basic dignity, of the person is permanent, whereas secondary dignity or disgrace is brought about by personal acts. The Gospel of Luke admonishes "Judge not, and you will not be judged; condemn not, and you will not be condemned; forgive, and you will be forgiven" (6:37). While we must evaluate with discernment the worth of behavior and acts (our own included), we are never to judge with condemnation the soul of any person (Jas 4:12; Rom 14:10–12). God alone can judge the person (*CCC*, §1861).

Body-Soul Unity as Gift of Life

Does It Make a Difference That Human Nature Is Whole and the Person a Unity?

There are different ideas of human nature in the history of philosophy. As discussed above, some involve materialist reductionism and others two-nature dualism, that is, separatist dualism. A Catholic model posits the human physical body–spiritual soul unity as an innate gift that is neither materialistic nor constituted by two natures or two substances. This unity is also called a "hylomorphic" unity, derived from the Greek words for matter (*hulē*) and form (*morphē*) (Aristotle, ca. 350 BC/1941e, I.7; Feser, 2006, pp. 219–228; Pakaluk, 2005, pp. 90–95). Personal unity remains even when there are certain types of change. For instance, a person remains a person even when he becomes musical. The underlying person loses his lack of being musical without losing his personhood, as Aristotle (ca. 350 BC/1941e) explains (I.7, 190a13–32). Moreover, all humans have a personal nature that is a whole, and through it we observe other people and experience our own selves as real, irreplaceable, and meaningful. Such experiences provide a basis for personalist and metaphysical judgments about the person being an inextrica-ble body-soul unity who is responsible and significantly (although not completely) free (see Chapter 16, "Volitional and Free"). The personal body-soul unity is also a mysterious gift and, in a Catholic vision, capable of life after death. This leads to a question: How is our notion of personal unity significant for how we flourish and languish?

How Is Body-Soul Unity Significant for Flourishing?

A Catholic philosophical Meta-Model of the person does not construe any one psychological, moral, or social function or flourishing as belonging purely to either the body or the soul. The premise that a person is a body-soul unity has implications for the interactions of the diverse human capacities and for the flourishing of the whole person (see Figure 1 above).

The Meta-Model recognizes bottom-up influences, that is, the effects of biological and neurological capacities on higher capacities, for example, the way that instincts, sensory perceptions, and emotions influence thinking, volition, and free choices. And through embodied activities, the person expresses, for example, spousal union, attentive friendship, and religious devotion. In this framework, the conscious and unconscious observable workings of the brain and nervous system function in support of intellectual and spiritual actions (Ashley, 2013; Beauregard, 2012; Beauregard & O'Leary, 2008).

The Meta-Model also recognizes top-down influences, that is, the effects of intellectual and spiritual capacities on lower capacities, for example the way that intentional goals and freely made decisions, as well as spiritual beliefs and divine grace, influence physical movements and emotions (see also top-down influences in Chapter 15, "Rational"). In accordance with this understanding, it is confusing to distinguish body and soul or mind and body as two different natures or substances (in a separatist dualism), as if the human body were not normally united to the soul even for unconscious neurological, cardiovascular, respiratory, and digestive movements (Życiński, 2006).

What Challenges Must a Body-Soul (Hylomorphic) Notion of Personal Unity Face?

Recent psychology and the mental health sciences, with their theoretical, empirical, and clinical applications, have pressed scientific studies into the service of understanding and healing the person. However, contemporary psychological science has tended to set methodological limits on psychology's field of study, and to focus only on the observable aspects of the person, generally the body half of the body-soul unity, to the exclusion of the *psuchē* or *psyche* (soul). For example, it has focused on genes and hormones, the brain and behavior, and the effect of environmental reinforcers on behavior or on particular drives, such as sex and aggression. Psychologists, for example, have turned to the neurosciences and to neuro-philosophers not only with a presupposition that the body

alone "produces" consciousness, but also with the expectation, one day, to be able to explain completely the human mind, soul, and morality in terms of brain function (Churchland, 2001, 2007). Not all neuroscientists, psychologists, or philosophers have opted for an eliminative materialism (for an example see Gazzaniga, 2006; Nagel, 2012). Moreover, some have openly critiqued the neglect of the fuller dimensions of the person, including the most significant ones, such as the person's basic dignity, capacity for responsibility and freedom, and the search for truth, goodness, and beauty (Tallis, 2011, 2013).

On the one hand, materialist-reductionist versions of evolutionary and naturalist views attempt to demonstrate that the human being is no different from other forms of evolved animal life on Earth (Dawkins, 2008; Dennett, 1991; Wilson, 1975; for arguments addressing general naturalist objections to a hylomorphic anthropology, see Goyette, 2009). Such versions assume that an evolutionary perspective will completely explain human origins and that the neurosciences will account for psychological function. They reduce the soul to the mind and the mind to an epiphenomenon of the brain, which itself is the product of environmental factors.

On the other hand, separatist dualism, another psychologically significant understanding of the person, construes body and mind (or body and spirit) as two separate natures or substances (Descartes, 1641/1996; Foster, 1989, 1991; Robinson, 2016: Swinburne, 1997). Adherents of a body-spirit separatist dualism seek to defend the spiritual dimension of the person (which includes the mental as well as a transcendent spiritual principle) against reductionist and determinist tendencies. However, these approaches express a weak notion of personal unity. They understand the physical and psychological dimensions as unreliable sources of knowledge about other human minds or the transcendent first principle (who is God; Rom 1:19–20).

Between these two extremes—of exaggerated reduction of the human to the body or exaggerated separation of the human body from the mind or spirit—there is a middle ground, expressed by a personalist vision of the person, a conceptualization of the person as necessarily a physical body–spiritual soul unity (Madden, 2013). Looked at from an ontological or metaphysical perspective, this vision is called a hylomorphic approach (Aquinas, 1273/1981). It is also called a prudential personalism, from an ethical perspective (Ashley, 2013; Wojtyła, 1993). The Meta-Model employs this classical yet expansive and constructive explanation of the person as a body-soul unity, which will be addressed in the following questions.

How Might Radical Materialism Be Rebutted?

There are numerous objections to the reductionist claim that humans are merely material beings (for an example of such arguments, see Nagel, 2012; and Tallis, 2011, 2013). First, recent psychological and neurological research suggests that bottom-up (emergentist) influences do not fully explain human experience. It identifies that there are also top-down mental (supervenient) influences that cannot be explained as originating in neurobiology itself. These empirical observations correlate with insights that originate from a philosophical perspective (see Życiński, 2006). These top-down movements are of several sorts and indicate an extra-neurological source at a mental or spiritual level (Beauregard & O'Leary, 2008; Doidge, 2007; Emmons & McCullough, 2004). Second, the health-inducing influence of everyday belief and meaningfulness is found in the well-documented placebo

effect, which suggests that mental expectations of change can actually change the body (Beauregard, 2012; Beauregard & O'Leary, 2008; Kohls, Sauer, Offenbächer, & Giordano, 2011). Such phenomena of change are due to more than an expression of urges or instincts; they depend on mental acts and even spiritual ones. Scientists have, furthermore, come to identify how, through first-person subjective experience, internal education, and disciplined practice, neural circuits are rendered more efficacious (myelinogenesis); brains can also be trained by higher sources, such as the mind (Beauregard, 2013; Beauregard & O'Leary, 2008; Doidge, 2007; Siegel, 2012, pp. 57–58, p. 399). A general understanding of the plasticity of human dispositions and the influence of other persons has been an essential aspect for conceptualizing virtues and pedagogy (Aquinas, 1273/1981, I-II, 49–54, especially 49.2 ad 3 and 49.4). Third, near-death and out-of-body experiences seem to suggest that there is more to life than the material aspect of the body (Alexander, 2012; Beauregard & O'Leary, 2008; Spitzer, 2015).

In sum, from the philosophical side, there are numerous arguments that support belief in the immateriality of human thought and language, choice, and the soul (Aristotle, ca. 350 BC/1941a; Ashley, 2013; Feser, 2008).

How Might the Meta-Model Reconcile Challenges to the Existence of the Soul?

There are other challenges to the classical notion of the body-soul unity that are found in anomalous experiences. At the psychological level, the existence of mental disorders, such as psychoses, raises questions about the possibility of having reliable contact with extra-mental reality. At the physical level, the existence of conjoined twins (for example, Abby and Brittany Hansel), who have some unique organs and other shared ones, raises questions about the unity of the body and soul. At the existential level, there are numerous people who deny the stability of human nature or the existence of God (Dawkins, 2008; Dennett, 1995; Sartre, 1946/2007). Such cases express something of the mystery of the human condition and invite psychological, philosophical, and theological responses, to which we now turn.

We would suggest that the challenges voiced by materialist and two-nature dualist (separatist dualism) positions can be reconciled within the unified body-soul (hylomorphic) paradigm, inasmuch as there is a correlation between the functional material elements (including the vital organs, the brain, and the nervous system) and the essential element (the person's basic core of goodness and the formal gift of spiritual life itself).

The mystery of the human person is predicated on the gift of life (a person's being created in the image of God). This gift of life, with its body-soul unity, can be freely accepted or not in due time. There are two major aspects of this gift of human life: our response to the basis for one's own life and also how that gift is given to and received by others, such as parents, siblings, and friends. This understanding of the personal unity of matter and spirit, body and soul, is at the center of a Catholic view of the person and serves to resist the two impoverished notions of the human person found in materialist reductionism and separatist dualism.

Both materialist reductionism and separatist dualism are seen in contrast to the Meta-Model's first philosophical premise, which affirms that human beings are persons, who have a personal unity and a single human nature that unites spirit and matter (Ashley, 2006; John Paul II, 1998). Philosophically explained, the human

soul is so deeply united to the body that it is the body's substantial form (Aristotle, ca. 350 BC/ 1941d, I.1; Madden, 2013; Maritain, 1952, pp. 35–38; Oderberg, 2005, pp. 81–86; Dewan, 2006, pp. 152–166). This view is given theological support, for it is held as a dogma of faith (Council of Vienne, 1312/2012; Pius XII, 1950).

What Are the Specifically Spiritual Aspects of Personhood and Death?

Although there are significant signs of intelligence in higher life forms (such as primates and dolphins, who can be taught a simple form of syntax), there are unique characteristics, such as higher forms of syntactic language, found in *Homo sapiens sapiens* (MacIntyre, 1999). Metaphysical and religious affirmations, furthermore, point to the significance of the spiritual soul to explain these traits. Moreover, they indicate that there must be some further personal and spiritual dimension to life to explain the origin, responsible development, and purpose of mankind.

In the theological perspective, the Christian tradition holds that each human person is created by that first principle and ultimate end of life, who is called God. How does this affirmation serve to bolster a coherent vision of personal unity? First, the Christian tradition attributes the source of the personal soul to a personal God, who immediately creates the soul and on whom the human being is always dependent for the animation of the soul and its giving form to the body. The Second Vatican Council (1965a) affirms that this "spiritual and immortal soul" (§14) acts as the animating principle and substantial form of the living human body. As the Psalmist says: "For you formed my inward parts, you knitted me together in my mother's womb" (Ps 139:13). Second, the human, whose being created in God's image is a gift, is materially mortal, while having a spiritually immortal soul and *telos*. The nature of the spiritual human soul requires that it normally subsist in a body (Gen 1–2) yet that it survives the death of that body (Gen 3). The proper functioning of the body is required in order for the person to exhibit human intellectual and spiritual capacities in this life. At death, the soul leaves the physical body, but the person still remains dependent on God for his or her life. That is, the human person's spiritual and immortal soul survives the body's death because of a gift from God. However, it is with the resurrection of the body that a full

person is made manifest again (Ashley, 2013; *CCC*, §99). Third, from a classical philosophical and Catholic Christian perspective, the person is meant for contemplation of God in eternity (Aristotle, ca. 350 BC/1941a, X.7–8; ca. 350 BC/1941d, III.5; Lk 23:43; 1 Cor 15:35–53). This reason-based and faith-based position stands in contrast to models of materialist reductionism and separatist dualism, which offer limited accounts of human dignity and human freedom. Furthermore, it contrasts with determinist perspectives that deny both dignity and freedom.

Biological Living Beings

What Is the Place of the Body in Personhood?

The significance of the body for the person should be neither understated nor overplayed. Human persons are bodily, but not in a reductionistic way. Their bodies are *fully* personal, and their persons fully embodied, because of their personal unity of physical body and spiritual soul. The body is expressive and reveals much about the soul. For example, it makes manifest the significance and purpose of language and meaningful actions (such as work and service, leisure and rituals and liturgy), and it expresses interpersonal relationships as found in the family, friendship, and community.

How Might the Body Be a Primary Object for Science?

Scientific studies of the human species continue to advance our knowledge by charting the neurobiological and behavioral bases for human action and well-being. Many scientists have accepted deterministic, materialist, or reductionist descriptions of human action based on the biological, neural, and endocrinological sciences. Notable scientists had announced that a full

and determinative account of mankind would be in hand within a decade or so (Wilson, 1975, 1998). However, a fuller account of scientific advances need not reduce the spirit (soul) to the mind (intelligence understood to be an epiphenomenon of the brain), or the mind to the body (neurons and hormones). (For nonreductionist, scientific accounts see Beauregard, 2008, 2012; Nagel, 2012; Scruton, 2017; and Vitz, 2017.) The fact that reductionist accounts have not been able to satisfactorily account for human self-consciousness, language, intelligence, free choice, desire, and relationality suggests that either they need much more time before they are able to vindicate this aspiration, or that human persons cannot be reduced to mathematically quantified observations after all. If we are not reducible to our observable bodies alone, and if human beings are not completely determined in their actions, then, as obligatory as these sciences are for understanding physical mechanisms and psychological functioning, we also need other disciplines to understand the origin and end of the body as expressed in rationality, the will, human relationships, and ultimately in transcendence.

How Do the Body and Personal Flourishing Correlate?

As living beings, human persons experience their own and other people's pleasure and pain. Moreover, bodily health, as well as states of pleasure and pain, are recognized to influence, without being equated to, overall personal flourishing. A holistic study of human flourishing includes not only scientific observations of the body but also philosophical and theological considerations of meaning and the well-being of the whole physical body–spiritual soul unity. The capacities of this unity include perception, emotion, reason, will, and relationality. Humans have, as part of their nature, diverse types of inclinations, which include searches for higher meaning and transcendent realities (Spitzer, 2015). Our capacities include the ability to respond to the movements of grace and the Holy Spirit. This includes our inclination to protect, preserve, and improve our bodily and spiritual well-being. The desire for self-preservation through intentional acts reaches beyond natural capacities and mortal limits of the agent's body to other persons and to the divine Other. For example, parents desire not only their own health but also that of their children and other people. Their desire for health is a desire for survival, communion, and meaning, which is a personal desire that is also desired for all loved ones inside and outside the family. This embodied yet transcendent desire to continue living with others even reaches toward the flourishing of eternal life.

How Does the Catholic Christian View of the Person Understand the Wholeness of the Body?

The Catholic Christian perspective is rooted in Scripture and tradition (Vatican II, 1965b). It presents a view of the unity of the person that is attentive to the need for and importance of the body, in this life and the next (with the promise of a resurrected body). In an example of holistic anthropology, the Psalmist recognizes the interweaving of the heart, the soul, and the body in experiences of life such as suffering and pain but also flourishing: "Therefore my heart is glad, and my soul rejoices; my body also dwells secure" (Ps 16:9). In the spirit of the Old Testament books of Deuteronomy (6:4–5) and Leviticus (19:18), the Gospel of Luke (10:27) expresses the vocation of love as an embodied personal experience that involves heart, soul, mind, and strength (see also Ashley, 1985, 2006; John Paul II, 1993b; Vatican II, 1965a). These concepts and conceptual metaphors contribute to our understanding the person as called to communion. This integral view of the body as fundamental to an understanding of the person and personality is found in the Church's teaching on human love, chastity, and the sexual act, as seen in Paul VI's *Humanae vitae* (1968) and John Paul II's *Theology of the Body* (2006), as well as his remarks on the meaning of work (John Paul II, 1981). This Catholic Christian perspective contrasts with the materialist position that views the body as a machine or that views the body as totally disconnected from the nature of the person. It also contrasts with the political position that reduces the person's body to be an instrument of the economy.

Human Movement

How Do Humans Move?

There are two basic types of human movement: one observable and the other deep, interior, generally unobservable, and often spiritual. First, there is the observable movement of one's own body and of others. Such movement allows for human communication, as well as allowing us to engage in relationships, service to others, and meaningful leisure. This type of movement includes both self-expression and types of interpersonal relationships, such as speaking, shaking hands, hugging, kissing, dancing, and playing an instrument. There are also observable movements that express our virtues and vocations, such as acts of courage, suffering in patience, cooking for one's family, caring for the sick, kneeling in prayer, and saying the Mass. Alternatively, these movements may express vices and general languishing, as shown in hostile comments, physical attacks, and infidelity to one's spouse.

Second, underlying what can be sensed, perceived, and quantified, there are other deep, interior, and generally unobservable spiritual movements that underlie our responses to truth, goodness, beauty, and to even existence itself. Such human movement is replete with meaning. Random human movement is rare, and inactivity can be a sign of fear, depression, or indifference. While the primordial gift of love and life originates in both God and parents, persons are given the capacity to move themselves. We seek to partake in meaningful and free behavior, within the limits of an autonomy connected to truth. Purpose—at internal and external, conscious and nonconscious levels—motivates us to work, play, and love. We express the ultimate meaning of love in self-sacrificial gifts of time, resources, and even our own life.

Furthermore, we are moved by others. As John Donne (1624/2012) says, "No man is an island, / entire of itself / .... / any man's death diminishes me, / because I am involved in mankind; / and therefore never send to know for whom the bell tolls; / it tolls for thee" (p. 91). We are stirred by each life and moved by each death, because we are called not to remain indifferent to anyone but rather to be united by knowledge and love (Aquinas, 1273/1981, III, 2.10). Such is the vocation of the saints and the just (Sherwin, 2005, p. xvii).

It is an illness or ignorance to go unmoved by knowledge and by love. Both compelling cognitions and persuasive affections move us. Knowledge—perception of reality, memory, imagination, reason, and intuition—constitutes the first step in being moved by someone and toward someone. As Augustine states, one cannot love what one does not know (Augustine, 416/1963, X.1.1). Affective responses to this knowledge occur in felt, intended, willed, and intuitive inclinations and choices. All of these movements express goods to be sought or evils to be avoided, be they near or far.

How Do Bodily and Spiritual Movements Interact?

In a faith-based context, St. Paul highlights the diverse movements of the body (or the flesh) and the mind (or the spirit). The body-soul unity can be negatively influenced by disordered emotions and vices, such as rage, lust, and pride. St. Paul also recognizes that the body (as flesh) can seem a weight on the spirit, when we indulge disordered desires and cravings, for example (Gal 5:16, 19–21). The body-soul unity also has natural inclinations that are basically good, as found in desires for communion (with the mother and with the spouse), justice (with siblings, peers, and society), and truth (in understanding our lives and the world around us). Moreover, the body-soul unity can also be brought into willing service of virtue and the vocation to holiness (Rom 8), and be moved by the Spirit (Gal 5:22–23). For example, in his second letter to Timothy (2 Tim 4:6–7), Paul uses the image of a journey and a battle to represent the embodied vocation of mankind. He says, "For I am already on the point of being sacrificed; the time of my departure has come. I have fought the good fight, I have finished the race, I have kept the faith." Such effort is more than words. It is a movement of the whole person (body-soul unity) and a God-given strength. As the Psalmist says, "By you I can crush a troop, by my God I can leap over a wall" (Ps 18:29). There are many other similar images that communicate the effects of the Word of God and the movement of the Spirit in everyday actions.

Historically, Ecologically, and Culturally Located

How Do History, Ecology, and Culture Matter to Humans?

History, ecology, and culture inescapably influence the human person. People always relate to one another inasmuch as they are situated in a distinct time (historical context), a distinct physical place (ecological context), and a distinct society (cultural context). We live in a particular cultural setting (even when multicultural) and dialogue using particular languages (even when multilingual). Modern travel and means of communication open the door to the globalization of culture and the ability to sustain relationships at a distance. Nonetheless, local cultures and communities—especially mother, father (Vitz, 2011; Wilcox, 1999), family, and friends—constitute the primary influences in the development of the child and throughout the life of each individual (Bowlby, 1982, 1973). First-hand experiences of nature or the ecosystem are also significant resources that contribute to the economy, social life, recreation, and even to a sense of wonder about creation. It is this wonder that gives rise to the vocation to philosophize, to seek the origin of the universe (Aristotle, 1941a, I.2).

As influential as the sociocultural and physical environments are, they do not totally determine the individual. Rather, responsible freedom, meaningful creativity, and conscientious stewardship are possible and necessary in responding to one's vocations (that is, flourishing and holiness; vowed and non-vowed vocational states; and work, service, and meaningful leisure) and in meeting life's challenges.

How Does a Christian Approach Conceptualize History, Ecology, and Culture?

Time, in human experience, is inherent to earthly life. We know that life is limited in time. Vocations take time. In a real sense, wasting time is wasting life. And giving time in service to family, friends, and community is giving our life to others. Temporality—being in time—underlies our relationships, culture, work, rest, and providence. Both work and meaningful leisure lead to flourishing, especially when work supplies a family's basic physical needs, contributes to the good of society, and exercises stewardship over and respect for God's creation, so that leisure, in turn, can aim at the deeper needs for culture, contemplation, and worship (Pieper, 1952/2009).

In particular, liturgical practices, personal prayer, and spiritual exercises involve bodily gestures and physical places, symbols and images, songs and music, discipline and asceticism that express a deep commonality while also differing across time, place, and culture (Maritain, 1932/1972). By divine purpose, we find the meaning of God's personal self-revelation only with sensitivity to culture and history, nature and beauty.

Christianity is a deeply historical religion. The Gospels, along with the rest of the New Testament, call upon the Old Testament to be fully understood, as St. Augustine recounts (388/1887, Chapter 18). St. Paul says, "When the time had fully come, God sent forth his Son, born of woman, born under the law, to redeem those who were under the law, so that we might receive adoption as sons" (Gal 4:4–5). The Gospels recount the particular details of the life of Christ, from nativity to resurrection, so that he may be an effective model. St. Basil the Great refers to Christ's model, represented in the Gospels, as providing Christians with a "pattern of life" that each disciple follows (Basil the Great, ca. 375/1980, Chapter 15, §35). In some sense, the model of Christ's life as preserved in the biblical writings is analogous to the event of the incarnation itself. As the Second Vatican Council's *Dogmatic Constitution on Divine Revelation* (1965b) indicates, the Word of God is God's own word revealed in human words: "For the words of God, expressed in human language, have been made like human discourse, just as the Word of the eternal Father, when he took to himself the flesh of human weakness, was in every way made like men" (§ 13).

The basic nature of being a personal unity, however, undercuts neither the complex inter-connection of body and soul, nor the complicatedness of an individual person's journey, nor the complexity of one's historical context and ultimate aim in life. By human "person," the Meta-Model's personalist perspective denotes a unique, complete, wholly unified, living, spiritual being constituted by a material body that is informed by an immaterial, incorruptible, and immortal soul. Being "informed" means being given vitality; being "informed" means that the body is composed with the soul in such a way that all of its operations are, ontologically speaking, integrated in a unified activity that participates in the human person's overall natural orientation toward completion and fulfillment (*telos*). This completion and fulfillment is ultimately to be found in supernatural beatitude with Christ.

Much of this chapter has sought to explain the ramifications of this principle of the human vital principle (soul). It is our conviction that the person cannot be understood apart from a specific animating form, which philosophers have called the soul, or life force (MacIntyre, 2009), and which reductionist thinkers have tended to avoid discussing or to reduce to biological mechanisms (Schrödinger, 1944/2012). However, there are compelling reasons to believe that the human being is animated by a spiritual principle or soul. For example, human intellectual and spiritual capacities (especially abstract thought and syntactical language), free choice, social life, complex tool use, and religious worship are all activities that biological or neurological mechanisms cannot adequately explain (Ashley, 2006, 2013; Austriaco, Brent, Davenport, & Ku, 2016; Feser, 2008; Nagel, 2012; Schmitz, 2009).

Multiple Capacities

Does the Human Person Transcend His or Her Biological Bases?

As noted earlier, naturalist reductionist perspectives posit that human cognition and affection are simply the result of biological processes, the epiphenomenon of neurological circuitry (Dawkins, 2008; Dennett, 1995). Nevertheless it is important to keep in mind that such naturalist perspectives have their serious critiques within secular academia itself. For example, Nagel (2012), although he rejects theism, presents powerful arguments that neo-Darwinian theory (materialism) cannot explain the rise of consciousness, value, meaning, and morality. Furthermore, naturalist positions miss indications of how wisdom, love, and free will employ biological bases, but also transcend them.

In contrast to reductionist perspectives, the Catholic Christian vision of the person affirms that the human capacities for cognition (both sense perception and intellectual knowledge) and affect (both emotions and volition) manifest a capacity to transcend their biological bases (see Table 8.2). Many different theorists, most of whom are secular scientists, have made clear that they see human language as transcending basic animal awareness and giving rise to the unique power of human culture. Human language transcends the biological bases and preverbal bases of perceptual cognition (Berwick & Chomsky, 2016; Bikerton, 2014; Dietrich & Hardcastle, 2004; Klein & Edgar, 2002; Nagel, 2012; Polanyi, 1968; Scruton, 2014; Suddendorf, 2013; Vitz, 2017). Some others argue for a further type of transcendence, above normal human transcendence, that is exemplified in mystical and related experiences (Beauregard, 2012; Beauregard & O'Leary, 2008; Otto, 1958; Spitzer, 2015).

Hierarchical organizations or systems al-most always have top-down (Beauregard, 2012; Beauregard & O'Leary, 2008) *and* bottom-up influences on performance. Since the brain is hierarchically structured, we should expect to find both top-down and bottom-up influences in its activities. We are not totally determined in our responses to sense stimuli but are capable of meaningful and responsible love and choices that aim at a transcendent goal. Personal unity constitutes the existential basis that expresses itself in the multiple capacities of persons and their human nature that require yet also transcend their biological bases.

Concern for a person's mental well-being, for example, demands attention to the organic, cognitive, and affective aspects of the person at the levels of sensory and intellectual capacities. The model's metaphysical approach to experience affirms that there is a deep, natural, and transcendent intellectual-spiritual character to human capacities for knowing and loving. This intellectual character is spiritual because of the higher order mental-intellectual capacities, such as discursive reasoning, language-use, intuition, understanding, volition, or will. Furthermore, it depends on the fundamental way that God maintains the person and his capacities in existence. This character depends both on the continuous common gift of God that underlies all existence, goodness, and truth, and of course on our own personal participation in them as found in our human nature and committed life-callings (Ashley, 2006; Schmitz, 2007, 2009). Christian faith-informed reflection, moreover, affirms that the specific supernatural intellectual-spiritual character of faith, hope, and charity also depends on God's grace and the movements or gifts of the Holy Spirit (Aquinas 1273/1981, I-II, 68; Ashley, 2013; John Paul II, 1998). These are

Table 8.2. Structure of Human Capacities as Found in the Philosophical Premises of the CCMMP

	Cognitive Capacites	Affective Capacities
Intellectual Capacities	**Intellectual Cognition: Understanding & Reason** ⊙ Foundational–Theoretical: intuition and understanding ⊙ Discursive: reasoning and language about truth and the ordering of goods	**Intellectual Affect: Will or Volition** ⊙ Foundational: disposition of being drawn toward the good and repulsed by evil ⊙ Discursive: pursuit of and choices about goods and repulsion of evils

◄————► **Body–Soul Unity** ◄————►

	Cognitive Capacites	Affective Capacities
Sense Capacities	**Sensory-Perceptual Cognition: Preverbal Cognitive Capacities** ⊙ Higher-Order Perceptions & Systems: • Evaluative capacity • Imagination as a capacitiy • Memory as a process • Synthetic capacity ⊙ Primary (5) Senses: Vision, hearing, smell, taste, touch and pain (as well as vestibular and proprioceptive-kinesthetic senses)	**Sensory Affect: Emotion** ⊙ Emotions of Initiative (Irascible): affected by the difficult-to-attain good and difficult-to-repulse evil: • Fear & daring • Hope & despair • Anger ⊙ Emotions of Desire (Concupiscible): drawn toward the good; repulsed by evil: • Love and hate • Desire and repulsion • Joy (pleasure) & sorrow (suffering)

Organic and Neural Dimensions

See also Table 11.2 for a simplified expression of the contents of this table.

generally understood to be more specific in the individual person and situation. For example, in the history of Israel, God opened the Red Sea to free his people, and in the history of salvation, God opened St. Paul's heart to belief in Christ.

How Does the Philosophical Perspective on Cognition and Affection Preserve a Unified Vision of the Person?

The Catholic Christian Meta-Model's philosophical (wisdom-based) perspective seeks to broaden the use of reason in the study of and care for the person, family, and community. This broadened wisdom-based perspective recognizes that neither the neurosciences themselves (which involve a methodological reductionism) nor a philosophical emphasis on a disembodied human spirit (a separatist dualism) will give the whole account of human development, healing, and thriving (Życiński, 2006). Nonetheless, the perspective of the Meta-Model will acknowledge the true findings and insights that are expressed in the sciences. A wisdom-based approach will promote also consideration of how one responds to one's personal callings in life (to goodness and holiness, to committed states in life, and to work and service to others). It will encourage persons to seek to be aware of and responsible for their own mental health, moral flourishing, and spiritual state. This responsibility entails developing intentional plans to strengthen the multiple capacities that serve the everyday and ultimate ends of each person. Living out the practices associated with such plans cultivates personal resiliency. This responsibility also means knowing when, for nurturing or healing in each of these domains, one needs to call on the competence of particular experts, including parents and spouses, medical doctors and mental health practitioners, educators and ethicists, as well as spiritual directors and confessors.

The Bible likewise recognizes a faith-based, holistic vision of the person, and the use of the multiple human capacities: "You shall love the Lord your God with all your heart, and with all your soul, and with all your strength, and with all your mind; and your neighbor as yourself" (Lk 10:27; see also Deut 6:4–5; Lev 19:18).

Wholeness

How Does Human Wholeness Necessarily Include a Capacity for Transcendence?

The human person cannot be understood without references to his capacities to reach beyond himself to other persons and to God. Nor can the person be understood in terms of the transcendental quality of unity (*unum*), which underlies all that exists (Schmitz, 2009, pp. 11–14; Aquinas, 1259/1953, II.1.1). Nor can the person be understood apart from a recognition of the equality, difference, and complementarity of the sexes. Nor can the person be understood apart from an awareness of his capacity to act intelligently and in freedom. Consideration of work and recreation are also not enough. Although personal wholeness of the body-soul unity must include consideration of interpersonal, bodily, rational, and volitional domains, each person is unique in his or her own wholeness and his or her calls. The wholeness of this experience also involves, not merely an animal awareness, but the self-consciousness and awareness that transcend animal awareness. There is a still-higher level of transcendence, which is experienced however fleetingly in great love, goodness, truth, and beauty, and in religious and mystical experience (MacIntyre, 1999; Vitz, 2017). Near-death experience also clearly points to this transcendence (Alexander, 2012; Spitzer, 2015). In short, the human being receives the mysterious gift of life, which includes the capacity for self-transcendence and the vocation for communion with the ultimate good, who is God.

What Misreadings of Wholeness Threaten the Understanding of the Human Person?

As mentioned before, a whole and unified notion of the person avoids individualism (missing common human nature for interest in the uniqueness of each human being), materialism (denying the spiritual in order to credit the material), reductionism (taking partial observations of a phenomenon as the whole), determinism (focusing on necessity and limits without crediting genuine freedom), dualism (construing the distinctiveness of the human body and soul as separate natures, while losing sight of the wholeness of the person and the in-separability of human nature), and behaviorism (recognizing the importance of conduct without recognizing its internal mental origins and transcendent calling).

The whole view of the person will take what is positive in each of these misreadings—or rather, it will focus on the person with the expertise of each discipline and an eye open to what constitutes the whole truth of the person. Wholeness is served by all the disciplines, including the sciences, humanities, philosophy, and theology. From a faith-based perspective, John Paul II (1993a) recognizes that the work of the mental health professional draws near to

"the threshold of the human mystery" inasmuch as one approaches the wholeness of the person:

> The human person is a unity of body and spirit, possessing an inviolable dignity as one made in the image of God and called to a transcendent destiny. For this reason, the Church is convinced that *no adequate assessment of the nature of the human person or the requirements for human fulfillment and psycho-social well-being can be made without respect for man's spiritual dimension and capacity for self-transcendence.* (§2, emphasis in text)

The mystery is lost without reference to both transcendence and the whole person.

Conclusion

We will close this chapter with a special note on perspective and method. In the Meta-Model's philosophical vision of the person, we have chosen to start with personal wholeness in order to assure a point of departure that does not deviate toward a separatist dualism or a reductionism that would lead us very far astray

(Aristotle, ca. 350 BC/1941c, 271b10). Next, in analyzing the particular dimensions of the human person in the following chapters, we must continue to affirm that the human physical body and spiritual soul are one nature, inseparable (except through death), and always in relationship with other persons.

REFERENCES

Alexander, E. (2012). *Proof of heaven: A neurosurgeon's journey into the afterlife.* New York, NY: Simon & Schuster.

Aquinas, T. (1953). *The disputed questions on truth* (J. V. McGlynn, Trans.). Chicago, IL: Henry Regnery Co. (Original work composed 1256–1259)

Aquinas, T. (1981). *Summa theologiae.* (English Dominican Province, Trans.). Westminster, MD: Christian Classics. (Original work composed 1265–1273)

Aristotle. (1941a). *Metaphysics.* In R. McKeon (Ed.), *The basic works of Aristotle* (pp. 689–926). New York, NY: Random House. (Original work composed ca. 350 BC)

Aristotle. (1941b). *Nicomachean ethics.* In R. McKeon (Ed.), *The basic works of Aristotle* (pp. 935–1126).

New York, NY: Random House. (Original work composed ca. 350 BC)

Aristotle. (1941c). *On the heavens.* In R. McKeon (Ed.), *The basic works of Aristotle* (pp. 395–466). New York, NY: Random House. (Original work composed ca. 350 BC)

Aristotle. (1941d). *On the soul.* In R. McKeon (Ed.), *The basic works of Aristotle* (pp. 535–606). New York, NY: Random House. (Original work composed ca. 350 BC)

Aristotle. (1941e). *Physics.* In R. McKeon (Ed.), *The basic works of Aristotle* (pp. 218–394). New York, NY: Random House. (Original work composed ca. 350 BC)

Ashley, B. M. (1985). *Theologies of the body: Humanist and Christian.* Braintree, MA: The Pope John Center.

Ashley, B. M. (2006). *The way toward wisdom: An interdisciplinary and intercultural introduction to metaphysics.* Notre Dame, IN: University of Notre Dame.

Ashley, B. M. (2013). *Healing for freedom: A Christian perspective on personhood and psychotherapy.* Arlington, VA: The Institute for the Psychological Sciences Press.

Augustine. (1887). On the morals of the Catholic Church (R. Stothert, Trans.). In P. Schaff (Ed.), *Nicene and Post-Nicene Fathers, First Series, Vol. 4. Augustine—Anti-Manichaean writings* (pp. 41–63). Buffalo, NY: Christian Literature Publishing. (Original work composed 388)

Augustine. (1963). *The Trinity* (S. McKenna, Trans.). Washington DC: The Catholic University of America Press. (Original work composed 400–416)

Austriaco, N. P. G., Brent, J., Davenport, T., & Ku, J. B. (2016). *Thomistic evolution: A Catholic approach to understanding evolution in the light of faith.* Middletown, DE: Cluny Media.

Basil the Great. (1980). *On the Holy Spirit.* Crestwood, NY: St Vladimir's Seminary Press. (Original work composed ca. 375)

Beauregard, M. (2012). *Brain wars: The scientific battle over the existence of the mind and the proof that will change the way we live our lives.* New York, NY: HarperCollins.

Beauregard, M., & O'Leary, D. (2008). *The spiritual brain: A neuroscientist's case for the existence of the soul.* New York, NY: HarperCollins.

Berkeley, G. (2003). *A treatise concerning the principles of human knowledge.* La Salle, IL: Dover. (Original work published in 1710)

Berkman, J., & Titus, C. S. (Eds.). (2005). *The Pinckaers reader: Renewing Thomistic moral theology.* Washington, DC: The Catholic University of America Press.

Berwick, R. C., & Chomsky, N. (2016). *Why only us: Language and evolution.* Cambridge, MA: MIT Press.

Bikerton, D. (2014). *More than nature needs: Language, mind, and evolution.* Cambridge, MA: Harvard University Press.

Bowlby, J. (1973). *Attachment and loss: Vol. 2. Separation: Anxiety and anger.* New York, NY: Basic Books.

Bowlby, J. (1982). *Attachment and loss: Vol. 1. Attachment* (2nd ed.). New York, NY: Basic Books. (Original work published 1969)

Catechism of the Catholic Church (2nd ed.) [*CCC*]. (1997). Vatican City, Vatican: Libreria Editrice Vaticana.

Churchland, P. M. (2001). Toward a cognitive neurobiology of the moral virtues. In J. Branquinho (Ed.), *The foundations of cognitive science* (pp. 77–98). New York, NY: Oxford University Press.

Churchland, P. M. (2007). *Neurophilosophy at work.* New York, NY: Cambridge University Press.

Condic, M. (2009). When does human life begin? A scientific perspective. *The National Catholic Bioethics Quarterly, 9*(1), 129–149. doi:10.5840/ncbq20099184

Council of Vienne. (2012). *Constitution fidei catholicae.* In H. Denzinger & P. Hunermann (Eds.), *Enchiridion symbolorum: A compendium of creeds, definitions, and declarations of the Catholic Church* (43rd ed., pp. 289–290). San Francisco, CA: Ignatius Press. (Original work composed 1312)

Dawkins, R. (2008). *The God delusion.* New York, NY: Mariner Books.

Dennett, D. C. (1991). *Consciousness explained.* New York, NY: Little, Brown & Co.

Dennett, D. C. (1995). *Darwin's dangerous idea: Evolution and the meanings of life.* New York, NY: Simon & Schuster.

Descartes, R. (1983). *Principles of philosophy* (V. R. Miller & R. P. Miller, Trans.). New York, NY: Reidel. (Original work published in 1644)

Descartes, R. (1996). *Meditations on first philosophy: With selections from the objections and replies* (J. Cottingham, Trans.). Cambridge, United Kingdom: Cambridge University Press. (Original work published in 1641)

Dewan, L. (2006). St. Thomas, metaphysics, and formal causality. In *Form and being: Studies in Thomistic metaphysics* (pp. 131–166). Washington DC: The Catholic University of America Press.

Dietrich, E., & Hardcastle, V. G. (2004). Sisyphus's boulder: Consciousness and the limits of the knowable. Amsterdam, The Netherlands: John Benjamins.

Doidge, N. (2007). *The brain that changes itself: Stories of personal triumph from the frontiers of brain science.* New York, NY: Penguin.

Donne, J. (2012). *Meditation XVII. Devotions upon emergent occasions together with death's duel.* Ann Arbor, MI: The University of Michigan Press. (Original work published 1624)

Ellis, A. (1980). Psychotherapy and atheistic values: A response to A. E. Bergin's "Psychotherapy and religious values," *Journal of Consulting and Clinical Psychology, 48*(5), 635–639.

Ellis, A., & Ellis, D. J. (2011). *Rational emotive behavior therapy.* Washington, DC: American Psychological Association.

Emmons, R. A., & McCullough, M. E. (Eds.). (2004). *The psychology of gratitude* (Series in affective science). Oxford, United Kingdom: Oxford University Press.

Feser, E. (2006). *Philosophy of mind.* Oxford, United Kingdom: Oneworld Publications.

Feser, E. (2008). *The last superstition: A refutation of the new atheism.* South Bend, IN: St. Augustine Press.

Foster, J. (1989). A defence of dualism. In J. Smythies & J. Beloff (Eds.), *The case for dualism* (pp. 1–24). Charlottesville, VA: University of Virginia Press.

Foster, J. (1991). *The immaterial self: A defence of the Cartesian dualist conception of the mind.* New York, NY: Routledge.

Gazzaniga, M. S. (2006). *The ethical brain: The science of our moral dilemmas.* New York, NY: Harper Perennial.

Gazzaniga, M. S. (2011). *Who's in charge?: Free will and the science of the brain.* New York, NY: HarperCollins.

Goyette, J. (2009). St. Thomas on the unity of substantial form. *Nova et Vetera*, English Edition, 7(4), 781–90.

Huxley, T. H. (1917). Materialism and idealism. In C. D. Warner (Ed.), *Collected essays* (Vol. 1). New York, NY: Warner Library Co.

John Paul II. (1981). *Familiaris consortio* [Apostolic Exhortation, on the role of the Christian family in the modern world]. Vatican City, Vatican: Libreria Editrice Vaticana.

John Paul II. (1993a, January 4). Address of His Holiness John Paul II to the members of the American Psychiatric Association and the World Psychiatric Association. Vatican City, Vatican: Libreria Editrice Vaticana.

John Paul II. (1993b). *Veritatis splendor* [Encyclical, on certain fundamental questions of the Church's moral teaching]. Vatican City, Vatican: Libreria Editrice Vaticana.

John Paul II. (1995). *Evangelium vitae* [Encyclical, on the value and inviolability of human life]. Vatican City, Vatican: Libreria Editrice Vaticana.

John Paul II. (1998). *Fides et ratio* [Encyclical, on the relationship between faith and reason]. Vatican City, Vatican: Libreria Editrice Vaticana.

John Paul II. (2006). *Man and woman he created them: A theology of the body* (M. Waldstein, Trans.). Boston, MA: Pauline Books and Media.

Klein, R., & Edgar, B. (2002). *The dawn of human culture: A bold new theory that sparked the "big bang" of human consciousness.* New York, NY: Wiley.

Kohls, N., Sauer, S., Offenbächer, M., & Giordano, J. (2011). Spirituality: An overlooked predictor of placebo effects? *Philosophical Transactions: Biological Sciences, 366*(1572), 1838–1848.

Kuhse, H., & Singer, P. (1988). *Should the baby live?: The problem of handicapped infants.* Oxford, United Kingdom: Oxford University Press.

MacIntyre, A. (1999). *Dependent rational animals: Why human beings need the virtues.* Chicago, IL: Open Court.

MacIntyre, A. (2009). *God, philosophy, and universities: A selective history of the Catholic philosophical tradition.* Lanham, MD: Sheed & Ward.

Madden, J. D. (2013). *Mind, matter, and nature: A Thomistic proposal for the philosophy of mind.* Washington, DC: The Catholic University of America Press.

Maritain, J. (1952). *The range of reason.* New York, NY: Charles Scribner's Sons.

Maritain, J. (1972). *Distinguish to unite, or the degrees of knowledge* (G. B. Phelan, Trans.). London, United Kingdom: Geoffrey Bles. (Original work published 1932)

McAleer, G. (2012). *To kill another: Homicide and natural law.* New York, NY: Transaction Books.

Monod, J. (1971). *Chance and necessity: An essay on the natural philosophy of modern biology.* New York, NY: Knopf.

Nietzsche, F. (2006). *Thus spoke Zarathustra: A book for all and for none* (A. del Caro, Trans.). Cambridge, United Kingdom: Cambridge University Press. (Original work composed 1883–1885)

Nagel, T. (2012). *Mind and cosmos: Why the materialist*

neo-Darwinian conception of nature is almost certainly false. New York, NY: Oxford University Press.

Oderberg, D. S. (2005). Hylemorphic dualism. In E. F. Paul, F. D. Miller, & J. Paul (Eds.), *Personal identity* (pp. 70–99). New York: Cambridge University Press.

Otto, R. (1958). *The idea of the holy: An inquiry into the non-rational factor in the idea of the divine and its relation to the rational.* New York, NY: Oxford University Press.

Pakaluk, M. (2005). *Aristotle's* Nicomachean Ethics: *An introduction.* New York, NY: Cambridge University Press.

Piaget, J. (1929). *The child's conception of the world.* London, United Kingdom: Routledge & Kegan Paul.

Neisser, U. (Ed.) (1993). *The perceived self: Ecological and interpersonal sources of self-knowledge.* Cambridge, United Kingdom: Cambridge University Press.

Pieper, J. (2009). *Leisure: The basis of culture* (A. Dru, Trans.). San Francisco, CA: Ignatius Press. (Original work published 1952)

Pius XII. (1950). *Humani generis* [Encyclical, concerning some false opinions threatening to undermine the foundations of Catholic doctrine]. Vatican City, Vatican: Libreria Editrice Vaticana.

Polanyi, M. (1968). Life's irreducible structure. *Science, 160,* 1308–1312.

Robinson, H. (2016). Dualism. In E. N. Zalta (Ed.), *The Stanford encyclopedia of philosophy* (Fall 2017 ed.). Retrieved from https://plato.stanford.edu/archives/fall2017/entries/dualism/

Rogers, C. R. (2012). *On becoming a person: A therapist's view of psychotherapy.* Boston, MA: Houghton Mifflin Harcourt. (Original work published in 1961)

Sartre, J.-P. (2007). *Existentialism is a humanism* (C. Macomber, Trans.). New Haven, CT: Yale University Press. (Original work published 1946)

Schmitz, K. (2007). *The texture of being: Essays in first philosophy.* Washington, DC: The Catholic University of America Press.

Schmitz, K. (2009). *Person and psyche.* Arlington, VA: The Institute for the Psychological Sciences Press.

Schrödinger, E. (2012) *What is life?* New York, NY: Cambridge University Press. (Original work published 1944)

Scruton, R. (2014). *The soul of the world.* Princeton, NJ: Princeton University Press.

Scruton, R. (2017). *On human nature.* Princeton, NJ: Princeton University Press.

Sherwin, M. S. (2005). *By knowledge and by love: Charity and knowledge in the moral theology of St. Thomas Aquinas.* Washington, DC: The Catholic University of America Press.

Siegel, D. J. (2012). *Pocket guide to interpersonal neurobiology: An integrative handbook of the mind* (1st ed.). New York, NY: Norton.

Singer, P. (2011). *Practical ethics.* Cambridge, United Kingdom: Cambridge University Press. (Original work published 1980)

Snodgrass, J., & Thompson, R. (Eds.). (1997). *The self across psychology: Self-recognition, self-awareness, and the self concept.* New York, NY: New York Academy of Sciences.

Spitzer, R. (2015). *The soul's upward yearning: Clues to our transcendent nature from experience and reason.* San Francisco, CA: Ignatius Press.

Suddendorf, T. (2013). *The gap: The science of what separates us from other animals.* New York, NY: Basic Books.

Swinburne, R. (1997). *The evolution of the soul* (rev. ed.). Oxford, United Kingdom: Clarendon Press.

Tallis, R. (2011). *Aping mankind: Neuromania, Darwinitis and the misrepresentation of humanity.* Durham, United Kingdom: Acumen Press.

Tallis, R. (2013). *Reflections of a metaphysical flâneur and other essays.* Durham, United Kingdom: Acumen Press.

Vatican II, Council. (1965a). *Gaudium et spes* [Pastoral constitution on the Church in the modern world]. Vatican City, Vatican: Libreria Editrice Vaticana.

Vatican II, Council. (1965b). *Dei verbum* [Dogmatic constitution on Divine Revelation]. Vatican City, Vatican: Libreria Editrice Vaticana.

Vitz, P. (2011). The importance of fatherhood. In E. Metaxas (Ed.), *Socrates in the city: Conversations on "life, God, and other small topics"* (pp. 77–103). New York, NY: Dutton.

Vitz, P. C. (2017). The origin of consciousness in the integration of analog (right hemisphere) & digital (left hemisphere) codes. *Journal of Consciousness Exploration & Research, 8*(11), 881–906.

Vitz, P. C., & Felch, S. M. (Eds.). (2006). *The self:*

Beyond the postmodern crisis. Wilmington, DE: ISI Books.

Wilcox, W. B. (1999). Emerging attitudes about gender roles and fatherhood. In D. E. Eberly (Ed.), *The faith factor in fatherhood* (pp. 219–240). Lanham, MD: Lexington Books.

Wilson, E. O. (1975). *Sociobiology: The new synthesis.* Cambridge, MA: Belknap Press.

Wilson, E. O. (1998). *Consilience: The unity of knowledge.* New York, NY: Knopf.

Winnicott, D. W. (1958). *Through paediatrics to psycho-analysis.* London, United Kingdom: Hogarth Press.

Wojtyła, K. (1993). *Love and responsibility* (H. T. Willetts, Trans.). San Francisco, CA: Ignatius Press. (Original work published 1960)

Życiński, J. (2006). *God and evolution: Fundamental questions of Christian evolutionism* (K. W. Kemp & Z. Maślanka, Trans.). Washington, DC: The Catholic University of America Press.

Chapter 9

Man and Woman

Equality, Differences, and Complementarity, with Application to Vocations and Virtues, Especially Courage

CHRISTOPHER GROSS, LISA KLEWICKI, PAUL C. VITZ,
AND CRAIG STEVEN TITUS

ABSTRACT: This chapter proposes that men and women possess equal, innate dignity, while also possessing significant differences that serve as the foundation for their complementarity. In accordance with the Catholic Christian Meta-Model of the Person, this chapter examines the equality, difference, and complementarity of the sexes from the perspective of the psychological sciences, philosophy, and theology. It maintains that the psychological sciences, drawing from neuroscience and clinical observations, contribute to an understanding of the equality, difference, and complementarity of the sexes. It also provides examples of how this approach to treating men and women has implications for mental health practice. Considered from a philosophical perspective, since men and women are different, and because the person is a unity of both body and soul, sex difference affects many important areas of the person's life, among them the way in which individuals live out their vocations. Yet in their differences, men and women complement each other on physical and biological levels, in psychological and social tendencies, and in ethical and spiritual dispositions. From the theological perspective, men and women are both created in the image and likeness of God; therefore, they each share a basic human dignity and equality. However, this equality does not imply sameness. This chapter explores, as an example, the complementarity found in the masculine and feminine expressions of acquired natural and infused virtues and life-callings (vocations). Throughout, the chapter will focus on these two levels of callings and virtues, with special attention on courage (fortitude). Different expressions of vices in men and women are also briefly considered.

This chapter examines how men and women share a common human nature, are equal in dignity, and have important differences due to their creation as men and women, and that these differences are not random, but instead represent a purposeful complementarity. It employs a science-based, reason-based, and faith-based approach to discussing the sexes. The Meta-Model affirms that, in addition to similarities between men and women, there are important natural sex differences and a purposeful complementarity between males and females, as especially seen in the complementarity found in the male and female expressions of virtues and life-callings.

First, the chapter addresses the equality of dignity of the sexes. This equality is recognized in the disciplines of psychology, counseling, and other mental health fields within their respective codes of conduct (American Psychological Association [APA], 2017; American Counseling Association [ACA], 2014; National Association of Social Workers, 2017; American Association for Marriage and Family Therapy, 2015). It is also implicit in much recent neuroscience (Brizendine, 2006, 2010). Considered from the reason-based and realist metaphysical perspective of the Meta-Model, men and women share a common humanity or human nature, which gives them equal basic dignity and worth, and a shared basis for rights and moral responsibility (Wojtyła, 2011). From a theological perspective, the equality of the sexes is rooted in their relationship to God. Both men and women are created in the image and likeness of God (Gen 1:27), which serves as the ultimate foundation for their equality and dignity. Yet, God chose to enter difference and complementarity into human history by creating and distinguishing between man and woman.

The equality of the sexes has not always been recognized or reflected in practice and legislation. A deeply rooted notion of equality does not itself correct the discrimination that has arisen from presumptions that men were biologically and intellectually superior to women and, therefore, that women had fewer rights than men. For example, such presumptions are found in works of Aristotle (ca. 350 BC/1943, II, 3, 737a27–28) and Aquinas (1273/1981, III, 31.4; also I, 92.1).

The discovery that women and men contributed equally to the genetic makeup of the child was not known until the development of modern science. Prior to that discovery, men were assumed to be the only source or seed of the child. In part because of these presuppositions, historically in many cultures women have had fewer civil rights, such as the right to property ownership, to hold public offices, and to vote.

Historical injustices and philosophical errors, however, should not be taken to disprove the fact that from the beginning of the human race the natural moral law, which underlies the person's basic dignity, natural inclinations, conscience, practical reason, and call to goodness, has been and remains common to all people, both men and women. In an effort to advocate for equality, many feminists and some psychologists, philosophers, and theologians mistakenly have equated equality with sameness, ignoring or rejecting any differences between the sexes beyond obvious physical differences (William, 1982). Thus, they have sometimes seen the concept of complementarity as disparaging or in conflict with the idea of equal dignity. As we will explain later, this notion of sameness is inconsistent with the biological, neurological, psychological, and sociological evidence.

While affirming the equality of men and women, this chapter also proposes that there are important differences between the sexes. The differences are discerned in experience, specified by neuroscience, and supported by the Christian tradition. These sex differences are found in the expression of one's physical, psychological, moral, social, and spiritual capacities, as well as in the expression of one's life-callings (vocations) and virtues. These differences as well as shared capacities are grounded in our human nature, although some of the differences can be either highlighted or clouded by cultural practices.

In our discussion of difference, we seek to avoid biases and stereotypes, while at the same time identifying both common and distinct natural tendencies of each of the sexes. The avoidance of biases and stereotypes is accomplished by reflection on the fact that each person, man or woman, is ultimately a unique, unrepeatable creation who is willed by God and called through his or her uniqueness to know, love, and serve him in this world and the next.

These characteristics of sex differences include what is generally obvious, such as the biological and morphological differences of the body (genes, organs, hormones, as well as the development of the brain, dispositions, and behaviors). There are also the less obvious differences concerning styles of using language, processing emotions, solving problems, relating to others, and displaying skills (Baron-Cohen, 2003; Brizendine, 2006, 2010; Budziszewski, 2012; Buss, 2015; Christen, 1991; Ellis et al., 2008; Geary, 2010; Gurian, 2011; Harley, 2011; Larimore & Larimore, 2008; Norfleet, 2007, 2012; Rhoads, 2004; Tannen, 1990).

These differences also serve as the foundation for complementarity between the sexes, which is the focus of the third main section of this chapter. The contention of the Catholic Christian Meta-Model is that this complementarity is purposeful, involves a personal calling, is willed by God, and thus is not simply a result of randomness or evolutionary processes. There is a synthetic meaning in sex differences and sexual acts (Budziszewski, 2012). To say that males and females are complementary is to say that when taken together they provide a synergy that is a greater good than when they are considered as separate and different without respect to their relevance for the other. Complementarity speaks to the ordering of human nature and the human person toward different expressions of flourishing through vocations and in virtue. Such flourishing includes the specifically spousal vocations to procreation and unity, which support life-long commitments and family life and involve conjugal sexual acts, and which include parental vocation.

Complementarity also speaks to other vocational states, such as the vocation to being a single man or a single woman, and furthermore of those called to consecrated or priestly vocations. Complementarity is also present in the non-spousal relationships that include other types of friendship, shared activities, emotional bonding, and self-giving. Globally speaking, male and female complementarity can be studied at different levels, such as the physical (biology and neurosciences), the psychological (psychology and counseling), the social (sociology), the existing or ontological (metaphysics or ontology), the moral (ethics), and the transcendent revealed levels (spirituality and theology).

A full explanation of the equality, differences, and complementarity of the sexes will come neither from the sciences alone (for instance, from attachment theory or evolutionary theory), nor from fallen human nature alone, nor from revelation and spirituality alone (that is, God's original intent to create man and woman for each other in mutual self-gift). All these perspectives taken together, however, contribute to our understanding better how humans develop into flourishing men and women and how they are called to contribute to each other's growth, healing, and goodness at natural and transcendent levels and in the light of life-callings and virtues. Therefore, this chapter considers sex difference from a biological, psychological, philosophical, and theological perspective, examining the equality, difference, and complementarity of men and women according to each discipline.

Men and Women as Equal

Each of the Meta-Model's premises is informed by the reality that men and women are equal in dignity, and that they possess the same aspects of basic human nature. Each person is created, fallen, and redeemed, is a unified whole, fulfilled through vocations and in virtue, interpersonally relational, sensory-perceptual-cognitive, emotional, rational, and volitional and free. However, equality here is not synonymous with sameness. Men and women are equal in dignity and value, and thus they have an unalienable right to the same respect, even though they are different in the many ways that the basic aspects and capacities of their personhood are manifested. This section considers how such equality is understood and supported by biology, psychology, philosophy, and theology.

How Is Equality Between Men and Women Understood from a Psychological Perspective?

Most personality theories have not distinguished between equality and sameness of the person. This sameness of the sexes is implied by the fact that such theories make no distinctions based on whether a person is male or female. Important theories of this kind are those developed by Alfred Adler, Eric Erikson, Gordon Allport, Carl Rogers, Abraham Maslow, and Lawrence Kohlberg. Other theorists, as shown in textbooks on personality theory, whose concepts of the person are primarily unisex are Anna Freud, Margaret Mahler, Melanie Klein, D. W. Winnicott, Heinz Kohut, Harry Stack Sullivan, Karen Horney, Rollo May, Viktor Frankl, George Kelly, and Albert Bandura. These early founders of modern psychology range in theoretical orientation from psychoanalysts to existentialists to social psychologists to test-and-measurement

psychologists. While occasionally these theorists addressed gender issues, such as when criticizing Sigmund Freud, none of them introduced male and female difference into basic theoretical concepts. Thus, there has been an implicit and widespread assumption in psychology that there is no difference in men and women (a "no-difference" assumption).

One partial exception to the above list is Carl Jung (Jacobi, 1973, pp. 114–124; Sollod, Wilson, & Monte, 2009, pp. 164–165), who clearly identifies male and female archetypes as important to understanding a person. Nonetheless, in Jung's framework all persons are somewhat androgynous. In addition, although *animus* and *anima* are different, they are considered equally important for understanding individual personality and for their relevance to clinical practice.

The one significant exception to the preceding list of personality theorists is Sigmund Freud (Freud, 1961, pp. 26–30; 1931, p. 230; Sollod, Wilson, & Monte, 2009, pp 54–62.), who places sex differences at the center of one of his major concepts, the Oedipus complex. Freud emphasizes male psychology, as in the Oedipus complex, and in general appears to believe in male superiority.

Other evidence for the general tendency of psychology to assume that no difference exists between the sexes can be found in the original Binet IQ test that was developed around one hundred years ago. The authors of the test assumed men and women were equal in intelligence and constructed the overall IQ measure from a group of different subtests that often showed differences between males and females. However, these subtest scores were combined into a general score, and this average IQ score turned out to be the same for boys and girls or for men and women of the same age. This process thus masked the differences existing across the sexes.

The Diagnostic and Statistical Manual of Mental Disorders (DSM-5), the official manual of mental disorders, used by psychiatrists, psychologists, counselors, and many other mental health practitioners (American Psychiatric Association, 2013) assumes respect for the value and dignity of the person whether man or woman; there is no hint of male or female superiority, and hence equality in this general sense is assumed. Furthermore, the DSM assumes no sex differences exist between men and women with regard to mental disorders unless observation and research clearly demonstrate otherwise. (The many sex differences identified in the DSM are taken up in the next section.) For example, for many disorders, there is no mention of a possible difference, and thus the assumption of no difference or equality is implicit. In some major disorders, the no-difference assumption based on considerable research is made explicit, such as with schizophrenia (American Psychiatric Association, 2013, p. 102), which occurs almost equally in men and women. In such cases, the sameness or no-difference distinction between men and women is made according to both sexes' endorsement of a common, limited set of symptoms that are identified rather reductionistically as defining the whole experience of the psychological disorder, rather than as data to be considered at broader levels of analysis. For example, one could certainly wonder whether an infertile married couple's experience of depression is really identical for both the wife and husband even when they share some common symptoms such as sadness, deficits in sleeping, or loss of appetite.

As for neuroscience and, with it, medicine (except for the well-known observable physical and reproductive differences), the basic assumption has also been that there is no difference between the sexes—for example between male and female kidneys, blood, lungs, heart, and so on (recently basic, physiological differences between the sexes have been discovered; Ellis et al., 2008; MacDonald, 2018). And, of course, the American Medical Society certainly assumes that men and women are of equal value and that ensuring the health of either sex is equally important.

Within mental health practice, there too is assumed equal respect for the rights and welfare of men and women. For instance, the American Psychological Association's *Ethical Principles of Psychologists and Code of Conduct* states that psychologists strive to "safeguard the welfare and rights of those with whom they interact professionally" (APA, 2017, Principle A). The *Ethical Principles* go on to state that psychologists do not engage in discrimination based upon many factors, gender being one of them (APA, 2017, §3.01). This principle of non-discrimination is also contained in the *American Counseling Association Code of Ethics* (ACA, 2014, C.5). Thus, in helping people with whom mental health professionals work and avoiding harm to all persons, there is an implied concept of equal dignity among both men and women.

In addition, while psychology and counseling also stress the need to treat all people with dignity and respect, they also emphasize a need to build a therapeutic alliance with all clients. This therapeutic relationship is essential no matter what type of treatment modality one is using (van Kaam, 1966; Rogers, 1951). A key component of building a healthy therapeutic relationship with clients is treating all people with equal dignity and respect. This is especially true of the three basic elements that Carl Rogers (1951) proclaims for the good therapist:

genuineness, unconditional positive regard, and empathy. These three core conditions for doing person-centered therapy require men and women to be treated with equal dignity and respect. Nonetheless, it is common in the everyday practice of mental health professionals to take into account the sex of the therapist in decisions around the therapist-client fit. For example, in cases where a male child who has been abandoned long ago by his father and who is being raised by a single-parent mother, it is not uncommon to consider whether a male therapist might be advantageous.

How Is Equality Between Men and Women Understood from a Philosophical Perspective?

Arguing for female uniqueness and even superiority, some radical feminists deny that there is a common, basic human nature (Butler, 1999; Daly, 1968, 1984). However, the Catholic Christian vision of the person affirms that there is a common human nature. There are, at the same time, sexually differentiated expressions of that nature, namely male and female. The equality of the sexes is rooted in their shared human nature, but that shared nature is lived out in sexually differentiated bodies. Because the person is a unity of body and soul, our male and female bodies affect our souls—both the psychological and spiritual aspects of each person—and our souls affect our bodies (Chapter 8, "Personal Wholeness"). Men and women are seen as equal yet unique in their expressions of intelligence and in their use of reason and will (Chapter 15, "Rational," and Chapter 16, "Volitional and Free"). They also possess the same sensory-perceptual-cognitive and emotional abilities, although these are influenced by their sexually differentiated bodies.

Within each of these capacities, both men and women have the power to form either virtuous or vicious habitual dispositions through their actions and with the help of role models. For example, the virtue of courage (fortitude) perfects our initiative-taking emotions, especially fear and daring (Aquinas, 1273/1981, I-II, 23.4). Courage also has interpersonal, cognitive, and behavioral dimensions. These dimensions of the virtue enable us to accompany others in their challenges, recognize how to react well to obstacles, and act and endure to attain a difficult goal (see Figure 9.1 for an overview). Both men and women need the virtue of courage in order to flourish, and both are equal in their ability to develop this virtue. Similarly, both sexes can suffer from excess or defects in dimensions of the virtue of courage that cause them to act poorly.

While the analysis here focuses on the virtue of courage, it applies to all virtues. Since men and women share the same basic human nature and thus the same basic capacities, they can each acquire the virtues, including courage, temperance, justice, and prudence, that hone and refine those capacities. Every person, regardless of sex, is called to a flourishing life that is fulfilled through virtues (Aristotle, ca. 350 BC/1941, Book I; Peterson & Seligman, 2004).

How Is Equality Between Men and Women Understood from a Theological Perspective?

From the Christian, faith-based perspective, the two creation accounts in the book of Genesis provide foundational truths concerning the equality of dignity and differences of the sexes. These chapters of Genesis are not scientific observations (or quantified data) but rather faith- and wisdom-based accounts that give us information about the interpersonal relationships and vocations as well as the missions and purposes of each person. These accounts address

Figure 9.1. The Virtue of Courage: Basic Expression with Focus on Fear

Courage

Excess in Fear

Deficit in Fear

The virtue of courage engages reasoned initiative taking and endurance while employing the emotions, especially fear and daring, to address difficulty in attaining good or in avoiding evil.

Courage requires excellence in:

E1. Excess or too much fear (**emotion**): overly fearful.

E2. Excess fear in **relational** dimension, in goals and being a role model: not helping others to stand up for what is right in difficulty; withdrawing support.

E3. Excess in **congitive** expression of fear. Erroneous discernment or calculation in responding to difficulty because of fearlfulness.

E4. Excess of fear in **action**: cowardice or spinelessness when facing difficulty (imprudent behavior).

1. Balanced use of **emotions**, especially fear and daring, in attaining the difficult good.

2. Balanced use of pro-social skills, mentoring, and goals in attaining the difficult good, while accompanying others to face difficulty as well (**interpersonally relational**.)

3. Wisely recognizing what can be done to minimize, stop, or intelligently address the difficulty (**congitive**).

4. Good **action** is fitting to attain the difficult goal by initiative taking and enduring (prudent behavior).

D1. Deficit or too little fear (**emotion**): overly fearless.

D2. Deficit in **relational** dimension in terms of goals and being a role model: overconfidence in the group's ability to overcome adversity.

D3. Deficit in **cognitive** expression of fear. Erroneous discernment or calculation in responding to difficulty because of fearlessness and rashness.

D4. Deficit in **action**: recklessness when facing difficulty (imprudent behavior).

the call to flourishing and indicate the ways that humans may experience trauma, psychologically suffer, and morally fail. The first creation account demonstrates the equality of the sexes, while the second account identifies the differences (as we will discuss further, later in the chapter).

In the first creation account, God not only creates both man and woman, but he creates each in his own image. "God created man in his own image, in the image of God he created him; male and female he created them" (Gen 1:27). After their creation, both receive a common blessing and share a common mission: to care for offspring and be good stewards of the earth (Gen

1:28–30; see also John Paul II, 2006, pp. 134–137). After giving this blessing, God looks over all that he has created, including man and woman, and he declares all of creation "very good" (Gen 1:31). In being created in God's image, both man and woman are in their very nature good. Thus, the first creation account contains no support for the notion that men are superior to women; rather, it stresses, in a myriad of ways, the inherent equality of dignity and goodness of the sexes, as does all of Scripture (International Theological Commission, 2004, §36).

In addition to this basic human equality of men and women that comes from being created in the image of God, there is also the equality that comes in Baptism. As St. Paul says in his letter to the Galatians (3:28), in being one in Christ, there is neither "Jew nor Greek, there is neither slave nor free, there is neither male nor female; for you are all one in Christ Jesus." St. Paul does not mean that our maleness or femaleness no longer matters after Baptism. Rather, he is "affirming that no human differences can impede our participation in the mystery of Christ" (International Theological Commission, 2004, §35). Through the sacrament, we are all made

sons and daughters of God, regardless of our race or sex (Gal 3:27).

St. Paul also points to the equality of men and women in the sacrament of Marriage, encouraging both husbands and wives to be "subject to one another out of reverence for Christ" (Eph 5:21). As part of this mutual service (subjection and self-giving) and exercise of sanctification, he calls husbands to follow the example of Christ, particularly the unselfish love that Christ embodies on the cross. He also calls wives to follow the example of the Church, which follows Christ out of a similar unselfish love (Eph 5:22–28). Men and women are called to share equally in willingly offering service and guidance to each other. With their shared service and guidance, each spouse is called to self-giving love that serves their union and their growth in holiness (John Paul II, 1988, §24).

The call to goodness is universal, as is the call to work and to a vocational state as married, religious, or single (Chapter 10, "Fulfilled Through Vocation"). Men and women have an inherent equality that is based on their common nature and on their shared call to goodness, communion, and self-gift.

Men and Women as Different

The previous section considered, from psychological, philosophical, and theological perspectives, how men and women are equal. One of the central claims of this chapter is that being equal in dignity and rights does not mean sameness in other regards. Men and women are also different, having unique responsibilities and particular vocations. This section turns to consider the meaning, types, and extent of sex differences according to social constructionist, essentialist, and Catholic Christian perspectives.

Sex differences are undeniable, but positions differ concerning the origins and implications

of those differences. For example, social constructionists maintain that the only difference between men and women are superficial physical differences. For advocates of this position, other sex differences are a product of culture. They are not rooted in biology but are socially constructed (Gross, 2013). According to Nelson (1992), the

social constructionist approach emphasizes our active roles as agents, influenced by culture, in structuring our bodily realities. It recognizes that the concepts and categories we use to describe and define our experience vary considerably in their meanings over time and among different cultures and subcultures. (p. 46)

Social constructionists do not believe that there are any fixed characteristics of men and women beyond basic anatomy, which is of minor consequence. The apparent fixed characteristics that initially seem to be significant differences between men and women (for example, that women are more interpersonally attentive and sensitive) are just the product of socialization (Gross, 2013).

Social constructionism is built upon a distinction between sex and gender. While sex is merely biological, gender signifies how culture influences our views of masculinity and femininity, including the roles and characteristics that supposedly are appropriate for men and women (Gross, 2013; Miller & Swift, 1976; for a nonreductionist view, see Grabowski, 2003). According to the constructionist view, the lie of substantial sexual differences has been advanced by patriarchal cultures to justify the oppression of women. In reality, other than their physical differences, men and women are the same (Williams, 1982; Gross, 2013).

Essentialists maintain "that men have certain identifiable, fixed characteristics, and women have other identifiable, fixed characteristics, and that these identifiers are rooted in our very nature" (Storkey, 2001, pp. 25–26). There are different forms of essentialism. For example, strong essentialism holds that society has little impact on sex difference; rather differences are innate and largely determine behavior. Because the theory does not adequately account for how sex differences are influenced by culture, strong essentialism borders on biological determinism (Gross, 2013).

The Catholic Christian Meta-Model of the Person rejects both strong essentialism and social constructionism. It acknowledges that sex differences are innate and a part of the whole experience of the person, a part that society does not create. However, it also recognizes that cultural, environmental, and nurturing factors can reinforce, ignore, or downplay these differences (Christen, 1991; Gross, 2013).

How Is Sex Difference Understood from a Psychological Perspective?

Despite the widespread no-difference assumption found in the work of many important figures in psychology, significant sex differences have become much better understood in the last few decades, thanks to a large number of psychological and scientific studies. For example, these studies indicate that from infancy, girls are much more interpersonally oriented than boys (Sandberg & Meyer-Bahlburg, 1994). They look at faces more, smile and talk earlier, and are much more responsive to people in general. Studies also have shown that women—more than men—tend to *verbally* express themselves to other people, express emotions and seek emotional support, discuss problems, and encourage themselves (Tamres, Janicki, & Helgeson, 2002, p. 2). Moreover, while the most typical responses to stress have long been identified as "fight or flight" (Brizendine, 2010; Ong, 1981), recently a more female type of response to stress has been noted and called "tend and befriend" (Taylor et al., 2000). In this way, a woman reaches out to another to care for the person in distress, engaging them in relationship (Gilligan, 1982; Taylor et al., 2000). Taylor et al. (2000) identify in "tend and befriend" behavior the effect of the bonding hormone oxytocin, which will be discussed later in this chapter.

Because of their interpersonal orientation, girls show more emotional empathy than do boys, who display more cognitive empathy (Baron-Cohen, 2003). For example, Simner

(1971) found that infant girls cried longer than infant boys when exposed to the cry of another infant, but there was no sex difference in such crying when babies were exposed to a loud artificial noise. Thus, infant girls are able to distinguish the types of crying of others and show more empathy for another's pain.

Men tend to be better at spatial tasks than women are, desire to compete more, and generally are less emotionally empathetic. Studies "confirm that boys organize themselves into much larger social groups than do girls, engage in intergroup competition once such groups are formed, form within group hierarchies, and show within group differentiation and specialization" (Geary, 2010, p. 304; see also Eder & Hallinan, 1978; Lever, 1978). Still other research has shown that boys begin to show a preference for group-level activities over dyadic ones as early as 3 years of age, show strong bias against members of competing groups by 5 years of age, and consistently form larger groups than girls by 6 years (Geary, 2010, p. 304; see also Benenson, 1993; Rose & Rudolph, 2006). In many respects, the differences between men and women are shown by the strong evidence that men show a preference for objects and things; women, for people and relationships (Su, Rounds, & Armstrong, 2009).

Men also are reliably more aggressive, which can have the advantage of their being able to protect and advance a family's welfare, and they are also risk takers; furthermore, new approaches and ideas are more often pioneered by men (Charness & Gneezy, 2012; Harris, Jenkins & Glaser, 2006). On the down side, aggression, risky behaviors, and new ideas that are false, mistaken, or premature can result in death, personal failure, and so on. Young men are especially prone to risk taking, which is shown in statistics: The accidental death rates of young men are much higher than those of young women. In addition, men in many careers are more confident or even overconfident compared to women in the same careers (Schulz & Thöni, 2016).

For women, their spouses, their lovers, their children, and their friends are typically central to their sense of well-being, because they are much more focused on personal relationships. Women base their achievement on those positive interpersonal relationships, while men mostly seek achievement in the outside world. It is not surprising, then, that women are more fearful of social exclusion than men (Benenson et al., 2013).

Women's sexuality is also more interpersonal (Oliver & Hyde, 1993). While men can more easily separate sex and emotional intimacy, for women the two are more interconnected (Gross, 2013). Women seek companionship and intimacy as part of sexual relationships. Payne (2001) notes that even though some feminists have claimed that women can be as cavalier about sex as men, "males still see sexual intercourse as a way to achieve pleasure and please their partner, while females still view it as a way to achieve emotional closeness" (pp. 100–101). Regnerus and Uecker (2011) found similar positions among men and women in their research. They discovered that "women, on average, don't want to *have sex with*. They want to be made love to" (p. 152). They go on to add, "Being made love to implies a secure relationship and puts the focus on the benefits of the act" (Regnerus & Uecker, 2011, p. 152). For women (in comparison to men) there is a much stronger connection between physical, sexual intimacy and emotional intimacy (Gross, 2013).

While numerous studies have identified the emotional component of women's sexual desire, other studies have demonstrated that men's sexual desire typically is driven more by visual stimulation than by emotional intimacy (Gross, 2013; Wood, Koch, & Mansfield, 2006). This strong connection between visual stimulation and sexual arousal in men can be seen in the disproportionate male interest in pornography (Ogas & Gaddam, 2012). Men are also more likely to spend money on sexual products and activities, including prostitution, and they masturbate more frequently and at an earlier age. Aggression, in men, is also more strongly connected to sexuality than it is in women. This connection is shown in individual self-concepts, initiation of sex, and in coercive sex (Peplau, 2003).

How does neuroscience identify sex differences? There is now a large amount of evidence from biochemical and brain studies supporting the conclusion that women in general are much more people-oriented than men. Male and female brains appear to be wired differently in a way that supports the general sex difference interpretation (Ingalhalikar et al., 2014). Women's brains were found to be more connected across the corpus callosum, that is, women are highly connected across left and right hemispheres. These lateral connections indicate that women would generally be better at social skills, interpersonal remembering, and multitasking. Conversely, men's brains are much more connected between front and back regions of the brain and typically in only one hemisphere. Thus, men seem wired for perception and coordinated physical actions and not surprisingly have a better sense of direction (Pintzka, Evensmoen, Lehn, & Håberg, 2016).

Women also have better memories for episodic events, that is, events usually involving other persons and their activities and interactions with them (Herlitz & Rehnman, 2008). They also have better memories for faces. Women have richer autobiographical memories of experiences (Andreano & Cahill, 2009) and

a more detailed memory of them (Pillemer, Wink, DiDonato, & Sanborn, 2003). In addition, they are more accurate with respect to the dates of life events (Skowronski, Betz, Thompson, & Shannon, 1991). Again, we see evidence for women's unique interpersonal skills. Men have a better memory for facts and abstract ideas, such as the capital city of major countries or the value of pi to five decimals or Laffer's curve of tax rates and income (Gurian, 2011, p. 27). We thus see evidence for men's and women's strengths in differing memory skills.

Furthermore, men's brains are more modular than women's. Modularity means that men's brains appear to organize types of mental processing into more specific, localized brain areas than do women (Ingalhalikar et al., 2014; Tunç et al., 2016; Yeo et al., 2015). Modularity combined with a tendency to function much more in one hemisphere could explain why men are also more distressed at being interrupted (Vitz, personal communication, May 2018). They presumably need to travel a longer internal neural distance to address the interruption plus the effort needed to escape from their focus in a particular task-based module. For women, crossing the corpus callosum is much easier, and, being less module-based, they can more quickly move from one task to another even if they stay in the same hemisphere. From observation, women dealing with interpersonal relationships cope more easily with interruptions without showing irritation or hostility.

Another distinctively female characteristic is greater expressed emotionality (Geary, 2010, p. 259). The recent evidence from neuroscience gives it a much firmer foundation in the adult female body. This expressed emotionality is there from the start in girls, but it is greatly increased during puberty. It also is sometimes affected by a woman's monthly cycle. A variety of different behaviors have been found to vary with a woman's monthly cycle and its hormone-induced mood swings, as well as with other fluctuating hormones (see for further discussion, Durante, Rae, & Griskevicius, 2013; Eisenbruch, Simmons, & Roney, 2015; Grebe, Gangestad, Garver-Apgar, & Thornhill, 2013).

Some might argue that although women are more expressive of emotion, men are just as emotional but do not express it. There may be some truth to this, but even so it demonstrates a major difference in the behavior of men and women. There is also some neurological evidence that men are, on average, in fact less emotional than women. For example, we know that autism, much more common in men, reduces the ability to empathize and to understand that other people have emotions and intentions (Baron-Cohen, 2003). In addition, individuals with antisocial personality disorder, also more commonly male, often appear to have little capacity to empathize with others (American Psychiatric Association, 2013, pp. 660–662). These facts demonstrate certain sex differences, even if they should not be taken as the measure of the healthy male population.

One major male emotion that may qualify the generalization about women is the emotion of anger, which seems to be much more commonly expressed by men (Archer, 2004). While men tend to experience and express anger more directly, there is reason to assume that women experience anger as often as men but less frequently visibly express this emotion (Benenson et al., 2013; Ellis et al., 2008 Kring, 2000). In addition to different cultural influences on the expression of emotions and anger in particular, there are also indications that the aggressive male tendencies may lead to expressing anger in exaggerated ways, while caring female tenden-

cies may lead to more subdued expressions of anger (Benenson, 2013; Kring, 2000).

Another aspect of female emotionality is that women can change their emotional state more easily than men. This characteristic is probably another effect facilitated by the bridging of the corpus callosum. In addition, the female brain tends to find its resting state in the limbic system, which contains major emotional structures, while the male brain tends to find its resting state in the medulla oblongata, which is less associated with emotion and more focused on immediate behavioral response (Brizendine, 2006, 2010).

In understanding women's emotions, it is important to recall the bonding hormone oxytocin, which facilitates peaceful moods, trusting relationships, and interpersonal bonding. It is released during birth, nursing, and orgasm, as well as during exercise, listening to music, and many intimate interactions, such as hugs. Finally, the character of a woman's emotional life goes through a last hormone-induced change during and after menopause. This latter change typically involves a decline in preoccupation with others combined with a greater focus and concern with the self (Brizendine, 2006; Zak, 2012).

Cozolino (2006) presents evidence that a mother's attachment to her child is similar to an addiction, since biochemicals and brain structures similar to those in drug addiction are involved. "Research with primates suggests that the activation of the opioid systems of mother and child propels and regulates the attachment process. When [female] primates come together for contact, grooming, or play, endorphin levels increase in both parent and child" (Cozolino, 2006, p. 119; see also Keverne, Martensz, & Tuite, 1989). Also, "Human mothers often report feeling distress, anxiety, and sadness when [they are] separated from their newborns. In large part, this response is caused by the precipitous declines in endorphin levels that are triggered by separation" (Cozolino, 2006, p. 119). Many of a mother's rewards come from her response to her children and to others, but it is clear that important rewards hinge on her body, specifically on endogenous opioid hormones.

The female brain actually changes during pregnancy. The amygdala, so important in emotion and its regulation, and also the brain areas involved in response to faces, both actually get larger during pregnancy (this is part of what is sometimes called the "mommy brain"; see Brizendine, 2006, pp. 95–116). Not only does the birth of the baby trigger positive nurturing from the mother, but the mother has, not surprisingly, positive effects on the baby's nervous system before, during, and after birth. The mother's presence also has a positive effect on affect regulation and the amygdala in children (see Gee et al., 2014; Siegel, 2012). There is very recent evidence that pregnancy changes a woman's brain for up to two years (Hoekzema et al., 2016).

Men are also affected by hormones, such as testosterone. These effects often combine with other hormones as well (see Brizendine, 2010; Eisenegger, Hausehofer, & Fehr, 2012; Mazur & Booth, 1998; Shepherd, Farrington, & Potts, 2004).

What are the clinical implications of sex difference? The growing recognition of sex difference is clear in the evolution of the DSM. While the first DSM, which was published in 1952, makes no references to sex or gender differences at all, sex differences are prominently featured in the DSM-5 (American Psychiatric Association, 2013).

In this manual a large number of the mental disorders listed note either that a given disorder is more common in one sex or that the same disorder is manifested in different ways by each

sex. For example, there is a higher prevalence of depressive disorders in females (American Psychiatric Association, 2013, p. 167), and panic disorder, agoraphobia, and generalized anxiety are all more common in women (p. 216, p. 219, p. 224); also, anorexia nervosa and bulimia nervosa are much more common in females (p. 341, p. 347). In contrast, neuro-developmental disorders (American Psychiatric Association, 2013, p. 57), substance-related disorders (p. 495), and paraphilic disorders are much more common in men (pp. 688–703); in addition, men tend to suffer more frequently from disruptive, impulse-control, and conduct disorders (p. 461). It is also important to note that some disorders have different patterns of expressions in men and women. For instance, with dissociative identity disorders, females show more flashbacks, amnesia, hallucinations, and self-mutilation, while males display more criminal or violent behaviors (American Psychiatric Association, 2013, p. 295).

A recent article by Fossati et al. (2016) provides considerable support for this analysis of sex differences in the DSM-5. In their thorough evaluation of the DSM-5 alternative model of personality disorders involving different kinds of measures, they found many significant sex differences. For example, men showed more restricted affectivity, more withdrawal, and also more antagonism, for instance callousness and grandiosity. They also scored higher in risk taking, and they judged relationships as secondary. In contrast, women scored higher in anxiousness, emotional lability, agreeableness, neuroticism, and preoccupation with relationships.

Our analysis here is similar but with a slightly different emphasis. In general, when one examines sex differences in the DSM-5, men tend to show much more pathological external behavior, often violent or sexual, as expressed in neuro-developmental disorders, disruptive-impulsive disorders, substance abuse, and sexually deviant disorders; females generally show more emotion-based disorders, such as depression, anxieties, and eating and sleep-wakefulness disorders. Although, it should be noted, there is significant overlap between males and females in both generalities. These findings, along with the fact that some disorders take a different pattern of expression in each sex, negate the assumption that there are no significant mental or psychological differences between men and women.

With regard to the clinical treatment of male and female differences, the APA in 2007 published the *Guidelines for Psychological Practice with Girls and Women*, and the ACA in 2008 published *Girls' and Women's Wellness* (Choate, 2008). Such guidelines suggest that there is a difference between treating men and women, boys and girls. The 11 guidelines from the APA are to be followed in work with women and girls in mental health treatment. Specifically, the guidelines state that psychologists should be aware of the effects of identity development and unique life events on the development of girls and women. Furthermore, these guidelines include the necessity of the psychologist's awareness of interventions and approaches shown to be effective in treating issues of concern to women and girls. Moreover, the guidelines suggest that psychologists must familiarize themselves with and utilize relevant mental health, education, and community resources for girls and women (APA, 2007). The development of these documents for working with girls and women demonstrates that the APA and ACA are quite aware of the unique challenges that girls and women face as well as how mental health professionals ought to address the existence of important diversity issues when providing treatment for girls and women.

In addition to specific guidelines for treating

girls and women in the mental health field, there have been guidelines proposed for working with boys and men (APA Boys and Men Guidelines Group, 2018). Englar-Carlson, Evans, & Duffey (2014) also published *A Counselor's Guide to Working with Men* following research on the topic of the differences between men and women. Furthermore, when typically more traditional masculine styles are acknowledged and seen as strengths in the therapeutic relationship, boys and men will benefit more from the therapeutic encounter (Kiselica & Englar-Carlson, 2010; Englar-Carlson & Kiselica, 2013). In fact, Liu (2005) suggests that a therapist's being aware of masculine traits and incorporating them into therapeutic practice is important for clinical multicultural competency.

There are several disorders that require different types of treatment for men and women. For instance, with regard to panic disorder, the common psychological belief is that men's "fight or flight" response to stress or panic is universal across genders. Therefore, it is often treated in both men and women by using cognitive restructuring based upon the assumption that their fear, which caused the fight or flight response, is a misunderstanding of a benign situation or stimulus. Musslewhite (2017) proposes that since men and women respond to fear-inducing stimuli differently that their mental health treatment should also differ. She proposes that since women's response to fear usually involves a "tend and befriend" phenomenon that the psychological treatment of fear in women should focus more on the relational aspects of situations that cause stress and panic, as opposed to the cognitive restructuring used for men.

Substance-related addiction is another area in which mental health professionals are finding that there is a sex difference in the etiology (the study of causes), risk factors, patterns of consumption, and treatment outcomes. These differences, therefore, require different treatment for men and women (Greenfield & Grella, 2009; Handwerk et al., 2006; Vigna-Taglianti et al., 2016). In general, both drug and alcohol addictions are more common in men than in women (American Psychiatric Association, 2013: for alcohol use, see p. 493; for cannabis, p. 512; hallucinogenic drugs, p. 525; opioids, p. 543). However, Vigna-Taglianti et al. (2016) found that women with drug addictions were on average younger, had more family discord, including separations and divorce, had more psychiatric comorbid disorders, and reported higher use of sedatives other than alcohol, than did men with drug addictions. They concluded that since there were such significant differences in sociodemographics, drug-use patterns, and psychiatric symptoms that there is a need for sex-specific treatment protocols in order to improve treatment outcomes. Furthermore, Handwerk et al. (2006) found similar sex differences in adolescents in residential treatment facilities and, therefore, also concluded the need for different treatment options for boys and girls.

In the area of trauma and post-traumatic stress disorder (PTSD), there is often a sex difference identified in the treatment and subsequent outcomes for men and women. For instance, overall women tend to benefit more from psychotherapy than do men (Békés, Beaulieu-Prévost, Guay, Belleville, & Marchand, 2016). Békés et al. (2016) found that after women received the same treatment for PTSD as men did, their quality of life and ability to cope by seeking support from others were significantly improved, more so than men's. The study also found that, to cope with their symptoms, women used avoidance of traumatic stimuli more often than men.

Furthermore, Flemingham & Bryant (2012)

found that although men and women did not show a difference in response to treatment for PTSD immediately following the treatment, they did show significant differences at a six-month follow up. For instance, in the exposure-only cognitive-behavior therapy group, six months post treatment, men displayed more severe PTSD symptoms than did women in the same group. Men with PTSD were unable to maintain treatment gains as well as women. Flemingham & Bryant conclude that this longer-term difference in treatment outcomes is likely due to women's ability to recall, more strongly than men, both emotional memories that are tied to the traumatic event and those related to the extinction of the emotional memory following exposure treatment. This ability for emotional memory in women may facilitate emotional processing and, therefore, long-term treatment gains for women.

Men and women have been known through time to communicate differently. These differences in communication have led to popular books like *Men are From Mars, Women are From Venus* (Gray, 1994), which approach men and women differently. However, there is truth to these differences. Men and women often use different words to communicate the same message and even share different messages in order to obtain the same end of sharing themselves with the other (Tannen, 1990). Not only do men and women communicate differently, their tendency to understand each other's communication style is also different. For instance, Noller & Fenney (1994) found that with regard to understanding how the other is communicating, women perceived their husbands' nonverbal communication more accurately than men perceived their wives'.

In addition, men and women's differences in therapy extend to their differences in expressing intimacy. Hook, Gerstein, Detterich, & Gridley (2003) found that while both men and women valued intimacy, they expressed intimacy in different ways. Women displayed more comfort with more traditional measures of intimacy such as the tender feelings of love and affection than did men. In addition, McRae, Dalgleish, Johnson, Burgess-Moser, & Killian (2014) found that while both men and women were able to soften toward each other and build a deeper connection during couples' Emotion-Focused Therapy (EFT) sessions, women experienced their emotions more strongly in session. Finally, Greenberg and Goldman (2008) suggest that during couples therapy men and women express their desires differently. A man may offer advice as a way of coming closer to his wife, while the wife wants compassion and understanding to feel closer (Greenberg & Goldman, 2008). Thus, it is important for the therapist to understand that while men and women both desire intimacy, they may express it differently.

These examples illustrate that sex differences for men and women often necessitate different approaches in treatment and may result in different treatment outcomes. Beyond the disorders discussed here, there are many other addictions and disorders for which different approaches in treatment are preferable. Recognizing the differences between the sexes and accounting for them in treatment tends to produce better outcomes.

How Is Sex Difference Understood from a Philosophical Perspective?

Recently, there has been a renewed interest in virtue ethics; this interest is evident not only in theology and philosophy but also in psychology with the growth of positive psychology. The Meta-Model of the Person, drawing from the Catholic Christian tradition and the larger

philosophical tradition on virtue and vice, is a contribution to this recovery of virtue ethics. It offers an innovation that draws together virtue theory and the psychological sciences (including neuroscience). It also emphasizes that sex equality, difference, and complementarity are a proper dimension of virtue in theory and practice (Chapter 11, "Fulfilled in Virtue"). To this end, this section offers new philosophical reflections on virtue ethics in light of contemporary insights from psychology and neuroscience concerning differences between the sexes.

Sex difference has not been treated extensively or constructively in the philosophical recovery of virtue ethics. The scholarship has largely overlooked the possible impact that sex difference makes on the exercise and acquisition of virtue. Secular virtue theory, as in Fowers (2005), concentrates less on the moral dimension of individual acts and more on the developmental nature of person. A Catholic Christian approach to virtue is attentive both to the person and to the person's acts in light of what is morally good. Nonetheless, relatively little attention has been paid to the human person as male and female, nor to the sex differences' effect on men's and women's vocations. Furthermore, John Paul II's reflections on the meaning and importance of the body and the person as a whole invite critical reflection on the importance of sex difference in philosophical and theological anthropology. As we saw earlier, studies in neuroscience and psychology have demonstrated that there are important differences between the sexes, and a robust account of virtue must take these findings seriously and enter into dialogue with the other disciplines.

Because every person is a body-soul unity, sex differences influence how men and women live out their shared basic human nature and the common core of faith, hope, and charity (the theological virtues) and the infused and moral virtues, such as practical wisdom, justice, courage, and temperance. Therefore, not only are sex differences important for psychology and neuroscience to consider, they have bearing on the moral and spiritual lives of men and women as well. These differences are found in the masculine and feminine expressions of natural inclinations (which underlie the natural law precepts), vocations, and virtues and vices.

What impact does sex difference have on the acquisition and exercise of virtue? From a very general perspective of the equality of sexes, these differences seem to have no bearing on a Christian philosophical vision of the person. Every person is an individual substance of a rational, volitional, interpersonally relational, sensory-perceptual-cognitive, emotional, and unified nature (Chapter 2, "Theological, Philosophical, and Psychological Premises") with a common human nature and equal dignity and value. Furthermore, every human person is called to a life of flourishing, which is found in virtue and through vocation.

In becoming virtuous, both men and women need grace as well as human effort and a context of committed vocations. The infused virtues are rooted in the theological virtues of faith, hope, and charity, which are given to us by God at Baptism. However, we must cooperate with grace throughout our lives, even though ultimately these infused virtues can be increased in us only by God (Aquinas, 1272/2005).

By contrast, acquired virtues are developed through our repeating virtuous actions. The way in which acquired virtues are expressed is affected by our masculinity and femininity; this whole natural foundation of acquired virtue participates in the expression of the infused virtues and theological virtues (Sherwin, 2009), as nature is perfected by grace. By repeatedly choos-

ing the virtuous action that lies between the two extremes, or vices, the person develops a stable and firm disposition to the good (*Catechism of the Catholic Church* [CCC], 2000, §§1803–1804). For example, an individual acquires the cardinal virtue of courage by choosing the virtuous mean that moderates between cowardice and rashness (Aristotle, ca. 350 BC/1941, III.7).

Sex differences underlie the practice of virtue and need to be recognized in any virtue ethics, including an Aristotelian-Thomistic framework. If one takes into account the sex differences that have been made evident by psychology and neuroscience, then the way in which men and women manifest specific virtues may be different, and the temptations that lead each sex into certain vices may differ as well.

How do sex differences influence the capacities that underlie the virtues? As was previously mentioned, all human beings possess the same basic natural inclinations to goodness, life, family, society, and truth, but these inclinations are underdetermined. These seeds can be developed by the virtues, which enable us to pursue our natural inclinations in a way that allows us to flourish by shaping our human capacities in light of our vocations (Chapter 11, "Fulfilled in Virtue"). These natural inclinations can also become disordered and may lead to languishing and vice.

While the virtues are interrelated in a dynamic way, each virtue perfects a particular capacity (Aquinas, 1273/1981, I-II, 55.1). For example, the virtue of justice perfects our volitional capacity, and the virtues of temperance and fortitude perfect their underlying affective capacities. Thus, such capacities can be called the matter of a given virtue, and the virtues can be distinguished by the capacities in which they support growth.

Numerous contemporary studies, including the ones that we highlighted in the previous section, demonstrate sex differences with respect to the emotional, rational, volitional, and interpersonal capacities. While the virtues perfect the same capacities in both sexes, and men and women are both equally capable of becoming virtuous, there are different ways in which these capacities are expressed. These differences in the matter of the virtues along with differences in vocational commitments and responsibilities shape how particular virtues and vices, such as courage and lust, are expressed in men and women.

How is the virtue of courage expressed differently in men and women? Courage is the cardinal virtue that concerns the reasoned use of the emotions of fear and daring. (This section focuses on the acquired virtue of courage, while the infused virtue of courage will be considered in the theological section.) Courage is contrasted to exaggerated expressions of fear and daring as found in the vices of being overly fearless or overly fearful and of being reckless or cowardly (Aquinas, 1273/1981, II-II, 123.3). Aquinas (1273/1981) maintains that courage (fortitude) primarily concerns death, particularly death in battle (II-II, 123.4 & 123.4); more broadly, he points out that fortitude "helps to resist the assaults of all vices" (II-II, 123.2 ad 2).

The relationship between courage and war is found across time and cultures, and since most warriors throughout history were men, courage has been a virtue typically identified principally with men (Miller, 2000). Women, conversely, have been historically viewed as the opposite of courageous. Miller (2000) notes that "courage, manliness, manly virtue is defined less by what it is than by what it is never supposed to be: womanish or effeminate" (p. 233). However, if courage is examined in light of sex differences, then it becomes clear that both sexes frequently display the virtue of courage but in different

ways. This feminine expression of courage has been overlooked in the tradition developed by male thinkers.

Recall from the last section that compared to women, men tend to take initiative, being risk takers and more aggressive. Women are more interpersonal than men, frequently displaying more empathy and care. Therefore, it is not surprising that male and female expressions of courage are shaped by these differences (see Figure 9.2). Female expressions of courage tend to be characterized by empathy and focus on being with and for the other, while male expressions of courage often are oriented toward initiative taking and doing for the other. Feminine empathy expresses courage through the acceptance of the pain of the other, even of the possibility of the other's death and the pain that would cause. In accepting a child, the mother accepts also the pain of pregnancy and childbirth itself, including the possibility of the child's death or even her own. All of this derives from her feminine interpersonal character. St. Gianna Molla is an example of a wife and mother who accepted the risks and pain of childbearing. When pregnant, a tumor was found in her uterus. She chose to have the tumor removed, but to keep the child. She died of complications of the delivery by Caesarean section. Throughout the pregnancy and delivery, she showed herself a model of a mother courageously accepting the possibility of dying in the delivery of her child.

The different ways in which men and women express the virtue of courage can be seen more clearly if we consider heroism in a variety of settings and vocations. On the one hand, Becker and Eagly (2004) found that men were much more likely to perform courageous acts that involved initiative taking and risking their lives to save the life of a stranger, including saving people from fires, drowning, or criminal attacks.

Figure 9.2. Female and Male Expressions of the Virtue of Courage

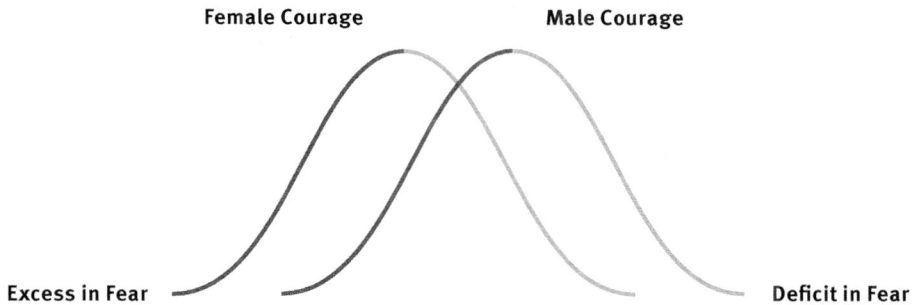

Female expression of courage tends toward:

- More empathetic expression of emotion.

- Focus on interpersonal relationships by being with the other.

- Understanding the emotions and needs of the other.

- Patiently enduring suffering (risking pain) for and with the other.

Male expression of courage tends toward:

- More initiative-taking expression of emotion.

- Focus on interpersonal relationships by doing for the other.

- Understanding the facts and outcomes for the other.

- Daringly taking intiative (risking harm) to protect the other.

On the other hand, they discovered that women were as likely or more likely than men to donate a kidney or volunteer to serve others through organizations such as Doctors of the World and the Peace Corps (Becker & Eagly, 2004). These latter types of heroism tend to express a different type of initiative, being less risky but requiring more perseverance and patience, which are associated with the virtue of courage (Aquinas, 1273/1981, II-II, 136 & 137). Rather than isolated acts of courage, they involve commitments that stretch over long periods of time as well as the opportunity to build relationships, especially family. For instance, in a survey of kidney donors who were biologically related to the recipients, women, more than men, viewed their donation as part of their duty to their family (Simmons, Marine, & Simmons, 1987; Becker & Eagly, 2004).

The findings of Simmons, Marine, and Simmons (1987) also cast light on how different vocational responsibilities and commitments between the sexes influence how virtues, including courage, are cultivated and expressed. For example, motherhood requires a unique expression of courage to accept new life as well as to be patient and persevere in interpersonal commitments. A mother risks her own well-being and sacrifices her own physical comfort during pregnancy and when giving birth. After the child is born, she needs not only patience and perseverance to care for a newborn, but possibly to care for older children as well. Of course, fathers also need patience and perseverance, but their expression of patience and perseverance, including their emotional and physical sacrifices, will be different. For instance, they will need to persevere in learning how to nurture and bond with the new child. Fatherhood often requires a unique expression of courage associated with initiative taking to protect and support his family. Furthermore, there are other ways that men and women display courage in other vocational states.

How is the vice of lust expressed differently in men and women? While differences in the emotional, rational, volitional, and interpersonal aspects of men and women affect the expressions of virtue, they also affect how vices are acquired and expressed. For example, men and women both lust, but they lust in different ways and for different reasons.

Even though our libertine culture promotes the notion that sex is just a casual physical activity in which both sexes willingly participate for pleasure, differences between men and women still persist. While men are moved to have sex by visual stimulation and the desire for physical pleasure, women are more likely to seek emotional closeness and intimacy in sex (Gross, 2013; Moir & Jessel, 1992). How do these differences inform our traditional understanding of the vice of lust?

Traditionally, the vice of lust has been defined as a disordered desire for sexual pleasure (*CCC*, 2000, §2351). Unchaste practices (acts of lust) include masturbation, fornication, pornography, prostitution, and rape (*CCC*, 2000, §§2352–2356). These lustful acts are related to the pursuit of physical gratification, and they are predominantly sins that males commit (Gross, 2013). As was previously mentioned, the use of pornography is more prevalent among men, as is masturbation (Das, 2007). Furthermore, almost all rapists are men (Greenfeld, 1997). Nonetheless, women do have sex outside of marriage, use pornography, masturbate, and develop sexual additions (Ferree, 2013).

A common understanding of lust and de-

scription of lustful acts largely ignores sex difference and fails to account for how and why women lust (Gross, 2013). Even though women engage in lustful acts, such as extramarital sex, they do so oftentimes seeking emotional intimacy or trying to overcome isolation, and not primarily seeking sexual pleasure (Carnes, 2001; Gross, 2013). Again, the vice for both sexes is the same (unchaste practices done for distorted sexual pleasure or for distorted emotional intimacy). What the vice is distorting is different in each sex.

There are two interrelated types of sex-related intimacy: physical intimacy (which includes sex) and emotional intimacy (which includes romance). With male lust, the female is used as a source of physical sexual pleasure; with female lust, the male is used as a source of emotional intimacy (Gross, 2013). This distorted desire that objectifies the other for the pleasure of romance may be expressed by reading erotic novels, such as *50 Shades of Grey*, or by talking about sex with friends. In these activities, women experience sexual pleasure that is akin to the sexual pleasure that men desire and seek through physical sex, because these activities produce pleasurable feelings from the increase in dopamine and oxytocin (Brizendine, 2006; Doidge, 2007).

Thus, the difference between male and female lust may lie either in the *means* chosen or the *intention* of the agent (Gross, 2013). For instance, women tend to opt for erotic novels, while men are drawn to visual pornography, as noted, but in both cases, there is a disordered desire for sexual stimulation and pleasure, although the means of achieving that shared end is different. And, while a man and a woman may choose the same immoral means, such as extramarital sex, their intention in choosing that object may differ (Gross, 2013): The man, in many instances, will have extramarital sex in order to fulfill an inordinate desire for physical pleasure, while the woman, oftentimes, will engage in extramarital sex because of an inordinate desire to satisfy her need for emotional intimacy. Additionally, women can engage in extramarital sex with other moral or immoral intentions, such as for financial security or notoriety. Even if the intention may be good, it does not justify an immoral act (Gross, 2013).

Through their actions, both men and women have the potential to form virtue or vice in themselves. However, because of the numerous differences between the sexes, which have been identified by neuroscience and psychology, virtues and vices may be expressed differently by each sex. For example, as noted, women's focus on interpersonal relationships often influences how they express virtues, such as courage, and influences their reasons for committing acts of vice, including lust. Conversely, masculine expressions of courage may involve more risk taking, and they are typically tempted into acts of lust through visual stimulation. While neuroscience, psychology, and philosophy must consider these differences, their origin, meaning, and significance can only be fully explained when the theological perspective is integrated. It is to that perspective that we now turn.

How Is Sex Difference Understood from a Theological Perspective?

According to biblical tradition, God has created humans as male and female, which involves a natural difference and complementarity. To be male or female is not a mere social convention or only necessary for the survival of the human race. Sex differences are willed by God for the establishment of interpersonal relationships (Gen 1–4) and committed vocations.

Both of the biblical creation accounts describe the creation of two sexes. The first chapter of Genesis emphasizes that man and woman are created in the image of God, with a common blessing, mission, and dignity (Gen 1:27), as mentioned earlier. The second chapter of Genesis describes the original solitude that man experienced, and it identifies that the man was not meant to be alone (Gen 2:23; John Paul II, 2006, pp. 146–156). Rather, the man needs the woman as "a helper fit for him" and as the wife with whom he is to be joined so that "they become one flesh" (Gen 2:18–25).

While both men and women must make an individual and "sincere gift of self" in order to discover themselves, the ways in which they give of themselves is influenced by their unique geniuses. For John Paul II (1989), the feminine genius is rooted in women's capacity for motherhood (Savage, 2015). That capacity involves receptivity not only to new life but also to the other. This openness to the other can be seen in *physical motherhood*, during which mothers share their bodies with another person, as well in an openness to caring for and suffering with the other who is not one's offspring (Congregation for the Doctrine of the Faith, 2004, §13). This type of *emotional motherhood* and receptivity can be lived out in a vocation to the single life or by those who are married but have been unable to conceive children. It is also present in religiously vowed women, such as in the case of a mother superior's emotional care of her novices, or in the case of someone like St. Teresa of Calcutta who emotionally and physically cared for the poor.

A *spiritual maternity* also orients women toward the other; it is experienced by women who embrace virginity for the sake of the kingdom of God (Congregation for the Doctrine of the Faith, 2004, §13, John Paul II, 1988, §21; Savage, 2015, p. 88), as well as by any women who nurture the spiritual life of others. In these other types of motherhood, motherhood finds "forms of full realization" even when there is "no physical procreation" (Congregation for the Doctrine of the Faith, 2004, §13).

The capacity for motherhood and the receptivity to the other that it includes influences the whole person; it influences the physical, emotional, and spiritual lives of women (Congregation for the Doctrine of the Faith, 2004, §13). Through their vocation to the single life, or marriage, or the consecrated life, women maintain a readiness to pour themselves out for the other (John Paul II, 1988, §21). Savage (2015) notes that "from the beginning, the horizon of all womankind includes persons" (p. 88). Unlike Adam, Eve is never alone, and she never experiences solitude. From the moment of her creation, she is in the presence of another human person and in human relationship (Gen 2:22–24; Savage, 2015).

While all human beings are called to live for the other, women are more immediately attuned to this call because of their unique capacity for motherhood, and, therefore, they serve as a reminder of this call (Congregation for the Doctrine of the Faith, 2004, §21). "Woman's genius is to keep constantly before us the fact that the existence of living persons, whether in the womb or walking around outside of it, cannot be forgotten while we frantically engage in the tasks of human living" (Savage, 2015, p. 89).

The other-centeredness that informs the feminine genius can be seen in the universal call to holiness as well as in the vocation to work and service and leisure. Women excel at a number of different types of work and service. They are particularly drawn to helping professions, including nursing, education, social work, and mental health professions (American Psychological Association Center for Workforce Studies, 2015; Stein, 1996, p. 114; Ingersoll, Merrill,

& Stuckey, 2014; Salsberg et al., 2017; United States Department of Labor, 2003). They also have significant contributions to make in any environment in which they work, including the corporate and political worlds (John Paul II, 1988). In all these areas, a woman can contribute "the feminine gifts of empathy and adjustment [that] enable her to participate, understand, and stimulate" (Stein, 1996, p. 115).

Just as the feminine genius is rooted in woman's capacity for motherhood, the masculine genius is rooted in man's capacity for fatherhood, which may be fulfilled in *physical, psychological, social* (including social identity and skills), or *spiritual* ways (Allen, 2004; Congregation for the Doctrine of the Faith, 2004, §13; Stein, 1996).

Whereas the highest expression of the feminine genius is Mary, who offers herself as "handmaid of the Lord" (Lk 1:38) and willingly accepts her vocation as mother and wife (John Paul II, 1995, §10), Joseph is the paradigm of the masculine genius as father and husband (John Paul II, 1989; Savage, 2015). Like Mary, Joseph makes a total gift of self to the Holy Family with his life and work, following God's call to holiness (Mt 1:19–25; John Paul II, 1989, §8).

Throughout the Gospels, Joseph humbly and obediently serves God and his family (John Paul II, 1989, §17; Savage, 2015). When the angel of the Lord comes to Joseph and explains to him what has happened to Mary and how he should proceed, Joseph wakes up and "does as the angel of the Lord commanded him" (Mt 1:24). This is the beginning of "Joseph's way" (John Paul II, 1989, §17). This way involves especially doing rather than speaking; it is centered on action in faith.

Joseph's righteousness, dedication, courage, and faithfulness are manifest through extraordinary acts, such as protecting his family by taking them to Egypt to escape Herod, but these qualities are also evident in his routine acts of love and service (Mt 1:19 & 2:13–14). Joseph accepted the daily responsibility of providing for his family as well as of educating Jesus in the Mosaic Law and a trade (John Paul II, 1989, §16).

This image of Joseph as a humble, dedicated, and hardworking father is exemplified by his trade as a carpenter (Mk 6:3). John Paul II notes, "Work was the daily expression of love in the life of the Family of Nazareth. The Gospel specifies the kind of work Joseph did in order to support his family: he was a carpenter" (John Paul II, 1989, §22); he goes on to add, "This simple word [work] sums up Joseph's entire life" (§22).

Joseph's life of physical work reflects the charge that man was given from the beginning. Before the fall and prior to the creation of woman, Adam was placed in the garden of Eden and commanded by God to cultivate and care for it (Gen 2:15; Savage, 2015, p. 87). This command remains after the fall of man, but now man is forced to toil and sweat to eat from the land as he battles thorns and thistles (Gen 3:17–18).

In the second creation account, after God tells Adam to care for the land, he also allows Adam to name the various creatures that God creates (Gen 2:19–20). Just as Adam is given the power to name, Joseph is given the honor and power to name Jesus (Mt 2:21; Savage, 2015, p. 151).

Based on the creation accounts in Genesis and the paradigmatic examples of Mary and Joseph, what can we conclude about the masculine genius, and how does it differ from the feminine genius? The feminine genius is rooted in being for the other, whereas the masculine genius is rooted in doing for the other, but at the same time, men are called to be for others as they do things, and women are called to do things as they are devoted to others.

How are infused virtues and spiritual vocations expressed differently in men and women? As we previously mentioned in the section on equality, St. Paul is clear on the equality that comes through Baptism: "All are one in Christ Jesus" (Gal 3:28). Yet, this equality does not mean that sex differences or the unique geniuses of the sexes are erased through God's grace. Grace heals and perfects nature, "according to its mode" (Aquinas, 1273/1981, I, 62.5; I-II, 109.3).

The infused virtues and the call to holiness given to men and to women at Baptism perfect the same capacities, but the emotional, rational, volitional, and interpersonal differences in men and women remain. These differences continue to shape and influence how the infused theological and moral virtues are expressed in men and women, who are both equally capable of growing in holiness.

Infused virtues have a supernatural end: love of God in the beatific vision. They enable followers of Christ to behave as "'fellow-citizens with the saints, and of the household of God' (Eph 2:19) and differ from the acquired virtues, whereby man behaves well in respect of human affairs" (Aquinas, 1273/1981, I-II, 63.4). As mentioned earlier, traditionally, the highest act of acquired courage is considered to be death in battle in defense of the common good (Aquinas, 1273/1981, II-II, 123.5). In the Catholic Christian faith, which is the foundation and principle of the Meta-Model, the highest act of infused courage is considered to be martyrdom, when one defends the Christian faith and is ready to give one's life for God and others (Aquinas, 1273/1981, II-II, 124.3).

While the virtue particularly concerns facing death well, in battle or childbirth, more broadly speaking, infused courage is "a graced strength in difficulty to face fear and anxiety" in different situations (Titus, 2006, p. 271; see also Aquinas,

1273/1981, II-II, 124.3). Courage, like the other cardinal virtues, has associated virtues that may accompany its exercise and that are given to us by God at Baptism. Classically, courage faces difficulty with the help of two sorts of associated virtues, which address initiative taking and endurance. The second group includes the virtues of patience and perseverance. Patience allows us to endure pain inflicted by others without being overwhelmed by sorrow (Aquinas, 1273/1981, II-II, 136.4). If we lack patience, sorrow might drive us to turn away from the good (Aquinas, 1273/1981, II-II, 136.4). Perseverance is persistence in the pursuit of a difficult good until the virtuous end is accomplished (Aquinas, 1273/1981, II-II, 137.1). Perseverance helps the person not to give up when courage is required not just for a moment but over an extended period.

Since both male and female saints have displayed infused courage through heroic acts, including martyrdom, how can one begin to describe the different ways in which the infused virtue is lived out differently in men and women? It is important to recall here the principle that was mentioned in the last section—grace does not destroy nature but heals and perfects it—which applies to sex differences, vocations, and virtues. All of the infused virtues, including courage, perfect our capacities and enable us to do, know, and believe things that we otherwise could not because of the deforming effects of sin and our various human limitations (Titus, 2006, p. 270). As Cessario (2006) notes, "The grace of the infused moral virtues shapes and energizes our human operative capacities, intellect, will, and sense appetites" (p. 5). As mentioned earlier, the Meta-Model identifies thirteen dimensions of virtue that include not only the significance of

sex differences in forming human dispositions, but also how vocations and transcendence influence acquired and infused expressions of virtue (Chapter 11, "Fulfilled in Virtue"). Thus, the virtues are exercised by women and men who have not only biological and psychological differences but also different vocations and personal experiences. As we mentioned in an earlier section, women tend to be more focused on interpersonal relationships by being with others, and therefore, their expressions of courage tend to be characterized by empathy. Conversely, men tend to be more focused on interpersonal relationships by doing for others, through being problem-focused and taking more physical risks, and thus, male expressions of courage are oriented toward initiative-taking. These natural differences can still be seen in expressions of infused courage, because they are not removed by grace but rather they are informed by the exemplarity of the message and lives of Christ and the saints.

For instance, the impact of these differences on infused virtue and vocation can clearly be seen in the life of Edith Stein (St. Teresa Benedicta of the Cross). The courage, patience, and perseverance that Stein displayed were gifts from God, but those gifts transformed and transfigured her natural capacities, virtues, and vocation to holiness and religious life (Barron, 2007, p. 290).

This section has considered sex differences from the neuroscientific, psychological, philosophical, and theological perspectives. These differences and the unique geniuses each sex possesses affect how they express the virtues and live out their vocations. Now, we turn to examine how the differences of man and woman can function together in a complementary way.

Men and Women as Complementary

Complementarity occupies the middle ground between two erroneous positions concerning sex difference (Congregation for the Doctrine of the Faith, 2004, §1). Some thinkers have promoted an antagonistic relationship between the sexes, arguing that the only way in which women can have power and equality is to make men their enemies (Daly, 1968, 1984). In contrast, other thinkers, in order to defend equality, have denied all differences other than basic bodily differences (Ruether, 1993). Neither of these positions comprehends both the equal intrinsic dignity possessed by both men and women, and the numerous sex differences between them. However, complementarity recognizes equality between men and women, their differences, and the dynamic, synergistic way in which these differences can work together.

Complementarity is more than the sum of sex differences. It is a multiplication of the differences that elevates both men and women and their relationships to new levels of fruitfulness. Complementarity does not diminish the dignity of each man and woman; the person does not have less dignity as an individual (Allen, 2006). In addition, complementarity does recognize that we are created for interpersonal relationships. While men and women are called to true friendship with the same sex, relationships between men and women are unique in that they bring together complementary differences in a way not found in same-sex friendships. Masculine and feminine differences can work in a synergistic way for each sex to facilitate cooperation and growth in a multitude of different areas, from moral development to parenting (Allen, 2006; Stein, 1996; Gilligan, 1982; John Paul II, 1989). These differences and their synergy are expressed not only in marriages but also potentially in all male and female interactions, including in the workplace, in friendships, and in our vocations as brothers and sisters and sons and daughters.

How Is Complementarity Between Men and Women Understood from a Psychological Perspective?

There is a substantial amount of evidence of male and female difference that, interpreted within an evolutionary framework, strongly implies complementarity (Buss, 2015; Geary, 2010). That is, each sex specializes in certain necessary biological and social tasks to create an environment better suited for human survival. For example, women tend naturally to be more nurturing and emotionally attentive, and therefore, they typically are the primary interpersonal caregivers for babies and children (Bjorklund & Jordan, 2013). Conversely, men more naturally tend to be more involved in outside activities that provide security and resources for the family and that often require more risk-taking behavior (Bjorklund & Jordan, 2013). Compared to that of other primates, human growth and development occurs over a greatly extended period. If they are to develop in a healthy physical and psychological way, children need the unique gifts that both parents provide (Bjorklund & Jordan, 2013). Together, these characteristics provide a much better chance of survival and flourishing than any one average human could ever accomplish. However, human beings are also extremely resilient and can flourish even in situations, such as after divorce or the death of a mother or father, where two parents are not present (Wilcox et al., 2011).

One aspect of complementarity is that women and men model different strengths for each other, and in the case of marital relationships men and women can become more like each other. For instance, men can become more able to have emotionally charged conversations and able to be grow in empathy, and women can become more focused on how to solve their marital problems. Both spouses come to understand each other's perspectives, not only to tolerate differences better but also to appreciate and incorporate them into their lives. Men don't become women, and women don't become men. However, they both are enriched. For example, if the father watches the mother with the first child, he will likely become different with the second—and in the case of tragedy, would be more equipped to fulfill some aspects of the mother's role if, after having a number of children, the wife died and he were a single parent.

There is also evidence, from an evolutionary perspective, for the complementary long-term mating strategies of men and women (Buss, 2015; Fisher, 2004, Trivers, 1972). Buss's (2015) evolutionary interpretation focuses on *why* women select a mate: to provide for the welfare of their children, as well as her own welfare. It also focuses on *how* men obtain mates: through social power, often based on money or physical prowess, and through status, striving in political and business structures, activities that normally result in attaining resources. In this interpretation, men commonly compete with men in such a way as to provide the resources women and their children need, while women typically compete with women through their beauty and attractiveness for the men with desirable resources.

From the perspective of evolutionary psychology, moreover, male and female differences very often work together in a complementary and synergistic way. Synergy involves two persons working together and producing some-

thing that cannot be created by either one alone. There is a special type of synergy that arises from male and female differences, and this synergy is visible in the evolutionary interpretation of sex differences (Buss, 2015; Fisher, 2004; Geary, 2010; Trivers, 1972). One should always keep in mind, however, that these differences can also be barriers to men's and women's understanding each other and can be serious sources of friction and disagreement.

Positive synergy is probably best illustrated by the creation of a family and its generational history, because a child is the fruit of this synergistic complementarity of man and woman, and the family seeks to support the needs of each of its members and of the whole (Allen, 2006). Synergy can also be seen in the workplace, friendships, and the religious life. An example of the synergy that occurs within the family can be seen at times of family crisis. For example, a case when in a snowstorm a tree may hit the house or block the driveway. The father gets out his chainsaw and takes the tree off the house or frees the driveway. He then covers the hole in the house or drives for needed supplies. The mother guides the children to a safe room, comforts them, prepares food, and distracts the children by telling stories. In much smaller crises, less dramatic but similarly differential responses occur. The father tends to care for those inside the home by engaging in activities outside of the home that involve his strength and willingness to take risk, and the mother tends to care for those inside of the home by courageously offering compassion, comfort, and empathy while also working to care for their physical needs. In these situations, the synergy is expressed in the successful response to the entire crisis, because both sexes contribute their unique gifts to support the survival and flourishing of the family. This does not mean that when either masculine or feminine genius is not present in a crisis that either men or women are completely incapable of fulfilling the full set of needs required by the situation. But in doing so the challenge is experienced as extremely demanding since it requires going beyond what is experienced as natural tendencies and skills.

How does the complementarity between men and women influence clinical and work practice? There are areas of life in which the complementarity of men and women can influence outcomes in a synergistic manner such that having both a male and female presence will enhance an otherwise all-male or all-female group. These areas include the workplace, friendships, and clinical practice. Arguden (2012) proposes that, in the workplace, the inclusion of women on professional organizational boards is helpful to sustain performance and viability for the company they represent. He states that women add to the masculine presence on these boards by uniquely addressing the needs of customers, employees, shareholders, and the community.

Among the types of friendships, Baumgarte & Nelson (2009) found that among college students, men and women who preferred opposite-sex friendships rated those friendships as higher in closeness, trust, caring, having common interests, and providing them personal benefits than those college students who preferred same-sex friendships. In addition, Bleske and Buss (2000) discovered that friendships with the opposite sex enhanced both friends' self-esteem.

Not only do male-female relationships in the workplace and in friendship have a unique quality that is not found in same-sex workplace or friendship relationships, this interactive effect of male-female relationships also can be seen in individual and marital therapy. Within individual therapy, it is important to understand not only the individual but also the interpersonal system

in which the client lives. Asking questions about this social system when treating the individual becomes essential. For instance, when an individual client presents with a specific set of symptoms, it becomes important to ask about his or her interpersonal system to understand how the client is affected by those around him or her. Asking questions about friendships and a potential romantic partner or spouse becomes paramount to treatment of an individual because the therapist has both the individual client in the therapy room and the client's interpersonal system, whether that system is supportive or not.

Within the realm of marital therapy, it is important for the therapist to focus on both the husband and the wife. The therapy should promote the unique characteristics or gifts that each brings to the fulfillment, flourishing, and mutual respect of the couple. For instance, women tend to present with the interpersonal issues and emotional needs of the couple. Women's attention to these issues and needs can be beneficial for the husband. However, when women present emotionally important issues in intense, forceful, and even confrontational ways, they run the risk of their husbands' being emotionally flooded and unable to process the material or sustain a discussion (Gottman, 1999). Conversely, men tend to be more comfortable with discussing problem-solving strategies (Guerney, 1977; Scuka, 2005). Although this can be an important aid for the couple in order to bring about positive change, if the husband is too focused on finding a solution and does not take some time for empathetically understanding his wife first, the solutions may not take into account each of their needs and may be very unsatisfying for his wife. When these strengths and weaknesses are taken together in a complementary way, though, they can greatly enhance the relationship. For instance, when women begin the communication by sharing the positive aspects of what they want to accomplish both emotionally and practically, men are less emotionally overwhelmed and more able to open themselves up to the emotional state of the relationship (Gottman, 1999). Conversely, when men genuinely acknowledge the wife's emotional desires, she feels understood and becomes more able to hear his practical suggestions to solve the problems. Thus, the influence of each expands the other's perception of the relationship such that their interpersonal sharing of emotions and problem-solving can lead to true understanding of each other's needs, forgiveness, practical solutions, and the teamwork and mutual motivation to make individual-level changes and implement mutual solutions. Ultimately, this complementarity results in both partners' appreciating and incorporating at least some of what may be more natural qualities of their spouse and may foster an increasing sense of trust and unity in their marriage.

How Is Complementarity Between Men and Women Understood from a Philosophical Perspective?

A robust philosophical account of complementarity must include physical complementarity but move beyond it to include other types of complementarity, especially psychological, moral, and spiritual complementarity (CCC, 2000, §2333). Furthermore, while affirming difference and the synergy that arises out of it, a proper understanding of complementarity must also affirm the equality of the sexes. To this end, any account of complementarity must avoid what Allen (2006) calls fractional complementarity. This view is represented in the Enlightenment understanding of sex difference, particularly the thought of Immanuel Kant (1797/1974). This view of complementarity holds that there are real differences between the sexes, but each sex

is incomplete. "Each provides only a fraction of one whole person" (Allen, 2006, p. 90). For example, while women contribute intuition, men contribute reason, and together they produce one mind (Allen, 2006). This understanding of complementarity may be expressed with the formula $\frac{1}{2} + \frac{1}{2} = 1$. The problem with fractional complementarity is that it denies the dignity, wholeness, and personal unity of each individual. It exaggerates sex difference to such a degree that it fails to recognize the human nature and capacities that men and women share. In addition, this understanding of complementarity frequently hides a deeper misogyny, in which women are seen as different from but also inferior to men (Allen, 2006).

By contrast, as we explained earlier in this chapter, the Meta-Model holds that men and woman are equal in intrinsic dignity and worth but also different. While sharing many characteristics, men and women are not identical at the levels of the physical body and spiritual soul (which together include emotional and psychological characteristics). As we observed in the previous section concerning the psychological sciences, these differences can work together in a synergistic way to create much more than either the man or woman could alone.

A nuptial view of complementarity can be expressed with the formula $1 + 1 = 3$ (Schiltz, 2015). The synergy that comes from complementarity can be seen in the conjugal act, when man and woman, in their wholeness and uniqueness, come together to create a third person. When the husband and wife come together to create a new life, their genes are united in one individual, contributing equally to create someone who is new, unique, and different than each parent individually.

The product of constructive comprehensive complementarity can be seen in any context where men and women work together, including within the family, in other vocations, and in areas of work (Schiltz, 2015). For instance, one part of the equation, focusing on the contribution of women, involves "the presence of women in higher echelons of the hierarchical structures" where they exercise "an extremely positive influence on the behavior of their male colleagues by restraining, disciplining, and elevating the latter's behavior" (Carbone & Cahn, 2007, pp. 52–53). The contribution of a male-created hierarchy with its problem-solving capacities and emotional stability can be enhanced by women's contribution to the existing male components. In general, hierarchy, risk taking, and isolated rationality are often likely to cause interpersonal harm, while the feminine genius can introduce attentiveness to interpersonal relationships, sustained commitments, and emotional intelligence. These interactions and collaborations can produce something dynamic and different than either sex working alone, and they are important for a healthy, harmonious society (CCC, 2000, §2333).

In addition to the benefits of complementarity for society, at the level of the individual, it is also significant for how relationships and modeling by the opposite sex may assist a given man and woman in cultivating virtues into their lives and avoiding vice. As we previously noted, both men and women can acquire and grow in virtue, but they may express a virtue differently. Seeking to grow in virtue, men and women can learn from each other. For example, through their interactions with women, men may learn to be more compassionate and attentive to interpersonal relationships, while women, through their interactions with men, may become more independent and less fearful of social exclusion (Noddings, 1984; Gilligan, 1982). This process doesn't mean that sex differences evaporate. On the contrary, each sex maintains its own unique genius, but complementarity allows them to grow in virtue, avoid vice, and to flourish in a way that neither could do alone. A closer examination of the virtue of courage will demonstrate how men and women not only express the virtue differently but do so in a complementary way.

How can female and male complementarity be seen in the acquired virtue of courage? The virtue of courage, which helps us face difficulties well, has emotional, interpersonal, cognitive, and behavioral dimensions (see Figure 9.1). The emotional dimension of courage fosters the good use of fear and daring and prevents us from being overwhelmed by extremes of fear or daring. The cognitive dimension enables us to recognize what can be done in the face of the difficulty or danger. The interpersonal dimension of courage helps us to accompany others when they encounter difficulties and challenges, as well as to accept the pain that accompaniment often brings.

As we saw in the section on difference, men and women tend to express the virtue of courage differently (see Figure 9.2). At the emotional level, female courage tends to accent more the empathetic expression of emotion, for instance, they tend to patiently endure suffering for and with the other. Masculine courage tends to accent more initiative-based expressions of emotion, for instance, in using the emotion of daring to take initiative to protect the other. These different modes or expressions of courage are still complete expressions of the virtue. Each expression of courage includes cognitive, emotional, and interpersonal elements, but simply stresses different dimensions of the virtue. Furthermore, these different expressions of courage are complementary and assist each sex in developing courage and resisting vice. For instance, the feminine accent on the interpersonal aspect of the virtue focuses on being with the other, while the masculine accent on the interpersonal aspect of the virtue focuses on doing for the other. These foci remind men and women that courage cannot remain an individualistic virtue but involves helping others stand together and stand up for what is right.

Similarly, the masculine and feminine accents on the cognitive dimension of the virtue complement each other. The feminine expression of courage focuses on understanding the emotions and needs of the other, and the masculine expression focuses on understanding the facts and likely outcomes for the other. Both emphases can be applied to encourage men and women to be attentive to what can be done to minimize, stop, or even use the difficulty. Without the other sex's expression of the virtue, each sex is more likely to miss the mark and be deficient or excessive in any of these dimensions. For instance, male recklessness can be moderated by female caution, while female fearfulness can be moderated by male confidence.

How Is Complementarity Understood from a Theological Perspective?

From a theological perspective, complementarity flows out of a synergistic understanding of sexual equality and difference that is found in the two creation accounts in the book of Genesis. As Pope Francis (2014) points out: "To reflect upon 'complementarity' is nothing less than to ponder the dynamic harmonies at the heart of all Creation. This is a big word, harmony. All complementarities were made by our Creator, so the Author of harmony achieves this harmony" (§1). This harmonious complementarity that is willed by God between the sexes can be seen in both accounts of creation in Genesis.

The first creation account establishes that both sexes are equal, since both are created in the image and likeness of God, but they are unique creations (Gen 1:27). Together they are given the charge to be fruitful and multiply, a charge that neither could have fulfilled alone (Gen 1:28). Their difference calls them into relationship, and in relationship, they can "multiply, fill the earth and subdue it" (Gen 1:28).

In the second creation account, God creates all kinds of wild animals and birds, but "none proved to be the suitable partner for the man" (Gen 2:20). It is only with the creation of woman that man finds a suitable partner, recognizing someone similar to him but also distinct and different (Gen 1:23). By recognizing that "it is not good for the man to be alone" (Gen 2:28), God "affirms that, 'alone,' the man does not completely realize his essence. He realizes it only by existing '*with someone*'—and, put even more deeply and completely by existing '*for someone*'" (John Paul II, 2006, p. 182).

John Paul II (2006) sees in our masculinity and femininity a call to communion and self-gift that is realized in a unique way through marriage but is relevant to all persons and vocations. The human body contains "the 'spousal' attribute, that is, the *power to express love: precisely that love in which the human person becomes a gift* and—through this gift—fulfills the very meaning of his being and existence" (John Paul II, 2006, p. 186). While sharing the common dignity of being human persons, both men and women must make an individual and "sincere gift of self" in order to discover themselves (Vatican II, 1965, §24; cited in John Paul II, 1988, §10). The complementarity of such gifts conveys the nuptial significance of the person. The nuptial "disinterested gift of self" is typified not only in marital love but also in celibate forms of self-giving (Wojtyła, 1993, p. 322; see also Eph 5:28–33; Groeschel, 1985).

The spousal character of the person points

men and women toward their fundamental vocation, which is holiness and flourishing that comes through self-gift (Farnan, 2015). The other sex is essential in living out this vocation. Early in life, in infancy and childhood, the person is shaped by the vocation and genius of the other sex, when, for example, children experience and witness their mothers and fathers living out their vocations (Farnan, 2015). Beyond childhood, the vocations of man and woman continue to "complement each other in a way that enables the person to discover the richness of his or her humanity" (Farnan, 2015, p. 162). In marriage, this complementary dimension of vocations is seen in a unique way as the two persons become one (Gen 2:24), and each spouse grows in virtue and holiness through making a sincere gift of self to his or her spouse as well as to the rest of the family. Outside of marriage, men and women continue to complement one another in their vocations to holiness, as can be seen in the different ways they practice their faith and follow Christ. They also complement each other in their vocation to work and service both inside and outside of the Church.

As was previously mentioned, sex differences do not always function in a synergistic complementarity. Sex differences involve something of both the original order (original unity and friendship) and the disorder or the effect of sin (manipulation and abuse) (John Paul II, 2006, p. 143). Like the rest of creation, sex differences are affected by the fall, which puts enmity between man and woman (Gen 3:15). While sex difference was willed by God from the beginning, the friendship between the sexes as well as their particular geniuses were wounded by the fall.

For instance, men may have difficulty understanding and expressing the personalist norm through the body, because of their tendency to use women through lust, jealousy, meanness, vi-olence, and forgetfulness (Wojtyła, 1993, p. 283). These distortions of masculinity have had and continue to have negative consequences for women, families, and societies (Farnan, 2015). Conversely, women's other-centeredness can lead them into unhealthy relationships in which they fail to consider their own well-being or they manipulate others in a harmful way. Women's desire for emotional intimacy also can lead them to act and dress immodestly to attract the attention of men (Barger, 2003; Gilligan, 1982). However, the geniuses of men and women were not destroyed by the fall; they can be healed and perfected through grace. (For more on how original sin affects the relationship between men and women, see Chapter 18, "Fallen.")

How can female and male complementarity be seen in the infused virtue of courage? As we mentioned earlier, the infused virtues are given to us by God. Infused courage is among these gifts and takes a special form when we follow Christ, who is the exemplar of all the virtues. Courage involves taking initiative with daring action in the face of immediate danger. Courage also involves being empathetic and patient, and persevering in the midst of fear and suffering so as to achieve the difficult good. Barron (2007) points out that with infused courage "there is both a supernatural motivation for the person's courage (love of Christ) and a supernatural power or form to it (Christ's own love now infused into the person)" (p. 281). Christ's initiative taking involved embracing the humiliation, judgment, punishment, and finally the cross, which he took willingly in the face of certain death. His patience and perseverance involved his preparation for the cross as well as the way in which he endured and remained faithful to his mission until the end. His empathy was shown in his ability to forgive those who put him to death.

Figure 9.3. Female, Male, and Synergistic Expressions of the Virtue of Courage

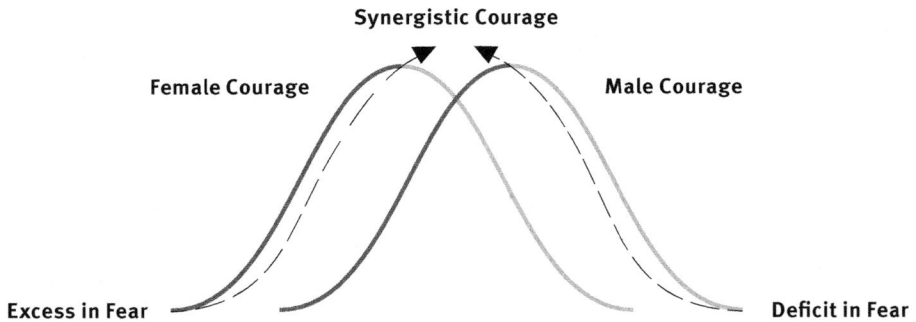

Synergistic complementarity of male and female expressions of courage

Through interpersonal interactions male and female expressions of courage tend to synergistically complement each other, especially at emotional, interpersonal, cognitive, and behavioral levels (see Figures 9.1 and 9.2).

Female expression of courage tends toward:	**Male expression of courage tends toward:**
• More empathetic expression of emotion.	• More initiative-taking expression of emotion.
• Focus on interpersonal relationships by being with the other.	• Focus on interpersonal relationships by doing for the other.
• Understanding the emotions and needs of the other.	• Understanding the facts and outcomes for the other.
• Patiently enduring suffering (risking pain) for and with the other.	• Daringly taking intiative (risking harm) to protect the other.

The extraordinary displays of courage among the holy men and women of the Church often appear similar. However, grace does not erase masculinity and femininity or the synergy that can come through complementarity. In the life of grace, male expressions of courage tend toward initiative-taking and daring, while female expressions of courage tend toward patience and perseverance. When considered together, these expressions of courage display a synergistic complementarity (see Figure 9.3). The complementary expressions of courage create a new, synergistic expression of courage that is beyond what either sex can accomplish alone.

For example, like St. Edith Stein (St. Teresa Benedicta of the Cross), mentioned above, St. Maximilian Kolbe was killed at Auschwitz, and, like Stein, he comforted, consoled, and prayed with and for others who were also condemned to death alongside him. Kolbe's sacrifice also involved dramatic initiative-taking, which is a characteristic of the masculine genius. In a heroic act, he voluntarily substituted his life for that of another man, who was condemned to die.

As noted earlier, from a theological perspective, Mary is the highest expression of the feminine genius, and Joseph is the paradigm of the masculine genius. In the Gospels, both are called to courage, but they each live out the virtue in light of their unique geniuses and in complementary ways. When the angel of the Lord appears to Joseph in a dream, the angel implores him, "Do not be afraid" (Mt 1:20). Similarly, when the angel Gabriel appears to the Virgin Mary announcing that she will bear a son, he tells her, "Do not be afraid" (Lk 1:30). Both of their acts of courage are animated by charity, belief that the angel is from God, and hope that the difficult task will bring forth fruit. However, their acts of courage are different. Joseph's courage and faith, including his firm hope and initiative-taking, are clear when he takes Mary as his wife and later immediately responds to the angel in the dream by leading his family to Egypt to escape Herod's plan. Mary's faithfulness and courage, including her patience and perseverance, are evident in her acceptance of motherhood and trust in Joseph as they flee to Egypt. Joseph's courage is rooted in the masculine genius of doing for the other, and Mary's courage is rooted in the feminine genius of being for the other. Both expressions of courage surround the Incarnation, participate in God's salvific plan in a complementary way, and are needed for its fulfillment.

It is important to recall that virtues have different dimensions (Chapter 11, "Fulfilled in Virtue") including the vocational and transcendent dimensions, and the synergy that comes from complementarity takes different forms in light of those different dimensions and different vocations (Chapter 10, "Fulfilled Through Vocation"). For example, synergy can be found in the behavioral or performative dimensions of infused courage that is found in the everyday life of families, where the courageous acts of moth-

ers and fathers complement each other because of faith, hope, and charity. Both mothers and fathers sacrifice and give of themselves out of love for Christ. These sacrifices can be unique and can be complementary.

This synergy can also be found in the perfective and corrective dimensions of the infused virtue of courage (Chapter 11, "Fulfilled in Virtue"). In our hypersexual culture, men and women will need the gift of infused virtue of courage (along with temperance) to live chaste lives. Men and women, through their unique geniuses, can assist each other in growing in these virtues. For example, Eberstadt (2012) discusses the unique perspective that women have on pornography. Women do not use visual pornography to as great an extent as men but nevertheless are harmed by it (Ferree, 2013). This harm can either be direct, through exploitation, or indirect, through their partners' use of it. Thus, women have a unique perspective on the evils of pornography (Eberstadt, 2012). Because of divine grace and the moral guidance of the Church, women are supported by infused courage. They fulfill their calling by being for others, as well as by doing for others, for instance, by standing up against pornography publicly, speaking to the harm that it does to interpersonal relationships, and proclaiming the beauty of the Gospel's vision of chastity. In short, women can draw men's attention to the harm that pornography does to interpersonal relationships—an aspect that men frequently overlook, dismiss, or deny.

However, because of the same divine grace and the moral guidance of the Church, men must proclaim the complementary message. Since men are the primary users, makers, and financial beneficiaries of pornography, men are called to condemn pornography courageously. They must defend the dignity of women, draw attention to pornography's addictive qualities, explain how it distorts men's natural sexual life, and emphasize the importance of infused chastity. Even though women do not tend to use visual pornography, they are often consumers of erotic romance literature, and they have to resist it as well. Men can help women to see that excessive desires for romance to find the perfect prince charming, for the glamor of the rich and successful man, or for emotional intimacy of the ideal soul-mate can objectify the other and create harmful and unhealthy expectations. Men and women will have distinct messages informed by their unique geniuses, the vision of the person in the Gospel, and their love of Christ. Together their synergy creates awareness, strengths, and virtues unlikely to be developed solely on their own. They can help each other grow in holiness and gain a more robust understanding of the harm of lust, the importance of virtue, and the grace needed to live chastely.

Recall that synergy involves two persons working together to produce something that neither could create alone. In the infused virtue of courage, masculine-feminine synergy can be found in complementary expressions of the virtue. However, permeating all of these expressions and underlying this synergy are the particular geniuses of men and women, which have been healed and perfected by grace. Because of the unique genius found in the feminine expression of courage, women tend more to suffer with the other. This suffering comes in many forms, including the suffering that arises from being more deeply rooted in interpersonal relationships and thus being closer to the spiritual, physical, psychological, and moral pain of the other. Infused courage for women, then, oftentimes is expressed in the patience and perseverance to withstand and act through this suffering in order to remain with and sacrifice for the other (John Paul II, 1988, §19). Conversely, because of the unique genius found in the masculine expression of courage, men tend to take more initiative and physical risks. Together, these different geniuses produce different expressions of the virtue of courage (acquired and infused). As the virtue of courage is formed by charity and lived out in faith and hope, men and women provide each other with a more robust and dynamic understanding of the infused virtue that enables both sexes to flourish in their vocations, including the universal call to holiness.

This section has considered the significance and horizon of sex difference and complementarity. When masculine and feminine differences work together in a complementarity manner, they produce synergy and something greater than either could produce without the influence of the other. This complementarity does not diminish the dignity of men or women but instead elevates it by reminding both sexes of our call to communion and gift of self.

Conclusion

From the perspective of the Catholic Christian Meta-Model of the Person, sex difference has implications for how we flourish as individuals and together. While men and women are both created in the image and likeness of God and share the same human nature and dignity, they are biologically, psychologically, and spiritu-ally different. These biological, psychological, and spiritual differences influence how men and women flourish by shaping their vocational responsibilities as well as how they exercise the virtues within those vocations. In addition, these differences influence how men and women languish, how they express vice, and how they respond to treatment and therapy.

Sex differences also serve as the foundation of male-female complementarity. Male and female persons have nuptial significance and thus complement each other at the level of physiology and neurobiology, at the level of psychological and social tendencies, and at the level of ethical and spiritual dispositions. The complementarity between the sexes can produce a synergistic effect. When men and women work together, cooperate, and allow themselves to be shaped by the other sex, they produce something greater than either could produce alone, including fuller expressions of the virtues and of their callings, which reflect the strengths of both man and woman.

REFERENCES

Allen, P. (2004). Philosophy of relation in John Paul II's new feminism. In M. Schumacher (Ed.), *Women in Christ: Toward a new feminism* (pp. 67–104). Grand Rapids, MI: Eerdmans.

Allen, P. (2006). Man-woman complementarity: The Catholic inspiration. *Logos: A Journal of Catholic Thought and Culture, 9*(3), 87–108.

American Association for Marriage and Family Therapy (2015). *AAMFT Code of ethical principles for marriage and family therapists.* Washington, DC: Author. Retrieved from https://www.aamft.org/Documents/Legal%20Ethics/AAMFT-code-of-ethics.pdf

American Counseling Association (ACA). (2014). *ACA code of ethics.* Alexandria, VA: Author. Retrieved from www.counseling.org/resources/aca-code-of-ethics.pdf

American Psychiatric Association. (2013). *Diagnostic and statistical manual of mental disorders* (5th ed., text revision). Washington, DC: Author.

American Psychological Association (APA). (2007). Guidelines for psychological practice with girls and women. *American Psychologist, 62*(9), 949–979. Retrieved from www.apa.org/about/policy/girls-and-women-archived.pdf

American Psychological Association (APA). (2017). *Ethical principles of psychologists and code of conduct.* Washington, DC: Author. Retrieved from www.apa.org/ethics/code/ethics-code-2017.pdf

American Psychological Association (APA) Center for Workforce Studies. (2015). Demographics of the U.S. psychology workforce. Retrieved from https://www.apa.org/workforce/publications/13-demographics/index.aspx

American Psychological Association (APA), Boys and Men Guidelines Group. (2018). APA guidelines for psychological practice with boys and men. Retrieved from http://www.apa.org/about/policy/psychological-practice-boys-men-guidelines.pdf

Andreano, J. M., & Cahill, L. (2009). Sex influences on the neurobiology of learning and memory. *Learning and Memory, 16*(4), 248–266. doi:10.1101/lm.918309

Aquinas, T. (2005). *Disputed questions on the virtues* (E. M. Atkins & T. Williams, Eds.; E. M. Atkins, Trans.). Cambridge, United Kingdom: Cambridge University Press. (Original work composed 1272)

Aquinas, T. (1981). *Summa theologica* (Fathers of the English Dominican Province, Trans.). Westminster, MD: Christian Classics. (Original work composed 1265–1273)

Archer, J. (2004). Which attitudinal measures predict trait aggression? *Personality and Individual Differences, 36*(1), 47–60. doi:10.1016/S0191-8869(03)00050-3

Arguden, Y. (2012, June 7). Why boards need more women. *Harvard Business Review.* Retrieved from https://hbr.org/2012/06/why-boards-need-more-women

Aristotle. (1941). *Nicomachean ethics.* In R. McKeon (Ed.), *The basic works of Aristotle* (pp. 935–1112). New York, NY: Random House. (Original work composed ca. 350 BC)

Aristotle. (1943). *Generation of animals.* (A. L. Peck, Trans.). Cambridge, MA: Harvard University Press. (Original work composed ca. 350 BC)

Barger, L. (2003). *Eve's revenge: Women and a spirituality of the body.* Grand Rapids, MI: Brazos Press.

Baron-Cohen, S. (2003). *The essential difference: Men, women, and the extreme male brain.* London, United Kingdom: Allen Lane.

Barron, R. (2007). *The priority of Christ: Toward a*

postliberal Catholicism. Grand Rapids, MI: Brazos Press.

Baumgarte, R., & Nelson, D. W. (2009). Preference for same versus cross-sex friendships. *Journal of Applied Social Psychology, 39*(4), 901–917. doi:10.1111/j.1559-1816.2009.00465.x

Becker, S. W., & Eagly, A. H. (2004). The heroism of women and men. *American Psychologist, 59*(3), 163–178. doi:10.1037/0003-066X.59.3.163

Békés, V., Beaulieu-Prévost, D., Guay, S., Belleville, G., & Marchand, A. (2016). Women with PTSD benefit more from psychotherapy than men. *Psychological Trauma, 8*(6), 720–727.

Benenson, J. F. (1993). Greater preference among females than males for dyadic interaction in early childhood. *Child Development, 64*(2), 544–555. doi:10.2307/1131268

Benenson J. F., Markovits, H., Hultgren, B., Nguyen, T., Bullock, G., & Wrangham, R. (2013). Social exclusion: More important to human females than males. *PLoS ONE, 8*(2), e55851. doi:10.1371/journal.pone.0055851

Bjorklund, D. F., & Jordan, A. C. (2013). Human parenting from an evolutionary perspective. In W. B. Wilcox & K. K. Kline (Eds.), *Gender and parenthood: Biological and social scientific perspectives* (pp. 61–90). New York, NY: Columbia University Press.

Bleske, A. L., & Buss, D. M. (2000). Can men and women be just friends? *Personal Relationships, 7,* 131–151.

Brizendine, L. (2006). *The female brain.* New York, NY: Broadway.

Brizendine, L. (2010). *The male brain.* New York, NY: Broadway.

Budziszewski, J. (2012). *On the meaning of sex.* Wilmington, DE: ISI Books.

Buss, D. (2015). *Evolutionary psychology: The new science of the mind.* New York, NY: Pearson Education.

Butler, J. (1999). *Gender trouble: Feminism and the subversion of identity.* New York, NY: Routledge.

Carbone, J., & Cahn, N. (2007). Behavioral biology, the rational actor model, and the new feminist agenda. In D. Gold (Ed.), *Law & economics: Toward social justice* (pp. 189–235). Bingley, England: Emerald Group Publishing.

Carnes, P. J. (2001). *Out of the shadows: Understanding sexual addiction.* Center City, MN: Hazelden.

Catechism of the Catholic Church (CCC) (2nd ed.). (2000). Vatican City, Vatican: Libreria Editrice Vaticana.

Cessario, R. (2006). *Christian faith and the theological life.* Washington, DC: The Catholic University of America Press.

Charness, G., & Gneezy, U. (2012). Strong evidence for gender differences in risk taking. *Journal of Economic Behavior and Organization, 83*(1), 50–58. doi:10.1016/j.jebo.2011.06.007

Choate, L. H. (2008). *Girls' and women's wellness: Contemporary counseling issues and interventions.* Alexandria, VA: American Counseling Association.

Christen, Y. (1991). *Sex differences: Modern biology and the unisex fallacy* (N. Davidson, Trans.). Piscataway, NJ: Transaction.

Congregation for the Doctrine of the Faith. (2004). Letter to the bishops of the Catholic Church on the collaboration of men and women in the Church and in the world. Vatican City, Vatican: Libreria Editrice Vaticana.

Cozolino, L. (2006). *The neuroscience of human relationships: Attachment and the developing social brain.* New York, NY: Norton.

Daly, M. (1968). *The Church and the second sex.* Boston, MA: Beacon Press.

Daly, M. (1984). *Pure lust: Elemental feminist philosophy.* Boston, MA: Beacon Press.

Das, A. (2007). Masturbation in the United States. *Journal of Sex & Marital Therapy, 33*(4), 301–317.

Doidge, N. (2007). *The brain that changes itself: Stories of personal triumph from the frontiers of brain science.* New York, NY: Penguin.

Durante, K. M., Rae, A., & Griskevicius, V. (2013). The fluctuating female vote: Politics, religion, and the ovulatory cycle. *Psychological Science, 24*(6), 1007–1016. doi:10.1177/0956797612466416

Eberstadt, M. (2012). *Adam and Eve after the pill: Paradoxes of the sexual revolution.* San Francisco, CA: Ignatius Press.

Eder, D., & Hallinan, M. T. (1978). Sex differences in children's friendships. *American Sociological Review, 43*(2), 237–250. doi:10.2307/2094701

Eisenbruch, A. B., Simmons, Z. L., & Roney, J. R. (2015). Lady in red: Hormonal predictors of women's clothing choices. *Psychological Science, 26*(8), 1332–1338. doi:10.1177/0956797615586403

Eisenegger, C., Hausehofer, J., & Fehr, E, (2012). The role of testosterone in social interaction. *Trends in Cognitive Sciences, 15,* 263–271.

Ellis, L., Hershberger, S., Field, E., Wersinger, S., Pellis, S., Geary, D., … & Karadi, K. (2008). *Sex differences: Summarizing more than a century of scientific research.* New York, NY: Psychology Press.

Englar-Carlson, M., Evans, M. P., & Duffey, T. (Eds.). (2014). *A counselor's guide to working with men.* Alexandria, VA: American Counseling Association.

Englar-Carlson, M., & Kiselica, M. S. (2013). Affirming the strengths in men: A positive masculinity approach to assisting male clients. *Journal of Counseling & Development, 91*(4), 399–409. doi:10.1002/j.1556-6676.2013.00111.x

Farnan, T. (2015). The dignity and vocation of men. In M. Hasson (Ed.), *Promise and challenge: Catholic women reflect on feminism, complementarity, and the Church* (pp. 155–177). Huntington, IN: Our Sunday Visitor.

Ferree, M. (2013). Females: The forgotten sex addicts. In P. Carnes & K. M. Adams (Eds.), *Clinical management of sex addiction* (pp. 255–270). New York, NY: Routledge.

Fisher, H. (2004). *Why we love: The nature and chemistry of romantic love.* New York, NY: Owl Books.

Flemingham, K. L., & Bryant, R. A. (2012). Gender differences in the maintenance of response to cognitive behavior therapy for posttraumatic stress disorder. *Journal of Consulting and Clinical Psychology, 80*(2), 196–200. doi:10.1037/a0027156

Fossati, A., Somma, A., Borroni, S., Maffei, C., Markon, K. E., & Kreuger, R. F. (2016). A head-to-head comparison of the Personality Inventory for DSM-5 (PID-5) with the Personality Diagnostic Questionnaire-4 (PDQ-4) in predicting the general level of personality pathology among community dwelling subjects. *Journal of Personality Disorders, 30*(1), 82–94. doi:10.1521/pedi_2015_29_184

Fowers, B. J. (2005). *Virtue and psychology: Pursuing excellence in ordinary practices.* Washington, DC: American Psychological Association.

Francis. (2014, November 17). Address at opening of Colloquium on Complementarity of Man and Woman. Retrieved from https://zenit.org/articles/pope-francis-address-at-opening-of-colloquium-on-complementarity-of-man-and-woman/

Freud, S. (1961). The ego and the id. In J. Strachey (Ed. & Trans.), *The standard edition of the complete psychological works of Sigmund Freud* (Vol. 19, pp. 12–66). London, United Kingdom: Hogarth. (Original work published 1923)

Geary, D. C. (2010). *Male, female: The evolution of human sex differences* (2nd ed). Washington, DC: American Psychological Association.

Gee, D., Gabard-Durnam, L., Telzer, E., Humphreys, K., Goff, B., Shapiro, M.,… Tottenham, N. (2014). Maternal buffering of human amygdala–prefrontal circuitry during childhood but not adolescence. *Psychological Science, 25*(11), 2067–2078. doi:10.1177/0956797614550878

Gilligan, C. (1982). *In a different voice: Psychological theory and women's development.* Cambridge, MA: Harvard University Press.

Gottman, J. M. (1999). *The marriage clinic: A scientifically based marital therapy.* New York, NY: Norton.

Grabowski, J. S. (2003). *Sex and virtue: An introduction to sexual ethics.* Washington, DC: The Catholic University of America Press.

Gray, J. (1994). *Men are from Mars, women are from Venus: A practical guide for improving communication and getting what you want in your relationship.* New York, NY: Harper-Collins.

Grebe, N. M., Gangestad, S. W., Garver-Apgar, C. E., & Thornhill, R. (2013). Women's luteal-phase sexual proceptivity and the functions of extended sexuality. *Psychological Science, 24*(10), 2106–2110. doi:10.1177/0956797613485965

Greenberg, L. S., & Goldman, R. N. (2008). *Emotion-focused couples therapy: The dynamics of emotion, love, and power.* Washington, DC: American Psychological Association. doi:10.1037/11750-000

Greenfeld, L. (1997). Sex offenses and offenders: An analysis of data on rape and sexual assault. U.S. Department of Justice, Bureau of Justice Statistics. Retrieved from https://bjs.gov/content/pub/pdf/SOO.PDF

Greenfield, S. F., & Grella, C. E. (2009). What is "women-focused" treatment for substance use disorders? *Psychological Services, 60*(7), 880–882. doi:10.1176/appi.ps.60.7.880

Groeschel, B. (1985). *The courage to be chaste*. Mahwah, NJ: Paulist Press.

Gross, C. (2013). *Men and women becoming virtuous: An examination of Aquinas's theory of virtue in light of a contemporary account of sexual difference* (Doctoral dissertation). Retrieved from Proquest Dissertation & Theses Global database (UMI No. 3564679).

Guerney, B., Jr. (1977). *Relationship enhancement*. San Francisco, CA: Jossey-Bass.

Gurian, M. (2011). *How do I help him?: A practitioner's guide to working with boys and men in therapeutic settings*. Spokane, WA: Gurian Institute Press.

Handwerk, M. L., Clopton, K., Huefner, J. C., Smith, G. L., Hoff, K. E., & Lucas, C. P. (2006). Gender differences in adolescents in residential treatment. *American Journal of Orthopsychiatry, 76*(3), 312–324. doi:10.1037/0002-9432.76.3.312

Harley, W. F., Jr. (2011). *His needs, her needs: Building an affair-proof marriage*. Grand Rapids, MI: Revell Publishing.

Harris, C. R., Jenkins, M., & Glaser, D. (2006). Gender differences in risk assessment: Why do women take fewer risks than men? *Judgment and Decision Making, 1*(1), 48–63.

Herlitz, A., & Rehnman, J. (2008). Sex differences in episodic memory. *Current Directions in Psychological Science, 17*(1), 52–56.

Hoekzema, E., Barba-Müller, E., Pozzobon, C., Picado, M., Lucco, F., García-García, D.,... Vilarroya, O. (2016). Pregnancy leads to long-lasting changes in human brain structure. *Nature Neuroscience, 20*(2), 287–296. doi:10.1038/nn.4458

Hook, M. K., Gerstein, L. H., Detterich, L., & Gridley, B. (2003). How close are we? Measuring intimacy and examining gender differences. *Journal of Counseling & Development, 81*(4), 462–472.

Ingalhalikar, M., Smith, A., Parker, D., Satterthwaite, T., Elliott, M., Ruparel, K.,... Verma, R. (2014). Sex differences in the structural connectome of the human brain. *Proceedings of the National Academy of Sciences, 111*(2), 823–828. doi:10.1073/pnas.1316909110

Ingersoll, R., Merrill, L., & Stuckey, D. (2014). *Seven trends: The transformation of the teaching force, updated April 2014*. CPRE Report (#RR-80). Phila-delphia, PA: Consortium for Policy Research in Education, University of Pennsylvania.

International Theological Commission. (2004). *Communion and stewardship: Human persons created in the image of God*. Vatican City, Vatican: Libreria Editrice Vaticana.

Jacobi, J. (1973). *The psychology of C. G. Jung*. New Haven, CT: Yale University Press.

John Paul II. (1988). *Mulieris dignitatem* [Apostolic letter, on the dignity and vocation of women]. Vatican City, Vatican: Libreria Editrice Vaticana.

John Paul II. (1989). *Custos redemptoris* [Apostolic exhortation, on the person and mission of Saint Joseph in the life of Christ and of the Church]. Vatican City, Vatican: Libreria Editrice Vaticana.

John Paul II. (1995, June 29). *Letter to women*. Vatican City, Vatican: Libreria Editrice Vaticana.

John Paul II. (2006). *Man and woman he created them: A theology of the body* (M. Waldstein, Trans.). Boston, MA: Pauline Books and Media.

Kant, I. (1974). *Anthropology from a pragmatic point of view* (Mary J. Gregor, Trans.). The Hague, Netherlands: Martinus Nijhoff. (Original work published 1797)

Keverne, E. B., Martensz, E. B., & Tuite, B. (1989). Beta-endorphin concentrations in cerebrospinal fluid of monkeys are influenced by grooming relations. *Psychoneuroendocrinology, 14*, 155–161.

Kiselica, M. S., & Englar-Carlson, M. (2010). Identifying, affirming, and building upon male strengths: The positive psychology/positive masculinity model of psychotherapy with boys and men. *Psychotherapy: Theory, Research, Practice, Training, 47*(3), 276–287. doi:10.1037/a0021159

Kring, A. M. (2000). Gender and anger. In A. H. Fischer (Ed.), *Studies in emotion and social interaction. Second series. Gender and emotion: Social psychological perspectives* (pp. 211–231). New York, NY: Cambridge University Press. doi:10.1017/CBO9780511628191.011

Larimore, W., & Larimore, B. (2008). *His brain, her brain: How divinely designed differences can strengthen your marriage*. Grand Rapids, MI: Zondervan.

Lever, J. (1978). Sex differences in the complexity of children's play and games. *American Sociological Review 43*(4), 471–483. doi:10.2307/2094773

Liu, W. M. (2005). The study of men and masculinity as an important multicultural competency consideration. *Journal of Clinical Psychology, 61*(6), 685–697. doi:10.1002/jclp.20103

MacDonald, H. (2018, August 17). Gender is a construct—Except when it is not. *City Journal.* https://www.city-journal.org/html/gender-construct-16117.html

Mazur, A., & Booth, A. (1998). Testosterone and dominance in men. *Behavioral and Brain Sciences, 21*(3), 353–363.

McRae, T. R., Dalgleish, T. L., Johnson, S. M., Burgess-Moser, M., & Killian, K. D. (2014). Emotion regulation and key change events in emotionally focused couple therapy. *Journal of Couple & Relationship Therapy, 13*(1), 1–24. doi:10.1080/153 32691.2013.836046

Miller, C., & Swift, K. (1976). *Words and women.* Garden City, NY: Doubleday.

Miller, W. I. (2000). *The mystery of courage.* Cambridge, MA: Harvard University Press.

Moir, A., & Jessel, D. (1992). *Brain sex: The real difference between men and women.* New York, NY: Dell Publishing.

Musslewhite, K. (2017). *A reconceptualization of panic disorder in women over 45: Taking into consideration the integral complementarity of men and women.* (Unpublished doctoral dissertation). Institute for the Psychological Sciences, Divine Mercy University, Arlington, VA.

National Association of Social Workers. (2017). *Code of ethics of the National Association of Social Workers.* Retrieved from https://www.socialworkers .org/About/Ethics/Code-of-Ethics/Code-of-Ethics-English

Nelson, J. (1992). *Body theology.* Louisville, KY: Westminster/John Knox Press.

Noddings, N. (1984). *Caring: A feminine approach to ethics & moral education.* Berkeley, CA: University of California Press.

Noller, P., & Feeney, J. A. (1994). Relationship, satisfaction, attachment, and nonverbal accuracy in early marriage. *Journal of Nonverbal Behavior, 18*(3), 199–221.

Norfleet, J. A. (2007). *Teaching the male brain: How boys think, feel, and learn in school.* Thousand Oaks, CA: Corwin Press.

Norfleet, J. A. (2012). *The parent's guide to boys: Help your son get the most out of school and life.* Austin, TX: Live Oak Book Company.

Ogas, O., & Gaddam, S. (2012). *A billion wicked thoughts: What the internet tells us about sexual relationships.* New York, NY: Plume.

Oliver, M. B., & Hyde, J. S. (1993). Gender differences in sexuality: A meta analysis. *Psychological Bulletin, 114*(1), 29–51.

Ong, W. (1981). *Fighting for life: Contest, sexuality, and consciousness.* Ithaca, NY: Cornell University Press.

Payne, K. (2001). *Different but equal: Communication between the sexes.* Santa Barbara, CA: Praeger.

Peplau, L. A. (2003). Human sexuality: How do men and women differ? *Current Directions in Psychological Science, 12*(2), 37–40. doi:10.1111/1467-8721.01221

Peterson, C., & Seligman, M. E. P. (2004). *Character strengths and virtues: A handbook and classification.* New York, NY: Oxford University Press.

Pillemer, D. B., Wink, P., DiDonato, T. E., & Sanborn, R. L. (2003). Gender differences in autobiographical memory styles of older adults. *Memory, 11*(6), 525–532. doi:10.1080/09658210244000117

Pintzka, C. W., Evensmoen, H. R., Lehn, H., & Håberg, A. K. (2016). Changes in spatial cognition and brain activity after a single dose of testosterone in healthy women. *Behavioural Brain Research, 298*(B), 78–90. doi:10.1016/j.bbr.2015.10.056

Regnerus, M., & Uecker, J. (2011). *Premarital sex in America: How many young Americans meet, mate, and think about marrying.* New York, NY: Oxford University Press.

Rhoads, S. E. (2004). *Taking sex differences seriously.* San Francisco, CA: Encounter Books.

Rogers, C. (1951). *Client-centered therapy.* Boston, MA: Houghton-Mifflin.

Rose, A. J., & Rudolph, K. D. (2006). A review of sex differences in peer relationship processes: Potential trade-offs for the emotional and behavioral development of girls and boys. *Psychological Bulletin, 132*(1), 98–131. doi:10.1037/0033-2909.132.1.98

Ruether, R. R. (1993). *Sexism and God-talk: Toward a feminist theology.* Boston, MA: Beacon Press.

Sandberg, D. E., & Meyer-Bahlburg, H. F. (1994). Variability in middle childhood play behavior: effects of gender, age, and family background. *Archives of Sexual Behavior, 23*(6), 645–663.

Salsberg, E., Quigley, L., Mehfoud, N., Acquaviva, K.,

Wyche, K., & Sliwa, S. (2017). Profile of the social work workforce. Washington, DC: The George Washington University Health Workforce Institute. Retrieved from https://www.cswe .org/Centers-Initiatives/Initiatives/National -Workforce-Initiative/SW-Workforce-Book -FINAL-11-08-2017.aspx

Savage, D. (2015). The nature of woman in relation to man: Genesis 1 and 2 through the lens of the metaphysical anthropology of Aquinas. *Logos: A Journal of Catholic Thought and Culture, 18*(1), 71–93.

Schiltz, E. (2015). The promise and the threat of the "three" in integral complementarity. In M. Hasson (Ed.), *Promise and challenge: Catholic women reflect on feminism, complementarity, and the Church* (pp. 155–177). Huntington, IN: Our Sunday Visitor.

Schulz, J., & Thöni, C. (2016). Overconfidence and career choice. *PLoS ONE, 11*(1): e0145126. doi:10.1371/journal.pone.0145126

Scuka, R. (2005). *Relationship enhancement therapy.* New York, NY: Routledge.

Shepherd, J., Farrington, D., & Potts, J. (2004). Impact of antisocial lifestyle in health. *Journal of Public Health, 26*, 347–352.

Sherwin, M. (2009). Infused virtue and the effects of acquired vice: A test case for the Thomistic theory of infused cardinal virtues. *The Thomist, 73*, 29–52.

Siegel, D. J. (2012). *Pocket guide to interpersonal neurobiology: An integrative handbook of the mind* (1st ed.). New York, NY: Norton.

Simmons, R. G., Marine, S. K., & Simmons, R. L. (1987). *Gift of life: The effect of organ transplantation on individual, family, and societal dynamics.* New Brunswick, NJ: Transaction Books.

Simner, M. L. (1971). Newborn's response to the cry of another infant. *Developmental Psychology, 5*(1), 136–150. doi:10.1037/h0031066

Skowronski, J. J., Betz, A. L., Thompson, C. P., & Shannon, L. (1991). Social memory in everyday life: Recall of self-events and other-events. *Journal of Personality and Social Psychology, 60*(6), 831–843.

Sollod, R. N., Wilson, J. P., & Monte, C. F. (2009). *Beneath the mask: An introduction to theories of personality* (9th ed.). Hoboken, NJ: Wiley.

Stein, E. (1996). Spirituality of the Christian woman. In L. Gelber & R. Leuven (Eds.), *Essays on woman: The collected works of Edith Stein* (2nd ed.,

pp. 87–128) (F. M. Oben, Trans.). Washington, DC: Institute for Carmelite Studies Publications.

Storkey, E. (2001). *Origins of difference: The gender debate revisited.* Ada, MI: Baker Publishing Group.

Su, R., Rounds, J., & Armstrong, P. I. (2009). Men and things, women and people: A meta-analysis of sex differences in interests. *Psychological Bulletin, 135*(6) 859–884.

Tamres, L. K., Janicki, D., & Helgeson, V. S. (2002). Sex differences in coping behavior: A meta-analytic review and examination of relative coping. *Personality and Social Psychology Review, 6* (Part 1), 2–30. doi:10.1207/S15327957PSPR0601_1

Tannen, D. (1990). *You just don't understand: Women and men in conversation.* New York, NY: Ballantine.

Taylor, S. E., Klein, L. C., Lewis, B. P., Gruenewald, T. L., Gurung, R. A., & Updegraff, J. A. (2000). Biobehavioral responses to stress in females: Tend-and-befriend, not fight-or-flight. *Psychological Review, 107*(3), 411–429. doi:10.1037/0033-295X.107.3.411

Trivers, R. (1972). "Parental investment and sexual selection." In B. Campbell (Ed.), *Sexual selection and the descent of man: 1871–1971* (pp. 136–179). Chicago, IL: Aldine.

Titus, C. S. (2006). *Resilience and the virtue of fortitude: Aquinas in dialogue with the psychosocial sciences.* Washington, DC: The Catholic University of America Press.

Tunç, B., Solmaz, B., Parker, D., Satterthwaite, T. D., Elliott, M. A., Calkins, M. E., ... Verma R. (2016). Establishing a link between sex-related differences in the structural connectome and behaviour. *Philosophical Transactions of the Royal Society of London, 371*(1688). doi:10.1098/rstb.2015.0111

United States Department of Labor. (2003). Quick facts on registered nurses. Retrieved from https:// www.dol.gov/wb/factsheets/Qf-nursing.htm

van Kaam, A. (1966). *The art of existential counseling: A new perspective in psychotherapy.* Denville, NJ: Dimension Books.

Vatican II, Council. (1965). *Gaudium et spes* [Pastoral constitution on the Church in the modern world]. Vatican City, Vatican: Libreria Editrice Vaticana.

Vigna-Taglianti, F. D., Burroni, P., Mathis, F., Versino, E., Beccaria, F., Rotelli, M., ... Bargagli, A. M. (2016). Gender differences in heroin addiction and treatment: Results from the VEdeTTE cohort.

Substance Use & Misuse, 51(3), 295–309. doi:10.3109/10826084.2015.1108339

Wilcox, W. B., Anderson, J. R., Doherty, W. J., Eggebeen, D, Ellison, C. G., Galston, W. A., … Wallerstein, J., et al. (2011). *Why marriage matters: Thirty conclusions from the social sciences* (3rd ed.). New York, NY: Institute for American Values.

Williams, W. W. (1982). The equality crisis: Some reflections on culture, courts, and feminism. *Women's Rights Law Reporter, 7*(3), 175–200.

Wojtyła, K. (1993). The family as a community of persons (T. Sandok, Trans.). In A. N. Woznicki (Ed.), *Catholic thought from Lublin: Vol. 4. Person and community: Selected essays* (pp. 315–327). New York, NY: Peter Lang. (Original work published 1974)

Wojtyła, K. (2011). *Man in the field of responsibility* (K. Kemp & Z. M. Kieroń, Trans.). South Bend, IN: St. Augustine's Press. (Original work published 1991)

Wood, J., Koch, P., & Mansfield, P. (2006). Women's sexual desire: A feminist critique. *Journal of Sex Research, 43*(3), 236–244. doi:10.1080/00224490609552322

Yeo, B. T., Krienen, F. M., Eickhoff, S. B., Yaakub, S. N., Fox, P. T., Buckner, R. L., Asplund, C. L., Chee, M. W. (2015). Functional specialization and flexibility in human association cortex. *Cerebral Cortex, 25*(10), 3654–3672. doi:10.1093/cercor/bhu217

Zak, P. (2012). *The moral molecule: The source of love and prosperity.* New York, NY: Penguin.

Chapter 10

Fulfilled Through Vocations

CRAIG STEVEN TITUS, WILLIAM J. NORDLING,
AND PAUL C. VITZ

ABSTRACT: From within the Catholic Christian Meta-Model of the Person, this chapter asks how vocations contribute to the unique ways that the person flourishes or languishes. It proposes a triadic structure of vocations: call, response, and change (with positive or negative effects). It considers how the person is fulfilled through vocation understood at three levels and through two perspectives. The three levels are: vocations to goodness, justice, or holiness; vocational states; and work, service, and meaningful leisure. The two perspectives are a faith-based perspective (theology and the narrative of redemption) and a reason-based perspective (philosophy and science, including mental health theory and practice), which are used at each level of vocation, with special emphasis on implications for psychology and mental health practice. First, from a philosophical perspective, the chapter explores the supposition that by nature each person experiences a desire for goodness and a call to flourish. From a theological perspective, it explores the Christian supposition that the call (or vocation) to holiness enhances the call to goodness and flourishing, since it is made personal by God, who puts a desire in the human heart for growth in holiness and for communion. Second, the chapter philosophically explores the supposition that vocations take on further meaning because of intentional commitments to and practices in vowed and non-vowed vocational states (single, married, and religious or ordained service). Theologically, it then explores the Christian supposition that these vocational states are rooted in the divine gift of grace. Third, it explores philosophical and theological suppositions about the meaning and flourishing that are found in work, service, and meaningful leisure.

What does it mean to be called to goodness? And to holiness? What does it mean to be called to vocational states, such as being married in a family or ordained as a priest? What does it mean to be called to productive work in construction or service to one's nation in politics? How does the assumption that the human person experiences callings (or vocations) by na-ture and by grace provide a basis for understanding human flourishing and languishing? What are the implications for mental health practice?

The desire to flourish is a powerful influence in human life. The Catholic Christian Meta-Model of the Person (CCMMP) recognizes that this desire requires both subjective experience and an objective source of attraction, namely, the callings of goods such as life, family, friendship, and other social relationships, as well as truth and beauty. Human beings are drawn toward the source of purpose and meaning, which is the end or goal of human life. The nature of such goods is not merely that they generously and freely give of themselves, as the neo-Platonic dictum would express it: "Goodness is diffusive of itself" (*bonum est diffusivum sui*) (Pseudo-Dionysius, cited by Aquinas, 1273/1981, I-II, 94.2; I, 19.2). Rather, intrinsic goods serve as an invitation to encounter, service, and communion. This teleological or purposeful reality informs the basic callings, responses, and changes inherent to vocations. The person approaches his end (*telos*) in a narrative wherein vocations and virtues inform each other in a dialogical process. Virtues find roots in vocations, and vocations find expression in virtues, as they are interconnected through concrete practices (such as the just, caring, and competent practices of a mental health practitioner) and interpersonal relationships (such as being mother or father, son or daughter, friend or neighbor).

In this chapter, we will be attentive to the reason-based (philosophical) and faith-based (theological) understandings of vocation, as well as to indications of how a Catholic Christian conceptualization of vocation has theoretical and practical implications for ethics and mental health practice. We will investigate how dialogue and commitment underlie particular vocations. The natural inclinations are seeds of the virtues, vocations, and flourishing that constitute the call to a good life. The virtues themselves are understood as ways of ordering our response to the call of love (*ordo est amoris*), as St. Augustine would have it (427/1958, XV.22). The vocations and virtues frame the human understanding of and response to the persistent longing for more, the experience of restlessness

that endures throughout this life (Augustine, 401/2007, I.1.2).

Within the Catholic Christian faith-based dimension of this vision of the person, vocation has a redemptive character closely tied to its narrative. Redemption is needed because of the alienation from God, and the harm to others and society, caused by original, personal, and social sin. It is Christ who offers the Christian a frame for redemption and for the greatest love, which is based in communion and involves laying "down one's life for one's friends" (Jn 15:13). This love concerns not only the disciples (Mt 4:19; Mk 1:17), for every Christian is also called to follow Christ in this greatest love (Mt 16:24). In the Old Testament, the definitive response to the call from God is "Here am I, Lord." God calls Abraham (Gen 22:1), Moses (Ex 3:4), Samuel (1 Sam 3:4), the other prophets, and his beloved people. In the present age, the call is extended through Christ to all people, who are called to holiness, communion, and purpose (Mt 28:19). From this perspective, to lay down one's life is rooted in union and sacrament, which are the foundation for the many services and sacrifices called for by committed loving relationships, as among friends, family, and neighbors. In particular this chapter will explore the Christian supposition that the vocational states are rooted in Baptism for all, the sacraments of Matrimony and Ordination for the married and ordained, consecration or promises for religious men and women, and the commitment to the goods available through single life (such as charity and chastity).

We will also explore the meaning of vocation, by asking: What difference do vowed and non-vowed vocational states make for understanding oneself and others? This question has parallel and complementary foci, which are essential to our relationships to ourselves, others, and the world. Two truths stand out clearly. First, we cannot understand another person without some sense of the vocations that are operative in his or her life. Second, we cannot fully understand ourselves and our relationships with others and the world without an awareness of how our vocational commitments shape our self-understanding and character. We presume, in this chapter, that vocations are dialogical and are best understood within the narrative of one's interpersonal relationships, ethical and religious principles and practices, practical reason and choices, as well as related feelings, instincts, and inclinations. And on the theological level, we posit that such a philosophical understanding of nature, vocation, and flourishing is complemented by a Catholic Christian understanding of grace. Grace is God's active presence and his gifts that underlie life and the offer of salvation and all that is good. It not only brings new motivation to the vocation, but also transforms its content and goal, providing additional gifts that enable the living out of one's vocation. For each topic treated, the chapter will first engage the philosophical idiom, before engaging theological reflections as well.

People Are Fulfilled Through Personal Vocations

Often, the term "vocation" is associated with a work profession or a religious calling. However, if we, without neglecting work or the religious dimension, first focus on the larger phenomenon, we discover that callings or vocations are charged with meaning and direction for one's life. According to Wojtyła (1993), "The question 'what is my vocation?' means 'in what direction should my personality develop, considering what I have in me, what I have to offer, and what others—other people and God—expect of me?'" (p. 257). "Vocation" comes from *vocare*,

which is Latin for "to call." The call that underlies a vocation is not simply someone else's cry for help. Rather, it is an announcement of real desire for true flourishing and potential communion with God. It is an invitation to engage in the particular and unique task that meets God's purpose for our life. It involves the attraction to and desire for the goodness, truth, beauty, existence, of a person, a relationship, or a belief. Moreover, if the call is significant enough, people will spend their whole lives in its company and at its service, as is the case of the calls found in conjugal commitment and in enduring causes, such as justice and holiness. As Wojtyła (1993) adds: "That a particular person has a particular vocation always … means that his or her love is fixed on some particular goal" (p. 256) (see also other Catholic personalists and phenomenologists, such as Nédoncelle, 1966; Marcel, 1951/2010; and Stein, 1996). Failure to respond to the higher calling and ultimate meaning will lead to languishing, as affirmed not only by a Catholic approach to the person, but also by humanistic theorists, for example, Buber (1923/1971), Frankl (1959, 1969), Fromm (1950, 1956), and Maslow (1968, 1987).

What Is the Structure of a Vocation?

A vocation is dynamic. It requires both passive moments and active movements. It has a narrative character, historical background, metaphysical context, and an ultimate goal. Furthermore, a philosophical analysis of the experience of vocations reveals a triadic structure: call, response, and change. When we live out our vocational calls successfully, rooted in the narrative into which we are born (e.g., as son or daughter), we grow in love, wisdom, and justice (Hauerwas, 1981).

First, we are called by the other, that is, we receive a call, a vocation. Someone as a source of goodness attracts us and creates an encounter. For example, we meet another person and are shown the possibility of developing an enduring friendship based on worthwhile values and goals (Aristotle, ca. 350 BC/1941a), such as belief in God or the import of being good fathers or mothers (Jn 15:13). Without knowledge, encounter, and initiative, we do not do anything, speak to others, or make commitments. A human call (that is, a vocation) is established when a good discloses itself, through the very nature of a thing or through the intentional communication of others and God. Certain calls beckon almost irresistibly for a personal meeting, since to ignore it would diminish us. In particular callings, we find instances of the good, truth, relationality, beauty, and existence (Schmitz, 2009) in the spouse, child, friend, and stranger. We also find them in God and in the natural world. In creation, the good that calls out may not be a person as we know it. In order to have an effect, though, the call must be both communicated and recognized. The source of the call must be perceived as attractive and suitable to the person's goals. In this sense, a call is primarily received.

Second, once we have encountered the call as an invitation, we have a choice. We can ignore the call, reject it, or accept it. In everyday life, we can reject many types of callings without ill effect, and in some case things that seem like callings may be distractions or temptations. However, in responding negatively to the fundamental types of callings aimed at our perfection and redemption (that is, the transcendent, vocational states, and work, service, and meaningful leisure), in rejecting the call we have received—we attempt to refute reality and the natural moral order (natural law). We undermine the *potential* of the call, and thus we languish. In responding positively, in accepting it, we appropriate the

call. It becomes personal. And, since we enter into and share the call with the call-giver, the call becomes a source of shared goodness and relationship between us. An active positive response to the call elicits reciprocity, mutuality, and a receptive affirmation. The dialogue begins, and the vocation takes form such that a friendship is started. The "I" responds to the "you," and they become a "we" (Buber, 1923/1971). A future lies open. In the case of future spouses, the possibilities of friendship, courtship, engagement, and marriage present themselves. In the case of a career, the possibilities of working as a craftsman, creating as a writer, or taking initiatives as an entrepreneur present themselves. There are ethical implications that depend on the nature of the commitment and of the agents (specifically as persons), such as the ethical responsibilities of being a spouse, parent, employee, and so on. While there are many types of affirmative response, the basic response of interest and commitment sets the groundwork for further developments.

Third, responding changes us. Positive responses to true callings result in growth, negative ones in self-diminishment. As we give of ourselves through pursuit of the call and chosen response, we are transformed by the encounter and the dialogue, in our acts and in who we become as sons and daughters, brothers and sisters, husbands and wives, fathers and mothers, colleagues and friends. The external call and mutual end becomes internalized and transforms our actions. The goal or purpose (*telos*) of vocations is thus the perfecting of persons and relationships. This active, engaged, transformative sense of "having a calling" requires types of receptivity and active self-gift that embed each person in the particular vocation. We are changed with a view to building a larger project with a greater end that involves a new or renewed commitment, relationship, and action. For example, marriage involves a calling and dialogue in which fidelity must be lived. In an ideal setting, the man and the woman freely prepare for and choose the flourishing that the marriage vocation offers. In other words, they get to know each other deeply, they offer or accept the proposal of marriage, they engage in the serious courtship that prepares for marriage, and they commit themselves to communion and mutual self-giving and to serving the family in love. Or, by contrast, they allow selfishness and self-centeredness to dominate, they fail to give of self and receive from their spouse, or they fail to be honest and faithful.

This triad of call, response, and change underlies the peculiarities of each level of the vocational experience, which will be discussed in this chapter as pertaining to (a) calls to flourishing and goodness, (b) calls to committed forms of life, and (c) calls to work, service, and meaningful leisure.

What Are the Three Levels of Vocation?

In the strict and basic sense, to have a "vocation" is to respond to the call to flourishing and goodness. This response characterizes a person's life, especially through the gift of self, personal encounter, and communion or, on the contrary, through the closing of oneself, narcissism, and indifference (Aquinas, 1265–73/1981, II-II, 23.1; Wojtyła, 1993). A closer look reveals that, as mentioned above, there are three large fields of vocation (calls to flourishing, to vocational state in life, and to work, service, and meaningful leisure) and two perspectives (philosophical and theological) to consider.

First, from a philosophical perspective, there is each person's basic *call to flourishing or goodness* as a human person. Such human flourish-

ing springs from an ultimate origin and points toward an ultimate end. For from the Christian philosophical perspective, the attempt to live a good life is anchored in calls from and responses to God. Second, there is the call that concerns a person's *vocational state in life*. Each person is born with a spousal meaning to his or her body, even while still single (Wojtyła, 1993). Some people experience a clear call to the *single* life and commit themselves to the good of relationship, charity, and chastity, with family, friends, and neighbors. Others choose to commit themselves uniquely to another person (i.e., their spouse), and to the fruit of this union (i.e., children), through *marriage*, in which the spouses promise their lives and commit their time to each other. Other people choose to devote their lives to people, the Church, and God through *consecrated or ordained life*. Third, there is the level of vocational call that touches on a person's *work, service, and meaningful leisure* throughout life. Such work includes both the formal labor and the informal service (such as volunteer work) that occupy a person's time and attention. Needed rest and meaningful leisure also provide for restoration and self-development. Across all of these levels there is a free yet "proper course for every person's development to follow" (Wojtyła, 1993, p. 256). The negative responses to these three levels of vocation lead to self-centeredness and social withdrawal, noncommittal relationships and abandoned families, and half-hearted service and undiscovered meaning in work and rest; in short, such negative responses lead to languishing.

From the theological perspective of the Catholic Christian Meta-Model of the Person, there are questions that arise from the spiritually transcendent dimension of vocations. Looked at from this perspective, "vocation" is perceived as a religious phenomenon: God calls or invites people to holiness, to a particular vocational state, or to a particular work; people respond (or not) to the calling; and they are changed in the process. Coming from this perspective, we posit that the spiritual vocation elicits types of communion and self-giving that are transformed by grace, that is, by God's presence, will, and word, which strengthens, frees, and sanctifies us in the image of his Son through the Holy Spirit. We do not posit that the spiritual or theological dimension will be perceived by all. For example, an experience of faith and hope can bring meaning to the mother of suffering children, whom she experiences as a gift of God, while she receives strength and understanding to care for them, even when their lives are short or different than expected. However, a non-believer may not understand the difference that theological faith and hope bring. So although there is but one reality, the experience is shaped, first at the natural level, by one's discernment of and response (or non-response) to vocational calls, and second, by whether such calls are responded to from a perspective of faith.

What Are the Differences Between Everyday and Ultimate or Final Vocations?

A call or vocation attracts us because of the good or value that it embodies or promises. On the one hand, a vocation can contribute to one's own and other people's flourishing, since each unique manifestation of personal and societal justice, patience, service, and self-giving is part of a larger whole. On the other hand, a vocation can refer to the very source of flourishing, as when a vocation to service seeks the common good, or a vocation to ordained ministry seeks the good of others and participation in God's offer of salvation to the world.

A basic philosophical and phenomenological treatment of vocation can identify the common

experiences of call and response, which we constantly encounter, and which have both everyday and ultimate import. There are the everyday instances of call and response and change; for example, parents experience a call to care for children, especially when the latter are hungry or frightened, sad or confused. Parents in turn experience flourishing in their calling as they respond to the needs of their children in responsible and loving ways. In short, by responding to the needs of their children, they exercise love and increase their ability to be other-centered and to sacrifice for the good of others; or instead, by neglecting their children, they become more self-centered and narcissistic.

In many cases, there is also the ultimate vocation, through which people sense the existence of a unique source of life: God. We propose that this vocation is of great importance and is commonly and personally experienced even in the midst of contradictory voices. For example, the New Atheists claim that there is no meaning to human life, or that the desire for meaning, truth, and God is an epiphenomenal illusion that has some evolutionary, survival advantage for the human race (Dawkins, 1976; Dennett, 1995; Hitchens, 2007) and that can be attributed to a "God molecule" or "God gene" (Hamer, 2005). However, this rejection of ultimate meaning and vocation is challenged by neuroscientists such as Beauregard (2012), who refute the scientific accuracy of claims that a so-called God gene or God molecule could explain much important about faith and religion or be anything but the embodied, neurological capacity for religious experience. At one level, the neurological experiments reported by Beauregard (2012; Beauregard & O'Leary, 2008) demonstrate the possibility that top-down, self-conscious executive functioning (efficacious volition) serves to modify strong emotions, such as sadness or sexual attraction. At a further level, also in a nonreductionist manner, top-down personal experiences also manifest further change that believers call grace (see section on Nature and Grace in Chapter 19, "Redeemed").

Moreover, philosophers, such as Nagel (2012) and Feser (2008), address the challenges of the New Atheists by drawing upon human experience and reason to show the reasonableness of belief in the existence of a nonreductionist source of ultimate meaning and, therefore, an ultimate vocation. Consideration of the existence of an ultimate being—the source of existence, goodness, truth, beauty, and family and other relationships—does not leave a person indifferent; it has implications for ethics and mental health practice. This ultimate level of vocation is dialogical and participatory, a communion. It is a foundational call to relationship with God, lived out in holiness, love, goodness, and gratitude, and given shape by the different levels of vocation found in a person's vowed or non-vowed vocational state and life work, as will be explained.

How Are Vocations Significant for Psychology, Mental Health Practice, and Ethics?

The CCMMP identifies personal and interpersonal vocations as essential for understanding the person in any setting, for example, as client or clinician. The Meta-Model also recognizes that mental health professionals, for example, can acquire the capacity to explore the various levels of vocational calls that they and their clients experience and to utilize them to offer motivation, meaning, and direction for their clients and therapeutic work: by taking the client's vocations into account in assessment and intervention, by helping the client to understand better his or her vocations so as to provide intrinsically

meaningful and motivating therapeutic goals, and by helping the client draw upon his or her own vocational resources, with good effects for treatment outcomes (Chapter 20, "Principles for Training"). The clinical response to the suffering that challenges the basic natural vocation or call to flourishing is not abstract (Miller, 2004). Rather it is found in the practices, for example, that enable a therapist or friend to serve as a relay of hope for the depressed person, or as a source of courage for the person suffering from an anxiety disorder, or as a support in self-control for the person attracted to mind-altering substances. This is the natural level of vocation, which is called flourishing.

Thus, understanding a person's vocations is just as foundational as understanding his virtues. Vocations support a person's search for relationship and meaning, which are, in psychology, mental health practice, and ethics, key measures of flourishing. A vocation is the means by which a person concretely participates in the dialogue of seeking an end for which it is worth freely giving of his very limited time: in a real sense, these vocations are means by which persons give their very lives. As mentioned earlier in this chapter and in the next chapter, on virtues, a vocation requires a dynamic view of the person and the virtues in order to take its full shape as an appropriate response and change. Understanding how various vocations underlie and constitute a good life of virtue and flourishing is the interest of (a) *psychology*, which concerns the theoretical responses to the questions of how to find a "why to live for" (Frankl, 1959), how to find relief from suffering, and what makes a person flourish; (b) *psychotherapy*, which concerns the therapeutic responses that free people from disorders (or support them in coping with what cannot be changed) and that free them for fuller engagement in the practices that contribute to the flourishing found in their callings; and (c) *ethics*, which concerns the context of the natural moral law and the ethical responses that build up virtuous character and the freedom for excellence

and flourishing (Ashley, 2013; Berkman & Titus, 2005; John Paul II, 1993; Pinckaers, 1995). For more on the moral determinations and development, see Chapter 11, "Fulfilled in Virtue."

Vocation to Goodness: Philosophical Perspective

The Catholic Christian Meta-Model of the Person supposes that a basic relational and dialogical structure underlies all levels of vocation. Everyone is called to goodness, that is, to seek what is good and resist what is evil. Human callings involve being attracted to and perfected by true goods found in knowledge, existence, love, family, friendship, community, truth, and beauty. Each vocation is made personal when, upon encountering a particular person or good, the one called responds. The response assumes an attraction, attachment, and, ultimately, gift of self that leads to and motivates personal development, healing, moral action, flourishing, and communion.

What Is the Basic Vocation of Mankind?

What is the human person's most basic vocation? From a philosophical view and an evolutionary perspective, survival of the person and the species (*homo sapiens sapiens*) are basic needs that people strive for consciously and unconsciously. Evolutionary psychology frames its conception of human agency and relationships in terms of survival and reproduction. The need to protect oneself and pass on one's genes does explain something of human experience. In fact, this basic knowledge existed before the science of genetics. But the theory of evolution fails seriously when, shortsightedly, it assumes mere materialistic determinism. For example, Richard Dawkins (1976) has popularized a version of evolutionary theory that assumes that genes

have a tendency not only to survive but to be selfish, even more so than conscious individual humans. In seeking to survive, genes influence humans (through instincts) to naturally select partners who will improve the gene pool.

Dawkins's interpretation, however, assumes a relativist, reductionist, and deterministic perspective, which does not result from observation, but sets a limit on what can be understood as human purpose and flourishing; that is, this assumption sets the principle of survival of the fittest above the vocation to love and be just (Feser, 2008), which more fully develops as one ages, even as one loses the capacity for reproduction. A biological reductionist interpretation of evolution, thus, has no interest in our human flourishing or in our happiness. A complex view of evolution based on a classical philosophical perspective posits that people are called to more than simple survival (Nagel, 2012; Schönborn, 2007). They are called to a type of flourishing—as individuals, families, and a whole—that is intrinsically teleological, nondeterministic, and nonrelativist. Recent re-conceptualizations of flourishing, in positive psychology, have tried to widen the notion of happiness that is narrowed by the assumptions made by Dawkins and other New Atheists. For example, Seligman (2012) has corrected his own thought by widening his conceptualization of flourishing. He identifies five factors, which expand his baseline of understanding flourishing: positive emotion, engagement, relationship, meaning, and accomplishment. However, positive psychology seems to focus on these factors as functional mental health concepts (Peterson, 2006, p. 238; Kristjansson, 2013), without recognizing the related and necessary side that is largely personalist, clearly ethical (connected to natural moral law), and commonly religious.

The merely "natural vocation" or desire to survive and reproduce does not explain significant things that human beings value. Nor does a functional mental health concept of flourishing adequately include what humans value as worthwhile. Other goods—such as truth, goodness, justice, family life, and community—underlie our desires for love and acceptance and give meaning to our efforts at overcoming suffering and fear and at flourishing on everyday and ultimate levels. Reproduction is not the most basic of callings. Goodness is. Truth is. Committed relationship is. Humans are called to know truth, to love goodness, to serve other people, to contemplate beauty, and to flourish as a consequence. These transcendent desires are at the heart of reality and human experience. Such an understanding of the person often leads clients in psychotherapy, who begin with goals such as ending suffering, to ultimately conclude with therapeutic goals aimed at doing what is right and just, healing relationships, and seeking meaning, even when short-term or even long-term suffering may be required of them.

What Do Experiences of Languishing and Unhappiness Say About Flourishing?

Both languishing and flourishing speak of our call to be a whole person in relationship with others. They speak of our capacities to know and love other people and the way we are fulfilled or not through vocations and in virtues. Although the Meta-Model's approach is positive—that is, it aims at flourishing—we posit that understanding languishing is necessary in order to better understand flourishing. Certain types of languishing and suffering can be caused by defects, accidents, and trauma at biological, psychological, social, and spiritual levels, for which the person is not personally responsible. Languishing also can be caused by persons' intentionally not affirming the goods or appreciating the beauty that they encounter. This denial of good leads to compromised choices and maladapted senses of what is right or pleasurable. For example, regardless of personal mitigating factors, failing to respond to the call to goodness can often be traced to disrespect for life, lack of self-control, self-serving deeds, hateful words, indifference or lack of empathy toward others, wrathful attacks on the innocent, and other vices. Certain "calls" should be ignored, such as the call of pseudo-friends to crime, the call of temptation, and the call to follow the effects of past sin. Such skewed calls contribute to languishing and vice that influence persons' everyday well-being and direct them away from their vocation, flourishing, and ultimate redemption.

How Might an Account of Vocation Need Reference to Virtues?

Rather than to languishing, vice, and ill health, the basic calling of the person is to flourishing (what is called holiness, in the theological approach; see below). As discussed in the next chapter (Chapter 11, "Fulfilled in Virtues"), flourishing is understood in accord with the potential of human nature. Flourishing requires the realization of biopsychosocial health, ethical goodness, and spiritual holiness. These three aspects (health, goodness, and holiness) must be clearly distinguished from one another and attended to seriously: emphasis on any one of these aspects without the others results in unbalanced flourishing. Human flourishing can be understood through the practical wisdom and practices that underlie the acquisition of the virtues (Mac-Intyre, 1999; Guardini, 1998; Moncher & Titus, 2009). As demonstrated throughout the rest of this chapter, to understand the way that a person flourishes or languishes through vocations, we need recourse to complex accounts of the virtues and details of that person's life. This account of flourishing will include reference to the practices of reason (philosophy) and faith (religion), as well as their implications for mental health practice widely speaking.

The vocation to flourish requires capacities for virtue, especially the capacities to know and to love. Reason tells us that humans have a nature that, although rather malleable, has a stable core, which serves as a basis for the articulation of ethical norms and the development of legal structures (International Theological Commission, 2015). Knowledge of evil acts always to be avoided and good practices to follow provides a basis for family life, educational initiative, and societal laws and customs (John Paul II, 1993, §§80–82). For example, a person can have clarity in knowing that intrinsically evil acts such as murder and adultery are never to be done, regardless of circumstances or intention, and that good practices like fidelity in marriage are always to be respected. Far from stifling personal creativity and distinctness, a person's vocation is a unique combination of call, response, and change that is lived out through his or her responsible, just, and loving personal relationships with family, friends, community, and God (Cullen, 2012). The natural and graced aspect of every vocation—to goodness or flourishing; to the single, married, religious, or priestly life; and to work—involves a building up of the person's human nature. The response to one's callings enriches the very structures of human nature, by both perfecting and healing the person through the qualities of courage, fidelity, patience, self-control, friendliness, and the other virtues.

Vocation to Holiness: Theological Perspective

What Difference Does a Call to Holiness Make?

Some people have claimed that everyday goodness and Christian holiness have the same object but simply different types of motivation. This is the Kantian approach, which empties the object of religion in order to focus on good will or benevolence. This position, however, is not compelling. Although such a view may give comfort through its ecumenism and support of the valuable commonalities of various ethical systems and religious traditions, it minimizes and distorts important, even vital, differences among them in how one views the nature of the human person and human callings. The Catholic Christian Meta-Model supposes that both dimensions, the objective and the personal, are significant to understanding goodness and holiness. A Christian vocation is differentiated not only by personal motivation or charity, but also by the intentional object (i.e., the aim or goal of the vocation), which is God's providential plan of salvation through Christ Jesus, sanctification through the Holy Spirit, in the context of the Church community of faith and sacramental practices.

The first of our levels of "vocation," in the proper theological sense, involves the divine call to holiness, love, and flourishing, which requires the personal response that characterizes people's lives, especially through communion and the "gift of self." In addition to ethical goodness though, the Second Vatican Council (1964) teaches that all Christian believers are called to a life of holiness in following Christ (§39). Providentially, God calls each person to specific types of knowing, loving, and serving God, others, and self (Lk 10:27). This personal Christian call communicates the unique role that the person is asked to carry out in the divine plan (Eph 2:10; 1 Thess 4:3; 2 Tim 1:9; Grisez & Shaw, 2003). This theological vision of vocation also is rooted in the belief that Christ is the center of human history, although not in a way that is personally known by non-believers. Moreover, this first level of vocation is experienced in the goodness of creation and the responses that even non-believers make in respecting and admiring the nature of creation and of other persons. In this context, the Second Vatican Council (1964) affirms that God also offers grace to non-Christian believers, as well as to agnostics and atheists, who search for goodness and justice in the world (Vatican II, 1964, §16). All humans are called to respond to their vocations and to seek goodness through a virtuous life.

Admittedly, this divine call often occurs in the face of languishing, evil, and hatred, which contrast flourishing, holiness, and love. We sense that our negative experiences, however, are not the last word. They mysteriously contain an invitation to their contrary. Even when awakened by the absence of flourishing, holiness, and love, vocation entails love, service, sacrifice, and the exercise of virtue—all of which are perfective of the person and the person's relationships. People of faith typically interpret vocations as a personal "call" from God.

According to the Second Vatican Council (1964, §§39–40), the "universal call to holiness" springs from God's call and grace. Jesus' teaching and example expresses the call to a purpose or end (telos): "Be perfect [téleioi] as your heavenly Father is perfect [téleiós]" (Mt 5:48). At the most basic level, this divine dynamic call is to

be humbly united with God, in whose image we were created. The fundamental vocation of the Christian and of all mankind (even those who neither know the Judeo-Christian tradition nor have an experience of Christ) is to be united to God. At the core of this call to holiness is charity, which animates the virtues and the good life. The vocation to goodness and holiness, moreover, is available to all those who recognize the call to goodness as it is represented in the parable of the Good Samaritan (Lk 10:30–38) and as it is found in the virtues of charity and justice, in the gifts of the Holy Spirit, and in the wisdom of the Beatitudes (Mt 5:3–12).

Is Flourishing Immediate or Progressive?

There are different types of perfection or completeness for the human person. However, in every case, God is the primary referent for what can be considered perfection. God is the transcendent first and final principle of human joy (beatitude), completeness (holiness), and love (charity). The Christian life has the goal of perfecting charity, as a progressive union with God and others. There are degrees of charity and of all the virtues; we all start as beginners, but progress as intermediates, in order to attain traits of a mature or advanced Christian; the dynamic perfect virtue we strive for will be the state of the blessed in heaven (Aquinas, 1273/1981, II-II, esp. 24.9). It should be stated that the term "perfect" is often used in Catholic theology to describe the last stage of development (Tanquerey, 1930). However, since this term is often taken as static, this text will use the terms "advanced" and "mature" to identify the dynamic and humble aspect of this stage of continuing development. Every Christian is bound to God's precepts and commandments, not only the beginner but also the intermediate and the mature. The basic precept, which informs every more particular precept and practice, is that of the twofold love of God and neighbor (Mt 22:37; Mk 12:30; Lk 10:27; Eph 2:10; 1 Thess 4:3). The state of the mature is the goal for every Christian's expression of love. These three stages can be further understood in what mystical theology has identified as asceticism (purification), illumination, and sanctification (union) (Pinckaers, 1995, pp. 354–378; see also Garrigou-Lagrange, 1948). These three stages of growth and their implications are treated further in this volume (Chapter 19, "Redeemed"). Such progression of growth is mirrored in psychotherapy by clients who become less self-centered, more self-mastered, more loving and relational, and more forgiving as therapy proceeds (Enright, 2012; Enright & Fitzgibbons, 2014; Worthington, 2003; Worthington et al., 2014).

These theological insights have many implications for the psychological studies, which have recently shown that healthy spiritual practices (spirituality) and psychosocial functions positively correlate with human flourishing (McEntee, Dy-Liacco, & Haskins, 2013). Moreover, a growing body of research suggests a positive empirical correlation between mental health and intrinsic religious or spiritual practices such as belief, prayer, church attendance, moral principles, and so on (Koenig, King, & Carson, 2012). Unfortunately, this chapter does not have space to elaborate; however, the importance and relevance of the research is worth mentioning.

How Does a Person Pursue Perfection Without Perfectionism?

Mental health practitioners, spiritual directors, ethical counselors, and people in their everyday interactions need to understand how the spiritual call to "perfection" (goodness and holiness) accompanies the basic processes of grace, growth, and healing in the human psyche and in human relationships. Inasmuch as human beings are in the process of overcoming the effects of sin, they participate in two levels of growth and purification. First, there is the graced *growth* needed to overcome many of the effects of ignorance, original sin (e.g., tendencies to hatred, pride, envy, and narcissism), and social disorders (e.g., family dysfunction, cultural prejudice, poverty resulting from injustice). Second, there is the *healing* needed to overcome the effects of particular personal and interpersonal sin and the corresponding disordered dispositions (e.g., particular acts of hatred and the tendency to repeat hateful acts). In either case (growth or healing), well-intentioned efforts may be undercut by excess—such as, by destructive perfectionism and scrupulosity, or alternatively, complacent narcissistic views that undermine an evaluation that one is in need of growth.

According to the Five Factor Model of personality traits, perfectionism is a maladaptive form of extreme conscientiousness (Widiger, 2017; Widiger & Costa, 2012). It is the harmful tendency to always want to better oneself or to perform flawlessly. It often involves overly critical evaluations of oneself and of others. Nevertheless, striving for perfection (goodness and holiness) may also be conceptualized in a positive manner. To discern the positive ways forward and the negative traps on the journey toward flourishing, some thinkers have distinguished between "normal and neurotic perfectionism" (Hamachek, 1978).

Human "perfection" without perfectionism can be understood from the explicitly theological perspective of development, healing, and sanctification. Spiritual perfection (completeness and holiness) without negative or neurotic perfectionism is a process wherein a person humbly follows the humble Christ, through charity, and in an ordered love, to his vocation or life goal (*telos*) (Mt 19:21; Vatican II, 1964, §40). The traps to seeking such flourishing include spiritual scrupulosity and over-conscientiousness, when a person expects perfection in exaggerated terms and timing (Santa, 2007). Furthermore, scrupulosity perfectionism is found in the anxiety that continually judges oneself wanting. A person fears to transgress the ethical code, break a moral law, upset a friend, or offend God. Such fear of punishment or alienation is a source of anxiety that often arises out of uncertainty about being loved. From the Catholic Christian perspective, "perfect love casts out fear" (1 Jn 4:18). Thus, the fear of punishment (servile fear) is replaced by filial reverence and respect (filial fear). Moreover, the spiritual discernment characterized by humble prayer and attentiveness is a safeguard against neurotic perfectionism. The virtue of humility helps us both to understand our own limitations and to recognize our human dignity as God's children, while we patiently work toward the perfection that God wills for us and assists us in attaining. Humility also teaches us more about ourselves and God's plan of salvation and sanctification than does a frenetic race to flourish on our own terms.

Vocational States: Philosophical Perspective

The second level of vocation concerns the vocational states and their implications for flourishing, ethics, and mental health. Although everyone is born single, and some people remain so throughout life, there are four vocational states (some vowed, some non-vowed) that involve the commitment that marks one's life and way of relating to other people. The four vocational states are found in being single, married, ordained, and religiously consecrated to the service of God and others. In this section we will attend to the philosophical side of these states, before discussing their theological aspects in the section that follows.

What Is the Nature of the Call to Being Single?

The call to flourishing is intrinsic to the single person and motivates him or her, manifesting itself in a unique way because of the nature of being single (that is, non-vowed to a vocational state—not married, not ordained as a priest, not publicly and religiously consecrated to God). We will identify several ways of responding to the call to be single. It should be noted that, before making any "state of life" commitments, each person is born single. Generally all of childhood and adolescence are spent in the single state of life, in which the child or adolescent is called to obedience and honoring of parents, to serving as a role model for siblings, to developing friendships with siblings and peers, to work at attaining an education and skills, as well as to other service to the family through chores. Children are also called to age-appropriate leisure, which is normally a form of play. At all ages they are called to relationship with God and goodness, and they are called to develop virtues.

During the time of maturation, as well as throughout one's life, being single is a foundational state full of potential, development, and flourishing. The foundational state of being single informs ethical, family, and social responsibilities and opportunities, for it marks out the ways of being in the world and for others. Single people are called to be bonded in charity and justice to family, friends, and community. If they respond to this call, they receive from others (parents, siblings, and friends), give of themselves, and then participate in human flourishing; by contrast, if they reject the call, they live selfishly and suffer because they are exceedingly turned in on themselves and thus inattentive to God and neighbor.

At an early age and in some conditions, people are not aware of the implications of being single. They simply live it (for example, most children and adolescents). In other situations, people more intentionally identify with being single. On the one hand, there are people who do not enter or remain in another "state of life" through no choice of their own, but nonetheless they *accept* being single, as in the case of the widow who accepts her new state. On the other hand, there are people who are single, having received a calling to that state. They *consciously choose the single life* and contribute to family, friendships, community, and work in unique ways because they are intentionally single (Novak & Simon, 2011, p. 171). Further examples of being single include the 7-year-old boy, who is single and participating in the vocation to his family as son, brother, and student; the 23-year-old man and woman who are seriously courting with a view to getting married; and the 76-year-old woman who has lost her spouse. Each of these persons has responsibilities that are inherent to being single, which vary according to his or her age and personal development. At all times, each human person is called to promote flourishing (one's own well-being, as well as that of family, friends, and neighbors), and the common good. But the vocation of being single further informs the basic call to goodness.

Being single involves being interpersonally relational. The single state does not mean being isolated nor does it mean indifference to others. In addition, the single person is embodied and sexually differentiated at conception (Bachio-chi, 2013; Brizendine, 2006, 2010; Garcia, 2010; Rhoads, 2004). Consciousness of being single and male or female, and of the complementarity of being male or female, is significant for self-understanding, ethical behavior, and mental health (Budziszewski, 2009, p. 16; John Paul II, 2006, §23:5). At any time, single people have a responsibility to respond to the call to wholeness or integrity of life, by which they develop competences or virtues that support the flourishing of their character as single, for example, in promoting justice and generosity in the world, serving neighbors and relatives as surrogate parents for those in need, and offering their lives in other ways that are unique to the opportunities and commitments of a single person. Furthermore, single people who are discerning or who have conscious intentions of one day entering married, religious, or priestly life will want to begin intentionally cultivating the virtues and habits needed within these vowed vocational states, although for the time being from within a non-vowed single state. Although all of the virtues are required for fulfilling one's vocational calling, each vocational state colors the way that a given virtue is developed and expressed. For example, the courage to discuss difficult issues with one's spouse is different than the courage shown by the priest who must correct a penitent. But both forms require a type of moral courage.

Throughout the different stages of the life of a single person, new challenges are the occasion to acquire virtues and consolidate character, as when there is need of hope in the face of loneliness, illness, or death. From the beginning of life, the single person acquires virtues and strengths (e.g., love, practical wisdom, justice, courage, patience, self-control, and so on) through concrete practices such as eating together with siblings; generously sharing resources with those in need;

praying in and outside the family; sharing hobbies and playing games and sports with neighbors; and participating in educational, cultural, and leisure activities (Pieper, 1952/2009); as well as giving oneself in formal work and informal service. Aspects of these practices must be adapted to the particularity of being single, being male or female, and having certain strengths or preferring certain activities, as well as to age and circumstances. It is necessary to keep in view the good that is sought after by every child, youth, and adult as single per se, as well as the good they seek in preparing for other vocations, such as marriage or religious consecration or priestly ordination. For example, the family practices that help children acquire a well-rounded character while younger must be adjusted to help adolescents adapt to embodied and environmental challenges. Puberty presents new challenges and requires practices that cultivate purity, modesty, chastity, and justice. The educational settings and peer environment of a single person can serve, on the one hand, to bolster virtues such as self-control and patience or, on the other, to bolster vices such as pride or envy. Furthermore, as single persons enter adulthood, they need to further adapt their practices related to work and leisure. Their practices should engender the acquisition of virtues and the attainment of their goals in life and prepare them for other possible vocations of commitment and service. In short, integral formation first requires one to become a good person, and a good man or woman, not being selfish but being ready to sacrifice and to be communal, because all vocations have these characteristics. It then requires formation of one's specific vocational state and one's vocation to work and service to others, as we will see shortly.

What Is the Structure of the Call to Married Life?

There is a core to marriage, even in the midst of laws and practices that improperly attribute the name "marriage" to polygamous, polyamorous, or same-sex unions. A core to marriage—from a nonrelativist, Catholic Christian, philosophical perspective—affirms that marriage is a natural institution that is based in the generative nature of the complementarity of one man and one woman, the call to lifelong loving commitment to a spouse, openness to children and caring for them, and mutual support to each other's flourishing (Girgis, Anderson, & George, 2012). A strong case has been made that faithful and indissoluble marriage supports the couple, the family, and society (Waite & Gallagher, 2000). Indeed, the absence of the husband or wife, the lack of commitment or the breaking of marital vows, and the separation of father or mother from the family have been shown in different ways to cause distress and difficulty for families and their members at the levels of economic security, physical health and longevity, mental health and emotional well-being, and crime and domestic violence (Sullins, 2015; Wilcox et al., 2011; Wilcox & Dew, 2013).

The call to a sacramental married life involves fixing love on a particular good and a particular person. As Wojtyła (1993) says: "A person who has a vocation [to marriage] must not only love someone but be prepared to give him or herself for love" (p. 256). The self-gift of marriage involves a man and a woman becoming one with a twofold goal that is unitive and procreative (Augustine, 401/1955; Paul VI, 1967). They commit to love each other for life and to be open to new life. The desire for family life concerns not only connectedness with parents and siblings in the family of origin, but also the new family that a man and woman create in married life.

A spousal desire needs to be nurtured for a couple to be ready for marriage. They need to know and understand each other: they need to know that they are both free from prior inhibiting commitments, know that they intend to be faithful and understand that the marriage union involves a lifelong commitment of shared life, understand spousal generativity, know that they are open to the gift of children, and understand the requirements of parenthood. This knowledge and understanding prepares the couple to give full and free consent to the marriage vows and unreservedly commit to the potential spouse. A marriage requires preparation over time that begins distantly in the family of origin, more proximately in dating, most concretely in the attachment developed through courtship, and finally in wedding arrangements and planning for the new life in common (Hazan & Shaver, 1987; Mikulincer & Phillip, 2007).

Furthermore, the mutual self-gift of committed conjugal love requires giving what is due within the couple and with God (Wojtyła, 1993, p. 245). This justice involves a horizontal justification between the man and woman, who are called to love each other as persons, rather than use each other as mere objects of pleasure or utility. This justice also involves a vertical justification that recognizes the order of creation, which renders the conjugal relationship just before God. As Wojtyła (1993) says: "Man is just towards God the Creator when he recognizes the order of nature and conforms to it in his actions" (p. 246). Both these dimensions affirm the uniqueness of each person, the complementarity of male and female, and the way that certain roles can be shared while others cannot (Savage, 2015).

Recent psychological and sociological studies confirm that the roles of men and women are complementary at certain levels and flexible at other levels (Bachiochi, 2013; Garcia, 2010; Rhoads, 2004; Vitz, 2018). For example, there is a need for both mother and father to contribute to childrearing (Anatrella, 2009; Sullins, 2015; Wilcox et al., 2011). The contributions of contemporary married mothers and fathers seem to function well, across diverse work-family strategies inside and outside the home and across diverse cultures (Wilcox & Dew, 2013). Furthermore, psychological studies have demonstrated the relevance of conceptualizing parenthood as a calling. The positive sense of being called to childrearing has been correlated with good outcomes and a sense of personal fulfillment and of contributing to the greater good (Coulson, Oades, & Stoyles, 2012a, 2012b). The mental health studies continue to attest to the challenges that face the call to married life, since there is no uneventful childhood, adolescence, adulthood, or death. The state of the family has implications, for better and for worse, for personal, spousal, and family flourishing and languishing. Last, there is no ideal marriage, since spouses and families usually exhibit a need for further development and healing (Francis, 2016; John Paul II, 1994a; Wilcox et al., 2011).

What Is the Natural Structure of Binding Promises and Religious Vows?

From a philosophical perspective, a vow, oath, or binding promise aims at an end, goal, or good, and is based upon the nature of the person's capacities for freely committing himself to everyday and ultimate ends. Not all promises are publicly acclaimed, as in the case of personal vows or consecrations expressed through devotion and piety to God. Nor are all promises the same. Examples include promises to be truthful (solemn oath in court of law), to respect the dignity of the person (Hippocratic Oath), to enter a covenant bond of marriage for life (marriage vows). A public oath may also make reference to God, as when one swears "to tell the whole truth, so help me God" or when one promises to be bound to God for life through a particular religious community (religious vows as a Dominican, Franciscan, or Jesuit). These vows constitute a change in life that binds and commits the person to aim at these goods according to the nature of the good, the promise, and the interpersonal context. The valid consent of promises and vows change the person; it often ushers in a way of life and the basis for ongoing transformation.

From a Christian philosophical perspective, it is reasonable and highly laudable to commit oneself to the right ordering of love toward other people and toward God. Such commitments underlie both the structure of justice (family, civic, natural, or spiritual) and every form of true religion (from natural desires for God to revealed religion, as in Christianity). Binding promises are all the more comprehensible when the promise is made toward a higher source and for a higher good. From a non-believing or non-Christian perspective, various nonreductionists have argued that goodness and intelligence have an ultimate source, which has been called Mind or God (Beauregard, 2012; Beauregard & O'Leary, 2008; Nagel, 2012; Spitzer, 2010). When one recognizes that the ultimate source of life has called one into a unique relationship and service, a person is motivated to respond personally to that source. To experience attraction to ultimate goodness is to begin to understand the human desire to commit oneself intentionally to this source of good. A full, personal response to the Creator can take many forms and can be largely ultimate, spiritual, and religious. The call to the transcendent is open to all people of good will, not only to devout Christians.

Recognition of the source of life, goodness, and truth elicits in a significant number of people a committed response that influences their whole life. This response, at one level, involves a response in justice—the response that is due to the source of life. From an ultimate perspective, a response in justice is expansive and generous, rather than reductive and calculating. Philosophically speaking, it is also a response of a natural religious sort (Pieper, 1952/2009). People are known to commit their life's work to justice, truth, and care. Aquinas (1273/1981, II-II, 81) understands this kind of natural religious phenomena to be, in part, a moral virtue related to justice. This is often called the virtue of religion, which links the person and the community to the transcendent through acknowledgement and respect, work and service, gratitude and worship. Inasmuch as religious or spiritual practices express a just relationship with the transcendent, a person can understand philosophically something of the call to commit oneself to knowing, loving, and serving.

Vocational States: Theological Perspective

This chapter now addresses the theological aspects of vocation to vowed and non-vowed vocational states, which constitute the second level of personal and unique vocations through which persons explicitly participate in the call of the Kingdom of God and intentionally cooperate in the redemptive work of Jesus Christ. Humans are called to live committed lives both when single and in marriage, priesthood, and religious consecration (Vatican II, 1964, §§39–47). It is through accepting and assenting to their vocational states that people can collaborate in God's work of redeeming and sanctifying both themselves and others. A discussion of discernment will lead to a discussion of the vocational states.

What Are Some Criteria for Discerning Vocations?

Discernment is critical to the process of identifying one's call to a vowed or non-vowed vocational state and engaging in it wholeheartedly. From a Catholic Christian perspective, prayer is one of the most significant elements in discernment (Benedict XVI, 2008, §3). An element that is common to spirituality and discernment is the meaning found when someone "allows himself to be led by the Spirit" (Torrell, 2003, p. 200). It involves learning both to be led by the Holy Spirit, who assures one's life course, and to be led by sage counsel, one's own conscience, and communal support (Spitzer, 2008; Torrell, 2003). Biblical discernment distinguishes the true from the false, the authentic from forgery (Dubay, 1997). According to St. Paul, spiritual discernment distinguishes the spirit of life from that of death, goodness from evil, and the spirit of adoption in Christ from the way of the "flesh" (Rom 8:4–12). The Catholic Christian tradition is home for diverse models of discernment that are biblical (Dubay, 1997), patristic (Rich, 2007), Benedictine (Marett-Crosby, 2003), Cistercian (Bertrand, 2001), Franciscan (Songy, 2012), Thomist (Torrell, 2003), Ignatian (Gallagher, 2005; Spitzer, 2008), Carmelite (Larkin, 1998), and so on. It should be noted that something similar to the process of discernment also occurs within the context of psychotherapy as clients become more aware of their interior life (e.g., emotions, connections to others, core beliefs, moral decision-making) and seek awareness of how they need to change and to make important life decisions. For now, however, what follows will explore what discernment within the Christian tradition encompasses, focusing on certain elements of Aquinas's and Ignatius's approaches to discernment, because of their influence within the Catholic tradition.

Discernment, according to Aquinas (1273/1981), calls upon the dynamic interconnection of charity and practical reason in a life that seeks God in truth. A Christian seeks the direction and judgment perfected by grace and the sevenfold Gift of the Holy Spirit (Wisdom, Understanding, Counsel, Fortitude, Knowledge, Piety, and Fear of God [Is 11:2–3; *Catechism of the Catholic Church* (CCC), 2000, §1831]). Discernment of a vocational state—or any important decision—requires being cognitively and affectively disposed to and moved by the Holy Spirit (Aquinas, 1273/1981, II-II, 52.2 ad 3; John Paul II, 1993, §28).

There are three major steps: (a) counsel and intention, (b) deliberation and consent, and (c) decision and choice. First, how does a person discern a vocational state or work goal, for example, becoming a mental health practitioner? Beyond perceiving something in general and simply wishing for it, the person needs to rightly discern the good goal or end that is worthwhile and possible to attain. In order to judge whether he can accomplish or attain it, he will need to discern what has been given him in his inclinations toward life, truth, goodness, family, and society and in his biopsychosocial and spiritual capacities, temperament, and gifts. He will need to take counsel from others about which middle-term goals to pursue at present (e.g., options for life work and service training) with a view to intending a more long-term goal (e.g., becoming a mental health professional).

Second, he needs to deliberate about the various good means that might lead to the desired end (e.g., finding competent training programs). He will need to identify the viable means, consenting to the most appropriate one (e.g., a specific program). The end, however, is not yet attained by deliberation and consent.

Third, he needs to decide to use the specified means (the course of studies and clinical experiences), with a view to actually choosing to do so (actually applying himself in order to attain the goal for his life work, in this case) (Aquinas, 1273/1981, II-II, 47.10; I-II, 65.2). The end is still not attained unless there is the execution of the plan, applying it, performing it, and coming to completion that gives flourishing or languishing. Through prayer and attentiveness to thinking and feeling (i.e., virtuous movements of knowing, understanding, wise choosing, counseling, being courageous, and so on), the person must continue to discern his personal vocation (e.g., as father or workman) and those vocations that concern groups for which he is responsible (e.g., family or business). This view of discernment requires the person's engagement with diverse communities over time. Discernment is both sustained and motivated by the family, friends, and communities of faith and service. It is lifelong.

Ignatius of Loyola's model of discerning personal vocations identifies conditions for discernment that require all of the following: (a) moral choices; (b) confidence; (c) good motivations; (d) unselfish detachment; (e) an honest attempt; (f) real action; and (g) a continuous effort at discerning God's will (Ryan, 2007, pp. 11–16; Spitzer, 2008). The process of discerning a vocational state calls for further criteria. *First*, according to St. Ignatius (1524/1964), the person should focus on his ultimate end, namely, "to praise, reverence, and serve God" and pray for help to know God's will (as cited in Ryan, 2007, p. 16). *Second*, the person must consider his own personal gifts and the needs of other people. *Third*, he should evaluate the positive and neg-

ative aspect of each option. *Fourth*, he should discern the affective state or the desire of the heart, that is, how he is affected by the option under consideration in terms of spiritual consolation or desolation (Gallagher, 2005). Human affects tend to go smoothly when moving from good to better or from bad to worse, but become troubled when changing direction. The implications of this complex insight reveal the need for a careful and complex reading of the affective life of the person in the context of discernment and spiritual development. *Last*, morally acceptable options alone are the subject of Christian discernment. Then, once careful consideration has led to the more attractive option, the person is at peace and must put the object of discernment into practice (Ryan, 2007, pp. 16–18).

Is There a Christian Vocation to Be Single?

Although most people choose to become married or consecrated or ordained, all humans are born single and many die single. The commonly misunderstood vocational state of being single is called into focus when considering the Christian difference to vocations (see earlier in this chapter for a philosophical treatment of the call intrinsic to being single). While it is unquestionable that each person, singles included, is called both to: (a) goodness and holiness and (b) work and service, at times it has been unclear in the Catholic tradition as how to describe the state of being single. We propose to distinguish the non-vowed vocational state (the single state) and vowed vocational states (married, ordained, and consecrated states). We believe that this distinction is consistent with Church teaching and tradition.

In the presentation of the Catholic Christian tradition, often "states of life" are rooted in a public choice or commitment that creates an obligation to a person or a thing (*CCC*, 2000, §2230; Vatican II, 1964, §13, §35, §43) and are considered "a stable social situation, recognized by society, and, therefore, juridically determined" (Bonino, 2002, p. 347). These definitions cover marriage, priestly ordination, and religious consecration (publicly recognized states of perfection constituted by the evangelical counsels) as states of life, but they do not cover being single per se.

In the midst of these reasons for not identifying being single as a proper "state of life" and the reasons set forth in our treatment of vocation, it is necessary to present reasons that being single is nonetheless to be considered a vocational state, the *basic vocational condition,* or even the *foundational state of vocation* that invites a response to God's will. This section will describe five reasons, from a Christian perspective, for holding that each person is also called to the vocational state of being single at some point in life. These distinctions will help avoid the erroneous belief that there is any time in a person's life that God is not calling the person to himself and to loving service to family, friends, neighbors, and society. This divine calling elicits generous responses that bring increasing psychological, moral, and spiritual maturation throughout one's life.

First, when considering a person's experiences of true flourishing, *the call to holiness cannot be separated from a basic vocational foundation or "specific state of life."* The Second Vatican Council (1964) clearly connects the call to holiness to the vocational state of being single, as when praising the example "offered by widows and single people, who are able to make great contributions toward holiness and apostolic endeavor in the Church" (§41). Because of grace and through the sacrament of Baptism, persons are called to follow Christ as the model of holiness; but Jesus

Christ was not abstractly holy. Therefore, single people are called to holiness, but in ways specific to being single—not as pseudo-married nor as pseudo-priests. The personal vocation to exist and to be holy is played out in a personal way through encounters and commitments, as the single, non-vowed child, adolescent, and adult interact with and serve their families, friends, and neighbors. It is in such contexts that God calls, humans respond, and growth continues to occur as a function of the basic vocational condition of being single. From conception, persons move toward the good, and in time, with adequate development, actively seek it. They also begin to concretely respond to the call of values and goodness in their lives, even though often mistakenly, as when an adolescent seeks to form community and friendship by joining a gang, in contrast to the adolescent who commits himself to positive civic projects and organizations.

Second, single persons are called to be *distinctively interpersonal, as seen in familial, social, and ecclesial links.* While being individuals, single persons are also sons and daughters, brothers and sisters. Such interpersonal relationships are the foundation for participating in the vocations of parents and family in a way that is particular to the non-vowed vocational state, not only during childhood but also throughout their lives. They flourish or languish because of the impact that receiving and giving parental, filial, and familial, love, caring, service, and justice have on them. Single people also participate in a unique way in the mission of the Church. They are called to accept the gifts (e.g., grace, spiritual and social support) that God offers through the Church. They are called to contribute to its flourishing as well. They are called to the fullness of charity, chastity, and generous service that is fitting to their being single; they are open to and working for the good of others and the common good, which is how they find meaning in life. Through this participation in the vocations of others and the Church, they flourish, for, when in contact with others, single people learn the ways of perceiving, receiving, and giving that are informed by the vocations of their family and community of faith. Novak and Simon (2011) describe a particular openness, chaste and delightful love, and joy, as well as vulnerability, which can accompany the single state (p. 172).

Third, the non-vowed single state is *embodied in ways that are common to all yet distinctly expressed in those who are single*. In his teaching on the theology of the body, John Paul II (2006, §23:5) reminds us that the body is as important for the single person and the vowed celibate as it is for the married person. Celibate persons, both single and consecrated, are also called to understand the spousal meaning of the body, to be conscious of being male or female, which influence their vocational lives and behavior (John Paul II, 1988a, 1989). For example, the non-vowed single person's life of chastity takes a different form than that of the consecrated celibate's chastity. Inasmuch as a single man may be preparing for a vocation to marriage, it is appropriate that he appreciate the feminine sensitivity, loving care, fidelity, and beauty of a prospective wife; likewise, it is appropriate that a woman appreciate the masculine courage, capacity to provide, devotion, and strength of a prospective husband. These acts of chaste imagination and conversation are not in principle sexually distorted or illicit for the non-vowed single person, while they would be for the consecrated celibate, if experienced in the same way (Budziszewski, 2012). According to John Paul II, the whole person is always attracted to others as a sign of our fundamental call to God through holiness. God calls non-vowed single people to respond to the invitation to be a sign of chastity

and generosity in service and to contribute to the transformation of the world and the lives of others, by giving themselves in ways distinct to the single state (Vatican II, 1965b).

Fourth, the fact that some people transition in and out of being single does not disqualify being single as a vocational state. It is a common trait of the proper "states of life" (with the exception of priesthood and solemn vows) that people sometimes change them. For example, although in the sacrament of Marriage spouses consent to an indissoluble unity, their vows promise fidelity "until death do us part." Consider St. Elizabeth Ann Seton, who, after growing and developing in the non-vowed single state, was called to the vowed married state of life; then she was widowed and again was single for some time, before she entered a vowed religious state of life and founded a congregation. It would seem an error to say that Mother Seton was not living in a vocational state at any point throughout her life, including her time in the single state and in widowhood.

Fifth, all vowed and non-vowed vocational states are gifts from God that also require a response from people (a) in the form of *acceptance* (when the state is given, e.g., widowhood) or (b) in the form of vowed *commitment* (when an option is open, e.g., to pursue religious life or marriage), or (c) in the form of a time of *preparation* for further commitments and for fidelity to one's non-vowed and vowed vocations. There is a need to *prepare* and *practice* for the full expression of any state, including being single. Culture, the family, and the Church are not always perfect sources of formation. But, even with their imperfections, they are necessary for discerning, answering, and living out one's vocational calls. As noted earlier, the heart of vocational discernment and fidelity is found in prayer (Benedict XVI, 2008) and practical wisdom; its longevity is grounded in the family, fraternal support, and divine grace. This is true for all vowed and non-vowed vocational states, including the single one.

In sum, the Christian perspective identifies that humans are always called to flourishing, the concrete quest for goodness and holiness, through non-vowed and vowed vocational states and in service to God and others. God uniquely calls each vowed and non-vowed person and empowers each in diverse ways to actively and passively prepare for, discern, answer, and live out vocations.

What Is the Christian Difference in the Vocation to Marriage?

The vocation to marriage originates in a special type of love between man and woman, who in their complementarity aim at the endurance and growth of their unitive and procreative love. The man and woman become husband and wife through a public exchange of vows, which are an indissoluble commitment to lifelong spousal unity, exclusive fidelity, mutual support, and openness to having and educating children, throughout which they work toward each other's growth in holiness. Married love is a permanent communion and constant gift of self aimed at a twofold goal of being and further becoming both spouse and parent (Gen 1 & 2; Mt 19:1–12; Mk 12:1–12; John Paul II, 1981a, 2006; Paul VI, 1967; Pius XI, 1930). The relationship of spouses involves a mutual submission to each other in self-giving and sacrificial love, respect, and service; these will be expressed somewhat differently in men and women (Eph 5:21–33). Within St. Paul's wide teaching about the family as domestic Church, the spouses will find compelling ways to share responsibility for teaching (instruction), sanctifying (prayer), and leading (bringing order to family life), while the family

continues to remember the primacy of Christ. (Eph 5:32; John Paul II, 1981a, §21; Vatican II, 1964, §11). According to Wojtyła (1993), conjugal love presupposes justice between the two persons and God (pp. 245–249). The theological perspective brings a grace-based dimension to understanding the horizontal justification, in which the man and woman love each other as persons, rather than use each other as mere objects of pleasure or utility. The grace of the sacraments of Baptism and Marriage help them to rightly order their actions as persons with a human nature and personal commitments and goals. The vertical justification renders the conjugal relationship just before God, for the man and woman recognize the role of grace and the order of nature and conform to them in action (Wojtyła, 1993, p. 246).

A Catholic Christian model affirms that the Creator has instilled the potential for the marriage vocation in the nature of man and woman. The two creation accounts of Genesis demonstrate the divine intention that (a) human beings be in a right relationship with God and neighbors, and (b) man and woman be made for union based on complementarity and commitment (Gen 1 & 2). Each person is embodied, which includes his or her sexual differentiation as male or female. The loss of original justice through man's first sin of disobedience, however, has had tragic consequences both for personal integrity and for the relationship of the sexes and for the primal vocation to love (Gen 3; Aquinas, 1273/1981, I-II; 1270/2003, IV.1 & IV.8). These consequences include the desire to dominate the other sex rather than to serve, the tendency to seduce and manipulate, the propensity to use force and violence, and so on. The destruction of the original harmony results in the loss of a certain aspect of the person's control over the body. It also disfigures the union of man and woman with tensions of lust and domination (Gen 3:7–16; *CCC*, 2000, §400). Nonetheless, the calling to interpersonal relationships, the process of growth, and the vocation to fruitfulness, although "burdened by the pain of childbirth and the toil of work," which were the result of sin, are now surprisingly the possible means of redemptive sacrifice (Gen 3:16–18; *CCC*, 2000, §1607; cf. John Paul II, 1988b, 1989).

The essence of marriage is not undercut by its diverse cultural and legal expressions, nor by the difficulties of those who experience genital ambiguity or gender misidentification (Francis, 2016, §56). In a nonrelativist approach, a Catholic Christian model of the person affirms that matrimony has found perennial interest and support in every culture, even if notable challenges and shortfalls exist. All world cultures recognize that marriage supports not only the family, but also society itself, and, of course, the Church (Girgis, Anderson, & George, 2012; International Organization for the Family [www.profam.org]; Waite & Gallagher, 2000; Wilcox et al., 2011). As the Second Vatican Council (1965a) affirms: "The well-being of the individual person and of both human and Christian society is intimately linked with the healthy condition of that community produced by marriage and family" (§47.1). The personal calling to married life is noble and demanding, as it implies constant sacrificial self-gift, generativity, and growth as spouses and usually as parents.

The depth of the above-mentioned characteristics of a Catholic Christian marriage is significant and involves the interior, spiritual, and psychological life of each spouse. The mere external signs of a sacramental marriage—that is, a public exchange of wedding vows, much less cohabitation—are not enough to develop a flourishing marriage (Byrd, 2009). For example, psychological studies have shown that the

commitment to marriage—as an internalized and confirmed desire for the relationship to persist rather than as simply an external behavioral inclination to stay in relationship—is positively correlated with stable marriages (Schoebi, Karney, & Bradbury, 2012). Furthermore, there are certain factors and practices that significantly predict stable marriages, such as personal commitment to marriage (Johnson, Caughlin, & Huston, 1999), covenant commitment (Cade, 2010), commitment to the spouse as a person (Clements & Swenson, 2000), parenthood, especially for mothers and married fathers (Kamp Dush, Rhoades, Sandberg-Thoma, & Schoppe-Sullivan, 2014), as well as social, moral, and religious values, practices, and supports to staying married (Collins, 1998; Nelson, Kirk, Ane, & Serres, 2011). These factors are predictive of marriage stability without being determinative or comprehensive.

What Is the Christian Difference in Consecrated and Ordained Vocations?

The *locus classicus* for all vocations to consecrated and ordained life is found in the Gospel of Matthew where Jesus said to the rich young man: "If you wish to be perfect, go, sell your possessions, and give the money to the poor, and you will have treasure in heaven; then come, follow me" (19:21). Christian vocations are gifts that come from God through the Church; however, religious and ordained callings require a specific response to the universal call to holiness (John Paul II, 1984; 1992, §35; 1994b; see also Cole & Connors, 1997; Council of the Major Superiors of Religious Women, 2009). Since the time of Christ, women and men have responded to his invitation to follow him. Based on the encounter of Christ in faith, the special and specific state of religious life connects the person to

God in the Church community. In effect, union with God the Father, conformity to Christ, and sanctification though the Holy Spirit are, together, the very definition of the Christian perfection found in charity and sought in consecrated religious life. The evangelical counsels—namely, voluntary poverty, chastity, and obedience—have proven to be "a certain type of instrument for attaining perfection" and for the self-giving love spoken of by Christ (Aquinas, 1273/1981, II-II, 184.3). These three counsels require a two-fold movement that serves both the good of the person and the mission of the Church (Congregation for Catholic Education, 2008). First, there is the leaving behind (giving away to the poor, detaching from house and family, and so on). Second, there is following Christ, not just with physical steps, but with spiritual devotion and an organized life of prayer and sacrament (Mt 19:7; Aquinas, 1273/1981, II-II, 184.3 ad 1).

This ultimate goal of Christian perfection, laid out in the original plan of love, includes each person not only as created in the image of God but also as marked by his or her spousal nature. The spousal meaning of the body has its ultimate meaning at the end of time in the beatific vision, where its fulfillment is found in the redeemed and chaste state, where God is "all in all" (1 Cor 15:28; also Mt 22:30). The chaste state of the body describes well the way that humans will relate to God and others in heaven. Jesus Christ is once again an example: this time, for his chaste celibacy and devotion to God the Father and to all people. The Second Vatican Council (1964) furthermore says that the evangelical counsels are signs of the coming Kingdom of God (§§43–48). They were lived in an exemplary manner by Jesus, who was the model of obedience, chastity, and poverty for all Christians. The counsels presuppose Baptism and constitute the consecrated person's response to God's call as a further gift

to God and to the Church and the world. In *Vita Consecrata*, John Paul II (1996) says:

> The consecrated life is at the very heart of the Church as a decisive element for her mission, since it "manifests the inner nature of the Christian calling" and the striving of the whole Church as Bride towards union with her one Spouse. (§3)

There is also a special role for those men called to priestly ordination in the Church, who are called to internalize "the type of life shown by Jesus the Good Shepherd, Head and Bridegroom of the Church" (Congregation for Catholic Education, 2008, §5). The vocation to Holy Orders is directed toward the salvation of others (which makes it similar to the sacrament of Matrimony). It is a school of perfection in following Christ (which makes it similar to the consecrated religious life). The service of bishops, priests, and deacons contributes to their personal salvation, inasmuch as they serve others. As the Second Vatican Council affirms: they "are consecrated by Holy Orders, are appointed to feed the Church in Christ's name with the word and the grace of God" (Vatican II, 1964, §11.2; see also *CCC*, 2000, §1535; John Paul II, 1992). Christ has designated three services (*tria munera Christi*) that priests fulfill: "teaching (*munus docendi*), divine worship (*munus liturgicum*) and pastoral governance (*munus regendi*)" (*CCC*, 2000, §1592; also John Paul II, 1992, 2003; Vatican II, 1964).

In addition to the myriad challenges of human integration, the priest's public office to fulfill these three services within the Church will inform the priest's self-understanding and be occasions where he might well need special healing, normal growth and development, and fraternal support (1 Pet 5:1–4). In particular, John Paul II (1992) emphasizes that the priestly vocation to follow Christ requires a complete formation and attentiveness to discernment at human, spiritual, intellectual, and pastoral levels (§§43–59). Benedict XVI (2006) specifies further the need to be "capable of cultivating an authentic spiritual paternity" (§6).

The vocational perspective of the Meta-Model and mental health practice serve each other. First, knowledge of the theological perspective on the dynamics of vocations to religious life and priesthood has implications for mental health practice. Activities and practices related to the vocation of the consecrated religious and ordained priesthood influence the clinician's and client's conception of the body, duty, friendship, and flourishing, as well as the way virtues are lived out. The way the priest or the consecrated religious experiences communal expectations and personal ideals (about hope, chastity, patience, and perseverance, for example) is both uplifting and challenging. At times, the vocation may seem a burden that requires continuous discernment, training, sacrifice, and support if the person is to faithfully live its demands.

Second, the psychological sciences give knowledge about the person that is helpful for understanding the search for and response to vocations. For example, studies of the psychological processes involved in discerning a vocation to the Catholic priesthood have shown the significance of stages of self-understanding as a man progresses in his knowledge of the nature of ordained ministry (Hankle, 2009). The sacrament and the vows result in an ontological change in the nature of the ordained man. This change gives greater light and self-understanding than any study of the functional dimension of career or life style. Hankle (2009) conceptualizes the goal of discernment of a priestly vocation, from the candidate's side, as how well a man has associated his sense of self with priesthood. These psychological observations demonstrate nuances that can be put at the service of the discernment needed to determine vocations to the priesthood. However, as gifts of God, the vocations to and discernment of religious life and the priesthood do not, strictly speaking, fall within the competence of psychology (Congregation for Catholic Education, 2008, §5). Nonetheless, the psychological sciences can be of assistance, as when identifying psychological problems, including:

> excessive affective dependency; disproportionate aggression; insufficient capacity for being faithful to obligations taken on; insufficient capacity for establishing serene relations of openness, trust and fraternal collaboration, as well as collaboration with authority; a sexual identity that is confused or not yet well defined. (Congregation for Catholic Education, 2008, §8)

The psychological sciences can also help a person's vocational response to be freer, by helping the person overcome relational, cognitive, and emotional barriers, thus enhancing the human qualities needed in discernment of one's call to the priesthood and also in the actual duties of the priest.

Work, Service, and Meaningful Leisure: Philosophical Perspective

What difference does a Catholic Christian perspective on vocations have for understanding and experiencing human work, service, and meaningful leisure? What implications does it have for ethics and mental health practice? This section will explore how human work and service, and rest and leisure conceived as a third area of vocation, uniquely influence human flourishing. Contemporary mental health practitioners readily conceive of vocation as pertaining to work, as when they address vocational discernment, career training, and the perceived meaning of one's occupation or job satisfaction. In this chapter, however, we aim at synthesizing such factors into a larger notion of work seen as vocation, for we conceptualize this call as interconnected with the foundational call to goodness or holiness and different vocational states. We will ask how personal and interpersonal ways of being, doing, and making correlate in a synthetic model of the person, and we will explore what implications result from the Meta-Model's personalist, realist, and theological suppositions. In short, work and service are not simply something we do but are part of being a person and are closely related to both our vocational call to holiness and our particular vocational state. Work is meant to be transformative. It is meant to be meaningful and perfecting. When it does not have these qualities, it may be either that the person is suffering from a biopsychosocial or spiritual disorder (for example, inordinately pursuing power, prestige, and pleasure), or that the work itself and the work environment are not respectful of the proper dignity of the person (John Paul II, 1981b; 1991).

What Is Work?

For the purposes of this section, *work and service* is defined as intentional and purposeful efforts aimed at a result, done in or outside the household, regardless of remuneration. The Meta-Model's definition, moreover, requires existential and teleological wisdom. There is more to work than is found in the simple distinctions between a *job* as compensated, *toil* as necessary and wearisome, and *work* as purposeful (Green, 1968; Homan, 1986). From early efforts in the home as children, humans more or less con-

sciously engage in work and service to flourish and to support family life. This calling entails natural and spiritual purposes in the context of a community of persons. As a positive human effort, work is rooted in the intelligibility and meaning of life. Importantly, it is to some extent self-transcending (more than self-serving), teleological (aimed at a future goal), intentional (conscious of the good pursued), and free (willingly chosen in pursuit of a good). Therefore, human efforts are considered demeaning or negative if the aforementioned characteristics are missing, or if the effort employs evil means or aims at an evil end (e.g., oppressing others, or physical or emotional abuse) instead of aiming at life and true progress (e.g., the flourishing of workers, families, and society).

There are different approaches to understanding the nature of work and calling. For instance, in the philosophical literature, the notion of calling underlines various aspects of a general analysis of work. Some of the properties of work that vocation underlies include work as a necessary curse or burden, as a possible source of freedom, as a commodity to be bought or sold, as a useful activity, as personally fulfilling, as a contribution to society, as a basis of caring for others, and as a source of personal identity (Budd, 2011, p. 14). In the field of education, work and vocation are related to career choice and to personality itself. Various factors are recognized as bearing on a person's choice of a work vocation: "(1) faith/spirituality, (2) interpersonal relationships, (3) encounters with others, (4) values, (5) critical life events contributing to self-definition, (6) understanding of passion, gifts, and talents, and (7) developmental issues and one's capacity for self-authorship" (Dahlstrand, 2010, p. 4).

The mental health field looks mostly at psychological factors bearing on occupational choice. These factors include personality characteristics (e.g., the Big Five; Widiger, 2017; Widiger & Costa, 2012), and recently spirituality has been recognized as a leading factor used in career discernment (Dreher, 2012; Hall, Burkholder, & Sterner, 2014; Homan, 1986). Additionally, those who take a phenomenological approach to being called to work have identified psychological realities (Terranova, 2006), and have created a calling and vocation questionnaire, which integrates three pertinent dimensions: "(1) a transcendent summons, (2) deriving or expressing meaning or purpose through work, and (3) a prosocial orientation in work" (Eldridge, 2011). In the present section we offer our synthetic Meta-Model for integrating such contributions. In our Catholic Christian approach, we seek not only to identify work-related phenomena, but also to offer a synthetic approach to work and service that is largely personalist and realist, in a philosophical vein, and that offers an even larger understanding through a theological perspective, covered in the next section.

From the personalist perspective of John Paul II (1981b), there are three interrelated dimensions of work (§10). First, there is the *personal* dimension, which identifies experiences of self-gift, self-determination, personal abilities, and commitment. Second, human work most often serves as the *foundation for and expression of family life*. Personal and family dimensions significantly support each other. In particular, a person learns to work in the family, which is sustained by its members; and the family as a community exists because of the work of its members, who are naturally inclined to contribute to the family. Third, a notion of work would be incomplete if it did not include *society* at large. Human work is framed by historical, legal, economic, civic, cultural, and religious factors. The complexity of work comes from both subjective and objective dimensions within personal, fa-

milial, and social dimensions. For example, in appraising the ethics of the call to work in general and the dignity of particular kinds of work, John Paul II (1981b) says:

> Work is a good thing for man—a good thing for his humanity—because through work man *not only transforms nature*, adapting it to his own needs, but he also *achieves fulfilment* as a human being and indeed, in a sense, becomes "more a human being." (§9; italics in the original, citing Vatican II, 1965a, §38)

Such fulfillment through the call to work is found in the development of industriousness or initiative (Aquinas, 1273/1981, II-II, 129.3), courage, justice, and the other virtues that support person, family, and society. Work by its nature is a difficult good that requires cognitive and emotional formation, initiative to plan and realize worthwhile ambitions, patience in the face of setbacks, and perseverance in the prolonged process of bringing projects to fruition. Work and service deserve to be compensated in justice and to be recognized as honorable, in the case of noteworthy and generous efforts, and gracious gifts of time and resources.

Do Humans Work to Be at Leisure?

In addition to working for pay and for recognition, humans also work so as not to work. According to Aristotle (ca. 350 BC/1941a), "we are busy that we may have leisure" (1177b4) and much human action is predicated on leisure (ca. 350 BC/1941b, 1337b33). The ancient Greek and Roman cultures contrasted work to leisure, they defined work as the lack of leisure (Greek: *a-scholia*; Latin: *neg-otium*). According to Pieper (1952/2009), work and leisure, however, can be understood only in the larger context of human needs and flourishing. Work serves leisure, culture, art, and worship. It is contrasted to the need for celebration, rest, and faith. Divinely established festivals and periods of rest from labor allow people to focus on what is ultimate (love of God and neighbor). As Aristotle held, perfect flourishing (*eudaimonia*) comes through the highest virtue: the contemplative activity of "taking thought of things noble and divine, whether it be itself also divine or only the most divine element in us" (ca. 350 BC/1941a, 1177a15–16).

Pieper (1952/2009) recognizes that a "work for work's sake" mentality, which he found in post–World War II Marxism and in National Socialism, uses the person for the ends of production and makes the claim that labor is the entirety of life. This mentality can be found in modern societies as well, in attempts to maximize productivity at work and success in sports, even through risky or illegal pharmacological substances that are supposed to enhance performance. This same theme can also be identified in the "entertainment for entertainment's sake" and "art for art's sake" mentalities, which do not motivate people toward any ultimate goal. The result of valuing only useful work or aesthetic pleasure (cut off from ultimate notions, such as love and faith) is a totalitarian, relativistic, and deconstructive concept of culture and the person. Such ideologies remove work from the scope of the goal or *telos* of individual perfection and flourishing and the goal or *telos* of relationship and interpersonal love.

Pieper argues that a rich notion of leisure responds to the deficits in contemporary notions of flourishing. Leisure is based upon the flourishing found in interpersonal communion and self-gift. It requires sacraments and sacrifices. Sacrament mediates communion with other people and with the invisible through the visible. Self-gift values the greatest gift of oneself that is love's achievement (Jn 15:13). Against materialist interpretations of work, moreover, a realist conception of leisure, contemplation, and worship expresses a transcendent goal and awareness of human needs. It provides a basis for culture as well as a way to humanize labor and put aims of justice in the context of ultimate flourishing. In this approach, work is understood in relation to leisure, which is more than a simple absence of work and a simple notion of self-care and rest, since it disposes the person to encounter beauty and truth, and to wonder about ultimate meaning and belonging.

What Are the Enriching and Challenging Aspects of Work?

When work is fitting for the common good, it benefits not only the workers and their families, but also business associates and friends, as well as the rest of mankind and the world. Nevertheless, work and service are engaged in for different reasons and experienced in diverse ways. The goals that people seek to attain through human work usually include supporting oneself and one's family, but other goals influence the perception of the meaning of work, such as the goals of contributing to the health of individuals, the well-being of local communities, the enrichment of civic culture, and the common good of all people.

Work has subjective and objective aspects, both of which are also personal and interpersonal. As John Paul II (1981b) says, human labor, whether manual or intellectual, is always a subjective, personal act of "the whole person, body and spirit" (§24) that puts the person in contact with others. Persons and groups of persons, however, may languish when excluded or mistreated at work and when the work environment is detrimental to the person because of physical dangers, psychological stressors, ethical conflict, or spiritual discord.

There are negative and positive tendencies that influence the experience of work. On the *negative side*, there is the disordered tendency toward self-focus and pride, envy and greed, as well as indifference and injustice. Moreover, individuals and corporations can be exclusivist, discarding workers to maximize profit, or short-sighted, neglecting stewardship of the environment and the common good of all. Work can also be a source of frustration, for example, when conditions expose the worker's life to physical danger, psychological trauma, or moral compromise, and when salaries are inadequate to support the worker's family.

On the *positive side*, there can be a virtuous tendency to be drawn into new social responsibilities by work. Work can be inclusive, linking people, communities, and nations in socioeconomic and cultural ties and friendship. Work can be an occasion for self-gift, where people employ their talents and efforts at the service of others and find meaning in their efforts and their associations. For example, people are drawn to the goods of the health and helping professions, committing themselves to be trained accordingly. Such intentional preparation allows persons to find meaning in their service to those in need. There are types of work that do entail danger and stress, but that are willingly chosen in the service of others. These types of work demand a high level of virtue, and often self-sacrifice.

What Is the Origin and Nature of Work as a Calling?

The call to work is not simply a divine command. Nor is it simply a natural duty or requirement of just relationships with neighbors. There is a sense of inter-human responsibility (natural law) that grows out of the goodness shared through human labor. People encounter other people in the context of service received and service rendered, from the earliest moments of life. People naturally feel gratitude. They imitate the work of others. Such natural gratefulness for the work of others inclines people to work and give of themselves in turn. The call to work involves a nuanced response: pay is due the worker, recognition is due the benefactor, and gratitude is due all around (Aquinas, 1273/1981, II-II, qq. 106 & 107). Gratitude and justice are incomplete, though, unless the person not only gives in turn but also works in turn. Work supports life and thus is a life-giving action. On the contrary, to willingly withhold one's work to support self, family, community, and society, or to be intentionally not grateful for the work of others is life negating. Furthermore, there are other forms of work that are intrinsically life negating, for example, sex-trafficking or selling illicit drugs.

Being able to express gratefulness is a basic psychological strength as well as a moral virtue. Gratitude is activated through the experience either of receiving just payment and recognition or of receiving gracious gifts. And in particular, dispositions to work and serve others are built up through acts of self-giving work that have meaning and that benefit the worker, his family, and his community.

Pieper (1952/2009) furthermore argues that, even in demeaning work, man is revived from the fatigue of active toil by rest, contemplation, and worship; these acts require an openness to the source of life and a receptivity that activates us and makes us flourish (pp. 4–26). Through these experiences, we receive renewed vitality, a glimmer of the ultimate, and bonding to the source of goodness. But the active nature of work also requires receptivity. Active work builds on the gift inherent in all knowledge and love. Aquinas (1259/1953, II.15.1) accords receptivity a fundamental role in two basic aspects of knowledge: (a) intellectual vision (*intellectus*) and (b) discursive reason (*ratio*). Intellectual vision is founded on the receptivity of the essential insight (*simplex intuitus*), intuition, or basic understanding of the goodness, beauty, and interrelationship of oneself, the world, and God. The basic experience of an other founds the receptivity of intuition. Discursive reason develops out of the perception, experience, and encounter of the person. The intuition is received. It is a gift, which once received provides principles and context for the discursive work of analysis, observation, imagination, critical judgment, and synthesis. For example, such work is required in the mental health practices of empathy, observation, assessment, diagnosis, case conceptualization, and treatment. By contrast, mere acceptance of subjectivist views (which define truth as that which the individual determines for him or herself) does not acknowledge receptivity. Subjectivism has led modern thinkers to overemphasize the intellectual work of the philosopher or the psychologist and the utility of work. It also underemphasizes the roles that nature, and especially the nature of the person, and of God, play as objective sources that inform work expressed, for example, in culture, art, healing, or ethics.

What Does Psychology Say About Callings and Work?

"The concept of the person as embedded in [a multidimensional] vocation is undeveloped in the mental health field" (Chapter 20, "Principles for Training"), and the principle of viewing the person as embedded in vocation is emphasized neither in personality theory nor in psychotherapy. Nonetheless, the field of psychology does study "vocation and calling" as pertaining to work and self-actualization more than to the other levels of vocation (especially holiness, states of life, and moral goodness). For example, counseling psychology defines a "calling as an approach to work that aligns with a sense of personal meaning, is motivated by prosocial values, and arises from a transcendent summons" (Duffy, Bott, Allan, Torrey, & Dik, 2012, p. 50). This definition is noteworthy, even though the article in which it is found mentions family as a barrier to job satisfaction and gives no substantiation for its mention of "transcendent summons" (which might have restricted personal or social meanings). Such studies focus on "career commitment and work meaning" when researching vocational outcomes (Duffy et al., 2012, p. 51). From a therapeutic perspective, the researchers notably suggest that aiding clients to better perceive their work as a calling may enhance "career commitment, work meaning, and subsequent work satisfaction" (Duffy et al., 2012, p. 58).

A positive psychology perspective (Seligman, 2012) on workplaces offers further insights on work as a calling. For example, researchers have identified topics, in addition to the popular foci of job satisfaction and commitment, that contribute to desired outcomes at work. In particular, Luthans and Youssef (2009) identify capacities that constitute "positive organizational behavior" and "psychological capital," especially *self-efficacy* in motivation and action, *hope* in agency and pathways to a goal, *optimism* in the style one uses to explain the situation, and *resiliency* in the face of difficulty and responsibility (pp. 582–583). These and other positive psychological capacities provide significant indicators about how people flourish in the workplace.

Some psychological work also identifies existential qualities related to human work, qualities such as authentic existence (Homan, 1986), that contribute to an understanding of the person and flourishing (Eldridge, 2012; Terranova, 2006). The scope of the Catholic Christian

Meta-Model of the Person would suggest that further work on the calling of mental health practitioners to address existential suffering would also be beneficial. For example, studies could address how mental health practice in-cludes a self-giving type of practical wisdom in the face of suffering that might be dehumanized if not expressed as empathetic, other-focused, and self-giving (Miller, 2004).

Work, Service, and Meaningful Leisure: Theological Perspective

What Is the Meaning of the Call to Work and Service?

From a theological Catholic Christian perspec-tive, we will explore how human work finds its origin in natural necessity, divine command, and grateful response, as a participation in the beau-ty of divine work and an imitation of God's per-petual initiative and creativity (Chenu, 1963). According to the book of Genesis, initially man and woman were intended to cultivate and protect the Garden of Eden. They were to be stewards of the earth, other creatures, and them-selves. In the first creation account, we hear the admonition: "Be fruitful and multiply, and fill the earth and subdue it; and have dominion over the fish of the sea and over the birds of the air and over every living thing that moves upon the earth" (Gen 1:28). The second creation account says: "The Lord God took the man and put him in the garden to till and keep it" (Gen 2:15). Al-though the work took effort, we conjecture that it was done with a certain ease (an original ease) and served as a source of strength and meaning. Work was done in imitation of God from the be-ginning, as a response to the call to be stewards of the earth. Therefore, as John Paul II (1981b) argues, work should not be considered a pun-ishment. In working, mankind serves "his own humanity, which requires work in order to be maintained and developed" (§16).

The book of Genesis specifies that pain and toil were attached to childbirth and to tilling the soil because of sin: "By the sweat of your face you shall eat bread until you return to the ground, for out of it you were taken; you are dust, and to dust you shall return" (Gen 3:19). The consequence of sin is the loss of original jus-tice and original ease with oneself, with neigh-bor, and one's environment, but not the loss of the possibility of self-control, interpersonal love, and the fruitfulness of the earth. Furthermore, since the coming of Christ and his conquering of sin, work now potentially becomes a redemp-tive activity.

In the Bible, the law and the prophets seek to protect human persons from the abuse of work. For instance, Sabbath rest and devotion (Ex 20:8–11; Deut 5:14; see also John Paul II, 1998), sabbatical year (every seventh year) debt cancel-lation (Deut 15:1–4), and just practices regarding proper and timely payment of laborers (Deut 25:4) are practices meant to give work spiritual, ethical, and covenantal context. Outside of the covenant relationship with God, work eventu-ally becomes either a source of pride and pre-sumption or an empty execution of divine laws or a form of exploitation. God does not dispense with work, but rather renders it fruitful, so that the vinedresser will taste the fruit of his labor and the builder will live in his dwelling. Bibli-cal wisdom literature praises a whole range of human occupations (that of scribes, farmers, artisans, smiths, potters, and builders), which have their own social worth for the community, city, and nation. The Book of Wisdom (14:2–3) identifies three factors in successful work: desire for gain in planning the effort, the wisdom of the artisan in building it, and divine providence in bringing the project to fruition. This admiration for work is highlighted by numerous rebukes for idleness and by the folly of idol makers, who relate to their own works as to gods. Without putting excessive confidence in human possibilities, mankind is called to personal effort, engagement, and choice in actualizing work.

The New Testament presents Jesus Christ as the eternal image of the Father, the Word and Wisdom through whom God created all things (Lk 2:40; Jn 1:1–3). His apostolate is expressed as work: for example, harvesting and fishing (Mt 4:19). Christ's works are crowned by his salvific sacrifice (the work of the cross), in which humans are called to participate (Jn 15:13). Every person's own work is related to that of the Church and Christ (Vatican II, 1965b, §1). Moreover, work has meaning and dignity that are expressed in its various dimensions. At a personal level, work is a means to express talents and realize goals. At an embodied level, it is the normal way to meet basic needs. At a relational level, it is a way to support family and to contribute to the larger community and the common good. At a redemptive level, it is a participation in the divine plan of creation and redemption (John Paul II, 1981b, §6, §10).

The baptized Christian is called to a special kind of vocation to work and service that participates in the mission or work of the Church. This special call to work and service is called, by Catholics, an apostolate (Vatican II, 1965b). An apostolate is the service and work, occupations and professions that constitute the way through which people live out their call to holiness and justice to serve society and the Church (Vatican II, 1964a, §§39–42; also John Paul II, 1988a, §16). Notably, apostolic work contributes to the common good at large, the well-being of local communities, as well as the ongoing support of person and family, and the sanctification of the family's members. In addition, through such work a person is able to reach beyond family and friends to love his neighbor, welcome the stranger, care for the poor, and respect the enemy. John Paul II (1988a, §15) identifies that the baptized have an apostolic mission. They are called to participate in the apostolate of Jesus Christ and the Church, by bringing the Gospel message out of the parish and home and into the workplace and public square. The scriptural image is the call of laborers to work in the vineyard (Mt 20:1–16). The fruits are the very works that God makes possible through the faithful witness to love of God and neighbor (charity and justice) in daily life and activities among neighbors, friends, and colleagues. These fruits are possible only when the laborer remains in Christ, as a branch must remain attached to the vine to produce fruit, so must the believer abide in Christ in order to live out the mission to be fruitful in the world (Jn 15:1–17).

The Catholic Christian Meta-Model of the Person also has implications for the conceptualization and practice of work in the mental health profession. The model highlights the providential nature of the encounter between the client and mental health practitioner. Both client and clinician respect each other for their consciences and differences, as well as for their common call to right relationships, flourishing, and holiness. The type of self-gift and love in this service setting recognizes that God works through both of them. While mental health practitioners are instruments of grace and healing, they will also be held accountable for the service they render and for their intentional participation in the healing process (Mt 25:31–46; see also Chapter 20, "Principles for Training").

How Does a Christian View of Work Disclose Three Types of Rest?

As discussed above, people work in order to attain higher purposes, not only to support themselves and families, but also for leisure, worship, and contemplation. When turning to an explicitly theological Catholic Christian view of work, we can identify three types of rest: everyday rest, Sunday or Sabbath rest, and ultimate or eternal rest (beatific vision).

First, as discussed above, in order to care for themselves and their families, people need respite from manual labor and intellectual activities, be they intense or tedious. Everyday needs include nutrition and sleep, which revive each person physically, psychologically (Pilcher & Huffcutt, 1996), and spiritually (Pieper, 1952/2009), and social interactions, such as spending time with family and friends in leisure and recreational activities. Thus, this everyday type of rest is not only personal but also interpersonal.

The Christian tradition recognizes Sunday or Sabbath rest as another type of rest that is spiritual in source, practice, and extent. Sabbath rest is a gift from God (Ps 127:1–2). It is rooted in the example of God, who is credited as being Creator of the multitude of beings in the heavens and the earth, but also as having rested (Gen 2:2–3). God completes creation by another type of activity, that of rest. And God blesses this Sabbath day for rest (Gen 2:3). Humans are commanded to imitate God in keeping holy the Lord's Day (Ex 20:8–11; Deut 5:12–15), to grow in love and union with God and others. The New Testament associates the work of God as Creator and as Redeemer, giving the Lord's Day (Sunday) the purpose of sanctifying time and people's lives. It is more than a time of simple relaxation.

In his apostolic letter on keeping the Lord's Day holy, John Paul II (1998, §72) emphasizes the need for rest for body and soul. Rest means refraining from unnecessary work and celebrating the Eucharist (Mass, Divine Liturgy, the Lord's Last Supper), seeking spiritual enrichment and interpersonal communion, and acclaiming the primacy of God through efforts of mercy, charity, and apostolic activity. John Paul II (1998) also identifies a call to a contemplative gaze on the beauty of what has been accomplished in the orders of creation and redemption. True beauty and refreshment are found in Jesus Christ, who says: "Come to me, all who labor and are heavy laden, and I will give you rest" (Mt 11:28).

A third type of rest is found in God's presence and the beatific vision. Participation in this type of rest is already experienced in the presence of Christ and the Holy Spirit through worship and contemplation, as well as in the invitation to enter into God's rest and eternal joy. This joy-filled rest serves as the object of Christian hope and is symbolically identified as the wedding feast of the Lamb, proclaimed in the book of Revelation. This ultimate rest identifies the fulfillment of the nuptial love that Christ has for the Church and that God has for all people. It extends an invitation to enter into God's joy, which makes all things new (Rev 19–21; Eph 1:10).

Conclusion: Vocation to Love and Self-Gift

This chapter identifies a Catholic Christian frame for understanding how human nature and grace underlie a vocational narrative of call, response, and change (toward flourishing or toward languishing), with the special consideration of a mental health context. Callings and responses (conscious or otherwise) bring about changes in free agency and interpersonal relationships. The basic (philosophical) and faith-based (theological) perspectives proposed in this chapter offer complementary reflections. This model of call, response, and change can aid mental health practitioners in attending to the significance of vocations for their clients and themselves. The client is always embedded in several vocations, which influence short-term objectives, medium- and long-term goals, and one's ultimate end. The psychotherapist is no different. The clinician must recognize both his client's and his own moral and spiritual strengths and weaknesses, and the need for spiritual and vocational development.

The three types of vocation interrelate with each other and with the virtues: (a) the basic vocation to flourishing (vocation to goodness, justice, and holiness) needs to be considered in the light of a person's being called to express all the virtues to some real degree, but especially to express charity; (b) the relational and committed vocations (vocational states) each provide a specific application of the virtues; and (c) a person's life work (specific work and service commitments) and meaningful leisure activities are context for the practice and development of the virtues, including justice. These vocations inform the way we develop virtues, as we will see in the next chapter.

All these vocations cannot be understood without awareness of the uniqueness and unity of the person, plus recognition of the person's sensory-perceptual-cognitive, emotional, relational, rational, and volitional and free dimensions. A vocation-based model accompanied by experience (and knowledge of the model's virtue-based component) will aid mental health practitioners to be mindful of the difference vocational callings make for understanding, assessing, and treating clients.

The ultimate form of vocation, in the Catholic Christian Meta-Model of the Person, is the vocation to love, which is found in the call to holiness, to each vocational state, and to the many forms of service and gratitude, which vary according to the diversity of persons, family, and society. From this Christian perspective, Christ's call to the greatest love, "to lay down one's life for one's friends" (Jn 15:13), is central to each baptized person's vocation to the gift of self and holiness throughout life. It is expressed by the martyr literally, lived by the religious and ordained in concrete generative ways of loving God and others, manifested by the single person in a life of generosity and service, and foundational to the married person in the life of a family. It also underlies a Christian viewpoint on the right relationships and self-gift expressed in work, service, and meaningful leisure.

REFERENCES:

Anatrella, T. (2009). Disappearing fathers, destabilized families. *Communio: International Catholic Review, 36*, 309–328.

Aquinas, T. (1953). *The disputed questions on truth* (J. V. McGlynn, Trans.). Chicago, IL: Regnery. (Original work composed 1256–1259)

Aquinas, T. (1981). *Summa theologica* (Fathers of the English Dominican Province, Trans.). Notre Dame, IN: Christian Classics. (Original work composed 1265–1273)

Aquinas, T. (2003). *On evil* (B. Davies, Ed.; R. Regan, Trans.). New York, NY: Oxford University Press. (Original work composed 1266–1272)

Aristotle. (1941a). *Nicomachean ethics*. In R. McKeon (Ed.), *The basic works of Aristotle* (pp. 935–1112). New York, NY: Random House. (Original work composed ca. 350 BC)

Aristotle. (1941b). *Politics*. In R. McKeon (Ed.), *The basic works of Aristotle* (pp. 1127–1316). New York,

NY: Random House. (Original work composed ca. 350 BC)

Ashley, B. M. (2013). *Healing for freedom: A Christian perspective on personhood and psychotherapy*. Arlington, VA: The Institute for the Psychological Sciences Press.

Augustine. (1955). *The good of marriage* (C. T. Wilcox et al., Trans.). In R. J. Deferrari (Ed.), *Fathers of the Church: Vol. 27. Treatises on marriage and other objects* (pp. 3–52). Washington, DC: The Catholic University of America Press. (Original work composed 401)

Augustine. (1958). *The city of God* (G. G. Walsh, D. M. Zema, G. Monahan, & D. J. Honan, Trans.). New York, NY: Image Books. (Original work composed 427)

Augustine. (2007). *Confessions* (2nd ed.) (M. P. Foley, Ed.; F. J. Sheed, Trans). New York, NY: Hackett. (Original work composed 397–401)

Bachiochi, E. (2013). Women, sexual asymmetry, and Catholic teaching. *Christian Bioethics, 19*(2), 150–171. doi:10.1093/cb/cbt013

Beauregard, M. (2012). *Brain wars: The scientific battle over the existence of the mind and the proof that will change the way we live our lives*. New York, NY: HarperCollins.

Beauregard, M., & O'Leary, D. (2008). *The spiritual brain: A neuroscientist's case for the existence of the soul*. New York, NY: HarperCollins.

Benedict XVI. (2006, May 25). Meeting with the clergy (Warsaw, Poland). Vatican City, Vatican: Libreria Editrice Vaticana.

Benedict XVI. (2008, April 16). Responses of his Holiness Benedict XVI to the questions posed by the bishops [Address, National Shrine of the Immaculate Conception, Washington, DC]. Vatican City, Vatican: Libreria Editrice Vaticana.

Berkman, J., & Titus, C. S. (Eds.). (2005). *The Pinckaers reader: Renewing Thomistic moral theology*. Washington, DC: The Catholic University of America Press.

Bertrand, D. (2001). Bernardine discernment: Between the Desert Fathers and Ignatius of Loyola. *Cistercian Studies Quarterly, 36*(3), 325–336.

Bonino, S. T. (2002). Charisms, forms, and states of life (IIa-IIae, qq. 171–189). In S. J. Pope (Ed.), *The ethics of Aquinas* (pp. 340–352). Washington, DC: Georgetown University Press.

Brizendine, L. (2006). *The female brain*. New York, NY: Broadway Books.

Brizendine, L. (2010). *The male brain*. New York, NY: Broadway Books.

Buber, M. (1971). *I and thou* (W. Kaufmann, Trans.). New York, NY: Touchstone. (Original work published 1923)

Budd, J. W. (2011). *The thought of work*. Ithaca, NY: Cornell University Press.

Budziszewski, J. (2009). *The line through the heart: Natural law as fact, theory, and sign of contradiction*. Wilmington, DE: ISI Books.

Budziszewski, J. (2012). *On the meaning of sex*. Wilmington, DE: ISI Books.

Byrd, S. E. (2009). The social construction of marital commitment. *Journal of Marriage and Family, 71*(2), 318–336. doi:10.1111/j.1741-3737.2008.00601.x

Cade, R. (2010). Covenant marriage. *The Family Journal, 18*(3), 230–233. doi:10.1177/1066480710372072

Catechism of the Catholic Church (*CCC*) (2nd ed.). (2000). Vatican City, Vatican: Libreria Editrice Vaticana.

Chenu, M. D. (1963). *The theology of work: An exploration*. New York, NY: Gill.

Clements, R., & Swensen, C. H. (2000). Commitment to one's spouse as a predictor of marital quality among older couples. *Current Psychology, 19*(2), 110–119.

Cole, B., & Connors, P. (1997). *Christian totality: Theology of the consecrated life* (rev. ed.) New York, NY: Alba House.

Collins, C. L. (1998). *Early marital attraction, barriers, and alternatives as predictors of later marital status* (Doctoral dissertation). Retrieved from PsycINFO. (Order No. AAM9824905)

Congregation for Catholic Education. (2008). *Guidelines for the use of psychology in the admission and formation of candidates for the priesthood*. Vatican City, Vatican: Libreria Editrice Vaticana.

Coulson, J. C., Oades, L. G., & Stoyles, G. J. (2012a). Parents' subjective sense of calling in childrearing: Measurement, development and initial findings. *The Journal of Positive Psychology, 7*(2), 83–94. doi:10.1080/17439760.2011.633547

Coulson, J. C., Oades, L. G., & Stoyles, G. J. (2012b). Parent's conception and experience of calling in child rearing: A qualitative analysis. *Jour-*

nal of Humanistic Psychology, 52(2), 222–247. doi:10.1177/0022167810382454

Council of the Major Superiors of Religious Women. (2009). *Foundations of religious life: Revisiting the vision.* Notre Dame, IN: Ave Maria Press.

Cullen, C. M. (2012). The natural desire to see God and pure nature: A debate revisited. *American Catholic Philosophical Quarterly, 86,* 705–730.

Dahlstrand, J. A. (2010). *The caller and the called: How young adults understand vocation in their lives* (Doctoral dissertation, Loyola Univ. Chicago). Retrieved from http://ecommons.luc.edu/luc_diss/148

Dawkins, R. (1976). *The selfish gene.* New York, NY: Oxford University Press.

Dennett, D. C. (1995). *Darwin's dangerous idea: Evolution and the meanings of life.* New York, NY: Simon & Schuster.

Dreher, D. E. (2012). Vocation: Finding joy and meaning in our work. In T. G. Plante (Ed.), *Religion, spirituality, and positive psychology: Understanding the psychological fruits of faith* (pp. 127–142). Santa Barbara, CA: Praeger.

Dubay, T. (1997). *Authenticity: A biblical theology of discernment.* San Francisco, CA: Ignatius.

Duffy, R., Bott, E., Allan, B., Torrey, C., & Dik, B. (2012). Perceiving a calling, living a calling, and job satisfaction: Testing a moderated, multiple mediator model. *Journal of Counseling Psychology, 59,* 50–59. doi:10.1037/a0026129

Eldridge, B. M. (2011). *Structure of calling and vocation across gender and age cohort* (Doctoral dissertation). Retrieved from PsycINFO. (Order No. AAI3419038)

Eldridge, B. M. (2012). Development and Validation of the Calling and Vocation Questionnaire (CVQ) and Brief Calling Scale (BCS). *Journal of Career Assessment 20(3),* 242–263.

Enright, R. (2012). *The forgiving life: A pathway to overcoming resentment and creating a legacy of love.* Washington, DC: American Psychological Association.

Enright, R. D., & Fitzgibbons, R. P. (2014). *Forgiveness therapy: An empirical guide for resolving anger and restoring hope.* Washington, DC: American Psychological Association.

Feser, E. (2008). *The last superstition: A refutation of the New Atheism.* South Bend, IN: St. Augustine Press.

Francis. (2016). *Amoris laetitia* [Apostolic Exhortation on love in the family]. Vatican City, Vatican: Libreria Editrice Vaticana.

Frankl, V. (1959). *Man's search for meaning.* New York, NY: Washington Square Press.

Frankl, V. (1969). *The will to meaning.* New York, NY: New American Library.

Fromm, E. (1950). *Psychoanalysis and religion.* New Haven, CT: Yale University Press.

Fromm, E. (1956). *The art of loving.* New York, NY: Harper & Brothers.

Gallagher, T. M. (2005). *The discernment of spirits: An Ignatian guide for everyday living.* New York, NY: Crossroad.

Garcia, L. (2010). Authentic freedom and equality in difference. In Erika Bachiochi (Ed.), *Women, sex, and the church: A case for Catholic teaching* (pp. 15–33). New York, NY: Pauline Books.

Garrigou-Lagrange, R. (1948). *The three ages of the interior life, prelude of eternal life* (M. T. Doyle, Trans.). St. Louis, MO: Herder.

Girgis, S., Anderson, R. T., & George, R. P. (2012). *What is marriage?: Man and woman : A defense* (1st American ed.). New York, NY: Encounter Books.

Green, T. F. (1968). *Work, leisure, and the American schools.* New York, NY: Random House.

Grisez, G., & Shaw, R. (2003). *Personal vocation: God calls everyone by name.* Huntington, IN: Our Sunday Visitor.

Guardini, R (1998). *Learning the virtues that lead you to God.* Manchester, NH: Sophia Institute Press.

Hall, S. F., Burkholder, D., & Sterner, W. R. (2014). Examining spirituality and sense of calling in counseling students. *Counseling and Values, 59(1),* 3–16.

Hamachek, D. E. (1978). Psychodynamics of normal and neurotic perfectionism. *Psychology: A Journal of Human Behavior, 15(1),* 27–33.

Hamer, D. (2005). *The God gene: How faith is hardwired into our genes.* New York, NY: Anchor.

Hankle, D. D. (2009). The psychological processes of discerning the vocation to the Catholic priesthood: A qualitative study. *Pastoral Psychology, 59(2),* 201–219. doi:10.1007/s11089-008-0190-6

Hazan, C., & Shaver, P. (1987). Romantic love conceptualized as an attachment process. *Journal of Personality and Social Psychology, 25,* 511–524.

Hitchens, C. (2007). *God is not great: How religion poisons everything*. New York, NY: Hachette.

Homan, K. B. (1986). Vocation as the quest for authentic existence. *The Career Development Quarterly, 35*(1), 14–23. doi:10.1002/j.2161-0045.1986.tb00757.x

Ignatius of Loyola. (1964). *The spiritual exercises of St. Ignatius* (A. Mottola, Trans.). Garden City, NY: Image Books. (Original work composed 1522–1524)

International Theological Commission, (2015). In search of universal ethic: A new look at the natural law. In W. Mattison (Ed.), *Searching for a universal ethic: Multidisciplinary, ecumenical, and interfaith responses to the Catholic natural law tradition*. Grand Rapids, MI: Eerdmans.

John Paul II. (1981a). *Familiaris consortio* [Apostolic exhortation, on the role of the Christian family in the modern world]. Vatican City, Vatican: Libreria Editrice Vaticana.

John Paul II. (1981b). *Laborem exercens* [Encyclical, on human work]. Vatican City, Vatican: Libreria Editrice Vaticana.

John Paul II. (1984). *Redemptionis donum* [Apostolic exhortation, to men and women religious on their consecration in the light of the mystery of the redemption]. Vatican City, Vatican: Libreria Editrice Vaticana.

John Paul II. (1988a). *Christifideles laici* [Apostolic exhortation, on the vocation and the mission of the lay faithful in the Church and in the world]. Vatican City, Vatican: Libreria Editrice Vaticana.

John Paul II. (1988b). *Mulieris dignitatem* [Apostolic letter, on the dignity and vocation of women]. Vatican City, Vatican: Libreria Editrice Vaticana.

John Paul II. (1989). *Custos redemptoris* [Apostolic exhortation, on the person and mission of Saint Joseph in the life of Christ and of the Church]. Vatican City, Vatican: Libreria Editrice Vaticana.

John Paul II. (1991). *Centesimus annus* [Encyclical, on the hundredth anniversary of *Rerum Novarum*]. Vatican City, Vatican: Libreria Editrice Vaticana.

John Paul II. (1992). *Pastores dabo vobis* [Apostolic exhortation, on the formation of priests]. Vatican City, Vatican: Libreria Editrice Vaticana.

John Paul II. (1993). *Veritatis splendor* [Encyclical, on certain fundamental questions of the Church's

moral teaching]. Vatican City, Vatican: Libreria Editrice Vaticana.

John Paul II. (1994a, February 2). *Gratissimam sane* [Letter to families]. Vatican City, Vatican: Libreria Editrice Vaticana.

John Paul II. (1994b). *Ordinatio sacerdotalis* [Apostolic letter, on reserving priestly ordination to men alone]. Vatican City, Vatican: Libreria Editrice Vaticana.

John Paul II. (1996). *Vita consecrata* [Post-synodal apostolic exhortation, on the consecrated life and its mission in the Church and in the world]. Vatican City, Vatican: Libreria Editrice Vaticana.

John Paul II. (1998). *Dies Domini* [Apostolic letter, on the importance of Sabbath rest]. Vatican City, Vatican: Libreria Editrice Vaticana.

John Paul II. (2003). *Pastores gregis* [Apostolic exhortation, on the bishop, servant of the Gospel of Jesus Christ for the hope of the world]. Vatican City, Vatican: Libreria Editrice Vaticana.

John Paul II. (2006). *Man and woman He created them: A theology of the body* (M. Waldstein, Trans.). Boston, MA: Pauline Books and Media.

Johnson, M. P., Caughlin, J. P., & Huston, T. L. (1999). The tripartite nature of marital commitment: Personal, moral, and structural reasons to stay married. *Journal of Marriage and Family, 61*(1), 160–177.

Hauerwas, S. (1981). *A community of character: Toward a constructive Christian social ethics*. Notre Dame, IN: Notre Dame University Press.

Kamp Dush, C. M., Rhoades, G. K., Sandberg-Thoma, S., & Schoppe-Sullivan, S. (2014). Commitment across the transition to parenthood among married and cohabiting couples. *Couple and Family Psychology: Research and Practice, 3*(2), 126–136. doi:10.1037/cfp0000006

Koenig, H. G., King, D., & Carson, V. B. (Eds.). (2012). *Handbook of religion and health* (2nd ed.). New York, NY: Oxford University Press.

Kristjansson, K. (2013). *Virtues and vices in positive psychology: A philosophical critique*. Cambridge, United Kingdom: Cambridge University Press.

Larkin, E. (1998). *Silent presence: Discernment as process and problem*. Denville, NJ: Dimension.

Luthans, F., & Youssef, C. M. (2009). Positive workplaces. In S. J. Lopez & C. R. Snyder (Eds.),

The Oxford handbook of positive psychology (pp. 579–588). Oxford, United Kingdom: Oxford University Press.

MacIntyre, A. (1999). *Dependent rational animals: Why human beings need the virtues.* Chicago, IL: Open Court.

Marcel, G. (2010). *Homo viator: Introduction to the metaphysic of hope* (E. Craufurd & P. Seaton, Trans.). South Bend, IN: St. Augustine Press. (Original work published 1951)

Marett-Crosby, A. (2003). *The Benedictine handbook.* Collegeville, MN: Liturgical Press.

Maslow, A. (1968). *Toward a psychology of being.* London, United Kingdom: Van Nostrand.

Maslow, A., & Frager, R., Fadiman, J., McReynolds, C., & Cox, R. (Eds.) (1987). *Motivation and personality* (3rd ed.). New York, NY: Longman. (Original work published 1954)

McEntee, M. L., Dy-Liacco, G. S., & Haskins, D. G. (2013). Human flourishing: A natural home for spirituality. *Journal of Spirituality in Mental Health, 15,* 141–159.

Mikulincer, M., & Phillip, P. R. (2007). *Attachment in adulthood: Structure, dynamics, and change.* New York, NY: Guilford Press.

Miller, R. B. (2004). *Facing human suffering: Psychology and psychotherapy as moral engagement.* Washington, DC: American Psychological Association.

Moncher, F., & Titus, C. S. (2009). Foundations for a psychotherapy of virtue: An integrated Catholic perspective. *Journal of Psychology and Christianity, 28*(1), 22–35.

Nagel, T. (2012). *Mind and cosmos: Why the materialist neo-Darwinian conception of nature is almost certainly false.* New York, NY: Oxford University Press.

Nédoncelle, M. (1966). *Love and the person.* New York, NY: Sheed & Ward.

Nelson, J. A., Kirk, A. M., Ane, P., & Serres, S. A. (2011). Religious and spiritual values and moral commitment in marriage: Untapped resources in couples counseling? *Counseling and Values, 55*(2), 228–246. doi:10.1002/j.2161-007x.2011.tb00034.x

Novak, M., & Simon, W. E. (2011). *Living the call: An introduction to the lay vocation.* New York, NY: Encounter Books.

Paul VI. (1967). *Sacerdotalis caelibatus* [Encyclical, on the celibacy of the priest]. Vatican City, Vatican: Libreria Editrice Vaticana.

Peterson, C. (2006). *A primer in positive psychology.* New York, NY: Oxford University Press.

Pieper, J. (2009). *Leisure: The basis of culture* (A. Dru, Trans.). San Francisco, CA: Ignatius Press. (Original work published 1952)

Pilcher, J. J., & Huffcutt, A. I. (1996). Effects of sleep deprivation on performance: A meta-analysis. *Sleep, 19*(4), 318–326.

Pinckaers, S. (1995). *The sources of Christian ethics* (M. T. Noble, Trans.). Washington, DC: The Catholic University of America Press. (Original work published 1985)

Pius XI. (1930). *Casti cannubii* [Encyclical, on Christian marriage]. Vatican City, Vatican: Libreria Editrice Vaticana.

Rhoads, S. E. (2004). *Taking sex differences seriously* (1st ed.). San Francisco, CA: Encounter Books.

Rich, A. D. (2007). *Discernment in the Desert Fathers.* Bletchley, United Kingdom: Paternoster.

Ryan, P. S. J. (2007). How to discern the elements of your personal vocation. *Fellowship of Catholic Scholars Quarterly, 30,* 11–18.

Santa, T. (2007). *Understanding scrupulosity: Questions, helps, and encouragement.* Liguori, MO: Liguori Publications.

Savage, D. (2015). The nature of woman in relation to man: Genesis 1 and 2 through the lens of the metaphysical anthropology of Aquinas. *Logos: A Journal of Catholic Thought and Culture, 18*(1), 71–93. doi:10.1353/log.2015.0007

Schmitz, K. (2009). *Person and psyche.* Arlington, VA: The Institute for the Psychological Sciences Press.

Schoebi, D., Karney, B. R., & Bradbury, T. N. (2012). Stability and change in the first 10 years of marriage: Does commitment confer benefits beyond the effects of satisfaction? *Journal of Personality and Social Psychology, 102*(4), 729–742. doi:10.1037/a0026290

Schönborn, C. (2007). *Chance or purpose: Creation, evolution, and a rational faith.* San Francisco, CA: Ignatius Press.

Seligman, M. E. P. (2012). *Flourish: A visionary new understanding of happiness and well-being.* New York, NY: Atria Books.

Siegel, D. J. (2012). *Pocket guide to interpersonal neurobiology: An integrative handbook of the mind* (1st ed.). New York, NY: Norton.

Songy, D. (2012). *Spiritual direction for priestly celibacy.*

Rome, Italy: Pontifical Theological Faculty Tere-sianum.

Spitzer, R. (2008). *Five pillars of the spiritual life: A practical guide to prayer for active people.* San Francisco, CA: Ignatius Press.

Spitzer, R. J. (2010). *New proofs for the existence of God: Contributions of contemporary physics and philosophy.* Grand Rapids, MI: Eerdmans.

Stein, E. (1996). *Essays on woman: The collected works of Edith Stein* (2nd ed.) (L. Gelber & R. Leuven, Eds.; F. M. Oben, Trans.). Washington, DC: Institute for Carmelite Studies Publications. (Original work published 1932)

Sullins, D. P. (2015). Emotional problems with children of same-sex parents: Different by definition. *British Journal of Education, Society and Behavioural Science, 7*(2), 99–120.

Tanquerey, A. (1930). *The spiritual life: A treatise on ascetical and mystical theology.* Charlotte, NC: Saint Benedict Press.

Terranova, L. E. (2006). *The experience of being called to serve: A phenomenological study of vocation* (Doctoral dissertation). Retrieved from PsycINFO. (Order No. AAI3218527)

Torrell, J.-P. (2003). *Saint Thomas Aquinas: Vol. 2. Spiritual master* (R. Royal, Trans.). Washington, DC: The Catholic University of America Press.

Vatican II, Council (1964). *Lumen gentium* [Dogmatic constitution on the Church]. Vatican City, Vatican: Libreria Editrice Vaticana.

Vatican II, Council. (1965a). *Gaudium et spes* [Pastoral constitution on the Church in the modern world]. Vatican City, Vatican: Libreria Editrice Vaticana.

Vatican II, Council. (1965b). *Apostolicam actuositatem* [Decree on the apostolate of the laity]. Vatican City, Vatican: Libreria Editrice Vaticana.

Vitz, P. C. (2018). Men and women: Their differences and their complementarity: Evidence from psychology and neuroscience. Unpublished manuscript, Divine Mercy University, Arlington, VA.

Waite, L., & Gallagher, M. (2000). *The case for marriage: Why married people are happier, healthier, and better off financially.* New York, NY: Doubleday.

Widiger, T. A. (2017). *The Oxford handbook of the Five Factor Model.* Oxford, United Kingdom: Oxford University Press.

Widiger, T. A., & Costa, P. T. (2012). Integrating normal and abnormal personality structure: The Five-Factor model. *Journal of Personality, 80*(6), 1471–1506. doi:10.1111/j.1467-6494.2012.00776.x

Wilcox, W. B., Anderson, J. R., Doherty, W. J., Eggebeen, D, Ellison, C. G., Galston, W. A., ... Wallerstein, J, et al. (2011). *Why marriage matters, third edition: Thirty conclusions from the social sciences.* New York, NY: Institute for American Values.

Wilcox, W. B., & Dew, J. J. (2013). No one best way: Work-family strategies, the gendered division of parenting, and the contemporary marriages of mothers and fathers. In W. B. Wilcox & K. K. Kline (Eds.), *Gender and parenthood: Biological and social scientific perspectives* (pp. 271–303). New York, NY: Columbia University Press.

Wojtyła, K. (1993). The problem of vocation (H. T. Willetts, Trans.). In *Love and responsibility* (pp. 219–261). San Francisco, CA: Ignatius Press. (Original work published 1960)

Worthington, E. L., Jr. (2003). *Forgiving and reconciling: Bridges to wholeness and hope* (rev. ed.). Downers Grove, IL: InterVarsity Press.

Worthington, E. L., Jr., Lavelock, C., Van Tongeren, Tongeren D. R., Jennings II, D. J., Gartner, A. L., Davis, D. E., & Hook, J. N. (2014). Virtue in positive psychology. In K. Timpe & C. A. Boyd (Eds.), *Virtues and their vices* (pp. 433–458). Oxford, United Kingdom: Oxford University Press.

Chapter 11

Fulfilled in Virtue

CRAIG STEVEN TITUS, PAUL C. VITZ, WILLIAM J. NORDLING,
MATTHEW R. McWHORTER, AND
CHRISTOPHER GROSS

ABSTRACT: This chapter will focus on the contribution that the classical, wisdom-based approach of the Catholic Christian Meta-Model of the Person makes for understanding virtue and flourishing. The Meta-Model identifies the advantages of an integrated view of the virtues in facing difficulty, frailty, sin, and vice, while respecting normative human nature and duty, the dignity and uniqueness of each person, the differences of the sexes, the common good, and the movement of grace. Furthermore, it identifies thirteen dimensions of the virtues, as (1) performative; (2) perfective and corrective; (3) purposeful; (4) ethical; (5) influenced by personal uniqueness, equal innate dignity, sex difference and complementarity; (6) connective, relational, and developmental; (7) learned through role models; (8) moderating; (9) preventative; (10) nonreductionist; (11) applied; (12) vocational; and (13) open to the transcendent and to God. A comparison table of the ideas of Aquinas and Seligman with respect to these dimensions is made. The virtues perfect the natural inclinations and capacities, by participating (along with the natural moral law and its precepts) in the realization of human goals and vocations. From a Christian theological perspective, the chapter discusses how the development of virtue also draws on spiritual inclinations, transcendent vocations, and divine grace; and, on the contrary, how selfish and evil choices produce tendencies toward moral and spiritual disorders and vices. This chapter also presents a classification of the moral, intellectual, and theological virtues, while outlining the associated virtues connected to them and the vices contrasted to them. It draws upon theory, research, and practices that are associated with psychological function and dysfunction, moral character strength and weakness, as well as spiritual maturity and languishing or vice.

Humans flourish or languish as a result of the types of commitments they do or do not make to living a good life. In the classical, wisdom-based approach of the Catholic Christian Meta-Model of the Person, the good life is understood through the qualities expressed in the personal and interpersonal dimensions of the virtues and life-callings (vocations). In this model, as seen in this chapter and throughout the volume, the virtues are understood to underlie flourishing human experience—for example, the love of a mother for her newborn, the hope of a father for his struggling children, the initiative-taking of the woman starting a business in the face of economic instability, the courage of the fireman in the midst of service, the faith of the young woman confronted with doubt, the patience of a priest in the trials of assisting the needy, the mercy of parents at the return of a prodigal son, and the integrity of the elderly person who persists in caring for others. Such vocation-embedded virtues, although often challenging and difficult, are the means by which people encounter the meaning and purpose of life (also see Chapter 10, "Fulfilled Through Vocation"). The contrary experiences and tendencies are examples of vices that lead to languishing, which is the result of giving in to indifference, despair, short-sightedness, fear, distrust, impatience, avoidance, intransigence, and especially self-centeredness. Languishing involves a disintegrative movement of the person, who suffers from the negative influence of such actions and attitudes on his own development and interpersonal relationships.

The history of mankind is a history of contemplating, desiring, and practicing virtue; it is also a history of imagining, plotting, and enacting vice. This chapter examines the contributions that virtues offer for understanding people and mental health practice. It conceptualizes virtues as leading to flourishing (usually through persistent effort and difficulty) and vices as bringing suffering (often with short-term benefits that may be considerable). It is our thesis that this virtue-based model—informed by experience, science, and reason, on the one hand, and a Christian approach to Scripture and tradition, on the other—prepares us to better understand the personal mixture of virtuous and vicious dispositions that stimulate our contradictory desires. For instance, while seeking the good through virtues such as justice,

self-control, and patience, humans often experience a mixture of desires, some of which tend toward unjust, self-serving, and impatient deeds.

The recent renewal of virtue theory has stimulated and enriched theological, philosophical, psychological, and empirical scholarship. Contributions have been made, according to the perspectives and methods of different disciplines, from *psychology* (Kinghorn, 2016; Linsley & Joseph, 2004; Lopez & Snyder, 2009, 2014; McMinn, 2017; Peterson & Seligman, 2004; Van Slyke, 2014; Worthington et al., 2014), from *counseling* (Harris, Thoresen, & Lopez, 2007; Plante & Thoresen, 2012), from *philosophy* (MacIntyre, 2007, 1999; Miller, 2014; Pieper, 1966, 1957/1998; Russell, 2013; Slote, 2010; Timpe & Boyd, 2014), from *theology* (Cessario, 2002, 2008; Hauerwas, 1981; Kaczor, 2015; Pinckaers, 1978, 1995; Ricœur, 1992), and from other human sciences.

Contributing to this renewal, the Catholic Christian Meta-Model of the Person is virtue-based, drawing on contemporary psychological and human science sources, on ancient, medieval, modern, and contemporary philosophical sources, and on Christian theological and philosophical sources. This chapter presents the Meta-Model's view of the person—a unified person who is interpersonal, embodied (with sensory-perceptual cognition and emotions), intellectual, cognitive and volitional, moral (responsible and free), vocational, and spiritual (transcendent)—as aimed at flourishing through a good life of virtue.

As one part of the Meta-Model of the Person, this chapter addresses several questions: What contribution does a multidimensional virtue-based approach to flourishing make to a synthetic model of the person? Are all conceptual frameworks of virtue the same? What implications does a virtue-based model have for mental health practice? And how does the practice of virtue influence persons according to their being relational and to their vocations?

This chapter will explore the viability of an integrative multidimensional model that understands virtue as having the following thirteen properties in an integrated and often overlapping manner. Virtues are: (1) **performative** (act-based); (2) **perfective and corrective** (agent-based); (3) **purposeful** (teleological and reason-based); (4) **ethical** (moral norm–based); (5) **influenced by personal uniqueness, equal innate dignity, sex difference and complementarity** (based in personal individuality, including common and distinctive characteristics); (6) **connective, relational, and developmental** (holistic and interpersonal process–based); (7) **learned through role models** (based in exemplars and sources that model goodness and truth); (8) **moderating** (seeking a middle ground of excellence between two extremes); (9) **preventative** (strength-based); (10) **non-reductionist** (contextual and open to evidence); (11) **applied** (in need of being applied to research and practice); (12) **vocational** (calling-based); and (13) **open to the transcendent and to God** (seeking goodness, truth, and beauty, and their transcendent source). These properties are not independent, and we need to keep in mind that these dimensions have overlapping aspects. It is these thirteen properties that constitute the main expression of the integrative nature of the Meta-Model's treatment of the virtues.

After a description of the first three dimensions of the CCMMP's approach to virtue, this chapter addresses how the natural inclinations (toward self-preservation, sexual union and child rearing, seeking truth and goodness, and life in society) serve as seeds for the development of understanding and respecting the normative dimension of the person and the precepts of the natural law. It addresses the most basic human in-clination, which is ultimate flourishing, and how it relates to the development, health, and healing of the person. The above-mentioned thirteen dimensions of virtue are presented while comparing Christian virtue theory and other virtue theories, such as that of positive psychology (Peterson & Seligman, 2004). Finally, the chapter discusses moral disorders, evil, and vice as negative contrasts to moral character, goodness, and virtue and flourishing.

What Does a Virtue-Based Model of the Human Person Comprise?

The term "virtue" has been understood in quite diverse ways. Most ethical models claim to be either anchored in virtue theory or contrasted to it. Some ethical models explicitly employ virtue language: for instance, certain flourishing-based, agent-based, act-based ethics of care (medical or professional ethics; Pellegrino & Thomasma, 1996), moral rationalist (Kant, 1788/1993), and moral sentimentalist (Hume, 1740/2000) approaches. Other ethical models distance themselves from virtue concepts or render them secondary, as in utilitarian and consequentialist approaches to "measuring" and comparing goods.

Immanuel Kant's (1724–1804) duty-based (deontological) approach is an example of an ethics that present-day proponents often contrast with virtue theory, especially with a virtue theory that is associated with utilitarian approaches to happiness (Fowers, 2005; van Deurzen, 2008). Kant does explicitly critique happiness (eudaemonic) approaches to ethics (Kant, 1785/2011, §442; 1788/1993, §114) and also implicitly critiques modern utilitarian approaches. (For Kant's doctrine of a kingdom of ends, which serves as an implicit critique of utilitarianism, see Kant, 1785/2011, §433–§435; for commentary on Kant's doctrine, see Wojtyła, 1993, p. 37). However, in one of his later works (1797/1964), Kant devotes

the concluding section to "The Doctrine of Virtue" and identifies virtue as "the moral strength
of a man's will in fulfilling his duty" (p. 66) in
spite of contrary emotions. More often than not,
though, Kant's ethics are presented as duty-based
rather than virtue-based. The history of virtue is
complex, and the priority of either duty or virtue in time (development) or in primacy (end)
will need to be treated elsewhere (see MacIntyre,
2007; Titus, 2013b). This chapter posits that overly simplified or indistinct references to virtue, like
the one found in Kant, are inadequate. Virtue is
more than a good act done out of duty or proper
sentiment, more than a good habit or an ethical
norm. Virtue must also be understood in light of
the developmental, normative, and ultimate dimensions of human life. Our claim is that a multidimensional virtue-based model overcomes the
weaknesses and objections just mentioned, and
it is more effective in ethical considerations and
mental health applications.

We begin by focusing on three of the principal dimensions of the virtues: good acts,
fitting dispositions, and ethical and spiritual
norms. The term "act" is preferred to "behavior"
because it implies both internal and external
action (both intending to feed the hungry person and really providing food to him), in ways
that the term "behavior" does not. First, acts
are signs of either virtue or vice. The *act-based
dimension* distinguishes the good acts of virtue
from the compromised acts of vice (Aristotle,
ca. 350 BC/1941a, V.1–3). Second, in their dispositions to act, agents demonstrate tendencies
toward virtue or vice. The *agent-based dimension*
identifies the person's capacities, dispositions,
or character traits that are engaged in action.
Third, virtues are made possible by the presence
of reason, as found in the person, in positive relationships, in law, and in integral flourishing.
Reason also helps develop psychological, moral,

and spiritual standards for the purpose of exercising virtuous acts. The *reason-based dimension*
involves the good standards from which virtues
draw and at which they aim.

These three dimensions are the foundational
dimensions of the virtues, namely, the act-based
(performative), agent-based (perfective and
corrective), and reason-based (purposeful) dimensions (see Table 11.1 for an overview). These
three dimensions aid in overcoming the traps not
only of anthropologically and developmentally
static visions of virtue, but also of supposedly
value-neutral, relativistic, and non-normative
ones (Fowers, 2005; Halwani, 2003; Schimmel,
1997). The three dimensions will each be considered in the following introductory discussion,
after which we will proceed to the first main section of this chapter, which treats the topic of natural inclinations and the natural law. These three
dimensions will be treated again (along with the
other ten dimensions of the virtues) in the fourth
section below, entitled, "Virtues: Their Types
and Connection." The other ten dimensions of
the virtues will also be explored more fully in the
discussion of the virtues that are found in Chapters 12–16 of this work.

What Is the Act-Based Dimension of Virtue? (Performative)

First, the person flourishes through the virtues
in the acts that the person performs; for example, caring for a sick spouse, giving to a neighbor
in need, or being honest at work. The act-based
dimension explores the virtuous agency found
in a person's concrete good actions. In the virtuous act, the person finds the middle ground of
excellence (competence, fittingness, coherence)
between extremes of excess or deficit in the exercise of human capacities such as reasoning,
willing, feeling, and relating to other persons.
Acts have to be guided by reason and the gold-

Table 11.1. Three Basic Dimensions of Virtue in the Meta-Model of the Person

Dimension	Aspect of virtue	Contribution	Goal	Condition or cause
Act-based (performative)	Acts	Good acts, both internal (e.g., intention) and external (e.g., overt behavior)	Free and responsible moral acts	Efficient (volition behind the act)
Agent-based (perfective & corrective)	Habits or habitual dispositions	Capacities modified (personal & relational): -cognition (reason) -volition (will) -affect (emotions)	Moral and spiritual development and character	Material (embodied capacity) & Formal (spiritually unifying and intelligible cause)
Reason-based (purposeful)	Reasonable standards and values, vocations and relational goals, moral norms, and spiritual aims	Objective reasons, norms, values, vocations	Personal flourishing and spiritual beatitude	Final (goal, aim, purpose, or *telos*)

en mean. Even in the acts of care and service we must seek the golden mean: one cannot serve another person 24 hours a day, 7 days a week and at the expense of other important commitments. We know that people must use reason to determine how to act in a way that is truly good and virtuous. To approach a middle ground of excellence (the golden mean) in what we do is neither automatic nor easy, as Aristotle (ca. 350 BC/1941b) says concerning right anger, generosity, and initiative:

> so, too, any one can get angry—that is easy—or give or spend money; but to do this to the right person, to the right extent, at the right time, with the right motive, and in the right way, that is not for every one, nor is it easy; wherefore goodness is both rare and laudable and noble. (1109a27)

His construal of a good action is demanding, for people desire and seek a holistic goal to which they can devote their life. A good act involves more than a functional mean (too much emotion or too little emotion) or a mathematical mean (quantified arithmetically). The act is virtuous because it personifies the good of being a whole person seeking greater wholeness or integrity as relational, embodied, rational, volitional, and free. In the more explicit language of the Meta-Model, the act must also respect people's vocational commitments and responsibilities to grow in goodness, to serve family, to work for others, and to care for themselves and worship God in meaningful leisure, cultural, and religious activities.

What Is the Agent-Based Dimension of Virtue? (Perfective and Corrective)

Second, one good act does not guarantee the next. It is necessary also to consider the agent-based dimension of virtue—the human capaci-

Table 11.2. Human Capacities

	Cognitive Capacities	Affective Capacities
Intellectual Capacities	Reason	Will
Sense Capacities	Sensory-Perceptual Cognition	Emotion
Organic and Neural Dimensions		

ties, operational dispositions (*habitus*, engrained in our capacities for action), and character traits that influence acts. The agentive aspect of virtue is influenced not only by an individual's experience and uniqueness, but also by the sex differences and vocational dimensions of the person and his or her relationships, as will be made clear in the other chapters of this volume, especially Chapter 8, "Personal Wholeness," Chapter 9, "Man and Woman," and Chapter 10, "Fulfilled Through Vocation." In a dynamic way, virtuous acts are influenced by operative or habitual dispositions (including temperament and character traits), and, at the same time, habits are influenced by virtuous acts. Virtuous dispositions (operative habits) are the means through which a person tends, in duty and in love, toward the end of virtue. For example, patient acts of a mother for her sick child or of a father for his anxious son are influenced by a person's own dispositions to act. These dispositions shape, for better or for worse, the person's next act. One of the founders of neuropsychology, Donald Hebb (1949), observes that, in a sense, "neurons that fire together wire together" (for more recent treatment of this phenomenon, see Shatz, 1992, and Doidge, 2007, p. 427). The neural connections needed for particular acts form neural

dispositions to perform such acts again. A more popular way of referring to this experience is "practice makes perfect."

Dispositional capacities yield four types of knowledge and love, which can be found within any vocation—let us take, for example, the human vocation of marriage: (1) *sensory-perceptual cognitions* (and higher-order perceptions, including memory, imagination, and evaluations, e.g., repulsion at the thought of infidelity); (2) *emotion*, or sensory affect (including the habits to feel certain ways about things, e.g., anger at the injustice and deceit expressed in infidelity), (3) *reason*, or intellectual cognition (including intuition, discerning, discursive judgment, and decisions, e.g., discerning the way to avoid extramarital affairs), and (4) *volition or will*, intellectual affect (including intention, choice and consent, e.g., not just intending fidelity, but also choosing effective ways to practice it and consenting to remain faithful to one's spouse). In coming chapters, especially in Chapters 13–16, we will describe how these capacities can be analyzed in two pairs of capacities: the sensory and intellectual and the cognitive and affective (see Table 11.2).

Fuller versions of this table are found below. An organic basis or structure underlies these human capacities.

Above all, virtue involves the good and fitting use of the mind or intellect (reason and will), yet it also involves the acts and dispositions of all these human capacities at both conscious and other levels. Even when a person's capacities are well disposed to goodness, however, one must (a) discern the good to be intentionally aimed at (for instance, to start a new clinic); (b) deliberate about the particular means to that end (e.g., what is needed in terms of office space, collaborators, and investment); and (c) make a particular choice to act morally (e.g., rent an office for the clinic, hire a collaborator, and invest the funds). Nevertheless, even with well-formed dispositions and experience, the exercise of virtuous acts and the cultivation of virtuous dispositions are neither easy nor automatic.

What Is the Reason-Based Dimension of Virtue? (Purposeful and Normative)

Third, there is the reason-based dimension. The virtues are informed by the person's final purpose, goal, or end (*telos*)—included in human nature, the common good, natural law, and divine law—which leads to a person's flourishing. These purposeful goals are norms that we find through our intellectual efforts, through the experience of our human nature, and through the order of natural law (on the natural law, see

Aquinas, 1273/1981; Budziszewski, 2009, 2012; Levering, 2008, also see Chapter 15, "Rational"). Christian theological sources address these ends, goals, and norms in terms of the flourishing that comes of being children of God and in terms of the ethical teaching found in the Old Testament (law and prophets), the New Testament (moral exhortations), Catholic moral teaching, and other precepts that are specified through practical reason (International Theological Commission, 2014; Pinckaers, 1995; Spitzer, 2015a, 2015b, 2016, 2017). Conscious knowledge of these norms and ends, concerted efforts to live them in duty and in love, and even nonconscious inclinations toward these ends guide human judgment and action toward good and away from evil. Such norms (for example, to protect the marriage bond) need further specification in the type of *just acts* (support between spouses), *integrity* (in remaining faithful in spousal intimacy), and *patience* (in the midst of the illness of a spouse or the tantrum of a child) that need to be embodied in acts and in related dispositions to act. The purposeful dimension of virtue is active even when a person is only partially aware of it and even when one performs the acts merely out of duty. The tendencies of vice are also active, but in another way, as we will see at the end of this chapter.

Inclined Toward Flourishing and God

What Is the Most Basic Human Inclination?

Throughout time, every people and each person has sought flourishing (Aquinas, 1273/1981; Augustine, 401/2007; Haidt, 2006; Seligman, 2011). This search does not mean that people have consistently found the way to full and true flourishing at any of these times, or that they have not injured themselves and others in the process.

Arguably, "happiness" (from the Old English root "happ," an accidental state) indicates a more subjective emphasis, while "flourishing" tends to indicate a richer and more stable way to understand the goal and purpose of human life. Disordered approaches to flourishing do not fully satisfy, nor do mundane ones that simply involve money, prestige, power, physical health, or pleasure (Aquinas, 1273/1981, I-II, 2). Such goods may satisfy, but only temporarily. Their luster fades with time and even very quickly in many cases. Just as for an addict, the effects of adaptation and satiation set in, so a person seeking merely earthly goods needs increasingly more to experience even short-term satisfactions and even to appear happy. Likewise, disordered desire for everyday goods will not quench that deepest desire of our hearts. Ultimate flourishing, within the Catholic Christian Meta-Model, depends upon positive and loving relations with God and others.

What Is the Importance of Subjective and Objective Flourishing?

The question arises as to the place for subjective and objective happiness and flourishing in psychological, ethical, and even metaphysical views. Contemporary thought in general and psychological thought in particular tends to focus on subjective flourishing, although attentiveness to the objective and the interpersonal dimensions are on the rise (Seligman, 2002, 2011). Importantly, Kant's critique of purely subjective appreciations of happiness (1724–1804) has influenced contemporary thought. For example, according to van Deurzen (2008), the sway of Kantian critiques can be found in contemporary psychology's distrust of happiness in psychotherapy.

While classical philosophical thought has focused on an objective ontological and ethical frame, criticizing simplistic hedonism (as did Plato in the *Philebus*, ca. 360 BC/1961), modern philosophical thought focuses more on subjective experiences, including those of happiness, from relativist positions such as social constructivism (Butler, 1988, 1999; Fowers, 2005; Singer, 2011) or existentialism (de Beauvoir, 1949/2011; Sartre 1946/2007). A combination of hedonism

and empiricism is found in British utilitarianism, which seeks to quantify and maximize happiness or pleasure (Bentham, 1789; Mill, 1861/1957). Forerunners to hedonism are found in Epicureanism, although Epicurus (writing in the third to second century BC) sought to diminish the expectation and experience of pleasure in order to be content with little (1994). A strong version (and interpretation) of hedonism is perhaps more current at present in practice than in theory, that is, in the experiences of consumerism, narcissism, and sensual license. It is hard to argue that attaining physical or psychological pleasure and avoiding pain alone is a stable basis for flourishing. Nor can pleasure as mere physical health, short-term well-being, or calculated forms of enjoyment be considered a solid basis for flourishing.

Furthermore, contemporary humanistic personality theories have affirmed either an innate movement toward goodness and growth (Fromm, 1956; Rogers, 1961/2012; Rousseau, 1762/1979) or innate tendencies to cognitive development (Piaget, 1932/1997) and to moral and prosocial judgment (Kohlberg, 1981). These theories can be seen as charting various aspects of natural tendencies toward flourishing (even though, for example, Rogers's denial of a normative role of reason seriously deforms his theory; see Vitz, 1994). In a more positive light, these psychologies parallel in part the classical tradition's understanding of basic inclinations as tending to prosocial flourishing. Adler (2013) was perhaps one of the first psychologists to emphasize contributions to society as necessary for personal mental health. More recently, for example, Erikson (1994) recognizes the innate need for meaning and self-gift through generativity (the penultimate stage in adult development). Instead of a vague notion of social welfare, and in contrast to stagnation, adult generativity involves contributing concretely to the upbringing of the next generation of children (even when one is without one's own offspring).

In recent times, the turn to measure subjective experience has even reduced human happiness to the "remembering self's" memories of pleasant experiences (Kahneman, 2011). Seligman (2011), however, has attempted to widen the modern consideration of flourishing to include five elements (under the acronym PERMA): positive emotion, engagement, positive relationships, meaning, and achievement. Nonetheless, the result does not yet include a convincing objective moral standard or ethically normative reference (Titus, 2017). In contrast, the Meta-Model and the classical approach explicitly identify the objective and communal dimension of the quest for flourishing as the basic measure for evaluating different subjective experiences (Aristotle, ca. 350 BC/1941b, IX & X). People need these moral standards, because they do not flourish alone, nor do they flourish without God (Aquinas, 1273/1981, I-II, 3.8; Pieper, 1957/1998).

Does a Natural Desire to See God Underlie the Most Basic Desire for Flourishing?

In a philosophical idiom, and based on the evidence of introspection, every human person experiences the basic inclination toward the good that will make them flourish. Such is the basic structure of the will. Even when we realize that what we have is as good as it gets—a good marriage, good friendships—it is not enough. We still seek a greater good, even an absolute one, who is God. This inclination ultimately aims at the transcendent source of the world's cosmic origin and of every gift, a source that alone promises, as the end of our longings, to make us flourish truly and fully. That ultimate source

and the end of all things is God. As the personal Creator of all, God is also the source of this inclination. Because of his absolute and eternal goodness, this desire for the good is an indelible and a natural desire to see God (Rom 1:20; Aquinas, 1273/1981, I-II, qq. 1–5; Cullen, 2012; de Lubac, 1946/1998; Feingold, 2010; Życiński, 2006). The attraction to goodness expresses the capacity to be moved and to move—to receive and to give—that underlies all tendencies to temporal flourishing (e.g., to family life, professional work, and civic engagement; Peterson & Seligman, 2004), to moral rectitude and altruism (e.g., to love and justice; Post, 2007), and to eternal beatitude (e.g., to religion and the loving contemplation of God; Koenig, King, & Carson, 2012; Pieper, 1957/1998). This basic inclination underlies the intelligent and free action that seeks personal healing, moral development, and spiritual growth (Aquinas, 1273/1981, II-II, 94.2). The natural desire for God is expressed not only in existential, phenomenological, and artistic ways, but also in scientific attempts to recognize the limits of physics and the beginning of the metaphysical order (Spitzer, 2010; Schmitz, 2009).

In a psychological idiom, many people experience an existential discontent in life as a negative contrast experience to this natural desire for God. People ask: "Is this all that there is?" or "Is this as good as life gets?" Psychological experience of the desire for more and the desire for God is often unknowingly present in an experience of disquiet and unrest. This phenomenon of languishing, which has been likened to *acedia*, or sloth (Keyes, 2002), might best be seen as more than a simple lack of mental flourishing and more like a deep existential malaise. Recognition of such languishing can be an important moment that leads a person to be more open to friends or therapeutic attempts to heal. Even when concealed by disability, misconstrued by addiction, or masked by atheistic claims, the need for God and for flourishing is the basis for therapeutic interventions that seek to disentangle our deepest longings for goodness from particular disordered desires. Important aspects of this unknown search for God are found in the work of Frankl (2000, 1959/2006).

In a theological perspective, the origin and end of flourishing (i.e., beatitude) is found in the love of God, who loves us first, and in our love of neighbors. This love of God is both friendship-love (Jn 15:13) and filial love (Jn 1:12). It is more than pleasure and is ultimately *agapē*, or self-giving love (Benedict XVI, 2005; John Paul II, 2006). The effects of sin, however, continue to distance humans from God and others and to strongly trouble the person. God's love for us and our love of God, neighbor, and self in truth serve as means to remedy disordered

desires for flourishing, to resist temptations, and to reconcile sinners in their continued effort to overcome the effects of sin (Gallagher, 1999). This love also rectifies self-centeredness, inasmuch as it is other-centered while being foundationally God-centered. The desire for true beatitude is rooted in a perception of this true love, which is never quenched until one lovingly contemplates God face to face. Thus, St. Augustine (401/2007) prayerfully speaks of restlessness: "For Thou hast made us for Thyself and our hearts are restless till they rest in Thee" (I.1.2). This relational tendency is a substantial element of what it means to be a human being who is made in "the image of God" (Gen 1:26–27; Mt 5:8; Acts 17:27; Aquinas, 1273/1981, I, 35.3 ad 3; Vatican II, 1965, §19). This is discussed later in the theological section (Chapter 19, "Redeemed").

Natural Inclinations, Natural Law, and the Personalist Norm

The personalist norm and natural law together contribute to our understanding of the course of moral character, spiritual maturity, and personal flourishing. They provide an account of ethical dysfunction and spiritual languishing, as well. The natural law and the personalist norm also make a significant contribution to our understanding of the interrelation between professional ethics, Christian philosophical ethics, and Catholic moral theology. They are particularly significant because of their implications for everyday life. The Meta-Model seeks to articulate the roles the natural law and the personalist norm play in supporting ethical and moral judgments, in general, and, more specifically, in professional ethics within the mental health field (as seen later in this chapter).

Ethical perspectives founded on a personalist

vision are sometimes understood to be at odds with those founded on natural law and metaphysics. On the one hand, radical versions of personalism (for example, Fowers, 2005; Nussbaum, 1986; Singer, 2010; Singer, 2011) focus on value and individuality, while neglecting the importance of human nature and natural law for the field of ethics. On the other hand, static versions of natural law are legalistic or biological, neglecting an existential, metaphysical, and developmental approach to the person, value, and virtue.

The Catholic Christian Meta-Model of the Person recognizes the need for both the natural law tradition and personalism, which both set the human person, created in the image of God, as a norm for understanding one's self and for interacting with others (Wojtyła, 2011). In different ways, a Catholic Christian approach to natural law and personalism emphasize the person, the interpersonal, virtues, norms and natural law, a metaphysical basis, and a personal rational participation in the divine law, as we will now see.

How Does the Person Serve as a Criterion for a Moral Norm?

The dignity of the person underlies moral claims, in a Catholic Christian vision. Human persons are self-possessing moral agents. They are called to be responsible subjects, who must, as much as possible, take charge of their lives through seeking truth and making practically wise and good decisions. They each necessarily have distinct ends and goals. Because of this inherent dignity and vocational call to attain their everyday and ultimate ends, they cannot be used instrumentally, as mere objects or as mere means to someone else's ends. Karol Wojtyła (1993) states that:

> Whenever a person is the object of your activity, remember that you may not treat that person as only the means to an end, as an instrument, but must allow for the fact that he or she, too, has or at least should have, distinct personal ends. (p. 28)

Consideration of the person as worthy of just treatment demands a notion of what and who the person is. This principle presupposes a deep tie between freedom and truth; that is, freedom of conscience to do the good is possible only in light of the truth of the person and of his or her life journey and ultimate end, which informs our understanding of how to relate to each person. For example, we should not reduce a personal subject to being the mere object of pleasure, as happens in prostitution, in pornography use, and in the hookup culture. Nor should we reduce a person to being merely an object for material gain, as in the exploitation of clients or workers.

The key to the personalist norm is to respect each person's vocation to freely participate in an action, with the stipulation that each act be fitting for the human persons involved. This norm forbids "intrinsically evil" acts—such as sex trafficking, torture, murder, prostitution, and theft (John Paul II, 1993, §80; see also Vatican II, 1965, §27). It also shows how love and service transform an action—as when pleasure is uplifted through the self-giving love of marriage, or when service is unselfishly and freely rendered in professional work.

Professional ethics, in the mental health profession, use such principles and values, for example, when therapists are mandated to report sexual and physical abuse of children, as well as clients who endanger themselves or others. Mental health professionals are also called to be honest (and even charitable) in their dealings with clients.

How Does a Prudential Personalism Contribute to Moral Action?

The Catholic Christian vision entails a person-, virtue-, natural law-, and duty-based ethical approach that may be called a prudential personalism (Ashley & O'Rourke, 1997, 2013). Such an ethical approach is rooted in the basic human experience of the need for relationships and personal reason, will, and emotion in moral agency or behavior. This prudential personalism involves natural law as a human intelligent participation (using intuition, reason, emotion, and volition) in the wisdom inscribed in the cosmos and the normative dimension of reality, which is ultimately based in the wisdom of the ultimate source and end of all that exists.

Natural law is found in the order and purpose (*telos*) of human inclinations, relationships, actions, and vocations, always in the perspective of the final end, as the law that is written in the human heart, in each person's inner being. The Meta-Model of the Person recognizes that the natural law cannot be reduced to the precepts that attempt to formulate it in words. The direction of the natural inclinations, which underlie the natural law, is neither always easy to discern nor always easy to apply to complex everyday settings, especially when people are distracted, or even conflicted, by self-interest, pleasure, and fear. That is why it is necessary to see it in the context of a virtue approach, such as a prudential personalism.

From a faith-based perspective, the natural law is defined, for example by Aquinas (1273/1981, I-II, 94.2), as an intelligent participation in eternal law, that is, in divine wisdom and love. St. Paul talks about how non-believers, who do not have a covenant of law, show by the good that they may do "that what the law requires is written on their hearts, while their conscience also bears witness and their conflicting thoughts accuse or perhaps excuse them" (Rom 2:15; see also Rom 1:19–20). Here St. Paul is speaking of the way that all people have this capacity and may be just, wise, and caring, although as it is for everyone not without difficulty and error. Furthermore, the divine origin of the natural law is affirmed, protected, and clarified in the moral and spiritual content of Divine Revelation, especially as found in certain Decalogue prescriptions, which can be summed up as a calling to love God and to love your neighbor as yourself (Ex 20:1–17; Lev 19:18; Mt 22:38–39; Rom 13:9; see also Aquinas, 1273/1981, I-II, 100.1).

The Catholic Christian Meta-Model of the Person, in the form of a prudential personalism, also recognizes the range of human woundedness, disintegration, and difficulty, as well as of the effects of the fall, pride, and sinfulness. These common signs of human moral and spiritual weakness harm the wise use of the will, emo-

tions, and interpersonal support. They often obstruct the person's capacity to know and be aware of what the natural moral law would demand and its application in moral action (John Paul II, 1993, §36; Aquinas, 1949, a.7 ad 10).

What Role Do Natural Inclinations Play in the Natural Law?

This chapter began with a wisdom-based treatment of three dimensions of virtues (act-based, agent-based, and reason-based dimensions). These dimensions cannot be fully understood without making explicit the ethical, as a significant dimension of virtue. It is posited that a teleological, norm-based, and multidimensional frame of virtue (a prudential personalism) offers a fuller conceptual vantage point from which to understand the human action, flourishing, and languishing, that is the ethical dimension (Ashley & O'Rourke, 1997, MacIntyre, 2009). The question is how best to ground a compelling argument for understanding the ethical dimension of virtues in light of (a) natural inclinations, and (b) the moral precepts of the natural law and the personalist norm, which include moral and spiritual purpose, goals (*telos*), and flourishing.

Using the Meta-Model of the Person, this chapter seeks to make the case that a dynamic treatment of natural inclinations, norms or law, callings, and virtues helps to better understand human flourishing. The philosophical side of this approach draws upon the sources of a realist, natural law-based, and personalist view of the person. The Catholic theological side of this approach draws upon sources found in the Bible and Church teaching (the Magisterium), and from its notable thinkers such as Augustine, Aquinas, and John Paul II. Without these sources and this deep view, the analysis of virtue and vice would be static and thin. While a fuller debate on natural law (Budziszewski, 2009, 2012;

George, 2001; Hittinger, 2007; International Theological Commission, 2014; Levering, 2008; Pinckaers, 1995) and the personalist norm is recorded in other works (Wojtyła, 1993), we propose an approach to the natural inclinations that underlie human activity and that serve as the seeds for natural law precepts, virtuous acts and dispositions, and ethical judgments (prudential personalism). For a fuller understanding of this issue, we need to treat also disordered desires, loss of goals, and disengagement from vocations, which underlie vicious acts and dispositions.

What is a natural inclination? The Meta-Model of the Person recognizes that the natural inclinations are the most basic teleological tendencies toward goodness that underlie all derivative articulations of goodness. The natural inclinations underlie, and are more profound than, the neurological processes and biological urges. They manifest the transcendental properties of existence (*esse*). These properties are unity (*unum*), truth (*verum*), goodness (*bonum*), relationality (*aliquid*), and beauty (*pulchrum*) (Schmitz, 2007, p. 15; 2009, pp. 11–14; Aquinas, 1259/1953, II.1.1). These transcendental qualities are the basis for the physical, psychological, ethical, and metaphysical tendencies found in human natural inclinations (see Figure 11.1). These natural inclinations are the seeds both of the natural law precepts and of the virtues (Aquinas, 1273/1981, I-II, 51.1 & 63.1).

These natural inclinations are found in the most basic human experience. We intuit them and rationally infer their existence through our experience of the personal and substantial unity of human body and soul as rooted in the gift of existence (Spitzer, 2010). The person does not create himself, but is a given (Giussani, 1997). Moreover, the endowment of our existence cannot be understood without reference to its dependence on the primal, ultimate, or divine

source. The fact that human existence is intrinsically a gift makes each human person relational by his or her very nature, as well as by his or her personal history and family (as having and being mother, father, sibling, friend, and so on). Within the integrity, harmony, and radiance of existing things and interpersonal relations, beauty is also made manifest. These existential, relational, and attractive qualities can be understood rationally, to a point; for human life is taken up largely in the ongoing search to know one's origin, reality, and end in a fuller way, through subjective meaning and objective truth. This search goes hand in hand with the desire to freely express love through giving of self, being morally upright, and embracing the fullness of spiritual goodness (Ashley, 2006).

The perennial realist philosophical tradition (Aristotle, the Stoics, and so on) and the Catholic-Christian tradition recognize that humans are thus inclined to seek goodness, existence, truth, family life and society, and beauty in their lives. At an intelligible level, there is an order to the universe, and human beings can rationally participate in the laws of the universe, which not only provide guidance for our lives but also lead us toward an end that is beyond our own capacity to attain without divine assistance (Aquinas, 1273/1981, I-II, 5.5). St. Paul expresses a conviction that humans can have a natural (non-revealed) level of knowledge about the truth concerning creation and God's existence, because of the way reality manifests itself in human experience as an intelligible gift. He says:

> For what can be known about God is plain to them, because God has shown it to them. Ever since the creation of the world his eternal power and divine nature, invisible though they are, have been understood and seen through the things he has made. (Rom 1:19–20)

Figure 11.1. Natural Inclinations: Seeds of Natural Law, Virtue, and Vocation

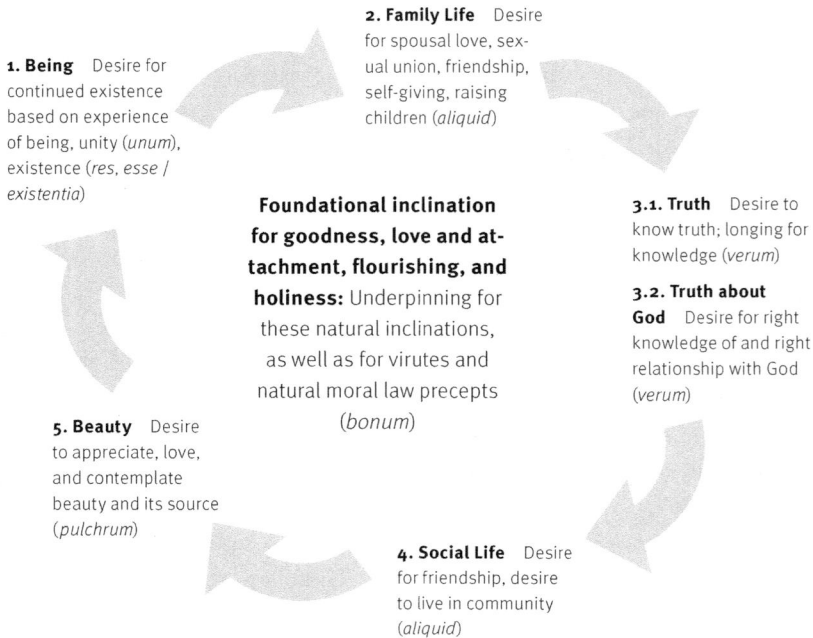

1. Being Desire for continued existence based on experience of being, unity (*unum*), existence (*res, esse / existentia*)

2. Family Life Desire for spousal love, sexual union, friendship, self-giving, raising children (*aliquid*)

Foundational inclination for goodness, love and attachment, flourishing, and holiness: Underpinning for these natural inclinations, as well as for virutes and natural moral law precepts (*bonum*)

3.1. Truth Desire to know truth; longing for knowledge (*verum*)

3.2. Truth about God Desire for right knowledge of and right relationship with God (*verum*)

5. Beauty Desire to appreciate, love, and contemplate beauty and its source (*pulchrum*)

4. Social Life Desire for friendship, desire to live in community (*aliquid*)

(Sources: Aquinas, 1273/1981, I–II, 94.2; Ashley, 2006; Schmitz, 2007, 2009)

St. Paul also acknowledges that the law written in the heart of man is morally significant:

> When Gentiles who have not the law do by nature what the law requires, they are a law to themselves, even though they do not have the law. They show that what the law requires is written on their hearts. (Rom 2:12)

St. Paul thus considers that the basis for law is written in human nature. He uses the metaphor "written on their hearts" to evoke a deep and complete reality, which serves as a foundation for rational reflections leading to knowledge of God (pre–Divine Revelation), to natural moral law (human intelligent participation in eternal law, in divine wisdom and love), and to judgment of practical reason and conscience (prudential personalism, applied through the virtues in life-callings).

What Is More Basic: Order or Disorder in the Inclinations?

Psychopathology, existential anxiety, and tendencies toward injustice and indifference exhibit introspective and behavioral evidence that all persons experience some of the many disorders that plague the human condition (Chapter 18, "Fallen"). When we look deeper, though, we find that such disorders involve some underlying order that has been negatively influenced by the misuse of freedom or the contingency of actual human experience, including the effects of sin (original, personal, and social sin), of trauma, or of physiological and neurological disorders. Through experience and reflection, people recognize that there are deeper tendencies that are basically good. Both mind and matter are intrinsically good. This is the position of classical Catholic Christian philosophy, which holds that even in the midst of human and natural disorders, the basic structure of the universe is ordered and good (MacIntyre, 2009). As prevalent as disorder and evil may be, neither is equal to or more fundamental than order and goodness. This position holds that basic natural inclinations serve to draw humans throughout life toward flourishing. In this classical perspective, true happiness or flourishing implies attending to the needs found in the foundational natural inclinations to goodness and love: continued existence; spousal love, sexual union, and family; truth; friendship and social life; and beauty. These inclinations are the seeds for precepts of the natural law and of the virtues, as already mentioned. Admittedly, the denial of this hopeful perspective often plagues people who suffer from addiction, depression, anxiety, self-deception, broken and abusive families, or trauma.

Select aspects of natural inclinations are found in certain psychological theories, for example, client-centered psychology, an approach that isolates as the singular motivation for human life the notion of self-actualization, can be considered a partial form of the inclination to flourishing (Rogers, 1961/2012). Social psychology, influenced by the Darwinian theory of survival of the fittest, can be considered a partial form of the inclination to self-preservation and the inclination to social life (Tallis, 2011, 2014). Positive psychology, focused on flourishing and the development of the human capacities

in virtues, can be considered a relatively large, but still partial form of the basic inclination to flourishing and the inclinations to social life (Peterson & Seligman, 2004; Lopez & Snyder, 2009, 2014). An evidence-based approach, like that of the Meta-Model, seeks to identify and affirm the truth that is present in such perspectives without limiting itself or distorting its own synthetic effort.

How Do Natural Inclinations Serve as the Basis of Natural Law?

According to the classical realist tradition, the good serves as the end that motivates every action (Aquinas, 1273/1981, I-II, 27.1, 29.2, 29.1; Cicero, 44 BC/1991). The need for the good underlies our basic desire to love and to be loved, and it is important for each vocation. It underlies our human cognitive and affective capacities that receive and give in their own ways. As seeds of the virtues that may stagnate in growth, require healing, or be misused, the natural inclinations are nonetheless basically good. They are at first general in themselves (as inclinations) and need to be developed in particular precepts and virtues and callings. The natural inclinations serve as a basis for the precepts of natural law, because they express a rational participation in the cosmic or divine order. The natural inclinations also serve as a basis for the virtues, because they direct the virtues at intellectual, moral, and spiritual levels. Humans use (a) *intuition* to grasp first principles that underlie these virtues (such as, good is to be done), (b) *induction* to come to understand, from particular instances and experience, how a conclusion or precept supports the practice of virtue (such as, based on the experiences of fraud and theft, it is bad to steal), and (c) *inference* to deduce from principles and precepts the practice of virtue (such as, the deduction from the precepts of justice that

Table 11.3. Basic Natural Inclination and First Precept of the Natural Law

Basic Natural Inclination	First Precept of Natural Law for the Person (first principle of practical reason)
To do what is good and to be repulsed from what is evil, as the basis for flourishing.	Good is to be done and pursued; and evil is to be avoided

being disposed to fairness and equity will help people to act well and society to flourish).

The natural inclinations also ground our intuitive and inferential knowledge of intrinsically evil acts, which are never to be done (John Paul II, 1993, §80; Vatican II, 1965, §27). Nonetheless, natural inclinations are often misused, as when they develop into false precepts and particular vices. Natural inclinations are not moral actions themselves. Rather, to become practical precepts and moral actions, the natural inclinations require rational judgments and intentional choices of prudence, well-formed conscience, as well as the consideration of personal callings (relationships and commitments).

Since general natural inclinations must be specified in practice according to the context and characteristics of the person who experiences them, they must regard not only the biological sex and culture of the individual, but also his or her sociological, psychological, and physiological circumstances (Ashley, 2013, p. 291).

The most basic principle and general natural inclination about practical matters is: "Good is that which all things seek after." In turn, the first practical precept is: "Good is to be done and pursued, and evil is to be avoided" (Aquinas, 1273/1981, I-II, 94.2; also quoted in International Theological Commission, 2014; Pinckaers, 1995, pp. 406–456). The first level of basic natural inclinations and the first practical precept

are intuited (see Table 11.3). They are abstract and in need of specification and development into virtues. For example, we are called to pursue a good life (developing justice, friendliness, patience, and fidelity to commitments and vocations) and refrain from bad deeds (taking innocent human life, committing adultery, giving false witness, and stealing other people's property) (MacIntyre, 2009; Vatican II, 1965, §27; Wojtyła, 1993, §80).

The first practical precept requires the further specification found through the natural inclinations and their related general and secondary precepts. Secondary precepts of the natural law are determinations of the general precepts and are applied to particulars of the individual person, family, others, and culture. The ordering of the foundational natural inclinations serve as the basis to allow reason to arrive at general precepts and more particular secondary precepts, which are either negative (such as "do not steal!") or positive (such as "be truthful!"). Aquinas (1273/1981, I-II, 94.2) presents a way of organizing these precepts starting with what is common to all things that exist, then what is common to all animals, and finally what is proper to human society.

Within this global organization, the natural inclinations have been divided into six broader inclinations (with samples of the associated precepts and virtues). First, humans tend to care for and protect their own lives, but need virtue strengths to resist pressures toward suicide and euthanasia, for instance ("Do not kill yourself!"; respect for life). Second, there is a natural desire to love and seek love and to seek sexual union and the care of offspring ("Care for the needs of your spouse and children!"; spousal and parental love). Third, humans seek to know what is rational and true ("Do not deceive others!"; truthfulness). Fourth, humans seek to know the ultimate cause of life, that is, God ("Love and honor God!"; gratitude, religion). Fifth, they desire to live in society ("Restore property to its rightful owner!"; justice). Sixth, they also have a natural desire to appreciate beauty ("Be aware of and appreciate beauty!"; wisdom, truth); this sixth domain of the natural law is attributed by John Paul II (1993, §51) to Aquinas (1273/1981, I-II, 94.2). These precepts of the natural law, as for human law (civic law), are conceived in the light of training people in the good life (virtue, vocation, and flourishing).

See Table 11.4 on the relationship between the natural inclinations and the different precepts of the natural law (and associated virtues). This table represents the trajectory of the precepts from the general to the secondary levels. However, it is not exhaustive, and there is need for a next step, which involves the use of practical wisdom (prudential personalism) to apply the precepts and to develop ethical reflections for particular domains, such as the family, business, or mental health practice (with the professional ethics that will be discussed later in this chapter).

How Is the Inclination to Self-Preservation Shown?

The basic inclination toward the good of one's own nature is shared by every substance, which tends to preserve its own existence. A rock, a tree, and a bobcat, each must have molecular in-tegrity. The strengths and weaknesses of a substance are due to its nature. For example, iron ore naturally resists losing its solid state of structural integrity until its temperature approaches its melting point. Animals express more complex types of self-preservation. Humans naturally resist threats, such as physical and psychological attacks on their personal integrity. These phenomena are studied in the same way as are the natural protective reactions to blink in the face of bright light, pull away from excessive heat, and so on. In addition, humans usually seek to sustain life by loving, eating, sleeping, and engaging in other activities that are vital for survival. Even emotional expressions, such as anger, can help to resist threats. Such life-preserving inclinations are found in nonconscious, preconscious, and conscious movements. Support for this inclination to self-preservation seems to be universal and is certainly found even in materialist evolutionary theory.

This inclination to self-preservation is shown also in the primary precepts to care for oneself and to protect oneself from harm, and in the secondary precepts that require one to feed oneself and that forbid self-mutilation and suicide. Such self-preserving inclinations, however, do not function in a way that is automatic or absolute. On the one hand, people acquire other inclinations and desires that distort these natural inclinations, as in the case of an eating or sleeping disorder, the desire to harm oneself, or the choice to end one's life. On the other hand, people override this natural inclination in order to make intentional sacrifices for the sake of a higher inclination to family, society, and religion. For example, a person can supplant a desire to preserve one's body from fatigue, injury, or death. Consider a mother who sacrifices sleep for the good of a child in need of care, or a soldier who sacrifices his life for the good of others.

Table 11.4. Natural Inclinations and Precepts of the Natural Law

Natural Inclinations: *Basic, normal, and in need of development in virtues*	General or Primary Precepts: *that express the person's call to act*	Positive Secondary Precepts *(and related virtues): dynamic, overlapping, and incomplete list. These precepts admit of different cultural expressions.*	Negative Secondary Precepts *(and related virtues): dynamic, overlapping, and incomplete list. While some of these precepts admit of different cultural expressions, others concern intrinsically evil acts, which are never to be done.*
1. Natural inclination to stay alive; to stay healthy, body and soul; to resist dangers and threats to existence	1. Seek to preserve one's own life.	Respect human life and dignity of person (justice) Care for one's own body and soul (preservation and flourishing) Be moderate in food and drink (temperance) Love others as yourself (friendship love)	Do not kill yourself: suicide, euthanasia Do not harm yourself: unnecessary self-endangerment, self-mutilation Do not take innocent life: murder, genocide, abortion (respect life and dignity) Do not torture (justice and respect) Do not abuse food or drink (temperance)
2. Natural inclination to sexual union, to care for offspring	2. Seek the goods of sexual intercourse and raising offspring	Be faithful to husband or wife; open to life (marital love). Care for the needs of children (parental love) Honor your mother and father (filial piety, humility, justice) Care for family members (familial piety, justice) Care for the children of others (justice) Be chaste according to your vocational state (chastity) Be modest in dress and action (modesty)	Do not engage in adultery, incest, rape, fornication, same-sex acts, prostitution, masturbation, pornography, artificial contraception, sterilization (chastity; justice) Do not lust for others—students, patients, or neighbors (chastity)
3.1. Natural inclination to what is rational and true	3.1. Seek good according to reason	Follow reason (prudence) Be truthful (honesty, justice) Seek wisdom, understanding, and knowledge (intellectual virtues)	Do not deny the existence of truth (truth) Do not deceive others (truth) Do not let disordered fear stop one from doing what is good and true (fortitude, hope)

(table continues)

Table 11.4 (*continued*)

3.2. Natural inclination to a right relationship with God	3.2. Know the truth about God	Know, love, be grateful to, and worship God (faith, filial love, gratitude, justice, religion)	Do not deny the existence of God (truth) Do not hate or blaspheme God (religion) Do not worship false gods (religion, devotion)
4. Natural inclination to the goods of human society	4. Live in society	Treat others the way you want to be treated (justice) Love neighbor (friendship love) Be courageous (fortitude) Be thankful (gratitude) Restore property to its rightful owner (justice) Respect the aged (justice) Punish wrongdoing (justice)	Do not steal (justice) Do not exploit workers: slavery, degrading living and working conditions (justice) No arbitrary imprisonment (justice) No human trafficking (justice) Do not commit incest or rape (justice) Do not envy your neighbor's goods Do not coerce others (justice, truth)
5. Natural inclination to contemplate beauty	5. Seek to appreciate the beauty of nature, of other human beings, and of the ultimate source of all beauty.	Be aware of the beauty of nature Be aware of the beauty and goodness of other human beings Be aware of the beauty and goodness of human art (music, literature, painting) Contemplate God's beauty	Do not be indifferent to the beauty of creation (wisdom, charity) Do not objectify others through lust or pornography (chastity) Do not be closed to the absolute and transcendent source of beauty and life (wisdom)

(Sources: Ex 20:2–17; Dt 5:6–21; Aquinas, 1273/1981, I-II, 94.2; Ashley 2009; Budziszewski, 2009; Hittinger, 2007; John Paul II, 1993, §51 & §80; Kaczor, 2002; Levering, 2008; Pinckaers, 1985/1995, pp. 406–456; Vatican II, 1965.)

How Is the Inclination to Sexual Union and the Family Shown?

Over and above simple self-preservation, all animals are instinctively inclined to preserve their future offspring. Humans and other animals exhibit an inclination to sexual intercourse and education of offspring. Nevertheless, the human way to preserve the species involves using the good of human rational nature expressed in the interpersonal self-giving of a man and a woman who make the commitments necessary for family life. Human sexual union and procreation have characteristics both similar and dissimilar to those of nonrational animals. Human coupling and reproducing are not simply instinctive activities, nor is human monogamy simply genetic and hormonal (as in certain species of prairie dogs; Young & Alexander, 2012). The human family is built upon natural inclinations that become further specified by commitments, practices, and prohibitions that embody and protect marital fidelity, exclusive monogamy and tenderness, as well as responsible paternity and maternity (John Paul II, 2006; Paul VI, 1968; Pius XI, 1930). The inclination to family life is shown, for example, in the primary precepts to honor marital commitments and to welcome children, and in the secondary precepts that govern the duties and rights of spouses and children (Chapter 10, "Fulfilled Through Vocation," and Chapter 12, "Interpersonally Relational"). In short, there is much evidence that human procreation is more complex than a simple biological drive.

How Is the Need for Truth, God, Community, and Beauty Shown?

In a more or less direct way, humans rule their inclinations by reason. Humans can display an intentional control over themselves and a conscious stewardship over creation (Benedict XVI, 2009a, 2010; Francis, 2015). Humans are inclined to know and love the truth, for it is one of their greatest goods. Even when unaware that they are doing so, people seek the truth about themselves, others, the world, and the source of ultimate meaning, including the truth about God (Aquinas, 1259/1953). This desire for truth permeates theoretical and practical realms. It is the touchstone for the sciences, ethics, and psychotherapy.

By reason and by love, humans also are inclined to live in society. They seek vital contact with other human beings, in practical, social, communal, and governance matters, as well as for business, sports, culture, and art. The goods associated with these social domains are protected and promoted by the formulation of and respect for just practices, precepts, rules, and laws. Such external principles become internal though the practice of the virtues, as is seen in the precept "be thankful" (which is supported by a developed virtue of gratitude) or "do not exploit workers" (which requires the virtues of fairness and justice).

Finally, humans recognize beauty in the clarity and ordering of nature, human efforts, and the divine (John Paul II, 1993, §51, §73; see also Benedict XVI, 2009b; John Paul II, 1999; Laracy, 2011). The inclinations to truth and social life and beauty are shown, for example, in the primary precept to be honest (not to lie); in the secondary precepts to be truthful in figuring and paying taxes, to follow traffic laws when driving, and to give strangers correct directions; and in the appreciation of natural, human, and moral beauty.

How Does the Commandment to Love (the Golden Rule) Relate to the Personalist Norm and the Natural Law?

The personalist norm and natural law are manifest in different, often partial, ways in other formulations, for example, the Golden Rule, the principle of beneficence, or the Kantian categorical imperative (see Wojtyła, 1993). In a Christian perspective, the personalist norm is found in and transformed by the command of love, which is found in the law and the prophets: "You shall love your neighbor as yourself" (Lev 19:18) and "Thus says the Lord of hosts, Render true judgments, show kindness and mercy to one another" (Jer 7:9). In its negative form, the law of love and the personalist norm are called the silver rule (do not do to others what you would not have them do to you) and can be likened to the principle of nonmaleficence (i.e., do no harm) (Spitzer, 2011).

There is further transformation of the personalist norm and the precepts of the natural law in a Christian vision of the person, which is influenced by the Gospel exhortations as found in the Sermon on the Mount:

> Do to others as you would have them do to you.... But love your enemies, do good, and lend, expecting nothing in return. Your reward will be great, and you will be children of the Most High; for he is kind to the ungrateful and the wicked. Be merciful, just as your Father is merciful. Do not judge, and you will not be judged; do not condemn, and you will not be condemned. Forgive, and you will be forgiven; give, and it will be given to you. (Lk 6:31, 35–38; see also Mt 7:12)

The Gospel of Luke (as well as the Gospel of Matthew) is very concrete and demanding about the implications of this command or exhortation, which is fulfilled only in mercy and fully self-giving love (John Paul II, 1980). Of course, this expression of love may not be accompanied by positive emotion, but it does require a willed desiring of the good for the other, often through self-giving and sacrifice.

How Does a Catholic Christian Meta-Model Relate to Professional Ethics?

There are several codes of professional ethics related to mental health practice, such as those of the American Psychological Association (2016), the American Psychiatric Association (2013), the American Counseling Association (2013), the National Association of Social Workers (2008), and the American Association for Marriage and Family Therapy (2015). They generally identify core values, aspirational principles, and professional codes of ethics. For instance, the general principles of the American Psychological Association (2016) and the American Counseling Association (2013) are almost identical: beneficence, nonmaleficence, fidelity and responsibility, integrity, justice, respect for peoples' rights

and dignity, and autonomy. These general principles are aspirational, guiding mental health professionals in more a global view of their therapeutic work than the professional ethical codes or principles, which provide concrete standards and best practices for specific areas where ethical considerations and conflicts arise in the everyday clinical settings. For example, the American Psychological Association's (2016) ethical principles address resolving ethical issues, competence, human relations, privacy and confidentiality, advertising and other public statements, record keeping and fees, education and training, research and publication, assessment, and therapy.

How might the Catholic Christian Meta-Model of the Person bring light to understanding and applying such an impressive list of general principles and down-to-earth codes of ethics? How do the virtues and precepts of natural law interact with the principles of professional codes? What are the sources of authority in discerning how to apply these principles wisely?

First, the Meta-Model and these codes work on related but different levels. As we have seen, the Meta-Model explicitly offers an ethical perspective based on the natural law, the person, and flourishing that provides a philosophical and theological framework for realist ethics and Christian morality. The codes of professional ethics do not identify a particular philosophical or theological frame, even though they do adopt the ambient secular one. Civil law, building codes, traffic laws, likewise, to be intelligible, require a certain notion of being a person, family, or society in order to make, promote, and enforce laws. For instance, civil society has its own governance (legislative, executive, and judicial), yet it is not the sole source of ethical principles. It is the reality of the person and interpersonal relationships, and the conformity or divergence to these realities that make principles of civil law (or professional ethics) just or not. This is, of course, from a realist personalist–natural law perspective, which takes the person as the basic moral criteria.

The Meta-Model's personalist and natural law foundation, furthermore, has roots in both reason-based and faith-based principles, values, and virtues, as is explicated throughout this chapter and the rest of the volume. The Meta-Model gives an explicit basis for the needed practical wisdom (virtue of prudence) to adjudicate particular human moral actions and the application of professional principles and practices, while being attentive both to the client's and to the therapist's beliefs and conscience, and to each person's life goals.

It is not enough to say that practical wisdom—a prudential personalism—is needed for the application of professional principles (Ashley, 2013; Ashley & O'Rourke, 1997). Several further distinctions need to be made in order not to confuse the competencies of the reason-based ethics, faith-based morality, and professional codes. Their specific competencies are found in addressing (1) the depth of philosophical anthropology, (2) the breadth of ethical issues, and (3) applications to professional codes of ethics, Christian ethics, and moral theology.

First, in terms of assumptions and depth, what are the theoretical foundations or assumptions that guide the conceptualization of professional codes of ethics? That is, is their supporting ethical theory made explicit or not? It has been argued elsewhere that even basic ethical principles such as dignity and respect for the person (which are affirmed by these professional codes) may be narrowed when applied from within reductionist worldviews and value systems (Titus, 2017). To grasp the importance of basic assumptions, we should ask: What difference would it make to apply these codes of ethics from (a) a *utilitarian rule-based approach* (which merely seeks to maximize good or pleasant consequences), (b) a *duty-based approach* (which limits itself to emphasize the good will [or intention] and the use of a categorical imperative [a universal moral obligation]), (c) an *emotivist approach* (which exaggerates the importance of the subject's emotional state as the highest moral criteria), or (d) a *prudential personalism* (in which the person and natural moral law, virtue, and duty are employed, taking the person as created in the image of God and in need of a community—and grace—to live well)? The psychologists Handelsman, Knapp, & Gottlieb (2009), for instance, have argued that professional codes tend to be limited by rule-based and utilitarian approaches, which exclude attention to the therapist's self-awareness and moral character, and to the client's or the therapist's ethical and religious perspectives and consciences.

Second, in terms of breadth, are the codes of ethics and their principles adequate to cover the full range of ethical issues? The professional codes of ethics, while being valid and helpful in clinical practice, may benefit from other principles: a fuller understanding of respect for the innate dignity of each person from conception to death, regardless of the person's health or state; support for the conscience and moral responsibility of both client and clinician; respect for the individual's freedom for flourishing and happiness (which is not simply a freedom from outside interference or from disease and disorder, but also a freedom for excellence and moral character). A fuller notion of ethical issues would require not only the consideration of principles and acts, but also a more robust understanding of ethical and spiritual dispositions: the ethical norms, virtues, and vocations, as well as their religious, spiritual, and transcendent dimension.

Third, in terms of application, how might a wider notion of the principles of professional ethics, along with the support of natural law precepts and the personalist norm, promote applications in professional contexts? Unlike secular utilitarian approaches, which are disconnected from callings and goals of everyday and transcendent sorts, a wider view, as found in the Meta-Model's perspective on mental health practice, may provide further applications because of its being rooted in common natural inclinations, existential commitments, metaphysical foundations, transcendent ends, and personal vocations. This perspective, for example, leads the therapist to safeguard or promote novel practices that (a) respect the human being as a person with purpose (self and others), (b) recognize the value of therapeutic applications of forgiveness and reconciliation, (c) promote working toward social justice, and (d) acknowledge the value of worshiping the source of the universe, who is called God by Christians (United States Conference of Catholic Bishops, 2009).

Development, Health, and Illness

What Light Does a Developmental Perspective Shed on the Person?

The capacities of the human person, as described so far, are evident only over time as people interact in the family and with their social environment and religious community. Thus, people develop capacities that allow them to enrich the life of the mind and the heart. Already at conception, the basic elements of life are present, both the genetic code and the spiritual soul (which serves as a type of spiritual "code" and animates the person from conception). Thus, we can reasonably affirm that the human person comes into existence when his or her living body-soul unity comes into existence. Moreover, modern biology affirms that the form of the unique body of all persons is found in their original code (DNA) and becomes alive at conception (Chapter 5, "Basic Psychological Support"). The unique animated human form is not found in the ovum or the sperm prior to that point. Conception is an event in which a new life form becomes present. Afterward, there is a development of this same living being. There are, of course, times during life when the personality and consciousness of the person are hidden—before birth, or when asleep, in a coma, or under anesthesia. People develop their multiple capacities of human nature over time through physical growth and relationships (especially those relationships that involve family, marriage, friends, society, and religion), moral practices and decisions (through which the person seeks to be just and to contribute to the common good), and virtues and vocations (through which the person overcomes a divided heart, social discord, and religious indifference, as well as participates in flourishing and communion) (Rist, 2009).

What Does a Teleological Perspective Add to the Notion of Health?

Recently, positive psychology has made a substantial case that psychological health and well-being is not simply an absence of illness (Lopez & Snyder, 2009; Peterson & Seligman, 2004). Instead, positive psychology argues that psychological health—a flourishing life—requires the development and the living-out of virtues. By including a positive notion of virtue and character strengths in modern psychology, this movement has brought the teleological perspective into psychology as well, a major change.

It invites an expanded conception of health, because it holds that considerations of normalcy as a statistical notion (e.g., rates of soldiers who develop PTSD or who commit suicide) are reductionistic measures of the person. Health is a larger idea that includes flourishing in physical, psychological, interpersonal, ethical, and spiritual domains. The World Health Organization (2012) offers a definition of health as "a state of complete physical, mental and social well-being, and not merely the absence of disease" (p.1). This definition, however, can be complemented by considerations of spiritual or religious well-being, which often outstrip "physical, mental, and social well-being" and cannot be reduced to a psychological or sociological analysis. (On the positive effects of religion, see Koenig, King, & Carson, 2012.) The consideration of a person's true flourishing and ultimate beatitude must become a teleological and existential perspective that embraces long-term goals, interpersonal vocations, and the ultimate purpose of life. In short, the largest sense of well-being and healthy development must involve the lifelong process of integrating the person's mental, social, ethical, and spiritual capacities, commitments, and virtues with a view to everyday and ultimate life goals and vocations.

Can a Person Flourish in the Face of Limitations?

Indeed, all people seek to flourish in the face of limitations: physical illness, psychological disorders, as well as harmful social and cultural influences. In short, flourishing is not an absence of limitations. Flourishing can be constituted not only by the partial manifestations of well-being and integral human development but also by the positive acceptance and resilient use of our limitations, disappointments, and sufferings. Thus, in many respects, flourishing means

the overcoming of limitations. A developmental model of health can specifically appreciate healthy flourishing in terms of attaining various physical, emotional, cognitive-affective, relational, and spiritual states and goals. A developmental model of flourishing can also grasp the competing, and sometimes conflicting, aspects of flourishing. An ethical and spiritual framework puts limitations, unattained short-term goals, and competing values in a larger context. For instance, the ethical businessman may opt for short-term economic disadvantage in order to be just and generous with his employees and customers. The larger context of the call to human flourishing also requires the recognition of the risk of dying in service of other people and because of the nature of one's vocation—consider the fire fighter who risks his own life for the sake of others.

How Does Wholeness Correlate with Holiness?

The wholeness of mind and body (flourishing at biopsychosocial levels) does not simply equate to holiness (flourishing at a spiritual and religious level). For example, some geniuses have lived in debauchery or at the service of ill-intentioned projects, while others have not. Some psychologically challenged individuals have lived in generous self-giving service, while others have not.

Grace builds up and perfects nature (Aquinas, 1273/1981, I, 1.8 ad 2 & 62.5). The well-being of mind and the health of body serve the person who is responding to a call to holiness in grace. However, imperfect health seems to be the occasion for some people to grow in holiness. There are many examples of saints who, while suffering physical illness or psychological disorders, have generously devoted their lives to others in answer to the call to holiness. In all cases, holiness has more to do with drawing from the ultimate source of goodness and truth, who is God, rather than from human strengths per se.

Without denying the complexity of human well-being, the Psalmist uses the image of a tree to depict the state of the righteous person who flourishes because God's gifts enable him to love God, others, and himself: "He is like a tree planted by streams of water, that yields its fruit in its season, and its leaf does not wither. In all that he does, he prospers" (Ps 1:3). Likewise, in the context of development, St. Paul speaks about

the need for growth and intentional commitment: "When I was a child, I spoke like a child, I thought like a child, I reasoned like a child; when I became a man, I gave up childish ways" (1 Cor 13:11). Paul is talking about growth in holiness. The adult character that he promotes is focused on self-giving and enduring love that is patient and kind, rather than a character that is envious, boastful, arrogant, rude, or self-serving (1 Cor 13:4–8). The relation between health and holiness is explored more fully in Chapter 12, "Interpersonally Relational."

Virtues: Their Types and Connection

Virtue theory gives the Meta-Model further bases for talking about the purpose-oriented flourishing of the person. A fuller understanding of human nature demands an existential, expansive, and interconnected view of the virtues. This fuller understanding also requires a narrative account of human nature and the person. It is at the same time a normative account that integrates natural and divine law, the personalist norm and duty, as well as the common good and divine grace (see also Budziszewski, 2009; Levering, 2008; Wojtyła, 1993). In short, a narrative, normative moral framework is necessary for understanding the integration and expression of the virtues. This frame demands a view that interrelates (1) how the workings of the virtues are connected (as when practical reason serves one's courageous defense of one's family) or disconnected (as when one is loving with one's wife, but not courageous to defend her) and (2) how the virtues are complete or incomplete at psychological, ethical, and spiritual levels (e.g., expressing not only faith among fellow believers, but also love to an enemy) (1 Cor. 13:1–3; Aquinas, 1273/1981, II-II, 25.8; Titus, 2010, 2013a, 2017).

The present section employs the Catholic Christian Meta-Model's multidimensional vision of the person to understand how virtues underlie psychological, moral, and spiritual growth, healing, and flourishing. Later in this chapter, another section also addresses how vices, even those that may seem to be beneficial (in the short term), are inevitably associated with disorder, pathology, and languishing.

What Is Virtue?

We now address two particular definitions of virtue, namely, that of the positive psychology movement (Peterson & Seligman, 2004) and that of Aquinas (1273/1981), and we will go on to offer the Meta-Model's synthetic approach to virtue.

The positive psychology movement defines and evaluates particular virtues and character strengths, using sources that are based on both Western and Eastern traditions, according to ten criteria. Virtues, character strengths (subvirtues), and situational themes must (1) lead to flourishing by a good life; (2) correspond with moral values; (3) not diminish others; (4) have a non-felicitous opposite; (5) be a character trait or be trait-like; (6) be conceptually identifiable; (7) be supported by a consensus; (8) be identifiable in prodigies and (9) in selective absences; and (10) be supported by cultural, institutional, and social practices (Peterson & Seligman, 2004, pp. 17–28). This rather thorough list, however, is more functional and mechanistic than personalist, synthetic, and normative. Peterson and Seligman (2004) admit that they do not fully treat ethical judgments and ultimate applications, which are the tasks of philosophers and theologians (pp. 88 & 269–270). In short, they do not propose a moral or ethical framework for evaluating conflict in real-life applications of the virtues.

Aquinas (1273/1981), by contrast, says that virtue "denotes a certain perfection of a capacity" (I-II, 55.1), which is aimed toward a purpose, goal, or end of the action and the person. Virtue is an operative disposition (*habitus*) that tends to that which is best, that is, the end or goal of the person (I-II, 55.1). It is perfective of both the person and his acts. It is purposeful according to the type of virtue, be it intellectual, moral, or theological. Specifically referring to the virtues that are given by God (infused by grace), Aquinas identifies a further level of perfection and purpose: "virtue is a good quality of the mind, by which we live righteously, of which no one can make bad use, which God works in us, without us" (I-II, 55.4). The inclusion of grace in the definition of virtue has been an ongoing contribution to Christian virtue theory (Aquinas, 1273/1981, I-II, 55.4; Augustine, 395/2010, II.19; *Catechism of the Catholic Church* [CCC], 1997, §§1810–1813; Cessario, 2002, 2008; Hauerwas, 1981; John Paul II, 1993; Pinckaers, 2005; Sherwin, 2009).

Aquinas's (1273/1981) contribution to virtue theory is not only his definition of virtue, but also a multidisciplinary method, which includes not only philosophy and theology but also premodern psychology, that is, a philosophical psychology. His strategy, similarly to that of modern thinkers such as Benedict XVI (2006) and MacIntyre (2007), requires the scholarly treatment of sources, theories, and findings in a premodern approach that has a wider notion of virtue than that found in modern rationalism. Aquinas's definition of virtue is an offshoot of his vision of the person and his method of theological and philosophical reflection. His approach employs a structured model that identifies the anthropological, realist, rational, and existential bases for responsible and free discernment, agency, and flourishing (Pinckaers, 2005). From within the conviction that truth is one (MacIntyre, 1990, 1999, 2009), Aquinas's position draws upon the diverse authorities found in Sacred Scripture, Church teaching, patristic writings (e.g., those of Augustine and Gregory the Great), philosophical reflections (e.g., those of Aristotle, Plato, and the Stoics), and premodern scientific tradition.

What Are Aquinas's and Seligman's Contributions to a Multidimensional Understanding of Virtue?

Drawing from both Aquinas and Seligman, the Meta-Model employs findings from contemporary sources, including positive psychology, as well as presuppositions and reflections from a classical Christian perspective. Using the thirteen dimensions, previously introduced, the Meta-Model delineates virtue by considering (1) the acts that the virtues occasion (*performative* dimension); (2) the capacities and dispositions that practice of the virtues forms (*perfective and corrective*); (3) the good ends that make the person flourish, at which the virtues are aimed (*purposeful*); (4) the rational moral standards the virtues employ (*ethical*); (5) the unique expression of virtue proper to each person and influenced by the equal innate dignity as well as differences and complementarity of the sexes (*influenced by personal uniqueness, common dignity, and sex difference and complementarity*); (6) the way the virtues are progressively connected among themselves and require interpersonal connection with others (*connective, relational, and developmental*); (7) the way the virtuous dispositions and acts are influenced by exemplars in modeling goodness and truth (*learned through role models*); (8) virtue as a middle ground of excellence between two extremes of excess and deficit (*moderating*); (9) the strengths that the virtues provide to face ills and vices (*preventative*); (10) the openness to nonreductionist or holistic evidence that can inform the study of virtue (*nonreductionist*); (11) the application of virtue in research and practice (*applied*); (12) the callings—to goodness and holiness; to single, married, religious, or ordained life; and to work—that are interdependent on the virtues (*vocational*); (13) and the openness to transcendent goodness, truth, and beauty and to God that transforms the virtues (*open to the transcendent and to God*). Table 11.5 identifies the dimensions of virtue with an indication about the strengths and weaknesses of Aquinas's and Seligman's individual contributions.

What Are the Implications of an Interactive Multidimensional Understanding of Virtue for Mental Health Practice?

To show how the previously mentioned dimensions work in an interactive way, we address the virtue of practical wisdom (also called prudence, right practical reason, or "wisdom," as it is called by Seligman). Right practical reason develops the human capacity to reason when a person seeks to attain reasonable goals through fitting action, as when a mother and father both use their capacities to discern and take counsel, make judgments, and concretely act in raising

their children to be honest and caring members of a family, society, and church. Prudence underlies the virtuous pursuit of all goods and flourishing. It involves a process that refines, corrects, and perfects not only reason and the whole range of cognition, but also the will and the whole range of affection, as shown throughout the following chapters.

The thirteen above-mentioned dimensions of virtue have implications not only for mental health practice, but also for philosophy and theology. The dimensions are overlapping, and they need to be interpreted with respect to different types of virtue, which pertain to nature and graced nature. Therefore, the theological virtues based on grace (faith, hope, and charity) can be distinguished from the acquired virtues based on nature (practical wisdom, justice, courage, and temperance). It is important to understand that the thirteen dimensions pertain to all the different virtues, in spite of their differences. In the sections that follow, we provide both a short philosophical description of each dimension and note some implications for psychology and mental health practice. Many of the thirteen dimensions are well understood by mental health practitioners, as aspects of curative factors in mental health practice. However, it is the holistic awareness of these dimensions that provides a clear nonreductionist understanding of the person.

1. Performative (act-based dimension): Human acts are both visible and not-so-visible signs of virtue and vice. The characteristics of any visible human act are rooted in the non-visible life of instinct, intuition, cognition, volition, emotion, and interpersonal relationship. External acts and practices are means by which we communicate values and goals; for example, the devotion of a mother or the fortitude of a rescue worker

Table 11.5. Aquinas's and Seligman's Comparative Contributions to the Dimensions of Virtues

Dimensions	Characteristics	Contributions
1. Performative (Act)	The free acts of virtue that are a. involved in creating virtuous dispositions and b. influenced by virtuous habits	Aquinas. Strong (5): nature of person and act. Seligman. Strong (5): biopsychosocial study of virtuous acts
2. Perfective and corrective (Agent)	The dispositions that a. are formed by virtuous acts and b. contribute to virtuous acts	Aquinas. Strong (5): anthropology of dispositions. Seligman. Very good (4): scientific study of habit formation
3. Purposeful (Reason-based and teleological)	The virtue's good ends a. that make the person flourish and b. at which virtues aim	Aquinas. Strong (5): personal and interpersonal, philosophical and theological ends and flourishing. Seligman. Moderate (3): connection with human nature and flourishing
4. Ethical (Moral and norm-based)	The rational moral standards that the virtues employ	Aquinas. Strong (5): natural law ethics and moral theology. Seligman. Moderate (3): moral value; delegates moral adjudication
5. Influenced by personal uniqueness, equal innate dignity, and sex difference and complementarity	Based in personal individuality, including equal or common innate dignity, sex differences and complementarity	Aquinas. Moderate (3): recognition of the differences of the sexes, limited by reliance on ancient biology; limitation counteracted by theological understanding of the person and grace. Seligman. Very good (4): sex differences considered in the study of each character strength; but lack of considering the complementarity of the sexes.
6. Connective, relational, and developmental	Holistic, dynamic, and interpersonal process-based	Aquinas. Very good (4): aiming at a whole person. Seligman. Moderate (3): integrity, but limited
7. Learned through role models	Based in exemplars and sources that model goodness and truth	Aquinas. Very good (4): psychological, metaphysical, and theological levels. Seligman. Moderate (3): at the level of psychological function
8. Moderating (Measured)	Seeking a middle ground of excellence between extremes of excess and deficit	Aquinas. Very good (4): level of personal and theological flourishing. Seligman. Very good (4): study of psychological function
9. Preventative (Strength-based)	The virtue-based character and interpersonal strengths that face ills and vices	Aquinas. Very good (4): interpersonal and person strengths. Seligman. Moderate (3): limited interest in opposites

(table continues)

Table 11.5. (*continued*)

Dimensions	Characteristics	Contributions
10. Nonreductionist (Contextual)	Contextual and open to evidence, including from scientific, evidence-based, value-based, and truth-seeking sources	Aquinas. Fair (2): observation, non-experimental approach Seligman. Very Good (4): empirical studies
11. Applied (Research and practice)	Applications of virtue-based theory and practices to mental health and other disciplines enhance flourishing	Aquinas. Very good (4): ethical and spiritual practice Seligman. Very good (4): applied to therapy and practice
12. Vocational (Calling-based)	Informed by the callings: to goodness and holiness; to single, married, religious, or ordained life; and to work that underlies the virtues	Aquinas. Very good (4): three calls are operative Seligman. Moderate (3): partial consideration—work
13. Open to the transcendent and to God	Seeking goodness, truth, and beauty and their first transcendent source (God), which transforms the virtues	Aquinas. Strong (5): special strength, both nature and grace Seligman. Moderate (3): transcendence, but not God

Note: This table uses the Likert scale: (1) weak/absent, (2) fair, (3) moderate, (4) very good, (5) strong (judged by the authors, N=3).

is shown in the caring and courageous performance of particular tasks and duties. Each act is a building block for more complex acts, commitments, and virtues. Another example can be found in the vocation to marriage, which does not come to be and flourish through internal thoughts and feelings alone, but requires a public exchange of vows and continued visible support and fidelity.

[*Implications for mental health practice*: The performative dimension of virtue identifies the import of acts, practices, and goals used in therapy. Cognitive-Behavioral Therapy, for example, has incorporated this emphasis on behavior and performance as foundational for change. The emphasis on actual behavior remains, in all types of therapy, equally important for the development of virtue and its implications for other types of therapy.]

2. Perfective and corrective (agent-based dimension): "Virtue" is more than a virtuous act or behavior. Virtue also includes the person's dispositions and habits at conscious and other levels. Personal and interpersonal acts are corrective and perfective of human growth and flourishing. Human dispositions can tend toward either the good life or compromised goals. The use and development of agent-based dispositions are an important positive property of virtues, one that has potential therapeutic implications. Of course the negative property of vices has therapeutic ramifications as well. As mentioned before, the neurosciences have described something of these dynamics in Hebb's postulate (1949): "Neurons that fire together wire together" (Shatz, 1992).

[*Implications for mental health practice*: The perfective and corrective dimension of virtue emphasizes sources of development, continuity, and change that are harbored in the acting person. The work of Bandura (2001, 2006) and positive psychology studies (Peterson & Seligman, 2004) have identified the importance of willpower or self-regulation in life, including its implications for helping people who are facing psychological problems. The formation of destructive dispositions, on the contrary, is especially clear in addictions and sometimes in depression.]

3. Purposeful (teleological and reason-based dimension): Purposefulness implies the implicit and explicit rationale, the finality and calling, and the direction of the virtues. First, in general, the basic purpose of human life is intuited. For instance, we intuit that human life is good and is directed toward the goals inherent in the virtues, that is, toward relationships in justice and fairness, love and caring, patience and hope. Second, the particular purposes of the virtues are inferred through rational discourse and in social narratives. We rationally investigate how to attain the goals of the virtues in the context of our vocations, such as in the call to family life. The members of the family are taught to deliberate (provide reasons) on why and how to do good acts and to attain the dispositions of virtues. In practice, the family thus serves as a tradition in which goals are chosen, means are employed, and reasons are given to realize the important human aims and purposes need for flourishing, such as love, justice, and hope (MacIntyre, 1999).

[*Implications for mental health practice*: The purposeful and directive dimension of virtue emphasizes how human intelligence is intrinsically driven by goals, as shown by the types of finality and vocation necessary for flourishing. Psychotherapy often entails encouraging clients to reach larger goals by giving them practice in reaching smaller goals and by helping them to use reason to set new goals that are more practical and attainable, evaluating and correcting as need be, based on what is possible and good.]

4. Ethical (morally normative dimension): The ethical dimension of a virtue acknowledges that virtues must protect not merely a relative good (good exclusively for me), but also the common good (connecting me to other people). The ethical dimension of a person's virtue must be informed not only by knowledge of and commitment to local law, natural law, divine law, human nature, and the common good, but also by the person's natural inclinations, vocations, interpersonal relationships, and commitments. Practical wisdom (prudence) and conscience must be practiced to guide virtuous action and serve to judge it wisely.

[*Implications for mental health practice*: This ethical dimension of the virtues is evident in the principles and particular ethical codes of the mental health professions. Through training and practice, the mental health practitioner internalizes the virtues, and this greatly safeguards the client against unethical practice.]

5. Influenced by personal uniqueness, equal innate dignity, and sex difference and complementary (based in personal individuality, including common and distinctive characteristics): This dimension of the distinctiveness of each person is inscribed in the equal or common dignity, and the differences and complementarity of the sexes. The individuality of each person influences the development toward goals that are common to all human beings (for instance, goodness, flourishing, friendship). At the same time, the nuptial meaning of the person influences, in particular ways, the development of all the virtues throughout life, but especially the interpersonally relational ones, such as male and female expressions of caring and loving, justice and fairness.

[*Implications for mental health practice*: The personal uniqueness and sex difference dimension of the virtues implies considering each virtue and vocation in connection with the individuality, sex difference, and interpersonally sexual (nuptial) character of each person. For example, this dimension specifies the expression of the virtues that tend toward a fatherly type of courage (such as, addressing external threats to the family with initiative-taking) and that tend toward a motherly type of courage (such as, addressing external threat to the family with empathically suffering with and caring for others) (John Paul II, 2006; Scheler, 2008; Stein, 1996; Wojtyła, 1993; see also Gilligan, 1982; Kohlberg, 1981; also Chapter 9, "Man and Woman").]

6. Connective, relational, and developmental (interpersonal and holistic process dimension): Virtues are necessarily connective and developmental. Each virtue needs to be completed through a developmental interconnection of the virtues. Virtues are also intrinsically interpersonal, and they make constant reference to family and society, as found in care, justice, courage, and friendship.

[*Implications for mental health practice*: The interconnection of the virtues and their interpersonal nature facilitates psychological health, ethical goodness, and holiness, as when the refugee's earthly hope draws support from both everyday and theological hope, from patience, and from courage in resisting and confronting difficulty. This interconnection is especially served by reason (practical wisdom) and love (virtue of charity). Each particular virtue implies further personal and interpersonal development, in the process of becoming virtuous that continues throughout life.]

7. Learned through role models (based in exemplars and sources that model goodness and truth): The intra- and interpersonal connectivity of the virtues has implications for understanding how virtue and vice are learned through role modeling. There are the imitative or modeling effects of acts; that is, people tend to emulate what another person does. A person's witnessing virtuous practices can tend to strengthen the virtue observed. For example, a brother's courage evokes courage in other siblings. Something similar is found with vice (Girard, 1976). There are two types of role modeling: the everyday and the extraordinary. Relationships with everyday role models influence our learning virtue. They include parents, siblings, neighbors, and colleagues, who mentor us through their example in service and caring. Extraordinary role models influence us because they have a unique importance identified by a person's nation, culture, or religion; they include heroes such as George Washington or Martin Luther King, Jr., or saints such as St. Paul (1 Cor 11:1) or St. Thérèse of Lisieux.

[*Implications for mental health practice*: While the imitation of virtue and vice has neural bases, for example, the effects of mirror neurons (Cozolino, 2010, 2014; Iacoboni, 2008, 2009; Rizzolatti & Sinigaglia, 2008), the mimetic potential of actions and character suggests implications of exemplarity at further physical, psychological, moral, and spiritual levels (Girard, 1976; Zagzebski, 2017). Everyday exemplars have a special influence on us. We emulate the virtues and vices of parents, brothers, sisters, friends, mentors, and colleagues, because of their relationship with us. Extraordinary role models elicit a more distant but nonetheless powerful mimetic desire. We emulate the lives great people, heroes, and saints because of the historical influence of the civic, cultural, and religious realms, which identify them. This mimetic capacity is especially relevant for the character development of children, though it is active throughout life.]

8. Moderating (middle ground of excellence): Each virtue is contrasted with opposing vices, as a middle ground of excellence (virtue) between two extremes of excess and deficit. Such virtues are moderating when considered in accordance with their related emotions, cognitions, volitions, and interpersonal relations. For example, when observing an unjust injury committed against another, either (a) one can focus destructive wrath at the perpetrator, thus multiplying the wrong, or (b) one can respond with indifference to the unjust injury, thus implicitly supporting the injustice. The virtue of morally just anger is a middle ground between these two extremes.

[*Implications for mental health practice*: Virtue, seen as a range between extremes, widens one's understanding of well-being by demonstrating a graduated model of physical, psychological, moral, and spiritual well-being.]

9. Preventative (strength-based dimension): In the midst of difficulty and frailty, virtue strengths serve as resilience factors in resisting both the present and future onslaught of disorder, ills, and vice. Virtue strengths and practices also promote post-trauma growth.

[*Implications for mental health practice*: At the relational level, virtues such as patience, compassion, self-control, as well as forgiveness and reconciliation, both prevent further interpersonal conflicts and heal interpersonal relationships. A preventative influence is seen in the resilience research on the strengthening effect in overcoming difficulty of the virtue of hope (Masten, Cutuli, Herbers, & Reed, 2011; Rand & Cheavens, 2011).]

10. Nonreductionist (evidence-based dimension): Virtue theory and practice are nonreductionist when they are open to research and evidence-based practices that inform a developmental understanding of virtue and when they are open to higher-order meaning and a teleological vision of human growth and healing.

[*Implications for mental health practice*: Constructive results from research and effective psychotherapeutic practice may be used to better identify the working of intellectual, moral, and spiritual virtue strengths, and to promote their growth. For example, research on curative factors in psychotherapy and counseling research has found the therapeutic value and positive effect on relationships that is found in the practice of the virtue of empathy (which is associated with the virtues of charity and patience). Moreover, studies on the practices of the virtues are being employed in the clinic settings. For instance, the positive effect of forgiveness and gratitude can be the basis for therapeutic applications (Emmons & McCullough, 2004; Enright & Fitzgibbons, 2014; Worthington, 2003).]

11. Applied (research and practice): Applications of virtue theory and virtue-based practices are commonplace, even when they are not explicitly recognized as such. For example, communications skill training requires that couples learn empathy, self-control, prudence, and justice, as they dialogue in a cooperative manner that seeks the true goodness of both spouses.

[*Implications for mental health practice*: For example, the therapist shows practical wisdom, patience, empathy, and other virtues in intake interviewing, diagnosis, respecting diversity, implementing treatment, as well as in planning the end of treatment. These very same virtues are seen as qualities that the therapist hopes clients will learn or embody as part of their recovery.]

12. Vocational (calling-based dimension): Virtues become manifest, comprehensible, and directed in the context of a person's vocational commitments: (1) the call to flourishing, goodness, justice, and holiness; (2) the call to vocational states (single, married, religious, and ordained); and (3) the call to work, service, and meaningful leisure.

[*Implications for mental health practice*: A virtue's developmental and therapeutic potential for growth and healing is weakened if not considered in the context of the person's vocational states. The virtue of patience, for example, demonstrates its value for a married man in relating to his wife, children, and colleagues. For further implications on vocations, see Chapter 10, "Fulfilled Through Vocation."]

13. Open to the transcendent and to God (seeking goodness, truth, and beauty and their transcendent source): A Catholic Christian model, based on vocations and virtues, considers God's role in the human exercise of virtue in two ways: by nature and by graced-nature. First, while both nature and grace call for a type of transcendence, natural transcendence is limited to reaching beyond oneself and one's family and society for well-being. Human nature is full of potential, as

can be seen in the dynamics of the acquired virtues (which positively develop human nature for a good life in society). Second, graced-nature is the realization of the potential of nature in ways that are possible only as gifts of God (theological and infused virtues, and the gifts of the Holy Spirit), that is, a type of transcendence that only God can realize (Chapter 17, "Created in the Image of God," and Chapter 19, "Redeemed."

[*Implications for mental health practice*: The natural types of faith, hope, and love are essential curative factors. To even seek out psychotherapy, the client must have hope that suffering can be diminished and healing achieved. They must have faith in the competency of the mental health professional. And the therapist has to express a sense of caring, while the client must experience this caring. These virtues encourage practices of the mind and the heart that enable and encourage the client to further natural and transcendent growth, healing, and flourishing. Of course, divine grace is a gift of God that is neither under human control nor dependent on clinical practice.]

This multidimensional description of flourishing in virtue will become more concrete as we look at the types of virtues, their particularities, the way in which they relate to each other, and the way that they underlie the calling of each man, woman, and child. The rest of this chapter and volume address how these dimensions of virtue contribute to strengthening the Meta-Model's conceptualization of the person.

What Are the Different Types of Virtue?

The virtues are classically differentiated into three major types: theological, moral, and intellectual. First, there are **theological virtues** of faith, hope, and charity or love, which animate the other virtues with a divine perspective. The three theological virtues are contrasted with vices such as unbelief, despair and presumption, and hatred and indifference. The theological virtues, their associated infused virtues (those virtues that are animated by the virtues of faith, hope, and charity) with the supporting gifts of the Holy Spirit and precepts of the Decalogue, as well as their contrasting vices, are discussed in Chapter 19, "Redeemed." Second, there are **moral virtues** (also called the cardinal moral virtues) of prudence (practical wisdom), justice, fortitude (courage), and temperance (self-control). Third, there are **intellectual virtues**, which are often assumed, but which have special importance in this course of study that promotes integrative thought and practices. There are two types of intellectual virtues: (1) theoretical virtues of wisdom, intuition, and inferential knowledge or science, and (2) practical virtues of art and practical wisdom (prudence). Seligman's list (Peterson & Seligman, 2004), for instance, does not make the distinction between these three categories of virtues that traditional virtue theory does, nor does Seligman include the ultimate dimension that involves the theological virtues (although he hints at it with the category of transcendence).

While Aquinas (1273/1981) and the positive psychology movement (Peterson & Seligman, 2004) are methodical when analyzing virtue in order to then form a synthetic understanding of it, many thinkers treat the virtues in a less systematic way. For instance, it is common for authors to treat one virtue in isolation. They also tend to treat one dimension of the virtue or to maintain a restricted focus. In particular, they use a simple list of virtues or anecdotal treatment of them, as in the popular treatment of Guardini (1998) or the therapeutic treatment of Kleponis (2015), or the pedagogical treatment

of Lickona (2004). These approaches highlight virtues—such as mercy, forgiveness, humility, hope, obedience, religion, and leisure or rest—that are sometimes underestimated in the contemporary intellectual world. Such writers contribute greatly to the understanding of virtue, but do not focus on the larger context of virtue, as we are doing here.

The Meta-Model of the Person aims to understand the virtues in an expansive and interconnected way, while also highlighting each virtue within the present discussion. In the chapters that follow, the virtues will thus be studied according to the ends that they seek to attain (diverse modes of flourishing), while being organized according to the capacities that they develop and perfect (such as cognitive and affective inclinations and capacities). Thus, prudence is treated in conjunction with the rational capacity (Chapter 15); justice, with the volitional capacities (Chapter 16); and fortitude and temperance, with the embodied or emotional capacities (Chapter 14). Furthermore, since every virtue is intrinsically relational, the virtues are also addressed in conjunction with our interpersonal capacities (Chapter 12). In addition, all the virtues are treated in conjunction with the callings or vocations described throughout the volume. Nonetheless, it is important to provide a global introduction to the moral virtues and to offer suggestions about their implications for men and women in everyday life and in the mental health field.

What Are the Cardinal Moral Virtues?

The four cardinal moral virtues concern moral action. They are classically considered to be prudence or practical wisdom, justice, courage or fortitude, and temperance or self-control (see Table 11.6). There are three configurations of these virtues, which are complicated because

Table 11.6. The Cardinal Moral Virtues

Moral Prudence (practical wisdom about moral action)→ Virtues of practical intellectual capacities, as seen in practical discernment, judgment, and willed action. The virtue of **prudence** is the use of practical moral reason (practical wisdom) by persons and in groups to direct human action toward their everyday and ultimate goals using good means.

[*See also Table 11.7 and below for a discussion of the intellectual virtues, which include the theoretical aspect of prudence or practical wisdom.*]

Sample associated virtues: good counsel, sound memory of relevant actions, intelligence, reason, caution; types of prudence: family prudence, business prudence, therapeutic prudence, and so on.

Sample contrastive vices: Negligence, false prudence, presumption, and so on.

Sample psychological disorders or distortions: narcissism, attribution bias, impulsivity, weakness of will.

Justice (fairness)→ Virtues of affect, volition, and free will to do what is right and just to others, giving what is due to each and to all in equity. **Justice** and its associated virtues perfect with steady resolve the interpersonal and volitional capacities to give to all subjects "their due in equality" (Aquinas 1273/1981, II-II, 80) as persons (commutative justice), as members of families (familial justice), as partners in trade and as citizens (legal justice), as communities (distributive, economic, social, and retributive justice), and in front of God (religion, worship). Justice and Catholic social teaching make reference to such principles as common good, rights and duties, subsidiarity, participation, solidarity, freedom, environment, and peace.

Sample associated virtues: restitution, respect of persons, gratitude for kindness, being truthful, friendliness, fairness, as well as the honest practices of work, social justice, and so on.

Sample contrastive vices: murder, adultery, injury, indifference (sloth), theft, unjust practices, ingratitude, lying, flattery, covetousness, stinginess, and so on.

Sample psychological disorders or distortions: rationalization, self-serving bias, antisocial personality, and other forms of narcissism, bigotry, self-hatred.

Fortitude (courage) → Virtues of emotions related to the good that is difficult to reach or the evil that is difficult to avoid, concerning emotions such as fear and daring, hope and despair, and anger. **Fortitude** grows through personal and interpersonal practices that apply practical wisdom to situations that evoke emotions related to difficulty.

Sample associated virtues: patience, perseverance, initiative-taking (natural virtue of hope), generosity.

Sample contrastive vices: fearfulness and lack of daring, fearlessness and foolhardiness, vainglory, presumption and ambition, impatience, obstinacy, and so on.

Sample psychological disorders or distortions: workaholic, lethargy or procrastination, many anxiety disorders, aspects of depression and despair, giving in to negative peer pressure.

Temperance (self-control) → Virtues of emotions related to the good, where self-control is needed to manage attraction to a good or repulsion from the lack of good or from something actually bad. **Temperance** grows through personal and interpersonal practices that apply practical wisdom to situations that evoke emotions related to desire.

Sample associated virtues: self-regulation (concerning desire for food and mind-altering substances or activities), humility, modesty, chastity, clemency.

Sample contrastive vices: pride, wrath, lust and adultery, gluttony, greed, envy, and unhealthy curiosity.

Sample psychological disorders or distortions: addictions, impulsivity, extreme expressions of anger, aspects of narcissism, eating disorders, promiscuity, certain cognitive aspects of depression, lack of self-care.

of the effects of disorder and sin on the human person. First, there are the moral virtues that are acquired by intelligent effort through virtuous practices (acquired moral virtues). Second, there are moral virtues that are gifts of God and that depend on the theological virtues and are focused on a supernatural end (infused moral virtues) (Aquinas, 1273/1981, I-II, 63.3; Pieper, 1966; Sherwin, 2009). And last, there is the mutual influence of the infused moral virtues on the acquired virtues, and the acquired virtues on the infused virtues. This mutual influence depends on the state of the acquired virtue (as disposition) and the collaboration with grace. For example, some people "experience difficulty in their works, by reason of certain ordinary dispositions remaining from previous acts" (Aquinas 1273/1981, I-II, 65.3, ad 2). In short, the effects (dispositions and memories) of our previous actions or behavior do not immediately disappear after a change in heart, but commonly continue for some time. When humans collaborate with grace in acts of moral virtue, there is a growth in the underlying disposition of the acquired virtues.

The cardinal moral virtues (prudence, justice, fortitude, and temperance) are understood best in the light of their mutual necessary connections. Plato (ca. 360 BC/1961a, ca. 360 BC/1961b), Aristotle (ca. 350 BC/1941b, ca. 350 BC/1941c), and other Greek and Roman thinkers articulated a conception of human flourishing in terms of the cardinal moral virtues (see Pieper, 1966). The content of these virtues, however, has been found in philosophical and religious traditions across human cultures (Peterson & Seligman, 2004). Each of the cardinal moral virtues, as articulated in the Western tradition, is an entry point to a wide range of other acquirable virtues and character strengths related to the interaction of cognition, affect,

and action. The cardinal virtues are major moral virtues, but by no means the only ones. They are called "cardinal" (from the Latin *cardo*, for "hinge"), because a group of associated virtues hinges on each of them. For example, the virtue of prudence or practical wisdom is further characterized by the associated moral virtues of discernment, judgment, and willed action. Moreover, these associated moral virtues are applied to the different types of prudence needed by each man and woman as well as by various groups; for example, there are different types of practical wisdom, such as that needed in family life, in civic engagements, and in economic activity (Aquinas, 1273/1981, II-II, 48–51).

The virtue of prudence is the use of practical reason (practical wisdom) by men and women (as persons) and in groups, to direct human action, using good means, toward their everyday goals (such as being a good mother or father) as well as their ultimate goals (eternal life). On the natural plane, prudence is the center of the development of every virtue, inasmuch as reason and cognitive capacities (such as perception, memory, imagination, discernment, judgment, and so on) are required in human action. Practical wisdom also requires the other moral virtues, and it is exercised with some nuance by individuals and in groups. The exercise of prudence benefits from goodwill (justice) and well-trained emotions (courage and temperance), which protect it from potential hindrances that distract humans from unbiased reasoning about the course of true flourishing. For example, humans develop prudence in the practice of particular virtues in specific contexts, as when the members of a family learn to reason rightly through the practice of mercy, forgiveness, and reconciliation after experiencing wrongdoing and mistakes inside and outside the family.

Justice, and its associated virtues, perfects

with steady resolve the interpersonal and volitional capacities: it seeks to give to all subjects "their due in equality" as persons (commutative justice), as members of families (familial justice), as partners in trade and as citizens (legal justice), as communities (distributive, economic, and social justice), and in front of God (religion, worship) (Aquinas, 1273/1981, II-II, 80; CCC, §§2401–2463; Pieper, 1966, pp. 71–74). All are true forms of justice. Each one involves the differences of the particular person (being man or woman) and particular vocational states (being called to be son or daughter, husband or wife, and so on). Its opposite, injustice, underlies many *human disorders*. For instance, when family, caregivers, or educators cause traumas and abuse, or when they do not provide protection against these injustices, a person can experience deep attachment wounds, mistrust, and resentment, with their associated negative influences. It is because the human person is fundamentally a relational being, who needs justice in family, friends, business, and social settings, that such injustices deeply wound the person.

Fortitude or courage, with time and intentional effort, perfects the disposition of our emotions that face difficulties, fears, and dangers. Through personal and interpersonal practices fortitude expresses practical wisdom to face fearful difficulties—not only grave physical harm, but also moral and interpersonal fears, such as fears of rejection and criticism, as well as fears of being judged. Also, people can be afraid of a positive challenge just as much as of a negative threat. To bring about the good that one seeks, whether preserving life or meeting a positive challenge for growth, one needs courage and the virtues associated with it. The development of virtuous dispositions related to fear and daring—courage—makes the person more attentive to the implications of reason and inter-

personal relationships. The person develops a disposition to feel fear rightly and, when experiencing fear, to act courageously in accordance with right judgment.

The virtues associated with courage (listed here in parentheses) require taking initiatives that challenge our imagination and resources (natural hope and generosity), as well as holding on to the intended good in the midst of inevitable suffering (patience and perseverance). For example, when people are in pain or suffering because of a physical ailment or psychological disorder, the development of patience helps them to avoid seeking relief through extreme medical interventions, euthanasia, or suicide. Such virtues related to courage involve emotion in the performative, purposeful, ethical, and preventative dimensions of virtue.

The vices involve emotion in contrasting ways. On the one hand, fear, when well-founded and moderated, helps one to focus on finding its source and removing its sting. On the other hand, immoderate or unfounded fear disturbs reasoning about the situation, upsets one's sense of what is real versus imaginary, and disrupts one's capacity to give and take counsel. Vices associated with the lack of courage include extreme fearlessness (recklessness and presumption) or fearfulness (cowardice) (Aquinas, 1273/1981, II-II, 130–133 & 135; Pieper, 1966; Titus, 2006). The virtue of fortitude, its associated virtues, and its contrasted vices are also treated in Chapter 14, "Emotional."

Temperance (self-regulation or self-control) is the capacity to attend to interpersonal love and to other human goods, in spite of a temptation of disordered desires of various kinds, such as extreme forms of attraction or repulsion concerning food, drugs, and sex. This capacity implies facing a disordered desire for pleasure or an extreme fear of pain that would distract us from greater goods (Aristotle, ca. 350 BC/1941b, VI.5, 1140b12). Through this virtue we manage our desires—such as those for recognition and sex, as well as for food and mind-altering substances or activities—through the associated character strengths, such as modesty, integrity, humility, chastity, sobriety, and so on (Aquinas 1273/1981, II-II, 141). Such self-mastery is gained by the discipline of intentional and interpersonal practices. Temperance or self-regulation is undercut, for example, in addictions (especially those that involve drugs and sex), eating disorders, or extreme forms of rage. The virtue of temperance, self-regulation, or self-control is treated also in Chapter 16, "Volitional and Free," and Chapter 14, "Emotional."

What Are the Intellectual Virtues?

The intellectual virtues concern the differentiation and integration of human cognitive capacities, especially intuition, knowledge, judgment, and belief. There are theoretical and practical intellectual virtues that are operative in intellectual work and are of special interest to anyone who seeks to understand the interplay of science, ethics, metaphysics, faith, and their practical applications. The intellectual virtues are in many respects different from, and cannot be reduced to, (1) the cognitive capacities underlying abstract reasoning or (2) moral prudence, which involves both evaluative judgment and moral action. The three classic theoretical intellectual virtues are wisdom, understanding, and knowledge or science. In addition, there are the practical intellectual virtues called art (or techné), and intellectual prudence (or the theoretical aspect of practical wisdom) (Aquinas, 1273/1981, I-II, 57–58; Roberts & Woods, 2007; Zagzebski, 1996, 2009).

Are the Virtues Necessarily Connected?

On a theological note, charity is the unifying factor for the whole of the Christian life. As the most enduring and pervasive of virtues, charity love (agapé, friendship love: see Aquinas, 1273/1981, II-II, 23; Benedict XVI, 2005; Lewis, 1960; Pieper, 1997) unites the following domains: interpersonal (love of God and neighbor), emotional (sensory affect in attractions and the embodied overflow of charity), rational (knowledge of the person as the basis of intentional loving), and volitional (completion of the work of love with free self-giving action). Charity informs the other virtues with a fuller potential, as can be understood when self-control is expressed as a type of chastity aimed at preparation for the sacrament of Marriage. This potential is understood, from a Catholic perspective, through two main sources: (1) natural reason (nature) that is applied to experiences of reality, research, and theory, and that is ordered to each person, family, and the common good; and (2) faith-informed reason (grace) that draws from Sacred Scripture and Church teaching, and that is aimed at ultimate flourishing and supported by divine grace.

Development of the virtues is needed, since flourishing and the good life is the reward of the continual practice of virtue (for example, love demands the further practice of love; justice, further justice). Given the effects of original, social, and personal sin, as well as acquired disordered dispositions, people express a mixture of tendencies and character traits, both strengths and weaknesses (Miller, 2014; Peterson & Seligman, 2004). Natural deficits furthermore can be the basis for the particular way a virtue may have to be developed. People can tend to seek good and truth expansively, even if they suffer from a lack of positive development, inconsistent par-

Table 11.7. The Intellectual Virtues

Wisdom (theoretical insight) → Theoretical intuition about ultimate meaning and principles. Example: intuitively grasping the meaning of flourishing, goodness, existence, truth, beauty, as well as of family life and other relationships.

Understanding (theoretical reasoning about insights or research) → Theoretical reason about application of the principles of ultimate meaning. Examples: (1) reasoning about the significance of vocation and interpersonal relationships for flourishing, (2) conceptualizing the meaning of authority or legitimacy, such as the meaning of research on human attachment or anxiety, in the context of everyday and ultimate flourishing, (3) reasoning about the need for a new product and the best way to finance, develop, and market it, and (4) reasoning about the meaning of the ultimate goodness of the divine gift of life and the means to protect it.

Science (theoretical investigation and empirical research) → As a virtue, science is primarily the disposition of the mind to know reality. Secondarily, it is an issue of scientific method, object of study, and types of knowledge. The humanistic types of knowledge (or science in the classical sense of the word) include discursive investigation or study through narrative, dialogical, and deductive approaches, based on an experience of reality and in search for the conditions and causes of things. The empirical and natural scientific types of knowledge use scientific methods, inductive reasoning, and evidence-based investigation. Of course, the major expression of this latter category of knowledge is found in physics, chemistry, biology, and the other natural sciences, as well as mathematics, which has its own role. Still other somewhat different examples arise from the human sciences, using both qualitative and quantitative methodologies.

Art and *technē* (applied practical knowledge and skills) → Practical reason applied to making things. Example: the expert knowledge of the architect, carpenter, cook, or any artist or artisan, who applies best practices and personal skill to a particular need, plan, or situation.

Intellectual Prudence (theoretical aspect of practical wisdom)→ Theoretical reasoning in the service of moral action. The theoretical aspect of prudence is needed for the practical application of prudence in moral action (*see previous description of the virtue of prudence in Table 11.6*).

enting at home, negative influences outside the home and through the media, or even traumatic experience of abuse or war.

The deep underlying effect of good practices (such as fidelity in marriage, and commitment at work and in community service) is to draw a person's life together morally and spiritually. In particular, the basic virtues, associated virtues, and practices deepen the interconnected paths of intellectual, moral, and spiritual development. For example, courage (a basic virtue) and hope and perseverance (two of its associated virtues) must be formed through certain practices, such as training in emergency situations. The firefighter practices courage and initiative-taking (hope). His professional calling requires it. Similarly, mothers and fathers do so because of their parental calling. Even though it can rightfully be said that each virtue primarily perfects one of the human capacities, the virtues interrelate in a dynamic connection of intellectual, moral, and theological strengths that are needed for a person's complete practice of virtue. Both the secular and the Christian therapist require everyday hope in their work with clients. The Christian therapist's and client's vocations and commitments are further supported and motivated by theological hope, which potentially adds new power and meaning to facilitate the healing process. From a Christian perspective moreover, even a secular therapist is also influenced by the ultimate nature of reality and its ultimate hope that life has meaning and that personal life continues after death (for example, directly through an afterlife or indirectly in one's children and through the effects of one's actions).

The progressive connecting effect of virtues often is spectacular (as in recovery from addiction or the reconciliation of a married couple). However, mostly the work of virtue is humble, seen in small advances, and always in need of both human and divine action, for it is the divine and human collaboration of grace perfecting nature.

Whence Come the Virtues?

As mentioned earlier, the natural inclinations are the "seeds of the virtues" (Aquinas, 1273/1981, I-II, 51.1; cf. I-II, 63.1). Basic acquired virtues and their associated virtue strengths are rooted in the natural inclinations, which constitute the pathways of intellectual, moral, and spiritual development (MacIntyre, 1999). The virtues involve the development of (1) basic inclinations to goodness (existence; loving attachment, family life, and society; truth; and beauty), (2) the anthropological capacities (to be interpersonally relational, emotional, rational, or volitional and free), and (3) life goals (flourishing involved in everyday callings and one's ultimate calling).

No one virtue stands on its own. The virtues are fully developed only when they are practiced in concert with the other intellectual, moral, and theological strengths. For example, true courage requires the application also of the virtues of prudence, justice, and temperance, each in right measure: virtues disconnected from one another are virtues misunderstood. Virtues separated from the good are false. Each complete virtue requires the work of practical reason (the virtue of prudence) in order to aim at a good end (e.g., supporting one's family) and to use a good means (e.g., honest work). A thief who suppresses extreme fear of losing his life or of getting caught is not truly courageous—though modern philosophy would like to credit him with that virtue—for his motivation, both to steal and to feign true courage, is dishonest. Such contrived views of courage originate when the virtues are not understood as tending toward a whole. True virtues contribute to covering the whole range of goodness and must be purposeful and normative, connected to each other, ethical, and distinguished from vices.

In the theological arena, there are further assumptions that explain the performative, perfective, purposeful, ethical, preventative, connective, and transcendent dimensions specific to the virtues of faith, hope, and charity (love). Through God-focused knowing and loving, the theological virtues unify a person's life in service of an ultimate purpose or goal, which for the Christian is life with God, the angels, and redeemed humankind. On the journey of life, it is especially charity love that connects all the virtues, especially as they pertain to salvation, and express the fruit of the Spirit (Gal 5:22–26). As St. Paul says, "Love is patient and kind; love is not jealous or boastful; it is not arrogant or rude.... Faith, hope, and love abide, these three; but the greatest of these is love" (1 Cor 13:4–5, 13). The theological virtues are discussed more extensively in Chapter 19, "Redeemed."

Moral Disorders and Evil

The Meta-Model recognizes that human action—good or bad behavior—has implications for the development of moral character and human relationships, whether perfective or defective, leading to flourishing or languishing. This section offers a Catholic perspective on the nature of moral disorders and weakness, their relation to evil and sin, and their particular effects on cognitive and affective capacities.

What Do Moral Disorders Have to Do with Evil?

In order to conceptualize moral disorder and its destructive nature, and to account for related experiences of languishing, it is necessary to address the question, "What is evil?" and to distinguish types of evil, including those that are not moral evil—that is, those that are not morally attributable to someone's fault or error. In general, evil is not a "who." It is a "what." Or even more, evil is a "not"—a loss, privation, disorder, or lack of something that should properly belong to a person or a thing. For example, the fact that an autistic child may lack empathy is an evil, but the child, of course, is not evil. Within psychology, such deficits are considered not as evil, but rather as a disorder. In both philosophy and psychology, this type of evil is understood as a deprivation. In this case, the child is certainly not blameworthy; rather the child instead suffers from the disorder. Moreover, it is an evil (philosophy) or disorder (psychology) to be lacking the cognitive and affective capacities to reason or to experience empathy. In certain cases, evil is the intended disorder of an activity; and such intentionally disordered action can be the cause of further evil, often by others. Those to whom evil is done do evil in return. The types of evil are distinguished according to the types

of loss, privation, and action involved. In particular, there are material, psychological, moral, and spiritual evils.

A *physical evil* is the disorder, deformity, or destruction of something (e.g., a genetically caused deformity) or a natural disaster (e.g., a tsunami) (*CCC*, §§310–311). Moral responsibility should not usually be attributed to physical evil, although some people attribute it to God, since he is omnipotent and omniscient. However, although God is the first transcendent cause of existence and of life, God created humans and a cosmos that are neither eternal nor indestructible and that suffer loss, corrosion, and death. For example, earthquakes caused by the shifting of tectonic plates are a part of the geophysical nature of our planet.

There are different types of *psychological disorder* or evil at physical, cognitive, affective, behavioral, and interpersonal levels; these disorders can be caused by (a) developmental and neurological disorders, (b) abuse and trauma; (c) one's own present choices; and (d) the effects of one's past choices and vice. These psychological disorders, because they can be caused by various biopsychosocial and spiritual conditions, often overlap. For example, depression can be caused, entirely or in part, by a chemical imbalance or by physical abuse, abandonment, or trauma; it can interact with certain types of temperaments and can be affected by moral and spiritual conditions, such as by vice, as will now be illustrated.

A *moral and spiritual evil* is the voluntary thoughts, words, or deeds that are against reason and human nature or that counter the natural and divine law. However, for moral and spiritual evil and disorder to be considered a personal sin, the individual must actively, knowingly, and freely choose the evil. The degree of responsibility differs according to the seriousness of the evil, the fullness of knowledge, and the completeness of consent. Ratzinger (1995), from a philosophical and theological viewpoint, makes a provocative comment about the human capacity to do and observe moral and spiritual evil. He notes: "people recognize the good only when they themselves do it. They recognize the evil only when they do not do it" (p. 63). From a psychological viewpoint, Menninger (1974) laments the disappearance of attention to sin and wrongdoing in contemporary psychology and in people's consciousness. It has been noted, however, that psychology does record the effects of moral disorder, although those effects are often separated from explicit considerations of moral responsibility and spiritual consequences (Álvarez-Segura et al. 2017; Álvarez-Segura, Echavarria, & Vitz, 2017). Noteworthy exceptions can be seen in the aspirational principles of the ethical codes of conduct for various mental health professions, self-help movements such as Alcoholics Anonymous, and recent models of forgiveness therapy (Enright & Fitzgibbons, 2014; Worthington, 2003), which also identify moral and spiritual dimensions of mental health practice.

Sacred Scripture serves the Christian tradition as a source for identifying evil-related phenomena: deceit, disobedience, and distrust (Gen 3:1–5; Jn 8:44); pursuit of false "goods" and temptation (Gen 3:6; Mt 6:13; 2 Cor 11:12–15); the avoidance of responsibility (Gen 3:12–13; Jn 3:20); and disordered acts (Gal 5:19–21; Eph 5); as well as the consequences of choosing moral evil (Gen 3:16–19; Mt 7:17–18; Jn 5:29; Rom 1:18–32).

When people make evil choices, they are attracted to something or someone in a disordered way. For instance, serial killers are attracted to killing—the acts are evil, although the disordered attraction is perhaps based on some form of imaginary justice or on psychopathology, such as the psychopathic or sociopathic lack of empathy. Killing, or adultery, or cheating is perceived as good or as bringing some good consequence to the author of the act. Persons with such disordered attractions are often influenced by a prior interpretation or choice, such as learned behaviors in the family, which lead them to construe their lives, other people, relationships, and surroundings in partial and distorted ways. For example, a business colleague's evil choice may in part be the result of his defensively interpreting a situation (rejecting a plan in order to oppose a colleague), denying reasonable compromises or making unreasonable ones (resisting good options to collaborate for self-serving purposes), rationalizing evil as good or as good enough (not resisting unethical business or clinical practices), and basing decisions on ideology rather than on truth. Past evil choices can lead to moral disorders at the personal, familial, and social level, as humans acquire a tendency to inordinately seek gratification (licentiousness and substance abuse), power (injustice and divisive groups), and recognition (jealousy and quarrels) (Gal 5:19–21). For example, overpowering emotions and disordered cognitions or volitions impede human flourishing, as when a person despairs of ever reaching a difficult goal and thus unreasonably chooses to abandon a commitment at work, in marriage, or in friendship.

What Do Moral Disorders Harm?

With positive psychology becoming mainstream psychology, there is a growing interest and need to address not only the bioneurological, psychological, or sociological elements of development and health of the virtues and character strengths, but also the moral and spiritual ones (Beauregard, 2012; Beauregard, & O'Leary, 2008). The theories and findings of Piaget (1932/1997), Kohlberg (1981), and Gilligan (1982) have made some contributions to exploring the place of moral cognition and caring in human well-being, but they have in various ways been critiqued and surpassed by Hoffman (2001) in understanding empathy. Peterson and Seligman (2004), from their perspective as psychologists, admit that philosophy has a competence that psychologists do not have in the ethical domain. Such an admission should lead mental health professionals to want to consult with professional ethicists and philosophers in complex situations. Observation and introspection demonstrate that the ethical component of all intentional action affects personal and social well-being. When people freely choose to inordinately seek self-gratification, power, and recognition, they morally disorder their critical capacities, which influence not only their own moral character but also the other people around them. For example, a person caught up in narcotic addiction or in violent anger has difficulty respecting other people and personal commitments. Clinicians should be interested in knowing how immoral acts may lead to moral disorders at cognitive, affective, and even interpersonal levels, where such disorders impede human flourishing and even promote languishing.

Are Moral Disorders Found in Our Cognitive Capacities?

Both the intuitive and the discursive cognitive capacities are significant in moral judgments. First, intuitive "judgments" precede the rational cognitive judgments, as these first "judgments" (i.e., intuition) commonly, quickly, and roughly distinguish many perceptions as morally good or evil. Moreover, humans are intuitively attracted to certain acts and repelled from others. For example, a mother's caring for a child is intuitively perceived or judged as good; in contrast, the mutilation of a child is judged as repulsive. This type of intuited discernment is hard to train or un-train, but nonetheless, it is influenced by the repetition of moral or immoral activity. Intentionally performing intrinsically disordered or evil acts can form nonconscious dispositions toward repeating such acts. Aquinas (1259/1953, II.14.1; 1273/1981, I, 78.1; 1272/2003) identifies this capacity for pre-discursive dispositions as the evaluative capacity (which in Latin is called *vis cogitativa* or *ratio particularis*). At least in part, it is what neuropsychology calls the intuitive cognitive system or "fast thinking" (Kahneman, 2011; Evans & Stanovich, 2013). (See also Chapter 13, "Sensory-Perceptual-Cognitive.")

From an objective moral perspective, human acts influence human dispositions to act. Through freely and consciously chosen acts or through acts that are part of a local culture, humans can acquire evil dispositions. Examples of this are the gratifications that are linked with overeating, pornography use, abuse of power, excessive impatience, sedentary comfort, and so on. People thus come to habitually misconstrue good and evil, for example, in confusing which pleasures, values, and goods to pursue (such as those that come from proper nutrition, initiative, or marital fidelity) and which pains and evils should be rejected (such as those that come from gluttony, moral indifference, or adulterous affairs). Disordered cognitive acts and dispositions also disorder our memories and imagination, which then tend to be preoccupied with power, food, money, and sex.

Second, and more evidently, moral disorders can deform human rational capacities to discern and judge. Uncertainty about what is true and inconsistency in judgments of what is good negatively influence moral action and interpersonal relationships. Moral disorders influence what philosophers call the human capacity to make right practical judgments (i.e., prudence and its connection with the other virtues and with conscience), and what cognitive psychologists call "core beliefs" (Ellis, 1980; Ellis & Ellis, 2011). When rational acts are turned repeatedly toward compromised good and intrinsic evil, rational dispositions to act (and core beliefs) are disordered, and the human conscience is weakened (Rom 1–2; Aquinas, 1273/1981, II-II, qq. 53–55; Aristotle, ca. 350 BC/1941b; John Paul II, 1993; Vatican II, 1965).

Are Moral Disorders Found in Our Affective Capacities?

The affective capacities are also morally significant at sensory (emotion) and intellectual (will) levels. First, sense affects include emotions or feelings, sentiments, moods, and temperaments (Chapter 14, "Emotional"). Emotions have moral value because they participate in the good of reason by identifying goods (feeling rightly attracted to or repulsed by something), by helping one to act in a fitting way, and by promoting good interpersonal relationships. Disordered emotions can also negatively influence human cognition, free agency, and social interaction. Examples of disordered affect are found in tendencies (1) not to act courageously because of fear of personal embarrassment or derision, for instance, as when not standing up for one's ethical and religious convictions in a public context; (2) not to serve true justice because of either ex-

cessive anger or indifference to the wrong that has been committed; and (3) not to invest time and energy in a hope-filled initiative (aimed at a worthwhile and possible but arduous goal) because of sadness or depression (Aristotle, ca. 350 BC/1941b).

Second, the will or volition (and the intellectual affect more generally) is influenced by moral and immoral acts. For example, compromised acts (evil taken as good) can contribute to the development of a weak will and divided heart (Rist, 2009). Moreover, when suffering from a weakened will or a divided heart, people do not always do the good that they both desire and know that they should do.

Considered from the Christian, biblical perspective, disordered desires distract one from the type of self-gift and self-mastery by which we love God and others. St. Paul identifies the misdeeds that come from disordered desires: "fornication, impurity, licentiousness, idolatry, sorcery, enmity, strife, jealousy, anger, selfishness, dissension, party spirit, envy, drunkenness, carousing, and the like" (Gal 5:19–20). Such disordered desires and acts distract one from the truth and from the freedom needed to do what is good. It is the personal relationship with and commitment to the Word of God that provides a spiritual foundation for remedying such desires, as Jesus says to his followers: "If you continue in my word, you are truly my disciples, and you will know the truth, and the truth will make you free" (Jn 8:31–32).

Vice

What Is a Vice?

Vice can be approached through the same thirteen dimensions used to study virtues (see above). The vices are (1) **deformative**, not per-

formative (at the level of acts); (2) **defective**, not perfective or corrective (of the agent's character and dispositions); (3) **negatively-purposeful**, not purposeful (indecisive and anti-communal);

(4) **unethical** or **amoral**, not ethical (immorally teleological and egotistical); (5) **distortive of person and sex difference**, not influenced by personal uniqueness, equal innate dignity, sex difference and complementarity (exaggeration or denial of personal uniqueness; denial of equal dignity, sex differences, and complementarity); (6) **disruptive**, not connective, relational, or developmental (pseudo-holistic, fixated, or neglectful of personal relationships); (7) **learned through disordered role models**, preventing the influence of good exemplars that model true good (exemplars that model only apparent goods); (8) **extreme**, not moderating (conformed to an erroneous, weak, or extreme measure); (9) **degenerative and disintegrative**, not preventative (not strength-based); (10) **reductionist**, not holistic (missing the greater and higher evidence for understanding virtue); (11) **misapplied**, disordered applications of apparent goods in everyday and professional contexts; (12) **anti-vocational**, not vocational (not committing to personal goodness and holiness, vocational states, and work); and (13) **non-transcendent**, closed to the transcendent and to God (not seeking, but avoiding higher goodness, truth, and beauty and their transcendent source). See also the treatment of the dimensions of vice in Chapter 18, "Fallen." Vice is a mixture of the above dimensions. Vice is the disordered development of a good human capacity (agent-based and perfective dimension). The evil of vice manifests itself through a spectrum of contrasting extremes (excess and deficit) expressed in human emotional, volitional, and rational capacities, which are relational. Psychology and the human sciences can identify some of the languishing that is caused by acts and standards that are not adaptive to the person and family, such as psychological abuse, physical violence, and inadequate parenting

(Wilcox et al., 2011). As in the case of virtue, vice is complex and should not be reduced to any of the thirteen dimensions. For example, while a vice may be found in a single act (on intrinsically evil acts, see John Paul II, 1993, §80; Vatican II, 1965, §27), the effect of evil in vice is further understand with reference to how it distorts the person's dispositions, and so on.

There are diverse ways to talk about vices, for example, as vicious disorders of affect, cognition, and action. There are vices that contrast each virtue as its extremes. They involve an excess, loss, or lack concerning what is ethically due to all persons involved, our commitments and callings, and our ultimate end in life. For example, a justly felt expression of anger (a virtuous, constructive, or righteous anger) is meaningful and helpful to recognize and express (see Figure 11.2). This just anger is contrasted with extreme expressions of the emotional energy that underlies it (Axis A). In the subjective consideration of the emotional act, the extreme of the apathetic attitude toward the unjust violence done to innocent people is a lack of what is due. This lack is contrasted with destructive rage that unleashes violence in disproportion to the original offense and without calling on competent authority. Beyond such an analysis of the subjective side, the notion of the mean between extremes (lack and excess) must also be applied to consider the objective norm and situation as a real base to measure the individual's perception and judgment. In the Christian context, the mean of virtue should be discerned in reference to natural moral law and divine law (Aquinas, 1273/1981, I-II, 63.4).

Axis B identifies the extremes caused in the judgment of injustice done and the expression of felt anger concerning it, because there are self-distorting and other-distorting influences that deform ethical judgments and psychologi-

Figure 11.2. Anger as a Mean of Subjective Act (Axis A), Objective Norm (Axis B),
and Dispositional State (Axis C)

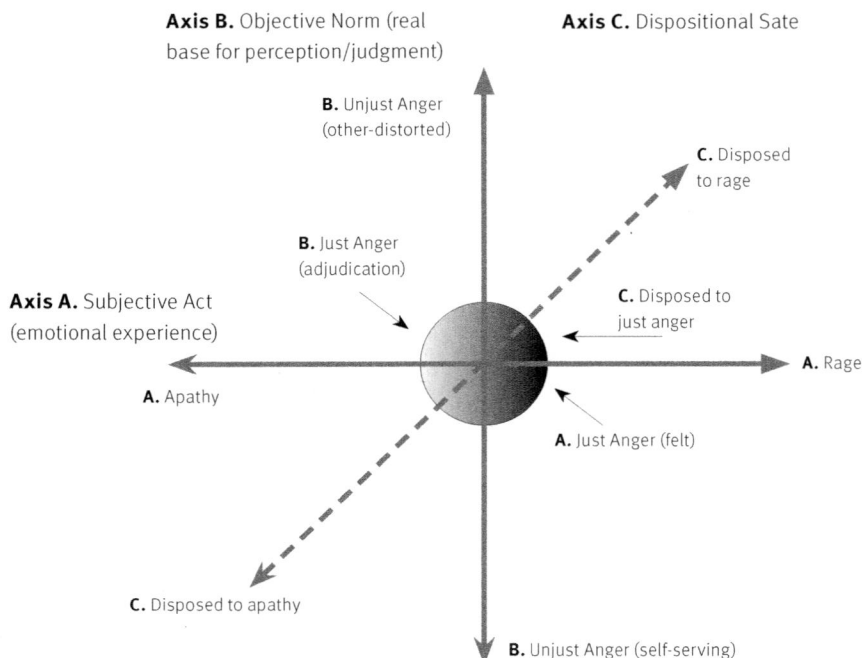

Axis B. Objective Norm (real base for perception/judgment)

Axis C. Dispositional Sate

B. Unjust Anger (other-distorted)

C. Disposed to rage

B. Just Anger (adjudication)

Axis A. Subjective Act (emotional experience)

C. Disposed to just anger

A. Rage

A. Apathy

A. Just Anger (felt)

C. Disposed to apathy

B. Unjust Anger (self-serving)

cal mechanisms. Axis C considers the person's disposition or acquired tendency to express a range of anger-related emotions when faced with injustice, ranging from rage to apathy. To remain in the virtuous middle ground requires being disposed to a righteous anger that will stand up to injustice, and use a good measure of anger in ways that are corrective of the evil, preventative of further injustice, and indicative of a balanced mean between extremes. Figure 11.2 explicitly touches on only three of the virtue-vice dimensions, while the discussion within this chapter integrates several other dimensions, such as vocation and transcendence.

How Are Virtue and Vice Distinct?

Vices are habitual dispositions that are formed progressively, through freely choosing various excesses of desire, will, or judgment. In forming vices, there is a multidimensional range between virtue and opposite extremes of vice. Inasmuch as a person is inclined to one vicious excess or lack, it is difficult to find the mean (Aristotle, ca. 350 BC/1941b, 1109a20–30; also Aquinas, 1273/1981, I-II, 64.1–3). This is seen in the types of disorder that can progressively influence someone's emotion, will, and knowledge. As Aristotle (ca. 350 BC/1941b) describes, there is a difference of completeness between (1) the virtue of chastity (whole virtue informing emotion, will, and reason), (2) the semi-virtue of continence (lacking emotional virtue, but retaining strength of will and rightness of reason), (3) the partial-vice of incontinence (lacking ordinate emotion and falling into disordered choices, while the person retains knowledge of what is good), and (4) unchastity (fully vice at the levels of emotion and will, as well as of perception, cognition, and reasoning) (1145a15–1152a35). An example of this range between extremes concerning temperance in eating styles is outlined in Figure 11.3.

Another example of the virtue-vice range is found between truth and deceit, seen through the influence of jealousy and lying. At the topmost level, as shown in Figure 11.3, the virtue of truthfulness involves the emotional, volitional, and rational search for the truth and respect for other people. The second level reveals emotions related to jealousy (envy, resentment, distrust, covetousness, and so on) toward a colleague,

which can be troubling. A person may be able to do what is right in the midst of an emotional struggle, as when jealous emotions hinder but do not stop honest evaluation of a colleague. At the third level, through an intentional choice (a failure of the will, an ill-will, or a divided heart), a person may not only struggle emotionally, but actually choose not to tell the truth, for instance, in regard to the excellent performance of a fellow-worker. At the fourth level, that concerning vicious knowledge and perception, through repeatedly choosing to misrepresent a colleague's work, a person may begin to think that the jealous lie is the honest truth. At this state, the vice has touched the person's acts and dispositions globally at the level of emotions, free will, and reasoned judgment. The dynamic range from virtue to pseudo-virtue (the mixture of vice and virtue) to vice covers not only human embodied (emotional), volitional and free, and rational states, but also other factors, especially the interpersonal and vocational.

Figure 11.3. Temperance in Eating as an Excellence Demanding Reason, Will, and Emotion

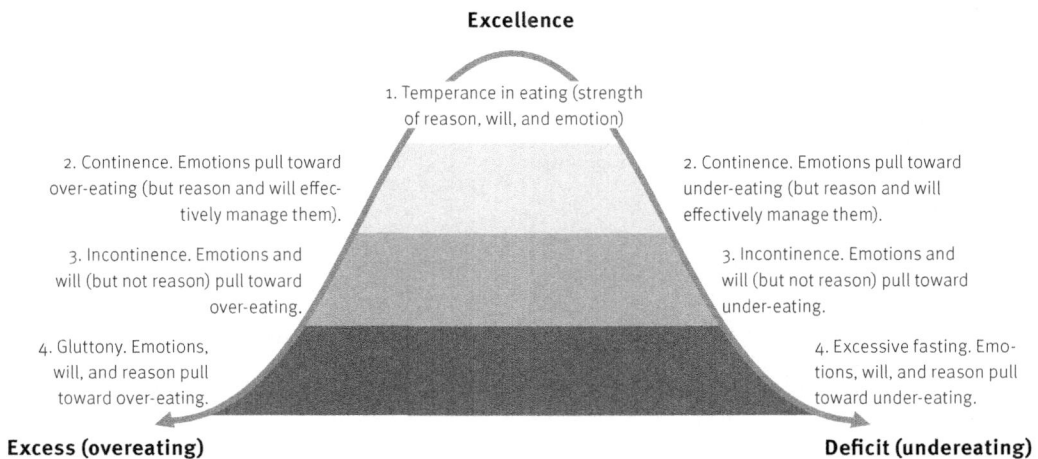

How Do the Vices Interrelate?

Distinctions about the common usage of terms apply to the virtues, as stated previously, as well as to vices. For example, "pride" can mean a proper sense of self-respect or a vicious sense of self-importance. Pride, in its vicious forms, is conceptualized as the vice whereby an individual puts himself at the center of the universe or on a pedestal above others and even above God. It is narcissistic and destructive. The vice of pride, according to the Christian tradition, is seen as the root of all sin (Sir 10:15; Cassian, 426–429/1997; Gregory I, 595/1844–1850; Aquinas, 1273/1981, I-II, 84.2; II-II, 162.7). It blinds people to recognizing that they have received all the goods at their disposal, for they have received life itself and even love. Moreover, it undercuts a foundational principle of life—that in order to flourish one must give generously what one has received gratuitously. The prideful posture is radical especially when a person does not realize that his or her very life (including resources, talents, family, and friends) is a gift that must be shared in order to be truly enjoyed. Pride, as has been interpreted as underlying Adam and Eve's original sin (Gen 3), is seen to transgress the law established by God. Moreover, it is thought to express doubt in God's love for mankind (John Paul II, 2006).

The traditional treatment of the vices, which comes from the early Church Fathers, recognizes seven capital sins or deadly vices (1 Jn 5:17), usually in addition to the primordial sin or vice of pride. They are called "capital" because they lead to other sins and vices (Cassian, 426–429/1997, 420–429/2000; Evagrius of Pontus, ca. 379/2006, ca. 390/2009; Gregory I, 595/1844–1850; see also DeYoung, 2009). The vices can be translated and put in the following order, from more spiritual to more material: vanity, envy, indifference, avarice, wrath, lust,

and gluttony, which is the order and formulation of Gregory I (595/1844–1850; XXXI.45.87–88). The vices influence not only individuals, but also the external environment and people, who pass their vices on to their associates.

Does Psychology Inevitably Face Moral Issues?

Humans commonly experience themselves as personal unities, that is, as being whole persons. Except in severe types of divided heart (for example, weakness of will) or psychological disorder (such as schizophrenia), people have introspective evidence about the meaningfulness of life. They recognize that they are whole beings who are fulfilled by virtues and through vocations, and they are embodied, interpersonally relational, rational, and volitional and free. They even experience a desire for further wholeness in the face of negative experiences of brokenness and weakness. They recognize that their emotional states have moral and spiritual meaning. Such experiences also suggest that psychological capacities and moral virtues or vices are enmeshed. Since human beings are foundationally moral and spiritual creatures, psychology will need to address moral and spiritual issues in one way or another. Likewise, since human beings are psychological creatures, ethics must address psychological issues (psychological capacities, being ordered or disordered, strengths or weaknesses).

It has been argued that not all approaches to ethics are as psychologically nuanced as a virtue-based approach (Casebeer, 2003; Fowers, 2005), which outstrips the simpler ethical systems that are utilitarian (Bentham, 1789; Mill, 1861/1957), deontological (Kant, 1785/2011), emotivist (Hare, 1952; Hume, 1740/2000), or consequentialist (McCormick, 1985). Simplistic correlations of ethical principles and psychology miss the fact that personal, freely chosen, moral evil is not the cause of all psychological disorder. Nonetheless, freely chosen evil does create further brokenness at personal and social levels. Moral evil is the lack of some good that ought to be present in a person's judgment, choice, action, or disposition to act. It reflects voluntary action that lacks the ethical responsibility or spiritual maturity appropriate to the person's situation in life, as when as a husband and father of a family chooses to enter into an adulterous affair.

The previously mentioned vices are called "cardinal vices," since they are the roots of sin and of other flaws found in one's character. The existence of moral evil complicates the human development and healing of each child, adolescent, and adult. For example, disordered emotions (such as immoderate hatred, extreme impatience, and destructive jealously) must be addressed as evil, that is, as expressing a lack of some good that should be present in someone's emotional states at personal and interpersonal levels. Such evil is a personal, psychological, and spiritual reality. Other such types of immoral acts and dispositions, at rational and volitional levels, also lack the moral ordering that should be present. Personal responsibility for such disorders and evil depends on many factors. Nonetheless, because moral evil influences people's capacity to know themselves and to interact with others in healthy and holy ways, it is necessarily an issue in psychotherapy.

What Responses Do Vices Elicit?

The experience of moral vice is personally disruptive and calls for justice for the injured that is meted out by proper authorities; it also calls for mercy and compassion from others, and remorse from the perpetrator. It necessitates efforts at forgiveness, reconciliation, and healing at interpersonal, social, and religious levels. The first step toward healing is to experience mercy and compassion toward the person who was wronged but also toward the wrongdoer. As an affective bond, mercy is expressed in empathy toward the one who suffers. As an effective action, mercy overcomes indifference, transforms hatred, and halts the cycle of revenge.

Furthermore, the perpetrator rightly feels remorse or guilt after a misdeed (Enright & Fitzgibbons, 2014). When humans freely and knowingly choose moral evil, they need the experience of measured remorse (John Paul II, 1993). Without due remorse, conscience is mistaken or dulled. Proper remorse or guilt is grounded in the accurate assessment of one's responsibility and the nature of the deed. It should not lead to scrupulously belaboring the error or sin, but, rather, it should awaken the desire to correct what can be corrected and to be reconciled with those who are harmed, when this is appropriate. Where a personal seeking of forgiveness is no longer possible (if the offending person died), one can pray for them, that is, at least in some Christian practice (Catholic and Orthodox). Inasmuch as the feeling of proper remorse is tied to a correct conscience, there is a need to train one's cognitive and affective exercise of judgment and sense of conscience. A well-trained conscience discriminates between excessive and deficient senses of guilt or remorse, between laxity and scrupulosity (John Paul II, 1993). It thus knows the difference between strict justice and mercy.

For the Christian, evil and guilt are not the last words. Nor is the meting out of just punishment. Mercy is necessary for all parties, and pardon brings relief. Forgiveness and, when possible, reconciliation lead to redemption and peace, and contribute to both spiritual and psychological flourishing. Christ's capacity to save and reconcile is foundational to the Gospel and

Christian life (Lk 15; Mt 1:21). As John Paul II (1984) says: "Sin is an integral part of the truth about man.... [However] sin is countered by the truth of divine love, which is just, generous and faithful, and which reveals itself above all in forgiveness and redemption" (§13; see also John Paul II, 1980). God both demands justice and offers love and mercy. Christ brings both. (A more extensive theological treatment of the phenomena of moral disorder, evil, and sin are treated in Chapter 18, "Fallen.")

Prevention

A brief acknowledgment of the preventive role that virtue can play will put this chapter in the perspective of the pathway to flourishing. In the Catholic Christian Meta-Model of the Person, integral human development toward flourishing is not simply an end to be sought in itself. The integral development found in a person's authentic desire for wholeness, brought about by connecting the virtues, also serves to prevent the further brokenness that is caused when a person freely chooses evil or experiences new trauma. Nevertheless, even though when one is forewarned one is forearmed, and even with a well-trained mind, will, emotions, and supportive family, there is great difficulty in living a good life. The wholeness of vision must be completed with a wholeness of heart and with a coherent community and, as the Catholic Christian will confess, with the great support of divine grace. Theological and spiritual practices that support this wholeness include communal celebration of the sacraments, the reading of Sacred Scripture, personal prayer, and self-giving service, as well as the honoring of one's vocational states.

The Catholic Christian Meta-Model of the Person provides a frame for identifying the positive potential and deeper truths that are the foundation for attaining moral integrity, resisting moral disorder, and advancing in spiritual maturity. The fragmentation of a person's moral integrity (moral action and virtue) leads to particular traps; awareness of such traps can help to avoid or minimize the danger. For instance, the virtuous life is facilitated by an awareness of the major moral errors found in the following positions: *Relativism* denies the existence of the objective truth, which prudence and the other moral virtues recognize as moral standards. *Emotivism* construes ethical judgments as simply expressions of a person's positive or negative emotions about a situation, rather than as conclusions objectively rooted in reason (natural and divine law) and the reality of the person (human nature, value, and the personalist norm). *Subjectivism* holds that a person's perception, knowledge, or judgment is necessarily correct, rather than recognizing the possibility of error and being aided by humility and right practical judgment. *Consequentialism* adjudicates an act's goodness by its consequences alone. Furthermore, it denies that any acts are intrinsically evil. A Catholic viewpoint, however, identifies three founts for moral judgment: (1) the subject's intention or the end of one's motivation, (2) the nature of the act (the object of the act), and (3) the circumstances (the special qualities that depend on who is involved, what the situation is, when it is done, and so on) (*CCC*, §§1750–1754; John Paul II, 1993, §§74–78). All three sources of moral judgment contribute ethical weight; any one of these sources can render the whole act evil. For example, a good intention (reducing medical costs) might be used to justify an evil act (euthanasia). Last, *materialism* reduces the human person to biological determinants, such as genetic and neural processes or psychological capacities. A full view of the person and his or her potential for flourishing through the connection of all the virtues must recognize the body-soul unity of the person, and the person's aim or *telos*, as well as any biological and psychological influences or causal factors.

Flourishing is circumscribed in this chapter's discussion of virtue, but it also requires a fuller treatment of the types of flourishing that are found in the committed life of callings or vocations. Virtue finds its fuller meaning and expression in the context of a person's and family's callings and vocations, which is the topic of the previous chapter, and in the focus on the person as relational, which is the topic of our next chapter.

REFERENCES

Adler, A. (2013). *The practice and theory of individual psychology* (Vol. 133). New York, NY: Routledge. (Original work published 1924)

Álvarez-Segura, M., Echavarria, M. F., Lafuente, M., Zeiders, C., Antonín, P., & Vitz, P. C. (2017). Defense mechanisms: Determined or ethical choices or both? *European Journal of Science and Theology*, 13(3), 5–14.

Álvarez-Segura, M., Echavarria, M. F., & Vitz, P. C. (2017). A psycho-ethical approach to personality disorders: The role of volitionality. *New Ideas in Psychology*, 47, 49–56.

American Association for Marriage and Family Therapy (2015). *AAMFT code of ethical principles for marriage and family therapists*. Washington, DC: Author.

American Counseling Association (2014). *ACA code of ethics*. Alexandria, VA: Author.

American Psychiatric Association. (2013). *The principles of medical ethics: With annotations especially applicable to psychiatry*. Washington, DC: Author.

American Psychological Association. (2017). *Ethical principles of psychologists and code of conduct*. Washington, DC: Author.

Aquinas, T. (1949). *On charity* (L. Kendzierski, Trans.). Milwaukee, WI: Marquette University Press.

Aquinas, T. (1953). *The disputed questions on truth* (J. V. McGlynn, Trans.). Chicago, IL: Regnery. (Original work composed 1256–1259)

Aquinas, T. (1981). *Summa theologiae* (English Dominican Province, Trans.). Westminster, MD: Christian Classics. (Original work composed 1265–1273)

Aquinas, T. (2003). *On evil* (B. Davies, Ed.; R. Regan, Trans.). New York, NY: Oxford University Press. (Original work composed 1266–1272)

Aristotle. (1941a). *Metaphysics*. In R. McKeon (Ed.), *The basic works of Aristotle* (pp. 689–926). New York, NY: Random House. (Original work composed ca. 350 BC).

Aristotle. (1941b). *Nicomachean ethics*. In R. McKeon (Ed.), *The basic works of Aristotle* (pp. 935–1112). New York, NY: Random House. (Original work composed ca. 350 BC)

Aristotle. (1941c). *On the soul*. In R. McKeon (Ed.), *The basic works of Aristotle* (pp. 535–603). New York, NY: Random House. (Original work composed ca. 350 BC)

Ashley, B. M. (2006). *The way toward wisdom: An interdisciplinary and intercultural introduction to metaphysics*. Notre Dame, IN: University of Notre Dame Press.

Ashley, B. M. (2013). *Healing for freedom: A Christian perspective on personhood and psychotherapy*. Arlington, VA: The Institute for the Psychological Sciences Press.

Ashley, B. M., & O'Rourke, K. D. (1997). *Health care ethics: A theological analysis* (4th ed.). Washington, DC: Georgetown University Press.

Augustine. (2007). *Confessions* (2nd ed.) (M. P. Foley, Ed.; F. J. Sheed, Trans.). New York, NY: Hackett. (Original work composed 397–401)

Augustine (2010). *Augustine: On the free choice of the will, on grace and free choice, and other writings* (P. King, Ed. & Trans.). Cambridge, United Kingdom: Cambridge University Press. (Original work composed 395)

Bandura, A. (2001). Social cognitive theory: An

agentic perspective. *Annual Review of Psychology, 52*, 1–26.

Bandura, A. (2006). Toward a psychology of human agency. *Perspectives on Psychological Science, 1,* 164–180.

Beauregard, M. (2012). *Brain wars: The scientific battle over the existence of the mind and the proof that will change the way we live our lives.* New York, NY: HarperCollins.

Beauregard, M., & O'Leary, D. (2008). *The spiritual brain: A neuroscientist's case for the existence of the soul.* New York, NY: HarperCollins.

Benedict XVI. (2005). *Deus caritas est* [Encyclical, on Christian love]. Vatican City, Vatican: Libreria Editrice Vaticana.

Benedict XVI. (2006, September 12). *Faith, reason and the university: Memories and reflections* [The Regensburg address]. Vatican City, Vatican: Libreria Editrice Vaticana.

Benedict XVI. (2009a). *Caritas in veritate* [Encyclical, on integral human development in charity and truth]. Vatican City, Vatican: Libreria Editrice Vaticana.

Benedict XVI. (2009b). Address for the meeting with artists. Vatican City, Vatican: Libreria Editrice Vaticana.

Benedict XVI. (2010). Message for the world day of peace. Vatican City, Vatican: Libreria Editrice Vaticana.

Bentham, J. (1789). *An introduction to the principles of morals and legislation.* Mineola, NY: Dover.

Budziszewski, J. (2009). *The line through the heart: Natural law as fact, theory, and sign of contradiction.* Wilmington, DE: ISI Books.

Budziszewski, J. (2012). *On the meaning of sex.* Wilmington, DE: ISI Books.

Butler, J. (1988). Performative acts and gender constitution: An essay in phenomenology and feminist theory. *Theatre Journal, 40*(4), 519–531.

Butler, J. (1999). *Subjects of desire: Hegelian reflections in twentieth-century France.* New York, NY: Columbia University Press.

Casebeer, W. D. (2003). Moral cognition and its neural constituents. *Nature Reviews Neuroscience, 4*(10), 840–847.

Cassian, J. (1997). *The conferences* (B. Ramsey, Trans.). Mahwah, NJ: Newman Press. (Original works composed 426–429)

Cassian, J. (2000). *The institutes* (B. Ramsey, Trans.). Mahwah, NJ: Newman Press. (Original works composed 420–429)

Catechism of the Catholic Church (*CCC*) (2nd ed.). (1997). Vatican City, Vatican: Libreria Editrice Vaticana.

Cessario, R. (2002). *The virtues, or the examined life.* New York, NY: Continuum.

Cessario, R. (2008). *The moral virtues and theological ethics* (2nd ed.). Notre Dame, IN: University of Notre Dame Press.

Cicero. (1991). *On duties* (M. T. Griffin & E. M. Atkins, Eds.). Cambridge, United Kingdom: Cambridge University Press. (Original work composed 44 BC)

Cozolino, L. (2017). *The neuroscience of psychotherapy: Healing the social brain* (3rd ed.). New York, NY: Norton.

Cozolino, L. (2014). *The neuroscience of human relationships: Attachment and the developing social brain* (2nd ed.). New York, NY: Norton.

Cullen, C. M. (2012). The natural desire to see God and pure nature: A debate revisited. *American Catholic Philosophical Quarterly, 86*(4), 705–730.

de Beauvoir, S. (2011). *The second sex.* New York, NY: Vintage. (Original work published 1949)

de Lubac, H. (1998). *The mystery of the supernatural* (R. Sheed & J. Pepino, Trans.). New York, NY: Herder and Herder. (Original work published 1946)

deYoung, R. K. (2009). *Glittering vices: A new look at the seven deadly sins and their remedies.* Grand Rapids, MI: Brazos Press.

Doidge, N. (2007). *The brain that changes itself: Stories of personal triumph from the frontiers of brain science.* New York, NY: Penguin.

Ellis, A. (1980). Psychotherapy and atheistic values: A response to A. E. Bergin's "psychotherapy and religious values." *Journal of Consulting and Clinical Psychology, 48*(5), 635–639.

Ellis, A., & Ellis, D. J. (2011). *Rational emotive behavior therapy.* Washington, DC: American Psychological Association.

Emmons, R. A., & McCullough, M. E. (Eds.). (2004). *The psychology of gratitude.* Oxford, United Kingdom: Oxford University Press.

Enright, R. D., & Fitzgibbons, R. P. (2014). *Forgiveness therapy: An empirical guide for resolving anger* and restoring hope. Washington, DC: American Psychological Association.

Epicurus. (1994). *The Epicurus reader: Selected writings and testimonia* (B. Inwood, Trans.). Indianapolis, IN: Hackett Publishing. (Original work composed third to second century BC)

Evagrius of Pontus. (2006). *On thoughts.* In R. E. Sinkewicz (Trans.), *Evagrius of Pontus: The Greek ascetic corpus* (pp. 136–182). Oxford, United Kingdom: Oxford University Press. (Original work composed ca. 379–399)

Evagrius of Pontus. (2009). *Talking back: A monastic handbook for combating demons* (D. Brakke, Trans.). Trappist, KY: Cisterian Publications. (Original work composed ca. 390–399)

Erikson, E. (1994). *Identity: Youth and crisis.* New York, NY: Norton. (Original work published 1968)

Evans, J. S. B. T., & Stanovich, K. E. (2013). Dual-process theories of higher cognition: Advancing the debate. *Perspectives on Psychological Science, 8*(3), 223–241.

Feingold, L. (2010). *The natural desire to see God according to St. Thomas Aquinas and his interpreters.* Naples, FL: Sapientia Press.

Fowers, B. (2005). *Virtue and psychology: Pursuing excellence in ordinary practices.* Washington, DC: American Psychological Association.

Francis. (2015). *Laudato si'* [Encyclical, on care for our common home]. Vatican City, Vatican: Libreria Editrice Vaticana.

Frankl, V. E. (2000). *Man's search for ultimate meaning.* Cambridge, MA: Perseus Publishing.

Frankl, V. E. (2006). *Man's search for meaning* (I. Lasch, Trans.). Boston, MA: Beacon Press. (Original work published 1959)

Fromm, E. (1956). *The art of loving.* New York, NY: Harper & Row.

Gallagher, D. M. (1999). Thomas Aquinas on self-love as the basis for love of others. *Acta philosophica, 8*(1), 23–44.

George, R. P. (2001). *In defense of natural law.* Oxford, United Kingdom: Oxford University Press.

Gilligan, C. (1982). *In a different voice: Psychological theory and women's development.* Cambridge, MA: Harvard University Press.

Girard, R. (1976). *Violence and the sacred* (P. Gregory, Trans.). Baltimore, MD: Johns Hopkins University Press. (Original work published 1972)

Giussani, L. (1997). *The religious sense* (J. Zucchi, Trans.). Montreal, Canada: McGill-Queen's University Press.

Gregory I. (1844–1850). *Morals on the book of Job* (Vols. 1–3). Oxford, United Kingdom: J. H. Parker. (Original work composed 595)

Guardini, R. (1998). *Learning the virtues that lead you to God.* Manchester, NH: Sophia Institute Press.

Haidt, J. (2006). *The happiness hypothesis: Finding modern truth in ancient wisdom.* New York, NY: Basic Books.

Halwani, R. (2003). *Virtuous liaisons: Care, love, sex, and virtue ethics.* Chicago, IL: Open Court.

Handelsman, M. M., Knapp, S., & Gottlieb, M. C. (2009). Positive ethics: themes and variations. In S. J. Lopez & C. R. Snyder (Eds.), *The Oxford handbook of positive psychology* (pp. 105–113). Oxford, United Kingdom: Oxford University Press.

Hare, R. M. (1952). *The language of morals.* Oxford, United Kingdom: Oxford University Press.

Harris, A. H. S., Thoresen, C. E., & Lopez, S. J. (2007). Integrating positive psychology into counseling: Why and (when appropriate) how. *Journal of Counseling & Development, 85*(1), 3–13.

Hauerwas, S. (1981). *Vision and virtue.* Notre Dame, IN: University of Notre Dame.

Hebb, D. O. (1949). *The organization of behavior.* New York, NY: Wiley.

Hittinger, J. (2007). *The first grace: Rediscovering the natural law in a post-Christian world.* Wilmington, DE: ISI Books.

Hoffman, M. L. (2001). *Empathy and moral development: Implications for caring and justice.* Cambridge, United Kingdom: Cambridge University Press.

Hume, D. (2000). *A treatise of human nature.* Oxford, United Kingdom: Oxford University Press. (Original work published 1740)

International Theological Commission. (2014). *Sensus fidei in the life of the Church.* Vatican City, Vatican: Libreria Editrice Vaticana.

Iacoboni, M. (2008). *Mirroring people: The new science of how we connect with others.* New York, NY: Farrar, Straus and Giroux.

Iacoboni, M. (2009). Imitation, empathy, and mirror neurons. *Annual Review of Psychology, 60,* 653–670.

John Paul II. (1980). *Dives in misericordia* [Encyclical, on divine mercy]. Vatican City, Vatican: Libreria Editrice Vaticana.

John Paul II. (1984). *Reconciliatio et paenitentia* [Apostolic exhortation, on reconciliation and penance]. Vatican City, Vatican: Libreria Editrice Vaticana.

John Paul II. (1993). *Veritatis splendor* [Encyclical, on certain fundamental questions of the Church's moral teaching]. Vatican City, Vatican: Libreria Editrice Vaticana.

John Paul II. (1999, April 4). *Letter to artists.* Vatican City, Vatican: Libreria Editrice Vaticana.

John Paul II. (2006). *Man and woman he created them: A theology of the body* (M. Waldstein, Trans.). Boston, MA: Pauline Books and Media.

Kaczor, C. (2002). *Proportionalism and the natural law tradition.* Washington, DC: The Catholic University of American Press.

Kaczor, C. (2015). *The gospel of happiness: Rediscover your faith through spiritual practice and positive psychology.* New York, NY: Image.

Kahneman, D. (2011). *Thinking, fast and slow.* New York, NY: Farrar, Straus and Giroux.

Kant, I. (1964). *The doctrine of virtue* (M. J. Gregor, Trans.). New York, NY: Harper & Row Torchbooks. (Original work published 1797)

Kant, I. (1993). *Critique of practical reason* (L. W. Beck, Trans.). New York, NY: Pearson. (Original work published 1788)

Kant, I. (2011) *Groundwork of the metaphysics of morals: A German-English edition* (M. Gregor & J. Timmermann, Ed. and Trans.). Cambridge, United Kingdom: Cambridge University Press. (Original work published 1785)

Keyes, C. L. M. (2002). Complete mental health: An agenda for the 21st century. In C. L. M. Keyes & J. Haidt (Eds.), *Flourishing: Positive psychology and the life well-lived* (pp. 293–312). Washington, DC: American Psychological Association.

Kinghorn, W. (2016). The politics of virtue: An Aristotelian-Thomistic engagement with the VIA classification of character strengths. *The Journal of Positive Psychology,* 1–12. doi:10.1080/17439760.2016.1228009

Kleponis, P. (2015). *Integrity restored.* Steubenville, OH: Emmaus Road.

Koenig, H. G., King, D., & Carson, V. B. (Eds.). (2012). *Handbook of religion and health* (2nd ed.). New York, NY: Oxford University Press.

Kohlberg, L. (1981). *Essays on moral development: Vol. 1. The philosophy of moral development: Moral stages and the idea of justice.* New York, NY: Harper and Row.

Laracy, M. (2011). *The role of the experience of beauty in psychotherapy* (Doctoral dissertation, The Institute for the Psychological Sciences). Retrieved from ProQuest Dissertations & Theses Global. (Order No. 3453653).

Levering, M. (2008). *Biblical natural law: A theocentric and teleological approach.* Oxford, United Kingdom: Oxford University Press.

Lewis, C. S. (1960). *The four loves.* New York, NY: Harcourt Brace.

Lickona, T. (2004). *Character matters: How to help our children develop good judgment, integrity, and other essential virtues.* New York, NY: Touchstone.

Linsley, P. A., & Joseph, S. (2004). *Positive psychology in practice.* Hoboken, NJ: Wiley.

Lopez, S. J., & Snyder C. R. (Eds.). (2009). *The Oxford handbook of positive psychology* (2nd ed.). Oxford, United Kingdom: Oxford University Press.

Lopez, S. J., & Snyder C. R. (Eds.). (2014). *Positive psychology: The scientific and practical explorations of human strengths* (3rd ed.). Los Angeles, CA: Sage.

MacIntyre, A. (1990). *Three rival versions of moral enquiry: Encyclopaedia, genealogy, and tradition.* Notre Dame, IN: University of Notre Dame Press.

MacIntyre, A. (1999). *Dependent rational animals: Why human beings need the virtues.* Chicago, IL: Open Court.

MacIntyre, A. (2007). *After virtue: A study in moral theory* (3rd ed.). Notre Dame, IN: University of Notre Dame Press. (Original work published 1981)

MacIntyre, A. (2009). Intractable moral disagreements. In L. S. Cunningham (Ed.), *Intractable disputes about the natural law: Alasdair MacIntyre and critics* (pp. 1–52). Notre Dame, IN: University of Notre Dame Press.

Masten, A. S., Cutuli, J. J., Herbers, J. E., & Reed, M. G. (2011). Resilience in development. In S. J. Lopez & C. R. Snyder (Eds.), *The Oxford handbook of positive psychology* (2nd ed., pp. 117–131). Oxford, United Kingdom: Oxford University Press.

McCormick, R. A. (1985). *Health and medicine in the Catholic tradition: Tradition in transition.* New York, NY: Crossroad.

McMinn, M. R. (2017). *The science of virtue: Why*

positive psychology matters to the Church. Grand Rapids, MI: Brazos Press.

Menninger, K. (1974). *Whatever became of sin?* New York, NY: Hawthorn Books.

Mill, J. S. (1957). *Utilitarianism.* Indianapolis, IN: Bobbs-Merrill. (Original work published 1861)

Miller, C. B. (2014). *Character and moral psychology.* New York, NY: Oxford University Press.

National Association of Social Workers. (2008). *Code of Ethics of the NASW.* Washington DC: Author.

Nussbaum, M. (1986). *The fragility of goodness: Luck and ethics in Greek tragedy and philosophy.* Cambridge, United Kingdom: Cambridge University Press.

Paul VI. (1968). *Humanae vitae* [Encyclical, on the regulation of birth]. Vatican City, Vatican: Libreria Editrice Vaticana.

Pellegrino, E. D., & Thomasma, D. C. (1996). *The Christian virtues in medical practice.* Washington, DC: Georgetown University Press.

Peterson, C., & Seligman, M. E. P. (Eds.). (2004). *Character strengths and virtues: A handbook and classification.* New York, NY: Oxford University Press.

Piaget, J. (1997). *The moral judgment of the child.* New York, NY: Free Press. (Original work published 1932)

Pieper, J. (1966). *The four cardinal virtues.* Notre Dame, IN: University of Notre Dame Press. (Original work composed 1949–1959)

Pieper, J. (1997). *Faith, hope, love* (R. Winston & C. Winston, Trans.). San Francisco, CA: Ignatius Press. (Original work published 1986)

Pieper, J. (1998). *Happiness and contemplation.* South Bend, IN: St. Augustine's Press. (Original work published 1957)

Pinckaers, S. T. (1978). *Le renouveau de la morale.* Paris, France: Téqui.

Pinckaers, S. T. (1995). *Sources of Christian ethics.* Washington, DC: The Catholic University of America Press. (Original work published 1985)

Pinckaers, S. T. (2005). *The Pinckaers reader: Renewing Thomistic moral theology* (J. Berkman & C. S. Titus, Eds.). Washington, DC: The Catholic University of America Press.

Pius XI. (1930). *Casti connubii* [Encyclical, on Christian marriage]. Vatican City, Vatican: Libreria Editrice Vaticana.

Plante, T. G., & Thoresen, C. E. (2012). Spirituality, religion, and psychological counseling. In L. Miller (Ed.), *Psychology and spirituality* (pp. 388–409). Oxford, United Kingdom: Oxford University Press.

Plato. (1961a). *Philebus* (R. Hackforth, Trans.). In E. Hamilton & H. Cairns (Eds.), *The collected dialogues of Plato: Including the letters* (pp. 1086–1150). Princeton, NJ: Princeton University Press. (Original work composed ca. 360 BC)

Plato. (1961b). *Republic* (P. Shorey, Trans.). In E. Hamilton & H. Cairns (Eds.), *The collected dialogues of Plato: Including the letters* (pp. 575–844). Princeton, NJ: Princeton University Press. (Original work composed ca. 360 BC)

Post, S. G. (Ed). (2007). *Altruism and health: Perspectives from empirical research.* Oxford, United Kingdom: Oxford University Press.

Rand, K. L., & Cheavens, J. S. (2011). Hope theory. In S. J. Lopez & C. R. Snyder (Eds.), *The Oxford handbook of positive psychology* (2nd ed., pp. 323–344). Oxford, United Kingdom: Oxford University Press.

Ratzinger, J. (1995). *From the beginning: A Catholic understanding of the story of creation and the fall* (B. Ramsey, Trans.). Grand Rapids, MI: Eerdmans.

Ricœur, P. (1992). *Oneself as another.* Chicago, IL: University of Chicago Press (Original work published 1990)

Rist, J. (2009). The divided self: A classical perspective. In C. S. Titus (Ed.), *The psychology of character and virtue* (pp. 21–41). Arlington, VA: The Institute for the Psychological Sciences Press.

Rizzolatti, G., & Sinigaglia, C. (2008). *Mirrors in the brain: How our minds share actions and emotions* (F. Anderson, Trans.). New York, NY: Oxford University Press.

Roberts, R. C., & Woods, W. J. (2007). *Intellectual virtues: An essay in regulative epistemology.* Oxford, United Kingdom: University of Oxford Press.

Rogers, C. R. (2012). *On becoming a person: A therapist's view of psychotherapy.* Boston, MA: Houghton Mifflin Harcourt. (Original work published 1961)

Rousseau, J. (1979). *Emile: Or on education* (A. Bloom, Trans.). New York, NY: Basic Books. (Original work published 1762)

Russell, D. C. (Ed.) (2013). *The Cambridge companion*

to virtue ethics. Cambridge, United Kingdom: Cambridge University Press.

Sartre, J. P. (2007). *Existentialism is a humanism* (C. Macomber, Trans.). New Haven, CT: Yale University Press. (Original work published 1946)

Scheler, M. (2008). *The nature of sympathy*. London, United Kingdom: Routledge

Schimmel, S. (1997). *The seven deadly sins: Jewish, Christian, and classical reflections on human psychology*. Oxford, United Kingdom: Oxford University Press.

Schmitz, K. (2007). *The texture of being: Essays in first philosophy*. Washington, DC: The Catholic University of America Press.

Schmitz, K. (2009). *Person and psyche*. Arlington, VA: The Institute for the Psychological Sciences Press.

Seligman, M. E. P. (2011). *Flourish: A visionary new understanding of happiness and well-being*. New York, NY: Atria Books.

Seligman, M. E. P. (2002). *Authentic happiness: Using the new positive psychology to realize your potential for lasting fulfillment*. New York, NY: Atria Paperback.

Shatz, C. J. (1992). The developing brain. *Scientific American, 267*, 60–67.

Sherwin, M. S. (2009). Infused virtue and the effects of acquired vice: A test case for the Thomistic theory of infused cardinal virtues. *The Thomist, 73*, 29–52.

Singer, P. (2010). *The life you can save: How to do your part to end world poverty*. New York, NY: Random House.

Singer, P. (2011). *Practical ethics*. Cambridge, United Kingdom: Cambridge University Press. (Original work published 1980)

Slote, M. (2010). *Moral sentimentalism*. Oxford, United Kingdom: Oxford University Press.

Spitzer, R. J. (2010). *New proofs for the existence of God: Contributions of contemporary physics and philosophy*. Grand Rapids, MI: Eerdmans.

Spitzer, R. J. (2011). *Ten universal principles: A brief philosophy of the life issues*. San Francisco, CA: Ignatius Press.

Spitzer, R. J. (2015a). *Finding true happiness: Satisfying our restless hearts*. Vol. 1 of *Happiness, suffering, and transcendence*. San Francisco, CA: Ignatius Press.

Spitzer, R. J. (2015b). *The soul's upward yearning: Clues to our transcendent nature from experience and reason*. Vol. 2 of *Happiness, suffering, and transcendence*. San Francisco, CA: Ignatius Press.

Spitzer, R. J. (2016). *God so loved the world: Clues to our transcendent destiny from the revelation of Jesus*. Vol. 3 of *Happiness, suffering, and transcendence*. San Francisco, CA: Ignatius Press.

Spitzer, R. J. (2017). *The light shines on in the darkness: Transforming suffering through faith*. Vol. 4 of *Happiness, suffering, and transcendence*. San Francisco, CA: Ignatius Press.

Stein, E. (1996). *Essays on woman: The collected works of Edith Stein* (2nd ed.) (L. Gelber & R. Leuven, Eds.; F. M. Oben, Trans.). Washington, DC: Institute for Carmelite Studies Publications. (Original work published 1932)

Tallis, R. (2011). *Aping mankind: Neuromania, Darwinitis and the misrepresentation of humanity*. Durham, United Kingdom: Acumen Press.

Tallis, R. (2014). *Reflections of a metaphysical flâneur and other essays*. New York, NY: Routledge.

Timpe, K., & Boyd, C. A. (Eds.). (2014). *Virtues and their vices*. Oxford, United Kingdom: Oxford University Press.

Titus, C. S. (2006). *Resilience and the virtue of fortitude: Aquinas in dialogue with the psychosocial sciences*. Washington, DC: The Catholic University of America Press.

Titus, C. S. (2010). Moral development and connecting the virtues: Aquinas, Porter, and the flawed saint. In R. Hütter & M. Levering (Eds.), *Ressourcement Thomism: Sacred doctrine, the sacraments, and the moral life* (pp. 330–352). Washington, DC: The Catholic University of America Press.

Titus, C. S. (2013a). The use of developmental psychology in ethics. Beyond Kohlberg and Seligman? In F. Doridot et al. (Eds.), *Ethical governance of emerging technologies development* (pp. 268–288). Hershey, PA: IGI Global.

Titus, C. S. (2013b). Vertus. In E. Gaziaux, D. Müller, & L. Lemoine (Eds.), *Dictionnaire encyclopédique d'éthique chrétienne* (pp. 2073–2093). Paris, France: Cerf.

Titus, C. S. (2017). Aquinas, Seligman, and positive psychology: A Christian approach to the use of the virtues in psychology. *Journal of Positive Psychology, 12*(5), 447–458.

United States Conference of Catholic Bishops (USCCB). (2009). *Ethical and religious directives for Catholic health care services* (5th ed.). Washington, DC: Author.

van Deurzen, E. (2008). *Psychotherapy and the quest for happiness.* London, United Kingdom: Sage.

Van Slyke, J. A. (2014). Moral psychology, neuroscience, and virtue: From moral judgment to moral character. In K. Timpe & C. A. Boyd (Eds.), *Virtues and their vices* (pp. 459–480). Oxford, United Kingdom: Oxford University Press.

Vatican II, Council. (1965). *Gaudium et spes* [Pastoral constitution on the Church in the modern world]. Vatican City, Vatican: Libreria Editrice Vaticana.

Vitz, P. C. (1994). *Psychology as religion: The cult of self-worship* (2nd ed.). Grand Rapids, MI: Eerdmans.

Wilcox, W. B., Anderson, J. R., Doherty, W. J., Eggebeen, D, Ellison, C. G., Galston, W. A., … Wallerstein, J., et al. (2011). *Why marriage matters: Thirty conclusions from the social sciences* (3rd ed.). New York, NY: Institute for American Values.

Wojtyła, K. (1993). *Love and responsibility* (H. T. Willetts, Trans.). San Francisco, CA: Ignatius Press. (Original work published 1960)

Wojtyła, K. (2011). *Man in the field of responsibility* (K. W. Kemp & Z. M. Kieroń, Trans.). South Bend, IN: St. Augustine's Press. (Original work published 1991)

World Health Organization. (2012). Health. Retrieved May 24, 2012. http://www.who.int/topics/mental_health/en/

Worthington, E. L., Jr. (2003). *Forgiving and reconciling: Bridges to wholeness and hope* (rev. ed.). Downers Grove, IL: InterVarsity Press.

Worthington, E. L., Jr., Lavelock, C., Van Tongeren, D. R., Jennings, D. J., Gartner, A. L., Davis, D. E., & Hook, J. N. (2014). Virtue in positive psychology. In K. Timpe & C. A. Boyd (Eds.), *Virtues and their vices* (pp. 433–458). Oxford, United Kingdom: Oxford University Press.

Young, L., & Alexander, B. (2012). *The chemistry between us: Love, sex, and the science of attraction.* New York, NY: Penguin.

Zagzebski, L. (1996). *Virtues of the mind.* Cambridge, United Kingdom: Cambridge University Press.

Zagzebski, L. (2009). *On epistemology.* Belmont, CA: Wadsworth.

Zagzebski, L. (2017). *Exemplarist moral theory.* Oxford, United Kingdom: Oxford University Press.

Życiński, J. (2006). *God and evolution: Fundamental questions of Christian evolutionism* (K. W. Kemp & Z. Maślanka, Trans.). Washington, DC: The Catholic University of America Press.

Chapter 12

Interpersonally Relational

CRAIG STEVEN TITUS, PAUL C. VITZ, AND
WILLIAM J. NORDLING

ABSTRACT: This chapter explores the philosophical premise that the human being is interpersonally relational. The influence of individualism in contemporary psychology, philosophy, and spirituality puts human interpersonal relatedness and community second to the right of the individual to autonomy. Different types of individualism are found in the writings of psychologists, such as Rogers (1961/2012), and philosophers, such as Sartre (1946/2007) and Nietzsche (1885/2006). However, the Christian and classical philosophical tradition affirms that "life in its true sense ... is a relationship" (Benedict XVI, 2007, §28). Representatives of other schools of psychology, such as Adlerian, Sullivanian, and later interpersonal therapies, attachment theory, family systems, Emotion-Focused Therapy, and positive psychology, have placed much more emphasis on relationships than have individualist approaches. This chapter recovers and defends a classical and Christian philosophical notion of the person as relational by nature and as expressing undeniable interpersonal features. The person should be considered relational, since persons (a) flourish through interpersonal receiving and giving, (b) are centered in love, and (c) have a natural desire to be in an interpersonal relationship with the source of being, namely, God. Human interpersonal relationships, moreover, have different significant characteristics according to whether they are spousal, parental and filial, brotherly and sisterly, or that of friends or community.

Based on a classical Christian philosophical vision of the person, this chapter offers dialectical, narrative, and experiential support for understanding the person as inherently relational. The person, even in his or her weaknesses, manifests signs that only in social contexts is flourishing stable and long-lasting. Giving and receiving are the basis— on every level, from sensory-perceptual-cognitive and emotional to intellectual and spiritual—for practices of justice and love.

This chapter also explores how the deep natural desires for family and social contact lead toward explicit but varied interpersonal relationships (1) with parents, siblings, spouses, and children, inside the home; (2) with friends, colleagues, and strangers, outside the home; and (3) ultimately with the source of being and interpersonal relationship (whom Christians and others call God).

In contrast, modern and contemporary psychology and philosophy have had a strong individualist bias, which is found in the works of Freud and much of the neo-psychoanalytic tradition, including Jung's self-realization (individuation) (1981) and the works of Nietzsche (1885/2006), Rogers (1961/2012), and Sartre (1946/2007). Since the Enlightenment, the focus on the individual has brought a heightened attention to the study of the person (see, for example, Locke, 1689/1980, Chapter 8, §§95–99, pp. 52–53). But it has also precipitated short-sightedness concerning social theory, communal practice, and the basic relationality of human beings (Lee, 2012; Schmitz, 2009). Sociological studies have suggested that individualist biases and social policies contribute to the breakdown of the family and other social units and supports (Putnam, 2001; Wilcox et al., 2011). These individualist biases, as personally and socially expressed, often manifest a social skepticism and reduce understanding interpersonal phenomena to be the result of behavioral imprinting or evolutionary pressures. In this line of thought, Dawkins (2008) posits that interpersonal phenomena are merely the result of genetic and environmental pressures that promote kin or species survival, determined self-serving tendencies, or indiscriminate and superficial social behaviors.

Much of the social impact of this individualistic bias has occurred through changes in law, in which the autonomous individual and his choices for actualization are emphasized at the expense of the others involved. This understanding of law and legal rights has strongly influenced the decision on abortion, no-fault divorce, and same-sex marriage (Alvaré, 2015; Bradley, 2012).

From the origins of modern psychology, the exclusive focus on the single isolated individual or patient, without any inclusion of the significant others in the person's life, implicitly emphasized the autonomous individual. Only since marital and family therapies became readily available (well past the middle of the twentieth century) have we seen the inclusion of couples and family members together in therapy sessions.

As is seen in this chapter, the Catholic Christian vision of interpersonal relationships offers a constructive contrast to such individualist views. The chapter addresses the natural qualities of receiving, giving, and being interpersonal, as found in various self-sacrificial activities of parents, teachers, firemen, and military personnel. It focuses on the nature of one of the most basic experiences of human life, namely, love, the epitome of which is found in unselfish giving and, from a Christian perspective, in a Christ-like, sacrificial laying down of one's life for others. The chapter also addresses the major human relationships with spouses, family, friends, communities, and God.

Receptive and Interpersonal

Persons cannot be fully understood without adequate consideration of their basic relationality, being a person in relation to other persons (see Figure 12.1). The person is by nature in relationship, as an intentional subject (an "I") in relation to another intentional subject (a "You") (Buber, 1923/1971), who together manifest a community (a "We"). More than a grammatical construct, the plurality of I and you manifest the reality of community, pointing toward the primordial, creative, and ultimate communion of persons. A humble and generous interpersonal receptive and giving stance toward people, the cosmos, and God underlies flourishing. However, the

Figure 12.1. Philosophical Premises of the Catholic Christian Meta-Model of the Person

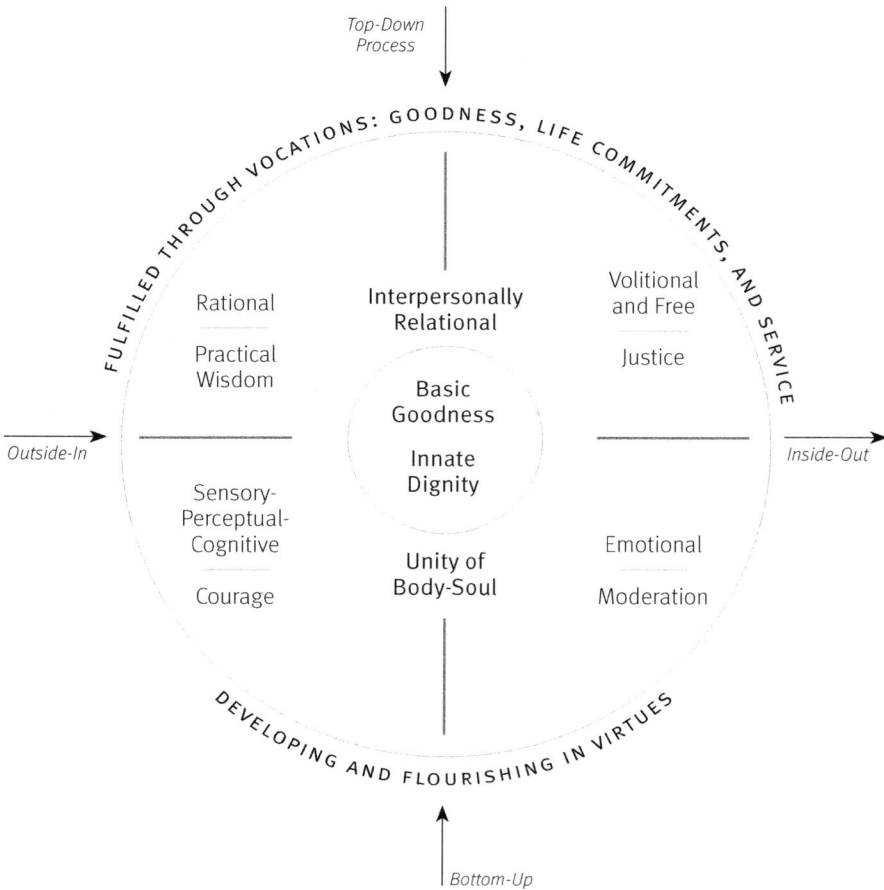

pervasive effects of individualism and rationalism have negatively influenced not only the basic notions of the person in modern Western culture, but also in present notions of family life and social cohesion.

What Is the History of the Notion of the Person

As already noted, the original biblical and Greek notions of the human being are solidly rooted in being interpersonally relational and in an in-

telligent and free search for the common good and for personal flourishing (Benedict XVI, 2005). The life of political and religious communities structure the life of persons and families and society (Bellah, Madsen, Sullivan, Swidler, & Tipton, 2007). The biblical narrative tells of the creation of human beings in the context of a family (Adam and Eve) and of a people uniquely chosen and called by God to enter into a covenant relationship of love and respect (Abraham, Isaac, Jacob, Moses). The two tablets of the Ten

Commandments outline the types of relationships that the First, or Old Testament, Covenant promoted, namely, relationships with God and with parents, families, friends, neighbors, and even with strangers.

Greek philosophers, such as Plato (*Republic*) and Aristotle (*Nicomachean Ethics* and *Politics*), as well as the Bible (St. Paul's letter to the Ephesians, Chapter 5) and the early Christian writers, such as Augustine (*City of God* and *Confessions*) and Gregory the Great (*Morals on the Book of Job*), express interpersonally relational ways of thinking and acting, and even feeling.

The late Middle Ages and the modern era, with the advent of nominalism and romanticism, spelled a focus on the individual as an autonomous agent in need of being freed from the control of family, state, and religion. This modern individualist tendency has undercut a deeper understanding of the relational nature of the person (Taylor, 2007). The loss of a communal vision of the person and the radical turn to the subject can be traced through the work of many thinkers, such as Descartes (1641/1996), Hume (1740/2000), and Kant (1788/2002). And individualism has become a central tenet of modern thought, political theory, and psychology, as already mentioned. Modern thought has changed the notion of community and person. It has had a negative impact on the rights and duties that were inherently part of such relationships as marriage and family. For example, the introduction of "no-fault" divorce has greatly weakened the natural institution of marriage, which by its nature is lifelong and indissoluble (Fagan & Churchill, 2012; Wilcox et al., 2011).

The Catholic Christian Meta-Model of the Person makes a contribution to the recovery and defense of a vision of the human being as interpersonally relational, intelligent, and free, by nature of existing and being ordered toward

flourishing, goodness, truth, spousal and family life, society, and beauty (metaphysics and ontology). Our deepest desires concern becoming united to persons to whom we are committed in love.

Is the classical notion of the person relational?
There is a definition of the person that has served as a constant reference, even though it has been interpreted in quite opposing ways. This popular source for defining the person is proffered by the Christian philosopher Boethius. His undisputed classical definition of a person has been misinterpreted in three ways: in non-relational, individualist, and rationalistic ways (Clarke, 1993, 2009). Boethius's (ca. 513/1973a) definition reads: "A person is an individual substance of a rational nature" (Chapter III). His mention of "individual substance," however, in no way should be read to override the very interpersonal framework of the classical and Christian perspective that Boethius in fact defended with aid from prosocial Greek philosophers (such as Aristotle, ca. 350 BC/1941b, 1253a2) and the Bible. Boethius (ca. 519/1973b) affirms that the name "person" itself refers to the relation of human persons in community and to the divine persons in the one God. Considering the divine persons, Boethius says: "Every word that refers to the person signifies relation" (as cited by Aquinas, 1273/1981, I, 29.4 sc). Aquinas builds upon Boethius's definition, explaining how the word "person" in God signifies a relationship between one divine person and the other persons. In this respect, Aquinas argues that the word "'person' means relation not only by use and custom ... but also by force of its own proper signification" (Aquinas, 1273/1981, I, 29.4). Aquinas's insight here into the meaning of the word "person" (as inherently denoting a relationship) serves a critical role in contemporary personalist

trains of thought and in correction of individu-alistic perspectives (Clark, 1993). A person finds a unique dimension of meaning in community and relationship (Wojtyła, 1991/2011). From his Christian perspective, Aquinas (1273/1981) iden-tifies relationship as an integral aspect of what it is to be a person, and this is found in a special way in the Christian understanding of God: the mutual loving and self-giving relation among Fa-ther, Son, and Holy Spirit is of the very Essence of God (I, 39.1), the God in whose image we are made.

From a philosophical or reason-based per-spective, thinkers (such as Wojtyła, 1961/1993b, 1974/1993d) observe that a human person is by nature relational and rooted in community and in the common good. Thus, failures of commu-nities, broken families, and disruptive relation-ships have a harmful impact on a person because of the basic desire and need for experiences of unity and communion.

From a faith-based perspective, within the Christian tradition, Roman Catholic, Orthodox, and other Christian communions have consis-tently understood that the human person is re-lational by nature, as created in the image of the triune God (Augustine, 426/1991; Boethius, ca. 519/1973b; Gregory Nazianzen (ca. 381/1894); Zizioulas, 1985/1997). The greatest command-ment—to love God and to love neighbor—is an explicit affirmation of the relational nature of human beings. Moreover, human relationality is manifest in the capacities, virtues, and char-acter that govern the moral, social, and spiritual aspects of living well. For example, the human person manifests inherent relational capacities and vocations, exemplified by newborns' imme-diate responses to and attachment to their moth-er. These tendencies develop and influence the way the child will be caring, just, and loving in later interpersonal relationships.

What Are Some Undeniable Human Social Features?

It is only because of social collaboration, par-enting, and friendship that humans can survive infancy and make progress in childhood and adolescence. The major accomplishments of the human race are rooted in our relationships: lan-guage and literature, arts and science, civic or-der and laws, and so on. Moreover, there are the other unpremeditated factors that evidence our prosocial instinctual and unconscious capaci-ties (such as the higher order perceptions and evaluative capacities; see Chapter 13, "Sensory-Perceptual-Cognitive"). There are also the resid-ual results of prosocial self-conscious past choic-es, regular practices, and training (Commission on Children at Risk, 2003; MacIntyre, 1999). For example, in a mother's prosocial kindness and compassion, shown in her feelings, intent, language, and behavior, we find different indica-tions of a basic positive social capacity (nature), expressing natural inclinations toward the di-verse forms of family and social relationships.

Although cogent arguments can identify neurological, behavioral, evolutionary, and determinant influences on human social na-ture, an analysis of the underlying psychologi-cal states and moral intentions reveals that the self-conscious and unconscious foundations for human relational acts cannot satisfactorily be reduced to neurobiology, survival instincts, or cultural conditioning (Beauregard, 2012; Beauregard & O'Leary, 2008; Cozolino, 2010, 2014; Siegel, 2012). Indeed, personal self-reports reveal how common is our experience of proso-cial reasoning and the importance of our rela-tional commitments (Commission on Children at Risk, 2003; Goleman, 2006; Hoffman, 2001). Furthermore, representatives of social schools of psychology have tended to put importance on the interpersonal dimension of psychology and psychotherapy: see, for example, Vygotsky (1962, 1978), on how interpersonal interaction is the basis for developing conscious cognition; see the schools of object relations (Winnicott, 1964), interpersonal psychology (Sullivan, 1953), and family therapy (Bowen, 1985; Greenberg & Johnson, 1988) on the representation of family relationships in psychological well-being; see attachment theory (Bowlby, 1973, 1969/1982, 1988; Ainsworth, Blehar, Waters, & Wall, 1978; Cassidy & Shaver, 1999) on styles of attachment and on well-being; and see positive psychology (Lopez & Snyder, 2009) on interpersonal virtues, such as compassion, empathy, forgiveness, gratitude, and love.

Do We Receive Before We Give?

A full examination of humans as relational beings requires recognizing that human beings are intrinsically receptive. There are different levels of receiving (and giving) though. First, from conception, we receive our basic genetic code, nutrition, and care from our mothers and fathers. At the same time and at the most basic level, from a Christian perspective, our spiritual souls are the direct gift from God, who gives the "breath of life" (Gen 2:7). Each person's human nature is constituted of a body-soul unity, which is a gift from God, with contributions from the mother and the father (Vatican II, 1964, §14.1; see also Chapter 8, "Personal Wholeness," as well as Chapter 5, "Basic Psychological Support").

Second, beyond this fundamental level of receiving life, we also continue to receive support for life and the means of growth and healing throughout life. However, we receive in our early years love and care from our mother or mother-figure, and then from other family members, where our attachment needs are normally met. The ongoing reception of the inter-personal gifts of other people (thoughts, words, and deeds) contributes to the formation of our character and personality throughout life. However, our receiving is incomplete if we do not express gratitude for the gifts and give what we have received to others in turn. That is, we must not only receive from God and others what we need to live and to live well, but we must also give in turn to live and to live well, as we see next (Acts 20:35; 2 Cor 9:7; Aquinas, 1273/1981, II-II, 106.1–3).

Is it necessary to give in order to flourish? One of the most basic interpersonal acts is to express gratitude for gifts that have been received and, in a related way, to give freely in turn, and not only to those who have given freely to us. There are particular types of expressions of gratitude for the gifts given by parents, family, friends, and God. More than merely expressing vital interdependency or a social duty, the communication of gratitude and the act of giving in turn together constitute a pathway to flourishing (MacIntyre, 1999). Human acts serve personal flourishing only inasmuch as they serve interpersonal flourishing. There is no truly solitary act or happiness. Each person is called to serve the good of other persons and the common good, even when caring for himself. In contrast, there is also an exaggerated accent that can be put upon giving. If giving is raised to be more important than receiving, there can be a masochistic, self-destructive drive, or a "work for work's sake" mentality, which can be associated with a disregard for others as well as a disregard for receptive contemplation (Pieper, 1952/2009).

Receptivity, giving, and gratitude are significant in family life and friendship, as well as throughout the therapeutic process. For example, the therapeutic relationship requires a receptive stance for empathy and a self-giving element on the part of both client and therapist. People may find it difficult to accept what other people offer, and that difficulty can have a number of causes, including a dearth of attachment, acceptance, and love at home and in their communities. When a patient lacks self-confidence and trust in others, he or she may have difficulty receiving the empathetic support offered in the therapeutic process (as well as at home and in friendship). The initial task of the therapist is to establish trust in the therapeutic alliance and to restore the patient's self-worth and confidence in others. Likewise, a friend's goal is to establish trust that more freely receives the gifts and shares the goods that constitute human flourishing. Furthermore, depression and other signs of languishing may have roots in short-circuited receptivity and giving. For example, it has been proposed that a person suffering from ruminative depression may benefit from a shift in attitude toward being thankful for what he or she has received and from intentional acts of gratitude (Gudan, 2010).

Both receptivity and action are emphasized in the Christian understanding of self-giving love. Nonetheless, from the beginning to the end, the ultimate priority is placed on reception. It is God who first gives life and all good things when he creates. He continues to hold all creation in existence and to give profoundly of himself to all human beings, especially through the Son's incarnation and crucifixion, and through the sacraments (Jas 1:17). We have to receive before we can give ourselves to others totally in the way that God gives himself totally in Christ. Active participation in this interpersonal principle recognizes both material and spiritual needs, according to the first letter of John: "But if anyone has the world's goods and sees his brother in need, yet closes his heart against him, how does God's love abide in him? ... Let us not love in word or speech but in deed and in truth" (1 Jn 3:17–18). Receptivity and self-giving are interrelated by nature, as a duty to be open to receive from and give to others, and in full flourishing these are expressed in love or charity.

Centered in Love

The person is centered in love, which is the most basic of human dispositions and actions. This general principle may be widely accepted, but for different reasons. From a Catholic Christian vision of the person, we need to ask about love's roots and how love is involved in human vocations, character, and behavior.

What Are the Sources of Love?

Even if psychological, philosophical, and spiritual approaches to the person may widely accept the significance of "love" for mankind, they bring different expertise for understanding the source, development, and end of love. Experience gives us a notion of the basic dy-

namic of the desire for the good; this dynamic can be philosophically understood as the basic natural and supernatural framework for love. "Love" is also identified as *friendship* (Jn 15:13; Aristotle, ca. 350 BC/1941a; Aelred of Rievaulx, ca. 1166/1974), *altruism* (Post, 2007), *eros* or *romanticism* (Nygren, 1930/1982; Scruton, 1986), and *charity* or *agapē* (Benedict XVI, 2005; Lewis, 1960; Pieper, 1997). In these different ways, love is a certain kind of "union and bond" (*unio et nexus*) of feeling and will between the lover and the loved (Aquinas, 1273/1981, I-II, 26.2 ob 2 & ad 2).

Psychological theories identify the diverse causal mechanisms and functioning that underlie the cognitive, emotional, behavioral, and bio-physiological processes that in diverse ways have been associated with love. For example, attachment theory (Bowlby, 1969/1982, 1973) offers insights on the difference between being securely or insecurely attached to one's mother (or primary care giver). Attachment theory identifies the biological, cognitive, and social aspects of the development of interpersonal attachment. There are indications that attachment styles (secure or insecure) make a difference for relationships across the lifespan (Mikulincer & Shaver, 2007).

In one way or another, the flourishing or languishing of interpersonal love can be understood through the lens of character and the virtues and vices (such as justice and injustice, perseverance and unpredictability, self-control and self-indulgence, forgiveness and hatred). It also underlies a person's vocations (call to basic goodness; call to marriage and family; and call to work and service). A person's sense of inherent goodness and dignity develops and is affected by the love that he receives and the love that he perceives throughout life. The state of one's loving interpersonal relationships and self-understanding (or identity) depends on experiencing and expressing love, and it can also be seen as significant in therapeutically addressing disorders of anxiety, depression, and addiction, among others.

What Is the Nature of Interpersonal Love?

From a Christian philosophical viewpoint, the highest expression of interpersonal communication is centered in love. This love involves sacrificial self-giving (John Paul II, 2006). It is symbolized, in the spiritual and romantic traditions, as emanating from the "heart" or the center of the person. The prophet Jeremiah announces

that God will write the law on the heart of the people (Jer 31:33). This law and greatest commandment is to love God with "all your heart, and with all your soul, and with all your might" (Deut 6:5; Mt 22:37; Mk 12:29–30; Lk 10:27). Moreover, St. Paul says that hope is founded in "God's love [which] has been poured into our hearts through the Holy Spirit who has been given to us" (Rom 5:5).

In order to understand further the nature of love, we need to distinguish emotive attractions from voluntary commitments. While having a unity of purpose, love takes different forms depending on the type of interpersonal relationship at hand (for example, between wife and husband, mother and son, father and daughter, between friends, between strangers, and between the person and God). The love understood as charity informs and interconnects the other virtues, while being served by them as well, especially the virtues that concern marital, family, friendship, civic, and religious relationships, through justice, religion, chastity, courage, and obedience (Chapter 11, "Fulfilled in Virtue"). Relationships that overemphasize pleasure, utility, and need, or even rights, can lead to ethical compromise and suffering. However, relationships that give due focus to the other as person bring true flourishing and healing (Chapter 25, "Virtue in Mental Health Practice").

What Are the Basic Four Names of Love?

We experience affection (*storgē*) toward the basic goodness of other people and things (Lewis, 1960). We find security in attachments to parents and loved ones (Hazan & Shaver, 1987; Mikulincer & Shaver, 2007; McEntee, Dy-Liacco, & Haskins, 2013). We receive and give love in friendship (*philia*), according to a typology of pleasure, utility, or virtue-based friendship (Aristotle, ca. 350 BC/1941a). We exchange the gift of love in courtship and marriage (*eros*). In the deepest human form of love, we love each other and mutually give of ourselves in the virtue of charity or friendship-love (*agapē*) (Jn 15:13; Aquinas, 1273/1981, II-II, 23.1). This *agapē* love is made concrete in committed relationships that represent mutual self-gift, such as between husband and wife, brother and sister, Christian friends, or between the consecrated or ordained person and God and the Church.

Although some thinkers find an inevitable conflict between *eros* and *agapē* (Nygren, 1930/1982), others find that the digressions of love (in our affections, friendships, sexual relations) can be purified by true love or *agapē*. For example, they identify how, at the highest level, *eros* and *agapē* need each other (Nédoncelle, 1966), and how *eros* serves to draw people out of themselves in attraction to another, while *agapē* completes love through committed and purified self-gift (Benedict XVI, 2005). Moreover, they identify how the spousal vocation of each person—the call to be attentive to being man or woman—involves a movement of *eros* and a completion of *agapē* that underlies each vocational state. The differences of man and woman are lived out initially in the distinct vocation to be a boy or girl (as a son or daughter within a family, as a young male or female in chaste relationships, as a young man or woman in courtship, as a married couple, and then as a widow or widower). Moreover, the differences of man and woman are lived out in the special call to religious life and priesthood. In these vocations, persons must also be attentive to being man or woman in their commitment to God and others through chaste love and service (John Paul II, 2006, p. 528). The spousal meaning of human life is fulfilled in all of these callings and ultimately in communion with God. The relationship between man and woman is addressed in Chapter 9, "Man and Woman." And the distortions of love are treated throughout the volume (Kolodziejczak, 2006).

What Is Emotional Love?

While love is relational by nature, not every instance of "love" has the same origin, development, or end. Charity love, or *agapē*, requires a commitment of the will that is not simply sentimental love or affection (Wojtyła, 1960/1993a). But, in general, human emotional love is an important aspect of human affectivity that develops through three stages called love, desire, and joy (delight or pleasure) (Aristotle, ca. 350 BC/1941a; Aquinas, 1273/1981, I-II, 25.2).

First, the knowledge of a good thing or person attracts us. It creates emotional love, according to its meaning and vocation. We are attracted to the good as it discloses its own goodness to us, and we become attached (connected) and bonded (integrated) to it in turn. Nevertheless, every gift that is given, but not yet fully received, involves an imperfect love. Love must grow through experiences of presence, absence, and renewed presence, as well as through attachment, detachment, and deepened attachment. The splendor, truth, and revelation of the good create desire and drive. This process of attraction and being drawn out of oneself underlies the first attachment of love. We long to be fully united with the radiant other.

Second, this desire stirs us to act. We plan, work, sacrifice, and sometimes risk our very lives to attain or to be united to the source of love. We desire not simply to be in relationship with a personal source of love but to be united with the beloved permanently.

Third, until we actually receive the promised gift, neither will our thirst be assuaged nor our whole person be at rest. When the good is received, it can be given in turn (John Paul II, 2006). In the two movements of being drawn out of self (to receive from the other) and of giving of self (what has been received), we are capable of loving not only natural goods and persons but also divine ones (Benedict XVI, 2005). The other alternatives are resentment (of the love as thwarted desire), forgetfulness (of the love as eclipsed from our mind and affections), indifference (to the love that is present or promised), or despair (of the previously hoped-for love as impossible).

What Does Psychology and Mental Health Practice Say About Love?

Contemporary psychologies of love have sought to explicate the importance of love for growth and flourishing in human life (Titus & Scrofani, 2012, pp. 120–122). Notable examples of secular theories are those of Erikson (1968/1994), Bowlby (1982, 1988), Fromm (1956), May (1969), as well as Hazan and Shaver (1987). Erikson (1968/1994) construes human growth as progressing in stages from individuality toward mutuality and, finally, community, where love finds a fuller expression. The attachment theory of Bowlby (1982, 1988) and Ainsworth, Blehar, Waters, and Wall (1978) identifies the qualitative significance of interpersonal attachment for receiving and giving love across the lifespan. They note the special importance found in the mother-child dyad, and their typology of attachment (secure, anxious-avoidant, anxious-preoccupied, disorganized) provides a basis for understanding a psychology of love. Of special interest are the empirical findings about the range of love, from selfish to sacrificial. This range affects psychological capacities for relationship or isolation; secure or insecure attachments; and the expression of love, indifference, and hate (Titus & Scrofani, 2012).

Studies on ordered and disordered love serve as a reference point for dialogue between secular and Christian approaches about understanding love (Kolodziejczak, 2006; Lee, 2012; Sodergren, 2009).

What Does a Christian Notion of Love Offer?

In the fullest sense, including the diverse kinds of human knowledge and affect, love perfects the will and other affective capacities as love perfects the whole person interpersonally. Such fullness or perfection is always in process and in need of further purification, as attractions and friendships and romance need to be purified by self-giving (Benedict XVI, 2005).

In the Christian tradition, the perfect love of complete self-gift is epitomized in the life, death, and resurrection of Jesus, who is the ultimate model of charity love. This highest form of love is discussed in terms of the gift of the theological virtue of charity (love) and the way that this highest love informs the moral infused virtues, such as patience, justice, and courage. St. Paul describes the characteristics of this Christian love:

> Love is patient and kind; love is not jealous or boastful; it is not arrogant or rude. Love does not insist on its own way; it is not irritable or resentful; it does not rejoice at wrong, but rejoices in the right. (1 Cor 13:4–13)

The Gospel of John makes friendship-love (*agapē*) the greatest form of self-gift: "Greater love has no man than this, that a man lay down his life for his friends" (Jn 15:13). This gift of self is found in every vocation. For example, there is the sacrifice found in the mother's persistent care for her child across the lifespan. There is the self-gift of the husband and father, who takes a second job in order to pay for his child's education. Such self-giving love's epitome is found in God, who is love and who shares divine love. The first letter of John equates love and God: "He who does not love does not know God; for God is love" (1 Jn 4:8). Benedict XVI (2005) highlights biblical anthropology's capacity to express a full notion of love that knits together emotional attraction and volitional self-gift. The theme of love and its place in development and healing is found throughout the rest of this chapter and this volume as well (see especially Chapter 10, "Fulfilled Through Vocation," Chapter 16, "Volitional and Free," and Chapter 17, "Created in the Image of God". For a more complete treatment of the theological virtue of charity love, see Chapter 17, "Created in the Image of God," and Chapter 19, "Redeemed.")

Relationship with God

A classical perspective and a Christian worldview recognize that humans are innately social and religious beings. That some people express antisocial behavior, anti-religious views, and agnostic beliefs does not disprove this point. Humans naturally tend to the goods of family, friendship, society, and life with God, which each in their own way contribute to flourishing and health (Koenig, King, & Carson, 2012; McCauley, 2011).

Is It Natural to Desire God?

We are naturally religious (McCauley, 2011). By our intellectual and affective nature, we not only seek to know ourselves, but we also long to know others. We seek to know the meaning of our life and reality itself. We are attracted to the absolutely first origin of all things and the final end of human flourishing, who is called God (Feser, 2017).

However, some thinkers deny that there is a personal, super-intelligent origin of love, who is called God (Dawkins, 2008; Dennett, 1995; Freud, 1927/2012). Although religious belief is relatively high in America, the influence of atheists (Feser, 2008) and the influence of secular psychology have made this a secular age (Taylor, 2007). Research, moreover, has suggested that other negative influences on belief in God come through defects in one's parental relationships, especially when parents are absent or abusive, or through neurological impairments (such as autism) that affect the capacity to have relationships (Vitz, 2013). Nonetheless, through the experiences of beauty, harmony, and personal goodness, and through the gift of faith, other people come to express belief in God or at least hope in his existence (Eph 2:8).

What Is the Natural Desire for God?

The desire for the ultimate and the absolute is not only expressed in revealed religion and grace-based theology (Cullen, 2012; de Lubac 1946/1998; Feingold, 2004; Long, 2010). This natural desire is also implicitly found in experiences of beauty and wonder and in the sense of meaning, in communion, and in the I-Thou relationship (Buber, 1923/1971). The natural desire for God is furthermore implicitly expressed in the arts and sciences and personal narratives, which express the personal desire for "more" (Giussani, 1997), for the ultimate, and for the transcendent (Heschel, 1954), while being a means for other people also to vividly experience this desire at intellectual and affective levels.

Over the last 70 years, advances in contemporary physics have provided a rational basis that complements traditional "proofs" for the existence of God (Davies, 2004; Feser, 2017; Spitzer, 2010). In addition to the classical approaches that identify God as the origin and goal of our natural inclinations and desires for goodness, truth, existence, relationship, and beauty (classical metaphysics), there are also complementary expressions that refer to our desire for God and understanding of God as "a unique, unconditioned, unrestricted, absolutely simple, super-intelligent, continuous Creator of all else that is" (Spitzer, 2010, p. 3).

The natural desire for God serves a special role in human experience. It is linked to the deepest longing for true flourishing. At the center of all natural inclinations to goodness (continued existence, love and family life, social harmony, and truth and beauty) is the implicit desire not only to know but also to be in communion with God. This desire is manifest in the longing for the Creator of all (first cause), the One who sustains life (efficient cause), the Source of meaning and order (formal cause), and the One toward whom we are attracted as the ultimate end of our life (final cause) (Aquinas, 1273/1981, I, 2.1–3; 1259/1953). Yet this natural desire is limited: the created human mind is finite, and, despite a person's strivings, he or she cannot even by way of revelation know the essence of God directly in this life (Aquinas, 1273/1981, I, 12.13 ad 1). Apart from receiving the beatific vision, the created lover can know the divine beloved only "in a mirror dimly" (1 Cor 13:12).

At the same time, the natural desire for God, when it is healed and elevated by grace, manifests a thirst for more, for ultimate personal fulfillment and communion. When the natural desire for God becomes explicit, the human person is not satisfied merely with knowledge that God exists, but desires even more to know what God is (Aquinas, 1273/1981, I-II, 3.8; 1265/1975, Chapter 50) as well as who God is (as a personal God of belief). The person so inclined and en-

flamed with love continuously strives to express what limited and indirect understanding can be attained of the essence of God in this life (Gregory of Nyssa, ca. 390/1978, §239, p. 116). In the words of Augustine (401/2007), "Our hearts are restless until they rest in God" (I.1.2).

What Is the Origin of Religious Practice?

There are natural and revealed sources of religious practice (Schmidt, 1935). First, the deep feeling of awe we feel when confronted with the order of the cosmos and the beauty of nature is a natural experience of wonder (Eliade, 1981; Otto, 1917/1958). This experience is communicated by natural symbols and expressed through particular rituals and practices (Bellah, 2011; Douglas, 1970/2003; Heschel, 1954). It draws mankind further toward the truth about creation and accompanies a natural desire to worship and thank God. This desire is the foundation of the diverse expressions of natural types of religion and spirituality (Maritain, 1932/1959, pp. 268–270). Religious practices express our need for contact with the ultimate source and end of life.

Second, a Catholic Christian perspective recognizes a revealed source of religious practice: a call to a personal relationship with God. The history of salvation is revealed as not only a source of spiritual (faith-based, theological) knowledge but also a basis for graced religious experience and practice. It is through prayer, through reading Scripture and celebrating the sacraments, and through other expressions of the gifts of faith, hope, and love that we worship, respect, and love God in a personal and communal way. As the Gospel of John says, "To all who received him, who believed in his name, he gave power to become children of God" (Jn 1:12). According to Christian revelation, the ultimate foundation of interpersonal relationships is the triune God, who is a unity (one God) in a community of love (three divine persons). In sum, while the desire for God underlies human nature, which is created for the "more" that God alone can offer, this desire is satisfied by God through revealed Christianity. The desire for God is also expressed through particular Christian vocations, with the three levels of callings (Chapter 10, "Fulfilled Through Vocation"). Negative, disordered, and hateful experiences, besides expressing real brokenness, can constitute a contrastive experience of the need for God. They also can be inadvertent vehicles to developing resilience and to generating hope for a divine offer of salvation.

Spousal Relationships and the Spousal Meaning of the Body

How Are Humans Made for Marriage?

Marriage has been practiced in different forms throughout history, most notably in monogamy and polygamy. The relationship between spouses is the primary natural bond among all social relationships (Augustine, 401/1955, Chapter 1). Marriage requires and builds upon the difference and the complementarity of the sexes. It is based on the meaning of the body as male or female with its inclination toward sexual union and personal commitment, and toward the care of offspring. Such a desire and tendency has moved many people to enter into commitments of marriage and to give themselves in sacrificial ways.

This mutual attraction, with personal commitment and communion, between man and woman is now often taken up and included in the nuptial vocation of man and woman (John Paul II, 2006, p. 257). Both the man and the woman are changed by their interaction of becoming husband and wife, father and mother. For example, even neuroscience demonstrates how marriage and childbearing influences the neurobiology of the mother and father in complementary ways (Wilcox & Kline, 2012, 2013).

The complementarity and difference of the attraction to the opposite sex need not be reduced to the physical or neurological level. It is not simply instinctive or the product of the sexual urge as expressed in the emotions and imagination. This attraction to the other sex is also directed by moral character and spiritual values, as well as by family and friends. This attraction is influenced by interpersonal relationships, that is, whether the man and woman are related as spouses or future spouses, parent and child, friends (of the same or different sexes), business associates, or strangers in the street (Budziszewski, 2012). These signs of natural inclinations to marriage are confirmed when the sexual attraction of spouses takes on a committed expression. Furthermore, from the nature of human dependency, especially but not exclusively at birth, and of the self-giving required to form a family that supports the needs of the young and the old, the healthy and the ill, marriages thrive best through lifelong indissoluble commitments between one man and one woman (Carlson & Mero, 2007; Maher, 2004; Waite & Gallagher, 2000; Wilcox et al., 2011).

For a further treatment of men and women as naturally made for marriage, and of marriage as a vocation and a sacrament, see Chapter 9, "Man and Woman", Chapter 10, "Fulfilled Through Vocation," and Chapter 19, "Redeemed."

What Is the Catholic Understanding of Marriage?

The Christian tradition understands that the nature of human love and the needs of spouses and of offspring support the practice of marriage as a lifelong, indissoluble, covenantal commitment between one man and one woman, through a mutual and total gift of self (in a true union). Spousal love is a unique type of interpersonal love formalized in a monogamous marriage that is open to the gift of new life (procreation) and committed to caring for children and the other goods of family (John Paul II, 2006; Müller, 2014). The husband and wife are called to be unique helpers and companions for each other in full flourishing, at natural and graced levels.

God did not make man to be alone but rather intended that man and woman should leave father and mother in order to be joined faithfully to each other and become one flesh in marriage (Gen 2:18–24; Mt 19:3–12; John Paul II, 2006). God has intended from the beginning that marriage should be lifelong, faithful, and fruitful. According to the Catholic tradition (Paul VI, 1968, §12), each act of married intercourse should have a double significance: openness to new life (procreation, including the care and education of the children) and the marriage union (mutual charity, aid, and support, as well as a valid outlet for sexual desire and enjoyment). Paul VI (1968) says: "Husband and wife, through that mutual gift of themselves, which is specific and exclusive to them alone, develop that union of two persons in which they perfect one another, cooperating with God in the generation and rearing of new lives" (§8).

Procreation, therefore, is not the sole end of the institution of marriage (Vatican II, 1965, §50; Burke, 2015, pp. 60–61). The bond of marriage remains and contributes to the well-being of the spouses even when children are not forthcoming (Augustine, 401/1955, Chapter 15). Growing in the nuptial bond constitutes the unitive meaning or purpose of the institution of marriage (Paul VI, 1968, §12). The unitive meaning of the relationship pertains to the natural companionship and friendship of the spouses (Augustine, 401/1955, Chapter 3).

God provides graces in the sacrament of Marriage for the spouses to face the challenges to their relationship, such as the challenges to intimacy, fidelity, and family. The sacrament of Marriage raises the natural institution of marriage to a new level of perfection, protecting it against attempts to redefine it or minimalize the nature of its indissoluble commitment. The spouses are images of God not only as unique persons but also together, as a spousal community (Chrysostom, ca. 400/1986, p. 75). This vision of the Christian couple is not static, but requires the active participation of the couple to respond to the call to marriage as a means to their flourishing and sanctification (O'Leary, 2007; Ouellet, 2005/2015; Petri, 2016; Scola, 2000/2005; Whitehead, 2007).

What Are the Grounds for Understanding Marriage as Indissoluble?

In order to understand the indissolubility of a sacramental marriage, it is helpful to observe the unique character it has as a participation in God's covenant with all humanity (*Catechism of the Catholic Church* [CCC], 2000, §1601, §1639). Thus, a sacramental marriage itself is a relationship that can be understood as a covenant between the spouses. In accordance with its covenantal character, those who enter into the bond of marriage do so with irrevocable personal consent (Vatican II, 1965, §48). This irrevocable consent, when freely given, even in the midst of uncertainty and imperfections, is indissoluble for the length of the earthly life of the couple who give it (CCC, 2000, §1601, §1605, §1614, §1638; see also Augustine, 401/1955, Chapter 15; Burke, 1999, pp. 18–31; John Paul II, 1995a). Scripture points not only to the original intention of fidelity and permanency (Gen 2:24; Mt 19:5) but also to the way in which the covenant bond makes the unity of husband and wife a sign of the unity of Christ and the Church

(Eph 5:32; *CCC*, 2000, §1661, §2365). In this respect, the self-offering of the spouses to one another takes on a Eucharistic dimension, that is, the sacrament of Marriage participates in a certain manner in Christ's self-offering to the Church through the sacrament of the Eucharist (Vatican II, 1965, §48; *CCC*, 2000, §1621). The sacramentality of a Christian marriage in this regard is even more important than the spouses' ability to have offspring (Augustine, 401/1955, Chapter 18). In accordance with the character of marriage as a sacrament of service, each spouse works to help the other grow toward ultimate salvation (*CCC*, 2000, §1534).

The Christian tradition uses spousal imagery to express the primacy of God's loving relationship to his people (see the books of Isaiah and Hosea) and of Christ's relationship to the Church, as well as the divine intention about monogamous marriage (Mt 19:3–12; Eph 5). The person's most primal relationship—as expressed in union, communion, and self-gift—is to God. The spousal imagery specifies a relationship with God, who calls each person to a faithful and exclusive self-gift at the ultimate level (John Paul II, 2006, p. 395).

Different aspects of the spousal union are expressed in the chastity appropriate to each vocational state: single chastity (abstinence), conjugal chastity (fidelity and periodic abstinence), and vowed chastity (consecrated chastity or celibacy). Some people, in witness to the Kingdom of God and in explicit commitment to Christ, vow themselves to celibate self-giving (Mt 19:12). Through consecrated celibacy, human persons love and serve God, the Church, and other people (Chapter 9, "Man and Woman" and Chapter 10, "Fulfilled Through Vocation"). These vocations are not a denial of the spousal meaning of the body but an affirmation of it. Celibacy in this sense is not a negation of human sexuality, but rather it makes one available for others in a similar but unique type of self-gift. It allows the gift of self to be readily extended to people in need within the community who would otherwise not receive it. It is a sacrifice of the goods of marriage (including natural procreativity and sexual union) for the sake of giving one's self entirely to the spiritual mission of Christ and the Church (John Paul II, 2006, pp. 418–419, 431–432).

Family

The "reciprocal self-giving" of spouses in conjugal love is oriented toward the generation of children and the realization of the family community (Congregation for the Doctrine of the Faith, 1987, II, A, §1; Wojtyła, 1993c). Family is a major source of life and hope, in which husband and wife, mother and father, sons and daughters, brothers and sisters, and extended family support one another in their personal and familial challenges to grow and flourish. It is also a place of complicated interpersonal problems: among spouses (for instance, violence, estrangement, and divorce), be-

tween parents and children (for example, authoritarianism, abuse, carelessness, and control issues), and among siblings (for example, rivalry), all of which call for family-focused reflections, policies, and sometimes therapies.

How Is the Family a School of Life?

The family comprises privileged interpersonal relationships that are the first school of life and virtue for its members (Benedict XVI, 2005). Parents are the primary educators for children.

This includes not only forming children with respect to culture, but also providing a moral and religious education (Eph 6:4; *CCC*, 2000, §2221, §§2225–2226). Humans usually express a natural need for family, which, when healthy, contributes to the physical, psychological, social, and spiritual well-being of the family members and the larger community. Humans experience natural inclinations to establish families (Aquinas, 1273/1981, I-II, 94.2); that is, they desire the goods of marriage, procreation, and the education of children (as expressed in the previous section; see also Chapter 10, "Fulfilled Through Vocation"). Family is the basic unit of society. It is also the most basic unit of the Church and has thus been called "the domestic church" (Atkinson, 2014; *CCC*, 2000, §1656; John Paul II, 1994; Vatican II, 1964, §11).

How Does Family Contribute to Flourishing?

From the perspective of ultimate flourishing and meaning, the family, as the most basic social unit, provides the foundation for emotional, intellectual, moral, and spiritual development. From the perspective of psychosocial research, we can find (partial) indications of what renders a family successful in its psychosocial and religious mission (inside and outside of itself). For example, family strengths—found in exclusive and lifelong commitment—confront threats to the common good and the person. Family weaknesses—lack of commitment, cohabitation instead of marriage, no-fault divorce, lack of mutual self-gift, lack of paternal involvement or of the nurturing presence of mother—challenge the capacity of family members to care for one another and to contribute to society (Waite & Gallagher, 2000; Wilcox et al., 2011). Even from a psychological perspective, children serve as anti-narcissists, because of their ongoing need

for parental self-sacrifice. Furthermore, the family systems model recognizes not only the positive place of the family in promoting the development and healing of individuals in the family, but also the negative ways that the family, when broken by violence, abuse, neglect, and divorce, contributes to the psychological disorders of its members (Bowen, 1985; Kerr & Bowen, 2003).

How Does the Family Involve a Religious Vocation?

From a Christian perspective, parents seek to form their children so that they will be able to respond to their vocations, which are ways of participating in human and spiritual flourishing and of growing in truth, goodness, and love. Parental love serves as "the visible sign of the very love of God, 'from whom every family in heaven and on earth is named'" (John Paul II, 1981, §14). Children, in turn, contribute to their parents' growing in holiness, for the parents must cultivate patience, forgiveness, compassion, and kindness (*CCC*, 2000, §2227). As the Second Vatican Council (1964) affirms: "The well-being of the individual person and of human and Christian society is intimately linked with the healthy condition of that community produced by marriage and family" (§47).

What Is Responsible Parenthood?

From a Catholic perspective, responsible parenthood requires the development of the spousal virtues (charity, chastity, fidelity, and family prudence) that are necessary for a Catholic response to contemporary challenges to family integrity (Paul VI, 1968, §§ 7–18). Parents are called to take responsibility for the care and well-being of children already born into the family as well as those who may be born in the future. To respond to such challenges requires that husband and wife grow in the spousal virtues and receive support from both inside and outside the family. It involves fertility awareness and responsible family planning. Ultimately, responsible parenthood entails becoming accountable for the expression of their conjugal love (Wojtyła, 1993a/1960; 1979, pp. 22–27). Specifically, responsible parents must understand the goods of marriage and the family in the face of difficulty, confusion, and lack of societal support; make a firm commitment to actively seek these goods in the face of weakness; and master their emotions in the face of fear, temptation, and even provocation. According to Paul VI (1968):

> The question of human procreation, like every other question which touches human life, involves more than the limited aspects specific to such disciplines as biology, psychology, demography or sociology. It is the whole man and the whole mission to which he is called that must be considered: both its natural, earthly aspects and its supernatural, eternal aspects. (§7)

He goes on to warn that widespread use of artificial contraceptive methods will bring the lowering of moral standards, the rise of infidelity, the decrease in men's respect for women, government coercive use of reproductive technologies, and belief in absolute autonomy over one's own body (Paul VI, 1968, §17). Sadly, the social data vindicates Paul VI's remarkably accurate predictions, which were ridiculed at the time (Eberstadt, 2012; Smith, 1993).

How Does a Catholic Vision Serve the Family?

In the midst of many challenges to the family, John Paul II (1995b) outlines the responsibility of mental health professionals and other social scientists to assist husbands and wives in their marriages and the whole family in their life together:

> Marriage and family counseling agencies by their specific work of guidance and prevention, carried out in accordance with an anthropology consistent with the Christian vision of the person, of the couple and of sexuality, also offer valuable help in rediscovering the meaning of love and life, and in supporting and accompanying every family in its mission as the "sanctuary of life." (§88)

The Holy Family— Jesus, Mary, and Joseph —give us indications about the need for love and obedience (Lk 2:51; John Paul II, 1981). In this Christian view, the family and marriage contribute to the goals of personal growth, mutual sanctification, and the glorification of God (Vatican II, 1965, §48.2). Benedict XVI (2011) calls Christians to make their "home a real nursery of virtues and a serene and luminous place of trust, in which, guided by God's grace, it is possible to discern wisely the call of the Lord who continues to invite people to follow him."

Friends

What Is the Purpose of Friendship?

Friends contribute to one another's flourishing, for human friendship constitutes one of the primary ends of human existence. In the broad sense, friendship underlies every interpersonal relationship, although in very distinct ways. The friendship of spouses is not that of business associates, though all types of friendship may be rooted in a life of virtue. Friendship underlies the relationships of affection, companionship, and intimacy that are grounded on a mutual gift of self and a common sharing of the good in ways other than through sexual love (Knobel, 2016). Friendship is a unique form of love (*philia*). This friendship-love is expressed whenever a genuine friendship develops: "friendship without love is impossible" (Aelred of Rievaulx, ca. 1166/1974, Book III, §2).

What Types of Friendship Are There?

Aristotle distinguished virtue-based friendships—in which friends mutually share a desire and life-project for the good—from friendships that consist only in pleasure or utility (ca. 350 BC/1941a, Book VIII–Book IX). In contrast to exclusively deontological (duty-based), rule-based, or consequentialist ethics, a virtue-based approach to morality that searches for true flourishing and friendship avoids getting bogged down in calculations of utility and pleasure or in an exclusive focus on duty and obligation. The notion of virtue-based friendship involves openness to others and commitment to their good as our own. It is also attentive to moral duties, the common good, and the call to holiness. It is not egocentric, but it involves types of love that are compatible with marriage and family, as well as professional commitments and society. Even in the secular world of military service, the man who lays down his life for his comrades is recognized as expressing a very high level of virtue, both courage and friendship; likewise in secular family life, a woman who sacrifices her life for her children is equally admired.

How Does Christianity Make a Difference in Friendship?

From a clearly Christian perspective, friendship is related to morality and spirituality inasmuch as the ultimate goal that enlightens and motivates human acts is friendship with God and the flourishing and beatitude that it promises. Benedict XVI (2008) says that "Christian ethics is not born from a system of commandments, but rather is the consequence of our friendship with Christ." Christ's call to the "greatest" love, to "lay down one's life for one's friends" (Jn 15:13), is, first, central to the universal vocation of the baptized person's gift of self; second, expressed by the martyr literally; third, lived by the religious and ordained in another way, as witnesses to the Kingdom of God and in service to the Church; and fourth, foundational to the married couple, as the basis for their mutual self-gift and self-surrender for the good of spouse and children (Jn 15:15).

Communities

What Is the Purpose of a Community?

As prosocial beings, humans need communities not only to express their relational needs but also to express their personal identity and interiority. Human persons cannot live and thrive without economic, sociocultural, civic and political, and faith-based communities. On the one hand, communities shape persons without totally determining them. The educative influence of a society is indicative of its health and its future. On the other hand, all humans are called to contribute to their communities. In so doing, they express responsibility for one another and for their society as a whole. For example, the specialization of economic activities often involves the vocation to work; if everyone were a baker or a shoemaker or a miner or a teacher, most human flourishing would be made impossible.

These basic insights into the purpose of a community are enriched as we look at the individual, family, and social systems the community comprises and on which it depends as a whole (Bronfenbrenner, 2004). The community necessarily has ethical and spiritual aspects as well. The ethical is especially needed in the context of law and social interactions. The spiritual is needed to find meaning and purpose for the individual and the society.

What Are the Major Threats to Community?

Individualistic, terrorist, anarchistic, and totalitarian practices not only endanger society as a whole and threaten communities in particular, but also jeopardize the well-being of individuals and their families. Antisocial acts and dispositions are found in the disregard for one's commitments (irresponsibility), the disrespect for social norms (immorality), the exaggeration of one's own importance (narcissism), and the denial of objective moral truth (relativism). Likewise, aggressiveness, recklessness, and the failure to appreciate social goods represent tendencies that counter the communal vocation of mankind and in various ways constitute or contribute to psychological, moral, and spiritual disorders that can be considered antisocial. In all of these ways, antisocial dispositions lead to alienation of the person from the community, whereas prosocial dispositions lead to participation in the community (Wojtyła, 1976/1993c, pp. 252–258).

Besides general descriptions of the threats to community life, there are also related psychopathologies, such as antisocial personality disorder, social anxiety disorder, depression, and addictions. For example, people with social anxiety disorder can be influenced by a disproportionate fear of being negatively evaluated in social settings such as meeting new people or speaking in public. Obviously, this sort of social anxiety can undercut prosocial functioning.

What Are the Foundations for Community?

According to MacIntyre (1999), for communities to advance, each person must recognize that he or she has both a rational and an animal dimension, that is, both an intellectual and an instinctual level. The use of reason and the expression of intentions constitute vast resources that people deploy for social planning and actions. Nonetheless, since they are physically, economically, and psychologically vulnerable, and since disability pervades human life, each person is dependent on others in different but real ways throughout life. Each person must rely on social relationships in order to acquire and sustain virtues. At the heart of the interpersonal structure of virtue is found friendship (friendship-love) that serves as the principal bond between the members of a society. This bond underlies the common good of each community and of the community of communities. Friendship-love enables unconditional commitments not only at the familial level but also at more expansive social, economic, and political levels.

Human social nature is constituted with others, for "no person is as such alone in the universe, but is always constituted with others and is summoned to form a community with them" (International Theological Commission, 2004, §41). As socioeconomic beings, a human person "actualizes the essentially social element in his constitution as a person within familial, religious, civil, professional, and other groups that together form the surrounding society to which he belongs" (International Theological Commission, 2004, §42).

What Is a Christian Approach to Community?

The vitality of human society depends not only on justice but also on truth and even joy (John

Paul II, 1993). As Aquinas (1273/1981) says, "As man could not live in society without truth, so likewise, not without joy" (II-II, 114.2 ad 1). Ultimate justice, truth, and joy are the ends of a Christian approach to community. Furthermore, the Church's social teaching is built upon the principles of subsidiarity, common good, solidarity, and family (Leo XIII, 1891; John Paul II, 1991; Benedict XVI, 2009; Francis, 2015). For example, the principle of subsidiarity involves respecting the hierarchy of social groups for the level of social organization that is appropriate for a particular social problem (Schumacher, 1973/2010), as, for instance, when families and local communities implement a proximate and practical solution before more abstract state and federal policies are applied (Pontifical Council for Justice and Peace, 2004).

Moreover, Catholics understand that the Church is the community that gathers all nations and all communities together in answering the divine call to the Kingdom of God (Mt 6:33). St. Paul applies the metaphor of the body (with its members that serve one another) to the Church. As members of the Body of Christ, Christians express their gifts and render services all under the headship of God (Eph 4:4–13). This image of the body has Christological, ecclesiological, and moral dimensions (Pinckaers, 2005) that represent an image of community that finds its fullness in the inner life of God who is a unique and singular community (one God, three Persons) and who calls all people to communion (Jn 14:16).

Conclusion

In sum, the Catholic Christian vision understands the person as innately interpersonal. In the midst of rich and important cultural and religious differences, we are called to discover the common humanity found in every person. Human persons are always in relationships. Even the most individualistic person, and certainly the hermit (who prays for the world), is always embedded in and indebted to relationships.

Humans are always embedded in their families and their relationships with the parents and siblings and friends who cared for them, whether well or poorly. In addition, every person's language is embedded in society and relationship. Each person learns a mother tongue, and that language was formed by others in the countless years before he was born.

In a faith-based view, from our family of origin to our eternal home with God, each person is embedded in interpersonal relationships that evoke the giving and receiving found in love and service. Strained and broken relationships are still relationships, even if less obviously so. Once a man is a father, he is always a father. Likewise, once a woman is a mother, she is always a mother. Once a boy is a brother and a girl a sister, they are always so. Although some attachments are more tentative, like those of friends or colleagues, there is always the basic relationship found in being human, sharing human nature, and participating in the common good of all.

REFERENCES

Aelred of Rievaulx. (1974). *Spiritual friendship*. Kalamazoo, MI: Cistercian Publications. (Original work composed ca. 1163–1166)

Ainsworth, M. D. S., Blehar, M. C., Waters, E., & Wall, S. (1978). *Patterns of attachment: Assessed in the strange situation and at home*. Hillsdale, NJ: Erlbaum.

Alvaré, H. M. (2015). Religious freedom versus sexual expression: A guide. *Journal of Law and Religion, 30*(3), 475–495.

Aquinas, T. (1953). *The disputed questions on truth* (Vol. 2) (J. V. McGlynn, Trans.). Chicago, IL: Regnery. (Original work composed 1256–1259)

Aquinas, T. (1975). *Summa contra gentiles. Book three: Providence, part II* (V. J. Burke, Trans.). Notre Dame, IN: University of Notre Dame Press. (Original work composed 1265)

Aquinas, T. (1981). *Summa theologiae* (English Dominican Province, Trans.). Westminster, MD: Christian Classics. (Original work composed 1273)

Aristotle. (1941a). *Nicomachean ethics*. In R. McKeon (Ed.), *The basic works of Aristotle* (pp. 935–1112). New York, NY: Random House. (Original work composed ca. 350 BC)

Aristotle. (1941b). *Politics*. In R. McKeon (Ed.), *The basic works of Aristotle* (pp. 1127–1316). New York, NY: Random House. (Original work composed ca. 350 BC)

Atkinson, J. (2014). *Biblical and theological foundations of the family: The domestic church*. Washington, DC: The Catholic University of America Press.

Augustine. (1955). *The good of marriage* (C. T. Wilcox, Trans.). In R. J. Deferrari (Ed.), *Fathers of the Church: Vol. 27. Treatises on marriage and other subjects* (pp. 3–52). Washington, DC: The Catholic University of America Press. (Original work composed 401)

Augustine. (2007). *Confessions* (2nd ed.) (M. P. Foley, Ed.; F. J. Sheed, Trans). New York, NY: Hackett. (Original work composed 397–401)

Augustine. (1991). *The Trinity* (E. Hill, Trans.). Hyde Park, NY: New City Press. (Original work composed 399–426)

Beauregard, M. (2012). *Brain wars: The scientific battle over the existence of the mind and the proof that will change the way we live our lives*. New York, NY: Harper Collins.

Beauregard, M., & O'Leary, D. (2008). *The spiritual brain: A neuroscientist's case for the existence of the soul*. New York, NY: Harper Collins.

Bellah, R. N. (2011). *Religion in human evolution: From the Paleolithic to the Axial Age*. Cambridge, MA: Belknap.

Bellah, R. N., Madsen, R., Sullivan, W. M., Swidler, A., & Tipton, S. M. (2007). *Habits of the heart: Individualism and commitment in American life* (3rd ed.). Oakland, CA: University of California Press.

Benedict XVI. (2005). *Deus caritas est* [Encyclical, on Christian love]. Vatican City, Vatican: Libreria Editrice Vaticana.

Benedict XVI. (2007). *Spe salvi* [Encyclical, on Christian hope]. Vatican City, Vatican: Libreria Editrice Vaticana.

Benedict XVI. (2008, November 26). General audience. Vatican City, Vatican: Libreria Editrice Vaticana.

Benedict XVI (2009). *Caritas in veritate* [Encyclical, on integral human development in charity and truth]. Vatican City, Vatican: Libreria Editrice Vaticana.

Benedict XVI. (2011, January 2). *Angelus*. Vatican City, Vatican: Libreria Editrice Vaticana. Retrieved from http://w2.vatican.va/content/benedict-xvi/en/angelus/2011/documents/hf_ben-xvi_ang_20110102.html

Boethius. (1973a). A treatise against Eutyches and Nestorius. In *The theological tractates* (H. F. Stewart & E. K. Rand, Trans.) (pp. 72–129). Cambridge, MA: Harvard University Press. (Original work composed ca. 513)

Boethius. (1973b). The Trinity is one God not three Gods. In *The theological tractates* (H. F. Stewart & E. K. Rand, Trans.) (pp. 3–31). Cambridge, MA: Harvard University Press. (Original work composed ca. 519)

Bowen, M. (1985). *Family therapy in clinical practice*. Lanham, MD; Jason Aronson.

Bowlby, J. (1973). *Separation: Anxiety and anger*. New York, NY: Basic Books.

Bowlby, J. (1982). *Attachment and loss: Vol. 1. Attachment* (2nd ed.). New York, NY: Basic Books. (Original work published 1969)

Bowlby, J. (1988). *A secure base: Clinical applications*

of attachment theory. London, United Kingdom: Routledge.

Bradley, G. V. (2012). *Essays on law, religion and morality*. South Bend, IN: Saint Augustine's Press.

Bronfenbrenner, U. (2004). *Making human beings human: Bioecological perspectives on human development*. Thousand Oaks, CA: Sage.

Buber, M. (1971). *I and thou* (W. Kaufmann, Trans.). New York, NY: Touchstone. (Original work published 1923)

Budziszewski, J. (2012). *On the meaning of sex*. Wilmington, DE: ISI Books.

Burke, C. (1999). *Covenanted happiness: Love and commitment in marriage*. New York, NY: Scepter Publishers.

Burke, C. (2015). *The theology of marriage: Personalism, doctrine, and canon law*. Washington, DC: The Catholic University of America Press.

Carlson, A. C., & Mero, P. T. (2007). *The natural family*. Dallas, TX: Spence.

Cassidy, J., & Shaver, P. R. (Eds.). (1999). *Handbook of attachment: Theory, research, and clinical applications*. New York, NY: Guilford.

Catechism of the Catholic Church (CCC) (2nd ed.). (2000). Vatican City, Vatican: Libreria Editrice Vaticana.

Chrysostom, J. (1986). *On marriage and family life*. Crestwood, NY: St. Vladimir's Seminary Press. (Original work published ca. 390–400)

Clarke, W. N. (1993). *Person and being, and St. Thomas*. Milwaukee, WI: Marquette University Press.

Clarke, W. N. (2009). *The creative retrieval of Saint Thomas Aquinas: Essays in Thomistic philosophy, new and old*. New York, NY: Fordham University Press.

Commission on Children at Risk. (2003). *Hardwired to connect: The new scientific case for authoritative communities*. New York, NY: Institute for American Values.

Congregation for the Doctrine of the Faith. (1987). *Donum vitae* [Instruction on respect for human life]. Vatican City, Vatican: Libreria Editrice Vaticana.

Cozolino, L. (2010). *The neuroscience of psychotherapy* (2nd ed). New York, NY: Norton.

Cozolino, L. (2014). *The neuroscience of human relationships: Attachment and the developing social brain* (2nd ed.). New York, NY: Norton.

Cullen, C. M. (2012). The natural desire to see God and pure nature: A debate revisited. *American Catholic Philosophical Quarterly, 86*(4), 705–730.

Davies, B. (2004). *An introduction to the philosophy of religion* (3rd ed.). Oxford, United Kingdom: Oxford University Press.

Dawkins, R. (2008). *The God delusion*. New York, NY: Mariner Books.

de Lubac, H. (1998). *The mystery of the supernatural*. New York, NY: Herder and Herder. (Original work published 1946)

Dennett, D. C. (1995). *Darwin's dangerous idea: Evolution and the meanings of life*. New York, NY: Simon & Schuster.

Descartes, R. (1996). *Meditations on first philosophy: With selections from the objections and replies* (J. Cottingham, Trans.). Cambridge, United Kingdom: Cambridge University Press. (Original work published in 1641)

Douglas, M. (2003). *Natural symbols: Explorations in cosmology* (2nd ed.). New York, NY: Routledge. (Original work published 1970)

Eberstadt, M. (2012). *Adam and Eve after the pill: Paradoxes of the sexual revolution*. San Francisco, CA: Ignatius Press.

Eliade, M. (1981). *A history of religious ideas* (3 Vols.) (W. Trask, Trans). Chicago, IL: Chicago University Press.

Erikson, E. (1994). *Identity: Youth and crisis*. New York, NY: Norton. (Original work published 1968)

Fagan, P. F., & Churchill, A. (2012). *The effects of divorce on children*. Washington, DC: Marriage and Religion Research Institute.

Feingold, L. (2004). *The natural desire to see God according to St. Thomas and his interpreters*. Washington, DC: The Catholic University of America Press.

Feser, E. (2008). *The last superstition: A refutation of the New Atheism*. South Bend, IN: St. Augustine's Press.

Feser, E. (2017). *Five proofs of the existence of God*. San Francisco, CA: Ignatius.

Francis. (2015). *Laudato si'* [Encyclical, on care for our common home]. Vatican City, Vatican: Libreria Editrice Vaticana.

Freud, S. (2012). *The future of an illusion*. Peterborough, Canada: Broadview Press. (Original work published 1927)

Fromm, E. (1956). *The art of loving*. New York, NY: Harper & Row.

Giussani, L. (1997). *The religious sense* (J. Zucchi, Trans.). Montreal, Canada: McGill-Queen's University Press.

Goleman, D. (2006). *Social intelligence: The new science of human relationships*. New York, NY: Bantam Books.

Greenberg, L., & Johnson, S. (1988). *Emotionally focused therapy for couples*. New York, NY: Guilford.

Gregory Nazianzen. (1894). Select orations of Saint Gregory Nazianzen (C. G. Browne & J. E. Swallow, Trans.). In P. Schaff & H. Wace (Eds.), *S. Cyril of Jerusalem, S. Gregory Nazianzen* (Vol. 7, p. 424). New York, NY: Christian Literature Company. (Original work composed ca. 379–381)

Gregory of Nyssa. (1978). *The life of Moses* (A. J. Malherbe & E. Ferguson, Trans.). New York, NY: Paulist Press. (Original work composed ca. 390)

Gudan, E. (2010). *Gratitude-based interventions for treating ruminative depression* (Doctoral dissertation, The Institute for the Psychological Sciences). Retrieved from ProQuest Dissertations and Theses. (Accession Order No. 3444447)

Hazan, C., & Shaver, P. (1987). Romantic love conceptualized as an attachment process. *Journal of Personality and Social Psychology, 25*, 511–524.

Heschel, A. J. (1954). *Man's search for God: Studies in prayer and symbolism*. Santa Fe, NM: Aurora Press.

Hoffman, M. L. (2001). *Empathy and moral development: Implications for caring and justice*. Cambridge, United Kingdom: Cambridge University Press.

Hume, D. (2000). *A treatise of human nature* (D. F. Norton & M. J. Norton, Eds.). Oxford, United Kingdom: Oxford University Press. (Original work published 1740)

International Theological Commission. (2004). *Communion and stewardship: Human persons created in the image of God*. Vatican City, Vatican: Libreria Editrice Vaticana.

John Paul II. (1981). *Familiaris consortio* [Apostolic exhortation, on the role of the Christian family in the modern world]. Vatican City, Vatican: Libreria Editrice Vaticana.

John Paul II (May 1, 1991). *Centesimus annus* [Encyclical, on the hundredth anniversary of *Rerum novarum*]. Vatican City, Vatican: Libreria Editrice Vaticana.

John Paul II. (1993). *Veritatis splendor* [Encyclical, on certain fundamental questions of the Church's moral teaching]. Vatican City, Vatican: Libreria Editrice Vaticana.

John Paul II. (1994, February 2). *Gratissimam sane* [Letter to families]. Vatican City, Vatican: Libreria Editrice Vaticana.

John Paul II. (1995a, February 10). *Address to the Tribunal of the Roman Rota*. Vatican City, Vatican: Libreria Editrice Vaticana.

John Paul II. (1995b). *Evangelium vitae* [Encyclical, on the value and inviolability of human life]. Vatican City, Vatican: Libreria Editrice Vaticana.

John Paul II. (2006). *Man and woman he created them: A theology of the body* (M. Waldstein, Trans.). Boston, MA: Pauline Books and Media.

Jung, C. (1981). *The archetypes and the collective unconscious* (2nd ed.) (G. Adler & R. F. C. Hull, Trans.). Princeton, NJ: Princeton University Press. (Original work published 1968)

Kant, I. (2002). *Critique of pure reason* (W. S. Pluhar, Trans.). Indianapolis, IN: Hackett. (Original work published 1788)

Kerr, M. E., & Bowen, M. (2003). *One family's story: A primer on Bowen theory*. Washington, DC: Bowen Center for the Study of the Family, Georgetown Family Center.

Kolodziejczak, G. C. (2006). *Distortions of love as distortions of the self from a psychological perspective* (Unpublished doctoral dissertation). Arlington, VA: Institute for the Psychological Sciences.

Knobel, A. (2016). Aristotle, true friendship, and the 'soulmate' view of marriage. *Public Discourse*, June 1. Retrieved from http://www.thepublicdiscourse.com/2016/06/16819/

Koenig, H. G., King, D., & Carson, V. B. (Eds.). (2012). *Handbook of religion and health* (2nd ed.). New York, NY: Oxford University Press.

Lee, S. L. (2012). *Essential elements of love, personhood, and attachment: From metaphysics to psychological theory and psychotherapy* (Doctoral dissertation, Institute for the Psychological Sciences). Retrieved from ProQuest Dissertations and Theses. (Accession Order No. 3503185)

Leo XIII (1891, May 15). *Rerum novarum* [Encyclical,

on capital and labor]. Vatican City, Vatican: Libreria Editrice Vaticana.

Lewis, C. S. (1960). *The four loves.* New York, NY: Harcourt, Brace and Company.

Locke, J. (1980). *Second treatise of government.* Indianapolis, IN: Hackett. (Original work published 1689)

Long, S. A. (2010). *Natura pura: On the recovery of nature in the doctrine of grace.* New York, NY: Fordham University Press.

Lopez, S. J., & Snyder, C. R. (Eds.). (2009). *The Oxford handbook of positive psychology.* Oxford, United Kingdom: Oxford University Press.

May, R. (1969). *Love and will.* New York, NY: Norton.

MacIntyre, A. (1999). *Dependent rational animals: Why human beings need the virtues.* Chicago, IL: Open Court.

Maher, B. (Ed.). (2004). *The family portrait* (2nd ed.). Washington, DC: Family Research Council.

Maritain, J. (1959). *Distinguish to unite, or the degrees of knowledge* (G. B. Phelan, Trans.). London, United Kingdom: Geoffrey Bles. (Original work published 1932)

Maslow, A. (1987). *Motivation and personality* (3rd ed.) (R. Frager, J. Fadiman, C. McReynolds, & R. Cox, Eds.). New York, NY: Longman. (Original work published 1954)

McCauley, R. N. (2011). *Why religion is natural and science is not.* New York, NY: Oxford University Press.

McEntee, M. L., Dy-Liacco, G. S., & Haskins, D. G. (2013). Human flourishing: A natural home for spirituality. *Journal of Spirituality in Mental Health, 15,* 141–159.

Mikulincer, M., & Shaver, P. R. (2007). *Attachment in adulthood: Structure, dynamics, and change.* New York, NY: Guilford.

Müller, G. (2014). *The hope of the family: A dialogue with Cardinal Gerhard Müller.* San Francisco, CA: Ignatius Press.

Nédoncelle, M. (1966). *Love and the person.* New York, NY: Sheed & Ward.

Nietzsche, F. (2006). *Thus spoke Zarathustra: A book for all and for none* (A. del Caro, Trans.). Cambridge, United Kingdom: Cambridge University Press. (Original work composed 1883–1885)

Nygren, A. (1982). *Agape and eros.* Chicago, IL: University of Chicago Press. (Original work published 1930)

Ouellet, M. (2015). *Mystery and sacrament of love: A theology of marriage and the family for the new evangelization* (M. K. Borras & A. J. Walker, Trans.). Grand Rapids, MI: Eerdmans. (Original work published 2005)

O'Leary, D. (2007). *One man, one woman: A Catholic guide to defending marriage.* Manchester, NH: Sophia Press.

Otto, R. (1958). *The idea of the holy* (2nd ed.) (J. W. Harvey, Trans.). London, United Kingdom: Oxford University Press. (Original work published 1917)

Paul VI. (1968). *Humanae vitae* [Encyclical, on the regulation of birth]. Vatican City, Vatican: Libreria Editrice Vaticana.

Petri, T. (2016). *Aquinas and the theology of the body.* Washington, DC: The Catholic University of America Press.

Pieper, J. (1997). *Faith, hope, and love.* San Francisco, CA: Ignatius Press.

Pieper, J. (2009). *Leisure: The basis of culture* (A. Dru, Trans.). San Francisco, CA: Ignatius Press. (Original work published 1952)

Pinckaers, S. (2005). The Body of Christ: The Eucharistic and ecclesial context of Aquinas's ethics (M. T. Noble, C. S. Titus, M. Sherwin, & H. Connelly, Trans.). In J. Berkman & C. S. Titus (Eds.), *The Pinckaers reader: Renewing Thomistic moral theology* (pp. 26–45). Washington, DC: The Catholic University of America Press. (Original work published 2000)

Pontifical Council for Justice and Peace. (2004). *Compendium of the social doctrine of the Church.* Vatican City, Vatican: Libreria Editrice Vatican.

Post, S. G. (Ed.) (2007). *Altruism and health: Perspectives from empirical research.* Oxford, United Kingdom: Oxford University Press.

Putnam, R. (2001). *Bowling alone: The collapse and revival of American community.* New York: NY: Touchstone Books.

Rogers, C. R. (2012). *On becoming a person: A therapist's view of psychotherapy.* Boston, MA: Houghton Mifflin Harcourt. (Original work published in 1961)

Sartre, J. P. (2007). *Existentialism is a humanism*

(C. Macomber, Trans.). New Haven, CT: Yale University Press. (Original work published 1946)

Schumacher, E. F. (2010). *Small is beautiful: A study of economics as if people mattered.* New York, NY: Harper. (Originally published 1973)

Schmidt, W. (1935). *The origin and growth of religion* (2nd ed.) (H. J. Rose, Trans.). London, United Kingdom: Methuen.

Schmitz, K. (2009). *Person and psyche.* Arlington, VA: The Institute for the Psychological Sciences Press.

Scola, A. (2005). *The nuptial mystery* (M. K. Borras, Trans.). Grand Rapids, MI: Eerdmans. (Original work published 2000)

Siegel, D. J. (2012). *The developing mind* (2nd ed.). New York, NY: Guilford.

Scruton, R. (1986). *Sexual desire: A moral philosophy of the erotic.* New York, NY: Free Press.

Spitzer, R. J. (2010). *New proofs for the existence of God: Contributions of contemporary physics and philosophy.* Grand Rapids, MI: Eerdmans.

Smith, J. E. (1993). Paul VI as prophet. In J. E. Smith (Ed.), *Why* Humanae Vitae *was right: A reader.* San Francisco, CA: Ignatius Press.

Sodergren, A. (2009). *Attachment and morality: A Catholic perspective* (Unpublished doctoral dissertation). Institute for the Psychological Sciences, Arlington, VA.

Sullivan, H. S. (1953). *The interpersonal theory of psychiatry.* New York, NY: Norton.

Titus, C. S., & Scrofani, P. (2012). The art of love: A Roman Catholic psychology of love. *Journal of Psychology and Christianity, 31,* 118–129.

Taylor, C. (2007). *A secular age.* Cambridge, MA: Belknap Press.

Vatican II, Council. (1964). *Lumen gentium* [Dogmatic constitution on the Church]. Vatican City, Vatican: Libreria Editrice Vaticana.

Vatican II, Council. (1965). *Gaudium et spes* [Pastoral constitution on the Church in the modern world]. Vatican City, Vatican: Libreria Editrice Vaticana.

Vitz, P. C. (2013). *Faith of the fatherless: The psychology of atheism* (2nd ed.). San Francisco, CA: Ignatius Press.

Vygotsky, L. S. (1962). *Thought and language.* Cambridge, MA: MIT Press.

Vygotsky, L. S. (1978). *Mind in society.* Cambridge, MA: Harvard University Press.

Waite, L., & Gallagher, M. (2000). *The case for mar-riage: Why married people are happier, healthier, and better off financially.* New York, NY: Doubleday.

Whitehead, K. D. (2007). *The Church, marriage, and the family.* South Bend, IN: St. Augustine's Press.

Wilcox, W. B., Anderson, J. R., Doherty, W. J., Eggebeen, D, Ellison, C. G., Galston, W. A., … Wallerstein, J., et al. (2011). *Why marriage matters: Thirty conclusions from the social sciences* (3rd ed.). New York, NY: Institute for American Values.

Wilcox, W. B., & Kline, K. K. (2012). *Mother bodies, father bodies: How parenthood changes us from the inside out.* New York, NY: Broadway.

Wilcox, W. B., & Kline, K. K., (2013). *Gender and parenthood: Biological and social scientific perspectives.* New York, NY: Columbia University Press.

Winnicott, D. W. (1964). *The child, family, and the outside world.* Redding, MA: Attison.

Wojtyła, K. (1979). *Fruitful and responsible love.* New York, NY: Seabury.

Wojtyła, K. (1993a). *Love and responsibility* (H. T. Willetts, Trans.). San Francisco, CA: Ignatius Press. (Original work published 1960)

Wojtyła, K. (1993b). Thomistic personalism (T. Sandok, Trans.). In A. N. Woznicki (Ed.), *Catholic thought from Lublin: Vol. 4. Person and community: Selected essays* (pp. 165–75). New York, NY: Peter Lang. (Original paper presented in Polish, 1961)

Wojtyła, K. (1993c). The family as a community of persons (T. Sandok, Trans.). In A. N. Woznicki (Ed.), *Catholic thought from Lublin: Vol. 4. Person and community: Selected essays* (pp. 315–327). New York, NY: Peter Lang. (Original work published 1976)

Wojtyła, K. (1993d). The person: Subject and community (T. Sandok, Trans.). In A. N. Woznicki (Ed.), *Person and community: Selected essays* (pp. 219–261). New York, NY: Peter Lang. (Original work published 1974)

Wojtyła, K. (2011). *Man in the field of responsibility* (K. W. Kemp & Z. M. Kieroń, Trans.). South Bend, IN: St. Augustine's Press. (Original work published 1991)

Zizioulas, J. D. (1997). *Being as communion: Studies in personhood and the Church* (Contemporary Greek theologians series, No. 4). Crestwood, NY: St. Vladimir's Seminary Press. (Original work published 1985)

Chapter 13

Sensory-Perceptual-Cognitive

MATTHEW R. MCWHORTER, PAUL C. VITZ,
AND CRAIG STEVEN TITUS

ABSTRACT: This chapter addresses the sensory-perceptual-cognitive capacities of the person from a Christian philosophical perspective—in particular, from the viewpoint of the Catholic-Christian Meta-Model of the Person. A close analysis of these embodied aspects of human nature and experience makes apparent the importance of sensation, perception, cognition, memory, imagination, and basic kinds of evaluation for understanding a person. Consideration is given to human primary sense capacities and higher-order perceptual capacities as well as to how they relate to cognition, emotion, and volition, in dialogue with neuroscience, psychological theory, and clinical practice. How persons develop cognitive dispositions is also explored. This chapter discusses the sensory-perceptual-cognitive dimension of human knowledge in an integrated classical, realist, philosophical framework. While psychology and the neurosciences inform this chapter with respect to understanding brain functions, these sources are placed within the larger context of the Catholic-Christian philosophical tradition and its understanding of the person.

The human person is a whole. As a whole, one perceives and understands the world, other people, and oneself. We do injustice to the person when we deny that the person is a body-soul unity (Chapter 8, "Personal Wholeness"). We also do injustice to the person when we deny or neglect to explore knowledge and consciousness. Since persons are multidimensional, we do further injustice when their multiple capacities are not recognized or when they are under-examined.

The present chapter analyzes the range of sensory-perceptual-cognitive capacities that underlie and contribute to human understanding. It is an exercise in a classical philosophical psy-chology, which is a vision of the person (human anthropology) that is informed by the thought and methods of a realist understanding of the world and human life (Aquinas, 1273/1981; Aristotle ca. 350 BC/2000c; MacIntyre, 1999; Popper, 1983; Wojtyła, 1979). In keeping with the Meta-Model's multidisciplinary and multilayered understanding of the person, we are attempting to bring the findings of neuroscience (Kolb & Whishaw, 2009; Siegel, 2012; and so on) into a useful interaction with this realist tradition. This philosophical and psychological vision thus contains elements of neuroscience, a realist theory of knowledge, and examples from mental health practice.

Beginning with Gustav Fechner and Wilhelm Wundt in the nineteenth century, contemporary psychology has adopted an experimental methodology for understanding the sensory-perceptual-cognitive and basic emotional functions of the person (Ashley, 2013b, pp. 21–22; Ashley, Deblois, & O'Rourke, 2006, p. 137; Wundt, 1904). From the empirical observations of human behavior and cognition, the field has taken a strong interest in the neurological basis for mental capacities (on the theoretical orientation of neuropsychiatry, see Beck, 1979, pp. 8–9). A common tendency, though, is to treat human experiences of cognition and affection merely as neurochemical events or as bottom-up movements, emergent effects arising out of the material and biological substrate of the person (Murphy, 1998; Siegel, 2012; Życiński, 2006). In general, much of contemporary psychotherapy proceeds on the philosophical bias of reductive materialism (Ashley, 2013b, p. 25). In extreme forms of such reductionist and materialist approaches, pharmacological treatments may be seen as wholly adequate solutions for all psychological disorders (Życiński, 2006). But recently, scientists have been developing important nonreductive approaches in the fields of mental health theory, research, and practice (Beauregard & O'Leary, 2008; Enright & Fitzgibbons, 2014; Worthington, 2003; Worthington, 2005). Positive psychology, with its emphasis on the will, offers another nonreductive perspective (Peterson & Seligman, 2004).

In contrast with strictly materialist approaches, what follows is a nonreductive Catholic Christian consideration of the person's sensory-perceptual-cognitive capacities, one that examines not only the material and physiological aspects of the person but also the mind and self-consciousness, understood as nonmaterial, or spiritual. Sensory-perceptual-cognitive activities can be distinguished from the higher intellectual capacities of the person and from nonmaterial self-consciousness (Aquinas, 1265/2001, 60.2). While sensations, perceptions, and cognitions all contribute to human flourishing, the examination of these capacities alone is not sufficient to explain fully how and why persons perceive and evaluate the world around them and interact with one another. While human knowledge begins with sensations, it does not end there (Chapter 15, "Rational," and Chapter 16, "Volitional and Free").

The present chapter is the first of four steps in analyzing types of human knowledge and affect. These four chapters address the person as sensory-perceptual-cognitive, emotional, rational, and volitional and free, acknowledging various ways of knowing and loving. In this chapter, the sensory-perceptual-cognitive character of the person will be examined in detail. We consider, first, how a person's sensory capacities enable that person to be receptive to and interact with the outside world. We then provide a brief overview of the particular sensations associated with each of the five primary senses. Next, we examine the activities associated with the higher order perceptual capacities, such as remembering and basic evaluations of experience. Fourth, we treat the question of ordered and disordered (or positive and negative) cognitive-affective dispositions resulting from the conditioning of the higher order perceptual capacities (Chapter 14, "Emotional"). Throughout the chapter, we discuss how the sensory-perceptual-cognitive dimension of the person enables one to have an active encounter with the world.

Receptive to the External World

A person interacts with his or her physical environment and all of reality through a hierarchy of capacities. In the case of sensation, the activity of each sensory capacity is an activity of the person as a body-soul unity. The person's experience of sensation involves a determinate physiological change, such as when the retinal elements respond to brightness and color (de Anna, 2000, p. 48). The higher order perceptual capacities, as physio-psychological capacities, receive from, react to, and engage the surrounding physical world. Specialized sensory receptors that are unique to each sense capacity contribute to the realization of each particular kind of sensation (Kolb & Whishaw, 2009, p. 198). These sensory receptors can be exteroceptive— oriented to sensible properties that are outside the body of the person (such as the shape of an exterior thing)—or interoceptive—oriented to sensible properties physiologically interior to the body of the person (such as abdominal pain or headache) (Kolb & Whishaw, 2009, p. 201). Sense receptors also include specialized neurons in the brain (Goldstein, 2010, pp. 26–27).

Instinctive bio-physiological reactions at the reflex level (such as the dilation of the pupil of the eye in low light) function in a manner that is pre-volitional (that is, independent of the exercise of the will). In a similar way, natural inclinations respond to sensations of objects in the external world around a person. These include the inclination to self-preservation (reacting to sensations of food and drink) and inclinations involving other attractions to sensed objects (such as attractions to other persons in association with enjoyment of the good of community), which emerge prior to the will's consent. Some of these natural inclinations for basic needs and goods in the external world are (a) common to all things (self-preservation); others are (b) shared between human beings and other animals (sexual union and rearing offspring); and still others are (c) proper to human nature (natural inclinations to know the truth, especially about God, and to live with others in a rationally ordered community, as well as to appreciate beauty) (Aquinas, 1273/1981, I, 5.4 ad 1; I-II, 94.2; II-II, 145.2; John Paul II, 1993, §51). The failure to fulfill these properly human inclinations through interacting with persons and objects in the external world can lead to psychological disorders. Such inclinations, however, often remain hidden under such disorders. Further, these inclinations underlie the ethical precepts, vocations, and virtues by which we rationally promote moral and spiritual flourishing (see the section "Natural Inclinations, Natural Law, and the Personalist Norm" in Chapter 11, "Fulfilled in Virtue").

The Five Primary Senses

The five primary senses of the body (vision, hearing, smell, taste, and touch) are at times called "exterior" senses. The word "exterior" here indicates that such senses enable the person to be oriented to the properties of things existing outside of that person in the surrounding physical environment. However, these primary senses at times involve sensations that are responses not only to exterior stimuli, but also to stimuli that are physiologically interior to the person's body (such as hunger) (Kolb & Whishaw, 2009, p. 201). To acknowledge that distinction, reference here will be made strictly to the five "primary" senses rather than to "exterior" senses.

Each of the five primary senses is oriented toward a single kind of sensible property (Ashley, 2013b, p. 154). Whether the sensed property is external to the body (the sound of an orchestra) or internal (abdominal pain), it is a reality that is present to the sense capacity: sensation involves knowing what is proximate to the person now, in this temporal moment (Aquinas, 1269/2005b, p. 158). A sensible property is a specific quality (for example, brightness, sound, scent, flavor, temperature, or pain) that affects or acts upon the sensory capacity (Aquinas, 1268/1994a, §§383–384; Macdonald, 2007, p. 346). The sensory capacity is directly receptive of—or immediately affected by—that specific sensible quality (Aquinas, 1266/2005c, q. 13). The act of sensation is in itself receptivity: "to sense is to be affected in some manner" (Aquinas, 1269/2005a, p. 185). For example, activated chemical receptors partially enable taste and smell; activated photoreceptors partially enable vision (Bear, Connors, & Paradiso, 2007, p. 252, p. 290). The *experience* of sensation, however, remains a remarkable event with a special quality (on basic awareness or *qualia* 1, see Vitz, 2017, and Chapter 6, "Person as an Integrated Laminate") that transcends our physical explanations of neurological activity.

Each receptive element in a sensory capacity may be said to be "naturally fitted" to be acted upon by a specific sensible property or specific sensory stimulus (Aquinas, 1268/1994a, §387). Such sensible properties effect sensation when conditions are appropriate (Aquinas, 1273/1981, I, 78.3 ad 2). The sensory capacity itself is passive in the face of these sensible properties: "the sensible object imprints its likeness upon the sense" (Aquinas, 1269/2005a, p. 198). The likeness that is received by means of sensation can be called an "impression" (Aquinas, 1269/2005a, p. 185). At times, this is also called a sense intention

(Aquinas, 1273/1981, I, 78.3; Macdonald, 2007, pp. 347–348). In order to emphasize the dynamic character of a sense capacity, one might speak of its intentional orientation (Kenny, 1994, p. 34) or its "directionality," which concerns how the sense capacity points toward the stimulus that activates it (Tellkamp, 2007, p. 276).

Each healthy primary sense has a kind of cognitive certitude with respect to the specific sensible property to which it is oriented. The knowledge of a healthy primary sense cannot be "false" when considered in relation to the sensible property that is being sensed (Aquinas, 1268/1994a, §384, §630; Aristotle, ca. 350 BC/2000c, 427b13). At the same time, the physiological organ system that enables a person to have sensation can itself suffer from pathology (for example, hallucinations associated with psychoses or drug use). The person's sensations may consequently be judged to be abnormal in comparison with the sensations of other persons whose organ systems exemplify an accepted standard of healthy functionality. Further, any primary sense can prove fallible in the accuracy of its sensation if that sense capacity is used in isolation in an attempt to discern a common sensible property (such as attempting to ascertain the cause of a sound by using one's sense of hearing only) (Aquinas, 1268/1994a, §385).

Although a sense impression can be said to "represent" an objective property of an exterior reality (for example, the sensation of the heat of a fire), this must be carefully understood in order that one realize how a person's sense capacities enable him to experience the reality of the world around him. This is the starting point of a realist philosophy. A sense impression does not stand in between the sense capacity and the sensed object, so to mediate the latter to the former. This philosophical position (called "representational realism," exemplified by the philosopher

John Locke [2008]) contrasts with the realism of the Catholic-Christian Meta-Model of the Person. Locke's position is open to the skeptical charge that such an impression in fact obscures or blocks access to reality—a flaw that eventually leads to the "phenomenalism" and anti-realism exemplified by the philosopher David Hume (BonJour, 2010, pp. 124–125; Sokolowski, 2008, pp. 157–161). For the Meta-Model, the individual sense impression is the very activity of sensation. In other words, the sense impression is not an entity inserted in between the sense receptor and its object; rather, it is the structure of the sensation itself, a structure in real accord with the sensed property (Aquinas, 1273/1981, I, 85.2; de Anna, 2000, pp. 48–49; Decaen, 2001, p. 186).

That is, there is a certain kind of structural unity between the activated sense capacity and the sensible property that is sensed (Aquinas, 1273/1981, I, 87.1 ad 3). The unity or identity under consideration here, however, is the identity of sensation as a sensed or experienced, structural, or a coded identity, not an ontological one; in other words, the sense capacity does not become ontologically identical with the real property (they are not one being or one entity), but only experienced as identical (Aristotle, ca. 350 BC/2000c, 425b27–28; Aquinas, 1268/1994a, §590; Esfeld, 2000, p. 327). The likeness that is impressed upon the sense, although enabling the sensory capacity to become unified with the sensed property, has its own ontological status, as a structure or internal code, distinct from that real property: the sensible property really exists in nature, whereas its likeness, which is imprinted upon the sensory capacity, depends upon the occurrence of the real stimulus for its existence (Aquinas, 1268/1994a, §553; Aquinas, 1269/2005b, p. 156; Haldane, 1983, p. 235; Tellkamp, 2007, p. 276). When the exterior elements of a sensible property are replicated in

a primary sense as an internal code, the mode of being that those elements have as replicated differs from their existence in objective reality (Aquinas, 1268/1994a, §418; Burnyeat, 2001, pp. 132–133). In this way, it is helpful to keep in mind that "whatever is known is known in the mode of the knower" (Aquinas, 1273/1981, I, 14.1 ad 3). In realist terms, the external stimulus is reality itself. The sensation is an interior code of external reality. In this contact, the reality of the stimulus is present in the coded sensation.

Furthermore, it remains the case that there is a genuine structurally coded unity that occurs between the sense capacity and the real sensible property. In other words, the bodily senses enable one to know and interact with the surrounding world in its reality. At the moment of sensation, the person knows the present reality, which is sensed in such a way that the qualitative experience of that sensation *contains within itself contact with reality*. It is in this respect that the present approach to understanding sensory-perceptual capacities exemplifies a philosophical realism. Should one appeal to occurrences of illusion or mistaken identity as grounds for doubting the reliability of the senses (see Descartes, 1641/2000, p. 105), one might reconsider that such events are indicative rather of a failure of the human processing of sensation at a higher cognitive level, not a failure at the level of sensation. The very fact that a person can come to recognize a previous judgment to be wrong indicates that he has access to reality, which corrects his misapprehension (for a discussion of this observation as grounds for a scientific realism, see Popper, 1975, 1983; also Almeder, 1996). Reality and sensation of reality are prior in time to thought about reality.

We turn now to consider briefly each of the primary senses. The *sense of vision* or *sight* is primarily an exteroceptive system, oriented to sensible properties that are outside the body of the person (Kolb & Whishaw, 2009, p. 213). Vision is receptive of singular or discrete sensible properties (such as an object's brightness) as well as of common sensible properties (such as shape and size). Visual sense data can at times be interoceptive as when physical manipulation of the eye produces interior visual sensations (for example, the experience of phosphenes) or when one suffers visual hallucinations. Sensations of sight are processed in the visual cortex region of the occipital lobe (Goldstein, 2010, pp. 26, 74).

The *sense of hearing* is also primarily an exteroceptive system, oriented to real sensible properties that are outside the body (Kolb & Whishaw, 2009, p. 213). The sense of hearing is receptive of the discrete sensible property of sound, including aural qualities such as shrillness or mellifluence. Sounds can be described in terms of their pitch, intensity, and timbre (Goldstein, 2010, pp. 264–268). The sense of hearing can also at times be interoceptive, as when one hears the shifting of interior fluid (for example, in the Eustachian tube), experiences an anomalous transduction (as with the pathology of tinnitus—see Bear, Connors, & Paradiso, 2007, p. 376), or experiences aural hallucinations sometimes precipitated by drugs or severe psychopathology. Aural sensations are processed in the auditory cortex, which is located in the temporal lobe of the cerebrum (Goldstein, 2010, p. 26, pp. 280–281).

The *olfactory sense* or *sense of smell* is receptive of the discrete sensible property of odor or scent, including associated characteristics such as pungency and noxiousness. Sensations involving scent are based on the encounter with minute particles of the thing sensed; these are processed in the olfactory cortices (Goldstein, 2010, p. 364). Meanwhile, sensations involving taste, also based on small particles of the thing tasted, are received in the nucleus of the solitary tract located in the brain stem and then are transmitted to the thalamus and processed in the frontal lobe of the brain (Goldstein, 2010, pp. 368–367). Smell and taste are intimately interconnected.

Last, the *tactile sensory capacity* or *touch* is the most pervasive and basic sense and is common to all animals (Aquinas, 1273/1981, I, 91.1 ad 3; Ashley, 2013b, p. 155; Goldstein, 2010; Kolb & Whishaw, 2009). Since this sensory capacity is spread out along the entire nervous system and includes multiple receptors throughout the skin, it is at times also referred to as "the cutaneous senses" or as "the cutaneous system" (Goldstein, 2010, pp. 329–352). The "sense of touch" or "hapsis" (which involves tactile sensations of pressure and density) is only one mode of this multifaceted system, which also includes nocioception (the sensation of pain or uncomfortable temperatures) (Kolb & Whishaw, 2009, p. 213). The same sensory system also includes a person's proprioceptive sense, which involves general bodily awareness and the sensation of bodily position in space (Goldstein, 2010, p. 330). Touch is unique among the five primary senses in that it is responsive to more than one discrete kind of sensible property (for example, by means of touch one senses both pressure and temperature) (Aquinas, 1268/1994a, §384; Macdonald, 2007, p. 346). Tactile sensations are processed in the somatic sensory cortex, located in the parietal lobe of the brain (Goldstein, 2010, p. 26; Ashley, 2013b, p. 155).

Higher-Order Perceptions or Perceptual Cognitions

The discussion now moves from consideration of sensation to the topic of perceptions. The words "sensation" and "perception" are at times used synonymously (see, for example, Aquinas, 1273/1981, I, 78.3 ad 3 & 91.1 ad 3; III Supp., 92.2 ad 7). But the two words can also be distinguished. The higher order perceptual capacities include the synthetic capacity (basic consciousness or awareness), imagination, memory, and a basic evaluative capacity. The synthetic capacity is a higher-order perceptual capacity that differentiates and sorts individual sense impressions received through the primary senses and also apprehends whole things, whole persons, and so on. The imagination is a perceptual capacity that stores these impressions (Aquinas, 1266/2005c, q. 13). Memory is a perceptual capacity that recalls stored impressions (Aquinas, 1266/2005c, q. 13). Finally, the elementary evaluative capacity is a perceptual capacity that recognizes individual things and persons and also appraises them (for example, in terms of potential harm or utility; many animals have a similar kind of capacity) (Aquinas, 1266/2005c, q. 13). The higher-order perceptual capacities process and evaluate sense data that is received from the five primary senses (Aquinas, 1273/1981, I, 78.4; Ashley, 2013b, pp. 158–173). In what follows, we will examine each of these higher order perceptual capacities in turn. As with the treatment of the primary senses above, here too we will give brief consideration to research in contemporary neuroscience that complements our philosophical inquiry.

The Synthetic Capacity

The first higher-order perceptual capacity is the synthetic capacity, which includes with its operation the awareness of the object perceived. This capacity enables a person, and many animals, to interact with a whole and complete object, such as a human face or a cat. This capacity has been called "the common sense," for it involves a primordial receptivity that is a kind of common root and foundation of the five primary senses (Aquinas, 1268/1994a, §602; di Martino, 2008, p. 88; McLuhan, 2015, p. 9). The phrase "common sense" will not be used here because of the different meaning that this phrase has in popular English usage (Ashley, 2013b, pp. 166–167).

Unlike a primary sense, the synthetic capacity does not receive individual or discrete impressions of one particular kind of sensible property (such as visual properties only or aural properties only). Rather, the synthetic capacity is receptive of *all* of the individual impressions originating from the five primary senses (Aquinas, 1273/1981, I, 1.3 ad 2, & 57.2; Aquinas, 1268/1994a, §390; regarding 57.2, see di Martino, 2008, p. 95). In this respect, the synthetic capacity is receptive of everything (Aristotle, ca. 350 BC/2000b, 449a18). The primary senses each contribute their specific kind of sensation to the synthetic capacity for further engagement and processing (Aquinas, 1269/2005b, pp. 156–157).

A significant activity of the synthetic capacity is to differentiate between the various kinds of sense data that a person encounters (Aquinas, 1268/1994a, §390, §§601–614; Aquinas, 1266/2005c, q. 13; Aristotle, ca. 350 BC/2000c, 426b14–427a16). For example, the synthetic capacity is able to distinguish brightness from sweetness, or the feeling of warmth from an unpleasant smell. This activity is neurological, not intellectual, in that it involves the differentiation of discrete sense impressions, not the differentiation of intelligible structures or patterns (Aquinas, 1268/1994a, §601). This activity of differentiation can be described as a kind of negative perceptual judgment or negative "assertion" (as for example with a cube of processed sugar when it is tasted: "the sweetness of this thing differs from its whiteness") (Aristotle, ca. 350 BC/2000c, 426b22, 428a1; also Aquinas, 1268/1994a, §604). It is important to underscore that this activity of the synthetic capacity is pre-intellectual and pre-linguistic. The fact that the two sensations need to be differentiated indicates that both, though sensed by separate capacities, are grasped in a single act of perception (Aquinas, 1268/1994a, §604). The synthetic capacity thus in some manner has multisensory awareness (Aristotle, ca. 350 BC/2000c, 426b22; also Aquinas, 1268/1994a, §604). Because the major function of this capacity is to enable a person to perceive diverse sensible properties together as a whole thing, its primary activity is called synthetic.

This capacity involves awareness of a real whole that in turn structures the discrete sense properties as parts. It is, as some thinkers observe, a "gestalt sense" (de Haan, 2014, p. 404).

There are idealist and realist ways of understanding the activity of the synthetic capacity. The idealist perspective interprets the synthetic capacity as an internally generated structure applied to sensation. This account supposes that diverse and separated sensations are informed by an *a priori* psychological structure that originates absolutely and entirely from within the knower (Kant, 1787/1996, I, Part II, Book I, Chapter 2, Section 2, §§15–20 [B129–146]; Book II, Chapter 1 [B176–177]).

The realist perspective, affirmed by the Meta-Model, proposes that the synthetic capacity responds to structures of sensation existing in the real object of which it is aware. In other words, the synthetic capacity does not create the structure that enables its perception. The holistic structure that informs the synthetic capacity is itself an *object* of perception (Aquinas, 1259/1954, 15.1 ad 3; Aquinas, 1273/1981, I, 1.3 ad 2). In this respect, the synthetic capacity is receptive and passive in relation to the real sensible whole that it perceives (Aquinas, 1268/1994a, §612). Nevertheless, after a person perceives the holistic structure of an object, such structures are preserved as memories and can be recalled so to facilitate recognition of the same or similar objects.

The real whole, then, which structures the activity of the synthetic capacity, is ontologically prior to the synthetic capacity's perception of it and exists independently of that capacity. The conditions of reality (explored by ontology) are prior and independent of persons who perceive and know reality. The reason that the synthetic capacity never perceives opposite parts in the same whole simultaneously and in the same respect (for example, one never perceives "this apple is sweet and not sweet" at the same time) is not because this violates the rules of a logic stipulated in advance and imposed upon human consciousness (see Kant, 1787/1996, I, Part II, Book II, Chapter 2, Section 2 [B195–197]). Rather, the perception of such opposites simultaneously does not occur because such opposites do not coexist simultaneously and in the same respect as parts of concrete ontological wholes in reality.

One should not appeal to fallibility in perception (again, for example, the experience of mistaken identity of another person or perceptual illusions) as grounds for doubting the ability of the synthetic capacity to contact real physical wholes. Here again, one must observe that such errors are errors of recognition that occur at a higher level of processing (namely, in the activity of the evaluative capacity, discussed below); they are not errors of the synthetic capacity. It is rather the synthetic capacity that enables reality to later correct the rare times when the evaluative capacity is subject to illusion.

Because of its ability to be in contact with complex objects in reality, the synthetic capacity is also able to differentiate real objects from products of the imagination. This capability can be exercised upon awakening from sleep in order to differentiate the content of dreams from real sensations (Aquinas, 1273/1981, I, 84.8 ad 2; Ashley, 2013a, pp. 315–316). In this way, the synthetic capacity enables a person to discern whether the holistic structure is originating from real sensory input or from the imagination or memory, and thus also to be conscious of the difference between reality and fantasy. However, evaluation of this content may also occur at a higher cognitive level. The synthetic capacity—with the help, in humans, of higher processing levels—is also able to identify that a primary sense is operating: in other words, by means of the synthetic capacity, one perceives that one sees, or hears, or tastes (Aquinas, 1273/1981, I, 78.4). Furthermore, the synthetic capacity also enables a person to perceive that he or she lives (insofar as one's awareness of sensation is an indication that one is alive) (Aquinas, 1268/1994a, §390).

Sensations of the primary senses are sent to the thalamus for processing, then they are further processed by the primary and secondary sensory cortices and ultimately by the association cortex, where sensory information is even further processed (Stillings et al., 1995, p. 293). The synthetic capacity integrates the various kinds of sense data originating from the primary senses in a manner that is evocative of the processing and integration that occurs in the association cortex (Ashley, 2013a, pp. 317–318; Ashley, 2013b, p. 167, p. 333; de Haan, 2014, p. 403; Kenny, 1994, p. 34; Macdonald, 2007, pp. 369–370; Pasnau, 2002, p. 198; Peghaire, 1943, p. 132;

Tellkamp, 2012, p. 611). Our consideration of the integrating activity of the synthetic capacity in comparison with the integrating activity of the association cortex relates to an open question in philosophical neuroscience (called the "binding problem"), which concerns how the various discrete elements of sensation are synthesized in the brain to yield unified experience (Kolb & Whishaw, 2009, pp. 17, 263). The synthetic capacity, understood as integrating sensations in this way, is unlikely to be an isolated cortical center having the specific function of uniting various kinds of sense data, because no such center has as yet been identified in anatomical neural research. Rather, the synthetic capacity understood in this way would more likely comprise a network of intercortical connections that include the association cortex (Kolb & Whishaw, 2009, p. 263). If we assume this theoretical perspective, the synthetic capacity could be understood as a complex perceptual capacity that is dependent upon reciprocal interaction among the frontal, parietal, temporal, and occipital lobes in order to realize its function of synthesizing discrete visual, aural, and tactile sense impressions.

Some thinkers also affirm that, because of its integrative function, the synthetic capacity should be identified with basic awareness, sentience, or animal consciousness (Peghaire, 1943, p. 123). The word "consciousness" in this way can be treated broadly as a synonym for "cognition" in the most general meaning of the word (Ashley, 2013b, p. 154). The word "consciousness" can also be used more strictly as a synonym for "sentience," that is, basic animal consciousness or awareness (Aristotle, ca. 350 BC/2000c, 427a16; on this form of sense knowledge in contrast with intellectual knowledge, see Aquinas, 1273/1981, I, 85.3). Consciousness as understood in the present realist perspective is not reduced to an epiphenomenal product of brain activity (Kolb & Whishaw, 2009, p. 652).

With respect to basic consciousness, our consideration of the synthetic capacity again relates to an open question in philosophical neuroscience, namely, the problem of identifying the neural correlates of elementary consciousness. As noted above, if the synthetic capacity (associated with a network of intercortical connections) is a complex perceptual-cognitive capacity that enables unified and integrated sense experience, then this capacity correlates with—or is—basic awareness or consciousness (Goldstein, 2010, p. 39). This elementary form of awareness is distinct from and not reducible to the biological and material processes of primary sensation, which it integrates. In the present discussion, one may go further and propose that basic consciousness as described here is qualitatively distinct from the neurobiological correlates associated with its own activity (on basic consciousness, see Vitz, 2017). At the same time, this basic awareness is an expression of the unity of an animal's experience. With respect to humans, recent studies in neuroscience that consider fMRI scans of comatose patients have suggested that the neural network associated with basic awareness may involve a small region of the brainstem (the rostral dorsolateral pontine tegmentum) and two cortical regions (the ventral anterior insula and the pregenual anterior cingulate cortex) (Fischer et al., 2016). In this respect, the insular cortex and cingulate cortex might also participate in the network of intercortical connections involving the association cortex, discussed above.

Sentience or animal consciousness does not necessarily involve self-consciousness (Ashley, 2013b, p. 152). This is evident when we understand the basic kind of consciousness as a kind of reflectivity of sensed objects (Wojtyła, 1979,

pp. 31–34). But consciousness construed as a mirror is incomplete when considered only in and of itself without its orientation toward perceived objects (Wojtyła, 1979, p. 38). A mirror does not reflect itself; a mirror reflects objects that are ontologically distinct from the mirror itself. Thus, the perception of self-consciousness (self-reflection or self-knowledge) belongs to a different capacity, one that is bound up with language (Wojtyła, 1979, p. 36 & p. 304 endnote 17; regarding self-consciousness and language [*qualia* 2], see Vitz, 2017; also Chapter 6, "Person as an Integrated Laminate"). While general animal consciousness includes awareness of interoceptive physiological sensations (such as pain), self-consciousness is something more than merely the awareness of perception (which is the activity of the synthetic capacity as described above, for example, perceiving that one is seeing or hearing). Rather, self-consciousness involves perception of one's self as the agent who is perceiving (Ashley, 2013b, pp. 195–196). This particular activity, however, need not be construed as entirely nonmaterial. Contemporary neuroscience, for example, has identified the medial prefrontal cortex as operative in cognitive exercises involving self-reference (Heatherton et al., 2006, p. 18; Pfeifer, Lieberman, & Dapretto, 2007, p. 1324).

The Memory Capacity

First-order individual sense impressions originating from the primary senses as well as second-order impressions originating from the synthetic capacity are stored and recalled by means of the capacity of memory (Aquinas, 1266/2005c, q. 13). The memory under consideration here is a higher-order perceptual-cognitive capacity involving neurological activity. Our presentation, if not otherwise specified, will be of simple memory, which is similar in many ways to that found in higher animals. This sensory-perceptual memory is different, and at a lower level, than the intellectual memory, that is, the nonmaterial memory that belongs to the intellect of the soul and that can subsist without the body (Chapter 8, "Personal Wholeness," and Chapter 15, "Rational"; also see Aristotle, ca. 350 BC/2000c, 430a18; regarding the intellectual memory, see Aquinas, 1273/1981, I, 79.6–7; Aquinas, 1259/1954, 10.2, especially ad 1). The present consideration focuses only on this sensory-perceptual storage and retrieval capacity that has neural correlates and not on the memory that belongs to the higher capacity of the intellect that transcends such neural correlates.

One's act of remembering involves the basic awareness of consciously reliving a past perception (this includes a *reactivation* of associated neural pathways). One can go so far as to say that in some way such a reliving also involves the reactivation of the past awareness; this accounts for the disconcerting psychological symptoms associated with re-experiencing events of trauma or intense shame (Keyes, Underwood, Snyder, Dailey, & Hourihan, 2018; Linley, & Joseph, 2004; Schore, 2002; Sokolowski, 2000, p. 68, p. 71). When considering memory, one should differentiate between short-term memory and long-term memory (Kolb & Whishaw, 2009, pp. 434, pp. 513–518; Stillings et al., 1995, pp. 40–41). One can also differentiate between explicit memories and implicit memories: while an explicit memory is the conscious recall of an experienced event, an implicit memory is exemplified by a spontaneous response to a perception (Kolb & Whishaw, 2009, p. 493; Siegel, 2012, pp. 88–90). Such responses can occur in ways of which a person is unaware (for example, a person might spontaneously fear a hospital upon seeing one, yet without understanding

why). An implicit memory is also exemplified by an acquired skill or habit, which we will discuss, with respect to cognitive dispositions, below (Kolb & Whishaw, 2009, p. 493, p. 705). Often, with implicit memories there may also be explicit memories intertwined with the emotional response (Bear, Connors, & Paradiso, 2007, p. 582; Siegel, 2012, pp. 88–90). Explicit memories are dependent upon a neural circuit involving the hippocampus, the rhinal cortex in the temporal lobe, and the prefrontal cortex in the frontal lobe, while implicit memories are dependent upon the entire neocortex and structures within the basal ganglia (Kolb & Whishaw, 2009, p. 499, p. 510).

The Imaginative Capacity

The perceptions of the synthetic capacity along with their constitutive sensations are preserved in a different perceptual capacity, called the imagination (Aquinas, 1273/1981, I, 78.4). This higher order capacity enables a person to produce mental copies or replicas of sensations and perceptions. These replicas can then be perceived in turn (as, for example, when one evokes a mental image of a tree before one's "inner eye" after having seen a real tree with one's bodily eyes). Such replicas are akin to residual "likenesses" of primary experiences, much like the impression of an image left in wax or a sketch of an object (Aristotle, ca. 350 BC/2000a, 450a31). They are at times called "phantasms" (Aristotle, ca. 350 BC/2000c, 428a1). Here they will be called "mental images" (with the caveat that this phrase refers also to replicated sounds, tastes, odors, and sensations of touch, as well as the whole objects grasped by the synthetic capacity).

It is the synthetic capacity that perceives a mental image produced by the imagination (Aristotle, ca. 350 BC/2000a, 450a10–11). When the awareness of the synthetic capacity perceives a mental image as its object, the image is faint and weakened in comparison with perception of a real object (Aristotle, ca. 350 BC/1994, 1370a29). At the same time, such replicas can be just as efficacious as present realities for eliciting affect in a person (such as desire or aversion) (Aquinas, 1268/1994a, §669). Elements of objects previously perceived (such as the "gold" or "wingedness" of a statue of an angel) can be retained in the imaginative capacity itself. The imaginative capacity enables a person to combine such retained elements into new designs. In this way, entirely imaginary combinations can be constructed (such as a centaur or a winged horse) (Aquinas, 1273/1981, I, 78.4). While the retentive function of the imaginative capacity is common to persons and other animals, this combining function is a unique human capacity (Wolfson, 1935, p. 122).

Imagination is properly characterized as a higher-order perceptual capacity and not as a primary sense, because it can be activated when sensible realities are no longer physically present: mental images can be recalled by a person after primary sensation has ceased (as occurs in dreams) (Ashley, 2006, p. 205). While, as mentioned above, the sensations of the primary senses are never false (considered strictly in orientation to specific sensible properties), the syntheses of the imagination can be false in comparison with reality (Aristotle, ca. 350 BC/2000c, 428a5–13, 428b18; see also Aquinas, 1268/1994a, §§641–647, §661; Frede, 2001, p. 163).

Just as the imagination differs from the primary senses, so also does its mode of combining retained mental images differ from the activity of other human capacities, such as the ability to form opinions. The formation of imaginative fantasies can involve a kind of free play of invention (Aquinas, 1268/1994a, §633). While the imagination and the cognitive capacity, which

forms opinions, both produce combinations that are either true or false in correspondence with reality, an opinion that attains to the status of a belief results from a person's obtaining conviction of its truth by way of a reasoning process. In contrast, the formation of imaginative combinations does not presuppose a reasoning process. This is evident from the fact that animals other than humans can possess some kind of basic imaginative capacity, but they lack both the ability to combine images in original ways as well as the ability to reason (Aristotle, ca. 350 BC/2000c, 428a19–25; also Aquinas, 1268/1994a, §§649–650).

The imaginative capacity of the person can also be differentiated from his or her memory. It is helpful to outline this difference, since the imagination and memory are easily confused (Sokolowski, 2000, p. 69). A contemporary philosophical approach distinguishes these two capacities by way of a phenomenological analysis (that is, by way of an introspective consideration of realities in light of how they are experienced). This analysis juxtaposes the mode of consciousness operating when a person is focused on a present object (what might be called perceptual attentiveness) with the mode of consciousness present when the person is focused on interior awareness, such as memories or fantasies (Sokolowski, 2000, pp. 71–75; Sokolowski, 2008, pp. 140–141). Furthermore, the mode of consciousness operative when one is focused on products of the imagination is different from the mode of consciousness present when one is focused on memories. The imagination represents realities for consciousness, whereas memory recalls stored perceptions of past realities (Sokolowski, 2000, p. 67).

A further difference between the imagination and memory is the realism associated with perceptions stored in memory. In psychologically healthy persons, certainty is typically absent with respect to affirming the reality of the products of one's imagination (Sokolowski, 2000, p. 71). Only a very limited realism can accrue to the imaginative capacity. This is found when one fantasizes about possible futures that might occur. While such imaginative projections into the future may enable a person to make decisions, fear of merely imagined possibilities can also lead to groundless anxiety (Sokolowski, 2000, pp. 73–74).

A final comment should be made about the relationship between the imagination and mental health. When a person is healthy, his or her intellect regulates the use and influence of the imaginative capacity. In other words, the active use of the combinative power of the imagination (to produce a composite image that affects the person in some way) is in healthy persons always subordinate to that person's intellect and volition (Aristotle, ca. 350 BC/2000c, 427b19; also Aquinas, 1268/1994a, §633). Yet the imaginative capacity may become the predominant influence upon a person in times of sickness, sleep, serious psychological illness, or with the emergence of strong passions such as anger (Aristotle, ca. 350 BC/2000c, 429a7–9; also Aquinas, 1268/1994a, §670). With respect to this point, it would be helpful to observe the connection between the imagination and emotional responses to stimuli; however, this topic will be treated in the next chapter.

The Evaluative Capacity

An elementary or basic evaluative capacity is found at the highest level of sensory-perceptual processing. At this higher level, the evaluative capacity can exert a top-down influence on both the imagination and the synthetic capacity. In humans, this capacity interacts with the intellectual capacity, which is higher still, but also distinct from it (the evaluative capacity is at times called the "cogitative" capacity: see Klubertanz, 1952). Inquiry into the nature and functioning of this capacity is one area of contemporary research that stands to benefit greatly from the effort to integrate philosophy with the psychological sciences (especially in connection with cognitive theory and therapy) (Ashley, 2013c, pp. 290–291).

A similar evaluative capacity can be found in most higher animals, which proceed by way of instinctive estimation. Consider, for example, a bird's attraction to food or a sheep's natural inclination to avoid wolves (Aquinas, 1273/1981, I, 78.4; Ashley, 2013b, pp. 171–173; Ashley, 2013c, p. 291). This capacity in animals is activated by individual sense impressions that produce automatic and instinctive evaluations. These evaluations arise without deliberation on the part of the animal (Aquinas, 1259/1954, 24.2; Cates, 2009, p. 114). For example, an animal can by instinct avoid a harmful predator. In this respect, certain animals also manifest a kind of animal intelligence when they reach correct evaluative judgments (Aquinas, 1268/1994a, §629; Aquinas, 1272/1993, §1215; Aquinas, 1269/2005a, Chapter 1, p. 184; Aquinas, 1259/1954, 24.2, 25.2; for the example of dolphin intelligence, see Bearzi & Stanford, 2010; MacIntyre, 1999, pp. 21–28; Pryor & Norris, 1991). Such judgments can, in higher animals, involve evaluation of what means are most conducive for obtaining desired ends (for example, dolphins when hunting fish for food may change their course of action when an initial attempt proves unsuccessful) (MacIntyre, 1999, pp. 25–26).

The evaluative capacity in humans is much more complex. This capacity is "evaluative" in that it enables a person to discern and assess objects of consciousness, for example, "this animal is to be avoided" (*hostile*) or "this animal is be approached" (*friendly*) (Aquinas, 1259/1954, 25.2; Cates, 2009, p. 120). This assessment can involve certain reactions that occur on the basis of natural inclinations (for example, the natural inclination for self-preservation is manifested in the desire to nurse found in mammals). But the evaluative capacity in humans develops over time. Children, for example, are typically unable to evaluate the benefit or harm of most objects in an adequate manner. This is because the natural inclinations of persons are largely undetermined with respect to their realization in practical activities (for example, one may experience a natural inclination to satisfy hunger but be uncertain whether a particular substance can be eaten as food); specific applications of general natural inclinations are always subsequent to education (culture) and the acquisition of life experience; this knowledge is applied in practical activity as the evaluative capacity develops (Ashley, 2006, pp. 433–434; Ashley, 2013c, p. 291). Contemporary neuroscience observes that this perceptual evaluative capacity in particular involves the prefrontal region of the frontal lobe of the cerebrum (Kolb & Whishaw, 2009, p. 430). In accordance with the neurological constitution of this capacity, its use and realization varies from person to person, as do physiological differences (Aquinas, 1265/2001, 75.16).

The functions of the human evaluative capacity can be sorted into three primary categories: recognition, appraisal, and recollection. With respect to recognition, the evaluative capacity proceeds in a manner that "compares and contrasts" particular forms in order to identify a present individual, for example, when a person recognizes a friend in a crowd of people (Aquinas, 1266/2005c, q. 13). The evaluative capacity's process of recognition can also function in a discursive manner, including a number of mental operations such as questioning, compar-

ison, and referencing memory (Aquinas, 1964, §1255; Aquinas, 1272/1993, §1255; Peghaire, 1943, pp. 137–138). These operations enable a kind of analysis of a present sensible object and its properties. This analysis refers to stored memories for the purpose of judging sameness, difference, and similarity. This process occurs, for example, when the person compares a present object, which is grasped by means of the synthetic capacity (awareness), with a memory. Through the application and comparison of memories with such objects, the person is able to judge whether the present individual is the same as, different than, or similar to the memory. When the present reality is judged to be the same as a stored memory, an act of recognition occurs: this particular thing or person is known. The evaluative capacity may be understood, therefore, to grasp the unique character of this individual object, such as this person or this toy (Aquinas, 1268/1994a, §396, §398). There is an important difference between the evaluative capacity and the synthetic capacity (awareness): the synthetic capacity integrates discrete sensations into the unified experience of awareness, whereas the evaluative capacity recalls affection (emotions) and cognition related to the present objects by means of referencing memory.

Certain higher animals are also able to recognize and identify individual objects and individual people (MacIntyre, 1999, pp. 27, 41). But the evaluative capacity is a more developed capacity in humans, which enables humans to recognize the distinctive characteristics of other persons. By this capacity, one is able to grasp *who* another person is, for example, one's brother or cousin, based on higher-level properties. One can thereby refer to the "Socrates-ness" of Socrates (Aquinas, 1266/1932, q.8 a.3). Another distinctively human use of the evaluative capacity is the recognition of what the individual object or thing is (for example, to recognize Socrates as a man, that is, as human) (Aquinas, 1268/1994a, §398; Black, 2000, pp. 67–68).

Further, not only does the evaluative capacity of a person separate individual perceptions from one another through its process of comparison (for example, perceiving one person as harmful and another as helpful), but it can also synthesize individual perceptions together (Aquinas, 1259/1954, 10.5; Aquinas, 1265/2001, 73.14; Peghaire, 1943, p. 137) (for example, when a person is perceived to be dangerous but at the same time perceived to be contained). This is a synthesis of perceptions, not a synthesis of sensations (the latter occurs by way of awareness or the synthetic capacity, as discussed above). In this activity of synthesis, the evaluative capacity is similar to the imagination.

With respect to appraisal, the evaluative capacity, by way of its synthesis of perceptions, is able to form a value judgment (for example, "this tool will be useful for my project") (Aquinas, 1266/2005c, q. 13; Ashley, 2006, p. 205; Ashley, 2013b, p. 171). But, whereas lower-level perceptual syntheses (awareness) are not subject to fallibility, the evaluative process is fallible, as is evident when someone misidentifies a present reality or when a person makes decisions on the basis of false judgments concerning individual matters (for example, "I must flee since this man is pursuing me," when in fact there is no pursuit). One can misjudge reality with respect to any evaluative function (for example, in the case of mistaken identity or of persons suffering from delusions). While one should always judge carefully, since one's judgment can be in error, this observation does not necessarily warrant adopting an epistemology of universal doubt (Maritain, 1932/1995, p. 82).

The evaluative capacity has its own unique structure that informs its process of appraising objects (for example, "this substance is *harmful*" or "that tool is *useful*"). It is not derived from the primary senses or the synthetic capacity (basic awareness) (Aquinas, 1273/1981, I, 78.4, 81.2 ad 2; Allers, 1941b, pp. 212–213; Peghaire, 1943, p. 133; Gasson, 1963, p. 9). Also, while the synthetic capacity enables one to differentiate sweet from warm, it does not enable one to appraise a perceived object as useful. As found in animals, an evaluative perception of usefulness can result from an instinctive reaction to an object of awareness (as when a bird reacts to straw and uses it to build a nest). Yet, in humans, the evaluative capacity's perception of value can result from a higher level process of investigation and deliberation (Aquinas, 1266/2005c, q. 13; Aquinas, 1266/1953, a.13, p. 330).

Through its activities of recognizing individuals and assessing them, the evaluative capacity can trigger a subsequent affective reaction in response to a recognized individual (Aquinas, 1273/1981, I, 81.3). For example, recognition of a caregiver can trigger a simple positive affective reaction (Siegel, 2012, pp. 88–90); similar responses do occur in animals, upon recognition of their care-providers. In a more complex way, a person may be grateful for a particular job, which they are performing in pursuit of the expected income it should bring (Ashley, 2013b, p. 178). Yet, as mentioned above, evaluations of sensed objects can also arise from the imagination (Aquinas, 1273/1981, I, 81.3 ad 2). The imagination, therefore, can also elicit an affective reaction in response to an object (whether a present reality or a fantasy).

A further function of the evaluative capacity involves its ability to facilitate the recall of a perception stored in memory. This evaluative procedure is often referred to as "recollection" or "reminiscence" (Aristotle, ca. 350 BC/2000a, 451a18; also Aquinas, 1269/2005a, p. 184; Aquinas,

1273/1981, I, 78.4; Aquinas, 1266/2005c, q. 13). Recollection differs from recovery of a memory (Aristotle, ca. 350 BC/2000a, 451a20–21, 451b8). Recollection is a discursive process by which we recover prior cognitions for a purpose (such a cognition may be a sensation of a primary sense or a higher order perception), as when, faced with several options, we recollect the safer path home (Aristotle, ca. 350 BC/2000a, 451b2–5; also Aquinas, 1269/2005a, pp. 208–209).

In the tradition of Aristotle, the evaluative capacity is called the "passive intellect" (Aquinas, 1265/2001, 60.1), a term that will not be employed here. Instead, we will refer to it as a higher-order cognition, one that has some similarity to and some interaction with the intellectual capacity. Both capacities apprehend objects that are only incidentally related to the objects of primary sensation (Aquinas, 1268/1994a, §396; Lisska, 2007, pp. 6–7). But the evaluative capacity can be differentiated from the intellectual capacity in several ways. First, the evaluative capacity is an organic and neurological capacity, whereas the intellectual capacity is nonmaterial (Tellkamp, 2012, p. 627; Vitz, 2017). This difference leads to a difference in operation: the evaluative capacity knows reality by way of comparing particular perceptions of concrete realities, whereas the intellectual capacity knows reality by way of comparing universal intelligible patterns that are separated from matter (Aquinas, 1273/1981, I, 78.4; Aquinas, 1265/2001, 60.1).

A second difference between the evaluative capacity and the intellectual capacity is that the evaluative capacity serves a preparatory function for the intellect by providing mental images from the imagination and the memory (Aquinas, 1265/2001, 60.1, 73.16, 73.28, 81.12; Lonergan, 1997, p. 184). Such mental images are stored in the imagination and memory, but they are not stored in the intellect (Aquinas, 1265/2001,

73.14; Barker, 2012a, p. 218). In other words, mental images originate from physiological and neurological sources and are retained in neurological structures (namely, in the memory and imagination) (Aquinas, 1273/1981, I, 89.1; Aquinas, 1265/2001, 81.12; Cohen, 1982, p. 201; Egnor, 2017).

A common characteristic of the evaluative capacity and the intellectual capacity is that, just as the evaluative capacity acts upon and influences the emotions (inasmuch as higher cortical functions can supervene upon the limbic system), so too does the intellectual capacity act upon and affect the evaluative capacity (Aquinas, 1273/1981, I, 81.3 & 78.4 ad 5; Cates, 2009, p. 116). It is in virtue of being affected by the intellectual capacity (a top-down influence) that the evaluative capacity (a bottom up inclination) can be understood as "participating" in the nonmaterial dimension of the person and in reason (Aquinas, 1273/1981, I, 78.4; Aquinas, 1268/1994a, §397; Pasnau, 2002, p. 254). In this respect, the evaluative capacity recognizes what an individual is, that is, the common nature of a thing. The evaluative capacity informed by the intellect in this way can influence the interpretation given to the primary senses (for example, when particularizing the universal understanding one has of "humanity" and combining this with the individual perception of "Socrates" as an example of humanity). The evaluative capacity thus serves to instantiate universal knowledge stored in the intellectual memory. In this way, a person can recognize Socrates both as "Socrates" and as "human," as mentioned above (Aristotle, ca. 350 BC/1997, 100b2; also Aquinas, 1272/1970, II.20, p. 239; Lonergan, 1997, p. 43; see also Aristotle, ca. 350 BC/2005, 184a25; Aquinas, 1269/1999, I.1, §§9–11).

The evaluative capacity's recognition of the universal (humanity) in the particular (Socrates), however, does not involve the evaluative capacity's knowing the universal nature as such separate and apart from particular objects (Peghaire, 1943, p. 140). Rather, the evaluative capacity mediates universal intelligible patterns to the synthetic capacity (basic awareness) in a manner that is always particularized and individuated (Aquinas, 1259/1954, 10.5 ad 4; Aquinas, 1273/1981, I, 20.1 ad 1 & 81.3; Ashley, 2013c, p. 291). For example, when one knows with one's intellect in a universal way that curry is always savory (all things being equal), and when the synthetic capacity recognizes that this present individual thing is curry, then the evaluative capacity assesses the present reality in light of the universal knowledge. A common property, "savory," is thereby recognized as present in this individual object. The evaluative capacity mediates between the highest level of sensory-perceptual-cognition and nonmaterial intellectual activity.

The evaluative capacity plays a similar role when mediating universal ethical judgments to concrete situations (for example, one should not steal this present item from its owner, since in general it is immoral to steal) (Allers, 1941a, p. 106; Aquinas, 1273/1981, I, 86.1 ad 2; Pasnau, 2002, pp. 254–255). For this reason, the evaluative capacity is also understood to be the human capacity that serves the deliberation necessary when making an ethical decision about a particular action (here one can see the interaction between deliberation, recollection, and the comparison of individual things) (Aristotle, ca. 350 BC/2000a, 453a13–14; also Aquinas, 1269/2005a, p. 230). In this respect, the evaluative capacity can be developed with the virtue of practical wisdom (Aquinas, 1273/1981, II-II, 49.2). As with the application of universal ethical judgments, the evaluative capacity also applies the general expectations of human fore-

sight to particular circumstances ("it is cloudy outside and I hear thunder; this typically means it will rain, therefore I should avoid a road that is subject to flooding") (Aquinas, 1259/1954, 10.2 ad sc 4).

The different functions of the evaluative capacity and the intellectual capacity lead to a noteworthy distinction in epistemology, which has methodological importance, namely, a distinction between experiential knowledge and intellection (Aquinas, 1271/1926, §18; Aquinas, 1272/1995, §18; Barker, 2012b, p. 61). Experiential knowledge involves an attentive engagement with and observation of individual sensory-perceptual-cognitive realities (Aquinas, 1273/1981, I, 114.2; Barker, 2012b, p. 46). Conversely, intellection occurs when the person grasps and understands a universal nature (such as, humanity). The activity of any human capacity occurs in accordance with a structure derived from reality. Such structuring occurs at each hierarchical level of activity (sensation, perception, and understanding). In this way, just as the sensation of a sense capacity occurs in accordance with a sense impression, and just as the perception of a higher-order perceptual capacity involves a holistic structure of its own that can be stored in memory, so also does the understanding of the intellectual capacity occur in accordance with its own distinctive structure (Aquinas, 1273/1981, I, 84.4 & 85.1).

In contrast to the intellect, which knows by way of universal intelligible patterns separated from material objects, the lower evaluative capacity enables a knower only to have experiential knowledge of a concrete commonality that is discerned to be present in numerous perceptions of the same thing, event, or person (Aquinas, 1272/1970, II.20, p. 237; Aquinas, 1272/1995, §17; Barker, 2012b, pp. 57–63). This concrete commonality known by the lower evaluative capacity is inseparable from the particular sensory-perceptions in which it is found.

A person is genuinely said "to understand" only by virtue of his intellect, which considers reality by way of universal intelligible patterns (Aquinas, 1265/2001, 73.15). Although comparisons made during the process of evaluation can enable subsequent acts of understanding or insight that are strictly nonmaterial, the evaluative capacity always remains focused upon distinct concrete objects (Lonergan, 1997, p. 56); it is always oriented toward and grounded in particular individual things (p. 53). An example that contrasts experiential and intellectual knowing may be found in the following scenarios: with his properly human evaluative capacity, a physician observes that a certain medicine is the common factor that healed a particular group of his patients of an ailment; with his intellect, the same physician judges that this medicine will—universally speaking—heal *any* person suffering from that ailment, all things being equal (Aquinas, 1272/1970, II.20, p. 237). These two kinds of cognitive processing are distinct and operate at different levels of knowing. Yet they are also related, in that the lower level contributes to the activity of the higher level: just as the evaluative capacity's experiential knowledge of a concrete commonality depends upon the integration of many perceptions (memories and mental images), so does the intellect's universal knowledge by way of a separate intelligible pattern depend upon integrating many instances of experiential knowledge (Aquinas, 1273/1981, I, 58.3 ob 3; Aquinas, 1272/1995, §18; Aristotle, ca. 350 BC/1997, 100a4; Aristotle, ca. 350 BC/2003, 980b28).

Only when the intellect grasps a complete universal can the principles of the arts and sciences become fully established in the human mind (Aquinas, 1272/1970, II.20, p. 237; Aristotle, ca. 350 BC/1997, 100a4–100b4; see also Aqui-

nas, 1265/2001, 60.12–14). The evaluative perception of a commonality is "almost the same" as intellection by way of a universal; evaluative perceptions in fact can enable a person to have general success in practical activities (Aquinas, 1272/1995, §17). Such is apparent when a person who has firsthand experiential knowledge (without having studied the science) can encounter success in his or her practical activities, whereas another person who does not have firsthand experiential knowledge might fail (although having studied the science at length) (Aquinas, 1272/1995, §20, §22). It would not be wrong to compare one's intellectual capacity and one's evaluative capacity in the same way that one might compare theory and praxis, science and application, philosophical contemplation and the active moral life.

At this point, one is now better able to understand how the intellect is dependent upon the evaluative capacity and also how the evaluative capacity is said to prepare mental images for the intellect's consideration: the evaluative capacity prepares mental images when by its function of recognition it discerns particular features that are common to multiple perceptions and experiences. Once a person, by means of his evaluative capacity, recognizes that there is a common feature that is present in multiple perceptions of the same reality, he is then able to use his intellect to isolate that common feature and consider the intelligible structure or pattern itself, apart from perception and sensation. It is in this respect that one reaches the apex of natural human knowing. A person's intellect in this function, however, remains dependent upon the initial preparatory activity of the evaluative capacity (just as the evaluative capacity is dependent upon a person's memory and imagination, and these perceptual capacities are dependent in turn upon the bodily senses). Importantly, different evaluative preparations of mental imagery (recognition of different commonalties) will necessarily lead to different acts of understanding (Aquinas, 1273/1981, II-II, 173.2; Lonergan, 1997, p. 184). Variations in evaluative perception will therefore lead to various perspectives, differentiate the sciences, and inform diverse worldviews.

In sum, through the interplay of the evaluative capacity and the intellect, one may consider the application of universal principles to particular cases, as when one uses one's imagination to picture a singular triangle that conforms to universal geometrical principles, or to picture a moving object that proceeds in accordance with the universal principles of physics, or to imagine in the interpersonal realm an act of self-sacrifice in conformity to the universal calling of spouses in marriage (Aquinas, 1272/1993, §1214; Ashley, 2006, p. 205).

Cognitive Dispositions

Sensory-perceptual-cognitive capacities can be trained and developed with repeated actions. The synthetic capacity, for example, can be conditioned to acquire skill in differentiating nuanced degrees of color or flavors (Aquinas, 1272/1993, §1215). A similar process occurs with the evaluative capacity: through recurrent assessments of perceptions, through similar behavioral responses, and through repeated evaluative operations, the person gradually develops various dispositions. Some dispositions incline the person to act in an ordered manner, which contributes to the realization of personal flourishing, or, conversely, to act in a disordered manner, which leads the person away from health and the good life (Chapter 14, "Emotional"). For example, in an emergency room a young doctor may initially be repulsed by the sight of severe injuries. However, with experience, such repulsions often fade, and the doctor is able to assess and offer helpful intervention, as the result of a new disposition.

Conditioning, which occurs through life experience, can lead to the acquisition of predispositions that influence a person when appraising objects of perception. In this respect, a person may experience automatic or reflex attraction to (or repulsions from) other people, objects, and kinds of behaviors (for example, the habitual desire for chocolate upon seeing it). Such acquired automatic appraisals can be understood as "pre-rational" in multiple ways. For example, an automatic appraisal is pre-rational when the values of parents are internalized by a child and used when that child chooses to pursue certain goods or to behave in a certain manner without deliberation (Ashley, 2006, p. 434; Lambert & McShane, 2010, p. 122, footnote 34).

Such judgments in turn influence emotions and contribute to the later rational development of moral virtues at a still higher mental level. They can often corroborate rational judgments and choices, and in general they motivate the person in an "upward" direction (that is, they involve inclinations "from below"). For example, when a person observes child abuse in a market, he or she may react automatically with anger, which corroborates the rational judgment that such behavior is immoral. But to react spontaneously to a particular deed with an evaluative judgment (for example, that it is repulsive) does not in itself (as a simple evaluative perception) constitute a complete moral act. In the example of viewing child abuse, the initial evaluation would lead to a further cognitive act involving the application of a universal ethical norm (John Paul II, 1993; Titus, 2013).

Through top-down processes, such as guidance from the intellect and reflection upon experience, the evaluative capacity can also be formed with a virtuous disposition that leads to human flourishing, namely, the moral virtue of prudence, which includes associated dispositions of providing good counsel and respecting law (Aquinas, 1272/1993, §§1214–1215, §1255). The cardinal moral virtue of prudence, while properly a virtue of the intellect, contributes to the healthy exercise of the evaluative capacity (Aquinas, 1273/1981, II-II, 47.3 ad 3; I-II, 50.4 ad 3 & 56.5).

In a similar way, through frequent exercise of memory (that is, through reflection), a person can develop skill in recollection (Aristotle, ca. 350 BC/2000a, 451a12–14; see also Aquinas, 1269/2005a, pp. 203–204). The evaluative capacity can be conditioned in its mode of recollection to follow a particular sequence of thoughts for the recovery of a valued memory (Aristotle, ca. 350 BC/2000a, 451b10–452a1; also Aquinas, 1269/2005a, pp. 211–214). Furthermore, such conditioning can involve the development of dispositions such as those involving an athletic ability or refined manual skill. These acquired dispositions may be understood as implicit or body memories as discussed above (Ellis, 2004; Ellis & Ellis, 2011; Beck, 1979; Kolb & Whishaw, 2009, p. 705).

The evaluative capacity can also be disposed in such a way that it can contribute to the onset of psychopathology (Journet, 1924, pp. 37–38; Ripperger, 2013, p. 280). Disordered cognitive evaluations can interfere with a person's interpretation of experience and can elicit undue affective responses. Psychotherapy is particularly concerned with addressing such dysfunctional cognitive dispositions, volitions, and emotional states that do not contribute to the flourishing and well-being of the person (Ashley, 2013b, p. 317). From a philosophical point of view, psychological illness can with some probability be primarily associated with the higher evaluative capacity (Ashley, 2013c, p. 291). Dysfunctional patterns of thought often occur in conjunction with disordered affective states and behaviors, which can lead to cognitive schemas that develop into psychological pathologies (Ashley, 2013b, p. 334). Psychotherapy serves to facilitate change with respect to these dysfunctional schemas or patterns (Sperry & Sperry, 2012, pp. 71–72).

Conclusion: The Basis for Active Knowledge and an Active Encounter with the World

As is clear from the preceding section, sensory-perceptual-cognitive capacities involve a spectrum of basic cognition. This spectrum rises from the five primary senses up through the higher order perceptual-cognitive capacities and ultimately to the nonmaterial capacities of the person, which involve one's higher intellect and use of language. While distinct, these various kinds of cognition are all oriented to reality. The sensation associated with each activated primary sense is a primordial kind of cognition. The level of cognition associated with the higher-order perceptual-cognitive capacities is more refined than what is found at the level of the primary senses, just as the nonmaterial intellect of the person (or "universal reason") enables a cognition that is still higher than that which occurs at the level of the perceptual-cognitive capacities (Aquinas, 1273/1981, I, 78.4). On the basis of sensory-perceptual-cognitive experience, the person has an active encounter with the real world.

REFERENCES

Allers, R. (1941a). The intellectual cognition of particulars. *The Thomist, 3*(1), 95–163.

Allers, R. (1941b). The *vis cogitativa* and evaluation. *The New Scholasticism, 15*(3), 195–221.

Almeder, R. F. (1996). *Blind realism: An essay on human knowledge and natural science.* New York, NY: Rowman & Littlefield.

Aquinas, T. (1926). *In metaphysicam Aristotelis commentaria* (M.-R. Cathala, Ed.). Turin, Italy: Marietti. (Original work composed ca. 1271)

Aquinas, T. (1932). *On the power of God: Quaestiones disputatae de potentia dei* (English Dominican Fathers, Trans.). Eugene, OR: Wipf & Stock. (Original work composed 1265–1266)

Aquinas, T. (1953). *Quaestio disputata de anima* (P. P. M. Calcaterra & T. S. Centi, Eds.). In P. Bazzi, M. Calcaterra, T. S. Centi, E. Odetto, & P. M. Pession (Eds.), *Quaestiones disputatae* (Vol. 2, pp. 277–362). Rome, Italy: Marietti. (Original work composed 1265–1266)

Aquinas, T. (1954). *Truth* (3 Vols.) (R. W. Mulligan, J. V. McGlynn, R. W. Schmidt, Trans.). Indianapolis, IN: Hackett. (Original work composed 1256–1259)

Aquinas, T. (1964). *In decem libros Ethicorum Aristotelis ad Nicomachum* (R. M. Spiazzi, Ed.). Rome, Italy: Marietti. (Original work composed 1271–1272)

Aquinas, T. (1970). *Commentary on the* Posterior analytics *of Aristotle* (F. R. Larcher, Trans.). Albany, NY: Magi Books. (Original work composed 1271–1272)

Aquinas, T. (1981). *Summa theologiae* (English Dominican Province, Trans.). Westminster, MD: Christian Classics. (Original work composed 1273)

Aquinas, T. (1993). *Commentary on Aristotle's* Nicomachean ethics (C. J. Litzinger, Trans.). Notre Dame, IN: Dumb Ox Books. (Original work composed 1271–1272)

Aquinas, T. (1994a). *Commentary on Aristotle's De anima* (K. Foster, Trans.). Notre Dame, IN: Dumb Ox Books. (Original work composed 1267–1268)

Aquinas, T. (1995). *Commentary on Aristotle's* Metaphysics (J. P. Rowan, Trans.). Notre Dame, IN: Dumb Ox Books. (Original work composed ca. 1270–1272)

Aquinas, T. (1999). *Commentary on Aristotle's* Physics (R. J. Blackwell, R. J. Spath, & W. E. Thirlkel, Trans.). Notre Dame, IN: Dumb Ox Books. (Original work composed 1268–1269)

Aquinas, T. (2001). *Summa contra gentiles. Book two: Creation* (J. F. Anderson, Trans.). Notre Dame, IN: University of Notre Dame Press. (Original work composed 1260–1265)

Aquinas, T. (2005a). Commentary on Aristotle's *On Memory and Recollection* (E. M. Macierowski, Trans.). In K. White and E. M. Macierowski (Eds.), *Commentaries on Aristotle's "On sense and what is sensed" and "On memory and recollection"* (pp. 167–260). Washington, DC: The Catholic University of America Press. (Original work composed 1268–1269)

Aquinas, T. (2005b). Commentary on Aristotle's *On sense and what is sensed* (K. White, Trans.). In K. White and E. M. Macierowski (Eds.), *Commentaries on Aristotle's "On sense and what is sensed" and "On memory and recollection"* (pp. 1–165). Washington, DC: The Catholic University of America Press. (Original work composed 1268–1269)

Aquinas, T. (2005c). *Questions on the soul* (J. H. Robb, Trans.). Milwaukee, WI: Marquette University Press. (Original work composed 1265–1266)

Aristotle. (1994). *Rhetoric* (J. H. Freese, Trans.). Cambridge, MA: Harvard University Press. (Original work composed ca. 350 BC)

Aristotle. (1997). *Posterior analytics* (E. S. Forster, Trans.). Cambridge, MA: Harvard University Press. (Original work composed ca. 350 BC)

Aristotle. (2000a). On memory and recollection. In W. S. Hett (Trans.), *On the soul, Parva naturalia, On breath* (pp. 285–313). Cambridge, MA: Harvard University Press. (Original work composed ca. 350 BC)

Aristotle. (2000b). On sense and sensible objects. In W. S. Hett (Trans.), *On the soul, Parva naturalia, On breath* (pp. 205–283). Cambridge, MA: Harvard University Press. (Original work composed ca. 350 BC)

Aristotle. (2000c). On the soul. In W. S. Hett (Trans.), *On the soul, Parva naturalia, On breath* (pp. 1–203). Cambridge, MA: Harvard University Press. (Original work composed ca. 350 BC)

Aristotle. (2003). *Metaphysics, I–IX* (H. Tredennick, Trans.). Cambridge, MA: Harvard University Press. (Original work composed ca. 350 BC)

Aristotle. (2005). *The physics: Books I–IV* (P. H. Wicksteed & F. M. Cornford, Trans.). Cambridge, MA: Harvard University Press. (Original work composed ca. 350 BC)

Ashley, B. M. (2006). *The way toward wisdom: An interdisciplinary and intercultural introduction to metaphysics.* Notre Dame, IN: University of Notre Dame Press.

Ashley, B. M. (2013a). Anthropology: Albert the Great on the cogitative power. In I. Resnick (Ed.), *A companion to Albert the Great* (pp. 299–324). Leiden, The Netherlands: Brill.

Ashley, B. M. (2013b). *Healing for freedom: A Christian perspective on personhood and psychotherapy.* Arlington, VA: The Institute for the Psychological Sciences Press.

Ashley, B. M. (2013c). Mental health and human well-being. In R. Cessario, C. S. Titus, & P. C. Vitz (Eds.), *Philosophical virtues and psychological strengths: Building the bridge* (pp. 281–291). Manchester, NH: Sophia Institute Press.

Ashley, B. M., Deblois, J., & O'Rourke, K. D. (2006). *Health care ethics: A Catholic theological analysis* (5th ed.). Washington, DC: Georgetown University Press.

Barker, M. J. (2012a). Aquinas on internal sensory intentions: nature and classification. *International Philosophical Quarterly, 52*(2), 199–226.

Barker, M. J. (2012b). Experience and experimentation: The meaning of *experimentum* in Aquinas. *The Thomist, 76*(1), 37–71.

Bear, M. F., Connors, B. W., & Paradiso, M. A. (2007). *Neuroscience: Exploring the brain* (3rd ed.). New York, NY: Lippincott, Williams, & Wilkins.

Bearzi, M., & Stanford, C. B. (2010). *Beautiful minds: The parallel lives of great apes and dolphins.* Cambridge, MA: Harvard University Press.

Beauregard, M., & O'Leary, D. (2008). *The spiritual brain: A neuroscientist's case for the existence of the soul.* New York, NY: HarperCollins.

Beck, A. T. (1979). *Cognitive therapy and the emotional disorders.* New York, NY: Meridian Books.

Benedict XVI. (2005). *Deus caritas est* [Encyclical, on Christian love]. Vatican City, Vatican: Libreria Editrice Vaticana.

Black, D. (2000). Imagination and estimation: Arabic paradigms and Western transformations. *Topoi, 19,* 59–75.

BonJour, L. (2010). *Epistemology: Classic problems and contemporary responses* (2nd ed.). New York, NY: Rowman & Littlefield.

Burnyeat, M. F. (2001). Aquinas on 'spiritual change' in perception. In D. Perler (Ed.), *Ancient and medieval theories of intentionality* (pp. 129–153). Leiden, The Netherlands: Brill.

Cates, D. F. (2009). *Aquinas on the emotions: A religious-ethical inquiry.* Washington, DC: Georgetown University Press.

Cohen, S. M. (1982). St. Thomas Aquinas on the immaterial reception of sensible forms. *The Philosophical Review, 91*(2), 193–209.

de Anna, G. (2000). Aquinas on sensible forms and semimaterialism. *The Review of Metaphysics, 54,* 43–63.

de Haan, D. D. (2014). Perception and the *vis cogitativa*: A Thomistic analysis of aspectual, actional, and affectional precepts. *American Catholic Philosophical Quarterly, 88*(3), 397–437.

Decaen, C. A. (2001). The viability of Aristotelian-Thomistic color realism. *The Thomist, 65*(2), 179–222.

Descartes, R. (2000). *Meditations on first philosophy.* In R. Ariew (Ed.), *Philosophical essays and correspondence* (pp. 97–141). Indianapolis, IN: Hackett. (Original work composed 1641)

di Martino, C. (2008). *Ratio particularis: Doctrines des sens internes d'Avicenne à Thomas d'Aquin, contribution à l'étude de la tradition arabo-latine de la psychologie d'Aristote.* Paris, France: Librairie Philosophique J. Vrin.

Egnor, M. (2017, June 29). A map of the soul. *First Things.* Retrieved from https://www.firstthings.com/web-exclusives/2017/06/a-map-of-the-soul

Ellis, A. (2004). *The road to tolerance: The philosophy of rational emotive behavior therapy.* New York, NY: Prometheus Books.

Ellis, A., & Ellis, D. J. (2011). *Rational emotive behavior therapy.* Washington, DC: American Psychological Association.

Enright, R. D., & Fitzgibbons, R. P. (2014). *Forgiveness therapy: An empirical guide for resolving anger and restoring hope.* Washington, DC: American Psychological Association.

Esfeld, M. (2000). Aristotle's direct realism in *De anima. The Review of Metaphysics, 54,* 321–336.

Fischer, D. B., Boes, A. D., Demertzi, A., Evrard,

H. C., Laureys, S., Edlow, B. L., ... Geerling, J. C. (2016). A human brain network derived from coma-causing brainstem lesions. *Neurology, 87*(23), 2427–2434.

Frede, D. (2001). Aquinas on *phantasia*. In D. Perler (Ed.), *Ancient and medieval theories of intentionality* (pp. 155–183). Leiden, The Netherlands: Brill.

Gasson, J. A. (1963). The internal senses—functions or powers? Part I. *The Thomist, 26*(1), 1–14.

Goldstein, E. B. (2010). *Sensation and perception* (8th ed.). Belmont, CA: Wadsworth Cengage Learning.

Haldane, J. J. (1983). Aquinas on sense-perception. *The Philosophical Review, 92*(2), 233–239.

Heatherton, T. F., Wyland, C. L., Macrae, C. N., Demos, K. E., Denny, B. T., & Kelley, W. M. (2006). Medial prefrontal activity differentiates self from close others. *Social Cognitive and Affective Neuroscience, 1*(1), 18–25.

John Paul II. (1993). *Veritatis splendor* [Encyclical, on certain fundamental questions of the Church's moral teaching]. Vatican City, Vatican: Libreria Editrice Vaticana.

Journet, C. (1924). Les maladies des sens internes. *Revue Thomiste, 7*(25), 35–50.

Kant, I. (1996). *Critique of pure reason* (W. S. Pluhar, Trans.). Indianapolis. IN: Hackett. (Original work composed 1787)

Kenny, A. (1994). *Aquinas on mind*. New York, NY: Routledge.

Keyes, B. B., Underwood, L. A., Snyder, V., Dailey, F. L. L., & Hourihan, T. (2018). Healing emotional affective responses to trauma (HEART): A Christian model of working with trauma. *Frontiers in the Psychotherapy of Trauma and Dissociation, 1*(2): 212–243.

Klubertanz, G. P. (1952). *The discursive power: Sources and doctrine of the* vis cogitativa *according to St. Thomas Aquinas*. St. Louis, MO: The Modern Schoolman.

Kolb, B., & Whishaw, I. Q. (2009). *Fundamentals of human neuropsychology* (6th ed.). New York, NY: Worth.

Lambert, P., & McShane, P. (2010). *Bernard Lonergan: His life and leading ideas*. Vancouver, British Columbia: Axial Publishing.

Linley, P. A., & Joseph, S. (2004). Positive change following trauma and adversity: A review. *Journal of Traumatic Stress 17*(1), 11–21.

Lisska, A. J. (2007). A look at inner sense in Aquinas: A long-neglected faculty psychology. *Proceedings of the American Catholic Philosophical Association, 80*, 1–19.

Locke, J. (2008). *An essay concerning human understanding*. New York, NY: Oxford University Press.

Lonergan, B. (1997). *Verbum: Word and idea in Aquinas*. Toronto, Ontario: University of Toronto Press.

Macdonald, P. A. (2007). Direct realism and Aquinas's account of sensory cognition. *The Thomist, 71*, 343–378.

MacIntyre, A. (1999). *Dependent rational animals: Why human beings need the virtues*. Chicago, IL: Open Court.

Maritain, J. (1995). *Distinguish to unite, or the degrees of knowledge* (G. B. Phelan, Trans.). Notre Dame, IN: University of Notre Dame. (Original work published 1932)

McLuhan, E. (2015). *The sensus communis, synesthesia, and the soul*. New York, NY: BPS Books.

Murphy, N. (1998). Supervenience and the non-reducibility of ethics to biology. In R. J. Russell, W. R. Stoeger, & F. J. Ayala (Eds.), *Evolutionary and molecular biology: Scientific perspectives on divine action* (pp. 463–489). Berkeley, CA: Center for Theology and the Natural Sciences.

Pasnau, R. (2002). *Thomas Aquinas on human nature*. New York, NY: Cambridge University Press.

Peghaire, J. (1943). A forgotten sense, the cogitative according to St. Thomas Aquinas. *Modern Schoolman, 20*, 123–140.

Peterson, C., & Seligman, M. E. P. (Eds.) (2004). *Character strengths and virtues: A handbook and classification*. New York, NY: Oxford University Press.

Pfeifer, J. H., Lieberman, M. D., & Dapretto, M. (2007). "I know you are but what am I?!": Neural bases of self- and social knowledge retrieval in children and adults. *Journal of Cognitive Neuroscience, 19*(8), 1323–1337.

Popper, K. R. (1975). *Objective knowledge: An evolutionary approach*. London, United Kingdom: Oxford University Press.

Popper, K. R. (1983). *Realism and the aim of science*. New York: Rowman & Littlefield.

Pryor, K., & Norris, K. S. (1991). *Dolphin societies:*

Discoveries and puzzles. Berkeley, CA: University of California Press.

Ripperger, C. (2013). *Introduction to the science of mental health.* Lincoln, NE: Sensus Traditionis Press.

Schore, A. N. (2002). Dysregulation of the right brain: A fundamental mechanism of traumatic attachment and the psychopathogenesis of posttraumatic stress disorder. *Australian and New Zealand Journal of Psychiatry, 36*(1), 9–30.

Siegel, D. J. (2012). *Pocket guide to interpersonal neurobiology: An integrative handbook of the mind.* New York, NY: Norton.

Sokolowski, R. (2000). *Introduction to phenomenology.* New York, NY: Cambridge University Press.

Sokolowski, R. (2008). *Phenomenology of the human person.* New York, NY: Cambridge University Press.

Sperry, L., & Sperry, J. (2012). *Case conceptualization: Mastering this competency with ease and confidence.* New York, NY: Routledge.

Stillings, N. A., Weisler, S. E., Chase, C. H., Feinstein, M. H., Garfield, J. L., & Rissland, E. L. (1995). *Cognitive science: An introduction* (2nd ed.). Cambridge, MA: MIT Press.

Tellkamp, J. A. (2007). Aquinas on intentions in the medium and in the mind. *Proceedings of the American Catholic Philosophical Association, 80,* 275–289.

Tellkamp, J. A. (2012). *Vis aestimativa* and *vis cogitativa* in Thomas Aquinas's *Commentary on the Sentences. The Thomist, 76*(4), 611–640.

Titus, C. S. (2013). Reasonable acts. In R. Cessario, C. S. Titus, & P. C. Vitz (Eds.), *Philosophical virtues and psychological strengths: Building the bridge* (pp. 81–114). Manchester, NH: Sophia Institute Press.

Vitz, P. (2017). The origin of consciousness in the integration of analog (right hemisphere) and digital (left hemisphere) codes. *Journal of Consciousness Exploration & Research, 8*(11), 881–906.

Wojtyła, K., (1979). *The acting person* (A. Potocki, Trans.; A.-T. Tymieniecka, Ed.). Boston, MA: D. Reidel. (Original work published 1969)

Wolfson, H. A. (1935). The internal senses in Latin, Arabic, and Hebrew philosophical texts. *The Harvard Theological Review, 28*(2), 69–133.

Worthington, E. L., Jr. (2003). *Forgiving and reconciling: Bridges to wholeness and hope* (Rev. ed.). Downers Grove, IL: InterVarsity Press.

Worthington, E. L., Jr. (Ed.) (2005). *Handbook of forgiveness.* New York, NY: Routledge.

Wundt, W. (1904). *Principles of physiological psychology* (E. B. Titchener, Trans.). New York, NY: Macmillan.

Życiński, J. (2006). *God and evolution: Fundamental questions of Christian evolutionism* (K. W. Kemp & Z. Maślanka, Trans.). Washington, DC: The Catholic University of America Press.

Chapter 14

Emotional

CHRISTOPHER GROSS,

CRAIG STEVEN TITUS, PAUL C. VITZ, AND

WILLIAM J. NORDLING

ABSTRACT: This chapter considers the person's emotional capacities from a Catholic Christian philosophical perspective. As an expression of the unity of body and soul, emotions not only are influenced by sensory-perceptual cognitions and higher intellectual and linguistic capacities, but they can also influence these aspects of the person in turn. Emotions also play a prominent role in personal self-understanding, interpersonal relations, moral action, and the spiritual life. While emotional capacities are inherently good by nature, particular emotions can be morally good or evil (depending on their relation to reason and will) and particular emotional dispositions can lead to flourishing or to languishing (depending on how they are formed). By bringing neuroscience and psychological theory into conversation with Christian philosophy, this chapter explores different understandings and terms for emotions, including the traditional term "passions," which is used by Augustine, Aquinas, and the *Catechism of the Catholic Church* (*CCC*) (2000). It also describes how the person's emotional capacities can be shaped by virtue, participate in reason, be influenced by charity and other spiritual experiences, and thus contribute to true flourishing.

Why do some people prolong their anger in states of rage, while others forgive? Why do some people seek sexual pleasure and emotional affection outside of their conjugal commitment, while others remain faithful? Why are some people compulsively attracted to food, alcohol, or drugs, while others control their desires in these matters? Why are some people caught in spirals of fear, while others express bravery? There are reasons behind such emotionally charged behaviors and tendencies. Some of these actions seem motivated by unrestrained emotion, while others seem to be rooted in rea-

son and accompanied by controlled emotion. Given the prominent role that emotions play in creating a flourishing life, an understanding of the emotions is important for many disciplines that seek to understand the person; these include the disciplines of psychological and social sciences, neuroscience, law, and even theology.

Throughout history, the role of the emotions in the moral life has been of great interest to those studying the human condition. For example, the traditional term for emotions has been "passions," and, in his work *The City of God*, Augustine (427/1972) sketches the dispute between the Aristotelian Peripatetics and the Roman Stoics regarding the role of emotions in human life (IX.4). Aristotelians held that even the virtuous person experiences emotion, but in the virtuous, emotions are governed by reason, that is, by wise judgments. In line with the Aristotelians, the positive psychology movement also recognizes the need to develop virtuous emotional dispositions (Peterson & Seligman, 2004) as does Emotion-Focused Therapy (Greenberg & Johnson, 1988; Greenberg, 2012); dialectical behavior therapy (Linehan, 1993) speaks of this process in terms of emotion regulation skills. The Roman Stoics, on the contrary, maintained that the virtuous man is unaffected by his emotions because he has eradicated them. For the Stoics, according to Augustine, the emotions only interfere with the acquisition and exercise of virtue. Some cognitive-behavioral theories reflect the view of the Stoic inasmuch as they see emotions as the basis for irrational cognitions and behavior (Ellis, 2004; Beck, 1979)

For his part, Augustine contends that the emotions are an important part of the human person and the moral life. Indeed, contrary to the Stoics, Augustine (427/1972) insists that something distinctively human is missing from our moral actions if they are performed without emotions such as compassion (IX.5). However, following the Aristotelians as well as Scripture, he also maintains that emotions must be controlled and trained to prevent man from becoming a slave to them (Augustine, 427/1972, IX.4).

Drawing on Augustine and Aristotle, Aquinas (1273/1981) devotes significant attention to emotion in his *Treatise on the Passions* (I-II, 22–48). Like Augustine, Aquinas holds that emotional capacities are an important part of our human nature and are fundamentally good (I-II, 24.4). However, depending on how they interact with reason and will, emotions can be morally good

or evil. They involve either acts, such as expressions of anger, or dispositions, such as a tendency to anger (I-II, 24.1). In total, Aquinas discusses eleven different emotions, including fear, anger, and love or desire, and the virtues that are necessary in order to properly moderate them and bring about the person's flourishing (I-II, 23.4).

Aquinas's fundamental conclusions concerning the goodness of our emotional capacities as well as our need to have mastery over them are supported by both commonplace and clinical experience. Common human experience demonstrates that feelings such as extreme rage or complete indifference are harmful to the person as well as to his relationships with others. Thus, for those who continually struggle with overly intense or impoverished emotions, one goal of virtually all contemporary psychotherapies is to help persons integrate emotions, so that personal (rational and volitional, but also interpersonal) well-being can be attained (Gondreau, 2013, p. 148).

By recovering and drawing on the wisdom of Augustine, Aristotle, and Aquinas, and by incorporating insights from contemporary psychology, this chapter seeks to explain the proper relationship between reason and emotion as well as to clarify the positive potential place that emotions have in the moral life. The Catholic Christian Meta-Model of the Person holds that the emotional capacities are inherently good, as they are natural aspects of the person (Chapter 2, "Theological, Philosophical, and Psychological Premises"). Emotional capacities are part of the person's body-soul unity, which is a gift from God. The emotions influence the whole of human life, including self-understanding, interpersonal relationships, moral action, the spiritual life, and the free pursuit of goals. However, while the emotional capacities are inherently good in the order of nature, particular emotions become good or bad in the order of morality depending on how they are evoked by and interact with reason and will. Some emotions are considered bad in themselves: shamelessness, envy, and malice (desiring evil) (Aristotle, ca. 350 BC/1941, 1107a9–19). Emotions that are considered good, inasmuch as they have been informed by reason, include courage, modesty, and temperance. In order to contribute to flourishing, the person's emotional capacities must be formed by moral virtues.

To explain how the person forms these emotion-based virtues and why the emotions are significant in moral action, this chapter proceeds as follows. The first part defines an emo-

tion and distinguishes it from temperament and moods, and the second section examines the role of the emotions in moral action and spiritual life according to the Meta-Model, as compared to reductionist approaches. Sections three and four discuss the relationship between the emotions and bottom-up as well as top-down influences. The fifth section considers how morally responsible persons are for their emotions, while the final sections discuss how emotional capacities are formed by virtue or can be deformed by vice, and how emotion-based virtues can transform or heal vice.

What Is an Emotion?

Any attempt to integrate the insights of theology, philosophy, and psychology regarding emotional capacities immediately encounters a significant obstacle concerning language.

Thomas Dixon (2003) points out that the word "emotion" was not prominent until the eighteenth and nineteenth centuries, when it became a popular word and category in psychological writings. Prior to that period, the phenomena that are now commonly referred to as emotions were discussed in terms of passions, affections, or sentiments (Dixon, 2003). Initial attempts to link emotion as treated in Aquinas with modern psychology are found in the works of Magda Arnold and Robert Edward Brennan (Arnold, 1960; Brennan, 1941; see also Shields & Kappas, 2006).

Aquinas (1273/1981) refers to movements of the sensory affect (sense appetite), which he frequently calls passions. He, furthermore, distinguishes them from affections of the intellect (intellectual appetite), which he calls the will (III, 15.4 & I-II 22.3; see also Lombardo, 2011, pp. 75–77). John of Damascus (ca. 745/1958) defines a passion as,

a movement of the appetitive faculty [affective capacity] which is felt as a result of a sensory impression of good or evil. It may also be defined in another way: passion is an irrational movement of the soul due to an impression of good or evil. (II.22)

Aquinas (1273/1981) states that a movement of the sensory affective capacities is always accompanied by a bodily change (I-II, 22.2 ad 3). Thus, when one experiences fear or anger, one's heart may race or hands shake. These bodily changes more properly belong to the affections of the sense appetite than to the affections of the will and also may be more evident with the passions (Aquinas, 1273/1981, I-II, 22.3; Lombardo, 2011, pp. 75–77; Miner, 2009, p. 35). However, the affections of the will also are accompanied by some bodily change, at least at the neurological level, because human persons are a unity of body and soul (Aquinas, 1273/1981, I-II, 22.1). Properly speaking, only God and the angels, who are without physical bodies, can experience affections, such as anger, without some bodily change (Aquinas, 1273/1981, I, 82.5 ad 1; I-II, 22.1 & 22.3; Siegel, 2012, §AI-27). While they are distinct, intellectual affections (will, intention, choice) and sensory affections (passions) are not completely disconnected. Aquinas (1273/1981) points out that affections in the will often overflow into the sense appetite and excite the passions, such as the joy of contemplation overflowing to ease sorrow (I-II, 38.4 ad 3 & 77.6; Lombardo, 2011, pp. 89–93) or the joy of understanding sorrow in the context of new meaning (Frankl, 1959).

The more modern category of emotion is broader and more difficult to define than either passion or affection in Aquinas's thought. Dixon (2003) pessimistically notes that "the over-inclusivity of 'emotion' has made it impossible for there to be any consensus about what an emotion is" (p. 246). This difficulty in narrowing down what the word "emotion" signifies has been exacerbated by the fact that interests in the emotions have extended well beyond religion, philosophy, and psychology to include other fields such as neuroscience and law.

Despite this challenge, the word emotion is still useful, particularly in this work of integration (Damasio, 1994). As mentioned above, the term is used by multiple disciplines, and it is broad enough to include passion and affection. Therefore, all of the passions that Aristotle or Aquinas treat in detail would certainly be considered emotions by any definition of the term. However, in light of Dixon's concerns and the varied uses of the term, it is important to explain emotion as it will be used for the remainder of this chapter.

We distinguish the person's capacity for emotion from acts of emotion and from a disposition of that capacity. Through their emotional capacity, humans affectively sense the meaning of reality in dialogue with their sensory-perceptual cognitions, which is the first step in general intelligence with the support of emotions (emotions involve a basic step in the knowledge of the outside world, for example, approach or avoidance). A person's

understanding and reasoning about truth is related to emotions. For instance, the truth of good and bad is already found in early infancy in the formation of the internal representation of the good mother and the bad mother, that is, when the mother is seen as all good and loving or all bad and cruel. Our emotions also affect our ability to express goodness to others, and there are many emotions, such as fear, daring, and desire, that have social and spiritual influences. The capacity for emotion itself is inherently good. An emotion is the personal bodily affective response to reality. Through an emotion, people are moved by the values and intelligibility that they experience. This emotional movement is influenced by their rational judgments as well as by social forces and divine grace. Particular expressions of emotions are good, neutral, or evil. Over time and with repeated emotional acts, the person's emotional capacities acquire good or evil dispositions, which influence future emotional responses.

This definition recognizes that emotions involve movement (Wojtyła, 1979, p. 224). Depending on whether the stimulus is perceived as attractive or repulsive, emotions "evoke motion" (Siegel, 2012, §AI-27). They prepare the person to turn freely toward the sensed value or away from it (Wojtyła, 1979, p. 251; see also, Frijda, 1986, p. 71). For example, when the person experiences disgust, he turns away from the object of disgust or seeks its removal (Scarantino, 2016, p. 22). This definition also acknowledges that the emotions (or sensory affective capacities) interact with the person's sensory-perceptual cognition, as well as his reason and will and interpersonal capacities, as shown in Table 14.1 (Siegel, 2012, §AI-27; Miner, 2009, pp. 65–82). One however should keep in mind the fact that many emotions are experienced unconsciously. Often psychotherapy is about trying to make the person consciously aware of irrational emotions.

Table 14.1. Structure of Human Capacities as Found in the Philosophical Premises of the CCMMP

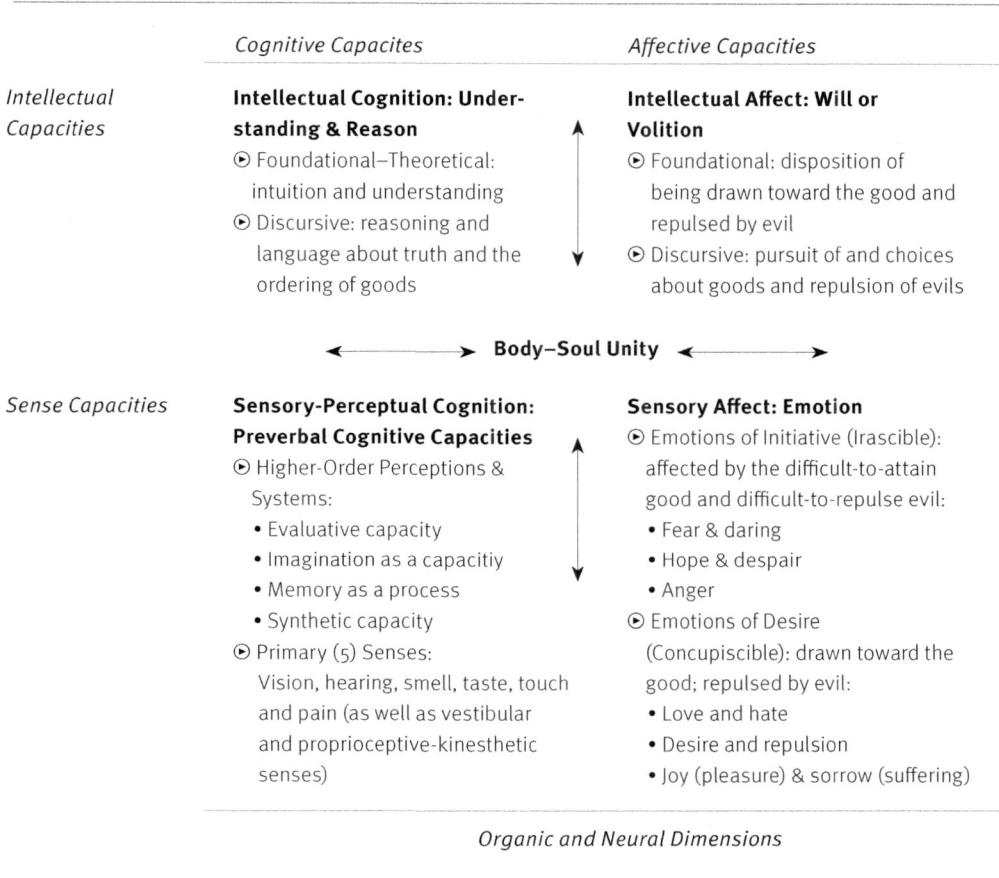

	Cognitive Capacites	*Affective Capacities*
Intellectual Capacities	**Intellectual Cognition: Understanding & Reason** ⊙ Foundational–Theoretical: intuition and understanding ⊙ Discursive: reasoning and language about truth and the ordering of goods	**Intellectual Affect: Will or Volition** ⊙ Foundational: disposition of being drawn toward the good and repulsed by evil ⊙ Discursive: pursuit of and choices about goods and repulsion of evils

⟷   **Body–Soul Unity**   ⟷

	Cognitive Capacites	*Affective Capacities*

Sense Capacities	**Sensory-Perceptual Cognition: Preverbal Cognitive Capacities**
	⊙ Higher-Order Perceptions & Systems:
	  • Evaluative capacity
	  • Imagination as a capacitiy
	  • Memory as a process
	  • Synthetic capacity
	⊙ Primary (5) Senses:
	  Vision, hearing, smell, taste, touch and pain (as well as vestibular and proprioceptive-kinesthetic senses)
		Sensory Affect: Emotion
		⊙ Emotions of Initiative (Irascible): affected by the difficult-to-attain good and difficult-to-repulse evil:
		  • Fear & daring
		  • Hope & despair
		  • Anger
		⊙ Emotions of Desire (Concupiscible): drawn toward the good; repulsed by evil:
		  • Love and hate
		  • Desire and repulsion
		  • Joy (pleasure) & sorrow (suffering)

Organic and Neural Dimensions

How Does the Meta-Model's Account of the Role of the Emotions in the Moral Life Differ from Reductionist Approaches?

Unfortunately, until the recently renewed interest in virtue ethics, Aquinas's treatment of the emotions—as being able to participate in reason as well as the theological and philosophical framework in which he places them—have largely been overlooked by philosophers, particularly those outside of the Catholic moral tradition (as described by MacIntyre, 2007). For example, Chandra Sripada and Stephen Stitch (2004) contend that "from Plato's time until the closing decades of the 20th century, the dominant view was that the emotions are quite distinct from the processes of rational thinking and decision making, and are often a major impediment to those processes" (p. 133). Robert Solomon (1993), in his book *The Passions: Emotions and the Meaning of Life*, makes similar claims (p. 10). These latter philosophers are also at odds with contemporary neuroscience (Damasio, 1994; LeDoux, 1998).

In part, these omissions are due to the extensive influence of the philosophers of the Enlightenment, who offer two radically different views on the importance of the emotions; both of these positions stand in stark contrast to Aquinas's view (Gondreau, 2013, pp. 175–182). Distrusting emotions and seeking to insulate reason from their influence, Descartes and Kant champion different forms of emotional rationalism (Barad, 1991). For Descartes (1649/1989), the emotions only disturb the tranquility of the soul, and for Kant (1797/1996), they interfere with one's ability to perform one's moral duty. For these philosophers, the emotions have little positive role to play in the moral life (Sherman, 1997). Hobbes (1651/1994) and Hume (1740/2000), on the contrary, elevate the emotions above reason and argue that reason should be a slave to the emotions. According to Hobbes's and Hume's emotivism, the emotions serve both as the source of moral judgments and as our motivation to act (Barad, 1991).

While the Meta-Model's analysis of emotions differs significantly from the views of these Enlightenment philosophers, it also needs to be distinguished from other approaches to emotions found in the biopsychosocial sciences. Within these sciences, there are at least six theoretical traditions on emotion: neo-Darwinian, Jamesian, cognitive, socioconstructivist, developmental, and neuroscientific (Evans & Cruse, 2004). Besides exhibiting different presuppositions about approaches to emotions and human flourishing, these perspectives appraise emotions in quite different ways: either as the highest good (Epicureanism and hedonism), as irrational (Plato, Hegel, Ellis), as suspicious (Buddhism, Freud, Kant), as the center of piety—feeling complete dependence on the divine (Schleiermacher)—as a reliable guide (Rogers, Hume), or as basically good capacities in need of training (Aquinas, Augustine, Seligman). At points these perspectives intersect with or complement the Meta-Model's understanding of emotions, but at other points they diverge from it considerably. For instance, like the socioconstructivist theory of emotions, we would acknowledge that one's emotional capacities are shaped by family experiences and culture (Teske, 2003, p. 195). But, with Evans (2001) and Ekman (1992), we reject the more radical socioconstructivist claim that our emotional experiences are almost completely dictated by culture.

The Relationship Between Emotion and Bottom-Up Influences

Emotions in Aquinas's anthropology are divided in two large categories: emotions of desire and emotions of initiative-taking (Aquinas, 1273/1981, I, 81.2; Ashley, 2013, p. 174–175). The emotional capacity of desire (concupiscible) seeks what is pleasurable and avoids what is harmful. The initiative-taking capacity (irascible) concerns overcoming obstacles in order to attain goods a person desires and to avoid harmful things. Thus, the emotions of desire are love and hate, attraction and aversion, and joy and sorrow. These emotions are elicited in the presence or absence of a good. The five initiative-taking emotions are hope and despair, fear and daring, and anger (Aquinas, 1273/1981, I-II, 23.4). These emotions enable us to take initiative to attain a difficult good or to patiently wait for the prudent time to act, but they can also cause us to turn away from the difficult good, as in the case of crippling fear or despair. It is important to note, as Robert Miner (2009) points out, that a sensory affective capacity is a passive capacity that requires "something else to activate it" (p. 69). What activates these capacities?

Emotions can be elicited by sense stimuli and higher order perceptions, especially the evaluative capacity (pre-rational or subconscious evaluations), from the bottom-up, as emergent phenomena arising from sensory-perceptual cognition, which influences the sensory affective capacities. The imagination, frequently working with information provided by the primary senses and other higher-order perceptions, may activate the emotions (Aquinas, 1273/1981, I, 81.3 ad 2; I-II, 9.1 ad 2; Fritz-Cates, 2009; Miner, 2009, pp. 65–69). (For an overview of all the higher-order perceptual capacities, including imagination, see Chapter 13, "Sensory-Perceptual-Cognitive"). This activation of the emotions can also occur as soon as sensory apprehension occurs, without any reasoning or exercise of discursive thinking (Aquinas, 1273/1981, I, 81.3 ad 2; Aquinas, 1272/1993, VII.6, §1388, §1393). For example, a person who loves steak may smell charcoal burning, recall the last steak, imagine another one, and immediately experience the desire to find and grill another steak (Miner, 2009, p. 68).

The affective sensory capacity can also be moved by the evaluative capacity (Aquinas 1273/1981, I, 81.3; Loughlin, 2001, p. 46). To illustrate this point, Miner (2009) provides the following example (pp. 79–81): A young child gets burned by placing her hand on a hot stove, and the next month, she burns herself again on a kerosene heater. A few months later, she is standing outside by a campfire, experiences fear, and decides not to touch it, even though she has no experience of seeing or being near a campfire. She makes this decision and experiences a healthy fear, because her evaluative capacity, informed by sensory memory, enables her to judge that the campfire is hot and dangerous. Notice that the emotion itself does not arise in this case as an instinct; rather, it is elicited on the basis of her past individual experiences that inform memory, imagination, and the evaluative capacity, experiences that further specify and direct her natural inclination to avoid pain (Ashley, DeBlois, & O'Rourke, 2006, p. 147).

The Relationship Between Emotion and Top-Down Influences

Emotions do not only arise from the bottom-up sensory-perceptual-cognitive capacities. They also are elicited by intellectual judgments and choices and spiritual sources, from the top down, that is, as supervenient phenomena (Elliot, 2006; Fritz-Cates, 2009: Kahneman, 2011; Pinckaers, 2005). For instance, upon rationally understanding the evil and injustice of a policy and practice, such as abortion on demand, we feel righteous anger, or by choosing to dwell on a sexual encounter ingrained in one's memory, one can stoke sexual desire. There is also a special kind of spiritual emotion that overflows from the theological virtues, which are poured into us by God. While charity and hope perfect the will, and faith perfects the intellect, these virtues influence the whole person, including our emotional capacities. For example, in the midst of conflict or difficulty, the virtues of faith, hope, and charity, and other experiences of transcendence, can bring about comfort and encouragement, and our friendship with God (charity) can give rise to experiences of profound joy and peace (Aquinas, 1273/1981; Dickens, 1859/1989; Frankl, 1959; Lewis, 1961; Lombardo, 2011).

These examples give the appearance that

the emotional capacities impelled by difficulty (irascible) and governed by desire (concupiscible) necessarily obey reason and will. This interpretation of reason and will is at best only partially true, as a result of the specific nature of the relationship between the higher (intellectual, linguistic) and lower (sensory) capacities. When the will commands a part of the body to move, then it moves (unless it is impaired, for example, by injury or fatigue). It cannot resist. However, the reason and will possess only partial control over emotions. Like free citizens, the lower powers are subject to rule but also can resist commands. Gondreau (2013) describes this limited freedom of the lower powers as a kind of "quasi-autonomy" (p. 164). While the emotions (sensory affective capacities) cannot be dominated by reason, they can participate in reason either occasionally, by merely following the command of reason, or more consistently, when they are shaped by virtue (Aquinas, 1273/1981, I, 81.3 ad 2; Aristotle, ca. 350 BC/1941, I.13). For instance, both humans and lower animals, when desiring to cross a room, experience that their bodies move in response to their desire. But in the midst of experiencing fear, when going into a house on fire, a person with the virtue of courage is able to act in spite of his or her emotion. Given their quasi-autonomy, when the emotions impelled by desire or difficulty are brought about by bottom-up influences, the person may become overwhelmed by emotion and may be either blinded to reason or actively reject it (Aquinas, 1273/1981, I, 81.3 ad 2; see also Aquinas, 1268/1947, Chapter 224).

How does this disobedience of the lower powers influence reason? Properly speaking, the emotions (sensory affective capacities) cannot move the will directly; rather, they interfere with the proper functioning of the intellect and will in three different ways (Aquinas, 1981, I-II,

77.1). First, the emotions can distract the intellect, so that the individual does not consider the morality of his action (Aquinas, 1981, I-II, 77.1; DeYoung, McCluskey, & Van Dyke, 2009, p. 102). DeYoung et al. (2009) give the example of "an agent who seeks pleasure by engaging in gossip without stopping to think about how he might damage someone's good name" (p. 102). Second, the passion can make an apparent good attractive to an agent, which apart from the emotion would not be appealing (Aquinas, 1273/1981, I-II, 6.4 ad 3 & 77.1; DeYoung et al., 2009, p. 102). For instance, a man may be docile and not inclined to violence. However, under the influence of strong anger, punching someone who has insulted him might seem like a good or at least justifiable act. Third, emotions may overwhelm reason completely. One may figuratively be blinded by passion and become bereft of reason, such as in extreme cases of fear, desire, or anger (Aquinas, 1273/1981, I-II, 6.7 ad 3; Cessario, 2001, p. 112). We see this kind of blinding emotion frequently in drivers who experience extreme road rage and endanger their own lives as well as the lives of others. It can also occur with respect to individuals suffering from diverse psychopathologies, such as depression or anxiety.

When the person voluntarily and repeatedly chooses to follow distorted attractions and repulsions of the lower capacities rather than the guidance of reason, there is an acquired disordered disposition in the person (Hartel, 1993, p. 189). This rebellion reduces the person's true freedom as he becomes enslaved to his emotions, and it moves the individual away from flourishing (Augustine, ca. 397/1998, VIII.5.10). According to Augustine, in the beginning, man was created by God at peace within himself; the lower capacities obeyed the higher capacities without rebelling (Augustine, 427/1972, XIV.19;

see also Aquinas, 1272/2003, 4.2, p. 205). However, as a result of original sin, man frequently finds himself at war with himself and experiences strong emotions that influence the will to act against the guidance of reason (Gondreau, 2013, p. 165; see also Aquinas, 1272/2003, 4.2, p. 205; Augustine, 427/1972, XIV.19). Yet even though our sensitive appetite is wounded by sin, its inherent natural goodness is not destroyed. Our emotions have an important role to play in our moral actions, but they need to be properly disposed and brought under the rule of reason and prudent judgment by the formation of a virtuous character and particular virtues. Before examining how our emotional capacities are perfected through virtue and deformed through vice, the next section considers the person's moral responsibility for his or her emotions.

Emotions and Moral Responsibility

Emotions are multidimensional and can be considered from different perspectives, including philosophical, psychological, and neuroscientific. This section focuses on the moral dimension of emotions, which admittedly does not exhaust the meaning of emotions but is an important dimension for understanding human free action. People typically speak and conceive of emotions as forces or energies that simply happen to us, which we cannot control and for which we are not responsible. However, virtue ethics, rooted in natural law and the Aristotelian-Thomistic tradition, such as is used in the Meta-Model, offers a more nuanced position about how emotions issue from and relate to good capacities (Aquinas, 1273/1981, I, 81.2; Augustine, 427/1972, XII.5). Emotions in themselves are considered good or evil only when engaged by reason and will (CCC, 2000, §1767). They can be morally good or bad depending on how they influence moral choices and how they are evoked and used by reason and will. As we saw in the prior section, we can willfully evoke emotions that are good or bad, morally speaking. For example, a couple could promote a morally good emotion by intentionally fostering calm so that they may come to mutual understanding and forgiveness. On the contrary, a husband would be promoting a morally bad emotion by fostering resentment and a selfish anger that would block communication with and forgiveness of his wife, or by not keeping angry feelings at the level where constructive communication can occur. For instance, even love can be evil, as when one loves heroin or when one loves in a disordered way, such as in an adulterous relationship. In this context, St. Augustine (427/1972) maintains that emotions are evil if what is desired or loved is evil and good if what is desired or loved is good (XIV.7). Inasmuch as acts, dispositions, and practices voluntarily evoke and foster moral and spiritual emotions from the "heart," we are responsible for them (Mk 7:21; CCC, 2000, §§1762–1775). It is important to acknowledge two further points about the morality of emotions. First, voluntary emotions can be evaluated as morally good or bad regardless of whether or not the person performs an exterior action motivated by an emotion (Mt 5:28; Mattison, 2008, p. 82). For instance, one can feel hatred toward Jews but never actually carry out an action of hatred against them. Setting aside issues concerning the individual's culpability for acquiring such a disposition, the very act of choosing to hate is still, objectively speaking, morally wrong (Vitz, 2018; Chapter 11, "Fulfilled in Virtue").

Second, emotions can arise out of rational choices either directly or indirectly. The person can use his reason and will to excite emotion either in a positive or negative way (Cessario, 2001, p. 112). For instance, the person may choose to recall and dwell on an incident from the past in order to stir up his anger again. Virtuous actions, in contrast, may produce affections in the will that overflow and excite emotion indirectly. Aquinas (1273/1981) gives the example of joy, which may overflow from the will into the emotions when one performs an act of justice (I-II, 59.5). These second movements are morally good or bad depending on the moral consequences of the decision they effected. There are also top-down influences from outside the person, for example, there are demonic forces (Blai, 2017; Gallagher, 2005; Lhermitte, 2013; see also Chapter 18, "Fallen") and disordered choices of other people that can influence the person's emotions (Chapter 12, "Interpersonally Relational").

While voluntary emotions can be evaluated as morally good or bad, a person is not responsible for the kind of emotion that is a first movement and that arises prior to the will's consent (Aquinas, 1273/1981, I-II, 89.5; Mattison, 2008). These pre-volitional emotions arise spontaneously out of initial evaluations (whether the evaluation of sensation, imagination, or the proper evaluative capacity). In response to an evaluation, one may experience sudden joy at seeing a beautiful sunset, anger at a perceived slight, or impatience in a traffic jam. These types of first movements occur without any intentional cooperation of will, and they are not originating from a stable and firm disposition within the person. People can also be considered not responsible for certain emotions when they have been raised to have them from childhood. There are examples of such negative emotions for which we are not responsible, identified and understood in Scripture: "Be angry but sin not" (Ps 4:4); "Be angry but do not sin; do not let the sun go down on your anger" (Eph 4:26; see also Vitz, 2018).

However, it should be noted at this point that not all pre-volitional movements reside outside of the person's control. There are unconscious emotions that we are not responsible for. But we are responsible for unconscious emotions that originally we consciously chose or consciously accepted. As a person ages and forms himself through choices, there are other pre-volitional movements that are not entirely spontaneous, but rather arise from a morally good or bad disposition that a person has developed within himself (Mattison, 2008). To return to the example above, if an individual reads anti-Semitic literature, builds up the vice of hatred within himself, and then feels hatred when driving past a synagogue, he is responsible for that movement of hatred, even though it arises without rational reflection or deliberate consent in that moment. Similarly, with virtuous dispositions: When a virtuous man sees an attractive young woman enter the room, he sees her full humanity and dignity rather than an object that can satisfy him sexually. His pre-volitional emotional response is praiseworthy, and it arises from the virtue of chastity that he possesses (Mattison, 2008, p. 63). Since emotional dispositions that are morally good or bad contribute to or detract from the person's flourishing, the next section examines in greater detail how the person builds up virtue or vice within his emotional capacities.

Emotional Capacities, Virtue, and Vice

Recent neurobiological research (LeDoux, 1998) suggests that human emotionality plays a more significant role in moral action than had been previously thought. In effect, the research suggests that intentional acts need emotional support for concentration, consistency, and execution. For instance, in framing a just anger that sustains the intentional effort to correct an injustice, there are two extremes: (a) exaggerated anger or rage that can blind us to how to correct the injustice, and (b) an inadequate anger or indifference that tends to prevent us from paying enough attention to the injustice and our part in rectifying it. Damasio (1994) goes so far as to suggest that without emotions human beings would not be able to act rationally. Put in a constructive perspective, well-ordered emotions aid humans to act according to rational principles and to their vocations.

Aristotle (ca. 350 BC/1941) holds that moral virtue involves not only right action but *right feelings* about moral action: "the man who abstains from bodily pleasures and delights in this very fact is temperate" (II.3, 1104b4–6). One of the distinguishing features of the truly virtuous man is properly disposed emotions. Aristotle compares the virtuous man, who does what is right and feels good about doing it, to the man who struggles with bad emotions and the man who gives in to them. The man who is self-controlled (continent) often does the right thing, but he frequently has to fight against his emotions, which are pulling him toward a negative choice. The weak man (incontinent person) is also at war with himself, but he does not possess even the same self-control. He knows what is right, but he is unable to resist his passions and gives in to the bad emotion and consequent acts. The vicious person does not even possess

this struggle within himself. He chooses to do what is wrong and feels good about it (Aristotle, ca. 350 BC/1941, VII.1–4; Sokolowski, 1982, pp. 57–58).

Even though human beings share a common nature, an individual's emotional capacities are shaped by a variety of influences and personal experiences. Culture, family, friends, religion, as well as sex difference all contribute to the formation of one's emotions (Goleman, 2005; Brizendine, 2007, 2010; Gilligan, 1982; Rhoads, 2004). Emotions are also influenced by one's individual experiences, as the story of the toddler and the fire in the previous section indicates. A person's emotions are also affected by God's grace in the infused moral virtues and the gifts of the Holy Spirit. However, human beings also shape their emotions through their own decisions and actions.

As mentioned above, while persons are not morally responsible for emotions that emerge as entirely spontaneous pre-volitional movements, humans can, through formative practices and choices, develop stable emotional dispositions ordered in accord with true flourishing. The emotions are put into the service of natural law and right reason by the cardinal virtues temperance and fortitude (courage), which order the emotional capacities of desire and initiative-taking emotional capacities respectively. The associated virtues of courage include patience, perseverance, and hope, or initiative-taking, and generosity. The associated virtues of temperance include chastity, humility, and meekness. Explaining the need for and domain of each virtue, Aquinas (1273/1981) writes that courage "is chiefly about fear of difficult things which can withdraw the will from following reason" (II-II, 123.3), while "temperance, which denotes a kind of moderation, is chiefly concerned with those emotions that tend towards sensible goods, [namely] desire and pleasure and consequently with the sorrows that arise from the absence of those pleasures" (II-II, 141.3). (See also Chapter 11, "Fulfilled in Virtue.")

Since the act of choosing is exclusively the domain of the will, these virtues do not strictly speaking elicit a right choice. However, they facilitate moral action by ingraining the emotional capacities to tend toward the true good and toward obeying God, right reason, and the guidance of the will; and by ordering the emotions, they remove obstacles to virtuous action and help bring about a life of flourishing (Cessario, 2002, p. 163). Furthermore, virtuous emotions also can draw reason's attention to a virtuous act that should be performed, as when out of compassion for another's misery, a person is moved to consider offering assistance (Aquinas, 1273/1981, I-II, 24.3 ad 1; Augustine, 427/1972, 9.5).

Conversely, through their choices, human beings can deform the emotional capacities of desire and initiative-taking by acquiring vices, which lead to languishing. To illustrate this point, Mattison (2008) offers the following example (p. 85): A father may frequently feel enraged at his children's behavior even when they are doing nothing wrong. At first, when he begins to experience this anger, he attempts to suppress it. However, after a while rather than restraining himself (showing self-control), he allows his anger to consume him, and he proceeds to yell and scream at his children. Soon his disordered anger is not limited to his children; he begins to lash out at his wife, his friends, and other family members over perceived offenses as well. The father is clearly intemperate, suffering specifically from the vice of excessive anger. His disordered anger leads to bad acts, adversely affects his relationships with those he loves, and inhibits his ability to flourish.

Goleman's 2005 work on emotion confirms and reinforces the importance of properly forming our emotions. Inspired by the psychological findings of Mayer and Salovey (1989) as well as by Aristotle's view of emotions, Goleman highlights the significance of what he refers to as emotional intelligence. Emotional intelligence includes being able to constructively use one's emotions, empathetically understand the emotions of others, and employ emotions to support successful relationships (p. xxiii). According to Goleman, emotional intelligence is necessary not only for one's physical well-being but also for one's flourishing in a family, community, and profession. Deficiencies in emotional intelligence make the individual susceptible to a number of vices, including impatience, gossip, and jealousy (p. xxiii).

Reshaping Emotions

Once our emotional capacities are formed well or poorly, usually when we are young, it is difficult to change them. But as adults, we are often called to change them. This is especially needed in psychotherapy with emotions such as hatred, anxiety, and depression. Virtues and vices, including those concerning the lower sensory affective capacities, profoundly alter a person's character. Aristotle (ca. 350 BC/1941, 1152a30–34) and Aquinas (1273/1981) both liken the "operative disposition" of virtue and vice to a kind of second nature aimed at moral action (I-II, 55.4). Aquinas (1273/1981) states that a disposition "is like a second nature, and yet it falls short of it" (I-II, 53.1 ad 1). There is hope in the case of vice, if there is still the possibility of change toward virtue. Moreover, a partially formed disposition can be understood in one sense as a character of the person that is less permanent, more unstable, and more easily changed (Aquinas, 1273/1981, I-II, 49.2 ad 3) than is a fully formed disposition that can be changed, but only with difficulty.

Even with the help of God's grace, change is difficult for the individual whose emotional capacities have been disordered by vice. Though grace heals the sinner of the vice, often some trace of that past behavior still remains in the person in the form of the negative effects of acquired vice (Aquinas, 1272/2005, a. 10 ad 16). When contrary dispositions continue to hinder the individual in the life of grace, he struggles with his emotions and holds on by sheer willpower instead of experiencing the ease of a well-established virtue (Aquinas, 1272/2005, a. 11 ad 15).

Sherwin (2009) offers the Venerable Matt Talbot as the embodiment of the kind of person who Aquinas envisions when he acknowledges the power and deep-seated nature of vice. Talbot, an Irish laborer, suffered from intemperance; he was an alcoholic from his mid-teens to his conversion at 28. He then gave up alcohol and dedicated his life to God and service of the poor. Despite his conversion, his former lifestyle tugged and beckoned; he remembered the taste, the pleasant mental state that it brought, and his old friends. Particularly in the beginning of his new Christian life, he felt a strong desire to drink and return to his old practices. While divine grace gave him the infused moral virtue of temperance, influences of his old acquired vicious dispositions still remained. Nevertheless, with the help of God's grace, over an extended time, he was able to overcome even this desire for his former life (Sherwin, 2009).

Relatively recent findings in neuroscience concerning the plasticity of the brain confirm the insights from Aristotelian-Thomistic virtue ethics concerning the difficulty of overcoming vice. Research has demonstrated that the brain "can change its own structure and function through thought and activity" (Doidge, 2007, p. xix). While it would seem as if this power of the brain would make conquering vice easier, Doidge points out, "Once a particular plastic change occurs in the brain and becomes well established, it can prevent other changes from occurring" (p. xx). He refers to this phenomenon as "the plastic paradox" (Doidge, 2007, p. xx).

To illustrate the plasticity of the brain, Doidge (2007) turns to the rampant rise of internet pornography and corresponding increase in pornography addiction (pp. 103–109). Because neurons that fire together wire together, users of pornography wire images into the pleasure centers of their brains (pp. 108–109). Over time, what they previously found sexually exciting, such as sex with girlfriends or spouses, becomes less exciting. They have to take their pornography experiences into their sexual relationship, recalling as they are having intercourse the images that they have viewed. Eventually, as users become sensitized to the images, they crave pornography intensely and need even more graphic images to produce the same effect, even though they may not actually like pornography (pp. 108–109). In more traditional language, the pornography user has misused his sexual desire and built up the vice of lust in himself. His transformation will require him to move from the vice, through lack of control, to self-control, which supports the virtue of chastity. He needs to make progress by first reordering his cognition to know that chastity is good and lack of control is not, which will require moving from the vice of lust to the disposition of self-control. Next, he will need to reorder his will to make chaste choices. Finally, he will also benefit by acquiring a chaste desire (temperance, in particular chastity). Throughout this transformation, the disordered cognitions, choices, and emotions must be changed to motivate and support virtue instead of lust.

Since this process is extremely difficult, the person will be greatly aided by virtuous practices and friends, and by different forms of psychotherapy, including Cognitive-Behavioral Therapy (Ellis, 2004), experiential therapy, and Emotion-Focused Therapy (Greenberg, 2012; Greenberg & Johnson, 1988), as well as by God's mercy and grace (Mattison, 2004, pp. 172–175; Mattison, 2008, pp. 87–90).

Conclusion

A Catholic view understands the importance of reason, will, interpersonal relationships, and divine grace in the life of emotion. We have a limited capacity to control our particular emotions. But emotions do participate in reason either (a) when a person freely wills to follow the command of reason and develops the emotional moral dispositions to do so, or (b) when spontaneous pre-volitional movements—which arise from acquired emotional dispositions—embody reason. Emotions are either morally good or evil depending upon how they participate in and are influenced by reason and will. In the Gospels, Jesus' own expression of emotions, such as anger (Jn 2:15) and sorrow (Jn 11:35), give a model of the integration of emotion, reason, and will (Gondreau, 2007, 2009; Titus, 2009). Calling upon the wisdom of the Catholic Christian tradition, the *Catechism of the Catholic Church* (2000) associates emotions with growth in "moral perfection [which] consists in man's being moved to the good not by his will alone, but also by his sensitive appetite [emotions], as in the words of the psalm: 'My heart and flesh sing for joy to the living God' (Ps. 84:2)" (§1770).

REFERENCES

Aquinas, T. (1947). *Compendium theologiae* (C. Vollert, Trans.). St. Louis, MO: Herder. (Original work composed 1268)

Aquinas, T. (1981). *Summa theologiae* (English Dominican Province, Trans.). Westminster, MD: Christian Classics. (Original work composed 1273)

Aquinas, T. (1993). *Commentary on Aristotle's* Nicomachean Ethics (C. J. Litzinger, Trans.). Notre Dame, IN: Dumb Ox Books. (Original work composed 1272)

Aquinas, T. (2003). *On evil* (R. Regan, Trans.). New York, NY: Oxford Univeristy Press. (Original work composed 1266–1272)

Aquinas, T. (2005). *Disputed questions on the virtues* (E. M. Atkins & T. Williams, Eds.; E. M. Atkins, Trans.). Cambridge, United Kingdom: Cambridge University Press. (Original work composed 1272)

Aristotle. (1941). *Nicomachean ethics*. In R. McKeon (Ed.), *The basic works of Aristotle* (pp. 935–1112). New York, NY: Random House. (Original work composed ca. 350 BC)

Arnold, B. M. (1960). *Emotion and personality: Vol. 1. Psychological aspects.* New York, NY: Columbia University Press.

Ashley, B. M. (2013). *Healing for freedom: A Christian perspective on personhood and psychotherapy.* Arlington, VA: The Institute for the Psychological Sciences Press.

Ashley, B. M., Deblois, J., & O'Rourke, K. D. (2006). *Health care ethics: A Catholic theological analysis* (5th ed.). Washington, DC: Georgetown University Press.

Augustine. (1972). *The city of God* (H. Bettenson, Trans.). New York, NY: Penguin Books. (Original work composed 427)

Augustine. (1998). *Confessions* (H. Chadwick, Trans.). New York, NY: Oxford University Press. (Original work composed ca. 397)

Barad, J. (1991). Aquinas on the role of emotion in

moral judgement and activity. *The Thomist, 55*(3), 397–413.

Beck, A. T. (1979). *Cognitive therapy and the emotional disorders.* New York, NY: Plume.

Blai, A. C. (2017). *Possession, exorcism and hauntings.* Steubenville, OH: Emmaus.

Brennan, R. E. (1941). Modern psychology and man. *The Thomist: A Speculative Quarterly Review, 3*(1), 8–32.

Brizendine, L. (2007). *The female brain.* New York, NY: Broadway Books.

Brizendine, L. (2010). *The male brain: A breakthrough understanding of how men and boys think.* New York, NY: Three Rivers Press.

Catechism of the Catholic Church (*CCC*) (2nd ed.). (2000). Vatican City, Vatican: Libreria Editrice Vaticana.

Cessario, R. (2001). *Introduction to moral theology.* Washington, DC: The Catholic University of America Press.

Cessario, R. (2002). *The virtues, or the examined life.* New York, NY: Continuum International Publishing.

Damasio, A. R. (1994). *Descartes' error: Emotion, reason, and the human brain.* New York, NY: Putman.

Descartes, R. (1989). *The passions of the soul* (S. Voss, Trans.). Indianapolis, IN: Hackett. (Original work composed 1649)

DeYoung, R. K., McCluskey, C., & Van Dyke, C. (2009). *Aquinas's ethics: Metaphysical foundations, moral theory, and theological context.* Notre Dame, IN: University of Notre Dame Press.

Dickens, C. (1989). *A tale of two cities.* New York, NY: Bantam Classics. (Original work published 1859)

Dixon, T. (2003). *From passions to emotions: The creation of a secular psychological category.* Cambridge, United Kingdom: Cambridge University Press.

Doidge, N. (2007). *The brain that changes itself: Stories of personal triumph from the frontiers of brain science.* New York, NY: Penguin Books.

Ekman, P. (1992). An argument for basic emotions. *Cognition and Emotion, 6,* 169–200.

Elliott, M. A. (2006). *Faithful feelings: Rethinking emotion in the New Testament.* Grand Rapids, MI: Kregel Publications.

Ellis, A. (2004). *The road to tolerance: The philosophy of rational emotive behavior therapy.* New York, NY: Prometheus Books.

Evans, D. (2001). *Emotion: The science of sentiment.* Oxford, United Kingdom: Oxford University Press.

Evans, D., & Cruse, P. (Eds.). (2004). *Emotion, evolution, and rationality.* Oxford, United Kingdom: Oxford University Press.

Frankl, V. E. (1959). *Man's search for meaning.* New York, NY: Washington Square Press.

Frijda, N. H. (1986). *The emotions.* Cambridge, United Kingdom: Cambridge University Press.

Fritz-Cates, D. (2009). *Aquinas on the emotions: A religious-ethical inquiry.* Washington, DC: Georgetown University Press.

Gallagher, T. M. (2005). *The discernment of spirits: An Ignatian guide for everyday living.* New York, NY: Crossroad.

Gilligan, C. (1982). *In a different voice: Psychological theory and women's development.* Cambridge, MA: Havard University Press.

Gondreau, P. (2007). The passions and the moral life: Appreciating the originality of Aquinas. *The Thomist, 71*(3), 419–450.

Gondreau, P. (2009). *The passions of Christ's soul in the theology of St. Thomas Aquinas.* Scranton, PA: University of Scranton Press.

Gondreau, P. (2013). Balanced emotions. In R. Cessario, C. S. Titus, & P. C. Vitz (Eds.), *Philosophical virtues and psychological strengths: Building the bridge* (pp. 139–200). Manchester, NH: Sophia Institute Press.

Goleman, D. (2005). *Emotional intelligence: Why it can matter more than IQ* (2nd ed.). New York, NY: Bantam Books.

Greenberg, L. S. (2012). Emotions, the great captains of our lives: Their role in the process of change in psychotherapy. *American Psychologist, 67*(8), 697–707.

Greenberg, L. S., & Johnson, S. M. (1988). *Emotionally focused therapy for couples.* New York, NY: Guilford.

Hartel, J. (1993). *Femina ut Imago Dei in the integral feminism of St. Thomas.* Rome, Italy: Gregorian and Biblical Press.

Hobbes, T. (1994). *Leviathan* (E. Curley, Ed.). Indianapolis, IN: Hackett. (Original work composed 1651)

Hume, D. (2000). *A treatise of human nature* (D. F. Norton & M. J. Norton, Eds.). New York, NY: Oxford University Press. (Original work composed 1740)

John of Damascus. (1958). An exact exposition of the orthodox faith. In F. H. Chase, Jr. (Trans.), *Writings* (pp. 165–406). Washington, DC: The Catholic University of America Press. (Original work composed ca. 745)

Kahneman, D. (2011). *Thinking, fast and slow.* New York, NY: Farrar, Straus and Giroux.

Kant, I. (1996). *The metaphysics of morals* (M. Gregor, Ed. & Trans.). Cambridge, United Kingdom: Cambridge University Press. (Original work composed 1797)

LeDoux, J. (1998). *The emotional brain: The mysterious underpinnings of emotional life.* New York, NY: Simon & Schuster.

Lewis, C. S. (1961). *A grief observed.* New York, NY: HarperCollins.

Lhermitte, J. (2013) *True or false possessions? How to distinguish the demonic from the demented.* Manchester, NH: Sophia Institute Press.

Linehan, M. M. (1993). *Skills training manual for treating borderline personality disorder.* New York, NY: Guilford.

Lombardo, N. (2011). *The logic of desire: Aquinas on emotion.* Washington, DC: The Catholic University of America Press.

Loughlin, S. (2001). Similarities and differences between human and animal emotion in Aquinas's thought. *The Thomist, 65*(1), 45–65.

MacIntyre, A. (2007). *After virtue: A study in moral theory* (3rd ed.). Notre Dame, IN: University of Notre Dame Press.

Mattison, W. (2004). Virtuous anger?: From questions of *vindicatio* to the habituation of emotion. *Journal of the Society of Christian Ethics, 24*(1), 159–179.

Mattison, W. (2008). *Introducing moral theology: True happiness and the virtues.* Grand Rapids, MI: Brazos Press.

Mayer, J. D., & Salovey, P. (1989). Emotional intelligence. *Imagination, cognition, and personality, 9*(3), 185–211.

Miner, R. (2009). *Thomas Aquinas on the passions: A study of Summa theologiae Ia2ae 22–48.* Cambridge, United Kingdom: Cambridge University Press.

Peterson, C., & Seligman, M. E. P. (2004). *Character strengths and virtues: A handbook and classification.* New York, NY: Oxford University Press.

Pinckaers, S. (2005). Reappropriating Aquinas's ac-

count of the passions. In J. Berkman and C. Titus (Eds.), *The Pinckaers reader: Renewing Thomistic moral theology* (pp. 273–287). Washington, DC: The Catholic University of America Press.

Rhoads, S. E. (2004). *Taking sex differences seriously.* San Francisco, CA: Encounter Books.

Scarantino, A. (2016). The philosophy of emotions and its impact on affective science. In L. F. Barrett, M. Lewis, & J. M. Haviland-Jones (Eds.), *Handbook of emotions* (4th ed., pp. 3–48). New York, NY: Guilford Press.

Sherman, N. (1997). *Making a necessity of virtue: Aristotle and Kant on virtue.* Cambridge, United Kingdom: Cambridge University Press.

Sherwin, M. S. (2009). Infused virtue and the effects of acquired vice: A test case for the Thomistic theory of infused cardinal virtues. *The Thomist, 73*(1), 29–52.

Shields, S. A., & Kappas, A. (Eds.). (2006). *Magda B. Arnold's contributions to emotion research and theory.* London, United Kingdom: Psychology Press.

Siegel, D. (2012). *Interpersonal neurobiology.* New York, NY: Norton.

Sokolowski, R. (1982). *The God of faith & reason: Foundations of Christian theology.* Washington, DC: The Catholic University of America Press.

Sripada, C., & Stich, S. (2004). Evolution, culture, and the irrationality of emotions. In D. Evans & P. Cruse (Eds.), *Emotion, evolution, and rationality* (pp. 113–158). Oxford, United Kingdom: Oxford University Press.

Solomon, R. (1993). *The passions: emotions and the meaning of life* (2nd ed.). Indianapolis, IN: Hackett.

Teske, J. A. (2003). The social construction of the human spirit. In N. Gregersen, W. Drees, & U. Görman (Eds.), *The human person in science and theology* (189–212). Edinburgh, Scotland: T&T Clark.

Titus, C. S. (2009). Passions in Christ: Spontaneity, development, and virtue. *The Thomist, 73*(1), 53–87.

Vitz, P. C. (2018). Addressing moderate interpersonal hatred before addressing forgiveness in psychotherapy and counseling: A proposed model. *Journal of Religion and Health, 57*(2), 725–737.

Wojtyła, K. (1979). *The acting person* (A. Potocki, Trans.; Tymieniecka, A.-T., Ed.). Boston, MA: D. Reidel. (Original work published 1969)

Chapter 15

Rational

CRAIG STEVEN TITUS, PAUL C. VITZ,
AND WILLIAM J. NORDLING

ABSTRACT: This chapter focuses on the philosophical premise that the person is rational and seeks to know himself, others, the external world, and God. It affirms that human knowledge has limits and is completed by love. Signs of human intelligence and rationality are found in syntactical language and interpersonal narratives about the meaning of life, multifaceted social relationships and economic interactions, complex tool use and developed science, self-consciousness and intentionality, conscience and ethical free agency, as well as in culture and art. This chapter first investigates the human desire to know truth about mankind and about the cosmos, in particular about humanity's origin, development, and end. It also affirms that humans are fallible and acquire knowledge progressively, even learning from mistakes. Second, the chapter considers the context of self-consciousness in being supported by nonconscious—biological (bottom-up) and spiritual (top-down)—influences. Third, diverse types of sensory-perceptual and intellectual cognitions are seen in rational discourse, ethical judgments, and reasonable practices, in the light of both nature and grace. Fourth, belief is treated as a kind of "knowledge with assent" that admits of everyday and religious types. Next, the nature and limits of direct and indirect self-control are explored, as are rational virtues and vices with their intellectual, linguistic, moral, and faith-based dimensions. Last, the desire for beauty (even in the midst of deformity, brokenness, and darkness) is considered as a disclosure of reality and a call to contemplate the ultimate source of integrity, harmony, and radiance. In sum, the chapter addresses the epistemological, metaphysical, ethical, and spiritual dimensions of human rational intelligence.

Mankind has been identified with its achievements, and its achievements, with reason or intelligence. The major achievements of intelligence include syntactical language and complex tools, cultures and art, literature and stories, as well as technological breakthroughs and scientific discoveries, economic and medical progress, and therapeutic advancements. These accomplishments are rooted in instinct and urges as well as in intuition and rational intelligence. At the more personal and hidden level, mankind's achievements are also found in each person's self-understanding and interpersonal relations, especially with family, friends, and community. Of course, there is a downside to human history as well, as found in wars and injustices, indifference to those in need, biases against certain races and cultures, as well as shortsightedness at personal, family, and communal levels. Affirming that humans are rational and intelligent thus does not deny the presence of ignorance and distorted cognitive schemas, for example, narcissistic, envious, and aggressive motives, that are not in accord with reason. The very capacity to identify both achievements and failures, moreover, is rooted in human rational intelligence.

Among the issues that this chapter and the rest of the volume address is the argument that the intellectual dimension of human experience draws heavily and even depends in certain ways upon sensory-perceptual-cognitive and emotional dimensions of intelligence, even at nonconscious levels, as well as upon interpersonal experience. At the same time, neither the intellectual nor the sensory can be reducible to each other (see Table 15.1 and Chapters 13, "Sensory-Perceptual-Cognitive," and Chapter 14, "Emotional," which explicate the bottom two cells of Table 15.1, as well as Chapter 16, "Volitional and Free," which corresponds to the upper right-hand cell). In particular, the person's capacity to spiritually know and love distinguishes intellectual cognition (the mind's capacity for understanding, wisdom, and knowledge) from intellectual affect (the capacity for choice, love, and justice), and both of these are distinguished from sensory-perceptual cognition and emotion. Yet all of these capacities belong to a single and unified person. In the next chapter, on the person as volitional and free, we focus on the intellectual affect, that is, the heart or the will. In observing that the person is rational and in explaining how this is so, the current chapter affirms another significant aspect of a Catholic Christian Meta-Model's multidimensional paradigm of the person that should not be understood without referring to the unity or wholeness of each person.

This chapter first addresses the intellectual cognitive dimension of the natural inclinations that feed into the capacity for reason and knowledge of truth. These are expressed in continuity with the sometimes nonconscious biopsychosocial inclinations for knowledge. Second, it addresses the nature of the objects of knowledge and how they contribute to flourishing. It also identifies the context of self-conscious, preconscious, and nonconscious knowledge and memories, by contextualizing the discussion in terms of emergent (biological; bottom-up) and supervenient (spiritual; top-down) sources (Aquinas, 1273/1981, I 79.3 & 84.1; Aquinas, 1268/1994a, §397; Ashley, 2006, p. 434). Third, it distinguishes how human cognition varies from the sensory-perceptual to the intellectual, with special consideration for the influence of grace, especially infused knowledge such as faith. In particular, it takes into consideration how human reason seeks truth in the midst of the challenges due to relativism. Next, belief is presented as the knowledge, with volitional assent, that can be manifest in everyday beliefs as well as ultimate or religious belief. The next two sections of the chapter address self-control, practical reasoning (the virtue of prudence) along with its associated virtues and opposing vice, and the influence that Christian principles and grace have on practical moral reasoning and action. Last, it identifies the source of beauty, its uniqueness, and its capacity to disclose reality and to invite contemplation. The chapter, in union with the rest of the volume, offers a basic or philosophical frame for understanding human intelligence and reason in light of the person as a spiritual body-soul unity, as fulfilled in vocation, flourishing in virtue, interpersonally relational, sensory-perceptual-cognitive, emotional, and volitional and free (see Figure 15.1, for the context of this chapter in the whole of the Meta-Model's reason-based premises).

Table 15.1. Structure of Human Capacities as Found in the Philosophical Premises of the CCMMP

	Cognitive Capacites	Affective Capacities
Intellectual Capacities	**Intellectual Cognition: Understanding & Reason** ⊙ Foundational–Theoretical: intuition and understanding ⊙ Discursive: reasoning and language about truth and the ordering of goods	**Intellectual Affect: Will or Volition** ⊙ Foundational: disposition of being drawn toward the good and repulsed by evil ⊙ Discursive: pursuit of and choices about goods and repulsion of evils

← → **Body–Soul Unity** ← →

Sense Capacities	**Sensory-Perceptual Cognition: Preverbal Cognitive Capacities** ⊙ Higher-Order Perceptions & Systems: • Evaluative capacity • Imagination as a capacitiy • Memory as a process • Synthetic capacity ⊙ Primary (5) Senses: Vision, hearing, smell, taste, touch and pain (as well as vestibular and proprioceptive-kinesthetic senses)	**Sensory Affect: Emotion** ⊙ Emotions of Initiative (Irascible): affected by the difficult-to-attain good and difficult-to-repulse evil: • Fear & daring • Hope & despair • Anger ⊙ Emotions of Desire (Concupiscible): drawn toward the good; repulsed by evil: • Love and hate • Desire and repulsion • Joy (pleasure) & sorrow (suffering)

Organic and Neural Dimensions

What Are the Basic Types of Human Intelligence and Reasoning?

Humans express intelligence in different ways. First, we communicate through language in narratives, which are vehicles of personal and interpersonal meaning and purpose. Each person lives out his own personal story, but each personal story is interwoven with family narratives. Family narratives include accounts of friends and foes, and of journeys that lead us away from home and that return us home again. There are also the ultimate cosmic and faith-based narratives that communicate the knowledge of the source of life, its present meaning, and its ultimate fulfillment (Hauerwas, 1981a, 1981b). Throughout such narratives, there are the basic (philosophical) and technical (scientific) narratives or discourse that have particular grammars or ways of using reason to attain knowledge (MacIntyre, 1984, 1990, 1999). These grammars

Figure 15.1. Philosophical Premises of the Catholic Christian Meta-Model of the Person

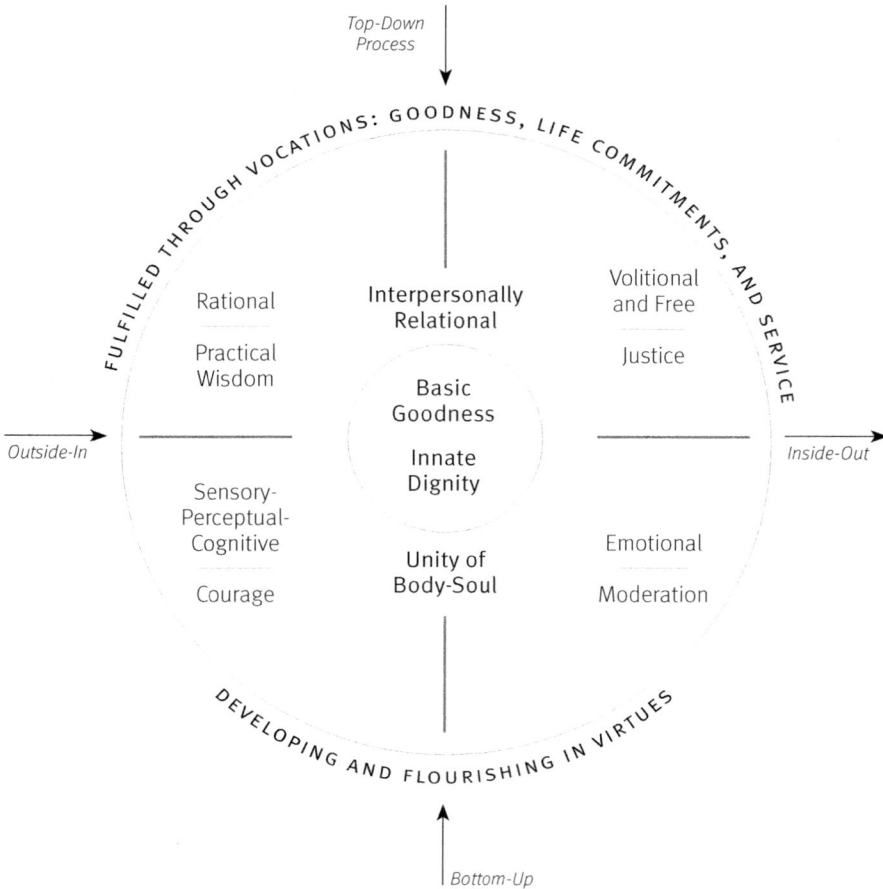

Top-Down
Process

FULFILLED THROUGH VOCATIONS: GOODNESS, LIFE COMMITMENTS, AND SERVICE

Rational

Practical
Wisdom

Interpersonally
Relational

Basic
Goodness

Innate
Dignity

Unity of
Body-Soul

Volitional
and Free

Justice

Sensory-
Perceptual-
Cognitive

Courage

Emotional

Moderation

Outside-In

Inside-Out

DEVELOPING AND FLOURISHING IN VIRTUES

Bottom-Up

of discourse include inductive, deductive, and mixed and applied methods.

We express formal and conceptual discursive rationality when in the midst of experiences of human flourishing we grasp reality and formulate concepts, principles, and theories about how to promote flourishing (Dewan, 1995; Seligman, 2004, 2012; Wojtyła, 1979, pp. 14–15). For example, we observe the flourishing of a couple who are caring and faithful to each other and who are devoted to family. Then, we grasp the potential conditions (such as, public commitment), principles (such as, loving care and fidelity) and theories (such as, attachment theory) that help to explain flourishing between spouses and within the family.

Also we deductively reason from logical principles, natural moral law precepts, faith-based principles and precepts, and evidence or empirically-based principles to conclusions about what is logical, ethically right, or morally good, and what are validated therapeutic practices. We reason deductively from abstract principles (such as, the principle of non-contradiction) to more concrete conclusions (such as, non-self-contradicting arguments). In the field of mental health and marital flourishing, for example, we take the rational principles found in faith-based traditions that are related to the institution of marriage to guide our discernment and action about spousal fidelity and openness to new life in the family. The living-out of these principles may require further therapeutic means that promote the aims of marriage concretely, such as increasing mutual respect and care in a particular couple, through Relationship Enhancement Therapy.

These methods or ways of thinking and communicating—induction, deduction, and combinations of the two—are simple as principles yet result in complex types of discourse and narrative. They are useful in distinguishing how our conscious and nonconscious, and instinctual and intuitive cognitive capacities identify the disclosure of being (ontological contemplation) as well as how our emotional capacities respond to the goodness of being (affective affirmation). These ways of thinking also contribute to understanding purpose (both discovering meaning and, at another level, making meaning), driving our actions, and accounting for our intentions and motives.

What Do the Psychological Sciences and Philosophical Reflection Add to an Understanding of Intelligence and Reason?

Psychology has had great interest in the human capacity for reasoning, as shown in its many ways for measuring reason as conceptualized by the term intelligence. Various types of measures or tests of intelligence have been developed; examples include the Stanford-Binet cognitive

ability assessment score and the Intelligence Quotient and Weschler Adult Intelligence Survey (WAIS-III). Recently, researchers have sought to measure distinct types of intelligence (Deary, 2001), including cognitive (Neisser, 2014), volitional (Baumeister & Tierney, 2011), emotional (Salovey & Mayer, 1989; Goleman, 1995, 2006; Siegel, 2012), and social intelligence (Siegel, 2012). However, there are types of intelligence, such as interpersonal and spiritual types of intelligence, that evade empirical measure and reduction to quantifiable mental or neural activities (Aquinas, 1265/2001, II.60.2). A complex approach to individual capacities and skills has been charted in terms of "multiple intelligences" (Gardner, 2006), which is not focused on mental abilities alone.

Furthermore, a Catholic Christian philosophical view of personal unity and a broadened understanding of rationality and responsible freedom affirm that our intellectual capacities underlie not only the personal quest for truth, but also the interpersonal quest for flourishing that is possible only when founded on family life and community engagement (see Chapter 16, "Volitional and Free," on freedom of excellence). As mentioned before, the wider range of intelligence is found throughout human history in its sciences and technology (Ashley, 2006, 2013); its economies, culture, and art; its work and meaningful leisure (Pieper, 1952/2009); as well as its contemplation and religion and divine worship (Aquinas, 1273/1981; Augustine, 401/2007; Bellah, 2011).

Human experience is full of self-conscious, intelligent efforts to understand the meaning of one's life and the cosmos. At the core of these experiences, though sometimes nonconsciously, is the inclination for existence, goodness, truth, relationship, and beauty (Schmitz, 2009). They all contribute to our everyday and ultimate flourishing. We often seek these transcendental properties of being for their own sakes, rather than for their utility. For example, there is a gratuity and limited utility—or even added accountability—in seeking justice (from which one does not visibly benefit, but which rather demands that one give to the other who is due something), in contemplating truth or solving mathematical formulae (without any practical benefit or monetary profit), in acknowledging the dignity of all mankind (which increases one's responsibilities toward others); or in seeking transcendent experiences of nature (which provide passing wonder and a hint of undying joy). We even sometimes seek these properties at our own peril or that of mankind, for example, in beauty (skiing in off-slope powder), discovery (expeditions to the South Pole), or knowledge (in nuclear research).

Because of our self-conscious intelligence and desire for knowledge, we pursue factual truth about the cosmos, and we receive personal disclosures made by other human beings and also, for many, by God. In its fullest human measure, self-conscious intelligence includes types of knowledge and love, that is, both intellectual cognition (intuition and reason) and intellectual affect (will). The rise of human consciousness appears to have occurred rather suddenly some 50,000 years ago (Vitz, 2017). It almost certainly involved the development of the human capacity for language and apparently has continued to develop to more sophisticated levels since its beginning. The uniqueness of this language-based human self-consciousness separates us widely from even the most advanced animals (Berwick & Chomsky, 2016; Bikerton, 2014; Deacon, 1997; Klein, 1999; Suddendorf, 2013).

Rational Inclinations

Humans have a natural desire and need for knowledge. We desire to know the world, other persons, and ourselves, of course, in tandem with our need for love, intentionality, and freedom (Sherwin, 2005). We ask questions. Where do we come from? Where are we going? Is there a purpose in life in general? Is there a purpose and meaning in my life? The thirst for quantifiable science is a part of this yearning, but so is the desire for qualitative knowledge of other persons, for interpersonal empathy, and for self-understanding.

What Roles Do the Natural Inclinations Play in Knowledge and Reason?

Among the natural inclinations that human beings experience, the natural desire for knowledge serves as a seedbed for the intellectual,

moral, and theological-infused virtues related both to knowledge and to love (see Chapter 11, "Fulfilled in Virtue"). Our curiosity is linked to a natural sense of responsibility for our thoughts and actions. It informs a desire to know what to do ethically and the judgment of conscience (guided in part by the moral virtue of prudence; Aquinas, I-II, qq. 47–56; *Catechism of the Catholic Church* [CCC], 2000, §§1783–1789, §1806). And conscience is in need of training. For example, we naturally want to know not only what persons are (because of their human nature) and how we flourish as persons and in families and communities (personal experience and vocations). We also want to know what we are called to do (what we ethically should do), and why we sometimes act in ways that hurt others and ourselves and even those whom we love the most.

These human experiences of seeking to know more to flourish demonstrate that the human mind is not only interested in survival (though, of course, there are conscious and nonconscious human activities—of the neural, hormonal, and other human systems—that make survival possible), it is interested also in knowledge of the world, self, and others. Furthermore, we are interested in ultimate transcendence and God. If the mind were simply a byproduct of survival or an epiphenomenon of "the selfish gene" (Dawkins, 1976/2016), it would only make statistical calculations of the survival value or utility of each action and person.

We not only seek knowledge in order to prolong life and to bring about physical and psychological healing, but we also work in service of freedom, peace, economic prosperity, as well as spiritual healing and reconciliation. These qualities, however, cannot be reduced to survival, even when they have survival value (Nagel, 2012). While rightfully concerned for the survival of the individual, the family, or the gene pool, we also devote our lives to the exploration of the meaning of life in theoretical, practical, and personal ways. We seek truths commonly known about the world and ultimate truth beyond any utility. We seek beauty beyond its survival value and ethical truth, even when others oppose it strongly and even though it may come at an emotional cost to us. Furthermore, humans give their lives in spite of the cost, for instance, as parents for their children, as soldiers for their country, and as martyrs for their faith.

It is our understanding, in light of a Catholic Christian philosophical position, that the natural inclination for knowledge and truth (and the cognitive aspects of the other natural inclinations, as seen in the last two chapters as well as the next one) serves a constructive role not only in human knowledge and contemplation,

but also in motivation and free agency, meaning and aesthetics, ethics and responsibility. In addition, rational inclinations are present in our search for everyday flourishing and ultimate beatitude (Aquinas, 1273/1981, I-II, 94.2; Levering, 2008; Pinckaers, 1995; Schmitz, 2009). We seek to know the truth, which is not simply the accurate relationship of the mind to reality. Truth is also found through the disclosure of being and the discovery of the meaning of existence, the personal knowledge of other humans, the metaphysical knowledge of the ultimate source of existence and truth (who is God), and the ethical demand engendered by the nature of each person and his or her vocational commitments. An important part of our dedication to truth and knowledge is our desire and work to preserve and teach them for the good of others and of society.

How Does the Basic Drive for Knowledge Influence Interpersonal Agency?

Our natural inquisitiveness to know the truth is unsatisfied with theoretical responses about human nature, theories about survival value, or scientific information about brain function. We seek not only to know the world and human beings but also to interact with them. This desire is not a simple unfolding of innate knowledge, nor is it satisfied with scientific data and partial explanations. Rather, this desire underlies the search to discover who people are, the meaning of our relationship with them, and the purpose of our lives. The natural desire for knowledge and truth leads toward the fuller meaning of human life at rational, interpersonal, ethical, metaphysical, and mystical levels. In so doing, it makes claims on how we act, how we engage ourselves, and who we become (Wojtyła, 1979, 1993). This natural desire functions as a seed of virtue and a way to know the direction offered by natural moral law. The natural desire grows, from underdeveloped inclinations, to intuition of what is good and right and what is not, to what is our end, to discernment about the means to that end, to responsible acts, to virtuous dispositions, to moral and spiritual maturity. This desire is also deeply interpersonal, for knowledge is acquired in interpersonal relationships as well as in communities and their narratives.

Philosophically speaking, natural moral law is found through the human rational participation in ordered objective reality. Theologically speaking, the rational participation in the natural moral law is also a rational participation in the eternal law (Rom 1:19–20 & 2:14–15; Aquinas, 1273/1981, I-II, 91.2). Its divine origin is confirmed and clarified in Divine Revelation, for example, in the two tablets of the Decalogue (Ex 20:1–17; see also Chapter 17, "Created in the Image of God," particularly the section, Divine and Moral Order). St. John Paul II (1993) identifies how at creation God gives mankind wisdom and love as well as a "final end, through the law which is inscribed in" the heart (1993, §12; cf. Rom 2:15); and, in accord with the classical tradition, he calls it the natural law.

Knowledge of the natural moral law has a direct influence on human agency. This knowledge is transformative and performative. Knowing the truth about reality shows us true goods to be pursued and promotes virtuous acts and true flourishing. Natural law underlies the desire for moral or spiritual virtues that positively build up relationships with others and with the source of reality (Chapter 11, "Fulfilled in Virtue," especially the section, Natural Inclinations, Natural Law, and the Personalist Norm). The drive to know is intertwined with the drive to do what is good and to flourish, which are in accord with the nature of the person. The basic precept of

the natural moral law is this: do the good, and avoid evil (Aquinas, 1273/1981, I-II, 94.2). The secondary precepts involve those duties and virtues that forbid murder and protect life, that prohibit adultery or promiscuity and promote fidelity, that prevent the abandonment of parents and endorse honoring them, and so on. These precepts are confirmed by Catholic Christian tradition, as found in the Decalogue (Ex 20:1–17), the Sermon on the Mount (Mt 5, 6), and St. Paul's moral exhortations (Gal 5; Eph 5), as well as magisterial sources such as the documents of the Second Vatican Council (1965b) and the encyclicals of St. John Paul II (1993). At a theological level, the secondary precepts (duties and virtues) that concern God include not neglecting worship of God, but recognizing God; not taking God's name in vain, but honoring it; not disregarding the Sunday or Sabbath day of rest, but using it to pursue meaningful leisure, including, especially, the worship of God.

The fact that the precepts of law are rooted in natural inclinations does not mean that the precepts are obvious to everyone (Aquinas, 1273/1981, I-II, 94.4; Austriaco, 2011). However, the existence of culpable ignorance (not having moral knowledge that one should have), misunderstandings, denial of truth, dysfunctional cognitive schemas, and other disorders of reason disproves neither the fact that humans have a natural inclination to know the truth about moral flourishing or the fact that this knowledge makes claims on how we act ethically and spiritually. However, these counterexamples do lead to the conclusion that we must be seriously attentive to the physical, psychological, social, ethical, and spiritual causes of personal development and decline, healing and disorder, and cognition and ignorance.

Is Human Knowledge Simply a Matter of Neurology?

The cognitive neurosciences have recently made important discoveries about the correlation between the activity of brain regions and human experience, including moral action. One of the significant discoveries has been that different brain circuits support fast intuitive (perception, intuition, and emotion) as opposed to slower reflective (rational discursive) cognition (Kahneman, 2011). Thus, the neurosciences have identified how emotion is intertwined with cognition and cognition with emotion. For example, in the perspective of childhood and adult development, recent studies show that the underlying particular and global neural circuits for moral agency include not only higher order cognitions but also empathy and emotions (Decety & Howard, 2013). There are particularly significant studies on the childhood development of both moral cognition and emotion. For example, even young children have notions of fairness and commitment in their play and interpersonal interactions (Hamlin, 2013). The neurosciences will inevitably continue to identify connections: the way that the neurological system is integrated throughout the brain and the body (Siegel, 2012); the regions of the brain that support the expression of intellectual intuition, moral cognition, and morally relevant emotion (Siegel, 2012); and even neural correlates to prayer and infused belief (Beauregard, 2012).

Although helpful in various ways, the correlation of neural regions and knowledge has sometimes been expressed in latently reductionistic ways (Damasio, 2010). Such a tendency holds that a brain model will explain the whole person and the person's experiences of perception, emotion, thought, and will (Churchland, 2001). This tendency erroneously attributes to a part of the organism (the brain) what can properly be ascribed only to the whole (the person). This logical error has been called the mereological fallacy (Bennett & Hacker, 2003, p. 73). What are some of the indications that there is more to humans than biological and neurological function? Some neuroscientists recognize that the brain does not completely explain mankind's behavior or intelligence. For example, Gazzaniga (2006) says: "Neuroscience will never find the brain correlate of responsibility, because that is something we ascribe to humans—to people—not to brains" (p. 101). In addition to not being able to explain the person's self-understanding and freedom, neural activities alone cannot explain the influence of divine grace in these activities (Beauregard & O'Leary, 2008; Egnor, 2017). Furthermore, the failure of mechanistic naturalism and determinism (Życiński, 2006) to explain human self-consciousness and rational intelligence, free will and moral intentionality, value and meaning, and the mind itself has led some philosophers to look for principles of order in the cosmos that are teleological in form rather than mechanistic (Nagel, 2012). Admitting that human knowledge is not simply a matter of neuroscience does not discredit biological and neurological sciences. Rather, it sets forth a principle that opens further conversation in the light of understanding the wholeness of the person and human rational capacities.

Objects of Knowledge

Human beings have limited knowledge of things and limited ways of knowing them. We come to receive knowledge in our human mode of being and knowing (Aquinas, 1259/1994b). We, nonetheless, can come to know many things accurately, which often takes not only effort and thought, but also tools to gain some types of knowledge. For example, a particle's speed (if not its position, at the same time) can be known (Heisenberg principle). The normal process of a human zygote's development can be known. And a mother and child's attachment styles can be known. All of these types of knowledge, however, have different characteristics and some limitations.

To gain knowledge of objects requires different questions and methods of study. It also requires recognizing that what we want to know (our questions) determines how we come to know the object of knowledge (methods). A method that is not fit for an object will at best reveal only part of its being or qualities. The more complex a thing, the more complex the methods of study will be needed. For example, the complexity increases from the study of minerals (chemistry) to the study of cats (anatomy, biology, zoology) to the study of human persons (neurology, medicine, psychology, sociology), their moral agency, and ultimate end (philosophical and theological anthropology, ethics, and moral theology).

A particular human being's knowledge is formed by the real thing as an object of study, depending on the way that the object, including persons, discloses itself and on the methods and tools at hand to help in the process (Sokolowski, 2000).

Human knowledge, globally speaking, can be distinguished as sense knowledge, higher order perceptual cognitions (synthetic capacity, memory, imagination, evaluative capacity), intellectual knowledge (intuition and reason), and scientific knowledge (distinguished according to the scientific method's focus on objects). These types of knowledge can be conscious or non-

conscious, as when repressed memories cause certain psychopathologies or when serious trauma is experienced before memories can be coded for language (that is, before age 4) (Schore, 2002). Human knowledge furthermore involves not only the dyad knowledge-ignorance, but also the nuances that distinguish belief, opinion, and doubt (review Table 15.1).

What Types of Knowledge Aid Human Flourishing?

The knowledge needed for human flourishing is more moral, more personal, and commonly simpler and more available than the knowledge that specialists exhibit. Experts and specialists seek refined expressions of aesthetic, philosophical, scientific, and spiritual knowledge. They contribute to a larger comprehension of humanity and the cosmos (Ashley, 2006; Maritain, 1932/1959). However, not every person is expert in any particular field of knowledge, let alone all of them. What humans need to begin to flourish in everyday life is more humble than that. We can flourish even in the midst of types of ignorance and forgetfulness. The massive amount of information available that can tax our attention on life priorities, moreover, leads to the recognition that there are even advantages to ignorance (ignorance, for example, of the personal lives of celebrities) or to not knowing everything at once. Even if they would not describe their search this way, all persons seek a general understanding of what it is to be a human person (human nature and human flourishing) and of that to which they are called to devote their lives (vocations). For example, to flourish we must understand our vocations and the basic knowledge required for living them out well. Such a quest involves personal self-knowledge and knowledge of others, but it also requires interpersonal relationships with individuals (especially family members, friends, work colleagues, etc.) and with God (whom many people explicitly believe in). Without knowledge of their personal, interpersonal, and ultimate vocations, however, humans feel lost in history and in their own story. Moreover, humans seek practical knowledge of how to advance in their particular vocations at everyday levels (e.g, as a husband or wife, father or mother, and mental health professional or one in need of therapy) as well as at ultimate levels (e.g., through goodness, justice, and holiness in relationship with God). This practical knowledge, which overcomes languishing while promoting flourishing, is shared in families, among friends, in schools, in religious communities, and through the ministrations of mental health professionals.

Do We Know More Than That of Which We Are Immediately Conscious?

We become aware of the world through different sources over time. Sensate knowledge of others and ourselves serves as a basic building block for more complex types of knowledge. The conscious level, which involves the types of sensory-perceptual and intellectual cognition of which we are aware, is only a fraction of our knowledge. Conscious knowledge is informed by instincts, sensations, higher-order perceptions (such as imagination, memory, and lower-order evaluations), as well as intuition and understanding, theoretical reasoning, and practical judgments involving concepts, persons, and reality. For example, conscious knowledge of the moral principle that life should be protected is rooted both (1) in the instinctive and biological (bottom-up) knowledge of the goodness of existing things that we have experienced through the senses and the higher order perceptions, and (2) in the spiritual, intuitive, and intellec-

tual (top-down) understanding of the goodness of existing things as coming from the ultimate source of goodness and life.

The terms conscious and nonconscious (including preconscious) are used to understand human knowledge and experience. Psychology has focused on the bottom-up development of knowledge and consciousness. The Catholic Christian Meta-Model of the Person recognizes not only an emergent (bottom-up) but also a supervenient (top-down) movement in developing knowledge and consciousness. The supervenient influences on nonconsciousness and consciousness are the human intellectual and spiritual levels, including grace and the way that grace perfects nature (Aquinas 1273/1981, I, 1.8 ad 2). The preconsciousness of the spirit refers to the top-down spiritual knowledge of concepts and use of intellect, as well as the presence and working of divine grace (Maritain, 1953, p. 108).

Personal knowledge is accumulated and becomes nuanced through experience as we seek to unite sensory-perceptual cognition and intellectual knowledge of ourselves and others. In part it also draws from nonconscious levels, which originate both at a supra-rational level (from the preconscious of the spiritual domain) and at the sub-rational level (from the nonconscious of the automatic and instinctual domain). The human sensory-perceptual cognition (such as memory, imagination, and evaluation) and intellect are united within the human soul, through which we access intuitions about the truth of reality, and through which, in reasoning, we organize knowledge of the external senses, internal imagination, as well as concepts and ideas.

As implied, conscious knowledge depends on sources that are not all conscious, at least not at first and not without reflection, hindsight, and the help of other people. We become aware of nonconscious (or preconscious) perceptions and evaluations based on their effects, not only with basic awareness (the synthetic capacity) but also with the help of others and in bottom-up and top-down patterns of cognition.

In a bottom-up movement, for example, starting with the reality that is encountered and sensory perception of it, we experience an injury, suffer physical pain, perceive danger by nonconscious sub-rational evaluation of the situation, feel repulsion or fear, focus our attention on the source of the pain and danger, become conscious of the injury, danger, and repulsion, and start to think about appropriate action to avoid further injury to self and others, including ways to find a safe haven and the assistance needed for medical care and safety.

In the other direction, in a top-down movement of rational deliberation and choice, while trying to keep a clear and cool head, we first have an intuition about the need to preserve one's life (safety, and health) and we then desire it. We recognize that there is some possibility to attain safety and we then intend to pursue it. We deliberate about ways to protect our life and we then consent to them. We decide on particular means to safety and we then choose to do one. Finally, we execute the plan actually negotiating, fleeing, attacking, and so on (Aquinas, 1273/1981, I-II, 11–17; Clayton & Davies, 2006; Murphy, 2006).

We also influence nonconscious cognitive and affective habits (such as our emotions and behaviors) in a top-down manner. For example, our cognitive distortions, dysfunctional schemas, or other cognitive disorders can cause dysphoric emotion; however, we can use our rational thoughts, with the aid of cognitive therapies, to calm and help to correct such distortion (Beck, 1979; Ellis & Ellis, 2011). Furthermore, our conscious activities can also become nonconscious or acquired patterns of thought. We

intentionally shape our cognitive and rational dispositions. For example, we can form cognitive dispositions to resist anxiety through training in cognitive scripts and self-calming skills, and through focusing our attention on an object that does not produce anxiety, panic, or anger.

How Does Conscious Knowledge Involve Other Types of Knowledge?

There are two types of nonconscious (including preconscious) knowledge at two different levels—bottom-up (emergent) and top-down (supervenient)—that influence consciousness, as we have already mentioned. First, there is the bottom-up human intelligence that also involves automatic instinctual as well as habituated types of nonconscious knowledge. This sub-rational knowledge influences human sensory-perceptual cognition, emotions, and rational judgments (Ashley, 2013; Kahneman, 2011; Maritain, 1959). Nonconscious influences and knowledge can be rooted in the experiences of youth and the traumas of life. Although unrecognized, they may influence our cognitive and affective lives. Nonconscious sources of knowledge include not only basic instinct but also the rapid evaluation of a thing's or a person's attractive or repulsive characteristics. This judgment is enabled by the evaluative capacity (Aquinas, 1273/1981, I, 78.4; Ashley, 2013; Tellkamp, 2012; see also Chapter 13, "Sensory-Perceptual-Cognitive"). Such an evaluation can inform the intelligence of our emotions as well as our further rational reflections about the person or thing. This has been called emotional intelligence and social intelligence (Damasio, 2010; Goleman, 1995, 2006). However there is more to full human intelligence, as we shall see next, unless we reduce the mind to a simple creation of the brain or a bottom-up epiphenomenon (Davies, 2006; Murphy, 1998; Pinker, 2009; Życiński, 2006).

Second, it is assumed here that there are several levels of top-down structure and activity. There are nonconscious or preconscious influences that are manifest in the human intellectual capacities and activities. Moreover, there are preconscious and supra-rational influences that are the result of grace and the gifts of the Holy Spirit. These divine influences are preconscious in the sense of being ontologically prior to or above consciousness (Augustine, 401/2007, VII.17). The preconsciousness of the Spirit affects the intellectual and spiritual capacities for knowing and loving (Aquinas, 1273/1981, I, 79.3 & 84.1; Aquinas, 1268/1994a, §397; Ashley, 2006, p. 434). Such influences involve, for example, being illuminated by receiving the gift of understanding (*CCC*, 2000,§1831) or being inspired to affirm truths that transcend the capacity of one's natural intellect (Aristotle, 1941c; Pinckaers, 2005, p. 387; Vatican II, 1965a, §§7–11). Such top-down influences may be only indirectly ascertained (Vatican II, 1965b, §36).

How our conscious knowledge involves these other types of knowledge is apparent when spiritual influences reach our affectivity. We experience an interplay between felt emotion, willed love, and spiritual and religious affect, which can overflow into emotion. Thus, we can experience spiritual joy, intellectual peace, and emotional pain at the same time. For example, imagine a daughter, who loves her father and who has faith in God and an afterlife. She may, at the time of his death, feel real emotional pain at the loss of her father, as well as a spiritual joy and peace in the hope of God's granting him eternal rest and beatitude (see Chapter 19, "Redeemed," Chapter 14, "Emotional," and Chapter 16, "Volitional and Free").

How Does Psychology Understand the Growth and Development of Persons?

The quest for knowledge about the self can be understood psychologically (by way of developmental theories), philosophically (by way of metaphysics, epistemology, and an ethics based on the natural law), and theologically (by way of a religious exploration of divine law and revelation).

From a psychological perspective, there are different approaches to understanding the development of the self, which consider cognition, family and sociocultural influences, as well as implications for emotion and behavior. Piaget (1929) calls attention to human cognitive development. Kohlberg (1981, 1984; Kohlberg, Boyd, & Levine 1990) extends Piaget's work to focus on cognitive moral development, especially understood as the judgment of justice. Vygotsky's (1962, 1978) influence contributes to a widening of the study of development to include a sociocultural perspective. Gilligan (1982) explores how care for others is also significant in moral agency, and how without it we do not understand moral development in women (care is also pertinent for men, as we will discuss throughout the volume). Bowlby (1982, 1988) and his students (Ainsworth, Blehar, Waters, & Wall, 1978; Hazan & Shaver, 1987; Mikulincer & Phillip, 2007) recognize the importance of attachment styles in learning, in agency, and in interpersonal relations throughout the lifespan. Erikson (1979, 1994) and Hoffman (2001) also contribute to a further notion of growth that involves not only cognitive but also social and emotional development. In particular, Erikson's stages of development involve interpersonal stages that move from egocentric, through latency, to true relationality. Gardner (2006), furthermore, seeks to widen the notion of intelligence and cognition to that of "multiple intelligences," including skills at musical, visual, linguistic, logical-mathematical, bodily, interpersonal, intrapersonal, naturalistic, and existential levels (pp. 8–21). Most recently, positive psychology presents an outline of human psychological flourishing in terms of virtues and character strengths (Peterson & Seligman, 2004; Lopez & Snyder, 2009).

Psychological ways of coming to self-knowledge involve different aspects of experience, such as reading literature or engaging in discussions about oneself with family and friends. Psychotherapy provides a major contemporary contribution to leading clients to self-knowledge, as does reading about psychology and its findings, and reflecting on successes and failures in one's life.

How Is the Person Known from Philosophical and Theological Perspectives?

From philosophical and theological points of view, the quest for knowledge of the self can be construed in four anthropological dimensions that serve a higher-level synthesis of knowledge about the self and others, placing this knowledge in a rational context.

First, humans know themselves through personal recognition of their own existence, cognitions, and affections. The Delphic maxim "Know yourself!" is one of the most ancient philosophical aphorisms (Plato, ca. 370 BC/2001, 229e). It expresses a commonly experienced thirst for wisdom (Rom 12:2–3; Gal 6:3) that is deeper than the particular knowledge of music and the arts, or sciences and math, or psychology and sociology. It involves personal, ethical, and sapiential dimensions.

Second, knowledge of others leads to a deeper understanding of oneself than can be had alone. Mankind is social by nature and calling. We learn about ourselves through coming to understand our being male or female, through

interactions with our families, and in responding to our basic vocations to flourishing. There is not only the interpersonal knowledge that comes through the first smiles and signs of affection of the mother and the education of parents, but also the systematic and scientific knowledge of the person in relationship that is found through the social sciences and psychology (MacIntyre, 1999).

Third, experience of reality (the book of nature or creation) provides a basis for intuitional knowledge and metaphysical judgment about existence, goodness, truth, relationship, beauty, and the source of them all, namely God (Rom 1:19–20; Aquinas, 1273/1981; Maritain, 1959; Schmitz, 2009).

Fourth, experience of Divine Revelation (the book of the Word of God) communicates more precise information about God, the human vocation, salvation history, natural moral law, and divine law (Lk 8:10; John Paul II, 1998, §4, §9, §19; Vatican II, 1965a). This knowledge of God leads to further intra- and interpersonal understanding, especially concerning the personal character of the calling to ultimate flourishing (2 Pet 1:2–9).

What Is the Importance of the Desire for and Knowledge of God?

There is great moral and clinical importance to the fact that humans seek truth about their own flourishing, through self-knowledge and experience, as well as through the types of cognition found in the arts and literature, the sciences and technology, philosophy, and Divine Revelation. A Christian perspective on the knowledge of good and evil does not stop with the practical knowledge (and natural inclination) that good is to be pursued and evil avoided (Jn 14:15). Nor does this perspective limit itself to subjective knowledge. At the basis of human cognition is a restless desire for truth, including an interpersonal union with the source of truth. In his *Confessions*, St. Augustine (401/2007) addresses God personally as this source, exclaiming: "Our hearts are restless until they rest in you" (I.1.2). Moral knowledge, found in the Christian tradition's commandments and moral doctrine, is rooted in the knowledge of God through Jesus Christ and in the Holy Spirit (John Paul II, 1993, §§6–27). The belief that God calls each person by name for a life of faith and goodness has great

moral, clinical (Frankl, 1959/2000) and empirical (VanderWeele, 2017a, 2017b) significance. For example, although theological hope is primarily rooted in faith, it provides more than information about salvation. For hope becomes "performative," making believers live differently. Faith lived in hope offers new meaning for the life journey, as well as a source of joy and peace even in the midst of trials and suffering (Benedict XVI, 2007, §§1–2)

Sensory-Perceptual-Cognitive and Intellectual Knowledge

Humans do not invent objective moral standards, the truth of things, or the order of the universe. We comprehend them only in part and not by human reason alone. But, in the complex process of human knowing we discover something of the objective truth and standards that serve as the basis for reasonable action and more concrete laws and customs (on divine order and natural law, see Chapter 17, "Created in the Image of God"). To establish a wider understanding of intelligence, one needs to resist narrow modern rationalism and relativism. In particular, one needs to acknowledge that, often, secularized approaches presuppose that faith-based and metaphysical worldviews are insignificant for valid knowledge about the human person; the effect of the secularized presupposition is the inherent or outright denial of metaphysically nonreductionist worldviews, such as those held by many mental health professionals and social scientists, such as Bandura (1997, 2006), Beauregard (2012), Frankl (1959), Fowers (2005), Giorgi (1970), and Romanyshyn (1982), as well as many positive psychologists, such as Joseph and Linley (2006), and Lopez and Snyder (2009).

Viable responses require a nonreductionist approach that integrates scientific, historical, and

cultural sources of knowledge (Benedict XVI, 2006). Such a quest for a broader scope of understanding recognizes that human intelligence involves an often unperceived interplay of receiving and giving of facts, knowledge, and understanding or wisdom. As discussed earlier in this volume, we are human body-soul unities, thus also rational animals. Our way of knowing is influenced by sensory and intellectual cognitions. There are (a) natural inclinations (such as toward truth and beauty), (b) sensations (such as tactile appreciation of the child's temperature), (c) higher-order perceptions (such as evaluations about what is dangerously hot for a child), as well as (d) instances of intellectual knowledge further informed by basic experience and reason (such as taking the child's temperature and calling the doctor), and, (e) as Christians maintain, God's grace.

The process of knowing is not simply an acquisition of the meaning of the world and its structure. Rather knowledge is also tied to loving, loving particular people (for example, loving the child when he is sick and cantankerous or one's mother and father even when they have acted in unlovable ways), and aiming at very particular goals (for example, enjoying Mendelssohn's Italian Symphony or seeking therapeutic help for depression).

Why Distinguish Sensory-Perceptual-Cognitive and Intellectual Knowledge?

To resist reducing the person to the mind and the mind to the body, we need to credibly identify the spiritual body-soul unity of the person as a source of both sensory-perceptual and intellectual-linguistic knowledge. If humans were simply material beings, that is, if each person were not a spiritual body-soul unity, we would not need to distinguish sensory-perceptual cognition from intellectual knowledge. We would have only sensory-perceptual-cognitive capacities by which we sense colors, perceive colored things, and are repulsed by such things that are dangerous or attracted to those that are beneficial. Or, if we were materialist, we might maintain that there is a higher neural structure that explains our foundational understanding of truth and attraction to the good, human relationality and other immaterial realities. But it has been convincingly shown that the human body-soul unity is the most helpful way to understand how it is that we experience more than sensory-perceptional cognition and emotion and their neural correlates (Beauregard & O'Leary, 2008; Nagel, 2012; Vitz, 2017). Through observation and rational judgment, we can identify the first causes and principles (Aristotle, ca. 350 BC/1941a) of the intellectual (including linguistic) and spiritual dimension of each person, which provide a meaning-based and purpose-directed (teleological) account for more of what we prize as persons.

To say that a person is a spiritual body-soul unity (hylomorphic unity) is different than saying a person is a mind, or a heart, or a soul, or a body, or a spirit (Chapter 8, "Personal Whole-

ness"). Nonetheless, the primary sensory capacities and higher-order perceptual capacities are seen to be the foundation of sensory-perceptual knowledge (bottom-up), and the intellectual (including linguistic) and spiritual (including God's grace) capacities are seen to be the source of intellectual knowledge (top-down).

What is sensory-perceptual knowledge? Sensory-perceptual cognition pertains to sensing and perceiving particular things. For example, through our primary senses, we know that that object is red (rose), that sound is loud (Mozart), that smell is pungent (Gorgonzola), that taste is bitter (chocolate), and that object is rough (sandpaper). But also through cognitive perceptions, we have memories of a person, images of the person in a new setting, and attractions to what is useful and repulsion at that which is dangerous for the person (Chapter 13, "Sensory-Perceptual-Cognitive").

Sensory-perceptual-cognitive knowledge is attained through the external senses of touch and proprioceptive cues, sight, hearing, taste, and scent, which are five different ways of receiving information about the world. It also involves the higher-order perceptual-cognitions—such as the synthetic capacity, imagination, memory, and the evaluative capacity—which are further ways to receive and process the basic information of reality (Ashley, 2013). Of particular interest, the evaluative capacity is the higher-order perception of a person or thing as, in its own way, being delightful or painful, attractive or repulsive.

What Is Distinctive About Self-Conscious Intellectual Knowledge?

What is intellectual knowledge? Taken as a whole, human sensory-perceptual cognition of things and people is complemented by the self-conscious intellectual (intellection, conception, and language) knowledge that is rooted in reality, as well as in the basic experience and knowledge of each person's interior life (Pinckaers, 1995, pp. 48–82; Vitz, 2017). Intellectual cognition involves knowing universal features of experienced realities (such as humanity, or justice, or beauty) which once apprehended (intellection) can be conceptualized (inner words and principles) and expressed by way of language (outer words and speech) (Aquinas, 1273/1981, I, 27.1; Aquinas, ca. 1272/2010, I.1, §25–§29; Dewan, 1995). This kind of cognition is the basis for human culture (creation and appreciation) and complex tools (science and use). A realist vision of sensory-perceptual-cognitive and intellectual-linguistic knowledge relies upon the unique type of spiritual (intellectual and graced) experiences and interpersonal relationships that humans have (Beauregard & O'Leary, 2008). This realist view of knowledge affirms that human knowledge is objective, yet at times fallible (Popper, 1975).

Human knowledge and rationality are different than that of other animals, as evidenced in our capacity for syntactical language, complex tool use, self-conscious and intentional free agency, science, the preservation of knowledge, and certain social relationships (Berwick & Chomsky, 2016; Bikerton, 2014; Deacon, 1997; Klein, 1999; Suddendorf, 2013; Vitz, 2017). Furthermore, according to Sokolowski (2000, p. 158) and a realist phenomenology, we have access, through our intellects, to different aspects of reality. We can intuit and rationally determine factual truth about the cosmos and make rational judgments about human nature. We can also partake in the personal reception and disclosure of aspects of the truth of each person and God. Our deep interior life, represented by such self-conscious intellectual knowledge and love, relies in various ways on sensory-

perceptual-cognitive knowledge and basic spiritual experience. Our intellectual knowledge can be intuitive (involve insight and understanding), discursive (be reached by reasoning), or infused (involve graced belief) (Lonergan, 1992).

Based on our sensory-perceptual-cognitive knowledge that is sub-rational and our pre-ideational and contemplative experience of reality (Pinckaers, 1995) and because of our intellectual capacities, we intuit the truth and beauty of a person or thing (for a fuller presentation of epistemology and metaphysics, see Aristotle, ca. 350 BC/1941a; Ashley, 2006; Maritain, 1959, 1953; Popper, 1975; Schmitz, 2009). Experience of such properly intellectual knowledge (of being, truth, goodness, relationship, beauty) underlies a philosophical (and Catholic) conviction that humans are composed of a spiritual soul-body unity. We are neither simply matter nor pure spirit (as angels are). Human beings, rather, have a unified intellect that is both intellectually receptive and rationally active in coming to grasp and understand persons and things (Aquinas, 1268/1994a; Aristotle, ca. 350 BC/1941c; McInerny & O'Callahan, 2014). The active receptivity and receptive activity of the intellect, although united, are called "possible intellect" and "agent intellect," respectively, by Aquinas (1270/1968). Our intellectual or spiritual capacities appreciate reality through intuiting or inferring the thing or person's existence, nature, potential, and relationships (Aquinas, 1265/2001, II.60.22).

Intellectual understanding (*intelligere*) involves basic insight (*simplex intuitus*) into experience, received through the bodily senses, about the nature, truth, goodness, and beauty of things, ourselves, and the world, ultimately leading one to consider our first Source (Aristotle, ca. 350 BC/1941a; Aquinas, 1273/1981, I, qq. 84–87). Through intellectual understanding, we intuit the validity of truths: "a thing cannot be and not be at the same time" (principle of non-contradiction), and "good is to be done and evil avoided" (first principle of practical reason). Intuition provides basic principles of self-conscious knowledge, which are refined and applied through discursive reasoning (Aquinas, 1259/1994b, II.15.1; Ashley, 2013; Lonergan, 1992; Pieper, 1952/2009, p. 11).

What Is the Nature of Rational Discourse (Including Moral Discourse)?

Self-conscious and intentional rational discourse (*ratio*) exercises reflective cognition rooted in reality and in our basic experience and knowledge of that reality. One kind of rational discourse is involved when one takes counsel and reflects upon courses of practical action (Aquinas, 1273/1981, II-II, 49.5). Rational discourse also exercises the intellect's inferential capacity by way of logical deduction. Deduction moves from principles and hypotheses to applications and practices. In a complementary movement, the intellect can form generalizations and hypotheses based on experience and observations (Popper, 1975; Robinson, 2007). While the rational discourse of deductive reasoning is distinct from the rational discourse of hypothesis formation, scientific reasoning requires both processes (O'Donohue, 2013; Oskawa, 2002). In a similar way practical reasoning requires the formation of hypotheses about moral action and situations and a kind of deduction from moral principles (Aquinas, 1273/1981, II-II, 49.5 ad 2; Aquinas, 1272/2003, 3.9 ad 7; Osborne, 2012, p. 282).

In short, reasoning moves from experience to forming hypotheses that explain the experience. Psychological theories are constituted in this way when based upon practical experiences, empirical evidence, and cases of sound

mental health as well as psychopathology. For example, observations of people who are able to overcome difficulty when provided resources and hope leads to insights about the resiliency effect of secure versus insecure attachment (Ainsworth, Blehar, Waters, & Wall, 1978; Bowlby, 1982, 1988). Such observations lead also to the formation of hypotheses in psychology. For example, hope is built on cognitive pathways and personal agency and leads to resiliency in the face of difficulty (Snyder, 1994; Rand & Cheavens, 2009).

Deductive reasoning is another aspect of the complex use of reason in science, psychotherapy, ethics, and culture. For example, discursive reason is operative in the scientific method when it tests (verifies or disproves) a hypothesis through measured observations. Such tests often involve first making a deductive inference regarding what outcomes would logically follow should a hypothesis be true, then structuring an experiment to discern the presence of those outcomes (as when blood analyses are conducted in order to verify or falsify a medical diagnosis) (Copi & Cohen, 2005, p. 527). Deduction is also operative when mental health professionals apply to clients' treatment evidence-based therapeutic practices, intuited philosophical truths about mankind, or psychological theories about the development of persons. A similar process is found in moral reasoning. For instance, in professional ethics (American Psychological Association, 2010; American Counseling Association, 2014), a mental health professional adheres to principles, such as "beneficence and non-maleficence," "fidelity and responsibility," and "justice," and applies these in practice when deductively concluding that he must refer a client to another professional because of a conflict of interest.

What Is the Nature of Grace-Informed Knowledge?

There is a knowledge that is possible only through the experience of faith. The Christian considers this knowledge to be infused by the gift of grace. God gives a knowledge of himself that is both a loving knowledge and a knowing love. Faith-based knowledge elicits a graced assent of the intellect and consent of the will in response to the encounter with God, who reveals himself and informs us of the truth about the world and about ourselves (Aquinas, 1273/1981, II-II, 6.1; Francis, 2013; Pieper, 1997). For example, through infused faith and charity, the intellectual attention of our mind and the loving desire of our will are unified and enabled to begin to approach God, the First Truth to be known and the greatest Good to be loved. We can also know truths about God and his works, such as the truth about God as a triune interpersonal communion, about God's creating the world, about God's redeeming mankind through Jesus Christ, and about the necessity of justice and forgiveness for flourishing (Chapter 19, "Redeemed"). As unaided human reasoning is not immediately aware of nonconscious biological activity (such as the activity of neurotransmitters and hormones), so also it is not immediately aware of nonconscious movements of grace (CCC, 2000, §2005). Nonetheless, a Catholic Christian model recognizes that such knowledge—naturally known and divinely revealed—can influence human action. With the help of natural and faith-based knowledge, we reason about the reality of being (ontology) and about rational ways of relating to particular beings (ethics). For example, through Divine Revelation as a graced event mediated through contact with the Word of God (Scripture and the Magisterium; Vatican II, 1965a), we encounter the models of the saints and a global narrative that provide the basis for us to relate to people not simply as objects (sources of warmth or nutrition or pleasure) but as persons manifesting their own dignity, who are made in the image of God (Gen 1, 2), and who are called to a new life in God through Christ (2 Cor 5:27).

What Kinds of Truth Can Human Reason Attain?

Through intellectual cognition, we seek to know the truth about ourselves, other persons, and the world itself. When taken in its entirety, this capacity is not only subjective and personal but also objective with respect to the common knowledge the intellect grasps about the human condition, the universe, and the ultimate origin and end of all that exists. According to John Paul II (1993), the human intellectual vocation is tied to two factors: truth and freedom. Through knowledge, understanding, and dedication to the truth, humans express not only a freedom from ignorance (which is always only partial) but also a freedom to fulfill humbly their vocation, such as to pursue love, goodness, and holiness; to found families and raise children; and to work for constructive ends, including participation in the healing of those in need (Chapter 16, "Volitional and Free").

Although the scientific community seeks a fuller understanding of factual truth, in general, the disclosure of truth of each person is limited and ongoing. The quest for factual truth and personal truth is inadequate for understanding the person without the search for the ultimate source of being. Knowledge of the nature of mankind, the beauty of each person, and the expanse of the universe is incomplete without an acknowledgement of their transcendent first and ultimate source (White, 2009). However, the full knowledge of the transcendent source and end of life and truth, who is God, cannot be attained with unaided human reason. It requires divine self-revelation that is not a human accomplishment but rather a gift of God (Ex 3:14–15; Jn 14:6; 1 Cor 2:9–13). Even if human knowledge of truth is limited, there is one source of truth, God, who is also the source of existence, goodness, communion, and beauty. A Catholic perspective humbly offers insights on how all truth participates in the one source of absolute truth, each according to its nature (John Paul II, 1998; MacIntyre, 1990, p. 200; Wojtyła, 1993, 2011).

Can Thought When Closed to the Transcendent Satisfy the Human Longing for Truth and Meaning?

John Paul II (1998) maintains that any true philosophy that contributes to human knowledge of truth will not be closed to the reality of the transcendent (§81). However, arguments for moral relativism, materialist determinism, and nihilism are usually predicated on challenges about whether humans can know objective transcendent truth and meaning. These arguments may attract our attention, especially when espoused by a scientist (e.g., Dawkins, 2008) or a psychologist (e.g., Ellis, 1980). They may contain a kernel of truth and much scientific data. But these arguments are not ultimately convincing for most people because they exhibit a significant ignorance or neglect of human existential, moral, and spiritual nature (Beauregard & O'Leary, 2008; Nagel, 2012; McGrath, 2004; Ratzinger, 2007). In the face of materialist interpretations, persons long for a fuller account of human nature that includes consideration of

flourishing, responsibility, and freedom. This longing is a response to the inadequacy of materialist interpretations (Nagel, 2012; Feser, 2008; Spitzer, 2010, 2015); it is expressed in widespread metaphysical and religious searches for understanding the meaning of our life. Scientific data is limited to particular fields of observing sensory or measurable phenomena. In a similar way, accounts of subjective experience are also limited (Kahneman, 2010). The interest of scientific data, clinical studies, and statistical research (quantitative findings), along with narrative accounts of the client's experience (qualitative reports) should not prevent humans from seeing that there is more to truth than the behavior that can be measured empirically or recounted in narrative (Bruner, 1986, 1990, 1991; Geertz, 1973; Hauerwas, 1981a, 1981b; MacIntyre, 1984, 1990, 1999). What must be recovered is the realization that the person as rational can move beyond the measurement and classification of observable phenomena to a deeper level of knowing reality, which grasps its fundamental structures (Vatican II, 1965b, §15). In this regard, there are depths of interpersonal, moral, and spiritual character that can be apprehended and understood. We experience a foretaste of deeper meaning and fuller truth (especially ultimate truth), freedom (particularly a freedom for excellence), and flourishing (even eternal beatitude), as we long for more than what our limited experience has given us. Truth, freedom, and flourishing motivate us in this world. Ultimate truth, freedom, and flourishing both motivate us in this world and direct us toward the next.

Types of Belief

As mentioned earlier in this chapter, belief is one type of knowledge. It should be distinguished from others, such as sensory-perceptual cognition, and theoretical and practical knowledge. In addition to such types of firm assent, belief should also be differentiated from doubt (i.e., lacking a cognitive inclination to affirm either one judgment or another that contradicts it), suspicion (inclining to affirm one option but with only slight motivation), and opinion (inclining to affirm an option yet while still fearing that it may be wrong) (Aquinas 1273/1981, II-II, 2.1; see also, Aristotle, ca. 350 BC/1941c; Augustine, 401/2007; Popper, 1975; Zagzebski, 1996, 2009). In the case of belief, there is a need to attend not only to the object of knowledge, but also to the methods of approaching the particular objects of belief and to the authority of the witnesses to belief. This section will offer an understanding of belief that is larger than the contemporary analytical philosophical notion of belief, which is defined in this school as the attitude that one holds when considering something to be true (Schwitzgebel, 2015). Furthermore, although there are different meanings and nuances given to the term "belief," we will propose one that may clarify an important aspect of this type of multifaceted human cognition.

What Type of Belief Is Found in Cognitive Psychotherapy?

To prepare for a discussion of philosophical and theological insights on belief, we will first distinguish among cognitive psychology's various notions of belief. For example, in cognitive therapy (CT), there are "core beliefs," or cognitive schemas, beneficial beliefs versus dysfunctional ones, and automatic thoughts, which emerge from such belief systems (Dobson, 2012, pp. 16–17, 56–57). Core beliefs concern convictions about the characteristics and potential of people and reality (Young, Klosko, & Weishaar, 2006). They underlie the way that we perceive reality, understand ourselves, and interpret other people. Such persons and events can be interpreted accurately or misinterpreted (Dobson, 2012, pp. 64–65). Cognitive therapy seeks to capitalize on beneficial core beliefs. It presupposes that we can modify core beliefs by

cognitive interventions. Such can be described as "cognitive restructuring" or "schema change" (Dobson, 2012, p. 57, pp. 83–92; see also Sperry & Sperry, 2012, pp. 71–72). During therapeutic treatment of a client, both cognitive therapy and Rational Emotive Behavioral Therapy (REBT) evaluate the influence of beliefs on a person's emotional experiences and behavior (for CT, see, for example, Young, Rygh, Weinberger, & Beck, 2007, pp. 259–260; for REBT, see Ellis & Ellis, 2011). Such core beliefs can give rise to psychopathologies, such as phobias (Beck, 1979, p. 168). A person may not always be aware of the influence such core beliefs have on his or her thought processes and behavior—the beliefs may be nonconscious in the sense described above (Jones & Butman, 2011, p. 217). Rational Emotive Behavioral Therapy distinguishes rational from irrational beliefs, the latter of which are considered dysfunctional, biased, and erroneous cognitions (see Ellis, 1980; Ellis, 2001, p. 81; Ellis & Ellis, 2011). Focused therapeutic interventions seek to alter distorted core beliefs that confirm social isolation, narcissism, pessimism, and distrust. Lastly, it should be noted that some researchers in cognitive psychotherapy employ the notion of "automatic belief systems" to describe what otherwise might be called instinct, intuitions, pre-discursive judgments, and cognitive dispositions (Martin & Santos, 2014).

What Is Belief?

There are two main types of belief that will be discussed here: everyday and religious beliefs. From a philosophical perspective, belief is complex action involving conscious and nonconscious dimensions of the person, as well as interpersonal relations. It is a type of knowledge, but more, as well. The different sorts of human belief employ diverse ways that we assent, choose, and judge concerning an object that is in some way unsure for us at present. We distinguish "belief" from scientific knowledge (even though some scientific knowledge is theoretical or hypothetical and as such can be considered a "scientific belief"), and we distinguish this philosophical notion of belief from that of the psychological "core beliefs" just mentioned.

There are two common elements that distinguish this understanding of philosophical belief. According to Pieper (1997), "To believe always means to believe someone and to believe something" (p. 29). We commonly experience within ourselves and within others the desire to speak truthfully about what we know. We readily believe in and trust personal testimonies. This capacity for belief underlies almost all social interaction. Belief requires conviction in someone's truthfulness and knowledge, which is needed to ascertain the truth at hand and to assent to it. In addition, when we believe someone and something, we engage our whole conscious being, expressing a claim on knowledge accepted by one's free will and even one's emotions. Such belief engages a forward-leaning love, a commitment that moves us through an empathetic connection to the other (Pieper, 1997, p. 35). Doubt, on the contrary, is a hesitation about the veracity or knowledge presented by the other, which calls into question normal human communication. According to Ratzinger (2004), belief and doubt are closely related in the person—the believer always carries a sliver of doubt, and those who do not believe also carry a sliver of doubt (pp. 46–47). Doubt should not be confused with healthy pondering of reality or contemplating truth. Furthermore false beliefs, that is, beliefs that are at odds with reality and with one's commitments, can be destructive of flourishing, for example, the false belief that lying will contribute more to flourishing than honesty.

What Is an Everyday Belief?

We can distinguish everyday beliefs from religious beliefs. An everyday belief is not empirically verifiable as is knowledge about the periodic table of elements, nor identifiable as formally valid as is a mathematical equation, such as $2 + 2 = 4$. An everyday belief, rather, involves affirming an assertion that we cannot validate without relying upon some authoritative witness (Ratzinger, 2006, pp. 79–82), as when someone states "dinner upset my stomach." The source of such belief is usually the credibility of the witness or the example of another person. For example, if I have confidence in John, I will believe it when he says "I am suffering" or "I am sorry." Such everyday beliefs can also emerge from one's ability to evaluate personal experience, as when one apprehends the intention of another person based on perceived signs and behaviors (for example, I might judge based on body language that someone is being dishonest and therefore not believe his claims of being injured by someone else). Everyday beliefs concern a whole range of knowledge and depend on the type of authority attributed to a particular witness, including one's own authority as an interpreter of personal experience. Developing in the virtues helps one to reflectively evaluate such beliefs. For example, prudence assists one to evaluate the best means one believes will lead to one's goals (CCC, 2000, §1806), while charity guides one to give favorable interpretations to the intentions of others (CCC, 2000, §2478).

What Is a Religious Belief?

Religious belief emerges in a manner that is like the development of everyday beliefs, but there are important differences. One such difference is that religious beliefs are not oriented toward mundane matters but rather address ultimate questions about reality and human purpose. In general, religious beliefs guide the attention of a person's mind toward the transcendent. In the theistic religions, this can involve entering into a relationship with God, who transcends human history.

Positive psychology (Peterson & Seligman, 2004) has recognized that religious beliefs and practices are rooted in human transcendence and that "they inform the kinds of attributions that people make, the meanings they construct, and the ways they conduct relationships" (p. 600). The overall beneficial influence of committed religious belief and practice has been well documented in recent decades (Koenig, King, & Carson, 2012; Ross & Wagner, 2012; VanderWeele, 2017a, 2017b).

Considered from a Christian perspective, furthermore, religious belief or faith is a gift of grace (a theological virtue) through which humans assent to God's existence and enter into a relationship with him (CCC, 2000, §1814; Francis, 2013; see "Faith" in Chapter 19, "Redeemed]"). Religious faith, informed by charity, leads one to ponder God with loving assent, trusting his authority (Augustine, 429/1992, 2.5; Pieper, 1997, p. 50). In particular, someone who seeks an understanding of the realities affirmed through religious belief continues to "think about while affirming" God's nature and existence and the truths revealed by God (Aquinas, 1273/1981, II-II, 2.1; CCC, 2000, §158). It is because someone willingly assents to the truthfulness of God's revelation that he believes in Jesus Christ as the Son of God and the head of the mystical body, the Church, or believes that the human person is created in the image of God. A person's assent by way of religious belief and experience is enabled directly through the infused grace of faith and supported by the gifts of the Holy Spirit who connects one to Christ (CCC, 2000, §152).

The content of faith is communicated indirectly through human witnesses (Rom 10:17). There are different types of witness: the Sacred Scriptures, the Apostolic tradition, the Magisterium of the Church, the lives of believers, and the words of friends. Even with the support of such witnesses, though, there is a distance that remains between the intellect's assent through belief and the intellect's direct knowledge of something. In this life, knowledge of God is indirect, proceeding by way of nature (Wis 13:5; Rom 1:20) and by way of graced assent to revelation (CCC, 2000, §153). We continue to ponder God, but we may have doubts about the degree to which we understand God, even though we have no doubt about God's existence or his love for us (Ratzinger, 2004).

The distance between the pondering of faith and our reception of the direct beatific vision of God creates a longing for a more complete understanding of the truth (Augustine, 401/2007). As Aquinas says, "The cognition of belief does not quiet the craving but rather kindles it" (1265/1975, 40.5; as cited in Pieper, 1997, p. 53). Different types of unrest of mind and heart can be found in the midst of theological faith, just as everyday belief can be affected by psychopathology and sin. Moreover, the disquiet and anxiety of psychopathology can be caused when a person doubts the goodness of other people.

According to John Paul II (2006), a type of doubt about the nature of God's gift is at the heart of original sin. Genesis (Chapter 3) recounts how Adam and Eve chose to disobey God, once they were led to suspect that God was holding something back from them. In the order of redemption, from a Christian perspective, true peace is found in God alone, even though doubts and disquiet may be present. The journey deeper into that peace can involve a constructive type of temporal unrest but not mistrust of God. This unrest can be used constructively when it provides a pathway to many types of growth and healing that are made possible through faith and openness to the movement of the Holy Spirit (see the section "What Are the Gifts of the Holy Spirit?" in Chapter 19,

"Redeemed"). The phenomena of spiritual suffering, including dark nights of the soul, such as those of St. John of the Cross (1579/2010) or St. Teresa of Calcutta (2007), show how a deeper connection with God can be forged even in uncertainty or in spiritual dryness and darkness.

Rational Control and the Loss of Control

There are numerous negative influences that deflect our thoughts and actions away from our intended goals. We experience only a limited range of free action and consistency in cognition, because of internal and external influences. For example, our emotions can influence our thoughts about other people. Gottman (1999) speaks about "negative sentiment override," which is when negative emotions, such as hatred or mistrust, serve to filter out the positive interaction in our interpersonal relationships. For instance, these emotions can cloud the communication between spouses or between parents and children. In this way, a person fails to see the positive dimensions of his wife's or her husband's words, deeds, or intentions. In severe cases, even memories can become distorted. There is also a "positive sentiment override" when positive emotions filter out the negative interpersonal interactions. Moreover, biological, psychological, or sociological disorders can lead to the loss or diminishing of a person's rational capacity to control his or her emotions, cognitions, or actions. This loss or reduction of control is also the result of what Christians recognize as the lingering effects of personal, social, and original sin.

What Are the Limits and Advantages of Self-Control?

In the fallen condition of humanity, the acquisition of the virtues that allow us to master our

actions using reason require the assistance of the other capacities as well. While practical wisdom is complete only with rational action, it needs also the support of virtues of the will and virtues of the emotional capacities. For example, the virtues of the emotions (such as temperance, or self-control) require not only time and effort to develop, but also the aid of reason as well as of the will, emotion, and the assistance of others. Although growth in virtue benefits from the help of God's grace (CCC, 2000, §1811), the development of self-control is usually accompanied by an ongoing interior struggle (Rom 7:15–25). Nonetheless, it is common experience that humans can develop the ability to exercise responsible thought and carry out free acts. Guided by right reason (but not without effort nor without the support of the will and emotion), human persons can directly and indirectly control their thoughts and actions. Biblical and classical sources (Rom 1–2; Aristotle, ca. 350 BC/1941c; Plato, ca. 360 BC/1961a) and recent studies (Bandura, 1997; Damasio, 2010; Kahneman, Slovic, & Tversky, 1982) concur that humans can regulate themselves in this way, although self-control can be incomplete and not meet one's own or others' expectations. Further, the ability to control oneself is not necessarily proportionate to measures of intelligence. For example, an empirical study on "self-discipline" in adolescents (Duckworth & Seligman, 2005) found that levels of self-control among eighth-grade students were a better predictor of grade performance than IQ. The study concluded that the children who did not exercise self-disciple achieved a more limited development of their intellectual potential.

What Are Direct Means of Rational Self-Control?

Humans have a large area of control, including both bodily locomotion and moral agency. For example, we can consistently and justly choose to return what is due to a neighbor, and we can choose to bill a client reasonably and honestly. We commonly seek to develop rational beliefs, skills, and virtues that dispose us to act freely to achieve our goals and flourishing. Even though the intellectual capacity is characteristic of the human species, its reasoned applications are personal. It is expressed in the various moral pathways possible for constructive efforts, problem solving, and solution building, as well as in cultural diversity or the individual disorders that accompany them. Nonetheless, there are times when we react more with automatic patterns that do not exhibit free rational choices, as when a couple continues in often-repeated harmful interactions with one another. An important moment for persons as rational occurs when,

for example, the couple obtains insight about negative patterns of interaction. This awareness or insight can lead to significant positive change, as evidenced in a number of psychotherapy models including Emotion-Focused Therapy, Cognitive-Behavioral Therapy, and Rational Emotive Behavioral Therapy, and mindfulness approaches (Chapter 16, "Volitional and Free").

What Are Indirect Means of Self-Control?

There are other aspects of self-control that human beings can influence only *indirectly* (Gondreau, 2013). We have only indirect rational control of emotions and sense perceptions, as well as the evaluations that arise from them and the imagination. For example, when confronted with an injustice, we can redirect our attention to another object to calm our emotions, or, instead, we can focus on the injustice to excite our anger and agency. Our passions, feelings, and moods are internal movements that interact with and influence multiple dimensions of our personhood, conscious reason being only one of them. For example, we can be pulled in different directions by external stimuli and by our biological states (see Chapter 14, "Emotional").

Rational Virtues and Vices

The natural inclinations to know and to love are the seedbed for not only the intellectual and moral virtues but also the related vices. Being underspecified in themselves, the natural inclinations must be cultivated through experience, study, and practice in order that the person might develop the beliefs and enduring strengths of mind and heart called intellectual and moral virtues (Aristotle, ca. 350 BC/1941b; DePaul & Zagzebski, 2003; Pakaluk, 2005). The

development of the virtues can be identified in what cognitive therapy calls healthy cognitive schemas, automatic thoughts, and adaptive behaviors, including self-care (Dobson, 2012, pp. 78–83; Beck, 1979, pp. 31–33; Beck, Rush, Shaw, & Emery, 1979, pp. 12–13; Young, Klosko, & Weishaar, 2006). Positive psychology calls such schemas and patterns of behavior "character strengths" and "virtues" (Peterson & Seligman, 2004). Because of the nature of intellectual and moral dispositions, we become what we think, will, and feel, for better and for worse. Becoming virtuous is a challenge for each person, both clinician and client. When approaches to psychotherapy and counseling emphasize a client's growth in character strengths or virtues, psychology can have a direct impact on the client (Harris, Thoresen, & Lopez, 2007).

There is a special challenge for mental health professionals, when they are exposed to personal psychological sufferings (e.g., depression, narcissism, and substance abuse). There is also a special challenge in responding to the client's moral and spiritual suffering, disorder, and weakness, found in related vices (e.g., hatred of self and others) (Langberg, 2006). Empathetically bonding with such clients can at times be both intellectually and emotionally fatiguing as well as morally and spiritually toxic. It is a challenging situation, where some therapists may identify with and adopt some of the negative attributes of their clients. Therapists should strive to resist the effect that these negative attributes can have on them and to develop virtues in their own lives to assist them in their professional clinical work (Meara, Schmidt, & Day, 1996).

How Do the Virtues and Vices of Practical Reasoning Develop?

As a result of using our intelligence to repeatedly pursue flourishing (or, the contrary, to repeatedly pursue patterns of thought and behavior that lead to languishing), we become disposed to act well (or to act in a disordered way). On the applied, or moral, side, right practical reason informs the process of intending good ends (both everyday and ultimate) and seeking fitting means to attain those goals (Aquinas, 1273/1981, II-II, 47.2). For example, a husband remains faithful to his wife by excluding acts that compromise his commitment but also by

performing positive acts that reaffirm his love. Such a right use of practical reason is developed by the cardinal moral virtue of practical wisdom or prudence, as well as by its associated virtues, which aid in being rightly disposed to discern and counsel, adjudicate, and perform moral action in accord with our ethical commitments and spiritual goals (Titus, 2013). For example, in the context of marriage, a man and woman together discern and choose, as a fitting goal, to value fidelity concretely by avoiding adulterous temptations and by rejecting and correcting immoral thoughts, thus remaining faithful to one another in thought, word, and deed. A spouse's intellectual and practical commitment to fidelity will become a disposition that nonetheless requires moral effort (and spiritual support and grace) if he or she is to be truly faithful for life. By the same token, the repetition of unfaithful thoughts, words, and deeds form the opposite habits, which facilitate the repetition of these actions and the creation of a vicious disposition.

What Skills and Strengths Does Practical Reasoning Require?

In order to reason well when faced with practical challenges in the midst of contingency, we need to persistently decipher information, plan for goals, solve problems, seek solutions, and find meaning. In this repeated process, we grow by learning from errors and by correcting misjudgments. We do so not as isolated individuals but with the support of others. Practical reasoning requires the use of capacities and skills. For instance, the members of a family will need to use memory (of promises to be faithful), intelligence (about good goals at which to aim), shrewdness (in facing challenges to family solidarity), reason (about good means to common goals), caution (about dangers that threaten bonding), and good counsel (of exemplars who are practically wise) (Aquinas, 1273/1981, II-II, 50). We also need practical skills and strengths to oppose vices (imprudence and negligence) and to avoid false appearances of practical reason (guile, deceitfulness, and fictional solicitude about the future). In psychological terms, rationalizations, denials, and defense mechanisms give a resemblance of truth, but only a resemblance. We learn to exercise our rational capacities virtuously in families and communities that lead us from being dependent to independent, while recognizing our continued interdependence (MacIntyre, 1999). This apprenticeship is mediated through the intelligible practices (for example, participating in communal worship) that constitute familial, social, cultural, and religious experience. There are specific cognitive dispositions and associated practices in these different areas of practical wisdom. What differentiates these various dispositions of practical wisdom is the end or goal to which each disposition is oriented (Aquinas, 1273/1981, II-II, 47.11). For example, the effective and good use of practical reasoning for the good of one's family requires a set of cognitive dispositions different from (although interrelated with) those dispositions needed to reason for the good of the state in politics or for the good of the client in psychotherapy. To the extent that practical goals can be judged to have different degrees of value and goodness, a person's cognitive dispositions that are oriented toward higher ends can be understood to take precedence above the other dispositions and to regulate them (Aquinas, 1273/1981, II-II, 47.11 ad 3). For example, the good of one's family may be judged to be greater than the good of one's business.

To learn practical reasoning requires cognitive-affective competence, social support, and moral norms, in contextualized practices. Excluding the presence of grave cognitive-affective defects and with an adequate quality of bonding with and education from parents, educators, and other exemplars in their community, children usually can develop toward the mature rationality and good judgment often found in adults (MacIntyre, 1999). Experience, practice, and discipline are needed though. The prevalence and complexity of reasoning and its relationship to willing and emotions puts it at the center of virtue theory, without making virtue rationalistic or easy. In virtue theory, the positive development of this rational potential also depends on the moral norms that guide our judgment and action toward true goods and away from what is evil. These norms are rooted in natural moral law and divine law.

How Is Christian Infused Practical Reasoning Different?

A person's conscience is the foundation of moral judgment. Conscience is a moral compass (Francis, 2013, §35). A person's conscience, however, must be formed and practiced. This formation occurs in part by growing in the virtue of practical wisdom or prudence, which is the immediate guide of conscience (*CCC*, 2000, §1806). Practical wisdom is, simply understood, "right reason" with respect to human acts to be performed (Aquinas, 1272/1999b, a. 1 ad 3 & a. 2). A person can begin to acquire practical wisdom through life experience (Aquinas, 1273/1981, II-II, 47.14 ad 3). The exercise of such acquired prudence involves civil law and also the natural moral law (Aquinas, 1273/1981, II-II, 48.1), the latter being written in the human heart (Rom 2:14; Vatican II, 1965b, §16).

At the same time, the human ability to grasp the natural moral law and also to acquire the virtue of practical wisdom has been adversely affected by human fallenness (Aquinas, 1273/1981, I-II, 85.3; *CCC*, 2000, §1811, §1960; John Paul II,

1993, §36; Chapter 18, "Fallen"). Christ's sancti-fying grace is needed to restore and justify fallen human nature, after which a person might again benefit more completely from having "right rea-son" (consider, for example, the effect theologi-cal charity has upon the rational discernment of social justice) (CCC, 2000, §1889). Christ's sanc-tifying grace also provides, to the person who responds to God's offer of redemption, a divine law of love, which orients human life toward supernatural beatitude in Christ (Mt 22:37–40; Aquinas, 1273/1981, I-II, 91.4 ad 1). In association with receipt of this divine law (which involves the grace of the Holy Spirit within the heart of the person—Jer 31:33; Rom 5:5; Heb 10:16; CCC, 2000, §1966), the person receives also the grace of a special kind of moral virtue (Aquinas, 1272/1999a, a. 10). Among these infused moral virtues is a unique Christian practical wisdom that helps a person to exercise his or her moral reasoning with reference to the divine law and the goal of beatitude (Aquinas, 1273/1981, I-II, 63.4; II-II, 47.14 ad 3). In this respect, Christian practical reasoning is unique in that it is enabled by God's grace, animated by theological charity, and is oriented to an ultimate spiritual end.

From this discussion, it is evident that good practical reasoning depends upon consideration of many different sources (for example, the nat-ural moral law, civil law, the divine law) as well as upon the development of virtuous charac-ter strengths, as is suggested in the writings of the positive psychology movement (Joseph & Linley, 2006; Peterson & Seligman, 2004). Good moral reasoning requires good character

as well as good interpersonal support; it is not an isolated intellectual act by which one could automatically come to correct conclusions. Further, good moral reasoning is not mechani-cal—as if produced on a calculator or using an algorithm—for it also draws upon interpersonal commitments and personal callings, as well as emotions and experience.

Anyone who has faced a conflict of interest or a difficult case can witness that such situa-tions require that we inform our consciences and draw upon the competency and wisdom of others, as well as on our own. While Christians always remain imperfect in many ways, they do seek to follow Christ, and they do avail them-selves of practices that are cultural, philosophi-cal, and religious in origin, in order to develop their moral and spiritual character. In the forma-tion of personal conscience, Catholic Christians will specifically call upon the resources of the living tradition. They also practice their faith through prayer, liturgy, sacraments, and acts of mercy and charity. In addition, they seek the counsel of others: wise friends, spiritual direc-tion, study of the lives of the saints, and above all the guidance of the Holy Spirit (Jn 14:26; CCC, 2000, §1811; Cessario, 1996, pp. 162–169; John of St. Thomas, 1644/2016; Pinckaers, 2005, pp. 385–395; see also Chapter 19, "Redeemed"). Jesus' Sermon on the Mount (Mt 5–6) and St. Paul's moral exhortations provide the principles that serve to form consciences, practical reflections, and moral acts, for example, in service to the poor and in defense of life (John Paul II, 1995, §93; Pinckaers, 2005, pp. 321–341).

Beauty

Being rational enables persons to experience beauty in a profound way. In fact, humans are made for beauty. The search for beauty arises

as a natural inclination (John Paul II, 1993, §51) and leads a person beyond himself into a rela-tionship with what is beautiful. This inclination means that persons are aesthetic by nature. This sense is developed through culture, which enables one to appreciate beauty and grow more attuned to it. Humans are attracted to beauty in its many forms, such as nature, culture, music, dance, and fine art (Scruton, 2011, 2012).

Persons contemplate beauty in its coming to be and in its passing away. This transitory nature of much beauty (for example, a sunrise or piece of music) also draws people to seek the beauty that is ever-present and eternal. In a similar way, scientists can find beauty in the natural order and the grandeur of the cosmos (Dubay, 1999). For example, a scientist might ponder the marvel of photosynthesis and the order inherent in the periodic table of elements.

Furthermore, inspired by the wonder of beauty, people seek to make beautiful things. They imitate what they observe and seek to replicate the beauty they have discovered and, thus, to contribute something of themselves in so doing. This nonreductionist notion of beauty enables us to seek its deeper levels, such as those that are encountered in each person, family, and culture, and in the environment. These basic affirmations about beauty lead us to ponder several questions: From where does the human thirst for beauty come? What is unique about the many aspects of human beauty? And how does beauty demand a response such as contemplation and praise of its origin?

What Is the Basis of the Human Thirst for Beauty?

Beauty, luminosity, harmony, and integrity are qualities of all that exists, even when these qualities are hidden from direct view. A person can thirst for beauty just as he thirsts for life itself. Beauty is found in the goodness of all that exists, in all that is true, in all that is good in interpersonal relationships. In general, those familiar with any particular art form tend to be in agreement about the best examples of that art form, although with innovations some time is needed for a consensus to develop. Beauty, as Pieper argues in *Leisure, the Basis of Culture* (1952/2009), is both received and created. Beauty is based in reality—real people, real relationships, real things. Our measure of beauty is found in the form or pattern that we not only see and remember, but imagine and conceptualize in new ways. Beauty and orderliness (as well as ugliness and deformity) relate to the form of the thing. Plato (ca. 360 BC/1961b, ca. 360 BC/1961c) speaks of a realm of the forms, including "Beauty." Each beautiful thing participates in ultimate beauty. Aristotle (ca. 350 BC/1941a, ca. 350 BC/1941d), on the contrary, talks of the beauty in the things themselves. There is no separate realm where the forms of things exist; rather, each thing communicates a form that is shared by other like-things. Aquinas's Christian notion of beauty attributes beauty to the exemplary cause of all beauty, who is God. His account can be understood to recognize beauty as a transcendental feature of being and of real things, inasmuch as people and things participate in a transcendental pattern of beauty (Maritain, 1930/2016; Schmitz, 2009; Scruton, 2011, 2012).

Beauty is a metaphysical reality of being. Through our imagination and ideas, we can appreciate the beauty that we encounter and that we imagine. Nature itself provides inspiration and measure for beauty. When we contemplate beautiful things, persons, and actions, the intelligibility of beauty is given to us, even when we must perform a duet or build a chair. Through our basic experience, we sense, imagine, and intuit beauty. We do not only receive the form of beauty from reality. We also actively create beauty in different human ways. We use our imagination and ideas to bring forth novelty in thought, word, and things, for example in the work of the writer, painter, poet, carpenter, cook, architect, and film-maker.

There are three qualities that classically have been seen to constitute beauty. First, the measure for beauty is disclosed in the person's or symphony's wholeness or integrity. We recognize the aesthetic value of a whole being, according to the nature and structure of the thing: a horse (not just its left ear), a child (and not just his bloody knee), even a married couple (not just a man and a woman). Second, beauty is found in a person's or a building's proportion or harmony. We are attracted by the shape and texture of the thing, action, or person. For example, the beauty of justice is found in the right proportion of what is due, based on commitments, human nature, and interpersonal relationships. Third, beauty is found in a person's or a sunset's radiance or luminosity. We even talk about a radiant smile that signifies a state of pleasure or joy, as in the faces of the bride and groom on their wedding day or of long-lost friends on a surprise meeting (Aquinas, 1273/1981, I, 5.4 ad 1; II-II, 145.2; Sevier, 2015, pp. 103–104).

What Is Unique About Human Beauty?

True human beauty is not primarily a matter of physical appearance, even though physical beauty is commonly perceived as one of the most familiar sources of attraction, and physical deformity is often simplistically identified as repulsive. Rather, the deepest qualities of beauty are found and produced in the virtues that make a person flourish, such as the self-giving love of a mother for her child, the fidelity of spouses throughout 40 years of marriage, or the patience and wisdom that reestablishes friendship after a dispute among neighbors (Maritain, 1953). According to the Catholic Christian tradi-

tion, the beauty that is deeper than appearances (Prov 31:30; 1 Pet 3:4) is found in the good wife (Eccl 26:16), in the wisdom symbolized by the old man's beard (Prov 20:29), and in moral and spiritual uprightness (Aquinas, 1273/1981, II-II, 145.2). These moral and spiritual qualities of beauty are found preeminently in the Son of God, who manifests "the beauty of the Lord" (Ps 27:4; Aquinas, 1273/1981, I, 39.8).

How Does Beauty Demand Contemplation?

Beauty demands admiration, which arises as a spontaneous reaction to that which is beautiful (Gilson, 1965/2000, p. 20). In a sense, admiration for the beautiful is a response to a kind of vocation (Scarry, 1999, p. 126n7). In other words, what is beautiful calls out to be recognized, appreciated, and loved by rational creatures. The experience of created beauty leads us to contemplate its very existence and its source, be it a person and his or her actions, or some other part of reality, or ultimately the supreme source of all that is beautiful. By its nature, beauty invites human beings to practice the task of being open and receptive to God through experience of created realities and to focus their attention on the depth and source of beauty (Wis 13:5; CCC, 2000, §32). In particular, it is the luminosity, harmony, and integrity that draw us toward transcendental beauty and its divine source. Beauty demands, more than simple admiration, a contribution and investment. It invites a creative and communal effort to realize beauty in new cultural forms, relationships, and personal life.

At contemplative and creative levels beauty can be therapeutic (Laracy, 2011). Its contemplation answers a deep call for communion with the source of true beauty. Creating beauty, moreover, in one's life and works responds to the

God-given vocations through which human persons actively participate in the gift that constitutes the flourishing of the whole person (body and soul) and of his or her relationships. According to Pieper (1952/2009), the experience of physical, moral, and spiritual beauty creates a thirst for the absolute source of beauty. Each disclosure of beauty in persons, relationships, and reality at large leads us to seek and hope to contemplate the ultimate source of all integrity, proportion, and radiance. Such contemplation facilitates flourishing of persons.

Conclusion

The Catholic Christian Meta-Model envisages each person as rational. Each person is an agent moved by rational inclinations, knowledge, belief, self-control, virtue, vocation, and beauty in ways that are truly human and uniquely personal. The approach of the Meta-Model involves neither a rationalism (in the tradition of Descartes) nor a pragmatic idealism (in the tradition of Kant). Rather, the Meta-Model seeks to understand persons as rational agents capable of experiencing and knowing reality and of participating in interpersonal relationships. Throughout this volume, and here also in the focus on being intellectual and rational, we are reminded of the wholeness and relationality of persons. The discussion above shows how reflecting on beauty gives rise to such a consideration of personal and interpersonal wholeness. The experience of beauty occurs in the context of the disclosure of reality and the disclosure of persons. Such disclosures clarify human knowledge about the cosmos as well as self-consciousness and self-understanding. In this approach, the human experience of reality is clarified by intelligible principles, and intelligible principles are clarified by experience. There is, furthermore, the clarification that comes when the psychological sciences enter the picture and when theological reflection offers support, as we have seen in this chapter and will continue to see throughout this volume. The three-way dialogue of philosophy, theology, and psychology in this chapter, while primarily involving a philosophical perspective, employs a receptive language that seeks to integrate insights from personal experience, religion, and the sciences. This conversation will continue in the next chapter, which focuses on the person as volitional, who is an agent of free will and change.

REFERENCES

Ainsworth, M. D. S., Blehar, M. C., Waters, E., & Wall, S. (1978). *Patterns of attachment: Assessed in the strange situation and at home.* Hillsdale, NJ: Erlbaum.

American Counseling Association. (2014). *ACA code of ethics.* Alexandria, VA: Author.

American Psychological Association. (2010). *Ethical principles of psychologists and code of conduct, including 2010 amendments.* Washington, DC: Author. (Original work published 2002)

Aquinas, T. (1968). *On the unity of the intellect against the Averroists* (B. Zedler, Trans.). Milwaukee,

WI: Marquette University Press. (Original work composed 1270)

Aquinas, T. (1975). *Summa contra gentiles, book three: Providence, part II* (V. J. Bourke, Trans.). Notre Dame, IN: University of Notre Dame Press. (Original work composed 1265)

Aquinas, T. (1981). *Summa theologiae* (English Dominican Province, Trans.). Westminster, MD: Christian Classics. (Original work composed 1265–1273)

Aquinas, T. (1994a). *Commentary on Aristotle's De Anima* (Rev. ed.) (K. Foster & S. Humphries, Trans.).

Notre Dame, IN: Dumb Ox Books. (Original work composed 1268)

Aquinas, T. (1994b). *Truth* (J. V. McGlynn, Trans.). Indianapolis, IN: Hackett. (Original work composed 1256–1259)

Aquinas, T. (1999a). Disputed question on the virtues in general. In R. McInerny (Trans.), *Disputed questions on virtue* (pp. 1–104). South Bend, IN: St. Augustine's Press. (Original work composed 1271–1272)

Aquinas, T. (1999b). Disputed question on the cardinal virtues. In R. McInerny (Trans.), *Disputed questions on virtue* (pp. 105–140). South Bend, IN: St. Augustine's Press. (Original work composed 1271–1272)

Aquinas, T. (2001). *Summa contra gentiles, book two: Creation* (J. F. Anderson, Trans.). Notre Dame, IN: University of Notre Dame Press. (Original work composed 1260–1265)

Aquinas, T. (2003). *On evil* (R. Regan, Trans.). New York, NY: Oxford University Press. (Original work composed 1270–1272)

Aquinas, T. (2010). *Commentary on the Gospel of John, chapters 1–5* (F. Larcher & J. A. Weisheipl, Trans.). Washington, DC: The Catholic University of America Press. (Original work composed ca. 1272)

Aristotle. (1941a). *Metaphysics.* In R. McKeon (Ed.), *The basic works of Aristotle* (pp. 689–926). New York, NY: Random House. (Original work composed ca. 350 BC)

Aristotle. (1941b). *Nicomachean ethics.* In R. McKeon (Ed.), *The basic works of Aristotle* (pp. 935–1112). New York, NY: Random House. (Original work composed ca. 350 BC)

Aristotle. (1941c). *On the soul.* In R. McKeon (Ed.), *The basic works of Aristotle* (pp. 535–603). New York, NY: Random House. (Original work composed ca. 350 BC)

Aristotle. (1941d). *Poetics.* In R. McKeon (Ed.), *The basic works of Aristotle* (pp. 1455–1487). New York, NY: Random House. (Original work composed ca. 350 BC)

Ashley, B. M. (2006). *The way toward wisdom: An interdisciplinary and intercultural introduction to metaphysics.* Notre Dame, IN: University of Notre Dame Press.

Ashley, B. M. (2013). *Healing for freedom: A Christian perspective on personhood and psychotherapy.*

Arlington, VA: Institute for the Psychological Sciences Press.

Augustine. (1992). On the predestination of saints (J. A. Mourant & W. J. Collinge, Trans.). In R. J. Deferrari (Ed.), *Fathers of the Church: Vol. 86. St. Augustine: Four anti-Pelagian writings* (pp. 218–270). Washington, DC: The Catholic University of America Press. (Original work composed 428–429)

Augustine. (2007). *Confessions* (2nd ed.) (M. P. Foley, Ed.; F. J. Sheed, Trans). New York, NY: Hackett. (Original work composed 397–401)

Austriaco, N. P. G. (2011). *Biomedicine and beatitude: An introduction to Catholic bioethics.* Washington, DC: The Catholic University of America Press

Bandura, A. (1997). *Self-efficacy: The exercise of control.* New York, NY: Freeman.

Bandura, A. (2006). Toward a psychology of human agency. *Perspectives on Psychological Science, 1,* 164–180.

Baumeister, R. F., & Tierney, J. (2011). *Willpower: Rediscovering the greatest human strength.* New York, NY: Penguin.

Beauregard, M. (2012). *Brain wars: The scientific battle over the existence of the mind and the proof that will change the way we live our lives.* New York, NY: HarperCollins.

Beauregard, M., & O'Leary, D. (2008). *The spiritual brain: A neuroscientist's case for the existence of the soul.* New York, NY: HarperCollins.

Beck, A. T. (1979). *Cognitive therapy and the emotional disorders.* New York, NY: Plume.

Beck, A. T., Rush, A. J., Shaw, B. F., & Emery, G. (1979). *Cognitive therapy of depression.* New York, NY: Guilford.

Bellah, R. N. (2011). *Religion in human evolution: From the Paleolithic to the Axial Age.* Cambridge, MA: Harvard University Press.

Benedict XVI. (2006, September 12). *Faith, reason and the university: Memories and reflections* [The Regensburg address]. Retrieved from http://w2.vatican.va/content/benedict-xvi/en/speeches/2006/september/documents/hf_ben-xvi_spe_20060912_university-regensburg.html

Benedict XVI. (2007). *Spe salvi* [Encyclical, on Christian hope]. Vatican City, Vatican: Libreria Editrice Vaticana.

Bennett, M. R., & Hacker, P. M. S. (2003). *Philosophical foundations of neuroscience*. Oxford, United Kingdom: Blackwell.

Berwick, R. C., & Chomsky, N. (2016). *Why only us: Language and evolution*. Cambridge, MA: MIT Press.

Bikerton, D. (2014). *More than nature needs: Language, mind, and evolution*. Cambridge, MA: Harvard University Press.

Bowlby, J. (1982). *Attachment and loss: Vol. 1. Attachment* (2nd ed.). New York, NY: Basic Books. (Original work published 1969)

Bowlby, J. (1988). *A secure base: Clinical applications of attachment theory*. London, United Kingdom: Routledge.

Bruner, J. S. (1986). *Actual minds, possible worlds*. Cambridge, MA: Harvard University Press.

Bruner, J. S. (1990). *Acts of meaning*. Cambridge, MA: Harvard University Press.

Bruner, J. S. (1991). The narrative construction of reality. *Critical Inquiry, 18*, 1–21.

Catechism of the Catholic Church (CCC) (2nd ed.). (2000). Vatican City, Vatican: Libreria Editrice Vaticana.

Cessario, R. (1996). *Christian faith and the theological life*. Washington, DC: The Catholic University of America Press.

Churchland, P. M. (2001). Toward a cognitive neurobiology of the moral virtues. In J. Branquinho (Ed.), *The foundations of cognitive science* (pp. 77–98). New York, NY: Oxford University Press.

Clayton, P., & Davies, P. (2006). *The re-emergence of emergence: The emergentist hypothesis from science to religion*. Oxford, United Kingdom: Oxford University Press.

Copi, I. M., & Cohen, C. (2005). *Introduction to logic* (12th ed.). Upper Saddle River, NJ: Prentice Hall.

Damasio, A. (2010). *Self comes to mind: Constructing the conscious brain*. New York, NY: Vintage.

Davies, P. C. W. (2006). Preface. In P. Clayton & P. Davies (Eds.), *The re-emergence of emergence: The emergentist hypothesis from science to religion* (pp. ix–xiv). Oxford, United Kingdom: Oxford University Press.

Dawkins, R. (2016). *The selfish gene* (4th ed.). New York, NY: Oxford University Press. (Original work published 1976)

Dawkins, R. (2008). *The God delusion*. New York, NY: Mariner Books.

Deacon, T. W. (1997). *The symbolic species: The co-evolution of language and the brain*. New York, NY: Norton.

Deary, I. J. (2001). *Intelligence: A very short introduction*. Oxford, United Kingdom: Oxford University Press.

Decety, J., & Howard, L. H. (2013). The role of affect in the neurodevelopment of morality. *Child Development Perspective, 7*, 49–54. doi:10.1111/cdep.12020

DePaul, M., & Zagzebski, L. (Eds.). (2003). *Intellectual virtue: Perspectives from ethics and epistemology*. Oxford, United Kingdom: Oxford University Press.

Dewan, L. (1995). St. Thomas and pre-conceptual intellection. *Etudes maritainiennes/Maritain Studies, 11*, 220–233.

Dobson, K. S. (2012). *Cognitive therapy*. Washington, DC: American Psychological Association.

Dubay, T. (1999). *The evidential power of beauty: Science and theology meet*. San Francisco, CA: Ignatius Press.

Duckworth, A. L., & Seligman, M. E. P. (2005). Self-discipline outdoes IQ in predicting academic performance of adolescents. *Psychological Science, 16*, 939–944. doi:10.1111/j.1467-9280.2005.01641.x

Egnor, M. (2017, June 29). A map of the soul. *First Things*. Retrieved from https://www.firstthings.com/web-exclusives/2017/06/a-map-of-the-soul

Ellis, A. (1980). Psychotherapy and atheistic values: A response to A. E. Bergin's "psychotherapy and religious values." *Journal of Consulting and Clinical Psychology, 48*(5), 635–639.

Ellis, A. (2001). *Overcoming destructive beliefs, feelings, and behaviors*. Amherst, NY: Prometheus Books.

Ellis, A., & Ellis, D. J. (2011). *Rational emotive behavior therapy*. Washington, DC: American Psychological Association.

Erikson, E. H. (1994). *Identity: Youth and crisis*. New York, NY: Norton. (Original work published 1968)

Erikson, E. H. (1979). *Identity and the life cycle*. New York, NY: Norton. (Original work published 1959)

Feser, E. (2008). *The last superstition: A refutation of the New Atheism*. South Bend, IN: St. Augustine's Press.

Fowers, B. J. (2005). *Virtue and psychology: Pursuing excellence in ordinary practices*. Washington, DC: American Psychological Association.

Francis. (2013). *Lumen fidei* [Encyclical, on faith]. Vatican City, Vatican: Libreria Editrice Vaticana.

Frankl, V. E. (2000). *Man's search for ultimate meaning.* Cambridge, MA: Perseus Publishing. (Original work published 1959)

Gardner, H. (2006). *Multiple intelligences: New horizons.* New York, NY: Basic Books. (Original work published 1993)

Gazzaniga, M. S. (2006). *The ethical brain: The science of our moral dilemmas.* New York, NY: Harper Perennial

Geertz, C. (1973). *The interpretation of cultures: Selected essays.* New York, NY: Basic Books.

Gilligan, C. (1982). *In a different voice: Psychological theory and women's development.* Cambridge, MA: Harvard University Press.

Gilson, E. (2000). *Arts of the beautiful.* Champaign, IL: Dalkey Archive Press. (Original work published 1965)

Giorgi, A. (1970). *Psychology as a human science: A phenomenologically based approach.* New York, NY: Harper & Row.

Goleman, D. (1995). *Emotional intelligence: Why it can matter more than IQ.* New York, NY: Bantam Books.

Goleman, D. (2006). *Social intelligence: The new science of human relationships.* New York, NY: Bantam Books.

Gondreau, P. (2013). Balanced emotions. In R. Cessario, C. S. Titus, & P. C. Vitz (Eds.), *Philosophical virtues and psychological strengths: Building the bridge* (pp. 81–114). Manchester, NH: Sophia Institute Press.

Gottman, J. M. (1999). *The marriage clinic: A scientifically based marital therapy.* New York, NY: Norton.

Hamlin, J. K. (2013). Moral judgment and action in preverbal infants and toddlers: Evidence for an innate moral core. *Current Directions in Psychological Science, 23*(3), 186–193.

Harris, A. H., Thoresen, C. E., & Lopez, S. J. (2007). Integrating positive psychology into counseling: Why and (when appropriate) how. *Journal of Counseling & Development, 85,* 3–13.

Hauerwas, S. (1981a). *A community of character: Toward a constructive Christian social ethics.* Notre Dame, IN: University of Notre Dame Press.

Hauerwas, S. (1981b). *Vision and virtue.* Notre Dame, IN: University of Notre Dame Press.

Hazan, C., & Shaver, P. (1987). Romantic love conceptualized as an attachment process. *Journal of Personality and Social Psychology, 25,* 511–524.

Hoffman, M. L. (2001). *Empathy and moral development: Implications for caring and justice.* Cambridge, United Kingdom: Cambridge University Press.

John of St. Thomas. (2016). *The gifts of the Holy Spirit.* Middletown, DE: Cluny Media. (Original work composed 1644)

John of the Cross. (2010). *The collected works of St. John of the Cross* (K. Kavanaugh, Trans.). Washington, DC: ICS Publications. (Original work published 1579)

John Paul II. (1993). *Veritatis splendor* [Encyclical, on certain fundamental questions of the Church's moral teaching]. Vatican City, Vatican: Libreria Editrice Vaticana.

John Paul II. (1995). *Evangelium vitae* [Encyclical, on the value and inviolability of human life]. Vatican City, Vatican: Libreria Editrice Vaticana.

John Paul II. (1998). *Fides et ratio* [Encyclical, on the relationship between faith and reason]. Vatican City, Vatican: Libreria Editrice Vaticana.

John Paul II. (2006). *Man and woman he created them: A theology of the body* (M. Waldstein, Trans.). Boston, MA: Pauline Books and Media.

Jones, S. L., & Butman, R. E. (2011). *Modern psychotherapies: A comprehensive Christian appraisal* (2nd ed.). Downers Grove, IL: IVP Academic.

Joseph, S., & Linley, P. A. (2006). *Positive therapy: A meta-theory for positive psychological practice.* London, United Kingdom: Routledge.

Kahneman, D. (2010). The riddle of experience vs. memory [Video file]. Retrieved from: https://www.ted.com/talks/daniel_kahneman_the_riddle_of_experience_vs_memory?language=en

Kahneman, D. (2011). *Thinking, fast and slow.* New York, NY: Farrar, Straus & Giroux.

Kahneman, D., Slovic, P., & Tversky, A. (Eds.). (1982). *Judgment under uncertainty: Heuristics and biases.* Cambridge, United Kingdom: Cambridge University Press.

Klein, R. (1999). *The human career.* Chicago, IL: University of Chicago Press.

Koenig, H. G., King, D., & Carson, V. B. (Eds.). (2012). *Handbook of religion and health* (2nd ed.). New York, NY: Oxford University Press.

Kohlberg, L. (1981). *The philosophy of moral development: *Moral stages and the idea of justice*. New York, NY: Harper & Row.

Kohlberg, L. (1984). *The psychology of moral development: The nature and validity of moral stages*. New York, NY: Harper & Row.

Kohlberg, L., Boyd, D., & Levine, C. (1990). The return of stage 6: Its principle and moral point of view. In T. Wren (Ed.), *The moral domain: Essays in the ongoing discussion between philosophy and the social sciences*. Cambridge, MA: MIT Press.

Langberg, D. (2006). Spiritual life of the therapist: We become what we habitually reflect. *Journal of Psychology and Christianity, 25*(3), 258–266.

Laracy, M. R. (2011). *The role of the experience of beauty in psychotherapy* (Doctoral dissertation). Retrieved from ProQuest Dissertations & Theses Global. (Order No. 3453653).

Levering, M. (2008). *Biblical natural law: A theocentric and teleological approach*. Oxford, United Kingdom: Oxford University Press.

Lonergan, B. (1992). *Insight: A study of human understanding*. Vol. 3 of F. E. Crowe & R. M. Doran (Eds.), *Collected works of Bernard Lonergan*. Toronto, Canada: University of Toronto Press.

Lopez, S. J., & Snyder, C. R. (Eds.). (2009). *The Oxford handbook of positive psychology*. Oxford, United Kingdom: Oxford University Press.

MacIntyre, A. (1984). *After virtue: A study in moral theory* (2nd ed.). Notre Dame, IN: University of Notre Dame Press. (Original work published 1981)

MacIntyre, A. (1990). *Three rival versions of moral enquiry: Encyclopaedia, genealogy, and tradition*. Notre Dame, IN: University of Notre Dame Press.

MacIntyre, A. (1999). *Dependent rational animals: Why human beings need the virtues*. Chicago, IL: Open Court.

Maritain, J. (1953). *Creative intuition in art and poetry*. New York, NY: Pantheon Books.

Maritain, J. (1959). *Distinguish to unite, or the degrees of knowledge* (G. B. Phelan, Trans.). London, United Kingdom: Geoffrey Bles. (Original work published 1932)

Maritain, J. (2016). *Art & scholasticism*. Tacoma, WA: Cluny Media. (Original work published 1930)

Martin, A., & Santos, L. R. (2014). The origins of belief representation: Monkeys fail to automatically represent others' beliefs. *Cognition, 130*(3), 300–308.

McGrath, A. (2004). *The twilight of atheism: The rise and fall of disbelief in the modern world*. New York, NY: Doubleday.

McInerny, R., & O'Callahan, J. (2014). Saint Thomas Aquinas. In E. N. Zalta (Ed.), *The Stanford Encyclopedia of Philosophy* (Summer 2018 Edition). Retrieved from https://plato.stanford.edu/entries/aquinas/

Meara, N. M., Schmidt, L. D., & Day, J. D. (1996). Principles and virtues: A foundation for ethical decisions, policies, and character. *The Counseling Psychologist, 24*(1), 4–77.

Mikulincer, M., & Shaver, P. R. (2007). *Attachment in adulthood: Structure, dynamics, and change*. New York, NY: Guilford Press.

Murphy, N. (1998). Supervenience and the nonreducibility of ethics to biology. In R. J. Russell, W. R. Stoeger, and F. J. Ayala (Eds.), *Evolutionary and molecular biology: Scientific perspectives on divine action* (pp. 463–489). Berkeley, CA: Center for Theology and the Natural Sciences.

Murphy, N. (2006). Emergence and mental causation. In P. Clayton & P. Davies (Eds.), *The re-emergence of emergence: The emergentist hypothesis from science to religion* (pp. 227–243). Oxford, United Kingdom: Oxford University Press.

Nagel, T. (2012). *Mind and cosmos: Why the materialist Neo-Darwinian conception of nature is almost certainly false*. New York, NY: Oxford University Press.

Neisser, U. (2014). *Cognitive psychology: Classic edition*. New York, NY: Psychology Press.

O'Donohue, W. (2013). *Clinical psychology and the philosophy of science*. Cham, Switzerland: Springer International Publishing.

Osborne, T. (2012). Practical reasoning. In B. Davies & E. Stump (Eds.), *The Oxford handbook of Aquinas* (pp. 276–286). New York, NY: Oxford University Press.

Oskawa, S. (2002). *Philosophy of science: A very short introduction*. Oxford, United Kingdom: Oxford University Press.

Pakaluk, M. (2005). *Aristotle's* Nicomachean Ethics: *An introduction*. New York, NY: Cambridge University Press.

Peterson, C., & Seligman, M. E. P. (Eds.). (2004). *Character strengths and virtues: A handbook and classification*. New York, NY: Oxford University Press.

Piaget, J. (1929). *The child's conception of the world*.

London, United Kingdom: Routledge & Kegan Paul.

Pieper, J. (1997). On faith: A philosophical treatise. In *Faith, hope, love* (R. Winston & C. Winston, Trans.) (pp. 13–86). San Francisco, CA: Ignatius Press. (Original work published 1962)

Pieper, J. (2009). *Leisure, the basis of culture* (A. Dru, Trans.). San Francisco, CA: Ignatius Press. (Original work published 1952)

Pinckaers, S. (1995). *The sources of Christian ethics.* (M. T. Noble, Trans.). Washington, DC: The Catholic University of America Press. (Original work published 1985)

Pinckaers, S. (2005). *The Pinckaers reader: Renewing Thomistic moral theology* (J. Berkman & C. S. Titus, Eds.) Washington, DC: The Catholic University of America Press.

Pinker, S. (2009). *How the mind works.* New York, NY: Norton. (Original work published 1997)

Plato. (1961a). *Republic.* In E. Hamilton & H. Cairns (Eds.), *The collected dialogues of Plato: Including the letters* (pp. 575–844). Princeton, NJ: Princeton University Press. (Original work composed ca. 360 BC)

Plato. (1961b). *Greater Hippias.* In E. Hamilton & H. Cairns (Eds.), *The collected dialogues of Plato: Including the letters* (pp. 1534–1559). Princeton, NJ: Princeton University Press. (Original work composed ca. 360 BC)

Plato. (1961c). *Symposium.* In E. Hamilton & H. Cairns (Eds.), *The collected dialogues of Plato: Including the letters* (pp. 526–574). Princeton, NJ: Princeton University Press. (Original work composed ca. 360 BC)

Plato. (2001). *Phaedrus.* In H. N. Fowler (Trans.), *Euthyphro, Apology, Crito, Phaedo, Phaedrus* (pp. 405–579). Cambridge, MA: Harvard University Press. (Original work composed ca. 370 BC)

Popper, K. R. (1975). *Objective knowledge: An evolutionary approach.* London, United Kingdom: Oxford University Press.

Rand, K. L., & Cheavens, J. S. (2009). Hope theory. In S. J. Lopez & C. R. Snyder (Eds.), *The Oxford handbook of positive psychology* (pp. 323–343). Oxford, United Kingdom: Oxford University Press.

Ratzinger, J. (2004). *Introduction to Christianity* (J. R. Foster, Trans.). San Francisco, CA: Ignatius Press.

Ratzinger, J. (2006). *Christianity and the crisis of cultures.* San Francisco, CA: Ignatius Press.

Ratzinger, J. (2007). Relativism: The central problem for faith today. In J. F. Thornton & S. B. Varenne (Eds.), *The essential Pope Benedict XVI: His central writings and speeches* (pp. 227–240). New York, NY: Harper One. (Original work published 1996)

Robinson, D. N. (2007). *Consciousness and mental life.* New York, NY: Columbia University Press.

Romanyshyn, R. D. (1982). *Psychological life: From science to metaphor.* Austin, TX: University of Texas Press.

Ross, G. A., & Wagner, M. (2012). A cohort analysis of happiness among young adults. In S. R. Sharkey (Ed.), *Sociology and Catholic social teaching: Contemporary theory and research* (pp. 129–144). Lanham, MD: Scarecrow Press.

Salovey, P., & Mayer, J. D. (1989). Emotional intelligence. *Imagination, Cognition, and Personality 9*(3), 185–211. doi:10.2190/dugg-p24e-52wk-6cdg

Scarry, E. (1999). *On beauty and being just.* Princeton, NJ: Princeton University Press.

Schore, A. N. (2002). Dysregulation of the right brain: A fundamental mechanism of traumatic attachment and the psychopathogenesis of posttraumatic stress disorder. *Australian and New Zealand Journal of Psychiatry, 36*(1), 9–30.

Schmitz, K. (2009). *Person and psyche.* Arlington, VA: The Institute for the Psychological Sciences Press.

Schwitzgebel, E. (2015). Belief. In E. N. Zalta (Ed.), *The Stanford Encyclopedia of Philosophy* (Summer 2015 edition). Retrieved from https://plato.stanford.edu/archives/sum2015/entries/belief/

Scruton, R. (2011). *Beauty: A very short introduction.* Oxford, United Kingdom: Oxford University Press.

Scruton, R. (2012). *The face of God: The Gifford lectures.* London, United Kingdom: Continuum.

Sherwin, M. S. (2005). *By knowledge and by love: Charity and knowledge in the moral theology of St. Thomas Aquinas.* Washington, DC: The Catholic University of America Press.

Seligman, M. E. P. (2004). *Authentic happiness.* New York, NY: The Free Press.

Seligman, M. E. P. (2012). *Flourish: A visionary new understanding of happiness and well-being.* New York, NY: Atria Books.

Sevier, C. S. (2015). *Aquinas on beauty.* Lanham, MD: Lexington Books.

Siegel, D. J. (2012). *Pocket guide to interpersonal neurobiology: An integrative handbook of the mind* (1st ed.). New York, NY: Norton.

Snyder, C. R. (1994). *The psychology of hope: You can get there from here.* New York, NY: Free Press.

Sokolowski, R. (2000). *Introduction to phenomenology.* New York, NY: Cambridge University Press.

Sperry, L., & Sperry, J. (2012). *Case conceptualization: Mastering this competency with ease and confidence.* New York, NY: Routledge.

Spitzer, R. J. (2010). *New proofs for the existence of God: Contributions of contemporary physics and philosophy.* Grand Rapids, MI: Eerdmans.

Spitzer, R. J. (2015). *Evidence for God from contemporary physics: Extending the legacy of Monsignor Georges Lemaître.* South Bend, IN: St. Augustine's Press.

Suddendorf, T. (2013). *The gap: The science of what separates us from other animals.* New York, NY: Basic Books.

Tellkamp, J. A. (2012). Vis aestimativa and vis cogitativa in Thomas Aquinas's *Commentary on the Sentences. The Thomist, 76,* 611–640.

Teresa of Calcutta. (2007). *Mother Teresa: Come be my light: The private writings of the saint of Calcutta.* New York, NY: Doubleday.

Titus, C. S. (2013). Reasonable acts. In R. Cessario, C. S. Titus, & P. C. Vitz (Eds.), *Philosophical virtues and psychological strengths: Building the bridge* (pp. 81–114). Manchester, NH: Sophia Institute Press.

VanderWeele, T. J. (2017a). Religious communities and human flourishing. *Current Directions in Psychological Science. 26*(5), 476–481.

VanderWeele, T. J. (2017b). On the promotion of human flourishing. *PNAS, 114*(31), 8148–8156.

Vatican II, Council. (1965a). *Dei verbum* [Dogmatic constitution on Divine Revelation]. Vatican City, Vatican: Libreria Editrice Vaticana.

Vatican II, Council. (1965b). *Gaudium et spes* [Pastoral constitution on the Church in the modern world]. Vatican City, Vatican: Libreria Editrice Vaticana.

Vitz, P. C. (2017). The origin of consciousness in the integration of analog (right hemisphere) & digital (left hemisphere) codes. *Journal of Consciousness Exploration & Research, 8*(11), 881–906.

Vygotsky, L. S. (1962). *Thought and language.* Cambridge, MA: MIT Press.

Vygotsky, L. S. (1978). *Mind in society.* Cambridge, MA: Harvard University Press.

White, T. J. (2009). *Wisdom in the face of modernity: A study in Thomistic natural theology.* Naples, FL: Sapientia Press.

Wojtyła, K. (1979). *The acting person: A contribution to phenomenological anthropology* (A.-T. Tymieniecka, Ed.; A. Potocki, Trans.). Boston, MA: D. Reidel. (Original work published 1969)

Wojtyła, K. (1993). Thomistic personalism (T. Sandok, Trans.). In A. N. Woznicki (Ed.), *Catholic thought from Lublin: Vol. 4. Person and community: Selected essays* (pp. 165–75). New York, NY: Peter Lang. (Original paper presented in Polish, 1961)

Wojtyła, K. (2011). *Man in the field of responsibility* (K. W. Kemp & Z. M. Kieroń, Trans.). South Bend, IN: St. Augustine's Press. (Original work published 1991)

Young, J. E., Klosko, J. S., & Weishaar, M. E. (2006). *Schema therapy: A practitioner's guide.* New York, NY: Guilford.

Young, J. E., Rygh, J. L., Weinberger, A. D., & Beck, A. T. (2007). Cognitive therapy for depression. In D. H. Barlow (Ed.), *Clinical handbook of psychological disorders: A step-by-step treatment manual* (pp. 250–305). New York, NY: Guilford.

Zagzebski, L. (1996). *Virtues of the mind.* Cambridge, United Kingdom: Cambridge University Press.

Zagzebski, L. (2009). *On epistemology.* Belmont, CA: Wadsworth.

Życiński, J. (2006). *God and evolution: Fundamental questions of Christian evolutionism* (K. W. Kemp & Z. Maślanka, Trans.). Washington, DC: The Catholic University of America Press.

Chapter 16

Volitional and Free

CRAIG STEVEN TITUS, WILLIAM J. NORDLING,
AND PAUL C. VITZ

ABSTRACT: This chapter philosophically addresses from the viewpoint of the Catholic Christian Meta-Model of the Person (CCMMP) how persons are subjects of committed love, free will, and moral action. It describes the importance of not only seeking "freedom from" negative influences and disorders, but also cultivating a "freedom for" excellence and a life of spiritual and moral virtue in accord with one's vocational state. It argues that humans, even when negatively influenced by other people, trauma, and the effects of sin, remain largely responsible for their acts and moral character. The volitional and free dimension of moral action can be more fully analyzed as (1) wishing for some good, (2) intending a particular goal, (3) assenting to the most viable option, (4) choosing the best means to obtain the goal, (5) making ready to apply the means, and then (6) completing the action. Performing good free actions requires interpersonal support, which enables people to positively and morally order their cognitions, affections, friendships, and spousal commitments through the practice of virtues such as justice and charity love. Furthermore, persons are capable of creativity and self-control within the limits of their volitional or executive capacities and interpersonal resources. In addition to exploring the philosophical underpinnings of moral responsibility, this chapter also draws upon psychological theory concerning the nature of the will and freedom. Furthermore, it addresses related theological presuppositions, such as the universal calling of all people to love God, neighbor, and self and to cooperate freely with God's will and grace in order to develop a disposition toward true freedom and charity love.

We live, and make great sacrifices, for love and freedom, but not just any type of affection or any idea of liberty. We are capable of consciously wanting and even offering our lives for specific values and beliefs as well as for the love of particular people. At one level, we readily affirm that, through the exercise of our affections, volition, and choices, we have some measure of freedom as well as a capacity for love, justice, and responsibility. We even extend great efforts to defend political liberty—for example, the civil freedom of religious practice or the freedom of personal expression. Beyond these civil freedoms and associated civil rights, there is a more foundational moral freedom, which is based upon human nature itself and to which there is a human right regardless of culture and civil law. Nonetheless, criticism of the belief in the existence of true human freedom, the right to freedom, and the meaningfulness of human choice and love has been expressed in association with the deterministic views found in many disciplines, including evolutionary biology (Dawkins, 2008; Wilson, 1975, 1998), psychology (Freud, 1930/2010; Skinner, 1971, 1976; Watson, 1913), philosophy (Churchland, 1995; Democritus ca. 370 BC/2010; Dennett, 1991, 2006; Hobbes, 1651/2008; La Mettrie, 1747/1994), the neurosciences (Libet, 1985, 2004), and, in some cases, also theology (Calvin, 1543/2002, 1536/2008). These current and ancient trends presuppose a deterministic view of the human will or at least maintain serious doubts about human freedom and meaning, purpose, and finality. Other modern thinkers, like David Hume (1740/2000), subscribe to another position called compatibilism, which argues that causal determinism and human free will are not mutually exclusive (Pinker, 2009).

This chapter will explore the Catholic Christian Meta-Model's philosophical approach to integration, focusing on the person as volitional and free (see Table 16.1, upper right hand quadrant). It will identify the Meta-Model's presuppositions about the will (that is, volition) and explore the person's volitional potential in terms of inclinations and instincts, responsibility and self-determination, as well as types of love and creativity. This chapter will also explore the human capacity for a positive freedom for excel-

lence, which is ordered to the development of moral character and spiritual maturity.

For a graphic contextualization of this chapter in the Meta-Model's reason- and will-based premises, see Figure 16.1. In the previous chapter, we explored rational intelligence, which is another significant facet of the Meta-Model's multidimensional vision of the person, and which is a prerequisite of love. Furthermore, our reflection on volition and will needs to keep in mind the unity of the person and interpersonal relationality, as also represented in Figure 16.1.

We should also mention that the epitome of human volition and freedom for excellence is charity love. The term "love" has many meanings. It involves the different types of affect, ranging from emotional affect to intellectual affect: it can refer to the basic affection that many have for animals and food, or it can refer to the quality of the will found in committed friendship love, spousal love, and charity love. Of course, love and knowledge accompany one another: We cannot love what we do not know. And authentic love is basically willing the good of the other, according to the nature of the person. The good will of love is differentiated because of the nature of the interpersonal relationship, which makes certain social acts and commitments fitting and others not. Since friendship, spousal, and charity loves are basically interpersonal, we have treated them more extensively in Chapter 12, "Interpersonally Relational."

What Is the Will?

The will has been called—by different disciplines—volition, free will, willpower, self-control, internal locus of control, self-regulation, motivation, and executive function. It has also been understood in diverse ways. In psychology, the will is referred to as self-regulation or

willpower, which is seen as an internal force or energy that a person exerts in moving him- or herself to action (Baumeister & Tierney, 2011). Recent studies suggest that willpower may be limited by a person's lack of resources pertaining to incentives or motivation, acquired

Table 16.1. Structure of Human Capacities as Found in the Philosophical Premises of the CCMMP

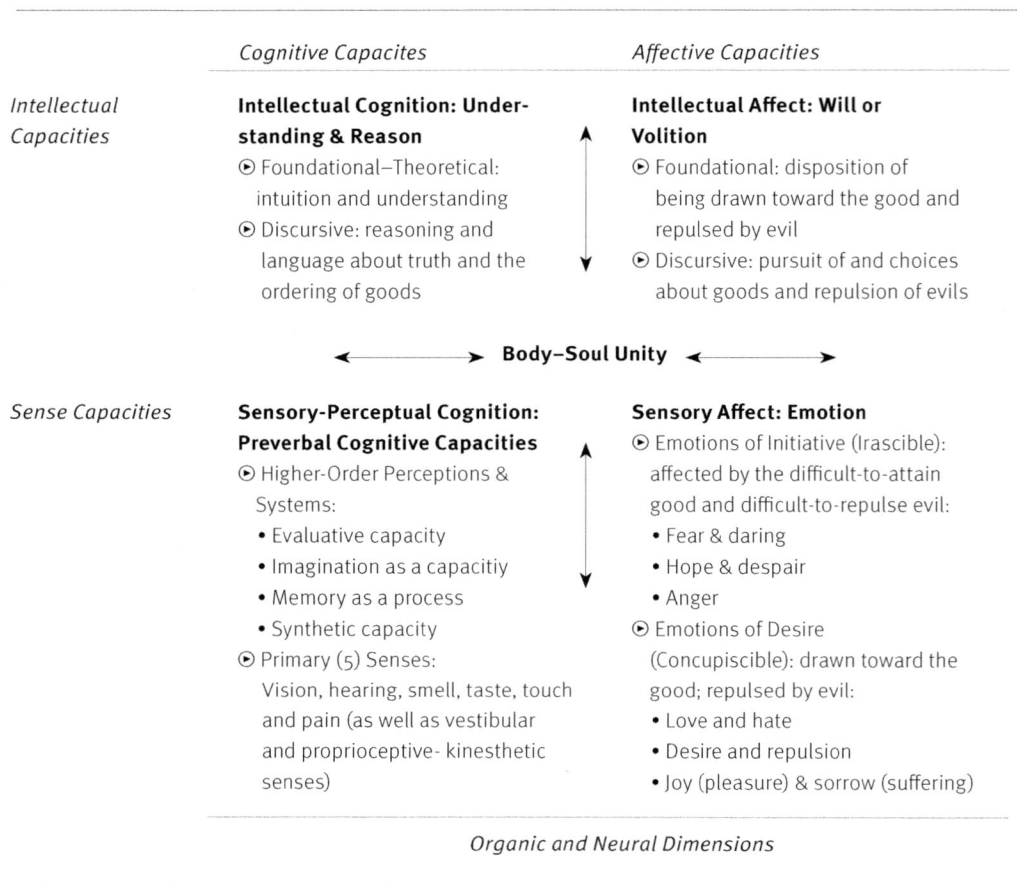

	Cognitive Capacites	Affective Capacities
Intellectual Capacities	**Intellectual Cognition: Understanding & Reason** ⊙ Foundational–Theoretical: intuition and understanding ⊙ Discursive: reasoning and language about truth and the ordering of goods	**Intellectual Affect: Will or Volition** ⊙ Foundational: disposition of being drawn toward the good and repulsed by evil ⊙ Discursive: pursuit of and choices about goods and repulsion of evils

◄──────► Body–Soul Unity ◄──────►

	Cognitive Capacites	Affective Capacities

Sense Capacities	**Sensory-Perceptual Cognition: Preverbal Cognitive Capacities**
	⊙ Higher-Order Perceptions & Systems:
	  • Evaluative capacity
	  • Imagination as a capacitiy
	  • Memory as a process
	  • Synthetic capacity
	⊙ Primary (5) Senses:
	  Vision, hearing, smell, taste, touch and pain (as well as vestibular and proprioceptive- kinesthetic senses)
		Sensory Affect: Emotion
		⊙ Emotions of Initiative (Irascible): affected by the difficult-to-attain good and difficult-to-repulse evil:
		  • Fear & daring
		  • Hope & despair
		  • Anger
		⊙ Emotions of Desire (Concupiscible): drawn toward the good; repulsed by evil:
		  • Love and hate
		  • Desire and repulsion
		  • Joy (pleasure) & sorrow (suffering)

Organic and Neural Dimensions

self-control strengths, physical reserves (Hagger, Wood, Stiff, & Chatzisarantis, 2010), and executive functions (Barkley, 2012; Cozolino, 2010, 2014; Naglieri & Goldstein, 2014). Furthermore, much of modern psychology has denied or ignored free will. For example, Freud (1915/1961) has an energy or pressure model of action, which arguably is deterministic. His model focuses on the unconscious pressure caused by the instincts of libido and aggression and by defense mechanisms that determine behavior, as when a person acts on sex urges. Meanwhile, Skinner (1971, 1976) is a well-known example in modern psychology of a thinker who maintains the assumption that environmental factors, especially reinforcements, determine all animal and human behavior.

In Catholic-Christian philosophy, however, the will is understood to be the intellectual affective capacity. It is closely related to reason

Figure 16.1. Philosophical Premises of the Catholic Christian Meta-Model of the Person

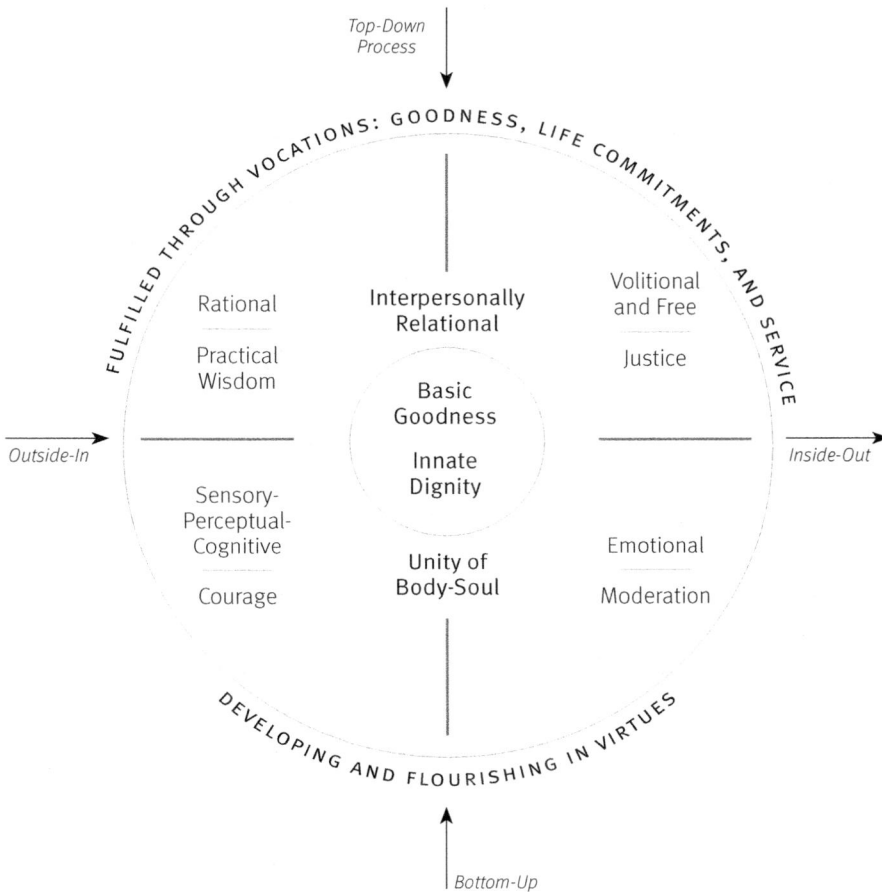

Top-Down Process

FULFILLED THROUGH VOCATIONS: GOODNESS, LIFE COMMITMENTS, AND SERVICE

Outside-In

Rational

Practical Wisdom

Interpersonally Relational

Basic Goodness

Innate Dignity

Unity of Body-Soul

Volitional and Free

Justice

Inside-Out

Sensory-Perceptual-Cognitive

Courage

Emotional Moderation

DEVELOPING AND FLOURISHING IN VIRTUES

Bottom-Up

and the emotions. Like the emotions, the will is drawn toward good things and repulsed by bad things. The human intellect, taken as including both knowledge and will, has a nonmaterial transcendent dimension, which is sometimes called spiritual. The work of the spiritual intellect is the interrelated effort of the capacities of knowing and loving or reasoning and willing (Sherwin, 2005).

As was described in the previous chapter,

we have an intellectual and spiritual capacity to know and to reason. This *intellectual cognitive capacity* is exercised at both theoretical and practical levels. It starts when we intellectually apprehend something as good, judge it to be worth pursuing, deliberate on the means to attain it, decide how to put the means into action, command the deed to be done, and then perform the actual deed (Cessario, 2013, pp. 118–120).

We also have an intellectual and spiritual capacity to will and to love. This *intellectual affective capacity* completes the action planned out in intellectual cognition. Through it, we move from theoretical levels to practical actions, employing reason in a sort of dialogue with the will. The will follows reason as it wishes for the good end perceived, intends to attain it, consents to the various possible means, chooses a particular means, applies it to the present situation, and then actually completes the deed (Aquinas, 1273/1981, I-II, 11–17; Cessario, 2013, pp. 113–114). These two intellectual capacities, reason and will, can be differentiated by the fact that we do not will or love that which we do not know (or that of which we are unaware). For example, a person becomes aware that his mother is sick, identifies the possibility of visiting her, and chooses the means to do so. But knowing that one's mother is ill requires more than intention and choice in order to arrive at her bedside. It requires intelligent and freely willed action.

What Is Free Will?

The person is naturally inclined to will goodness in general, even though he may not will a good thing in practice. The person wills to attain good things and to be united with other people through the interconnection of embodied, intellectual, and spiritual movements of attraction, intention, choice, consent, and enjoyment or love, as mentioned above. According to Aristotle (ca. 350 BC/1941a, 1109b30–1115a3), voluntary actions can be freely chosen, with knowledge of the circumstances and of the end desired, and with due deliberation about the means to attain the end. They are more than evaluative reactions of attraction or repulsion. They are more than the capacity to fix one's attention on an object. Rather, a person's voluntary movements start from the sensory-perceptual cognition of an object of desire, continue as the person uses practi-

cal reason to find a way to attain the object, and finish when he actually chooses and executes the plan (Aristotle, ca. 350 BC/1941b, 433a18–20).

For Aquinas (1273/1981; I-II, 6.1; also qq. 8–19), volition is a human act that springs from an intrinsic principle of attraction toward a goal or end. The person desires the goal as good and as contributing to flourishing. Voluntary acts are elicited when a person wills an end, either (1) immediately, such as the intention to help someone in distress; (2) through other means, such as when a person chooses to empathize with someone in pain, which influences one's emotions to feel mercy toward that person; or (3) through the influence of emotion, when the emotions indirectly move one to choose, such as when pity influences the choice to be merciful (Aquinas, 1273/1981, I-II, 24.3 ad 1). In sum, this understanding of the movements of the will involves the whole, unified person, including the embodied, interpersonal, intellectual, and spiritual capacities. Observation of only one of these capacities offers limited results, as when, observing interpersonal behavior alone, one notices external information but not the internal subjective states of desire or reason.

Free will is not simply synonymous with the volitional capacity itself. Rather, free will results from the joint exercise of a person's reason and will together (Aquinas, 1273/1981, I, 83.1, ad 3). A classical approach to free will recognizes that the will's movements range from interior volitions to exterior actions and are informed by cognitions that specify objects for intentional choice and for focusing one's attention. This understanding is explicated in the sequence of volitional movements that contribute to a complex act. For example, the complex act involved in marriage (for convenience, we will focus on the man's perspective, while recognizing that both spouses are called to a sincere gift of self in the sacrament, and we will leave aside, for the sake of the discussion at hand, the emotional and interpersonal aspects of the act) would include such affective steps as (1) *affection for a good*: for example, consider a man who discerns that he is called to marry; (2) *intention*: he resolves to find a woman to whom he can give himself in the sacrament of Marriage; (3) *approval*: he then must discern who, among his acquaintances, would be the best spouse and friend; (4) *choice*: he then must choose a woman with whom he feels called to enter into a deeper relationship, courting her and asking her to marry him; (5) *application*: he needs to follow through with his plan by preparing materially, psychologically, and spiritually for married life; and finally (6) *enjoyment of the result*: he actually marries the beloved and starts a family and thus experiences the joy and suffering (at the intellectual level of the will) and the pleasure and pain (at the sensory level of emotion) that come as the affective aspect of the actual act.

As already noted, these six steps of the will all have cognitive, emotive, and interpersonal facets. Insights on the course of more protracted, planned, and conscious movements (such as this example of getting engaged and then married, or other examples such as planning and starting a business) can be complemented by the recognition that an act often involves more spontaneous moments of self-movement, as when simply becoming fascinated by someone's charm or admiring someone's strength. Arguably, the human will is more complex than simply the ability to make choices. At its root, volition is the basic intellectual orientation to the good as desirable, that is, the rational desire for something attractive or for someone loveable (Aquinas, 1273/1981, I-II, 6.1). We are naturally drawn to a good person, to a good value or belief, as well as to the source of all goodness. Our

flourishing is tied up with seeking goodness and avoiding evil, seeking particular goods and avoiding particular evils. This natural inclination manifests an essential reality that underlies our spiritual or intellectual desires for love and goodness.

Furthermore, between the spiritual longings for ultimate good and the actual attainments of particular goods, there are also the free and discursive movements that sometimes seem quasi-spontaneous (pulling a child away from immediate danger) or interminable (preparing for retirement). Will is internally displayed in love, empathy, intention, desire, and joy. In overt interactions between knowing and loving and between nonconscious and conscious activities, we also exercise mastery of our capacities to be attracted to the particular good of a person, value, or belief. However, we exercise free will only within the limits and potential of human nature and relationships, since our callings and commitments influence our knowledge, love, and service of neighbor, self, and God (Aquinas, 1273/1981, I-II, qq. 6–19; Hoffmann, 2013).

What Is So Significant About Free Will?

Free will is an important part of any understanding of the person. For instance, some level of free will is required if we are to account for interpersonal love, ethical decision making, sociopolitical intentionality, financial and legal responsibility, and spiritual capacities. Both materialist and nonmaterialist neuropsychologists agree that consideration of free will is important for understanding the person and society, but they offer diametrically opposing reasons. Materialists deny that there is free will or that it is meaningful (La Mettrie, 1747/1994; Dennett, 2003). By this denial they dehumanize the person as well as relationships and fail to provide a compelling account of moral responsibility. Nonmaterialists, on the contrary, recognize that, without free will, human life is perhaps meaningless (Beauregard, 2012; Beauregard & O'Leary, 2008; Gazzaniga, 2011; Nagel, 2012). They even presuppose that the meaning of responsibility and love is based on the possibility and extent of free will.

The Catholic Christian Meta-Model and the nonmaterialists reject the assumption that humans are purely instinctual, simply machine-like, or indistinguishable from other animals. Also, the recent understanding of human self-consciousness and its intrinsic link to language has made clearer the type of transcendence that humans experience and has affirmed the realm in which human free will operates (Berwick & Chomsky, 2016; Bikerton, 2014; Vitz, 2017). Without free will, we would live predetermined lives. If everything were predetermined, for example by our instincts, we would not have the same sense of accountability for our actions. The legal system (laws, trials, and contracts) and economic practices (ownership, financial transactions, and initiative taking) as well as moral praise and blame would be fictitious.

In the psychological literature, there are further indications about the importance of commitment and responsibility for one's free actions. For example, several psychological studies (Baumeister, Masicampo, & DeWall, 2009; Rai & Holyoak, 2013) have shown that denying the existence of free will has a negative correlation with honesty. For example, one study suggests that there is a higher prevalence of cheating in an experimental group that has first been given a text to read that denies free will than occurs in a group given a text that affirms free will and responsibility (Vohs & Schooler, 2008).

In the philosophical perspective of the Meta-Model, the reality of free will is central to understanding the human heart and self-consciousness. After all, interpersonal commitments, life-callings, and moral responsibility are meaningful because we are free agents, who can freely say yes or no to life and love. A genuine sense of responsibility and interpersonal relationships rests upon a meaningful and realist understanding and expression of free will. If we deny that we experience weakness and that at times we have disordered desires to do what we do not truly want to do, we risk failing to acknowledge the importance of the will, its inevitable need for training and growth, and its need for interpersonal and communal support as well as periods of rest. Without a recognition of the reality of free will, the notions of virtue and commitment are meaningless.

How Can Freedom Be Doubted?

If we could never take the long way home or stop to admire the sunset when we desired, we would doubt our free will. Similarly, if we found a script of our every action, we would feel like puppets. Such a script is not forthcoming. Nonetheless, materialists support the belief that science will eventually provide this script, casting doubt on free will or radically restricting its import. Even though we commonly experience ourselves as moral agents and subjects of free choice, many theoretical psychologists, influenced by Pavlov, Watson, Skinner, and Freud, also express misgivings about free will. Many theoretical psychologists have been influenced by determinist, positivist, and materialist perspectives that hold that scientific laws of cause and effect radically constrain the possibility of freedom or completely impede it. In short, freedom does not exist, for many materialists, because of internal genetic and neurological forces and external social pressures.

Other thinkers deny both free volition and deliberate intention, holding them to be epiphenomenal illusions. For instance, neuroscientist

Benjamin Libet's (1985, 2004) research found that humans physically move their bodies (for example, push a button) and anticipate social situations (for example, greet one's neighbor) even before being aware of such movements or even intending them. However, had Libet performed a more explicit analysis of the chain of nonconscious and conscious activity, he would have noted that activities prior to the motor cortex were not monitored by his experiment. Bennett and Hacker (2003) remark that Libet's experiment has confounded parts of the person for the whole, namely, the functioning of the motor cortex for the whole person's free will (for other refutations of Libet's conclusions see Gallagher 2005a, 2005b; Kahneman, 2011).

Further doubts about free will and freedom are voiced by neurophilosopher Paul Churchland (1995), philosopher and cognitive scientist Daniel Dennett (1991, 2003, 2006), and evolutionary biologist Richard Dawkins (2008). They view experiences that are called "freedom" as an epiphenomenal illusion, as not grounded in the reality of science, or as merely due to the effects of evolutionary natural selection in the midst of a determined world. They understand science and ethics to be "two self-contained systems played out among the same entities in the world," but using different rules and different games (Pinker, 2009, p. 55). However, how can free will be denied in one game (science) yet retained in the other (ethics)? That is, how can studies involve the same interpersonal subjects in both determined and nondetermined cases? This high profile group of scientists, called the New Atheists, expresses doubts not only about free will and an objective basis for ethics but also about the existence of any objective or ultimate meaning beyond the laws of physics, chemistry, and evolution by natural selection. This chapter, in what follows, offers a critique of the position of the New Atheists, while making a case in support of the freedom of the person as an object of study and a subject of action (for further arguments in support of free will see especially Feser, 2008; Nagel, 2012; McGrath, 2004, 2011; Titus, 2017).

What Are Some Psychological Supports for Believing in Free Will?

At the end of the nineteenth century, psychology still accepted the concept of free will. For example, William James (1890/1981) addressed a whole chapter to the will in his work on the principles of psychology, and he clearly supports free will, which is shown in his understanding of religion. Very roughly, the decline of psychology's explicit belief in free will came during the century after James. This decline came about because of deterministic influences in psychology, science, and philosophy. For example, the first two major paradigms within modern psychology—the psychoanalytic tradition (e.g., Freud) and the behavioral tradition (e.g., Pavlov, Watson, and Skinner)—both expressed types of materialist determinism and naturalist reductionism.

In science, reductionist and deterministic influences also came from advances in genetics and subatomic physics (seeking explanations at ever lower levels) and in the adoption of the experimental method and evolutionary theory as the only bases for legitimate knowledge, including knowledge about the person. In philosophy, reductionist influences came in the rejection of metaphysics, as found in versions of skeptical empiricism, early analytic philosophy (early Wittgenstein), and logical empiricism (Ayers), and in the various reductions found in the field of ethics, such as relativism, social constructivism, emotivism, and utilitarianism (e.g., Singer, 2011; Kuhse & Singer, 1988).

However, since the 1980s, psychology has begun to reappropriate a theoretical understanding of free will. In opposition to the strict determinists, there are major psychologists who provide reasons to believe in human freedom. Social cognitive theorist and psychologist Albert Bandura (1997, 2001), for example, has conducted studies that indicate that humans do exercise free will. His studies have focused on self-efficacy and the sense of being free to move oneself and to do things. Bandura (2006) states: "People are self-organizing, proactive, self-regulating, and self-reflecting. They are not simply onlookers of their behavior. They are contributors to their life circumstances, not just products of them" (p. 164). He has shown that individuals can directly change their own motivation and influence their own well-being, through intentionality, forethought, self-reactiveness, and self-reflectiveness (Bandura, 2001). Moreover, his studies have demonstrated that consciousness of and belief in free will makes a difference in how one acts. Furthermore, researchers Snyder, Rand, and Sigmon (2002) demonstrate that persons who express hope in their strengths and resources, such as their capacity for initiative-taking, and who believe that they can achieve their goals, are more effective, successful, and healthy compared to persons with low expectations of self-efficacy or free will.

Although free will was neglected theoretically for several decades, a real interest in free will is found in psychotherapeutic approaches. For example, cognitive behaviorists, in theory and practice (Beck, 1979; Ellis & Ellis, 2011), express confidence in the client's capacity to change. Such free ability to change is presupposed when a client is asked to identify and distance himself from automatic thought patterns and deterministic patterns of behavior (Beck, 1979, p. 243). Existentialist psychologists have

also expressed confidence in the contribution that free will makes to meaning in life (Frankl, 1959/2006; Maslow, 1987; May, 1969). Attentiveness to the importance of intense emotions has also demonstrated that the will is operative when someone freely uses techniques to overcome acquired maladaptive interpersonal behaviors (Ellis & Ellis, 2011). For example, couples who are emotionally polarized can freely choose to use techniques, such as mindfulness and self-soothing, to change what were once automatic dysfunctional responses (Gottman, 1999). The neo-psychoanalytic perspective expresses belief in free will, as, for example, in the informal psychoanalytic saying "where id was, ego will be," or in the therapeutic goal of bringing the unconscious to consciousness. And if we consider free will from a medical perspective, psychopharmacological approaches are able to increase human freedom by reducing harmful or pathological emotions and behaviors.

In addition to the reappropriation of the free will in secular psychology, since the 1970s, there have been a number of Christian integrative approaches to psychology (the current volume included), which assume that human free will is an essential part of personality theory and psychotherapy (Johnson, 2010; McMinn, 2017; McMinn & Campbell, 2007; Stevenson, Eck, & Hill, 2007).

Neurobiologist Mario Beauregard (2012) demonstrates the vacuity of the materialist position, arguing that the field of neuroscience has not disproven freedom or the spiritual nature of the soul (pp. 116–118; see also Beauregard & O'Leary, 2008). When presuming that freedom and the soul do not exist, materialists face inconsistencies at the level of human experience. For instance, without free will, how can one account for the creativity and inventions that are found in culture and technology (Beauregard &

O'Leary, 2008, p. 231)? Without free will, how can one account for the development of artistic expression, not to mention scientific efforts and technical applications? On the contrary, when we assume that there is a meaningful degree of human freedom, we can account better for human experience and for the type of ethics and responsibility that are constructive of personal flourishing and the common good of families and societies (Ashley, 2013).

Capacity for Freedom

The capacity for freedom can further be seen in terms of a basic philosophical distinction that informs two different understandings concerning freedom and human nature. Either (a) the capacity for freedom and choice (born of reason and will) is anchored in the affirmation of a human nature that provides an interpersonal foundation for moral norms, vocations, and virtue; or (b) the capacity for freedom is unanchored as a result of a denial of human nature (and of natural law and interpersonal subjectivity), which is considered irrelevant for our freedom. In other words, either freedom is rooted in, measured by, and oriented to the truth of a person's humanity (especially as exercised in interpersonal relationships), or freedom is created by the individual (for an example of the latter understanding, see Sartre, 1946/2007), who is indifferent to any norm beyond himself, to any truth beyond the truth he creates (John Paul II, 1993).

How Can One Respond to the Denial or Limitation of Freedom?

The denial or misuse of freedom is deeply disturbing to our understanding of interpersonal subjectivity. Some thinkers have placed restrictions on freedom in theory and practice, calling into question the way we are invited to relate to others in truth, justice, and love. Pieper (1952/2009) critiques such restrictions of free will as found in totalitarian ideologies. Pinckaers (1995) outlines the historical shifts of other thinkers who have framed free will as a "freedom of indifference" (that is, thinkers who have construed freedom as merely the right to be able to choose one way or another, whether good or evil, independent of the truth of the matter and the truth of the person) (pp. 327–353). Certain contemporary atheists and agnostics, especially influenced by particular schools of naturalism, existentialism, and libertarianism, exhibit this understanding of human freedom by denying both the moral significance of human nature and the existence of God (de Beauvoir, 1949/2011; Sartre, 1946/2007).

Furthermore, it has become common to view autonomy and power, even the power over one's own body, as main moral values and political principles. For instance, the notion of self-determination, without a moral notion of human nature, can lead to practices in which "might makes right." For different reasons, these beliefs express a misuse of freedom or seek to restrain its scope by denying significant moral goals. For example, proponents of euthanasia or assisted suicide, in invoking a person's freedom and autonomy, deny the value of human life and the objective moral responsibility to uphold it (regarding this denial applied also to abortion, see Dennett, 1995; Singer, 2011, p. 5). Such thinkers conceptualize freedom as the right to do as one pleases in privacy, among consenting partners, or when not infringing on the rights of another person. In the name of rights and freedom, such thinkers deny the human moral responsibility to protect the rights and freedom of others, for this concept of a freedom of indifference presumes falsely that there is an absolute private sphere, in which actions can be pursued without impact on oneself, other people, and the common good. It effectively undercuts the human call to an ultimate and true flourishing by denying the relationship between moral action and self-determination (Wojtyła, 1979).

A response to this notion of freedom as an exercise in indifference to the reality of human nature and moral truth can be found in the affirmation of a "freedom for excellence" (Pinckaers, 1995, pp. 354–378). This freedom requires two kinds of interrelated freedoms: (1) freedom from those things that block personal flourishing and (2) freedom for pursuing those things that contribute to personal flourishing. These interrelated freedoms are served by a hierarchy of vocations and virtues in the quest for ultimate purpose and meaning.

How Can a Fuller Understanding of Freedom Serve the Pursuit of Excellence?

The assumption that human nature and true human flourishing serve as normative sources for our exercise of the will requires an understanding of the capacity of freedom for excellence. This complex notion of freedom develops in two interdependent ways. First, we seek "freedom from" negative things that hinder our health and development and that cause psychological pathology, physical illness, and moral and spiritual disorder. Second, we seek "freedom for" positive things that promote our health and development and that cause psychological healing, physical well-being, and moral and spiritual flourishing.

Modern approaches have conceptualized these two types of freedom as incommensurable, in part because of the possible misuse of a positive notion of freedom. Isaiah Berlin (1958) critiqued "positive" freedom because it had been abused in the totalitarian regimes of the Second World War. That freedom can be abused, however, does not mean that every type of "positive" freedom involves abuse. Rather, positive freedom requires properly formed conscience aimed at an objective good. A classical, Catholic vision of the person understands that these two movements are both essential to a freedom for excellence, which pursues a life of flourishing in the context of a hierarchy of goods. Negative and positive expressions of freedom (freedom from and freedom for) both bear upon natural goods and goals, but furthermore benefit from a recognition of the fuller meaning natural goods take on in the context of our ultimate goals, especially spiritual or theological ones. This is evident, for example, in how theological hope and charity bring further meaning to the natural love that parents have for their children (McInerny, 2006; Weigel, 2002).

What Is "Freedom From"?

Although all true freedom requires a type of proactive effort, the first element of the freedom for excellence is "freedom from" those things that inhibit, depress, coerce, oppress, or harm individuals at physical, emotional, psychological, and spiritual levels. In a sense, this is a negative freedom, a freedom to avoid harm. It rejects what stands in the way of flourishing. There are many restrictions that are unfitting for the flourishing of the person and society. Humans need to liberate themselves from those things that significantly restrict them from attaining natural goods or that have rendered them passive in the effort to achieve difficult goods (Ashley, 2013; Pinckaers, 1995, 2005). A politician, for example, should seek freedom from oppression and injustice that offend people and the civil common good (Berlin, 1958). Of special interest for the psychologist is the process of a person's becoming free from psychological disorders or free from outside influences that cause disease and suffering and threaten interpersonal relationships. In the face of distorted loves (broken families and alienated friends) and other difficulties (a conflict between one's career and one's family), we often experience undue fear that restricts our capacities to fittingly reason, choose, feel, and relate even to people who are most dear to us, such as our spouses, children, parents, and so on. In order to have peace of mind, we need to be freed from being over-controlled by fear. However, this is not the only movement of the capacity of freedom. In this way, a major goal of traditional psychotherapy is to increase the client's freedom—"freedom from."

What Is "Freedom For"?

Second, and most fundamentally, there is the more active facet that is the freedom for excellence, which requires a freedom for flourishing. Through this positive understanding of freedom, humans grow in their capacities to know truth and reality, to choose good, and to avoid evil (Pinckaers, 1995, 2005). They thereby develop in the moral virtues, especially practical wisdom, justice, courage, temperance, and so on, in pursuit of their callings or vocations. Positive psychology (Peterson & Seligman, 2004) is consistent with the idea of positive freedom to the degree that it promotes a freedom through the flourishing found in the virtues, a freedom that is tied to true goods and fitting practices. Positive psychology has also admitted that a fuller conception of flourishing comes only with the aid of philosophical reflection and religious practice (Peterson & Seligman, 2004). A completed and higher-order positive psychology (let us call it a "Meta-Positive Psychology") will recognize that the person flourishes through a freedom for excellence (positive freedom) that express-

es a normative and hierarchical interconnection of the desire and pursuit of existence, goodness and love, truth, beauty, family, and other interpersonal relationships. From the perspective of the Catholic Christian Meta-Model, the epitome of this flourishing is self-giving, even mutual self-giving, which can often be expressed in forgiveness (Enright & Fitzgibbons, 2015; Worthington, 2003), reconciliation, altruism (Post, 2007), generosity, and the self-sacrifice shown by spouses, parents, friends, and others.

Through the exercise of the freedom for excellence, humans become ever more intimately linked to truth (John Paul II, 1993, §34) and self-gift (Jn 15:13; Aquinas, 1273/1981, II-II, 23.1), which prevent this greater "freedom for" from being simply reduced to a "freedom from." The freedom to be able to give of oneself willingly and generously can also be understood philosophically and theologically.

From the theological perspective of the Catholic Christian vision of the person, moral and spiritual truth is the foundation for freedom. In the Gospel of John, Jesus correlates truth and freedom, saying: "You will know the truth, and the truth will set you free" (Jn 8:32). This freedom is based not primarily on learning new concepts. Rather, it emerges primarily as the gift of God and secondarily as the achievement of the person who grows in God's grace. First, freedom from undue fear or disordered loves permits a steady understanding of the implications of the truth that the person is created in the image of God and redeemed in Christ. Second, freedom for committed relationships and deep peace promote adherence to the fullness of this truth. We must practically and willingly adhere to truth once we have found it, once it has been given to us in the encounter with God (Vatican II, 1965a, §3). Both spiritual truth and freedom are needed for flourishing and peace, as St. Paul says:

Whatever is true, whatever is honorable, whatever is lovely, whatever is gracious, if there is any excellence [*aretē*], if there is anything worthy of praise, think about these things. What you have learned and received and heard and seen in me, do; and the God of peace will be with you. (Phil 4:8–9)

This Christian freedom finds its flourishing in an encounter with Christ, who leads us to the Father through the Holy Spirit. Such freedom constitutes the flourishing that is partial at present but, in Christian hope, is seen as being completed at the end of time.

Volitional Inclinations

The Meta-Model presupposes that humans have a series of natural inclinations that underlie our experience of reality (see especially Chapter 11, "Fulfilled in Virtue," and Chapter 15, "Rational"), including our experience of goodness and the freedom to choose it. At the most basic level, we experience an inclination to flourish. Springing out of this most basic desire to flourish is the desire for the good. Following Aristotle, Aquinas, and classical philosophy, the Model presupposes that the human tendency toward the good is manifest in different volitional inclinations. But there are different philosophical perspectives on our attraction to good and evil and our natural desires, which propose different notions of volitional inclinations, as we will now see.

How Deep Is Our Desire for Goodness?

The presuppositions of materialist naturalism tend to treat as relative the import of good and evil. They make the awareness of good and evil and our attraction toward and repulsion from them a result of evolutionary pressures that merely favor the existence of the individual's offspring or of the group (Hauser, 2006). In this view, the moral mind and its sense of good and evil or right and wrong are simply the result of evolutionary processes of natural selection. The logic of reductionist evolutionary theory has no interest in transcendent truth and spiritual beauty (Nagel, 2012; McGrath, 2011; Życiński, 2006).

It pays very little attention to personal flourishing, post-reproductive adulthood, and lifelong committed love, except inasmuch as parents and parents of parents support the survival of children and the children of children.

A classical view of the person, such as is adopted in the Meta-Model, on the contrary, is attentive to order and purpose within evolutionary patterns and to personal, daily, and ultimate flourishing without the limitations of relativist, reductionist, and determinist presuppositions (Schönborn, 2007; Życiński, 2006). It holds that it is reasonable to think that the world "originated in a very complicated process of evolution" that does not deny the place of God or reason (Ratzinger, 2002, p. 139). This view is intrinsically nondeterministic, recognizing that there is a universal moral and teleological sense or inclination to seek what is good and to avoid what is evil. A consideration of natural law would reveal that there are teleological and moral inclinations toward goodness, existence, sexual union and family, truth (including truth about God), society, and beauty (Aquinas, 1273/1981, I-II, 94.2). It manifests a transcendent movement toward flourishing through a person's vocations and virtues. However, this approach recognizes that the person and the universe are ordered not only by such human inclinations and basic natural moral laws; the Creator of the universe is the source from which the person and the universe come and the end to which they point. Even in the midst of distorted biases and evil choices, the classical perspective recognizes that the human heart and mind are ordered toward goodness, love, justice, and eventually God (Aquinas, 1273/1981, I, 2.3; Schönborn, 2007; Spitzer, 2010). The questions arise, though: How do these moral inclinations influence human freedom and responsibility? How profound is our natural inclination toward goodness and away from evil?

In the midst of historical contingency and natural selection, the laws of nature and the natural moral law manifest the nondeterministic ordering of the universe. As a basic expression of the natural moral law, natural inclinations underlie the order of reality and of human knowledge and love. Of particular importance is the natural inclination of the human affective powers toward goodness, which concerns the diverse levels of love and types of affection and friendship. Research shows that humans are "hardwired to connect," (Commission on Children at Risk, 2003), that is, they are naturally inclined to love and seek the goods of parental attachment, bonding with friends, spousal relationships, and family life (Brizendine, 2006, 2010; Hazan & Shaver, 1987; Lee, 2012; McEntee, Dy-Liacco, & Haskins, 2013; Mikulincer, 2013). This affective inclination is a pathway to flourishing. We cannot, however, be happy with only an inclination, let alone with one that would overshadow our freedom. The simple inclination to bond with and feel affection for parents, family, friends, and community is a step toward the actualization of those goods and relationships. However, especially as adults, we must intentionally pursue these human goods, because they are merely the "seeds of the virtues" that potentially become virtues only when pursued well (Aquinas, 1273/1981, I-II, 51.1; Aristotle, ca. 350 BC/1941b).

How Do Natural Inclinations Become Distorted and Restored?

As seeds, the natural inclinations are underdetermined; they require our free and formative efforts if we are to flourish in accord with our life commitments and vocations (Levering, 2008; Pinckaers, 1995, 2000). Although the natural inclinations remain basically good, they suffer from types of distortion at a secondary level. For example, they are subject to developmental disorders (caused by biological deformation, trauma, and lack of secure attachment), neurocognitive disorders, (caused by deficits in decision-making and error-correction capacities), and moral distortions (caused by evil choices, narcissism, hatred, acting out of fear, and lack of forgiveness). In the context of family, friends, therapy, and community, such distortions may be remediated and healed over time. Each person is more or less aware that the distortions are grafted on to something that is more basic than the distortion itself; however, that awareness will vary according to psychological context (mild anxiety versus severe fear or psychosis) and metaphysical perspective (realist versus reductionist views), and so on. The Meta-Model, following Aquinas (1273/1981, II-II, 94.2) and other natural law personalists (Levering, 2008), posits that each person's common human nature and unique personhood reliably retain access to the natural inclinations toward goodness, existence, family, community, truth, and beauty. Furthermore, the distortions, as negative contrasts, often point toward the flourishing that can be attained through free and personal efforts; through collaboration with others and God.

Does God Overpower Our Free Will?

Nonreductionist neuroscientists, such as Beauregard (2012; Beauregard & O'Leary, 2008), have argued that there is no contradiction between a religious point of view and human freedom, that is, that believers are free in the midst of affirming religious belief. However, it is a further step of philosophy in dialogue with neuroscience (Beauregard & O'Leary, 2008) to explain how persons can be truly moved to desire divine goods both by their own free will and by divine grace, without doing violence to their will.

From the Christian perspective, humans are motivated by what they prize. As the Gospel of Matthew says: "Where your treasure is, there will your heart be also" (Mt 6:21). When the treasure is an object of faith, hope, and love, we can notice the particularity of our own choice at the same time as we feel the pull and support of a spiritual source—what Christians call divine grace. For example, I choose freely to love my neighbor as myself in serving her in her need (Mt 22:39), even while being called to do so through my conscience and while being influenced by my emotion of pity, and while being supported in my free choice by a higher source of strength and goodness. In hindsight, we can recognize both that we might have done otherwise and

that our actual free choice was supported by the guidance and support of someone more, that is, God. There can be a transformation of the will as the result of divine and human collaboration. Without giving up our own capacity to will or our necessity to engage ourselves, we seek to follow Christ's prayer—"not my will, but yours, be done" (Lk 22:42; also Mt 26:42 & 6:10)—and, in so doing, unite our will with God's will. The divine aspect of free purposeful or teleological movements (freely seeking the good of love) is recognized by the Christian as the movements of the Holy Spirit that have been called by different names: spiritual instincts, spiritual impulses, spiritual gifts, or the *instinctus* of the Holy Spirit (Aquinas, 1273/1981, II-II, 52.2 ad 3; Pinckaers, 2005). Such a theology of grace, however, does not dispel all the mystery behind how the inclinations tend toward spiritual goods and how we freely act while being supported in the good that we do. Rather, it modestly situates both human and divine involvement in personal agency, while anchoring freedom in truth and recognizing a broad notion of freedom that includes such possibilities as positive change from psychotherapy.

Moral Responsibility and Prudential Personalism

When addressing ethics, volition, and freedom, we enter directly into a discussion of the nature of moral responsibility for evil and for good, the responsibility that concerns oneself, others, and the whole of creation. This responsibility is largely a product of the conditioned dispositions and the process of practical reasoning or practical wisdom (i.e., prudential personalism), which requires consideration of interpersonal relationality, natural moral law and its principles, choices and actions, as well as emotion. The different levels of a person's responsibility for himself, others, and for groups of others include his

responsibility for his family and for those whom he serves through his vocations. These aspects of responsibility govern how a person's acts affect his own life and the lives of others, as well as how a person needs other people in order to become responsible and to act responsibly with some reliability.

How Responsible Are We for Our Own Actions?

There are three levels of practical wisdom or personal moral responsibility that a person has: responsibility for oneself, for one's committed relationships, and for the common good. In order to be responsible, a person has to be able not only to formulate moral intentions, identify pertinent moral and spiritual principles, fix appropriate goals, evaluate acts, and anticipate the outcomes, but also to respond or act in a timely way. Even if we are responsible for ourselves, there are limits to our responsibility. The type and extent of our responsibility are connected to the limits of our knowledge and understanding, to our intentions and choices, and to our own power to do things. From the outside, there is the influence of others upon us, as well as the circumstances of our acts, especially such factors as who is involved, when an act happens, where it takes place, and how the act produces good and evil effects.

What Are the Three Sources of Morality?

The three major elements of moral responsibility, called the three sources of morality, are of particular salience in the moral evaluation of actions (Ashley & O'Rourke, 1997; *Catechism of the Catholic Church* [CCC], 2000, §§1750–1754; John Paul II, 1993, §§71–78). The three sources of morality are the intention, the action itself, and the circumstances (see Table 16.2). The goodness of these three sources is manifested in the natural and divine law, the person (or human nature), and the person's vocations. We must use our conscience and the virtue of practical wisdom to ascertain the pertinence of these and other principles (such as professional codes and civic laws). We should also be aware of the person's conditioned dispositions (virtues and vices) and psychological well-being, which must be considered in the assessment of the person's moral culpability for or the praiseworthiness of an action.

The **intention** is the purpose or ultimate end that moves the person to seek a good or moral action. Why does he or she want to do something, in general? Or what is his intention for seeking to do an action? For example, in light of the great commandment and the personalist norm, the remote intention of a person may be to love God, neighbor, and self (Ex 20:1–17; Lev 19:18; Deut 6:5; Mt 22:36–40; Mk 12:28–34; Lk 10:25–28; John Paul II, 1993). In addition to these remote ends, there are also the closer or more proximate goals, such as to strengthen the marital bond of a couple in therapy or to aid a mother and father in discerning together how to care for their children's need. Neither the remote intention (last end) nor the closer intention (choice of proximate end or means) alone constitutes the full moral action (Aquinas, 1273/1981, I-II, 12.3). Nonetheless, such intentions are essential to direct the action and judge the circumstances. For example, general intentions express the desire to care for the client, but also need the specification of the appropriate means to these ends, which may include the choice and application of appropriate evidence-based practices, as found in Cognitive-Behavioral Therapy, attachment therapy, couples therapy, and so on.

The **action** bears upon a purpose (a moral object) that accomplishes the person's intentions. The act, or action, takes on its moral character from the object to which it is immediately oriented (for example, an act of "theft" bears upon the "property of another"; or "adultery" bears upon the "spouse of another"). It is a particular kind of moral action that is chosen to be performed. The same kind of physical act can be present in acts that differ morally as a function of the actual moral conditions (for example, the physical act of sexual intercourse is present both in conjugal relations and in adultery). Likewise, the same general kind of moral act may be present in different moral contexts (for example, the same act of concern for another is present both

Table 16.2. Three Sources of Morality (Intention, Action, and Circumstances)

A. INTENTION (end)	Purpose or ultimate end that people seek to achieve (why they do something). (John Paul II, 1993, §§71–78).
	Criteria for good drawn from the normative measure of natural law, the person (human nature), vocations, and the divine law.
	For example, theistic and other Christian intentions would include to love and serve God and neighbor, as well as the other intentions that specify this ultimate end of life and action.
	What is the intention or what are the intentions for doing the action?
B. ACTION (moral object)	Moral character of the act that they seek to perform to achieve the purpose (John Paul II, 1993, §§71–78).
	Acts must never be intrinsically evil, that is, an act must be consistent with the vocation to goodness and holiness of the person as being created in the image of God (Vatican II, 1965, §27; John Paul II, 1993, §§79–80).
	Nor may an evil means be justified by a good intention or goal (Rom 3:8; *CCC*, §1759).
	What is the moral character of the action that is being chosen?
C. CIRCUMSTANCES	Circumstances of the act (when, where, how) and of the person (psychological, sociological, including vocational commitments).
	When is it being done? Where is it being done? Who are the persons involved? What are their vocational responsibilities (concerning family, job, and so on)? How is the action being done—is it influenced internally by fear or externally by force?
	[See Tables 16.3 and 16.4 for further principles applicable when there are both good and evil effects (a double effect) or involvement in the evil done by someone else.]

Sources for Table 16.2: Rom 3:8; *CCC*, 2000, §§1750–1754; John Paul II, 1993, §§71–80; Vatican II, 1965, §27.

in the clinical act of expressing empathy for a client or in the family when a parent is expressing care for children).

In moral acts, what a person understands himself to be doing is important: the person must also desire and specify the action as a fitting way to achieve more ultimate ends (John Paul II, 1993, §§71–78). A type of act may be considered, at this first level of analysis, with respect to whether it is in accord with human nature. Persons are called to do thoroughly good actions (acts of service, care, generosity, and so on), while being aware of and avoiding acts that are intrinsically evil. A person must never do an act—such "as any type of murder, genocide, abortion, euthanasia or willful self-destruction, whatever violates the integrity of the human person, such as mutilation, torments inflicted…" (John Paul II, 1993, §§79–80, quoting Vatican II, 1965b, §27)—that is inconsistent with his being created in the image of God or with his moral and spiritual calling to justice, goodness, and holiness.

Furthermore, the choice of an evil action or means can never be justified by an appeal to a good intention or goal (Rom 3:8; *CCC*, 2000, §1759). For example, a good intention to support a client and respect his autonomy, responsibility, and dignity does not justify indifference to or encouragement of the client's immoral behavior (abuse, addiction, and intrinsically evil acts). An intention and an act that affirm the autonomy, responsibility, and dignity of the person need not also affirm the client's decision if the decision is harmful or unethical.

To consider prudentially (with practical wisdom) the intentions and the nature of the person's acts helps to identify how personal responsibility for action involves being a moral agent. In a Catholic Christian vision of the person, the moral agent not only knows why he is doing something (for example, he performs an act to praise God or to seek selfish recognition), but also knows the type of moral action that he is doing. For example, the act of empathetic listening can serve various moral purposes, such as seeking to find out information that will lead a clinician to understand the client and permit a correct diagnosis with a view to healing. Or such listening can lead to unprofessional small talk in order to get extra payment.

The **circumstances** are further moral details that are related to the moral action. They can mitigate or increase responsibility. There are two kinds of circumstances: those that pertain to the person and those that pertain to the moral act.

First, person-based circumstances (to whom) pertain to the psychological, sociological, and vocational situation of the moral agents. In the clinical setting, for instance, who is the moral agent that is being considered: the clinician or the client, as an individual or a couple? Is the moral agent married, a parent, employed, and so on? What are his or her vocational responsibilities concerning family, job, and so on?

Second, action-based circumstances pertain to how, when, and where the action is done. In the clinical context, for instance, how is the act of psychotherapy being carried out? Is the clinician exerting pressure on the client, internally by fear or externally by force?

The act is also specified further because of how the therapy is given. For instance, how has the therapist established an informed consent agreement, including reference to the therapist's worldview and value-system? How has the therapist and this agreement respected both his or her own and the client's own conscience. Furthermore, are there clearly foreseeable good effects for the client? Is it probable that the treatment will relieve the symptoms? Are there any clearly foreseeable evil effects of clinical intervention? If so, how does the clinician foresee avoiding them in order not to cause evil, such as depression, mental disorder, or self-harm? Is it foreseeable that the client will misuse the new competencies gained in therapy?

Thus, the three sources of morality help people to identify (a) the intention or ultimate end that they seek to achieve (why they do something); (b) the actual act that they choose to perform (what they want to do, which is the means to the good end); and (c) the significant circumstances that encircle the act (who is involved, how, when, and where will the act take place, what are the secondary effects of the action, especially possible bad effects). All of these three aspects of the act must be good in order for the act to be considered good. A good intention or a good ultimate end (a) is not enough. A good action or proximate end (b) is not enough. And good circumstances, such as a good consequence or a good effect of the act (c) are not sufficient to constitute a morally good act.

An action is evil when it lacks something that is due by way of justice and charity that would make the act a moral act and worthy of choice by a person who is an image of God. However, when a person is not morally responsible for being ignorant of the evil nature of the action or of a bad effect that comes from the action, it is possible that there is no imputation of guilt (Chapter 18, "Fallen"). For example, a person lends his neighbor a chainsaw to cut up a fallen tree; he mentions the possible dangers and is told by the neighbor that he is familiar with chainsaw use. Nevertheless, the neighbor misuses the chainsaw and cuts his leg badly. Such an unforeseeable outcome does not bring culpability with it.

Furthermore, there is a lessened culpability when the result of an action is not intended but nonetheless arises due to inadvertence. For example, there is culpability, but of a lesser degree, when for example the person inadvertently fails to verify the neighbor's competence in chainsaw use. However, even though the person may not be fully responsible for the action, the objective evil of the external act exists and remains, that is, the evil of the cut leg.

In upcoming sections of the chapter, we will address the principles that clarify the morality of an action that has both evil and good effects (double effect; Table 16.3) and the morality of being involved in the evil done by someone else (Table 16.4).

How Are We Interpersonally Responsible?

Personal responsibility is always in some way interpersonal. For example, we are accountable in justice for what we owe another person, including owing the truth about reality and the truth about what is common knowledge, such as information on life-threatening behaviors (Aquinas, 1273/1981, II-II, 47). There are at least three kinds of explicitly interpersonal responsibility. First, a designated leader has *personal responsibility for a group*; for instance, a father or a mother has a responsibility for the well-being of the family and each member. This requires the exercise of domestic prudence for each parent (Aquinas, 1273/1981, II-II, 48.1). Second, there is also *shared responsibility* of spouses, or of business, government, or church leaders, for the effects of their actions on the family, workers, citizens, and church members. This responsibility extends to the individual members of such systems or groups, as well as to its members as a group (for example, the public at large), and even to the environment (Benedict XVI, 2005; Francis, 2015). Third, there is the *collective responsibility* of the group for collective actions and collective intentions (Smiley, 2017).

The Meta-Model assumes that society is based on the conviction that individuals, families, and society itself should develop their capacities to be responsible (the virtue of practical reason). Society requires people who are capable to work together with others to *seek good ends* (purposeful or teleological goals fitting for the person, family, and society), *plan good acts* (through intentional deliberation), and *perform good actions* (actual judgments, choices, and deeds).

The rule of law, furthermore, depends on the human capacity to act responsibly. Society seeks to make people more responsible through civic education and practices, law and policy, sentences and punishments, as well as rewards and honors (George, 1995; Hittinger, 2007). For example, laws about alcohol use and driving also have the pedagogical effect of teaching young people their need to attend to the safety of others (Lickona, 1991, 2004).

Our interpersonal responsibility requires us to evaluate responsibility for our actions and those of others. Often our own actions influence the actions of others, for good or for ill. Evaluation of a person's own moral responsibility involves not only an adequate knowledge of the person, the act, and the effects of the act, but also the recognition of how our actions contribute to others' actions. In the Meta-Model, we start by acknowledging the person's commitments and vocational states, as well as his formal and informal work and service. For example, being a married person makes a difference in how one emotionally and physically interacts with other people. Such a substantial evaluation also requires the same knowledge about the other people who are significantly involved in the action. In family therapy the therapist needs to know the characteristics of each spouse, and also of the other members of the family who can be influenced by therapeutic interventions.

How Might We Be Responsible for Both Good and Bad Consequences (the Double Effect) of a Voluntary Act?

Recall, from just above, that the three sources of morality indicate that the intention (purpose, goals, or ends) and the action (the means chosen to obtain that goal), as well as the circumstances, all must be good. When there are good and bad effects or consequences of a voluntary action (a moral double effect), we need another level of analysis, which involves so-called double-effect principles (Table 16.3). The first double-effect principle is that the action being done

must be rationally specified as a good act or, at least, as morally neutral (Ashley & O'Rourke, 1997, pp. 191–193). It must not be intrinsically evil. For example, the act of providing filial therapy, which improves the communication and interpersonal relationship between a mother and a daughter, is good, that is, if it is clinically appropriate for the clients and within the competency of the practitioner, and so on.

Second, the intention that people seek to achieve (the reason they do something) must be good (Ashley & O'Rourke, 1997, pp. 188–189). The intended remote end must seek the good end that drives the action. For example, the clinician must have an adequate, good remote end that serves his client, such as the good of improved mother-daughter relations for his clients; his intended remote end should not be simply the fee that he will collect.

Third, evil should never be done as a means to achieve some other good (Rom 3:8; Aquinas, 1273/1981, II-II, 64.7; CCC, 2000, §1789, §1756). For example, one should not shoot one's neighbor to bring "peace" to the neighborhood. That is, when both good and evil remote effects follow from a person's act, care must be taken that one does not seek to use the evil effect as a means to obtain the intended good effect. Even though the evil remote effect may be anticipated, it cannot be intended in any way, but merely tolerated. The evil effect must either follow the good effect or occur simultaneously; it cannot precede the good effect (Ashley & O'Rourke, 1997, p. 191). For example, the therapist provides the woman and daughter filial therapy, which is a significant good. However, in the process, the therapist also foresees that as the relationship with her daughter improves, the woman might become alienated from her husband, who declined to participate in therapy. This alienation is an evil secondary effect. For the therapist, however, this foreseen bad effect is out of his control, unintended, and causally remote enough from the therapy that he is providing. And of course, the bad effect might not even happen.

Finally, we must use practical wisdom to understand whether the circumstances are important moral conditions that clarify the object of the act (Aquinas, 1273/1981, I-II, 18.10). Practical wisdom must also assure that the foreseen and desirable good effect is greater than or equal to the foreseen yet merely tolerated evil effect (Ashley & O'Rourke, 1997, p. 191–193). This double-effect principle relates to practical reasoning about the circumstances of an action; one must recognize who is affected by the action and what moral difference one's life-callings make. Concerning the above-mentioned example of the woman seeking filial therapy, she should rationally consider the circumstances. She should consider how her marital vocation (married with three children), her work calling (air traffic controller), and where she needs to be (out of the home until midnight) relate to the remote effects, both the intended good results of working hard (salary, job satisfaction) and also the unintended bad results of working hard (having less time for her husband, daughter, and other children, and socio-religious practices).

As a final point in relation to moral double effect, consideration must be given also to those circumstances under which a person may still be morally responsible for unintended bad consequences even when the aforementioned four principles are satisfied. First, a person should act in a way involving neither negligence nor the kind of culpable ignorance that is present when a person fails to educate himself as he ought when he responds to a vocational calling (for example, a father may be culpable for his child's unforeseen and unintended death if the father's ignorance is the result of negligence or

of a failure to acquire obligatory healthcare information) (CCC, 2000, §1736). With new vocational commitments come obligatory vocational responsibilities. Furthermore, a person should always take due care to avoid any unintended bad effects where such can be avoided; failure to choose a safer or better course of action when such is available may also result in the imputation of some amount of culpability for unintended bad effects (as, for example, when a woman who is pregnant takes an abortifacient medicine, though she does not intend the abortion, when an alternate medication is available to take that is not abortifacient) (CCC, 2000, §1737; Aquinas, 1273/1981, I–II, 18.5). Last, whenever one acts in a reckless or imprudent manner and selects a means disproportionate to the intended end (as when a person ingests a substantive dose of an opiate only to alleviate a mild headache), this too may occasion moral responsibility regardless of that person's intention (Aquinas, 1273/1981, I–II, 19.8; II-II, 64.7).

How Might We Be Morally Responsible for Evil Done by Someone Else?

A further type of moral double effect concerns a person's involvement in a bad decision or evil thing that is done by someone else. This situation is often called the problem of "cooperation in moral evil," but it must also be seen in the light of the possible involvement in the good done by others as well (Table 16.4). For example, we may, wittingly or not, become involved in the dishonesty, disrespect for life, or violence done by another person. When we, as mental health professionals, face the issue of how we are involved in the good and the evil actions of others, we need to ask: Are there good reasons (comparing the good done and the evil that might occur) for supporting and treating a person whose decisions and behavior are unethical?

Table 16.3. Analysis of an Action that Has Both Good and Evil Effects
(Principle of Double Effect) with Example of Self-Defense

Action must be good	• Rationally specified. • Morally fitting to the intended good end. • Appealing to the pertinent moral norms. • Not intrinsically evil. • *For example, the use of force to rebuff an attacker (good action) protecting a child's life (good effect) and injuring the attacker (unintended bad effect).*
Intention must be good	• Aim at the good of the person. • Motivate the particular action. • Serve to measure the fittingness of the action. • Not seek the evil effect. • Only tolerate the bad effect. • Avoid the bad effect as possible. • *For example, a good intention would aim at protecting the child.*
Good effect must not be the result of evil effect	• The evil effects must not be immediately causally connected to the moral object of the action. • An evil means is not justified by a good intention or goal. • *For example, the good effect of the action of protecting the child's life is independent of the evil effect of injuring the assailant*
Practical wisdom must be used to discern effects	• Practical wisdom is used for moral discernment. • The good effects are morally greater than or equal to the evil effects. • This judgment of reason is not moral proportionalism. • Use of moral norms: natural and divine law, nature of person and family, vocational responsibilities, professional ethics, and so on. • Consideration of the influence on vocational responsibilities. • *For example, the life of the innocent child (or adult) has intrinsic value, as does the life of the assailant; a father or mother should protect his or her child from danger.*

Sources for the rationale behind Table 16.3: Ashley & O'Rourke, 1997; Austriaco, 2011; *CCC*, 2000, §§1750–1754; John Paul II, 1993, §§71–80; Vatican II, 1965, §27. See also Table 16.2 on the Three Sources of Morality.

In the midst of a discussion of evil and sin, we need to outline the limits and criteria for permitting our cooperation in the evil that is primarily done by another person (Ashley & O'Rourke, 1997, pp. 193–199; Austriaco, 2011 pp. 263–275; Congregation for the Doctrine of the Faith, 2008; Di Camillo, 2013). More is needed than simply identifying moral principles and exercising prudence (prudential personalism) in order to make a moral decision about cooperating with evil (Aquinas, 1273/1981, II-II, 50.1–4). In addition to considering our intention (why we do something), our actions (what we do), and the circumstances of our actions (including our vocational responsibilities) (John Paul II, 1993; *CCC*, 2000, §1750), we must recognize

Figure 16.2. Involvement in Evil Action of Others

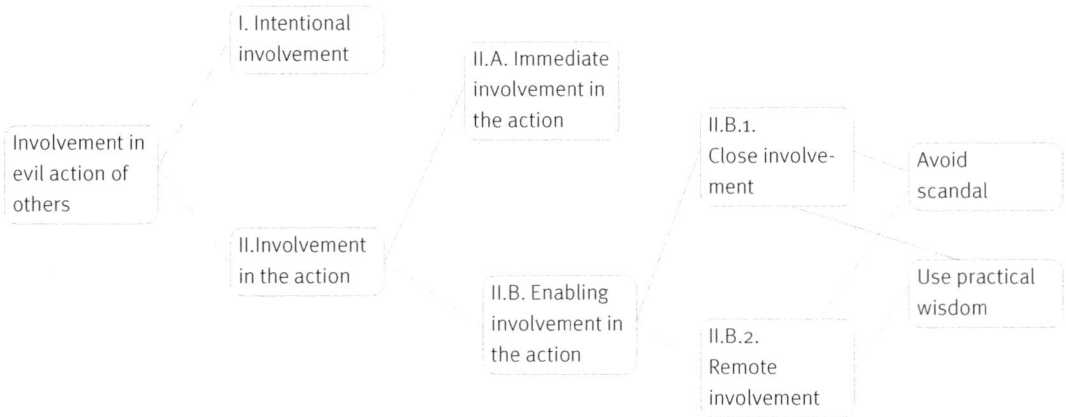

that moral actions often have both good and evil effects. In order to assess the effects of cooperating in the actions of others, we must again take into consideration all of the moral double effect criteria discussed above (Ashley & O'Rourke, 1997, pp. 191–193).

Furthermore, legitimate cooperation in the evil of others (1) should be an involvement only in the action (*material* cooperation) and never an intentional involvement (*formal* agreement) with the evil intention of the primary agent; (2) should be at most a *mediate* or nonessential involvement in the action and never an *immediate* or essential cooperation, which participates in the performance of the action; (3) should seek to avoid *scandal*; (4) should be as causally *remote* from the evil as possible; (5) should give *good reasons* for the involvement; (6) should also recognize that a purist approach that avoids any kind of association with an individual who does evil may well err at the other extreme: the

omission of good effects resulting from the cooperation.

The basic structure of moral responsibility, which calls upon the three sources of morality and the principles for dealing with moral double effect (discussed in previous sections), must be expanded when addressing the possible cooperation in the evil done by others in a clinical setting. The clinician must intend and do the good act of fulfilling his vocational requirements, which includes respecting the client as a child of God and as created in the image of God. The clinician must also support the client in her life-callings and must affirm her in a therapeutic alliance toward healing. This support for the client can be done without intending what the client might intend or doing what the client may do, if her intention and act is unethical or harmful. Furthermore, the clinician will seek to avoid scandal by voicing opposition to immoral action (Figure 16.2 and Table 16.4).

The above analysis offers distinctions that are useful to the understanding of a therapist's involvement with clients who intend to perform evil actions or who are habitually involved in immoral actions, which are beyond the particular focus of therapy. First, Catholic Christian therapists have a calling to heal. To achieve as much good as possible, it will often be necessary to be associated with and support people without intending or doing the evil that they may intend and do (the classic example being Jesus' frequent involvement with people known to be sinners). Concerns about the non-intended involvement in the evil done by another person (material involvement) need not stop one from being involved in good actions that are done as well. Simple association with people who are known to have broken the civil or moral law does not make one guilty of their crimes or sin (unless there is collusion). As mentioned above, there are possibilities of licit association with a person and unique opportunities for good in the clinical setting of supporting the person as a child of God in need of care and healing. For example, married spouses who are struggling to remain together after one spouse has committed repeated infidelities may need to strengthen their communication skills as well as work on forgiveness. The therapist will need to support the couple therapeutically and aid them (through experience-based practices, such as relationship enhancement techniques) to discern the value of their marriage commitment. They will also need to understand better the negative short- and long-term consequences of continued infidelities as well as what impact divorce would have upon them as persons and also on their children. There is a risk, though, that the unfaithful spouse may use these new skills to continue to commit acts of infidelity. The therapist can, however, work to support the couple therapeutically without agreeing with any immoral intentions, decisions, or behaviors. The therapist will also want to protect his or her own conscience, by informing the clients about his or her moral positions (when fitting), since letting the client know about one's opposition to divorce or infidelity may help to avoid scandal.

The need to be associated with people who do bad things is inevitable but not obvious. For example, Jesus associated himself with tax collectors and sinners, and even calls himself their friend (Mt 9:10–11; Lk 7:34; CCC, 2000, §554). His aim was not only to truly love all people, but to announce the Kingdom of God—a call to conversion and the forgiveness of sins (Mt 26:28; Lk 15:7). St. Augustine (ca. 423/1956), also, distinguished persons from their deeds, calling for a love of all people and a hatred of all sin (p. 46). Such authoritative examples further confirm that there are reasons and principled ways to seek non-compromising and non-scandalous involvement with other people, without excusing the bad choices and evil that may be done by the other.

How Does Mental Health Practice Influence Responsibility?

Some people have criticized mental health professionals for providing excuses for willful misdeeds and for extending a deterministic viewpoint on human agency. However, from a Catholic Christian perspective, therapy and counseling have multiple roles. When working with clients, therapists must look to the past, identify the source of disorder and remove undue blame, but not in a deterministic or reductionist way. This "negative psychology" must explore how a person's action may be due to past traumas and motives, of which a person may not be aware, since the person is influenced by childhood and prior experience. However, therapists

Table 16.4. Discerning the Moral Involvement in Evil Acts Done by Others, with Brief Examples

Preliminary principles for understanding moral involvement in evil acts done by others:

- Use practical wisdom to discern the morality of the situation and the good to be attained.*

- Identify vocational responsibilities, and apply CCMMP moral principles to the clinical task (for example, the three sources of morality and the principle of double effect).

- Offer therapeutic support to the client, but recognize supporting a client therapeutically does not require one morally to endorse or affirm every choice or action of a client.

- Consult the relavent professional code of ethics (APA or ACA) regarding how to interact with the client.

- Avoid scandal and distance oneself from the evil done by the other person.†

- Depending on the level of involvement, there must be good or even grave reasons to be associated with an evil act done by another person.

A. Intentional Involvement (Formal Cooperation): Being intentionally involved in the evil act that someone else is undertaking; affirming the end or means chosen by the other person—for example, a pro-choice therapist encouraging a client to have an abortion. This type of cooperation is always illicit.

B. Involvement in the Action (Material Cooperation): Not intending or affirming the evil that the other person is doing, but being involved in some way that helps the person who does the immoral acts—for example, providing therapy for a woman who has stated that she intends to have an abortion. There are multiple types of material cooperation; some are licit, some are not.

1. Immediate Involvement in the Action (Immediate Material Cooperation): Being immediately involved in the evil act of the other person and making the act possible even though one does not agree with the evil act—for example, a pro-life therapist (bracketing his own ethical principles) supporting and encouraging a client's decision to have an abortion. This type of cooperation is always illicit.

2. Enabling Involvement in the Action (Mediate Material Cooperation): Being involved in a way more or less causally proximate or remote from the immoral act, but still enabling the act to occur in some way, while not agreeing with the evil act. There are two types of mediate material cooperation; their licitness depends upon their circumstances.

a. Close Involvement (Proximate Mediate Material Cooperation): Being closely involved with the act, but not necessary for its completion—for example, facilitating a therapy session for a pregnant couple (Bob and Betty) both of whom have stated in the last therapy session that they find the conception of their child untimely, since they both wanted to pay off debts and get promo-

tions before having a child. Betty has stated that she wants an abortion and will not change her mind. However, she wants psychological help to feel better about the abortion, and she wants Bob's agreement as well. The therapist hopes that facilitating a fuller discussion between the couple (without supporting the wife's desire to have an abortion) will result in their deciding together to keep the child. Proximate mediate material cooperation may be illicit (if there is not a serious reason for the involvement). For the act to be licit, the therapist must have a viable and serious reason for involvement (such as realizing that if the couple goes to a pro-choice therapist, they may well be influenced to elect to abort). Also, the therapist must have good intentions: the act must be aimed at (a) the goodness of keeping the child and (b) strengthening the marital bond. The act must have a good object: the therapist must be able (a) to lead the couple to explore keeping the child and (b) to faciliate a discussion that will strengthen the marital bond.

(table continues)

b. Remote Involvement (Remote Mediate Material Cooperation): Keeping a significant causal distance from the immoral act, for example, facilitating a therapy session for a pregnant couple (Carter and Cathy) both of whom stated in the last therapy session that they find the conception untimely, since they both wanted to pay off debts and get promotions before having a child. Cathy moreover has stated that she is confused but believes that she wants an abortion. Carter has stated that he wants to keep the child. They would like to see the therapist again before making a final decision.

The therapist hopes to help the couple discern a way to keep the child. This case may be easier to discern as licit involvement (than the case of Bob and Betty), since Carter does not want an abortion and Cathy has not stated a commitment to have one. Nonetheless, Cathy and even Carter may come away from the therapy session deteremined to have an abortion. Therefore, the therapist must use practical wisdom in leading the session. Furthermore, the therapist will need to be careful in both types of involvement not to cause scandal.

---

* Practical Wisdom: To make licit a proximate mediate material involvement (case of Bob and Betty) or a remote material involvement (Carter and Cathy) with the evil that is done by another person, reasons should be identified as to how good is being defended and evil is being avoided in the particular instance. There must be a grave and serious reason for proximate involvement and a good reason for remote involvement. In both these cases, the therapist can must foresee the different possibilities that may play into a couple's deciding not to keep the child or that may tend to compromise their marital bond.

† Avoid Scandal: Danger of scandal may also cause mediate material involvement to become illicit. As for the above examples, there is the possibity that people be scandalized by a therapist's involvement in such a case. The therapist will want to avoid scandal by voicing opposition to the immoral action. In Carter and Cathy's case, the therapist could state his or her conscientious objection to the act as immoral. Such statements are best done in the context of ongoing informed consent.

Sources for the rationale behind the above presentation: Ashley & O'Rourke, 1997 (pp. 195–199); Austriaco, 2011 (pp. 263–275); Congregation for the Doctrine of the Faith, 1997, 2008; Di Camillo, 2013.

should not create a sense of victimhood in the client or look only at the past (Vitz, 2005). The effect of good therapy is to release patients from a pathological deterministic path and therefore to increase their freedom.

Psychology and mental health practice must also look to the potential freedom and responsibility that can be found in the midst of limitations. While the client may first self-refer for therapy because of intrusive symptoms and because of the desire to overcome problems that have made life painful, a Catholic Christian approach to mental health seeks, like most psycho-

therapy, to uncover the causes of the symptoms. Furthermore, as supporting a "positive psychotherapy" or a goal-driven (teleological) view of the person, the CCMMP also addresses the horizons of flourishing, freedom, and responsibility, as well as the spiritual freedom and grace that open up in therapy. Therapy awakens, and responds to, the client's desire for greater freedom to pursue faithfully the commitments and vocations that constitute pathways to flourishing. The psychotherapist thus intends not only to treat disorders and promote freedom from pathology, but also to increase flourishing and freedom for responsible thinking, choosing, feeling, and relating to other people (Ashley, 2013). In short, the therapist might say: "Now, with my help, you understand your problem. And now, also, with my help, what are you going to do about it?"

What Are the Limits of Responsibility and Accountability?

From an ethical and a theological perspective, such as that provided by the Catholic Christian Meta-Model of the Person, one can ask whether seeking to heighten people's awareness of their moral accountability might give them a disordered sense of personal guilt. While open honesty and condemnation of certain acts may be needed at many levels, St. Paul in his letter to the Romans (Chapter 7) humbly recognizes his own culpability. More than a personal confession, though, he identifies a troubling human tendency to do wrong, even the wrong that one does not want to do. St. Paul says: "For I know that nothing good dwells within me, that is, in my flesh. I can will what is right, but I cannot do it. For I do not do the good I want, but the evil I do not want is what I do" (Rom 7:18–19). His theological perspective leads him to affirm that lingering effects of sin can trouble a person at embodied, psychological, and spiritual levels.

He is, however, also hopeful for the power of God to help each person. In his writings, he frequently exhorts members of those early Christian communities to live moral and spiritual lives, to be responsible for themselves and each other (Gal 5; Eph 6 & 7). To take responsibility for one's acts, one must discern and judge what is right or wrong and who is responsible. Knowledge of culpability, in this Christian perspective, should become a turning point or an opportunity for change. To take responsibility for oneself,

one's family, and one's larger commitments is both to uphold justice and to seek to right our wrongs and bring about reconciliation. But what is the difference between condemning an act (one's own included) and condemning a person for his or her acts?

While one can distinguish good acts from evil behavior, and while the rule of law will need to bring wrongdoers to justice, no one has the right to condemn the soul of any human person (*CCC*, 2000, §1861). Even people who have done evil retain their basic human dignity. There remains the reality that they are created by God and loved by God. This Christian perspective (Lk 6:37; Rom 14:10–12; Jas 4:12) is exemplified in Jesus's treatment of the woman caught in the act of adultery. First, Christ does make obvious the fact that humans are responsible for sin (Jn 8:10–11). Yet without condemning the person or condoning the deed, he expresses an affirmation and an exhortation: "Neither do I condemn you; go, and do not sin again" (Jn 8:11). Furthermore, there is the responsibility that we have to help a brother or sister who is doing wrong (Mt 18:15). Such fraternal correction, which when done in truth, humility, and charity, can serve not only the person in question, but also his family and community.

What Are the Therapist's Moral Responsibilities in Professional Settings?

The above-mentioned moral insights and principles require special attention when being prudentially applied in professional settings. In the CCMMP perspective, like that of many other approaches, mental health and other professional settings have therapeutic, ethical, and transcendent dimensions. Each school of thought explicitly or implicitly stands on a worldview and value system that comprises a set of presuppositions (Ashley, 2000; Bergin, 1980; Ellis, 1980; Hicks, 2014; O'Donohue, 2013; Parrott, 1999; Smith, 1978). Some schools provide frames for understanding the person through the lenses of psychology and therapy (therapeutic orientation), the moral nature of existence (natural moral law), and a faith-based approach to the person and God (divine law). Even those schools that deny universal human nature (materialist reductionism), and deny the common foundation for natural moral law (moral relativism), and deny the existence of an ultimate end of life (secular atheism) require their own type of implicit ultimate viewpoint. Because of such presuppositions, there is no value-neutral approach to the mental health sciences.

Worldviews and value systems, furthermore, influence therapeutic and moral applications (Hamilton, 2013; Miller, 2001; Vohs & Schooler, 2008). In the clinical setting, for instance, the timing and context of therapy must first be focused on the client's safety and therapeutic progress. Without imposing values, therapists seek to help the client to attain his or her therapeutic goals, as well as moral progress and true freedom. It would be ethically reductionist and unjust to deny the importance of moral issues in therapy. Even the attention to the client's safety (in cases such as suicidal ideas, cutting, or eating disorders) is rooted in an objective view of the person, professional ethics, and natural moral law. Moreover, a client's psychological health and spiritual well-being are both closely interrelated, as seen in the therapeutic benefit of empathy and forgiveness and in the ethical and religious benefit of love and mercy. The therapist will seek to aid clients in healing and growth through a gradual therapeutic transformation, which will help them to live out more freely their true callings and moral responsibilities (John Paul II, 1981, §34; 1993, §119; see also Ashley, 2013; Hoffman, 2001; Kolodziejczak, 2006; Sodergren, 2009; Wachtel, 2013; see also Chapter 11, "Fulfilled in Virtue" and Chapter 18, "Fallen").

Self-Determination

Each person has some capacity to shape his own life. Through intentional acts, either good or bad, he shapes his moral and spiritual character. Nonetheless, each person is neither alone in shaping his character nor predisposed to just one possible life outcome.

How Can I Change Who I Am?

Psychological studies have shown that although our family members, neighbors, and culture influence us, we are not strictly determined genetically (i.e., hardwired) nor environmentally (i.e., softwired) (Doidge, 2007). Nevertheless, our nature, surroundings, and past influence the present and the future by constituting more or less enduring traits of our interpersonal dispositions of mind, will, and emotion. For example, when a person has lied repeatedly, that person is more likely to be dishonest in the future. And even when people try to stop lying (or try to change any negative disposition), many may regress or recidivate, because their character is difficult to change after repeating maladaptive behaviors or even because of a biologically based disorder.

The importance of choice becomes all the more evident when we realize that by repeating a particular type of choice (not only high profile negative and addictive ones, but also healthy and good ones), we acquire some facility at making such a choice again. This type of limited self-determination is facilitated through our conscious intentions, as well as our personal, cultural, and religious practices, which shape our volitional capacities. Indeed, there is now general psychological support for affirming the human potential to make significant positive change (Amen, 1998; Beauregard, 2004: Beauregard & O'Leary, 2008; Doidge, 2007; Seligman, 1993); such potential can be seen in a change in men's response to pornography (Beauregard, Lévesque, and Bourgouin, 2001), in women's voluntary suppression of sadness (Lévesque et al., 2003), and in persons' acquiring virtue by exercising acts of will (Peterson & Seligman, 2004). As Seligman (2002) says: "To be a virtuous person is to display, by acts of will, all or at least most of the six ubiquitous virtues" (p. 137).

How Is Freedom a Goal to Be Pursued?

The classical philosophical perspective and that of the Meta-Model are nuanced about free will, in positing that we are free, yet limited. Contrary arguments against human freedom often take an all-or-nothing stance: Humans are absolutely free, or we are machines. Freedom, however, is a gift to all, which, through the development of virtue and our responses to our vocational calls, expands as we become more morally and spiritual mature (Pinckaers, 1995). Such growth in true freedom requires that we face our limitations, weakness of will, and lack of resources. Within the notion of a bounded freedom, the very exercise of relative self-control (autonomy, self-determinacy, and flourishing) evidences not only free will but also the need to develop this motivational capacity to seek the goods that are consistent with what it is to be a human being (Aristotle, ca. 350 BC/1941a). Admittedly, our decisions and behaviors can be overridden by undesired compulsions, intrusive thinking, or

overpowering emotions, or they can be blocked by external force. Obsessive compulsive disorders, for example, reduce a person's capacity to act freely. Moreover, external violence, fear, ignorance, passion, weakness of will, and addiction can impede the exercise of one's own decisions (Dunnington, 2010). Nonetheless, we are not, for the most part, completely dominated by these conditions. Rather, we have reasons to hope that people can develop a freedom for excellence in due time with the help of family, friends, religious community, psychologists and counselors, and God (Pinckaers, 1995, 2005). We will more fully discuss limitations to human freedom in the last section of this chapter.

How Do We "Create" Ourselves? And What Part Does God Play?

Using a paradoxical image, St. Gregory of Nyssa says that in a certain manner we "create … ourselves as we will, by our decisions" (ca. 390/1978, II.2–3). He explains that, in a sense, we are our own parents, introducing a mixture of good and evil into our habitual dispositions. However, this limited type of self-determination is influenced by us and by other human beings, where we are co-responsible for good (with the help of divine grace), and we are morally responsible for evil (on our own and because of the influence of others).

God is continuously involved in the life and formation of each person. Recognizing that through spiritual sacrifice a person becomes holy and acceptable to God, St. Paul exhorts the Christians in his letter to the Romans: "Do not be conformed to this world but be transformed by the renewal of your mind, that you may prove what is the will of God, what is good and acceptable and perfect" (Rom 12:2). God does not force himself upon us, but rather aids our efforts at flourishing in the present and gives us a foretaste of ultimate flourishing and goodness. At two levels, through nature and graced-nature, God calls and enables us to participate in goodness, existence, family and social life, as well as truth and beauty. All of these ways of participating in goodness involve types of love, as we shall now see.

Creativity

Human intelligence and will are one source of human creativity. The attractive nature of reality, which engenders a sense of wonder, meaning, and beauty, is another source. Human creativity, furthermore, is born of necessity and of leisure, both of which can serve the highest and the most ordinary ends and purposes. The importance of creativity can be seen in procreation, artistic contributions, conflict resolution in interpersonal relationships, entrepreneurial innovations, scientific and technological advances, problem solving at social and communal levels, as well as in everyday playfulness and humor. Finally, God's unique capacity to create from nothing (*ex nihilo*) is the basis for all other types of creativity.

Is Creativity Necessarily Good?

Although creative talents are often used for good, they can also be used for evil. In our creativity we can inadvertently damage other goods. We pursue one approach while destroying or displacing a source of goodness, as when technology promotes the loss of face-to-face contact. We use creativity to design massively destructive means to protect ourselves, such as nuclear warheads. There are notable examples of humans who have used their talents and political genius for evil and antisocial ends in the name of a seemingly prosocial agenda. Examples include Adolf Hitler and Joseph Stalin. Moreover, some studies have identified a positive correlation between creativity and immorality (Simonton, 2004), even claiming that "creativity can lead people to behave unethically" (Riddle, 2012, para. 3). The studies suggest that a dispositional creativity used to justify one's behavior can lead to unethical acts, such as dishonesty and cheating (Gino & Ariely, 2012). Likewise, a person might rationalize doing unethical things in the name of such ingenuity or originality ("it is good for business;" "it is needed to save the nation").

However, we would posit that the positive correlation between creativity and immorality, suggested in such studies, is not due to any creative potential itself. The gift of creativity, like the gift of free will, helps us to truly flourish only when used in the light of truth and for the sake of the good. On the contrary, the use of creativity can be deformed by pride, hatred, greed, and other antisocial motives, as well as by ignorance. At the same time, the capacity to imagine unethical actions or to rationalize evil behavior does not determine the individual to carry out the misdeed, no matter how seemingly glorious or original. Importantly, commitment to truth, goodness, justice, and love serves as ethical protection against the misuse of freedom and creativity, especially for those who are rooted in both duty and virtue, and who seek the prosocial help of others and the grace of God (see also Chapter 15, "Rational," the section on Beauty).

What Is Unique About God as Creator?

Humans are creative and are recognized as such. Almost by necessity, works created by humans draw attention to their author or creator. Anonymous masterpieces are rare. Likewise, the beauty and order in the cosmos are masterpieces. They speak of an author (Wis 13:5). Nonetheless, this analogy and conclusion is foreign to the New Atheists (Dawkins, 2008; Dennett, 1991, 2006), as stated earlier. Reflecting on the creativity of the human will always lead back to a consideration of the uniqueness and primacy of the creativity of God. The uniqueness of God as Creator is often lost in arguments about whether the universe can be explained better by referring to chance, and humanity by evolution and natural selection, or whether the universe can be explained better by referring to creation, design, and purpose (Schönborn, 2007; Życiński, 2006). There are significant philosophical and theological cases being made that a materialist, neo-Darwinian evolutionary approach fails to explain human freedom, mind (rational intellect), and transcendence (Nagel, 2012; McGrath, 2011; Życiński, 2006). Moreover, positive constructive approaches are calling upon the sciences and philosophy to provide a basis for understanding the possibility of a unique cause and absolute end to reality. Nonetheless, there are agnostics (Nagel, 2012), Catholics (Feser, 2017; Ratzinger, 2002; Schönborn, 2007; Spitzer, 2010; Życiński, 2006), evangelicals (McGrath, 2011), and others, who, through the study of the cosmos, using biology, physics, other sciences, and philosophy, have reasoned that there must be an absolute source of the universe, which some of them call God.

It is a biblical view that God's capacity to bring things and people into being from nothing (*ex nihilo*) is absolutely unique (Aquinas, 1273/1981, I, 45.5 & 65.3). As the first transcendent cause, God created the goodness of the universe and the existence of each person (Hütter, 2012, p. 200). Nonetheless, God gives to humans the ability to participate freely in a type of co-creative agency and stewardship. The book of Genesis, for example, reports that God created the universe and mankind and that what God created was "very good" (Gen 1:31). Analogically, humans are able to envisage new things and produce them in a way that participates in a type of the divine creativity of God, who has given a mission to mankind: "Be fruitful and multiply, and fill the earth and subdue it" (Gen 1:28). This calling to a kind of creativity that reflects the creativity of God implies responsible stewardship over the earth and the promotion of justice among people (Gen 2:15). Thus, human creativity serves the physical, psychological, and spiritual needs of mankind and the earth, as mentioned earlier.

Limitations

Although free in significant ways, humans experience disconcerting limitations to our freedom and self-control. We intend to do one thing yet actually do another. We speak out for justice yet fail to be fair. We vote for programs to help the poor yet do not evaluate whether the programs truly benefit those in need. We often will something good yet are unwilling to sacrifice to obtain it. We promote care and concern in public yet lack it in the family. There are the personal disorders, the self-serving biases, the social pressures, and the effects of sin that we encounter as so many reasons for inconsistency and as causes that restrict our flourishing.

What Are the Limits to Human Freedom?

There are many acquired negative factors that limit freedom, which have been charted in different terms. First, there are *physical and biological* problems and disorders, such as physical disabilities and injuries. Second, there are *psychological* problems and disorders, such as depression, anxiety, and compulsion, which occur on a spectrum ranging from common difficulties to full-fledged psychopathology. Third, there are the *political and economic* limits that are hidden in political pressure and economic policy that serve a *de facto* standard of "political correctness" instead of the civil common good. Last, there are the *ethical and spiritual* problems, such as the effects of sin and vice: pride, jealousy, hatred, indifference, and so on. Of course, there are other limitations, such as our existential finitude (we are not eternal) or the historical-cultural character of our experience (we are born and die at particular times and places), and so on.

An integrated philosophical view of the person will seek to identify these levels as well as the moral character and interpersonal skills needed for ultimate flourishing. It will seek also to recognize the weaknesses and disorders that challenge such flourishing.

What Are the Nature and Levels of the Will's Involvement in Self-Control?

As stated earlier, the biological, psychological, and sociological sciences speak of the will in terms of volition, free will, willpower, self-control, self-regulation, executive function, or motivation. Psychology now conceptualizes the factors that lead to the failure of the will in terms of ego depletion (Baumeister, Sparks, Stillman, & Vohs, 2008), limited resources (Vohs et al., 2008), quality of motivation (Muraven, 2012), lack of self-care and compassion fatigue (Figley, 2002), and limited physical energy stores or physical fatigue (Inzlicht & Schmeichel, 2012). Recent studies provide evidence that

self-control can be strengthened or replenished by the following factors: rest and positive affect or emotion (Baumeister, 2002); positive mood (induced by humor or receiving gifts) (Tice, Baumeister, Shmueli, & Muraven, 2007), implicit positive emotion and rest, (Ren, Hu, Zhang, & Huang, 2010), as well as rest and exposure to nature (Chow & Lau, 2015). We might propose other factors for strengthening self-control, such as interpersonal-vocational commitments, models and mentors, values and virtues (hope), and contemplation.

The resource model of self-control presupposes that exerting the will serves to deplete the limited resources needed for free and consistent acts (Hagger et al., 2010). The limits to willpower can be understood in terms of the resources that a person needs to have on hand to make free decisions correctly and coherently. The aforementioned studies focused on three bases that support willpower: incentives (motivation), training (self-control practices), and physical energy (measured by glucose levels). The ongoing research continues to investigate the types and levels of resources needed to act freely and make sound judgments. Relatedly, psychological research on willpower demonstrates that task performance is affected by certain beliefs regarding willpower. For example, Job, Dweck, and Walton (2010) found that, when fatigued or when resource-depleted, participants who believed that willpower is not a limited resource tended to perform the same or better on a subsequent task compared to those who believed that willpower is limited.

From the philosophical view of the Meta-Model, these studies suggest important findings as well as limitations to the research. First, it would be important to differentiate the type of self-control that is exerted and the way in which the will is involved. Experiments on self-control in consumer behavior or eating habits do not often identify underlying moral choices and spiritual commitments. We would expect more coherence in choices that involve explicit personal and religious conviction, based on moral and spiritual principles and long-term goals, than in choices that involve fashion or consumer behaviors driven by changing vogues and economic pressures. In contrast to relativist assumptions, a value-rich goal will motivate more than an incidental one. For example, goals linked to interpersonal commitments, ethical principles, and spiritual aims are more likely to motivate than goals linked to less vital commitments. Research on hope and goal-setting has found that human action required that goals be identified, pathways to those goals be found, and agency be initiated along the pathways to the goals (Rand & Cheavens, 2009; Snyder, 1994).

Second, under concern for self-care, the psychotherapy and counseling literature addresses not only the limits of personal resources used in expressing compassion to those in need or making decisions while under stress, but also the phenomena of finding, strengthening, and restoring one's resources. Such research on self-care also illustrates the psychological side of the ethical considerations and spiritual principles about the need for rest, leisure, and worship (Ex 20:8–11; Pieper, 1952/2009). Third, the Meta-Model leads us to investigate what difference is found when we understand the limits of human freedom but also the limitations in our other human capacities.

Furthermore, developmental and clinical issues influence self-control. Continual growth in secure attachment (Bowlby, 1982, 1988) and in dispositions of self-control (Erikson, 1994, p. 109) is important for everyone. We may experience immature levels of skills and capacities as a result of our genetic heritage, our family and environment, and our particular choices. Moreover, there are acquired disordered dispositions or clinical phenomena or pathologies that influence the will and need remediation or healing, such as attention-deficit / hyperactivity disorders; obsessive-compulsive disorders; disruptive, impulse-control, and conduct disorders; and substance-related and addictive disorders (American Psychiatric Association, 2013).

Self-knowledge and diagnosis can lead to overcoming some of these limitations through intervention and treatment. Knowing that we are deficient in self-control can be a step toward initiating practices and finding proper support—in family, friends, or therapy—to manage better our desires for wealth, recognition, and pleasure. Being diagnosed as suffering from social anxiety disorder, for example, can be a step toward committing oneself to treatment, which will strengthen one's courage to face fears.

At the same time, wisdom and insight are needed to recognize which limitations must be accepted and how to change our perspective on them. Such insights about limitations apply also to the world of personal work and resource management, where practical wisdom is needed to know how to find meaning in one's job and be generous regardless of one's situation.

The current secular models of diagnostic criteria, furthermore, offer insights into biological, psychological, and sociological pathologies (American Psychiatric Association, 2013; World Health Organization, 2015). However, as the positive psychology movement has argued, a purposeful schema for understanding human flourishing is needed as a complement for such secular models. The Meta-Model's integrative approach, for its part, broadens the context for understanding the nature of human limitations and potential for freedom, inasmuch as it offers a psychological, philosophical, and theological vision of the person. The Meta-Model explicitly offers moral norms and identifies the place of the family and community in adjudicating moral principles and cooperating in mutual spiritual support.

How Is Spiritual Strength Found by Recognizing Weakness?

As a closing note, we will consider the exercise of the will with a faith-based focus. From a theological perspective that uses psychological insights and ethical principles, we can revisit St. Paul's account of his own struggles with weakness, sin, and evil and his experience that strength is perfected in infirmity. In his description of inner struggle, he says: "For I do not do the good I want, but the evil I do not want is what I do" (Rom 7:19). This sense of helplessness is contrasted with the vocation to the life of the Spirit that, through the grace of God, gives peace and righteousness (Rom 8:9–11).

This life of grace is the divine gift that provides strength in weakness. This gift also underlies the virtues needed to do good and to reject evil. After requesting the healing of his own weakness, St. Paul receives a message from God: "My grace is sufficient for you, for my power is made perfect in weakness" (2 Cor 12:9). This assurance gives Paul a basis from which to acknowledge his own weaknesses, so that the power of Christ may rest upon him. His insight is not that human beings are incapable of good, but that we require the constant support of others, especially God, to be morally just and coherent. If we add the above-mentioned insights about the benefits of rest, leisure, and worship, we have the conceptual and affective tools to recognize fundamental goodness, as well as our limits, with true humility.

REFERENCES

Amen, D. G. (1998). *Change your brain, change your life*. New York, NY: Three Rivers Press.

American Psychiatric Association. (2013). *Diagnostic and statistical manual of mental disorders* (5th ed., text revision). Washington, DC: Author.

Aquinas, T. (1981). *Summa theologiae* (Fathers of the English Dominican Province, Trans.). Westminster, MD: Christian Classics. (Original work composed 1273)

Aristotle. (1941a). *Nicomachean ethics*. In R. McKeon (Ed.), *The basic works of Aristotle* (pp. 935–1112). New York, NY: Random House. (Original work composed ca. 350 BC)

Aristotle. (1941b). *On the soul*. In R. McKeon (Ed.), *The basic works of Aristotle* (pp. 535–606). New York, NY: Random House. (Original work composed ca. 350 BC)

Ashley, B. M. (2000). *Choosing a world-view and value-system: An ecumenical apologetics*. New York, NY: Alba House.

Ashley, B. M. (2013). *Healing for freedom: A Christian perspective on personhood and psychotherapy*. Arlington, VA: The Institute for the Psychological Sciences Press.

Ashley, B. M., & O'Rourke, K. D. (1997). *Health care ethics: A theological analysis* (4th ed.). Washington, DC: Georgetown University Press.

Augustine. (1956). Letter 211. Letter of Aurelius Augustine to the consecrated virgins. In W. Parsons (Trans.), *Letters 204–270: Volume V* (pp. 38–51). Washington, DC: The Catholic University of America Press. (Original work composed ca. 423)

Austriaco, N. P. G. (2011). *Biomedicine and beatitude: An introduction to Catholic bioethics*. Washington, DC: The Catholic University of America Press.

Bandura, A. (1997). *Self-efficacy: The exercise of control*. New York, NY: Freeman.

Bandura, A. (2001). Social cognitive theory: An agentic perspective. *Annual Review of Psychology, 52*, 1–26.

Bandura, A. (2006). Toward a psychology of human agency. *Perspectives on Psychological Science, 1*, 164–180.

Barkley, R. A. (2012). *Barkley deficits in executive*

function scale—Children and adolescents. New York, NY: Guilford Press

Baumeister, R. F. (2002). Ego depletion and self-control failure: An energy model of the self's executive function. *Self and Identity, 1*, 129–136.

Baumeister, R. F., Masicampo, E. J., & DeWall, C. N. (2009). Prosocial benefits of feeling free: Disbelief in free will increases aggression and reduces helpfulness. *Personality and Social Psychology Bulletin, 35*, 260–268.

Baumeister, R. F., & Tierney, J. (2011). *Willpower: Rediscovering the greatest human strength.* New York, NY: Penguin Press.

Baumeister, R. F., Sparks, E. A., Stillman, T. F., & Vohs, K. D. (2008). Free will in consumer behavior: Self-control, ego depletion, and choice. *Journal of Consumer Psychology, 18*, 4–13.

Beauregard, M. (Ed.) (2004). *Consciousness, emotional self-regulation, and the brain.* Amsterdam, Netherlands: John Benjamins.

Beauregard, M. (2012). *Brain wars: The scientific battle over the existence of the mind and the proof that will change the way we live our lives.* New York, NY: HarperCollins.

Beauregard, M., & O'Leary, D. (2008). *The spiritual brain: A neuroscientist's case for the existence of the soul.* New York, NY: HarperCollins.

Beauregard, M., Lévesque, J., & Bourgouin, P. (2001). Neural correlates of conscious self-regulation of emotion. *Journal of Neuroscience, 21*(18), RC 165. doi:10.1523/JNEUROSCI.21-18-j0001.2001

Beck, A. T. (1979). *Cognitive therapy and the emotional disorders.* New York, NY: Plume.

Benedict XVI. (2005). *Deus caritas est* [Encyclical, on Christian love]. Vatican City, Vatican: Libreria Editrice Vaticana.

Bennett, M. R., & Hacker, P. M. S. (2003). *Philosophical foundations of neuroscience.* Oxford, United Kingdom: Blackwell.

Berlin, I. (1958). *Two concepts of liberty.* Oxford, United Kingdom: Clarendon Press.

Berwick, R. C., & Chomsky, N. (2016). *Why only us: Language and evolution.* Cambridge, MA: MIT Press.

Bikerton, D. (2014). *More than nature needs: Language, mind, and evolution.* Cambridge, MA: Harvard University Press.

Bowlby, J. (1982). *Attachment and loss: Vol. 1. Attach-ment* (2nd ed.). New York, NY: Basic Books. (Original work published 1969)

Bowlby, J. (1988). *A secure base: Clinical applications of attachment theory.* London, United Kingdom: Routledge.

Brizendine, L. (2006). *The female brain.* New York, NY: Broadway Books.

Brizendine, L. (2010). *The male brain.* New York, NY: Broadway Books.

Calvin, J. (2002). *The bondage and liberation of the will* (G. I. Davies, Trans.). Grand Rapids, MI: Baker Books. (Original work published 1543)

Calvin, J. (2008). *Institutes of the Christian religion* (H. Beveridge, Trans.). Peabody, MA: Hendrickson. (Original work published 1536)

Catechism of the Catholic Church (CCC) (2nd ed.). (2000). Vatican City, Vatican: Libreria Editrice Vaticana.

Cessario, R. (2013). *Introduction to moral theology* (rev. ed.). Washington, DC: The Catholic University of America Press.

Chow, J. T., & Lau, S. (2015). Nature gives us strength: Exposure to nature counteracts ego-depletion. *The Journal of Social Psychology, 155*(1), 70–85.

Churchland, P. M. (1995). *The engine of reason, the seat of the soul: A philosophical journey into the brain.* Cambridge, MA: MIT Press.

Commission on Children at Risk. (2003). *Hardwired to connect: The new scientific case for authoritative communities.* New York, NY: Institute for American Values.

Congregation for the Doctrine of the Faith. (2008). *Dignitas personae* [Instruction on certain bioethical questions]. Vatican City, Vatican: Libreria Editrice Vaticana.

Cozolino, L. (2010). *The neuroscience of psychotherapy* (2nd ed.). New York, NY: Norton.

Cozolino, L. (2014). *The neuroscience of human relationships: Attachment and the developing social brain* (2nd ed.). New York, NY: Norton.

Dawkins, R. (2008). *The God delusion.* New York, NY: Mariner Books.

de Beauvoir, S. (2011). *The second sex.* New York, NY: Vintage. (Original work published 1949)

Democritus. (2010). *The atomists: Leucippus and Democritus: Fragments* (C. C. W. Taylor, Trans.). Toronto, Canada: Toronto University Press. (Original work composed ca. 370 BC)

Dennett, D. C. (1991). *Consciousness explained*. New York, NY: Little, Brown.

Dennett, D. C. (1995). *Darwin's dangerous idea: Evolution and the meanings of life*. New York, NY: Simon & Schuster.

Dennett, D. C. (2003). *Freedom evolves*. New York, NY: Viking Press.

Dennett, D. C. (2006). *Breaking the spell: Religion as a natural phenomenon*. New York, NY: Viking Press.

Di Camillo, J. A. (2013). Cooperation with moral evil: Forging collaborative arrangements. *Ethics and Medics, 38*(7), 1–4.

Doidge, N. (2007). *The brain that changes itself: Stories of personal triumph from the frontiers of brain science*. New York, NY: Penguin.

Dunnington, K. (2010). *Addiction and virtue: Beyond the models of disease and choice*. Downers Grove, IL: IVP Academic.

Ellis, A. (1980). Psychotherapy and atheistic values: A response to A. E. Bergin's "psychotherapy and religious values." *Journal of Consulting and Clinical Psychology, 48*(5), 635–639.

Ellis, A., & Ellis, D. J. (2011). *Rational emotive behavior therapy*. Washington, DC: American Psychological Association.

Enright, R. D., & Fitzgibbons, R. P. (2015). *Forgiveness therapy: An empirical guide for resolving anger and restoring hope*. Washington, DC: American Psychological Association.

Erikson, E. (1994). *Identity: Youth and crisis*. New York, NY: Norton. (Original work published 1968)

Feser, E. (2008). *The last superstition: A refutation of the New Atheism*. South Bend, IN: St. Augustine's Press.

Feser, E. (2017). *Five proofs of the existence of God*. San Francisco, CA: Ignatius.

Figley, C. R. (2002). Compassion fatigue: Psychotherapists' chronic lack of self care. *Journal of Clinical Psychology, 58*, 1433–1441. doi:10.1002/jclp.10090

Francis. (2015). *Laudato si'* [Encyclical, on care for our common home]. Vatican City, Vatican: Libreria Editrice Vaticana.

Frankl, V. E. (2006). *Man's search for meaning* (I. Lasch, Trans.). Boston, MA: Beacon Press. (Original work published 1959)

Freud, S. (1961). *Beyond the pleasure principle*. New York, NY: Norton. (Original work published 1915)

Freud, S. (2010). *Civilization and its discontents*. New York, NY: Norton. (Original work published 1930)

Gallagher, S. (2005a). *How the body shapes the mind*. Oxford, United Kingdom: Clarendon Press.

Gallagher, S. (2005b). Intentionality and intentional action. *Synethesis Philosophica, 40*, 319–326.

Gazzaniga, M. S. (2011). *Who's in charge?: Free will and the science of the brain*. New York, NY: HarperCollins.

George, R. P. (1995). *Making men moral: Civil liberties and public morality*. Oxford, United Kingdom: Clarendon Press.

Gino, F., & Ariely, D. (2012). The dark side of creativity: Original thinkers can be more dishonest. *Journal of Personality and Social Psychology, 102*, 445–459.

Gottman, J. M. (1999). *The marriage clinic: A scientifically based marital therapy*. New York, NY: Norton.

Gregory of Nyssa (1978). *The life of Moses* (A. Malherbe & E. Ferguson, Trans.). Mahwah, NJ: Paulist Press. (Original work composed ca. 390)

Hagger, M. S., Wood, C., Stiff, C., & Chatzisarantis, N. L. D. (2010). Ego depletion and the strength model of self-control: A meta-analysis. *Psychological Bulletin, 136*, 495–525.

Hamilton, R. (2013). The frustrations of virtue: The myth of moral neutrality in psychotherapy. *Journal of Evaluation in Clinical Practice, 19*(3), 485–492.

Hauser, M. D. (2006). *Moral minds: How nature designed our universal sense of right and wrong*. New York, NY: Ecco.

Hazan, C., & Shaver, P. (1987). Romantic love conceptualized as an attachment process. *Journal of Personality and Social Psychology, 25*, 511–524.

Hütter, R. (2012). *Dust bound for heaven: Explorations in the theology of Thomas Aquinas*. Grand Rapids, MI: Eerdmans.

Hicks, D. J. (2014). A new direction for science and values. *Synthese: an International Journal for Epistemology, Methodology and Philosophy of Science, 191*(14), 3271–3295.

Hittinger, R. (2007). *The first grace: Rediscovering the natural law in a post-Christian world*. Wilmington, DE: ISI Books.

Hobbes, T. (2008). *Leviathan*. Oxford, United Kingdom: Oxford Classics. (Original work published 1651)

Hoffman, M. L. (2001). *Empathy and moral develop-

ment: Implications for caring and justice. Cambridge, United Kingdom: Cambridge University Press.

Hoffmann, T. (2013). Free choices. In R. Cessario, C. S. Titus, & P. C. Vitz (Eds.), *Philosophical virtues and psychological strengths: Building the bridge* (pp. 117–138). Manchester, NH: Sophia Institute Press.

Hume, D. (2000). *A treatise of human nature.* Oxford, United Kingdom: Oxford University Press. (Original work published 1740)

Inzlicht, M., & Schmeichel, B. J. (2012). What is ego depletion? Toward a mechanistic revision of the resource model of self-control. *Perspectives on Psychological Science, 7,* 450–463.

James, W. (1981). *The principles of psychology.* Cambridge, MA: Harvard University Press. (Original work published 1890)

Job, V., Dweck, C. S., & Walton, G. M. (2010). Ego depletion—is it all in your head? Implicit theories about willpower affect self-regulation. *Psychological Science, 21*(11), 1686–1693. doi:10.1177/0956797610384745

John Paul II. (1981). *Familiaris consortio* [Apostolic exhortation, on the role of the Christian family in the modern world]. Vatican City, Vatican: Libreria Editrice Vaticana.

John Paul II. (1993). *Veritatis splendor* [Encyclical, on certain fundamental questions of the Church's moral teaching]. Vatican City, Vatican: Libreria Editrice Vaticana.

Johnson, E. L. (2010). *Psychology and Christianity: Five views.* Downers Grove, IL: IVP Academic.

Kahneman, D. (2011). *Thinking, fast and slow.* New York, NY: Farrar, Straus & Giroux.

Kolodziejczak, G. (2006). *Distortions of love as distortions of the self from a psychological perspective.* (Unpublished doctoral dissertation). Arlington, VA: Institute for the Psychological Sciences.

Kuhse, H., & Singer, P. (1988). *Should the baby live?: The problem of handicapped infants.* Oxford, United Kingdom: Oxford University Press.

La Mettrie, J. O. de. (1994). *Man: A machine.* La Salle, IL: Open Court. (Original work published 1747)

Lee, S. L. (2012). *Essential elements of love, personhood, and attachment: From metaphysics to psychological theory and psychotherapy* (Doctoral dissertation). Retrieved from ProQuest Dissertations and Theses. (Accession Order No. 3503185)

Levering, M. (2008). *Biblical natural law: A theocentric and teleological approach.* Oxford, United Kingdom: Oxford University Press.

Lévesque, J., Eugène, F., Joanette, Y., Paquette, V., Mensour, B., Beaudoin, G., Leroux, J. M., Bourgouin, P., Beauregard, M. (2003). Neural circuity underlying voluntary suppression of sadness. *Biological Psychiatry, 53,* 502–510.

Libet, B. (1985). Unconscious cerebral initiative and the role of conscious will in voluntary action. *The Behavioral and the Brain Sciences, 8,* 529–566.

Libet, B. (2004). *Mind time: The temporal factor in consciousness.* Cambridge, MA: Harvard University Press.

Lickona, T. (1991). *Educating for character: How our schools can teach respect and responsibility.* New York, NY: Bantam.

Lickona, T. (2004). *Character matters: How to help our children develop good judgment, integrity, and other essential virtues.* New York, NY: Touchstone.

Maslow, A. (1987). *Motivation and personality* (3rd ed.) (R. Frager, J. Fadiman, C. McReynolds, & R. Cox, Eds.). New York, NY: Longman. (Original work published 1954)

May, R. (1969). *Love and will.* New York, NY: Norton.

McEntee, M. L., Dy-Liacco, G. S., & Haskins, D. G. (2013). Human flourishing: A natural home for spirituality. *Journal of Spirituality in Mental Health, 15,* 141–159.

McGrath, A. (2004). *The twilight of atheism: The rise and fall of disbelief in the modern world.* New York, NY: Doubleday.

McGrath, A. (2011). *Darwinism and the divine: Evolutionary thought and natural theology.* Malden, MA: Wiley-Blackwell.

McInerny, R. (2006). *Praeambula fidei: Thomism and the God of the philosophers.* Washington, DC: The Catholic University of America Press.

McMinn, M. R. (2017). *The science of virtue: Why positive psychology matters to the Church.* Grand Rapids, MI: Brazos Press.

McMinn, M. R., & Campbell, C. D. (2007). *Integrative psychotherapy: Toward a comprehensive Christian approach.* Downers Grove, IL: InterVarsity Press.

Mikulincer, M., & Phillip, P. R. (2007). *Attachment in adulthood: Structure, dynamics, and change.* New York, NY: Guilford Press.

Miller, R. B. (2001). Scientific vs. clinical-based

knowledge in psychology: A concealed moral conflict. *American Journal of Psychotherapy, 55*(3), 344–356.

Muraven, M. (2012). Ego depletion: Theory and evidence. In R. Ryan (Ed.), *The Oxford handbook of human motivation* (pp. 111–126). New York, NY: Oxford University Press.

Nagel, T. (2012). *Mind and cosmos: Why the materialist neo-Darwinian conception of nature is almost certainly false.* New York, NY: Oxford University Press.

Naglieri, J. A., & Goldstein, S. (2014). Assessment of executive function using rating scales: Psychometric considerations. In *Handbook of executive functioning* (pp. 159–170). New York, NY: Springer.

O'Donohue, W. (2013). *Clinical psychology and the philosophy of science.* Cham, Switzerland: Springer International Publishing.

Parrott, C. (1999). Towards an integration of science, art and morality: The role of values in psychology. *Counselling Psychology Quarterly, 12*(1), 5–24.

Peterson, C., & Seligman, M. E. P. (Eds.). (2004). *Character strengths and virtues: A handbook and classification.* New York, NY: Oxford University Press.

Pieper, J. (2009). *Leisure: The basis of culture* (A. Dru, Trans.). San Francisco, CA: Ignatius Press. (Original work published 1952)

Pinckaers, S. (1995). *The sources of Christian ethics.* (M. T. Noble, Trans.). Washington, DC: The Catholic University of America Press. (Original work published 1985)

Pinckaers, S. (2005). *The Pinckaers reader: Renewing Thomistic moral theology* (J. Berkman & C. S. Titus, Eds.). Washington, DC: The Catholic University of America Press.

Pinker, S. (2009). *How the mind works.* New York, NY: Norton. (Original work published 1997)

Post, S. G. (Ed.). (2007). *Altruism and health: Perspectives from empirical research.* Oxford, United Kingdom: Oxford University Press.

Rai, T. S., & Holyoak, K. J. (2013). Exposure to moral relativism compromises moral behavior. *Journal of Experimental Social Psychology, 49,* 995–1001.

Rand, K. L., & Cheavens, J. S. (2009). Hope theory. In S. J. Lopez & C. R. Snyder (Eds.), *The Oxford handbook of positive psychology* (2nd ed., pp. 323–343). New York, NY: Oxford University Press.

Ratzinger, J. (2002). *God and the world: A conversation with Peter Seewald.* San Francisco, CA: Ignatius Press.

Ren, J., Hu, L., Zhang, H., & Huang, Z. (2010). Implicit positive emotion counteracts ego depletion. *Social Behavior and Personality, 38*(7), 919–928.

Riddle, T. (2012, April 24). How creativity connects with immorality: Are creative types more likely to cross moral boundaries? *Scientific American.* Retrieved from http://www.scientificamerican.com/article/how-creativity-connects-immortality/

Sartre, J. P. (2007). *Existentialism is a humanism* (C. Macomber, Trans.). New Haven, CT: Yale University Press. (Original work published 1946)

Schönborn, C. (2007). *Chance or purpose: Creation, evolution, and a rational faith.* San Francisco, CA: Ignatius Press.

Seligman, M. E. P. (1993). *What you can change and what you can't: The complete guide to successful self-improvement.* New York, NY: Knopf.

Seligman, M. E. P. (2002). *Authentic happiness: Using the new positive psychology to realize your potential for lasting fulfillment.* New York, NY: Atria Paperback.

Sherwin, M. S. (2005). *By knowledge and by love: Charity and knowledge in the moral theology of St. Thomas Aquinas.* Washington, DC: The Catholic University of America Press.

Simonton, D. K. (2004). *Creativity in science: change, logic, genius, and Zeitgeist.* Cambridge, United Kingdom: Cambridge University Press.

Singer, P. (2011). *Practical ethics.* Cambridge, United Kingdom: Cambridge University Press. (Original work published 1980)

Skinner, B. F. (1971). *Beyond freedom and dignity.* Indianapolis, IN: Hackett.

Skinner, B. F. (1976). *About behaviorism.* New York, NY: Random House.

Smiley, M. (2017). Collective responsibility. In E. N. Zalta (Ed.), *Stanford Encyclopedia of Philosophy* (Summer 2017 Edition). Retrieved from http://plato.stanford.edu/entries/collective-responsibility/

Smith, M. B. (1978). Psychology and values. *Journal of Social Issues, 34*(4), 181–199.

Snyder, C. R. (1994). *The psychology of hope: You can get there from here.* New York, NY: Free Press.

Snyder, C. R., Rand, K. L., & Sigmon, D. R. (2002). Hope theory: A member of the positive psychology family. In C. R. Snyder & S. J. Lopez (Eds.), *Handbook of positive psychology* (pp. 257–276). New York, NY: Oxford University Press.

Sodergren, A. (2009). *Attachment and morality: A Catholic perspective.* (Unpublished doctoral dissertation). Arlington, VA: Institute for the Psychological Sciences.

Spitzer, R. J. (2010). *New proofs for the existence of God: Contributions of contemporary physics and philosophy.* Grand Rapids, MI: Eerdmans.

Stevenson, D. H., Eck, B. E., & Hill, P. C. (Eds.). (2007). *Psychology & Christianity integration: Seminal works that shaped the movement.* Wilsonville, OR: Christian Association for Psychological Studies.

Tice, D. M., Baumeister, R. F., Shmueli, D., & Muraven, M. (2007). Restoring the self: Positive affect helps improve self-regulation following ego depletion. *Journal of Experimental Social Psychology, 43*(3), 379–384.

Titus, C. S. (2017). Aquinas, Seligman, and positive psychology: A Christian approach to the use of the virtues in psychology. *Journal of Positive Psychology, 12*(5), 447–458.

Vatican II, Council. (1965a). *Dignitatis humanae* [Declaration on religious freedom]. Vatican City, Vatican: Libreria Editrice Vaticana.

Vatican II, Council. (1965b). *Gaudium et spes* [Pastoral constitution on the Church in the modern world]. Vatican City, Vatican: Libreria Editrice Vaticana.

Vitz, P. C. (2005, March). Psychology in recovery. *First Things*, 17–21.

Vitz, P. C. (2017). The origin of consciousness in the integration of analog (right hemisphere) & digital (left hemisphere) codes. *Journal of Consciousness Exploration & Research, 8*(11), 881–906.

Vohs, K. D., Baumeister, R. F., Schmeichel, B. J., Twenge, J. M., Nelson, N. M., & Tice, D. M. (2008). Making choices impairs subsequent self-control: A limited resource account of decision making, self-regulation, and active initiative. *Journal of Personality and Social Psychology, 94*, 883–898.

Vohs, K. D., & Schooler, J. W. (2008). The value of believing in free will: Encouraging a belief in determinism increases cheating. *Psychological Science, 19*(1), 49–54. doi:10.1111/j.1467-9280.2008.02045.x

Wachtel, P. L. (2013). *Therapeutic communication: Knowing what to say when* (2nd ed.). New York, NY: Guilford Press.

Watson, J. B. (1913). Psychology as the behaviorist views it. *Psychological Review, 20*(2), 158–177.

Weigel, G. (2002, March 1). A better concept of freedom. *First Things*, 14–20.

Wilson, E. O. (1975). *Sociobiology: The new synthesis.* Cambridge, MA: Belknap Press.

Wilson, E. O. (1998). *Consilience: The unity of knowledge.* New York, NY: Knopf.

Wojtyła, K. (1979). *The acting person: A contribution to phenomenological anthropology* (A-T Tymieniecka, Ed.; A. Potocki, Trans.). Boston, MA: Reidel. (Original work published 1969)

Wojtyła, K. (1993). *Love and responsibility* (H. T. Willetts, Trans.). San Francisco, CA: Ignatius Press. (Original work published 1960)

World Health Organization. (2015). *International statistical classification of diseases and related health problems* (10th rev.) (ICD-10). Retrieved from http://apps.who.int/classifications/icd10/browse/2015/en

Worthington, E. L., Jr. (2003). *Forgiving and reconciling: Bridges to wholeness and hope* (Rev. ed.). Downers Grove, IL: InterVarsity Press.

Życiński, J. (2006). *God and evolution: Fundamental questions of Christian evolutionism* (K. W. Kemp & Z. Maślanka, Trans.). Washington, DC: The Catholic University of America Press.

Part IV

Theological Support

Chapter 17

Created in the Image of God

CRAIG STEVEN TITUS, PAUL C. VITZ,
AND WILLIAM J. NORDLING

ABSTRACT: The Catholic Christian Meta-Model of the Person can be understood from different perspectives. In the previous two parts, we have explored the psychological and philosophical supports for the Model. This part supplies support for the Meta-Model's specifically theological or faith-based premises, and some of its application to diverse disciplines and the sciences. In three chapters, it explores some of the foundations for faith-based approaches to the person as created in God's image, fallen and influenced by the effects of sin, and offered a way of redemption. First, this chapter identifies a synthetic, theological definition of the person and a brief overview of the development of a Christian understanding of the concept of person. It addresses the assumptions, sources, exemplars or role models, and methods needed for a deeper discussion of the theological premises in the context of Christian philosophy and contemporary sciences. Then it focuses on the gift of being created in the image of God as the foundation for understanding (1) reality and our capacity for knowledge of reality and for love of God and neighbor, (2) the origin and extent of basic human dignity, as distinguished from acquired merit or blame, (3) the differentiation of the sexes, (4) the gift of love as foundational for every gift and for the final goal of human life, (5) the spiritual source of the unity and uniqueness of each person, (6) interpersonal relationality, the emulation active in the call to communion, (7) human longings and exemplarity in the development of moral character and spiritual flourishing, and (8) the nature of divine and moral order. It affirms that mankind is called to the flourishing, goodness, holiness, acts of self-giving, and communion with God and others that is possible only with divine grace and the involvement of other people. Such callings include vocational states (married, single, consecrated, or ordained), as well as work, service, and meaningful leisure. Examples from the mental health field are offered.

What difference does it make to be created in the image of God? From a Catholic Christian perspective, each human person is created by God from love and for love (Zundel, 1939/2012). This belief is based on the creation accounts (Genesis, Chapters 1 and 2), which communicate the ultimate origin and final purpose of mankind. In the first chapter of Genesis, God indicates that human beings are created as relational: God refers to himself as a communion of persons, stating that human beings are made "in our image, after our likeness" (1:26, RSV, Second Catholic Edition). God affirmed that mankind should both take care of creation and benefit from it. Mankind, furthermore, was created as male and female so as to be fruitful in procreating new life and caring for their offspring. The revelation that each human person is created in the image of God is central to the Catholic Christian understanding of human life and love, family and flourishing (Cassuto, 2005; Wenham, 2000).

The patristic tradition, furthermore, emphasizes the significance of being created in the image of God. St. Augustine (426/1991) affirms that the Trinity (and consequently the human person, who is created in God's image) is relational (V.5.6). This relationality is in one respect intrapersonal (as reflected in the interaction that occurs between the human person's capacities of memory, intelligence, and will) (Augustine, 426/1991, X.11.18). It is in another respect interpersonal (as reflected in the human person's love of another) (Augustine, 426/1991, VIII.10.14 and IX.2.2). St. John Damascene, furthermore, holds that the divine image implies that man is "an intelligent being endowed with free-will and self-movement" (Damascene, ca. 749/1999, Book II, Chapter 12; cited by Aquinas, 1273/1981, I-II, prologue; see also *Catechism of the Catholic Church* [*CCC*], 1997, §1705).

First, this chapter will explicitly address the faith-based assumptions, sources, and methods that ground the Catholic Christian Meta-Model of the Person. Then the chapter will briefly address how simply being a person means sharing a common goodness and dignity, but also necessarily having a unique goodness and dignity. Then it addresses what being created in the image of God implies for the equality and differences of men and women. The divine source of the created human provides a faith-informed

rationale for human dignity and value not found in present secular understandings of the person (Singer, 2011; Kuhse & Singer, 1988). Indeed, contemporary psychotherapy has no foundational rationale for human dignity and value, although wisely it is often assumed. As a preparation for the three faith-based chapters (Created, Fallen, and Redeemed), we will address the value that theological principles bring to understanding the indelible dignity and other basic characteristics of the person. For mental health practitioners, the chapters provide a narrative-based personality theory and other essential attributes of the person, all of which have significance for a psychological understanding of the person and applications in mental health practice. For example, love is at the center of understanding the person for theology and for much of contemporary psychology, including attachment theory, marital therapy, forgiveness therapy, and positive psychology (Post, 2007; Post & Neimark, 2007). This chapter then addresses how the unique unity of the person implies interpersonal relationality and communion with God and neighbor. Natural and divine types of transcendence, which have been touched on elsewhere, are discussed here more completely, as providing a basis for understanding human flourishing. Last, it identifies the significance of divine and moral order for understanding the highest form of personal flourishing.

Faith-Based Assumptions, Sources, Exemplars or Role Models, and Methods for the Meta-Model

Earlier in this volume (Chapter 7, "Methodology and Presuppositions"), we posited that the understandings of human and social sciences inevitably are founded on a worldview and value system, both in theory and in practice. That is, we argued that mental health practitioners make assumptions about the person and meaning, health and illness, the influence of role models, flourishing and languishing, and so on. For instance, there are particular schools of psychology and counseling that are materialist. These schools hold that there are only brains and behavior, and they even explain human mental life and the moral order as simply based on matter. In contrast, there are nonmaterialist positions (Nagel, 2012), including the Catholic Christian position, that hold that an authentic study of the person should include not only brain and behavior, but also nonmaterialist understandings of minds and ethics.

We have desired to make explicit our own theological presuppositions, sources, and methods that we use and the implications that we understand to follow upon them, especially as they pertain to the person as an object of study as well as a subject of free action. Ours is a specifically Catholic Christian approach to the major sources that constitute the theological perspective on the person. It is widely shared, for the most part, by other Christians. In particular, the approach explores the human being through a tripartite ordering of salvation history in which mankind: (1) is created by God out of love and for love; (2) suffers weakness and death because of the effects of sin; and (3) is offered redemption through Jesus Christ, sanctification through the working of the Holy Spirit, and beatitude by God. This journey is marked by particular vocations (goodness, justice, mercy, and holiness; vowed and non-vowed vocational states; and life work, service, and leisure) and the gifts of faith, hope, and love. This synthetic theological approach engages the influence of personal narratives, role models, historical knowledge, and transcendent salvation history.

We assume, with two provisos, that theology, psychology, and philosophy can collaborate in conceptualizing the person. First, we affirm the primal place of theology's sources, identified as the Word of God, Sacred Scripture, tradition, and the Magisterium (Vatican II, 1965a). At the same time, we recognize that faith-based reflection on the sources of God's self-revelation (theology) is a systematic and synthetic, personal and communal-ecclesial effort. This effort draws from the distinct analyses of psychology and philosophy (based in experience and reason) and from these disciplines' efforts to gain knowledge and understanding of the person. Theology needs contributions from psychology and philosophy to understand the goodness and weaknesses of human nature as well as the potential for growth and healing (International Theological Commission, 2012; Vatican II, 1965a).

Second, while God and his active presence in human lives are the proper objects of the study of theology, we explore how Catholic theology (as a worldview and value system) provides a coherent frame for a positive vision of psychological and philosophical understandings of the person. This expansive approach is founded on confidence in objective truth and reality rather than on the hubris of human limited efforts and knowledge. In particular, it is grounded in the truth of God, revealed through the example of Jesus Christ and the movement of the Holy Spirit. Therefore, the Meta-Model employs an integrative multidisciplinary approach to the sciences, philosophy, and theology. It is confident in its revealed faith-based sources (whose competence includes normative doctrinal and moral areas), while giving credit to the scientific disciplines for their important and unique contributions.

In this volume the theological premises are addressed after the philosophical ones. Nevertheless, there are significant theological developments and references found in the previous section's discussion of the eight philosophical premises (conceptualizing the person as a personal unity, fulfilled through vocations, flourishing in virtues, interpersonally relational, sensory-perceptual-cognitive, emotional, rational, and volitional and free). These premises identify the natural personal dimensions for

flourishing in one's vocations. Philosophy engages ultimate issues, but theology does so even more, as will be shown. (For a fuller coverage of the methodology of integrating theology, philosophy, and psychology, see Chapter 7, "Methodology and Presuppositions").

The Image of God, Interpersonal Relationality, and the Sexes

In a Catholic Christian vision of the person, as just affirmed, men and women are interpersonally relational by nature. They possess equal dignity and goodness, as well as a common vocation to holiness. Men and women also deserve equal respect as human persons from conception until death. At the same time, they embody differences that are not only personal, but also physiological, psychological, and spiritual. These differences between men and women are sometimes difficult to decipher because of the overlap between male and female characteristics and human adaptability. Furthermore, beyond differences, there is also a male and female complementarity that is found in the midst of men and women's ongoing relationships, such as being mother or father, and that complementarity is significant for understanding each person (Allen, 2014; Bachiochi, 2013; Brizendine, 2006 & 2010; Ong, 1981; Rhoads, 2004; Stein, 1932/1996; Schumacher, 2004; Chapter 9, "Man and Woman").

How Are the Sexes Equal yet Different?

In a theological perspective, St. John Paul II (2006) has offered commentary on the book of Genesis and how being created in the image of God underlies the equality, difference, and complementarity of man and woman (p. 163). The two creation accounts of the book of Genesis communicate the significance of the divine image for men and women alike. Each sex has

different and complementary contributions to the flourishing of mankind and the stewardship of the earth. The first creation account states: "In the image of God he created them; male and female he created them" (Gen 1:27). While receiving shared dignity, man and woman express specific characteristics of the divine image and have particular callings (Savage, 2015). For example, women and men are called to express their vocations to be spouses and to motherhood or fatherhood not only biologically, but also in psychological, social, and spiritual ways (John Paul II, 2006, p. 432; Stein, 1932/1996).

The second creation account of Genesis describes in greater detail what is fitting for the vocation of man and woman. Men and women have distinct ways of following the call of God (Stein, 1932/1996). From the beginning of their existence, they each are marked by their vocations to be daughters or sons (of God and of their parents), husbands or wives, mothers or fathers (John Paul II, 1988, §22), as well as brothers or sisters. These distinctions are played out in men and women as they are called in their own ways to respond to three major vocations and missions, which are all shaped by the divine image: (1) to search for flourishing in justice, goodness, and holiness, a task that will inevitably need to take account of the person and situational peculiarities of being a man or a woman; (2) to pursue one's chosen vowed or non-vowed vocational states (married, single, consecrated, or ordained), a task that also involves recognition of sex differences in context, especially in marriage and ordination; and (3) to work in service for the good of one's family and community and to be responsible stewards of the earth.

The equality of and distinctions between the sexes and their complementarity are the basis of authentic efforts to develop one's feminine or masculine character, such as the differences in the feminine and masculine expression of patience, caring, courage, and justice. These distinctions touch on the different ways in which men and women experience individual flourishing and the ways in which they contribute to the flourishing of the family, community, and society. Understanding differences related to the sexes does not overshadow the uniqueness of each person and the complementarity of the sexes. Elsewhere in this volume can be found further discussions of these vocations (Chapter 10, "Fulfilled Through Vocation"), as well as the virtues (Chapter 11, "Fulfilled in Virtue") in relation to sexual differentiation (Chapter 9, "Man and Woman").

How Does the Image of God Make the Human Person Relational?

The human person is not always understood as relational in psychological theory or philosophical approaches. Nominalist and Enlightenment thinking, individualistic ideology in modern psychology (Rogers, 1961/2012), and much of early biological science have led to an exaggerated focus on the individual at the expense of his or her relationality and participation in real communities of family, friends, society, and the Church (for the critique of this phenomenon, see Vitz, 1994; also Pinckaers, 1995, p. 351; Atkinson, 2014). There are exceptions particularly in recent decades to this focus on isolated individuals, as found in attachment theory (Bowlby,

1973, 1982, 1988), interpersonal psychotherapy, family systems theory (Bowen, 1978), positive psychology (Peterson & Seligman, 2004); and interpersonal neuroscience (Siegel, 2012a, 2012b; Schore, 2002). This misconception of the relational nature of the human person and mankind as a social animal has also necessitated a retrieval of Catholic Christian sources (Clarke, 1992, 2009), as mentioned earlier.

From the beginning, the Old Testament demonstrates God's interpersonal character through his relationship to Adam and Eve, to Abraham, the prophets, David, and the whole people of Israel. For example, God dialogues face to face with Moses and he makes a covenant with the people (Ex 34:34). The divine image, however, is not completed with the creation of Adam, Eve, and all mankind or with God's self-revelation to the people Israel. It is in the revelation of the Father's love through Jesus Christ that the fullness of the image of God is made manifest and further perfected (Col 1:15; von Balthasar, 2013). This revelation of God's love and image present in Christ "fully reveals man to man himself" (Vatican II, 1965b, §22).

Furthermore, the Christian tradition has used the concept of "person" to communicate the conviction that humans are marked in their being or basic reality (ontologically) by the indelible image of God, who is both perfect unity and perfect community. The Godhead is one divine substance and three personal relations, which Christians call Father, Son, and Holy Spirit. The Trinity of personal relations manifests the one God's dynamism of love that creates, redeems, and sanctifies. By analogy, the divine image establishes the human person as necessarily relational, that is, as "essentially dialogical or relational in its ontological structure" (International Theological Commission, 2004, §45). This relational structure is significant for notions of psychological health, moral well-being, and spiritual flourishing, all of which demand transformation, fidelity, creativity, and self-giving or sacrifice. The affirmation that each human is created in interpersonal relationality and for interpersonal relationality (with parents, spouses, family, friends, community, and God) leads to further questions about the dynamic nature of these types of relationality. Nonetheless, it is inaccurate to speak of a psychologically healthy autonomous individual without speaking of relationships, which the Christian tradition identifies as finding their summit in interpersonal self-giving love (Chapter 12, "Interpersonally Relational").

How Does the Relational Nature of the Image of God Develop in Human Persons?

Human relationships progress as they contribute to personal and interpersonal wholeness of oneself and others. Humans will not however completely flourish until the end of time, when brought into the loving, eternal presence of God (Emery, 2010). In between the present and eternity, there is the pathway of growth that is common to all, yet unique to each person, as can be seen in the various role models of sanctity found in each saint and every pilgrim on the way to God (consider the similarities and differences among St. Peter, St. Paul, St. Mary Magdalen, St. Gregory of Nazianzus, St. Gregory of Nyssa, St. Monica, St. Augustine, St. Francis, St. Teresa of Ávila, St. Ignatius of Loyola, and St. Thérèse of Lisieux, to name just a few).

The image of God is not a static thing. It can be understood as the dynamic pathway of the one who is "the way, the truth, and the life" (Jn 14:6). Thus also the relationships of each human person and family must grow in the characteristics that are Christ-like. These characteristics include love and care, justice and kindness, commitment and self-giving. Growth in spiritual strengths is rooted in the virtues of faith, hope, and love, as St. Paul reminds us (1 Cor 13:13). This life of the Spirit (Rom 8) offers both strength and direction for life's journey as well as a foretaste of the flourishing intended by God. Christ was an exemplar of both perfection in his divinity and development in his humanity. In different ways, he grew not only in physical stature but also in psychological and moral virtue through his obedience to his parents, participation in family life, learning a trade, and observation of the Jewish practices of his time (Lk 2:51–52; Aquinas, 1273/1981, III, 7.2 ad 2; I-II, 61.5; Gondreau, 2002; Titus, 2009).

Likewise, our relationships are neither static nor solitary. For example, even though one who becomes a mother or father is always a mother or father, there are continual changes in parental-filial relations. Moreover, the inner life of a family, as rich as it may be, will stagnate if it does not also reach out beyond one's family to serve those in need (Benedict XVI, 2009; Post & Neimark, 2007). Furthermore, families must face challenges to the physical, mental, and spiritual well-being of their members in order to experience positive growth. It is through the trials of life, which happen largely in our relationships, that we are tested, purified, and perfected in the image of God (1 Pet 1:7–8; 1 Cor 10:13).

How Do Nature and Grace Influence Top-Down Processes?

The integrated Christian perspective, as laid out in this volume, recognizes the various conditions, causes, influences, and actions that affect the person's interface with the world and with God. There are top-down, bottom-up, outside-in, and inside-out capacities and movements that contribute to the value, meaning, and purpose of human life that is created in the image of God. Each of these processes will now be described in more detail, with attention to both nature and graced-nature, both of which are involved in bottom-up and top-down processes.

First, there are two types of top-down processes and movements (of the intellect and of grace), which follow the hierarchical structure of the person's body-soul unity, from the spiritual and intellectual (reason and will) at the top, to the sensory (sensory-perceptual cognition and emotions) and organic at the bottom. Top-down movements start with the spiritual and intellectual capacities (moral, aesthetic, and religious) that are influenced by nature and grace (Davies, 2006; Życiński, 2006).

By *human nature*, the person exercises top-down capacities, by which one's intellect influences one's judgments, emotions, behavior, and relationships. They are the ways that meaning and goals (final causes) and motivations such as free will (efficient causes) influence a person. For example, when the intellect knows objective and ultimate life goals, there is a top-down movement that directs and motivates the person; for example, a mother and father who seek to raise their children in a just and caring way. These top-down causes influence the whole person and distinguish humans—who use their intellect and will in parenting—from non-human creatures driven solely by instinct and behavioral conditioning (Levinas, 2000; Murphy, Ellis, & O'Connor, 2009; Pinckaers, 1995: Życiński, 2006).

By *grace-informed nature*, the person cooperates in the graced top-down processes (divine movements) that further influence intellect, will, emotion, behavior, and relationships. Divine grace perfects the person (grace perfects nature), his reason and will, as he pursues everyday goals and ultimate meaning. For example, there are graced movements that influence the mother and father's self-giving practices (which, for example, aim at being just to siblings who are in conflict or at caring for the sick child). For the Christian, such practices are perfected by the imitation of Christ's self-giving love and by the gifts of the Holy Spirit, such as the gifts of counsel and wisdom, as well as the infused moral virtues. Grace influences the top-down processes at multiple levels: (1) higher cognitions (as when parents correct their own distorted beliefs about their children), (2) free will (as when parents choose to motivate the child to pursue healthy and holy ways of living), as well as (3) interpersonal relationships and narratives (as when parents as a couple interact to discern moral action and religious practices to promote flourishing and communion in the family) (Beauregard, 2012; Hall, 2007a & 2007b; Segal & Solomon, 2013).

How Do Nature and Grace Influence Bottom-Up Processes?

Second, bottom-up capacities and conditions underlie the experiential features of human life that emerge from embodied organic and neurological, sensory-perceptual-cognitive, and emotional experience. By *nature*, a person's potential for growth and change (the material cause) is a basis for actual change, that is, the material potency of the person must be actualized. The causes that actualize the progressive emergence of complex and coherent life are not just the genetic and epigenetic factors that contribute to forming the body-soul unity of the person. As just mentioned, there are also spiritual-intellectual causes that influence the body-soul nature of the person. These formal and efficient causes make possible transcendence, intellect, volition, and free will, as found in the mother loving her child and the father willing to work long hours. Although growth sometimes may apparently derive from random causes and instincts, growth and action have deeper origins, including that found in the natural inclinations toward self-preservation, family life, social life, goodness, truth, and beauty (Schmitz, 2009; Życiński, 2006; on natural inclinations, see Chapter 11, "Fulfilled in Virtue").

By *grace*, bottom-up capacities can be developed or perfected. This can be observed in the lives of many saints, when faith helps to transform the bottom-up tendency of being fearful or hateful to being peaceful or loving. Grace, thus, perfects nature, including the natural inclinations that are seeds of virtues (Aquinas, 1258/1987, 2.3, p. 48). In this process, the natural inclinations participate in the person's faith-informed reason, not only when one responds to reality through particular virtuous acts of the will, but also when a person becomes more disposed to act in like virtuous ways. Therefore, we can speak of how grace influences the bottom-up capacities and how grace (especially the infused moral virtues) shapes our acquired moral virtues, when there is collaboration between grace and our moral actions (Aquinas, 1273/1981, I-II, 65.3 ad 2; Sherwin, 2009). Nonetheless, there may be a long time needed for this new growth, especially when a person is overcoming engrained habits, such as addictions (Doidge, 2007, pp. 103–109; Dunnington, 2010).

The person may also suffer from a tendency not to do good acts (Aquinas, 1273/1981, I-II, 65.3 ad 2 & 53.1 ad 1; Sherwin, 2009). This happens because the bottom-up capacities have been negatively influenced by disordered actions, as mentioned above in the case of addictions. Nevertheless, bottom-up capacities can be perfected by good actions, including influences of family life. For example, a mother or a father experiences instinctual affections for, attraction to, and attachment to their offspring. These bottom-up conditions are raised or perfected by the parents' committed love expressed in patience, justice, and care for their children. Of course, damage or aging of natural capacities, because of accidents or degenerative mental conditions, can limit the expression of cognitive capacities that once reflected a higher level of expression. For example, Alzheimer's disease can damage a person's memory, attention, and other cognitive capacities, including learned virtues.

Goodness and Dignity

What Is the Origin and Extent of Human Dignity?

A Catholic-Christian view recognizes that human goodness and dignity involve a deeper origin and a more extensive end than can be understood by the methodology of a secular psychological or philosophical view (Chapter 8, "Personal Wholeness"). The creation accounts of the Bible (Gen 1 & 2) affirm that everything created by God, at the most profound level of existence, expresses goodness and has dignity. Humans, furthermore, created in the *imago Dei*, merit being called "very good" (Gen 1:31). Such an affirmation recognizes the value of the gift of human life and renders praise to the Giver of the gift.

Each human shares the value of being a person with the same basic dignity. The Second Vatican Council (1965b, §24) teaches that because of our capacities to know, love, and serve God in a personal way, we have a special status in creation. Each human is unique and created for his or her own sake but also shares in a communal destiny. This is not to discredit the value of other animals (Mt 10:29; as seen in the poem of St. Francis of Assisi), for whom we are called to practice a trustworthy stewardship (Gen 1:26; Benedict XVI, 2009; Francis, 2015). Rather, it links our dignity and our intelligence with the ethical responsibility that we have concerning other persons and the rest of creation.

Since God is the continuous source of human life and dignity, each person retains a basic goodness and dignity. In the beginning, God endowed Adam and Eve with the special grace of friendship-love of God, which coordinated the various capacities of a person into a unified harmony oriented to God. This order is called "original justice" (Aquinas, 1273/1981, I-II, 82; John Paul II, 2006). Even after the fall and the loss of original justice (i.e., the loss of mankind's first friendship with God), human beings preserve their basic dignity (Gen 3). Our psychological, ethical, and spiritual failures do not annul our value, nor do the fragility and inconsistency of life deny that there is a basic dignity common to all humans. Each person is basically good, that is, has the same basic God-given dignity. This basic goodness and dignity also create obligations among human persons. This dignity remains the same even when, as an embryo, a person is not viable outside the mother's womb, and even when, suffering with dementia, an aged man cannot recognize his spouse or coherently converse with her. Another expression of this common Catholic Christian obligation among persons is the obligation to pray for others, even for the dead.

In growth and healing, the person experiences not only the effects of sin and weakness (including disordered desires, distractions, and weakness of will) but also the effects of good actions and grace (including patience in suffering, forgiveness and reconciliation, and unselfish giving). The effects of graced actions enable the person to grow in dignity and goodness in the form of virtue, atonement, and sanctification. We see this added dignity in the lives of the saints and martyrs, who have been conformed into a more perfect likeness of Christ. This added dignity is due, in part, to the person's own effort and, at the same time, primarily to God the Father's provident plan, Christ's salvific merit, and the Holy Spirit's sanctifying grace (Aquinas, 1273/1981, I-II, 114.1; von Balthasar, 1990).

What Is the Significance of Human Life?

The study of the goodness and dignity of humans, from a Catholic Christian vision of the person, leads to a deeper understanding of our nature. Explicitly, it recognizes not only our bodily structure and those characteristics that come from nature but also our origin and purpose (end, or *telos*), as fundamental aspects of our nature. We are not the creators of our own nature, nor is our nature the result of random chance. Humans cannot truly justify by themselves their own goodness and dignity apart from an ultimate origin and end. This vision of our end or purpose, as a gift from God, is part of our Catholic Christian Meta-Model. (Our bodily human nature is discussed more fully in the psychological chapters of Part II, especially in Chapter 8, "Personal Wholeness," Chapter 9, "Man and Woman," and Chapter 13, "Sensory-Perceptual-Cognitive".)

However, making materialist assumptions about human nature, some writers express theories of evolutionary psychology (Wright, 2001, 2009) that inspire notions of an impersonal, non-transcendent god, who is not yet fully God, and who will, perhaps, become God only at the end of further evolutionary pressures and events (Seligman, 2002, pp. 257–260). Although some contemporary thinkers expound materialist assumptions (Dawkins, 2008; Dennett, 1995), humans, more generally, seek to know the origin and purpose of their existence, goodness, and dignity. And many people come to believe in God, or the transcendent, as the source and end of human life and the universe (Aquinas, 1273/1981, I, 12.12; Feser, 2017; Spitzer, 2010). Furthermore, the Catholic Christian vision presents a nonmaterialist and nonreductionist vision of the person, while holding the validity of not only scientific theories and findings of evolution, but also the theological accounts of human dignity and experience (Austriaco, Brent, Davenport, & Ku, 2016; Benedict XVI, 2006; Chaberek, 2015; John Paul II, 1998, 1996; Pius XII, 1950; Schönborn, 2007; Życiński, 2006). Furthermore, the study of creation—or nature—and of salvation history both point to a source of life and an end for living that is beyond each one of us and beyond our species. An open-minded, inquisitive investigation of creation (the book of nature) and salvation history (the book of Divine Revelation), in different ways, reveals something of God and his providence.

Philosophical inquiry, psychological studies, and the other disciplines offer their own types of knowledge, based in experience, systematic observation, and reasoned reflection about human nature. This type of evidence leads in various ways to knowledge of the sources of the goodness and weakness that we find in humans. Focused observation, study, and reflection about psychological development, dysfunction, and healing are especially helpful for understanding the import of human goodness and dignity (Chapter 7, "Methodology and Presuppositions"). These findings can enrich theology at the level of understanding human growth and healing, as is elaborated later.

Catholics believe that the Word of God makes God the Father known, especially in the life, death, and resurrection of Jesus Christ (Lk 8:10; John Paul II, 1998, §4, §9, §19; Vatican II,

1965a) and through the gift of the Holy Spirit (Is 11:2; Lk 24:49; Jn 20:22; Acts 2:1–13). Furthermore, the Christian scriptural and theological tradition indicates that humans are relational, sensory-perceptual-cognitive, emotional, rational, and free. Creation first and foremost concerns God's bringing the existence of created things out of nothingness and maintaining them (CCC, 1997, §290, §296, §301; Aquinas, 1273/1981, I, 44.1). And the unified structure of the human person (his or her ontology) comprises these inherent conditions (relationality, embodiment, and spirituality as found in rational and volitional activities). Although influenced by the disordered effects of the fall from original justice and grace, humanity is meant for ultimate flourishing in response to God's callings, as Pope St. John Paul II (2006) argues in his papal catechesis, *Man and Woman He Created Them: A Theology of the Body*. Thus, scientific, philosophical, and theological types of knowledge enrich our personal understanding of the basic dignity and the acquired dignity of the human person. This includes the dignity that an individual attains through particular experiences of suffering and holiness, following Christ.

What Are Some Differences Between a Catholic and a Reductionist View of Creation?

From a Catholic Christian perspective, basic human dignity and worth come from being created in the image and likeness of God, not from anything that a person does to merit recognition or honor. From a secular perspective, by contrast, there is no such foundation for assuming that all humans have a basic dignity and value (Chapter 4, "Modern Personality Theories"). Rather, from this perspective, human dignity is rooted strictly in a functional anthropology, where dignity is based not on who the person is (the image of God), but on what the person can do independently at present, and on relativistic and social constructivist criteria; as such, human dignity is frail and unreliable and unavailable for many.

An example is a reductionist evolutionary or genetic notion of humanity that presupposes that the universe is closed to a transcendent first source, continuous interaction, and final end. Such a materialist reductionism assumes that mankind is simply the result of random chance interacting with principles that promote survival, such as natural selection (variation, heredity, and environment); this view is found in Darwin's final version of On *the Origin of Species* (1859/2009). In certain of their formulations, such materialist, reductionist presuppositions have further assumed that human life and the human species are of relatively limited value, especially when humans are young, disabled, or old (Kuhse & Singer, 1988; Singer, 2011).

What Are the Current Challenges to Human Dignity?

The value of the person is roundly threatened when, as a result of the vulnerability of their stage of development or illness or age, individuals lose the protection of law and the respect of the community. Legislation permitting abortion (*Roe v. Wade*, 1973) and physician-assisted suicide (the state of Oregon's Death with Dignity Act of 1997) are two of the ground-breaking examples of the loss of respect for basic personal dignity in American culture. These legislations and practices express, at the very least, confusion about the dignity of the person, about

the hierarchy of rights and obligations within natural law, about the existence of the right to life, and about respect for social obligations to protect and honor life, one's own life included. They seem to reduce dignity to autonomy. It is not hard to imagine as a society ages that the cost of maintaining large numbers of elderly will become very heavy. Hospitals and other institutions will be tempted to prescribe euthanasia particularly with elderly who are confused and do not have family protection.

Another danger of such anti-life laws is that their effects are magnified because of the human mimetic tendency. For example, it is a familiar observation that publicized crimes produce copycat crimes. The same is found in suicides and other actions that do not honor the basic value of human life. The importance of this mimetic phenomenon has been thoroughly identified by René Girard (1976).

In *Evangelium Vitae* (The Gospel of Life), John Paul II (1995) reiterates the Catholic tradition's affirmation of the "value of the person from the moment of conception" and throughout life (§45). In defending the unborn in the initial phase of existence and denouncing the manipulation of language to obscure the deliberate killing of the innocent, he says, "No word has the power to change the reality of things" (§58). With respect to acts of civil legislation such as those mentioned above, he also states that we are called to work "to ensure that the laws and institutions of the State in no way violate the right to life, from conception to natural death, but rather protect and promote it" (§93).

Gift of Love

What Is the First Gift?

We are made from and for divine and human love. Love and life are gifts that are received

even before we are consciously aware of them. Reception of such gifts elicits, with time, the capacity to see these two gifts for what they are: the basis for every other gift. The first gift is God's gift of creation, which he saw as good (Sokolowski, 1995, p. 9). Then, God created human persons, Adam and Eve, whom he saw as very good (Gen 1:31; Hayes, 2001, p. 26). Each person's life is a pure gift of love from the first source of love, for "God is love" (1 Jn 4:8). God, moreover, continues to sustain the gift of the person, which contains the image and presence of the Giver. As the letter of James says: "Every good endowment and every perfect gift is from above, coming down from the Father of lights" (Jas 1:17; also Jn 17:11–22).

How Can We Actively Receive the Gift of Life?

At one level, the gift of life is one-sided, particular to a person and place, and received in an entirely passive way. However, we are also invited to *actively* participate in the reception of the gift of life and the continuous gift of love. Early on, there is loving in return, which is one aspect of this active reception (for example, the child returns the love of his mother). Later, at a more mature level, there is the expression of gratitude for the gift of life and love. Then comes promoting and protecting life, service to others, and sharing the good things that one has received, which is a third, more active response (Aquinas 1273/1981, II-II, 106). The gift of love, thus, must be actively received, thankfully acknowledged, and freely given in turn. These three—returning love, gratitude, and giving—constitute the foundation for active reception and self-giving (Ps 138; 2 Cor 9:15; Col 3:14–17). Active reception of existence itself is a mystical stance involving an awareness of how one's own life depends on God and on others, including in a special way the gift as received through parents and others who love us. Such a stance toward life and love will not settle on survival or work or consumption as the ultimate meaning of life. Rather, it uplifts our attention toward the source of life through worship of the ultimate, personal source of life and love (Pieper, 1952/2009).

How Do We Give Love?

Our active response to God's gift of grace involves giving of ourselves in many ways. The responses involve the gifts, practices, and actions that lead to moral goodness and spiritual holiness as found in virtue strengths (especially faith, hope, and charity), moral character, and spiritual maturity. Other responses that are gifts are those that fulfill our commitments in our vocational states. These include self-gift of friendship and mutual self-giving and service as found in married love. Finally, we give love to others through the meaning of work both inside and outside the home. The full range of our giving and receiving is both an active receiving of the gift of love and also a fitting response to this gift. For example, the pursuit of physical health alone is inadequate for true human flourishing. If one focuses solely on the physical (strength, surface beauty, and so on), a person's flourishing will be only partial, because this focus omits worship of God and giving for the good of others. Such a focus on the body makes physical well-being a distraction rather than a gift to employ in one's common journey toward the ultimate end of life.

What Effect Does Self-Giving or Self-Serving Have on the Person?

The gifts of love are missed and misappropriated when not recognized or given in return, with the relevant commitments to God and other persons. Individuals make choices to be self-serving or self-giving. However, love cannot be hoarded, or, at least, not to good effect. Love must be offered gratuitously not only in return to its true source but also to others, that is, as a free gift. Opposite practices and lifestyles are practically narcissistic, since selfish love is a false love and an unfruitful endeavor, focusing on the self while eclipsing God and others. To give primary emphasis to one's self over God is idolatrous, and such a mindset sets up a wall to other persons. It is self-serving as well as ultimately stultifying and ignoble. For instance, in the therapeutic relationship, disordered self-serving love establishes a barrier between the client and the therapist. Recent thinkers have proposed that

training in virtues can be introduced into psychotherapy as particular ways of healing psychological disorders (Joseph & Linley, 2006; Linley & Joseph, 2004; Peterson & Seligman, 2004). Trautman (2006), for example, has proposed that practices that embody the virtue strengths of altruism and self-knowledge can be therapeutic for narcissistic personality disorder. And Gudan (2010) has proposed a way in which gratitude may underlie a remedy for moderate levels of ruminative depression.

Unity of Person and of Persons

What Is the Spiritual Source of a Person's Unity?

The dignity of the person is rooted in the personal unity of a material body and spiritual soul. It is this personal unity that is grounded in the divine breath or "inspiration." There is a great mystery in the spiritual nature of all human life. The book of Genesis (2:7) relates this special dependence of both matter and spirit in the second creation account: "Then the Lord God formed man of dust from the ground, and breathed into his nostrils the breath of life; and man became a living being." This narrative imagery evokes a whole "living being," called man or mankind ('ādām), who is taken from the ground ('ādāmāh) (John Paul II, 2006, p. 147). The wordplay between "mankind" and "ground" is typical of the early biblical tradition, which highlights mankind's relation to the ground, from which he is formed. The image is also found in the book of Jeremiah (18:6), which describes this divine effort as that of a potter working clay. The image of divine breath creates a sense of unity that is possible only because of the transformative action of God in creation. We are not talking here about a separatist, dualistic (two substance) notion

of body and soul. Rather, this living being is a whole. It is simultaneously nonmaterial and physical: soul and body, that is, hylomorphic (Chapter 8, "Personal Wholeness").

Is a Person Necessarily Interpersonally Relational?

God is also the source of the distinction between man and woman found in the second creation account (Gen 2:23), which is especially expressive of their relationality and complementarity. The man ('ādām) expresses the fact that no other creature would suit him. God counters by creating a helpmate taken from Adam's side, expressing the equality and difference of man and his helpmeet. Adam marvels at the difference that she makes, that is, how she responds to his needs and longings, as he says: "This at last is bone of my bones and flesh of my flesh; she shall be called Woman ['iššāh, or *ishshah*], because she was taken out of Man ['îš, or *ish*]" (Gen 2:23; John Paul II, 2006, p. 139). The distinction of the sexes undercuts neither the reality that each man and woman is a living human being nor the fact that they become "one flesh" in marriage (Gen 2:24). More than a metaphor, being "one flesh" involves an interpersonal unity made real by the sacrament of marriage (Mt 19); it is a sign (signified through word and action) that brings about what is signified. A child who is half of each parent also expresses this "one flesh" reality (Chapter 9, "Man and Woman").

Communion with God

What Is the Basis for Communion with God?

As stated above, God has revealed himself to be a knowing and loving communion of persons. The one God is at the same time a Trinity (Augustine, 426/1991). The divine initiative of creating human beings in the image of God provides the basis for the divine initiative of re-uniting each person with God. We are capable of being in communion with God because he has fashioned humanity in the communal *imago Dei*. Moreover, he provides the gratuitous gift of grace that also redeems and sanctifies us (Rom 6:22; 2 Thess 2:13; Aquinas, 1273/1981, I-II, 111.5). Jesus Christ communicates the divine intent that humans should share in the communion of the Trinity. As Jesus prays in the Gospel of John: "Holy Father, keep them in your name, which you have given me, that they may be one, even as we are one" (17:11), and "that they may all be one; even as you, Father, are in me, and I in you, that they also may be in us" (17:21). God is undivided in the divine nature yet a communion of three persons (2 Pet 1:4).

How Does Being Created in God's Image
Correlate with Being in
Communion with God Through Jesus Christ?

God has been present to mankind in a special way since the incarnation of Jesus, who reveals God in human form. God is far more easily understood in a human form. And Christ has revealed man to himself (Vatican II, 1965b, §22). Christ is the model for each person's life and vocation. He is the way, the truth, and the life for each person (Jn 14:6). That we need a model is the result of our enormous mimetic capacity (Girard, 1976).

Being created in the image of God is neither the end of the story nor the end of each person's life journey (Marcel, 2010; Pieper, 1994). Nevertheless, the Christian narrative of faith does have an ending that gives meaning to its whole course. Psychologists have also recently found the importance of narrative for basic human understanding (Bruner, 1986, 1990, 1991; McAdams, 1988; Shafer, 1992; Sacks, 1998; Spence, 1982; McLeod, 1997, 2004.

We are called to grow in the image of God, which is shown to us in Jesus Christ, and to enter personally into communion with God (Aquinas, 1273/1981, I, 93.4; Torrell, 2003, p. 90, p. 175). The call to communion with God is rooted in the very existence of each person, who feels in the depth of his or her being a need for communion with the ultimate source of being, life, truth, and love. This reality is the basis for our hope, especially when hope is linked with God's love and our faith in God's promise to fulfill this longing. The call to communion also involves a person's natural desire to see God (a topic discussed among theologians: see Cullen, 2012; de Lubac, 1946/1998; Feingold, 2004; Pinckaers, 2005). As Augustine observes, each person feels restless until he or she rests in God (401/2007, I.1). This call to communion with God reverberates throughout human history by way of the divine Word of God (Jn 1:1–5).

Catholics and Orthodox Christians recognize God's presence in the sacrament of the Eucharist, the body and blood of Christ. Through the sacrament, Jesus Christ is really and substantially present and a true source of faith, reconciliation, and support for believers. There is also a special presence of God through the seven gifts of the Holy Spirit, who, since his special manifestation at Pentecost, guides the Church, all those who believe in Christ, and all people of good will (Acts 1 & 2; Aquinas 1273/1981, I-II,

106.1; Augustine, 412/1887, Chapter 36; John Paul II, 1986; Journet, 1960; Vatican II, 1964, §16). Furthermore, we must wait for the coming of Christ and God's Kingdom (Mt 28). But, in the meantime, the Holy Spirit provides comfort, guidance, hope, and protection for the pilgrimage of life (Lk 24:9; Benedict XVI, 2009).

Communion with Others

How Do Marriage and Generativity Begin?

As the second creation account of Genesis (2:7) indicates, God formed man ('ādām) and breathed life into him, making man both of the earth and of God. In looking among the other creatures, man found neither an equal partner nor another creature who would serve his deep personal needs for communion and friendship. This experience of loneliness in original solitude was overcome, however, when God created Eve to be Adam's wife and "a helper fit for him" (Gen 2:18; John Paul II, 2006, pp. 146–147). As partners in original unity, they became spouses and parents, which are intertwined qualities. She became his spouse as well as "the mother of all the living" (Gen 2:18–20). God created man ('îš, or *ish*) and woman ('iššāh, or *ishshah*) in order that they enter into communion and friendship not only with each other but also with other persons and, above all, with God (John Paul II, 2006, p. 147; Chapter 10, "Fulfilled Through Vocation").

The nuptial meaning of persons and their bodies—the basic structure to receive and give, to know and love—serves to inform every vocation to both married and celibate life (John Paul II, 2006, p. 431). Even though not everyone is called to the married state, we are all called to understand this state and to participate in spiritual kinds of generativity that are learned because

of role models. Paternity and maternity are first experienced in family life. However, these relationships are also expressed in the public square through service to people other than one's own children. Often, grandparents, aunts and uncles, teachers, coaches, religious, priests, therapists, and other mentors who are childless have a great influence on others. Their generosity and devotion is generative and even parental in nature.

What Are the Principal Types of Interpersonal Communion?

There are types of interpersonal communion that necessarily constitute human flourishing: for example, spousal, parental and filial, brotherly and sisterly interpersonal communion, and that of friends. These dyads (and systems) require different priorities at different times during a person's lifespan. If one of the relationships is missing, though, it is often a sign of brokenness and solitude rather than of autonomy and independence.

For instance, if spouses do not grow in their commitment, alienation may replace communion. Even if unmarried, a mature adult who is not conscious of the spousal nature of his masculinity or her femininity will not be able to understand important aspects of interpersonal relationships (John Paul II, 2006; Wojtyła, 1979 & 1993). For example, if a man does not understand that men and women are different yet complementary, he will not appreciate women and femininity. Nor will he understand much of his own longing.

Furthermore, growth in the virtues of chastity, modesty, and fidelity involves both masculine and feminine interpersonal characteristics as well as personal ones. An individualistic and asexual account of such character strengths attends only to a shallow consideration of a person's emotions or behavior. On the contrary, a fuller account, like that of the Meta-Model of the Person, will consider the spousal nature of each person (whether actually married or not) and his or her vocational commitments as well (John Paul II, 2006; Wojtyła, 1993). In this context, development and healing need a right or-

dering of emotion, volition, cognition, action, and interpersonal relationships that facilitate virtue strengths and are important expressions of each person's masculinity or femininity.

For instance, the parent-child relationship serves as a constant human theme. More than merely an acknowledgement of lineage, the relationship of parent to child and child to parent is the basic structure underlying the reality of the gift of life (receiving), on the one side, and the source(s) of life (giving), on the other. In being created by God and "co-created" by parents (Wojtyła, 1993, p. 56), people are called to remain in relation with their source of life (progenitors) in gratitude, and with their lineage (progeny, offspring, children), in service—all throughout being called to communion in love.

Flourishing

How Does Being Created Include a Call to Flourishing?

The beauty, wonder, and ordering of the universe indicates not only a divine origin of creation but also a divine call, goal, or finality in heaven for humans. This calling, as it concerns human beings, demands personal development, a communal journey, and a God-centered narrative. It is more than the continuation of the species *homo sapiens*, the filling of earth, and stewardship over its creatures (Gen 1:28), or the perpetual inheritance of a people (Gen 18:18). From the beginning, God created humans in His own image and called us individually and communally to flourish. Indeed, he called the whole human race to flourish in this world and the next.

Some of this call to flourish is found in our yearnings for betterment of family, community, and the world. This longing also expresses particular desires that motivate a person's effort for survival, desire for family, and service to soci-

ety (Chapter 12, "Interpersonally Relational"). However, it is only in the revelation of the full plan of salvation, in the New Testament revealed through Jesus Christ (Mk 1:15; Lk 22:18), that the nature of the eternal life and beatitude intended for humans becomes clear (Mt 19:29; Jn 3:15–16; Chapter 19, "Redeemed").

At present, there is already an imperfect type of flourishing, a foretaste of eternal life, and this flourishing is manifest through the interpersonal accepting and giving of love. The whole range of flourishing (*beatitudo*) depends on interpersonal relationships and on human capacities to know, love, and act that are proportionate to our natural ends and that are made possible and elevated by grace toward our supernatural end (Aquinas, 1273/1981; Feingold, 2004; Long, 2010).

This inherent potential, being created in the image of God, is sustained and realized only through the support of God, who is the source of existence and of all that is good and, thus, ordered to human natural ends (God as the creator and sustainer of creation). God is also the source of saving grace, infused virtues, and the seven gifts of the Holy Spirit (God as source of redemption and sanctification). The ultimate flourishing is offered in the beatific vision, in communion with God, and in being a new creation in Christ (2 Cor 5:17). As the first letter of John says (3:2): "When he is revealed, we will be like him, for we will see him as he is."

How Does Flourishing Involve Natural Transcendence?

Humans manifest the inclination to flourish through the attraction of natural and supernatural gifts and promises, which are found in two sorts of transcendence (Pinckaers, 2005, pp. 359–368). One type of transcendence is that individuals rise above the natural drives and desires that serve their own needs. This is a natural bottom-up expansive transcendence of the natural inclination to goodness and flourishing that moves up through instincts toward conscious and self-conscious efforts. For example, the deeper inclination to self-preservation is manifest in the human basic animal instincts (such as the drives for physical survival, procreation, immediate care of offspring, and pleasure), which are taken up into human efforts to love others as persons and to seek truth and justice. Humans transcend their own needs and desires in unselfish acts, generous gifts, and sacrificial love. Such self-transcendence or altruism is more than a social focus on basic desires. It is also a metaphysical reality.

This natural self-transcendence of the basic instincts reaches beyond individual needs to the social realm (such as raising families, serving in the military, building homes, planting crops, and so on). Natural self-transcendence is found not only in intentional acts but also in the resultant dispositions consciously or otherwise embodied in the acquired virtues, such as justice, courage, self-control, and right practical judgment, which make serving others possible and often pleasant.

There is moreover a natural metaphysical transcendence. The very nature of the universe speaks of another level of ultimate causes that point to its origin, recognize a constant presence, and indicate a purposeful end. The Catholic Christian Meta-Model of the Person affirms that the multiple dimensions of reality or nature are a universe rather than a multiverse: there is a wholeness to reality, even if, without revelation, we can identify only part of it.

These deeper and higher levels of investigation associated with metaphysical or ontological knowledge go beyond those of the other sciences (such as physics, chemistry, and biology), since those sciences do not explain themselves, but proceed on the basis of presuppositions about reality and its end. Natural metaphysical transcendence goes beyond (*meta*) our common experiences to seek their ultimate origin (God) and the ultimate end of our natural desires for flourishing, goodness, truth, and beauty, and for spousal, family, and social relations.

How Does Flourishing Require Divine Transcendence and Closeness?

The other type of transcendence, divine transcendence, occurs through revelation and grace. Humans transcend everyday experiences and investigations of reality to reach for the origin and ultimate source of life. In the Catholic Christian vision of the person, humans have a supernatural end that is distinct from their natural end, while being united to it (Long, 2010). Human natural self-transcendence is itself transcended as human nature is further perfected by grace. Through the revelation of Jesus Christ, God the Father calls each person into intimate relationship (friendship), through the Holy Spirit's further transforming human relationships and perfecting the image of God in us. This ultimate flourishing is known through a revealed narrative that is both unique (the journey of salvation and sanctification of each person and each family) and communal (the journey of the whole of salvation history into communion with God).

The narrative is Trinitarian. God the Father's goodness and generosity are the source and fulfillment of life and love. Jesus Christ admonishes his disciples and followers in the Sermon on the Mount: "Be perfect, as your heavenly Father is perfect" (Mt 5:48). The sending of the Holy Spirit is the means by which we are elevated to participate in the divine transcendence and friendship. This elevation is also manifest in humble human action—in the confidence behind the gift of the widow's two mites (Mk 12:42) and in the struggle, identified by St. Paul, to overcome imperfection (Rom 7 & 8; 2 Cor 12:9). For humans, this call to ultimate or divine transcendence and flourishing, far from being an oppressive and impossible perfectionism, is welcome, the reward for their self-giving love, and a progressive completeness of the image of God in us (see Gregory of Nyssa, 1978; John Paul II, 1981, §17; Chapter 19, "Redeemed").

Divine and Moral Order

What Types of Presupposition Underlie Belief in the Divine and Moral Order?

Metaphysical atheists presuppose that there is neither natural nor divine moral law existing in the cosmos and underlying human society (Dawkins, 2008; Dennett, 1995). Methodological atheists, however, adopt a reductionist stance for the sake of scientific investigation, but not in denial of other valid types of knowledge that are non-scientific, such as knowledge of moral values, natural moral law, metaphysical claims, and religious doctrines.

Agnostics, for their part, deny that we can know with certainty that there is a God who is the source of cosmic order; nonetheless some agnostics are relativists while others affirm an aspect of moral order known through reason (Nagel, 2012). Some evolutionists presuppose that the idea of a moral order has evolved simply because of its utility for the continuance of the species (Hauser, 2006; Seligman, 2002). In contrast, some theists affirm the divine order that is known through faith but deny that humans can know the moral order through reason (as critiqued by Benedict XVI, 2006; Dougherty, 2010).

In contrast to all the above, Catholics, the Orthodox, and a significant number of other Christians affirm that reason and faith identify a moral and divine order in the universe, an order that each person can come to know, at least in part. Through reason, mankind can know the natural moral law as one that God has set in place in creation (Rom 1:20, 2:14; John Paul II, 1993, §54; Vatican II, 1965b). Through the gift of faith and the divine encounter with mankind, God reveals the divine order in salvation history, the offer of redemption, and the promise of eternal beatitude (Francis, 2013).

How Do We Know the Moral Order?

While faith may not be openly given to all, everyone at least has the call to be a man or woman of goodwill and to discover how to live in accord with the natural moral law, which is our rational participation in the eternal law (Rom 2:14). St. Paul affirms that through the observation of creation and the use of reason, humans can know the natural moral law. He goes so far as to say that everyone can discern God's action in created things: "Ever since the creation of the world [God's] invisible nature, namely, his eternal power and deity, has been clearly perceived in the things that he has made" (Rom 1:20; see also Aquinas, 1273/1981; John Paul II, 1998; Vatican I, 1870, Chapter 2, §1).

This confidence that humans can know the natural moral law does not deny that humans, as individuals and as societies, have misconstrued this law and have even made laws that contravene it. The fallen condition of humanity often prevents persons from apprehending moral truths that are in principle knowable by natural reason (John Paul II, 1993, §36).

Contravening laws can occur when a person uses practical reason to draw false inferences from the general principles of the natural moral law (Aquinas, 1273/1981, I-II, 94.4; MacIntyre, 2009, pp. 313–352). When human authorities contravene the law of God, people are called (by conscience formed by the higher law) to disobey. In these cases, St. Peter exhorts that: "We must obey God rather than any human authority" (Acts 5:29; see also CCC, 1997, §2242). Furthermore, the Gospel of Mark brings correction to possible simplistic interpretations of this message (12:17): "Render to Caesar the things that are Caesar's, and to God the things that are God's"

In What Way Does the Divine Moral Order Differ from the Natural Moral Order?

Our natural reason is imperfect because of our fallen condition. And we cannot attain perfect flourishing even when living in full accord with the natural moral law. Thus, the Catholic Christian tradition recognizes a need for the more complete moral knowledge that comes from God, namely the revealed divine law, as found in the Decalogue (Ex 20:1–17), the Sermon on the Mount (Mt 5–7), and the rest of the biblical and magisterial tradition. We need reason and revelation, both the natural and divine moral law, to understand the distinctness of each law and the transcendent relationship of all moral laws to the eternal law, who is God (Budziszewski, 2009; Levering, 2008).

Moreover, with the advent of new technologies and because of the challenges of reductionist ideologies and worldviews, the Magisterium offers clarity by presenting trustworthy determinations about doctrinal and moral matters, regarding the application of the moral law to specific questions, for example concerning bioethics, warfare, economics, and social teaching (International Theological Commission, 2012; John Paul II, 1993).

Even though the implications of understanding persons as created in the image of God are often obscured by the effects of the fall and by personal sin, investigation into the nature of this image remains very relevant for the study of the human sciences, especially for psychology and clinical practice. Theological considerations of being created in the image of God provide a positive contrast to the many negative experiences of human moral and spiritual evil observed in everyday life and clinical practice (see Chapter 18, "Fallen"). These considerations also highlight that human nature healed by grace can respond to divine callings and to inclinations that draw each person out of himself to others and to God (Chapter 19, "Redeemed").

REFERENCES

Allen, M. P. (2014). Gender reality. *Solidarity: The Journal of Catholic Social Thought and Secular Ethics, 4*(4), 1–36.

Aquinas, T. (1981). *Summa theologiae* (Fathers of the English Dominican Province, Trans.). Westminster, MD: Christian Classics. (Original work composed 1273)

Aquinas, T. (1987). *Faith, reason, and theology: Questions I-IV of his commentary on the De Trinitate of Boethius* (A. Maurer, Trans.). Toronto, Canada: Pontifical Institute of Mediaeval Studies. (Original work composed 1257–1258)

Atkinson, J. (2014). *Biblical and theological foundations of the family: The domestic church*. Washington, DC: The Catholic University of America Press.

Augustine. (1887). Treatise on the spirit and the letter. In P. Schaff (Series Ed.), *Nicene and Post-Nicene Fathers: Vol. 5. Augustine—Anti-Pelagian writings* (pp. 80–114). Grand Rapids, MI: Eerdmans. (Original work composed 412)

Augustine. (1991). *The Trinity* (E. Hill, Trans.). Hyde Park, NY: New City Press. (Original work composed 399–426)

Augustine. (2007). *Confessions* (2nd ed.) (M. P. Foley, Ed.; F. J. Sheed, Trans). New York, NY: Hackett. (Original work composed 397–401)

Austriaco, N. P. G., Brent, J., Davenport, T., & Ku, J. B. (2016). *Thomistic evolution: A Catholic approach to understanding evolution in the light of faith*. Middletown, DE: Cluny Media.

Bachiochi, E. (2013). Women, sexual asymmetry, and Catholic teaching. *Christian Bioethics, 19*(2), 150–171.

Beauregard, M. (2012). *Brain wars: The scientific battle over the existence of the mind and the proof that will change the way we live our lives*. New York, NY: HarperCollins.

Benedict XVI. (2006, September 12). *Faith, reason and the university: Memories and reflections* [The Regensburg address]. Vatican City, Vatican: Libreria Editrice Vaticana.

Benedict XVI. (2009). *Caritas in veritate* [Encyclical, on integral human development in charity and truth]. Vatican City, Vatican: Libreria Editrice Vaticana.

Bowen, M. (1978). *Family theory in clinical practice*. North Vale, NJ: Aronson.

Bowlby, J. (1973). *Separation: Anxiety and anger*. New York, NY: Basic Books.

Bowlby, J. (1982). *Attachment and loss: Vol. 1. Attachment* (2nd ed.). New York, NY: Basic Books. (Original work published 1969)

Bowlby, J. (1988). *A secure base: Clinical applications of attachment theory*. London, United Kingdom: Routledge.

Brizendine, L. (2006). *The female brain*. New York, NY: Broadway Books.

Brizendine, L. (2010). *The male brain*. New York, NY: Broadway Books.

Bruner, J. S. (1986). *Actual minds, possible worlds*. Cambridge, MA: Harvard University Press.

Bruner, J. S. (1990). *Acts of meaning*. Cambridge, MA: Harvard University Press.

Bruner, J. S. (1991). The narrative construction of reality. *Critical Inquiry, 18*, 1–21.

Budziszewski, J. (2009). *The line through the heart: Natural law as fact, theory, and sign of contradiction*. Wilmington, DE: ISI Books.

Cassuto, U. (2005). *A commentary on the book of Genesis, part 2: From Adam to Noah* (I. Abrahams, Trans.). Skokie, IL: Varda Books. (Original work published 1964)

Catechism of the Catholic Church (*CCC*) (2nd ed.). (1997). Vatican City, Vatican: Libreria Editrice Vaticana.

Chaberek, M. (2015). *Catholicism and evolution: A history from Darwin to Pope Francis*. Kettering, OH: Angelico Press.

Clarke, W. N. (1992). Person, being, and St. Thomas. *Communio, 19*(3), 601–618.

Clarke, W. N. (2009). *The creative retrieval of Saint Thomas Aquinas: Essays in Thomistic philosophy, new and old*. New York, NY: Fordham University Press.

Cullen, C. M. (2012). The natural desire to see God and pure nature: A debate revisited. *American Catholic Philosophical Quarterly, 86*(4), 705–730.

Damascene, J. (1999). On the orthodox faith. In H. Dressler, R. P. Russell, T. P. Halton, R. Sider, & M. J. Brennan (Eds.), *The Fathers of the Church: Saint John of Damascus: Writings* (Vol. 37) (F. H. Chase, Trans.). Washington, DC: The Catholic University of America Press. (Original work composed ca. 743–749)

Darwin, C. (2009). *On the origin of species* (6th ed.). New York, NY: Cambridge University Press. (Original work published 1859)

Davies, P. C. W. (2006). Preface. In P. C. Davies & P. Clayton (Eds.), *The re-emergence of emergence: The emergentist hypothesis from science to religion.* Oxford, United Kingdom: Oxford University Press.

Dennett, D. C. (1995). *Darwin's dangerous idea: Evolution and the meanings of life.* New York, NY: Simon & Schuster.

Dawkins, R. (2008). *The God delusion.* New York, NY: Mariner Books.

de Lubac, H. (1998). *The mystery of the supernatural.* New York, NY: Herder & Herder. (Original work published 1946)

Doidge, N. (2007). *The brain that changes itself: Stories of personal trimuph from the frontiers of brain science.* New York, NY: Penguin Books.

Dougherty, J. P. (2010). *Wretched Aristotle: Using the past to rescue the future.* Lanham, MD: Lexington Books.

Dunnington, K. (2010). *Addiction and virtue: Beyond the models of disease and choice.* Downers Grove, IL: IVP Academic.

Emery, G. (2010). *The Trinitarian theology of Saint Thomas Aquinas* (F. A. Murphy, Trans.). New York, NY: Oxford University Press.

Feingold, L. (2004). *The natural desire to see God according to St. Thomas and his interpreters.* Washington, DC: The Catholic University of America Press.

Feser, E. (2017). *Five proofs of the existence of God.* San Francisco, CA: Ignatius.

Francis. (2013). *Lumen fidei* [Encyclical, on faith]. Vatican City, Vatican: Libreria Editrice Vaticana.

Francis. (2015). *Laudato si'* [Encyclical, on care for our common home]. Vatican City, Vatican: Libreria Editrice Vaticana.

Girard, R. (1976). *Violence and the sacred* (P. Gregory, Trans.). Baltimore, MD: Johns Hopkins University Press. (Original work published 1972)

Gondreau, P. (2002). *The passions of Christ's soul in the theology of St. Thomas Aquinas.* Münster, Germany: Aschendorff.

Gregory of Nyssa. (1978). *The life of Moses* (A. Malherbe & E. Ferguson, Trans.). Mahwah, NJ: Paulist Press.

Gudan, E. (2010). *Gratitude-based interventions for treating ruminative depression* (Doctoral dissertation, The Institute for the Psychological Sciences). Retrieved from ProQuest Dissertations and Theses. (No. 3444447.)

Hall, T. W. (2007a). Psychoanalysis, attachment, and spirituality, Part I: The emergence of two relational traditions. *Journal of Psychology and Theology, 35,* 14–28.

Hall, T. W. (2007b). Psychoanalysis, attachment, and spirituality, Part II: The spiritual stories we live by. *Journal of Psychology and Theology, 35,* 28–42.

Hauser, M. D. (2006). *Moral minds: How nature designed our universal sense of right and wrong.* New York, NY: Harper Perennial.

Hayes, Z. (2001). *The gift of being: A theology of creation.* Collegeville, MN: Liturgical Press.

International Theological Commission. (2004). *Communion and stewardship: Human persons created in the image of God.* Vatican City, Vatican: Libreria Editrice Vaticana.

International Theological Commission. (2012). *Theology today: Perspectives, principles and criteria.* Vatican City, Vatican: Libreria Editrice Vaticana.

John Paul II. (1981). *Familiaris consortio* [Apostolic exhortation, on the role of the Christian family in the modern world]. Vatican City, Vatican: Libreria Editrice Vaticana.

John Paul II. (1986). *Dominum et vivificantem* [Encyclical, on the Holy Spirit in the life of the Church and the world]. Vatican City, Vatican: Libreria Editrice Vaticana.

John Paul II. (1988). *Mulieris dignitatem* [Apostolic letter, on the dignity and vocation of women]. Vatican City, Vatican: Libreria Editrice Vaticana.

John Paul II. (1993). *Veritatis splendor* [Encyclical, on certain fundamental questions of the Church's moral teaching]. Vatican City, Vatican: Libreria Editrice Vaticana.

John Paul II. (1995). *Evangelium vitae* [Encyclical, on the value and inviolabilityof human life]. Vatican City, Vatican: Libreria Editrice Vaticana.

John Paul II. (1996, October 22). *Message to the Pontifical Academy of Sciences: On evolution.* Retrieved from http://www.ewtn.com/library/PAPAL DOC/JP961022.htm

John Paul II. (1998). *Fides et ratio* [Encylical, on the

relationship between faith and reason]. Vatican City, Vatican: Libreria Editrice Vaticana.

John Paul II. (2006). *Man and woman he created them: A theology of the body* (M. Waldstein, Trans.). Boston, MA: Pauline Books and Media.

Joseph, S., & Linley, P. A. (2006). *Positive therapy: A meta-theory for positive psychological practice.* London, United Kingdom: Routledge.

Journet, C. (1960). *The meaning of grace.* New York, NY: P. J. Kenedy and Sons.

Kuhse, H., & Singer, P. (1988). *Should the baby live?: The problem of handicapped infants.* Oxford, United Kingdom: Oxford University Press.

Levering, M. (2008). *Biblical natural law: A theocentric and teleological approach.* Oxford, United Kingdom: Oxford University Press.

Levinas, E. (2000). *Alterity and transcendence.* New York, NY: Columbia University Press. (Original work published 1995)

Linley, P. A., & Joseph, S. (2004). Positive change following trauma and adversity: A review. *Journal of Traumatic Stress 17*(1), 11–21

Long, S. A. (2010). *Natura pura: On the recovery of nature in the doctrine of grace.* New York, NY: Fordham University Press.

MacIntyre, A. (2009). From answers to questions: A response to the responses. In L. S. Cunningham (Ed.), *Intractable disputes about the natural law: Alasdair MacIntyre and critics* (pp. 313–352). Notre Dame, IN: University of Notre Dame Press.

Marcel, G. (2010). *Homo viator: Introduction to the metaphysic of hope* (E. Craufurd & P. Seaton, Trans.). South Bend, IN: St. Augustine's Press.

McAdams, D. P. (1988). *Power, intimacy, and the life story.* New York, NY: Guilford.

McLeod, J. (1997). *Narrative and psychotherapy.* London, United Kingdom: Sage.

McLeod, J. (2004). The significance of narrative and storytelling in postpsychological counseling and psychotherapy. In A. Leiblich, D. P. McAdams, & R. Josselson (Eds.), *Healing plots: The narrative basis of psychotherapy* (pp. 11–28). Washington, DC: American Psychological Association.

Murphy, N., Ellis, G. F. R., & O'Connor, T. (Eds.). (2009). *Downward causation and the neurobiology of free will.* Cham, Switzerland: Springer-Verlag Berlin Heidelberg.

Nagel, T. (2012). *Mind and cosmos: Why the materialist neo-Darwinian conception of nature is almost certainly false.* New York, NY: Oxford University Press.

Ong, W. (1981). *Fighting for life: Contest, sexuality, and consciousness.* Ithaca, NY: Cornell University Press.

Peterson, C., & Seligman, M. E. P. (2004). *Character strengths and virtues: A handbook and classification.* New York, NY: Oxford University Press.

Pieper, J. (1994). *Hope and history* (D. Kipp, Trans.). San Francisco: Ignatius Press. (Original work published 1967)

Pieper, J. (2009). *Leisure: The basis of culture* (A. Dru, Trans.). San Francisco, CA: Ignatius Press. (Original work published 1952)

Pinckaers, S. (1995). *The sources of Christian ethics* (M. T. Noble, Trans.). Washington, DC: The Catholic University of America Press. (Original work published 1985)

Pinckaers, S. (2005). Aquinas on nature and the supernatural. In J. Berkman & C. S. Titus (Eds.), *The Pinckaers reader: Renewing Thomistic moral theology* (pp. 359–368). Washington, DC: The Catholic University of America Press. (Original work published 1992)

Pius XII. (1950). *Humani generis* [Encyclical, concerning some false opinions threatening to undermine the foundations of Catholic doctrine]. Vatican City, Vatican: Libreria Editrice Vaticana.

Post, S. G. (Ed.). (2007). *Altruism and health: Perspectives from empirical research.* Oxford, United Kingdom: Oxford University Press.

Post, S., & Neimark, J. (2007). *Why good things happen to good people: The exciting new research that proves the link between doing good and living a longer, healthier, happier life.* New York, NY: Broadway Books.

Rhoads, S. E. (2004). *Taking sex differences seriously* (1st ed.). San Francisco, CA: Encounter Books.

Roe v. Wade, 410 U.S. 113 (1973).

Rogers, C. R. (2012). *On becoming a person: A therapist's view of psychotherapy.* Boston, MA: Houghton Mifflin Harcourt. (Original work published 1961)

Sacks, O. (1998). *The man who mistook his wife for a hat: And other clinical tales.* New York, NY: Touchstone.

Savage, D. (2015). The nature of woman in relation to man: Genesis 1 and 2 through the lens of the metaphysical anthropology of Aquinas. *Logos: A Journal of Catholic Thought and Culture, 18*(1), 71–93.

Schmitz, K. (2009). *Person and psyche.* Arlington, VA: Institute for the Psychological Sciences Press.

Schore, A. N. (2002). Dysregulation of the right brain: A fundamental mechanism of traumatic attachment and the psychopathogenesis of posttraumatic stress disorder. *Australian and New Zealand Journal of Psychiatry, 36*(1), 9–30.

Schönborn, C. (2007). *Chance or purpose? Creation, evolution, and a rational faith* (H. P. Weber, Ed.; H. Taylor, Trans.). San Francisco, CA: Ignatius.

Schumacher, M. (Ed.). (2004). *Women in Christ: Toward a new feminism.* Grand Rapids, MI: Eerdmans.

Segal, D. J., & Solomon, M. (2013). *Healing moments in psychotherapy* (Norton Series on Interpersonal Neurobiology). New York, NY: W. W. Norton.

Siegel, D. J. (2012a). *Pocket guide to interpersonal neurobiology: An integrative handbook of the mind* (1st ed.). New York, NY: Norton.

Siegel, D. J. (2012b). *The developing mind* (2nd ed.). New York, NY: Guilford.

Seligman, M. E. P. (2002). *Authentic happiness.* New York, NY: The Free Press.

Shafer, R. (1992). *Retelling a life: Narration and dialogue in psychoanalysis.* New York, NY: Basic Books.

Sherwin, M. S. (2009). Infused virtue and the effects of acquired vice: A test case for the Thomistic theory of infused cardinal virtues. *The Thomist, 73*(1), 29–52.

Singer, P. (2011). *Practical ethics.* Cambridge, United Kingdom: Cambridge University Press. (Original work published 1980)

Sokolowski, R. (1995). *The God of faith and reason: Foundations of Christian theology.* Washington, DC: The Catholic University of America Press. (Original work published 1982)

Spence, D. (1982). *Narrative truth and historical truth: Meaning and interpretation in psychoanalysis.* New York, NY: Norton.

Spitzer, R. J. (2010). *New proofs for the existence of God: Contributions of contemporary physics and philosophy.* Grand Rapids, MI: Eerdmans.

Stein, E. (1996). The separate vocations of man and woman according to nature and grace (F. M. Oben, Trans.). In L. Gelber & R. Leuven (Eds.), *Essays on woman: The collected works of Edith Stein* (2nd ed.; pp. 59–85). Washington, DC: Institute for Carmelite Studies Publications. (Original work published 1932)

Titus, C. S. (2009). Passions in Christ: Spontaneity, development, and virtue. *The Thomist, 73*(1), 53–88.

Torrell, J. P. (2003). *Saint Thomas Aquinas: Vol. 2. Spiritual master* (R. Royal, Trans.). Washington, DC: The Catholic University of America Press. (Original work published 1996)

Trautman, L. J. (2006). *Virtue as a support for psychological health in the treatment of narcissistic personality disorder* (Unpublished doctoral dissertation). The Institute for the Psychological Sciences, Arlington, VA.

Vatican I, Council. (1869–1870). *Dei filius* [Dogmatic constitution on the Catholic faith]. Retrieved from http://www.ewtn.com/library/COUNCILS/V1.htm

Vatican II, Council. (1964). *Lumen gentium* [Dogmatic constitution on the Church]. Vatican City, Vatican: Libreria Editrice Vaticana.

Vatican II, Council. (1965a). *Dei verbum* [Dogmatic constitution on Divine Revelation]. Vatican City, Vatican: Libreria Editrice Vaticana.

Vatican II, Council. (1965b). *Gaudium et spes* [Pastoral constitution on the Church in the modern world]. Vatican City, Vatican: Libreria Editrice Vaticana.

Vitz, P. C. (1994). *Psychology as religion: The cult of self-worship* (2nd ed.). Grand Rapids, MI: Eerdmans.

von Balthasar, H. U. (1990). *The glory of the Lord: A theological aesthetics: Vol. 7. Theology: The new covenant* (B. McNeil, Trans.). San Francisco, CA: Ignatius Press. (Original work published 1969)

von Balthasar, H. U. (2013). *Theo-Drama: Theological dramatic theory: Vol. 3. Dramatis personae: Persons in Christ.* San Francisco, CA: Ignatius Press. (Original work published 1978)

Wenham, G. J. (2000). *Story as Torah: Reading the Old Testament narrative ethically.* Grand Rapids, MI: Baker Academics.

Wojtyła, K. (1979). *The acting person: A contribution to phenomenological anthropology* (A-T Tymieniecka, Ed.; A. Potocki, Trans.). Boston, MA: Reidel Publishing. (Original work published 1969)

Wojtyła, K. (1993). *Love and responsibility* (H. T. Willetts, Trans.). San Francisco, CA: Ignatius Press. (Original work published 1960)

Wright, R. (2001). *Non-zero: The logic of human destiny*. New York, NY: Vintage.

Wright, R. (2009). *The evolution of God*. New York, NY: Little, Brown.

Zundel, M. (2012). *The splendour of the liturgy*. Delia, KS: St. Pius X Press. (Original work published 1939)

Życiński, J. (2006). *God and evolution: Fundamental questions of Christian evolutionism* (K. W. Kemp & Z. Maślanka, Trans.). Washington, DC: The Catholic University of America Press.

Chapter 18

Fallen

CRAIG STEVEN TITUS,

MATTHEW R. MCWHORTER,

AND CHRISTOPHER GROSS

ABSTRACT: In this chapter, the implications of a Catholic Christian vision of the person as fallen (that is, as influenced by the effects of sin and evil, including original, personal, and social sin, as well as demonic evil) are explored, along with their effects on flourishing. Using examples from contemporary psychological theories, this chapter addresses the following questions and explores the implications of the Catholic Christian Meta-Model of the Person for understanding disorders and trials: How does being emotionally wounded, morally troubled, and spiritually fallen affect the person's flourishing? How are the effects of evil communicated by the imitation of behavior and desire that negatively influence flourishing? How does a denial of sin and evil, or a simplistic vision of them, change one's vision of interpersonal relationships? What difference does the Catholic Christian teaching on the fundamental goodness of human nature and of each person make for understanding the persistent and ongoing influence of sin and evil? The chapter also presents the scriptural and theological principles that address sin and evil, their origins, their causes, as well as their consequences. Experiences of suffering, shame, and guilt are analyzed as potentially destructive or constructive. Furthermore, the chapter recognizes that spiritual troubles can be used to attract attention, or they can be confused with psychological issues. Throughout, the chapter identifies some moral implications of a Catholic Christian vision of the struggle with and cooperation in evil (including demonic evil), human fallenness, weakness, and suffering.

What do "the fall" and "fallen" mean for understanding the continuous struggles with human sin and evil? The term "fall," a conceptual metaphor, primarily signifies an ontological change in humanity—the loss of an original state of friendship and justice between God and mankind. It confirms that there is a disordering of the mind and heart, in relation to oneself, to others, and even to God. Adam and Eve fell from the original state of grace when they disobeyed God. The fall is synonymous with what Christians call original sin, which is unlike other sins, since it is not merited but rather inherited as part of the human condition.

This chapter will address the following questions: What difference does a Catholic Christian account of the fall from a state of original grace and friendship with God make for understanding the person's ongoing struggles between flourishing and languishing? (See Gen 3:10–24; Rom 5:19.) How do people, because of fallen human nature and personal limitations, exhibit a need for both effort and grace to *do what is good* (for example, in general, to act in such a way as to respect the basic dignity of other people) and *to avoid evil* (for instance, in particular, to not be unfaithful to one's spouse)? How does a fallen state require that people come to understand their disordered dispositions, such as tendencies to react, feel, and think in ways that lead toward injustice, hatred, indifference, impatience, and so on? In the midst of these important questions, we ask the most basic one: What difference would it make if the negative influence of sin, evil, and disorder on the person were ontologically more foundational than goodness, justice, and redemption?

Human life is commonly experienced as a mixture of flourishing and languishing, consolation and desolation, pleasure and pain. We find joy, success, and goodness as well as suffering, failure, and evil woven not only into great literature, but also into our own lives and families. Some literary narratives represent evil victorious, such as Shakespeare's *Hamlet* or Marlowe's *Doctor Faustus*. Other narratives represent good victorious, such as Tolkien's *The Lord of the Rings* or Lewis's *Chronicles of Narnia*. Many narratives, including those of most people, involve complex journeys from tragedy to flourishing, flourishing to tragedy, and then back again. Throughout these stories, our aspirations for goodness, love, growth, and completeness guide us to flourishing. These aspirations, however, contrast with the occurrences, even continuing occurrences, of evil, indifference, isolation, weakness, and imperfection that make us languish. Good and evil and the persistence of evil and sin are complex and not easy to understand.

The psychiatrist Karl Menninger (1973) states that one of the best-documented facts is that humans are weak, wounded, and influenced by sin. The darkness of human nature—genocide, serial killers, abortion, terrorist attacks, sexual trafficking, hateful gossip, and harmful ideologies and social practices—theologically is recognized as the results of sin (Lee & Theol, 2014; Mullen, 2007). There is also the common, more everyday sin and evil found in addiction, domestic violence, bullying, adulterous betrayal, and lying, as well as the many consequences of such psychological states as envy, greed, lust, common selfishness, and rage.

Focused observation, clinical practice, and recorded history, all offer support for the view that human experience is replete with weakness, brokenness, fallenness, and sin. We often miss the moral and spiritual mark in ourselves and our interpersonal relationships, or we even do not aim at the right goal. Different interpretations of the person, however, have placed spiritual, moral, and psychological infirmity and vulnerability at a more or less fundamental level.

The present chapter predominantly makes reference to both Scripture and tradition in an integrative effort in dialogue with philosophy and psychology. It posits the basic question of what difference a Catholic Christian perspective on fallenness, sin, and evil makes for understanding the human condition and freedom. Toward this end, this chapter first presents the Christian view of fallenness and original sin. It then considers, in light of such ultimate meaning or the lack thereof, the disorders and trials or suffering that humans inevitably face. It also explores the consequences that sin has on human action, freedom, and responsibility. Most importantly, the chapter explores how the basic goodness of human nature remains even after the fall, and how the effects of the fall and of sin continue in time. Finally, it identifies the types of evil and describes the struggle not to cooperate significantly with evil.

What Is Fallenness?

In the Catholic Christian view of salvation history, the term "fallen" supposes that, in the beginning, God created the world and human beings as "very good" (Gen 1:31), yet humans have lost that original state of innocence, justice, friendship with God, and grace (Gen 3:10–24; Rom 5:19; Aquinas, 1273/1981, I-II, 82.1–4). After the fall from that first graced state, humans, to promote healing and flourishing, have aspired to a goodness that now needs further divine aid, personal effort, and interpersonal support (*Catechism of the Catholic Church* [CCC], 2000, §1811). The influence of original sin and of the fall from that first state of grace is apparent in common personal struggles, which show up in difficulties in work, suffering in relationships, and a sense of futility in life.

What Are the Common Explanations of Fallenness and Evil?

Every worldview and value system has an account of the origin and extent of human weakness and disorder (Haidt, 2006; Chapter 4, "Modern Personality Theories"). The meaning or meaninglessness one finds in the experience of suffering and evil is different depending on how evil and disorder are perceived. Here are several common representative schools of thought about the nature of evil.

First, nihilists and atheistic existentialists deny that there is meaning in life, or they view evil as the existential basis of reality and human life. There is simply a lack of any objective or common meaning that would make things good. Rather, the meaning of human nature, relationships, and acts are merely constructed through each individual's will (Sartre, 1946/2007; Nietzsche, 1885/1989).

Second, some monist schools (pantheism; Advaita Vedanta Hinduism) view evil as an illusion that should be relativized and ignored. There is ultimately only one type of being, a Self, which can be separated from the cycle of empirical causes and effects among which evil might arise (Embree, 1972, p. 50; Deutsch & Dalvi, 2004, pp. 9, 162, 248, 278–280).

Third, good-evil dualists (e.g., Zoroastrianism; Manichaeism) view evil as a fundamental co-principle standing in opposition to goodness. There are two equal forces in existence, one good and one evil (Augustine, ca. 405/1994, Chapter 41).

Fourth, the Jewish, Catholic, and Orthodox Christian traditions view evil as the loss of the original goodness of creation or the moral privation of what should be. God is good, and creation is fundamentally good (Maimonides, 1190/1964). Evil was caused by pride (disordered love of self) and disobedience (a choice of one's own will over the will of God). Allegiance to one's own self and not to the will of God remains at the heart of original sin. Nonetheless, through God's own plan, the victory over evil is already assured, although it will be apparent only at the end of time (Chapter 19, "Redeemed").

What method does this chapter use to understand the Catholic Christian vision of fallenness? This chapter presents the Catholic Christian Meta-Model of the Person, at the theological level, as a biblically informed vision of human origin, growth, and final or ultimate end, a model that is normative and objective, but also developmental and subjective. Even though this chapter adapts theological method rooted in revelation, it must also convincingly address the interpretation of evil behavior and human fallenness in a careful study of human languishing and suffering. Such a full understanding of the fallen condition aims to acquire more than a simple knowledge of perceptions, emotional phenomena, and abstract reflections on suffering. It seeks to know the real or actual experience, growth, and healing associated with one's personal psychology and worldview (be it that of the therapist or the client). It particularly seeks connections between (a) human experiences of suffering and evil, (b) the etiology suggested by the human sciences, and (c) spiritually formed worldviews, including but not limited to those that are Christian in origin (Frankl, 1959/2006, 2000). In sum, this chapter will use the Meta-Model to seek a fuller vision of the disordered or fallen condition by examining the origin, meaning, and consequences of evil and sin, with the help of different disciplines.

How Does the Bible Illustrate Original Grace?

According to the two Genesis creation accounts, Adam and Eve first experienced a deep and basic harmony and integrity in a condition of moral innocence and original grace and justice, when the moral law could have been rejected. Prior to that time, they experienced a period that was somewhat analogous to the human child before he becomes morally responsible at about age six, when they are innocent of the law itself (Rom 5:13; Vitz, 2017).

For an unknown length of time, they enjoyed peace and friendship with God and each other. They existed in this condition of "original innocence," and "original justice" (Aquinas, 1273/1981, I-II, 82–83; John Paul II, 2006), as well as "original holiness" (*CCC*, 2000, §404). Upon creating them, God pronounces that they are "very good" (Gen 1:31). This state had four attributes: (1) the human being's will was naturally obedient and responsive to God, (2) the other capacities of knowing and loving (cognition and affect) were

ordered toward God as their final goal, (3) Adam and Eve unselfishly loved each other, and (4) they also were good stewards of the rest of creation (Aquinas 1273/1981, I-II, 82.3). Because of this just and loving ordering, their efforts were easy, prompt, and joy-filled. Their emotions were subjugated to their will, their will to their reason, and the whole person was loving and obedient to God (*CCC*, 2000, §376, §400). Even given this ideal situation of original justice, though, Adam and Eve still needed grace to steadfastly assure the allegiance of their minds and wills to God (Aquinas, 1270/2003, 5.1, ad 13; Chapter 17, "Created in the Image of God").

How Does the Book of Genesis Illustrate Original Sin?

The third chapter of the book of Genesis gives the account of the first human sin, describing it as a prideful disobedience to God, who had set very clear limits on the first human persons in the first covenant. From a theological point of view, John Paul II (2006) affirms that the Genesis account of the first sin and ensuing shame (Gen 3:1–5) must be understood in the normative context of God's gift of love and the original covenant. In this reading, the first step toward sin was doubt. John Paul II (2006), in his *Man and Woman He Created Them: A Theology of the Body*, explains that sin is introduced in the human heart by a doubt about "the deepest meaning of the gift, that is, about love as the specific motive of creation" (26.5, p. 237). Consequently, pride enters when love is weakened by doubt. Adam and Eve are led to distrust God and to think that he is holding out on them.

How Does the Rest of the Bible Illustrate Fallenness?

This Genesis account is only the first of the many faces of evil and types of sin that Scripture chronicles. There are the examples of a tendency to evil: deceit, disobedience and distrust (Gen 3:1–5; Jn 8:44); compromised "goods" and temptation (Gen 3:6; 2 Cor 11:12–15; Mt 6:13); and avoidance of responsibility (Gen 3:12–13; Jn 3:20). The Old Testament book of Ecclesiastes, moreover, is pessimistic about the human capacity for goodness, as when it states:

> What has a man from all the toil and strain with which he toils beneath the sun? For all his days are full of pain, and his work is a vexation; even in the night his mind does not rest. This also is vanity. (Eccl 2:22–23)

This account graphically focuses on what goes wrong in human experience, as well as on the fragility of life. The Book of Job, likewise, demonstrates how the loss of family and the abandonment of friends cause suffering, yet also how such painful experiences are the occasion to express faith in God. Such suffering is the basis for a long and painful trial by which Job is found righteous (Job 42:7–17). The example of Job, as that of the prophets and saints, is not pointless, since it shows how faith in God enables humans to resist sin and endure evil (Isa 52–53).

In the New Testament as well, the weakness, disorder, illness, and death that humans experience is a sign of human limitation and universal fallenness. These shortcomings and limitations have become, however, an opportunity for something positive. The Easter liturgy of the Roman Rite proclaims that from the evil of the fall comes the offer of salvation: "O happy fault that earned so great, so glorious a Redeemer!" (*Roman Missal*, 2012, Easter Proclamation [Exsúltet], p. 472). The New Covenant puts new emphasis on God's plan of salvation, through the life, suffering, death, and resurrection of Jesus Christ. In the Catholic Christian perspective, meaning can be found in the midst of suf-

fering and good in the midst of evil (Rom 8:28), even though suffering itself is not considered good. Experiences of brokenness or fallenness even serve as opportunities for growth, conversion, purification, and sacrificial self-giving.

As will become apparent in the next chapter on the Christian understanding of redemption, the experience of suffering and fallenness has a bidirectional potential. It can be destructive or salvific. It can lead to hatred and resentment or mercy and reconciliation. It can be a source of self-destruction or purification; and, moreover, it may also lead to cursing God or to praising him. For example, the first letter of St. Peter says,

> In this you rejoice, though now for a little while you may have to suffer various trials, so that the genuineness of your faith, more precious than gold which though perishable is tested by fire, may redound to praise and glory and honor at the revelation of Jesus Christ. (1 Pet 1:6–7)

This confident message is also expressed in St. Paul's belief that God supports each person in his trials, when he says: "God is faithful and will not let you be tried beyond your strength" (1 Cor 10:13). This confidence in God, nonetheless, raises questions about how to understand the evil, disorder, and trials that humans do experience on a regular basis.

How Does the Catholic Christian Tradition Further Understand the Fall and Original Sin?

St. Augustine identifies Adam and Eve's disobedient pride as the origin of the fall (427/2002, XIV.13). Incited by the wickedness and pride of the tempter, Adam and Eve chose to believe that they could take the place of God and gain something in the process. The apparent gain turns out to be a real loss. According to the book of Sirach, pride is the root of sin, while humility is its remedy (10:13 & 10:28). The effect of pride is the disordering, deforming, and disfiguring of human capacities. Augustine affirms a contrastive relationship between (a) the primacy of pride, as a sinful stance that spawns other disordered acts and dispositions such as avarice and envy, and (b) the primacy of love, as a virtuous stance that informs every virtue (Cavadini, 1999, p. 680).

Adam and Eve, the first spiritual and moral agents of the human race, represent both the particularity and universality of mankind (Vatican II, 1965, §13.1; CCC, 2000, §390). On the one hand, they were individual persons and responsible for their own actions. They are like us, sharing a common human nature that is vulnerable because of the sin of others. However, it was because of Adam and Eve's unique situation and their particular choices that mankind has experienced the depth of the spiritual wound caused by "original sin," described above. They set in motion choosing the self instead of God, a kind of response that the rest of humanity quickly adopted.

The condition of original justice ended with the sin of Adam and Eve, as just mentioned. Because of their sin of pride and disobedience, in which they lost trust in God's goodness and abused their freedom, they fell from this privileged state. The first act of sin of Adam and Eve became a wounded condition of human nature (at the level of an ontological state), for themselves and the rest of the human family. Original sin is thus a condition—it is a "sin" only by analogy (CCC, 2000, §404). In an existential mood, Augustine (401/2007, VII.7.11) speaks of the mystery of lawlessness associated with original sin as unsolvable. It has introduced a residual disordering at personal, interpersonal, and social levels (CCC, 2000, §385).

From the disobedience of the first humans, the state of original sin continues to plague the human race (Rom 5:12). The origin of sin therefore cannot be adequately comprehended simply as a developmental issue or as a weakness of will or as an inadequate social structure (CCC, 2000, §387). To the question "what is the origin of sin," St. Augustine himself says: "I sought whence evil comes and there was no solution" (401/2007, VII.7.7). Original sin was the personal sin of Adam and Eve. However, it is passed on as a fallen state to human beings, who receive original sin "with human nature, 'by propagation not by imitation'" (Paul VI, 1968, §16; CCC, 2000, §419). Just as the good of human nature is communicated to all as a result of the "unity of the human race," so is the disorder of original sin transmitted to all on the same basis (Aquinas, 1270/2003, 4.1), that is, with the exception of Mary and Jesus, who are preserved from original and actual sin (see Chapter 19, "Redeemed"). Original sin is a state that is contracted rather than a sinful act that is committed (CCC, 2000, §404, §419, §§385–409). As such, it affects mankind in general. The origin of sin and the nature of original sin are comprehensible only in the frame of creation and free will. They are a lack of the moral ordering that should be found in human inclinations, cognition, affection, actions, and relationships. "For evil is the absence of the good, which is natural and due to a thing" (Aquinas, 1273/1981, I, 49.1). Since the effects of original sin continue (even after the forgiveness of sin through the sacraments of Baptism and Reconciliation), there is a continual spiritual struggle or battle, which will be discussed later in this chapter.

What Are the Results of Original Sin?

There are at least five results of original sin. First, the event of Adam and Eve willfully turning away from God upset the original communion of the first man and woman with God. No longer could they walk together with God. But rather they had fear of the One who was their beatitude (Gen 3:8–10). In turn, all mankind lacks original justice, that is, the original harmony with God. Interpersonal conflict, jealousy, and injustice came into existence with the fall.

Second, original sin as the loss of original grace entails a loss of humanity's original intra-personal harmony. It is a source of continued struggle with disordered passions. For Adam and Eve, and for all men and women, original sin has also disordered the other capacities of the soul so that they no longer are simply ruled by reason and love; this disorder influences the will, actions, bodily inclinations, and desires (Aquinas 1273/1981, I-II, 82.3, 83.3, 83.4). Anxiety, fear, and depression entered the world with the fall. In particular, fear of the gods replaced the previous harmonious love of God.

At the same time, the human will, for example, is not thereby so ruined that it can will nothing but evil (for an alternate view, see Calvin, 1536/1960; Luther, 1525/1962, p. 203). In the Catholic Christian view, the divine resemblance in mankind is wounded and disfigured (Gen 3:16–19), and the human attractions and mind are influenced by a type of wound and vulnerability (Aquinas, 1273/1981, I-II, 85.3). The natural inclinations or roots of virtue remain something good and positive in humanity; but because of the fall, these inclinations encounter obstacles (Aquinas, 1273/1981, I-II, 85.2). These good natural inclinations experience four wounds, which inhibit the easy acquisition of the four cardinal natural moral virtues. Instead of easily acquiring prudence, the human intellect is prone to ignorance; instead of easily acquiring justice, the human will is prone to acts of selfishness and malice. And instead of easily acquiring fortitude and temperance, the human emotions are prone to cowardly moral weakness and disordered sen-

sual desires (Aquinas, 1273/1981, I-II, 85.3; CCC, 2000, §37).

Third, the fall meant the loss of the gift of immortality, which brings the death of the body (Wis 1:13, 2:23–24). However, even though the body dies, the soul continues existence until it is united to its glorified body at the resurrection. At the beginning God creates each human soul as spiritual and immortal (CCC, 2000, §382 & §366; on the soul, see Chapter 5, "Basic Psychological Support"). God's special protection originally preserved humans from suffering death (Rom 5:12; Aquinas, 1273/1981, I-II, 85.6; CCC, 2000, §402, §999), that is, God did not intend human persons to consciously experience death (Gen 3:3) or the sufferings and miseries that derive from the fall (CCC, 2000, §403), or various pathologies and difficulties that came with the loss of the body's full submission to the soul (Aquinas, 1273/1981, I-II, 85.5 ad 1).

Fourth, this fall affects interpersonal relationships, with the loss of original unity and original innocence (John Paul II, 2006). For example, it entails the increase of a woman's pain in childbirth and a disordering of her good desire for her husband. For Adam and other men, the fall entails difficulty in labor, for the earth and external reality do not always cooperate with man's will (Gen 3:16–17).

Fifth, original sin brought about the universal condition of sin—personal sins (immoderate anger and hatred), social sins (racism) and structural sins (unjust laws). It negatively affects the individual, married couples, friends, and all social relations in their rapports within and among themselves and with God; moreover it affects families, communities, and nations. As sin, it also requires the forgiveness, justification, and sanctification offered through Baptism (Augustine, 396/1953; CCC, §403, §1250).

The fall constitutes the basis for grave struggles, trials, and quests for meaning in a world that holds the potential for both flourishing and languishing. It introduces a new need for grace for our healing and positive development (Aquinas, 1273/1981, I-II, 109.7; 1270/2003, 5.1 ad 13).

However, one need not assume or conclude from the narrative of the Catholic tradition that the wounding of human nature is as deep (or deeper) than the good instilled at creation. Indeed, a Catholic and Orthodox approach to the Christian tradition has interpreted evil as a serious troubling of the divine image in mankind, which causes damage to our relationship with God (as well as with others and our selves)

and introduces the experience of tendencies toward evil that do not come from God (Vatican II, 1965, §13.1). Nonetheless, this troubling struggle does not obliterate the image of God in the human person: Original sin does not destroy God's capacity either to forgive the human person and grant salvation (justification) or to heal the effects of sin and to elevate the acts of the virtues (sanctification). Furthermore, despite our wounded nature, every person retains a basic dignity that can never be removed (Gen 1:27–28; Aquinas, 1273/1981; International Theological Commission, 2004, §22).

Disorder and Human Trials

The biopsychosocial sciences, in the medical model of diagnosing pathology, have been attentive to human suffering and weakness. They use notions of dysfunction, abnormality, disorder, and pathology to measure and diagnose individuals. For example, the mental health profession focuses on the suffering and difficulty related to insecure attachment, irrational beliefs (automatic or core beliefs), anxiety, depression, or addiction. Its diagnostic handbooks, *Diagnostic and Statistical Manual* (DSM-5) (American Psychiatric Association, 2013), *Psychodynamic Diagnostic Manual* (PDM) (Lingiardi & McWilliams, 2006), and *International Statistical Classification of Diseases and Related Health Problems* (ICD-10) (World Health Organization, 2015) offer criteria to identify human pain, suffering, and disorder. Mental health practitioners have also ventured to categorize internal experience and external behavior, emotional and social function, and personality patterns and disorders (Lingiardi & McWilliams, 2006). These diagnostic approaches employ neuroscience and empirical bases for their criteria and approaches.

There is, however, a wider type of assessment, or understanding the person (which is not properly a clinical diagnosis) that is possible with a Catholic Christian Meta-Model. For instance, there are vocational and personal flourishing assessments that bring a further vision to bear on personal suffering and weaknesses (see Chapter 21, "Case Conceptualization," Chapter 23, "Enriching Psychodiagnostics," and Chapter 24, "Psychological Assessment").

What Difference Does the Meta-Model Make for Understanding Disorder and Trials?

The Catholic Christian vision of the person integrates spiritual narrative (faith-based), philosophical dialectic (reason-based), and mental health (psychology and counseling-focused) perspectives in a comprehensive Meta-Model of the person. The Model frames personal and interpersonal flourishing and suffering in a wider worldview and value system than any of the many partial theories currently existing in the mental health field. This more comprehensive frame serves (a) in integrating the truths of modern theories and practices, (b) in ascertaining their limitations, (c) in offering integrative contributions that safeguard against these limitations and (d) in bringing innovation to understanding the person who is facing trials and disorder; for example, these innovations come through considering vocations, virtues, body-soul unity, and our divine-based dignity.

First, the theological and philosophical frame of the Catholic Christian vision of the person allows for dialogue with different disciplines about the truth of the person's fallenness; for example, modern (secular) mental health theory and practice offers important knowledge about human psychological disorders and languishing through its personality theories, assessment tools, approaches to diagnosis, and treatment modalities. These mental health theories offer knowledge about the development of compulsion, depression, anxiety, and addiction, and many other disorders.

Second, the Meta-Model helps to identify what is lacking in common uses of these modern approaches. For example, it identifies the lack of a systematic and consistent moral framework. In addition, it identifies a similar lack of systematic and consistent understanding of spiritual life. Furthermore, the Meta-Model also makes clear that the moral and spiritual life are far more central to understanding the person than most contemporary psychological theories admit. Contemporary psychological theories and practice, in addition, largely ignore the existence of evil. For example, they have a limited knowledge of moral injuries, objective guilt, and struggles with evil. They also tend to overlook resources that can aid healing, such as forgiveness and reconciliation, also the virtues, faith prayer, sacraments, and so on.

Third, the Meta-Model, because of its focus on the whole person, safeguards clinicians from

reducing the person to explanation by a partial theory or to being simply understood through a diagnostic category. Instead, the failures and the suffering of the person are always considered in the larger theological, philosophical, and psychological context.

Fourth, the Meta-Model opens the way for new approaches and innovations rooted in the Catholic Christian vision of the person as fallen (and redeemed, as we will see in the next chapter). For example, it opens the way also for a fuller understanding of meaning in suffering.

What Causes Human Suffering?

Suffering is rooted in human experiences of physical pain, moral evil, psychological disorder, relational losses and conflicts, and spiritual trials. It is also rooted in the lack of hope, joy, or flourishing. Much personal suffering is caused by a lack of purpose and fulfillment. Such suffering can be insignificant or unceasing. It can be trivial or salvific. Every person and community must face experiences of pain, meaninglessness, and languishing. And every worldview and value system must address suffering, loss of meaning, and lack of flourishing.

No matter how suffering is understood, hope or despair makes the difference in what is bearable. For example, existentialist and nihilist approaches, such as that of Jean-Paul Sartre (1946/2007), start by presuming that suffering and meaninglessness constitute the deepest level of human experience. Nihilism ultimately leads to a relativist perspective that denies the possibility of finding objective meaning and hope in the midst of suffering. Freud (1930/2010), for his part, held that the work of psychotherapy (psychoanalysis) was to help people move from misery to attaining an everyday sort of suffering.

To understand teleological, vocational, and virtue approaches to the whole range of human suffering, we need to consider its spiritual dimension (based on Christian Scripture and tradition), which presupposes that flourishing, beatitude, and joy constitute the deepest reality and provident goal of human life. This goal can be experienced in part at present and in full at the end of time. Hope, both natural and ultimate (theological) hope, is foundational. Even in the midst of inevitable spiritual suffering, psychological distress, and physical death, this teleological perspective on suffering helps to explain why experiences of languishing are repugnant to our deepest desire for flourishing: they contrast genuine longings for true goods, such as existence and life; harmonious marriage, family, and social relations; truth and beauty; and, ultimately, communion with God (Ashley, 2013; Schmitz, 2009).

The simple lack of many of these goods (or a distorted search for them) is often the cause of suffering, despair, loneliness, and anxiety. When humans pursue goods in a disordered way, even attempts to remedy human pain, suffering, and languishing can become paradoxical. For instance, self-preservation, pleasure, and marital relations are real goods to be desired, sought, and enjoyed. These goods, however, are not ultimate goods (Aquinas, 1273/1981, I-II, 1–5; Spitzer, 2015). A disordered approach for these goods (trying to make ultimate what is not) causes further types of suffering.

When Does Suffering Have Meaning?

Some suffering, pain, or discomfort can intentionally be chosen to serve a good, such as in therapeutic medical procedures, purposeful sacrifices (difficult work for the benefit of family harmony, educational goals, and sport activities), self-discipline (to develop the virtues needed for one's vocations and to focus attention on God, loved ones, and important life goals), or the personal recollection and acknowledgement of one's own wrongdoing (in order to make forgiveness possible and reconciliation effective) (John Paul II, 1984a; Enright & Fitzgibbons, 2014; Worthington, 2006).

Beyond a nuanced description of suffering, there are the ethical-spiritual issues related to how to make sense out of suffering, when to permit it, and how to limit it (Frankl, 1959/2006, 2000; John Paul II, 1984b; Lewis, 1944, 1961). Considered from a Catholic perspective, pain and suffering are evils that in most cases should be avoided or minimized, especially when the suffering is intense and diminishes the expression of our natural capacities. At the same time, suffering has taken on new meaning in God's saving plan through the redemptive suffering and death of Jesus Christ, which he freely accepted in completion of the Father's plan of salvation. In particular cases, it should not be surprising that Christians seek to share in Christ's redeeming sacrifice by choosing to unite themselves with the suffering Christ, by bearing inevitable pain, or when suffering persecution because of opposing abortion, physician-assisted suicide, or euthanasia (Congregation for the Doctrine of the Faith, 1980; also Austriaco, 2011).

The Catholic Christian view recognizes that inevitable pain, suffering, and languishing can be transformed through finding everyday and ultimate meaning in them and in life in general (Frankl, 1959/2006, 2000; John Paul II, 1984b). Such meaning is found in the practice of virtue and commitment to one's vocations, which point not only to a joy that fulfills a person, but also to love that has a cost. For example, there is meaning in the suffering that is inevitably associated with *love* (*agapē*) as found in self-giving and self-sacrificial acts of maternal patience or paternal courage—the gift of self in family or friendship, in the face of limited time and resources, but also in the light of real benefit. There is meaning that is brought by *forgiveness* as found in family settings where real wrongs occur and where forgiveness involves releasing the other from his or her debt; the painful sacrifice opens the door to peace and reconciliation (John Paul II, 1984a). There is also that *compassion* that creates dialogue and establishes communion, which is courageously bought at the price of suffering along with the other person, and which is the backbone of finding meaning in every vocational state and calling to work and service (Benedict XVI, 2005).

We suffer not only pain but also fear about pain and suffering. It is common that people near the end of life suffer from an acute fear of having to experience unbearable pain or a protracted dying process. They fear being perceived as a burden or financial drain on family, friends, and society. The responsibility of the caregivers is to respect the person, preserve the patient's quality of life as much as possible, and protect the person from the burdens of protracted extraordinary care and let natural death occur (United States Conference of Catholic Bishops, 2009; also Austriaco, 2011).

For the Christian, suffering, in its various forms, can be associated with the suffering of Christ. When one intentionally joins oneself to Christ, one's own suffering takes on new meaning (John Paul II, 1984b; Congregation for the Doctrine of the Faith, 1980). The spiritual association with the person of Jesus Christ puts one's physical and mental suffering in the context of

God's presence, mercy, and plan of salvation. Furthermore, engaging in transformational religious practices, such as participation in the sacraments (sacrifice of the Mass), provides a means whereby this new meaning can be experienced and expressed (CCC, 2000, §1368).

A Christian approach to suffering involves a practical and prudential judgment about the nature of the suffering and about how to protect the goods of life and relationship, including quality of life. In this view, the mental health practitioner will want to be present to clients in their suffering. Therapists will implicitly and, when appropriate, explicitly help clients to search for meaning in their suffering. With Christian clients, therapists will bring the search for meaning into the client's narratives with God about being created with dignity, being called and chosen, and aiming at an ultimate and eternal end. For example, a Christian approach to a suffering client may involve the therapist's empathic understanding of the client's experience of seemingly endless dark nights (existential and spiritual emptiness) where life may seem meaningless (as, for example, in the lives of St. John of the Cross and St. Teresa of Calcutta). Additionally, a mental health practitioner's work may involve assisting a client to prepare for bodily death. There are modern therapies that seek to respect the person's dignity at the end of life, for example, dignity therapy (Chochinov, 2012). Nonetheless, such approaches would require a further spiritual application to explicitly incorporate a Christian vision of death and salvation.

Consequences of Sin

Unless suffering from an extreme form of mental pathology, humans have some real control over their moral actions and some sense of their freedom and responsibility (Álvarez-Segura, Echa-

varría, Lafuente, Zeiders, Antonín, & Vitz, 2017; Álvarez-Segura, Echavarría, & Vitz, 2015, 2017). To an important degree, our choices come from within ourselves and return there to shape each person. This "within" is not only the cognitions, emotions, memory, and imagination. It is also the spiritual center of the person, which engages the will and our own choice of good or evil. Second, our choices are also influenced by others, that is, by our interpersonal relationships and by the thoughts, words, and actions of other people, including their sinful influence on us. Third, in addition to interpersonal influences, there are also environmental influences, which include sinful practices that are passed on through culture, customs, and laws. This section asks, in particular, how sin—both the sins of others and our own sins—can influence our lives and the lives of others. In order to help us better understand the consequences of sin on the human person, it identifies the meaning of the diverse types of sin and their relationship to freedom (Aquinas, 1273/1981, I-II, 71.6 & qq. 71–89).

What Are the Consequences of Original Sin?

The consequences of sin and evil are revealed in the Judeo-Christian scriptural narratives (Gen 3:16–19; Mt 7:17–18; Jn 5:29; Rom 1:18–32), as mentioned earlier. Even though the first humans were created with a freedom intended to foster a life of truth, justice, and love, they turned away from God. They disrupted their original unity with each other and their original innocence before God. Not only the divine likeness in mankind, but also the idyllic relationships between Adam and Eve, and between them and God, were disfigured by the original disobedience.

This disobedience was really a choice to serve the self, and with this choosing the self over God come all other evils. Adam and Eve chose to serve the self as a god, the first idol, following the serpent's words "you shall be like God" (Gen 3:5). Although these relationships and the image of God in mankind were not destroyed

by this prideful disobedience and self-worship, the disorder it created has remained with mankind in various ways (Cessario, 2013, p. 29; Vitz, 1994). The consequences of original sin, and of every sin, pit mankind against God, person against person, each person against himself, and mankind against nature (Francis, 2015). This situation, which began with doubting God, led human beings to doubt others, themselves, and even the value of their own life. For example, in the face of God's providence, the Israelite people tested and spoke against God (Ps 78:18–19), and the apostles argued among themselves about who was greatest (Mk 9:33–37).

The disordered desire associated with original sin has been termed "concupiscence" or "the tinder of sin" (CCC, 2000, §1264). Importantly, however, the term "concupiscence" is used to refer to much more than just disordered sexual desires. It also involves the general disorder that is caused by original sin and that is passed on to each person by the mere fact of sharing in human nature (CCC, 2000, §1426). The general disordering that resulted from original sin is associated with four capacities, wounds, and virtues, as mentioned briefly above. Because of original sin, (a) reason remains wounded by ignorance and in need of the virtue of practical wisdom; (b) the will remains wounded by malice and in need of the virtue of justice; (c) the emotions related to the good that is difficult to reach or the evil that is difficult to avoid (that is, the irascible appetite) remain wounded by our weakness and in need of the virtue of fortitude; and (d) the emotions related to attraction to a good or repulsion of something that is evil (that is, the concupiscible appetite) remain wounded by disordered desire (concupiscence) and in need of the virtue of temperance or moderation. The fundamental goodness of the person and the capacities persist even in the midst of this type of disorder. These disordered tendencies remain also within human persons who are baptized (*CCC*, 2000, §1426; Aquinas, 1273/1981, I-II, 85.3; Hardon, 2005, p. 88; Augustine, 427/2002, XIV.1; see also Chapter 5, "Basic Psychological Support," on how genetic inheritance from a person's two parents often resembles the spiritual trans-generational transmission of the effects of sin).

What Is the Meaning of Sin?

The meaning of sin is not easily captured in a definition or in a description of its origin or types. Nor is it possible to reduce sin to a personal mistake, a developmental imperfection, a psychic flaw, bad social influences, and so on. Sin is connected with the everyday negative consequences of sin, for example, as when a child imitates a parent's inability to moderate anger. But first and foremost sin must be understood in relation to God's positive response and plan of salvation through which love and mercy overcome the effects of sin. As John Paul II (1984a) says: "Sin [is] an integral part of the truth about man.... [However,] sin is countered by the truth of divine love, which is just, generous and faithful, and which reveals itself above all in forgiveness and redemption" (§13). One of the most important, although counterintuitive, notions of a Christian understanding of sin is found in St. Paul's affirmation: "Where sin increased, grace abounded all the more" (Rom 5:20; see also Lk 15; Mt 1:21 & 26:28; 1 Jn 8–9; Rom 5:20–21). He intimates that mercy and grace are stronger than sin. They even precede it in God's provident generosity (*CCC*, 2000, §1846). John Paul II (1986) also observes how God's mercy brings the person into a new orientation toward acts of sin. He speaks of conversion away from sin as requiring a "convincing of sin" and redemption. Being convinced of our sins involves discovering a twofold gift: the gift of the truth of conscience

and "the gift of the certainty of redemption [through] the Spirit of truth [who] is the Consoler" (§31.2; see also Vatican II, 1965, §16).

A Catholic Christian notion of sin is rooted in the New Testament. There, one encounters several lists of sins, which are identified as "works of the flesh" (Gal 5:19–21), wickedness that suppresses the truth (Rom 1:28–32), acts of wrongdoing that distance one from the Kingdom of God (1 Cor 6:9–10), and that are rooted in misguided cravings (Jas 4:1–5) and in worldly love (1 Jn 2:15–17). In contrast to these indications of sin and its effects, Scripture also affirms God's plan of salvation (Mt 1:21; Jn 1:29; Acts 13:23; 1 Jn 2:1). Furthermore, patristic sources, especially Gregory of Nyssa, John Chrysostom, St. Augustine, and St. Gregory the Great, as well as later doctors of the Church, such as St. Thomas Aquinas (1273/1981), and the teaching Magisterium of the Church (John Paul II, 1984a; Benedict XVI, 2009) all provide further reflections and accounts of human struggles for good in the face of disordered and evil acts and habitual dispositions. For example, according to St. John Cassian (1997, 2000), the seven capital vices, or deadly sins (which are also called the eight deadly thoughts), are the particular weaknesses and sins linked to spiritual immaturity. They have been named: pride (the root), vainglory, envy, sloth, avarice, wrath, lust, and gluttony (Aquinas, 1273/1981, II-II; deYoung, 2009, p. 29). They are called "capital" because they give rise to other sins as well. Sin, furthermore, is typified as original sin, social sin, and personal sin, and characterized in terms of seriousness (venial or mortal sin), as we will now see.

What Are the Different Types of Sin?

Taking a robust theological view from St. Augustine (400/1887, Chapter 22), the *CCC* (2000) defines sin as "an utterance, a deed, or a desire contrary to the eternal law" (§1871), and thus contrary to God, since eternal law is understood as God himself, who is eternal wisdom (Wetzel, 1999). Not every sin is the same in its sources or effect. For example, a sin differs with respect to whom it offends, the virtue it opposes, or the commandment that it violates. The Catholic Christian tradition defines sin as a voluntary intention, desire, or action (including thought, word, deed, and omitted action) that is against reason, truth, law, and love (CCC, 2000, §1853).

While all sin inordinately turns us to a finite good and harms our friendship with God, not every sin turns us away from God. Sin that turns us away from God and severs our friendship is considered mortal sin (Aquinas, 1273/1981, I-II, 72.5 ad 1). For a sin to be mortal, it must meet three conditions: grave matter (such as murder), responsible knowledge of it, and deliberate consent to it (CCC, 2000, §1857; John Paul II, 1984a, §12; John Paul II, 1993, §69).

First, for a sin to be mortal, it must concern a grave matter, which is more or less serious, as murder is more serious than theft. The matter of mortal sins are described in the Ten Commandments, throughout Scripture (Mk 10:19; Mt 15:19-20), and in the Magisterium. A non-exhaustive summary of intrinsically evil acts involving grave matter is listed by the Second Vatican Council in its pastoral constitution, *Gaudium et spes* (1965, §27), and confirmed by St. John Paul II (1993, §80), as follows:

> Whatever is hostile to life itself, such as any kind of homicide, genocide, abortion, euthanasia and voluntary suicide; whatever violates the integrity of the human person, such as mutilation, physical and mental torture and attempts to coerce the spirit; whatever is offensive to human dignity, such as subhuman living conditions, arbitrary imprisonment, deportation, slavery, prostitution and trafficking in women and children; degrad-

ing conditions of work which treat laborers as mere instruments of profit, and not as free responsible persons: all these and the like are a disgrace, and so long as they infect human civilization they contaminate those who inflict them more than those who suffer injustice, and they are a negation of the honor due to the Creator.

Second, to commit a mortal sin, we must clearly know that what we are doing is seriously wrong, as when we know that an act breaks or weakens our foundational friendship-love with God. Responsible knowledge of an action is premeditated or it involves an actual awareness of the nature of the act, its foreseeable consequences, and one's responsibility for it.

Third, to commit a mortal sin, we must fully and freely will or consent to the wrong. There are numerous things that mitigate our volitional responsibility. The cooperation of the will is needed to intend, consent, and choose fitting actions. Conflicting desire and weakness of will can distract one from fully and freely willing something. Disordered affections and vices, which pursue disordered loves and only apparent goods, and extreme types of stress and fear can also dissipate the volitional focus needed for full responsibility. Moreover, distractibility and impulsivity can impair the focusing and functioning needed for responsible moral decision making (obsessive-compulsive disorder, attention-deficit/hyperactivity disorder, and so on).

Mortal sin is spiritual death for us, because we cut ourselves off from God. According to human nature and without cooperating with grace, this condition is incurable. We cannot rid ourselves of it. Catholic Christians are required to be reconciled, through the sacrament of Reconciliation, with God, the Church, and neighbor. The condition of mortal sin has been likened to addiction (Dyslin, 2008; May, 2007;

McCormick, 1989) or primary narcissism (Mc-Minn, 2008; Vitz & Gartner, 1989), wherein a person locks himself in a partial good in a distorted, selfish way. However, God's unbounded love and gratuitous mercy intervene by offering healing grace. Furthermore, mortal sin has been distinguished from "sin unto death," involving also final impenitence, which means turning away from God in the most radical way (Schoonenberg, 1965) or the sin against the Holy Spirit (Mt 12:31; Mk 3:28–29).

Venial sin, on the contrary, wounds our relationship with God, but does not turn us away from God, which absolutely differs from mortal sins (CCC, 2000, §§1855–1859; John Paul II, 1984a, §17). In venial sin, we disorder our acts and lives by inordinately turning toward good things without completely severing ourselves from God. We still have the fundamental principle of order, the order of love (ordo amoris), in our somewhat disordered acts and lives (Aquinas, 1273/1981, I-II, 72.5). This wounded situation of the person in venial sin is curable. In cases where such sins are repeated over time, combined with presumption and complacency, the person may be close to turning away from God as his ultimate end. Nevertheless, in freedom and grace, God calls each person to turn away from venial sin. When the person does repent, it is the divine grace of faith and love that primarily reorders a person's interior disorders. The regular remedy for such sin is found in the sacraments of Reconciliation and the Eucharist (John Paul II, 1984a) and other spiritual practices including almsgiving, prayer, and fasting (Mt 6:1–18).

What Is Social Sin?

In addition to the disorder introduced, by original and personal sin, into the relationship between humanity and God, social sin refers to the interpersonal and institutional sides of sin that divide brothers and sisters, families, socioeconomic classes, and races (John Paul II, 1984a, §§15–16; Congregation for the Doctrine of the Faith, 1984, §14–15). The recognition of social sin does not eclipse the fact that sin is primarily about a person's relationship to God. First, social sin is rooted in the disordering of original sin, mentioned above; that disordering influences our social inclinations and the structure of society and families. Without attending to the weakness and wounds of human nature, we can perpetrate errors in education and morals, family life, laws, politics, social action, and the economy (Benedict XVI, 2009, §34). Second, there is a twofold wound that sin perpetrates: personal wounds (as mentioned above) and social wounds (CCC, 2000, §408, §1887). Every personal sin is also social "insofar as and because it also has social repercussions" (John Paul II, 1984a, §15). Seldom is any personal sin truly victimless and private. Even sinful thoughts can have unexpected harmful effects. Analogously to human solidarity (and the communion of saints), each individual's sin affects other persons as a type of negative law and a communion of sin "whereby a soul that lowers itself through sin drags down with itself the church and, in some way, the whole world" (John Paul II, 1984a, §15). By choosing bad means (to a good end) or by misusing good means, we destabilize the proper everyday and ultimate order of values and create unjust structures. External factors, such as institutions, customs, and laws condition our knowledge, incite our choices, and influence our lives in good or bad ways. While individuals need conversion, these unjust structures require correction for the good of whole societies (CCC, 2000, §§1886–1887).

Catholic social teaching has addressed the social effects of sin. While every sin can be considered social, as just described, some sins constitute a direct attack on one's neighbor, through the content of the sin. These sins contravene love of neighbor; they override or neglect the justice due to persons and to interpersonal relationships; common examples are theft, slander, assault, religious persecution, and so on. The Magisterium has extensively addressed social justice and social sin in numerous encyclicals (Leo XIII, 1891; John Paul II, 1981, 1987, 1991; Benedict XVI, 2005, 2009) and discourses on topics such as corruption and the social ramifications of sin (Francis, 2013). It has also treated issues of involvement in the moral evil done by others (Congregation for the Doctrine of the Faith, 2008; John Paul II, 1995, §74; Chapter 16, "Volitional and Free").

What Is the Measure of Sin and Evil?

To consider the different ways that we can sin, we need also to differentiate the three sources of morality: the act understood in relation to (1) its object, (2) the intention, and (3) the circumstances (CCC, 2000, §§1750–1754; John Paul II, 1993). First, the nature of the related object of the act, that is, the object that constitutes what the person is doing, apart from intention or circumstances. It is necessary to identify those objects of the moral act that are "incapable of being ordered" to God and that are incapable of doing justice and respect to the human person made in God's image. John Paul II (1993) calls them intrinsically evil acts, for example, "homicide, genocide, abortion, euthanasia and voluntary suicide" (§80), to name a few (see also Vatican II, 1965, §27). In addition to what is done, there is the person's intention underlying the act, that is, why one does something. In different ways, what one does and why one does it (object and intention) forms the subject and has social consequences. The complexity of sin, its causes, and

its consequences, are relevant in different ways for the psychotherapist, moral theologian, and the spiritual director, as we will see.

As mentioned earlier, Augustine (388/1887) identifies God's eternal wisdom as the theological norm or measure for distinguishing moral acts. This norm has its counterpart based in human reason and law. Aquinas (1273/1981) adds that while theologians define sin "as an act against God, moral philosophers however define sin as contrary to reason" (I-II, 71.6 ad 5). Sin is a harmful reality, even if it is not an ontological thing.

In both moral theology and moral philosophy, or ethics, the matter of sin is voluntary acts, and its form is the lack of due measure (a privation of a measure that should exist according to the nature of the persons and things involved). Augustine (427/2002, XII.7) affirms that sin is not a thing in its own right, but a deficiency or privation of a good that should be present. The underlying measure of the good can be specified ultimately as the law of love—the loving wisdom and wise love of God, which is communicated through its participation in human reason (natural law) and through the grace of the Holy Spirit (the New Law of love). (On the relationship of natural law, the person, and human action, see Chapter 11, "Fulfilled in Virtue").

In this frame, Wojtyła (1993) speaks of the personalist norm, in which the person serves as the rational criterion for determining the actions that respect each human being. He says,

> whenever a person is the object of your activity, remember that you may not treat that person as only the means to an end, as an instrument, but must allow for the fact that he or she, too, has or at least should have, distinct personal ends. (p. 28)

Aquinas (1273/1981), for his part, says that the criterion for evaluating will and love is human reason, although primarily it is also the eternal law, that is, God's reason (I-II, 71.6). However, this is not a rationalist construal of "reason," for it recognizes the place of love in ordered reason. The disorder of sin stems from inordinate self-love, which attaches itself to disordered ends, goods, and acts. Aquinas says, "Now [the fact] that someone inordinately desires some temporal good, comes from inordinate love of self" (1273/1981, I-II, 77.4). This moral evil, therefore, does not exist in the finite good thing per se, but in our disordered relation to it. Sin is not simply a matter of choosing evil instead of good, since "evil is never without some good of nature" (Aquinas, 1273/1981, I-I, 78.3). This affirmation is *not* to say that acts such as murder, rape, and pillaging have some moral good in them. Rather, in sin, some apparent good attracts us (Aquinas, 1273/1981, I-II, 75.2), that is, we desire the semblances of good and virtue, as when we chose an evil (for instance, fraud) with the intention to do good (for example, support one's family). In ways that will be developed later in this volume, certain aspects of psychopathology can be correlated with being too self-centered (for instance, narcissism, inordinate self-love; [DSM-5, p. 669]) or with being too other-centered in a way that is self-effacing (for instance, dependent personality disorder [DSM-5, p. 675; Horney, 1945]), while aspects of health and healing can be correlated with being God-centered and other-centered (including a rightly ordered self-love and self-care [VanderWeele, 2017a, 2017b; Koenig, King, & Carson, 2012]).

How Might Sin Display Human Freedom?

The notions of sin and freedom go together. However, they have come to mean several quite contradictory things. First, in common parlance, freedom is often understood as being able to

choose in a way that is not limited by other people or by a goal. This is a *freedom of indifference* that indicates that the will in itself has no natural orientation toward goods that are naturally fulfilling. The result is that "free will" means that one should not be guided by moral obligations, callings, or purposes linked to human nature or vocations. It is a freedom for selfish convenience. It is as if freedom involves the will simply overpowering any obstacle or quite arbitrarily choosing for the sake of choosing, with a denial of moral boundaries (Nietzsche, 1885/1989, I.19; Pinckaers, 1995, pp. 327–353; also Ashley, 2013, p. 214).

Second, there is another sense of freedom that implies a *freedom from* what makes us suffer or languish. This may be a freedom from political oppression, financial debt, or mental disorder (Berlin, 1969, pp. 122–131). A major thrust of psychotherapy is to free people from the mental traps and prisons set up by traumas, indifference, and other psychological harms. This type of freedom can also pertain to a desire to be free from sin.

However, people may even want a *freedom from* any moral norms and inhibitions, such as the Ten Commandments. This is a denial of the rules that are needed for a flourishing life. In ways, this is similar to a mathematician who frees himself from the rules of arithmetic, or the musician that frees himself from the rules of music, or the speaker who frees himself from grammar. In all these cases the result is a complete failure in each discipline.

Third, there is the most complex sense of freedom. It is a *freedom for* what makes us flourish; it is a *freedom for excellence*. This type of freedom is a choice and a developed disposition intimately tied to the truth of the person. It implies virtuous thoughts, choices, feelings, and ways of relating to other people (Ashley, 2006,

2013; Pinckaers, 1995, pp. 354–378; Chapter 16, "Volitional and Free"). Freedom for excellence is seen as a divine gift that potentially enables humans to choose the lasting goodness of communion with God. The failure of this type of freedom comes in choosing transitory or imaginary goods at the expense of our vocation to be with and for other people and God (International Theological Commission, 2004, §44).

John Paul II (1993) insists that freedom is protected by a calling to seek what is true and good and by informing, referencing, and following one's conscience (§§62–64). However, conscience is not an infallible judge: a person's conscience may be unformed or malformed. We can frequently make mistakes out of ignorance. We can be culpable for our ignorance when we do not take time or care to seek the truth, or when we have dulled our conscience through the habit of sin (CCC, 2000, §§1790–1792; Vatican II, 1965, §16). However, ignorance can also be involuntary (CCC, 2000, §1793). When not aware of our own ignorance (invincible ignorance), we need help to overcome it. Furthermore, if we are ignorant through no fault of our own, our conscience still has a dignity and still speaks in the name of truth (Newman, 1875/2001).

How Is Free Choice Related to Sin and Evil?

The different perspectives on the origin and nature of moral responsibility, freedom, and sin vary with respect to how one discerns the moral character of human action. For example, some schools of thought deny that humans have free will (deterministic naturalism) and moral responsibility (Pereboom, 2006). Others affirm that human beings must assume that human persons are responsible for all actions, regardless of the formation of their conscience (for a discussion of rigorism, see Cessario, 2013, p.

226). The voluntarist view—that the ethical value of an act is determined by the agent's will—involves misunderstandings about the place of free will in the choice of evil. Voluntarism holds that the will alone must be good for an act to be morally good. Some forms of ethical voluntarism do not take into account the action that is performed and maintain that a person's intention alone specifies an act as good or evil, that is, if the intention is good then the act is good; this view is also called intentionalism (Abelard, 1130/1995, pp. 20–24; William of Ockham, ca. 1324/1991, pp. 211–212).

Still other ethical viewpoints determine the morality of the act by merely measuring the positive and negative consequences (consequentialism; Bentham, 1780/2007, p. 2) or the benefits in terms such as happiness (utilitarianism; Mill, 1861/2001, p. 7). Although there are other ethical perspectives within the philosophical tradition, those listed constitute many of the major approaches. We will now move on to explore a more explicitly Catholic understanding that conceptualizes the origin and nature of sin and evil.

The Catholic understanding of evil is found primarily in Scripture, Augustine, and Aquinas. First, Augustine (427/2002) identifies that there is no ontologically existent "evil" in itself to choose, but rather that we choose in evil ways; he incisively states that "evil has no positive nature; but the loss of good has received the name 'evil'" (Book XI, Chapter 9). Since evil is a loss of good, it is not a rival of good. Otherwise, how could evil have come to be? Nonetheless, the effects of evil on persons and their acts are real privations, as seen in the objective loss of honesty in fraud or the loss of justice in family violence.

Second, the Catholic understanding of sin is optimistic in affirming that we seek apparent goods, that is, what seems to be good (and what may be a partial, real good). This optimism is found in Pseudo-Dionysius, who says "no one acts choosing evil" (Aquinas, 1273/1981, I-II, 72.1, citing Pseudo-Dionysius, ca. 450/1987, 4.14, 4.22). This position offers observations, for example, about the way that people rationalize evil. This position however should not be misunderstood to suggest that a person is always seeking what he or she judges to be morally good despite suffering from a malformed conscience. A person can freely choose to perform an act of evil (such as when having malicious intent to harm another) because that person judges such an act to be "good" (for example, for realizing unjust vengeance) and in such a choice can even reject the guidance of conscience toward the true good.

The way that evil acts unfold identifies also the ontological impact of evil action. We are not so much attracted to the privation (or the disorder), but to the good found in the pleasure (in adultery and lust), the taste (in gluttony), the self-worth (in pride), and so on. At an explicitly moral level, while the use of good things is necessary for life and is not a sin, some sins do involve the use of good things in an inordinate manner. Aquinas (1273/1981) says, "Every sin consists in the desire for some mutable good for which a human being has an inordinate desire" (I-II, 72.2). An inordinate desire is "contrary to human nature, in so far as it is contrary to the order of reason" (I-II, 71.2). As an example of rationalizing the choice of an apparent good, consider a thief who seeks a "good" in a way that is ultimately self-serving rather than serving justice. The thief conceptualizes what he will do with the spoils and rationalizes that he merits them, for instance because of the injustice of society or the inequality of the classes. If the thief has been educated in civic virtues though, he will know that he is doing something illegal and

wrong. He may even feel shame at some point and in a fleeting way. There are myriad ways that humans chose partial goods in an evil manner. However, as in this case of the thief, there are also many ways that one's conscience may be awakened. One may see the loss of the good involved in stealing and turn away from it to return to honesty and justice.

What Causes Sin?

Sin is influenced but not caused by the desirable good thing or person, for that which we desire inordinately is not the sufficient cause of personal or social sin. Nor do unjust structures (for example, unjust laws) cause us to sin, although they may help to explain some of our limitations of knowledge and freedom. There is no external thing or person that can necessarily force us to sin. Rather, we are the cause of sin through our disordered will, reason, and emotion. As Aquinas (1273/1981) explains: "the internal cause of sin is the will, as completing the sinful act, the reason, as lacking the due rule, and the appetite [emotion], as inclining to sin" (I-II, 75.3). For instance, although one may feel angry and then be tempted to fits of violent anger after being unjustly laid off from one's job, one is capable of reflecting upon the situation and the emotion before acting (including reflecting upon the different ways to take counsel and find support from others to right the wrong, and, when this is not possible, to choose to forgive). Sin is a loss of the good that is required by justice and charity. It implies intentionally and freely acting against the good or without full consideration of the loss caused by the internal or external action.

It is also important to note the complexity of the indirect effects of our feelings, thoughts, and acts of volition. The primary source of a bad moral act is the will, without which there would be no voluntary behavior. We can distinguish what is directly chosen from what is indirectly chosen. We usually directly will the good rather than the disordered consequence, which is only indirectly willed, although caused by our action. Therefore, a good intention is not enough to avoid causing sin and disorder (Aquinas, 1273/1981, I-II, 75.1). The will needs reason, virtuous habits, as well as natural law and divine law to give it direction in doing good and avoiding evil.

Furthermore, while feelings do not directly cause sin, they can incline us to certain sinful acts. When emotions are extreme, moreover, they can block our reasoning, will, and social interactions; for instance, rage may blind us to what we know to be the requirements of justice, weaken our will to do what is good, and distance us from social and spiritual aids to virtuous action.

There is a parallel between these causes of sin and the causes of some psychological disorders. One distinguishing factor is the moral responsibility one has for a psychological disorder versus for a sinful act. Most psychological disorders are not directly chosen, some however are acquired as dispositions after directly and repeatedly choosing a good thing in a disordered way. For example, the person who becomes addicted to substances or activities (such as heroin or gambling) may at first be seeking to overcome loneliness or boredom, more than inordinately seeking the pleasure or thrill of the acts. Thus, a person may actually take the first steps toward a substance-related or process-related addictive disorder for reasons that resemble more camaraderie or solidarity with a friend than debauchery or sin per se. Furthermore, a person's experience of their sin or psychological disorders should not be reduced to a simple choice or a medical disease (Dunnington, 2011). Rather, there is a difference between personal involvement in acquiring addiction or psychological disorders

and the personal involvement in freely chosen sinful acts. We must be aware of both psychological disorders and personal sin within a larger vision of what it takes to flourish in virtue and to languish in vice (Álvarez-Segura, Echavarría, Lafuente, Zeiders, Antonín, & Vitz, 2017; Álvarez-Segura, Echavarría, & Vitz, 2015, 2017).

Persons must be aware of the ways that they contribute to their psychological disorders, if they are to be responsible for change. The most common way that change occurs is through the choice to seek help and then to follow what help is provided. Likewise, people are called to become aware of the ways that they have contributed to their personal sin. With awareness, they become responsible for both repentance and seeking change. This change normally also requires the choice to seek help and forgiveness, as found through seeking feedback from others and through spiritual techniques such as the examination of conscience and the sacrament of Reconciliation.

What Difference Does Vice Make?

There are many senses of the term "vice." It can mean a single sinful act or temptation or a tendency to be tempted by some evil, such as pride and vanity. In popular literature, vice can be referred to as if it were harmless or fun (Last, 2014). At the same time, vice has been recognized as a serious deficiency in moral character or the fallout of failure in spiritual struggle.

This section of the chapter focuses on the meaning of vice in the spiritual or theological context of the fall from grace, as well as vice's psychological, social, and moral implications, as seen in the multidimensional approach to vice. As already addressed in Chapter 11, "Fulfilled in Virtue," the Christian literature of the Desert Fathers, patristic sources, and the perennial theological tradition present the typology of the vices in a spectrum from carnal to spiritual struggles. For example, St. Gregory the Great (ca. 586/1845) identifies the seven capital vices (or deadly sins) as vanity, envy, anger, indifference (sloth or apathy), greed, gluttony, and lust, with the vice of pride underlying them all (XXXI.45.87–88; see also Cassian, 1997, V.2; John Paul II, 1993; deYoung, 2009). These vices express traits of immoral character and spiritual immaturity; in addition they represent psychological weakness—for example, unjust anger often involves emotional dysregulation and, when acted on, demonstrates impulsivity and lack of self-control. Such vices are called capital (from *caput*, meaning "head" or "source" in Latin) because they are the source for many associated vices and sins.

Sin does not always become vice. There are different kinds of sin and different kinds of vice, as already mentioned (Chapter 11, "Fulfilled in Virtue"). Although vice has sin as its base, and a serious sin may mark someone for life (murder, adultery, apostasy), one act of sin does not make a vice in the fullest sense. Rather, vice is the result of repeated acts that lead to the development of a moral disposition. For instance, if one act of moral weakness or bad judgment may lead to immoderate overeating, such an act does not usually make one gluttonous.

A full, Christian, faith- and reason-based view of vice, as presented in the Meta-Model, identifies thirteen different dimensions. Vices contrast with virtues across these thirteen dimensions (Chapter 11, "Fulfilled in Virtue"; see also just below), although these dimensions often overlap and are indicative of different types of vices.

What Are the Thirteen Dimensions of Vice?

As discussed in Chapter 11, "Fulfilled in Virtue," vices are (1) *deformative of human acts*, instead of being performative. They are act-based. "Vice" refers to disordered acts in which the subject, or agent, chooses to do something that is against the right measure of reason (human reason and God's wisdom). But human acts are not the whole story of the vices.

Vices are also (2) *defective of the agent*; they deform the person who does evil acts. The diverse capacities of a person's character, which are plastic, will be negatively influenced by voluntary involvement in vices of thought, word, action, and omission. Analyzing willing involvement in bad actions must take into account the negative and positive exemplarity and influence of family, friends, and society.

Vices are (3) *negatively-purposeful*; they deform the purpose of the person, misdirecting them away from their basic calling to love God and neighbor. They can lead a person to pursue false goods; they thus express a sickness of ends (teleopathy). They are anti-communal. Instead of being directed by reason, a vicious character leads one to focus in a self-serving way, narcissistically, on one's own desires or on those of one's own family or clan to the detriment of the common good and the love of God and others, which is the person's final end.

Vices are (4) *unethical or amoral*; they are based on selfish ends and goals. They are not guided by legal, ethical, and moral principles, nor do they consider the intrinsic dignity and value of the person; they do not aim at the true good and full flourishing as the end of action.

Vices can be (5) *distortive of the person as man and woman and as complementary*; they either exaggerate or deny the uniqueness of the person as man or woman. As when a man embodies the character of machismo so much that he cannot be a loving husband and father. Or when all differences are so rejected that the distinctive characteristics of men and women are denied normal expression, and sameness reigns.

Vices are (6) *disruptive of the personality and interpersonal relationships*; they are pseudo-holistic. While seeming to knit together the person's cognitive and affective capacities as interpersonal, they really involve being fixated on particular strengths and the partial benefit that those strengths can offer.

Vices are (7) *impairing* of the positive influence of role models and exemplars. They prevent people from wanting to emulate good models. They distract people from goals involved in imitating people that have the character they want to develop. Furthermore, vices confuse fitting models with the exemplars who seek merely apparent goods.

Vices are (8) *extreme*. They deviate from the mean of virtue; they use an erroneous, weak, or extreme measure. For example, the virtue of meaningful leisure can be used to nurture one's friendships, participate in cultural activities and worship; whereas the vice is either excessive enjoyment of pleasure or alternatively lacking appreciation of the positive aspects of one's relationships, culture, and the transcendent.

Vices are (9) *degenerative and disintegrative*. They add weakness to weakness. Instead of being strength-based, they are a display of pseudo-strengths. For instance, they are based on selfish love (egotism) or indifference rather than self-giving love (charity). Vices, thus, can focus on the love of self rather than the diverse ways that one is called to give in charity to many people in one's life.

Vices are (10) *reductionist*; they are not holistic. Vices arise through an isolation of one aspect of the whole person; they reduce the fullness of flourishing to a particular pleasure or limited good and disordered end, such as found in alcohol abuse or gambling disorders.

Vices are (11) *misapplied*: they are disordered applications of "virtue" or apparent good in everyday and professional contexts. Such misapplications foster a partial vision of virtue, which when applied to reasearch or practice distorts one's understanding of the person, family, and flourishing. A misapplied notion of virtue often reduces the person to biological factors, simple reinforced behavior, social function, or political agenda.

Vices are (12) *anti-vocational*; they interfere with forming and keeping vocational commitments. Vices sidetrack a person's call to goodness, truthfulness, justice, and holiness. They compromise the vocational states by denying the value of being just and holy as a single person, or faithful in marriage, or obedient, poor, and chaste in the life of the consecrated or ordained. Vices commonly refute or distort the value of work, service, and meaningful leisure.

Vices tend toward being (13) *non-transcendent*; they are closed to grace and so to ultimate transcendence. They can be intertwined with agnostic and atheistic interpretations of life. When a person chooses a way of vice, the underlying pride tends egotistically to put the self in God's place, thus denying God in practice, even if not also in theory.

These thirteen dimensions of vice help us to understand the larger context of vice and the languishing that it produces. However, care must be taken to distinguish the spiritual, moral, and intellectual aspects of vices, as well as their distinction from forms of psychopathology.

Goodness Is Foundational and Evil Is Not

Vices are one of the many effects of sinning. The effects of sin on mankind and human nature (especially the effects of original sin) have been interpreted in quite different ways, which this chapter explores below from theological, philosophical, and psychological perspectives. To begin, however, we must start from the premise that goodness is foundational to reality and human nature, and evil is not. The Catholic Christian position is that even though evil is a serious loss or privation of goodness, human nature and reality are fundamentally good. The goodness of basic human dignity persists (as a continuous gift of God), as do the roots of the basic natural inclinations of the human person (Aquinas, 1273/1981, I-II, 85.1 & 85.2; Vatican II, 1965, §24). While human nature is distorted or obscured by sin and must face obstacles, it is still good and still called to flourishing. Our nature is healed and elevated with the aid of grace, the infused virtues, and the gifts of the Holy Spirit, as well as through personal participation and the assistance of social cooperation.

What Goodness Remains After the Fall?

The legacy of the fall is the loss of original harmony with oneself, other people, and one's environment, and the loss of original friendship with God, as discussed earlier in this chapter. There are differences among Christian thinkers concerning how the fall affected the fruitfulness of Adam and Eve or of the earth. In the Genesis account of creation, there are predictions and promises both of difficulty and of hope that result from the fall (Gen 3:16–19). The difficulties surround but do not overpower life, for there is the promise of marriage, children, and sustenance. There is also the foretelling of the good

news of the one who will overpower the serpent (evil), sin, and death; that is, there is the foretelling of a Savior (Gen 3:15).

There are three schools of thought about the influence of goodness and evil on mankind's search for flourishing and capacity to act. Without wanting to oversimplify the truths found in each of these positions, this chapter situates the Catholic Christian view in between two opposing views.

A *first position*, call it "human nature optimism," claims that the effects of "original sin" do not stop people from being able to consistently do what is right and good by their own effort. Human nature is not so damaged by the fall as to need grace to act rightly. Man can resist the negative influence of original sin by the native power of his free will. That is, although benefiting by cooperation with grace, mankind does not need divine grace to live a just and moral life. The noble and just non-believer is the case in point. The classic proponent of this position is Pelagius (fifth century/1997), although it is also found in naturalism and romanticism (Rousseau, 1762/1979), sentimentalism (Hume, 1740/2000), and client-centered psychology (Maslow, 1970; Rogers, 1959), and other naturalistic secular approaches. Pelagius argues that if mankind ought to do something, he should be able to do it. That is, if there are moral norms to be obeyed, then mankind should be able to follow them. Put succinctly, "ought implies can" (Brown, 2000, p. 342). St. Augustine critiques Pelagianism because it underestimates the effects of disordered desire and weakness of will as well as the effects of ignorance, especially ignorance of God's plan of salvation (Augustine, 395/1993, III.20.56–23.70).

Human nature optimism is built on the truth

that people have a common experience of self-efficacy. This view is challenged, however, by the universal experience that people frequently fail to honor their own moral intentions. From the psychological perspective, this position is also challenged, since mental and emotional disorders, as well as disordered habits, lead people to do what they do not want or intend to do (Bandura, 2006; Baumeister, Masicampo, & DeWall, 2009; Baumeister & Tierney, 2011).

A *second position*, call it "human nature pessimism," has two overlapping characteristics: (1) many Christian thinkers maintain that human beings are unable to perform any salvific works, such as charity, on their own, and, furthermore, (2) there are some Christian thinkers who believe that human nature is so radically damaged that humans cannot perform any naturally good moral actions without the assistance of divine grace.

Early Reformers, such as Martin Luther (1525/1962, p. 203), John Calvin, and Ulrich Zwingli, thought that the evil of original sin greatly deformed human nature. For example, Calvin (1536/1960) thought that the image of God was crushed by sin. He held that although God's image was not totally destroyed in humanity, it was left in a frightful state (I.15.4, II.1.5, II.2.12). The Westminster Confession in 1647 describes this state as being "wholly defiled in all the parts and faculties of soul and body" (Chapter 6.2) and "utterly indisposed, disabled, and made opposite to all good" (6.4), which has been called by later Calvinists "total corruption" or "total depravity" (Johnson, 2009).

A secular psychological version of human nature pessimism also holds that humans are fundamentally disordered in their inter- and intrapersonal lives. For instance, Freud proposed that oedipal motivations are the result of "original sin," and he often denied free will (1913/1950,

p. 153; see also Klein, 1975; for a discussion of Freud's views, see Vitz, 1988, pp. 166–169). This position, be it the theological or psychological version, is built on the truth that people have a common experience of moral weakness and failure. A variant of this position is that of Manicheanism (described by Augustine, 400/1887), as well as that of ancient religions, which posit good and evil as equally foundational and always at battle. According to this variant, evil, moreover, is as prevalent as good at the level of human nature, and there is neither moral responsibility nor free will.

A *third position*, call it "human nature realism," occupies the middle ground between human nature optimism and human nature pessimism; it recognizes that humans can perform some naturally good works after the fall, even though not without failure and not without human assistance. This position is supported by Catholic Christians, the Orthodox, Wesleyans, and some Evangelicals, who affirm that humans retain a basic goodness, dignity, and potential in their capacities, even though they have lost original justice and are influenced by disordered affects and ignorance (Aquinas, 1273/1981, I, 48.4; Pakaluk, Titus, Vitz, & Moncher, 2009). This view also affirms the need for divine grace for consistency in good action. It affirms that each person's goodness is foundational, while evil—at the ontological, psychological, moral, and spiritual levels—is not. Similar philosophical views of human nature are found in Platonic (Plato, ca. 360 BC/1980; Rist, 2009), Aristotelian (Aristotle, ca. 350 BC/1941), and Stoic thinkers (Cicero, 44 BC/1991; Aurelius, ca. 167/2002).

In a Catholic theological model, our creation, while needing the divine gift of redemptive and sanctifying grace, yet retains a basic level of dignity and goodness of nature, because humans were created in the image of God. We find three types of effects of sin on the good of human nature. First, the basic capacities of the human soul are intact; they "are the principles of which nature is constituted, and the properties that flow from them, such as the powers of the soul, and so forth" (Aquinas, 1273/1981, I-II, 85.1). They are not lost or diminished by sin. The human tendency toward evil is at another level. Second, however, as mentioned before, original justice and friendship (a right relationship with God and other people) was lost with the first sin. This good of nature awaits heaven to be fully recovered. Last, the basic natural inclination to virtue has been diminished as a result of the fall and by the sins that oppose virtue, such as injustice, hatred, and envy. Although it diminishes the expression of the inclination to virtue, sin does not altogether destroy it. For example, acting according to reason is the basis for morality. If sin were to take away the use of reason altogether, then one would not be capable of and responsible for sin (Aquinas, 1273/1981, I-II, 85.2). Thus, sin does not completely destroy the good of human nature found in reason.

The disorders brought about by sin must be identified and distinguished. Humans are inclined to goodness, even when they have false notions of goodness. For example, humans are naturally inclined to the goods of *sexual union, marriage, and family* (unity and openness to procreation), even in the face of false notions of fidelity or fruitfulness. That is, humans generally affirm the goodness of *fidelity* and admit it is wrong for a spouse to seek intimate conjugal affection outside of his or her marriage commitment. Such natural inclinations must be rationally, volitionally, and emotionally controlled in order to be made into virtuous dispositions. Likewise, humans are inclined to *generosity*, even in an ambient culture of greed and inattentiveness to others. The sight of people in dire need grounds the affective step of felt pity and compassion, making way for a further reflective and affective step of mercy that prepares for generous action.

In sum, the third position, "human nature realism," affirms that the effects of evil do disorder human cognitive and affective inclinations and capacities. Human nature is seriously wounded as a result of original sin and personal and social sins (which diminish the inclination to the particular virtues). But this disorder does not destroy the foundational basis, the root principles of human nature, and the basic dignity of the human person as created in the image of God. Nonetheless, as a whole, each individual person's human nature and capacities need to be healed and elevated by divine grace. As counterintuitive as it may seem, mankind's original error of sin is ultimately a happy error. God's offer of redemption through Christ transforms it (Rom 5:20; *Roman Missal*, 2012, Easter Proclamation [Exsúltet], p. 472).

How Does the Goodness of Creation Resist the Destructiveness of Sin?

The Catholic Christian Meta-Model of the Person posits that the nature of the original friendship with God was a gift. At the same time, the original justice was predicated on Adam and Eve's respecting God's command and the natural moral laws set down in creation (Gen 2:17). This relationship was also predicated on grace and the human nature that God created. Mankind's relationship with God should not be reduced to obedience to the law, even though the fulfillment of the law is love. Of primordial importance is that man and woman are created in the image of God (Gen 1:26–27) and called to righteousness, holiness, and an intimate friendship love with God, others, and self (Mt 5:48).

What did Adam and Eve do, when they abused the freedom that was given to them?

They broke the friendship and state of justice that God had established by creating them in his image. Their act of disobedience wounded and disfigured this divine likeness. Moreover, they fell from the original holiness and justice that was intended to be the heritage of the whole race. Instead of a heritage of holiness, justice, and unity, it is a human nature mixed with disorder that is thereafter communicated to persons.

The goodness of creation, although wounded and disfigured, resists the destructiveness of sin, because of the nature of creation as a gift of God. Furthermore, because of the gift of God, each human person still has basic dignity and should be respected for his or her fundamental worth and unique distinctness. As difficult as a particular person may be to interact with, especially in the midst of disrespectful or immoral behavior, he or she still has basic dignity and merits respect. The contingent side of each person's human nature is due to his or her positive or negative development of moral character and spiritual maturity, insertion in a family and society, and exercise of free will, as well as the influence of the gratuitous gift of grace. A clear understanding of the goodness of human nature and its potential does not directly translate into knowledge of the actual situation of a particular person though. The person must be discovered by other people, thus also by the therapist, in the diverse effects of stagnation and development, evil and good, illness and health, as well as in the midst of the person's explicit commitments and implicit intentions about life goals.

What Are the Barriers to Recognizing the Fundamental Goodness and Value of the Person?

The basic dignity, goodness, and specific value of each person have been seriously threatened in contemporary culture. Examples of these threats include terrorism and war (genocide, abuse of noncombatants by soldiers; disproportionate uses of power); unjust discrimination (against people of different races, cultures, religions, or sex); social and economic injustice (based on poverty and oppressive or unfair practices and damage done to the environment); rejection of the dignity of human life (hatred of our species or replacement of it by an allegedly superior form of a trans-human life), and other threats to life (including pro-abortion and pro-euthanasia practices). The Catholic Christian vision of the person is found, for example, in John Paul II's 1995 affirmation, not only of the "value of the person" (§45), but also of the duty to affirm the "right to life of every innocent person from conception to natural death" (§101). In defending the unborn in the initial phase of existence, as well as those who are infirm throughout their lifespans, he says that "no word has the power to change the reality of things: procured abortion is the deliberate and direct killing, by whatever means it is carried out, of a human being in the initial phase of his or her existence, extending from conception to birth" (1995, §58). Among all of these barriers listed here, there are many other barriers that could be listed that curtail affirming the value of human life. But the most basic way to meet these challenges is to proceed with the conviction that life is a gift and that each human person is foundationally good. Though this conviction does not preclude the right of a person or society (after prudent determination) to defend themselves against unjust and serious threats.

What Is the Catholic Difference in Understanding the Effects of Sin?

There are several clear differences that a Catholic Christian vision of the fall make for psychotherapy (Pakaluk, Titus, Vitz, & Moncher,

2009). First, on the theoretical side, there is the conviction that evil has neither the first nor the last word in human affairs. The goodness that is found in the image of God imprinted in human persons is more basic than the evil effects of original, personal, or social sin. Evil, as a privation of what should be, is introduced after creation without fundamentally countering what the book of Genesis affirms, namely that: "God saw everything that he had made, and indeed, it was very good" (Gen 1:31). The Psalmist (Ps 8:5) affirms that mankind has been made "a little lower than God, and crowned … with glory and honor." The New Testament, furthermore, affirms that God offers new life and an adoptive status of sonship to those he has justified by faith through Jesus Christ in the Holy Spirit (2 Cor 5:17). In so doing, God offers to redeem human nature and human persons, rather than destroy them. This view of creation and promise of redemption (to be treated in the next chapter) offers reason for peace, hope, and joy, which are significant for mental health.

Second, on the practical side, differences that the Catholic vision of the fall makes are found in how there is not necessarily a direct correlation between the effects of personal sin and psychological disorders. Although there is not necessarily a direct correlation, there are many harmful psychological and spiritual states that are connected in various complex ways, for example, how narcissism, hatred, and envy can be intertwined. Furthermore, the Meta-Model offers a nuanced theoretical understanding of guilt, which can have many practical implications for the subjective experience of guilt (such as distinguishing a neurotic sentiment of feeling guilty from a true subjective guilt) derived from objective moral responsibility.

What Is Guilt?

In a Catholic Christian understanding of the person, which is biblically-based, realist, personalist, Augustinian, and Thomist (Chapter 2, "Theological, Philosophical, and Psychological Premises"), guilt is a multifaceted reality, because of the nature of sin and human nature. Understanding guilt is further complicated because the awareness of sin and its effects have been greatly lessened in the public square, as lamented by Karl Menninger (1973) in his book *Whatever Became of Sin?* John Paul II (1984), furthermore, argues that sin sows the seeds of death and disorder that are manifest in a thousand guises, including the "loss of a sense of sin" and ignorance of one's right relationship with mankind's ultimate End, who is God (§18). He argues, nonetheless, that moral conscience is tenacious because of its origin in God, which normally assures that humans come to know sin. St. Paul finds reason for this belief because God's "eternal power and divine nature, invisible though they are, have been understood and seen through the things he has made" (Rom 1:20). Paul is furthermore convinced that "what the law requires is written on [the hearts of humans], to which their own conscience also bears witness; and their conflicting thoughts will accuse or perhaps excuse them" (Rom 2:15). Nonetheless, many people override and silence their conscience by rationalizations and small sins that lead to the likelihood of greater sins.

Importantly, there are objective and subjective dimensions of guilt. Objective guilt refers to the moral-spiritual state of the person in relation to his or her deeds. A person is objectively guilty of a sin for which he is morally responsible, involving some evil that the person knows to be evil and consents to as such, for example, unjust thoughts, words, and deeds, such as marital infidelity, murder, rape, and so on. When such an act is committed knowingly and willingly, the act is morally imputable to the person: the person is culpable, or morally responsible (he or she has objective guilt, because of an objectively immoral act). There are, however, numerous circumstances that can mitigate or nullify the imputation of this guilt, such as "ignorance, inadvertence, duress, fear, habit, inordinate attachments, and other psychological or social factors" (CCC, 2000, §1735; also CCC, 2000, §1793, §1860; John Paul II, 1993, §63, §70). Some psychological factors that mitigate responsibility include impairments or lack of empathy, as in extreme forms of narcissism, borderline personality disorder, psychopathy, and autism (Baron-Cohen, 2011).

Formally, sins are against right reason and divine law. They miss important goals and aims in life, such as honesty, respect for human life and the environment, or patience with spouses and children. Personal sins are against neighbors and God, who are objectively offended by the injustice. The evil of such deeds is objective, even when guilt for them is mitigated or forgiven. Newman (1875/2001) recognizes that the objective nature of guilt can be truthfully known through conscience, which can know the reality of guilt as a state or an objective fact. Nonetheless, objective guilt can be remedied by reparations and sacramental means (Cessario, 2008, 2013).

What Is the Subjective Experience of Guilt?

People feel guilty for different reasons, not all of which are based in reality. There are accurate and constructive cognitive judgments and affective appreciations of objective moral states. There are also extreme, even neurotic, subjective appreciations of moral states.

Subjective guilt is how the evil deed or state is understood, desired, and felt by the person. The person subjectively evaluates his own guilt at different levels. Such judgments, feelings, and evaluations can be appropriate and proportionate to reality. People can often judge and feel rightly that they are guilty, which is helpful for moral betterment (Bassett et al., 2011). However, they can also experience inappropriate and disproportionate guilt compared to their actual responsibility and objective reality. For example, some children report that they feel that they caused their parent's divorce, because of a bad behavior that they are responsible for, but which in fact had nothing to do with the divorce. Adults may also inappropriately still feel guilty after forgiveness. Other types of inappropriate guilt are the opposite extremes of scrupulosity or hyper-vigilance, and of laxity, hardness of heart, or indifference. These can also be more or less psychologically, morally, and spiritually dangerous, because they are a distortion of reality.

In addition, the knowledge of guilt and the accuracy of the sense of one's responsibility for evil is influenced by grace, reason, will, emotions (or sentiments), and higher-order perceptions, all of which can be used to identify the different phenomena related to guilt. Factors that influence our sense of guilt (objective and subjective) include the following.

First, through the intellect moved by grace, the deep spiritual sense and right appreciation of guilt comes from the "voice of God" that is heard in the heart of one's conscience (Rom 2:15). This is what St. Jerome called the spark of conscience (Green, 1991). It is the movement of the Holy Spirit.

Second, through the intellect informed by practical wisdom and right reason, a person makes a judgment of conscience and appraises the good or evil of an act, as well as his own responsibility and guilt for such deeds.

Third, through will and behavior, humans can

consent to this judgment of conscience or deny or ignore it. This consent or denial is an acknowledgement of responsibility or non-responsibility for a deed and its consequences.

Fourth, humans have a variety of emotional experiences of feeling of guilt. We have particular feelings about particular deeds and states; these feelings can be more or less accurate appreciations of our objective guilt. They can also vary due to biochemical and hormonal fluctuations, for example, that may cause depression, anxiety, or irritability. Individuals may have stable dispositions *to* feel guilty or not feel guilty. For example, some people have (a) tendencies to feel excessive guilt usually for small infractions or even without cause, that is, to feel overly responsible or even guilty when one is not guilty; this tendency is called scrupulosity or hyper-vigilance, a type of obsessive-compulsive disorder; others have (b) tendencies to lack feelings of accountability and guilt for evil actions, which are caused by laxity, hardness of heart, indifference (sloth, see Nault, 2015) or even the lack of empathy (Baron-Cohen, 2011); or (c) tendencies to feel guilt appropriately according to the truth of the matter and taking into account wise counsel.

Fifth, knowledge or sense of guilt is influenced through higher-order perceptions, such as when evaluative judgments are made about the moral attractiveness or repulsion of a particular act or a moral state. We can feel the moral repulsion of guilt, even when only thinking about committing such acts. For example, we can feel morally repulsed when merely imagining lying, cheating, or infidelity, because of the moral evil and guilt associated with such acts that we have done, are in the midst of doing, or are considering doing in the future.

Feeling guilty is not always accurate (true) or to a right measure, as when a person makes reparation, seeks interpersonal and sacramental

forgiveness and reconciliation for lying about a colleague, and yet still feels guilty about the event. What can be missing is the distinction between feeling guilty and feeling sorry, or contrition for what was done, as well as considerations of depression, and so on. Scrupulosity may be a combination of exaggerated and erroneous senses of responsibility and guilt (disordered perceptions, feelings, choices, and so on). For example, St. Alphonsus Ligouri was thought to suffer from scrupulous feelings of guilt throughout his life (Van Ornum, 2004). This psychological disorder, however, was not an indication of the state of his sanctity. From a psychological viewpoint, sometimes an exaggerated sense of guilt (or even a delusional one) can be linked to depression or obsessive compulsive disorder. In contrast, a hyposensitive experience of guilt and responsibility can be associated with remorselessness, amoral affect, anti-social disorders, and psychopathology.

What Are the Practical Implications of Guilt?

A right sense of guilt involves grounding subjective affect in the objective truth of one's moral and spiritual state. A just sense of guilt can be constructive, inasmuch as it motivates people to seek reconciliation and reparation (Aquinas, 1273/1981, I-II, 39.3). One critique of certain schools of contemporary psychology is aimed at the way they have underestimated the importance of a healthy sense of guilt. An early work of Albert Ellis (1980) represents a way of thinking that bases its approach to guilt on particular anthropological, theoretical, and therapeutic assumptions. According to Ellis (2008), the goal of Rational Emotive Behavioral Therapy (REBT) is hedonist, "socialized hedonism," or utilitarian: it seeks to help clients "to rid themselves of as much irrational thought as possible in order to minimize pain" (p. 3). However, inasmuch as Ellis (2008) claims that a person should be emotionally disconnected from his moral standards (p. 4), there is a very basic anthropological incongruity: mankind is encouraged to suppress moral feelings and subjective guilt, especially about sexual behavior. This is the nature of a rationalist, "purely intellectual approach to … moral behavior" (Ellis, 2008, p. 5). Although Ellis claimed that his position on guilt, sin, and divine law was based on extensive clinical experience, his interpretation of guilt and religion reflect pre-empirical and pre-theoretical presuppositions. Later in his life, Ellis's (2000) position became less anti-religious—but he still denied the reality of the state of objective guilt (and the differences between the types of guilt) and the existence of an objective moral order.

In contrast, according to the Catholic Christian Meta-Model, a philosophical, realist view of "guilt" and "responsibility" enriches the psychotherapeutic picture in terms of both theory and practice (Maritain, 1959). As already mentioned in this section, an integrated approach will recognize that the meaning even of the feeling of guilt (subjective experience of guilt) needs recourse to the reality of a person's acts and their interpersonal relationships (including objective guilt) in order to be understood.

Furthermore, a person's moral perspective (and broader worldview) influences his under-standing and experience of moral culpability and spiritual failure. In particular, beliefs about the nature of forgiveness and the goals of moral action influence not only a person's moral motivation, but also the notion of culpability and well-being. Between a morality that primarily focuses on rules and obligation, and one that primarily focuses on flourishing, beatitude, and holiness (Pinckaers, 1995), there are major differences in the intuitions, sentiments, and judgments concerning guilt. In the latter approach to morality, love and mercy are seen as primordial, but there is no denial of the enduring value of commands, law, and duty.

The aforementioned different notions of guilt invite us to use the term with care: guilt is a "subjective experience of guilt" or "objective guilt" or complex appreciation of both. Indeed, guilt can be a stimulus for personal and interpersonal, moral and spiritual growth. For example, many interpersonal mistakes are a source of objective guilt, and without them much interpersonal growth would not occur. Furthermore, in recognizing that we are called to a personal relationship to God in goodness and holiness, a true Christian experience of personal guilt (subjective experience of the objective reality) will involve a manifestation of two gifts (John Paul II, 1986, 31.2): the gift of the truth of conscience, and "the gift of the certainty of redemption." This later gift is addressed in the next chapter.

The Struggle with Evil

Evil is a negative phenomenon found in disordered interpersonal relationships and human acts. It is often easy to recognize, even if its source is difficult to trace. It is found in each person, family, community, and nation and can be seen in selfishness (pride); violence (anger); lust (impurity); injustice (greed); jealousy (envy); abuse of nutrition and mind-altering medications (gluttony); and indifference to God, neighbor, or self (sloth) (Gregory the Great, ca. 586/1845; deYoung, 2009). There is evil in the disordered thinking, intentions, and social structures that underlie sinful acts and vicious dispositions. The privation underlying evil and that which is brought about by evil is seen also in the influence of spiritual beings, both fallen angels and humans, who have chosen evil over good (*CCC*, 2000, §391).

In the moral and spiritual sense, however, evil is difficult to know truly, unless we have some distance from it. Cardinal Ratzinger (Pope Emeritus Benedict XVI) makes a provocative observation about our capacities to do and observe evil. He notes: "People recognize the good only when they themselves do it. They recognize the evil only when they do not do it" (1995, p. 63). An interior knowledge of goodness gets to the heart of reality, for goodness is the right ordering of our loves. Our emotions are conformed to our will, our will to our reason, and the whole person is subject to God. In contrast, the conformity involved in evil blurs the understanding of one's true nature and the destructive nature of evil. Inasmuch as moral evil involves choosing a disordered good, the focus on the apparent or partial good can blind one to the real evil present in the choice.

Earlier in this chapter, we briefly considered the origin of evil and sin. This section now addresses moral and spiritual evil at greater depth.

What Is the Origin of Evil and Disorder?

It is only after addressing the origin of creation and its goodness (Gen 1–2) that the Bible first addresses the origin of evil. God created the universe, in which he placed mankind, and found that it all was very good (Gen 1:31). He did not create moral or spiritual evil. Evil effects are realized through acts of sin, when creatures (angels and persons) to whom God gave free will subsequently made choices against his truth, goodness, and beauty. The third chapter of Genesis describes the disorders, trials, and difficulties that enter into the human condition as the re-

sult of original sin (Gen 3:16–19). As a result of disobedience, mankind suffers further trials tied to weakness and disorder; these trials constitute inevitable lifelong challenges for each and every person. For women, there are the added pains in childbearing and a disordered relationship with the husband (John Paul II, 2006, p. 254). God says to Eve, "your desire shall be for your husband, and he shall rule over you." This distortion of the original equality of the woman and the man suggests a change in relation between the two, at intimate and social levels. It also indicates that the subordinate place of women in Israelite society was a result of human sin (John Paul II, 2006, pp. 250–253; 622–630).

For men, there is the additional toil in cultivating the ground, the need to fight thorns and thistles, the inevitability of extended effort undertaken with sweat, and even the need to "master sin" (Gen 4:7). This state of laboriousness is life long and inevitably accompanied by sickness and death, as the book of Genesis reminds us: "By the sweat of your face you shall eat bread until you return to the ground, for out of it you were taken; you are dust, and to dust you shall return" (3:19). The difficulty in relating to each other and the inevitability of death, however, were not accompanied by a lack of fruitfulness (Gen 3:19, 3:23). Nevertheless, there was a promise of a redeemer and redemption (Gen 3:15). The announcement that an offspring of Eve will crush the serpent's head foretells a savior who will triumph over evil. The Catholic Christian tradition takes this text as the *proto-evangelium* (first Gospel), as witnessed by St. Paul (1 Cor 15:21–27), St. Irenaeus (ca. 185/1885, III. 23.7), and St. John Paul II (2006, §§142–146). The Christian notion of redemption, discussed in the next chapter, outlines God's intention to remedy the situation of sin and evil.

How Does Physical Evil Come to Exist?

Perennial questions about evil continue to puzzle mankind. Why is there evil? Who or what causes evil? And more precisely, since Christians believe that God is absolutely provident, good, and powerful, why did not God create a world where evil had no place? Moral evil, at least, is scandalous. It is hideous, but it is also seductive. In a Christian view, represented by Augustine (401/2007) and Aquinas (1273/1981, I, 49.1), as noted earlier, the phenomena of evil represent an absence or loss—the privation—of something that is due to a thing or a person at a particular time. In the absences of some aspect of a thing's integrity, we say that there is evil. However, evil is an analogous term. Evil is something different when it concerns physical things than when it concerns personal, moral, and spiritual agents.

Physical evil involves those aspects of nature that are destructive or disfiguring, such as natural disasters and bodily death (CCC, 2000, §§310-311). In the Catholic Christian vision, God has created the world in "a state of journeying" toward its ultimate perfection (CCC, 2000, §310). This journey involves both the constructive and the destructive forces of nature, including what can be considered natural or physical evil. Human accidents also fall into this category, inasmuch as road disasters and train crashes, for example, are not necessarily anyone's intentional responsibility, although they can result from social sin. Effects of physical evil need not derive from direct and intentional human or divine responsibility, but can arise merely as circumstances in which someone suffers from some kind of human error, material failure, or forces of nature. Death and destruction due to natural disasters, furthermore, are seen more as the generally foreseeable processes of nature or natural phenomena. In natural processes, the origination of certain beings is followed by the destruction of others. Plants sprout from seeds. They grow. They die. And then they serve as nutrition for other forms of life. Humans are conceived, grow, and die as well.

What Is Moral Evil, and What Are its Implications for Mental Health?

Moral evil is the intentional absence of what should be present in thought, word, and deed, which, of course, involves what is lacking in interpersonal relationships and emotions. It is the privation of the goodness due in the actions of each person in conformity with their dignity as an image of God (John Paul II, 1993, §72), which is the case whether the goodness be that of human nature (justice) or of grace (charity). Moral evil is found in any action (interior or exterior act) that intentionally lacks what is needed for cognitive and behavioral integrity. Furthermore, such moral integrity should be found in the person's mature character, free will, and emotional life, as well as when he or she acts in accordance with truth and goodness. This moral integrity is manifest in personal conscience and prudence (practical wisdom) exercised in accordance with civil authority, natural moral law, and revealed divine law. For example, there is privation (moral evil) when someone freely chooses to oppose a just law or the ruling of a legitimate authority or God.

The judgment of whether a moral act is good or bad requires that the agent know (1) what he or she is doing (the moral act as understood in light of its object) and (2) why he or she is doing it (intention of the act), as well as (3) how the object and intention of the moral action relate to the structure of reality, its laws, and interpersonal relationships (circumstances) (CCC, 2000, §1750). If any of these elements is evil, then the entire act is morally disordered. As Pseudo-Dionysius explains, "good results from a whole and entire cause, whereas evil results from a single defect" (Aquinas, 1273/1981, I-II, 71.5, ad 1, citing Pseudo-Dionysius, ca. 450/1987, Chapter 4).

Moral evil has many implications for psychology and mental health practice. Intentional wrongdoing is the most difficult of psychological, moral, and metaphysical conundrums, and it affects personal, psychological, social, and spiritual life. John Rist (2009) argues that the problem of premeditated moral evil must be explored in the context of the complexity and simplicity of the person and the relation of the material body and immaterial soul. Rist takes a realist approach and uses insights from Plato, suggesting that the divided heart (or soul-division) is caused by trying to live different lives at the same time. Rist suggests that the divided heart can be overcome by living only one kind of life, namely the life of truth, in which the love of wisdom is motivated by the desire that focuses one's life on truth. He identifies the greatest ethical mistake possible as the belief that one can create the moral universe. This type of narcissism is anti-realist. It substitutes one's own choice and desire for the "Form of the Good," that is, by setting the fulfillment of "my own will" in opposition to God (Rist, 2009, p. 22).

As the Catholic Christian Meta-Model of the Person recognizes, the ethical mistake and experience of inner division that Rist describes both have great impact on a person's mental health. Although we can sometimes find mental disorders whose source is primarily biologically based, often there is a "teleopathy" (sickness of *telos*) or a disorder of moral ends behind psychological disorder and problems of everyday living (Goodpaster, 2006). In short, often some level of human choice is involved in the development,

worsening, or maintenance of psychological difficulty. The person can suffer from a certain sickness of ends. What is right or wrong? What is just or unjust? What should a family do if it lacks the means for survival at the socioeconomic level projected by the media? And if it has a surplus? If persons lose sight of ethical everyday goals and fitting ultimate ends, they muddle along. They can even sink in an existential and moral quagmire without a reference point that would serve to lift them up or by which they might navigate morally. Some schools of contemporary psychology have sought to resolve cognitive dissonance about moral and spiritual ends by lowering the aim of the person or evacuating feelings of guilt (as seen earlier in this chapter). What can result is a stunted notion of human purpose and unfulfilling goals fixed mostly on short-term self-centered pleasure and comfort.

What Is Demonic Evil?

A further question about evil involves the problem of personified spiritual evil. Contemporary Western culture is often caught between a denial of demonic evil and a fascination with it. Both phenomena are dangerous and deform reality. According to the Catholic tradition, "the devil and the other demons were created naturally good by God, but became evil by their own doing" (*CCC*, 2000, §391; see also Lateran Council IV, 1215, cited in Denzinger & Hunermann, 2012, §800, p. 266). Although created good and for good purposes, the devils became evil by falling to the enticement of their own dazzling but limited intelligence and beauty. They turned from God to adore themselves; in pride and idolatry, they sought to put themselves in God's place.

Behind the fall of Adam and Eve is the same type of seduction, used by Satan (the serpent) to entice them to doubt God's goodness, envy God's greatness, and seek to become like God by their own means (John Paul II, 2006). The woman rationalized the disobedience in the garden by focusing on the fruit as good to eat, beautiful, and a source of wisdom. The price to pay was enormous. The master of lies did not remind her of the consequences, but persuaded her that God's warning was not true (Gen 3:5).

Demonic evil is attested in the Bible, where the devil is described as the deceiver and "father of all lies" (Jn 8:44), the ancient serpent (Gen 3; Rev 12:9), and the power of darkness (Eph 6:12) and a murderer (Jn 8:44). The word "devil" (*dia-bolos*) means him who "throws himself across" God's plan of salvation. In the last petition of the *Our Father* prayer—"But deliver us from evil" (also translated as from "the evil one," Mt 6:13; Mt 13:19)—the term "evil" refers to a person that the Gospel of John (17:15) and the *Catechism* (2000, §§2850–2854) identify as the evil one, the demon, Satan, the fallen angel.

Demonic Interference or Psychiatric Illness?

The psychotherapist and spiritual director will need to ask whether particular types of mental states, behavior, and conditions are issues of mental disorder or demonic activity or, often, both. Well-trained mental health professionals will want further training to distinguish demonic interference from such psychological disturbances as hallucinations, or obsessive-compulsive, histrionic, or psychotic disorders (Amorth, 1999; American Psychiatric Association, 2013; Gallagher, 2005; Lhermitte, 2013). There is need to differentiate the spectrum of demonic activity, which can be outlined as temptations (moral and spiritual); infestation (homes or places); oppression (effort to control an individual through fear or fascination); and, much less common, possession. Possession is identified by four phenomena that surpass the secular explanations of skilled

physicians, psychiatrists, and psychologists, namely, xenoglossolia (use of languages that the person has never acquired); superhuman strength; preternatural knowledge; and unfounded rage at sacred objects (Acosta, 2012; Amorth, 1999; Blai, 2017; Lhermitte, 2013; Kheriaty, 2012). The resolution of the spiritual side of these troubles can be found in (1) education (catechesis); (2) moral and spiritual conversion (rejection of involvement in evil); and, especially, (3) continuous liturgical and personal prayer (and, when needed, deliverance and exorcism prayer).

The authority and power of prayers of deliverance and exorcism is found in Jesus Christ and the spiritual authority that he entrusts to the Church (Mt 12:26; Mk 1:25–26, 3:15, 6:7 & 13, 16:17; Jn 12:31; CCC, 2000, §517, §550, §1673). As the *Catechism* (2000) says: "When the Church asks publicly and authoritatively in the name of Jesus Christ that a person or object be protected against the power of the Evil One and withdrawn from his dominion, it is called exorcism" (§1673). There is a range of prayers adapted to the situation of evil. There are the common and daily prayers, the epitome of which is the *Our Father*—as mentioned just above, its last appeal constitutes a prayer of delivery from evil and the evil one (CCC, 2000, §2846; §§2850–2854). There is also a simple exorcism that is performed in the celebration of Baptism, when the faithful renounce Satan (CCC, 2000, §1237). There are also special prayers for diverse types of infestation, oppression, and possession.

The Catholic Church recognizes that demonic interference is not to be confused with psychological or other sorts of illness. It recognizes, nonetheless, that spiritual troubles can be feigned (for emotional reasons, for example, attracting attention), or they can be disguised or intertwined with psychological weaknesses and disorders. In short, demonic effects and psychological pathologies can often coexist with each other. The Church requires that the medical sciences and spiritual experts each play their part in helping to determine the state of the person. In the rare case of actual possession, an exorcism is performed by a competent ecclesial authority in union with the local bishop and in the spiritual communion of the Church and its Lord (Code of Canon Law, 1983, canon 1172; CCC, 2000, §1673).

Conclusion

This chapter on the Catholic Christian vision of the person is perhaps the most important of all the chapters for the perspective that it brings to the human condition. It recognizes (1) that the good of human nature, as a root, is not diminished by sin, for basic human dignity and the natural inclination to virtue remain (Aquinas, 1273/1981, I-II, 85.1 & 85.2; Vatican II, 1965, §24); (2) that the good of human nature, however, is diminished in the capacity to attain its end because of many obstacles placed in its path by original, personal, and social sin; and (3) that original justice, that blessed relationship between God and the first humans, is lost. Thus the human condition, resulting from original sin, is diminished in its capacity to attain the goal of full flourishing. This result of original sin is multiplied in the personal and social sin perpetrated by individuals, families, and societies; it is found in the real suffering experienced in the midst of the lifelong battle against evil—the resistance to morally unacceptable involvement in evil—and in the pursuit of cooperation with good. In the midst of the negative consequences of sin and the fall, the Catholic Christian vision of the person, expressed in this chapter, affirms that the goodness of the person's basic dignity and natural capacities and inclinations are more foundational than the negative consequences of sin and evil.

It is therapeutically significant that each person be recognized as basically good, valuable, and dignified. That we are created in the image of God is a gift that retains its goodness even in the midst of our serious disorderedness and the need of grace for spiritual healing (justification) and development (sanctification). Clinician and client alike will be more spiritually and psychologically healthy if they seek forgiveness from God and neighbor, and willingly give forgiveness to those who offend them. The moral strengths and weaknesses of the human condition are found in each person in some measure. That each person is a good gift needs to be affirmed in the clinical setting, especially when the clinician may find it challenging to remain empathetic with clients who are difficult and disagreeable. With such difficult clients, it is often through empathy, compassion, and forgiveness that the clinician can avoid harmful countertransference and remain an effective source of healing.

As will be explored in the next chapter, there is need for God's grace to restore the right ordering of the person, that each person might grow in the wholeness and unity that is singularly God's continuous gift. Even in a secular context, the basic dignity of each person can be affirmed in the collaboration between clients and therapists. This collaboration is multidimensional in that it is interpersonally relational throughout (it emphasizes justice and caring); it is rational and employs right reason (through practical wisdom and faith); it is volitional and free (it calls each person to ethical responsibility), requiring true love (it requires charity, hope, and justice);

and it is concerned with personal unity, bodily integrity, and rightly ordered emotions (such as courage and temperance or self-regulation).

In the meantime, though, it can be affirmed that the fall and the wounds of the human condition find their context not only when we look backward to creation, but also when we look forward to the endpoint of the Christian conviction that God's redemption of mankind involves making "all things work together for good for those who love God, who are called according to his purpose" (Rom 8:28). The next chapter will complete the treatment of the fall by addressing the promise and the meaning of redemption, and its relevance and non-relevance to therapy.

REFERENCES

Abelard, P. (1995). *Ethics (or Scitote Ipsum)*. In (P. Spade, Trans.), *Ethical writings: His ethics or "know yourself" and his dialogue between a philosopher, a Jew, and a Christian*. Indianapolis, IN: Hackett. (Original work composed 1130)

Acosta, S. Y. (2012). *Diabolical or psychological: The differentiation of psychological diseases from diabolical disorders*. Bloomington, IN: Xlibris.

Álvarez-Segura, M., Echavarría, M. F., Lafuente, M., Zeiders, C., Antonín, P., & Vitz, P. C. (2017). Defence mechanisms: Determined or ethical choices or both? *European Journal of Science and Theology, 13*(3), 5–14.

Álvarez-Segura, M., Echavarría, M. F., & Vitz, P. C. (2015). Re-conceptualizing neurosis as a degree of egocentricity: Ethical issues in psychological theory. *Journal of Religion and Health, 54*(5), 1788–1799.

Álvarez-Segura, M., Echavarría, M., F., & Vitz, P. C. (2017). A psycho-ethical approach to personality disorders: The role of volitionality. *New Ideas in Psychology, 47*, 49–56.

American Psychiatric Association. (2013). *Diagnostic and statistical manual of mental disorders* (5th ed., text revision). Washington, DC: Author.

Amorth, G. (1999). *An exorcist tells his story*. San Francisco, CA: Ignatius.

Aquinas, T. (1981). *Summa theologiae* (English Dominican Province, Trans.). Westminster, MD: Christian Classics. (Original work composed 1265–1273)

Aquinas, T. (2003). *On evil* (R. Regan, Trans.). Oxford, United Kingdom: Oxford University Press. (Original work composed 1270)

Aristotle. (1941). *Physics*. In R. McKeon (Ed.), *The basic works of Aristotle* (pp. 218–394). New York, NY: Random House. (Original work composed ca. 350 BC)

Ashley, B. M. (2006). *The way toward wisdom: An interdisciplinary and intercultural introduction to metaphysics*. Notre Dame, IN: University of Notre Dame.

Ashley, B. M. (2013). *Healing for freedom: A Christian perspective on personhood and psychotherapy*. Arlington, VA: The Institute for the Psychological Sciences Press.

Augustine. (1887). The morals of the Catholic Church and Manicheism. In P. Schaff (Ed.) *Nicene and Post-Nicene Fathers, First Series: Vol. 4. Augustine—Anti-Manichaean writings* (pp. 41–63). Grand Rapids, MI: Eerdmans. (Original work composed 388)

Augustine. (1887). Against Faustus, a Manichee (R. Stothert, Trans.). In P. Schaff (Ed.), *Nicene and Post-Nicene Fathers, First Series: Vol. 4. Augustine—Anti-Manichaean writings* (pp. 155–345). Edinburgh, United Kingdom: T&T Clark. (Original work composed 400)

Augustine. (1953). To Simplician: On various questions. In J. H. S. Burleigh (Trans. & Ed.), *Library of Christian Classics* (Vol. 6, Bk. 1, pp. 370–406). Philadelphia, PA: Westminster Press. (Original work composed 396)

Augustine. (1993). *On the free choice of the will* (T. Williams, Trans.). Indianapolis, IN: Hackett. (Original work composed 395)

Augustine. (1994). Concerning the nature of good, against the Manichaeans (A. H. Newman, Trans.). In P. Schaff (Ed.), *Nicene and Post-Nicene Fathers, First Series: Vol. 4. Augustine—Anti-Manichaean writings* (pp. 351–365). Grand Rapids, MI: Eerdmans. (Original work composed ca. 405)

Augustine. (2002). *The city of God* (M. Dods, Trans.).

In P. Schaff (Ed.). *Nicene and Post-Nicene Fathers, First Series: Vol. 2. St. Augustine: City of God, Christian Doctrine* (pp. 1–511). Grand Rapids, MI: Eerdmans. (Original work composed 427)

Augustine. (2007). *Confessions* (2nd ed.) (M. P. Foley, Ed.; F. J. Sheed, Trans.). New York, NY: Hackett. (Original work composed 397–401)

Aurelius, M. (2002). *Meditations* (G. Hays, Trans.). New York, NY: Modern Library. (Original work composed ca. 167)

Austriaco, N. P. G. (2011). *Biomedicine and beatitude: An introduction to Catholic bioethics.* Washington, DC: The Catholic University of America Press.

Bassett, R. L., Pearson, E., Ochs, S., Brennon, J., Krebs, G., Burt, L., … Grimm, J. P. (2011). Feeling bad: The different colors of remorse. *Journal of Psychology and Christianity, 30,* 51–69.

Baron-Cohen, S. (2011). *The science of evil: On empathy and the origins of cruelty.* New York, NY: Basic Books.

Baumeister, R. F., Masicampo, E. J., & DeWall, C. N. (2009). Prosocial benefits of feeling free: Disbelief in free will increases aggression and reduces helpfulness. *Personality and Social Psychology Bulletin, 35,* 260–268.

Baumeister, R. F., & Tierney, J. (2011). *Willpower: Rediscovering the greatest human strength.* New York, NY: Penguin Press.

Bandura, A. (2006). Toward a psychology of human agency. *Perspectives on Psychological Science, 1,* 164–180.

Benedict XVI (2005). *Deus caritas est* [Encyclical, on Christian love]. Vatican City, Vatican: Libreria Editrice Vaticana.

Benedict XVI (2009). *Caritas in veritate* [Encyclical, on integral human development in charity and truth]. Vatican City, Vatican: Libreria Editrice Vaticana.

Bentham, J. (2007). *An introduction to the principles of morals and legislation.* Mineola, NY: Dover Publications. (Originial work composed in 1780)

Berlin, I. (1969). *Four essays on liberty.* New York, NY: Oxford University Press.

Blai, A. C. (2017). *Possession, exorcism and hauntings.* Steubenville, OH: Emmaus Road.

Brown, P. (2000). *Augustine of Hippo: A biography* (2nd ed.). Berkeley, CA: University of California Press. (Original work published 1967)

Calvin, J. (1960). *Institutes of the Christian religion* (F. L. Battles, Trans.). Philadelphia, PA: Westminster Press. (Original work published 1536)

Cassian, J. (1997). *The conferences* (B. Ramsey, Trans.). New York, NY: Newman Press.

Cassian, J. (2000). *The institutes* (B. Ramsey, Trans.). New York, NY: Newman Press.

Catechism of the Catholic Church (*CCC*) (2nd ed.). (2000). Vatican City, Vatican: Libreria Editrice Vaticana.

Cavadini, J. (1999). Pride. In A. D. Fitzgerald (Ed.), *Augustine through the ages: An encyclopedia* (pp. 679–684). Grand Rapids, MI: Eerdmans.

Cessario, R. (2008). *The moral virtues and theological ethics* (2nd ed.). Notre Dame, IN: University of Notre Dame Press.

Cessario, R. (2013). *Introduction to moral theology* (rev ed.). Washington, DC: The Catholic University of America Press.

Chochinov, H. M. (2012). *Dignity therapy: Final words for final days.* New York, NY: Oxford University Press.

Cicero. (1991). *On duties* (M. T. Griffin & E. M. Atkins, Eds.). Cambridge, United Kingdom: Cambridge University Press. (Original work composed 44 BC)

Code of Canon Law. (1983). Washington, DC: Canon Law Society of America.

Congregation for the Doctrine of the Faith. (1980). Declaration on euthanasia (*iura bona*). Vatican City, Vatican: Libreria Editrice Vaticana.

Congregation for the Doctrine of the Faith. (1984). Instruction on certain aspects of the "theology of liberation." Vatican City, Vatican: Libreria Editrice Vaticana.

Congregation for the Doctrine of the Faith. (2008). *Dignitas personae* [Instruction on certain bioethical questions]. Vatican City, Vatican: Libreria Editrice Vaticana.

Denzinger, H., & Hunermann, P. (Eds.). (2012). *Enchiridion symbolorum: A compendium of creeds, definitions, and declarations of the Catholic Church* (43rd ed.). San Francisco, CA: Ignatius Press.

Deutsch, E., & Dalvi, R. (2004). *The essential Vedānta: A new source book of Advaita Vedānta.* Bloomington, IN: World Wisdom.

deYoung, R. K. (2009). *Glittering vices: A new look at*

the seven deadly sins and their remedies. Ada, MI: Baker Academic.

Dunnington, K. (2011). *Addiction and virtue: Beyond the models of disease and choice.* Downers Grove, IL: IVP Academic.

Dyslin, C. (2008). The power of powerlessness: The role of spiritual surrender and interpersonal confession in the treatment of addictions. *Journal of Psychology and Christianity, 27*(1), 41–55.

Ellis, A. (1980). Psychotherapy and atheistic values: A response to A. E. Bergin's "psychotherapy and religious values." *Journal of Consulting and Clinical Psychology, 48*(5), 635–639.

Ellis, A. (2008). Rational Emotive Behavior Therapy: A twenty-three-year-old woman guilty about not following her parents' rules. In D. Wedding & R. Corsini (Eds.), *Case studies in psychotherapy* (7th ed., pp. 59–79). Belmont, CA: Thomson/ Brook/Cole.

Ellis, A. (2000). Can Rational Emotive Behavior Therapy (REBT) be effectively used with people who have devout beliefs in God and religion? *Professional Psychology: Research and Practice, 31*(1), 29–33.

Embree, A. T. (Ed.). (1972). *The Hindu tradition: Readings in oriental thought.* New York, NY: Vintage Books.

Enright, R. D., & Fitzgibbons, R. P. (2014). *Forgiveness therapy: An empirical guide for resolving anger and restoring hope.* Washington, DC: American Psychological Association.

Francis (2013). *Evangelii gaudium* [Apostolic exhortation, on the proclamation of the Gospel in today's world]. Vatican City, Vatican: Libreria Editrice Vaticana.

Francis. (2015). *Laudato si'* [Encyclical, on care for our common home]. Vatican City, Vatican: Libreria Editrice Vaticana.

Frankl, V. E. (2000). *Man's search for ultimate meaning.* Cambridge, MA: Perseus Publishing.

Frankl, V. E. (2006). *Man's search for meaning* (I. Lasch, Trans.). Boston, MA: Beacon Press. (Original work published 1959)

Freud, S. (1950). *Totem and taboo* (J. Strachey, Trans.). New York, NY: Routledge. (Original work published 1913)

Freud, S. (2010). *Civilization and its discontents.* New York, NY: Norton. (Original work published 1930)

Gallagher, T. M. (2005). *The discernment of spirits: An Ignatian guide for everyday living.* New York, NY: Crossroad.

Goodpaster, K. (2006). *Conscience and corporate culture.* Malden, MA: Wiley-Blackwell.

Greene, R. A. (1991). Synderesis, the spark of conscience, in the English Renaissance. *Journal of the History of Ideas, 52*(2), 195–219.

Gregory the Great. (1845). *Morals on the book of Job.* Oxford, United Kingdom: John Henry Parker. (Original work composed ca. 579–586)

Haidt, J. (2006). *The happiness hypothesis: Finding modern truth in ancient wisdom.* New York, NY: Basic Books.

Hardon, J. A. (2005). *History and theology of grace: The Catholic teaching on divine grace.* Ann Arbor, MI: Sapientia Press.

Horney, K. (1945). *Our inner conflicts: A constructive theory of neurosis.* New York, NY: Norton.

Hume, D. (2000). *A treatise of human nature.* Oxford, United Kingdom: Oxford University Press. (Original work published 1740)

International Theological Commission. (2004). *Communion and stewardship: Human persons created in the image of God.* Vatican City, Vatican: Libreria Editrice Vaticana.

Irenaeus. (1885). *Against heresies.* In A. Roberts, J. Donaldson, & A. Cleveland Coxe (Eds.), & A. Roberts & W. Rambaut (Trans.), *Ante-Nicene Fathers* (Vol. 1, pp. 315–567). Buffalo, NY: Christian Literature Publishing. (Original work composed ca. 175–185)

John Paul II (1981). *Laborem exercens* [Encyclical, on human work]. Vatican City, Vatican: Libreria Editrice Vaticana.

John Paul II. (1984a). *Reconciliatio et paenitentia* [Apostolic exhortation, on reconciliation and penance]. Vatican City, Vatican: Libreria Editrice Vaticana.

John Paul II. (1984b). *Salvifici doloris* [Apostolic letter, on the Christian meaning of human suffering]. Vatican City, Vatican: Libreria Editrice Vaticana.

John Paul II. (1986). *Dominum et vivificantem* [Encyclical, on the Holy Spirit in the life of the Church and the world]. Vatican City, Vatican: Libreria Editrice Vaticana.

John Paul II (1987). *Sollicitudo rei socialis* [Encyclical, for the twentieth anniversary of *Populorum progressio*]. Vatican City, Vatican: Libreria Editrice Vaticana.

John Paul II. (1991). *Centesimus annus* [Encyclical, on the hundredth anniversary of *Rerum novarum*]. Vatican City, Vatican: Libreria Editrice Vaticana.

John Paul II. (1993). *Veritatis splendor* [Encyclical, on certain fundamental questions of the Church's moral teaching]. Vatican City, Vatican: Libreria Editrice Vaticana.

John Paul II. (1995). *Evangelium vitae* [Encyclical, on the value and inviolability of human life]. Vatican City, Vatican: Libreria Editrice Vaticana.

John Paul II. (2006). *Man and woman he created them: A theology of the body* (M. Waldstein, Trans.). Boston, MA: Pauline Books and Media.

Johnson, A. S. (2009). *John Calvin, reformer for the 21st century*. Louisville, KY: Westminster John Knox Press.

Klein, M. (1975). Love, guilt and reparation. In R. E. Money-Kyrle (Ed.), *The writings of Melanie Klein* (Vol. 1, pp. 306–343). New York, NY: Free Press. (Original work published 1937)

Kheriaty, A. (2012). *The Catholic guide to depression*. Manchester, NH: Sophia Institute Press.

Koenig, H. G., King, D., & Carson, V. B. (Eds.). (2012). *Handbook of religion and health* (2nd ed.). New York, NY: Oxford University Press.

Last, J. V. (2014). *The seven deadly virtues: 18 conservative writers on why the virtuous life is funny as hell*. West Conshohocken, PA: Templeton Press.

Lee, J., & Theol, M. (2014). The human dark side: Evolutionary psychology and original sin. *Journal of Religion and Health, 53*, 614–629. doi:10.1007/a10943-013-9805-z

Leo XIII. (1891, May 15). *Rerum novarum* [Encyclical, on capital and labor]. Vatican City, Vatican: Libreria Editrice Vaticana.

Lewis, C. S. (1944). *The problem of pain*. New York, NY: Macmillan.

Lewis, C. S. (1961). *A grief observed*. New York, NY: HarperCollins.

Lhermitte, J. (2013) *True or false possessions? How to distinguish the demonic from the demented*. Manchester, NH: Sophia Institute Press.

Lingiardi, V., & McWilliams, N. (Eds.). (2006). *Psychodynamic diagnostic manual* (2nd ed.). New York, NY: Guilford.

Luther, M. (1962). The bondage of the will. In J. Dillenberger (Trans.), *Martin Luther: Selections from his writings* (pp. 166–203). New York, NY: Anchor Books. (Original work composed 1525)

Maimonides, M. (1964). *The guide for the perplexed* (S. Pines, Trans.). Chicago, IL: University of Chicago Press. (Original work composed in 1190)

Maritain, J. (1959). *Distinguish to unite: or, The degrees of knowledge* (G. B. Phelan, Trans.). New York, NY: Scribner. (Original work published 1932)

Maslow, A. (1970). *Motivation and personality* (2nd ed.). New York, NY: Harper and Row

May, G. G. (2007). *Addiction and grace: Love and spirituality in the healing of addictions*. New York, NY: HarperOne.

McCormick, P. C. M. (1989). *Sin as addiction*. New York, NY: Paulist Press.

McMinn, M. R. (2008). *Sin and grace in Christian counseling: An integrative paradigm*. Downers Grove, IL: IVP Academic.

Menninger, K. (1973). *Whatever became of sin?* New York, NY: Hawthorn Books.

Mill, J. S. (2001). *Utilitarianism* (2nd ed.). Indianapolis, IN: Hackett. (Original work composed 1861)

Mullen, J. T. (2007). Can evolutionary psychology confirm original sin? *Faith and Reason, 24*(3), 268–283.

Nault, J. C. M. (2015). *The noonday devil: Acedia, the unnamed evil of our times* (M. J. Miller, Trans.). San Francisco, CA: Ignatius Press.

Newman, J. H. (2001). Letter to the Duke of Norfolk. In The National Institute for Newman Studies (Ed.), *Newman Reader* (section 5, pp. 246–260). Retrieved from http://www.newmanreader.org/works/anglicans/volume2/gladstone/index.html (Original work composed 1875)

Nietzsche, F. (1989). *Beyond good & evil: Prelude to a philosophy of the future* (Walter Kaufmann, Trans.). New York, NY: Vintage Books. (Original work composed 1885)

Pakaluk, M., Titus, C. S., Vitz, P. C., & Moncher, F. (2009). Appreciative musings on 'normative thoughts, normative feelings, normative actions.' *Journal of Psychology and Theology 37*(3), 194–203.

Pereboom, D. (2006). *Living without free will*. New York, NY: Cambridge University Press.

Pinckaers, S. (1995). *The sources of Christian ethics* (M. T. Noble, Trans.). Washington, DC: The Catholic University of America Press. (Original work published 1985)

Plato. (1980). *Republic*. In E. Hamilton & H. Cairns (Eds.), *The collected dialogues of Plato: Including the letters* (pp. 575–844). Princeton, NJ: Princeton University Press. (Original work composed ca. 360 BC)

Paul VI. (1968). *Solmni hac liturgia* [Apostolic letter, credo of the people of God]. Vatican City, Vatican: Libreria Editrice Vaticana.

Pelagius. (1997). *The letters of Pelagius* (R. Van de Weyer, Ed.). Evesham, United Kingdom: Little Gidding Books. (Original work composed in the fifth century)

Pseudo-Dionysius (the Areopagite). (1987). *Divine Names*. In *Pseudo-Dionysius: The complete works* (C. Luibheid, Trans.). New York, NY: Paulist Press. (Original work composed ca. 450)

Ratzinger, J. (1995). *From the beginning: A Catholic understanding of the story of creation and the fall* (B. Ramsay, Trans.). Grand Rapids, MI: Eerdmans.

Rist, J. (2009). The divided self: A classical perspective. In C. S. Titus (Ed.), *Psychology of character and virtue* (pp. 21–41). Arlington, VA: Institute for the Psychological Sciences Press.

Rogers, C. (1959). A theory of therapy, personality, and interpersonal relationships, as developed in the client-centered framework. In S. Koch (Ed.), *Psychology: A study of a science*: *Vol. 3. Formulations of the person and the social context* (pp. 184–256). New York, NY: McGraw-Hill.

Roman Missal (7th ed.). (2012). (International Commission on English in the Liturgy Corporation, Trans.). Woodbridge, IL: Midwest Theological Forum.

Rousseau, J. (1979). *Emile: or, On education* (A. Bloom, Trans.). New York, NY: Basic Books. (Original work published 1762)

Sartre, J. P. (2007). *Existentialism is a humanism* (C. Macomber, Trans.). New Haven, CT: Yale University Press. (Original work published 1946)

Schmitz, K. (2009). *Person and psyche*. Arlington, VA: The Institute for the Psychological Sciences Press.

Schoonenberg, P. (1965). *Man and sin: A theological investigation*. South Bend, IN: The University of Notre Dame Press.

Spitzer, R. (2015). *Finding true happiness: Satisfying our restless hearts*. San Francisco, CA: Ignatius Press.

United States Conference of Catholic Bishops.

(2009). *Ethical and religious directives for Catholic health care services* (5th ed.). Washington, DC: Author.

VanderWeele, T. J. (2017a). Religious communities and human flourishing. *Current Directions in Psychological Science, 26*(5), 476–481.

VanderWeele, T. J. (2017b). On the promotion of human flourishing. *PNAS 114*(31), 8148–8156.

Van Ornum, W. (2004). *A thousand frightening fantasies: Understanding and healing scrupulosity and obsessive compulsive disorder*. Eugene, OR: Wipf & Stock.

Vatican II, Council. (1965). *Gaudium et spes* [Pastoral constitution on the Church in the modern world]. Vatican City, Vatican: Libreria Editrice Vaticana.

Vitz, P. C. (1988). *Sigmund Freud's Christian unconscious*. New York, NY: Guilford.

Vitz, P. C. (1994). *Psychology as religion: The cult of self-worship*. Grand Rapids, MI: Eerdmans.

Vitz, P. C. (2017). The origin of consciousness in the integration of analog (right hemisphere) & digital (left hemisphere) codes. *Journal of Consciousness Exploration & Research, 8*(11), 881–906.

Vitz, P. C., & Gartner, J. (1989). The vicissitudes of original sin: A reply to Bridgman and Carter. *Journal of Psychology & Theology, 17*, 9–12.

Wetzel, A. D. (1999). Sin. In A. D. Fitzgerald (Ed.), *Augustine through the ages: An encyclopedia* (pp. 800–802). Grand Rapids, MI: Eerdmans.

William of Ockham. (1991). *Quodlibetal questions* (A. J. Freddoso & F. E. Kelley, Trans.). New Haven, CT: Yale University Press. (Original work composed ca. 1322–1324)

World Health Organization (WHO). (2015). *International statistical classification of diseases and related health problems* (10th rev.) (ICD-10). Retrieved from http://apps.who.int/classifications/icd10/browse/2015/en

Wojtyła, K. (1993). *Love and responsibility* (H. T. Willetts, Trans.). San Francisco, CA: Ignatius Press. (Original work published 1960)

Worthington, E. L., Jr. (2006). *Forgiveness and reconciliation: Theory and application*. New York, NY: Routledge.

Chapter 19

Redeemed

MATTHEW R. MCWHORTER AND
CRAIG STEVEN TITUS

ABSTRACT: This chapter addresses redemption to aid in the understanding of the person and the therapeutic process. There are two levels to redemption. First, there is the natural level or domain for fulfilling people's hope for positive change. This level is assumed and often made explicit in mental health practice, as people come to therapy with the hope of some kind of natural fulfillment or redemption (Chapter 5, "Basic Psychological Support"). Second, there is also the transcendent domain of a deeper and ultimate redemption that is primarily God's work to bring about (a) a liberation from sin that overcomes the barriers that separate mankind from God (also called justification), and (b) the ongoing healing and transformation of the person by divine grace (also called sanctification). In addition to freeing people from the barriers that separate them from God, this transcendent redemption also offers liberation from the effects of the fall, which alienate people from others and self. This chapter sheds light on human fallenness and the need for healing. It addresses how Christian redemption bestows new dignity on a person. It also explores the natural domain of the human desire for God, its limits, and how this desire is fulfilled and elevated by God's grace. The gift of the Holy Spirit is discussed, in addition to the effects associated with his indwelling. Special attention is given to faith, hope, and charity at the natural and theological levels (1 Cor 13:13). These virtues underlie the development and sanctification of a person by engendering the transformation of human nature and its structures of knowing and loving. Further, this chapter examines the natural and transcendent aspects of prayer, sacraments, and religious practices in the healing, development, and sanctification of the person. Throughout this chapter, emphasis is given to the importance of both types of redemption and the human and divine contributions to the work of mental health professionals in helping their clients to flourish.

Suffering, depression, and anxiety require serious consideration at two levels: natural and transcendent. To understand these domains requires the contributions of the sciences and the mental health professions (McAdams, 2013), as well as of philosophy and theology. From both natural-existential and transcendent-wisdom-based perspectives, these disciplines ask: Is there meaning to be found in human suffering? (See, for example, Frankl, 2006; John Paul II, 1984.) At the natural level, suffering is of value only when a person overcomes it, and becomes stronger and wiser. In the natural domain, learning is the overcoming of failures that always involve some kind of suffering. The Catholic Christian Meta-Model of the Person (CCMMP) recognizes that both the natural and the religious-transcendent experiences of persons contribute to healing when a person is burdened by distress, disorder, and despair.

Beneath dysfunctional emotions, thoughts, behaviors, and relationships, there are natural inclinations in accordance with which each person longs to enter into personal peace and positive communion with others. Because of weakness and disorders in these capacities at the natural level, there is a need for both a natural healer and a transcendent mediator and healer. The transcendent mediator is a reconciler who shows the way from the brokenness found in human suffering, existential angst, and social sin, toward communion with the divine, others, and self. At the transcendent level, suffering can be of value even when it is not healed or left behind, since it has meaning in itself when it brings a person into unity with the transcendent mediator, unity with Christ through the cross. Of course, secular commentators on the origin, condition, and destiny of the person do not talk about transcendent redemption or its effect on human nature and psychopathology. Yet a person can naturally long for ultimate freedom—or to be redeemed—from those things that weigh us down or separate us from loved ones, especially God.

The previous two chapters of this volume have addressed questions, from both the natural and transcendent levels, such as: From where have we come? What is the source of evil or disorder that we face in our lives? We must now address further questions such as: How can the effects of evil and injustice be overcome? To where are humans ultimately headed? What is the supreme source of meaning, healing, flourishing, and communion for human beings? This chapter suggests responses to these questions from a Catholic Christian vision of the person, recognizing the interplay of the two levels but focusing on the transcendent domain.

From a Catholic Christian view of redemption, God not only creates, conserves, and orders all things (*Catechism of the Catholic Church* [*CCC*], 2000, §301), but in the face of the brokenness experienced by mankind, God also offers a remedy for disorder. The "curative" work of redemption, however, is not something that God simply does to us without our cooperation. God calls each person to receive grace but also to participate actively in his or her own redemption and flourishing. Each person is invited, as part of his or her vocation to holiness and as an expression of faith, hope, and charity, to partake in the unique redemptive and healing work that Christ has achieved and continues to offer (Congregation for the Doctrine of the Faith, 2000, §14; John Paul II, 1979; Vatican II, 1964, 1965a; World Lutheran Federation and the Pontifical Council for Christian Unity, 1999). While this view (namely, that Christ alone is the healer and savior of mankind) may seem exclusivist to some, no person is excluded from God's offer of transcendent redemption (Trent, 1547/1990, Canon 17). Rather, God "desires all men to be saved and to come to the knowledge of the truth" (1 Tim 2:4; see also Acts 17:30).

Obviously, however, when dealing with non-religious or non-Christian clients the issue of supernatural redemption is certainly not a topic for professional intervention. Respect for the client requires that such a value-based issue should in no way be forced, even implicitly, on a client by the power of the therapist. This position concerning the therapist's non-imposition of private values is well emphasized in the

American Psychological Association and the American Counseling Association codes of professional ethics (American Counseling Association, 2014; American Psychological Association, 2017). Of equal relevance is that the Christian position itself rejects any pressure that might violate the nature of the client's free will, especially since faith is understood as a free gift (Benedict XVI, 2006).

What Is Transcendent Redemption?

At the heart of the Catholic Christian doctrine of redemption is the mystery of how God brings life out of death and an order of love out of prideful disorder (Lk 24:21; Eph 1:7; Col 1:14). In so doing, he brings forth forgiveness of sin out of self-giving sacrifice (1 Pet 4:8). He offers the freedom of becoming his children to those who are trapped in the slavery of sin (Gal 4:5). Even in the midst of suffering and the effects of sin, human beings have an intuition of the ultimate and eternal life that exists beyond their reach. Despite our having this intuition that life is greater than death, experience also reveals that accessing eternal life is not of one's own doing. Rather, the offer of redemption is first and foremost a gift that one receives, a personal calling that one encounters and to which one responds.

What is transcendent redemption? The word derives from Hebrew culture, in which property can be designated to another but also bought back, or redeemed (Lev 25:23–55, 27:15; Ruth 4:3–4). With respect to the fallen human condition, one can observe all the many ways that persons experience suffering, including bodily death, disordered natural inclinations, loss of the interior harmony that God intended for persons, as well as loss of the original harmony that God intended between man and woman (CCC, 2000, §376). This disorder is not the original condition of humanity that God de-

sired persons to experience (God created us for eternal life, not for death—Wis 1:13, 2:23). Yet because of the effects of the fall, no person has the ability to restore himself or herself to that original condition (CCC, 2000, §1993). Through Jesus Christ, however, God calls all persons to be restored—to be redeemed or "bought back" from the effects of sin. Through his suffering and death, Christ has paid a ransom (Mt 20:28; Mk 10:45; 1 Pet 1:18–19; Rev 5:9) and has purchased fallen persons for a price (1 Cor 6:20, 7:23), in order that they be offered the opportunity to be restored and reunited with God. At the psychological level, a person can be brought back to wholeness, a kind of natural redemption, through the help of family, friends, and therapists, as well as through understanding and addressing the sources of the client's suffering, including the client's own contribution to it.

What Is the Meaning of Christ's Offer of Redemption?

The benefits from and participation in Christ's redemption can take many forms. Basically, though, one must become connected in some way to Jesus Christ in his life, death, resurrection, and glorification (Rom 6:3–5; Vatican II, 1965b, §22). Christ's death was the result of an act of murder (and therefore it was an act of moral evil) (CCC, 2000, §312). Nonetheless, Christ's death did not occur in vain but rather was received by God the Father as a voluntary sacrificial offering (CCC, 2000, §610). In this sense, Jesus is named the "Lamb of God" whose death serves as the sacrifice that overcomes human sin and disorder (Jn 1:29; Heb 9:15; Rev 7:14). This view of redemption illustrates how God is able to bring forth moral good from evil, order from disorder, and life from death (Rom 8:28; CCC, 2000, §311; Trent, 1547/1990, Canon 6).

When a person is moved by God's grace to accept the gift of Christ's redemption, he or she participates in God's work of healing (*CCC*, 2000, §457). Christ's suffering begins to heal that person's disordered inclinations (1 Jn 2:2; *CCC*, 2000, §604). Christ's redemption also recalls that person from disordered relationships. This work of reordering human capacities (through which a person is able, for example, to begin to regain control over thoughts and desires) and of restoring that person to a relationship with God is a work that is called justification (Rom 3:24–25). A person's capacities and relationships are "made right," and, in this regard, one can speak of a person being restored to the fullness of "right reason" and love.

In accordance with the fullness of right reason (in the natural domain), a person will again by nature love God above all things (Aquinas, 1273/1981, I-II, 109.3; Nicolas, 1960, p. 41). But with the help of God's elevating grace (in the transcendent domain), a person's renewed relationship with God can develop in a more profound way than what is possible simply by human nature alone. In this way, a person's restored relationship with God overcomes alienation and separation from God (Mk 15:37–38; Jn 14:9; Rom 5:10; 2 Cor 5:19–21; Heb 10:19–20; *CCC*, 2000, §457, §614). This renewed relationship is familial, in that a person who sets out upon the path of redemption receives adoption as a son or daughter of God (Gal 4:5; Eph 1:5). Further, a person who believes in Christ is redeemed from a debilitating fear of bodily death (Heb 2:14–15; *CCC*, 2000, §635).

The entry into this restored transcendent relationship with God can also be described as "salvation" (*CCC*, 2000, §457). From the Catholic Christian perspective, salvation is the gift of redemption in a process of sanctification that continues throughout life. In addition to restoring one's relationship with God, redemption also offers a way to repair a person's other relationships. In this respect, the effects of Christ's redemption extend also to restoring the original harmonious relationship God intended for men and women (*CCC*, 2000, §376). However, transcendent redemption does not mean that one will not experience physical or psychological suffering in this life (John Paul II, 2006, pp. 143–144, p. 462).

What Is Atonement for Sin?

Christ's death can be understood as a sacrifice that he himself offers to overcome human sinfulness and its effects (Eph 5:2; Heb 9:13–14, 10:22; Ocáriz, Mateo Seco, & Riestra, 2004, pp. 222–223). Christ's work of transcendent redemption is referred to as an atonement: through his sacrifice he serves as a substitute who exonerates mankind before God's justice (Anselm, 1098/2000, I.11; *CCC*, 2000, §615). In making atonement, Jesus Christ can be understood as the suffering servant in the prophecies of Isaiah (Isa 50:5–6 & 53:1–12; *CCC*, 2000, §615) or as the persecuted righteous man found in Hebrew wisdom literature (Wis 2:12–20). Christ takes our fallen human condition into his own suffering and death (Gal 3:13; 1 Pet 2:24; *CCC*, 2000, §612). One is thus saved from the just condemnation of God (Rom 5:9). God permits the Son to stand for the truth of who God is, at the expense of his physical life. God brings forth from the great evil of Christ's death the great goodness of grace to be imparted to others through their being forgiven and renewed. According to the Meta-Model, such forgiveness is needed in order for a person to be restored to the highest level of flourishing.

In Christ, death and suffering are transformed and become doors to everlasting life. Bodily death is the last word only to one's earthly story (1 Cor 15:55; Benedict XVI, 2007, §10). Bodily death is only a single part of a fuller life narrative in which God transforms the mortal story through the promise of the redemption and resurrection of a glorified body (Lk 21:28; Eph 5:2).

Does Redemption Give a New Dignity to a Person?

Beyond the dignity of being created in God's image and the natural goodness of existence, God the Father grants a new dignity to human nature through Christ's assuming a body and soul to his divine person in the incarnation (Gen 1:26–27; Cessario, 2013, pp. 28–29). Christ "fully reveals man to man himself and makes his supreme calling clear" (Vatican II, 1965b, §22). This additional dignity is extended to all persons who respond to God's offer of transcendent redemption. Through the gift of grace, human nature "has been raised up to a divine dignity in our respect too" (Vatican II, 1965b, §22).

Eternal Flourishing and Beatitude

Throughout this volume, we have been addressing the natural and the transcendental levels of the process of flourishing of the person. Now, especially in this section, we focus on the natural and transcendent domains of desiring to see God and of attaining ultimate flourishing and beatific vision.

Do We Naturally Desire to See God?

Mankind has been given a basic desire to know what God is (Chapter 12, "Interpersonally Relational"). There is a contemporary debate regarding this desire (see, for example, de Lubac, 1998; Donneaud, 2009; Feingold, 2004; Long, 2000, 2010; Milbank, 2014; Pinckaers, 2005a; for an overview of this debate, see Cullen, 2012).

It can be affirmed that persons experience a natural attraction toward the source and goal of all life (Feser, 2017) as well as to a reality that transcends everyday experience (Heschel, 1954). The basic inclination to seek God is therefore often implicit, as when one has a spontaneous desire to seek what is good (Leo XIII, 1897, §9). It is implicit also in everyday longings to be healthy and live well (for example, to have a flourishing family) (Aquinas, ca. 1259/1987, 1.3 ad 4). Further, this desire is implied in the existential languishing that one feels when alienated from God and from others.

This desire to know what God is becomes explicit if one seeks to know the primary transcendent cause of all effects and all being (Aquinas, 1272/1999b, a. 10; Aquinas, 1273/1981, I-II, 3.8). This desire proceeds further still, after judging that God exists, to desire also to know about God's essence, that is, what God is (Aquinas, 1273/1981, I-II, 3.8). The desire for this knowledge has been associated with the searchings of philosophical theology (Aquinas, 1265/1956, III.25, §9 & §11; Hütter, 2009, p. 568). This desire is not only a desire for philosophical knowledge: this desire is also effected by the love of friendship, since it belongs to human nature to love God beyond all other things (Pinckaers, 2010, p. 639).

At the same time, the natural desire for God does not extend to seeking supernatural beatitude in the sense of the glorification that results from a direct vision of God's essence (see discussion of the beatific vision below) (Aquinas, ca. 1268/2012, pp. 469–470 ; Hütter, 2007, p. 105). Further, this natural desire is limited, in need of development (i.e., it is underspecified), and uniquely realized by each person. It is limited in that the natural human intellect cannot direct-ly attain or understand what God is (Aquinas, 1273/1981, I, 12.13 ad 1). This desire can even be nearly extinguished, since a person's intellect can be darkened.

What Is Meant by "Happiness" and Flourishing?

Everyone desires "happiness" and even "true happiness," or ultimate flourishing (Augustine, 401/2007, X.23.33). The desire for God can be misunderstood as a search for a superficial hap-piness if happiness itself is understood in a dis-torted way. The history of modern thought and ethics has been predicated on misunderstood notions of flourishing. For example, the word "happiness" in the English language has a pecu-liar etymology. It is based on "hap," which means simply luck or fortune. Happiness has also been associated with utilitarian (Mill, 1861/2001) and subjectivist interpretations (Seligman, 2002). Recent efforts in positive psychology have tried to widen the meaning of happiness and well-being to include considerations of achievement and positive relationships in relation to flourish-ing (Seligman, 2012). But more than being mere luck, the result of empirical calculations, or the experience of egotistical satisfaction, the true happiness for which mankind longs is better

termed "beatitude" or ultimate flourishing. In the Catholic Christian Meta-Model, this beati-tude is found in receiving the beatific vision.

What Is the Beatific Vision?

The intimacy of communion with God is de-scribed as a kind of "vision" (Mt 5:8; 1 Cor 13:12). The vision of God is beatific because through it, each person directly encounters God and is consequently brought to ultimate completion and fulfillment (CCC, 2000, §163, §2548). This vision of God occurs at spiritual, intellectual, and existential levels (Jn 1:18; 1 Jn 4:12; Aquinas, 1259/1994, 26.10). It involves an expressive dy-namic kind of "sight" and also a "hearing" in the sense of understanding and knowing the divine Word who expresses everlasting love (Francis, 2013, §29–§30).

The first letter of John states that God will transform our state as a child of God into a greater divine likeness when he manifests him-self (1 Jn 3:2). God will configure each of us to the model, Jesus Christ, through the work of the Holy Spirit (2 Cor 3:18). However, it is only in the fullness of time and in receiving the beatific vision of the Godhead that we are complete-ly transformed. Living a life of faith, hope, and charity prepares us for reception of this "face to face" vision.

Nature and Grace

Of What Interest Is Grace to Mental Health Professionals?

Therapists have a unique opportunity to en-counter the effects of God's grace in the lives of clients, but also in their own calling as mental health professionals. They also have a unique opportunity to encounter spiritual wounds and the effects of sin. Because each client is at a

different place in his or her life journey, and be-cause God's callings can occur at different times in a person's life, the effects of God's grace in the lives of clients will admit of great diversity. The clinical encounter is concrete and existential: it occurs with a particular client who exists in a present context, at a certain point in his or her personal and spiritual development.

When dealing with a Catholic Christian client, it is important to discern how that client understands God to be present in his or her life, whether that client recognizes the availability of God's grace, and whether the client believes religious faith would be a source of support in reaching therapeutic goals. When a client explicitly identifies religious faith as a personal resource, the therapist should explore therapeutically pertinent details of the client's spiritual life, such as how the client understands the support offered through God's presence and the gift of grace, as well as the theological virtues of faith, hope, and charity. In the case of non-Christian clients, it is important to discern how a client of good will strives to live a moral life aimed at truth and flourishing at both natural and transcendent dimensions.

Grace pertains also to the professional life and work of mental health practitioners. Their acquired virtues, such as clinical practical wisdom (professional prudence), need to be understood in the context of human nature and God's grace. The acquired virtues are the natural basis of the therapeutic competency and professional activity. These acquired virtues can be transformed by God's grace. This therapeutic competency is enriched, for example, by the faith-based conviction that all persons have dignity and value, as well as by other faith-based convictions, such as the belief that the sacramental bond of marriage should be protected as much as possible. The acquired virtues can be transformed when a Christian therapist's occupational prudence (and his or her professional practice) becomes ordered by the love of God to the ultimate flourishing of self and others. There is thereby a unity within a therapist's personal identity as both a mental health professional and a Christian.

Why Do Humans Need Divine Grace?

At the center of Christ's work of transcendent redemption is God's grace, which assists persons in the struggle with the fallen condition of human nature. This fallen condition includes, as discussed above, being wounded by sin, alienation from God, subjection to fear of bodily death, and suffering mental and moral disorders (on this last point, see *CCC*, 2000, §1811). God's gift of grace recalls one from this condition. The Passion of Christ on the Cross is the source of all redeeming grace (Isa 61:10; Gal 3:27–27; Aquinas, 1273/1981, III, 62.5; Vatican II, 1965c, §4). Christ, as head of the Church, shares his grace with others for the sake of their redemption (Aquinas, 1273/1981, III, 8.5). Christ's grace also becomes intrinsic to the person when the Holy Spirit begins to indwell in the person who is being redeemed, joining him or her to the person of Christ and to his redemptive work (Aquinas, 1273/1981, I, 43.3).

Through grace, God calls humans to become children of God (Jn 1:12–18), adopted sons or daughters, who call God "Father" in union with the only "Son" (Rom 8:14–17). As can be seen in a Catholic theological approach to grace, a person can observe the lingering effects of sin even after he or she responds to God's redemptive call. Grace does not erase all of the effects of the fall. For example, one's body still dies, and one still suffers mental and moral disorders (*CCC*, 2000, §1264). In order to help persons contend with these effects, the Spirit's work of sanctification is ongoing (1 Thess 5:23). Christian life progressively advances by being freed from the influence of evil (in a process called "purgation"), enlightened by the message of the Gospel ("illumination"), and brought into deeper connection with God ("union") (Aquinas, 1273/1981, II-II, 24.9; Garrigou-Lagrange, 1938/2002; Martin, 2006; Pinckaers, 1995, pp. 362–368).

What Is Grace?

For a Catholic Christian, "grace" is understood, generally speaking, as a free gift bestowed by God, who works freely to give humans new transcendent life in the midst of the effects of sin and weakness (Rom 5:16; *CCC*, 2000, §1996, §1999). In addition to referring to a gift, the meaning of the word "grace" relates also to its origin (the well-wishing or love of the one who gives the gift) as well as to the effects of the gift that is received (including the person's gratitude for the gift) (Journet, 1960, p. 5). In this regard, Christian grace involves three elements: the giver, the gift, and the receiver of the gift. First, God is the source of life and every good gift, be it from creation and nature or from redemption and sanctification (Jas 1:17). Second, the gift that is received is God's own presence in the soul through the indwelling of the Holy Spirit (1 Cor 3:16–17 & 6:19; Ratzinger, 2005, pp. 46–50). Third, many graced effects are brought about within a person as a result of God's indwelling (such as virtues, charisms, and gifts, discussed below) (Journet, 1960, p. 6, p. 26).

What Does Grace Do to Human Nature?

As already noted, grace perfects a nature that has its own dignity (created in the image of God) and that has been wounded by sin (Aquinas 1273/1981, I, 62.5). In God's dispensation of grace, one must understand both the human nature that is healed (by way of healing grace) as well as how that healed nature is transformed (by way of transcendent sanctifying grace). Without knowledge of the fallen condition of human nature, which God heals, we fail to understand the genuine free gift of God's assistance (Rom 1 & 2; Vatican I, 1869–1870; Pius XII, 1950; Vatican II, 1965b). A proper understanding of human nature requires reference to both its wounded condition and to God's grace that heals this condition (de Lubac, 1998, p. 55). To refer to human nature as either wounded or healed is not to refer to a closed concept where human nature has its ultimate fulfillment or meaning independent of God (Goris, 2007, p. 74). Rather, such a consideration seeks to understand the humanity that Christ takes to himself.

The Meta-Model affirms that grace leads one to what is above human nature but that grace also works in a way that accords with nature. Grace helps one experience fully what one could not otherwise experience, what is "supernatural." Through grace, a person experiences that which transcends the limits of human nature, for example, the contemplation of God face to face in the beatific vision. The effects of grace are also called supernatural because they derive from a cause that is above the order of nature, namely, God (Aquinas, 1267/2002, §200). With grace, a person is enabled to perform supernatural actions associated with the three theological virtues (faith, hope, and charity, as discussed below) (1 Cor 13:13; *CCC*, 2000, §1841) and with the gifts of the Holy Spirit (also discussed below) (Aquinas, 1273/1981, I-II, 68.2; *CCC*, 2000, §§1830–1831).

Some thinkers have criticized the characterization of grace as "above" nature in the sense of being "extrinsic" to human nature (see Goris, 2007, p. 69, citing Maurice Blondel). However, if one does not affirm uncreated grace to be extrinsic to human nature, then one judges God to be a part of humanity (the error of panentheism) or simply equates God with humanity (pantheism) (Goris, 2007, p. 73). And if one does not affirm created grace (the effects resulting from God's presence) to be extrinsic to those kinds of activities and effects that arise in accordance with natural human capacities, then one makes grace something innate or something that can be acquired by one's own efforts. According to the Meta-Model, grace does not negate human nature, but rather transforms it according to the manner of nature (Aquinas, 1273/1981, I, 62.5; Scheeben, 1954, p. 49). The classic formulation states that "grace does not destroy nature, but perfects it" (Aquinas, 1273/1981, I, 1.8 ad 2).

What Is the Effect of Justification?

Justification refers to how God makes right (justifies) a person's relationship with him. God justifies human nature and forgives a person's sins. Justification is a gift of God, who, at the same time, calls a person to cooperate in this justification through faith (Rom 3:28; 5:1; Jas 2:24). In the initial stage of grace, prior to conferral of justification, a person receives preparatory grace, which begins to dispose that person to receive the subsequent grace of justification (Aquinas, 1273/1981, I-II, 112.2; CCC, 2000, §2001). This preparatory grace can arouse an explicit desire in a person to seek out the fullness of God's grace—for example, to desire Baptism in an explicit way (Journet, 1960, p. 29; Nicolas, 1960, p. 51; Scheeben, 1954, p. 324). It is God who initiates this preparatory process, drawing a person toward himself and also toward the fullness of right reason (Jn 6:44).

With God's work of justification, a person becomes more fully established in the life of grace (CCC, 2000, §654). How grace confers justification can be understood in two ways. First, there is the grace of God's work itself (operating grace, when God immediately affects the human heart). Second, there is the grace that moves the human will to respond freely to God's work (cooperating grace) (Aquinas, 1273/1981, I-II, 111.2; CCC, 2000, §2002; Nicolas, 1960, p. 58; Trent, 1547/1990, Canon 1). Although justification is instantaneous, God does not justify a person without his or her free consent and participa-

tion (Aquinas, 1273/1981, I-II, 113.7; CCC, 2000, §§2001–2002).

Since belief in God's offer of grace is itself a matter of faith, a person should neither expect to experience direct actual grace nor reduce God's work of justification simply to one's subjective belief or self-confidence (CCC, 2000, §2005, citing Trent, 1547/1990, Chapter 9, Canons 12–14). At the same time, persons can experience God's grace indirectly in its effects—for example, the new blessings that Christ brings into their lives. To understand justification, one should place emphasis upon the justice of Jesus Christ (Rom 5:18–19), which is shared with those who become connected to him and participate in his work of redemption (Rom 5:9 & 6:3–5). This connection, as stated above, is facilitated by a person's receiving and sharing in the Holy Spirit (CCC, 2000, §152).

One may understand the gift of justification by considering the beneficial effects of Baptism, which include entering into a restored relationship with God and so regaining access to the beatific vision (CCC, 2000, §1263). It is important to note that while the grace of God is not limited to participating in visible sacraments such as Baptism (CCC, 2000, §1257), grace is available in the sacraments in a special way (CCC, 2000, §1129, §2003).

What Is Sanctifying Grace?

In Christ, God not only restores but also elevates or divinizes human nature. God's grace in this respect is called sanctifying or deifying grace, or theosis (Nicolas, 1960, p. 48; Ware, 1979). God calls all redeemed persons to grow in grace and to participate more fully in his own divine nature (2 Pet 1:4). Those who are adopted as sons and daughters of God are in a way called "gods" (Ps 82:6; Jn 10:34–35), in some sense "becoming God" (CCC, 2000, §460, citing

Athanasius, 336/1971, Chapter 54, §3). However, this call must be carefully understood. It is not the case that through the process of divinization, the redeemed person becomes God in an essential (ontological) way (Pius XII, 1943, §78). Yet, when one loves God directly upon receiving the vision of God, the lover "becomes" the beloved not in an ontological but in an intentional way, that is, by becoming entirely fulfilled upon "seeing" God face to face (1 Cor 13:12). The process of divinization can also be described as "deiformity" (Aquinas, 1273/1981, I, 12.5 & 12.5 ad 3). In other words, it is a process whereby one becomes increasingly conformed to Christ (Rom 8:29), imitating him more in thought, word, and deed, eventually sharing in Christ's glorification (1 Jn 3:2). One must at the moment of bodily death continue to seek God's assistance, hoping to receive the gratuitous help called the grace of final perseverance (Aquinas, 1273/1981, II-II, 137.4; Augustine, ca. 429/1992a).

Who Receives Grace?

The clients whom a therapist encounters are at different levels of spiritual development and manifest the life of grace in different ways. A therapist will want to explore the Christian client's interest and participation in the spiritual life. Through his death on the cross, Christ suffered for all humans (1 Jn 2:2; CCC, 2000, §605). In other words, the atonement of Christ is not limited only to a select group of persons. It is offered to all people (1 Tim 2:4). The Catholic position and that of many other Christian denominations is that no one is predestined to be excluded from the offer of Christ's grace (Trent, 1547/1990, Canon 17). In some sense, Christ has united himself to each person (CCC, 2000, §618; John Paul II, 1979, §14). But it is unknown as a matter of faith who responds to God's call and who freely cooperates with the assistance of his

grace. We may go so far as to assume that God offers to each person some kind of preparatory grace, even if it is not clear whether all persons respond in a way that leads to personal justification (Nicolas, 1960, p. 22; Scheeben, 1954, p. 321).

The question regarding who receives baptismal grace must be explored very carefully. The grace of God is not limited to the sacraments, and he offers to all persons the opportunity to participate in Christ's redemptive work in a way known to God (CCC, 2000, §1257; Vatican II, 1965b, §22). This can occur, in fact, when a person who is unaware of the necessity of Baptism acts in accordance with right reason while under the influence of grace (Aquinas, 1273/1981, I-II, 89.6, as interpreted to refer to a kind of Baptism of desire; see Journet, 1960, p. 92). Whatever opportunity this may involve, it requires that one turn to God in some way (Aquinas, 1273/1981, I-II, 89.6 ad 3). As such, this act under the influence of grace must be understood as connected to Baptism, since Baptism is necessary for salvation (Mk 16:16; Jn 3:5; CCC, 2000, §1129, §1257, §1277).

We can affirm a kind of Baptism by way of implicit desire for those who would seek Baptism if they knew about its necessity (CCC, 2000, §1260). The criterion for possessing this knowledge is met when one hears the Gospel (CCC, 2000, §1257). Yet some persons are ignorant of this knowledge through no fault of their own (CCC, 2000, §1260). Such persons might respond to the offer of redemption in a way known to God alone, but this does not occur without receipt of God's grace (CCC, 2000, §1281). Under the influence of grace such a person will also be moved to develop a kind of implicit theological faith through belief in God's providence, to the extent that this is understood (Aquinas, 1273/1981, II-II, 2.7 ad 3; CCC, 2000, §848).

What Are the Virtues Associated with Grace?

With God's work of justification, the seeds of the theological virtues (stable dispositions to act in ways that exemplify faith, hope, and charity) are infused in the person (1 Cor 13:13; 1 Thess 5:8; CCC, 2000, §1813, §1991). Recall that virtues, including infused virtues, are stable dispositions that perfect innate human capacities (such as a person's will or one's emotions; Aquinas, 1273/1981, I-II, 71.1; CCC, 2000, §1803) and that such dispositions also require relating a capacity to an end or goal (Aquinas, 1273/1981, I-II, 49.1; Chapter 11, "Fulfilled in Virtue").

Because of their divine origin and purpose, infused virtues transcend the human virtues (both intellectual and moral virtues) that in principle can be acquired by personal effort. Further, the theological virtues orient a person directly toward Jesus Christ, in whom one has faith and hope, in whom one loves God, and in whom one performs acts of charity to help others (CCC, 2000, §1812). These virtues, which strengthen a person's dispositions, are also referred to as "habitual grace" (CCC, 2000, §153, §2000). Such graced dispositions bring about a new quality associated with that person's elevated ability to respond to the vocation to holiness and to enter into a more intimate relationship with God (Aquinas, 1273/1981, I-II, 110.3 ad 3; 1259/1994, 27.2 ad 7; CCC, 2000, §1812; Nicolas, 1960, p. 45). These effects of grace are signs of God's presence. The effects of grace are also signs of God's work that gradually transforms a person and enables him or her to imitate Christ (1 Cor 11:1; 2 Cor 3:18; Emery, 2011, p. 186). Examples of such signs are found in the lives of saints and holy Christians and include extensive self-giving (even to the point of martyrdom), and special knowledge and wisdom (including sometimes supernatural knowledge, counsel, and ability to heal). Such virtues are thus integral to the process of divinization described above. These theological virtues originate from God, lead one to God, and are—properly speaking—the virtues of Christ, whom one imitates as a model and to whom one is connected by way of the Holy Spirit (1 Cor 4:16; Eph 5:1; Phil 3:17).

Sanctifying or divinizing grace also endows a person with the seeds of Christian moral virtue—infused prudence, justice, temperance, and fortitude (Aquinas, 1272/1999b, a. 10). These infused moral virtues are not acquired by human effort but rather are received as a gift. They are "implanted" in the soul by the Spirit (Pinckaers, 2001, p. 71).

Why are such infused or transcendent moral virtues needed? First, they assure the action that is necessary for salvation, that is, they assure the expression of faith-filled hope and charity. Infused moral virtues order a person to the heavenly city of God and the communion of saints, whereas the acquired moral virtues order a person to the earthly city, the civil community (Gal 4:26; Aquinas, 1273/1981, I-II, 61.5; Augustine, 401/2007, XII.16; Cessario, 2009, p. 110).

While infused virtues assure actions that are needed for salvation, especially faith, they do not assure that one will become, for instance, a prudent and good accountant, which would require acquired knowledge and training. Further, the Christian moral virtues take as their rule the divine law, which perfects the judgment of right reason (Aquinas, 1273/1981, I-II, 63.2 & 63.4). Thus, the fitting mean between extremes that is found in Christian virtue can be different from the mean found in natural human virtues. Christian virtue can thus involve a different kind of action. For example, Christian temperance may, on certain points, be the same as an Aristotelian temperance with respect to eating a moderate amount of food as determined by right reason

(Aquinas, 1273/1981, I-II, 63.4 ad 2; 1272/1999b, a. 10 ad 8). Yet in other respects, Christian temperance in fasting not only (a) calls for the person's intention to participate in Christ's work of salvation, but it also (b) specifies the object of fasting to be informed by a twofold conversion, *toward* God by imitating Christ and *away* from the pleasure of eating by developing discipline over one's desires.

Another difference between infused and acquired virtues can be noted: an act of grave sin can immediately destroy the infused moral virtue (as when one rejects God's grace, which is the foundation for this transcendent type of virtue), but a grave sin does not immediately destroy the acquired moral virtue (as when one chooses once to get drunk and to endanger his or her own live and the lives of others) (Aquinas, 1273/1981, I-II, 73.1 ad 2; *CCC*, 2000, §2290). Furthermore, infused Christian moral virtue can be sacramentally restored by the Spirit in one who is repentant, whereas an acquired moral virtue cannot be reacquired in such a sudden way once it is lost through repetition, as in alcohol-related disorders (Aquinas, 1273/1981, I-II, 53.1 ad 3; American Psychiatric Association, 2013).

Christian moral virtues are needed because, while not all human actions prior to justification are sins (Trent, 1547/1990, Canon 7), it remains difficult for persons to acquire moral virtue, because of the fallen condition of humanity (*CCC*, 2000, §1811). Some amount of virtue might be acquired through education and formation. Consider, for example, the different forms of true but imperfect occupational prudence that are ordered to particular goals (such as acquired business prudence or the prudence of the therapist). These dispositions relate a person to true but particular human goals (such as the civil common good) and require the acquisition of some amount of right reason through life ex-

perience. These acquired virtues are true virtues in only a qualified sense. For the Christian, transcendent (true) virtues, strictly speaking, require charity and reference to God (Aquinas, 1273/1981, II-II, 23.7).

God's work of justification has a profound effect upon a person's acquired virtues. Such acquired virtues are redeemed, so to speak, through God's work of justification: an acquired virtue is "taken up" within its infused Christian counterpart, just as human nature is elevated by divine grace and human reason is taken up by theological faith (Pinckaers, 1995, p. 178; 2001, p. 71). The Christian remains a citizen of the earthly city, but is called to relate to the civil common good in a transformed manner (Aquinas, 1272/1999b, a. 9). He or she recognizes the fuller framework for understanding civic justice or laws and the nature of the commitments of vocational states, such as the permanence and indissolubility of marriage. In a similar way, the Christian therapist relates to his or her professional work in a transformed manner: professional work can now be infused with charity. For instance, consider the charity of the therapist mediated to a client by way of clinical practical wisdom (professional prudence) (Klubertanz, 1959, p. 571; Maritain, 1944, pp. 210–216; Mirkes, 1997, p. 197).

What Are the Gifts of the Holy Spirit?

In addition to effecting the Christian virtues (theological and moral), the indwelling Holy Spirit also effects several dispositions in a person that are referred to as the Spirit's "gifts" (Aquinas, 1273/1981, I-II, 68; Bonaventure, 1268/2008; *CCC*, 2000, §1830; Pinckaers, 2005b). There are also special charisms (such as an individual's ability to heal) that are given to certain people. However, the gifts of the Holy Spirit under consideration here are imparted in common to all justified persons. The gifts are infused simultaneously with the theological virtues, emerging from the latter as from roots (John of St. Thomas, 1644/2016, pp. 87–88). The gifts are wisdom, understanding, knowledge, counsel, fortitude, piety, and the reverential fear of God (Isa 11:2; Rev 5:6; *CCC*, 2000, §1831). As with Christ's own justice, which is imparted via God's work of justification (and as with the Christian virtues and grace itself), so too are the gifts first and foremost the gifts of Jesus, upon whom the Holy Spirit preeminently rests. In this way, just as one is connected by the Spirit to Christ, so is one connected to Christ's grace, virtues, and gifts.

One might observe that the names of certain gifts are the same as the names of particular virtues, such as wisdom (an intellectual virtue) or fortitude (a moral virtue). Ultimately, however, such gifts are not typically referred to as virtues. This is because there are important differences that distinguish these dispositions from the other Christian virtues. A first difference is that the gifts are given to supplement and further perfect the Christian virtues (*CCC*, 2000, §1831; Pinckaers, 2001, p. 89): the gifts of the Holy Spirit assist human capacities in those areas where human nature (even elevated with grace) continues to fall short in relation to the attainment of beatitude (John of St. Thomas, 1644/2016, pp. 85–86). The gift of knowledge, for example, helps one to distinguish what should be believed with theological faith, and the gift of understanding helps one to apprehend, to some extent, that to which one is giving assent (Aquinas, 1273/1981, I-II, 9.1). Arising from the theological virtues, the gifts in turn serve as a kind of origin for the Christian moral virtues (Aquinas, 1273/1981, I-II, 68.4; II-II, 19.9 ad 4; Pinsent, 2012, p. 477). For example, the Spirit, giving fortitude, inspires a person with confidence in God's promise of beatitude, and this in turn supports that person in performing virtuous acts of Christian fortitude ordered to the heavenly city (Aquinas, 1273/1981, II-II, 139.1).

A further differentiation between gifts and infused virtues can be noted in how a disposition associated with a gift is activated. God assists one to develop spiritually through the gifts. This development must be carefully understood. We have underscored the increased passivity of human initiative with respect to the exercise of a gift. Growth in the gifts requires docility before the presence of the Holy Spirit and obedience to his inspirations (*CCC*, 2000, §1831). This emphasis upon passivity and docility, however, should not suggest a disdain for human initiative, nor a misconstruing of human activity as a kind of obstacle to the Spirit, nor does it require a person to become passive in the sense of an inanimate object or a puppet, where a person might seek a total self-negation (Denzinger, 1687/2012, §2201–§2205).

Faith

What Interest Does Faith Offer to Mental Health Professionals?

The psychologist, counselor, and clinician should be interested in the personal act of faith itself and how the disposition of faith relates to his or her own as well as to the client's confidence in the source of truth and the search for freedom, hope, charity, and joy. These moral and religious strengths are of particular importance for psychotherapy. Some type of religious faith resides at the base of every client's worldview and value-system (Ashley, 2000; Hicks, 2014;

O'Donohue, 2013; see also Chapter 7 "Methodology and Presuppositions" and Chapter 16 "Volitional and Free"). This foundation leads to a number of beliefs that inform the client's perspective and practices, as well as his or her goals for healing. For example, a client's faith in Christ's transcendent redemption can support that client on the path of renewal, purify his or her conscience, and clarify the client's remorse for past actions (Heb 9:13–14; CCC, 2000, §654). This faith in God's offer of salvation bolsters everyday and ultimate hope, as will be discussed later. Moreover, the non-Christian and person of good will may also seek to discern what is true and good, confident that there is meaning in life.

A mental health professional, moreover, will benefit from acquiring competency to understand how to discuss religious faith with a client. He or she will also benefit from gaining experience in implicitly integrating religious faith as a therapeutic support, and in explicitly integrating faith in therapy when a client desires to do so (Tan, 1996). Faith has further practical implications: the practitioner's own religious faith influences how he or she understands and relates to a client. For example, Catholic Christian religious faith affirms the dignity of each client as created in the image of God (Gen 1:27). This basic tenet of religious faith also illuminates the professional ethical codes by enriching the clinician's understanding of his or her role when caring for a client. When religious faith is integrated with professional practice, the Christian virtues can become joined with the professional virtues of the clinician (Pinckaers, 1995, p. 180). A therapist's virtue of faith can inform his or her understanding of clients (case conceptualization) and enable a conviction that the suffering a client faces has meaning.

Faith is relevant for the mental health professional not because professional virtues are replaced by the theological virtues, but because they are instead transformed within a distinct Catholic Christian form of professional practice (CCC, 2000, §1810; Pinckaers, 1995, p. 179). The clinician who integrates religious faith into professional practice seeks to be open to the way in which God works through the therapy both to heal the client and to guide the client toward true flourishing. Taking Christ's virtues as a model allows clinicians to participate in the suffering of their clients and even to endure their abusive behaviors while remaining forgiving and loving. A Christian practitioner also will recognize the Holy Spirit's gift of counsel, which is offered to assist both practitioner and client with discernment.

What Are the Different Types of Natural and Transcendent Faith?

In general, the natural dimension of belief is a type of knowledge that needs to be differentiated from doubt, ignorance, opinion, and science (Chapter 15, "Rational"). The object of belief is unreservedly accepted as true and real. This occurs with everyday sorts of belief ("I believe you when you say you were sick last night") (Ratzinger, 2006, pp. 79–82). This kind of belief is present in the fidelity that underlies many natural relationships (such as marriage and friendship) and that supports the trustworthy nature of many civil relationships (such as that between therapist and client) (see Austriaco, 2011, p. 119).

The acceptance and affirmation of belief is present also in transcendent religious belief or faith ("I believe in God, the Father almighty, Creator of heaven and earth"). Christian faith, understood as a disposition enabling one to assent to the revealed Truth, who is God (Jn 14:6), and also to truths about God, is bestowed as a gift through which the believer personally encounters God (Eph 2:8). Such religious belief or faith requires hearing the proclamation of Christ (Rom 10:17). But this faith is not simply belief in content asserted about God (that is, truth-bearing statements). Rather, religious belief also extends directly to God as the First Truth, who is believed (Jn 14:6; Aquinas, 1273/1981, II-II, 1.1; Cessario, 1996, pp. 51–77). Theological faith enables one to adhere to God as the source of all truth (Aquinas, 1273/1981, II-II, 17.6) and so to trust God, who is the Truth itself.

Faith leads one to ponder truths about God within the context of assent, where, assenting to God's truth in love, one also reflects upon it, seeking understanding (CCC, 2000, §158). This intellectual search is not merely a desire to understand what God has revealed but ultimately to understand God, to know God—to love God with all of one's mind (Lk 10:27). The searchings of faith are ultimately fulfilled when one receives the beatific vision, when one encounters the First Truth directly (Aquinas, 1273/1981, II-II, 1.2 ad 3). In this way, religious faith believes God and believes in God, as well as believing truths communicated about God and his works (CCC, 2000, §1814, §1842). Abiding in this faith (and so in the relationship that it grows out of) is necessary for transcendent redemption (that is, for justification and sanctification) (Rom 5:1; CCC, 2000, §161). Faith involves an intimation or sense of the beatific vision to come, where faith will be set aside (Aquinas, 1272/1999a, a. 4 ad 10; CCC, 2000, §163). The assent of theological faith does not contradict what is true in any discovery of science or philosophy. John Paul II (1998, §79) reminds us that the relationship of faith and reason is parallel to the relationship between human nature and sanctifying grace. Faith presupposes reason (and perfects it), just as grace presupposes human nature in order to perfect it (Aquinas, 1273/1981, I, 1.8 ad 2).

What Is the Structure of Theological Faith?

The transcendent structure of faith is twofold, involving both the person and the community of the Church. With respect to the person, the act of faith is constituted by the interior act that is proper to faith, namely, "to ponder with assent," to lovingly contemplate God (Aquinas, 1273/1981, II-II, 2.1). Benedict XVI (2011) says: "there exists a profound unity between the act by which we believe and the content to which we give our assent" (§10). One can ponder only that which one understands to some extent. Thus, the act of religious belief requires some preceding knowledge on the part of the believer (Aquinas, 1273/1981, II-II, 8.8 ad 2; Augustine, ca. 429/1992b, 2.5). This includes knowing what one ought to believe with theological faith—and this knowledge is common to all Christian persons by way of the associated gift from the Holy Spirit (Aquinas, 1273/1981, II-II, 9.1 ad 2).

The act of faith is also a communal act—but this is more than the sociological event of being initiated into a community. Regarding personal belief as sharing in communal belief, Pope Francis (2013) says: "The individual's act of faith finds its place within a community, within the common 'we' of the people who, in faith, are like a single person" (§14; see also Ratzinger, 1987, pp. 15–55). The biblical experience of being called to be the people Israel (Ex 4:22) and to be one Body in Christ (1 Cor 12:12–27) involves "openness to the ecclesial 'We' [that] reflects the openness of God's own love, which is not only a relationship between the Father and the Son, between an 'I' and a 'Thou,' but is also, in the Spirit, a 'We,' *a communion of persons*" (Francis, 2013, §39). It is within the context of communal religious belief that personal religious belief emerges and is nourished.

Hope

What Interest Does Hope Offer to Mental Health Professionals?

Hope is one of the most prevalent factors in psychological and sociological research on overcoming difficulty (Rand & Cheavens, 2009). It is also an important factor in the success of therapy. For example, hope is one of the four therapeutic variables that are attributed to healing in therapeutic approaches (Larsen & Stege, 2010). Hope is also explicitly emphasized in particular therapeutic modalities, as in hope-focused marital psychotherapy and counseling (Ripley, Maclin, Hook, & Worthington, 2013).

The Catholic Christian Meta-Model brings further insight to the psychological importance of hope by making the presuppositions and goals of such therapies more evident, and by recognizing how hope relates to the ultimate goal of the whole person. Hope that one will obtain the ultimate end—the beatific vision—pertains first and foremost to a person's spiritual dimension. But this hope also has important effects upon a person's overall mental health. Thus, while a theological consideration of ultimate hope primarily concerns hope's relation to a divine goal that is difficult to obtain, this perspective leads to a psychological consideration of hope and how hope contributes to a person's agency, developmental growth, and resiliency. In this way, the Meta-Model affirms a synthetic view of hope (psychological, philosophical, and theological) that explicitly integrates the multiple dimensions of hope (emotion, temperament, natural virtue, and theological virtue). This synthetic approach will interest the psychologist, counselor, and clinician, because the person cannot be understood and should not be treated in a way that is removed from his or her natural and transcendent goals.

What Is Hope?

Hope revitalizes the human psyche and transforms a person. In hope, we are drawn forward and move ahead when much pulls us back. Hope is reason and desire together leading us to seek worthwhile goals that are difficult to obtain and that require great effort. For example, hope enables a parent to maintain a loving relationship with a child, even if the child is terminally ill or the parent is facing old age. In addition to the discussion on the virtue of hope found in Chapter 11, "Fulfilled in Virtue," hope will be examined here within the context of considering redemption, both natural and divine.

There are at least four ways to consider hope: an emotion, a temperament, a natural virtue, and a theological virtue. These four types of hope can be understood fully only in relation to concrete human actions that seek to overcome difficulties and obtain the goals for which one hopes. The common element that underlies all these types of hope is the difficulty that it takes to attain some real good. However, it is not the difficulty itself that gives us hope. There must also be trust in our own resources as well as in the assistance of others. Besides having this confidence in receiving help, we recognize that not only are other people trustworthy in their help, but also, for many persons, God serves as a major source of hope.

How Is Hope an Emotion?

Hope should be counted as one of the foundational emotions. Although not having a particular facial manifestation (Ekman, 1992, 2003), hope has been recognized, along with its contrasts (despair and presumption) in both classic philosophical psychology (Lombardo, 2011, pp. 154–158; Miner, 2010, pp. 215–230) and in personality theory (Erikson, 1950, 1982) as one of the major initiative-taking emotions. For cognitive psychologists Lazarus and Lazarus (1994), the feeling of hope precedes a positive outcome; it is "essentially an antidote to despair" that requires that we anticipate the object of hope without falling into an illusory false hope (p. 72). The danger of this latter kind of hope, however, according to Lazarus and Lazarus (1994) "is that the person will continue to seek what is denied and, therefore, fail to redirect his or her thoughts and energies toward a more realistic outcome" (p. 74).

What Is the Temperament Trait Called Optimism?

The emotion called hope is distinguished from an optimistic temperament. General hopefulness or optimism (Seligman, 1990, 1995) or "being upbeat" (Kagan, 1994, 2007) is widely recognized as a general temperament trait. Snyder, Harris, et al. (1991) define the optimistic temperament "as a generalized expectancy that good things will happen" (p. 571; see also Snyder, Irving, & Anderson, 1991). Lazarus and Lazarus (1994) describe it as "a positive expectation about what will happen" (p. 73). In various ways, studies on optimism and a hopeful temperament have been the foundation for the positive psychology movement (Peterson & Seligman, 2004; Snyder & Lopez, 2002). Snyder, Rand, and Sigmon (2002, p. 258) have conceptualized hope as a positive motivational state in which we consciously understand our own capacity both to plan pathways to meet goals and to use these pathways for action. Attention has also been given to the positive effects of optimism (Seligman, 1990, 1995), such as experiencing subjective and physical levels of well-being (Beauregard, 2012; Koenig, King, & Carson, 2012), as well as the way hopefulness facilitates healing in group psychotherapy (Yalom & Lesczc, 2005; Scrofani, 2013).

How Is Hope a Natural Virtue?

In addition to the emotion and the temperament trait, there is also a natural virtue of hope. As a Christian philosopher, Pieper (1997) differentiates everyday hope from the theological virtue that involves a "fundamental hope" (pp. 24–28). As a natural virtue, hope involves the rational, motivational, and relational structure of the whole person, who is capable of consciously aiming at a difficult good. Hope makes a contribution to seeking out such difficult goods and also contributes to the performance of virtuous human acts. For example, humans act with hope when they have confidence and courage in seeking difficult life goals, as when one seeks clinical training or enters into marriage and family life. Such hope requires initiative taking that overcomes extreme fear, engages appropriate levels of daring, and manages the challenges due to the honors that come with success (Titus, 2006, pp. 214–215). Hope can be practiced by anyone, no matter the size of his or her life project. For example, both an entrepreneur and a homemaker must take initiatives aimed at their respective desires and intentions to run a business or a home efficaciously. Of course, without acquiring skills for planning and executing plans, they would not accomplish what is necessary for a thriving business or a flourishing home.

What Is the Theological Virtue of Hope?

A fourth type of hope is the properly transcendent variety of hope, a fundamental hope that Christians call the theological virtue of hope (*CCC*, 2000, §1817; Cessario, 2002). The theological virtue differs from the other kinds of hope described above because of its origin, mode of development, and goal, all of which concern God. Theological hope enables one to adhere to God and seek his assistance (Aquinas, 1273/1981, II-II, 17.6). It is here that the topic of hope connects with consideration of transcendent redemption and the assistance of God's grace. In the context of Christian hope, human life is given new scope and meaning, human work becomes more than a job, and human suffering becomes more than enduring pain. The goal of holiness aims at personal goodness and eternal salvation in the midst of our everyday hopes and initiatives. We hope for salvation and eternal life with God because of the promises of Christ and the greatness of God (Mt 4:17; Rom 6:3–6).

God alone can fulfill the expectation of Christian hope. Hope is a gift of divine grace that goes hand in hand with faith and love. The belief that sin, death, and disorder are definitively overcome by Jesus' redemption (1 Cor 15:54–55) is more than information about the promise of salvation. It is good news that transforms, bringing a hope that saves (Rom 8:24). In this light, suffering and difficulties become opportunities to grow in virtue (Rom 5:3). Further, with a new and ultimate hope, a Christian person is called to go forth to serve others in justice and through works of charity. Instead of being simply informative, Christian hope can be understood as "performative" (Benedict XVI, 2007, §2). As Pope Benedict XVI (2007) states, "The one who has hope lives differently; the one who hopes has been granted the gift of a new life" (§2).

Love

As with hope, so too does the complexity of the phenomenon of love demand a clear approach involving precise distinctions and vocabulary. Love is omnipresent in a Catholic Christian vision of mankind and manifests itself at natural and transcendent levels of flourishing. In this section, an overview of love is provided and then special attention is given to the preeminent love that is manifested in God's work of transcendent redemption, namely, theological charity. Love is addressed also in Chapter 12, "Interpersonally Relational."

What Interest Does Charity-Love Have for to Mental Health Professionals?

Charity moves a Christian mental health practitioner to act lovingly to his or her client. Sacred Scripture is clear and specific about charity-love:

> Love is patient and kind; love is not jealous or boastful; it is not arrogant or rude. Love does not insist on its own way; it is not irritable or resent-

ful; it does not rejoice at wrong, but rejoices in the right. Love bears all things, believes all things, hopes all things, endures all things. (1 Cor 13:4–7)

Such qualities are easily experienced by clients as being therapeutic when either Christian or non-Christian mental health practitioners have and express them. These qualities facilitate the development and maintenance of the therapeutic alliance. They are all characteristics that convey the wisdom and concern of the clinician. Although this love the therapist has toward a client is a general disposition, it manifests itself in very specific instances: being patient with the borderline client who is emotionally volatile and often accusatory; being an instrument of peace between angry spouses; or engaging generously in *pro bono* work. When these qualities are embodied, the practitioner becomes a role model for other-centered relationships; when these qualities are acquired by the client in turn, they help lead that client toward inner peace and flourishing. Part of this flourishing comes as clients become less self-centered and more other-centered as they serve others at home and at work.

Although certainly not proselytizing or attempting to convert non-Christian clients, the Christian clinician, through modeling genuine love for the client, hopes for the transcendent and eternal well-being of each client. The practice of this kind of charity-love also benefits the mental health professional. For example, patience helps prevent therapist burnout by reducing an anxious desire for quick change in clients. Loving one's client gives great positive meaning and purpose to clinical work. Love makes clinicians accepting of their clients and their diversity and therefore greatly reduces power struggles and arrogance.

The Varieties of Love

Numerous Christian authors have offered treatments of human and divine love (Benedict XVI, 2005; Lewis, 1960; Pieper, 1997; Titus & Scrofani, 2012; Wojtyła, 1993). Several kinds of love can be identified relative to particular interpersonal relationships within which love is expressed (Lewis, 1960). There is the faithful love expressed between friends (*philia*), a social love or brotherly love (William of St. Thierry, ca. 1122/1981, Chapter 3, §17). A genuine love between friends precludes any use of one person by another (Aristotle, ca. 350 BC/1941, VIII.3). There is also the romantic sexual love (*eros*) that, when similarly purified of any use of one person by another, is expressed in a holy way between spouses (Wojtyła, 1993, pp. 180–181). Further, there is the affectionate love that is expressed between family members (*storgē*) (Aristotle, ca. 350 BC/2003, VIII.12; William of St. Thierry, ca. 1122/1981, Chapter 3, §16). These kinds of love, along with other natural bases of self-giving

love (such as altruism and philanthropy) are all elevated by God in divine love (*agapē*) (Jn 3:16).

What is seen throughout the different types of love is a driving force for flourishing and fulfillment. And such forces, so to speak, can be unified by that highest love, the divine love, which is charity. Charity purifies all the forms of human love and elevates them (CCC, 2000, §1827). For example, romantic love as a movement outward toward other persons (as found in attraction and *eros*) can be purified and conjoined with charity (the divine love) (Benedict XVI, 2005, §7). So too can friendship love be situated within the broader divine love (Jn 15:15–17; Aelred of Rievaulx, ca. 1148/1977, I.32). Understood in this way, the unification of the varieties of love can lead us to understand love as such in its simplicity. This unification occurs when love finds its origin and end in a single source and goal, namely, God.

What Is Christian Love or Charity?

Love in the Christian person is perfected with the transcendent divine love of theological charity (CCC, 2000, §1822). Theological charity enables one to adhere to God by way of a union of love and to follow the model of Christ's love as a pattern of living (2 Jn 6; Aquinas, 1273/1981, II-II, 17.6). This love has its origin in God, since God is love (1 Jn 4:16). This love flows from God to the human person (Rom 5:5). The Christian Gospel describes the great love that the one God shows to mankind (Jn 3:16). Here too, one should observe that the theological charity that is imparted to those who respond to God's offer of redemption is transmitted exclusively through the mediation of Jesus Christ. As Jesus, the Son of God, receives divine love from God the Father, so does he transmit this love in turn to those who follow and imitate him (Jn 15:9–11). In his own earthly life, described in the Gospel narratives, Christ exemplifies how one should respond to the call to love: he reveals mankind to itself, illuminating love as the definitive gift of self (Vatican II, 1965b, §22). Since man is created in God's image, the sole way for mankind to rediscover the meaning of human life is by recognizing the profundity of such a sincere gift of self (Vatican II, 1965b, §24). This divine love is transformative of a person (1 Cor 13:4–7).

Why Do We Need the Commandment to Love Others in Charity?

The gift of self that is expressed through charity occurs whenever one puts into practice Christ's greatest commandments, the exhortations to love God and neighbor (Mt 22:35–40; Jn 15:12; CCC, 2000, §1822). These commandments are at the center of the Hebrew focus on love of God: "Hear, O Israel: The Lord our God is one Lord; and you shall love the Lord your God with all your heart, and with all your soul, and with all your might" (Deut 6:4–5). Such love is also interpersonal: "You will love your neighbor as yourself" (Lev 19:18; cf. Mk 12:29–31; cf. 1 Jn 4:10).

The virtue of theological charity enables a person to perform acts of divine love that transcend the natural capacity of a person. Such an act is not itself the presence of God (Aquinas, 1273/1981, II-II, 23.2;1272/1984, a. 1). But this work of charity does manifest and signify the presence of God in a profound way that differs from any other act of love. As such, an act of theological charity is not simply philanthropy, that is, it is not a simple generous gift of time, money, or reputation for a good cause. Christian theological charity is an act of love performed in Christ and primarily out of love for God (Aquinas, 1272/1984, a. 4). One loves one's neighbor not only for the value he or she has as a person, but even more so, as another self (Aquinas,

1272/1984, a. 2 ad 6). One ultimately loves the presence of God within the other person (Aquinas, 1272/1984, a. 4).

When it is said that faith without works is a dead faith (Jas 2:17), this may be understood to indicate the great importance that works of charity have in the Christian way of life. God's work of justification does not consist only in bringing about a state of trust between himself and a person (Trent, 1547/1990, Canon 12). Rather, entering into a relationship with God also places one into a new relationship with others. One who receives God's love is called to transmit that love to others. In this way, works of charity manifest a living faith (CCC, 2000, §1815). Further, to seek God's help to grow in charity is essential to developing one's relationship with God. Even should a person remain in the Church in a visible and exterior way, should they lack charity interiorly, that person's connection with God (and so his or her state of salvation) stands in question (1 Cor 13:1–3; Mt 7:21; Vatican II, 1964, §14).

When considering all of the activities of Christian life, including prayer and worship, charity in action constitutes the greatest kind of act enabled by the theological virtues (1 Cor 13:13). Works of charity preserve one's state of justification and deepen it (Trent, 1547/1990, Canon 24). Such works contribute to personal growth in the spiritual life (CCC, 2000, §2013) and constitute acts of worship, offerings to God (Tob 4:11). These works bring one closer to God and help one to overcome any servile fear or terror one may have of God (1 Jn 4:18).

Just as the act of charity is the great Christian act, so is the virtue of charity the greatest virtue (Aquinas, 1272/1984, a. 2; CCC, 2000, §1826). In fact, charity "overflows," so to speak, into all of the other activities of a Christian person, uniting all of a person's virtues and organizing all of a person's activities in orientation to God (Aquinas, 1273/1981, I-II, 65.3; I-II, 73.1 ad 3; Aquinas, 1272/1984, a. 5). Without charity, in fact, there are no absolutely true virtues, strictly speaking (Aquinas, 1273/1981, II-II, 23.7; see also 1 Cor 13:1). Apparent theological virtues, those without charity, may appear to be virtuous but in truth are self-serving, prideful, or involve a high-level narcissism (Aquinas, 1273/1981, I-II, 65.4). Charity structures the life of faith and hope (Aquinas, 1272/1984, a. 3 ad 13). It interconnects all of a person's virtues (Aquinas, 1272/1999a, a. 2) and also transforms acquired virtues such as legal justice (*CCC*, 2000, §1889).

Charity even retains a certain kind of preeminence vis-à-vis all the gifts of the Holy Spirit as well (Aquinas, 1273/1981, I-II, 68.8 ad 1), connecting and unifying them (Aquinas, 1273/1981, I-II, 68.5 & 68.8 ad 3). Further, charity leads one to understand religious faith in a proper way. In other words, charity serves as a litmus test for affirming any understanding one has regarding a mystery of faith.

How Should Self-Sacrifice in Charity Be Understood?

The commandment to love that calls one to give oneself to others will also lead each person to some degree of self-sacrifice in his or her vocations. The element of self-sacrifice in charity constitutes one of the many challenges to understanding and applying theological charity in contemporary society (Titus & Scrofani, 2012,

pp. 127–128). A Christian notion of self-sacrifice does not deprecate the person. A genuine Christian charity will involve a proper love of self and of one's own body (Aquinas, 1272/1984, a. 7). A proper self-love in this sense is not a disordered self-centeredness, in which one loves one's self first and then God or one's neighbor. Rather, one loves God first and then in God one loves oneself as well as one's neighbor as another self. A Christian person does not hate his or her life in this world, although he or she is called to love God first and put following Christ before family or comfort (Lk 14:26). Growing in charity does not require a reckless disregard for one's own well-being while one grows in love of other people. Authentic charity will enjoin upon each person the practice of self-care that is needed for a healthy and flourishing life.

Charity goes beyond merely fulfilling one's duty or the strict minimum, because it gives to others more than what is due according to justice and the natural moral law. This may mean providing less for oneself in order to give more to another. It is here, then, that self-sacrifice has a place when a person is growing in charity. This proper self-sacrifice is motivated not by self-loathing or self-negation, but rather by love of others. At the apex of charity, one may even elect to give up one's own bodily life for the good of others, imitating the model of charity found in Christ and the saints (Jn 15:13).

Prayer and Sacraments

One who responds to God's offer of transcendent redemption and enters into a relationship with him must, as in any relationship, invest time and energy into that relationship in order that it be maintained, grow, and thrive. This occurs through the practice of prayer, both personal

and communal. For a Catholic Christian person, communal prayer is found in liturgical worship of God. Such liturgical worship also involves participation in rites that are called sacraments. The Catholic sacraments are seven outward, efficacious signs of inward, divine grace that were institued by Jesus Christ and entrusted to the Church (Lk 22:19–20; 2 Cor 5:17; CCC, 2000, §1210). These are Baptism, Confirmation, the Eucharist, Holy Orders, Matrimony, Penance or Reconciliation, and the Anointing of the Sick (CCC, 2000, §1210). In the section that follows, prayer, sacraments, and other religious practices are briefly examined. Then, attention is given to how these activities can provide therapeutic support for treating Catholic Christian clients.

How Can Prayer, Participation in the Sacraments, and Spiritual Direction Offer Support for the Therapeutic Process?

Psychotherapy comprises distinct practices, tasks, and goals that cannot be replaced by provision of ethical guidance, spiritual direction, or pastoral care. At the same time, the goals of psychotherapy, as established by the client, often involve moral decisions and the desire of the client to more fully live out his or her own values and vocation. In the case of Christian clients, often a client sees the need for spiritual development to occur in tandem with psychological development (Tan, 1996, p. 378; Walker, Gorsuch, & Tan, 2004, pp. 70–71).

The efficacy of the mental health practice can benefit from considering a client's core moral values and spiritual resources as strengths that are able to motivate and support positive change and growth toward flourishing (Miller, 2002, p. 2, p. 12). For example, when a client so desires, the incorporation of spiritual and religious practices can be included in a client's larger treatment plan (Hughes, 2011; Plante, 2009, pp. 69–72). Referring a client to outside religious or spiritual experts and encouraging him or her to take advantage of ministries and services in his religious community can be an appropriate part of a treatment plan.

Mental health clinicians frequently help clients discern vocational callings regarding career, marriage, and family life. In doing so, they should have a deep respect for the fact that these decisions are central to the core values and the spiritual lives of their clients (Gallagher, 2006). A Christian therapist's integration of religious practices into therapy often may be only implicit, as when he or she prays for clients outside of their presence (Tan, 1996, p. 368). In cases (perhaps infrequent for some therapists) in which one works with mental health practices that primarily serve the Christian community, this integration can become more explicit. For example, collaboration in the treatment of a client may involve not only the mental health professional, but also a spiritual director or a member of the clergy. Referral to an ethical, spiritual, or pastoral expert may be needed for a client when his or her specific moral or spiritual goals surpass what is appropriate for mental health practice (Ashley, 2013).

Further spiritual practices, such as the reading of Sacred Scripture, attendance at church services, prayer, and reception of sacraments, may be encouraged when such religious practices are clearly perceived by the client as supporting psychological healing. Moreover, discussion of these types of spiritual supports with a client needs to occur with proper care and timing (Brownell, 2015, pp. 94–96). It is important to grasp a client's own self-understanding of his or her religious faith, vocations, and sacraments even if the client maintains the same faith as the therapist (for instance, it is necessary to identify a Christian client's understanding of what it means to participate in a faith-based marriage). These spiritual practices, generally speaking, occur within (and cannot be separated from) the life of faith.

What Is a Catholic Christian Understanding of Prayer?

God assists each person to develop in the life of prayer whereby one learns to speak and listen to God in a way that is both personal and communal (or liturgical). Personal development in the life of prayer can be understood as a progression through three stages: vocal, meditative, and contemplative (Dubay, 2002, pp. 55–91). All three stages are unified in that they involve the recollection of the heart and focusing the attention of the mind on God (CCC, 2000, §2697, §2721). These stages can generally be correlated with the three stages of the spiritual life, namely, the purgative, illuminative, and unitive stages (Garrigou-Lagrange, 1938/2002; Martin, 2006; Pinckaers, 1995, pp. 359–374), as well as with the three stages of the moral life, which are discipline, progress in virtue, and mature self-mastery in charity (Pinckaers, 1995, pp. 359–374).

Vocal prayer is found in private and liturgical prayer (such as with recitation of the "Our Father" during Mass or with individual recitation of the breviary, the daily prayer of the Church). Vocal prayer also occurs with the recitation of other group prayers (such as blessings prior to mealtime), devotions (such as the rosary), and in spontaneous personal prayer (as with prayers involving petitions concerning personal needs or the needs of others—see Davies, 2012). Vocal prayer emerges from the embodied nature of persons and typically involves spoken language (CCC, 2000, §2703). Vocal prayer may also occur, however, by way of the mental recitation of words (for example, saying the "Our Father" in one's mind) (CCC, 2000, §2700).

In contrast to vocal prayer, meditative prayer is interior. It is cognitive and affective. Meditative prayer manifests the act of prayer as remembrance of God in a focused way (CCC, 2000, §2697). This form of prayer may also involve reflecting on emotions and affective states, as well as considering religious imagery or visualizations of biblical events (CCC, 2000, §2723). Meditative prayer begins to develop within repetitive vocal prayer (as when one visualizes events in the life of Christ while reciting the rosary) (CCC, 2000, §2708). When God leads one to grow in meditative prayer, the practice of guided visualization may transition into cognitive inquiry; meditative prayer then develops alongside of "faith seeking understanding" (Anselm, 1085/2008, Preface; see also CCC, 2000, §158, §2706). In this respect, meditative prayer can conjoin with study and engender reflection upon spiritual, theological, and biblical readings (CCC, 2000, §2705). The remembrance of God (i.e., the recollection of the heart) that is associated with meditative prayer does not involve merely thinking about God in terms of a notion or idea. Rather, this kind of prayer leads one's mental attention toward God who is approached as real, living, and present (Heb 4:12). As one's mind becomes more and more focused on God's real presence, meditative prayer begins to transition into contemplative prayer.

The practice of contemplative prayer further unites a person with Christ in the most intimate way (CCC, 2000, §2724). As a general theological principle, higher levels of development take up and preserve what is essential to lower levels. In this way, just as meditative prayer emerges from but preserves vocal prayer, so does contemplative prayer emerge from but preserve meditative prayer (CCC, 2000, §2709). In contemplative prayer, one seeks to locate the most intimate region of the self, where, in a stillness and silence apart from speech and thought, one is preoccupied no longer with one's own knowledge but rather seeks one's innermost being where one is united with God, who gives one existence (Ps 46:10; Prov 3:5; CCC, 2000, §300,

§2709, §2714). This is not only a union with God as Creator but a union that is facilitated by the special indwelling of the Holy Spirit. Here, the recollection of the heart reaches its fullest realization as a recollection of the entire self, which is then spiritually offered to God the Father through Christ (CCC, 2000, §2711). In this respect, contemplative prayer can be combined with spiritual exercises that help to facilitate the integration of the self (Finney & Malony, 1985, p. 112; Ignatius of Loyola, 1524/1964; Sacks, 1979). However, it must be strongly emphasized from a theological perspective that the focus of one's prayer is not upon the self but always upon the reality and presence of Jesus Christ (CCC, 2000, §2715). In this way, at the contemplative stage of prayer, one participates in Christ's redemptive work in a profound, even experiential way (CCC, 2000, §§2718–2719).

What Is a Catholic Christian Understanding of a Sacrament?

A sacrament is a means whereby grace is conferred by Christ to persons (CCC, 2000, §1114, §1123; Aquinas, 1273/1981, III, 62.1). Christ is present in the sacrament inasmuch as he works through the sacrament in accordance with his promise to remain present with his followers by means of the invisible outpouring of the Holy Spirit (Mt 28:20). As understood in the Catholic tradition, a sacrament is a rite instituted by Christ involving an efficacious sign that makes present the grace it signifies (CCC, 2000, §1131). In this respect, a sacrament signifies three real-

ities simultaneously: past events in the life of Christ during his incarnation, the present when a person receives grace, and the future (relative to the recipient of grace) in which all things will be renewed in Christ (CCC, 2000, §1115, §1130).

The performance of a sacramental rite does not simply signify the general availability of God's grace but in fact confers grace: the sacrament itself effects what it signifies, namely, the communication of God's grace (Aquinas, 1273/1981, III, 62.1 ad 1; CCC, 2000, §1127). The efficacy of the sacrament to confer grace does not depend upon the holiness of the person who performs the rite; rather, the efficacy of a sacrament derives primarily from Christ's work of redemption and only secondarily from the rite performed (Aquinas, 1273/1981, III, 62.5 ad 2). As means whereby grace is conferred, sacraments contribute to the ongoing sanctification of those who participate in these rites (CCC, 2000, §1123).

In sum, the preceding three chapters, covering the theological premises of the Catholic Christian Meta-Model, have presented the person as (a) created in the image of God, (b) fallen and suffering the effects of sin and evil, and (c) offered transcendent redemption and ultimate flourishing. They have also presented some basic reflections on the significance of these theological premises for understanding the person and the therapeutic process. The next part of this volume (Part V) will more explicitly address a variety of theoretical and clinical applications of the Catholic Christian Meta-Model of the Person.

REFERENCES

Aelred of Rievaulx. (1977). *Spiritual friendship* (M. E. Laker, Trans.). Kalamazoo, MI: Cistercian Publications. (Original work composed ca. 1148)

American Counseling Association. (2014). *Code of ethics.* Alexandria, VA: Author.

American Psychiatric Association. (2013). *Diagnostic*

and statistical manual of mental disorders (5th ed., text revision). Washington, DC: Author.

American Psychological Association. (2017). *Ethical principles of psychologists and code of conduct.* Washington, DC: Author.

Anselm of Canterbury. (2000). Cur Deus homo. In

J. Hopkins & H. Richardson (Trans.), *Complete philosophical and theological treatises of Anselm of Canterbury*. Minneapolis, MN: The Arthur J. Banning Press. (Original work composed 1098)

Anselm of Canterbury. (2008). *Proslogion*. Oxford, United Kingdom: Oxford University Press. (Original work composed 1095)

Aristotle. (2003). *Nicomachean ethics* (H. Rackham, Trans.). Cambridge, MA: Harvard University Press. (Original work composed ca. 350 BC)

Aquinas, T. (1956). *Summa contra gentiles, Book Three: Providence, Part I* (V. J. Bourke, Trans.). Notre Dame, IN: University of Notre Dame Press. (Original work composed 1265)

Aquinas, T. (1981). *Summa theologiae* (English Dominican Province, Trans.). Westminster, MD: Christian Classics. (Original work composed 1273)

Aquinas, T. (1984). *On charity* (L. H. Kendzierski, Trans.). Milwaukee, WI: Marquette University Press. (Original work composed 1271–1272)

Aquinas, T. (1987). *Faith, reason, and theology* (A. Maurer, Trans.). (Original work composed ca. 1259)

Aquinas, T. (1994). *Truth, Vol. 3, Questions XXI–XXIX* (R. W. Schmidt, Trans.). Indianapolis, IN: Hackett. (Original work composed 1256–1259)

Aquinas, T. (1999a). Disputed question on the cardinal virtues. In R. McInerny (Trans.), *Disputed questions on virtue* (pp. 105–140). South Bend, IN: St. Augustine's Press. (Original work composed 1271–1272)

Aquinas, T. (1999b). Disputed question on the virtues in general. In R. McInerny (Trans.), *Disputed questions on virtue* (pp. 1–104). South Bend, IN: St. Augustine's Press. (Original work composed 1271–1272).

Aquinas, T. (2002). *Aquinas's shorter Summa*. Manchester, NH: Sophia Institute Press. (Original work composed 1265–1267)

Aquinas, T. (2012). *Commentary on the letters of Saint Paul to the Corinthians* (F. R. Larcher, B. Mortensen, & D. Keating, Trans.). Lander, WY: The Aquinas Institute for the Study of Sacred Doctrine. (Original work composed ca. 1268)

Ashley, B. (2000). *Choosing a world-view and value-system: An ecumenical apologetics*. Staten Island, NY: Alba House.

Ashley, B. M. (2013). *Healing for freedom: A Christian perspective on personhood and psychotherapy*. Arlington, VA: The Institute for the Psychological Sciences Press.

Athanasius. (1971). De incarnatione. In R. W. Thomson (Ed.), *Contra gentes and De incarnatione*. New York, NY: Oxford University Press. (Original work composed 335–336)

Augustine. (1992a). On the gift of perseverance. In J. A. Mourant & W. J. Collinge (Eds.), *Four anti-Pelagian writings* (pp. 271–337). Washington, DC: The Catholic University of America Press. (Original work composed ca. 429)

Augustine. (1992b). On the predestination of the saints. In J. A. Mourant & W. J. Collinge (Eds.), *Four anti-Pelagian writings* (pp. 218–270). Washington, DC: The Catholic University of America Press. (Original work composed ca. 429)

Augustine. (2007). *Confessions* (2nd ed.) (M. P. Foley, Ed.; F. J. Sheed, Trans.). New York, NY: Hackett. (Original work composed 397–401)

Austriaco, N. P. G. (2011). *Biomedicine & beatitude: An introduction to Catholic bioethics*. Washington, DC: The Catholic University of America Press.

Beauregard, M. (2012). *Brain wars: The scientific battle over the existence of the mind and the proof that will change the way we live our lives*. New York, NY: HarperCollins.

Benedict XVI. (2005). *Deus caritas est* [Encyclical, on Christian love]. Vatican City, Vatican: Libreria Editrice Vaticana.

Benedict XVI. (2006, September 12). *Faith, reason and the university: Memories and reflections* [The Regensburg address]. Vatican City, Vatican: Libreria Editrice Vaticana.

Benedict XVI. (2007). *Spe salvi* [Encyclical, on Christian hope]. Vatican City, Vatican: Libreria Editrice Vaticana.

Benedict XVI. (2011). *Porta fidei* [Apostolic letter, for the indiction of the year of faith]. Vatican City, Vatican: Libreria Editrice Vaticana.

Bonaventure. (2008). *Collations on the seven gifts of the Holy Spirit* (Z. Hayes, Trans.). St. Bonaventure, NY: Saint Bonaventure University. (Original work composed 1268)

Brownell, P. (2015). *Spiritual competency in psychotherapy*. New York, NY: Springer.

Catechism of the Catholic Church (CCC) (2nd ed.). (2000). Vatican City, Vatican: Libreria Editrice Vaticana.

Cessario, R. (1996). *Christian faith and the theological life*. Washington, DC: The Catholic University of America Press.

Cessario, R. (2002). The theological virtue of hope (IIa IIae qq. 17–22). In S. J. Pope (Ed.), *The ethics of Aquinas* (pp. 232–243). Washington, DC: Georgetown University Press.

Cessario, R. (2009). *The moral virtues and theological ethics* (2nd ed.). Notre Dame, IN: University of Notre Dame Press.

Cessario, R. (2013). *Introduction to moral theology: Revised edition*. Washington, DC: The Catholic University of America Press.

Congregation for the Doctrine of the Faith. (2000). *Dominus Iesus* [Declaration on the Lord Jesus]. Vatican City, Vatican: Libreria Editrice Vaticana.

Cullen, C. M. (2012). The natural desire to see God and pure nature: A debate revisited. *American Catholic Philosophical Quarterly, 86*(4), 705–730.

Davies, B. (2012). Prayer. In B. Davies & E. Stump (Eds.), *The Oxford handbook of Aquinas* (pp. 467–474). New York, NY: Oxford University Press.

de Lubac, H. (1998). *The mystery of the supernatural* (R. Sheed, Trans.). New York, NY: Crossroad.

Denzinger, H. (2012). Errors of Michael of Molinos. In P. Hünermann (Ed.), *Enchiridion Symbolorum: A compendium of creeds, definitions, and declarations on matters of faith and morals* (43rd ed., §§2201–2205). San Francisco, CA: Ignatius. (Original work published 1687)

Donneaud, H. (2009). Surnaturel through the fine-tooth comb of traditional Thomism. In S.-T. Bonino (Ed.), *Surnaturel: A controversy at the heart of twentieth-century Thomistic thought*. Ave Maria, FL: Sapientia Press.

Dubay, T. (2002). *Prayer primer: Igniting a fire within*. San Francisco, CA: Ignatius Press.

Ekman, P. (1992). An argument for basic emotions. *Cognition and Emotion, 6*(3/4), 169–200.

Ekman, P. (2003). *Emotions revealed: Recognizing faces and feelings to improve communication and emotional life*. New York, NY: Times Books.

Emery, G. (2011). *The Trinity: An introduction to Catholic doctrine on the Triune God*. Washington, DC: The Catholic University of America Press.

Erikson, E. (1950). *Childhood and society*. New York, NY: Norton.

Erikson, E. (1982). *The life cycle completed*. New York, NY: Norton.

Feingold, L. (2004). *The natural desire to see God according to St. Thomas and his interpreters*. Ave Maria, FL: Sapientia Press.

Feser, E. (2017). *Five proofs of the existence of God*. San Francisco, CA: Ignatius.

Finney, J. R., & Malony, H. N., Jr. (1985). Empirical studies of Christian prayer: A review of the literature. *Journal of Psychology and Theology, 13*(2), 104–115.

Francis. (2013). *Lumen fidei* [Encyclical, on faith]. Vatican City, Vatican: Libreria Editrice Vaticana.

Frankl, V. (2006). *Man's search for meaning*. Boston, MA: Beacon Press.

Gallagher, T. M. (2006). *The examen prayer: Ignatian wisdom for our lives today*. New York, NY: Crossroad.

Garrigou-Lagrange, R. (2002). *The three conversions in the spiritual life*. Rockford, IL: TAN Books. (Original work published 1938)

Goris, H. (2007). Steering clear of Charybdis: Some directions for avoiding 'grace extrinsicism' in Aquinas. *Nova et Vetera: English Edition, 5*(1), 67–80.

Heschel, A. J. (1954). *Man's search for God: Studies in prayer and symbolism*. Santa Fe, NM: Aurora Press.

Hicks, D. J. (2014). A new direction for science and values. *Synthese: An International Journal for Epistemology, Methodology and Philosophy of Science, 191*(14), 3271–3295.

Hughes, B. (2011). *The creative use of spirituality to enhance psychotherapy*. Retrieved from https://www.counseling.org/resources/library/VISTAS/2011-V-Online/Article_101.pdf

Hütter, R. (2007). Desiderium naturale visionis Dei— Est autem duplex hominis beatitudo sive felicitas: Some observations about Lawrence Feingold's and John Milbank's recent interventions in the debate over the natural desire to see God. *Nova et Vetera: English Edition, 5*(1), 81–132.

Hütter, R. (2009). Aquinas on the natural desire for the vision of God: A relecture of *Summa Contra Gentiles* III, c. 25 après Henri de Lubac. *The Thomist, 73*(4), 523–591.

Ignatius of Loyola. (1964). *The spiritual exercises of St. Ignatius* (A. Mottola, Trans.). Garden City,

NY: Image Books. (Original work composed 1522–1524)

John of St. Thomas. (2016). *The gifts of the Holy Spirit.* Tacoma, WA: Cluny Media. (Original work composed 1644)

John Paul II. (1979). *Redemptor hominis* [Encyclical, on the Redeemer of man]. Vatican City, Vatican: Libreria Editrice Vaticana.

John Paul II. (1984). *Salvifici doloris* [Apostolic letter, on the Christian meaning of human suffering]. Vatican City, Vatican: Libreria Editrice Vaticana.

John Paul II. (1998). *Fides et ratio* [Encyclical, on the relationship between faith and reason]. Vatican City, Vatican: Libreria Editrice Vaticana.

John Paul II. (2006). *Man and woman he created them: A theology of the body* (M. Waldstein, Trans.). Boston, MA: Pauline Books & Media.

Journet, C. (1960). *The meaning of grace.* New York, NY: P. J. Kenedy.

Kagan, J. (1997). *Galen's prophecy: Temperament in human nature.* New York, NY: Basic Books.

Kagan, J. (2007). *What is an emotion? History, measures, and meanings.* Cambridge, MA: Harvard University Press.

Koenig H. G., King D. E., & Carson V. B. (2012). *Handbook of religion and health* (2nd ed.). New York, NY: Oxford University Press.

Klubertanz, G. P. (1959). Une théorie sur les vertus morales "naturelles" et "surnaturelles". *Revue thomiste, 59*(3), 565–575.

Larsen, D. J., & Stege, R. (2010). Hope-focused practices during early psychotherapy sessions: Part I: Implicit approaches. *Journal of Psychotherapy Integration, 20,* 271–292. doi:10.1037/a0020820

Lazarus, R. S., & Lazarus, B. N. (1994). *Passion and reason: Making sense of our emotions.* New York, NY: Oxford University Press.

Leo XIII. (1897). *Divinum illud minus* [Encyclical, on the Holy Spirit]. Vatican City, Vatican: Libreria Editrice Vaticana.

Lewis, C. S. (1960). *The four loves.* New York, NY: Harcourt, Brace.

Lombardo, N. E. (2011). *The logic of desire: Aquinas on emotion.* Washington, DC: The Catholic University of America Press.

Long, S. (2000). On the possibility of a purely natural end for man. *The Thomist, 64,* 211–237

Long, S. (2010). *Natura pura: On the recovery of nature in the doctrine of grace.* New York, NY: Fordham University Press.

Maritain, J. (1944). *Science and wisdom.* London, United Kingdom: Geoffrey Bles.

Martin, R. (2006). *The fulfillment of all desire: A guidebook for the journey to God based on the wisdom of the saints.* Steubenville, OH: Emmaus Road.

McAdams, D. P. (2013). *The redemptive self: Stories Americans live by* (rev. ed.). New York, NY: Oxford University Press.

Milbank, J. (2014). *The suspended middle: Henri de Lubac and the renewed split in modern Catholic theology* (2nd ed.). Grand Rapids, MI: Eerdmans.

Mill, J. S. (2001). *Utilitarianism and the 1868 speech on capital punishment* (2nd ed.). Indianapolis, IN: Hackett. (Original work published 1861)

Miller, G. (2002). *Incorporating spirituality in counseling and psychotherapy: Theory and technique.* Hoboken, NJ: Wiley.

Miner, R. (2010). *Thomas Aquinas on the passions: A study of* Summa Theologiae *1a2ae 22–48.* New York, NY: Cambridge University Press.

Mirkes, R. (1997). Aquinas's doctrine of moral virtue and its significance for theories of facility. *The Thomist, 61*(2), 189–218.

Nicolas, J.-H. (1960). *The mystery of God's grace.* Eugene, OR: Wipf & Stock.

Ocáriz, F., Mateo Seco, L. F., Riestra, J. A. (2004). *The mystery of Jesus Christ.* Portland, OR: Four Courts Press.

O'Donohue, W. (2013). *Clinical psychology and the philosophy of science.* Cham, Switzerland: Springer International Publishing.

Peterson, C., & Seligman, M. (2004). Hope. In C. Peterson & M. Seligman (Eds.), *Character strengths and virtues: A handbook and classification* (pp. 569–582). New York, NY: Oxford University Press.

Pieper, J. (1997). *Faith, hope, love.* San Francisco, CA: Ignatius Press.

Pinckaers, S. (1995). *The sources of Christian ethics* (M. T. Noble, Trans.). Washington, DC: The Catholic University of America Press. (Original work published 1985)

Pinckaers, S. (2001). *Morality: The Catholic view* (M. Sherwin, Trans.). South Bend, IN: St. Augustine's Press.

Pinckaers, S. (2005a). Aquinas on nature and the supernatural. In J. Berkman & C. S. Titus (Eds.), *The*

Pinckaers reader: Renewing Thomistic moral theology (pp. 359–368). Washington, DC: The Catholic University of America Press.

Pinckaers, S. (2005b). Morality and the movement of the Holy Spirit. In J. Berkman & C. S. Titus (Eds.), *The Pinckaers reader: Renewing Thomistic moral theology* (pp. 385–395). Washington, DC: The Catholic University of America Press.

Pinckaers, S. (2010). The natural desire to see God. *Nova et Vetera, English Edition, 8*(3), 627–646.

Pinsent, A. (2012). The gifts and fruits of the Holy Spirit. In B. Davies & E. Stump (Eds.), *The Oxford handbook of Aquinas* (pp. 475–488). New York, NY: Oxford University Press.

Pius XII. (1943). *Mystici corporis Christi* [Encyclical, on the mystical body of Christ]. Vatican City, Vatican: Libreria Editrice Vaticana.

Pius XII. (1950). *Humani generis* [Encyclical, concerning some false opinions threatening to undermine the foundations of Catholic doctrine]. Vatican City, Vatican: Libreria Editrice Vaticana.

Plante, T. G. (2009). Internal religious-spiritual tools. In *Spiritual practices in psychotherapy: Thirteen tools for enhancing psychological health* (pp. 65–81). Washington, DC: American Psychological Association.

Rand, K. L., & Cheavens, J. S. (2009). Hope theory. In S. J. Lopez & C. R. Snyder (Eds.), *The Oxford handbook of positive psychology* (2nd ed.) (pp. 323–333). New York, NY: Oxford University Press.

Ratzinger, J. (1987). *Principles of Catholic theology: Building stones for a fundamental theology.* San Francisco, CA: Ignatius Press.

Ratzinger, J. (2005). The Holy Spirit as communion. In *Pilgrim fellowship of faith: The Church as communion* (pp. 38–59). San Francisco, CA: Ignatius Press.

Ratzinger, J. (2006). *Christianity and the crisis of cultures.* San Francisco, CA: Ignatius Press.

Ripley, J. S., Maclin, V., Hook, J. N., & Worthington, E. L., Jr. (2013). The hope-focused couples approach to counseling and enrichment. In E. L. Worthington, E. L. Johnson, J. N. Hook, & J. Aten (Eds.), *Evidence-based practices for Christian counseling and psychotherapy* (pp. 189–208). Downers Grove, IL: Intervarsity Press.

Sacks, H. L. (1979). The effect of spiritual exercises on the integration of self-system. *Journal for the Scientific Study of Religion, 18*(1), 46–50.

Scheeben, M. J. (1954). *Nature and grace.* Eugene, OR: Wipf & Stock.

Scrofani, P. (2013, September 19). Hope in groups: Insights from group psychotherapy and aging. *The 2013–2014 John Henry Newman lecture series.* Lecture conducted from Arlington, VA.

Seligman, M. E. P. (1990). *Learned optimism.* New York, NY: Vintage Books.

Seligman, M. E. P. (1995). *The optimistic child.* New York, NY: Harper Perennial.

Seligman, M. E. P. (2002). *Authentic happiness: Using the new positive psychology to realize your potential for lasting fulfillment.* New York, NY: Free Press.

Seligman, M. E. P. (2012). *Flourish: A visionary new understanding of happiness and well-being.* New York, NY: Atria Books.

Snyder, C. R., Harris, C., Anderson, J. R., Holleran, S. A., Irving, L. M., Sigmon, S. T., ... Harney, P. (1991). The will and the ways: Development and validation of an individual-differences measure of hope. *Journal of Personality and Social Psychology, 60*(4), 570–585.

Snyder, C. R., Irving, L. M., & Anderson, J. R. (1991). Hope and health. In Snyder and Forsyth, (Eds.), *Handbook of social and clinical psychology: The health perspective* (pp. 285–305). Elmsford, NY: Pergamon Press.

Snyder, C. R., & Lopez, S. J. (Eds.). (2002). *Handbook of positive psychology.* New York, NY: Oxford University Press.

Snyder, C. R., Rand K. L., & Sigmon, D. R. (2002). Hope theory: A member of the positive psychology family. In C. R. Snyder & S. J. Lopez (Eds.), *Handbook of positive psychology* (pp. 257–276). New York, NY: Oxford University Press.

Tan, S-Y. (1996). Religion in clinical practice: Implicit and explicit integration. In E. P. Shafranske (Ed.), *Religion and the clinical practice of psychology* (pp. 365–387). Washington, DC: American Psychological Association.

Titus, C. S. (2006). *Resilience and the virtue of fortitude: Aquinas in dialogue with the psychosocial sciences.* Washington, DC: The Catholic University of America Press.

Titus, C. & Scrofani, P. (2012). Art of love: A Roman

Catholic psychology of love. *Journal of Psychology and Christianity, 31*(2), 118–129.

Trent. (1990). Session 6: Decree on justification. In N. P. Tanner (Ed.), *Decrees of the ecumenical councils: Vol. 2. Trent to Vatican II* (pp. 671–684). Washington, DC: Georgetown University Press. (Original work composed 1547)

Vatican I, Council. (1869–1870). *Dei filius* [Dogmatic constitution on the Catholic faith]. Vatican City, Vatican: Libreria Editrice Vaticana.

Vatican II, Council. (1964). *Lumen gentium* [Dogmatic constitution on the Church]. Vatican City, Vatican: Libreria Editrice Vaticana.

Vatican II, Council. (1965a). *Apostolicam actuositatem* [Decree on the apostolate of the laity]. Vatican City, Vatican: Libreria Editrice Vaticana.

Vatican II, Council. (1965b). *Gaudium et spes* [Pastoral constitution on the Church in the modern world]. Vatican City, Vatican: Libreria Editrice Vaticana.

Vatican II, Council. (1965c). *Nostra aetate* [Declaration on the relation of the Church to non-Christian religions]. Vatican City, Vatican: Libreria Editrice Vaticana.

Walker, D. F., Gorsuch, R. L., & Tan, S-Y. (2004). Therapists' integration of religion and spirituality in counseling: A meta-analysis. *Counseling and Values, 49*(1), 69–80.

Ware, K. (1979). *The Orthodox way*. Crestwood, NY: St. Vladimir Seminary Press.

William of St. Thierry. (1981). *The nature and dignity of love*. Kalamazoo, MI: Cistercian Publications. (Original work composed ca. 1122)

Wojtyła, K. (1993). *Love and responsibility* (H. T. Willetts, Trans.). San Francisco, CA: Ignatius Press. (Original work published 1960)

World Lutheran Federation and the Pontifical Council for Christian Unity. (1999). *The joint declaration on the doctrine of justification*. Vatican City, Vatican: Libreria Editrice Vaticana

Yalom, I. D., & Lesczc, M. (2005). *The theory and practice of group psychotherapy*. New York, NY: Basic Books.

Part V

Theoretical and Clinical Applications of the Meta-Model

Chapter 20

Principles for Training Catholic Christian Mental Health Professionals

WILLIAM J. NORDLING, HARVEY PAYNE,
AND CRAIG STEVEN TITUS

ABSTRACT: Use of the Catholic Christian Meta-Model of the Person (CCMMP) has a number of implications for the development of programs for training mental health professionals. A training program based on the Meta-Model aims to help students to see both the mental health practitioner and the client as embedded in a Catholic Christian vision of the person, with special focus on the vocational context of each, an objective rarely found in graduate training. It also aims to educate and form mental health professionals in ways that foster a deep respect for clients' innate dignity and their transcendent calling and end. The CCMMP-centered curriculum provides the students (1) a thorough grounding in the Catholic Christian Meta-Model of the Person; which would include specific areas of focus such as (2) the dignity and nature of flourishing for both client and the clinician; (3) the importance of the vocations of clients and clinicians; (4) the presuppositions that underlie the Meta-Model; and (5) the model's implications for ethical practice. Of significant import is the training of clinicians in (6) application of the Meta-Model when working with non-Catholic Christians, people of different faiths, and non-believers; (7) theories and practices existing in the mental health field that are consistent with the CCMMP; and (8) ways that mental health professionals can serve the Church. Contextually important to any training curriculum is (9) how the CCMMP influences the selection of students, the formation of the faculty, and the training of the staff.

When the training program for mental health professionals is based on a comprehensive multidisciplinary and faith-based vision of the person, such as the CCMMP, the goals, objectives and formative practices of its curriculum will have to be expanded beyond those found in secular training settings. This is mostly an additive process. After all, the existing criteria for accred-

This chapter is an expanded and revised version of a text that was originally published as "Training psychologists and Christian anthropology," by G. M. Sweeney, C. S. Titus, & W. Nordling, 2009, *Edification: Journal of the Society for Christian Psychology*, 3(1), 51–56. The co-authors of this chapter wish to express their appreciation to Dr. Gladys Sweeney, who contributed valuable insights on training in the original article on which this chapter is based.

itation are certainly to be maintained, and thus the CCMMP means not any reduction in the existing requirements but the addition of new ones. The CCMMP incorporates and builds upon best practice standards, state laws, and professional accreditations. These standards require rigorous training in such areas as the psychological sciences (e.g., human development, statistics, and research design), counseling or psychotherapy, ethics, and multicultural competence. A faith-based training program must not only achieve excellence in these areas as the program forms students, but must in addition help students understand and apply such knowledge and skills in accord with a Christian vision of the person. Mental health programs adopting an integrative Christian perspective in training have long believed that such an effort is both worthwhile and justified, since faith and science are seen as compatible and mutually enriching.

Even though there has been a secularization in culture and a disengagement of science from religion (Taylor, 2007), many different worldviews and value systems are inevitably present in the scientific and practical work of mental health professionals (Ashley, 2000, 2006; Bergin, 1980; Brugger et al., 2008; Jones, 1996; Shafranske, 2000). Moreover, the work of the mental health professional is not simply that of a technician applying knowledge and skills based on scientific findings, but is heavily influenced by a foundational understanding of people, and a more specific understanding of each particular client. Although for many clinicians one or more of the numerous personality theories within the field of psychology may guide their foundational understanding of the person, these theories are often partial views of the person and often contradict each other. To develop a functional working understanding of clients, mental health professionals are inclined to integrate other sources of knowledge including philosophical considerations (O'Donohue, 1989; O'Donohue & Kitchener, 1996) and religious traditions, as well as those derived from their own values and worldview. Because of this inevitable combination of sources of understanding, it is vital for clinicians to examine how their own understanding of people has been formed. In addition, the formation of one's view of the person should not be haphazard, but developed in a deliberative and disciplined manner.

The CCMMP posits that such a deliberative and disciplined approach should include rigorous introduction to what the disciplines of psychology, philosophy, and the Catholic tradition say about the person. Therefore, to learn how to apply the CCMMP in practice, mental health professionals need to be trained with special attention to (a) what philosophical and theological influences have formed their understanding of the person prior to entering the program, (b) education in the clear and well-developed Catholic Christian philosophical and theological traditions, and (c) the positive insights and limitations of other religious and secular worldviews. Also, training in the distinctly Catholic understanding of the person, marriage, and family, as well as Catholic ethical principles, as found in the Meta-Model, needs to be introduced early in the training curriculum. The curriculum necessarily includes the acquisition of knowledge and formative experiences in the nine following areas.

1. Thorough Grounding in the Catholic Christian Meta-Model of the Person

A central goal of an educational program that uses the CCMMP is to ground all aspects of the training program—its curriculum, program faculty, on-site clinical supervisors, dissertation advisors, administration, and support staff—in a thorough introduction to the vision of the person represented by the Catholic Christian Meta-Model of the Person. Necessarily, the program's faculty, clinical supervisors, and, of course, its students will need intensive formation (Scrofani & Nordling, 2011). Although this vision begins at an intellectual and theoretical level, it should quickly also get integrated into to process of training in clinical competencies and interpersonal skills. The CCMMP not only provides an understanding of the person in general and of specific clients, but also gives students or faculty members a better self-understanding. In short it should move from being knowledge for clinical application to understanding of self, and thus faculty and students alike can be personally transformed by this teaching. This transformation should result in becoming more empathetic with clients, more loving toward others (including one's own family), and not only freer *from* those things that disorder and disrupt thoughts and choices, but also freer *for* those things that compose callings, such as one's calling to be an effective mental health professional, a loving parent, a faithful spouse, a true friend, and a good neighbor.

The curriculum (courses and training experiences) of the training program should progress in an integrated way: the planning begins with the end of the training in mind (Wiggins & Mc-Tighe, 2005). Designing the whole program with the end in mind requires that educators stage learning activities in a sequential way aimed at increasing mastery of academic and clinical skill assessments that document the learning desired for graduates. This forward-looking design requires practical, experiential, authentic learning. In particular, this type of learning takes place through activities that the future mental health provider will be engaged in on a regular basis as a professional. When instructional design focuses on experience, learning becomes practical and authentic. The goal of authentic learning is especially attained through attention to case conceptualization as a learning activity (Herrington & Oliver, 2000).

With the goal of forming students, faculty, and staff, the program should be sequenced at three distinct levels. Level 1 requires the development of an understanding of the theological, philosophical, and psychological wisdom traditions that support the premises of the CCMMP. Level 2 is the integration of this understanding of the CCMMP with the theoretical and empirical knowledge base and evidenced-based clinical practices existing within the mental health field. Finally, Level 3, in the context of clinical coursework and actual clinical practice, requires learning how to apply a CCMMP-enriched approach to case conceptualization and treatment.

Level 1. Theological and Philosophical Training

The curriculum contains foundational faith-based (theological) and basic (philosophical) coursework that uses faith and reason in understanding human nature via the Meta-Model of the person. The philosophical and theological coursework provides an encounter with the best sources that draw from the Catholic Christian tradition (especially Sacred Scripture, patristic, magisterial, and other theological sources, as well as philosophical sources of wisdom), while identifying the levels of meaning and entering into dialogue with contemporary thought, theories, and research on the person and family. This training in theological and philosophical anthropology introduces the students to the study of the major themes of the Catholic Christian Meta-Model. In a faith-based or theological perspective, the study addresses the person as created (possessing innate dignity and meant to flourish), fallen (needing to face his or her own failings and limitations), and redeemed (called to hope for ultimate flourishing). In a perspective of basic experience and philosophy, the coursework addresses basic dimensions of the human person: a personal unity, relational, sensory-perceptual-cognitive, emotional, rational, and volitional and free, as well as being fulfilled through vocations (such as a call to goodness and holiness and the call to the single or married life) and flourishing in virtues (such as faith, hope, charity, courage, and patience). Other coursework focuses on the development of practical reason and moral character (virtue and vice), the vocations of relationship (especially marriage and family), and spiritual challenges, development, and maturity. One important aspect of student formation in this coursework is the use of actual client case stories to understand how the therapist can apply an abstract theory of the person to understand actual clients. Students are also introduced to how the rich vision of the person represented by the CCMMP changes the scope and depth of questions asked of the client, compared to the interpretations made by more reductionistic theories of the person. This practice of understanding clients' life narratives progresses to a more formal case conceptualization later in the curriculum. But, even at the early stage of training, the teaching allows the clinician-in-training

to understand how the CCMMP quickly moves beyond the theoretical level. Ideally the early-formative coursework in the CCMMP is team-taught so that the multidisciplinary nature of the Meta-Model is represented in the classroom: an instructor with philosophical and theological expertise is paired with an instructor who has expertise in the mental health field and experience in a Catholic integrative approach to clinical practice. Such instructor teamwork allows students both to appreciate the depth of theoretical knowledge they are acquiring, and simultaneously to see it as practical and applicable in their work. When students can learn from role models who identify with and use the CCMMP in their work, the course both counters the traditional views that faith, philosophy, and science must be separated, and also allows students to face the challenging task of learning to think philosophically and theologically.

Level 2. Scientific, Theoretical, and Clinical Training

The curriculum necessarily contains traditional coursework in the scientific and theoretical foundations of the field (for instance, human development, biological bases of behavior, cognition, and emotion) and coursework teaching clinical skills (for example, courses in psychopathology and diagnosis, interviewing, assessment, therapy and counseling) but unlike in secular training programs, these courses should be informed by the Catholic Christian Meta-Model of the Person. Specifically these courses examine how contemporary theories and clinical practice within the mental health field can be enriched and integrated with the understanding of the person provided by the Meta-Model. This addition creates a truly integrated Catholic approach to working with clients. This approach is consistent with best practice in the field as well as with the faith-based identity of the mental health professional.

Courses within a curriculum can adopt an integrative perspective to varying degrees based on the nature of the course. For example, a course in the areas of psychometrics, statistics, or research design would have much less direct connection to the Meta-Model than courses in counseling and therapy interventions. A course on marital psychotherapy, however, would have significant differences in the way that it is taught. The Meta-Model proposes a normative understanding of the person, marriage, and family that is in contrast to relativistic views, where marriage is seen as self-defined by the couple. Although students are taught to respect the autonomy and conscience of spouses within a marriage and to be aware that clients may not share a normative view of marriage, in their clinical work, they are guided by faith-based principles:

1. Marriage is between one man and one woman and involves an exclusive, lifelong commitment.
2. Building unity between the spouses is essential; although individual needs are important, the spousal relationship (marital bond) is the ultimate client.
3. Three essential aspects of marital therapy are (a) helping couples to be united in marriage, (b) helping couples to support each other in a self-giving way in daily life and in their vocation as parents, and (c) ultimately helping each other to grow in flourishing (or holiness, in a Christian perspective).
4. It is important to help couples to establish a balance between the time needed for children and family life, time needed for developing their spousal relationship, time for individual pursuits, and the demands of the workplace.

5. Therapeutic intervention includes both spouses' development of virtues, such as patience, empathy, compassion, courage, prudence, and forgiveness, since these support spouses' ability to be united with each other, to become loving and wise parents, and to be effective in their life of work and service.

This is not an exhaustive list of the way the Meta-Model influences how a course on marital therapy is taught, but it does allow some idea of how the Meta-Model makes a difference. Again, it needs to be emphasized that the Meta-Model provides a vision of the nature of healthy marriage, which guides the clinician's understanding of marital problems and their solutions and is used as a basis for collaboration in developing treatment goals. This collaborative process allows the Meta-Model to inform treatment while providing safeguards against the therapist's imposing this vision of the person on the client.

Level 3. CCMMP-Based Case Conceptualization

Coursework and formative training experiences through the curriculum utilize case conceptualization as a central approach to training in the CCMMP at both the theoretical and applied levels. Through the case conceptualization process, the student (and the therapist) should come to understand the problem (diagnosis), how the problem developed (case formulation), what can be done to resolve problems, and how to bring about healing and flourishing. The usual process of training in case conceptualization is systematic and progressive. The CCMMP's vision of the person is more comprehensive and nonreductionist than is one provided by any one of the current understandings of the person used, either singly or in combination, by secular schools of counseling or psychotherapy. The Meta-Model calls for the therapist to gather more comprehensive information about clients (Chapter 21, "Case Conceptualizaton"). This broader approach to case conceptualization augments and incorporates what exists in traditional approaches. The CCMMP is a framework that makes use of multiple personality theories and models of psychotherapy to understand the person and his or her problems and strengths in relation to each of the eleven dimensions of the person comprised in the Meta-Model. As was stated earlier, initial training in understanding the rich view of the person contained in the Meta-Model occurs in the predominantly theological and philosophical courses taught early in the curriculum. The initial linking of this understanding to actual clinical practice occurs through the use of case vignettes and studies in these courses, and even more so when the courses are team taught with a clinician.

More formal training in case conceptualization from a CCMMP framework occurs in early courses in interviewing, diagnosis, assessment, diversity, and counseling and psychotherapy. This sequence of courses is designed to introduce specific content and nuances of understanding and application of case conceptualization. The training process reinforces earlier knowledge and skills by using in-depth analysis and application of the CCMMP as a framework for enriched case conceptualization.

The clinical application of the CCMMP framework for case conceptualization begins in such coursework but comes to fruition as students apply it in their early experiences with clients. Ideally this occurs in their training program's clinic, where the faculty are not only accepting of the CCMMP, but skilled themselves in using it for case conceptualization. As students begin to participate in externships or practica outside of the university setting where

their training program is based, continued consultation about use of the CCMMP in case conceptualization occurs within coursework that students are taking concurrently with such practica. For those training programs that do not maintain a clinic to provide students with their earliest clinical experiences, a concurrent use of the CCMMP for case conceptualization in coursework can at least partially assure that the students become competent at utilizing it within their clinical experiences. Finally, the demonstration of the use of the CCMMP for case conceptualization is included as a component of comprehensive exams, thereby ensuring that this competency has been obtained.

Moreover, it is important to emphasize that the personalist approach of the Meta-Model toward work with clients is also applied at the level of the formation of each student. Therefore, considerable care and attention must be given to the quality of mentoring relationships, which are essential to the successful formation of each individual student. Such mentoring relationships include, among others, the teacher-student, supervisor-supervisee, and dissertation advisor-advisee. All of these relationships are opportunities to foster an integrated formation in knowledge and application of the CCMMP.

Outcome studies have clearly documented the therapeutic alliance—the relationship between therapist and client—as a salient predictive factor of positive results in therapy (Miller, Duncan, Sorrell, & Brown, 2005). However, research into the role of student-faculty relationships in the education of mental health providers is developing but sparse (Hagenauer & Volet, 2014), and no clear understanding of this relationship has emerged. But Bordin (1979) suggests that the research on therapist-client working alliance may be fruitfully applied to "all change situations," including teaching and the working alliance between students and teachers. Three important core processes relating to the working alliance identified by Bordin have applicability within the general training process described previously: (1) agreement on goals, (2) tasks—how relevant and powerful are the formative tasks needed to meet those goals, and (3) bonds—the human relationship (attachment) that develops out of trust in the mentors and their genuine interest in each student's formation experience. Given the high priority the CCMMP gives to interpersonal relationality, its vision of the person calls for attention to this working alliance. This vision of the person calls for a commitment to explore, expand, and research the philosophy and pedagogy of graduate-level training of mental health providers in light of this neglected area of the working alliance in the formation of students.

2. The Dignity and Flourishing of Client and Clinician

The second objective of a training program rooted in CCMMP is for students (and faculty) to acquire a comprehensive positive vision of the human person and the person's social environment. Through this process, students begin to understand their own innate goodness and dignity, and that of their clients. They gain insights into the nature of true freedom, the importance of values and virtues, as well as the importance of vocations in achieving true flourishing (Chapter 10, "Fulfilled Through Vocation"). Such a positive view of life and flourishing can only partially be understood even in the best of existing personality theories and models of therapy and counseling, because of the influence of contemporary worldviews that construe complete flourishing as possible without a relation to anything higher than the human person and society (Taylor, 2007). Insofar as the human sciences have disengaged themselves from ethics and religion, they require further insights on such meaningful aspects of human existence as moral development and spiritual growth, as well as strong notions of human dignity and of the call to ultimate flourishing.

At the beginning of a training program, the student is introduced to the basics of a Cath-

olic Christian vision of the human person in philosophical terms: the person is substantially whole, interpersonally relational, sensory-perceptual-cognitive, emotional, rational, and volitional and free. In addition, the person is understood to be fulfilled through vocations and flourishing in virtue. Furthermore, there is the basic theological conception of the person as being created, fallen, and redeemed. These insights and their theological and philosophical explications not only complement a psychological understanding of growth and healing but also positively influence them. In particular, the Christian belief that all human beings are created in "the image of God" (Gen 1:27, Revised Standard Version; see also John Paul II, 1998, §60) and called to holiness in Christ (Eph 5:25–27; 1 Pet 1:15–16; Vatican II, 1964, §§39–42) should open the eyes of future mental health professionals to the nature and dignity of the person—including, of course, themselves. It should also uphold the conviction that each person is loved by God, has intrinsic value, and is capable of redemption. In particular, the mental health professional in training should come to see psychological problems and disorders in the corrective context of the human vocation to self-giving—which involves not only giving, but also receiving other persons as gifts (John Paul II, 2006, pp. 194–198)—as it is understood in the Sacred Scriptures, especially in the Sermon on the Mount (Mt 5–7) and the Beatitudes (Lk 6) (for discussion, see Pinckaers, 1995). Flourishing based on sacrificial giving imitates Christ's gift of self (Jn 15:13) and seeks God's kingdom and holiness (Mt 5:25–27).

Mental health professionals will meet people who have been wounded and betrayed, and who have wounded and betrayed others as well. A deep understanding of the CCMMP helps students in training (and faculty) to see not simply a spouse-abuser, an alcoholic, or an addict merely in need of behavior modification, anger control, or cognitive restructuring. They can learn to see clients in terms of their basic human dignity and vocational callings, created by God, fallen in sin, and redeemed by God's love. Students can develop the ability, as much as possible, to see their clients in the way God sees them. Thus, they see the client as being made in the image and likeness of God and destined to live eternally. Students must be trained to perceive these aspects of ethical and spiritual challenge and promise as being essential to a full psychological understanding of the client, rather than dismissing such understandings as relevant only in the "realm of religion." Students should come to understand that the ethical and the spiritual aspects of the person have practical and therapeutic ramifications for the client, even if the client is a non-believer and the clinician never mentions God, religion, or such theological concepts directly. In short, the CCMMP is fundamentally a framework for a "series of lenses" that the clinician uses in the development of a comprehensive and very positive understanding of the client and in the application of therapeutic modalities and evidence-based practices. At times this complex understanding of the client may be translated into everyday language and shared with the client, but in other cases the value of the CCMMP is simply evident in its effect on the way the clinician views and interacts with the client.

Mental health professionals should be trained to see that freeing people *from* depression, addiction, obsession, and so on, serves as the means to the larger goal of *freedom for* the types of flourishing that are consistent with one's ultimate destiny and calling (Ashley, 2013). From a Judeo-Christian perspective, the path to flourishing can be summarized as loving God with your whole heart, soul, mind, and strength and loving your neighbor as yourself (Deut 6:42–5; Lev 19:18; Lk 10:27; Mk 12:30). Moreover, seeking *freedom for* is a type of flourishing. It is part of the virtuous life. *Freedom for* guides and practically motivates the person in bringing healing that overcomes particular obstacles to freedom and sets the stage for understanding the place of virtue and vocational callings in clinical work (Chapter 25, "Virtue in Mental Health Practice").

A similar understanding (with different presuppositions) is found in positive psychology (Peterson & Seligman, 2004), which illustrates that concepts like basic dignity of the person, freedom, character strengths and virtue, and the seeking of a meaningful life are concepts that are not restricted to a Christian worldview, but instead can be understood by and discussed with most clients (see Chapter 25, "Virtue in Mental Health Practice").

3. The Importance of the Vocational Callings of the Client and Mental Health Professional

The third objective of a training program rooted in the CCMMP is for students and faculty to acquire an understanding of the importance of personal vocations for clients, as well as for their own lives. Traditional Catholic Christian teaching notes that each person has a vocation, and that we can speak of the concept of "vocation" in three senses (John Paul II, 1988; Vatican II, 1964; Grisez & Shaw, 2003; Wojtyła, 1981).

For Christians, the *first* and foundational type of vocation is the call to become holy, develop in virtue, and live a good life consistent with one's faith (Vatican II, 1964, §§39–42). For all people, Christian or not, the basic calling involves striving to live a good and just life: seeking meaning, pursuing purpose, and acting in a manner consistent with one's conscience.

The *second* type of vocation involves freely seeking, preparing for, and accepting a state of life as single, married, religious (that is, consecrated life), or ordained. And for all people of goodwill—Christian believer or not—there is a desire to commit oneself to a life of love and service within relationships, family, and community.

The *third* type of vocation is the particular work and personal service to which God calls each person so that he or she can love and serve God and neighbor and can grow in holiness (John Paul II, 1981b). Again, most people seek meaning and fulfillment in their life work as they serve others and their community. Even when forced by circumstances to take on jobs and tasks that are not fully in line with what they feel called to do, people can still find meaning and solace in their sacrifices made to support themselves and loved ones, and to provide services needed by others. Even the father of psy-

chotherapy, Freud, seemed to intuitively touch on the importance of vocation when he spoke of the central importance in life of work and love. Nonetheless, the concept of the person as embedded in vocation is underdeveloped in the mental health field.

Given the central importance of these three types of vocation in the lives of both client and clinicians, a training program that utilized the CCMMP would teach the specific characteristics, responsibilities, and developmental challenges of these different vocations. For example, since marriage is the most common vocation, it is important that the training program include the Catholic Church's teaching on the nature of marriage and family life, using the relevant sources from Scripture and tradition (such as the documents of the Council of Trent in 1563/2017; and Vatican II, 1964, 1965; as well as Benedict XVI, 2005; Francis, 2016; John Paul II, 1981a, 1994; Leo XIII, 1880; Paul VI, 1968; Pius XI, 1930; *Catechism of the Catholic Church*, 1997). A training curriculum would also integrate this perspective through clinical experiences.

Finally, the training curriculum would provide opportunities for clinicians in training to reflect on the meaning of vocation in their own life—their personal call to holiness; the importance of discerning and developing in their state in life (such as through marriage and the central role of being mother or father); and the gifts and responsibilities that becoming a mental health professional brings (for example, accompanying their clients in finding meaning in their struggles, the privilege of watching their clients heal or accompanying the suffering of their clients).

In experiencing their work as a part of their Christian vocation, mental health professionals should develop an understanding that their encounter with the client is providential and not random. They are instruments for healing the person. Such a sense of vocation and service motivates therapists not only to observe the ethical principles existing within the mental health professions, but also to put into practice Christian love and self-giving for the good of the client. Thus, Catholic practitioners develop a sense of responsibility for the client and accountability to God for how one serves the person in need (Mt 25:31ff). As a result of the therapeutic process both client and therapist should experience transformation and personal growth.

4. Presuppositions (Worldviews and Value Systems) that Underlie Theory and Practice

A comprehensive training curriculum based on the CCMMP would not only include thorough training in the psychological sciences (such as human development, cognition and emotion, biological bases of behavior) and evidence-based interventions, but also provide training and analysis of the philosophical and theological presuppositions contained in a Catholic vision of the person, marriage, family and society. Basic training in philosophy, with special emphasis on philosophical anthropology, allows students to explore the concepts of human nature, natural moral law, virtue, and freedom. Students will also explore models of the flourishing life. Training in theological anthropology, furthermore, identifies those truths that revelation offers about being created, fallen, and redeemed and the impact of that knowledge on the relief of suffering through clinical practice. Students examine other world philosophies, cultures, and religions to develop respect for diversity, to understand their client's worldview, and to recognize the presuppositions on which their own worldview is founded. They examine also the presuppositions of both theory and practice within the mental health field. This disciplined study of worldviews, culture, religions, and human diversity trains practitioners to be capable of understanding and caring well for all clients.

5. Implications of the Meta-Model for Ethical Practice

All programs that train mental health professionals ensure that the developing clinician is knowledgeable about laws, ethical principles, and best practice standards pertaining to clinical practice that are promulgated at the state and federal levels. In addition, training must introduce students to practice guidelines, ethical codes, and best practice standards that are issued by national-level professional associations. A course on ethics, law, and mental health practice, therefore, introduces the students to their appropriate profession's ethical guidelines and principles, for example the American Psychological Association (2017) *Ethical Principles of Psychologists and Code of Conduct* (for a psychology program) or the American Counseling Association (2014) *Code of Ethics* (for a counseling program). Students must also have opportunities to apply such ethical principles in actual clinical practice to ensure that a mature and reliable capacity for ethical reasoning develops. Again, such training is present in all training programs.

However, the CCMMP-based approach has additional implications for the training of mental health professionals with regard to ethical practice, which augment the usual education and training in professional ethics provided in secular programs. These areas include (a) understanding the ethical dimensions of various worldviews and religions; (b) examining the relationship between contemporary professional ethical principles and Christian ethical principles, (c) training students to avoid a reductionist view of the client and treatment inconsistent with Christian ethical principles, (d) fostering the psychological, spiritual, and moral formation of the therapist, and (e) training students to act in accord with Christian ethical principles and their own conscience while respecting the conscience and values of the client.

a. Understanding the ethical dimensions of worldviews and value systems

As indicated earlier, one area of focus of a CCMMP-based approach to training in the area of ethics includes helping students to understand the ethical dimensions of worldviews and value systems that influence the theory, research, and practice of the mental health professions. To understand why people act purposely and in different ways, the Meta-Model posits that students need to understand not only neurobiological, psychological, and sociological factors, but also the philosophical (basic experience) and faith-based (religious and spiritual) principles and practices that frame and inform the ethical decision-making process. There are several types of respect for diversity that are relevant for ethical practice. These include not only being attuned to the uniqueness of each person but also the uniqueness of their commitments to faith traditions, philosophical presuppositions, and cultural communities. Building knowledge and respect for worldviews affords the therapist a deeper understanding of the client, which in turn allows for both the client's and therapist's worldviews to be utilized collaboratively, instead of remaining unexamined.

b. Examining the relationship between professional ethics and Christian ethical principles

The CCMMP-based training program integrates training in professional ethics and Christian ethics so that students can see how good professional practice from a secular perspective can be integrated into one's identity as a Christian. For example, one aspirational principle in many professional ethics codes is "to do no harm" to clients; some professional codes offer an even higher level aspirational principle of "beneficence" or "to strive to benefit" clients. A Meta-Model approach to training in ethics would link these principles to the imperative of "love of neighbor" and also to the dignity due to the client, who is created in the image and likeness of God. In addition, the program would help the developing clinician to see that this is not some abstract principle but is part of their lived identity as a Christian called by God to become a mental health professional. Another example of this added value of the Meta-Model is that it gives greater depth to understanding ethical principles such as "avoidance of undue influence." It links such admonitions to the Christian principle of respecting the conscience and freedom of the individual and the understanding that God has unique callings for each individual person that should be treated with respect by the mental health professional.

c. Training students to avoid reductionist theories and practices inconsistent with Christian ethical principles

The Meta-Model-based program trains students to recognize when the underlying anthropology or ethical stance represented in a particular therapeutic model may be deficient or inconsistent with the anthropology presented in the Meta-Model. In such cases the student is trained to avoid reductionist approaches to the concept of person and to choose treatment methods in accord with Christian ethical principles. For example, some therapeutic methods may emphasize simple elimination of symptoms instead of addressing the complex problems the person is facing. Another example would be a case in which discouraged marital therapy clients may believe that because of high levels of "incompatibility" they should part company. Although ultimately, clients have the right to follow their conscience and to make their own life decisions, the clinician should be guided by the Catholic view of marriage and family life that posits marriage as a lifelong committed and exclusive relationship in which spouses support and forgive each other and foster holiness. The Meta-Model trained clinician, guided by this view, would do everything possible to reduce such "incompatibility" and to help spouses overcome the difficulties that leave them isolated and distanced, and that prevent healing and the reemergence of love.

d. Fostering the psychological, spiritual, and moral formation of the therapist

Many training programs encourage students to participate in personal psychotherapy both to foster their own psychological growth and to assist them in developing an experiential understanding of the therapeutic process. However, a Meta-Model-based program also fosters an encouraging environment for the further development of a Christian identity, deepening one's spiritual life, building virtues and humbly recognizing one's shortcomings as a Christian. As will be explored in a later section of this chapter,

practices for psychological and spiritual development are seen as integral to the formation of mental health professionals, and, although such development is not forced on students in training, it is easy to see how these areas of development augment and complement the student's understanding of and capacity to act ethically in professional life.

Furthermore, there are particularly therapeutic virtues that clinicians must practice to promote effective therapeutic relationships with their clients (Pellegrino & Thomasma, 1993). The training program also must help students to acquire and put into practice virtue-based capacities and skills such as empathy, listening, communication, affirmation, encouragement, motivation, hope, constructive (and nonthreatening) confrontation, interpretation (both verbal and nonverbal), respect, sustaining patience, ethical rectitude, and so on. These skills are part of a wider notion of competence, and thus of ethics. Furthermore, in training programs based on Christian anthropology, clinicians seek also to understand the theological dimension of these clinical virtues. For example, the Catholic therapist not only seeks to instill "hope" for psychological healing, but also seeks to foster a larger hope that reaches toward a more complete and transcendent flourishing. Such hope supports expressing perseverance when self-sacrifice is necessary and possessing courage to do the right thing when this is difficult.

e. Training students to act in accord with Christian ethical principles and their own conscience while respecting the conscience and values of the client

Finally, a CCMMP-based training program prepares students to recognize both how to act in accord with Christian ethical principles and their own conscience when providing services, while also respecting the client's conscience and her capacity to make life decisions and her right to autonomy. This is a very complex balancing process that requires respect for the dignity of the person of the client and therapist alike. It is not possible in this brief section to really do justice to this topic. However, we do want to emphasize that the values of the client and moral issues are sometimes an important dimension of the client's problems and lack of flourishing, and that ignoring the moral dimension (values, positive character strengths and deficits) of the client's life may result in a harmful and unjust form of reductionism. However, such areas must be addressed prudently. Students are trained to understand that, when addressing moral issues, the quality of the therapeutic alliance, the timing and prioritization of the issue, and the client's desire to address moral aspects of the issue must be taken into account. For example, in the case of working with a client who is severely depressed and who is also aware of his or her own moral lapses, the clinician will first empathetically affirm the goodness and dignity of the person, who is a child of God, created by love

and for love. The clinician will also want to communicate a nonjudgmental approach toward the person of the client, without undercutting a path toward moral development and the benefit of change. The client might need considerable time and therapeutic work to understand the implications of her dignity, the injustice she is committing, or the inconsistency of her actions with her values or religious convictions. In a number of therapeutic situations, addressing the moral dimension of the client's life may not be prudent or feasible until late in the therapy, or, in cases where the client is not open to such exploration, the moral dimension may not be explicitly a part of therapy. However, in such cases, and indeed in any therapeutic relationship, when assisting a client to bring about therapeutic healing and change, the clinician is careful not to intend to cooperate in or do moral evil that the client may desire or actually do. A much more detailed theoretical foundation for how this sometimes challenging task can be accomplished is given in an earlier chapter of this book (Chapter 16, "Volitional and Free").

6. Considerations for Working with Non-Catholic Christians, Those of Different Faiths, and Non-Believers

Most Catholic mental health professionals will work with non-Catholic Christians, people of other religions, and non-believers throughout their careers. One aspect of working with clients of different faiths or non-believers is to train clinicians how to communicate to their clients in clear language the diagnosis, case formulation, and treatment plans that are based on a CCMMP framework. Principles and concepts such as dignity, flourishing, forgiveness, vocation, and responsibility (and related virtues such as faith, hope, love, and patience) can be

applied in work with clients from different worldviews and value systems. If communicated in straightforward, effective, and timely ways, these principles can be instruments for personal understanding and increased motivation for therapy. For instance, a Catholic mental health professional working with such clients will want to use natural law concepts and commonsense everyday experiences to help the clients become aware of the ways in which they are responding to the vocational calls that give meaning to their lives.

A Catholic clinician will also want to help clients avail themselves of resources from the client's own family, friends, and faith tradition that may help them heal and mature. For example, when working with a Jewish man who values his faith, but is considering having an extramarital affair, the clinician will not only emphasize psychological and ethical benefits of fidelity in marriage but also encourage the client to talk to Jewish married and faithful friends who might help him gain perspective, and possibly to his rabbi for additional guidance, so that he can benefit from resources in his own Jewish tradition and faith community.

7. Theories and Practices Within the Mental Health Field that Are Consistent with the CCMMP

In addition to a thorough introduction to theories and evidence-based practices existing in the field, the CCMMP-based training program includes training in theory and practices already existing or emerging within the field of Christian psychology and counseling. These include new theories, such as Christian personality theory (Chapter 4, Modern Personality Theories"; see also Chapter 17, "Created in the Image of God"), Christian spiritual developmental theory (Groeschel, 1984), Catholic understandings of cultural diversity (Benedict XVI, 2009), and Christian professional ethics (Ashley & O'Rourke, 1997). The program also includes training in existing therapy models such as affirmation therapy (Baars, 1979; Terruwe & Baars, 2016), integrative psychotherapy (McMinn & Campbell, 2007), forgiveness therapy (Enright & Fitzgibbons, 2015; Worthington, 2003; McCullough, 2008), Christian marital and family therapy (Nordling, 2005), and virtue theory and therapy (Chapter 25, "Virtue in Mental Health Practice").

An important means of students' developing their Christian identity as a mental health professional and keeping up with existing and emerging Christian mental health interventions is an affiliation with Christian professional associations. In a CCMMP-based training program, students are highly encouraged to affiliate with the Christian mental health professional community by joining existing professional associations, for example, the Catholic Psychotherapy Association, Christian Association for Psychological Studies, Society of Christian Psychology, American Association of Christian Counselors, or Society of Catholic Social Scientists. Students are also introduced to the main journals containing Christian scholarship in the area of Christian integrative approaches to mental health practice, for example, *Journal of Psychology and Christianity, Journal of Psychology and Theology, Journal of Christian Psychology*, and *Christian Psychology Around the World*.

8. Preparation of Mental Health Professionals to Serve the Church

An eighth goal of a CCMMP-based training program is to help mental health professionals develop expertise in areas of special interest for the Catholic Church. For example, the curriculum might offer an elective to train students in conducting vocational evaluations and mental health care supporting the unique vocations of ordained, religious, and consecrated members of the Church. The Catholic Christian Meta-Model of the Person promotes not only a positive view of the person, but also a positive view of the identity of clinicians and their scope of practice as a mental health professional. Accordingly, the CCMMP would advocate for mental health professionals' applying their training and skills not only to heal psychological disorders, but also to prevent problems from developing, and to enrich the lives of clients who are not "diagnosable" or in distress, but who are not fully flourishing. For example, students in training could be introduced to the importance of assisting with the design of marriage preparation or marriage enrichment programs in their parish, or at the diocesan level. The practicum training experience, for example, might provide the opportunity for students to provide basic education in psychological theory and counseling skills to support work with the ordained,

religious, and consecrated in the formation of priests and religious, and the work of marriage tribunals.

A CCMMP-based training program should also help mental health professionals learn how to work within Catholic systems and environments such as within parish structures (priest and staff, school, outreach programs), diocesan structures, seminaries, and religious communities.

Finally, mental health professionals should also be trained to work collaboratively with pastors and spiritual directors to address psychological issues impeding spiritual development. Although it is not the clinician's role to enter into spiritual direction, often the intersection between psychological and spiritual problems is apparent, so the ability to communicate with spiritual directors and, when appropriate, provide a referral for spiritual direction can be important.

9. Students, Faculty, and Staff: Selection and Formation

Because a CCMMP-based training program requires the integration of a Catholic vision of the person with clinical practice, it is, of course, important that both students and faculty within the program support this mission. Therefore there is a self-selection process operating both in terms of students that apply to the program, and faculty that apply to teach in the program. In the case of the Institute for the Psychological Sciences (IPS) and the School of Counseling at Divine Mercy University, students and faculty are interested in affiliating with its mental health professional training programs. They are open to a Catholic view of the person and welcome the opportunity to receive clinical training in the context of a faith-based community seeking to understand the Christian life and live out its values. Its students and faculty members also have

an interest in exploring, from a context wider than the current paradigm in the mental health field, what it means to flourish and to be human.

The psychology and counseling faculties, in addition, understand the common ground between contemporary psychology and counseling, with their many valid insights, and the Catholic Christian Meta-Model of the Person, with its view of the natural and transcendent (or graced) dimensions of human nature. The faculty within each training program has developed a multidisciplinary approach toward their respective clinical disciplines, and the philosophical and theological fields. Both training programs have faculty members who are trained in their respective mental health professions, as well as those with expertise in philosophy and theology.

To accomplish this synthetic goal of forming

students to practice from an integrated Catholic perspective requires close collaboration of the program faculty members in designing and implementing their respective courses. It also requires collaboration across programs as part of the common mission of Divine Mercy University. For example, faculty members meet regularly to specifically learn from one another's expertise and experience as part of the effort to integrate various levels of theoretical and applied counseling and psychology. The philosophical and theological faculty, for their part, openly engage in dialogue with the faculty of each training program about the various disciplines' approach to diagnosis, case formulation, and intervention, in order to enrich such understandings with insights from philosophy and theology. The faculty members themselves bring a diversity of theoretical orientations and experiences in working with clients from varying cultures, religious beliefs, and worldviews. They assist the philosophically and theologically trained staff to see how the truths conveyed by the CCMMP can be put into clinical practice with individual clients. This collaborative endeavor not only results in a fuller understanding of the person, but also supports practice that is increasingly consistent with the Meta-Model. In selecting faculty for a CCMMP-based program, faculty members and administrators must ensure that candidates for faculty positions demonstrate not only a solid Christian identity, but also a clear belief that it is possible to be true to this identity while using it in a way that enriches practice and while respecting the dignity and freedom of all clients.

Finally, it is important that the faculty member possess both an intellectual interest in and a capacity for multidisciplinary dialogue. Another vital characteristic of faculty members is that they be willing to avoid the over-identification with a particular specialization that is common in most universities. It is expected that each faculty member brings areas of specialization that enrich the program and allow for the wide variety of courses within its curriculum to be taught by faculty with expert content knowledge and skills. Nonetheless, each faculty member must also be willing to commit to the common mission of the program and the university, that is, the understanding and application of the CCMMP. Faculty who wish to focus primarily on their specialty and have little desire to examine it from an integrative perspective, or who, like many in academia, have the majority of their intellectual life centering on ventures and projects outside of the University, will likely not be able to develop the mature understanding of the CCMMP that is needed to contribute to its development and implementation within their training program.

Generally new faculty members enter the training program with general competence in the mental health field as well as a special area of expertise developed over their career. However, a new expertise in the CCMMP must also be added. Most faculty members will initially have a partial understanding of the CCMMP and its integration with mental health practice. By being open to making the CCMMP a new area of expertise, faculty will have the motivation to engage in the important learning process required to move from a partial to a sophisticated understanding of the Meta-Model of the Person. Furthermore, integrating this understanding into their identity will allow them to form students that in a similar way will function with integrity as both Christians and mental health professionals.

In a training program based on the CCMMP, formation of support staff is also very important. Such support staff are often involved in activities crucial to the success of the program, such as recruitment of students, student life, chaplain's services, and marketing. In many secular training programs, a basic understanding of the goals and objectives of the programs of the university is fairly easily obtained. However, in the case of a CCMMP-based training program, newly hired staff members may have little understanding of how such a program differs from secular ones. Since staff involved with recruitment and admissions are often the first point of contact with applicants to the program, it is vital that they correctly present the unique vision of the person that is at the foundation of the student's training. Likewise, training of staff-members involved in fundraising and development will allow them to motivate possible benefactors about the important and unique contribution that a Meta-Model-based program makes to the Church and the fields of counseling and psychology.

In addition to the primary focus of the CCMMP-based training program—namely, forming new mental health professionals through academic work and clinical experience—an important aspect of such formation is to ensure that opportunities for spiritual growth and support are available to its students, faculty, and staff, in a noncompulsory way. Ideally, this would include availability of a chaplain, daily Mass, the sacrament of Reconciliation, Eucharistic adoration, spiritual direction, experiences of serving others, and retreats. It is especially helpful if the chaplain has a special interest in or calling for working with mental health professionals and the mentally ill. Such spiritual resources allow students and faculty to grow in faith and to better understand their call to the mental health profession.

Conclusion

At the level of training objectives and practices, this chapter has identified nine goals of a CCMMP-based training program:

1. providing a broad and thorough grounding of students, program faculty, and clinical supervisors in the Catholic Christian Meta-Model of the Person;

2. bringing about an understanding of the dignity and the flourishing of client and clinician;

3. encouraging an understanding of the importance of the vocations of the client and mental health professional;

4. exploring the presuppositions that underlie the Meta-Model in theory and practice;

5. identifying implications of the Meta-Model for ethical practice;

6. forming mental health professionals to apply the Meta-Model when working

with non-Catholic Christians, people of different faiths, and non-believers;

7. training mental health professionals in existing theoretical models and practices within the mental health field that are explicitly Christian or consistent with a Christian worldview;

8. preparing mental health professionals to serve the Church in a way that is consistent with the Church's own vision of the person; and

9. selecting and forming the faculty and staff so that a consistent view of the person is present at all levels of the training program and the institution.

In conclusion, a formation program needs to include training not only at the levels of evidence-based and other sound psychotherapeutic theories and practices but also at the level of the wisdom traditions, worldviews, and value systems that influence both client and clinician. This means that training also attends to the enlarged sense of origins, transcendence, and finality supported by philosophical and religious views of the person and the world that offer presuppositions for mental health theory, research, and practice. The training program seeks to make clinicians aware not only of their own vision of the human person but also that of their client. Clinicians can be trained to recognize, respect, and engage (as appropriate) the worldview and value system of the client and of the clinical theory and technique that they use. The formation of mental health professionals (both students and faculty) capable of mastering both the understanding and application of the Meta-Model

requires collaborative efforts of a community of scholarship and faith working together.

Last, the vision of the person presented here recognizes that the Christian vocation makes certain claims on clinical practice and training. Instead of being a burden to the practice of the mental health profession, the Christian vocation provides insights into the strengths and weaknesses of individuals, families, and society that lead toward a fuller type of flourishing. As an extension of this vocation, students and faculty members alike seek basic training and ongoing intellectual and spiritual formation in order to integrate with increasing sophistication their role as a mental health professional with a Catholic Christian vision of the person.

REFERENCES

American Counseling Association. (2014). *ACA code of ethics.* Alexandria, VA: Author. Retrieved from www.counseling.org/resources/aca-code-of-ethics.pdf

American Psychological Association (APA). (2017). *Ethical principles of psychologists and code of conduct.* Washington, DC: Author. Retrieved from www.apa.org/ethics/code/ethics-code-2017.pdf

Ashley, B. M. (2000). *Choosing a world-view and value-system: An ecumenical apologetics.* New York, NY: Alba House.

Ashley, B. M. (2006). *The way toward wisdom: An interdisciplinary and intercultural introduction to metaphysics.* Notre Dame, IN: University of Notre Dame Press.

Ashley, B. M. (2013). *Healing for freedom: A Christian perspective on personhood and psychotherapy.* Arlington, VA: The Institute for the Psychological Sciences Press.

Ashley, B. M., & O'Rourke, K. (1997). *Health care ethics: A Catholic theological analysis.* Washington, DC: Georgetown University Press.

Baars, C. W. (1979). *Feeling and healing your emotions.* Gainesville, FL: Logos International.

Benedict XVI. (2005). *Deus caritas est* [Encyclical, on Christian love]. Vatican City, Vatican: Libreria Editrice Vaticana

Benedict XVI. (2009). *Caritas in veritate* [Encyclical, on integral human development in charity and truth]. Vatican City, Vatican: Libreria Editrice Vaticana.

Bergin, A. E. (1980). Psychotherapy and religious values. *Journal of Consulting and Clinical Psychology, 48,* 95–105.

Bordin, E. S. (1979). The generalizability of the psychoanalytic concept of the working alliance. *Psychotherapy: Theory, Research & Practice, 16*(3), 252–260.

Brugger, E. C., & the Faculty of the Institute for the Psychological Sciences. (2008). Anthropological foundations for clinical psychology: A proposal. *Journal of Psychology and Theology, 36,* 3–15.

Catechism of the Catholic Church (2nd ed.). (1997). Vatican City, Vatican: Libreria Editrice Vaticana.

Enright, R. D., & Fitzgibbons, R. P. (2015). *Forgiveness therapy: An empirical guide to resolving anger and restoring hope.* Washington, DC: American Psychological Association.

Francis. (2016). *Amoris laetitia* [Apostolic exhortation, on love in the family]. Vatican City, Vatican: Libreria Editrice Vaticana.

Grisez, G., & Shaw, R. (2003). *Personal vocation: God calls everyone by name.* Huntington, IN: Our Sunday Visitor.

Groeschel, B. J. (1984). *Spiritual passages: The psychology of spiritual development "for those who seek".* New York, NY: Crossroad Classic.

Hagenauer, G., & Volet, S. E. (2014). Teacher-student relationship at university: An important yet under-researched field. *Oxford Review of Education, 40*(3), 370–388. doi:10.1080/03054985.2014.921613

Herrington, J., & Oliver, R. (2000). An instructional design framework for authentic learning environments. *Educational Technology Research and Development, 48*(3), 23–48. doi:10.1007/BF02319856

John Paul II. (1981a). *Familiaris consortio* [Apostolic exhortation, on the Christian family in the modern world]. Vatican City, Vatican: Libreria Editrice Vaticana.

John Paul II. (1981b). *Laborens exercens* [Encyclical, on human work]. Vatican City, Vatican: Libreria Editrice Vaticana.

John Paul II. (1988). *Christifideles laici* [Apostolic exhortation, on the vocation and the mission of the lay faithful in the Church and in the world]. Vatican City, Vatican: Libreria Editrice Vaticana.

John Paul II. (1994). *Letter to families*. Boston, MA: Pauline Books and Media.

John Paul II. (1998). *Fides et ratio* [Encyclical, on the relationship between faith and reason]. Vatican City, Vatican: Libreria Editrice Vaticana.

John Paul II. (2006). *Man and woman he created them: A theology of the body* (M. Waldstein, Trans.). Boston, MA: Pauline Books & Media.

Jones, S. (1996). A constructive relationship for religion with the science and profession of psychology: Perhaps the boldest model yet. In E. Shafranske (Ed.), *Religion and the clinical practice of psychology* (pp. 113–147). Washington, DC: American Psychological Association.

Leo XIII. (1880) *Arcanum divinae sapientiae* [Encyclical, on Christian marriage]. Vatican City, Vatican: Libreria Editrice Vaticana.

McCullough, M. E., (2008). *Beyond revenge: The evolution of the forgiveness instinct*. San Francisco, CA: Jossey-Bass.

McMinn, M. R., & Campbell, C. D. (2007). *Integrative psychotherapy: Toward a comprehensive Christian approach*. Downers Grove, IL: InterVarsity Press.

Miller, S. D., Duncan, B. L., Sorrell, R., & Brown, G. S. (2005). The partners for change outcome

management system. *Journal of Clinical Psychology, 61*(2), 199–208.

Nordling, W. (2005, October). *Implications of a Catholic worldview for marital therapy*. Paper presented at the annual conference of the Society of Catholic Social Scientists. Steubenville, OH.

O'Donohue, W. (1989). The (even) bolder model: The clinical psychologist as metaphysician-scientist-practitioner. *American Psychologist, 44,* 1460–1468.

O'Donohue, W., & Kitchener, R. (Eds.). (1996). *The philosophy of psychology*. London, United Kingdom: Sage.

Paul VI. (1968). *Humanae vitae* [Encyclical, on the regulation of birth]. Vatican City, Vatican: Libreria Editrice Vaticana.

Pellegrino, E. D., & Thomasma, D. C. (1993). *The Christian virtues in medical practice*. Washington, DC: Georgetown University Press.

Peterson, C., & Seligman, M. E. P. (2004). *Character strengths and virtues: A handbook and classification*. New York, NY: Oxford University Press.

Pinckaers, S. (1995). *The sources of Christian ethics* (M. T. Noble, Trans.). Washington, DC: The Catholic University of America Press.

Pius XI. (1930). *Casti connubii* [Encyclical, on Christian marriage]. Vatican City, Vatican: Libreria Editrice Vaticana.

Scrofani, P., & Nordling, W. (2011). The Institute for the Psychological Sciences: An integrative Catholic approach to clinical training. *Journal of Psychology and Christianity, 30*(2), 121–127.

Shafranske, E. P. (2000). Psychotherapy with Roman Catholics. In P. S. Richards & A. E. Bergin (Eds.), *Handbook of psychotherapy and religious diversity* (pp. 59–88). Washington, DC: American Psychological Association.

Taylor, C. (2007). *A secular age*. Cambridge, MA: Belknap Press of Harvard University Press.

Terruwe, A. A., & Baars, C. W. (2016). *Psychic wholeness and healing: Using all the powers of the human psyche*. Eugene, OR: Wipf & Stock.

Trent, Council of. (2017). Teaching on the sacrament of marriage. Session 24 in N. P. Tanner (Ed.), *Decrees of the ecumenical councils* (Vol. 2, pp. 753–759). Washington, DC: Georgetown University Press. (Original work published 1547)

Vatican II, Council. (1964). *Lumen gentium* [Dogmatic

constitution on the Church]. In G. Baum (Ed.), *The teachings of the second Vatican council*. Westminster, MD: The Newman Press.

Vatican II, Council. (1965). *Gaudium et spes* [Pastoral constitution on the Church in the modern world]. In G. Baum (Ed.), *The teachings of the second Vatican council*. Westminster, MD: The Newman Press.

Vitz, P. C. (2006). The embodied self: Evidence from cognitive psychology and neuropsychology. In P. C. Vitz & S. M. Felch (Eds.), *The self: Beyond the postmodern crisis* (pp. 113–127). Wilmington, DE: ISI Books.

Wiggins, G., & McTighe, J. (2005). *Understanding by design*. Alexandria, VA: ASCD.

Wojtyła, K. (1981). The problem of vocation (H. T. Willetts, Trans.). In *Love and responsibility* (pp. 219–261). San Francisco, CA: Ignatius Press. Original work published 1960.

Worthington, E. L., Jr. (2003). *Forgiving and reconciling: Bridges to wholeness and hope* (rev. ed.). Downers Grove, IL: InterVarsity Press.

Chapter 21

Case Conceptualization

The Catholic Christian Meta-Model of
the Person as a Framework

SU LI LEE AND WILLIAM J. NORDLING

ABSTRACT: The case conceptualization process, which includes diagnosis, case formulation, and treatment planning, has received increasing attention in the mental health field over the past two decades. This chapter examines how the Catholic Christian Meta-Model of the Person (CCMMP) provides a comprehensive understanding of the person and an organizing framework for case conceptualization, a framework that incorporates a wide range of existing theories in the field, while avoiding the reductionism, relativism, determinism, and frequently narrow focus associated with these theories. In addition, this chapter demonstrates how the Meta-Model's inclusion of important dimensions of personhood, such as vocational commitments, virtues and character strengths, and spirituality can be used to improve the case conceptualization process. Finally, a brief illustration of case conceptualization using the CCMMP is given in order to demonstrate more concretely how the Meta-Model significantly expands and enriches case conceptualization and the associated intake process.

The Importance of Case Conceptualization for
Understanding the Client

Over the past two decades, much has been written about the clinical usefulness of case conceptualization. A number of authors have emphasized the use of broad-based approaches to case conceptualization that are applicable across theoretical orientations (Berman, 2015; Bornstein, 2018; Eells, 2007; Ingram, 2012; Frank & Davidson, 2014; Sperry & Sperry, 2012). Other authors have utilized case conceptualization with specific theoretical orientations such as psychodynamic therapy (McWilliams, 1999), cognitive therapy (Needleman, 1999), Cognitive-Behavioral Therapy (Kuyken, Padesky, & Dudley; 2009, Persons, 2008), Emotion-Focused Therapy (Goldman & Greenberg, 2014), acceptance and commitment therapy (Bach & Moran, 2008) or family therapy (Reiter, 2014). Other authors have emphasized the use of case conceptualization based on specific mental health disorders (Kress & Paylo, 2015; Sperry, Carlson, Sauerheber, & Sperry, 2015) or treatment populations (Manassis, 2014).

Regardless of the level or type of focus, research has shown that the use of clinical formulation by the practicing clinician often leads to a more systematic and intentional stance toward both *being with* and *treating* the patient. The difference between what is properly called conceptualization and what is simply formulation varies according to how researchers' operationalize their working definitions and to clinicians' own theoretical backgrounds. Sometimes these terms are used interchangeably, and at other times they may denote some difference. For example, Sperry and Sperry (2012) have used the term "case conceptualization" as a broad process that includes case formulation, diagnosis, and treatment planning. Consistent with the broad definition of case conceptualization in this chapter, "case formulation" will be used to denote the way the client's presenting issues and narrative are understood as a whole, while "case conceptualization" will be used more generally to encompass case formulation as well as diagnosis, treatment planning, and all that they entail.

Major Theories as "Filters" for Case Formulation

Historically, case formulation has been the process in which the client's narrative is understood through the lens of a given psychological theory, with all its assumptions. These assumptions can provide a comprehensive understanding of the person and an organizing framework for case conceptualization, a framework that can be viewed as a certain kind of filter through which pieces of information about the client are sieved, organized, and pieced together into a narrative picture. Some psychological theories provide a more static picture of the client, while others present a more dynamic one. For example, a strictly behavioral formulation (e.g., Martin & Pear, 2015) of a person presenting with chronic tardiness may be formulated into a more or less static narrative that places the tardiness in the context of antecedents and consequences. The client has habituated into the behavior of always trying to finish too many tasks for any given amount of time (this is both an antecedent to tardiness as well as a consequence, inasmuch as the client feels satisfaction thinking that he can accomplish a long list of things in a short time), and his tardiness to the next appointment has always been forgiven (the consequence)—until now. The response or consequence given by the client's new partner, however, is anger. The now-unhappy client, who has had the consequences changed on him, is now in therapy. The clinician's task, as the formulation would seem to suggest, is to change the behavior by changing the antecedent. Implicit within this formulation is the assumption that all behaviors have an antecedent and a consequence, and that changing either (or both) will lead to behavioral change. Of course, the other fundamental assumption is that therapy is primarily meant to change observable behaviors.

Another filter that can be applied to this same client is a psychodynamic lens, which would lead to a more dynamic picture (e.g., McWilliams, 1999; Westmeyer, 2003). There are many related but differing possible filters that could be applied, given that there are quite a few differences among the various psychodynamic schools. We will adopt a simple one here, which will suffice to show the differences between adopting a psychodynamic explanatory framework rather than a behavioral framework. In this case the same routinely tardy client finds it difficult to wait for an appointment to begin. In order to avoid this painful waiting, the client has developed the habit of never arriving early, and in fact generally arrives late enough that the person on the other end is almost certainly waiting for the client's arrival. Note here that a behavioral formulation is still possible at this point, that is, in order to avoid the painful wait (consequence), the patient arrives late. A psychodynamically oriented clinician may then, upon exploration of feelings, also discover that the pain of waiting has to do with the fear of losing control—the client cannot control when the other will arrive—and waiting generates the sense of helplessness, hence the perpetual tardiness to avoid losing control and feeling helpless. We see here that this creates a more dynamic picture of the client insofar as it brings insight to the theme of control, which is potentially related to many other areas of the client's personality and problems that may not be observable as behavior.

Another often-used filter in case formulation, referred to as the "medical model" (see, for example, Cuthbert, 2014, and Jablensky, 2005 for thoughts on this issue), is most clearly exemplified by the categorization of presenting issues and narratives into symptom clusters as found in the DSM-5. It is undoubtedly helpful in many instances to be able to group patterns of symptoms together and to assign a label or diagnostic category. Such diagnostic categories can improve reliability of diagnosis across mental health providers and can assist in many ways, such as assisting with important decisions surrounding a medication prescription to ease symptoms. In spite of such utility, this symptom-cluster model is often constrained to managing only symptoms and often fails to capture or account for many areas of life that are psychologically meaningful and significant to the client.

The point here is that each personality theory and model of therapy has its underlying assumptions about the human person and reality itself. These assumptions are not always explicitly stated, nor examined in their normal day-to-day use by clinicians. This does not, however, negate the fact that the assumptions are there, and that it is precisely these assumptions that are built upon when clinicians use their preferred explanatory models or filters for case formulation.

The Issue of Values Embedded in Case Formulation

It is also widely recognized in the mental health field that there is no such thing as engaging in psychotherapy with no values, that is to say, values as they relate to the human person and to reality (see, for example, Dunn, Callahan, Farnsworth, & Watkins, 2017, discussing how to address supervisor-supervisee value conflicts, and Farnsworth & Callahan, 2013, discussing this same issue between client and clinician). While not so long ago in the history of the field there was some hope that a clinician could be value-free while in session, this has been conclusively shown to be not only false, but impossible (Slife, 2004; Slife, Smith, & Burchfield, 2003; Smith, 2009; Tjeltveit, 2006).

Likewise, mental health professionals automatically apply their preferred explanatory models (and their accompanying assumptions about the person) in their clinical activities. This habitual use of a preferred theoretical orientation is a heuristic that allows for quicker entrance into and understanding of the clients' worlds and their problems, but at the cost of often overlooking other equally important areas not immediately (if at all) covered by the heuristic. As a corrective to this problem, many clinicians have chosen either to use more than one explanatory model while engaging in case formulation, or alternatively to use the emerging explanatory models that integrate two or more schools of thought into their own theoretical model. In addition, increasingly, mental health professional training programs adopt more than one explanatory model and generally include the Biopsychosocial Model (see Plante, 2012), a model that takes into consideration how both inherited nature and the environment affect the person as he or she is embedded in a community and in society at large (see Campbell & Rohrbaugh, 2006, and Peterson, Goodie, & Andrasik, 2015, for an overview). The very significant and currently much-discussed area of diversity falls into this last category of environment and society. In addition, many contemporary explanatory models also have the assumption of development, bringing in the idea that the human person develops in and through time, and that the person's surrounding environment also changes over time, which in turn affects the person's growth (Berk, 2010; Bowlby, 1969, 1973; McWilliams, 2004).

Developmental Perspectives and the Nature-Nurture Debate

It is also important to consider what a developmental model within a biopsychosocial framework means for understanding the person in general, and case formulation more specifically. In the longstanding nature-versus-nurture debate of human development, the term "nature" has historically been used to denote what was part of the human make-up, first in terms of our phenotypical traits, and, in the more recent century of scientific advancement, the genotype we carry. In other words, nature has to do with what is essential to being a human as opposed to another animal. The term nurture, on the other hand, had to do with environmental factors such as parental care and shaping as well as ex-

pectations of the surrounding community and society at large. More recently, however, this debate has taken a turn in which nature itself is often construed of as a byproduct of nurturing forces (Stern, 1985). For example, the idea that biological sex affects gender identity has now been part of political ideology (on both ends of the spectrum) long enough that these two realities (sex and gender) have been conflated, deconstructed, reconstituted, and in general muddled—for reasons other than for the sake of the individual suffering person. It is sometimes believed that, in the context of what it means to be male or female, nature is no more than a form of nurture. Even though medical science is now able to modify certain aspects of what has heretofore been considered the original biological sex, it is not able to change the sex at the level of the DNA or chromosomal sex or at the level of individual cells or even the structure and shape of the skeleton (Chapter 9, "Man and Woman"). This turn away from sex to gender is significant for clinicians not because we are political advocates (though some may be), but because it illustrates that the underlying assumptions of theories based on the Biopsychosocial Model are in flux, and that such change is not necessarily the result of systematic improvement of the theory over time, but instead is dictated by social and political forces, without reference to enduring human nature or what is good for the human person.

One may object at this point that what is "good" for the person varies and is entirely relative to context—a case for nurture and the annihilation of nature. The Catholic Christian Meta-Model of the Person (CCMMP) as presented throughout this volume, however, has strongly argued otherwise, namely, that there is a human nature, while also acknowledging the importance of nurturing influences. The Meta-Model also claims that the client as a human person is much more than what is captured in one or even a collection of existing personality theories and explanatory models. In addition, the CCMMP also argues that reality itself is not simply a creation of the human mind and derived from the

person's own hopes and fears. It is precisely this belief in the stability of the nature of the human person and in the broader reality in which the person exists that makes the CCMMP a realistic and useful framework for case formulation and conceptualization.

The CCMMP and Case Conceptualization: A Framework

Thus far we have spoken about case formulation in general, that is, piecing together the client's presenting concerns and history into a single, coherent narrative. Case formulation, while useful for understanding the client, can be further expanded into what has been distinguished as case conceptualization. Sperry and Sperry (2012) have developed a framework for case conceptualization that takes into account the important common questions asked and purposes for doing case conceptualization that are generally shared across the various explanatory models and models of counseling and psychotherapy. In addition, they have offered a concise working definition of case conceptualization as "a method and clinical strategy for obtaining and organizing information about a client, understanding and explaining the client's situation and maladaptive patterns, guiding and focusing treatment, anticipating challenges and roadblocks, and preparing for success" (p. 4).

This definition provides some valuable insights into assumptions about case conceptualization. First, it posits that the client at the initial session brings a narrative that must be understood. This narrative, as we have seen, often has to do with a presenting concern, which itself is embedded within a certain context that is unique to the client. Second, the definition implies that case conceptualization, as defined above, is, first of all, a method of organizing this information. As the organizing occurs, more in-

formation is often needed and gathered, which leads to a more extended narrative, a narrative that needs to come together in a coherent whole that yields understanding—the case formulation. The question remains, however, as to what is guiding the clinician to sieve out information that is considered important. Obviously, this question hinges on another question, which is, what kind of organization is the clinician trying to create? Or into what sort of framework is the patient to be placed to be understood in a coherent manner?

It is in the need for coherence and the corresponding framework that integration finds one of its most significant roles in case conceptualization. To oversimplify the many chapters that have gone before in this book, it is worth repeating that the CCMMP is an attempt to give a comprehensive account to the question of personhood. It is this account that provides the framework for organizing individualized information in the first stage of case conceptualization. To know what the most important and defining dimensions of personhood are (such as rational, volitional, interpersonal, vocation-focused, created, fallen, etc.) is to have, at the same time, the guiding compass as to the kind of information to be gathered. The Meta-Model framework, therefore allows us to know that learning about a married client's quality of the relationship with a spouse, parenting worries, negative self-concept, problematic or very positive childhood experiences of family, or addictions will likely provide more understanding than other types of information, such as the client's favorite shirt or the size of his shoes. Although this may seem obvious, often not much reflection occurs about what makes a clinician obtaining information think that a certain aspect of the person may be more important than another.

Presuppositions and the Avoidance of Reductionism

The utility of the CCMMP lies in its recognition that the clinician's view of the client's problem is directly related to the clinician's view of the person. For example, if a mental health professional assumes that sexual relations are nothing more than isolated physical acts, then a person who has sexual relations with several partners concurrently does not have a relational problem. In fact, if sex is understood simply as an act that brings physical gratification, and gratification is an end in itself (note that to view this as an end in itself is also a certain view of the person, or of reality more broadly), then this person could in fact be seen as fulfilling his physical and emotional needs in an appropriate way. This example may seem somewhat simplistic, but it points to several things. First, every clinical conceptualization begins with assumptions about the person and the world, that is, the reality of the world in which we find ourselves. It is within and with these assumptions that the clinician obtains what is considered necessary and helpful information, and then ultimately organizes this information into some coherent form. The Meta-Model provides a nonreductionistic account of these basic assumptions, or, more precisely, of the fundamental understanding of what it means to be a person.

Before proceeding further, it is worthwhile

to state here, as a related note to the issue of human nature, the other side of the coin. The Meta-Model argues for assumptions of the human person in a manner that suggests that there is, in fact, such a thing as human nature, which structures and provides direction to human life. This nature is a given and is stable across time, space, and all other manner of diversity. This may seem obvious, but is it really so in the mental health field? Take, for example, the sexual act. That the sexual act is an outward behavior common to both humans and most other higher life forms on earth is rarely, if ever, disputed. That the act is also an intrinsically relational act that not only joins two bodily organisms but in itself is also meaningful as a unitive gesture—spiritually or psychologically, or both—is, on the other hand, very much disputed in the culture at large, and in the field of contemporary mental health in particular. This latter understanding, however, has not always been under so much contention in the general culture at large, both in the Western as well as Eastern world, nor in the psychological world. The point here is not either to contest or defend the meaning or meanings of the sexual act. The point, rather, is to show that the assumption in the contemporary mental health field is that the questions that the clinician asks to find relevant information commonly involve assumptions about the nature of the person. If there were no basic stable elements of human nature, then the clinician would be greatly hampered in what to even ask, much less how to address the client's problems. The CCMMP argues in nonreductionistic terms that there is such a thing as human nature and that we can understand the various dimensions of this nature. Further, with this knowledge, we can come to know better who the client is and what he or she needs.

In order to organize seemingly discrepant

parts of the client's narrative into a whole, experienced clinicians know that they are implicitly using some theory of the person. The clinician's theory of the person is distinctive, formed by his or her therapeutic training and personal past, which provides an understanding of reality and of how people, in general, should live. This therapeutic orientation provides a structure to organize the information gathered by the clinician. Because existing therapeutic orientations tend to be narrowly focused, they typically omit important information about the person. This is true even in the case of some therapeutic models that attempt to integrate two or more theoretical orientations. This interpretative approach of clinicians, we propose, can be substantially broadened by the Catholic Christian Meta-Model of the Person. The Meta-Model itself, as has been reiterated in other parts of this book, provides a normative understanding of the nature of the person, which guides clinical understanding without being a clinical theory itself.

Identifying the Client's Problem and Formulating a Treatment Plan

The next part of case conceptualization, as spelled out by Sperry and Sperry (2012), is that of "understanding and explaining the client's situation and maladaptive patterns" (p.4). Assuming we have expanded our listening for information to all areas of personhood as espoused by the Meta-Model, this part of the task requires that we understand what constitutes maladaptive patterns. For instance, is having extramarital affairs maladaptive? Or can it be justified on the grounds of satisfying needs that one's spouse does not seem able to meet? Furthermore, maladaptive for whom? What if the patient is getting satisfaction out of the extramarital affair and the spouse knows nothing of it? There are various ways of answering these questions, but these ways all hinge on how one understands the nature of marriage. If marriage is a vocation and the call to be a husband (and father) brings with it the implicit need for fidelity, then satisfying the unmet needs with extramarital affairs will ultimately fail, both as a long-term and as a short-term solution, and is therefore maladaptive; in addition, such infidelity will inevitably be harmful to the personhood of both the husband and wife. However, if marriage is nothing but a contractual agreement that can be terminated at any time, then it may in fact not be functionally maladaptive in the short-term to have extramarital affairs. The Meta-Model guides the identification of what is truly maladaptive or otherwise.

The final part of the working definition of case conceptualization is: "guiding and focusing treatment, anticipating challenges and roadblocks, and preparing for success" (p. 4). As has been stated earlier, the CCMMP gives us a broad comprehensive understanding of the person. Although the Meta-Model can give broad guidance on the areas of the person needing development and healing, it does not give a specific diagnosis or particular evidence-based intervention to be utilized. Nevertheless, the Meta-Model does provide a key component to clinical success, which is that it provides the very basis for judging success. In other words, the idea of success is empty in itself. It can mean anything from symptom reduction (which seems to be the medical slant of conceptualizing cases with symptom clusters), to becoming more self-aware (such as is the case for many psychodynamic and psychoanalytic schools), to becoming more free in various ways. It may be argued that anything from symptom reduction to self-awareness and everything in between is in fact helping the client to become freer to live, to feel, to choose, to think. Although this is true, the CCMMP provides a framework to which the clinician can constantly refer in the evolving process of therapy with any given client to ensure that all the dimensions of the client's flourishing are attended to, if possible (for it is not always possible); the clinician need not be constrained by or limited to only certain aspects of the person's flourishing.

We begin to see here that the entire enterprise of case conceptualization hinges on the clinician's perspective on reality itself, including what constitutes the human person. This is precisely the value and utility of the Meta-Model. The CCMMP is a comprehensive understanding of the person, an approach that attempts to draw out, as a whole, the nature of the human person. If one accepts the premise that an understanding of personhood, as such, results in a less reductionistic and more thorough understanding of problems that a person is experiencing, it follows that utilizing the Meta-Model's vision of the person as a guide should result in a more comprehensive case conceptualization. It bears repeating that the CCMMP serves as an overarching framework of understanding and does not replace the explanatory models found in psychological theories. Rather, the clinician, from his or her own therapeutic orientation, benefits by using this framework to organize and understand the various foundational characteristics of their clients.

There are several advantages to the clinician entering into and understanding the Meta-Model. As already noted, a central advantage of the Meta-Model is that it provides a comprehensive understanding of the person. The development of this comprehensive understanding requires the clinician to integrate a number of the existing personality theories and therapy models in order to assess all of the fundamental dimensions or capacities of the person identified in the Meta-Model. Another advantage is the Meta-Model's role in anchoring developmentally-based biopsychosocial models to a stable (but not static) understanding of personhood. The nature/nurture difference in contemporary Western society has all but collapsed into the category of societal influence and unbounded relativism in postmodern thought. The basic assumption of the Meta-Model challenges this collapse, compelling the clinician to take another look at what are unchanging truths about the human person, truths that affect the way a given psychological issue ought to be approached. If there are no truths, no anchor that grounds psychological theories to the reality of the human person, then the related dimensions of psychological problems and health are ambiguous. Related to the issue of a stable sense of personhood is the attempt at a more holistic view of the person in case conceptualization. To put it another way, the CCMMP is a way of safeguarding the clinician from reductionist and relativist formulations of the client and his or her circumstances. It accomplishes this through an intentionally broad-based understanding of the various dimensions of the person, proposing these dimensions as equally significant and always present, though not necessarily equally relevant in any given clinical situation.

Given the dimensions of the human person articulated in the CCMMP, the Meta-Model also proposes to the clinician a view of the client's flourishing to consider in case conceptualization. Many psychological theories provide accounts of pathology and its development; some also provide the corresponding view of positive growth, strengths, and resilience given a goodenough or ideal situation. For example, attachment theory, as first articulated by John Bowlby and now vastly expanded in both clinical and research literature, hypothesizes the conditions for what was to be called "good enough" (Winnicott, 1971). It postulates certain mothering traits that predict the establishment of a secure attachment style in children, which subsequently leads to a secure state of mind in an adult (Main, Kaplan, & Cassidy, 1985).

This security is fundamentally a recognition that one's needs (and feelings) are manageable and acceptable and that these needs can reasonably be expected to be met. It teaches the child, and subsequently anchors the adult in the realistic confidence that others can be trusted. In this perhaps oversimplified explanation of an aspect of attachment theory, it becomes clear that the theory, by postulating what would make the infant feel safe and learn that the world and people around him are generally caring (or at least benign), also gives us an idea of the origins of pathology as well as what constitutes healthy development. Yet, as comprehensive as this theory attempts to be in the origins or interpersonal relations and the formation of the concept of self, it does not speak to the goal or *telos* of these relations beyond accepting the evolutionary explanation that human beings need others to survive.

It is perhaps in this area of flourishing that the CCMMP is most evidently helpful in clinical work generally, and in case conceptualization more specifically. The CCMMP goes a step further by bringing to evidence that the need for attachment, above and beyond physical survival, has to do with the very nature of the human person. Persons are created as gifts, and it is in the nature of gift that another is needed, first the Other that is God, and then the other that is those significant persons in one's life. Relation is intrinsic to what it means to be human (note the "nature" aspect is more than just physical nature). Further, it is not just any relation that will suffice for us to be satisfied; relations must take on certain properties, such as sacrifice and commitment, both of which are embedded within the context of vocation. It is precisely by exploring all these other aspects of the human person in relationship that one can be more fulfilled— that one can flourish more fully. It is here that we see that in the framework of the CCMMP, these dimensions can be introduced to fill in the gaps in various psychological theories. Sometimes filling the gaps may mean contradicting some of the underlying basic assumptions of certain psychological theories while maintaining the validity of many of the functional aspects of the theory, and even advocating the use of the clinical methods derived from them. At any rate, what is most significant is the idea that the CCMMP provides a larger framework in which psychological theories can be understood and utilized in case conceptualization.

A Midpoint Elaboration on the Implications of the CCMMP for Case Conceptualization

As has been examined in this chapter so far, case conceptualization is an essential clinical skill that consists of several related clinical activities: diagnosis, case formulation, and treatment planning. These clinical activities are dependent on information gained in the intake process and on additional assessment, and on information gained from the ongoing therapeutic process. Diagnosis answers the question, "what is the client's problem?" Case formulation answers the question, "Why did this problem develop?" Finally, treatment planning answers the question, "What can we do to help with the problem?" As has been stated earlier, the answers to all of these questions are influenced by our understanding of the nature of the person and reality itself.

The Catholic Christian Meta-Model of the Person offers a comprehensive framework for understanding the person. The Meta-Model posits that the person is a unified whole that is interpersonally relational, sensory-perceptual-cognitive, emotional, rational, and volitional (free). The person is created in the image of God, and thus possesses foundational goodness and dignity, and, although sinful and being influenced by the sin of others, is capable of developing virtue, living more consistently with personal values, and experiencing psychological and spiritual growth and healing. Ultimately the person is seen as experiencing various vocational callings that give meaning to life. Through responding to such calls by faithfully living out his or her commitments and lovingly serving others, the client can flourish.

Even the wide scope of these capacities and dimensions of the person may seem to leave out some important considerations of the person, but in fact each of these dimensions, when explored, as has been done in the earlier chapters of this book, produces an enriched view of the person. For example, the dimension of the person as being a unified whole touches on the person as a unity, having a body and soul, mind, and spirit (Chapter 8, "Personal Wholeness"). It touches also on issues of sexual identity, as well as exploring the similarities, differences, and complementary aspects of women and men. The interpersonal dimension of the person conveys not only the importance of family and friends, but also the social nature of the person as rooted in gift rather than simply survival. It speaks

also of the importance, in the life of the person, of community and environment, and the value of culture as embedded in the intrinsic need for beauty, and not simply entertainment. This comprehensive understanding of the person increases the ability of the clinician to engage in case conceptualization in a way faithful to the complexity of the client.

As we have indicated, the Meta-Model offers a more comprehensive framework for understanding the person than do those given by any single personality theory or therapeutic model existing in the mental health field at present, or even the existing integrative attempts within the field. As noted previously, however, the CCMMP is not a competing personality theory, but instead is a broad framework for understanding the person, and as such it does not seek to replace other personality theories or the explanatory models of the person given in the various schools of therapy. Instead it represents a synthetic way to integrate the truths contained in these theories to fill out its understanding of the various dimensions of personhood. For example, the Meta-Model's understanding of the person as "interpersonally relational" is developed and greatly enriched by the contributions of psychodynamic theory, interpersonal theory, attachment theory, Emotion-Focused Therapy, Relationship Enhancement Therapy, the Gottman Method, family systems theory, and Bowenian family therapy, to name just a few. In short, far from rejecting other explanatory models within the mental health field, the Meta-Model is a corrective against relying too heavily on any single personality theory or therapy model. Instead the Meta-Model requires that the clinician draw from multiple theoretical models in approaching case conceptualization.

Moreover, the Meta-Model also draws on insights regarding the person given by the longstanding Christian philosophical and theological traditions in their efforts to understand the person. This multidisciplinary approach to studying the person emphasizes aspects of the client's life that have not been addressed adequately, or that have been addressed only recently within the mental health field. Such areas include the vocational callings of the person, the importance of spirituality in the life of the person, the meaning of work, the importance of forgiveness, and the importance of virtues, values, and the moral life. In addition, the many existing personality theories and therapeutic models often give contradictory answers to fundamental questions about the person; the CCCMP, as a framework, is able to arbitrate answers to these fundamental questions while still acknowledging and incorporating what is valuable from each theory. For example, to the question "Does the person possess adequate freedom to change?" the CCMMP gives a qualified "Yes," thus leaving room for working on psychological problems that hamper the client's freedom, while also bearing the hope that the client has the capacity to be ever more free. The CCMMP incorporates the importance of both physical and social environments in the life of the person without seeing them as deterministic. It also recognizes that behavioral concepts such as modeling, shaping, and schedules of reinforcement are important both for an understanding of how human problems develop and for use in treatment interventions.

The comprehensive understanding of the person represented by the CCMMP results in an increase in the breadth and scope, as well as depth, of information about the client's life that must be gathered in order for the clinician to have confidence that the resulting diagnosis,

case formulation, and treatment planning does justice to the person and his or her problems. An adequate case conceptualization is seen as emerging from the use of the CCMMP as the general guiding framework, which tells us what basic dimensions of the client's life must be inquired about and understood. A well-trained and experienced clinician has knowledge of a variety of personality theories and therapeutic models that assist in the skillful questioning and exploration of the dimensions of the person needed to satisfy the demands of the CCMMP.

Before moving on to a brief example of case conceptualization, it should be noted that one advantage of the CCMMP is that it demands a disciplined comprehensive understanding of human problems, how they develop, and what can be done to bring healing and growth. Although it is true that the Catholic Christian Meta-Model of the Person is unique in a number of ways, it is also true that the mental health field includes well-trained, highly experienced, wise clinicians that over many years of practice and study have developed their own distinctive broad-based and rich understandings of the person, which include many elements of the CCMMP. However, it is also true that many clinicians, regardless of experience levels, tend to be restricted by excessive reliance on a few models of therapy. The advantage of the CCMMP's serving a foundational role in training (Chapter 20, "Principles for Training") is that it provides a common, well-defined understanding of the person that can be acquired and competently applied by mental health professionals early in their careers. It also enriches the understanding of mature clinicians.

Implementation of the CCMMP Framework into Case Conceptualization: A Brief Case Analysis

A brief case analysis will be used to give some illustration of how the CCMMP influences case conceptualization. This analysis is not meant to represent a comprehensive case conceptualization, as would be possible if all of the Meta-Model's dimensions of the person in Table 21.1 were to be explored. Instead, in a more modest way, this illustration seeks to present some of the ways in which the CCMMP is both similar to and different from traditional approaches to case conceptualization. In addition, it demonstrates how using the Meta-Model approach entails an integration of multiple explanatory frameworks. For example, in this case analysis, the case conceptualization uses elements of the broad CCMMP framework (especially its understanding of the nature of marriage and family life), the Biopsychosocial Model, cognitive-behavioral perspectives, character strengths and virtues, attachment and other interpersonal theories, family systems theory, marital communication theory, cultural diversity perspectives, and the importance of spirituality and the faith community.

Case vignette:

Mr. Juan Garcia and his wife, Belinda, arrived for their intake interview with Dr. Roberts to discuss problems that their son Enrique was experiencing in school.

Below are a very select group of the much larger group of questions that might be asked in a CCMMP-based interview aimed at gathering information for case conceptualization.

Question 1:

Can you share with me what your concerns are about your son?

This basic open-ended question would likely be a good opening question in many approaches to interviewing and case conceptualization. It is thus one that is shared with the CCMMP. It shows respect for the parents and their perspectives on the problem. In this case we find out that the Garcia family has recently moved to the East Coast from the West Coast, and Enrique, age 7, has had a difficult transition to his new school. Follow-up questions from the behavioral perspective reveal that within a week after beginning to attend his new school, Enrique has begun to complain of pain in his stomach, at which point Mrs. Garcia allows him to stay at home for the rest of the day, even though within an hour Enrique seems to be playing happily and is pain-free. Questions touching on the biopsychosocial dimensions result in an understanding that Enrique's pediatrician finds no physical cause for the stomach pains. Other questions yield information that the school environment is stressful as a result of tension among various ethnic groups, with violence and bullying being commonplace. Although Enrique denies he is bullied, he feels isolated because he has no friends, since he is new to the neighborhood

Table 21.1. A Psychological Vision of the Person Consistent with the Theological and Philosophical Premises of the Catholic Christian Meta-Model of the Person.

The following eleven psychological premises represent a psychological understanding of the person consistent with the theological and philosophical premises of the CCMMP and with the psychological sciences. They serve as an outline that will be augmented with sub-premises that further elucidate the Meta-Model's theoretical and clinical implications for psychology and counseling. Together with the CCMMP's theological and philosophical premises, they deepen and help fill out our understanding of the person, for use in mental health practice. (In parentheses is found the name of the corresponding theological and philosophical premise.)

....

I. The person has an essential core of goodness, dignity, and value and seeks flourishing of self and others. This dignity and value is independent of age or any ability. Such a core of goodness is foundational for a person to value life, develop morally, and to flourish. (Created)

II. The person commonly experiences types of pain, suffering, anxiety, depression, or other disorders in his or her human capacities and interpersonal relationships. The person is also distressed or injured by natural causes and by others' harmful behavior. People have varying levels of conscious and non-conscious distorted experience, which express that they do not respect and love themselves or others as they should. Moreover, they often do not live according to many of their basic values. (Fallen)

III. The person, with the help of others, can find support and healing, correct harmful behaviors, and find meaning through reason and transcendence, all of which bring about personal and interpersonal flourishing. In short, there is a basis for hoping for positive change in a person's life. (Redeemed)

IV. Each human being is a body-soul unified whole with a unique personal identity that develops over time in a sociocultural context. This unity pertains to the person's whole experience. For instance, physical abuse affects the person's bodily, psychological, and spiritual life. (A Personal Unity)

V. The person flourishes by discerning, responding to, and balancing three callings: (a) called as a person to live a value-guided life while focusing on love and transcendent goals; (b) called to live out vocational commitments to others, such as being single, married, or having a distinct religious calling; and (c) called to participate in socially meaningful work, service, and leisure. (Fulfilled Through Vocation)

VI. The person is fulfilled and serves others through the ongoing development of virtue strengths, moral character, and spiritual maturity, including growth in cognitive, volitional, emotional, and relational capacities. Through effort and practice, the person achieves virtues that allow the attainment of goals and flourishing. For example, a father or a mother who develops patience, justice, forgiveness, and hopefulness is better able to flourish as a parent. (Fulfilled in Virtue)

VII. The person is intrinsically interpersonal and formed throughout life by relationships, such as those experienced with family members, romantic partners, friends, co-workers and colleagues, communities, and society. (Interpersonally Relational)

VIII. The person is in sensory-perceptual-cognitive interaction with external reality and has the use of related capacities, such as imagination and memory. Such capacities underlie many of our skills allowing us to recognize other people, communicate with them, set goals, heal memories, and appreciate beauty. (Sensory-Perceptual-Cognitive)

IX. The person has the capacity for emotion. Emotions, which involve feelings, sensory and physiological responses, and tendencies to respond (conscious or not), provide the person with knowledge of external reality, others, and self. The excess and deficit of certain emotions are important indicators of pathology, while emotional balance is commonly a sign of health. For example, when balanced, the human capacity for empathy can bring about healing for self and others, while a deficit or excess produces indifference or burnout. (Emotional)

(Table continues)

577

Table 21.1 (*continued*)

X. The person has a rational capacity. This capacity involves reason, self-consciousness, language, and sophisticated cognitive capacities, expressing multiple types of intelligence. These rational capacities can be used to facilitate psychological healing and flourishing by seeking truth about self, others, the external world, and transcendent meaning. (Rational)

XI. The person has a will that is free, in important ways, and is an agent with moral responsibility when free will is exercised. For instance, the human being has the capacity to freely give or withhold forgiveness and to be altruistic or selfish. Increases in freedom from pathology and in freedom to pursue positive life goals and honor commitments are significant for healing and flourishing. (Volitional and Free)

and school. What is clear at this point is that Enrique is experiencing high levels of anxiety and that he is resisting separating from his mother to go to school. It is possible that, in some narrow approaches to diagnosis and case conceptualization, Enrique would be simply diagnosed as having an anxiety disorder and given medication. A less narrow, but still reductionistic perspective might see his separation anxiety and school refusal as fitting perfectly within a behavioral perspective, thus leading to a behavioral treatment plan using relaxation, cognitive restructuring, or a hierarchy of desensitization.

This initial question and its resulting follow-up questions illustrates that the Meta-Model as a broad orienting framework naturally shares commonalities with the personality theories and explanatory models, which it utilizes to understand Enrique and his problems. However the information gathered is contextualized differently. For example, the approach to questioning is guided by a deep respect for the vocation of Mr. and Mrs. Garcia as parents. Certainly the questions yield information about valuable dimensions of the person, such as emotionality (Enrique's anxiety), sensory-perceptual-cognitive factors (Enrique's psychosomatic symptoms), and interpersonal factors (social isolation at school). All of this information, however, is also seen in the context of how these factors limit Enrique's volitional capacities to freely act in ways that are flourishing.

Question 2:

How would you describe your approach to parenting? Are you (as his father and mother) in basic agreement on parenting? What is your relationship with your son like?

The Meta-Model sees parents as the primary source of the intellectual, psychological, moral, and spiritual formation of their children. The Meta-Model assumes that a core part of the personal identity of spouses, the feelings of oneness and success in marriage, and the healthy development of children depend upon cooperative parenting. In addition, the quality of mother-son and father-son relationships are seen as vital in the development of their children and also greatly influence their satisfaction as parents. Questions in this area uncover that Mr. and Mrs.

Garcia have very different parenting styles. Mr. Garcia believes Mrs. Garcia to be too permissive and not firm in the way she disciplines Enrique. Mrs. Garcia believes Mr. Garcia is too harsh. Neither of them finds it possible to discuss the differences. Mr. Garcia says he usually just gives in, since Mrs. Garcia gets very upset with his attempt to take an active and firm approach to parenting their son. Consequently, because of long work hours, tension between him and his son, and feeling marginalized in his role as father, Mr. Garcia feels more distant from his son than he would like. Mrs. Garcia also worries about this distance between father and son. In a separate interview, Enrique also expresses a wish for a closer relationship with his father. Although he feels very close to his mother, Enrique expresses considerable worry about his mother. He states "that she is always crying" and that she warns him when going to school or playing in the neighborhood "be careful out there, it's very dangerous!" Enrique notes that sometimes he just stays in to avoid worrying his mother.

With the understanding of the CCMMP, a clinician would then proceed to use different relational theories, such as family systems theory, marital communication theory, and attachment theory. Using this approach, the clinician engages in a broader diagnostic picture, which exceeds the simple diagnosis of separation anxiety with school refusal. The vocational perspective of the Meta-Model allows the clinician to see that long before Enrique's anxiety developed, Mr. and Mrs. Garcia had significant problems in their co-parenting. Contributing to their problems in co-parenting, and a problem in its own right, is the challenge that the spouses have in communicating with each other and working as a team. We also see that the relationship between father and son is distant and far from the warm relationship that would be good for both father and son. Furthermore, the anxiety that Enrique's mother is experiencing about Enrique's safety is likely also contributing to Enrique's problems in going to school.

In summary, Question 2 reveals the emphasis of the interest that the clinician utilizing the Meta-Model has in examining vocational and interpersonal factors as contributing to the development of problems, but also as likely ways that problems can be resolved and flourishing established. In this case, the Meta-Model promotes the clinician's interest in the vocational issues of the quality of co-parenting, the effectiveness of marital communication, as well as the importance of sex roles and sex complementarity in parenting. It also becomes clear that the clinician has expanded the interest from Enrique's emotional functioning to include also the emotional life of the mother's struggles with her own anxiety. Note that this broadening to the family-level is supported by the use of a family systems framework but is not identical to it, since the vocation-focused emphasis is something not present either in family systems theory or in the many existing marital therapy approaches.

Question 3:

What are some positive qualities and strengths that you see in your son?

The Meta-Model is not primarily a deficit- or pathology-based model of the human person. Although it is important to obtain a DSM-5 diagnosis and to understand the deficits that are present, the end goal of diagnosis, case formulation, and treatment planning is not simply the amelioration of problems but the attainment of flourishing. Positive character strengths, successful relationships, and other human goods such as health and intellectual strengths all help clients address problems and help facilitate flourishing, and so they must be understood and brought into the case conceptualization process. In this case, questioning of parents and Enrique himself reveal a young boy who had been able to establish good friendships and who had possessed general competence in his school performance prior to the move to the East Coast. From a vocational perspective, he has a number of strengths: basic sense of right and wrong, pro-social values, general respect for his parents, past success in school, a desire to do well in school, past ability to get along with teachers, ability to form friends at school and in his prior church community, a positive stance toward God and going to church, a prayer life, desire to help others in need, willingness to serve his family by doing chores. Although real problems exist currently with his non-attendance of school, lack of friends in his new school, and tension and distance in his relationship with his father, it is important not to lose sight of the strengths as they relate to his vocation as a son within a family and

as a student. In summary, Question 3 illustrates how the clinician employing the Meta-Model contextualizes existing problems through an analysis of the client's strengths and the end goal of flourishing rather than simply the absence of symptoms. In this case, the clinician sees the strengths in Enrique's past in terms of moral development (sense of right and wrong) and virtues (respect for parents), positive stance toward God (involvement in church and family prayer), and past ability to form friendships. Again, it should be noted that clearly many clinicians, especially those influenced by positive psychology, would see the importance of these character strengths. What is unique to the Meta-Model is how character strengths and other positive human capacities are explored in a disciplined and consistent manner for all cases, and in addition are considered within the context of each type of vocational calling: (a) successfully and responsibly living life as a spouse, father or mother, son or daughter, (b) living a morally good life and being in relationship with the Transcendent, and (c) being successful in one's life of sacrifice and services within the family, work world (or school environment, for Enrique), and community.

Question 4:

What is your marriage like? What are the things you like most about it? What are the things that you wish were different?

Using the CCMMP's vocational perspective, the clinician understands that Enrique's vocation as a son is embedded in the marital vocation of his parents, and that Enrique and his parents also share a common family life, and, of course, that Enrique's vocation as a son within his family is a preparation for his adult commitments. Confidence in the importance of taking a vocational

perspective allows the clinician to ask questions of the parents about their marital relationship, questions that are typically not examined in many situations where the individual child is seen as the only level of analysis. Questioning of the Garcia couple results in some very important information coming to light. Mrs. Garcia states unequivocally that she feels blessed to have Mr. Garcia in her life, and finds it hard to believe that he has stayed with her through all of the adversity they have faced as immigrants and the troubles that her own personal struggles have brought to the marriage. When questioned further, Mrs. Garcia shares that she has always felt very insecure in relationships. She tearfully recounts how her parents abandoned her when she was two years old and that she was raised by her grandparents. She smiles as she speaks about how much she loves her grandparents who are now deceased. Upon gentle questioning about her life growing up, she again teared up as she described that about three years before she met Mr. Garcia she had had a boyfriend who abandoned her when she became pregnant. She was committed to keeping the baby, but it died during childbirth. Mrs. Garcia stated that she still cries every night about the loss of that child. She states with determination "I will never lose another child again." As Mrs. Garcia tears up, Mr. Garcia reaches over to hold her hand. He comforts her saying, "I will never leave you" and "I will protect our son."

Mr. Garcia goes on to say that he values how strong and good his wife is given all she has been through. He does express, however, his frustration that her fears make her overprotective of their son, and sometimes put the couple at odds with each other. He states, "I want to be closer to my son, to be a real father to him, to help him understand what a man is, but most of the time there is no room for me to get into his life because of the long hours of my job and, when I am finally at home, the closeness of my son and wife." These answers to this question have exposed the deep existential issues existing in this family. We also see again that the problems this family is facing are not Enrique's alone. We see some very important individual issues in terms of attachment wounds and unresolved grief affecting Mrs. Garcia that are likely contributing to the anxiety experienced by the son. We see the deep desire for a more active role in fathering and the desire for a better father-son relationship expressed by Mr. Garcia; we see also the possibility that such active fathering and deepening of father-son relationship might also build confidence and decrease anxiety in his son. More involvement by Mr. Garcia may also relieve some of Mrs. Garcia's anxiety that she alone is responsible for meeting her son's needs and keeping him safe.

In summary, Question 4 again reveals the importance that the clinician places on vocational callings. True healing must enable Enrique to successfully live out his current vocational calling as a son, and Mr. and Mrs. Garcia to live out their vocational callings as spouses and parents. Such vocational callings involve the relational dimension of the person. Therefore, we see the clinician's desire to understand the father-son and mother-son relationships, as well as the early attachment difficulties that Mrs. Garcia has experienced.

Given the Meta-Model's premise that the person is a unified whole, the clinician also seeks to understand the rational dimension of family members. This is evidenced by the uncovering of important cognitions that are central to understanding the case and planning treatment. These include Mrs. Garcia's desperate and fearful cognition underlying her statement "I will never lose another child again" as well as Mr. Garcia's positive statements "I will never leave you [his wife]" and "I want to be close to my son."

Question 5:

Do you have a connection with any religion or faith tradition?

The Meta-Model posits that religion and faith traditions often are central to one's identity and that they can give meaning to life and support in the face of life's difficulties (Johnson, 2007; McMinn & Campbell, 2007; Rosmarin, 2018). For many believers, the practice of religion is in some senses secondary to their personal relationship with the Transcendent. The clinician using the CCMMP would be negligent not to explore this dimension and, of course, must be skillful and tactful in such exploration, especially in cases where the client or family members do not identify these areas as being important. In the current case, Mr. and Mrs. Garcia attended a Baptist church on the West Coast and felt like part of their faith community. Mrs. Garcia states that she was especially involved with her church. She had friendships with other women at the church who were mothers, and she had "safe" places to bring her son to play with other children while she visited these friends. Both parents share that they have a family prayer that they say together and that they read from the Bible on Sundays. Nevertheless, they have not yet connected with any church since their move. Such information reveals the family had found fulfillment, relationship, and support in their prior involvement with their church community, which is lacking at present. One can reasonably imagine that connection with a faith community would bring new resources not only for Enrique's problems, but for the Garcia family overall. Since it is possible that some or many of the members of their local faith community may also share cultural backgrounds and life experiences similar to those of Mr. and Mrs. Garcia,

reconnecting with a faith community may also relieve some of the intense isolation the family is experiencing.

In summary, Question 5 demonstrates how the clinician understands the importance that the relationship with the Transcendent and faith life may have for clients' lives. This dimension of the person is linked closely to the dimension of the person as interpersonal. This is seen in the case of the Garcia family in that religion and spiritual practices are intricately related to the interpersonal support they received in the past from their church community, which in this case is also closely related to their cultural identity. The clinician using the Meta-Model also understands that the vocational calling to relationship with the Transcendent is a reality that for many clients shapes their whole identity and that gives meaning, contentment, and purpose to marriage, family life, and career choice, as well as, more generally, to life's struggles and sacrifices.

Question 5 also illustrates that the clinician applying the Meta-Model in case conceptualization views all dimensions of the person as being interrelated and thus important to explore. This is why a mental health professional adopting the Meta-Model framework and engaging in case conceptualization can begin with what in more reductionistic approaches could seem like a simple case of separation anxiety, and end up inquiring about the individual, interpersonal, vocational, and spiritual flourishing of all individuals within the family, as well as the strengths and deficits within the couple-level and family relationships.

Summary of Insights from the Brief Case Conceptualization

Although the previous example was brief, and far from what a full case conceptualization would produce, nonetheless some valuable aspects of the use of the Meta-Model are evident.

First, the use of the CCMMP obliges mental health professionals not to begin to narrow their focus too early, as could easily occur if the purpose of the intake interview were simply aimed at arriving at a DSM-5 diagnosis with the preformed goal of symptom reduction. Since the Meta-Model requires many dimensions of the person to be explored, it serves to prevent the clinician from becoming too directed by a single personality theory or therapeutic model in what questions are asked, in settling on "the problem," and in explaining why the problem developed. In the case of Enrique, a quick diagnosis of "anxiety disorder," or a behaviorally limited account of why Enrique's school refusal was occurring, is avoided by the clinician's making a broader inquiry about the lives of both Enrique and his parents.

The scope of questioning is heavily influenced by the Meta-Model's demand that Enrique be viewed not just as an individual, but as intrinsically interpersonal and embedded in vocational callings. This expands the breadth of questioning to include the flourishing of Mr. Garcia, Mrs. Garcia, the Garcias' marriage, the father-son relationship, the mother-son relationship, and the whole family. As these areas are explored, it is evident that this broader inquiry into both the individual functioning of each of the family members, the relationships within the family, and the family as a whole add valuable understanding of the nature of not only Enrique's problems, but also those of others within the family.

This broadening of focus results in a rich-

er and more expanded understanding of the complexity of the person in terms of positive strengths and areas of flourishing that exist alongside psychological problems and areas of non-flourishing. In the current case, we see that indeed Enrique likely has an anxiety disorder, that non-attendance at school is a problem, that the relationship between father and son needs to be strengthened, that Mrs. Garcia has long-standing issues related to attachment, loss, and grief that affect her flourishing and that of her mother-son and spousal relationships, that the parents could use help both in their marital communication and in developing a cooperative co-parenting approach, and that the family is feeling isolated. At the same time we see a little boy who had flourished prior to the move and who wants closeness to his father. We see that Mr. and Mrs. Garcia both love each other and their son and are committed to each other, that they have some insight into their family's problems and are seeking help, and that they have spiritual resources available to assist them in addressing their problems.

This case also gives some example of how the use of the CCMMP framework in case conceptualization depends on the judicious use of the explanatory power of a number of personality theories and therapy models. For this case, within the matrix of the CCMMP framework (especially its understanding of the nature of marriage and family life), the clinician is able to utilize and consolidate the Biopsychosocial Model, cognitive-behavioral perspectives, character strengths and virtues, attachment and other interpersonal theories, family systems theory, marital communication theory, cultural diversity perspectives, and spirituality and the faith community.

The Meta-Model also shapes treatment planning and intervention. Although it is possible that the use of medication or behavioral techniques (or both) may prove useful for Enrique, by using the Meta-Model framework, we also see that using these interventions alone may not result in a lasting resolution of Enrique's anxiety. We can also be fairly certain that it would not address the broader problems that affect Enrique, namely the difficulties his parents have in cooperative parenting, the impact that his mother's anxiety and grief have on him and the family as a whole, and the distant relationship he has with his father. In fact, the rich understanding provided by using the Meta-Model as a framework for case conceptualization may also result in wiser decisions about the proper level (or levels) and timing of interventions. In the case of Enrique, the level of seriousness of his lack of attendance at school might result in the use of some behavioral techniques or medication immediately as a temporary solution, but it is also quite possible that some focus on the father-son relationship, marital communication and co-parenting, or grief work for Mrs. Garcia would be initiated concurrently. It might prove that the Garcia family would see reconnection with a faith community as a part of the solution to some of the anxiety and isolation the family is experiencing, and that this reconnection might be the easiest and quickest first step of a comprehensive treatment plan.

Concluding Remarks

A primary benefit of the use of the CCMMP framework is that it ensures that the clinician avoids the reductionism that is both a common and natural result of many factors, including (a) the longstanding history of reductionistic theoretical models in the mental health field, (b) the traditional way clinicians are trained in graduate school, (c) the emergence of so many areas of specialization that the "generalist" skills of the clinician are either lacking or diminished, (d) the tendency to overlearn and use only a few treatment models and to become overly limited by the information deemed important by these models, and (e) the lack of a truly comprehensive framework for understanding the person that can be applied to clinical work in a disciplined and consistent manner.

By avoiding such reductionism, the clinician is more able to do justice to clients by understanding them more fully, seeing the whole range of difficulties that need addressing, and offering a more complete treatment plan for assisting them in resolving problems and achieving flourishing.

REFERENCES

Bach, P., & Moran, D. (2008). *ACT in practice: Case conceptualization in acceptance and commitment therapy*. Oakland, CA: New Harbinger Publications.

Berk, L. E. (2010) *Exploring lifespan development*. Boston, MA: Allyn & Bacon.

Berman, P. (2015). *Case conceptualization and treatment planning: Integrating theory with clinical practice* (3rd ed.). Los Angeles, CA: Sage.

Bornstein, R. F. (2018). From symptom to process: Case formulation, clinical utility, and PDM-2. *Psychoanalytic Psychology, 35*(3), 351–356. doi:10.1037/pap0000191

Bowlby, J. (1969). *Attachment and loss: Vol. 1. Attachment*. New York, NY: Basic Books.

Bowlby, J. (1973). *Attachment and loss: Vol. 2. Separation: Anxiety and anger*. New York, NY: Basic Books.

Campbell, W. H., & Rohrbaugh, R. M. (2006). *The biopsychosocial formulation manual: A guide for* mental health professionals. New York, NY: Routledge.

Cuthbert, B. N. (2014). Research domain criteria: Toward future psychiatric nosology. *Asian Journal of Psychiatry, 7*, 4–5. doi:10.1016/j.ajp.2013.12.007

Dunn, R., Callahan, J. L., Farnsworth, J. K., & Watkins, C. E., Jr. (2017). A proposed framework for addressing supervisee-supervisor value conflict. *The Clinical Supervisor, 36*(2), 203–222. doi:10.1080/07325223.2016.1246395

Eells, T. (Ed.). (2007). *Handbook of case formulation* (2nd ed.). New York, NY: Guilford.

Farnsworth, J. K., & Callahan, J. L. (2013). A model for addressing client–clinician value conflict. *Training and Education in Professional Psychology, 7*(3), 205–214. doi:10.1037/a0032216

Frank, R., & Davidson, J. (2014). *The transdiagnostic road map to case formulation and treatment planning*. Oakland, CA: New Harbinger.

Goldman, R., & Greenberg, L. (2014). *Case formulations in emotion-focused therapy: Co-creating clinical maps for change*. Washington, DC: American Psychological Association.

Ingram, B. (2012). *Clinical case formulations: Matching the integrative treatment plan to the client*. Hoboken, NJ: Wiley.

Jablensky, A. (2005). Categories, dimensions and prototypes: Critical issues for psychiatric classification. *Psychopathology, 38*(4), 201–205. doi:10.1159/000086092

Johnson, E. L. (2007). *Foundations for soul care: A Christian psychology proposal*. Downers Grove, IL: IVP Academic.

Kress, V., & Paylo, M. (2015). *Treating those with mental disorders: A comprehensive approach to case conceptualization and treatment*. Boston, MA: Peareson Education.

Kuyken, W., Padesky, C., & Dudley, R. (2009). *Collaborative case conceptualization: Working effectively with clients in cognitive-behavioral therapy*. New York, NY: Guilford.

Main, M., Kaplan, N., & Cassidy, J. (1985). Security in infancy, childhood, and adulthood: A move to the level of representation. *Monographs of the Society for Research in Child Development, 50*(1-2), 66–104. doi:10.2307/3333827

Manassis, K. (2014). *Case formulation with children and adolescents*. New York, NY: Guilford.

Martin, G., & Pear, J. J. (2015). *Behavior modification: What it is and how to do it* (10th ed.). New York, NY: Taylor & Francis.

McMinn, M. R., & Campbell, C. D. (2007). *Integrative psychotherapy: Toward a comprehensive Christian approach*. Downers Grove, IL: InterVarsity Press.

McWilliams, N. (1999). *Psychoanalytic case formulation*. New York, NY: Guilford.

McWilliams, N. (2004). *Psychoanalytic psychotherapy: A practitioner's guide*. New York, NY: Guilford.

Needleman, L. (1999). *Cognitive case conceptualization: A guidebook for practitioners*. New York, NY: Erlbaum.

Peterson, A. L., Goodie, J. L., & Andrasik, F. (2015). Introduction to biopsychosocial assessment in clinical health psychology. In F. Andrasik, J. L. Goodie, & A. L. Peterson (Eds.), *Biopsychosocial assessment in clinical health psychology* (pp. 3–7). New York, NY: Guilford.

Persons, J. (2008). *The case formulation approach to cognitive-behavior therapy*. New York, NY: Guilford.

Plante, T. G. (2012). A levels-of-explanation approach: Using a biopsychosocialspiritual and evidence-based model. In S. P. Greggo & T. A. Sisemore (Eds.), *Counseling and Christianity: Five approaches* (pp. 60–83). Downers Grove, IL: InterVarsity Press.

Reiter, M. (2014). *Case conceptualization in family therapy*. Boston, MA: Pearson Education.

Rosmarin, D, H. (2018). *Spirituality, religion, and cognitive-behavioral therapy: A guide for clinicians*. New York, NY: Guildford.

Slife, B. D. (2004). Theoretical challenges to therapy practice and research: The constraint of naturalism. In M. Lambert (Ed.), *Handbook of psychotherapy and behavior change* (pp. 44–83). New York, NY: Wiley.

Slife, B. D., Smith, A. M., & Burchfield, C. (2003). Psychotherapists as crypto-missionaries: An exemplar on the crossroads of history, theory, and philosophy. In D. B. Hill & M. J. Kral (Eds.), *About psychology: Essays at the crossroads of history, theory, and philosophy* (pp. 55–69). Albany, NY: SUNY Press.

Smith, K. R. (2009). Psychotherapy as applied science or moral praxis: The limitations of empirically supported treatment. *Journal of Theoretical and*

Philosophical Psychology, 29, 34–46. doi:10.1037/a0015564

Stern, D. N. (1985). *The interpersonal world of the infant: A view from psychoanalysis and developmental psychology*. New York, NY: Basic Books.

Sperry, L., Carlson, J., Sauerheber, J., & Sperry, J. (Eds.). (2015). *Psychopathology and psychotherapy: DSM-5 diagnosis, case conceptualization and treatment* (3rd ed.). New York, NY: Routledge.

Sperry, L., & Sperry, J. (2012). *Case conceptualization: Mastering this competency with ease and confidence*. New York, NY: Routledge.

Tjeltveit, A. C. (2006). To what ends? Psychotherapy goals and outcomes, the good life, and the principle of beneficence. *Psychotherapy: Theory, Research, Practice, Training, 43*, 186–200. doi:10.1037/0033-3204.43.2.186

Westmeyer, H. (2003). On the structure of case formulations. *European Journal of Psychological Assessment, 19*(3), 210–216. doi:10.1027//1015-5759.19.3.210

Winnicott, D. W. (1971). *Playing and reality*. Oxford, United Kingdom: Penguin.

Chapter 22

The Curative Factors of Group Psychotherapy

Philip Scrofani and Margaret Laracy

ABSTRACT: Little is written about Christian faith and group psychotherapy, particularly with respect to dynamic group psychotherapy. This chapter reviews the available literature and examines six of Irving Yalom's (2005) curative factors in the light of the Catholic Christian Meta-Model of the Person and of the writings of recent popes John Paul II and Benedict XVI. The chapter also sets the stage for understanding the remaining five curative factors identified by Yalom.

Group psychotherapy is a drama that one lives through. Its purpose is to engage its members in such a way as to allow personal exploration and interpersonal communication that makes a positive difference in the members' lives. However, as with the drama of great novels, plays, or cinema, the way we engage with and assimilate human experiences is shaped by our worldview. This is true for group therapists and members alike.

Considerable attention has been given to the empirical investigation of the factors that affect psychotherapy outcome. Recently, researchers have gone beyond scientific examination to look also at the philosophical assumptions behind the theories, recognizing that no approach is truly value-neutral. There has also been a movement to integrate matters of religious faith with psychological and psychiatric issues (e.g., Vitz, 1997, 2009). This thrust is fueled by recent discoveries in medicine, rehabilitation, and psychotherapy that one's faith very likely contributes to the recovery process (Kilpatrick & McCullough,

1999; also Hill & Pargament, 2003; Koenig, 1997; Koenig, King, & Carson, 2012; Plante, 1999; Rayburn, 2004; VanderWeele, 2017). Religious belief interacts with counseling and psychotherapy in at least two ways. First, according to the growing body of empirical literature, religious faith and practice could play a positive role in reducing psychological symptoms and improving mental health among those seeking treatment. Second, since no treatment approach is value-neutral, the therapists' and patients' worldviews will shape expectations, experiences, and outcomes of psychotherapy. Both points are relevant to our discussion of group psychotherapy, though the latter is a greater focus of attention in this chapter.

Christian integrative approaches to mental health intervention have focused primarily on individual and family psychotherapy. Much less has been written about how a Christian view of the person influences group psychotherapy, despite group psychotherapy's 60-year tradition and its increasing popularity with managed care. In this chapter, first we review the change agents in group therapy as they are traditionally conceived, and then we use the CCMMP along with other sources of Catholic and Christian writings as a framework for reconceiving this work on the change agents (also referred to as curative factors) from a faith-based perspective.

Before proceeding, a note is in order: For the most part, we are addressing how Catholicism informs the perspective and work of the mental health professional. In other words, we are presenting how the practitioner, looking at his work and conceiving of his clients from the perspective of the Catholic Christian Meta-Model of the Person, can deepen his understanding of the factors that influence change in the group member. However, while it is true that when the group leader and group members share a specific faith perspective some aspects of group process may be enhanced, this chapter provides a perspective on psychotherapy groups regardless of the religious faith or background of the population being served.

Group Psychotherapy as a Valid Treatment Modality

Numerous studies report that most people who receive psychotherapy experience at least moderate improvement (Lambert & Bergin, 1994). The overall efficacy of group psychotherapy in comparison to other forms of psychotherapy has been supported in research (Kaul & Bednar, 1994). Irving Yalom, a pioneer in this arena, began with his studies at Stanford and culminated with his classic work entitled *The Theory and Practice of Group Psychotherapy*, now in its fifth edition (Yalom, 2005).

Yalom derived ideas from his clinical experience and from other well-established group therapists, who aided in creating "a variegated and internally consistent inventory of therapeutic factors" (Yalom, 2005). He then researched successful group participants who supplied data on what was most helpful to them. He utilized a Q sort methodology made up of 60 items that were ranked. He also drew from research on outcome measures. The resulting effect has been one of scholarly and scientific refinement that culminated in many scientific studies (Cabral, Best, & Paton, 1975; Kivlighan & Mullison, 1988; Kivlighan & Goldfine, 1991; Sullivan & Sawilowsky, 1993). A factor analytic study by Rohrbaugh and Bartels (1975) yielded 14 clusters that resembled Yalom's original factors and gave credence to the validity of the separate constructs. Eleven primary factors are identified by Yalom (2005): instillation of hope, universality, imparting information, altruism, the corrective recapitulation of the primary family group, development of socializing tendencies, imitative behavior, interpersonal learning, group cohesiveness, catharsis, and existential factors.

More recently, other researchers and clinicians have written extensively about the therapeutic elements and benefits of group psychotherapy (Bieling, McCabe & Antony, 2009; Burlingame & Baldwin, 2011; and Corsini & Wedding, 2011). Marcus (2006) wrote a definitive article on the interactional and process components that add precision to the analysis of change factors in groups. Any serious treatment of the therapeutic factors within group psychotherapy, however, begins by taking the initial constructs identified by Irving Yalom into consideration.

What Does the Faith Integration Add to the Scientific Literature?

Although the topic is not well developed, a few thought-provoking articles have appeared that provide an integrative perspective on Christian faith and group therapy. Pingleton (1985) addressed the topic of group counseling in the church, pointing out that groups are central to the church in action and asserting that the entire New Testament calls people to live "in loving community with one another" (p. 21). Drawing from Carter and Narramore's integration of psychology and theology (Carter & Narramore, 1979), Pingleton analyzed group work in church settings specifically and, in the process, attempted to relate twelve curative factors of group therapy (including eleven taken from Yalom, 2005) to Scripture. He drew from Getz (1975), who examined a series of twelve interpersonally-related injunctions given by St. Paul (Pingleton, 1985). Pingleton proposed that "the principle curative factors ... in group psychotherapy are functionally equivalent to the scriptural principles identified by Getz (1973)." For example, the Pauline injunction to be "devoted to one another" (Romans 12:10) was identified as equivalent to the curative factor of group cohesiveness (see Pingleton, 1985, Table 1).

Other authors have also attempted to integrate faith with group treatment. Tschuschke and Dies (1994) reported that traditional factors like self-disclosure in groups and a sense of cohesion among the members promoted greater positive change when combined with a shared and affirmed sense of faith. Alexis Abernethy (1999) examined members' statements about God and concluded that therapists should examine not only the metaphorical meaning of religious content but also the helpful interpersonal effects of the members' disclosures about their faith. Siwy and Smith (1988), building on Pingleton, added their own views on what makes group therapy a "Christian group therapy." Two of the principles that this study proposes on the integration of faith and group psychotherapy are, first, that the essential quality of a Christian oriented group begins with "the inner attitude of faith" held by the group therapist; second, that when therapists seek "the living God," the members in group experience a qualitative difference that goes beyond the cohesiveness achieved by traditional means.

Group Therapeutic Factors from a Catholic Integrative Perspective

Here, we will draw from a number of sources in our attempt to develop an integrative Catholic view of group psychotherapy. We begin by building on the guiding principles of therapeutic change developed and validated by Yalom. We then include material from Pingleton's work, Scripture, and the Catholic Christian Meta-Model of the Person (Chapter 2, "Theological,

Philosophical, and Psychological Premises"), which comes out of the Catholic Christian tradition and is informed by works such as those of Thomas Aquinas (1273/1981), John Paul II (1979; 1994a; 1998), and Benedict XVI (2005; 2009).

To organize our efforts and to assist the reader, we have listed all of Yalom's published therapeutic factors in sequence:

Instillation of Hope
Altruism
Universality
Imparting Information
Socializing Techniques
Imitative Behavior
Interpersonal Learning
Group Cohesiveness
Existential Factors [CCMMP: Spiritual
    Factors]
Corrective Recap of the Family Group
Catharsis

In the current chapter, we discuss six factors, presented in bold in the list above, which we judged to be most pivotal at this early stage of our work. These are hope, universality, altruism, corrective recapitulation of the family group, imitative behavior, and cohesiveness. While existential factors are not addressed as a distinct factor, existential-spiritual themes and issues are pertinent throughout the discussion. The remaining factors will be treated in subsequent writings.

Hope

Numerous therapists subscribe to the notion of hope, and some take it to the level of a virtue (Frankl, 2004; Larsen, Edey, & LeMay, 2007; Moncher, 2001; Peterson & Seligman, 2004; Titus & Moncher, 2009; Yalom, 2005; and Chapter 11, "Fulfilled in Virtue"). Hope is universally necessary to healing. In modern medicine, it is well documented that patients will not comply with a doctor's orders unless they expect to improve. The same expectation brings patients back to counseling and psychotherapy. A patient will weather the side effects of treatment if he has hope for a desired outcome.

Mental health professionals are communicators of hope. They provide a positive outlook that is communicated through the therapeutic relationship. They promote alternative ways of seeing and interpreting difficult situations that are broader and truer than the patient's perspective; they track and punctuate client progress; and they affirm the client's strength to patiently persevere in the pursuit of the hoped-for good. In groups, the effect of this therapeutic stance is amplified by the communal dimension, which can bolster hope in several ways. First, when preparing a patient for entry into a group, therapists prepare potential clients by citing the evidence of client improvement in group therapy and providing reasons for the efficacy of groups. Once in the group, members learn from the therapeutic culture and do for each other what the therapist does for them. They are encouraged by the progress and graduation of more seasoned members and by positive change in their contemporaries. Seeing firsthand the change in others powerfully bolsters the hope of group members. In effect, the group setting provides multiple sources of evidence that positive change can and does occur. All of this pertains to what we might call natural hope, which could be defined as the expectation that things will get better, that some desired good can and will be attained. This natural hope, while not yet elevated to the theological or supernatural level, is a real human good.

Among the philosophical (or natural) dimensions that constitute the human person are the sensory-perceptual-cognitive, emotional, rational, volitional and relational capacities (Chapter 2, "Theological, Philosophical, and Psychological Premises"). All of these dimensions are pertinent to the group setting and are embraced by the natural experience of hope. Emotions move us toward a perceived good, toward something that speaks of flourishing. Thus, emotions are indispensable in achieving human goods and fulfillment. Although emotions assist in identifying the good, it is largely our rationality that informs us of the good, providing direction and purpose to the will. Our natural and spiritual inclination toward relationship fosters support, mutuality, and love, as we seek fulfillment and flourishing. In a well-functioning group, therapist and members represent multiple resources for rationality, relationality, and a shared sense of emotion during hopeful striving. These are part of the natural realm, which can be known by reason and so are accessible to all without regard to religious orientation.

But what is Christian hope? Pingleton (1985, p. 25) points to St. Paul's directive to "encourage one another and build up each other" (1 Thess 5:11). Such mutual encouragement is not the fruit of positive thinking, however; it is reasonable precisely because of the person of Jesus Christ, whose action in history makes possible salvation, and whose presence in the world continues. St. Paul makes this foundation for hope explicit:

> "But since we belong to the day, let us be sober, and put on the breastplate of faith and love, and for a helmet the hope of salvation. For God has destined us not for wrath but for obtaining salvation through our Lord Jesus Christ, who died for us, so that whether we are awake or asleep we may live with him" (1 Thess 5:8–10, New Revised Standard Version).

Christian hope, then, beyond the expectation of some natural good (e.g., health, children, financial stability, etc.) is the expectation of the answer to the most fundamental human desires and existential needs, which are met in Jesus Christ. We can be confident, with St. Paul, that Jesus Christ will complete what he has begun (Phil 1:6), answering the human need for happiness. Hope in this sense is not something that we produce on our own, but is a gift. Along with faith and charity, it is a theological virtue.

We can ask, then, what does the virtue of hope in the natural sense become when the person of Jesus Christ, and the notion of God's infinite love through him, come into focus? Hope becomes capitalized and advances even when the natural world fails. There is a complete paradigm shift. We express hope because we have faith in Christ; and strong, fortified belief is central to our lives. The difference is that God is present even when the day is not beautiful. He is there when the challenges in life cause distress, fear, darkness, and depression. How is this so? Because beyond the natural world the Christian sees a supernatural world that represents his ultimate end and that can absorb all the hurts along the way. There is the possibility of seeing the greater truth of our existence more clearly, that while we are finite creators, we are made with an infinite desire and destined to live for eternity with the God who is infinite. We are created beings (Chapter 17, "Created in the Image of God"), made for eternity, at the core good, but burdened by our incompleteness, contingency (dependence on something greater), suffering, restlessness, and disorder as a result of the fall (Chapter 18, "Fallen"). Yet we are gifted with the hope of resting in God and experiencing healing by virtue of his redemption of us (Chapter 19, "Redeemed"). As Pope Benedict XVI (2007) noted in his encyclical on hope, Christians are marked by their knowledge "that they have a future"; even without knowing how the details of life will unfold, they are certain that "their life will not end in emptiness" (§2). Such a perspective varies widely from that of Yalom and other existential psychotherapists, who conclude that "we are meaning-seeking creatures thrown into a world that has no intrinsic meaning" (Yalom, 2005, p. 102). By the existentialist account, one can hope for improvement, but not for an answer to the human question about ultimate meaning.

When the group leader has Christian hope, however, the group culture becomes one that is open to ultimate questions and answers to those questions. Furthermore, when a supernatural view is acknowledged and shared in the group (rather than unendorsed, ignored, or rejected, as it might be in mainstream secular therapy settings), there is the subtle unfolding of our nature as human beings. This unfolding occurs by the affirmation of faith through the example of those present or by the witnessing of revelation among the members. This establishes a distinctive and powerful group culture, one that is open to the mystery of God and thus capable of sustaining and increasing hope. We humans have the potential for what we think of as a place of deliverance and healing. This concept includes what Winnicott calls a "holding environment" or a place of nurturing and safety (Winnicott, 1965; Winnicott & Khan, 1986), but it also suggests there is far more than we will ever conceive of on earth. One's fulfillment in life at the moment is important, but it is only part of a much bigger picture; such an understanding can be supported by faith, even when the full picture is not fully understood. Hope calls upon the natural and the psychological capacities for self-understanding and on grace or spiritual support to see that the suffering, the relief, and the final end are all part of a plan. To paraphrase C. S. Lewis's words in *The Lion, the Witch and the Wardrobe*, it is the difference between "Always winter and never Christmas" and the ever-present reality of Christ and his redemptive action. It is the difference between a Narnia without Aslan, a cold and barren place, and a Narnia with Aslan, who symbolizes Christ (Lewis, 1950), or, less metaphorically, the difference in a world that is without or with Christ and his Church.

A situation in a group member's life that is for the moment fraught with suffering and lacking an immediate solution, as in a difficult marriage, becomes transformed by the sudden awareness of the example of Christ as it is witnessed by the member himself as well as his fellow group participants. What seemed hopeless now becomes a courageous effort to sacrifice for a greater good—his or her vocational calling as spouse and as parent. There is the deep awareness that pain is temporary but glory is eternal. In this context, suffering bears a meaning given by theological hope.

Universality

Many people who seek psychotherapy feel alone and look at everyone else as far more intact, and often fail to see their own intrinsic goodness and dignity. The philosophical existentialists have emphasized the reality that we are alone in our particular suffering and fear. We live and we die alone. We are brought to the precipice of despair. The existential therapist more accurately recognizes the interpersonal nature of the person and understands that we feel less alone when we meet people in similar straits. The supportiveness of groups and their members works wonders at reducing isolation. Therapy groups reduce the obstacles within us that deepen isolation. Intimacy is a salve for aloneness. Suffering and loneliness can be talked about, understood, or just experienced together with other group members. This has an element of consensual validation, which combines both the rational and relational dimensions of our nature. The simple event of one group member saying to another "I've been through something like that" or "I also have those feelings" can serve to normalize one's painful experience and to decrease feelings of shame, embarrassment, and isolation.

The emphasis, in existentialist psychotherapy, on the pain, suffering, and aloneness of the human condition is a great contribution of existentialism and is one of the keys to achieving sound mental health. The denial of this dimension of human experience is an aspect of psychological distortion that burdens the personality. To face this dimension is an initial change toward mental health, because the recognition of our disorder orients us toward the truth of our incomplete and contingent nature. In a paradoxical way, clients become healthier when they break through the façade and illusion of self-sustaining peace. The emotional suffering that results, when properly directed, can move them toward the good and toward change.

A Christian philosophical perspective on universality encompasses the common human nature that underlies our experiences of unity and division, relationship and isolation. Human nature involves a wholeness and an interpersonal relationality; it is called to flourishing and vocation, but is also marked by brokenness and vice. A Christian theological perspective on human nature views the person as created in love by God (Chapter 17), fallen and so living with the wound of Original Sin (Chapter 18), and offered redemption in Christ (Chapter 19). Because of the wound of original sin, the human plight is greater and more inclusive than the mental health struggles of clients alone; it is a universal problem. Our pain is uniquely our own—and some are afflicted by serious psychological disorder—but we are all in a state of imperfection and suffering together. Yet Christianity also asserts that we have been offered redemption from this fallen state and that, through faith, we are incorporated into the mystical Body of Christ and his Church. In that way, we may feel lost and alone at times but are never substantially marginalized or forsaken. Highlighting the Christian notion of universality, Pingleton cites Romans 15:5–6, emphasizing the injunction to "be of the same mind with one another." This "same mind" is the mind of Christ, which brings unity to the members of the Church. So in our universality, Christ joins the believer's suffering to his own and to that of the whole Church. The universality makes us of one heart. Thus, all human beings share a common nature, one that is basically good, but nonetheless wounded; furthermore, believers are bound together by faith.

The group experience brings this universality into action. A therapist who does not appreciate this healing aspect of a person's faith or who intentionally tries to disqualify it looks past a source of great strength. A therapist who affirms this point of view in group clients helps to amplify the awareness of our shared state in Christ and helps to bring a sense of redemption to the experience. Group members who have Christian faith can recognize that just as they need Christ's mercy, so too are all members—whether religious or not—in need of the same help. Furthermore, when there is a shared faith among group members it powerfully contributes to a sense of universality. To be in the shared communion in the spiritual realm is to literally be "catholic or universal" in our faith. Catholics worldwide share in the same Church with the same truths and are bound to other Christians through faith in Christ. We are one. Our accidental differences become subordinate. As St. Paul said, "There is no longer Jew or Greek, there is no longer slave or free, there is no longer male or female; for all of you are one in Christ Jesus" (Gal 3:28).

The following case description is quoted by one of the authors to illustrate at least one way that this sense of universality through faith might be manifested in a group setting:

The situation occurred in group therapy many years ago, when racial integration was still relatively new. The therapist included a black woman in a group of mostly depressed and anxious white men and women with a variety of life problems. The members were relatively new and were already feeling a sense of isolation and shame because of their need for mental health services. The therapist was planning to add another African American patient shortly thereafter, so that neither would be marginalized or isolated by their ethnicity. During the process of preparation for the group, the second African American individual had a job transfer and never joined. The first African American woman was marginalized initially and it raised some tension in a group that was just beginning to feel a sense of togetherness and sharing. It was clear that her presence was a bit of challenge for several white members who grew up in the rural south; other members were cordial but also somewhat cautious. The woman herself was continually skeptical of the members' acceptance of her. Then, a white woman, whom the African American woman had seen many times at Catholic Mass, joined the group. They had no previous friendship but suddenly the gap was breached. They practically celebrated the connection. They spoke openly about their involvement in the Church and their faith. The other members experienced a sense of relief, and the entire tenor of the interaction changed. All the members became open about their faith and its place in their struggles. The religious bond was greater than the racial difference and became a catalyst for uniting everyone at a greater level of togetherness than the mere fact that they all had psychological issues to solve. It was also a revelation to the young therapist at the time, who in the years to follow ran dozens of long term groups in which he was privileged to see this faith-based universality expressed repeatedly to the greater good of the group culture.

Altruism (Charity)

Yalom introduces altruism with a Hasidic parable (Yalom, 2005). There are two identical banquet tables with a large stew pot in the center and spoons so long that they cannot be used to bring the stew to one's own mouth. In hell, the people at the table sit in frustration, remaining hungry. In heaven, they reach out across the table and feed one another. Yalom does not stop there. Altruism is more than a mutually beneficial interchange. It includes the implicit benefit of escaping self-absorption by focusing on the needs of others. Within the Catholic Christian Meta-Model of the Person, the concept of altruism is derived from the truth that flourishing is possible only through unselfish service to others.

Group therapy is an ideal place for cultivating altruism. Initially, members may be quietly frustrated or even threatened by the presence of others, at least in part because it means there is less time and self-focus for each of them (when viewed from a purely individualized perspective). In time, there is a shift in perception. They find satisfaction in the helping of others and, in the process, come to know themselves better.

Pingleton (1985) specifically explores the factor of altruism as an example to illustrate how the curative factors proposed by psychologists can be integrated with a perspective of faith. Yalom (1975) recognizes that clients receive "from the intrinsic act of giving" (p. 13), and Pingleton points to the parallel between this notion of altruism and the teachings of Christ, such as, "It is more blessed to give than to receive" (Acts 20:35). Pingleton highlights "the serving character of giving" (see for example, Mt 5–7; Lk 9; and Jn 13) and points out that servanthood should be motivated "by an altruistic *agape* love" (p. 25). Emphasized throughout is the continuity between Yalom's perspective and the Gospel teachings on love and service.

While there are indeed parallels between altruism and Christian love, the theological virtue of charity (or love) cannot be reduced to altruism. Between a secular understanding of altruism and a Christian understanding of love there is a significant discontinuity. Unlike human altruism, God's love is without limit, and we are invited to receive and participate in this charity. Here our discussion of love runs headlong into the virtue of charity: *ordo amoris, ordo caritatis* (the order of love is the order of charity). The Christian view of charity begins with and rests in God's grace. God's grace is seen as necessary for completion of charity. We do more than give to create a society of mutual benefit. We do more than give in order to transcend our own anxiety or loneliness. We go past self-absorption. The more we see the truth of our personhood, the more we are drawn away from self and toward giving in a Godly way. When we become more open to his grace, we give because giving does his will and reflects his divine life. In the Trinitarian model, the substance of relationship itself is charity, and since human beings are "imago Dei" (created in God's image), we can share in this attribute of God and in the very life of the Trinity.

In Catholicism, furthermore, we complement scriptural sources with theological writings and doctrine that has developed over time. The following excerpt, which is taken from an article by Titus and Scrofani (2012) on a Catholic view of love, has relevance here to our treatment of altruism and its elevation in charity:

While drawing on patristic, biblical and scientific sources, in differentiated ways, a Catholic perspective focuses primarily on biblical Christian tradition constituted by the revealed Word of God (the Bible) and the apostolic tradition of doctrinal and moral teaching. The biblical and magisterial teaching construe love: as a gift that once received, calls forth a kenotic movement of self giving, following the example of Christ (Jn. 4:10; Phil. 4:5–11; John Paul, 1979); as relational and focused on other persons (Mk. 13:29–31; Benedict XVI, 2005); ... as involving service to neighbor, the poor, and the common good (John Paul, 1981, 1991; Benedict XVI, 2005; 2009) as uniquely unitive ... and as ultimately uniting all in God (1 Cor. 15:28).

Drawing from authoritative doctrinal teaching ... we affirm the importance of Jesus Christ for Christian love, as expressed in the teaching of the Second Vatican Council (*Gaudium et spes* [*GS*], 1965, n. 22). It is Christ who is united to humankind ... "He worked with human hands. He thought with human mind. He acted by human choice and loved with a human heart" (§ 22). (p. 119)

Love as the ordering principle of all Christian virtue is depicted in unsurpassed fashion by St. Paul in his first letter to the Corinthians (13:1–13): "Love is patient, love is kind; love is not envious or boastful or arrogant or rude. It does not insist on its own way.... And now faith, hope, and love abide, these three; and the greatest of these is love." Recent work in Catholic theology shows the development of thought on love and its nature. In particular, John Paul II's (2006) theology of the body communicates a profound vision of this type of unselfish, complete self-giving (in body and spirit); this *agapē* is not only the essence of marriage but the essence of any complete relationship, because it is how God relates (see also Benedict XVI, 2005). It is the prototype for all relationships (except that the conjugal aspects are confined to marriage): husband with wife, mother with child, friend with friend, fellow communicants with one another, therapist with client, and, in the group context, potentially group client with group client (sacrificing and giving of self for the psychological health and spiritual salvation of others).

There is also scientific evidence that punctuates the value of unselfish giving. In a recent study, one of the authors examined the relationship between attachment, interpersonal transactions, and a relational style that is oriented toward the best interest of others, rather than self (the person variable). One repeated finding was that relating to others with their best interest in mind (rather than for self-serving motives) correlated with the healthier aspects of attachment and with more wholesome, positive interpersonal styles (Scrofani, 2012).

In group therapy, there are two well-documented altruistic processes or dynamics that can flourish and potentially develop into an authentic manifestation of Christian charity. The more primary dynamic occurs when the therapist demonstrates unselfish giving to particular members or to the membership at large. He finds and wills the development of each person's essential goodness and beauty, despite any psychological impediments, defenses, character defects, or even burdensome moral deficiencies the group member might exhibit, seeking to look at the group members as God sees them. The therapist goes to great lengths to provide the best of the therapeutic relationship to each member. He or she is empathetic, patient, understanding, facilitating, comforting, instructive, challenging, just, prudent, and interpersonally skilled. These qualities are modeled for the membership to cultivate the tenor of their work with each other. These are all healthy and integrated expressions of emotion, reason, and

interpersonal interaction that together promote the realization of truth and of the person. This requires a quiet sacrifice of self on the part of the therapist for the benefit of the members and a willingly chosen sharing in the pain and suffering of the client through deep empathy. Members with avoidant, ambivalent, or otherwise wounded styles of attachment, in the sense understood by Bowlby and others (Bowlby, 1982, 1988; Fraley & Shaver, 2000), can through the therapist have a corrective experience of what they needed but did not receive in their early lives. It is akin to the mother discarding her rest and comfort, her very self in the moment, for the sake of the child. When it requires absorbing an aspect of the client's suffering, this movement of the therapist toward the clients can be likened to the unselfish love portrayed in the writings of John Paul II (2006) and Benedict XVI (2005, 2007). In this sense, the attitude of the therapist is elevated beyond altruism to love: a free gift offered for the total good of the other without any claim on the outcome. The response from the group members is often one of gratitude in various forms as they perceive the good will and care of the therapist. The therapist becomes a role model for clients. He encourages the same gratuitous care among the members, and as they gradually begin to experience charity in their interaction, they become role models one for another. A culture of love can then be born in a therapy group, where the good of each one is respected and sought.

The second demonstration of altruism within groups is more dramatic and more definitively a manifestation of Christian charity. In this case, the therapist sacrifices himself for the sake of the group or particular members in a climate that is not receptive to good will or is even hostile and rebellious: When members become irritated with each other; when there is dissatisfaction and disappointment; or even when there is an unconsciously driven sense of rebelliousness; or when a desire to escape prevails. These "fight-flight" postures within the membership of groups have been well documented in the study of groups, beginning with Winfred Bion (1959). More will be written of this process later in the chapter. What matters at this point in the discussion is that these processes can lead to destructive interaction, like blaming, rejecting, splitting, scapegoating, or psychological banishment. It is here that the therapist can choose to step in and show fortitude, courage, and charity by drawing the fire of unbridled discontents to himself in order to save the membership from each other. It is seldom well received, leaving the therapist temporarily attacked, and it is often experienced as distressing to the therapist. This process is captured to some degree in actual, documented statements of a group therapist cited below (although this is admittedly a decidedly abridged depiction of what generally occurs over time in the buildup):

"The group is choosing to direct all its anger at Timothy, rather than face each of your frustrations from within."

"The group is choosing to pit the newer members against the old members, rather than to face the deep disappointment the shared membership is feeling."

"The group members see in Barbara what they avoid seeing in themselves, while also avoiding the anger they feel toward me [the therapist]."

This type of intervention often directs the anger toward the messenger and helps to redirect potentially destructive interactions away from more vulnerable members. Here the therapist does what is needed at the expense of his own emotional comfort and is often left temporarily alone and marginalized. It is a more intense, lonely, complex form of self-sacrifice than in the first type, where the altruism and charity are abundantly visible and graciously received. It is here proposed that the impact is greatest to the extent that the therapist can empty himself more completely. In this case, the therapist can truly seek to be like Christ in the sense that he allows himself to be scapegoated without turning and victimizing the others. As René Girard (2003) has shown in his work, Christ was anthropologically unique as the innocent victim who did not victimize; in this sense, only Jesus Christ was (and is) capable of freeing us from the cycle of violence. In an interview, Girard (2003) had the following to say:

The Gospels tell us that to escape violence it is necessary to love one's brother completely—to abandon the violent mimesis involved in the relationship of doubles. There is no trace of it in the Father, and all that the Father asks is that we refrain from it likewise. (p. 189)

It is this love that steps out of the human processes of scapegoating and sacred violence, and it is this love that the group therapist participates in when he allows himself to be immolated in the model of Christ, accepting and absorbing the violence of the group. The degree to which the group therapist identifies with the person of Jesus Christ, he can be an agent of peace within the social microcosm of the group. This dynamic will be revisited and developed more completely in the section on cohesiveness.

Corrective Recapitulation of the Family Group

According to Yalom, a vast majority of clients who enter group therapy have had unsatisfactory experiences in their family of origin, and a great deal of corrective personality restructuring takes place during the reenactment of these primordial interpersonal events. Support for his notion runs from Freud through Sullivan, from modified dynamic therapists through object relations theorists, and even through some of the modern proponents of interpersonal therapy, Emotion-Focused Therapy, and Cognitive-Behavioral Therapy. Clients experience various transferences or have habitual interpersonal coping mechanisms that must be worked through. There may be real, exaggerated, or imagined neglect and abuse from parents that is now expected or even erroneously re-experienced in the group. Dependent clients may seek excessive nurturance from the therapist and members. Fellow group members may be inappropriately seen as competitive or disagreeable siblings. Inappropriate sexual feelings may emerge.

The group becomes invaluably therapeutic when these familial themes are felt and manifested in group to the point that they can be identified, corrected, and replaced. The group community in a sense becomes a corrective family experience that the person can draw upon to forge healthier attitudes and interactions in everyday life.

A faith-based approach to therapy, however, has the potential to go beyond the goal of correcting what was wrong in the individual's interpersonal adjustment, moving the client toward human flourishing. This horizon of full flourishing can never leave out the fact of one's family of origin, whatever wounds there may be. Nonetheless, through faith, there is a possibility of a new experience of family within the life of the Church. Finally, what is made possible through faith is a new horizon in which group members could be opened to the experience—or at least the possibility and the hope—of a lasting love, which is in God. Let us turn to look briefly at this perspective on the family given by the Church and at the difference this understanding can bring to group therapy.

In the Catholic tradition, the unique and primordial place of the family in the life of the human person—the whole person and every person—is affirmed. In his *Letter to Families*, John Paul II (1994b) articulates the desire of the Church to stand at the side of man "as he follows the paths of his earthly life" (§1), and he proceeds:

> Among these many paths, *the family is the first and the most important*. It is a path common to all, yet one which is particular, unique and unrepeatable, just as every individual is unrepeatable; it is a path from which man cannot withdraw. Indeed, a person normally comes into the world within a family and can be said to owe to the family the very fact of his existing as an individual. When he has no family, the person coming into the world develops an anguished sense of pain and loss, one which will subsequently burden his whole life. (§2)

In introducing his letter in this fashion, John Paul II gave due weight to the value of our human, familial origin. One cannot escape the reality of one's mother and father, a fact that is revealed in psychotherapy through the manifestation of transferences. John Paul II further emphasized that the Church wishes to come alongside families, with particular attention to people who suffer the wounds of a broken or absent family. Mental health practitioners share the late pope's awareness of the legacy of one's family of origin as they encounter and seek to heal family wounds.

The life of the Church is, indeed, a great help to families. For Catholics, marriage is a sacrament, one that offers the grace of Christ to help spouses live the marital bond in love, in faithfulness, and with an openness to life. For those called to marriage, this vocation gives a shape to all of life. Spouses are not only commissioned to form a mutually enriching contract with each other from the viewpoint of worldly matters (companionship, sharing, support, pleasure, etc.) but are joined in Christ and commissioned to walk together toward him, accompanying each other to heaven. Furthermore, the family, as an extension of marriage, is presented as the "domestic church," in which the love of the two spouses bears fruit in new life. Children ask a daily sacrifice, one that is difficult to live, but that is possible to live through grace.

Despite this eternal horizon, family life is wounded by sin and weakness, with some families suffering deep wounds such as abuse and divorce. In Christ, however, a new family is born. Pingleton (1985) draws from St. Paul's letter to the Romans to link this therapeutic factor with a scriptural perspective. There we read: "For as in one body we have many members, and not all the members have the same function, so we, who are many, are one body in Christ, and individually we are members one of another" (Rom 12:4–5). In this sense, each Christian person belongs one to another and each has a role to play in building up this body. Within a therapy group that is open to the perspective of faith, each group member can take his place within a new communal reality. Each has a role to play in expressing the charity of Christ. No one is dispensable. The group therapist who recognizes this fact will seek to help each member participate fully in the group.

As clients' faith is affirmed in the group setting, a transcendent horizon opens up, one that points beyond the individual members and beyond the group as a whole. While any well-facilitated group is fertile ground for corrective experiences, this interpersonal reality, even when lived within the love of God, will be limited. Christians recognize God as their only complete Father, the source of all human fatherhood. Catholics can also embrace the life of the Holy Family when their worldly family falls short. Ultimately, it is through this love, which God manifests in Christ (in the fact of the Incarnation and in the life of the Holy Family), that the human need for a relationship of love can be met. When such a horizon is introduced into a group, there is a great possibility for its members to move not only out of maladaptive patterns but into the light of love. Thus, in acknowledging the limitations of each person—therapists and group members—and the limitations of the group therapy experience, a new horizon can be introduced, that of God's infinite love, toward which the corrective experience of the group can point. In this way, old family wounds are acknowledged and addressed through the interpersonal process, within the ambit of the new reality that comes through Christ (Rev 21:5).

Imitative Behavior

Group therapists can at times symbolically represent parental figures. Just as children identify with parents, so too do group members identify with therapists. Usually members pick up superficial habits exhibited by the therapist or other members early on. This is imitative. It can be very helpful if healthy attitudes and interpersonal techniques are communicated. Identification comes later and involves the incorporation of character traits into one's personality. To imitate is to copy or even try something out. To identify is to make it part of yourself. Therapists are obliged to be aware of this process, lest they unwittingly promote attributes in their clients that are not intended, or miss opportunities to encourage characteristics that are positive.

Christian spirituality develops through the therapist's personal formation and is communicated through the therapeutic relationship (McMinn, 1996). It is in large part unspoken, just as parental characteristics often are. Clients unwittingly emulate and adopt superficial behavior, deep personality characteristics, values, and even belief systems of the therapists (Scrofani, 1996). In turn, whether or not there is explicit treatment of Christian themes within a group, there is a possibility for group members to identify with and appropriate features of the therapist that mark him as a Christian. Consider here the example of charity given above in which the group therapist accepts the role of scapegoat without retaliating in order to serve the group. This becomes a model for group members, not only in terms of external behavior, but also in the interior form of the action and in the therapist's identification with Christ. Again we will benefit from turning briefly to the work of Girard (2003), who exposes the human being as a "mimetic" creature. We are made in such a way that we imitate and identify with others. Wanting what another wants leads to rivalry and violence; indeed, for Girard, it is mimetic rivalry that gives rise to and perpetuates violence. Through a complete imitation of Christ—not only by means of mimicry but through the identification with his gaze on reality and his relationship with the Father—our mimetic tendencies can be oriented in their proper direction. What all of this means for the group therapist is that Christ's person and his implicit personal witness are indispensable.

Catholicism is rich in outward signs that represent Christ, as the Word, so if the therapist is to be true to his identity and vocation as a Catholic mental health professional, it is better to employ these outward signs purposefully rather than to communicate unintended habits. There are a number of resources in Catholic faith tradition from which the therapist can draw, and toward which the therapist can point group members should an appropriate opportunity present itself. We have *communio sanctorum* (the communion of saints), that spiritual solidarity that binds together the faithful on earth, the souls in purgatory, and the saints in heaven in the organic unity of the one mystical Body in Christ, with a constant interchange of blessings. We have the example of the canonized saints, human beings like us, who lived, enjoyed the bounty of the world, and suffered within the context of their respective circumstances, societies, and cultures, just like us, but did so in a manner that we can all hope to achieve in some fashion (Scrofani, 1999). We have the example of Christ and his continuing presence in the life of the Church through a shared baptism and the whole sacramental life. A Catholic approach to group therapy when animated by the therapist becomes a powerful medium through which to share all these gifts and graces in subtle, unspoken ways by example and in various timely and appropriate forms of professing and witnessing.

Cohesiveness

Cohesiveness is the most complex and significant therapeutic factor in the facilitation of change because it operates inseparably at both the individual and group levels of intervention. Yalom (2005) writes that "cohesiveness is broadly defined as the result of all the forces acting on all the members such that they remain in the group, or, more simply, the attractiveness of a group for its members" (p. 55). Cohesiveness in group therapy is analogous to the therapeutic relationship in individual therapy, which is a key predictor of good therapeutic outcome (Yalom, 2005); and cohesiveness, as a group-based relational phenomenon, is as effective as the therapeutic relationship for predicting outcome. Research validating the power of cohesiveness has been abundant since the beginning of the scholarly study of therapeutic factors in group therapy. In a very early study, Yalom (1967) followed five outpatient groups and found that group cohesiveness and general popularity were the strongest predictors of success. Lieberman, Yalom, and Miles (1973) studied 210 subjects from groups representing ten theoretical orientations of group practice and found that individuals in groups who measured higher on attraction to the group (an aspect of cohesiveness) made the greatest gains. Other early studies also repeatedly found that acceptance of the person by the group was one of the most powerful elements within cohesiveness (Cabral et al., 1975), and the findings have been replicated over the years.

In this section of the chapter, we will cover three aspects of cohesiveness in group therapy. First, we will examine the role of acceptance in cohesiveness. Second, we will look at the interaction of self-esteem and public esteem. Finally, we will explore a unique phenomenon in group that can help define an aspect of a Catholic approach to group leadership not previously addressed in the literature.

Acceptance. In early stages of a group, cohesiveness is enhanced by the therapist's attending to the conditions that maintain the group, such as attendance, punctuality, boundary keeping, openness, and so forth. In time, however, the group becomes progressively more stable as an entity and openness begins to occur, fostering the ability to recognize and deal with that which is problematic within the members. Effectively, as the culture or atmosphere of the group stabilizes, it becomes open to the truth of each client's plight. According to Yalom (2005), personality differences, unusual histories, and any variety of problems can all be assimilated in group therapy, so long as cohesiveness is formed, and this cohesiveness hinges primarily and most centrally on what Yalom refers to as nonjudgmental acceptance and inclusiveness.

The notion of nonjudgmental acceptance requires some qualification from the position of a Catholic approach to group psychotherapy. At the extreme, the notion is here considered naïve, whether viewed from a secularist or a faith-based viewpoint. It is obvious that some behaviors and attitudes are not acceptable from either position (as in the case of reportable incidents like child abuse or intra-group violence). However, there are fundamental differences between the Catholic and secularist positions that must be addressed with respect to the matter of nonjudgmental acceptance. By and large, the mainstream group therapist will subscribe to the humanistic notion that persons and society decide on the norms of acceptable behavior according to a subjectivist view of matters. There is no objective standard by which to assess which psychological manifestations and behaviors are consistent with the nature of the human person, except for matters that are blatantly harmful. Relativism all but dominates.

The Catholic view, on the other hand, assumes that the person is *imago Dei* (made in the image and likeness of God). This perspective of the human person has been present throughout the Judeo-Christian tradition and has been a cornerstone of the Catholic vision of the person represented by the Meta-Model under development at DMU since 1999. Recently, there have also been efforts to develop Christian therapy models such as integrative therapy (McMinn & Campbell, 2007) and *imago Dei* therapy (Dilsaver, 2009). In a Catholic Christian view of the person, therefore, each and every whole person is accepted as a gift, good and beautiful, created by God with the dignity of being made in his likeness. However, truth and goodness are understood in terms of the nature of who we are as persons, the corresponding purpose of our existence and our final ends. All psychological and behavioral manifestations are ultimately assessed in these terms, based on the objective criteria present in the person, inscribed in human nature. This is called the natural moral law. St. Paul pointed to this when he said "When Gentiles, who do not possess the law, do instinctively what the law requires, these, though not having the law, are a law to themselves" (Rom 2:14). Clients may manifest behavior that is inconsistent or in conflict with their personhood. For instance, sex outside marriage, promiscuity, abortion, and adultery are not consistent with the good of the human being. The secularist position, lacking a clear proposal about human nature, tends to avoid judgment regarding these matters.

While relativism could appear more open and accepting than a natural moral law perspective, this is paradoxically not the case. Following one's own desires in an egoistic way fails to satisfy the person. It is in living in accord with the truth that one ultimately has the greatest experience of freedom. Furthermore, an interpersonal environment is most accepting when it sees weaknesses and flaws and fully embraces the person. Consider the scriptural example, in the Gospel of John, of Jesus' encounter with the Samaritan woman at the well. Jesus points to the fact that the woman has had five husbands, but this is not experienced as a condemnation, for she goes away full of joy, saying "'Come and see

a man who told me everything I have ever done! He cannot be the Messiah, can he?'" (Jn 4:29). She is seen in all her complexity, weakness, and beauty. This is a greater experience of acceptance than hearing someone say, "Do what you like. It's all the same." Regardless of perspective (secular or Catholic), delicate issues related to relationships, sexuality, and abuse are the very kind of issues that clients need to share in the group in an atmosphere that is open and invites honest, deep reflection and consideration.

The process of acceptance in a group, when guided by Catholic principles is aimed at the freedom to share and process, a *condicio sine qua non* of therapy (an essential or requisite condition), without necessarily lending agreement to the content of what is shared. When clients present their struggles openly to their fellow members, the aim is to reward their openness with greater acceptance. However, the solution is not to be accepting at every level but to be compassionate at every level, in full recognition that some things are destructive to one's nature. Just as Christ allowed his followers time to come to know and accept him (Giussani, 1997), so too in the therapy group, time can be permitted for a group member to come to recognize and judge for himself the ways in which his actions are harming himself and others. This allows the client to see the truth and assimilate that reality, honoring and respecting the limits that the person has at the time. There is no contradiction, then, between a willingness to judge the truth and goodness of human action and the total embrace of a person, even one who continuously falls into the same areas of weakness. Just as all therapists, secular or Christian, accept and respect the client but not the pathology, it follows for issues that have detrimental psychological, ethical, and moral implications that the solution is to love the actor but not the act.

This raises another problem at a higher level. Sometimes non-acceptance and judgmental rejection occurs in a different manner within the therapeutic context, and vital opportunities for cohesiveness are missed. Worse still, cohesiveness can be hampered or impeded. Despite the sincere effort of mental health practitioners to be value neutral, sometimes diversity in terms of choices, behaviors, life styles and worldviews are selectively accepted. It is well documented and not uncommon in many groups for many Christian traditions, particularly conservative Christian traditions, to be ignored or even scrutinized as regressive and harmful, while other views are accepted wholesale, even if, from the Judeo-Christian perspective of our created personhood, they are deemed harmful. If Christian identification and beliefs are avoided, ignored, explained away as metaphors, or labeled neuroses, Christian members may have trouble adding to the cohesiveness of the group and availing themselves to the agents of change, because of their adherence to these values. On the other hand, research has shown that group cohesiveness is strengthened if one's faith-based views are respected and encouraged to be openly shared as heartfelt beliefs (although other group members can have sincere disagreement and still be helpful as cohorts) (Abernethy, 1999; Plante, 1999; Tschuschke, 1994). In a Catholic approach to group therapy, there is a forum for all views, even when they are in conflict, predicated on the principle that the human person is inherently free. (This does not imply that all views and preferences are consistent with the Catholic position on the nature of the human person, nor does it mean that they are consensually validated by the therapist). Regardless of differences among members, the truth of their humanity and personhood is discoverable and, at the core, can represent a common goodness that serves to build up cohesiveness over the course of time. The most important aspect of cohesiveness is love and caring that overrides the frustrations of all differences. Any coercion or manipulation of the client would in itself be contrary to Christian love and an affront to the dignity of the client, who must be allowed the freedom to act in accord with conscience.

Self-esteem and public esteem. The second area for consideration with regard to cohesiveness is self-esteem. As in the case of the significance of the therapeutic relations in all forms of therapy, Yalom has expanded the understanding of self-esteem in group therapy, placing it in relationship with what he deems to be "public esteem." According to Yalom, self-esteem (one's evaluation of oneself) and public esteem (the group's evaluation of a particular member) are interdependent.

The current authors have attempted to develop this notion more completely. It begins with the premise that the more the group matters (the more a member is influenced by the cohesive factors in the group), the more the person subscribes to the group's judgments regarding his interpersonal adjustment. This works well if your self-image is the same or less than the group's image of you; in other words, if you let down your defenses and recognize your shortcomings. Conversely, if your self-image is greater than the group's (you need to inflate your view of self or you rigidly defend against any real deficiencies in adjustment), you have a negative situation and the group becomes a source of personal conflict for you. You will be less influenced by the group's judgments of what you need to understand and change about yourself. The member in question will remain in conflict with the group, will shun the group's evaluations and is likely to leave or to be hopelessly marginalized in the group. We are assuming, of course, that the group is objectively in touch with deficiencies that the client needs to improve, and this accurate assessment does occur when a group is developing properly.

On the other hand, when the group successfully identifies negative aspects of a person's adjustment, and he is open to his deficiencies, accepting the painful truth of them, he becomes less inflated, and moves to try to change. The group members then change their valence toward him and elevate their evaluation of him because of his openness. He is positive to them in return, receives their judgments as instructive and caring, and feels better about his more toned-down view of himself. Public esteem is increased (group evaluation of the person increases) and positively affects self-esteem. He feels acceptable in his deficiencies and develops a sense of self-respect for his efforts to change. As this process happens repeatedly, across many members, cohesiveness is multiplied. In balance theory, this phenomenon can be explained in simple, straightforward terms: Negatively balanced triangles lead to stagnation, negatively unbalanced triangles invite change, and positively rebalanced triangles are usually reflective of positive outcome (Heider, 1958).

The entire notion can appear counterintuitive on the face of it. In effect, when a person admits to his or her shortcomings in a therapy group, a paradox occurs. The group values the virtues of courage, honesty, and openness. Yet the group also wants a person to focus on and acknowledge the truth of his weaknesses and deficiencies, and this posture becomes the very process by which his badge of honor is partially forged. His acknowledgment then reflects courage and honesty, and another virtue altogether is born, that of humility. This virtue is seldom if ever talked about in the realm of mainstream, secular therapy. It is within Christianity that humility is prized. The ancient Greeks had a notion of the cardinal virtues (justice, temperance, fortitude, and prudence), but the virtue of humility would have been alien to some. In much of the ancient Greek world, to agree to a lower status in the face of your fellow citizens would have seemed folly. Yet Scripture informs us of the paramount importance of humility in Christ's own words: "All who exalt themselves will be humbled, and all who humble themselves will be exalted" (Mt 23:12). The theme is echoed in St. Peter's words: "Humble yourselves therefore under the mighty hand of God, so that he may exalt you in due time" (1 Pet 5:6).

Humility is not self-debasement or considering oneself as worthless. Rather, it is recognizing one's shortcomings and limitations with a sense of healthy self-awareness. It is seeing the truth of our imperfection. In a context designed for people to learn about and treat psychological difficulties, group members seem intuitively aware of the value of humility. From the Catholic viewpoint, humility is not only personal but is also a dimension of our ontological state: The human being cannot fulfill the infinite desire that he finds in himself. There seems to be in all human beings the intuitive awareness that we, the only living creatures that are made for eternity and that therefore yearn for eternity, cannot ever realize this desire without our Creator. We are suspended in a fallen, humbled state without him, who is our Redeemer; or in Augustine's (401/2007) words from his *Confessions*, we are "restless until we rest in Him" (I.1.1). Clinical experience and research long ago discovered that group members draw together, become cohesive, and begin to work together in earnest, partially through the realization and witnessing of each other's imperfection, their shared, incomplete nature. When group members acknowledge a universally shared state of humility, then the existential territory of self-centeredness, aloneness, suffering, pain, and death comes into view and our need for something greater than ourselves confronts us. Pride is defeated and our natural limits come into focus; this mortification paradoxically opens the door for deliverance. In a Catholic approach to group therapy, when members look that far, either they see darkness, despair, and stark existential resignation, or they see light; and when they see light, they see love; and when they see love, they see Christ. Group therapy members are affirmed when they see their need for God, and the group context itself amplifies and helps to make the experience intellectually, psychologically, and emotionally more visible.

Sacrifice and cohesiveness. The final area for consideration with regard to cohesiveness as an agent of therapeutic change involves the role of the group therapist during a pivotal phase of group development, during which dissatisfaction, rebellion, and anger emerge. Clinical experience and research reveal that cohesiveness is not to be equated to mere comfort. Negative experiences and feelings are inevitable between and among people. Unless unpleasant emotions like fear, aloneness, anger, competition, jealousy, dissatisfaction, and the like are openly and responsibly expressed and processed in the group setting, cohesiveness is hampered. This is because these sentiments are present at some level of consciousness and cannot be avoided. Unexpressed negative feelings smolder. Research shows that cohesiveness is strengthened by the intense but modulated manifestation of these feelings in interaction, when they are processed successfully (Yalom, 2005).

In secular approaches to therapy, this inevitability is explained as the result of our competing self interests. Our personal needs come up against the group's needs or the needs of other members, and there is conflict because we want satisfaction at both levels: We want our own needs met, but we also want to be in relation to others. Relationship requires being less self-focused. The more wounded the group membership, the more prevalent this conflict becomes.

In a Christian approach to therapy, all of this is true, but the roots of the conflict are not grounded exclusively within the adjustment difficulties of the client populations; rather they are grounded in the human condition. We human beings are fallen and finite. We are confronted with a penetrating awareness of the harsh, inescapable existential realities of life: discord, insecurity, pain, aloneness, and, ultimately, death. We are at the deepest levels aware of our incomplete state; ours is a created nature made for an eternal glory we can never fully achieve through our own efforts.

This existential reality is frequently experienced most acutely at the unconscious level or is at the very least kept in the deep recesses of consciousness in most of our experiences. The group environment, however, amplifies the experience so that it dawns on us more readily and it becomes part of a primitive group process. Within the group process, this inherent dissatisfaction is an opportunity for the group therapist to enact what we view as one of the paramount benefits and goods of group therapy: bearing the anger, disappointment, and rebellion of group members without fleeing or retaliating. We briefly alluded to this phenomenon near the end of the section on altruism, and we will expand upon it here. The way this process is managed and worked through has major implications for the Catholic view of group psychotherapy.

Let's begin with the idea that has already been addressed. Buried in all of us is an awareness of our existential limitations, as well as a desire to transcend them. This gives rise to the wish and the notion that someone, some thing, or some event will deliver us from ourselves and from our plight in the world. Something fundamental to our lives is missing. This sense of loss is intensified among the psychologically distressed, but it exists in all of us. The existentialists proposed that this awareness is the sanity of recognizing the pain of our natural plight in life. In everyday life, we may seek deliverance from this state in our political and economic leaders. For the therapy client, it is initially sought in the therapist, and to some degree the status and power of the therapist is elevated to almost mythical proportions so as to make the wish seem possible. We are children hoping to be nurtured, protected, saved, and fully satisfied. The emotion is invariably amplified in process groups and therapy groups at the unconscious level of primary group process, as it was first discovered by Bion (1959). There is invariably an unconscious wish that the group therapist and the group itself will solve all problems. The process has been repeatedly documented over decades of clinical observation and research, especially with respect to Tavistock-type process groups but also in dynamic group therapy.

Yalom (2005) and others have observed these processes in psychodynamic groups. He reports that regardless of leadership style, generally, after 10 to 15 sessions of group development, the myth is dispelled. At various levels of consciousness, members will silently or overtly experience an intensified dissatisfaction with their psychological state, their relationships within and outside the group, and their plight in the world. The view of the therapist also changes from someone occupying a superior position, to one who does not meet the clients' expectations and is now seen as either incompetent, inauthentic, withholding,

or, worst of all, uncaring. This disappointment is experienced at various degrees of intensity, depending on the group. Unrealistic expectations are dashed. In the deeper recesses of human desire, the client has not been delivered from life's struggles, fears, sadness, and suffering. The therapist has not set it all right.

The unrealistic expectations are essentially a flaw in the human character that is amplified in the group setting. It is also known from experience and research that if members avoid the direct expression of this disappointment, they may attack in veiled ways. Since the relationship toward the group therapist or leader is an ambivalent one (as it is in the case of one's parents), the anger generated over his or her not fulfilling wishes often remains unconscious for some and simply unspoken for others. There is the fear of embarrassment, rejection, expulsion, or being seen as rebellious, or even the very basic need to preserve the leader in order to keep the illusion that he and his group therapy methods will eventually succeed. However, the dissatisfaction is very real, and the emotions need to be directed or displaced in some fashion. Group members find scapegoats, drop out, or develop smoldering irritation that divides membership. It is a group-wide process or a "group as a whole" phenomenon that is above and beyond the effects of each member's individual personality deficits.

This is a property of all group life, and in non-therapeutic settings it is sometimes deflected by organizational leadership to escape attack. They may choose to displace it or to find scapegoats and adversaries to spare themselves. The greater good of the group or organization is subordinated for a lesser good in the leader to preserve power, pride, security, or status. This is ineffective management that hinders rather than facilitates program development and is also well documented in organizational psychology.

In the context of group therapy, the leader must address this "destructive" potential by opening up this disappointment in him. This is difficult for therapists who may also consciously or unconsciously try to sidestep the impact of negative group sentiment. We see here the roots of self-protective human failings and even the potential for evil in the social microcosm, as it has surely been observed in society at large throughout history.

Therapists who are not trained or not inclined to deal with group process frequently use more structured techniques of group therapy, where this group dynamic is less likely to occur. They target narrow, circumscribed goals. This methodology is acceptable in the right circumstance and has yielded good results for many clients at the functional level of intervention, when the emphasis is on removing symptoms or relieving pain. Dynamic therapists aim toward broader aspects of psychological adjustment and character formation and therefore must address group process in order not to neglect their clients.

Well-trained therapists frequently weather the storm by helping membership effect "enabling" rather than "restrictive" solutions (Whitaker & Lieberman, 1964). Enabling solutions allow an expression of anger and dissatisfaction in a manner that does not produce the feared consequence, that is, the fear of being punished by the therapist or, worse, the fear of psychologically injuring the therapist (in fantasy, destroying the leader, which would result in the group's being unprotected). When an enabling solution is achieved, negative emotions can be vented, disappointments and conflicts can be expressed, and the group eventually coalesces around the solution. Positive group development can take place.

The Catholic view of psychotherapy in general and group therapy in particular takes matters much further and, we believe, closer to the true and the good. When therapy is seen from the viewpoint of our full Catholic anthropology, and specifically from the vantage point of a therapist's vocation, the notion of sacrifice emerges. In an article by Nordling and Scrofani (2009), the notion of suffering with the client is brought to light: a fuller investment in one's client requires a fuller investment in the struggles of their personhood. One of the curative components involves a caring that makes emotional demands on the therapist, especially in times of crisis.

This is not a completely foreign notion to secular practitioners. Yalom alluded indirectly to this dynamic in his work (Yalom, 2005). Clients have reported that it is often the therapist's special, unselfish caring that made the difference; compassion means to experience life's suffering together with someone. For clients, it is a shouldering the burden with them.

However, the ante is increased considerably from the view of Catholic group therapy. Here the therapist not only tries for enabling solutions but, during the thick of the process, directs the anger toward himself or herself, rather than to allow the membership to smolder, use denial or displacement, turn on each other, leave, or scapegoat someone. This requires exceptional training and skill on the therapist's part, and it is also psychologically difficult and draining. The anger is real and the disillusionment of the members is a painful truth of life. A litany of complaints and attacks emerges, as in the following sequence:

Client: "We have been in group for three months and I am not getting better; nobody is helping me."

Client: "My situation with my wife has not improved. I am still depressed."

Client: "I continue to find the other members [or so-and-so] irritating, uncaring…. No one understands and I am alone."

Therapist: "The group members are consumed with despair and beginning to turn on themselves, each other, and the group itself, when they feel in their hearts that the therapist has let them down or sold them a bill of goods…."

The above is admittedly an oversimplified depiction of many interchanges that are initially blocked by members' denial of the therapist's responsibility, but when skillfully drawn out, eventually lead to the venting of frustration, disappointment, and doubt, which can even become intense anger with a bandwagon effect. During the process, therapists have reported personally feeling rejection, guilt, resentment, anxiety, and fear, all of which they are required to temper and control in themselves.

But from the standpoint of Catholic psychotherapy, the process should be amplified rather than reduced. Most of the virtues within the therapist are engaged, beginning with fortitude, temperance, and humility. In time, membership settles down, often subdued because there is the enlightened awareness that they have run smack into the harsh existential realities of life: There is no omnipotent therapist to offer them quick solutions, and, even more penetrating, there are no complete solutions. Life is by nature incomplete.

But the current authors have observed during their experience in groups that the clients in the end recognize the therapist's courage and charitable self-sacrifice, and something special is realized: In the midst of "disappointing them," the therapist has taken on and endured their suffering rather than allow them to injure themselves and their fellows. A great lesson is achieved, and the group culture is changed forever. Here we have cohesiveness in its highest form.

This does not imply that the growth is complete at that point, or that the same processes will not have to be revisited again. But it will never be revisited in the same way. The model of self-sacrifice presented by the therapist's mortifying herself or himself for a higher good is now part of the group history. In the experience of disappointment and incompleteness, they have all seen anger and despair. In the witnessing of the therapist's self-sacrifice, they all see charity and love; and when they see love they see Christ. It is precisely in the therapist's imitation of Christ that cohesiveness is maintained and deepened.

Summary and Future Objectives

As mentioned, few writers have addressed the integration of faith-based concepts within group psychotherapy in general, and with dynamic group psychotherapy in particular. In this chapter we have reviewed the significant literature on the topic and then examined Irving Yalom's curative factors from the perspective of traditional psychology and from a Catholic perspective. In the current effort, we focused on six of Yalom's key therapeutic factors, namely, hope, universality, altruism, the corrective recapitulation of the family group, imitative behavior, and cohesiveness.

The authors found that the theological, philosophical, and psychological premises for a Catholic Christian Meta-Model of the Person (Chapter 2), in concert with other authoritative sources in Catholic tradition, were particularly helpful in organizing the material. The effort allowed for a fuller and more complete view of the human person as seen in a relationally oriented treatment setting such as group therapy. It also gave a direction to the concept of flourishing, as it is seen from the Catholic perspective. A second project is in the planning stages to address the remaining curative factors, including imparting information, socializing techniques, interpersonal learning, existential factors, and catharsis, although some of these factors were at least partially addressed here.

REFERENCES

Abernethy, A. (1999). Group cohesion: Maximizing healing in group therapy. *Journal of Psychology and Christianity, 18,* 276–279.

Aquinas, T. (1981). *Summa theologica* (Fathers of the English Dominican Province, Trans.). Notre Dame, IN: Christian Classics. (Original work composed 1265–1273)

Augustine. (2007). *Confessions* (2nd ed.) (M. P. Foley, Ed., & F. J. Sheed, Trans). New York, NY: Hackett. (Original work composed 397–401)

Benedict XVI. (2005). *Deus caritas est* [Encyclical, on Christian love]. Vatican City, Vatican: Libreria Editrice Vaticana.

Benedict XVI. (2007). *Spe salvi* [Encyclical, on Christian hope]. Vatican City, Vatican: Libreria Editrice Vaticana.

Benedict XVI. (2009). *Caritas in veritate* [Encyclical, on integral human development in charity and truth]. Vatican City, Vatican: Libreria Editrice Vaticana.

Bieling, P. J., McCabe, R. E., & Antony, M. M. (2006). *Cognitive-behavioral therapy in groups.* New York, NY: Guilford.

Bion, W. (1959). *Experiences in groups and other papers.* New York, NY: Basic Books.

Bowlby, J. (1982). *Attachment and loss: Vol. 1. Attachment* (2nd ed.). New York, NY: Basic Books. (Original work published 1969)

Bowlby, J. (1988). *A secure base: Clinical applications of attachment theory.* London, United Kingdom: Routledge.

Burlingame, G., & Baldwin, S. (2011). *Group therapy.* Washington, DC: American Psychiatric Association.

Cabral, R., Best, J., & Paton, A. (1975). Patients' and observers' assessments of progress and outcome in group psychotherapy: A follow-up study. *American Journal of Psychiatry, 132,* 1052–1054.

Carter, J., & Narramore, B. (1979). *The integration of psychology and theology.* Grand Rapids, MI: Zondervan.

Corsini, R., & Wedding, D. (2011). *Current psychotherapies.* Belmont, CA: Brooks/Cole.

Dilsaver, G. C. (2009). *Imago Dei psychotherapy: A Catholic conceptualization.* Ave Maria, FL: Sapientia Press.

Kilpatrick, S. D., & McCullough, M. E. (1999). Religion and spirituality in rehabilitation psychology. *Rehabilitation Psychology, 44,* 388–402.

Frankl, V. (2004). *Man's search for meaning: An introduction to logotherapy.* Boston, MA: Beacon.

Fraley, R. C., & Shaver, P. R. (2000). Adult romantic attachment: Theoretical developments, emerging controversies, and unanswered questions. *Review of General Psychology, 4,* 132–154.

Getz, G. (1973). *Building up one another.* Wheaton, IL: Victor.

Getz, G. (1975). *The measure of a church.* Glendale, CA: Regal.

Girard, R. (2003). *The Girard reader* (J. G. Williams, Ed.). New York, NY: Crossroad Publishing.

Giussani, L. (1997). *The religious sense* (J. Zucchi, Trans.). Montreal, Canada: McGill-Queen's University Press.

Guissani, L. (1998). *At the origin of the Christian claim* (V. Hewitt, Trans.). Montreal, Canada: McGill-Queens University Press

Heider, F. (1958). *The psychology of interpersonal relations.* New York, NY: Wiley.

Hill, P. C., & Pargament, K. I. (2003). Advances in the

conceptualization and measurement of religion and spirituality: Implications for physical and mental health research. *American Psychology, 58,* 64–74.

John Paul II. (1979). *Redemptor hominis* [Encyclical, on the Redeemer of man]. Vatican City, Vatican: Libreria Editrice Vaticana.

John Paul II. (1994a). *Crossing the threshold of hope* (V. Messori, Ed.). New York, NY: Knopf.

John Paul II. (1994b, February 2). *Gratissimam sane* [Letter to families]. Vatican City, Vatican: Libreria Editrice Vaticana.

John Paul II. (1998). *Fides et ratio* [Encyclical, on the relationship between faith and reason]. Vatican City, Vatican: Libreria Editrice Vaticana.

John Paul II. (2006). *Man and woman he created them: A theology of the body* (M. Waldstein, Trans.). Boston, MA: Pauline Books & Media.

Kaul, T., & Bednar, R. (1994). Experiential group research: Can the cannon fire? In S. Garfield & A. Bergin (Eds.), *Handbook of psychotherapy and an empirical analysis* (4th ed., pp. 201–203). New York, NY: Wiley.

Kivlighan, D., & Goldfine, D. (1991). Endorsement of therapeutic factors as a function of stage of group development and participant interpersonal attitudes. *Journal of Counseling Psychology, 38,* 150–158.

Kivlighan, D., & Mullison, D. (1988). Participants' perceptions of therapeutic factors in group counseling: The role of interpersonal style and stage of group development. *Small Group Behavior, 19,* 452–468.

Koenig, H. G. (1997). *Is religion good for your health? The effects of religion on the physical and mental health.* New York, NY: Haworth Pastoral Press.

Koenig, H. G., King, D., & Carson, V. B. (Eds.). (2012). *Handbook of religion and health* (2nd ed.). New York, NY: Oxford University Press.

Lambert, M., & Bergin, A. (1994). The effectiveness of psychotherapy. In S. Garfield & A. Bergin (Eds.), *Handbook of psychotherapy and behavioral change: An empirical analysis* (4th ed., pp. 143–189). New York, NY: Wiley.

Larsen, D., Edey, W., & LeMay, L. (2007). Understanding the role of hope in counselling: Exploring the intentional uses of hope. *Counselling Psychology Quarterly, 20,* 401–416.

Lewis, C. S. (1950). *The lion, the witch and the wardrobe.* New York, NY: HarperCollins.

Lieberman, M., Yalom, I., & Miles, M. (1973). *Encounter groups: First facts.* New York, NY: Basic Books.

Marcus, D. K. (2006) Interpersonal feedback: A social relations perspective. *International Journal of Group Psychotherapy, 56,* 173–189.

McMinn, M. R. (1996). *Psychology, theology and spirituality.* Wheaton, IL: Tyndale House.

McMinn, M. R., & Campbell, C. D. (2007). *Integrative psychotherapy.* Downers Grove, IL: InterVarsity Press.

Moncher, F. J. (2001). A psychotherapy of virtue. *Journal of Psychology and Christianity, 20,* 332–341.

Nordling, W., & Scrofani, P. (2009). Implications of a Catholic anthropology for developing a Catholic approach to psychotherapy. *Edification, 3*(1), 76–79.

Peterson, C., & Seligman, M. E. P. (2004). *Character strengths and virtues: A handbook and classification.* New York, NY: Oxford University Press.

Pingleton, J. P. (1985). Group counseling in the church: An integrative, theoretical and practical analysis. *Journal of Psychology and Theology, 13,* 21–28.

Plante, T. (1999). A collaborative relationship between professional psychology and the Roman Catholic Church: A case example and suggested principles of success. *Professional Psychology: Research and Practice, 30,* 541–546.

Rayburn, C. (2004). Religion, spirituality and health. *American Psychologist, 59,* 52–53.

Rohrbaugh, M., & Bartels, B. (1975). Participants' perceptions of curative factors in therapy and growth groups. *Small Group Behavior, 6,* 430–456.

Scrofani, P. (1996). Moral relativism and psychotherapy. *New Oxford Rev., 63,* 13–16.

Scrofani, P. (1999). The saints and our psychological well being. In J. Varacalli (Ed.), *The saints in the lives of Italian-Americans* (pp. 190–202). Stony Brook, NY: ForumItalicum.

Scrofani, P. J. (2012). *Relationships between interpersonal behavior, attachment and person attributes using brief assessment instruments.* Unpublished manuscript, Institute for the Psychological Sciences, Arlington, VA.

Siwy, J. M., & Smith, C. E. (1988). Christian group

therapy: Sitting with Job. *Journal of Psychology and Theology, 14*, 318–323.

Sullivan, P., & Sawilowsky, S. (1993, February). *Yalom's factor research: Threats to internal validity.* Paper presented at the American Group Psychotherapy Association Convention, San Diego, CA.

Titus, C., & Moncher, F. (2009). A Catholic Christian positive psychology: A virtue approach. *Edification, 3*, 57–63.

Titus, C., & Scrofani, P. (2012). The art of love: A Roman Catholic psychology of love. *Journal of Psychology and Christianity, 31*(2), 118–129.

Tschuschke, V., & Dies, R. R. (1994). Intensive analysis of therapeutic factors and outcome in long term inpatient groups. *International Journal of Group Psychotherapy, 44*(2), 185–208.

VanderWeele, T. J. (2017). Religious communities and human flourishing. *Current Directions in Psychological Science, 26*(5), 476–481.

Vitz, P. (1997). A Christian theory of personality. In R. C. Roberts & M. R. Talbot (Eds), *Limning the psyche: Explorations in Christian psychology* (pp. 20–22). Grand Rapids, MI: Eerdmans.

Vitz, P. (2009). Reconceiving personality theory from a Catholic Christian perspective. *Edification, 3*, 42–50.

Whitaker, D., & Lieberman, M. (1964). *Psychotherapy through group process.* New York, NY: Atherton Press.

Winnicott, D. W. (1965). *The maturation process and the facilitating environment.* New York, NY: International Universities Press.

Winnicott, D. W., & Khan, M. M. R. (1986). *Holding and interpretation: Fragment of an analysis.* New York, NY: Grove Press.

Yalom, I. (1967). Prediction and improvement in group psychotherapy. *Archives of General Psychiatry, 17*, 159–168.

Yalom, I. (1975). *The theory and practice of group psychotherapy* (2nd ed.). New York, NY: Basic Books.

Yalom, I. (2005). *The theory and practice of group psychotherapy* (5th ed.). New York, NY: Basic Books.

Chapter 23

Contextualizing the DSM-5

Considerations for Enriching Psychodiagnosis

Philip Scrofani and

G. Alexander Ross

ABSTRACT: After reviewing the development of the latest, fifth edition of the *Diagnostic and Statistical Manual of Mental Disorders* (DSM-5) the authors of this chapter suggest that the diagnostic categories included in the manual can better capture the fullness of the human person if they are placed within the framework of the theological, philosophical, and psychological premises of the Catholic Christian Meta-Model of the Person (CCMMP; see Chapter 2, "Theological, Philosophical, and Psychological Premises"). An example of how the CCMMP can enrich the diagnostic approach of the DSM-5 is then illustrated: the chapter applies the Meta-Model's integrated approach to avoidant personality disorder, a condition that reduces a person's capacity for relationality or interpersonal life. The chapter also discusses the relational focus of the Meta-Model by drawing on interpersonal psychology, the findings of attachment theory, and the latest research on relational processes in order to bring a more dynamic perspective to the diagnostic process.

The revision of the *Diagnostic and Statistical Manual of Mental Disorders* (DSM-5) in 2013 and the 2015 release of the *International Classification of Diseases, Tenth Revision, Clinical Modification* (ICD-10-CM) have inspired numerous research reviews and theoretical papers on the subject. In this chapter, we join this effort by suggesting a means by which the diagnostic categories of the DSM can be used more effectively when placed within a conceptual framework that encompasses the fullness of the human person, including the transcendent (that is, the spiritual and religious) aspect of human desires and development. It is noted here that when the DSM-5 was published, the authors, in anticipation of the change from the ICD-9-CM to the ICD-10-CM, included the codes from both ICD versions with each DSM-5 diagnosis, along with any related

This chapter is an expanded and revised version of a text that was originally published as "Beyond DSM-IV-TR: Some considerations for psychodiagnostics from a Catholic perspective on the person," by P. Scrofani & G. A. Ross, 2009, *Edification: Journal of the Society for Christian Psychology*, 3(1), 64–68.

descriptive material. For purposes of brevity and to minimize any confusion, we will refer only to the DSM categories and codes in this paper.

The theological, philosophical, and psychological premises for a Catholic Christian Meta-Model of the Person (Chapter 2), which we will hereafter refer to as the Meta-Model, assert that a complete approach to mental health practice must be based on carefully considered notions of the dimensions and capacities of the person. Without such a fuller perspective or framework, the quality of diagnosis, treatment planning, and intervention is reduced. Here we intend to explore how the vision of the person proposed by the Meta-Model can supply a greater framework and context by offering a set of unifying principles regarding human privation and flourishing.

The Diagnostic and Statistical Manual as a Tool in Diagnosis

The DSM is a guide for systematically ordering symptoms into categories and classifying various categories into diagnoses. By describing in a systematic manner what the client is manifesting and experiencing, it provides the practitioner with information about how to classify the problem and what the prognosis is. It also provides guidance in the selection and use of appropriate clinical interventions.

Early attempts at understanding psychopathology are similar to the beginnings of most scientific disciplines: the organization of naturally occurring events into mutually exclusive and exhaustive subcategories that then become tools of communication. Such categorization helps a mental health professional to reliably understand, describe, predict, and attempt to alter the mental disorder experienced by a client.

The search for categories of psychological disorders began in antiquity and proceeded through the Middle Ages and throughout the nineteenth century. However, it was not until the twentieth century, and more particularly at the time the DSM was first being planned and organized, that the classification process began to reflect more closely the principles of experimental science. Even then, the process was in its early stages, or what might be called alpha taxonomy (Bruner, Goodnow, & Austin, 1965). As the first DSM took form in 1952, the categorization and descriptions of mental disorders were drawn often from theoretical constructs derived from psychoanalytic theory, such as personality structures, defense mechanisms, traits, and neuroses (Adams, Luscher, & Bernat, 2001). Because this approach was based more on theoretical constructs and less on observed symptoms, the DSM was criticized for lacking reliability and validity in its application.

The second revision of the DSM, the DSM-III (American Psychiatric Association [APA], 1980) represented a major change to the criteria for classification of mental disorders. There was an attempt to stay closer to observables for which there could be greater consensual validation. Methodological innovations included more explicit diagnostic criteria, a multi-axial system, and a descriptive approach that tended to be theoretically neutral. Task forces and working groups conducted a three-stage process that involved comprehensive review of published research, reanalysis of archived data, and extensive field trials (APA, 2000, p. xxvi). The cooperative work resulted in improvements in reliability and validity and in the facilitation of fruitful scientific research in areas ranging from the impact of medications to the identification of best practices for psychotherapy.

The Underlying Model of the DSM-IV and the DSM-5

The DSM-IV was a further improvement over previous versions of the DSM but still had shortcomings, some of which have been addressed in the DSM-5. For example, users of the DSM-IV have cited deficiencies in the categorization of personality disorders or have been concerned that relational disorders are inadequately addressed (First, Bell, & Cuthbert, 2002). Dissatisfaction with the Global Assessment of Functioning scale (GAF) of the DSM-IV led to efforts by the DSM-5 task force and the World Health Organization (WHO) to separate further the concepts of mental disorder and disability, or what is seen as impairment in social, occupational, and other important areas of functioning (APA, 2013b, p. 6). To address other shortcomings, in Section 3 of the DSM-5, the manual has added assessment tools, a cultural formulation interview, and conditions for further study (APA, 2013b, p. 11). The proposed measures are intended to assist case formulation and overall assessment of persons to allow for a more informed diagnosis and treatment plan. While we agree that these are areas that might be strengthened by introducing dimensional approaches in Section 3 of the DSM-5 and by removing the Global Assessment of Functioning scale, our principal dissatisfaction continues to be that in the DSM-5, mental disorders, with their psychological pain, disability, and suffering, are not examined in the full context of what constitutes a complete and thriving person.

To provide that context, one needs to clarify a positive model or conception of human flourishing, a goal or ideal that serves to guide the diagnostic and therapeutic process not only in a contrastive diagnosis (the privation of health), but also in the assessment of resources that put the symptoms into personal context and serve

as footholds in treatment. In any field, the identification of disorder, or pathology, requires at least an implicit model of health and well-being. Medical science, for example, provides numerous parameters of both normal and superior functioning that help medical professionals identify bodily systems that may need special intervention or treatment, or alternatively to describe the patient as healthy, or even exceptional.

In the DSM, such a model of well-being has not been clearly provided, and the DSM-5 shows little improvement in this respect over earlier versions. Indeed, several of the new assessment scales developed for the DSM-5 are even more "deficit" oriented than the DSM-IV-TR (Text Revision). For example, in the case of the DSM-IV-TR, at least some indication of psychological well-being could be found within the Global Assessment of Functioning scale, where the highest level of psychological well-being was summarized as follows: "Superior function in a wide range of activities, life's problems never seem to get out of hand, is sought out by others because of his or her many positive qualities. No symptoms" (APA, 2000, p. 34).

Although this description falls short of what would constitute a comprehensive understanding of the flourishing person as developed in the Catholic Christian Meta-Model of the Person, it does suggest something about the model that was implicit in the DSM-IV-TR. "Superior functioning in a wide range of activities" implies high performance in major domains of adjustment. The individual is actively engaged in the world in a variety of areas and interests, adaptable and properly functioning in varied settings. The statement, "life's problems never seem to get out of hand," suggests self-control; the individual is levelheaded in the face of problems and competent when facing the unexpected. The person "who is sought out by others because of his or her many positive qualities" is one who has meaningful relationships with others and is interpersonally attractive. Finally, "no symptoms" implies an absence of maladaptive features.

We can summarize this model of well-being by stating that it depicts an individual who has a high level of physical and mental functioning, who is highly adaptive to life, who has the ability to control or mitigate threats from external sources, and who is actively engaged in the social world through empathy and social relationships. The traits specified are undoubtedly good. How-

ever, because the vision of human flourishing in the DSM-IV-TR recognizes little or nothing of any transcendent origin or purpose of the client it is both materialistic and reductionistic of the person. Indeed, in the same vein, some authors (Wakefield, 1992, 1999) have proposed Darwinian theory as the sole foundation for models of human adjustment, where one's theoretical considerations concentrate on issues of adaptation, survival, and the potential for propagation of the species. Yet such a reductionist focus, by excluding the moral and spiritual aspects of the person, neglects much of the nature of the person and reduces the richness of psychological life.

A Catholic Anthropology as a Diagnostic Framework for the DSM

In spite of the limitations of its view of the person and its underlying model of well-being, the DSM project remains the most rigorous and best-researched diagnostic tool available to clinical psychology, and we have no wish to question its status as a foundational tool for the mental health disciplines. However, we believe that a fuller use of the DSM that better serves clients requires an approach that encompasses a more complete range of the dimensions and capacities of the person and a wider, more enriched vision of flourishing and health. Over the years, developmental and humanistic psychologists have suggested approaches that seek this goal. Maslow (1943) posed an increasingly transcendent hierarchy of needs. Erikson offered stages of development that span a lifetime and become oriented to the welfare of future generations (Erikson, 1979; Marcia, 1966).

In an important paper, Bergin (1980) claimed that religious values provide important parameters for examining human potential and flour-

ishing. We can paraphrase his proposed values and assumptions as follows: God is supreme; personal identity is derived from the divine; self-control is employed in the pursuit of absolute values; love is primary; service is central to growth; there is commitment to marriage, procreation, and family life; responsibility is essential; acceptance of guilt, suffering, and contrition are keys to change; forgiveness is important; and meaning and purpose can be derived from reason and intellect.

While Christians may differ on the content of certain values that promote human happiness, there can be little debate among them about the source of an appropriate model of human flourishing: the person of Jesus Christ. Christians of all traditions understand that they are called to imitate Christ in their lives. Indeed, the very label "Christian" means a follower of Christ. Catholic doctrine is clear about this point. John Paul II often quoted the Second Vatican Council: "The truth is that only in the mystery of the incarnate Word does the mystery of man take on light. Christ, the final Adam ... fully reveals man to man himself and makes his supreme calling clear" (Vatican II, 1965, §22).

Yet the critical methodological question is how to put into practice this model of flourishing and health, for it is not obvious how we can incorporate the exemplarity of Christ as a framework for understanding the diagnostic categories within the DSM-5. A promising means to put into practice a Christian model of the person and well-being is provided by the anthropological principles (theological, philosophical, and psychological) that are set forth in the Catholic Christian Meta-Model. These principles suggest a diagnostic process that broadly reflects a Christian understanding of psychological flourishing as well as psychological privation. Insofar as a Christian model of well-being captures the range and content of flourishing more fully than the DSM-5, it can serve as a more complete framework for contextualizing the content of diagnostic categories as the failure to realize some dimension or capacity of personhood. Again, the Meta-Model presents a rich view of the person, which includes three theological dimensions (created, fallen, and redeemed) and eight philosophical dimensions and capacities (unified whole, called to vocation, called to a life of virtue, interpersonal, sensory-perceptual-cognitive, emotional, rational, and volitional and free). In addition, all eleven of these dimensions also have their own

psychological correlates, which allow them to be more readily used in the mental health field.

While the three theological principles of the CCMMP underline the transcendent foundation of our anthropology, in this chapter, we use explicitly only the philosophical dimensions of the person identified in the model. Furthermore, we combine these dimensions and regroup them into five conceptual categories or domains for use in our diagnostic framework. We combine sensory-perceptual with emotional processes and will refer to this domain as *perceptual-emotional*. We also combine the principle of interpersonal-relational with portions of fulfillment through vocation and will refer to it simply as *relational*. The principle of *rational* and the principle of *volitional and free* stand alone as domains. We prefer to conceptualize these categories (composed of six Meta-Model principles) as four interrelated "domains" of human action. Finally, the fifth domain that we utilize in this scheme is the principle of *personal unity*, which underscores the importance of the interconnections between the aforementioned four domains. This approach also allows us to incorporate theological (or transcendent) aspects of human nature that emerge through insights found in the Christian tradition. In order to demonstrate the advantages of the use of the Meta-Model to better contextualize and enrich the DSM-5, we will now turn to an example of its application to a specific diagnostic classification, specifically the diagnosis of avoidant personality disorder.

The Framework Applied to Avoidant Personality Disorder

Most clinicians during the course of their careers will have occasion to treat people with avoidant personality disorder (APD). The DSM-5 characteristics that are cited for this condition are summarized as follows:

A pervasive pattern of social inhibition, feelings of inadequacy, and hypersensitivity to negative evaluation, beginning by early adulthood and present in a variety of contexts, as indicated by four (or more) of the following symptoms: (1) avoids occupational activities that involve significant in-

Table 23.1. Conceptualization of Avoidant Personality Disorder (APD) on Four Domains in Terms of a Flourishing and Languishing Continuum

	Perceptual-Emotional	Rational	Volitional	Relational
Human Flourishing	accurate perception of the sensible world and pre-conscious adjudication of what attracts and repels; enduring emotional dispositions ordered in accord with what is truly good for the human person	faculty to know oneself and to make discerning judgments about one's environment; accurate intuitive and discursive judgments about what is true, good, real, and beautiful	capacity to pursue intuitively and discursively what is good for oneself and for others through responsible and free choices and self-determination	receptivity and orientation toward other persons; natural sociability expressed in relationships and more broadly within vocations that involve family, friends, colleagues, and the larger community
Human Privation (APD)	fear leading to restraint even in intimate relationships; feelings of inadequacy that distort perception and inhibit the formation of new relationships	cognitive distortion and an avoidance of truth; underestimation of one's own worth	lack of will-power to take on the risks of dealing with others; unwillingness to face and correct one's weaknesses	avoidance of interpersonal contact; restraint shown even in intimate relationships; inhibition, especially in new social settings, that can also result in a failure to achieve success in vocational commitments and one's life work

terpersonal contact, because of fears of criticism, disapproval or rejection, (2) is unwilling to get involved with people unless certain of being liked, (3) shows restraint within intimate relationships because of the fear of being shamed or ridiculed, (4) is preoccupied with being criticized or rejected in social situations, (5) is inhibited in new interpersonal situations because of feelings of inadequacy, (6) views self as socially inept, personally unappealing, or inferior to others, (7) is unusually reluctant to take personal risks or to engage in any new activities because they may prove embarrassing. (APA, 2013b, p. 328)

From the perspective of the four domains of the slightly condensed Meta-Model described above, we can locate this disorder on a series of continua of human flourishing. That is, APD can be conceptualized as a particular manifestation along four dimensions defined by the four anthropological domains. Table 23.1 may help communicate this idea. In the table, manifestations of human flourishing in each of the four domains are located at the top, while indications of privation—as illustrated in this case specifically with symptoms associated with APD— are placed at the bottom. Manifestations of human flourishing are borrowed from the Meta-Model.

Highlighting first the domain of perceptual-emotional, we can focus especially on the emotions as a capacity that inclines us to move toward or away from perceived stimuli or environmental events. Human emotional flourishing is indicated by enduring affective dispositions ordered in accord with what is truly good for the human person. In contrast to this ideal, the DSM symptoms above indicate a serious privation in this area. Symptom 3 speaks of the emotion of fear leading to inordinate restraint even in intimate relationships. Symptom 4 mentions feelings of inadequacy that inhibit the person's ability to form new relationships. Other symptoms speak of fears of rejection or criticism. Furthermore, when individuals experience fear or anxiety repeatedly or with sufficient intensity with regard to specific stimuli, such as new social situations, they can become classically conditioned to the point that the distressed responses become habitual and lead even to tissue changes that involve disorder in central nervous system stimulation, as in the case of an overly reactive amygdala or changes in biochemical reactions and RNA transfer.

These manifestations of perceptual-emotional privation are echoed in the second domain, rationality. Human flourishing in the domain of rationality includes having a balanced and truthful view of oneself (and of the world and transcendent realities). The symptomology of APD outlined above indicates at the very least an avoidance of truth, manifested in both an underestimation of one's own worth and dignity and an unwillingness to face and correct one's true weaknesses. This cognitive distortion can lead to unwarranted expectations or conclusions about social events. "People will see me with a critical eye and will reject anything that is not perfect about me." "I will be trapped in my own embarrassment." This irrational schema interacts quite readily with the previous domain, affecting perceptions and emotions in the form of dysphoria or strong distress. Thus, on a continuum from flourishing to privation we have, at one end, a truthful appraisal of one's talents and character (or at least the desire for such), and at the other, a false appraisal of self that both underrates oneself and one's goodness, and hides from opportunities to correct the falsehood.

The symptoms of APD also demonstrate a privation of volition or diminishment of freedom, the third domain. A flourishing human volition is manifested in the enduring ability to exercise one's freedom in personally and interpersonally adaptive ways; in other words, a flourishing volition is self-mastery easily exercised in human relationships. In contrast, as we see in symptom 2, an individual may lack the will to engage in social interaction with others unless assured of their positive evaluation. Or, as is evident in symptom 7, the person with APD may lack the strength of will to take on the risks of dealing with others, significantly curtailing his or her opportunities for flourishing. The will to succeed and experience the fruits of life's challenges becomes attenuated. Over time, the repetitive experience of anxiety followed by avoidance of people and situations can become so habitual as to become an almost automatic reactive stance that bypasses even the awareness that one has freedom

Finally, the symptomology of APD is perhaps most closely associated with the fourth domain, relationality. This domain reminds us that humans are naturally social with strong inclinations and needs for life in society. We are inclined naturally toward self-communicative acts of giving and receiving. Love is the highest expression of interpersonal self-communication.

Love is central in being able to live out the three levels of vocational callings that give meaning to life: the distinct responses to a call to live out goodness (and for believers, to be in relationship with the Transcendent), the ability to successfully live out our commitments in non-vowed and vowed vocational states (for example, single life, marriage, or priesthood), as well as living a life of work and service within the family and work world. Yet, without exception, the APD symptoms listed above all manifest significant privation in this important domain. The avoidance of interpersonal contact, the restraint shown even in intimate relationships, the inhibition especially in new social settings, all demonstrate how far the individual is from a level of flourishing in the domain of relationality.

Interaction Among the Domains: The Principle of Personal Unity

As the CCMMP explains, the principles of the Meta-Model are irreducible and highly interdependent. The principle of personal unity highlights the nature of the human persons in their wholeness and identity. But the principle of the person as a unified whole also acknowledges the interaction and mutual influence of the four domains of human action. In clinical practice one often sees problems arising in one domain that manifest themselves in another as well. For example, the research literature provides many illustrations of the effects of relationality on the other domains. Attachment styles forged in early parental and family relationships predict adjustment in many aspects of a person's life (Bowlby, 1999; Fraley, Waller, & Brennan, 2000). Primary relationships, such as parent-child relationships, have been shown to have a profound impact on the neural systems that govern emotional control and susceptibility to psychopathology (Beach, Wambolt, & Kaslow, 2006).

Other researchers, following their own conceptual frameworks, have provided evidence-based schemes that illustrate further the interactive nature of the anthropological domains by examining quantifiable aspects of interpersonal behavior. For example, in work over the past thirty years, Benjamin (2003) has generated dimensions of interpersonal behavior that capture with some precision the interaction of the emotional elements of interpersonal behavior with the control elements. Work by Scrofani (2012) follows portions of Benjamin's scheme and introduces an additional dimension of interpersonal interaction. He combines aspects of the emotional components of interpersonal behavior with volition (through an expansion of Benjamin's control component). He then introduces a third dimension (which he labels the "person" dimension) that casts many aspects of giving and receiving into psychologically measurable terms. This allows us to measure how the relational environment might promote either privation or flourishing in a person. It also takes relationality beyond Benjamin's parameters to an ideal of interpersonal flourishing captured by John Paul II's concept of self-giving and expressed in religiously based commitments and service (marriage and consecrated life) and in divine worship (John Paul II, 2006), which are aspects of human vocations.

Reductionist explanations that locate the primary causal agent in only one of the domains do not capture accurately the interaction among the domains; nor do materialist models that exclude moral and spiritual aspects of affection, cognition, motivation, and relationships. Rather, we think it is more appropriate to conceptualize this interaction by drawing an analogy with music; that is, as a kind of "resonating" process in which "concordant" or "discordant" patterns in one domain either enhance or impede the harmonic performance in the others. It is the whole person that must be the concern of the effective clinical practitioner.

Conclusion

Each of the four domains delineates a level of human flourishing that serves as the ideal to which a given DSM symptomology is compared. In turn, the principle of personal unity underscores the interaction of these domains and the importance of treating the human person as a whole. By framing the diagnostic process in this manner, the objectives of diagnosis, case formulation, treatment planning, and clinical intervention are made explicit for the clinician and client. Rather than the vague sense of environmental adjustment characteristic of a materialist model of health, the anthropology underlying the Meta-Model embraces a level of authentic fulfillment as the natural end of the human person, while also providing a basis for understanding divine support in these domains. And because the goal is complete human flourishing (natural and grace-assisted) rather than merely relief of symptoms, the client understands more clearly why the hard work of overcoming psychological disorder is worthwhile.

REFERENCES

Adams, H. E., Luscher, K. A., & Bernat, J. (2001). The classification of abnormal behavior: An overview. In H. E. Adams & P. B. Sutker (Eds.), *Comprehensive handbook of psychopathology* (3rd ed., pp. 3–28). New York, NY: Kluver Academic / Plenum Publishers.

American Psychiatric Association (APA). (1980). *Diagnostic and statistical manual of mental disorders* (3rd ed.). Washington, DC: Author.

American Psychiatric Association (APA). (2000). *Diagnostic and statistical manual of mental disorders* (4th ed., text revision). Washington, DC: Author.

American Psychiatric Association (APA). (2013a). *Diagnostic and statistical manual of mental disorders* (5th ed., text revision). Washington, DC: Author.

American Psychiatric Association (APA). (2013b). *Desk reference to the diagnostic criteria from the Diagnostic and statistical manual of mental disorders* (5th ed., text revision). Washington, DC: Author.

Beach, S. R., Wambolt, M. Z., & Kaslow, N. J., (Eds.). (2006). *Relational processes and the DSM-V: Neuroscience, assessment, prevention and treatment.* Washington, DC: American Psychiatric Publishing.

Benjamin, L. S. (2003). *Interpersonal diagnosis and treatment of personality disorder* (2nd ed.). New York, NY: Guilford.

Bergin, A. E. (1980). Psychotherapy and religious values. *Journal of Consulting and Clinical Psychology, 48*(1), 95–105.

Bowlby, J. (1999). *Attachment and loss: Vol. 1. Attachment* (2nd ed.). New York, NY: Basic Books.

Bruner, J. W., Goodnow, J. I., & Austin, G. A. (1965). *A study of thinking.* New York, NY: Science Editions.

Erikson, E. H. (1979). *Identity and the life cycle.* New York, NY: Norton. (Original work published 1959)

First, M. B., Bell, C. C., & Cuthbert, B. (2002). Personality disorders and relational disorders: A research agenda for addressing crucial gaps in DSM. In D. J. Kupfer, M. B. First, & D. A. Regier (Eds.), *A research agenda for DSM-V* (pp. 123–200). Washington, DC: American Psychological Association.

Fraley, R. C., Waller, N. G., & Brennan, K. A. (2000). An item response theory analysis of self-report measures of adult attachment. *Journal of Personality and Social Psychology, 78*(2), 350–365.

John Paul II. (2006). *Man and woman he created them:*

A theology of the body (M. Waldstein, Trans.). Boston, MA: Pauline Books & Media.

Marcia, J. E. (1966). Development and validation of ego identity status. *Journal of Personality and Social Psychology, 3,* 551–558.

Maslow, A. H. (1943). A theory of human motivation. *Psychological Review, 50,* 370–396.

Scrofani, P. J. (2012). *Relationships between interpersonal behavior, attachment and person attributes using brief assessment instruments.* Unpublished manuscript, Institute for the Psychological Sciences, Arlington, VA.

Vatican II, Council. (1965). *Gaudium et spes* [Pastoral constitution on the Church in the modern world]. Vatican City, Vatican: Libreria Editrice Vaticana.

Wakefield, J. C. (1992). The concept of mental disorder: On the boundary between biological facts and social values. *American Psychologist, 47,* 373–388.

Wakefield, J. C. (1999). Evolutionary versus prototype analyses of the concept of disorder. *Journal of Abnormal Psychology, 108,* 374–399.

World Health Organization. (2015). *The ICD-10-CM classification of mental and behavioural disorders: Clinical descriptions and diagnostic guidelines.* Geneva, Switzerland: Author.

Chapter 24

Psychological Assessment

FRANK J. MONCHER AND

PHILIP SCROFANI

Abstract: This chapter reviews the implications of the Catholic Christian Meta-Model of the Person for the professional task of psychological evaluation and assessment. The Meta-Model identifies a more comprehensive set of foundational principles and groups of capacities or domains of the person and flourishing that can serve as a basis for enhancing the scope of psychological assessment. This expansion would include new areas for assessment, such as interpersonal relationships, vocational callings, virtue strengths, the ability to forgive, and the freedom of the will. This chapter also discusses some widely used instruments, such as MMPI-2, Rorschach, and Wechsler scales, in light of the Meta-Model's framework for understanding the person. Finally, it outlines a few specific applications that are unique in working from a Catholic Christian perspective or in a Catholic setting—in particular, the role of assessment in the vocational discernment process for clergy and religious, and in marriage tribunal cases.

The theological and philosophical premises of the Catholic Christian Meta-Model of the Person (CCMMP), presented in Chapter 2 of this volume, present a comprehensive framework of eight philosophical premises and three additional theological premises. These eleven premises have eleven psychological analogs. Some of these identify dimensions and capacities of the person that have not typically been examined in psychological assessment. This framework includes the person as a whole, fulfilled through vocations, fulfilled in virtue, interpersonally relational, sensory-perceptual-cognitive, emotional, rational, and volitional and free, as well as being created in the image of God, fallen, and redeemed. Note that this framework introduces new areas of assessment, such as vocational callings (Chapter 10), virtues and character strengths (Chapter 11), and the spiritual life of the client (Chapter 17), that not only provide for a fuller understanding of the client and his or her dignity, but also have usefulness in their own right, since they often can serve as the context of the entire assessment itself. This chapter will focus primarily on the new dimensions that are defined by the model, with less emphasis on areas typically examined in the assessment process.

This chapter is an expanded and revised version of a text that was originally published as "Implications of Catholic anthropology for psychological assessment," F. J. Moncher, 2009, *Edification: Journal of the Society for Christian Psychology*, 3(1), 69–75.

The assessment process. A comprehensive psychological evaluation requires a clinician to gather information from a variety of assessment procedures and to interpret the results of this investigation. A theological perspective offers a vision of humans as created by God "in the image" and "after the likeness" of God (Gen 1:26), and as such humans are good and "have special dignity and value as persons," suggesting that the clinician should approach the overall assessment process with a foundational emphasis on ensuring respect for the dignity of the person evaluated, as well as evaluating whether clients are aware of their own dignity. When some or even many dimensions of the person, included in the CCMMP, are omitted from the assessment process, the result can be a reduced and impersonal representation of the client that inadequately reflects the dignity of the whole person.

During the intake process, the assessment focuses on the Meta-Model's eight philosophical premises, reviewed below. First and foremost, the clinician must carefully choose a battery of instruments that evaluate each of the dimensions or major capacities of the person (Chapter 8, "Personal Wholeness"). The evaluation process would include inquiry about the client's vocation at multiple levels, and the client's virtue strengths and weaknesses. Developing a full understanding of the client's vocations and his or her virtue strengths and weaknesses generally cannot be fully accomplished in the intake process. These dimensions of the person need to be investigated and monitored throughout therapy.

Mental health professionals have traditionally relied upon the clinical interview, existing case records, behavioral observations, and the outcomes of psychological tests to gather information about patients. Depending upon the information sought, a wide variety of functional aspects of the person can be assessed, such as the cognitive capacities of children struggling in school, the behavior of adolescents who harm themselves, the emotional state of those who have attempted suicide, the personality of those with relationship problems, and the sensory-perceptual-cognitive ability of those who have suffered brain damage. In everyday practice, professionals at times limit their attention to addressing only the presenting problem and thereby fail to capture the fullness of the person's strengths and weaknesses. Other professionals expand the focus of their inquiry beyond the presenting problem to take a larger view of the person. But often such efforts result in the accumulation of a body of relevant information that is not discussed or evaluated in a connected manner, because there is no accepted, comprehensive understanding of the person into which to integrate the findings. The Meta-Model, however, provides a template for organizing clinical impressions, observations, and test results in a coherent, systematic framework, which can then be used to promote a fuller scope of interventions and also to provide an understanding of the priority of these interventions.

After organizing the gathered information, the clinician typically generates a psychological report conceptualizing the client. In order to capture a larger characterization of the person in a report, we propose that the traditional categories used in report writing be reorganized according to the Meta-Model's domains to more thoroughly reflect the person's unique life and narrative history. For example, when using a common division within a report, such as "personality functioning," care should be given to examining how the person's personality characteristics affect his or her vocational callings (e.g., as a spouse and parent), ability to relate with others satisfactorily in a work setting, and even spiritual flourishing and transcendent goals.

This synthesized history would not only include a discussion of and recommendations for the elimination of symptoms, but would also support the larger goals that the Meta-Model presents, such as vocational commitments, and virtue and character development for personal growth and flourishing.

Contributions of the Meta-Model Premises to Assessing Specific Dimensions of the Person

In this section, we will examine the importance of the following dimensions of the Meta-Model's vision of the person for assessment: personal unity, vocations, virtues, interpersonal relationships, sensory-perceptual cognition, emotion, reason and intellect, and volition and freedom.

Personal Unity (Wholeness)

A key contribution of the CCMMP is the importance of the unity or wholeness of each person. How does this unity affect the assessment process? Even though different dimensions of the person are measured, the information gathered must also be integrated or synthesized into an understanding of the person as a whole.

This occurs in part through ensuring that all data is always considered in light of the other data collected to contextualize information and to avoid contradictory conclusions that might arise if such data is viewed in isolation. For example, there may appear to be a contradiction between a client who has a high IQ score but lacks self-knowledge, until we understand their long history of emotional abuse by parent or a long history of addiction. In addition, the foundational principles of vocation and virtue provide context for a fuller understanding of the initial observations. For example, in a marriage the weakness or vice of failure to commit become very important in understanding marital difficulties. In contrast, the character strengths of patience and perseverance form a basis for hopeful resolution of marital conflict.

Vocations

As covered in Chapter 5 ("Fulfilled Through Vocations"), there are three basic vocational callings occurring in every person's life: (a) the call to goodness, justice, and holiness (that is, the goal of personal flourishing, which might be interpreted differently according to a person's particular religious faith); (b) the call to vowed and non-vowed vocational states, such as marriage, single life, the consecrated life and priesthood; and (c) the call to work and service, paid or unpaid, that benefits the family as well as the larger community. These vocational possibilities are assessed in a modest way by a variety of scales.

Although the mental health field has not conceptualized these three types of calling in the same way as the Meta-Model, nonetheless, some assessment instruments have been developed that aid in getting information in some of these areas. For example, there are some questionnaires that assess elements of the first type of vocational calling, namely personal flourishing. Focusing on the role of purpose in vocations (Peterson & Seligman, 2004) can help the clinician to understand aspects of the person's fulfillment (Eldridge, 2012; Terranova, 2006). There are also some assessment measures that examine aspects of the second type of vocational calling to committed states of life, such as marriage. For example, there are marriage preparation scales that assess capacities and readiness for marriage as a vocation (Prepare/Enrich Inventories [Olson & Olson, 1999]; FOCCUS Pre-Marital Inventory

[Williams & Jurich, 1995).].). There are also measures, found in the Gottman scales (Gottman, 1999) and Marital Satisfaction Inventory-R (Snyder, 1997), that are used to evaluate various marital qualities, such as positive communication and problem solving, commitment, affection, and respect. There have been protocols proposed for assessing the qualities needed for vocations to religious life and priesthood (Plante & Boccaccini, 1998). And finally, the call to work and service benefiting society is primarily assessed with tests of an individual's aptitude or interests consistent with certain occupations (e.g., Campbell, 1987). Although these assessments focus on aptitudes for different jobs, they do not address service in family life or other common unpaid social contributions.

Overall, then, the concept of understanding the vocation of a client in these three different ways provides a framework for understanding the person as whole. Therefore, information gathered about specific capacities or dimensions of the person, such as reason and intellect or volition and free will, must be taken in the context of vocation. For instance, a person's IQ is primarily relevant in the context of the person's capacity to function properly in their family, work, and other vocations.

Natural and transcendent virtues and character

Since the Meta-Model views the person as being fulfilled and flourishing through the virtues, it invites assessment of a client's virtues, both natural (e.g., prudence, justice, courage, temperance) and transcendent (i.e., faith, hope, and love). The importance of virtue is gaining attention in the positive psychology movement (Peterson & Seligman, 2004; Lopez & Snyder, 2009), and some research tools have been developed in an effort to measure virtue, for instance, the Values in Action Scale (Peterson & Seligman, 2004) and the Virtues Scale (Cawley, 1997). In practice, however, virtues are rarely examined in the assessment process. A mental health professional utilizing a Meta-Model framework would measure flourishing directly and practically, by assessing a person's vocations, as mentioned above, and especially by evaluating the virtues and how they are expressed in the person and his or her vocations.

Over the past two decades there have been advances in the development of theoretical frameworks for assessing the quality of the religious-spiritual life, resources, and experiences of clients. By spiritual resources here is meant the spiritual influence active within cognition, will, emotion, and relationship. Such work has attended to religious-spiritual functioning by providing deeper accounts of human experience, for example, by distinguishing three religious orientations: quest, intrinsic, and extrinsic orientation (Allport & Ross, 1967; Hill & Hood, 1999; Koenig, King, Carson, 2012; VanderWeele, 2017a, 2017b). Despite advances, there is an inherent challenge in assessing the spiritual life, for these qualitative dispositions of a person are neither directly observable nor quantifiable, and the intangible influence of spiritual resources (including friendships and support from one's faith community) is challenging to study using statistical methods to measure. Nevertheless, a person's spiritual life can be assessed indirectly through its effects as expressed in language and behavior. For example, Christianity has a long tradition of identifying goodness and holiness in terms of a person's living the virtues heroically and in fidelity to God's will. This assessment is made by observing the person's acts and words, which reflect the internal thoughts, intentions, and desires.

While the goal of psychological assessment

is not intended to discern a person's holiness, it can nonetheless allow a mental health professional to come to some understanding of clients' spiritual life through self-reports, and to understand the impact of their spiritual life on their psychological functioning by employing various inquiries and approaches. An example for assessment in the spiritual domain is found in Hodge (2007). One of the very first measures was based on the classic distinction between extrinsic and intrinsic religiosity (Allport & Ross, 1967; Donahue, 1985). There are also now a variety of measures of religiosity (e.g., Hill & Hood, 1999; VanderWeele 2017a, 2017b). In addition, there are many studies that show the strong effect of a religiously informed or practiced life on health, general well-being, and on recovery from trauma (e.g., Koenig et al., 2012). Although spiritual-religious experience transcends statistical measurement, its higher aspects should be acknowledged as vital to assessment and, for believers, should be used in developing a treatment plan that considers a client's complete range of strengths and weaknesses. It is therefore unfortunate that standard assessment methods rarely include even one measure of the person's spiritual life. We hope that the present Meta-Model will contribute to correcting this oversight.

Historically as well, some efforts have been made at measuring moral development from a cognitive perspective (Kohlberg, 1981), though the success of these efforts has been found wanting (Gilligan, 1982; Vitz, 1994). Consistent with the Meta-Model's account of the person, however, more recent work on moral development has begun to integrate self-control, empathy, and interpersonal factors (attachment) with cognition (e.g., Gibbs, 2003; Hoffman, 2000). While discussion of the development of additional measures is beyond the scope of this commentary, it is worth noting that methods of measuring a person's rational capacity to know themselves, God, beauty, and morality would enhance the mental health professional's ability to understand clients more fully (Laracy, 2011).

Interpersonal Relationship Capacities

The Meta-Model's vision of the person indicates the importance of assessing relational functioning, which would include evaluating clients' vocational callings, such as their relationships with spouse and children in the case of married clients. Assessment of interpersonal relationship capacities requires that the clinician understand the functioning of the person's family, as well as the person's interpersonal acts of giving and receiving love, relationship with God, friendships, and connections to others in the local community. Common assessment methods include measures of interpersonal style (e.g., SASB-IS; see Benjamin, 2003), some subscales of standardized personality inventories, social skills (e.g., through behavioral observations), attachment behavior (e.g., Adult Attachment Interview, George, Kaplan, & Main, 1985), and marital and family dynamics (e.g., Sound Marital House Questionnaires, Gottman, 1999; circumplex model, Olsen, Russell & Sprenkle, 1989). Each of these approaches provides insight into the relational aspect of a person's functioning and thus is beneficial to the overall understanding of the human person. However, critical aspects of relational functioning, reflected in the Catholic Christian vision of the person, are not fully addressed. For example, missing aspects include the core components of one's ability to give and receive love and to establish authentic and healthy friendships in one's community.

However, the Person Scale, developed by Scrofani (2019), represents an effort to evaluate aspects of relational functioning by assessing key areas of interpersonal behavior related to self-giving. Scrofani builds upon schemes developed by Schaefer (1965) and Benjamin (2003) and goes beyond their approaches in assessing the dyadic dynamics of interpersonal expression. Schaefer and Benjamin characterize the active relationality of participants as falling in the dimensions of affection (love to hate) and autonomy (freedom to control), with wholesome and healthy relationships occupying the interactive quadrant characterized by positive affection and an ideal balance of freedom and commitment. For instance in a parental or spousal relationship characterized by warm caring and respect for the other's autonomy, both parties feel wanted and yet have a healthy sense of their individuality. This secular conceptualization is consistent with Christian conceptions of human relationship and should be assessed accordingly. However, the Person Scale introduces a third dimension that captures the animating motives by which the "other" is valued in the dyadic relationship. This can range along the Person dimension from self-centered and self-serving exploitation of the other ("others exist for me"), through contractual or quid-pro-quo engagement of the other ("I give in proportion to what I receive"), to a committed respect for the intrinsic dignity of the other as a creature in the image of God who has inherent and fundamental rights and who is worthy of sacrificial self-giving through the example of Christ ("I choose to give to you freely out of unconditional love"). This last position goes beyond simply enacting the appropriate level of affection and autonomy but embraces the other solely on the basis of his or her personhood. Paraphrasing the view of St. John Paul II, "No person can be regarded as an object to be used." This high regard for the inherent personhood of the other is what allows the spouse to keep giving, even when the circumstances become difficult, or allows the mother to choose life, even when

the decision imposes upon her comfort and freedom. It brings a mutually enriching dynamic to any aspect of relationality within the network of one's vocational roles. When the husband sacrifices self for the welfare of his wife, there is the possibility of actualizing her potential not only to be a more secure person who feels cherished but also to elevate her own capacity for self-giving. The same occurs when a young child grows up seeing loving sacrifice in her parents. Through her vocation as a child worthy of love and called to holiness, she in time becomes an adult and her own potential to relate in kind has been enriched. Both the interpersonal relationships and vocational callings of the client are essential to his or her flourishing and should be an essential aspect of assessment.

Sensory-Perceptual-Cognitive Capacities

The Meta-Model framework suggests that assessment of the body's capacities would include the measure of a person's sensory, perceptual, imaginative, memory, and motoric capacities. Traditional methods of assessing these areas include a range of neuropsychological instruments—such as the Halstead-Reitan Sensory-Perceptual Examination (Reitan & Wolfson, 1993), and the Bender Visual-Motor Gestalt-II (Bender, 2003)—other measures of psychomotor functioning, attention, impulsivity, or organicity—such as subtests of standardized IQ tests. Each of these tests to varying degrees provides insight into the bodily aspect of a person's functioning at a specific point in time and context, and thus is beneficial to the overall understanding of a client. In particular, the Meta-Model's vision of the person makes clear that any evaluation of capacity for knowledge must account for a person's sensory, perceptual, and memory capabilities, demonstrating the interconnected elements of personal unity.

Emotional Capacities

An assessment of the person's emotional capacities would include a range of evaluations to assess clients' ability to experience and express their own emotions and to detect, process, and react in an appropriate manner to others' emotions. It would be critical to understand whether the person's emotional capacities are healthy, that is, whether they are reasonable responses to reality that promote flourishing. Specifically, it is important to evaluate whether the emotional experiences of the client foster the development and use of virtues and support success in one's vocational callings. For example, does a spouse's tempered anger toward his or her partner's excessive work habits motivate a discussion that results in a better balance and care for both the spousal relationship and for meeting parenting commitments? At the same time, when such a discussion is held, does the excessive anger of either spouse result in defensiveness, polarization, and inability to work together? Although no current assessment instruments completely assess the emotional life in the context of the client's vocational callings, a number do touch on important aspects of emotional functioning and can prove valuable in the assessment process. These include the Shedler-Westen Assessment Procedure-200 (SWAP-200) (Shedler, 2015); the Affective Regulation and Experience Q-Sort Questionnaire (Westen, Muderrisoglu, Fowler, Shedler, & Koren, 1997); Affective Communication Questionnaire (Meehan, Levy, & Clarkin, 2012).

There are also a many clinical assessment instruments developed to assess a client's emotional states in order to determine whether psychopathology is present. These include such measures as the Beck Depression Inventory (Beck, Steer, & Brown, 1996), the Rorschach Inkblot Test (Rorschach, 1921) or the MMPI-2 (Butcher, Dahl-strom, Graham, Tellegen, & Kaemmer, 1989) to name but a few.

Rational and Intellectual Capacities

The Meta-Model states that human persons are capable of knowing created order, themselves, God, moral norms, and beauty. Assessment of a client's rational functioning would include measuring his or her sensory, perceptual, cognitive, and intellectual abilities. However, the Meta-Model has a richer understanding of rationality. For example, it would include inclination of the client to seek truth and develop intellectual virtues, especially wisdom, understanding, and practical reason (or prudence) (Chapter 15, "Rational"). It would also include considerations of moral and aesthetic capacities, which are needed for human flourishing.

Traditional assessment methods include measures of IQ, academic achievement, cognitive processing style, and memory, which are used in parallel with measures of neuropsychological (sensory and perceptual) functioning. Although intellectual knowledge can be intuitive (spiritual), discursive (reasoning), or infused (faith-based), traditional measures are almost exclusively of reason or discursive knowledge. In other words, the majority of these types of tests would best be understood as attempts to measure a person's ability to know truth at the natural level. Knowledge relating to transcendent realities, moral norms, aesthetic beauty, and the development of virtue is typically untapped in these traditional clinical methods. In addition, current assessment processes generally also do not include knowledge of self, or the ability to know what others are experiencing and feeling (empathy), even though both of these types of knowledge are intricately involved in flourishing in one's vocational calling.

The Will and Its Capacity for Freedom

The Meta-Model's account suggests that assessment of volition and freedom would include measurements of the person's self-regulation, creativity, ability to give and receive love, and development of moral responsibility and virtues (e.g., justice, love, hope, etc.). Important contemporary psychologists, such as Albert Bandura (2006) and Roy Baumeister and J. Tierney (2011), revived a serious psychological understanding of agency, free will, and self-control. Traditional assessment methods for this area are more difficult to identify, because the psychological sciences have historically presumed a deterministic stance, denying the concept of free will (e.g., radical behaviorism and some biological approaches) or at least suggesting very severe limitations to freedom (e.g., classic psychoanalysis). However, there is some literature on efforts to measure self-control that show promise (see Tangney, Baumeister, & Boone, 2004, for a measure and a review). Also, measures of personality functioning and style (MMPI-2, Butcher et al., 1989; 16 Personality Factors [16PF], Cattell, Cattell, & Cattell, 2000; NEO-PI-R, Costa & McCrae, 1992; Rorschach Inkblot Test, Rorschach, 1921; Thematic Apperception Test [TAT], Murray, 1938) often have scales or interpretive schemes that capture some aspects related to the assessment of the volitional capacities of the client. Particular examples include measures of ego strength (MMPI), conscientiousness (NEO), self-control (16PF), and some interpretations of projective responses (Rorschach, TAT). Nonetheless, the development of a more sophisticated or precise way of assessing the Meta-Model's rich understanding of human freedom and its limitations still need to be developed.

Some Specific Applications of the Meta-Model Framework in Assessment Processes That Serve the Church

In addition to the traditional uses of psychological assessments for the diagnosis and treatment of mental disorders, there are two particular ways in which assessments informed by a Catholic Christian Meta-Model of the Person can be used to assist the work of the Catholic Church: (a) evaluation of applicants to the priesthood and religious life (see Chapter 2, "Theological, Philosophical, and Psychological Premises," Premise III.6–9 and Premise V); and (b) evaluation of petitioners and respondents in diocesan marriage tribunal cases, where annulments (declarations of nullity) are being adjudicated.

Applicants to religious life

Making a commitment to a religious community (e.g., to the Franciscans or the Dominicans) or to the diocesan priesthood requires not only deep religious faith, but also personal responsibility, an ability to cope with stress, and a considerable amount of public trustworthiness. These demands require that applicants be psychologically healthy in order to be considered for entrance. Discernment of a candidate's religious vocation in the Catholic Church involves not only natural but also transcendent aspects of his or her life. Concerning the natural aspects, the Church in recent times has relied upon clinical psychologists to support the work of formators (vocation directors, religious superiors, and bishops) in their work of discerning an applicant's readiness for religious life (Plante & Boccaccini, 1998). In his apostolic exhortation *Pastores Dabo Vobis*, John Paul II (1992) discusses at length the necessary human characteristics. Blanchette (1997), a priest and psychologist, states that evaluations of applicants for the religious life should screen for impulse control, motivational factors, interpersonal functioning, and personality strengths and limitations. The rationale for evaluation is often twofold: (a) to decide if the applicant has any grave psychological barriers to fulfilling the vocational requirements, and (b) to help the applicant and the vocation director, seminary rector, or religious superior gain a clearer understanding of the functioning of the applicant and identify areas that may be in need of formation (Plante & Boccaccini, 1998).

This type of psychological assessment, often called a "vocational evaluation," frequently consists of a structured clinical interview and a battery of tests including intelligence tests, personality tests, and self-report measures, and can usefully be organized by the anthropological categories outlined by the Meta-Model. Similar to a typical clinical evaluation, these vocational evaluations address areas of strength as well as areas of weakness or concern that might be addressed in formation (Graveline, 2006). However, vocational evaluations have unique considerations. For example, some research has demonstrated that individuals undergoing psychological evaluations for vocational screening tend to present in a socially desirable manner (Butcher, 1994; Detrick, Chibnall, & Rosso, 2001; Plante, Manuel, & Tandez, 1996; Putnam, Kurtz, & Houts, 1996), while other research suggests that these applicants actually do possess certain socially desirable or virtuous characteristics (Graveline, 2006). Sometimes, however, some characteristics generally seen as less socially desirable may in some instances be adaptive and useful for living out a specific religious vocation. For example, seminary training and community life in religious orders require individuals to have both a high level of integrity and the ability to live among diverse others in

community, along with the ability to adhere to schedules and be highly self-disciplined, which highlights the importance of the anthropological premises reflecting interpersonal relatedness and freedom of volition. Thus, psychological test results that indicate a somewhat elevated (nonclinical) degree of compulsiveness or similar characteristics, which may be seen as a problem for a lay person, may actually be helpful in living in a religious community. Therefore, results of vocational evaluation need to be interpreted carefully and require the psychologist to have adequate knowledge of the formation circumstances and life situations of priests or religious if the evaluation is to accurately reflect an applicant's suitability.

Catholic marriage tribunal courts

Psychological assessment has also been used by marriage tribunals to adjudicate cases of nullity. In circumstances where a civil divorce has already been procured, the Church is being asked to judge whether the persons had the capacity to offer consent and freely commit to the obligations of a sacramental marriage at the time vows were exchanged. The principle that "it is … consent that makes marriage" has always been a hinge of Church doctrine regarding marriage (Code of Canon Law, 1983, Canon 1057). Because consent is a human act that depends on rationality and the will, psychologists are asked "to instruct the judge regarding the existence, nature, origin, and seriousness of the psychic disturbance of the subject" (Wrenn, 2002) that might compromise the subject's reason or will.

Canon lawyers and jurists are instructed to choose psychologists "who adhere to the principles of Christian anthropology" (Stankiewicz, 2006). Such instructions are understood as an attempt to ensure that evaluations are based on (a) a conception of human nature in which human nature is open to transcendent values, and (b) a conception of human vocation in which vocation is open to a theocentric self-transcendence. Based on clear and appropriate understanding of human nature and vocation, those evaluations can then give proper value to the personal autonomy of responsibility and freedom (Rulla, 1986). Psychologists should be chosen who offer "a truly complete vision of the person" and who are not "closed to transcendent values and meaning which allow human beings to tend towards the love of God and of neighbor as their final vocation" (John Paul II, 1987, §2 and §4).

Although formal testing might not be employed, the psychologist serves as a *peritus* (Latin for "expert") and offers his professional opinion to the tribunal. This opinion is most useful when the mental health professional conducting the assessment has a deep understanding of vocational callings, volition or freedom, interpersonal relatedness, the emotions, and the virtues as developed in the Meta-Model's framework for understanding the person. This information is then used by the court to determine the validity of the marriage in question, and at times to rule on the capacity of an individual validly to consent to marriage in the future. In those cases in which there is a restriction (*vetitum*) on a future marriage due to a true incapacity, the psychologist may also play a role in further assessing the capacity of the person in the future. The psychologist may also be asked to make recommendations for interventions that might provide healing so that a person would become capable of assuming the essential responsibilities of marriage.

Conclusion

In summary, the position set forth by the Catholic Christian Meta-Model provides a new constructive framework for organizing psychological assessments. This Meta-Model framework requires the clinician to make a more comprehensive evaluation, which includes traditional areas assessed in psychological evaluations (e.g., intellectual functioning, personality features) but also incorporates areas not generally included in assessments (e.g., vocational callings, moral development and spiritual functioning, and virtue development). The Meta-Model approach to psychological assessment is an additive process that does not replace traditional practices.

First, the Meta-Model approach incorporates contemporary and widely used measures, since they provide much of the needed information about the person. For example, there are many established psychological tests measuring intelligence (WAIS, WISC), perceptual anomalies (Bender-Gestalt), personality traits (MMPI-2), different aptitudes, unconscious motivations (Rorschach Test), and other psychological characteristics. In the Meta-Model these measures are not interpreted in any markedly different way, as they fit easily within the Model's general framework.

Second, utilization of the Meta-Model framework in psychological assessment reveals gaps in what these measures assess when compared to the vision of the person as conceived by the Meta-Model. For example, the Meta-Model's understanding of rationality is much broader, and not adequately captured by the reduction of rationality to intellectual intelligence. It includes self-knowledge and empathy, knowledge of other people, practical wisdom, faith seeking understanding, discernment of vocations, and moral awareness (conscience).

Third, the Meta-Model points to a need for the development of additional measures that correspond to dimensions of the person not usually evaluated in psychological assessment (e.g., spiritual functioning, virtue strengths, ability to be self-giving).

Finally, grounding psychological assessment more rigorously in a coherent Catholic Chris-

tian model would facilitate the assistance that the mental health field provides to the Church for vocational evaluations and for marriage tribunal adjudications. However, more importantly, the wider understanding of vocation, virtue, and spiritual life will be the basis for new types of psychological assessment that more comprehensively address the situations of clients, who have various personal and family experiences, and a range of psychological needs.

REFERENCES

Allport, G. W., & Ross, J. M. (1967). Personal religious orientation and prejudice. *Journal of Personality and Social Psychology, 5*(4), 432–443.

Bandura, A. (2006). Toward a psychology of human agency. *Perspectives on Psychological Science, 1*, 164–180.

Baumeister, R. F., & Tierney, J. (2011). *Willpower: Rediscovering the greatest human strength.* New York, NY: Penguin Press.

Beck, A. T., Steer, R. A., & Brown, G. K. (1996). *Beck Depression Inventory* (2nd ed.). San Antonio, TX: Harcourt Brace.

Bender, L. (2003). *Bender Visual-Motor Gestalt Test* (2nd ed.). San Antonio, TX: Pearson Assessment.

Benjamin, L. S. (2003). *Interpersonal diagnosis and treatment of personality disorder* (2nd ed.). New York, NY: Guilford Press.

Blanchette, M. C. (1997). On screening seminarians through behavioral assessment and psychological testing. *Seminary Journal, 3*(1), 25.

Butcher, J. N. (1994). Psychological assessment of airline pilot applicants with the MMPI-2. *Journal of Personality Assessment, 62,* 31–44.

Butcher, J. N., Dahlstrom, W. G., Graham, J. R., Tellegen, A., & Kaemmer, B. (1989). *The Minnesota Multiphasic Personality Inventory-2 (MMPI-2): Manual for administration and scoring.* Minneapolis, MN: University of Minnesota Press.

Campbell, V. L. (1987). Strong-Campbell Interest Inventory. *Journal of Counseling & Development, 66*(1), 53–56.

Cattell, R. B., Cattell, A. K., & Cattell, H. E. P. (2000). *Sixteen Personality Factor (16PF) questionnaire* (5th ed.). Minneapolis, MN: Pearson Assessments.

Cawley, M. J. (1997). *The virtue scale: A psychological examination of the structure of virtue and the relationships between virtue, personality, moral development, and epistemological style* (Unpublished doctoral dissertation). The Pennsylvania State University, State College, PA.

Code of Canon Law. (1983). Washington, DC: Canon Law Society of America.

Costa, P. T., & McCrae, R. R. (1992). *NEO PI-R professional manual.* Lutz, FL: Psychological Evaluation Resources.

Detrick, P., Chibnall, J. T., & Rosso, M. (2001). Minnesota Multiphasic Personality Inventory-2 in police officer selection normative data and relation to the Inwald Personality Inventory. *Professional Psychology: Research and Practice, 32,* 484–490.

Donahue, M. J. (1985). Intrinsic and extrinsic religiousness: Review and meta-analysis. *Journal of Personality and Social Psychology, 48*(2), 400–419.

Eldridge, B. M. (2012). Development and validation of the Calling and Vocation Questionnaire (CVQ) and Brief Calling Scale (BCS). *Journal of Career Assessment 20*(3), 242–263.

George, C., Kaplan, N., & Main, M. (1985). *The Berkeley Adult Attachment Interview* (Unpublished protocol). University of California, Berkeley, CA.

Gilligan, C. (1982). *In a different voice: Psychological theory and women's development.* Cambridge, MA: Harvard University Press.

Gibbs, J. C. (2003). *Moral development and reality: Beyond the theories of Kohlberg and Hoffman.* Thousand Oaks, CA: Sage.

Gottman, J. M. (1999). *The marriage clinic.* New York, NY: Norton.

Graveline, P. (2006). *Social desirability and virtuous inclination in applicants for the religious life* (Unpublished doctoral dissertation). The Institute for the Psychological Sciences, Arlington, VA.

Hill, P. C., & Hood, R. W., Jr. (Eds.). (1999). *Measures of religiosity.* Birmingham, AL: Religious Education Press.

Hodge, D. R. (2007). The spiritual competence scale: A new instrument for assessing spiritual competence at the programmatic level. *Research on Social Work Practice, 17*(2), 287–294.

Hoffman, M. L. (2000). *Empathy and moral development: Implications for caring and justice.* New York, NY: Cambridge University Press.

John Paul II. (1987, February 5). *Allocution to the Roman Rota.* Vatican City, Vatican: Libreria Editrice Vaticana.

John Paul II. (1992). *Pastores dabo vobis* [Apostolic exhortation, on the formation of priests]. Vatican City, Vatican: Libreria Editrice Vaticana.

Koenig, H. G., King, D., & Carson, V. B. (Eds.). (2012). *Handbook of religion and health* (2nd ed.). New York, NY: Oxford University Press.

Kohlberg, L. (1981). *Essays on moral development: Vol. 1. The philosophy of moral development.* San Francisco, CA: Harper & Row.

Laracy, M. R. (2011). *The role of the experience of beauty in psychotherapy* (Doctoral dissertation). Available from ProQuest Dissertations & Theses Global. (Order No. 3453653)

Lopez, S. J., & Snyder, C. R. (Eds.). (2009). *The Oxford handbook of positive psychology.* Oxford, United Kingdom: Oxford University Press.

Meehan, K. B., Levy, K., & Clarkin, J. F. (2012). Construct validity of a measure of affective communication in psychotherapy. *Psychoanalytic Psychology, 29*(2), 145–165.

Murray, H. (1938). *TAT: Thematic Apperception Test.* Cambridge, MA: Harvard University Press.

Olsen, D. H., Russell, C. S., & Sprenkle, D. H. (1989). *Circumplex model: Systemic assessment and treatment of families.* New York, NY: Haworth Press.

Olson, D. H., & Olson, A. K. (1999). PREPARE/ENRICH program: Version 2000. Preventive approaches in couples therapy. In R. Berger & M. Hannah (Eds.), *Handbook of preventive approaches in couple therapy* (pp. 196–216). New York, NY: Brunner/Mazel.

Peterson, C., & Seligman, M. E. (2004). *Character strengths and virtues: A handbook and classification.* New York, NY: Oxford University Press.

Plante, T. G., & Boccaccini, M. T. (1998). A proposed psychological assessment protocol for applicants to religious life in the Roman Catholic Church. *Pastoral Psychology, 46,* 363–372.

Plante, T. G., Manuel, G., & Tandez, J. (1996). Personality characteristics of successful applicants to the priesthood. *Pastoral Psychology, 45,* 29–40.

Putnam, S. H., Kurtz, J. E., & Houts, D. C. (1996). Four-month test-retest reliability of the MMPI-2 with normal male clergy. *Journal of Personality Assessment, 67,* 341–353.

Reitan, R. M., & Wolfson, D. (1993). *The Halstead-Reitan Neuropsychological Test battery: Theory and clinical interpretation.* Tucson, AZ: Neuropsychology Press.

Rorschach, H. (1921). *Psychodiagnostik.* Bern, Switzerland: Bircher.

Rulla, L. M. (1986). *Anthropology of the Christian vocation: Vol. 1. Interdisciplinary bases.* Rome, Italy: Gregorian University Press.

Schaefer, E. S. (1965). Configurational analysis of children's reports of parent behavior. *Journal of Consultation Psychology, 29,* 552–557.

Shedler, J. (2015) Integrating clinical and empirical perspectives on personality. The Schedler Westen Assessment Procedure (SWAP). In S. K. Hupriich (Ed.), *Personality disorders. Toward a theoretical and empirical integration in diagnosis and assessment* (pp. 225–252). Washington, DC: American Psychological Association.

Scrofani, P. J. (2019). *Developing norms for Version I of the Person Scale.* Manuscript in preparation.

Snyder, D. K. (1997). *Marital Satisfaction Inventory, Revised (MSI-R).* Los Angeles, CA: Western Psychological Services.

Stankiewicz, A. (2006). Some indications about Canon 1095 in the instruction *Dignitas connubii.* In P. M. Dugan & L. Navarro (Eds.), *Studies on the instruction* Dignitas connubii. *Proceedings of the study day held at the Pontifical University of the Holy Cross, Rome.* Montreal, Canada: Wilson & LaFleur.

Tangney, J. P., Baumeister, R. F., & Boone, A. L. (2004). High self-control predicts good adjustment, less pathology, better grades, and interpersonal success. *Journal of Personality, 72,* 271–322.

Terranova, L. E. (2006). *The experience of being called to serve: A phenomenological study of vocation* (Doctoral dissertation). Retrieved from PsycINFO (Order No. AAI3218527).

Vitz, P. C. (1994). Critiques of Kohlberg's model of moral development: A summary. *Revista española de pedagogía, 52*(197), 5–35

VanderWeele, T. J. (2017a). Religious communities and human flourishing. *Current Directions in Psychological Science, 26*(5), 476–481.

VanderWeele, T. J. (2017b). On the promotion of human flourishing. *PNAS, 114*(31), 8148–8156.

Westen, D., Muderrisoglu, S., Fowler, J. C., Shedler, X., & Koren, D. (1997). Affect regulation and affective experience: Individual differences, group differences, and measurement using a Q-sort procedure. *Journal of Consulting and Clinical Psychology, 65*(3), 429–439

Williams, L., & Jurich, J. (1995). Predicting marital success after five years: Assessing the predictive validity of FOCCUS. *Journal of Marital and Family Therapy, 21*(2), 141–153.

Wrenn, L. G. (2002). *Judging invalidity*. Washington, DC: Canon Law Society of America.

Chapter 25

Virtue in Mental Health Practice

A Comparative Case Study

FRANK J. MONCHER AND
CRAIG STEVEN TITUS

ABSTRACT: This chapter discusses how a multidimensional understanding of virtue serves the practice of psychotherapy and counseling. It employs a broad understanding of virtue, as (1) guided by a pursuit of meaning and flourishing (purposeful dimension), (2) through the virtuous acts (performative dimension), which (3) transform inter- and intrapersonal capacities (corrective and perfective dimension). It recognizes that every theory concerning the person or evidence-based counseling practice—including personality theories and therapy models—inevitably draws from a worldview and value system for understanding flourishing. The chapter first compares two frameworks for the use of virtue in mental health practice, namely, a secular virtue approach (Peterson & Seligman, 2004) and a faith-based one (Catholic Christian Meta-Model of the Person [CCMMP], that is, the model presented in the present book). It discusses these views on themes such as the normativeness of human nature and especially how life callings and vocations are needed to understand the development and healing of the person. Next, it compares how secular and faith-based frameworks influence the application of virtue in diverse psychotherapeutic modalities and practices. A single case is presented from a secular perspective on virtue and vice and then from a Catholic Christian perspective; the two approaches to the same case are revisited throughout the chapter; similarities and differences between these frameworks are identified.

Two Frameworks for the Use of Virtue in Mental Health Practice

In this chapter, we will employ two different virtue-based frameworks—a secular and a Christian one—to conceptualize the same person. We will use a client case study approach that

This chapter is an expanded and revised version of the texts that were originally published as "Foundations for a psychotherapy of virtue: An integrated Catholic perspective," by F. J. Moncher & C. S. Titus, 2009, *Journal of Psychology and Christianity*, 28(1), 22–35; and "A Catholic Christian positive psychology: A virtue approach," by C. S. Titus & F. Moncher, 2009, *Edification: Journal of the Society for Christian Psychology*, 3(1), 57–63.

permits a more thorough understanding of the potential of the two virtue-based frameworks. Using a single case seen through two different but related lenses will help us to understand the significance of explicitly identifying presuppositions when choosing a practical framework for comprehending a person in a clinical setting. The case chosen for this study is based primarily on an actual patient of the first author who was seen in psychotherapy over the course of several months. She was referred by a colleague who responded to the patient's request for a therapist who shared and understood her faith commitments. In accord with ethical practice, certain descriptive facts and unessential details are disguised in order to protect anonymity. Let us introduce the case of Barbara, in general, before introducing the two frameworks used in the chapter:

Barbara is the oldest female of several children born into an intact family. She came from a middle class, Midwestern United States background, with a traditional family arrangement of father working outside the home and mother staying with the children. The family was raised in the Catholic Church but was not active outside of the Sunday obligation (a mostly external or cultural expression of the virtue of piety). Barbara often took on the role of protector (aspects of the virtue of justice) and guide (aspects of the virtue of practical wisdom or prudence) for her younger siblings, who were at times physically abused by her father. Her mother would disappear when the father erupted in rage and would even at times tell the father things that would predictably cause violence to her children. One remarkable aspect of the environment of her family life is that her parents were kind and gentle with people in the world, but angry and critical within the family. Barbara learned that it was dangerous to relax, to trust in others' goodwill, and so she developed an independent style and an assertive self-reliance, repressing her feelings as a habitual response that kept her emotionally safe. Prior to meeting the clinician, Barbara had studied at university and later entered a religious congregation of sisters. It is in this context of the client's commitment to consecrated or religious life that the following case is played out.

Barbara is the same person although she takes a religious name, Sr. Lydia, when she enters religious life. Nonetheless, she is understood differently in the clinical setting when she is viewed from the distinct frameworks of the single and the consecrated life. We aim to demonstrate that the primary skills used by mental health professionals to foster growth in therapy can be conceptually associated with the practice of the virtues, and that this is true both from the secular perspective (for example, positive psychology) and the Christian perspective on the virtues and vices. Although secular and Christian approaches sometimes do not use the same way of speaking about virtue, both provide skills and practices that are needed for understanding and developing virtues and correcting vices. For instance, in a secular perspective on temperance, there are different strategies to develop ego strength and self-control around areas of bodily needs (e.g., eating disorders), desires (e.g., unchaste interpersonal relationships), and pleasures (e.g., addictions). Most prominently, positive psychology considers temperance by drawing on the values accessible to reason to attain self-mastery illustrated by the lives of exemplary role models and heroes (Peterson & Seligman, 2004). In a Catholic Christian approach to psychology, Christian temperance, rooted in the love and service of God, neighbor, and self, seeks to attain self-mastery by giving unselfishly and is modeled on the life of Christ and the saints. Both secular (supposedly value-free) and Catholic Christian approaches can draw upon the psychological sciences' virtue theory through use of measures and scales, knowledge of correlates and consequences, and understanding enabling and inhibiting factors, developmental, and cultural issues for virtue-focused interventions. Gathering basic information about the person and particular issues and problems, strengths and weaknesses, can be common to both approaches. The frameworks, however, permit different considerations of what is normative for human nature (natural law), and also what is the ultimate transcendent dimension of the person (divine law and spiritual and religious practices).

A Comparison of Models: Non-Normative and Relativistic Models

Often models of counseling and psychotherapy seek to employ empirically supported theories and evidence-based practices, while not examining the underlying views of the person and values that are implied by such theories and interventions. Even when using a virtue approach to counseling and psychotherapy, much is assumed or ignored concerning the worldview or value system that underlies supposed value-free or secular accounts and approaches.

The Catholic Christian Meta-Model of the Person, on the contrary, explicitly offers a foundation for a positive developmental and therapeutic paradigm for using virtues in ther-

apy using multiple dimensions, three of which are virtuous (a) goal-based practices, (b) acts, and (c) character strengths and dispositions. Earlier in this volume (Chapter 11, "Fulfilled in Virtue"), we suggest that there is a holistic anthropological structure to the virtues, which is in rapport with the person's interpersonally relational, cognitive, and affective capacities. That chapter anticipates the present chapter's effort to demonstrate a positive correlation between symptom reduction and overcoming vices or stress, through the promotion of virtuous action, the development of character strengths, and the exercise of practices that promote them. We consider the use of virtue in psychotherapy, drawing from a virtue tradition that is *philosophical* (e.g., Aristotle, ca. 350 BC/1941; MacIntyre, 1981, 1999; Pieper, 1966, 1997, 1998), *theological* (e.g., Aquinas, 1273/1981; Hauerwas, 1981; John Paul II, 1998; Pinckaers, 1995, 2005; Titus, 2006), and *psychological* (Joseph, 2015; Joseph & Linley, 2006; Lopez & Snyder, 2009; Peterson & Seligman, 2004; Snyder & Lopez, 2007). From within the virtue tradition, we have also identified certain anthropological principles relevant to the task of psychotherapy that spring from theological and philosophical sources (Cessario, Titus, & Vitz, 2013; Moncher, 2001).

Inasmuch as we take an explicitly Catholic Christian perspective (a philosophical psychology), we differ in some ways from other recent efforts to reappropriate virtue in psychology, both those that assert a non-normative and value-free framework and those that take a relativistic approach to moral norms. We will compare the basic frameworks or meta-models that are used in current virtue approaches to mental health practice, beginning with the contributions of positive psychology.

The positive psychology paradigm of character strengths and virtues has attempted to remove itself not only from particular religious traditions but also from moral norms as such (e.g., Fowers, 2005; Joseph & Linley, 2006; Peterson & Seligman, 2004; Seligman, 2002; Snyder & Lopez, 2007). For example, Peterson and Seligman (2004) claim their "richer psychological content and greater explanatory power" is descriptive of character strengths, but without normative reference (p. 88). While seeking moral references for good character in a pre-empirical moral anthropology (through the construal of the nature of virtue and the notion of positive human nature), they distance the inner motivation of the virtues from moral considerations (laws and principles) and from the normativeness of human nature. Such a separation of virtue from ethical sources (the person, moral inclinations, sentiments, law, and principle) produces ambiguity in terms of both client goals and motivations for change, as well as the direction and focus of mental health interventions. For instance, the Christian virtue of courage is needed to overcome fear when facing the need to repair a difficult marriage, that is, overcoming fear to attain sometime good. The secular virtue of courage is simply about overcoming fear, whether the goal is something good or evil, for example, when a spouse who "courageously" overcomes the fear of family rejection to initiate an adulterous affair. While positive psychology may give clues for positive growth, it has not yet succeeded in understanding the full potential of virtue-focused interventions, because of its failure to include a moral framework (Titus, 2012, 2017; Tjeltveit, 1999).

Other virtue-based approaches in the mental health field view counseling and psychotherapy as moral discourse (Cushman, 1990, 1993) and affirm the necessity of moral borders, though they posit only relativist ones. Cushman (1993)

views the mental health professional as a resource for the client's discernment of moral issues, and claims that "it is the job of a psychotherapist to demonstrate the existence of a world constituted by different rules and to encourage patients to be aware of available moral traditions that oppose the moral frame by which they presently shape their lives" (p. 109). However, Cushman postulates an "empty self," which is filled by ambient historical, cultural, and moral contexts with only relativistic references. Consequently, the clinician is unable to offer guidance from an understanding of what is true about human nature objectively and most apt to foster growth toward flourishing.

What this volume's Catholic Christian Meta-Model of the Person expresses, by contrast, is confidence in the moral frame of natural and divine law and of the person, a frame that can offer moral guidance while respecting the uniqueness of the individual, as well as differences due to cultural and sex differences (Wojtyła, 1993). At the same time, this frame offers a basis to counter the secular tyranny of relativism (Benedict XVI, 2006). One philosophical belief of the Meta-Model is that reasoned, focused observation about the human person—as experienced in family, culture, and community—offers a deeper understanding of human nature as rooted in natural moral law. This focus on the person, though, requires a focus on the ultimate source and end (purpose) of the person and the individual experience of particular persons. Searching for true self-knowledge leads to the recognition that there is a source and end greater than oneself and mankind. This recognition reaches beyond the person, to other human persons and creatures, to the source of existence and goodness, that is, to the transcendent first principle, who is called God (Ashley, 2006; Spitzer, 2010). Such an investigation unveils the world as instantiating an orderliness that underlies the relative disorders of vices and the particularities of history; it even recognizes a theistic view of mind, intention, and purpose in which God creates laws (Nagel, 2012, pp. 21–22).

This chapter affirms the value of reason and basic natural yearnings (for goodness, truth, beauty), even when someone errs in their use. Moreover, still at a philosophical level, its theocentric vision provides reasons to hold (1) that humans have a duty to pursue moral norms, even when they often fail, and (2) that humans will find flourishing in virtue and self-giving, even if it be only partial flourishing (Benedict XVI, 2008; Budziszewski, 2009; Levering, 2008).

Furthermore, the theological aspects of this view of the human person explicitly draw upon a faith-based understanding, rooted in revelation as expressed in Sacred Scripture and tradition, particularly in a Catholic Christian perspective. This revelation of the ultimate origin and finality of human persons aids the therapist and the client in distinguishing the numerous well-ordered means of pursuing ultimate human ends, with the help of divine grace, from various disordered actions. This divine law further clarifies the natural moral law and offers a larger sense to flourishing (Benedict XVI, 2006; John Paul II, 1995; See also Chapter 7, "Methodology and Presuppositions").

Distinctions Between Secular and Catholic Virtue Approaches to Mental Health Practice

Catholic Christian and secular approaches sometimes differ in the content, categorization, and hierarchy of the everyday or acquired character and virtues, and the psychological strengths and practices needed to attain them. They differ even more when addressing properly transcendent or theological virtues. However, secular and religious presentations are not necessarily at odds concerning foundational issues of justice, respect, basic dignity, self-moderation, and so on; and in various psychosocial domains there is a possibility for dialogue, which enriches each other's perspectives; and in many areas, mutual understanding. Furthermore, it is commonly accepted that the content of the virtues are present and valued across cultures and religious traditions. However, these associated virtue strengths and practices are often expressed in differing ways because of individual differences (including sex and developmental age), cultural influences, religious beliefs, and civic structures. This distinction of basic virtues, associated virtues or character strengths, and practices requires another level of distinction about what constitutes harmful and immoral actions that lead to languishing (such as family violence and marital infidelity) versus beneficial and morally good actions that lead to a participation in flourishing (self-giving love and truthfulness).

Contemporary thought often misrepresents classical notions of ethical norms, sex differences, and the development of virtue. Virtues are commonly perceived in the light of extremes: Either (a) each virtue is perceived as an ideal norm that must be instantiated in the same way for every person or not be considered virtue at all, that is, virtue is seen as a static definition and as if one size fits all; or (b) each virtue is charted on a developmental path and process that is absolutely unique to each person or sex, therefore, lacking an ultimate normative grounding or goal. In contrast, in the Catholic Christian vision of the person and virtue, both universal normativeness and individual differences are held together in a balanced, integrated unity. Accordingly, this vision of the person offers a stable moral basis for guiding the clinician and mental health interventions.

An important characteristic of this Catholic Christian virtue tradition, which is also shared by the secular virtue approach, is the recognition of human potential for change and development, which are central to the process of therapeutic interventions. As in the positive psychology approach, we suggest that counseling and psychotherapy seek not only reduction of symptoms but also growth in the positive human capacities at three levels: character strengths and major virtues, associated virtues, and particular practices. In fact, this holistic approach recognizes the joint movement in symptom reduction and overcoming vices alongside virtuous practices and development. With due consideration of its neurobiological bases, psychological health ultimately is related to being able to choose "goods" that are objectively adequate for human flourishing and to pursue the good in action. At this level, there is a convergence between psychological well-being and what has classically been called natural acquired moral virtue (everyday virtue). As clients become increasingly free to act and make choices in their lives, encouraging the exercise of related virtues and practices can have a dramatic impact on their psychological health in terms of self-knowledge and self-mastery and also of self-acceptance and trusting that they are worthy of love (Ashley, 2013; Moncher, 2001). Furthermore, in order for clinicians to provide this encouragement coherently and effectively, it is important that they be focused on living and learning the developmental pathways of the character strengths, virtues, and practices of their own life as well.

Virtue Applied to Psychotherapy

To make the clinical application of virtue theory concrete and to differentiate a secular from a Catholic Christian approach to the utilization of virtue in counseling and psychotherapy, we present a case study of one person that is revisited throughout the chapter from two perspectives. We offer first a secular virtue approach (case of Barbara), then one grounded in the Meta-Model's use of virtue in the practice of psychotherapy, in which we include a special focus on a Christian understanding both of virtue and strength and of disorder and weakness (case of Sr. Lydia).

The Case of Barbara: Exposition of History and Background from a Secular Virtue Perspective

Barbara's self-reliance, which was developed in her childhood as an adaptive, resilient response to the difficulties within her family dynamic, led to a natural desire to leave home for college and begin life on her own. While she was concerned about the welfare of her younger siblings, left with her father and his anger, Barbara also had some sense that her emancipation could be an important example for her siblings to have to follow. She was accepted by two universities on scholarship, one a private, Catholic university and the other a large state university; Barbara chose the smaller faith-based school, which was closer to her family home. She desired to study fashion design and business, having both an artistic and a practical aspect to her motivations. She performed well in college and secured a desirable internship placement in New York City. However, as these dreams of hers were falling into place, Barbara also had been connecting with campus ministry and started to find attending church useful, since it provided a new social support network for her. In addition, the meditation practices helped her to cope better with her many stresses.

CCMMP Reflections on the secular virtue presentation: While Barbara's religious practice is respected from the secular therapist's perspective, it is conceptualized only on an everyday level of psychological function and mechanism. For instance, the clinician recognizes Barbara's religious experience as a potentially helpful coping resource of reliable social support and perhaps as a context for good self-care. Her clinician however fails to grasp that her religious experience also provides an organizing framework giving her life positive transcendent meaning, as well as meeting a natural need for belonging.

The Case of Sr. Lydia: Exposition of History and Background from a Catholic Virtue Perspective

Barbara's emancipation from her family and success in college is sown with seeds of potential virtues and influenced by transcendent significance. Her self-reliance was becoming cultivated, growing into a proper understanding of her human dignity and self-worth. Her expectation that her siblings would benefit from her example was infused with the virtue of hope. Furthermore, her emancipation can be understood as a manifestation of courage and fortitude. A faith-based perspective on Barbara's school choice opens the possibility of discerning how her decision to attend the private, Catholic university was motivated by the connection with her family's faith tradition. This hypothesis is confirmed when Barbara's growth in knowledge of Catholicism and her faith journey led her to consider consecrated religious life. To the dismay of her family and friends, Barbara turned down her internship opportunity and instead became a consecrated member of a Catholic religious congregation. As a religious, Barbara took the name of Sr. Lydia. Her adjustment went very well in many ways, as she quickly acclimated to the routine of the life, which was congruent with much of what she naturally had always desired in her family of origin. Furthermore, within her current "family" of the convent she was surrounded by others who were not dangerous to her physically or emotionally.

The Human Person and the Virtue Perspective

Any psychotherapy that seeks to have a stable vision of the person must answer some crucial questions: How does a general notion (such as virtue) accommodate diverse times and cultures, different developmental stages of life, and sex differences? Moreover, how do we explain human capacities for excellence or goodness, continuity, and creativity, along with the contrary human expressions of mediocrity or evil, instability, and unexamined repetition? Virtue-based anthropology attempts such an account by recognizing that the human person has an origin and a goal, as well as a need for personal development in the process, without denying diversity in defining strengths or virtues. First, contrary to some postmodern theories, the Meta-Model accepts from philosophical argument (e.g., Cessario et al., 2013; D. McInerny, 2006) and empirical findings (e.g., Ekman, 1992, 2003) that human persons have a nature. They have been given a structure that specifies the species by not only physiological traits (including DNA) but also uniquely human psychological and spiritual capacities, including basic natural and spiritual inclinations toward appropriate life goals, broadly-speaking. Second, it recognizes a developmental perspective that distinguishes various areas in which human beings need to grow, in order, third, to approach the goal of mature flourishing, becoming free and responsible. That is, the Meta-Model's vision identifies a structure of human origins, pathways for development, and adequate and positive expressions of maturity (Schmitz, 2009).

The Case of Barbara: Beginnings of Therapy (Secular Virtue Perspective)

Barbara entered therapy as a result of feelings of discontent in religious life, feeling frustrated that despite her efforts and success at living the vows of poverty, chastity, and obedience she continued to feel a serious lack of fulfillment. Barbara was able to express her autonomy by choosing to pursue religious life. However, her commitment to poverty, chastity, and obedience raised challenges for living in a healthy manner. These three areas need to be considered in terms of Barbara's psychological well-being. Her forgoing a good option for pursuing a career would have suggested normal initiative and right judgment. Her choosing to live chaste celibacy, however, seems unrealistic and unhealthy. And her living under the authority of another as an adult seems to indicate a dependent personality. These three areas indicate potential treatment objectives [from a secular perspective], with the goal of moving Barbara from a dependent lifestyle that eschews natural pleasures, to one in which she is more in tune with her own needs and becomes more focused on establishing her autonomous self.

The Case of Sr. Lydia: Beginnings of Therapy (Meta-Model Virtue Perspective)

Sr. Lydia entered therapy as a result of feelings of discontent in religious life, feeling frustrated that despite her efforts and success at living the vows she continued to feel lack of fulfillment. She experienced difficulty in shifting her stance in religious community relationships to allow for the more intimate relating appropriate to communal life. She was experiencing challenges in the process of transition and growth normally needed when choosing to live religious vows. However, Sr. Lydia was apparently lacking openness to the virtue of friendship (love), which would be helpful in her transition to religious life. Exploring this further in therapy and having Sr. Lydia solicit feedback from her superiors, it was hypothesized that in her efforts to live in community there was something amiss in how she was pursuing holiness. In particular, the call of the religious sister is not only to grow in love for God, but also to love her neighbor as herself. In the case of communal life this includes developing genuine friendships and cheerfulness in serving her community and the mission of her order, as well as in her interactions with the laity. Somehow, the everyday or natural virtues she was trying to enact were not bearing the expected fruit. Lydia's difficulty was conceptualized as a result of her not interiorly and freely forming the virtues, but instead as a result of her primarily performing the virtues out of duty to the exterior law (rules and practices of the religious congregation). Thus, she was expressing an emotional and virtue profile blocked at the early stage of spiritual virtue development (dependent on duty and external rules), with the incumbent difficulties, dryness, and lack of spontaneity. This conceptualization was put forth by the therapist in the context of their shared faith background, along with minimal, appropriate, yet significant self-disclosure of his [the first author's] own experiences of this process. This intervention normalized her experiences and also enabled Sr. Lydia to understand why she was exhausted when going about her daily routine in the convent trying to do the right things; she was reflexively and habitually repressing her emotional reactions as they arose, so as not to become overwhelmed by them and possibly behave inappropriately. As a result, she had tended to restrict her emotional life.

Learning Virtues and Vices

The Meta-Model recognizes that the character of human virtues can be understood only in the context of a person who is a unity (soul and body), who tends toward a greater wholeness (flourishing in the virtues), and who is in interpersonal relationship. This unity of person, development in virtue, and rootedness in community are found in five areas of the Meta-Model: sensory-perceptual-cognitive, emotional, interpersonally relational, rational, and volitional (Ekman, 1992, 2003; Evans & Cruse, 2004; Griffiths, 1997; see also Chapter 10, "Fulfilled Through Vocation," and Chapter 11, "Fulfilled in Virtue").

Dimensions of Virtue and Vice: An Act, a Disposition, a Rational Moral Standard

The notion of virtue has often been reduced by modern thinkers to refer simply to an act (a single choice or deed), to a disposition to act virtuously (a virtuous internal tendency), or to a rational moral norm for action. Virtue is also reduced to being found in the action of the virtuous person, apart from virtuous norms and practices (Fowers, 2005; McDowell, 1979). However, the basis of the Meta-Model's classical (Aristotelian-Augustinian-Thomist) approach is the conception of virtue understood as including these dimensions in a developmental way (at emotional, cognitive, volitional, and interpersonal levels) in a way that contributes long-term to the moral and spiritual flourishing of the human person. The Meta-Model of the person has identified thirteen dimensions that contribute to an understanding of the interplay of virtue and vice at everyday natural-acquired and transcendental-theological levels. These strengths and virtues are contrasted with vices and disorders (Table 25.1).

This chart illustrates a comprehensive set of the dimensions of the virtues, but this chapter

Table 25.1. Characteristics of Thirteen Dimensions of Virtues and Vices

Virtue Dimensions	Characteristics of Virtue	Vice Dimensions
1. Performative (Act)	The free acts of virtue that are: a. involved in creating virtuous dispositions, and b. influenced by virtuous habits	**1. Deformative**, not performative (at the level of acts)
2. Perfective and corrective (Agent)	The strengths or dispositions of the virtuous person, which: a. are formed by virtuous acts and b. contribute to virtuous acts	**2. Defective**, not corrective or perfective (of the agent's character and flourishing)
3. Purposeful (Reason-based and teleological)	The virtue's good ends: a. that make the person flourish and b. at which virtues aim	**3. Negatively-purposeful**, not purposeful (indecisive and anti-communal)
4. Ethical (Moral norm-based)	The rational moral standards that the virtues employ	**4. Unethical or amoral**, not ethical (immorally teleological and egotistical)
5. Influenced by personal uniqueness, equal innate dignity, sex difference and complementarity	Based in personal individuality, including equal or common innate dignity, sex differences and complementarity	**5. Distortive of person and sex difference**, not influenced by personal uniqueness, equal innate dignity, sex difference and complementarity (exaggeration or denial of personal uniqueness; denial of equal dignity, sex differences, and complementarity)
6. Connective, relational, and developmental	Holistic, dynamic, and interpersonal process-based	**6. Disruptive**, not connective, relational, or dynamic (pseudo-holistic, fixated, or neglectful of personal relationships)
7. Learned through role-models	Based in exemplars and sources that model goodness and truth	**7. Learned through disordered role models**, following exemplars that model real evil and only apparent goods (preventing the influence of exemplars that model true good)
8. Moderating (Measured)	Seeking a middle ground of excellence between two extremes	**8. Extreme**, not moderating (conformed to an erroneous, weak, or extreme measure)
9. Preventative (Strength-based)	The virtue-based character and interpersonal strengths that face ills and vices	**9. Degenerative and disintegrative**, not preventative (not strength-based)

(table continues)

Table 25.1. (*continued*)

Virtue Dimensions	Characteristics of Virtue	Vice Dimensions
10. Nonreductionist (Contextual)	Contextual and open to evidence, including from scientific, evidence-based, value-based, and truth-seeking sources	**10. Reductionist**, not holistic (missing the greater and higher evidence for understanding virtue)
11. Applied (Research and practice)	Applications of virtue-based theory and practices to mental health and other disciplines enhance flourishing	**11. Misapplied,** disordered application of apparent goods in everyday and professional contexts distort flourishing
12. Vocational (Calling-based)	Informed by the callings: to goodness and holiness; to single, married, religious, or ordained life; and to work that underlies the virtues	**12. Anti-vocational** (not committing to personal goodness and holiness, vocational states, and work)
13. Open to the transcendent and to God	Seeking goodness, truth, and beauty and their first transcendent source (God), which transforms the virtues	**13. Non-transcendent**, closed to the transcendent and to God (not seeking, but avoiding higher goodness, truth, and beauty and their transcendent source)

will mainly address the virtues as performative, perfective, purposeful, ethical, vocational, and open to the transcendent.

It should be noted that a practical approach to the virtues involves working on their particular matters or capacities (namely, emotions, interpersonal relationships, will, and reason—and the interaction thereof), as well as their formal qualities. The dialogue in a therapy of virtue will necessarily involve some precise terminology as one attempts to both explore the issues in the client's life and help the client understand better the nature of his or her strengths and weaknesses. This dialogue addresses the course of attraction and repulsion in sensory-perceptional cognitions; positive strength or disorder in emotions such as love and fear; the demands, limitations, and potential in interpersonal rela-tionships; and the types of choices and reasons that need to be pursued or avoided. Each type of capacity has multiple types of directionality and consequences, as well as links with the other capacities. For example, the emotions embody diverse manifestations: from exaggerated movements, to timid expressions, to well-managed dispositions. However, each expression of emotion involves some past or present interaction with reason, choices, and interpersonal relationships, as well as commitments such as those in marriage, single life, or religious life.

When well trained, the therapist discusses virtue and vice in everyday terms and experiences, such as patience in suffering, courage in anxiety, perseverance in difficulty, and so on. The timing with which a therapist introduces particular virtues and the practices needed to support them is important. Several factors must be considered. First, the patient's level of stress and general emotional health should be assessed. While a discussion of the matter of virtue may be needed, an explicitly normative language of virtue is most often not advised during times of crisis, as it would be difficult for the patient to process the information discussed. Second, a patient's ability to successfully enact intentions must be assessed, because some measure of self-control (volitional health) is necessary so that early success can be achieved to build upon in therapy. Third, cultural expectations that have influenced the client's understanding of fitting expressions of care, affection, anger, and fear—including masculine and feminine expressions of each—should be taken into account (Cates, 1996; Mattison, 2007; also Chapter 9, "Man and Woman"). Finally, the patient's history of spiritual guidance and religious experiences should be assessed. Care must be taken, since some clients have been problematically (though perhaps inadvertently) shamed by others who encourage religious and moral growth in order to overcome weakness, when a disorder at the natural or social level has been the real barrier to healing or growth.

The Case of Barbara: Character Strengths and Virtues (Secular Virtue Perspective)

Although Barbara manifested many character strengths that would be thought to assist her in coping with the challenges of living in her new community, she nevertheless was struggling at several levels. Barbara's healthy but underdeveloped natural inclinations are manifest in an example from her adolescence: she had arisen early one morning to clean house before going to basketball practice, had attended a full day of classes, and done homework during study hall while most peers were nonproductive. Following her game, she helped clean the bus and accidentally left her books in the process. Upon arriving home, she called the bus depot and learned she could not get her books until the end of the following school day, so she was unable to finish her homework. She put her younger siblings to bed and did further chores in the home. The next day, her teacher berated her in front of the class for not having her homework and being irresponsible, an example of "what's wrong with youth these days." Barbara calmly but firmly expressed to the teacher that it was inappropriate to talk to her in that manner and left class, reflecting on how she had not actually been irresponsible the day before but had simply made a mistake. Because of the violence and chaos in her home, she had adapted a style of not attending to her emotional state or that of others, instead repressing her feelings and focusing on actions. So here she knew, intellectually, that she had not committed the error of which she was accused and took reasonable actions to escape from the unjust accusation. However, she did not recognize that simple mistakes can have negative consequences as well. Furthermore, she did not process the event emotionally and obtain full satisfaction; rather, she remained bewildered and grew in cynicism about adults.

CCMMP Reflections on the secular virtue presentation: A secular therapy without an explicit anthropology might tend to focus on integrating the emotional and intellectual aspects of the above-mentioned experiences, assisting Barbara in having the experience of processing her feelings and thoughts concurrently. First, she would be encouraged to access and identify her feelings in the past and then experience them in the present. Next, she would be assisted to understand how they could connect with her cognitive understanding of her experience in the past. While the integration of emotion and reason is a worthy goal and would provide some relief to Barbara's difficulties, such interventions would fall short of helping Barbara understand her struggles of the interpersonal dimension of family life and the vocational dimension of her experience in the religious community.

The Case of Sr. Lydia: Character Strengths and Virtue (Meta-Model Virtue Perspective)

As a youth, despite lacking many elements of fuller formation and role modeling, Sr. Lydia possessed a proclivity toward virtuous choices in her acts and her understanding of what was right. Because Sr. Lydia had not acquired a disposition toward virtue in the complete sense though, she was unable to act fully (that is, with promptness, ease, and joy) at home, while attending university, or in her religious community. Her choices in her youth were inclined toward flourishing, but because of her lack of formation she was unable to connect more fully her desires and actions in a manner that embodied the ethical, growth-directed, moderating, vocational, and transcendent properties of virtue for which she longed. Based in a Christian understanding of the person, therapy could further incorporate the objective truth that undergirded her youthful spontaneous actions. For instance, it could allow her to begin to access those feelings of anger-related injustice in a manner that allows for purposeful and moderated choices that are more consistent with her vocation.

Transcendent Level and the Virtue Perspective

An explicitly Catholic Christian transcendent or theological vision of the person contrasts and, in other respects, agrees with secular views. This Meta-Model uses the transcendent scriptural and magisterial tradition for understanding the human person as: (1) created in God's image, (2) influenced by the effects of sin, and (3) offered redemption by God's initiative in Jesus Christ.

Of special interest is the influence of sin and vice (such as pride, hatred, jealousy, wrath, disinterest, and so on), which have disfigured human beings and the above-mentioned image and which result in many different kinds of personal and relational disorders. But in the human person, these disorders nonetheless remain secondary to the goodness of God's creation. For through God's good pleasure, his dynamic image and the basic human dignity still remain after sin. To understand this potential for both good and evil, for health and illness, for virtue and vice, we need to understand the whole person in the light of how the Good News of Christ influences our practices relating to our embodiment, interpersonal relationality, reason, and will (Chapter 18, "Fallen").

According to the Second Vatican Council (1965), instead of diminishing human nature, Christ "restores the divine likeness which had been disfigured from the first sin onward" (§22) Christ offers adoptive daughtership and sonship, a holiness in the Spirit, and a promise of blessedness. In this last regard, humans seek flourishing, especially transcendent or ultimate beatitude, as the primary goal of their lives. Although understandings of what makes us happy differ, the Catholic Christian vision revolves around the blessedness that is engendered by faith, hope, and love and that is founded in Christ's teaching on the Beatitudes (Mt 5; Lk 6; also Chapter 19, "Redeemed").

This theological vision of the person demands a teleological process of development of the virtues that resembles a secular vision in some ways. Both visions inform therapies that seek to overcome past and present negative and neurotic influences on the client. They both seek to help develop a wide range of the client's virtues to assure a more stable transformation toward flourishing. However, the Meta-Model's vision of the person also offers a complement to the secular virtue vision, inasmuch as the transcendent Christian message and divine grace further influence one's self-understanding, free will, emotion, and interpersonal relationality. Furthermore, the Meta-Model, with its virtue and vocation focus, offers explicit practices and goals both to overcome mental disorders and to promote everyday resilience and, finally, ultimate flourishing (Sherwin, 2009).

The Case of Barbara: The Acquisition of Natural Virtues (Secular Virtue Perspective)

Barbara's maturing and flourishing in virtue manifests challenges to her self-sufficiency, independence, and successful separation from her family of origin. While she was seemingly on a positive trajectory during her years in college, her choice to follow a religious vocation raises questions. Is she legitimately sublimating a call to marriage and family life for the life in the convent? Could her willing submission to the obedience of others and denying herself certain earthly pleasures and ambitions (in the convent), be self-damaging and a continuation of past neurotic patterns from her family experience rather than a virtuous pathway to flourishing? And could these choices undercut her autonomy and flourishing instead of promoting them?

CCMMP reflections on the secular virtue presentation: Until the concerns mentioned above by the clinician are adequately addressed the therapist may have difficulty formulating treatment goals that would support her desires for religious commitment.

A secular therapist may need to ponder how to integrate an approach that is consistent with

Barbara's type of love and self-giving that is less focused on material success, earthly pleasure, and her own needs. Moreover, both the secular and Christian therapists would be interested in Barbara's capacity to express virtuous autonomy and responsible freedom in such a religious commitment. They both would also be attentive to how she might make progress in the interpersonal relationships and virtues, instead of reverting to past unhealthy ways of coping with family dysfunction. For example, with respect to her family, it would be important to observe whether she has overcome her negative emotional reactions and is more at peace with her family through her work in therapy.

The Case of Sr. Lydia: Natural, Acquired, and Theological Virtues (Meta-Model Virtue Perspective)

Although Sr. Lydia's family members have often failed to serve as positive role models, she has been showing a promising pattern of growing theological virtues (faith, hope, and charity-love) and a capacity to stand on freely chosen principles that are consistent with religious life. Even before feeling the call to her religious vocation, Sr. Lydia did not repeat her other family members's pattern of mistreating one another. She instead spent her days and nights trying to bring order to the house and its activities. This might have been the result not only of a natural inclination to goodness and prosocial collaboration but also to the transcendent, infused virtue of hope. She certainly has shown signs of charity in the sense that she has demonstrated unselfish giving to others (for example, making sure younger siblings are cared for when mother is "too busy" to do so). When she reported praying to God that her life and death would be used for the conversion of her family (prior to knowing fully what this might mean), she showed signs of the virtue of faith. If these supernatural virtues were operative, however, there must have been some positive influence coming from the family beyond the negative ones. For example, there was the influence of attending Mass, for there she was exposed to Scripture and the prayers of the Liturgy. In a real sense, she must have received a basic education of Christ's model of self-giving and hope, as well as examples from the saints. Her parents insured that she received the sacraments and in doing so were instruments to transcendent grace. Theologically we can also speak of the effects of Baptism with its graces that develop over time under divine guidance.

Emotions and Virtue

Some philosophers and theologians have a great deal of suspicion concerning the emotions, as sometimes accommodating but unreliable at best (Kant), or as consistently disruptive or evil at worst (the Stoics). However, Aristotle and Aquinas and the Catholic tradition (*Catechism of the Catholic Church*, 1997, §1767) affirm both that emotional capacities are inherently good and that particular emotions are potentially positive energies, which are subject to developmental processes, that is, virtues can be positively formed in emotional capacities. Emotions express pre-rational or instinctive judgments that come through sense knowledge of various sorts. The emotions thus provide signs of intelligibility (within beings, interactions, and events) through attractions and repulsions, fears and hopes, angers and loves, and so on. Furthermore, the Aristotelian-Thomist approach to the emotions—which is a foundation for the Catholic tradition and the Meta-Model—also correlates emotional expression and development with reasoning, willing, and interpersonal relationships (Chapter 14, "Emotional").

Aquinas considers particular emotions to be good in two ways (1273/1981, I-II, qq. 58–60 & 24.3). First, as virtuously shaped emotive capacities, particular emotions express a participation in reason and can point us toward acting in ways that are consistent with freely chosen goals. They express intelligibility at a pre-rational or instinctive level. Emotions are good when, as reactions antecedent to reasoning, they make us conscious of reality and prepare us for a more complete reaction and moral action. Emotion and choice then serve moral flourishing (e.g., when we have an appropriate spontaneous reaction of anger at injustice). Second, emotions are good as felt reactions that also follow the intellectual evaluation of a situation. Emotions can be expressive of rational decisions. Emotions can thus participate in our life of reason and will (Gondreau, 2013). For example, when we choose to rectify an injustice, a balanced expression of anger can help us to act decisively while being restrained enough so that we do not overreact. Through a righteous or just expression of anger, we aim to rectify injustice, while finding a just and rational mean between excessively weak or exceedingly strong emotional displays. This conscious and virtuous display of emotion exemplifies the significance of being able to read the intelligibility of emotions. It also involves the active control of one's emotional energy. This active but indirect control is indicative of how we can acquire a virtuous tendency in our emotions (e.g., a tendency to a more tempered expression of anger). Such dispositions of emotion are an acquired participation in the more direct control that is possible through our use of reason and will, and through social influences (Cates, 1996; Gondreau, 2013; Mattison, 2007).

In contemporary psychological studies, emotion is construed as part of a rapid-action meaning system that informs individuals of the significance of events to their well-being (Kahneman, 2011). The accuracy, utility, or purposefulness of an emotion is affected by multiple factors associated both with the appraisal that gives rise to the emotion (i.e., its accuracy) and the response it generates (i.e., how modulated it is). Although emotions are not always useful, their benefits on average exceed their costs (Parrott, 2001). The Meta-Model's understanding of the person as presented here is consistent with theories of emotion that incorporate reason and will (see, e.g., Frijda, 1986; Lazarus, 1991; Levenson, 1999), since, understood in an integrated view of the person as capable of responsible action, emotion depends upon perception and appraisal.

Psychological literature provides a basis for our thesis that a priority on emotional, embodied healing is at times critical to the success of a therapy of virtue. Certain factors have been put forth as important elements in treatment outcome: the working alliance, the depth of experiencing, differences in individuals' capacity for engaging in treatment, and emotional processing, which includes both emotional experiencing and working with the emotional significance of events and relationships in therapy (Johnson, 2004; Pos, Greenberg, Goldman, & Korman, 2003). This last factor has gained attention as researchers of basic emotion processes appear to be moving toward a consensus that emotions are adaptive, emphasizing the utility of emotions as persons respond to events and circumstances. Emotions are viewed as informing people about their cares and concerns. They prepare the body for action, directing our thoughts to ways that will appropriately address the issues at hand. They can signal and manipulate other people in ways that suit the person's emotional needs (Parrott, 2001). Being disconnected from emotional experience, therefore, means being cut off from adaptive information (Pos et al., 2003).

Furthermore, virtually all theories of psychotherapy give central importance to dealing with clients' emotions in some manner: cognitive and behavioral approaches focus on control or elimination of anxiety or other unwanted emotions (Beck, 1979); alternatively, psychodynamic, interpersonal, and experiential approaches often implicate the avoidance of painful emotions in the etiology and maintenance of psychological disorder (Mackay, Barkham, Stiles, & Goldfried, 2002). Furthermore, multiple schools of

thought have found empirical support to show that facilitating in-session emotional experience is both potent and efficacious (Wiser & Goldfried, 1998). For example, standard reviews of humanistic and psychodynamic therapy outcomes suggest a strong relationship between emotional experiencing in the treatment session and positive therapeutic outcome (Orlinsky, Ronnestad, & Willutzy, 2004). Similarly, positive outcome in cognitive therapy has also been found to be correlated with emotional experience (Castonguay, Goldfried, Wiser, Raue, & Hayes, 1996; Wiser & Goldfried, 1998).

The Case of Barbara: Regarding Justice and Anger (Secular Virtue Perspective)

Barbara's limitations in recognizing the reason within her emotions and of integrating emotions with her reasoned judgment occurred when she worked a summer job while in college. She recounted that she happened upon an irate customer yelling at a fellow employee who was overwhelmed and apparently frightened. Barbara confronted the customer calmly, stating, "We don't allow anyone to speak in that tone here," followed by, "Perhaps it would be good if you leave." In her mind, this was a statement of justice or "how people should treat each other." In the crisis, Barbara performed reasonably, making behavioral choices based upon her logical discernment of the circumstance. However, she neither reported feeling the natural accompanying emotions nor recognized that underlying the customer's expressed anger may have been an even more pressing issue of justice. Barbara appears to miss the cues both of her own emotions and those of others, likely because she has learned not to attend to these sensations and sentiments; in her family experience, emotions would not be explored, cared for, or understood, but instead might be seized upon as a vulnerability and ridiculed at minimum, if not used against her.

Meta-Model Reflections on the secular virtue presentation: The secular perspective on emotion and virtue identifies how emotions are significant for everyday coping and flourishing. A Meta-Model perspective on virtue adds another view of positive and negative emotion. Christian faith, for example, also involves a call to seek and offer forgiveness. It can help one to work toward the correction and forgiveness of injustices that underlie experiences of anger, es-

pecially in interpersonal relations. The effect of a religious call to forgiveness may also promote feelings of love for one's neighbor and God. The theological virtue of charity can moderate problematic emotions, such as feeling negative bias or ambivalence toward others. An experience of the theological virtue of hope, for example, can bear fruit in a person's feeling hope that God will forgive them.

The Case of Sr. Lydia: Justice and Anger Revisited
(Meta-Model Virtue Perspective)

In therapy, Sr. Lydia reflected back on her time in college and her handling of the incident in which she attempted to achieve justice for her co-worker. In processing the events and identifying her emotions she began to realize the importance of being attuned to others' emotions and to her own, and thus gain a fuller understanding of the situation as an act of loving her neighbor. In this case, the angry emotional expression needed to be contextualized in regard to the different injustices that caused the anger within herself and in the customer. She learned that anger itself was not bad, especially that a righteous anger was appropriate and constructive. There are the examples of Christ's becoming angry at injustice; for example, he expressed a righteous anger to protect the Temple as a house of prayer (Mt 21:12). Furthermore, Sr. Lydia began to understand that both lack of anger and too much of it could hide injustice and be insensitive to the needs of others. Righteous anger becomes a way for a person to follow Christ: righteous anger not only requires a good intention, but can specify a conversion toward God by encouraging the person to imitate Christ and even use righteous anger to accomplish some good. In this context, she seemed to have humbly accepted that her family members' angry reactions were not typical of a healthy family, and that one could be angry without sinning (Eph 4:26). She could also begin to risk sharing of herself and her emotions in her religious community without the same fear of ridicule or rejection. Sr. Lydia became more in touch with her emotions and recognized prudently when and with whom to share them to foster healthy relationships, community life, and individual flourishing, at everyday and transcendent levels.

The Relationship Between Symptom Reduction and the Capacity for Virtue

Treatment goals that include virtue development in psychotherapy have been described generally as management of emotional life and related virtues so that the client can better live in relationships with others. Virtue development also leads toward further growth in rational, volitional, and interpersonally relational virtues (Moncher, 2001; see also Greenberg, 2004; Chapter 14, "Emotional"). Ultimately, the goal of virtue development is the ability to live a responsible, flourishing life, which is to say, the morally good life. In contrast, psychological symptoms and disorders inhibit freedom, since they promote compulsively consistent (dys)function. They are motivated by excessive fear, anxiety, or other emotion. They also do not facilitate success rationally in solving a problem or promoting social relationships. Moreover, symptoms and disorders can be used effectively to reduce the perception of psychological needs, and, once they are habitual, they allow less opportunity for the person to practice and to enjoy freedom from vice and freedom for expression of virtues such as love, courage, and patience.

Because the psychological symptoms of a person provide an apparent, albeit temporary and dysfunctional, solution to his or her difficulties, it is critical that these symptoms be understood and addressed prior to the therapist's considering how the individual might explicitly grow in virtue.

Further, while the nature of virtue as defined in this Catholic Christian Meta-Model has an objective character that cannot be changed by either the therapist or the client, the expression of a major virtue and character strength (and its associated virtues and practices) will vary cross-culturally. Therefore, the therapist must be aware of his or her own formation and cultural views about how particular virtues might be expressed. This includes not only ethnic or racial considerations but also sex considerations, as the expression of character strengths and practices acceptable for or tolerated of males and females will vary by culture (see Ashley, 2006; Dueck & Parsons, 2004). Growth of virtue in the client often assists him or her to cope with symptoms and contributes to psychological growth and healing. It also promotes resiliency and reduces future vulnerability.

A person cannot be more fully healed in virtue development or in psychological growth, without in some way at least seeking growth in the other. Therefore, it is helpful conceptually, for both the therapist and the client, to realize that failure to address psychological barriers creates a real obstruction to genuine work on growing in virtue strengths. In other words, not only is it important and helpful to assist clients in reducing emotional distress and related symptoms for their own comfort, it also is necessary to help them understand (rational virtue) and manage (volitional and interpersonal virtues) their emotional life (emotional virtues) in order to free them for growth in developing capacities that might now be underdeveloped or disordered. This process is classically called the connection

of the virtues, in which right practical reason and charity play roles in integrating the person's cognitions and affections (Aquinas, 1273/1981, I-II, 65.1–5; Titus, 2010).

Why and When Should There Be a Priority on Healing the Sensory-Perceptual-Cognitive and Emotional Capacities?

Within its concerns for overall psychological health—which include personal wholeness and interpersonally relational, cognitive, and volitional domains—psychotherapy often needs to give a priority to sensory-perceptual-cognitive and emotional healing for a number of reasons, among them the fact that biologically-based cognition and affection influence reason, will, and all practical action (Ashley, 2013; Lakoff & Johnson, 1999).

The emotions and the sensory-perceptual-cognitive capacities are the higher-order perceptions and pre-rational cognitions that include the synthetic, memory, imaginative, and evaluative capacities that underlie our pre-rational (and preconscious) attraction or repulsion to a person or thing. Lack of development or psychopathology at this embodied level negatively influences the human capacity to read emotions and to enact one's rational plans and desires with appropriate promptness, ease, and pleasure.

It is difficult for some and impossible for others to fully access this capacity to reason responsibly and choose freely without formative attention to their emotional life. "Training our emotions to respond to the direction of reason is a most difficult task, and its achievement is called virtue" (R. McInerny, 1999). Establishing emotional maturity, we would stress, is an ongoing, developmental process (Gondreau, 2013). However, again, this is not to suggest that emotions do not have their own unique, positive contribution to human understanding and flourishing. Rather, in a special type of intelligence, emotions participate in reason without being equated with its conscious processes or being under its direct control.

Second, on the clinical level, this Meta-Model of the Person provides a framework that points to a formulation that recommends a preferred sequence of intervention. Because we are interpersonally relational and emotional (at least *in potentia*) from the moment of conception (and the relational and emotional capacities develop prior to the rational and volitional aspects), often the more serious psychopathology occurs at the interpersonally relational and emotional levels. In other words, for a therapeutic process to continue to fruition, it must address the natural developmental processes and the healing of relational and emotional wounds in order to lay a firm foundation for the pursuit of growth in the free and responsible use of rationality and will. Clinicians observe that clients who struggle with psychological disorders (such as phobias, compulsive behavior, or addictions) routinely report a gap between their intellectual understanding of the events around them and their habitual emotional reactions to them. An important component of psychotherapy is the development of the client's ability to disengage from rapid, preconscious associations (found in his or her body and expressed in emotions) and to consider his or her perceptions and evaluations from a more objective and sophisticated perspective. However, this cannot be accomplished strictly through rational and discursive procedures. The automatic and habitual manner of a client's emotional life must be experienced and recognized by the client before he or she can become more insightful regarding himself or herself (Palmer, 2005).

Well-known theoretical work in experien-

tial-humanistic therapy outlines two ways in which emotions are relevant in treatment. First, providing an empathetic, validating relationship and a collaborative alliance creates the safe environment in which clients can experience their emotions. Second, engaging in evocative, explorative, and meaning-making reflections, as well as emotionally stimulating tasks, gives clients deeper and immediate contact with emotions and helps clients make sense of them. An empathic, strong, therapeutic alliance is needed to create a safe atmosphere such that it is possible to have a specific focus in the clinical task of understanding, accepting, and healing the emotional wounds that bind people to the past and prevent them from the free exercise of their will in the present and future. Therefore, it is not accidental that the "talking cure" that has developed in counseling and psychotherapy is person-to-person, that is, interpersonally relational, and that the therapeutic alliance is frequently identified as one of the common factors in positive therapy outcome (Lambert & Ogles, 2004). The therapeutic alliance includes not only a personal bond between therapist and client, in which the client views the therapist as caring, understanding, and knowledgeable, but also an agreement with regard to the goals of treatment and the means by which these goals are achieved, which should be appropriate to the dignity of the human person (Goldfried & Davila, 2005). The effectiveness of therapy is influenced greatly by the trust that the client has in the therapist and the therapist's character and motivations. At this point in the development of the clinical relationship, the therapist's character formation is an issue inasmuch as the client must trust that the therapist not only has general knowledge and skills, but also is a proper guide as the process moves toward healing and growth. The therapist's having a faith perspective (or even a more general recognition of spiritual resources) in common with the client often facilitates this process and accelerates the readiness of the patient to take the emotional and interpersonal risks necessary for healing (as was the case with Sr. Lydia).

The therapist's understanding of and attention to formation in growing virtue in his or her own life is necessary for the maintenance of an objective view of the client's need for growth in virtue. Rooted in the Christian vision of the person discussed here, clinicians should come to understand themselves as well as their clients in terms of the types of strengths, flourishing, and freedom that are necessary to actively pursue a good life. This approach stresses the importance of the personhood of the therapist in light of the traditional Catholic teaching on vocation (Chapter 20, "Principles for Training"). In addition to referring to the general call to holiness (Vatican II, 1964) and one's state in life (as single, married, consecrated religious, or ordained),

vocation also reflects the unique and personal work to which God calls each person.

For example, clinicians can love and serve God and neighbor through the profound gift and responsibilities that come with serving clients:

> In experiencing their work as a part of their Christian vocation, mental health professionals should develop an understanding that their encounter with the client is providential and not random.... Such a sense of vocation and service motivates therapists not only to observe the ethical principles existing within the mental health professions, but also to put into practice Christian love and self-giving for the good of the client. Thus, Catholic practitioners develop a sense of responsibility for the client and accountability to God for how one serves the person in need (Mt 25:31ff.). (Chapter 20, "Principles for Training," pp. 553–554)

In this way, the therapist's orientation toward his or her own growth and development is significant in the treatment process.

The Case of Barbara: Treatment Goals (Secular Virtue Perspective)

The goals of treatment with Barbara include helping her to integrate her emotional life with the consciously willed but internally forced "virtuous" external acts that came at a cost to herself; this cost arose because the acts were not supported by the emotions she experienced, which were primarily remnants from past unresolved conflicts and fears and also the result of underdeveloped virtues. Reaching this treatment goal requires: (a) healing the emotional wounds through a more accurate reflection of the reality of what she was living, along with (b) emotional and psychological forgiveness of her parents [as available in a secular perspective (Enright & Fitzgibbons, 2014)], and subsequently (c) separating clearly what was past and what is present, with respect to the meaning of the emotions she experiences and is coming to understand.

In the short term, she needs to access her feelings, allow herself to experience them, and, in an appropriate way, express them in the context of a trusted therapeutic relationship which prepares her to process more clearly her emotions outside of the therapy session. In the long term, she can achieve a more temperate ideal as is expected from her in the convent, but in order to facilitate this growth, she will first need to experience, reflect upon, and heal in the present the pain from the past. (This is typically an extensive process, and only the highlights of her transformation are noted throughout this chapter).

The Case of Sr. Lydia: Treatment Goals
(Meta-Model Virtue Perspective)

Further insight into a Meta-Model approach to treatment planning can be seen during a visit home, when Sr. Lydia experienced a difficult time with her family. Because of the shared faith background and understanding of the therapist and client, Sr. Lydia was able to trust the guidance suggested whereby she could risk being fully herself and fully emotionally attuned during the home visit. Sr. Lydia understood from the perspective of Christian ethics that distancing from or neglecting the care of her family, even while living clearly apart as a religious sister, was not the charitable or just approach to take. The therapist was able to empathize with her fear of risking opening herself to a genuine encounter with family members who might not be receptive, yet trusting in providence that opportunities that presented themselves should be acted upon.

Sr. Lydia was most interested in taking such a risk through connecting with her youngest sister, now a teenager. This relationship was also expressive of the other family-vocational relationships that Sr. Lydia wanted to strengthen. Her interest was at many levels, including concerning the youngest sister's everyday and spiritual well-being. However, her younger sister's only interest seemingly was shopping for clothing that was often, from Sr. Lydia's perspective, too revealing. This outing became a family affair, with the usual criticism, hostility, and anger being expressed between members. Further, there was an incident in which Sr. Lydia was being harassed by some men, and her father, who witnessed the event, chose not to defend her. At this point she chose to return to the car and wait for the others in order to process her emotions, allowing herself to identify the frustration she felt at not being able to spend time alone with her sister, which would have allowed for more intimate, serious sharing between the two. She also needed to reflect upon her frustration with her father's lack of protection when she was insulted by the men. Processing this, Sr. Lydia became aware that her "frustration" was in fact disguised hurt and sadness related to the wounds she experienced in her family-vocational relationships with her father, sister, and other family members. She realized that the scandal and injustice she experienced was coming from outside of her, that is, from her family members. Therefore, she became focused more on sadness for her loved ones who must be suffering greatly themselves to have treated her this way; she then was able to let go of her upset. In this way, her initial narrower focus on practicing the faith and protecting her modesty (an aspect of her calling as a consecrated religious sister) was refocused by her more foundational expression of the love she had for her family (an aspect of her calling to honor her parents and serve her siblings). In the midst of their continuing negative patterns of hostility and anger, she came to realize that she could love and forgive her family, with the help of God, even if her own love and that of her family was limited.

Psychotherapy as Preparation for Growth in Virtue

We have argued that the therapeutic process must at times prioritize healing emotional wounds to stabilize the person's foundation for growth in the capacity to become free and responsible. Because of the emotions' ability to motivate and energize, the cultivation of emotions in developing virtue is importantly correlated with the education of reason and the strengthening of the will. Although we may act badly under the influence of intense, conflicted emotions, emotions themselves are not inherently disordered, and an important range of virtue (such as perseverance, patience, courage, modesty, and hope) stems from the knowledge attained by an appropriate expression of emotion. Further, the mere repetition of external acts does not guarantee the growth of virtue. For example, parents raising their children may exercise appropriate control over anger much of the time, but may also at times lose their temper in an intense and unjust way. But growth is also possible, as they learn to put things in perspective and take a constructive emotional posture to children's provocative antics.

A parent who suddenly errs after long years of apparently virtuous behavior might do so for at least three reasons. First, it is possible he or she never had these habits and for years had been depending upon external factors for self-control (Klubertanz, 1965). Second, an especially difficult situation or strongly evocative event may occur, which presents a bigger challenge than usual to generally well-established virtuous habits. Third, a parent may also simply have a temporary moral lapse and willingly make a bad choice. In this case, the dysfunctional emotional outburst or isolated bad act or mistake neither destroys the general disposition to act well, nor demonstrates that the virtue habit never really existed. Nonetheless, the lapses illustrate that even virtuous dispositions, which generally lead to virtuous acts, require continuous growth in response to new and challenging situations, as we see in later events in Barbara/Sr. Lydia's therapy.

The Case of Barbara: Another Interpersonal Experience of Emotions (Secular Virtue Perspective)

Barbara had been on an assignment working with young children from disadvantaged homes, and she observed how they were spontaneous and intense in their expressions, both joyful and otherwise. She marveled at the clarity with which they expressed their emotions, recognizing their deep, bodily knowledge of their experienced emotions. During therapy, she reflected on how, despite these strengths, the children did not have the ability to modulate their emotions, as this had not been nurtured in their families. In contrast, Barbara, as an adult and with her growth in virtue, was learning to more consistently identify and make fitting responses. Further, having begun to discuss these issues in therapy, in this work with children she was able to recognize more clearly her own interior emotions.

As a result of her therapeutic work, she also reflected on her experiences of living in close quarters with consecrated religious sisters. She reported constantly feeling as if she was a burden to them, while not considering how they were a burden to her when they were in her space. This lack of attention to her own natural, affective reaction, she came to understand, could be traced back to how, in her family of origin, she was never comfortable coming into close proximity of others, always feeling as if she was going to be attacked or met with a negative response. With time she became aware of this.

The Case of Sr. Lydia: Another Interpersonal Experience of Emotions (Meta-Model Virtue Perspective)

These two experiences—being with the spontaneous emotionally intense children and experiencing herself to be a negative burden on other people without the natural recognition of the corresponding burden imposed—led Sr. Lydia to reflect on how it is typical for her to feel as she does during times of duress. Through processing this in therapy sessions with both her everyday and religious expressions of emotion accepted and validated by the therapist, she was able to discover that it is not shameful to have these feelings but that they are basically good, can be expressed appropriately, and help her to understand her emotions in the context of her spiritual life. Thus, she was able to allow herself private emotional release (such as, spontaneous crying during Eucharist adoration). Having allowed herself to process the everyday emotions and religious sentiments, she then felt self-possessed to go about her day, having neither denied her experience nor negatively acted it out, as was the norm in her family. She was able to recognize her different emotions more clearly now, noting when they were accurate and helpful and when they were not. This holistic approach to her emotion improved her interpersonal relationships with her family and her religious community. With time, her religious commitments to poverty, chastity, and obedience felt less imposed and more fulfilling, although she was still somewhat marked by her family's emotional patterns. This is an example of a growing capacity to recognize how she can internalize her everyday and religious life goals and progress in reading her emotions, in affective self-mastery, and in healthy spontaneity.

Conclusion

A multidimensional understanding of virtue and vice, strength and weakness serves mental health practice. The goals of healing and the possibility of at least partial healing or a healthy and resilient use of weaknesses is informed necessarily by a worldview and vision of the person. This chapter has pointed out that the perspective adopted by the clinician in therapeutic work—secular virtue perspective or Catholic-Christian virtue framework—has real implications for his or her understanding of and work with clients. All worldviews make assumptions about the nature of the person, such as certain assumptions about free will, emotions, relationships, and the virtues that strengthen these capacities. Even when a secular psychotherapy is uncritical of its first principles, it nonetheless is influenced by them. A secular use of virtue in psychotherapy will thus be strongly influenced by its own vision of the person, especially when such a vision is relativist or reductionist, or presumes itself to be value-free.

The Catholic Christian Meta-Model of the Person clearly states its assumptions about the nature and capacities of the person, and the role of virtue in helping persons to live a good life, to be in relationship with others and the transcendent, and to live out their life callings and commitments—in short, to flourish. The Meta-Model with its rich and comprehensive view of the person can therefore serve as a framework for clinical practice, and specifically in selecting and implementing evidence-based practices, including strength-based and virtue-based approaches.

In this chapter, we have explored in theory and practice via a double case study (1) how virtue theory, from a Christian perspective, provides an important part of this general framework for understanding the goals and means that contribute to the development of strengths and flourishing in the midst of weaknesses and struggles, and (2) how virtuous and contrary practices, vices, in and outside of therapy contribute to or detract from flourishing. Furthermore, the Meta-Model's focus on virtue and vice also helps us to understand what is most frequent, the mixture of positive growth and some degree of weakness (an intermediate state) in a life-long pathway punctuated with times of peace and others of struggle. The use of virtues in psychotherapy requires that a therapist be attentive to the importance of his or her own person (strengths and weaknesses) in the therapeutic relationship as well. Such a therapist will seek to employ the most effective psychotherapeutic interventions while being aware of the therapeutic potential of virtues as a resource for the client (such as his or her own or others' generosity and self-giving, pardon and reconciliation, courage and daring, patience and justice) in the midst of human weakness and pathologies.

Use of a coherent Catholic Christian vision of the person and virtue in mental health practice should assist the clinician to help clients to be freed from psychological disorders and problems of everyday living so that they can live a healthier life. In a Christian context it also promotes the freedom that participates more fully in the complete flourishing offered only by God. Even if the word "virtue" is never mentioned during the work with a given client, we believe that symptom reduction is facilitated by at least a preparation for, if not also growth in, character strengths and virtues as a coherent part of the practices of counseling and psychotherapy for all clients. The inclusion of virtue-based clinical interventions often contributes to symptom reduction, the development of acquired virtue strengths and practices, the elimination of vices, and a growth in freedom. For clients whose identity centers on living from a faith-based worldview, the utilization of virtue-based interventions also support them in the development of faith, hope, and charity-love, and other spiritual virtues.

REFERENCES

Aquinas, T. (1981). *Summa theologiae* (English Dominican Province, Trans.). Westminster, MD: Christian Classics. (Original work composed 1265–1273)

Aristotle (1941). *Nicomachean ethics* (W. D. Ross, Trans.). In R. McKeon (Ed.), *The basic works of Aristotle* (pp. 935–1112). New York, NY: Random House. (Original work composed ca. 350 BC)

Ashley, B. M. (2006). *The way of wisdom: An interdisplinary and intercultural introduction to metaphysics*. Notre Dame, IN: University of Notre Dame Press.

Ashley, B. M. (2013). *Healing for freedom: A Christian perspective on personhood and psychotherapy.* Arlington, VA: The Institute for the Psychological Sciences Press.

Beck, A. T. (1979). *Cognitive therapy and the emotional disorders.* New York, NY: Plume.

Benedict XVI. (2006, September 12). Faith, reason and the university: Memories and reflections [The Regensburg address]. Retrieved from http://w2 .vatican.va/content/benedict-xvi/en/ speeches/2006/september/documents/hf_ ben-xvi_spe_20060912_university-regensburg .html

Benedict XVI. (2008, April 16). Responses of his Holiness Benedict XVI to the questions posed by the bishops. Retrieved from http://w2.vatican .va/content/benedict-xvi/en/speeches/2008/ april/documents/hf_ben-xvi_spe_20080416_ response-bishops.html

Budziszewski, J. (2009). *The line through the heart: Natural law as fact, theory, and sign of contradiction.* Wilmington, DE: ISI Books.

Castonguay, L. G., Goldfried, M. R., Wiser, S., Raue, P. J., & Hayes, A. M. (1996). Predicting the effect of cognitive therapy for depression: A study of unique and common factors. *Journal of Consulting and Clinical Psychology, 64*(3), 497–504.

Catechism of the Catholic Church (2nd ed.). (1997). Vatican City, Vatican: Libreria Editrice Vaticana.

Cates, D. F. (1996). Taking women's experience seriously: Thomas Aquinas and Audre Lorde on anger. In G. S. Harak (Ed.), *Aquinas and empowerment: Classical ethics for ordinary lives* (pp. 47–88). Washington, DC: Georgetown University Press.

Cessario, R., Titus, C. S., & Vitz, P. C. (Eds.). (2013). *Philosophical virtues and psychological strengths: Building the bridge.* Manchester, NH: Sophia Institute Press.

Cushman, P. (1990). Why the self is empty: Toward a historically situated psychology. *American Psychologist, 45*(5), 599–611.

Cushman, P. (1993). Psychotherapy and moral discourse. *Journal of Theoretical and Philosophical Psychology, 13*(2), 103–113.

Dueck, A., & Parsons, T. D. (2004). Integration discourse: Modern and postmodern. *Journal of Psychology and Theology, 32*(3), 232–247.

Ekman, P. (1992). An argument for basic emotions. *Cognition and Emotion, 6*(3/4), 169–200.

Ekman, P. (2003). *Emotions revealed: Recognizing faces and feelings to improve communication and emotional life.* New York, NY: Times Books.

Enright, R. D., & Fitzgibbons, R. P. (2014). *Forgiveness therapy: An empirical guide for resolving anger and restoring hope.* Washington, DC: American Psychological Association.

Evans, D., & Cruse, P. (Eds.). (2004). *Emotion, evolution, and rationality.* Oxford, United Kingdom: Oxford University Press.

Fowers, B. J. (2005). *Virtue and psychology: Pursuing excellence in ordinary practices.* Washington, DC: American Psychological Association.

Frijda, N. H. (1986). *The emotions: Studies in emotions and social interaction.* Cambridge, United Kingdom: Cambridge University Press.

Goldfried, M. R., & Davila, J. (2005). The role of relationship and technique in therapeutic change. *Psychotherapy: Theory, Research, Practice, Training, 42*(4), 421–430.

Gondreau, P. (2013). Balanced emotions. In R. Cessario, C. S. Titus, & P. C. Vitz (Eds.), *Philosophical virtues and psychological strengths: Building the bridge* (pp. 139–199). Manchester, NH: Sophia Institute Press.

Greenberg, L. S. (2004). Emotion-focused therapy. *Clinical Psychology & Psychotherapy, 11*(1), 3–16.

Griffiths, P. (1997). *What emotions really are: The problem of psychological categories.* Chicago, IL: University of Chicago Press.

Hauerwas, S. (1981). *Vision and virtue: Essays in Christian ethical reflection.* Notre Dame, IN: University of Notre Dame Press.

John Paul II. (1995). *Evangelium vitae* [Encyclical, on the value and inviolability of human life]. Vatican City, Vatican: Libreria Editrice Vaticana.

John Paul II. (1998). *Fides et ratio* [Encyclical, on the relationship between faith and reason]. Vatican City, Vatican: Libreria Editrice Vaticana.

Johnson, S. M. (2004). *The practice of emotionally focused couples therapy* (2nd ed.). New York, NY: Brunner-Routledge.

Joseph, S. (Ed.). (2015). *Positive psychology in practice: Promoting human flourishing in work, health, education, and everyday life* (2nd ed.). Hoboken, NJ: Wiley.

Joseph, S., & Linley, P. A. (2006). *Positive therapy: A meta-theory for positive psychological practice.* London, United Kingdom: Routledge.

Kahneman, D. (2011). *Thinking, fast and slow.* New York, NY: Farrar, Straus & Giroux.

Klubertanz, G. P. (1965). *Habits and virtues: A philosophical analysis.* New York, NY: Meredith Publishing.

Lakoff, G., & Johnson, M. (1999). *Philosophy in the flesh: The embodied mind and its challenge to Western thought.* New York, NY: Basic Books.

Lambert, M. J., & Ogles, B. A. (2004). The efficacy and effectiveness of psychotherapy. In M. J. Lambert (Ed.), *Bergin and Garfield's handbook of psychotherapy and behavior change* (5th ed., pp. 139–193). New York, NY: Wiley.

Lazarus, R. S. (1991). Cognition and motivation in emotion. *American Psychologist, 46*(4), 352–67.

Levenson, R. W. (1999). The intrapersonal functions of emotion. *Cognition and Emotion, 13*(5), 481–504.

Levering, M. (2008). *Biblical natural law: A theocentric and teleological approach.* Oxford, United Kingdom: Oxford University Press.

Lopez, S. J., & Snyder C. R. (Eds.). (2009). *The Oxford handbook of positive psychology.* Oxford, United Kingdom: Oxford University Press.

MacIntyre, A. (1981). *After virtue: A study in moral theory.* London, United Kingdom: Duckworth.

MacIntyre, A. (1999). *Dependent rational animals: Why human beings need the virtues.* Chicago, IL: Open Court.

Mackay, H. C., Barkham, M., Stiles, W. B., & Goldfried, M. R. (2002). Patterns of client emotion in helpful sessions of cognitive-behavioral and psychodynamic-interpersonal therapy. *Journal of Counseling Psychology, 49*(3), 376–380.

Mattison, W. C. (2007). Interpretation of Jesus' prohibition of anger (Matt 5:22): The rise and fall of the person/sin distinction from Augustine to Aquinas. *Theological Studies, 68*(4), 839–864.

McDowell, J. (1979). Virtue and reason. *The Monist, 62*(3), 331–350.

McInerny, D. (2006). *The difficult good: A Thomistic approach to moral conflict and human happiness.* New York, NY: Fordham University Press.

McInerny, R. (1999). Preface. In Thomas Aquinas, *Disputed questions on virtues* (pp. vi–xix). South Bend, IN: St. Augustine's Press.

Moncher, F. J. (2001). A psychotherapy of virtue: Reflections on St. Thomas Aquinas' theology of moral virtue. *Journal of Psychology and Christianity, 20*(4), 332–341.

Nagel, T. (2012). *Mind and cosmos: Why the materialist Neo-Darwinian conception of nature is almost certainly false.* New York, NY: Oxford University Press.

Orlinsky, D. E., Ronnestad, M. H., & Willutzy, U. (2004). Fifty years of psychotherapy process-outcome research: Continuity and change. In M. J. Lambert (Ed.), *Bergin and Garfield's handbook of psychotherapy and behavior change* (5th ed., pp. 307–390). New York, NY: Wiley.

Palmer, C. A. (2005, October). *Dual-process models of cognition: Insights from psychology into our "higher" and "lower" natures.* Paper presented at the annual meeting-conference of the Society for Catholic Social Scientists, Steubenville, OH.

Parrott, W. G. (2001). Implications of dysfunctional emotions for understanding how emotions function. *Review of General Psychology, 5*(3), 180–186.

Peterson, C., & Seligman, M. E. P. (Eds.). (2004). *Character strengths and virtues: A handbook and classification.* New York, NY: Oxford University Press.

Pieper, J. (1966). *The four cardinal virtues.* Notre Dame, IN: University of Notre Dame Press. (Original work composed 1949–1959)

Pieper, J. (1997). *Faith, hope, love* (R. Winston & C. Winston, Trans.). San Francisco, CA: Ignatius Press. (Original work published 1986)

Pieper, J. (1998). *Happiness and contemplation.* South Bend, IN: St. Augustine's Press. (Original work published 1979)

Pinckaers, S. T. (1995). *The sources of Christian ethics* (M. T. Noble, Trans.). Washington, DC: The Catholic University of America Press. (Original work published 1985)

Pinckaers, S. T. (2005). *The Pinckaers reader: Renewing Thomistic moral theology* (J. Berkman & C. S. Titus, Eds.; M. T. Noble, C. S. Titus, M. Sherwin, H. Connolly, Trans.). Washington, DC: The Catholic University of America Press.

Pos, A. E., Greenberg, L. S., Goldman, R. N., & Korman, L. M. (2003). Emotional processing during experiential treatment of depression.

Journal of Consulting and Clinical Psychology, 71(3), 1007–1016.

Schmitz, K. (2009). *Person and psyche.* Arlington, VA: The Institute for the Psychological Sciences Press.

Seligman, M. E. P. (2002). *Authentic happiness: Using the new positive psychology to realize your potential for lasting fulfillment.* New York, NY: Free Press.

Sherwin, M. S. (2009). Infused virtue and the effects of acquired vice: A test case for the Thomistic theory of infused cardinal virtues. *The Thomist, 73,* 29–52.

Snyder, C. R., & Lopez, S. J. (2007). *Positive psychology: The scientific and practical explorations of human strengths.* Thousand Oaks, CA: Sage.

Spitzer, R. J. (2010). *New proofs for the existence of God: Contributions of contemporary physics and philosophy.* Grand Rapids, MI: Eerdmans.

Titus, C. S. (2006). *Resilience and the virtue of fortitude: Aquinas in dialogue with the psychosocial sciences.* Washington, DC: The Catholic University of America Press.

Titus, C. S. (2010). Moral development and connecting the virtues: Aquinas, Porter, and the flawed saint. In R. Hütter & M. Levering (Eds.), *Ressourcement Thomism: Sacred doctrine, the sacraments, and the moral life* (pp. 330–352). Washington, DC: The Catholic University of America Press.

Titus, C. S. (2012). The Christian difference of *habitus* in virtuous acts, dispositions, and norms. *Edification: The Journal of the Society of Christian Psychology, 6*(1), 37–41.

Titus, C. S. (2017). Aquinas, Seligman, and positive psychology: A Christian approach to the use of the virtues in psychology. *Journal of Positive Psychology, 12*(5), 447–458.

Tjeltveit, A. C. (1999). *Ethics and values in psychotherapy.* London, United Kingdom: Routledge.

Vatican II, Council. (1964). *Lumen gentium* [Dogmatic constitution on the Church]. In G. Baum (Ed.), *The teachings of the Second Vatican Council* (pp. 71–164). Westminster, MD: Newman Press.

Vatican II, Council. (1965). *Gaudium et spes* [Pastoral constitution on the Church in the modern world]. In G. Baum (Ed.), *The teachings of the Second Vatican Council* (pp. 439–556). Westminster, MD: Newman Press.

Wiser, S., & Goldfried, M. R. (1998). Therapist interventions and client emotional experiencing in expert psychodynamic-interpersonal and cognitive-behavioral therapies. *Journal of Consulting and Clinical Psychology, 66*(4), 634–640.

Wojtyła, K. (1993). *Love and responsibility* (H. T. Willetts, Trans.). San Francisco, CA: Ignatius Press. (Original work published 1960)

Chapter 26

Social Psychology

G. Alexander Ross

ABSTRACT: The Catholic Christian Meta-Model of the Person (CCMMP, also called the Meta-Model), which integrates the discipline of psychology with philosophical and theological teachings, was developed within the context of mental health practice. However, it can also be applied fruitfully to other areas of the social and psychological sciences. This chapter applies the model of integration to the field of social psychology, examining in particular the classic research topics of helping behavior and obedience to authority, and more recent work in the social psychology of flourishing. The chapter argues that the Meta-Model offers significant advantages to social psychology by its holistic treatment of the human person, its effective incorporation of the moral virtues, and its sensitivity to the fundamental needs, interpersonally relational nature, and vocations of the person.

Over the past several years, the faculty of Divine Mercy University, along with many other collaborators within and outside the university, have developed a view of the person that integrates the discipline of psychology with the understandings of the person seen in the philosophical tradition and in the theological teachings of the Catholic Church. This vision of the person, referred to as the Catholic Christian Meta-Model of the Person, is a Catholic anthropology—or conception of humankind—that serves as the foundation for teaching the psychological sciences and serves also in the formation of students as mental health practitioners. This Meta-Model guides the approach to psychology and counseling by identifying a synthetic integration of psychological, philosophical, and theological truths regarding the person that must be used if one is to treat the human being both comprehensively and holistically. While of great assistance in the formation of mental health practitioners and in clinical research, the Meta-Model can serve also as a foundation for the other areas of the social and psychological sciences. This chapter uses the Meta-Model to envisage social psychology from such a Catholic perspective.

A Summary of the Catholic Christian Meta-Model

Because the anthropological principles delineated by the Meta-Model are well articulated elsewhere in this volume, I present only a brief summary here. The theological foundation of the Meta-Model is laid by three principles that describe the ordering of salvation history within the Christian understanding of man's meaning and purpose. The first principle states that man, created by God in his "image" and "likeness," possesses an inherent goodness and dignity. This principle orients the work in psychology toward man's flourishing state intended by God; namely, to live in loving communion with God and other persons. At the same time, man suffers the effects of the disobedience of his first parents as well as his own sin (e.g., envy, hatred, self-interest). This second theological principle recognizes the effects of sin and sustains a realism that rejects utopian solutions to the disorders that plague human physical, psychological, and spiritual flourishing. The third theological principle states that man is restored to a right relationship with God, his fellow man, and himself through the redemptive passion, death, and resurrection of his Lord and Savior, Jesus Christ. This principle recognizes the overarching role of divine grace and our reliance on God. It also grants a real earthly hope that health and wholeness is possible at personal and social levels (family and community).

Building on these theological truths are the philosophical principles of the Meta-Model, through which the human being is understood as a body-soul unity that is expressed in eight analytically distinct yet always integrated dimensions of personhood: the person is a unity (personal wholeness), interpersonally relational, sensory-perceptual-cognitive, emotional, rational, volitional and free, fulfilled through vocation, and fulfilled in virtue (Chapter 2, "Theological, Philosophical, and Psychological Premises").

The *sensory-perceptual-cognitive* and the *emotional* dimensions of the Meta-Model point to the fact that man is an organic, living being—created as either male or female—who moves through, interacts with, and emotionally responds to the sensible world that surrounds him (Chapter 13, "Sensory-Perceptual-Cognitive";

Chapter 14 "Emotional"). The *rational* dimension is the expression of man's capacity to reason: to know himself, others, the world, and God. The human person can know and appreciate truth, goodness, and beauty; he has a rational inclination to seek truth and to find happiness (Chapter 15, "Rational"). The *volitional* dimension involves the capacity of man to exercise his free will to act with intentionality and through self-direction. Though man's freedom is conditioned by a variety of factors, he does display a self-determining moral character, creativity, and a capacity to give and receive love (Chapter 16, "Volitional and Free").

The *interpersonally relational* dimension is manifest through self-communicative acts of giving and receiving. Man thrives when embedded in enduring relationships, especially in the family, but also in friendship and in a great variety of forms of human community. Human society is necessary to man and "a requirement of his nature" (*Catechism of the Catholic Church* [*CCC*], 2000, §1879). Man's ultimate flourishing, however, is found only in God, since he "is created by God and for God" (*CCC*, §27; see also Chapter 12 "Interpersonally Relational").

The *vocational* dimension points to the fact that intrinsic to the person is his finding meaning, fulfillment, and flourishing through honoring life commitments and serving others. Working hand-in-hand with the vocational dimension, the *virtue* or moral dimension gives meaning to and provides the basic tools for flourishing (Chapter 10 "Fulfilled Through Vocation" and Chapter 11 "Fulfilled in Virtue").

Finally, while one can focus analytically on a single dimension of the person, human action normally entails mutual influence and interaction among all of them simultaneously, exemplifying the characteristic of personal unity or wholeness (Chapter 8, "Personal Wholeness").

Applications of the Meta-Model to Social Psychology

While the Meta-Model was developed with special attention to its clinical application, it can also be applied fruitfully to research and analysis in other areas of psychology and related disciplines. To illustrate such application, I will examine two areas of research in social psychology using the Meta-Model as described above. These illustrations are drawn from two classic research programs in social psychology: one is labeled "helping behavior" and the other, "obedience to authority." Though not attracting great interest in the current research in the field, these topics are significant and established elements of the literature on social psychology, as witnessed by their standard inclusion in textbooks. I suggest that it is worthwhile to examine them within the framework of the Meta-Model to see what additional insight may be gained from these research programs.

Helping Behavior

One of the best-known research projects in social psychology was inspired by the murder of a young woman in 1964. Journalists reported at the time that 38 people witnessed the attack that took the killer more than half an hour to complete, but no one intervened or called the police until after her death (Darley & Latané, 1968; see also Latané & Darley, 1968). Although a later examination of court records has indicated that much of the original reporting was inaccurate (Manning, Levine, & Collins, 2007), the case did serve to motivate the researchers to find an explanation for the apparent indifference among those who might have come to the aid of the young woman.

The central explanation that the researchers proposed, often called the "bystander effect," is based on the presence and number of onlookers in emergency situations. Their experiments demonstrated that, when an emergency occurs, an observer is less likely to respond and offer assistance when there are other observers present than when he alone is there to help. For instance, one of the earliest experiments placed subjects alone in a laboratory cubicle in which they overheard what they thought was an epileptic seizure by another participant. The subjects believed either that they alone heard the subject's plea for help, that one other person in another cubicle also heard it, or that four other persons also heard it. The results of this experiment found that 85% of the subjects who thought they alone heard the victim's plea left their cubicles to find help in the time allotted by the experiment, while 62% of those who believed there was one other bystander, and only 31% of those who believed there were four other bystanders, sought help for the victim (Darley & Latané, 1968, p. 380).

Because the experimenters' focus was on the decision of each subject either to help or not, it is the volitional domain within the Meta-Model (i.e., the subject's will) that would appear to be most important. However, the experiments in helping behavior are particularly interesting because they show dramatically how, within the unity of the human person, the dimensions interact with one another.

The description of the research above confronts immediately the rational capacity of the experimental subject. The subject, when faced with the unusual character of the emergency situation, deliberates about the nature of the situation. The subject's capacity to do so effectively is an indication of what, in the classical understanding of virtue and moral reasoning, is identified as practical wisdom or prudence. As with other natural virtues, practical wisdom can be learned as the individual develops good habits of prudential judgment that will be applied to new situations (Aquinas 1273/1981, I-II, 55.1; II-II, 47–56). The young age of the subjects (all were college students enrolled in introductory psychology) and the unusual character of the experimental situation suggest that few of the subjects had much experience with emergency situations. The formation of habitual patterns of effective response is a primary goal of the training of emergency response personnel, training that many people do not routinely receive. Nevertheless, some of the subjects might have developed a level of virtue that would guide them rightly even in this unusual setting.

Practical wisdom involves not only the good use of reason, but also the proper operation of the will and the control of the emotions (Titus, 2013, pp. 85–86). In other words, practical wisdom involves the integrated operation of not only the rational capacity, but also the volitional and the emotional capacities of the person. For example, is the action that is willed by the person based on a reasoned deliberation, or is it diverted by other factors such as being overwhelmed by high emotional arousal? The typical experimental setting used in the bystander research, evoking strong emotions in the subjects through the realistic enactment of the victim's trauma, engaged the emotional capacities of the subjects as they considered a course of action. Some of the emotions felt, such as fear for the safety or health of the victim, might well have supported the subject's action to offer help, for practical wisdom does not require that emotions be eliminated, but only that they be made subordinate to reason (Aquinas, 1273/1981, I-II, 59.2; Gondreau, 2013). Yet other emotions might have diverted the subject's will. For example, discomfort or fear of embarrassment in the ambiguous

situation might have hindered the subject's clear application of his reason, trapping him in uncertainty or doubt.

The interpersonally relational dimension also influences the exercise of practical wisdom. Of course, the victim himself (though in reality an actor) evokes the interpersonally relational capacity of the subject, and it is this victim who provides the principal motivation for the subject to take action. However, it is the presence or absence of other persons that is the principal focus for the experimenters. Among subjects who believed that others also witnessed the seizure, they believed that others would offer assistance to the seizure victim. This made the subjects' own assistance less crucial, since among the other witnesses some would presumably already have done so. This information in turn influenced the continuing deliberation in the rational capacity about the nature of the situation. In contrast, among those subjects who believed that they alone were available to help the victim, their relational status—as the (apparently) only person knowing of the victim's need—strengthened their will to intervene and offer assistance.

It is worth noting that practical wisdom is not the only cardinal virtue highlighted by the helping behavior research; the virtues of justice and courage (fortitude) are also called on in the experimental settings. Justice, the determination to give to others what is due them, is a strong motivation for the experimental subject to offer help to the victim of the epileptic seizure. Courage, the reasoned use of fear and daring and the firm will to do the good even in the face of difficulties, would help the subject to overcome the various social and other obstructions to the offering of that help.

A study undertaken several years after the original research on the bystander effect examined the interaction of group cohesiveness with the previously observed relationship between group size and propensity to help. Rutkowski, Cruder, and Romer (1983) assembled subject groups of six volunteers each and induced group cohesiveness in half the groups through a variety of group-building exercises. Each of the six-person groups was then broken into a two- and a four-person group and subjected to an experimental setting in which the individual subjects (alone and isolated from each other in separate cubicles) heard a person in another room fall and cry for assistance. The individuals who were members of the two-person groups believed that only one other person heard the cry; those in the four-person groups believed that three others heard it. In the low-cohesive groups, the pattern found in earlier research was repeated: subjects in the larger groups were less likely than those in the smaller groups to help. However, the behavior of the high-cohesive groups reversed this pattern; in these groups, the subjects who were members of the larger groups were significantly more likely than those in smaller groups to respond to the emergency.

The Rutkowski study is particularly interesting because it demonstrates how a fuller consideration of the interpersonal relationality clarifies the applicability of the bystander literature. First of all, it demonstrates that social groups can be an effective means to support the acquisition of the virtue of practical wisdom. Indeed, Titus discusses the positive influence of friends, mentors, teachers, and therapists in learning to judge with prudence (Titus, 2013, pp. 90–91). Practical wisdom is learned most readily with the guidance of skillful mentors and wise teachers. The study also suggests that the bystander effect, apparently operative only among collections of people who have no meaningful social ties to one another, gives a misleading impression of the influence of groups on an individual's actions.

As a result of the group-building exercises in the Rutkowski experiments, the members of the cohesive groups had begun to develop a shared identity and a rudimentary commitment to one another. Increasingly cohesive relationships among group members typically entail a growing self-identification of the members with the group, a greater commitment to its existence, its goals, and its actions. But such ties were entirely absent from the experimental groups that were labeled as "low-cohesive," the only ones that exhibited the bystander effect. Indeed, as their members had no interaction with one another, from a sociological perspective they were hardly interpersonally related with each other, and thus only nominally could be called a group.

The prior literature on the bystander effect utilized such nominal groups exclusively, collections of people who would not be likely to experience themselves as interpersonally related to group members and hence did not have any degree of self-identification with other members or the group. Yet, given the natural propensity of human beings to form social bonds, a more experimentally real design for the experiments would have specified real groups as the context for the subjects. Because the original research utilized a design that imposed an anonymous social context on the subjects, the research on the bystander effect has planted in the field of social psychology (especially in text books on the subject) the misleading impression that the presence of other persons inhibits helping behavior. As Manning and her colleagues note, "the story of the 38 witnesses in psychology tells of the malign influence of others to overwhelm the will of the individual" (Manning et al., 2007, p. 555). Such an impression conceals the beneficial effect of a cohesive, harmonious social context in facilitating an individual's growth in virtue and his propensity to help others, a propensity that the Church teaches is a natural disposition of man.

According to Catholic teaching, one aspect of the image and likeness of God imparted to man at his creation is "a certain likeness between the union of the divine Persons, and the unity of God's sons in truth and charity." "This likeness," the Fathers of the Second Vatican Council explain, "reveals that man, who is the only creature on earth which God willed for itself, cannot fully find himself except through a sincere gift of himself" (Vatican II, 1965, §24). Being created by God and in the image of God bestows on the person a nature that is fundamentally good (although now wounded by sin) and an innate dignity. The Church also posits here that being created in the image of God produces a natural, universal inclination toward self-gift that, though weakened by original sin, is inherent in the human person. It is not a result, therefore, merely of the presence of cultural and social influences, although of course these influences can strengthen or weaken this inclination. I should note that I use the term "inclination" here in an Aristotelian-Thomistic sense rather than in the usage more familiar within modern psychology (Aquinas 1273/1981, I-II, 94.2). That is, the Church's understanding is that the gift of self is a necessary element of the purpose or end of the human person, the end for which he was created. The Church is not proposing any particular psychological mechanism that acts to impel a human being to self-gift; instead, one might say this innate capacity for self-giving is a result of how we are made (formal cause—being made in the image of God) and the purpose for which we are made (final cause—flourishing through vocation and living a moral life).

Interestingly, one of the principal investigators of the earliest helping behavior research, Daniel Batson, offers an observation that sup-ports the Catholic Christian teaching that man is vocational in nature and thus must give of himself to others if he is to flourish. Batson and his colleagues (Batson, van Lange, Ahmad, & Lishner, 2007) observe that the research on the bystander effect did not seek to explain why people help others, but rather why they *fail* to help. In other words, the research was guided by the assumption that normally people *do* offer help to others in emergency situations, but that certain social conditions may suppress this normal tendency. Apparently, we naturally expect people to offer help to others in need.

There are the effects of sin that influence our natural, God-given tendencies to be in harmony with others and to help them when in need (CCC, 2000, §400). Examples include the pattern of alienation and isolation in the common structural arrangements of mass society. The social organization of modern work also imposes on man an artificial arrangement of social patterns aimed not toward the flourishing of the person through meaningful work, which allows a response to what the person feels called to do, but instead to the functional needs of the work environment. Extraordinary levels of geographical mobility have fractured families and communities, leaving many people isolated and without meaningful social ties or even the balance of work and family life that allow for the meeting of vocational commitments and meaningful leisure (e.g., self-development, prayer and worship, and family life). In such alienating circumstances, one might easily learn to turn inward in suspicion of others, rather than outward, in openness and willingness to give. By using only anonymous subjects unacquainted with each other, the experimental research designs testing the bystander effect reproduced this alienating environment. Furthermore, the social psychological literature on social facilitation helps us to understand why this effect is stronger in larger groups. The fundamental principle of social facilitation theory is that the presence of others enhances among subjects their dominant response (Zajonc, 1965). It would follow, therefore, that in an alienating environment, characterized by the isolation of one person from another, the presence of a greater number of persons would more strongly reinforce inward-directed thoughts and desires and suppress the willingness to help another.

Under more harmonious, cohesive social circumstances, a far more favorable pattern would be likely to appear. In short, the natural vocational-focus (and its commitment to be of service to neighbor) and the capacities for acting virtuously (e.g., assessing need and the best means to be of assistance) would be more salient and might thereby be reinforced by the presence of others. This is precisely what happened in the experiment by Rutkowski and his colleagues, as the subjects in the larger cohesive groups displayed the highest levels of helping behavior. Furthermore, these authors even suggest that stimulating community cohesiveness may be an effective strategy to promote prosocial behavior, citing a successful program that did just that (Rutkowski et al., 1983, p. 552). More recent research also confirms the positive benefit of higher levels of social cohesion on helping behavior (Lenzi et al., 2012).

From the perspective of the CCMMP, although even the normal day-to-day assistance that people give to others is a participation in the self-giving nature of our Creator, the fullest enactment of helping behavior in this life is illustrated by the lives of the saints and martyrs and it is modeled through their examples. For instance, at Auschwitz, St. Maximilian Kolbe's supernatural hope gave him the strength to offer himself in place of another prisoner who, in reprisal for the earlier escape of one of the prisoners, had been condemned to death. That hope sustained him over the next two weeks until he died, as he prayed with and encouraged the nine other prisoners condemned with him to a slow death of starvation in a prison bunker. Such models edify and encourage us. Through them, we can learn to practice virtuous acts of self-gift of which, with God's grace, we are capable, and which give meaning to life.

In summary, the "bystander effect" explanation for non-assistance to those in difficulty is reductionist. It misses the prosocial dimension of human nature. It assumes that humans express general indifference, understanding people as autonomous self-interested individuals. It furthermore makes asocial presuppositions that influence the conceptualization of social psychology experiments and the interpretation of social phenomena.

I suggest, however, that more can be understood about the person and groups when we put the interpretation of social interactions in a larger framework, such as that of the Meta-Model. For instance, experimental designs could be more socially informed especially by the explicit recognition of the person's and group's interpersonally relational, vocational, and virtue-based dimensions. In particular, the person could be better understood when greater credit is given to human social nature and the prosocial commitments (vocations) and character (virtues) that are modeled by and learned from family, friends, and society.

Future research design could thus use a framework that allows new variables, based on the CCMMP, to be identified in human action and social psychology experiments and, then, scored for analysis. Examples of such CCMMP-based variables could be as follows: (1) If we assume the lack of action is due not to indifference but instead to trauma-induced inaction resulting from exposure to the violent event, then this raises the relevance of courage and past experience with violence to understand helping behavior. (2) We might consider how being not an isolated individual, but being in a group of two or more, might strongly influence bystander behavior by buffering against anxiety and providing mutual support for positive helping. (3) We must recognize personal character as effecting bystander helping behavior, especially when people have developed virtues of helping others in daily life.

Obedience to Authority

Another classic area in social psychology to which the Meta-Model can be applied fruitfully is the study of obedience to authority. Made famous by Stanley Milgram (1963) through his experimental examinations of factors influencing the obedience of subjects to an authority figure, these studies illustrate well the interaction among the dimensions of the person described by the Meta-Model.

Ostensibly, the original Milgram experiment was a study of the effect of reinforcement on learning. The subjects were assigned the role of "teacher" and instructed by a lab-coated experimenter to administer a word-pair test to the "learner" and inflict increasingly painful electric shocks whenever the learner made an error. Although the shocks were only simulated, the realistic-looking scenario convinced the subjects that they were delivering shocks of dangerous levels to the learner, whom they believed was another volunteer subject of the experiment, but was actually an accomplice of the researcher. Unknown to the subject, the learner gave predetermined responses to the questions in a schedule that resulted in about three errors for every correct response. When the subject balked at delivering the more severe shocks, the experiment-

er instructed him to continue. Even with vehement, audible protests from the learner, 65% of subjects obeyed the experimenter's instructions and administered shocks to the highest level (ostensibly, 450 volts). A more recent replication of the Milgram research, attempting to avoid the ethical problems of the original work, displayed similar levels of obedience among the experimental subjects (Burger, 2009).

Milgram varied the experimental conditions and found that the degree of obedience to the experimenter varied with the physical distance between the experimenter and the subject and between the subject and the learner. For example, in the original condition, the subject and learner were in separate rooms, and the subject administered the shocks by pressing levers on the shock generator. However, in a modified condition that brought the two closer together, the subject was required to place the learner's hand on a shock plate for shocks above 150 volts; in this condition, the rate of obedience dropped from 65% to 30% (Milgram, 2009, p. 35). Bringing the subject and the learner closer together, therefore, reduced the level of the subject's obedience in doing the objectionable task.

In another modification, Milgram increased the physical distance between the subject and the experimenter. In the original condition, the experimenter was seated a few feet away in the same room with the subject as he instructed him to proceed with the task. In a modified condition, however, contact between the experimenter and the subject was made exclusively over a phone line. With this modification, the rate of obedience declined from 65% to 20.5% (Milgram, 2009, p. 60), showing that increasing the distance between the subject and the experimenter reduced the level of obedience in doing the objectionable task.

The dynamic characteristics of the obedience studies illustrate well the unified nature of the person and the interaction among the dimensions or capacities of the person that are present in complex human action. With special relevance to the rational capacity of the person, the experimental setting presents to the subject strongly contradictory normative requirements. On the one hand, an apparently legitimate authority—represented by the experimenter—demands that the subject obediently pursue a task. Yet the task ordered is inconsistent with the nature of the person in several ways. One, there is contradiction with the sense that each individual possesses innate dignity and that exposure to pain and humiliation is not in accord with such dignity and is not just. Second, since the person is intrinsically vocational and oriented toward loving service that brings about flourishing for both self and others, such punishing actions are aversive on both accounts. Finally, the experiment requires the subject to violate a standard of justice; namely, the principle not to cause harm to an innocent human being. The two normative standards operative in this context—to obey the command of a respected professional and to avoid harming another human being—have different sources of authority. The former standard is grounded in this case both in the general norm of respect for professional expertise and in the informal obligation that the subjects accepted by agreeing to participate in the experiment. The latter standard is grounded in human nature as possessing innate dignity and being oriented toward self-giving, and also is a principle of natural law regarding justice to our fellow men. The two standards confront each other in the rational domain, where the subject seeks to embrace both but finds that, in this setting, they involve a contradiction. First, the contradiction is between two interpersonal messages that inherently bring conflict without any deeper level of

analysis. In addition, the contradiction between the two standards brings a rational conflict: the subject is doing harm to an innocent person in order to cooperate with the experimenter and the assumed importance of the experiment. Furthermore, this contradiction is also at the metaphysical level in that there is an awareness that the dignity of the person being shocked is violated. The conflict is also at the existential and ethical level, since complying with the order to administer shocks conflicts with a vocational call to self-giving service and to justice.

Once having entered the experimental setting, the subject is impelled to act, and it is in the volitional domain that the conflict is made visible. Obedience to the commands of a legitimate authority is normally unproblematic and, perhaps, even habitual or unquestioned. But in the experimental setting, this normal action involves behavior that is deeply troubling to the subject. He is motivated here to step back from the situation and to reassess his action. This reassessment is either promoted or impeded by the relative distance to the two principal parties in the interpersonally relational domain: the experimenter acting as authority figure and the learner as innocent fellow volunteer. As recounted above, Milgram's manipulation of the relative physical distance between the subject and these two parties influences dramatically the course of action chosen by the subject.

One of the most interesting elements of Milgram's report of the experiments is his description of extreme tension and anxiety displayed by most subjects as they administered the shocks, a level of tension that Milgram claimed was "rarely seen in sociopsychological laboratory studies." "Subjects were observed to sweat, tremble, stutter, bite their lips, groan, and dig their finger-nails into their flesh. These were characteristic rather than exceptional responses to the experiment" (Milgram, 1963, p. 375). Thus, the conflict within the volitional dimension of the person is also manifest dramatically in both the sensory-perceptual-cognitive and emotional dimensions of the person.

Finally, the experiments highlight the reciprocal effect of the bodily action on the rational capacity of the subject: at the conclusion of the experiment, the subject reassesses his understanding of himself in light of his behavior. Milgram illustrates this with the following account: "On one occasion we observed a seizure so violently convulsive that it was necessary to call a halt to the experiment. The subject, a 46-year-old encyclopedia salesman, was seriously embarrassed by his untoward and uncontrollable behavior" (Milgram, 1963, p. 375). But such a critical reassessment of self is likely to have occurred in more than this single person, for many of the other subjects must certainly have reflected on the implications of their behavior during the experiment. After the experiment, how many of them might have considered the significance for their moral character of what they had been willing to do to a decent, blameless man merely at the dictate of "an authority who [had] no special powers to enforce his commands" (Milgram, 1963, p. 376)? Their decision to administer the shocks might readily have served as instigation to intense self-evaluation.

Milgram's obedience experiments are perhaps the best-known research studies in social psychology. Their notoriety may be due to the surprise generated by the higher than expected levels of obedience exhibited by the subjects. Milgram and a small sample of his colleagues and students had expected that few if any of the subjects would go to the highest level of shock (Milgram, 1963, p. 375). I suggest that such a large underestimate of the actual level of obedience is a result of a generally distrustful attitude toward obedience in modern Western societies, specifically in academic circles where there is distrust of religion and natural law. People in such cultures stress the importance of individualism, valuing autonomy and independence highly, and giving priority to their personal goals over the goals of their in-groups (Triandis, 2001). In contrast, people in collectivist cultures, such as those in many non-Western nations, are more prone to submit to authorities and defer to their in-group. Milgram and his colleagues, being themselves distrustful of authority, would have underestimated the degree of obedience that actually occurred.

Closely related to obedience is the concept of authority. From the Meta-Model perspective, the modernist understanding of authority, expressed starkly in the work of Niccolò Machiavelli (*The Prince*), exhibits a strongly voluntaristic character, viewing its exercise as based solely on the will of the superior, rather than on transcendent principles of truth or justice. The one in command issues orders simply because he wishes them to be done or finds them expedient. Within such a notion of authority, there is always a tension between law and freedom (Pinckaers, 1995, pp. 268–269), and living under obedience is seen as contrary to freedom (Ratzinger, 2010, p. 536). This voluntaristic understanding of authority is especially apparent in the modern, positivistic conception of law and the state, which locates the fundamental basis of the law in the ruling body rather than in a transcendent, objective source. That is, law is simply what the lawmakers say it is. Lost in this conception is the Aristotelian-Thomistic understanding of law as a dictate of reason ordered to the common good (Aquinas, 1273/1981, I-II, 90.1–2). Law ought to be "in accord with some rule of reason"; otherwise, law becomes lawlessness (Aquinas, 1273/1981, I-II, 90.1, ad 3).

The law's purpose cannot be the private good of the sovereign, but must be addressed to the common good of the polity.

The modernist, voluntaristic understanding of authority obscures the fact that ideally a superior ought always to exercise authority over his subordinate in justice and in love. Within the framework of the Catholic Christian Meta-Model of the Person, those exercising authority and requiring obedience should ensure that a respect for the innate dignity of the person, the vocational nature and commitments of the person, and the will and conscience of the person be taken into account. To exact obedience that actively degrades the subordinate without serious cause would be considered an illegitimate use of authority, for it prevents a just exercise of vocational commitments (e.g., responsibilities to spouses and children, or religious practice), or forces the subject to act against conscience.

Man is drawn to an obedience based on justice because together they sustain his dignity and freedom, but he is repelled by one based on the arbitrary will of another. It is unlikely that Milgram's experimental subjects entered the experiment knowing that they would be subject to the arbitrary power of the experimenters. The scientific credentials overtly displayed by the experimenters, and their polite and professional manner, would have reinforced in the subjects a sense of moral legitimacy and important purpose to the operation. Concealed from them was the fact that they would be commanded to do things simply because the experimenter wished to see whether they would comply, or that they would be placed in a position to act against the innate dignity of the person and their own conscience. Milgram, his colleagues, and his students, however, knew the true purpose of the experiment and the nature of the "authority" exercised by the experimenter. Because such arbitrary authority is so distasteful, they would have thought it unlikely that any one would have obeyed it under such circumstances.

As modern society embraces moral relativism and rejects the objective basis of values, authority becomes arbitrary. As C. S. Lewis wrote, "A dogmatic belief in objective value is necessary to the very idea of a rule which is not tyranny or an obedience which is not slavery" (Lewis, 1947, pp. 84–85). In a society that no longer defends the objective reality of its fundamental principles, obedience is not the free assent to the truth, but a coerced submission to the will of another.

As in the previous section above on helping behavior, the CCMMP might also suggest future research designs to examine obedience to authority. For example: (1) The importance to the human person of group attachments suggests that lone individuals are not the most appropriate subjects for the observation of human responses to authority. How does the presence of others with whom one has strong ties (co-workers, for example) influence obedience? (2) How does personal character or virtue influence one's response to and discernment of authority? (3) What are means by which properly ordered authority can be sustained within a social context heavily influenced by moral relativism?

Concluding Remarks

The Catholic Christian Meta-Model of the Person contains a set of philosophical, theological, and psychological premises. The philosophical and theological premises contained in the Meta-Model preserve the understandings about the person that have been developed in the wisdom traditions over the past three millennia. This multidisciplinary understanding of the person results in an enriched, more comprehensive and nonreductionistic vision of the person, which the Meta-Model presumes can make valuable contributions to the field of psychology and related human and social sciences. This chapter has illustrated how the use of the Meta-Model can be used to examine classic research areas within social psychology and in so doing develop new insights in these areas, as well as pointing to new research questions.

In concluding, the Meta-Model suggests three additional ways in which it may prove fruitful for the field of social psychology. The first of these is the holistic treatment of the person. The Meta-Model provides both a synthetic and an analytical framework that facilitates well the consideration of the person as a totality. Social psychology can easily fall into a reductionist error, concentrating on a truncated representation of the human being. An over-emphasis on human cognition, a preoccupation with an evolutionary explanatory model, or an exclusive focus on the neuropsychological leave out much of what is important in the human experience. Guided by a model that delineates the fundamental dimensions of personhood, the social psychologist has a tool that helps avoid such reductionism. Furthermore, the premises of the Meta-Model that emphasize the person as unity (body-soul), interpersonally connected, volitional, and flourishing through virtue and vocations protects the analysis from a materialist bias that views human beings and their social relationships from individualistic and deterministic perspectives.

Second, the Meta-Model offers to social psychology a means to incorporate into its analysis the moral virtues through a constructive synthesis of the dimensions of the person and his related vocations and virtues, whether acquired naturally or infused by grace. A consideration of vocation and virtue is avoided in social psychology because many assume that it threatens the objective, scientific status of the discipline. Though rarely used, the term virtue is considered to be merely another name for subjectively held values. It is assumed that facts and values must be clearly segregated, and only the former constitute legitimate data for scientific investigation. By contrast, the Meta-Model recognizes that, through his creation by God, man has a nature that is ordered to objectively verifiable ends; reaching true flourishing is a matter not just of pursuing whatever is subjectively desirable, but of developing virtuous behavior and honoring vocations and commitments that incline us in our daily lives always to seek our true good and the good of others. Social psychology based on the Meta-Model's vision of the person can be a tool to assist us in this effort.

Finally, a significant benefit for social psychology arises from the great sensitivity to the relational nature of man exhibited by the Meta-Model. Theologically, philosophically, and psychologically the Meta-Model emphasizes the inherent social nature of man. Saying that man is social does not refer only to the context in which the individual acts, but also to a fundamental element of man's nature. As the *Catechism* (2000) states: "Society is not for him an extraneous addition but a requirement of his nature" (§1879). Highly individualistic societies and social experimental designs, where much of social psychology is practiced, uncritically assume an atomistic, autonomous individual as the ideal. The acknowledgement in the Meta-Model of the intrinsic relational nature of man, and the ways in which true flourishing is possible only through committed relationship and service to others is a valuable corrective to this misconception.

REFERENCES

Aquinas, T. (1981). *Summa theologiae* (English Dominican Province, Trans.). Westminster, MD: Christian Classics. (Original work composed 1265–1273)

Batson, C. D., van Lange, P. A. M., Ahmad, N., & Lishner, D. A. (2007). Altruism and helping behavior. In M. A. Hogg & J. Cooper (Eds.), *The Sage handbook of social psychology: Concise student edition* (pp. 241–258). Thousand Oaks, CA: Sage Publications.

Burger, J. M. (2009). Replicating Milgram: Would people still obey today? *American Psychologist, 64*(1), 1–11.

Catechism of the Catholic Church (*CCC*) (2nd ed.). (2000). Vatican City, Vatican: Libreria Editrice Vaticana.

Darley, J. M., & Latané, B. (1968). Bystander intervention in emergencies: Diffusion of responsibility. *Journal of Personality and Social Psychology, 8*(4), 377–383.

Latané, B., & Darley, J. M. (1968). Group inhibition of bystander intervention in emergencies. *Journal of Personality and Social Psychology, 10*(3), 215–221.

Lenzi, M., Vieno, A., Perkins, D., Pastore, M., Santinello, M., & Mazzardis, S. (2012). Perceived neighborhood social resources as determinants of prosocial behavior in early adolescence. *American Journal of Community Psychology, 50*(1), 37–49.

Lewis, C. S. (1947). *The abolition of man.* New York, NY: Macmillan.

Manning, R., Levine, M., & Collins, A. (2007). The Kitty Genovese murder and the social psychology of helping: The parable of the 38 witnesses. *American Psychologist, 62,* 555–562.

Milgram, S. (1963). Behavioral study of obedience. *The Journal of Abnormal and Social Psychology, 67*(4), 371–378.

Milgram, S. (2009). *Obedience to authority: An experimental view.* New York, NY: Harper Perennial Modern Thought.

Pinckaers, S. (1995). *The sources of Christian ethics* (M. T. Noble, Trans.). Washington, DC: The Catholic University of America Press.

Ratzinger, J. (2010, Fall). Conscience and truth. *Communio, 37,* 529–38.

Rutkowski, G. K., Cruder, C. L., & Romer, D. (1983). Group cohesiveness, social norms, and bystander intervention. *Journal of Personality and Social Psychology, 44*(3), 545–552.

Titus, C. S. (2013). Reasonable acts. In R. Cessario, C. S. Titus, & P. C. Vitz (Eds.), *Philosophical virtues and psychological strengths* (pp. 81–114). Manchester, NH: Sophia Institute Press.

Triandis, H. C. (2001). Individualism-collectivism and personality. *Journal of Personality, 69*(6), 907–924.

Vatican II, Council. (1965). *Gaudium et spes* [Pastoral constitution on the Church in the modern world]. Vatican City, Vatican: Libreria Editrice Vaticana.

Zajonc, R. B. (1965). Social facilitation. *Science, 149,* 269–274.

TABLES & FIGURES

ABSTRACTS

Part I: The Meta-Model of Integration

1. Introduction to a Catholic Christian Meta-Model of the Person for Mental Health Practice

This chapter introduces the Catholic Christian Meta-Model of the Person (CCMMP) and its implications for mental health practice. In doing so, it begins to respond to five basic questions, which are answered more fully in the rest of the volume. (1) What is the Catholic Christian Meta-Model of the Person? (2) Why is the CCMMP's enriched vision of the person necessary for the mental health field? (3) How does the use of the Meta-Model enrich clinical practice in general? (4) How does the CCMMP's vision of the person benefit the client? And (5) how does the Meta-Model's vision of the person benefit the clinician's understanding of his or her identity as a Christian mental health professional? In addition to these questions, the chapter presents three foundational documents of the Meta-Model: (a) its *Definition of the Person*, (b) its *Psychological Premises*, and (c) its *Framework for Mental Health Practice*. Finally, this chapter orients the reader to the structure of the book and suggests strategies for its use by readers of different backgrounds.

2. Theological, Philosophical, and Psychological Premises for a Catholic Christian Meta-Model of the Person

This chapter presents an integrated Catholic Christian Meta-Model of the Person (CCMMP). The Meta-Model is a framework that explicitly employs major theological and philosophical premises (foundational principles) and briefly identifies the basic corresponding psychological premises. The Meta-Model proposes a view that is informed by Christian faith and by reason and the psychological sciences. The text outlines and organizes the distinctive qualities of complex human nature and the dynamic human person. The intention is to produce a richer and truer understanding of the person for the mental health field, one that will enhance theory, research, and practice. How it does this is addressed in the chapters that follow. This chapter also provides a specific, synthetic, Christian definition of the person using theological, philosophical, and psychological perspectives for a deep understanding of the person.

Part II: Psychological Support

3. The Advantages That the Catholic Faith Provides for Development of an Integrated Meta-Model of the Person for Psychology and Mental Health Practice

This chapter identifies major reasons the present situation in the field of psychology is favorable to how a Christian understanding of the person can be meaningfully integrated with contemporary secular psychology and mental health practice. Present advantages include the marked decline of secular confidence that the future would be necessarily secular, along with the growth of religion in most of the world, including the United States, and the absence, over the last several decades, of new major psychological theories hostile to Christianity and the growth of psychological theory and practice compatible with Christianity, including Cognitive-Behavioral Therapy, positive psychology focused on the virtues, the acceptance of forgiveness as a factor in psychotherapy, psychology's changed and more positive attitude toward spirituality and religion. Another advantage for faith and psychology integration is the present existence of many Christian psychotherapists and the many Christians who now use mental health services; both groups desire such an integration. In addition, this chapter presents the special advantages provided by a Catholic understanding of psychology: the explicit, readily available official Catholic theology, the clear, official Catholic moral positions, the well-developed Catholic integration with major philosophical traditions and the many varied Catholic cultures that work against any capture by a particular culture.

4. Modern Personality Theories: A Critical Understanding of Personality from a Catholic Christian Perspective

Major secular theories of personality (e.g., Freudian, Jungian, Rogerian) are briefly identified, and their typically unnoticed and undefended philosophical presuppositions made explicit (e.g., atheism, determinism, moral relativism, subjectivism). These presuppositions are contrasted with Christian presuppositions for understanding the person. The major characteristics of the person, as they are understood in a Catholic Christian perspective, are then identified and, when it's needed, briefly defended. These characteristics include embodiment, which is based on body-soul unity and takes account of male and female differences; interpersonal relationships throughout the life span; a significant amount of free will; reason, that is, human intelligence;

sensory-perceptual-cognitive experience, including imagination; emotions; vocations; and the virtues. The general relevance of such a Catholic Christian theory for understanding psychological problems, and finally its theological connections to Trinitarian theology are presented.

5. Basic Psychological Support for the Catholic Christian Meta-Model of the Person

This chapter identifies how contemporary psychology serves to support the major theological and philosophical properties of the Catholic Christian Meta-Model. The narrative theological premises of created, fallen, and redeemed are similar to narrative aspects of existing approaches to personality and psychotherapy. For example, we as persons are good but harmed by experience and can find healing and fulfillment through self-actualization. Some narrative psychologists describe successful therapy as constructing a new and redemptive life-story. The teleological premises of the Meta-Model parallel those found in positive psychology with its focus on virtue development and the emphasis on higher meaning found in existential psychology. The structural dimensions of the person also receive psychological support. For example, the idea of the person as a body-soul unity or whole is similar to many holistic psychologies. The emphasis on relationship parallels attachment theory and other contemporary interpersonal theories. Traditional scientific psychology has long studied and known the importance of the person's reason, that is, intelligence and language, as well as the importance of emotions and of sensory-perceptual-cognitive capacities. Recently, after neglect, the will is receiving a new emphasis as well.

6. The Meta-Model and the Concept of the Person as an Integrated Laminate

A hierarchical model of the concept of person is proposed. The model consists of different levels of abstraction and understanding. The levels include three objective, observable levels: biochemistry, neuroscience, and behavior; three subjective levels of personal experience: simple awareness (*qualia* 1), human self-consciousness (*qualia* 2), transcendent or mystical experience (*qualia* 3); and the following four higher, rational levels: psychological theory, sociocultural theory, philosophical theory, and theological theory. The emotional response of fear of snakes, the nature of a person's embodiment, and the nature of a person's interpersonal relationships are all described within the model, which is based on the converging, supporting evidence about these properties of the person in the fields of science, psychology, and other disciplines, especially philosophy and theology. The mutually supporting evidence is more than scientific consilience, for it includes a hierarchical connectedness, or integration, among the different levels, many of which are not kinds of natural science, and each of which has its own epistemology.

Part III: Philosophical Support

7. The Methodology and Presuppositions of the Catholic Christian Meta-Model of the Person

Every approach to psychological theory, mental health practice, and human flourishing is based upon a vision of the person. Very often, though, the conceptual basis and tradition for such a worldview or value system is only implicit. This chapter explicitly presents an outline of the realist methodology, presuppositions, and tradition that underlie the Catholic Christian Meta-Model of the Person presented in this volume. While drawing from a wide base of theoretical and practical support for an integrated understanding of the person, the chapter also presents the way that this Meta-Model serves to integrate three levels of input: (a) *psychological support*—how personality theories, empirical studies, and evidence-based mental health practices contribute to our knowledge of the person; (b) *philosophical support* (reason-based)—how existential meaning, considerations of truth and beauty, and ethical reflections on goodness, vocations, and interpersonal relationships further enrich our vision of the person; and (c) *theological support* (faith-based)—how the Catholic Christian vision of the person, especially concerning the performative dimension of belief in God, hope in an afterlife, and self-giving love, enriches even more our understanding of the person. This chapter outlines how these three hierarchical disciplines serve each other and point us toward a greater understanding of the person as an object of study and a subject for action.

8. Personal Wholeness (Unity)

This chapter provides philosophical reflection on the Catholic Christian Meta-Model of the Person, which serves as a framework for understanding all persons. The chapter defends the premise that each human being is a personal unity and individual substance, with unique human, moral, and spiritual goals or ends. Employing common experience (including spiritual experience) and philosophical discourse, the chapter endorses the reasonableness of the Catholic Christian vision of personal unity and explores some of its implications for mental health practice. The chapter presents a compelling view of the person's unity or wholeness, which comprises the physical body and the spiritual soul, as a philosophical source for understanding the gift of human life, personal identity, meaningfulness, and dignity. It assumes that men and women are equal in dignity, with significant differences, which makes for their complementarity. Their bodies have nuptial significance and complement each other at the level of physiology and neurobiology, at the level of psychological and social tendencies, as well as at the level of ethical and spiritual dispositions (argument and evidence for this case is made in Chapter 9, "Man and Woman"). The chapter moreover underscores the development over time of the organic whole and unique identity of each person, who also is culturally, historically, and ecologically situated. Last, it challenges the individualist, reductionist, relativist, and dualist approaches to the person, often found in certain strains of philosophy and psychology.

9. Man and Woman: Equality, Differences, and Complementarity, with Application to Vocations and Virtues, Especially Courage

This chapter proposes that men and women possess equal, innate dignity, while also possessing significant differences that serve as the foundation for their complementarity. In accordance with the Catholic Christian Meta-Model of the Person, this chapter examines the equality, difference, and complementarity of the sexes from the perspective of the psychological sciences, philosophy, and theology. It maintains that the psychological sciences, drawing from neuroscience and clinical observations, contribute to an understanding of the equality, difference, and complementarity of the sexes. It also provides examples of how this approach to treating men and women has implications for mental health practice. Considered from a philosophical perspective, since men and women are different, and because the person is a unity of both body and soul, sex difference affects many important areas of the person's life, among them the way in which individuals live out their vocations. Yet in their differences, men and women complement each other on physical and biological levels, in psychological and social tendencies, and in ethical and spiritual dispositions. From the theological perspective, men and women are both created in the image and likeness of God; therefore, they each share a basic human

dignity and equality. However, this equality does not imply sameness. This chapter explores, as an example, the complementarity found in the masculine and feminine expressions of acquired natural and infused virtues and life-callings (vocations). Throughout, the chapter will focus on these two levels of callings and virtues, with special attention on courage (fortitude). Different expressions of vices in men and women are also briefly considered.

10. Fulfilled Through Vocations

From within the Catholic Christian Meta-Model of the Person, this chapter asks how vocations contribute to the unique ways that the person flourishes or languishes. It proposes a triadic structure of vocations: call, response, and change (with positive or negative effects). It considers how the person is fulfilled through vocation understood at three levels and through two perspectives. The three levels are: vocations to goodness, justice, or holiness; vocational states; and work, service, and meaningful leisure. The two perspectives are a faith-based perspective (theology and the narrative of redemption) and a reason-based perspective (philosophy and science, including mental health theory and practice), which are used at each level of vocation, with special emphasis on implications for psychology and mental health practice. First, from a philosophical perspective, the chapter explores the supposition that by nature each person experiences a desire for goodness and a call to flourish. From a theological perspective, it explores the Christian supposition that the call (or vocation) to holiness enhances the call to goodness and flourishing, since it is made personal by God, who puts a desire in the human heart for growth in holiness and for communion. Second, the chapter philosophically explores the supposition that vocations take on further meaning because of intentional commitments to and practices in vowed and non-vowed vocational states (single, married, and religious or ordained service). Theologically, it then explores the Christian supposition that these vocational states are rooted in the divine gift of grace. Third, it explores philosophical and theological suppositions about the meaning and flourishing that are found in work, service, and meaningful leisure.

11. Fulfilled in Virtue

This chapter will focus on the contribution that the classical, wisdom-based approach of the Catholic Christian Meta-Model of the Person makes for understanding virtue and flourishing. The Meta-Model identifies the advantages of an integrated view of the virtues in facing difficulty, frailty, sin, and vice, while respecting normative human nature and duty, the dignity and uniqueness of each person, the differences of the sexes, the common good, and the movement of grace. Furthermore, it identifies thirteen dimensions of the virtues, as (1) performative; (2) perfective and corrective; (3) purposeful; (4) ethical; (5) influenced by personal uniqueness, equal innate dignity, sex difference and complementarity; (6) connective, relational, and developmental; (7) learned through role models; (8) moderating; (9) preventative; (10) nonreductionist; (11) applied; (12) vocational; and (13) open to the transcendent and to God. A comparison table of the ideas of Aquinas and Seligman with respect to these dimensions is made. The virtues perfect the natural inclinations and capacities, by participating (along with the natural moral law and its precepts) in the realization of human goals and vocations. From a Christian theological perspective, the chapter discusses how the development of virtue also draws on spiritual inclinations, transcendent vocations, and divine grace; and, by contrast, how selfish and evil choices produce tendencies toward moral and spiritual disorders and vices. This chapter also presents a classification of the moral, intellectual, and theological virtues, while outlining the associated virtues connected to them and the vices contrasted to them.

It draws upon theory, research, and practices that are associated with psychological function and dysfunction, moral character strength and weakness, as well as spiritual maturity and languishing or vice.

12. Interpersonally Relational

This chapter explores the philosophical premise that the human being is interpersonally relational. The influence of individualism in contemporary psychology, philosophy, and spirituality puts human interpersonal relatedness and community second to the right of the individual to autonomy. Different types of individualism are found in the writings of psychologists, such as Rogers (1961/2012), and philosophers, such as Sartre (1946/2007) and Nietzsche (1885/2006). However, the Christian and classical philosophical tradition affirms that "life in its true sense ... is a relationship" (Benedict XVI, 2007, §28). Representatives of other schools of psychology, such as Adlerian, Sullivanian, and later interpersonal therapies, attachment theory, family systems, emotion-focused therapy, and positive psychology, have placed much more emphasis on relationships than have individualist approaches. This chapter recovers and defends a classical and Christian philosophical notion of the person as relational by nature and as expressing undeniable interpersonal features. The person should be considered relational, since persons (a) flourish through interpersonal receiving and giving, (b) are centered in love, and (c) have a natural desire to be in an interpersonal relationship with the source of being, namely, God. Human interpersonal relationships, moreover, have different significant characteristics according to whether they are spousal, parental and filial, brotherly and sisterly, or that of friends or community.

13. Sensory-Perceptual-Cognitive

This chapter addresses the sensory-perceptual-cognitive capacities of the person from a Christian philosophical perspective—in particular, from the viewpoint of the Catholic-Christian Meta-Model of the Person. A close analysis of these embodied aspects of human nature and experience makes apparent the importance of sensation, perception, cognition, memory, imagination, and basic kinds of evaluation for understanding a person. Consideration is given to human primary sense capacities and higher-order perceptual capacities as well as to how they relate to cognition, emotion, and volition, in dialogue with neuroscience, psychological theory, and clinical practice. How persons develop cognitive dispositions is also explored. This chapter discusses the sensory-perceptual-cognitive dimension of human knowledge in an integrated classical, realist, philosophical framework. While psychology and the neurosciences inform this chapter with respect to understanding brain functions, these sources are placed within the larger context of the Catholic-Christian philosophical tradition and its understanding of the person.

14. Emotional

This chapter considers the person's emotional capacities from a Catholic Christian philosophical perspective. As an expression of the unity of body and soul, emotions not only are influenced by sensory-perceptual cognitions and higher intellectual and linguistic capacities, but they can also influence these aspects of the person in turn. Emotions also play a prominent role in personal self-understanding, interpersonal relations, moral action, and the spiritual life. While emotional capacities are inherently good by nature, particular emotions can be morally good or evil (depending on their relation to reason and will) and particular emotional dispositions can lead to flourishing or to languishing (depending on how they are formed). By bringing neuroscience and psychological theory into conversation with Christian philosophy, this chapter explores different understandings and terms for emotions, including the

traditional term "passions," which is used by Augustine, Aquinas, and the *Catechism of the Catholic Church* (CCC) (2000). It also describes how the person's emotional capacities can be shaped by virtue, participate in reason, be influenced by charity and other spiritual experiences, and thus contribute to true flourishing.

15. Rational

This chapter focuses on the philosophical premise that the person is rational and seeks to know himself, others, the external world, and God. It affirms that human knowledge has limits and is completed by love. Signs of human intelligence and rationality are found in syntactical language and interpersonal narratives about the meaning of life, multifaceted social relationships and economic interactions, complex tool use and developed science, self-consciousness and intentionality, conscience and ethical free agency, as well as in culture and art. This chapter first investigates the human desire to know truth about mankind and about the cosmos, in particular about humanity's origin, development, and end. It also affirms that humans are fallible and acquire knowledge progressively, even learning from mistakes. Second, the chapter considers the context of self-consciousness in being supported by nonconscious—biological (bottom-up) and spiritual (top-down)—influences. Third, diverse types of sensory-perceptual and intellectual cognitions are seen in rational discourse, ethical judgments, and reasonable practices, in the light of both nature and grace. Fourth, belief is treated as a kind of "knowledge with assent" that admits of everyday and religious types. Next, the nature and limits of direct and indirect self-control are explored, as are rational virtues and vices with their intellectual, linguistic, moral, and faith-based dimensions. Last, the desire for beauty (even in the midst of deformity, brokenness, and darkness) is considered as a disclosure of reality and a call to contemplate the ultimate source of integrity, harmony, and radiance. In sum, the chapter addresses the epistemological, metaphysical, ethical, and spiritual dimensions of human rational intelligence.

16. Volitional and Free

This chapter philosophically addresses from the viewpoint of the Catholic Christian Meta-Model of the Person (CCMMP) how persons are subjects of committed love, free will, and moral action. It describes the importance of not only seeking "freedom from" negative influences and disorders, but also cultivating a "freedom for" excellence and a life of spiritual and moral virtue in accord with one's vocational state. It argues that humans, even when negatively influenced by other people, trauma, and the effects of sin, remain largely responsible for their acts and moral character. The volitional and free dimension of moral action can be more fully analyzed as (1) wishing for some good, (2) intending a particular goal, (3) assenting to the most viable option, (4) choosing the best means to obtain the goal, (5) making ready to apply the means, and then (6) completing the action. Performing good free actions requires interpersonal support, which enables people to positively and morally order their cognitions, affections, friendships, and spousal commitments through the practice of virtues such as justice and charity love. Furthermore, persons are capable of creativity and self-control within the limits of their volitional or executive capacities and interpersonal resources. In addition to exploring the philosophical underpinnings of moral responsibility, this chapter also draws upon psychological theory concerning the nature of the will and freedom. Furthermore, it addresses related theological presuppositions, such as the universal calling of all people to love God, neighbor, and self and to cooperate freely with God's will and grace in order to develop a disposition toward true freedom and charity love.

Part IV: Theological Support

17. Created in the Image of God

The Catholic Christian Meta-Model of the Person can be understood from different perspectives. In the previous two parts, we have explored the psychological and philosophical supports for the Model. This part supplies support for the Meta-Model's specifically theological or faith-based premises, and some of its application to diverse disciplines and the sciences. In three chapters, it explores some of the foundations for faith-based approaches to the person as created in God's image, fallen and influenced by the effects of sin, and offered a way of redemption. First, this chapter identifies a synthetic, theological definition of the person and a brief overview of the development of a Christian understanding of the concept of person. It addresses the assumptions, sources, exemplars or role models, and methods needed for a deeper discussion of the theological premises in the context of Christian philosophy and contemporary sciences. Then it focuses on the gift of being created in the image of God as the foundation for understanding (1) reality and our capacity for knowledge of reality and for love of God and neighbor, (2) the origin and extent of basic human dignity, as distinguished from acquired merit or blame, (3) the differentiation of the sexes, (4) the gift of love as foundational for every gift and for the final goal of human life, (5) the spiritual source of the unity and uniqueness of each person, (6) interpersonal relationality, the emulation active in the call to communion, (7) human longings and exemplarity in the development of moral character and spiritual flourishing, and (8) the nature of divine and moral order. It affirms that mankind is called to the flourishing, goodness, holiness, acts of self-giving, and communion with God and others that is possible only with divine grace and the involvement of other people. Such callings include vocational states (married, single, consecrated, or ordained), as well as work, service, and meaningful leisure. Examples from the mental health field are offered.

18. Fallen

In this chapter, the implications of a Catholic Christian vision of the person as fallen (that is, as influenced by the effects of sin and evil, including original, personal, and social sin, as well as demonic evil) are explored, along with their effects on flourishing. Using examples from contemporary psychological theories, this chapter addresses the following questions and explores the implications of the Catholic Christian Meta-Model of the Person for understanding disorders and trials: How does being emotionally wounded, morally troubled, and spiritually fallen affect the person's flourishing? How are the effects of evil communicated by the imitation of behavior and desire that negatively influence flourishing? How does a denial of sin and evil, or a simplistic vision of them, change one's vision of interpersonal relationships? What difference does the Catholic Christian teaching on the fundamental goodness of human nature and of each person make for understanding the persistent and ongoing influence of sin and evil? The chapter also presents the scriptural and theological principles that address sin and evil, their origins, their causes, as well as their consequences. Experiences of suffering, shame, and guilt are analyzed as potentially destructive or constructive. Furthermore, the chapter recognizes that spiritual troubles can be used to attract attention, or they can be confused with psychological issues. Throughout, the chapter identifies some moral implications of a Catholic Christian vision of the struggle with and cooperation in evil (including demonic evil), human fallenness, weakness, and suffering.

19. Redeemed

This chapter addresses redemption to aid in the understanding of the person and the therapeutic process. There are two levels to redemption. First, there is the natural level or domain for fulfilling people's hope for positive change. This level is assumed and often made explicit in mental health practice, as people come to therapy with the hope of some kind of natural fulfillment or redemption (Chapter 5, "Basic Psychological Support"). Second, there is also the transcendent domain of a deeper and ultimate redemption that is primarily God's work to bring about (a) a liberation from sin that overcomes the barriers that separate mankind from God (also called justification), and (b) the ongoing healing and transformation of the person by divine grace (also called sanctification). In addition to freeing people from the barriers that separate them from God, this transcendent redemption also offers liberation from the effects of the fall, which alienate people from others and self. This chapter sheds light on human fallenness and the need for healing. It addresses how Christian redemption bestows new dignity on a person. It also explores the natural domain of the human desire for God, its limits, and how this desire is fulfilled and elevated by God's grace. The gift of the Holy Spirit is discussed, in addition to the effects associated with his indwelling. Special attention is given to faith, hope, and charity at the natural and theological levels (1 Cor 13:13). These virtues underlie the development and sanctification of a person by engendering the transformation of human nature and its structures of knowing and loving. Further, this chapter examines the natural and transcendent aspects of prayer, sacraments, and religious practices in the healing, development, and sanctification of the person. Throughout this chapter, emphasis is given to the importance of both types of redemption and the human and divine contributions to the work of mental health professionals in helping their clients to flourish.

Part V: Theoretical and Clinical Applications of the Meta-Model

20. Principles for Training Catholic Christian Mental Health Professionals

Use of the Catholic Christian Meta-Model of the Person (CCMMP) has a number of implications for the development of programs for training mental health professionals. A training program based on the Meta-Model aims to help students to see both the mental health practitioner and the client as embedded in a Catholic Christian vision of the person, with special focus on the vocational context of each, an objective rarely found in graduate training. It also aims to educate and form mental health professionals in ways that foster a deep respect for clients' innate dignity and their transcendent calling and end. The CCMMP-centered curriculum provides the students (1) a thorough grounding in the Catholic Christian Meta-Model of the Person; which would include specific areas of focus such as (2) the dignity and nature of flourishing for both client and the clinician; (3) the importance of the vocations of clients and clinicians; (4) the presuppositions that underlie the Meta-Model; and (5) the model's implications for ethical practice. Of significant import is the training of clinicians in (6) application of the Meta-Model when working with non-Catholic Christians, people of different faiths, and non-believers; (7) theories and practices existing in the mental health field that are consistent with the CCMMP; and (8) ways that mental health professionals can serve the Church. Contextually important to any training curriculum is (9) how the CCMMP influences the selection of students, the formation of the faculty, and the training of the staff.

21. Case Conceptualization: The Catholic-Christian Meta-Model of the Person as a Framework

The case conceptualization process, which includes diagnosis, case formulation, and treatment planning, has received increasing attention in the mental health field over the past two decades. This chapter examines how the Catholic Christian Meta-Model of the Person (CCMMP) provides a comprehensive understanding of the person and an organizing framework for case conceptualization, a framework that incorporates a wide range of existing theories in the field, while avoiding the reductionism, relativism, determinism, and frequently narrow focus associated with these theories. In addition, this chapter demonstrates how the Meta-Model's inclusion of important dimensions of personhood, such as vocational commitments, virtues and character strengths, and spirituality can be used to improve the case conceptualization process. Finally, a brief illustration of case conceptualization using the CCMMP is given in order to demonstrate more concretely how the Meta-Model significantly expands and enriches case conceptualization and the associated intake process.

22. The Curative Factors of Group Psychotherapy

Little is written about Christian faith and group psychotherapy, particularly with respect to dynamic group psychotherapy. This chapter reviews the available literature and examines six of Irving Yalom's (2005) curative factors in the light of the Catholic Christian Meta-Model of the Person and of the writings of recent popes John Paul II and Benedict XVI. The chapter also sets the stage for understanding the remaining five curative factors identified by Yalom.

23. Contextualizing the DSM-5: Considerations for Enriching Psychodiagnosis

After reviewing the development of the latest, fifth edition of the *Diagnostic and Statistical Manual of Mental Disorders* (DSM-5) the authors of this chapter suggest that the diagnostic categories included in the manual can better capture the fullness of the human person if they are placed within the framework of the theological, philosophical, and psychological premises of the Catholic Christian Meta-Model of the Person (CCMMP; see Chapter 2, "Theological, Philosophical, and Psychological Premises"). An example of how the CCMMP can enrich the diagnostic approach of the DSM-5 is then illustrated: the chapter applies the Meta-Model's integrated approach to avoidant personality disorder, a condition that reduces a person's capacity for relationality or interpersonal life. The chapter also discusses the relational focus of the Meta-Model by drawing on interpersonal psychology, the findings of attachment theory, and the latest research on relational processes in order to bring a more dynamic perspective to the diagnostic process.

24. Psychological Assessment

This chapter reviews the implications of the Catholic Christian Meta-Model of the Person for the professional task of psychological evaluation and assessment. The Meta-Model identifies a more comprehensive set of foundational principles and groups of capacities or domains of the person and flourishing that can serve as a basis for enhancing the scope of psychological assessment. This expansion would include new areas for assessment, such as interpersonal relationships, vocational callings, virtue strengths, the ability to forgive, and the freedom of the will. This chapter also discusses some widely used instruments, such as MMPI-2, Rorschach, and Wechsler scales, in light of the Meta-Model's framework for understand-

ing the person. Finally, it outlines a few specific applications that are unique in working from a Catholic Christian perspective or in a Catholic setting—in particular, the role of assessment in the vocational discernment process for clergy and religious, and in marriage tribunal cases.

25. Virtue in Mental Health Practice: A Comparative Case Study

This chapter discusses how a multidimensional understanding of virtue serves the practice of psychotherapy and counseling. It employs a broad understanding of virtue, as (1) guided by a pursuit of meaning and flourishing (purposeful dimension), (2) through the virtuous acts (performative dimension), which (3) transform inter- and intrapersonal capacities (corrective and perfective dimension). It recognizes that every theory concerning the person or evidence-based counseling practice—including personality theories and therapy models—inevitably draws from a worldview and value system for understanding flourishing. The chapter first compares two frameworks for the use of virtue in mental health practice, namely, a secular virtue approach (Peterson & Seligman, 2004) and a faith-based one (Catholic Christian Meta-Model of the Person [CCMMP], that is, the model presented in the present book). It discusses these views on themes such as the normativeness of human nature and especially how life callings and vocations are needed to understand the development and healing of the person. Next, it compares how secular and faith-based frameworks influence the application of virtue in diverse psychotherapeutic modalities and practices. A single case is presented from a secular perspective on virtue and vice and then from a Catholic Christian perspective; the two approaches to the same case are revisited throughout the chapter; similarities and differences between these frameworks are identified.

26. Social Psychology

The Catholic Christian Meta-Model of the Person (CCMMP, also called the Meta-Model), which integrates the discipline of psychology with philosophical and theological teachings, was developed within the context of mental health practice. However, it can also be applied fruitfully to other areas of the social and psychological sciences. This chapter applies the model of integration to the field of social psychology, examining in particular the classic research topics of helping behavior and obedience to authority, and more recent work in the social psychology of flourishing. The chapter argues that the Meta-Model offers significant advantages to social psychology by its holistic treatment of the human person, its effective incorporation of the moral virtues, and its sensitivity to the fundamental needs, interpersonally relational nature, and vocations of the person.

VOLUME EDITORS AND
CONTRIBUTORS

Paul C. Vitz, Ph.D. is Senior Scholar and Professor at the Institute for the Psychological Sciences, at Divine Mercy University. He is a co-founder of the IPS and has been an active part of it since its founding in 1999. He received his Ph.D. from Stanford University, where he majored in personality theory and experimental cognitive psychology. For many years he was Professor of Psychology at New York University, where he is now Professor Emeritus. He also was a professor at the John Paul II Institute for Marriage and Family, in Washington, D.C., from 1991 to 2001.

His primary areas of interest and research are personality theory and its integration with Catholic theology and philosophy; the nature and historical origin of human consciousness; the importance of fathers for the family; how men and women are equal in dignity but different and complementary; the psychology of atheism; the psychology of the virtues; identity; and hatred and forgiveness. He has recently returned to some of his early work in cognitive psychology, such as models of sequential pattern learning, and the study of perceptual images and their drawings.

He has published many articles, essays, chapters, videos, and op-eds. His books, with the first three translated into other languages, include *Faith of the Fatherless: The Psychology of Atheism* (2nd ed.); *Sigmund Freud's Christian Unconscious*; *Psychology as Religion: The Cult of Self-Worship*, (2nd ed.); *Censorship: Evidence of Bias in our Children's Textbooks*; *The Self: Beyond the Postmodern Crisis*; and *Modern Art and Modern Science: The Parallel Analysis of Vision*.

William J. Nordling, Ph.D., is Professor and clinical supervisor at the Institute for the Psychological Sciences (School of Psychology) at Divine Mercy University. He is one of the co-founding faculty members of the IPS (DMU) and for eighteen years served as Chair of the Department and then as Academic Dean. He received his Ph.D. in Clinical Psychology from the University of Maryland, College Park, and is licensed as a clinical psychologist. He also holds the credential of Registered Play Therapist—Supervisor through the Association for Play Therapy.

His areas of expertise include child, marriage, and family therapy, and he has conducted over two hundred training workshops and presentations in these areas. He is widely recognized as an expert in the area of play therapy, and is co-author of the award-winning textbook *Child Centered Play Therapy: A Practical Guide to Developing Therapeutic Relationships with Children.*

Prior to coming to the IPS in 1999, Dr. Nordling served as Clinic Director and Director of Certification Programs at the National Institute of Relationship Enhancement (NIRE). Dr. Nordling currently holds training faculty appointments in a number of training institutes around the world, including NIRE, Play Therapy Australia, and ChildPlayWorks (New Zealand). Dr. Nordling was a founding board member and served as president of the Catholic Psychotherapy Association. He was a founding board member of the Maryland Association for Play Therapy. He also served on the board and as president of the national-level Association for Play Therapy.

Craig Steven Titus, S.T.D., Ph.D., is Professor of Integration at the Institute for the Psychological Sciences and Director of the Department of Integrative Studies at Divine Mercy University, where he has worked since 2002. He received his Doctorate of Sacred Theology from the University of Fribourg, Switzerland.

His areas of expertise include virtue theory and the psychology of virtue; the integration of psychological sciences, philosophy, and theology; the nature of the human person; practical reason and moral character; and marriage and family life.

He previously worked at the University of Fribourg as Researcher, Instructor, Vice-Director of the St. Thomas Aquinas Institute for Theology and Culture, and Vice-Director of the Servais Pinckaers Archives. Dr. Titus has published numerous book chapters and journal articles, for example, in *Journal of Positive Psychology*; *Journal of Psychology and Christianity*; *Journal of Moral Theology*; *The Thomist*; *Edification: The Journal of the Society of Christian Psychology*; and *Revue d'Ethique et de Théologie Morale*. His book is entitled *Resilience and the Virtue of Fortitude: Aquinas in Dialogue with the Psychosocial Sciences*. He is also co-editor of *The Pinckaers Reader: Renewing Thomistic Moral Theology*, and editor of nine other books.

Contributors to the Catholic Christian Meta-Model of the Person

Christopher Gross, Ph.D., is Assistant Professor of Integrative Studies at the Institute for the Psychological Sciences, Divine Mercy University, where he has worked since 2015. He received his Ph.D. from the Catholic University of America, in Washington, D.C. His research has focused on Thomistic virtue ethics, philosophical anthropology, and bioethics. Dr. Gross has taught theology at several institutions, including the Catholic University of America and the Dominican House of Studies. His research has appeared in academic journals, such as *The National Catholic Bioethics Quarterly*.

Lisa Klewicki, Ph.D., is a licensed clinical psychologist, Associate Professor of Psychology, and Associate Psy.D. Program Director at the Institute for the Psychological Sciences at Divine Mercy University, where she has worked for nine years. She received her Ph.D. in Clin-

ical Psychology from the Graduate School of Psychology at Fuller Theological Seminary. She also received her M.A. in Theology from Fuller Theological Seminary. Dr. Klewicki's areas of expertise include the psychotherapeutic process; psychological assessment of children, adolescents, and adults; and the use of assessment as a therapeutic technique. In addition to teaching, she has been in part-time clinical practice for over eighteen years, focusing on providing psychotherapy and psychological assessments to a variety of clients.

Margaret Laracy, Psy.D., is a licensed clinical psychologist in private practice in Bethesda, Maryland. She received her Psy.D. from the Institute for the Psychological Sciences. Dr. Laracy has worked as a clinician for a number of years with expertise in individual, marital, and group psychotherapy. She is also currently a candidate with the Psychoanalytic Training Institute of the Contemporary Freudian Society. In addition to her clinical work, she is an adjunct assistant professor of psychology at the Pontifical John Paul II Institute for Studies on Marriage and Family, and she was an assistant professor at the Institute for the Psychological Science for four years.

Su Li Lee, Psy.D., is Assistant Professor of Psychology and clinical supervisor at the Institute for the Psychological Sciences at Divine Mercy University, where she has worked since 2012. She also works as a clinician for the Alpha Omega Clinic. Dr. Lee received her Psy.D. from the Institute for the Psychological Sciences and her M.Sc. in Experimental Psychology from the University of Sussex, in the UK. She is currently licensed as a clinical psychologist in the Commonwealth of Virginia. Her areas of clinical interest lie primarily in individual psychotherapy and behavioral health consultation, with a sub-specialization in the area of trauma work.

Matthew R. McWhorter, Ph.D., is Assistant Professor of Integrative Studies at Divine Mercy University, where he has worked since 2016. He received his Ph.D. in Theology from Ave Maria University. His areas of expertise include theological and philosophical anthropology, fundamental moral theology, and philosophical ethics. Dr. McWhorter has taught philosophy and theology at several institutes of higher learning, including Holy Spirit College, Ave Maria University, and the Catholic Distance University. He has also taught courses for the diaconate formation program in the Archdiocese of Atlanta. His research has appeared in academic journals such as *The Irish Theological Quarterly*, *The Heythrop Journal*, *Nova et Vetera*, *Studies in Christian Ethics*, and others.

Frank J. Moncher, Ph.D. consults as a clinical psychologist for the Diocese of Arlington, serving as the Victim Assistance Coordinator, Assessor in the Tribunal, and as the Director of Training in Catholic Charities. He is licensed as a clinical psychologist in Virginia and in Washington, D.C. Frank received his Ph.D. in Clinical-Community Psychology from the University of South Carolina in 1992, following which he spent several years on the faculty of the Medical College of Georgia. In 2000 he began to teach at the Institute for the Psychological Sciences, before beginning his work with the Diocese of Arlington in 2010. Concurrent with this, he has consulted with numerous religious orders and dioceses to provide psychological evaluations of aspirants and candidates. His research interests include the integration of Catholic thought into psychotherapy, child and family development issues, and integrated models of assessment of candidates for the priesthood and religious life.

Harvey Payne, Psy.D., is Dean of the School of Counseling, Associate Professor, and co-director of the Clinical Mental Health Counseling program at Divine Mercy University, where he has worked since 2014. He received his Psy.D. from the Massachusetts School of Professional Psychology and is a licensed clinical psychologist. His areas of expertise include the use of narrative to bridge Christian faith and psychology; the overlap of attachment theory and the Christian model of covenant relationships; professional ethics; and neurodevelopmental disorders. Dr. Payne has worked in the mental health field for over thirty years, primarily in organizations serving children and adolescents with a variety of life issues and disabilities. In addition to his work as a mental health provider, he has also functioned as an administrator, educator, and overseas consultant. Prior to joining

Divine Mercy University, he served as Dean of the College of Counseling at Columbia International University.

G. Alexander Ross, Ph.D., was Professor of Social Psychology at the Institute for the Psychological Sciences, where he was also Dean of Students. He has served for many years as a member of the Board of Directors of Divine Mercy University and the IPS. He received his Ph.D. in Sociology from the Ohio State University in 1976. His areas of scholarly interest have included the social response to natural disasters and other emergencies; historical demography; the integration of the social sciences with a Catholic anthropology; social change in the family and religion; and the social psychology of happiness. Dr. Ross has taught at institutions of higher learning in Michigan, Ohio, and Florida. His research has been published in several scholarly journals, including *Human Relations, Journal of Family History, Michigan Historical Review, Edification: Journal of the Society of Christian Psychology, Catholic Social Science Review*, and *Interdisciplinary Journal of Research on Religion*.

Philip Scrofani, Ph.D., ABPP, is Professor of Psychology and clinical supervisor at the Institute for the Psychological Sciences at Divine Mercy University, where he has worked since 2004. He received his Ph.D. from the Catholic University of America and is licensed as a clinical psychologist. He has been Board Certified by the American Board of Professional Psychology since 1990. His areas of expertise include clinical psychology, Cognitive-Behavioral Therapy, group therapy, and research review. Dr. Scrofani worked at the Commission on Mental Health Services as the Director of Psychology for twelve years, where he had oversight responsibility for approximately one hundred clinical psychologists and administrative responsibility for an APA-accredited psychology internship. He also served as the Director of Family Psychotherapy Training for five years. He continues to have a faculty appointment with the Psychiatry Residency Training Program for the Department of Mental Health in Washington, DC.

INDEX

culture (*cont.*)
    and the person, 28, 33, 62,
      159–61, 177, 435
    served by work, 236–37
    and the sexes, 176–77, 232
    and virtue, 653
    and vocation, 230
curative factors, 588

D

Damasio, Antonio, 68, 93
Darwin, Charles, 459
Dawkins, Richard, 119, 217
    on freedom, 415
de Lubac, Henri, 52
death, 148
    bodily, 516–17, 522
    and courage, 186
    and personhood, 155–56
    preparation for, 483
    result of the fall, 479, 503
    and the soul, 156
    spiritual, 486
"death with dignity," 149, 459
deduction and induction, 133, 263,
    374–75, 388
demonic activity, 506
Dennett, Daniel, 119
    on freedom, 415
dependence
    on community, 324
    on family, 318
    on God, 26, 73, 155–56, 261
    and independence, 397
    See also independence; inter-
      dependence
Descartes, René, 93, 360
desire
    baptism of, 25, 522
    for beauty, 399
    contadictory, 250
    disordered, 158, 256, 285, 292,
      482, 484, 491, 495; love as
      remedy for, 258
    for flourishing, 210, 606
    for God, 29, 32, 257, 316–18,
      384–85, 462, 517, 521
    for the good, 312, 420–21
    for knowledge, 376
    and love, 314–15
    natural and transcendent,
      218

    and natural inclinations, 129,
      157
    sexual, 178–79; disordered,
      188–89
    and vocation, 29, 212
despair, 315, 481, 529, 592, 605,
    608
determinism, 64, 126, 163, 217, 390,
    409, 415, 490
development
    of Christian identity, 556
    considered in case conceptu-
      alization, 568–69
    and flourishing, 272, 642
    health as, 30, 593
    of the human person, 73, 193,
      271–73, 321, 454
    influences on, 159
    intellectual, 383–84
    moral, 30, 626
    of practical reason, 396–97
    and vice, 293
    and the virtues, 31, 250, 279,
      286, 288, 298, 643, 653
    See also flourishing
diagnosis, 11, 12, 116, 567, 579,
    613
dialogue
    among disciplines, 130, 145,
      184, 401, 422, 481
    ecumenical, 51
    interpersonal, 71, 281, 483
    between secular psychology
      and CCMMP, 122, 132, 315,
      548, 639
    in therapy, 645
    in vocation, 213–16
    See also communication;
      integration
dignity, human, 21, 26, 43, 82,
    149–52, 313, 450, 456–59, 507,
    602, 671, 673
    after the fall, 121
    vs. autonomy, 459
    basic, 150, 434, 457, 495–96
    challenges to, 459
    equal, 170, 172
    and ethics, 259
    given by God, 23, 456–57,
      498, 623
    merited, 149, 150, 457
    and redemption, 517

    respecting the client's, 13–14,
      425, 551–52, 557
    and virtue, 278–79, 641
disability, 614
disciplines, 134–35, 138, 174–76
    contributions of each, 4–6,
      121, 250
    as distinct, 117, 130, 135
    integration of, 4–6, 10–11, 118,
      128, 451
    as lenses, 4, 6, 117
    See also premises
discourse, 120–24, 388–89
dishonor, 150
    See also shame
disobedience, 23, 119, 231, 362,
    475–78, 484, 498, 503, 664
disorder, 480–83, 590–92, 613
    affective, 292
    avoidant personality, 616–19
    cognitive, 291
    in community, 324
    as distortion of basic order,
      262–63, 478, 639
    and injustice, 285
    lack of virtues, 70
    as limiting freedom, 439,
      440, 652
    mental, 69, 173, 181–84
    moral, 289–92, 503–4; and
      evil, 31
    physical, 289
    prevention of, 559
    psychological, 289, 297, 333,
      492, 496. *See also* psycho-
      pathology
    remedy for, 551–52, 514, 552,
      593
    result of the fall, 22, 83, 479
    and sin, 289, 363, 484, 492
    and vice, 188–89
    in work, 238
    See also evil; pathology;
      suffering
dispositions, 274
    and acts, 291–92
    cognitive, 349–50, 382, 391,
      397
    and emotions, 364; disorder
      of, 362
    formation of, 366–68, 382, 396
    and grace, 284, 456, 523

virtues (*cont.*)
    purposeful, 278
    rational, 395–98; see also
      wisdom, practical
    and self-control, 394
    and the sexes, 174, 184–88,
      197, 464
    theological, 185, 275, 282,
      288, 361, 520, 649; charity,
      532–33; faith, 526–27; hope,
      529–30, 591
    theological perspective on,
      288, 647–48
    types of, 30, 281–82
    universality of, 639, 653
    and vice, 294–96
    and vocation, 211, 218–19,
      243, 281
    and willpower, 93
    See also character strengths;
      interpersonal relationality
Vitz, Paul, 82
vocation, 24, 28–29, 43, 69, 210–43,
  664
    assessment of, 624–25
    basic, 217–18, 229
    and beauty, 400–401
    to being single, 222–24,
      228–31
    CCMMF emphasis on, 12–13,
      15, 126, 553, 623–24, 648,
      674; in case conceptualiza-
      tion, 137, 578–83
    definition and etymology, 212
    deformed by vice, 494
    discernment of, 227–28, 234,
      629–30
    and family, 321, 463
    fitting human response to, 28,
      211, 213
    and flourishing, 91–92,
      217–19, 464
    to goodness and holiness,
      24, 28, 159, 191, 217–22, 273,
      497, 523, 553
    and grace, 212, 215, 219, 220,
      242
    to Holy Orders. *See* Holy
      Orders
    levels of, 214–15
    to love, 130, 619
    to marriage. *See* marriage

    and mental health practice,
      216, 234, 239–40, 629–30
    and pathology, 70, 234
    philosophical perspective
      on, 28–29, 217–19, 222–26,
      234–42
    purpose of, 213
    to religious life, 225–26,
      232–34, 314, 320,
      558–59
    rooted in sacraments, 211
    and self-gift, 315, 533, 668
    and the sexes, 171, 452; as
      complementary, 199;
      as equal, 176; feminine
      genius, 190
    to states of life, 24, 29, 222–34,
      553
    and telos, 69, 211
    theological perspective on,
      219–22, 226–34
    transformative, 213–14, 318
    ultimate, 215–16
    as understood by the Chris-
      tian faith, 131, 219–20, 631
    and virtues, 211, 218–19, 243,
      281
    to work, service, and
      meaningful leisure, 25, 29,
      234–42, 553
vocational evaluation, 630
volition, 41–42, 44, 93, 408–41,
  664–65
    assessment of, 629
    conflict in, 671–72
    definition of, 413
    privation of, 618
    See also will, free
voluntarism, 490, 672–73
von Balthasar, Hans Urs, 52
von Hildebrand, Dietrich, 55
vows
    marriage, 231
    religious, 225–26
Vygotsky, Lev, 72, 311, 383

W
Watson, John B., 119
weakness
    acceptance of, 602, 618
    moral, 496
    psychological, 69, 296, 493

    and sin, 451, 457, 474–75, 480,
      484–87
    and strength, 441
    and vice, 494
    of will, 70, 436, 478, 495
Weber, Max, 119
well-being
    See health
wholeness, 28
    and beauty, 400
    of the body, 157
    as health, 296, 298, 515
    and holiness, 272–73
    integration of domains, 28
    personal, 145–64, 253, 296, 331,
      372, 412, 574, 619, 643. *See*
      also body-soul unity
    served by the various disci-
      plines, 164
    and transcendence, 163
will, free, 41–42, 44, 65, 68,
  408–41
    assessment of, 629
    and choice, 413
    denial of, 496
    and dispositions, 254
    and emotions, 362, 666
    and grace, 422
    limitations, 42, 436, 438–41
    and love, 41, 74
    and marriage, 630
    and moral disorder, 292
    pathology of, 70
    perfected by love, 315
    and reason, 666
    in secular psychology, 93
    and self-determination,
      435–36
    significance of, 413–14
    and sin, 486, 491
    in therapy, 603
    and virtues, 65, 93, 419, 652
    wounded by the fall, 479,
      484
    See also freedom; intellectual
      affect; responsibility;
      volition
willpower, 278, 409
    limitations of, 439
    and virtues, 93
    See also self-control
Winnicott, D. W., 92, 172

Printed in Great Britain
by Amazon

83083084R00418